Define *Universe* and Give Two Examples

A Comparison of Scientific and Christian Belief

(teenagers are forbidden to read this book)

To the Palmyra Library
with thanks for the
great help you were
and are!
Barton E. Dahneke

Barton E. Dahneke

"Define *Universe* and Give Two Examples,
A Comparison of Scientific and Christian Belief"
Printed in the United States of America.

Library of Congress Control Number: 2005906608
Author information: Dahneke, Barton E. (Barton Eugene), 1939-
Keywords: Christianity, Philosophy, Religion, Science, Truth,
Conflict between Science and Religion.

Individuals or book retailers may purchase this book
by credit card or on approved credit at
http://defineuniverse.com
(for credit approval or mail-order information, see this web site).

ISBN 0-9660858-8-4 (hardback)

BDS Publications,
Barton Dahneke Scientific
930 Johnson Road
Palmyra, NY 14522
USA

Quotations from *Define Universe and Give Two Examples*

In human intellectual endeavor there exist three principal challenges. The first is perceiving reality, the second is discovering some system of reasoning by which reality is recognized, rationalized, made consistent, reasonable, and meaningful, and the third is selecting personal goals and purpose in life. ... We address these three challenges in this book.

Although ultimate questions are posed and answered herein with a claim that the answers are correct, *a principal objective of this book is discovery of a method capable of identifying truth.* The questions addressed and their answers are of highest interest and importance. But the essentially-related, general, philosophical problem of establishing truth is at least equally fascinating, important, and far-reaching in its impact.

More than an accounting of mere knowledge of each of the two views [science and Christianity] is attempted. To understand either, one must understand an interpretation, a significance, an essence, a valuation of import, or a *meaning* of the knowledge. Until one obtains a valid interpretation or an understanding of significance, import, essence, consequence, or meaning, one does not yet fully understand. ... comprehension of consequence, significance, or meaning represents a level of understanding deeper than a mere knowledge of facts. Any *complete* examination, comparison, and evaluation of science and Christianity must therefore be addressed at the level of meaning...

The single element missing in the scientific method, the element whose absence is fatal to obtaining absolute understanding, is an absolute *yes* answer, i.e., an adequate truth criterion. Therefore, any progress in science must occur by an incremental series of *no* answers, with each *no* answer requiring a ... new guess. And a *no* answer may appear at any time in the form of a single, established fact contradictory to a guessed theory or law so that the absence of a *no* answer may not be regarded as a *yes* answer. ... It was realization of this fact – that empiricism and reason are forever inconclusive – that caused the Greek philosophers to lament their inability to establish certain truth.

The "purifying rite" of renouncing religion in order to properly practice science indicates a lack of understanding of the independent natures of the two philosophies. In particular, it indicates a lack of knowledge of the inherent limitations of science and the complementary capability of Christianity in transcending these limitations in the discovery of truth and meaning. An exclusive focus on the meticulous, rigorous, scientific examination of only the objective, external, lowest-common-denominator, material facts leads to a denial of meaning and an ignorance or absence of awareness of real reality because important facts, the most meaningful ones, fall outside the domain-of-data of science. Science can't take us to meaning because the scientific paradigm is unaware of its realm.

To establish that a paradigm is valid, that its followers have not deluded themselves by their reasoning internal in their paradigm into falsely believing it provides truth, one must invoke an external proof, an *ostensible step.* This step externally and independently validates the system and breaks a circular chain of reasoning. In Christianity an ostensible step is available for the receiving but it seems to be unknown to most Christians and others.

While the scientific method may be viewed as a tedious, tentative, fact-by-fact unraveling of the truth of the universe, the doctrine of Christ may be regarded as jumping immediately to the bottom line, the axiomatic base, the philosophical foundation, the power of God, or "fire and the Holy Ghost." Only from this base and the access it provides to Omniscience and Omnipotence may absolutely correct understanding of facts and their meaning be established.

The need to identify the correct vision of reality has been indicated throughout this book, especially in Book II ... for the scientific view and in Book III ... for the Christian one. However, *we can relax any distinction with respect to scientific or Christian or other view of reality because reality, by its definition as the totality of all real things and events, is comprehensive, universal, and unique. Any means for discovering and establishing the nature of reality and its description – the truth – is universally useful to Christian, scientist, and all others alike.*

Contents

# indicates this section is science-and-math intensive.
part # indicates this section is partially science-and-math intensive.

Preface

In human intellectual endeavor there exist three principal challenges. The first is perceiving reality, the second is discovering some system of reasoning by which reality is recognized, rationalized, made consistent, reasonable, and meaningful, and the third is selecting personal goals and purposes in life. Perception and rationalization of reality are critical because only through them are purpose and meaning evaluated and selected. But, if purpose and meaning are to have assured and lasting value, an absolutely true understanding of reality is necessary. And absolutely true understanding lies far beyond the merely "consistent and reasonable." Other endeavors in life are less intellectual and more practical. While practical and intellectual functions of life are separable in some senses, they are not in others. We learn through practice. In fact, the most important insights, values, and meaning are discovered only through both "lived experience" and contemplation.

We address these three challenges in this book. In doing so we must answer at least one "ultimate question" pertaining to perception and rationalization of reality and its meaning. We therefore address the discovery and establishment of the real nature of reality and its description – absolute or universal truth. Many answers to ultimate questions have been proposed but establishing truth of a proposed answer has not been addressed nearly so often. Yet identifying or establishing truth is an essential requirement for determining value of an answer, especially one to an ultimate question which is the type simultaneously most important and most difficult to answer.

Because discovery and identification of truth are deep and far-reaching in their importance, we examine two prominent *philosophies*, *systems of belief,* or *paradigms* widely held as "standards of truth." (The terms philosophy, system of belief, and paradigm are used equivalently in this book and are thus interchangeable. For examples, one system of belief is science and many others may be generically categorized as religion.) In this book we consider the strengths and weaknesses of science on the one hand and of one type of religion, namely, Christianity, on the other. In each case we examine the utility and power of the philosophy for discovering and establishing truth utilizing the paradigm's own terms, beliefs, and practices.

Religion has often been regarded as a philosophical "weak sister" of science, a belief supported by widely encountered materialistic bias. We argue in this book on the basis of logic, reason, and faith that Christianity is instead by far the philosophically "stronger sister." Many have long held, solely on the basis of faith, the view that Christianity is the more powerful philosophy. Others would prefer a comparison based exclusively on facts, logic, and reason. However, no careful comparison can ignore any of the elements of facts, logic, reason, and faith, all essential components of both science and Christianity and, indeed, of any philosophy. Thus, our comparison considers and is based on facts, logic, reason, and faith.

Physics and mathematics are generally regarded as the most carefully and exactly developed subjects in all philosophy, as well as highly practical and useful tools. This conclusion is supported and celebrated in a summary of the history, nature, and utility of important discoveries in science and mathematics. But, philosophical weaknesses in science or materialism are now beginning to be widely recognized. Both theoretical and experimental discoveries in physics over the last four decades indicate long-held beliefs in this field must be rescued from contradiction or abandoned. Similarly, discoveries within the last 75 years have forced long-held certainties in mathematics to be abandoned. Unexpected failures of or uncertainty about long-held, fundamental beliefs in science and mathematics indicate the discovery of truth by logical deduction and scientific methodology is more difficult than had been supposed and no better than tentative. Such developments in two of the most carefully and rigorously developed fields in philosophy do not bode well for other areas of philosophy and they therefore merit careful examination.

Traditional understanding in religion is also being revised, suggesting here, as well, uncertainty in past or present belief and practice. Ideally, revision is driven by new information and newly deduced implications. New information has appeared over the last century or so through publication of scholarly studies (translations and analyses) of ancient documents to provide improved understanding of history and the Bible. The Dead Sea Scrolls[1] and the Book of Enoch[2] are examples. Likewise, as is being ever more widely recognized, the 170-year-old revelations and sacred writings of the "Mormon" prophet Joseph Smith, Jr., are having broad-scope impact on understanding of Biblical principles. If Smith's claim that he was appointed and empowered by God as His modern-day prophet and seer is valid, this impact should be expected, eventually influencing "non-Mormon" thinking because, quoting one of his revelations, "truth embraceth truth." Implications of some of Smith's profound teachings as well as those of many other Christian writers are examined herein. Thus, in examining the relationship of science and Christianity we draw from scientific and traditional Christian sources, from Smith's writings, from C. S. Lewis' insightful and delightful sermons and addresses, and from many others.

This book contains several parallel themes. It is unusual because of the unusual nature of either some of the individual themes or of their combinations. Themes and unusual features of this book are now delineated, but not in any order of appearance or priority since the themes are interwoven throughout.

- - - - -

(1) Christianity is described by contrasting it with science and mathematics, a powerful literary device that allows significance, utility, and dint of elusive, delicate-but-mighty concepts of Christianity to be better recognized, assimilated, and appreciated. This device is powerful because stark but subtle contrasts exist between both the scopes and capabilities of (a) science and mathematics and (b) Christianity.

(2) Popular-level accounts of recent results in mathematics and physics and some of the new philosophical positions they imply or support are presented. Necessary components of these accounts are histories of selected topics in mathematics and science. These accounts are useful for two reasons: they illustrate the nature, utility, and limitations of science and mathematics and allow significance of recent uncertainty in their traditional beliefs to be better appreciated. Similarly, certain corrupted Christian beliefs, the original uncorrupted beliefs, and justifications of their classifications are considered.

On balance, Christianity is supported and strengthened relative to science in these accounts. Indeed, by examination of both paradigms we shall discover that according to these paradigms the scientific method cannot provide any certain principle, theory, or law while, in contrast, the Christian paradigm can. However, the position taken is not "Christianity wins over science" nor can it be since the two positions are essentially complementary. Rather, the position taken is "Christianity and science together provide useful, complementary utilities." Nevertheless, we conclude on the basis of arguments presented that Christianity must be regarded as the stronger philosophical sister, the philosophy that should control motivation and direction.

(3) Science and Christianity are two topics often treated together and usually, in our time, the treatment attempts to harmonize and consolidate them rather than treat them as adversarial. Nevertheless, in their fundamental methods and practices they are inherently adversarial[3] and it is important to recognize consequent adversity and its origin, sometimes only perceived and sometimes real.

The natural adversarial relationship of science and religion is apparent in an evolution versus creation debate, the current-day version of a much earlier "scientific revolution" against religion now 400-years old. In medieval times the Catholic Church held an elaborate, rigid dogma that specified "correct" understanding of religion and philosophy (including science). Restrictions in "proper" thinking imposed by the Church were challenged simultaneously by a scientific revolution and a religious reformation in the sixteenth and seventeenth centuries. As a result of the latter movement many found themselves members of new Protestant churches. By this mechanism, restrictions in permitted thinking were relaxed. Catholic-Church dogma was eventually moderated, removing many limitations. One detail we address is that early restriction on freedom of thought imposed on Catholics should be regarded as unsanctioned fiat by individual leaders, contrary to official policy.

In any case, from this historical "conflict between science and religion" and the evolution-creation debate, there exists today a vague, widely-held notion that some essential, fundamental conflict occurs between science and religion and that religion is somehow fundamentally flawed. Sources of information that contribute to this notion are rigid religious dogmas on the one side and, on the other, public school curricula, news media reporting, and dozens of other information sources that generally contain a materialistic bias in presenting only scientific views on various issues. Indeed, in the United States and elsewhere a disestablishment of religious (Christian) knowledge and belief is occurring in government controlled functions.

As we shall discover by thorough comparative examination, *no conflict exists between careful conclusions of science and of Christianity*. Fundamental differences in these two paradigms make their conclusions essentially independent of one another. Because they employ *different methodologies* to deal with *different primary evidential realms*, science and Christianity as philosophical systems are only complementary despite their natural adversity. In fact, because these fundamental differences in the two paradigms remain largely unrecognized, communication in debates pitting science against Christianity is frequently no better than partial, making the two *seem* adversarial in the sometimes exercised exchanges about the "actual" meaning of this or that term or the "real" significance of one event or another.

To understand that the two philosophies complement one another, we examine how they differ, down to their very foundations. Upon understanding their philosophical bases and different primary realms of experience or evidence and the consequent differences in their philosophical capabilities and priorities, causes of misunderstanding and miscommunication between advocates of each become readily apparent. Miscommunication and apparent conflict will persist until such fundamental understanding of the two systems is broadly realized. Until then, science and Christianity will be discussed in a "common language" when "different vocabularies" are often being used. (We also touch in this book on a similar problem: difficulty in communication between Christians of different denominations.) The complementary relationship of science and a Christian view immediately and spontaneously emerges from the insights apparent from consideration of the two philosophies and their different evidential realms.

(4) More than an accounting of mere knowledge of each of the two views is attempted. To understand either, one must understand an interpretation, a significance, an essence, a valuation of import, or a *meaning* of the knowledge. Until one obtains a valid interpretation or an understanding of significance, import, consequence, essence, or meaning, one does not yet fully understand.

As *meaning* and *comprehension of meaning* are important themes in this book but may be somewhat obscure concepts to some readers, we consider an example or two to illustrate meaning and its importance.

One can recite the steps of the scientific method or the articles of belief of a particular faith without fully understanding either science or the faith. One may understand all the facts but not the meaning. To comprehend meaning one must first invest effort to discover the consequence, significance, and value of the facts. And such "lived-experience" effort becomes part of their significance. For instance, a common experience of a student learning statistical mechanics may be described as a threefold process. On first encounter, the formalism seems complex and confusing. On a second, it begins to make some sense. On a third, the student fully grasps the concepts and wonders what caused his or her original confusion. The significance of and satisfaction in the accomplishment reside not merely in the newly acquired ability to use statistical mechanics but also in the success of having accomplished a difficult task. Indeed, the more difficult and beneficial a task, the greater the personal satisfaction and meaning found in its accomplishment.

Realization of meaning in principles of faith also requires effort. In such cases understanding may come through a divine response to a supplicant's sincere application of a certain principle of faith. Until such application and response, any deep meaning of the principle remains entirely outside the individual's experience and beyond his or her vision. What was originally an intellectual object with no associated feeling and little significance was only afterward beheld, through newly discovered feeling and associated realization of significance, as important, powerful, and rich in meaning. And the individual's effort itself becomes the personal, enabling part of his or her newly discovered understanding. For instance, an important meaning of faith in Christ is obtained through service motivated by Christ-like love (charity).

Such motivation is declared by Paul[4] to be the highest aspiration and Christ Himself teaches that service leads to greatness in the words

> whosoever will be great among you, let him be your minister; And whosoever will be chief among you, let him be your servant: Even as the Son of Man came not to be ministered unto, but to minister, and to give his life a ransom for many.[5]

While the prescription of service is immediately understood, comprehension of the deeper meaning of faith-inspired service and its proper motivation – love of Christ and Christ-like love of others – are acquired only in experience and feeling obtained through the habit of giving service because of one's faith in Christ. To say "I have faith in Christ" is not enough to know Him and become Christ-like in desire. Only as we follow Him in effort or works do we become Christ-like in our nature.

These illustrations indicate that comprehension of consequence, significance, or meaning represents a level of understanding deeper than a mere knowledge of facts. Any *complete* examination, comparison, and evaluation of science and Christianity, or religion in general, must therefore be addressed at the level of meaning, as we seek to do in this book.

(5) To comprehend meaning, one must pay required costs in developing capacities that are the basis or *precursors* of *comprehension of meaning*. Comprehension of meaning is therefore generally unique, personal, and subjective, depending on the presence and strength of precursors developed by an individual. How, then, is one to comprehend meaning perceived by another? Generally speaking, one does not in any complete manner. But, to the extent one has developed the necessary precursors, one may perceive at least a partial sense of meaning perceived by another through shared experiences or by mentally and emotionally placing one's self in the other's situation. The more knowledge, values, beliefs, and feelings one shares with another, the more the shared situation and realization of the other, the truer the perception of that person's meaning – for only through an individual's knowledge, values, beliefs, feelings, and precursors is meaning generated and perceived.

With these thoughts we touch on the basis of meaning and, therefore, the basis of differences in meaning between science and Christianity or, for that matter, between any two philosophies, systems of belief, or paradigms. This basis was well articulated by American philosopher and psychologist William James who wrote

> The whole universe of concrete objects, as we know them, swims ... for all of us in a wider and higher universe of abstract ideas, that lend it its significance. As time, space, and the [luminiferous] ether [a quantity believed to exist in James' day] soak through all things, so (we feel) do abstract and essential goodness, beauty, strength, significance, justice, soak through all things good, strong, significant, and just.
>
> Such ideas, and others equally abstract, form the background for all our facts, the fountain-head of all the possibilities we conceive of. They give its 'nature,' as we call it, to every special thing. Everything we know is 'what' it is by sharing in the nature of one [or more] of these abstractions. We can never look directly at them, for they are bodiless and featureless and footless, but we grasp all other things by their means, and in handling the real world we should be stricken with helplessness in just so far forth as we might lose these mental objects, these adjectives and adverbs and predicates and heads of classification and conception.

> This absolute determinability of our minds by abstractions is one of the cardinal facts in our human constitution. Polarizing and magnetizing us as they do, we turn towards them and from them, we seek them, hold them, hate them, bless them, just as if they were so many concrete beings. And beings they are, beings as real in the realm which they inhabit as the changing things of sense are in the realm of space.[6]

The origin of differences in matters of philosophy is differences individuals hold in their abstract concepts, including differences in the assigned priorities of these concepts, by which all things receive their meanings.

After describing essential Christian precursors (abstract concepts) of meaning, the situations and qualities of several faithful Christians are described. These individuals proved their deep devotion to Christ by their responses to challenging situations they willingly faced. In reading these historical accounts the reader is invited to vicariously sense the meaning these Christians experienced by "adopting" one or more of them and attempting to perceive and feel the experience as they did.

(6) A principal theme of this book regards our personal opportunity and responsibility as *agents in search of truth* seeking the attitude and precursors required to most fully understand meaning. Awareness of meaning and feeling only thus obtained allows us to perceive Christ's devotion to us and leads to understanding of the deepest meaning of all – knowing Christ. Such knowledge is of highest importance because, as I propose and argue in this book, the order in human afterlife or the *order of heaven*, the governing principle of heaven, is *mutual devotion* based on one's knowledge of Christ. In heaven, and even on earth for heavenly-type persons, devotion to Christ and His Father and their devotion to us *motivates and controls behavior.*

(7) This book is primarily written for a very specific audience – my family, namely, my wife, our children and grandchildren and their spouses, and our nieces and nephews and their spouses and children, as well as later generations that will one day succeed them. In case any of them wonder what I believe and what I stand for, a written record now exists. My desire to make a statement to my family, of what I believe and why, has been the principal motivation for this book.

And perhaps others will find this book interesting and useful. I sincerely hope so. In this hope it is offered to the general public so any, especially of my engineer and scientist friends, may have an opportunity to read it. But most readers, including those of my family, will not fully plumb all the depths of this book in a single reading. This book was not written to entertain and distract but to inform, challenge, inspire, and motivate. Multiple readings of some sections and further study of science/ mathematics and, especially, of scripture are intended and advised.

- - - - -

If this book presents only one intellectual and spiritual vision, that of a Christian embracing powerful concepts provided by the Bible, Book of Mormon, and Joseph Smith, as well as by science and philosophy, I hope it is interesting and useful in providing this vision. My selection and treatment of concepts is certainly not traditional and my contrast-centered account of science and Christianity provides enhanced understanding of both. Preparation of this book for a knowledgeable audience, in particular, careful justification of conclusions for such an audience, forced me to find weaknesses and gaps in my data and thinking. Through research I have strengthened these weaknesses and closed these gaps. But I found no flaw in the basic philosophy I describe and, indeed, my faith in it has been reinforced through discovery that its scope and power are broader, deeper, and more compelling than I had realized.

This book is written for a reader having no special preparation in science or mathematics. Nevertheless, I have included interesting tidbits which will be new to most professional scientists, some even to expert physicists. The text is self-contained and fully explanatory. In endnotes and appendices I include formulas, figures, and tables to provide enhanced understanding for those capable in or tolerant of mathematics and science. If you are not mathematically inclined, just skip the few formulas in the text. You may generally do so with little penalty in understanding the essential gist of the material presented.[7] However, only high-school-level mathematics is utilized in the text, all higher-level mathematical treatment being restricted to endnotes and appendices. And in every case the discussion is at a basic level so that *an interested reader without special training may learn essential concepts of mathematics and physics.* Only brief discussions of general relativity, Bohr's atomic theory, Bell's theorem, and thermodynamics and entropy even approach being intense in a mathematical or scientific sense because in these cases a little effort returns a large dividend in insight. And yet even in these cases the mathematical formulas may be skipped. The equations are displayed and some details of them discussed but, beyond those details, understanding of the equations is not required.

Likewise, no knowledge of scripture is required. I have included many quotations and citations of scripture for the interested reader as well as interesting tidbits in the form of more complete interpretations of Bible passages that will be new to most Christians. Readers who have prepared will benefit from their effort and the quotations and citations are included for these readers and for all readers who wish to use them. Scriptural preparation or preparation in matters of faith is just as essential to understanding a Christian view of reality as preparation in mathematics and science is to understanding a scientific one. The level of *meaning* one perceives in reading this book and in life itself depends on preparation in matters of faith. But even the most unprepared reader will, because of contrasts we consider between science and Christianity, perceive a sense of the meaning we address if he or she makes an attempt.

While we're comparing Christianity and science we also compare Christianity and Christianity, viz., we compare a few orthodox Christian and "Mormon" beliefs against the Bible standard. However, multiple interpretations of Biblical texts are often possible so that an adequate truth criterion is essential to reaching a reliable conclusion in any such comparison. A powerful truth criterion exactly for such use is described herein. It is simultaneously Biblical, rational, and mystical (in the special way we use this last term[8]). In the spirit of both science and Christianity one establishes truth by examining the evidence *using a reliable truth criterion*, it being the key to discovery of truth. We shall argue that for rational and mystical alike, only one adequate truth criterion exists, the one described in this book.

A few comments on terminology are necessary. I use the terms *materialism* and *science* to represent materialism or empiricism based ultimately on objective, reproducible, material facts. But according to scripture, spirits, angels, and God are material, but more "refined" so as to be invisible to humans in our present state.[9]

Likewise, *omnipotence* is used in a classical Christian sense excepting that God will not do "just anything." If one accepts human free will or agency, one denies that God has all power, i.e., an individual has power to resist God and God will not force him or her. Also, "Mormons," for example, fundamentally reject *ex nihilo* creation, believing rather that God *organized* existing space and matter in His creation of the universe. Subtleties in our use herein of "God's omniscience" cause it to differ slightly from traditional Christian usage by, e.g., Boethius, Augustine, and Calvin.[10] Some Greek-influenced theologies based on reason can demonstrate certain propositions including the existence of God. But we argue that perception and reason alone, without help from a higher level, are insufficient to reach any indubitable conclusion.

In the interest of clarity I often repeat myself. This aspect of style derives from my disdain for lost or invisible antecedents that completely disrupt continuity and may introduce confusion. It thus derives from my scientific writing habit, which I can only partially abandon, in which clarity of expression, rigor, and instruction are regarded as the paramount qualities to be pursued rather than elegance of presentation.

The many references to the Bible refer to the King James Version. The Book of Mormon, Doctrine and Covenants, and Pearl of Great Price are also cited. All four books are published by The Church of Jesus Christ of Latter-day Saints, Salt Lake City, Utah, and these four books together are regarded by members of this church (the "Mormons") as the canonical body of scripture. The common element of the four books is their focus on Jesus Christ as the predicted Messiah who came among mankind two millennia ago and is about to come again. The latter, pending event gives great urgency to the topics addressed in the canonical body of scripture and in this book.

Square brackets [...] when used in a quotation contain my addition or suggestion.

I thank those who have assisted me as my teachers. In addition to my excellent, beloved teachers who taught me during my formal training, I regard the authors I have quoted and cited in this book as my teachers, especially those repeatedly cited.

I also thank my friends who have read drafts of all or part of this book and provided valuable advice and encouragement. These individuals are David Anderson, Timothy A. Bancroft, Jeffrey A. Clark, Barton S. Dahneke, Ellen Dahneke, Dale S. Dallon, David Day, John A. Fahnestock, William Evenson, Terryl Givens, H. T. Goodwill, Sarah Dahneke Hedengren, Richard Holzapfel, Mike Kearns, Truman G. Madsen, and Donald R. Snow. I also thank Timothy Bancroft, Jeffrey Clark, Sharon Clark, William Evenson, and Donald Snow for valuable guidance pertaining to source material. William Evenson was particularly generous in his help in both guiding me to important source materials and editing. I told him more than once that he should be writing this book instead of me because I think his book would be better. David Day was especially generous in leading me through the entire publication process, like a combination production editor and software instructor, for which I am grateful.

I especially thank the Silent Coauthor of this book for His responses to my many requests for help. Everything good and true came directly or indirectly from Him. The rest is my personal views and endnote speculations, so identified.

Read well, learn and follow truth, and receive joy.

B. E. D.
Palmyra, New York

References and Notes for the Preface.

[1] For information on the Dead Sea Scrolls see www.imj.org.il/shrine/.

[2] Laurence, Richard (editor and translator from the Ethiopic), *The Book of Enoch the Prophet,* Kegan Paul, Trench & Co., London, 1883. Charles, R. H. (editor and translator), *The Book of Enoch,* Clarendon Press, Oxford, 1893. Knibb, Michael A. (editor and translator), *The Ethiopic Book of Enoch,* Clarendon Press, Oxford, 1978. Milik, J. T., *Aramaic Fragments of Qumran Cave 4,* Clarendon Press, Oxford, 1976, 167. Nibley, Hugh, *Enoch The Prophet,* Deseret Book Co. and FARMS, Salt Lake City, UT, 1986.

The Book of Enoch was a part of both the Jewish and early Christian Bible, located after the Book of Job. It was by far the oldest of all books in the Bible, having been preserved during the flood by Noah in his ark. Jews abandoned it shortly after the time of Christ and Christians followed about halfway through the third century AD. It was banned from the sacred canon of scripture in the fourth century AD, a time of other radical changes in Christian belief. One instance of these radical changes is the Nicene Creed originating as Christian doctrine with the Roman emperor Constantine at the council at Nicaea he convened and presided over in 325 AD. Until the mid-third century AD, the Book of Enoch was regarded as authentic and sacred (see introduction to Laurence's translation for evidence on this claim). Ethiopian Christians, however, long retained this Book in their Bible and it was "rediscovered" there in 1773. Although it has been translated into English by the several translators listed above, the Book of Enoch is neither widely known nor appreciated among English speaking people, no doubt because of its unusual imagery. Nevertheless, Nibley cites 128 teachings of the New Testament that come from the Book of Enoch with many of these listed by Laurence in the introduction to his translation. Christ and His apostles often quoted Enoch. But in only one quotation in the New Testament, Jude 1:14-15, is the Book of Enoch actually mentioned in our present Bible.

[3] In science one observes, thinks, and deduces while in Christianity one is told what to believe and do. Only in the latter is discovery of *Who-what*-and-*why* reality and meaning encouraged or possible.

[4] *Bible,* 1 Corinthians 13.

[5] *Bible,* Matthew 20:26-28.

[6] James, William, *The Varieties of Religious Experience,* Mentor Books, New York, 1958, 60.

[7] Why include equations when they can be ignored? Because they give the reader an opportunity to learn about important topics: mathematics and science. I quote from British novelist C. P. Snow who wrote *The Two Cultures* (Cambridge University Press, 1964). C. P. Snow was trained at Cambridge as a physicist and then became a writer. He had a foot planted firmly in each of two cultures. "As a result of this cultural dichotomy, I believe the intellectual life of the whole of Western society is increasingly being split into two polar groups. ...

"At one pole we have the literary intellectuals who, incidently, while no one was looking, took to referring to themselves as 'intellectuals' as though there were no others. ... at the other, scientists; and, as the most representative, the physical scientists. Between the two lies a gulf of mutual incomprehension.

"The scientists' culture is intensive, rigorous, and constantly in action. Their culture contains a great deal of argument, usually more rigorous and almost always at a higher conceptual level than literary arguments ... scientists are very intelligent men. Their culture is in many ways an exacting and admirable one. ... Of books, though, there is very little; of novels, history, poetry, plays, almost nothing. It isn't that scientists are not interested in the psychological or moral or social life. In the social life they certainly are interested, more than most of us. In the moral, they are by and large the soundest group of intellectuals we have; there is a moral component right in the grain of science itself, and almost all scientists form their own judgements on the moral life. It isn't that they lack the interests. It is more that the whole literature of the traditional culture doesn't seem to them to be relevant to those interests. They are, of course, dead wrong.

"But what of the other side? The nonscientific culture is impoverished, too – perhaps more seriously, because it is vainer about it. The literary intellectuals still like to pretend that the traditional culture is the whole of culture, as though the natural cultural – the sciences – didn't exist; as though the exploration of the natural order were of no interest either in its own value or its consequences; as though the scientific edifice of the physical world were not, in its intellectual depth, complexity and articulation, the most beautiful and wonderful collective work of the mind of man. Yet most nonscientists have no conception of that edifice at all.

"As with the tone-deaf, they don't know what they miss. They give a pitying chuckle at the news of scientists who have never read a major work of English literature. They dismiss them as ignorant specialists. Yet their own ignorance and their own specialization is just as startling. ... Once or twice I have been provoked and have asked the company how many of them could describe the Second Law of Thermodynamics. The response was cold; it was also negative. ...

"I now believe that if I had asked an even simpler question – such as, 'What do you mean by mass or acceleration?', which is the scientific equivalent of saying, 'Can you read?' – not more than one in ten of the highly educated would have felt that I was speaking the same language. So the great edifice of modern physics goes up, and the majority of the cleverest people in the Western world have about as much insight into it as their neolithic ancestors would have had."

[8] Many regard mysticism as pathological. A careful treatment of mysticism, which still miscasts it as somewhat negative which I believe it is not, is found in Charles A. Bennett's essay *A Philosophical Study of Mysticism* (Yale University Press, 1923). See also William James' book *The Varieties of Religious Experience,* loc. cit.

[9] *Doctrine and Covenants* 131:7-8.

[10] I thank Truman G. Madsen for pointing out my unmentioned yet slightly unconventional use of "omnipotence," "omniscience," and other similar terms.

A pencil sketch of the author drawn by Eugene Legend on 23 March 1973.

Dedication

For Marilyn,

...

Barton,
Marshall,
Marit,
Christa,
Ellen,
Sarah,
Rachel,

...

Jacquelyn Renee,
Scott Jacob,
Theresa Marie,
Elizabeth Anne,
Jonathan Scott,
Jessica Lynn,
Samuel Jesse,
Rulon Christian,
Allison Mary,
Barton Andrew,
Madeline Angel,
Andrew Marshall,
Christian James,
Hannah Abigail,
Rachel Madison,
Eric John,
Isaac Marshall,
Mary Marit,
Asher Moss,
and other grandchildren I don't yet know, but also already love, and

...

Lani,
Susan,
and
Jesse.

Definitions of a few terms as they are used in this book.

agnosticism - belief that the existence of any ultimate reality (such as God) is unknown and possibly unknowable so that study of and belief in it are postponed.

atheism - disbelief in existence of deity or doctrine or dogma that there is no deity.

belief - a state or habit of mind in which trust is placed in some idea or object.

Buddhism - a religion or philosophy derived from teachings of Gautauma Buddha.

Christianity - the religion instituted by Jesus Christ based on His teachings as provided by Him and His authorized servants.

Hinduism - a body of social, cultural, and religious beliefs and practices native to the Indian subcontinent.

humanism - a doctrine, attitude, or way of life focused on human interests or values, especially in the philosophy asserting the dignity and worth of man and his capacity for self-realization through reason, usually excluding supernaturalism.

Islam - the monotheistic Moslem religion of which Mohammed was the prophet.

Judaism - a religion developed among the ancient Hebrews based on belief in one God who is creator, ruler, and redeemer of the universe.

materialism - a theory that physical matter is the only reality and that all being and phenomena can be explained as manifestations of matter. It is therefore focused on material rather than intellectual or spiritual being and phenomena.

mysticism - a mystical union or direct communion with ultimate reality or God.

omnipotence - an attribute of God denoting the state or quality of possessing almighty, unlimited, infinite power, authority, and influence except as (self-) restricted as described on page xiv.

omniscience - an attribute of God denoting the possessing of universal, absolute, unbounded, and infinite knowledge, awareness, and understanding.

paradigm - a pattern, set of rules (such as assumptions, axioms, and laws), or model one may utilize to understand reality and the universe or some portion thereof.

philosophy - a system of beliefs, concepts, and attitudes of an individual or group.

scholasticism - philosophy that dominated Western Christian civilization from the 9th to the 17th centuries. It was based upon patristic writings and, later, on Aristotelianism. This term is now also used to represent insistence upon traditional doctrines and methods.

science - systematized knowledge of the physical universe or some portion thereof.

secularism - indifference to, rejection, or exclusion of religion or religious concepts.

Book I:

Perception of Reality

Book I:

Perception of Reality

1. Introduction - Where Am I? Where or Who Do I Want To Be?

I recommend one of three strategies for a first-time read of this book. For the science-and-math tolerant I recommend a straight read beginning with the preface. For the science-and-math shy I also recommend a straight read but skipping all or part of the science-and-math-intensive sections marked with # or part #. If one wants to begin with an overview I recommend the preface and Chapters 1, 5, 12, 16, 17, and 19.

Teenagers are forbidden to read this book, for two reasons. First, I am merciless in pointing out inadequacies of teenagers (and most others). The second reason is revealed later. Nevertheless, if you are one of my children or grandchildren, this book was written for you.[1] I also had in mind my fellow engineers and scientists and those of the general public interested in a searching, critical comparison of science and Christianity. But, as you will see, a few parts are directed especially to my family.

We consider in this book the questions in the above title, beginning in the Preface. (Please read it now if you haven't already.) Adequate answers to these fundamental questions require truth. Hence, a principal topic of this book is *establishing truth*. In making choices it is not enough to know just any old truth. To make the best choices we must understand values and their meaning. Such choices thus depend on *understanding of meaning*, which reveals where one is, allows an informed choice of where or who one would like to be, and indicates how to get there. We therefore seek in this book an understanding of both truth and meaning.

To obtain an understanding of truth and meaning we must consider a hierarchy of facts, knowledge, understanding, meaning and the associated topics of perception and truth criterion. Because this scope is impossibly broad for a single volume, we limit consideration to two philosophies, paradigms, or systems of belief: science and Christianity, using contrasts between them to enhance under-standing of both.

To indicate different natures of these two perspectives, the title of this book presents a rhetorical enigma. *Universe* is defined as all things and phenomena, observed and postulated. How can it have multiple examples? It can and does. The universe is neither uniformly perceived nor analyzed; neither people nor their concept of reality is so simple. A diversity in perceptions of the universe or visions of reality occurs in the minds of people because people have differing philosophies, paradigms, or systems of belief. Different philosophies *dictate* different visions of reality.

We consider in this book two universes or visions of reality, namely, the objective universe considered in science, including only material things and processes, and the broad, complete universe considered in Christianity (and other religions) that includes the subjective and spiritual in addition to the objective and material. We call the former the *material universe* and the latter the *total universe*. Between materialists and others the very scope of the universe is differently regarded.

Throughout recorded history humans have contemplated the universe and reality and sought some set of principles, rules, laws, axioms, and assumptions by which they can be rationalized. Such a set of principles, rules, laws, axioms, and assumptions is called in this book a philosophy, paradigm, or system of belief or, simply, a *system*. If such a system is to provide fundamental, broad, and reliable understanding, its scope must be complete and its validity or truth must be established. Only then can the system be regarded as correctly representing reality by providing a reliable knowledge and description of it – the truth. We take for *truth* a knowledge of things as they were, as they are, and as they are to be.[2] Then *reality*, described by truth, is the sum of all real things and events as they were, are, and are to be.

While we no more than mention many philosophies and barely consider only a few besides the two classes we focus on, it is clear in even cursory examination that philosophy contains difficulty and danger. Indeed, we divide philosophies into a higher or lower category according to awareness of and willingness to address this difficulty and danger. Two classes of philosophy, *science* and *religion*, appear to be most capable in and are historically accepted for defining truth. Lacking ability in the author and space in a short book to thoroughly and broadly address either science or religion, we further limit our focus to physics and Christianity and the task is still formidable. Physics provides an excellent prototype of science and comparisons and contrasts between physics and Christianity often apply quite generally to science and religion. Vision of reality as provided by science or materialism and as influenced by different religious beliefs, particularly different Christian beliefs, are examined in Books II and III. However, we begin our search for truth considering pitfalls to be avoided, the difficulty and danger encountered in philosophy.

Recognizing Confusion in a Broad Spectrum of Human Thought

Many systems have been embraced by different individuals and cultures. Popular systems of today include religions such as Christianity, Judaism, Islam, Buddhism, Hinduism, etc. in all their many divisions and sects as well as various philosophical methods, movements, and schools of thought including naïve Baconianism, social constructivism, postmodern criticism, deconstructionism, falsificationism, holism, idealism, pessimistic induction, materialism and positivism in their various forms, naturalism, operationalism, pragmatism and humanism, anti-, conjectural, internal, ontological, and metaphysical realism, reductionism, epistemic relativism, relativism, unity of science, secularism, and supervenience.[3] Each method, school, or system is generally consistent with the facts recognized in it. Over time each, especially of the older systems, has been refined to remove inconsistency. Yet this spectrum contains different, apparently contradictory views of reality. *Internal consistency is necessary but not sufficient to establish the validity of a system*, a claim we shall hereafter illustrate and justify. To establish truth, powerful methodology must be discovered and used, methodology that for this reason is extremely valuable and important.

Different systems utilize knowledge contained in different sets of facts and (without surprise) a system is consistent with the basis or set or kind of facts the system utilizes. The function of a paradigm is to provide exactly such a result: knowledge and even understanding by and within the context of the paradigm. Thus, a scientific analysis or interpretation is consistent with science and a Christian analysis with Christianity. In the Western world these two systems are the ones most widely embraced and we focus on science and Christianity in this book. They sometimes appear to indicate different realities because they are based on different principles and laws (methodology) and they regard different evidence (kinds of facts) as "legitimate." Different evidence and different methodology lead to different conclusions. In general, different paradigms or systems reveal different visions of reality and the vision of reality one discovers therefore depends on the system one utilizes. C. S. Lewis described well this property of philosophical systems in his book *Miracles* wherein he states "What we learn from experience depends on the kind of philosophy we bring to experience."[4] We add that what we learn also depends on what scope of experience we consider, which may be implicitly restricted by a philosophy, paradigm, or system of belief.

Systems based in science have had considerable success in broadening knowledge of connections among observed facts. However, to be comprehensive in scope and reliable and to provide fundamental, deep understanding – down to the level of causation or of primary or first cause – a system must be based on *absolute or universal truth.* No system is universally accepted as able to provide broad, deep, and fully reliable understanding. A scientific paradigm, for instance, can provide knowledge of and relate many facts but neither understanding to such a broad and deep level nor absolute reliability.

We humans have developed a broad spectrum of thought. The primary challenge in considering this spectrum is not to discover which vision of reality results from one paradigm or another and what their relative merits are, although such knowledge is useful and to some degree necessary. Rather, the greatest need is to determine which paradigm, if any, provides true understanding of the real, one-and-only reality. To move beyond the common, inconclusive *no*-versus-*no* stalemates in debates over the nature of reality according to different paradigms, such as science-versus-religion debates, some method or system must be established as valid and used to obtain a reliable knowledge and description of reality – the truth.

While a chain of reasoning may seem to be consistent throughout a broad range of results, apparently providing compelling evidence of its truth, we argue that most such chains capable of forming the basis of a comprehensive paradigm are inevitably circular, i.e., the paradigm depends upon or refers to itself. A paradigm usually inherits a view of reality based on itself or on an earlier version of itself, as we shall see, or otherwise employs circular reasoning. The issue of circularity makes proof of veracity of a paradigm difficult if not impossible while the related question of veracity of the vision of reality the paradigm imposes makes such a proof essential.

An illustration may be useful here (more elaborate illustrations are provided in Chapters 10, 13, and 16 and in Appendix A). If a person denies that spiritual things and phenomena exist and incorporates this belief into his or her paradigm, this person will surely never be convinced otherwise by experience until he or she changes this belief or paradigm and the intuition based thereon. Because validity of experience is judged by paradigm, experience with the spiritual will be denied and explained away by invoking other possible (and impossible! – see Appendix A) explanations. The boon of a paradigm is the consistent, broad vision of reality it provides. Its bane is the restricted, incomplete, or incorrect vision it imposes.

To establish that a paradigm is valid, that its followers have not deluded themselves by their reasoning internal in their paradigm into falsely believing it provides truth, one must invoke an external proof, a *reality test* in science and an *ostensible step*[5] in Christianity, that externally and independently validates the system and breaks any circularity in reasoning. In science a continual comparison of thought and observation provides the reality test. In Christianity this same reality test and an additional ostensible step are available for the receiving, but the latter, more important test seems to be unknown to most Christians and others. In view of its importance in understanding reality, broad ignorance of it is an unfortunate consequence of history. We attempt herein a remedy of this unfortunate consequence by illuminating the availability, value, and necessity of this ostensible-step method.

Reliable knowledge of reality or demonstrated truth requires finding answers to deep or "ultimate" questions using a method by which the truth of the answers is established. Finding such a method and discovering where it leads are the stories of this book. The quest we pursue is discovering and verifying the one, universal reality and knowledge of it, the absolute truth.

A quest for absolute truth is, of course, far from trivial. It has been pursued in vain by many brilliant persons in their times over millennia. Ancient Greek philosophers recognized that a method for establishing truth or a *truth criterion* was essential to reliable knowledge; they also recognized they possessed no such method.

> *Anaxagoras* plaintively exclaims, 'Nothing can be known, nothing can be learned, nothing can be certain, [sense] is limited, intellect is weak, life is short.' *Xenophanes* tells us that it is impossible for us to be certain even when we utter the truth. *Parmenides* declares that the very constitution of man prevents him from ascertaining absolute truth. *Empedocles* affirms that all philosophical and religious systems must be unreliable, because we have no criterion by which to test them. *Democritus* asserts that even things that are true cannot impart certainty to us; that the final result of human inquiry is the discovery that man is incapable of absolute knowledge; that, even if the truth be in his possession, he cannot be certain of it. *Pyrrho* bids us reflect on the necessity of suspending our judgement of things, since we have no criterion of truth; so deep a distrust did he impart to his followers, that they were in the habit of saying, 'We assert nothing; no, not even that we assert nothing.' *Epicurus* taught his disciples that truth can never be determined by reason. *Arcesilaus*, denying both intellectual and sensuous knowledge, publicly avowed that he knew nothing, not even his own ignorance! The general conclusion to which Greek philosophy came was this – that, in view of the contradiction of the evidence of the senses, we cannot distinguish the true from the false; and such is the imperfection of reason, that we cannot affirm the correctness of any philosophical deduction.[6] (italics added)

Other, more modern thinkers have reached similar conclusions, as will later be described. But somehow most have forgotten this early understanding of the nature of human knowledge. We have progressed far in scientific knowledge in the intervening twenty-five centuries, and most people do not therefore recognize the continuing state of human ignorance of which the ancient Greek philosophers were so aware. An unrecognized state of ignorance of truth is *where most of us are*. And the most disabling ignorance is that which is unrecognized. Thinking one knows obviates a search for truth. Most people are unaware of or unconcerned about unnecessary ignorance of the most fundamental and essential kind of knowledge. The thinking of most still lags behind ancient Greek thought now twenty-five centuries old.

The universal and individual challenge of finding, establishing, and following absolute truth is the primary task we face in life and how well we meet it will be the measure of our success. Although awareness of this challenge dates to antiquity and its solution has been recognized as both essential and elusive in human attempts to discover a powerful and reliable philosophy, most people today are ignorant of and seem indifferent to the challenge, content to consider less demanding and less consequential matters. While such a state is natural, we refute any justification of it. Ignoring this challenge is a dereliction of personal duty and an infidelity to one's self and others. And, ironically, one does not have to remain in ignorance, if that is where one is. And most, like the ancient Greeks, are, whether they realize it or not or whether they care or not. Each person can discover and establish absolute truth through his or her own, direct experience.[7] Moreover, discovering truth for one's self is challenging but also pleasant, rewarding, stimulating, and even exciting.

Agents in Search of Truth

Among all creatures in the known universe, humans are unique. Inanimate objects such as rocks and trees merely follow natural laws with no apparent expression of either intelligence or choice.[8] Creatures such as insects, fish, fowls, and animals excepting humans, although they may possess intelligence and personality and have some ability to choose, live and make choices at least partly by instinct. Humans are unique in their high level of ability to reason, understand, communicate, and choose based on substantial acquired knowledge, learned from their own experience and that of others. The life of a man or woman is entirely governed by choices he or she makes. Certainly events and conditions not chosen (rejection, divorce, loss of parents, poverty, disease, injury, tragedy, death of a loved one, war, etc.) influence one's life, but one's reaction to them, the life actually lived, is chosen.

The freedom of choice resident to a unique degree in humans is most clearly manifest in a person's occasional practice of doing one thing in spite of cognizance or feeling that he or she should do otherwise. In contrast, a rock always falls downward, a tree always grows toward light, and many creatures know only by instinct when to hibernate or migrate and when to flee or fight. Only humans appear to be fully independent to choose based on their knowledge, understanding, and, ultimately, desire.

Understanding and choosing are important capabilities. Indeed, they are arguably the defining human attributes. A person's acts are always based on choice and often a choice is postponed until more complete understanding is obtained. One can therefore define a man or woman as an *agent in search of truth*, the term *agent* implying freedom to choose and the *in search of truth* representing a person's capability and desire to discover what is most useful and beneficial to choose.[9] And because what a man or woman chooses has great influence on who he or she becomes, a person's search for truth and an inner resolve to utilize fully the knowledge it provides are both consequential and urgent.

But many a person recognizes neither the consequential nature and urgency in his or her search for truth nor has he or she developed a resolve to fully utilize truth. We consider in this book several *ultimate questions* that illustrate the importance of both discovering and choosing. Ultimate questions pertain to human origin and, as a result, to who we are, what the purpose of our mortal existence is, and why our present behavior is so consequential and our choices so rich in opportunity.

These ultimate questions are not commonly spoken of in casual conversation in current Western culture because these questions and their answers are of a private, personal-belief nature. Consequently, both questions and answers are obscure to many. However, multiple answers to some ultimate questions have been proposed, with each implying its own set of priorities in understanding and behavior.

Awareness of ultimate questions is essential because it leads to a realization and appreciation of higher philosophy. The knowledge and intelligence generally sought and obtained in the world, that pertaining to worldly activities, does not insure appreciation of higher philosophy. To illustrate, I quote German physicist Max Born (1882-1970) who won the Nobel Prize in physics in 1954 and should have shared in the 1932 Prize as well (as we shall see). Because Born was Jewish he was at grave risk in Nazi Germany and wisely fled to England; but, though remote, he remained loyal and sympathetic to friends and colleagues in Europe during the Nazi regime. He wrote

> I had believed in science not only as a way to obtain knowledge of Nature and to apply it to a better material life, but as a way to wisdom, to distinguishing between sense and nonsense; and as most wickedness is based in nonsense, on irrational thinking, I had thought that a real scientist could not do base deeds. The scientists I admired and loved, like Franck, Einstein, Rutherford, Planck, von Laue, seemed to confirm my belief. But Lindemann did base things and opened the gates of hell for other men of his type, men efficient and clever, but not profound and wise, who later became leaders in science and its application to politics and war.[10]

A challenge, then, for one seeking wisdom and truth and trying to avoid "wickedness" and "base deeds" and their undesired consequences is to discover ultimate questions and their answers, both questions and answers presently known and unknown, and determine the truth and value they contain. This challenge is philosophical in its nature and must therefore be philosophically addressed.

To discover such questions and their answers requires reliable methodology with sufficient power to establish truth, methodology we refer to as reality-test or ostensible-step methodology. Consequently, we address the question "Does science and/or Christianity provide this power?" Although ultimate questions are posed and answered herein with a claim that the answers are correct, *the principal objective of this book is description and demonstration of methodology capable of identifying truth.* The questions addressed and their answers are of highest interest and importance. But the essentially-related, general, philosophical problem of establishing truth is at least equally fascinating, important, and far-reaching in its impact.

Purpose and Practice of Philosophy

Through my work and personal interest I have developed a taste and appreciation for fundamental, rigorous understanding. In my trade as a scientist rigor is no mere luxury. I illustrate this claim with an example from my own work on the measurement of particles found in powders, slurries, and aerosols. Because of their wide use, often in technically critical and economically important applications, such particles must sometimes be manufactured with multiple properties each meeting some specification. The ability to accurately measure such particles is important to the discovery of what the desired specifications should be as well as development of adequate manufacturing and quality control processes. In addition, detection and exclusion of contamination particles may be equally important.

A strategy for accurate measurement of particles requires *a reliable theory* relating, say, particle motion to particle properties such as size, mass, and shape, where the theory is utilized with measured motion of a particle to infer particle properties. If a particle species of interest is only rarely observed, such as in the case of low-concentration contamination particles, millions of particles must be measured to adequately detect and characterize the rare species. In some cases contamination can be detrimental or fatal to product performance at a level of only one particle per million. Measurement of individual particles must be rapid (at least thousands per second) to provide a statistically significant measure of a rare particle species in an acceptable measurement time. Therefore, the strategy must be robust and the theory accurate and reliable over a broad range of particle properties and measurement conditions.

In selecting a measurement strategy critical questions arise. Is an available theory relating particle properties and particle motion sufficiently accurate for the conditions of each particle measurement? If not, can a new theory that provides adequate accuracy and breadth of application be discovered? With these questions the problem becomes philosophical, identical, in principle, with many problems throughout science and philosophy. Because the challenge posed by such questions is philosophical, the search for correct answers is philosophical and this process should therefore follow good philosophical practice.

To answer the question "What constitutes good philosophical practice?" we first consider what philosophy is about. Of course different authors have different views on what philosophy is about. One author defined philosophy as the "misuse of a terminology invented just for this purpose."[11] Georg Wilhelm Friedrich Hegel provided a more serious but no more restrictive definition of philosophy as the investigation of things by thought and contemplation. While many have sought understanding of reality, others have merely arbitrarily defined reality and its meaning. The danger of such megalomania is substantial. This kind of philosophy has caused much confusion and contention, especially in or pertaining to religion in Biblically unsupported assumptions like *ex nihilo* creation.[12] One must be careful to reject arbitrary, personal opinion of *lower philosophy* in favor of more honest, critical, and complete examination of *higher philosophy* wherein truth is recognized to exist and sought by deduction from reality.

Another serious attempt to define philosophy, in this case used primarily in the realm of science, still falls short of the higher philosophy we seek in this book. We quote from *The Problem of Knowledge* by English philosopher A. J. Ayer.

> Philosophers make statements which are intended to be true, and they commonly rely on argument both to support their own theories and to refute the theories of others; but the arguments which they use are of a peculiar character. The proof of a philosophical statement is not, or only very seldom, like the proof of a mathematical statement; it does not normally consist in formal demonstration. Neither is it like the proof of a statement in any of the descriptive sciences. Philosophical theories are not tested by observation. They are neutral with respect to particular matters of fact.
>
> That is not to say that philosophers are not concerned with facts, but they are in the strange position that all the evidence which bears upon their problems is already available to them. It is not further scientific information that is needed to decide such philosophical questions as whether the material world is real, whether objects continue to exist when they are not perceived, whether other human beings are conscious in the same sense as one is oneself. These are not questions that can be settled by experiment, since the way in which they are answered itself determines how the result of any experiment is to be interpreted. What is in dispute in such cases is not whether, in a given set of circumstances, this or that event will happen, but rather how anything at all that happens is to be described.[13]

In his book Ayer takes the view of logical positivism or logical empiricism.[13] In positivism, language and thinking are both enhanced and constrained using analysis of language to clarify and thereby legitimize descriptions of material processes and objects in terms of objective, "absolute" facts. Facts regarded as absolute include an object's color, a tone's frequency, a body's length, etc. However, the goal of making description absolutely clear contains the curious and suspicious tendencies to render science both fully comprehensible and trivial. Science achieves these properties by being reduced to only objective principles and phenomena that are clearly describable. Such reduction renders science useless in addressing anything not already clearly known. Regarding positivism Werner Karl Heisenberg (1901-1976), another German Nobel Prize winning physicist, wrote the following.

> I should consider it utterly absurd ... were I to close my mind to the problems and ideas of earlier philosophers simply because they cannot be expressed in a more precise language. ... in the final analysis, all the old religions try to express the same contents, the same relations, and all of these hinge around questions about values. The positivists may be right in thinking that it is difficult nowadays to assign a meaning to such parables. Nevertheless, we ought to make every effort to grasp their meaning, since it quite obviously refers to a crucial aspect of reality. ... [B]ut positivists will object that you are making obscure and meaningless noises, whereas they themselves are models of analytic clarity. But where must we seek for [new] truth, in obscurity or in clarity?[14]

We address positivism further in later chapters. For the present we note only that how something is described is always open to question if its meaning is not understood, and deep meaning is not defined by objective facts, though it may be indicated by such facts to one who already understands such meaning. Ignorance of purpose, cause, and consequence allows a wide latitude in descriptions, all equally deficient in these properties. Indeed, without understanding of purpose, cause, and consequence there is no understanding of meaning.

Philosophy unconstrained by reality provides neither dependable methodology nor reliable conclusions. Conclusions in lower philosophy are adopted *arbitrarily* on the basis of individual preference with no concern for truth beyond the belief that one has discovered or defined it. But reality is not defined by individual preference, royal prerogative, or democratic majority. Neither is it unconstrained as sometimes imagined in discretionary, arbitrary lower philosophy. Rather, reality is constrained to be what it is.

The adverb *arbitrarily* is insulting in philosophy when it implies insufficient basis for belief and, indeed, some philosophy deserves to be insulted. Lower philosophy does not honestly and squarely address basis of belief. That is, lower philosophy generally fails to recognize and address the concept of *truth* and how it relates thereto. But what else is philosophy about? One author writes: "It is not possible to explain in advance what philosophy is about. The best way to learn philosophy is to read the works of great philosophers."[15] But how can one identify great philosophers if it is not possible to explain in advance what philosophy is about? Kenneth Baker, S. J., has provided a better description of philosophy:

> The philosopher attempts to put order in the whole of reality or to come up with some kind of a world-picture; he does not restrict his reflection to just one aspect of reality – he explicitly considers the totality. ... There are many different philosophies but most (if not all) philosophers have striven for the same end: to give some kind of meaning to man and his universe. True, they have arrived at many different conclusions (often contradictory) but they have studied the same object (reality) and have employed the same basic method (reflection on human experience). ... The vastness of the object and the end, however, seem to exceed the capacities of human intelligence. The philosopher by definition strives for wisdom, for ultimate truth in the midst of a changing world, but no one [mortal] yet [save One] has been able adequately to grasp the whole.[16]

German astronomer Johannes Kepler (1571-1630) introduced the concept that scientific theories must agree with facts (measured data) and not *vice versa*. It is a small step from this concept to the slightly more general one – philosophy (about reality) must agree with reality and not *vice versa*. Higher (e.g., natural) philosophy is about discovering reality and establishing truth therein. Anything less is merely a sterile "language game," to use a favorite term of Ludwig Wittgenstein. The above-quoted claims of Ayer that all evidence that bears upon their problems is available to philosophers and that their theories are not tested by observation and are neutral with respect to particular matters of fact are too "freewheeling" for application in natural philosophy (science) and suggest, in an extreme inference, an arrogant, visions-of-grandeur self-image of philosophers as elite thinkers with *carte blanche* license to make any pronouncements they desire, properly embellished with cleverness and grand language in which great philosophers write and speak, and such pronouncements cannot be challenged on the basis of experience or any test, especially if no attempt is made to relate philosophy to reality or truth. Danger in such lack of discipline is a plague in philosophy.[17] It is unfortunate and frightening that undisciplined, confused philosophy has influenced and provides a basis for much belief, especially in religion when such philosophy is mixed with scripture.

Another author states: "Well-confirmed scientific results are in no need of justification via some doctrinaire philosophical theory of what truth is. The results of science aren't so much true or false as they are trustworthy or untrustworthy."[18] Ultimately, "truth" and "trustworthiness" are obtained together or neither is obtained alone according to the "doctrinaire theory of truth" we adopt in this book, namely, that "truth is knowledge of things as they are, and as they were, and as they are to be."[2] In contrast to unconstrained lower philosophy, seeking truth serves to drive higher philosophy toward the definite, reliable, and testable.

The function of philosophy we adopt herein is *not* to produce arbitrary theories or discretionary opinions having no basis in or connection to truth. Neither do we pursue merely relative understanding of the nature of reality nor defend dogma simply because we are partial to it or its school nor devise criteria and methods precisely contrived to be sufficiently vague and indefinite to accommodate (hide) ignorance. In this book we take as the function of philosophy determination of reality, truth, the best purpose, cause and consequence, discovery of deepest and highest meaning. Lower philosophy ignores or denies absolute truth thereby removing any higher purpose in such philosophy. The tasks of higher philosophy are to establish truth and extend understanding of reality, which are one and the same task. Philosophy that ignores this task in favor of theory, opinion, or dogma chosen on a basis of personal prejudice or arbitrary discretion and limited to relative thinking only propagates ignorance by displacing discovery of truth.

A Straw-person Philosopher

As a foil we invent a straw-person philosopher imagined for the purpose of knocking him or her over, discredited and humiliated. In toppling our straw person (known in former times as a straw man) we can all be gratified that evil is defeated and truth and goodness prevail. However, the straw-person philosopher we construct is a little too close to us for comfort so we topple him or her rather gently.

Advocates of lower philosophy, those who ignore or deny absolute or universal truth as an obtainable objective, are content to declare that reality coincides with their own untested, accountability-blind views, what we shall call *truth by decree*. To illustrate, consider, say, humanists and Christians. Many humanists today eschew traditional values and judgements but claim to embrace love, loyalty, kindness, service, honesty, tolerance, and inclusion, all in some ideal, remote manner. Claims of humanist and Christian groups are revealed as artificial façades when the groups collide and the pastoral principles of love, tolerance, and inclusion claimed by both sides are revealed, by behavior of one or both, to actually be arrogance, intolerance, and subversion. Observing such collisions one might conclude that humankind is engaged in an escalating ideological war between those who embrace values like love of family, allegiance to national ideals of unity and freedom, belief in God, and development of personal virtues on the one side against those who, on a claimed basis of love, kindness, honesty, and tolerance, instead embrace and promote perversions of these virtues in the form of irreverence, intolerance, and arrogance or, what is worse, living exactly these attitudes in the form of same-sex marriage, abortion, promiscuous participation in unseemly acts, and proud, belligerent, and aggressive refutation of any criticism, judgement, or lawful inhibition of such practices or beliefs. We address this ideological war involving *all* humankind in some detail in Book III.

How can we evaluate the thinking of such opposing sides, embracing either traditional values or perversions thereof, and predict their impacts on reality, their true consequences and meanings? An answer to this question reveals the destitution in value of lower philosophy. Elitist philosophers, activist judges and officials, ... who assume *carte blanche* license and think without vision, discipline, or accountability can and, apparently in some cases, would undermine order and stability. Thoughtless abandonment of proven traditions and values will cause chaos in government and society. Without traditional families and values, who will bear and care for our children? With only an artificial façade of tolerance and with complete disdain for accountability and consequence, where is good and bad, right and wrong, law and order? And with hidden agendas seeking subversion and subjugation, where is real love, honesty, and truth?

In this book we seek a vision that sees beyond lower philosophy, a vision in which we establish truth and understand reality, cause, consequence, and meaning. Without demonstration of truth, any conclusion is uncertain and arbitrary at best and may lead to complete chaos and personal and societal disaster at worst. Without adequate philosophical basis our judgements are naïve, arbitrary, and made in some measure of ignorance. An occasional "real" philosopher might smugly think that with deep and broad knowledge of (lower) philosophy, i.e., opinions of others, he or she or some like person must be the auditor of reality.[17] We also find such an attitude among groups supporting ideologies, especially extreme ones, with truth-by-decree views often regarded as "politically correct" and their advocates described as "thought police." But, rather than a truth-by-decree view, reality itself is the best auditor of philosophy about reality. In philosophical and all thinking, arbitrary judgement or opinion based on insufficient knowledge is mere *prejudice*. Only with an adequate truth criterion, experiment, experience, and contemplation thereof are our judgments properly audited by reality and based on truth rather than prejudice.

One might think that because our above inference (about philosophers with an arrogant, visions-of-grandeur self-image of elite thinkers with *carte blanche* license to make any pronouncement which cannot be challenged on the basis of any perception of reality) was described as extreme that few or none would fit this category. In fact most, if not all, people do. Consider the following two examples.

<u>*Example i*</u>

In recent debates about cultural or sociological pertinence and value of science, now called the *science wars*, a battle line has formed between nonscientist sociologists, philosophers, and cultural scholars questioning the value of science on the one side and those questioning the competence of self-appointed, nonscientist judges of science on the other. Endearing himself to scientists worldwide, Alan Sokal, a physics professor at New York University, wrote and submitted an essay entitled "Transgressing the Boundaries: Toward a Transformative Hermeneutics of Quantum Gravity" to the journal *Social Text* which published it in 1996. Loaded with recherché terms of the postmodern genre in vogue among sociologists of science and literary theorists and containing impressive mathematical-physics theorems and terminology, Sokal addressed potential political and cultural consequences of quantum-gravity theory. Sokal later revealed his essay was a hoax combining quotations from eminent scholars in absurd contexts with his own laudative but inane text. If the editors of *Social Text* weren't embarrassed, they should have been. Others have also participated in the science-wars fray. Steven Weinberg summarizes some history describing several ideological influences that have contributed to the current science-wars status.[19]

Sokal and Belgian theoretical physicist Jean Bricmont coauthored a 1996 book entitled *Imposteurs Intellectuel* which exposes well-known French social scientists and humanists in their writing of nonsense in absurd substitutions of subjective obfuscation for empirical or any other knowledge while pretending to be informed about the science they criticize. This book precipitated a Left-Bank uproar. It was translated into English as *Fashionable Nonsense: Postmodern Intellectuals' Abuse of Science.*[20] In his review of this book, Glenn Branch wrote

> ... abuse of science is rampant in postmodernist circles, both in the form of inaccurate and pretentious invocation of scientific and mathematical terminology and in the more insidious form of epistemic relativism. When Sokal and Bricmont expose Jacques Lacan's ignorant misuse of topology, or Julia Kristeva's of set theory, or Luce Irigaray's of fluid mechanics, or Jean Baudrillard's of non-Euclidian geometry, they are on safe ground; it is all too clear that these virtuosi are babbling.
>
> Their discussion of epistemic relativism – roughly, the idea that scientific and mathematical theories are mere 'narrations' or social constructions – is less convincing, however, in part because epistemic relativism is not as intrinsically silly as, say, Regis Debray's maunderings about Gödel, and in part because the authors' own grasp of the philosophy of science frequently verges on the naïve. ...[21]

Such "scholars" as these postmodernists and epistemic relativists undermine the purpose of scholarship – discovering truth. They appear to have no concern in their truth-by-decree expositions that reality should inhibit or constrain their use of fancy terminology in narrations of humanist and social structures which, therefore, are probably entirely unrealistic. Their unjustified criticisms of science reveal a condemning lack of both rigor and responsibility in their thinking that shows a disregard for even minimum standards of scholarship.

A prominent-oceanographer friend has often been approached about oceanography research by young scuba divers who thought their diving expertise gave them valuable ability. His usual comment to them was that it takes two weeks to learn scuba diving but years to learn the sciences in oceanography. By this analogy applied to the science wars, socialists and cultural scholars need to learn science before they can responsibly comment on it; apparently none yet has.

<u>Example ii</u>

Uncomfortably closer to home, whenever one makes a decision in the absence of established truth regarding the decision and its consequences, one has likewise invoked lower philosophy and prejudice or a truth-by-decree attitude. Of course such decisions are routinely necessary because, generally, one has access to established truth on few, if any, issues. Prejudice is common, normal, and hardly fatal in the short term. But, it is a serious mistake to regard a truth-by-decree decision made in the absence of established truth as final. We all learn continually, some faster than others because of natural gifts, energy, and attitude. In a near absence of established truth, all should be ready to receive further knowledge and revise earlier-made decisions and choices whenever one discovers they result in a less-beneficial way. But to some, a decision made, even generations before, is a decision to be maintained. To such, as with rash science-wars critics of science, ignorance and prejudice will ultimately be fatal to understanding of reality.

Good Philosophy

With this background about philosophy and its practice and their inherent difficulties and dangers we can now venture a statement as to what philosophy is about, at least in this book, by answering some fundamental questions: What practice constitutes good philosophy in science? And, for that matter, what practice constitutes good philosophy in general?

Good philosophical practice in acquiring improved understanding requires, *first*, a foundation of sufficiently diverse and correct knowledge in the form of experience, i.e., data or facts. *Second*, to discover new insights and deeper understanding one must discover in these facts some previously unrecognized relationship, some new pattern, organization, or connection buried in and implied by the facts. The deeper and more comprehensive the pattern or organization, the deeper and more universal the knowledge it provides about the facts (for example, the relationship between particle motions and particle properties). But, alas, the deeper and more abstract the pattern, the deeper it is buried, and the more elusive is its discovery. *Third*, a reliable truth criterion must be used to test deductions, i.e., to establish their veracity, before they become conclusions. An adequate truth criterion, experiment, and experience are essentials in discovery of truth and making most-beneficial choices. Hence, these topics repeatedly occupy our attention in this book.

Why the proportionality between depth and elusiveness? In order to see previously unrecognized pattern or organization in experience or a set of data or collection of facts, one must view one's knowledge from a previously unappreciated and usually unimagined perspective. Previously unrecognized connections not apparent in an *old* (traditional, familiar, intuitive, concrete) perspective are only recognizable in a *new* (experimental, innovative, non-intuitive, abstract) perspective. Discovery usually involves adopting a new view, seeing experience or facts with a new vision. The more obscure a pattern or organization is in an old vision, the more innovative and abstract a new vision must be to permit its recognition. And, generally speaking, the more abstract the new vision, the more difficult it is to imagine and discover. Physicist Max Born, who we have already met, aptly captured this principle with the observation that "progress in physics has always moved from the intuitive to the abstract."[22]

Hard and Soft Science

In physics, good philosophical practice like that just described is used to seek fundamentally correct or "hard" theory that accurately predicts data or facts. Hard theory, both deep and reliable, is required to provide accuracy over a broad range of application. Otherwise, without depth and reliability, a theory is only superficially correct or "soft" and can perhaps be adapted to agree with many observations, such as by use of adjustable constants, but can never be used in applications requiring exact predictions involving many degrees of freedom (dependence on variation of many variables) over broad ranges of application.

Discovery of a hard-science theory is an exercise in philosophy (as is the discovery of a soft-science theory, but the former is preferred over the latter). The starting assets are the recognition and challenge of a problem or a need for improved understanding, observation of apparent causes, consequences, and other facts on which understanding is to be based and which must properly be related. Issues to be addressed in discovering cause-and-effect relationships are (1) quantities (facts) that vary with a quantity of interest and (2) whether such variation of one quantity is caused by variation of a second or merely correlated with it, e.g., jointly dependent on a third quantity. Descriptive science and merely correlated or statistical results are insufficient for fundamental, mechanistic understanding of a process or phenomenon, i.e., a cause-and-effect understanding of it. Mere description is superficial or soft, contingent knowledge devoid of deep understanding, i.e., merely correlated results do not *explain* connections in fundamental terms. Such correlations can be used to *describe* facts *sometimes* observed but do not provide generally reliable prediction. Finally, truth is only established by use of an adequate truth criterion or reality test.

Then, tools for philosophical discovery of truth are observation, inference, reason and analysis, logical deduction, rigor, and reliable testing against reality. A knack for understanding how things fit together, i.e., an intuition for the order encountered in the universe, is also invaluable. This knack is evident (by definition) in all the great scientific discoverers. The objective is to capture and distill at a deep, abstract level a regularity and pattern in, say, a cause-and-effect relationship among the facts in a succinct statement of truth – a theory, law, or principle – that provides accurate description, reliable prediction, and improved understanding of reality. The more fundamental and comprehensive the theory, law, or principle, the more broadly it applies but the more difficult is its discovery.

Connection, Pattern, and Organization among the Facts

To gain improved understanding of any class of phenomena, processes, or things we must recognize a broader range of pertinent facts and find deeper relationships among them, a more fundamental knowledge of their pattern and organization, a clearer vision of their connection or how they fit together. We describe by the term *paradigm* or *philosophy* or *system of belief* a vision of connection and knowledge of pattern and organization and, ultimately, meaning. It follows that to understand reality we utilize a paradigm, philosophy, or system of belief that connects a broad range of experience or facts. Indeed, a paradigm or philosophy or system of belief *imposes* a view of connection of facts and thus a vision of reality. Full description of real reality, or absolute truth, requires a paradigm, philosophy, or system of belief founded on a full range of absolutely true facts among which even the deepest connections are apparent or implied in the paradigm.

The quest for understanding reality is consequently a quest for a correct paradigm, philosophy, or system of belief. In seeking this system it would be simplest to initially ignore the details and neglect the minutia. As interesting as they are, they are mere details and minutia and we seek a comprehensive, overall picture, a universal connectedness. We eventually can ignore details. A complete, valid paradigm must provide the details through connections in its vision of reality. However, the details are initially important if not in deducing elements of the paradigm then in testing its validity, since a complete, valid paradigm must correctly contain and relate all details of reality.

To obtain a paradigm, to capture a vision of reality, we must either adopt it from among known candidates or build our own original. In the latter case we may adopt a set of defining principles, axioms, postulates, assumptions, and laws that form the basis of a vision of reality. Or, in a more empirical approach, we can construct a fact-by-fact mosaic image of reality. Or we may select some principles and use them together with at least one mosaic image as a combination of these approaches. Both science and Christian faith incorporate a combination.

Facts: the Basic Elements of Knowledge, Understanding, and Meaning

Discovery of a scientific theory begins by discovering which facts are valid and pertinent and then identifying connections between "cause facts" and "effect facts," thus allowing prediction of events by establishing the exact conditions under which they will be observed. *Facts* are the basic elements of *knowledge*, *understanding*, and *meaning*. *Knowledge* is the knowing of facts. *Understanding* implies the knowing of facts and their interconnections and organization, the regularities and irregularities of pattern that exist among them. A good scientific law provides some level of understanding. It reveals order and structure among a broad range of results apparently unrelated in an ignorance of the law. It allows prediction of future events from knowledge of the present. It provides deep, far-reaching insight into the nature of nature. A good example is the second law of thermodynamics (Appendix F) which states that natural processes in an isolated system spontaneously change the system from a state of greater order to a state of lesser order, e.g., isolated structures like buildings or agricultural systems not maintained spontaneously decay and collapse or revert to wild growth or desert.

Meaning goes beyond the objective, reproducible facts and their material cause-and-effect relationships that science exclusively considers (facts connected predominantly by *how* questions). Meaning also involves the understanding of other kinds of facts and their connections to underlying principles and the causes, purposes, and consequences represented by these facts (facts connected by *who*, *what*, and *why* questions). Neither scientific facts nor theories that reveal their connection, order, and structure can, by themselves, fully impart the deep meaning we address in this book. This meaning transcends these facts in scope, power, and consequence. While a wise person observes facts and comprehends their meaning in connections and consequences, a less-wise person sees the facts and understands only a lesser part of their meaning or only the facts themselves and nothing at all of any further meaning. The stimulation of awareness is similar, but the levels of awareness stimulated are different. Comprehension of deep meaning – universal connections and ultimate consequences – is the highest level of wisdom and awareness of truth and goodness (and their opposites) and the highest aspiration of a wise person. We address and seek understanding of meaning in this book.

Science may be economically motivated and may involve university, government-agency, or corporate visibility, not to mention personal satisfaction, reputation, and status of the scientist and of his or her laboratory. But a quest for meaning is personally motivated. For one person, meaning is a critical need; another may regard meaning as superfluous. Comprehension of deep meaning requires a high level of awareness, a level obtained only by deliberate cultivation. This awareness of meaning imparts insight into and appreciation for the personal, the sympathetic, the spiritual, and the eternal. Such meaning is manifest in feelings toward self and others. These things are very fundamental and yet may be far removed from one's immediate perception in one's routine, everyday experience. Meaning cannot be fully defined in terms of routine-everyday-material-related-facts experience. Personal, inter-human, and spiritual experience are not simply reproduced by recreating outward physical conditions, as are the reproducible facts of science, because qualities that transcend the physical are involved.

At the same time, manifestation of meaning may be continuous in one's thoughts and feelings. Things pertaining to meaning are intuitive once one learns an intuition based on meaning. Then, once one has developed a sense and feeling of meaning within one's self, manifestation of meaning is natural and spontaneous. Experience with the sympathetic, spiritual, and eternal may seem invisible, elusive, remote, and undependable but it is, after we come to know and repeatedly feel its meaning, the deepest, most real, intimate, reliable, comforting, and motivating of all experience.

Science deals with careful experimentation, accurate observation of reproducible facts, and the causes and effects found therein. Science leads to intellectual discovery, philosophical success, personal satisfaction and fulfillment, and, perhaps, financial reward. Inter-human, spiritual, and eternal matters related to meaning involve values and feelings of faith, purpose, trust, gratitude, allegiance, generosity, love, devotion, aspiring beyond self, personal growth, peace, and joy. Both scientific knowledge and spiritual insight are good. One does not have to choose between them – they are not mutually exclusive. They are centered in different realms, but one may pursue both in a quest for a more comprehensive vision of reality, one in which two visions of reality are both utilized and consolidated in a search for absolute truth. However, the two methods are not harmonized in any fundamental way.

Commitment and Meaning – C. S. Lewis

A scientist conditioned to appreciate a philosophical structure that rigorously connects and organizes the material facts of science recognizes beauty and elegance in philosophical methods and logical structures in other fields of knowledge. Indeed, "in my utterly unbiased opinion" (in case it isn't obvious, I employ this phrase and others to lighten the load of reading this book), philosophers who have training in mathematics and physics excel when they turn to other areas of philosophy. They implicitly bring from their training the requirements that (1) theory (philosophy) has the purpose of rigorously relating cause and effect or otherwise connecting the facts and (2) any valid theory must be consistent with reality, i.e., the philosophy must be verified as consistent with *all* observation. These are very demanding constraints that are not always observed in "casual" philosophy which, in comparison, often seems soft – vague, arbitrary, and frustrating in its failure to reach definite, verifiable, and useful conclusions.[23] On the other hand, who would deny that it is, first and foremost, philosophical ability that allows a successful scientist to achieve definite, practical, and useful theories of cause-and-effect ordering consistent with all known facts? Nevertheless, discovery of ever-deeper pattern and connection and rigorous consistency with all known facts as sought in science incorporating mathematics provides a high ideal for all philosophy.

Of course many notable philosophers were untrained in science and mathematics. As indicated by my frequent quotations from his writings, I hold C. S. Lewis (1898-1963), long a Reader at Oxford University and finally a Professor of Medieval and Renaissance Literature at Cambridge University, as a favorite not only because of the scope, depth, rigor, and analytical power of his thinking but also and especially because of his insights into meaning and the philosophical issues he therefore chose to address. How can this be? A literature professor who freely admitted lack of ability in mathematics (and not just for sake of modesty) but nonetheless possessed the rigor and analytical power of a mathematical physicist.[24] Lewis' God-given gifts of intelligence and expression were generous. In addition, he utilized rigor, high personal standards, and diligence (labor and practice) to reach a unique level of insight and a singular vision of truth and meaning in many aspects of philosophy and Christian thought.

It is sometimes said that a philosopher must not be a citizen of any one community of ideas, the concern being that such citizenship would be limiting to a full, unrestricted range of thought and perspective. Because Lewis subscribed fully to a Christian system of belief he was generally categorized by himself and others as a Christian apologist rather than a philosopher. But I do not subscribe to the thought that a philosopher should not be committed to a community of ideas. Indeed, as I urge repeatedly in this book, one may obtain knowledge without commitment, but commitment is required to obtain understanding of meaning. And the insight and power of Lewis' writings rest on his understanding of meaning derived from his Christian belief and practice. Other notable thinkers, such as French mathematician and philosopher René Descartes (1596-1650, pronounced "day-cart"), British empiricist John Locke (1632-1714), German mathematician, jurist, diplomat, historian, and theologian Gottfried Wilhelm Leibniz (1646-1716), radical Scottish philosopher David Hume (1711-1776), German scientist and philosopher Immanuel Kant (1724-1804), and American medical doctor, physiologist, psychologist, and philosopher William James (1842-1910), were all rigorous in their analysis of topics relating to knowledge, cognizance, and reason but, with only occasional exceptions, they ignored understanding of meaning. Each of these philosophers and many others thought broadly and deeply. But understanding of meaning is acquired only through belief *and* practice. Intellectual consideration alone, no matter how deep and penetrating, is insufficient to discover meaning. C. S. Lewis, for example, by belief and practice came to understand meaning in Christian values that is clearly reflected in his meaning-rich writings, especially apparent to believing and practicing Christians. Many other philosophers, in contrast, seem preoccupied with a lower knowledge comprised of empirical, sensory-fact experience, cultural and social phenomena, and merely relative knowledge. These philosophers do not address the depth of meaning regularly perceived and conveyed by Lewis. If they had perceived it they would have addressed it with priority because of its power. But deep meaning is invisible to one who has not yet discovered and thus lacks any intellectual or operational comprehension of it.

Since I regard commitment as an important requirement for obtaining understanding of meaning, I do not regard Lewis' embracing of Christianity as disqualifying him as a philosopher. Rather, contrary to the previously mentioned convention, I regard commitment as *required* to obtain and describe a full philosophical knowledge including an understanding of essence, significance, or meaning. By this reasoning, a philosopher who remains uncommitted necessarily limits his or her ability to perceive and communicate truly powerful ideas. Citizenship in a community of ideas is consequently essential to understanding the essence, significance, meaning, insight, and power of the ideas embraced by the community.

Without meaning, apologetic writing is tedious when all existing, remotely-connected points, however obscure, are visited. Such tedium inhibits communication. Lewis' writing focused on meaning is not tedious but is direct and compelling and simple, first-person declarative in style. I also focus on meaning and use a simple declarative style in this book (but I do not suggest my writing is equal to Lewis'). No point is exhaustively treated, to minimize tedium. Many philosophies have been mentioned and more could be. We resist that temptation to avoid another plague in philosophy: the diversity of thought it strives to encompass and the resulting confusion it contains, for lack of an adequate truth criterion. Instead, we focus on only two classes of philosophy: science (physics) and Christianity. Science is the focus of Book II and the Author of Christianity, correctly regarded as the Greatest Philosopher in the history of humankind, is, with His philosophy, the focus of Book III.

Preview of Topics Considered in this Book

We address perception of reality in Book I. Because of their essential, fundamental role in philosophy, we consider in Chapter 2 the nature of perception and the facts thereby accessible to humans and in Chapter 3 the influence of culture, the role of values, and the character of meaning. While objectivity is always sought in science, law, and other fields, we suggest in Chapter 4 that objectivity is rarely, if ever, fully achieved. In Chapter 5 we describe a scientific paradigm.

In Books I and II we consider the history of some of the principal discoveries and discoverers in mathematics and in an important area of physics, namely, *mechanics*. Mathematicians we consider are Euclid, Newton, Gauss, Riemann, Gödel, and others together with some of their mathematical discoveries. In science we consider Copernicus, Kepler, and Galileo and their discoveries regarding orbiting planets and falling bodies (Chapter 6), Newton and Newtonian mechanics (Chapter 7), Einstein and his theory of relativity (Chapter 8), and quantum mechanics and many of the contributors to its discovery (Chapter 9). These discoveries in mathematics and physics describe forces acting on bodies and their resulting motions. Their descriptions reveal the nature of science and of seeking and discovery of truth therein.

In Chapter 10 we address the role of faith in science. No matter what we choose to believe, in an absence of absolute knowledge, understanding, or truth our belief is an act of faith whether by a deliberate choice or simply acquiescing to tradition or expectation. We observe that those who argue against faith are equally dependent thereon and, despite and perhaps because of their rigorous skepticism and elaborate argument, don't recognize it. In the absence of absolutely established truth previous to adopting a paradigm, the question is not whether to invoke faith but in what to place faith. Indeed, sometimes an argument is so elaborate and complex its basis in faith is obscure until one looks closely as we do in this chapter.

In Chapter 11 we consider psychology, free will, and agency. Psychology is included because some have proposed that psychogenesis is a cause of Christian or religious conviction. We examine materialist psychology and refute this proposal since this psychology presently fails to suggest a way that psychogenesis can occur as a cause of Christian conviction. Moreover, in addressing the topics of free will and agency we identify an important consequence of these closely-related concepts. And in considering psychology we extend our vision beyond the material universe to a broader scope of vision retained thereafter.

We examine in Book III a Christian paradigm – the doctrine of Christ – which we introduce and justify in Chapter 12 and contrast with science thereafter. The predominantly personal but unlimited nature of experience, perspective, and awareness versus the confining influence of paradigm are addressed in Chapters 13 and 14. In each person's individual interaction with the universe, he or she encounters real opposition in trying to discover and follow truth, i.e., the universe is not passive. To live a virtuous life requires a battle against subtle forces opposing such effort. Becoming and remaining virtuous requires that one defeat the universe! Our discussion of the aforementioned ideological war begins in these chapters.

We discuss in Chapter 15 right, wrong, and other absolutes. Without God or some absolute power or reference there is no absolute and everything is merely relative. Absence of an absolute in human philosophy is revealed by shifting of values in various cultures of history. Science, invoking only consistency with observed reality as its truth criterion, can provide only relative (consistent) rather than absolute knowledge. Concern that our behavior be "ethical" is good, but only recognition of an Absolute Power and ethics He has decreed carries the weight of Absolute Power. Until a person addresses the question of an Absolute Power (God), he or she has not faced the most important ultimate question and is shirking responsibility as an agent searching for truth.

We collect and compare in Chapter 16 the inherent, consequential properties of science and Christianity. These properties include inherent flaws fatal to establishing absolute truth by scientific inquiry. In contrast, the Christian model – the doctrine of Christ – contains no inherent flaw and provides power to discover and establish absolute truth. The truth so established is initially restricted to answers to specified ultimate questions – Is Christ the Son of God and the Creator of the universe? – or a similar question. Answers to such questions impose broad implications revealing the fundamental nature of reality to the level of First Cause. Because reality is unique and comprehensive, reliable knowledge of its nature has universal value irrespective of how it is discovered.

Chapter 17 assesses the power of science and of Christianity to provide understanding of meaning. Examination of these two systems leads to the conclusion that science, in objectively addressing only the material universe, provides no power to understand meaning beyond the realm of objective, reproducible, lowest-common-denominator, material-related facts. Meaning on a material-universe level has little value compared to meaning on a total-universe level accessible through Christianity. Moreover, while science contains no adequate truth criterion (Chapter 5), no absolute *yes* answer, Christianity does (Chapter 12).

In Chapter 18 we further elaborate meaning by describing lived experiences of a few persons who discovered meaning and manifested it in their lives. Such discovery and its manifestation are inseparable. Finally, in Chapter 19, we pose a question that allows you, dear reader, to discover your present direction in the journey toward meaning; and, in this journey, direction, not position, is *the* important measure because direction indicates desire and intent.

Purpose and Fulfillment in Life

Since discussion of meaning addresses cause, purpose, and consequence, it addresses where a person is lead by understanding of meaning, how understanding of meaning affects intent and volition, and who that person is becoming. So, child, grandchild, or friend reading this book, I include herein what I have learned, what I believe, and what I stand for regarding that which we can and should become. The search for absolute truth and meaning and our attitude therein are so important I must make a few general observations at the outset about the search itself.

When we choose (or simply inherit, without much thought) a philosophy, system of belief, or paradigm (I include these terms repeatedly to make them familiar to you), it becomes the lens by which we view the universe. It becomes the truth we support. It becomes our driving force, our motivation, our vision of reality. And, just as the scientist wants his theories and measurements to be based on a fundamentally sound, universally-valid system of knowledge that faithfully represents reality, so does the wise person want his or her life to be based on and stand for truth and good meaning. The wise person wants to base his or her life on value and virtue because value and virtue lead to great consequences. He or she wants to stand for something worthy of his or her best efforts, because what we stand for is what defines and inspires our best efforts. The wise person wants to embrace belief and faith in a purpose larger than self that will lead to growth, virtue, blessing, and joy, not only for him- or her-self but also for others touched and brought along the way, such as his or her children. The wise person wants to build his or her philosophy of life on a solid foundation, a rock broader than the universe and deeper than time, which will stand and provide support no matter what may come, ever. Thus, the question of truth, philosophy, system of belief, paradigm becomes the primary issue with which we must be concerned. Until we squarely address this issue we have not discovered *why we are* or defined *for what we stand* or *who we are becoming*. We have not established our vision of reality – we are to large extent drifting wherever the current in a contrary universe takes us.

Our lives can stand for something great, and thereby they can be great. While Christ established "the way, the truth, and the life"[25] as our Guide and Example, each person determines his or her own path and, beyond that, shall, through his or her influence, help others find and follow the beneficial way or some other way. Each of us carries, with Christ, the responsibility for establishing truth. To do so and make one's life great, each person must learn the facts, understand their meaning, consider the options, make the choice for truth, embrace the challenge, and endure for the duration of the "ride." Then we are not just drifting. We are "paddling" mightily toward a worthy goal. If we paddle hard – even when the wind and the waves are against us – we will find fulfillment and joy because (1) paddling moves us forward toward our destination, (2) paddling develops strength and stamina, (3) such effort builds devotion, and (4) in our devotion to a cause larger than just us (for others and for Him whose approval and companionship we desire, whether or not we presently realize it) we will occasionally notice that, when the rapids are dangerous or the current overpowering or the wind irresistible, He will be in the boat paddling with us and He is the most powerful paddler in the entire universe (save One), and has absolute power over wind and waves. He is the Light that guides the willing to everlasting joy, since "no man cometh to the Father [and this joy] but by [Him]. "[25] As Guide, Example, and Light, He assists us in our desire and effort to follow Him.

In this introduction and overview our discussion has spanned the range from scientific theory to absolute, fundamental, philosophical truth and meaning. In concept this leap is not a large one but, as will be demonstrated hereafter, such a leap is beyond the up-to-now, unassisted ability of mere mortals and, indeed, the ability required for making such a leap is not fully recognized. In fact, the gulf which must be leaped seems to be growing as we must now abandon long-held certainties in science and mathematics (Chapters 3 and 10) causing mathematics and science to appear ever more tenuous. But absolutely reliable truth neither does nor can come through scientific inquiry, as we shall demonstrate in this book and as has been argued in others to be quoted. Absolute truth and meaning are only received and recognized through both of two means – first, they are a gift from God and, second, each individual establishes his or her own future truth (who that person becomes and the way things will be for him or her) by his or her own desires and choices. And absolute truth is required for absolute joy and absolute salvation. Along the way to these conclusions we focus on how we can receive truth from God and how we can recognize truth when we receive it, regardless of its source. Identifying or confirming truth, not diluted or contaminated by assumptions, ignorance, and flawed philosophy, is an essential philosophical tool.

Receiving truth and aligning one's priorities with those of the preeminent Author of Truth is wonderful and exciting. Only this process leads to "… the peace of God, which passeth all understanding."[26] Only following Christ leads to "… joy unspeakable and full of glory."[27] This is *where or who we want to be*. Toward this goal we want to travel; and we can know when we are moving toward this goal since the qualities of the goal are experienced to some degree in the journey toward it.

I attempt to describe my vision of both the journey and the goal in this book. My hope is that I can share my vision with you in a way that you, dear reader, can better learn to recognize and appreciate truth and discover and establish it for yourself. Finding and following truth are the first and highest-priority tasks we face in life and everything depends on how well we address these challenges! What we attain, who we become, depends on recognizing where we are and who we want to be and, therefore, where we must aim, to what level we must aspire. So, my family and those of you "listening in," read well, seek truth, and aim high, that you may come to and embrace a sure knowledge of truth in the only way possible for mortals – beginning with the gift and power of Christ who is the preeminent Author of Truth.

So What?

Conclusions reached in this book are presented in the following chapters as a series of eighteen propositions listed together in the final appendix. These propositions or conclusions are supported and justified by the material presented but *complete justification requires application of the described principles by the reader*. Obtaining knowledge in either science or Christianity requires effort and, far beyond mere knowledge, we pursue herein both demonstration of truth and understanding of meaning.

Establishing truth and meaning and where they lead is the story of this book, but truth and meaning are neither fully discovered nor completely understood without committed, personal effort on the part of the seeker. Our story is not only *what* the natures of truth and meaning are but also *how* to establish them for one's self. Understanding of truth and meaning are not acquired by mere reading – they are not simple knowledge – but reading certainly can educate and guide us in seeking them. Like life itself, the establishment of truth and meaning is a personal experience. To acquire truth and meaning, you, dear reader, have to *reach out and capture them for yourself.* Indeed, discovery of and allegiance to truth and meaning are the purposes and opportunities of life. I hope this book will help provide you with knowledge and motivation necessary to fully acquire, use, and profit from them.

Notes and References for Chapter 1.

[1] I have not kept a personal journal to pass on by which I would share things I have learned. So I herein relate to you what I have learned from my own experience and from experience of others. I have drawn liberally from experience and thoughts (writings) of others rather than just my own for important reasons, namely, the experience of others is often more interesting and it provides a broader basis of understanding as it is more diverse in time, location, personality, circumstances, and insights.

[2] *Reality* is the totality of real things and events. *Truth* is knowledge of things as they were, are, and are to be. (*Doctrine and Covenants* 93:24.) Therefore truth provides knowledge and description of reality.

[3] See, for examples, Russell, Bertrand, *History of Western Philosophy,* Simon & Schuster, New York, 1945; Kenny, Anthony, *A Brief History of Western Philosophy,* Blackwell Publishers, Oxford, 1998; and Klee, Robert, *Introduction to the Philosophy of Science,* Oxford University Press, Oxford, 1997. The introduction of Allan Franklin's book *Are there really Neutrinos?* (Perseus Books, Cambridge, MA, 2001, Chapter 1) contains insightful criticisms of modern, anti-science thinking revealed to be lacking in discipline, care, and basis. Franklin points out that much anti-science thinking exhibits an "intellectual arrogance" revealed in one case by boasting of an author that he is uninformed in science while criticizing it, a kind of science-bashing machismo (very brave). Preconceptions in both science and culture form the basis of criticisms of "social critics," having beliefs dominated by whim-of-the-moment, politically-correct dogmas usually devoid of careful thought and presented as the "cultural or social context of science." What has social context to do with establishing absolute truth for one's self? Is one restricted in such a search to the socially acceptable as defined by a few self-anointed elitists? If one acquiesces to such restriction he or she cares more about approval of others than He who dispenses truth and, with that priority, shall never receive it. The required attitude for establishing truth for one's self is an intense desire to know truth and a real intent to use it.

[4] Lewis, C. S., *Miracles, A Preliminary Study,* Macmillan, New York, 1947, 7. I recommend this book, particularly to scientists. It presents valuable insight on holding a broad view while being careful and even rigorous in evaluating evidence, a useful combination.

Archeologists might benefit from Lewis' instruction as their view must be nearly impossibly broad. When I visited the ruins of Chichén Itzá and Tulum on the Yucatán Peninsula of Mexico, my guides cited " archeologists' " conclusions about functions of some of the structures. In one instance, they explained that a purpose of the principal, nine-tier-pyramid temple at Chichén Itzá was to indicate the spring and fall equinoxes and thereby provide a semiannual fix for the Mayan calendar. This pyramid has long, steep staircases on opposing sides, each contained within a pair of walls. The bottom end of each wall is a sculpted snake's head. At the spring and fall equinoxes (21 March, 22 September) the tiers cause a series of shadows forming seven diamonds on the walls which, with the snake heads at the bottom, give the image of a huge snake descending the pyramid from the temple on top. The calendar dates are thus dramatically indicated. However, another interpretation is more compelling. On 6 April the full nine-diamond image of a descending snake appears. The builders of this structure were not novices – the difference between the seven-diamond and full nine-diamond images must have been anticipated by them. In another instance, one small structure at nearby Tulum contains a narrow, straight hole in one wall. On one spring and one fall day a shaft of sunlight penetrates this hole and illuminates the inside of another structure across a walkway. The spring day is 6 April. Again, this date must be deliberate because of the sophistication of the builders.

What is the significance of 6 April? *Doctrine and Covenants* 20:1 indicates Christ's birthdate in Bethlehem was 6 April in the year 1 BC during the Passover feast in very crowded Jerusalem (thus, no room in the inn in nearby Bethlehem). At this time many impressive signs and wonders were observed by the Book-of-Mormon people, supposedly concentrated in the Yucatán and Central American region. While the Mayans had largely abandoned Christianity by the time these

Yucatán structures were built, 6 April may have been remembered and adopted for another purpose, like the present date for Christmas was (I suspect no shepherds stay with their flocks in the fields at night near Bethlehem in late December; but they do during the lambing season in spring).

John P. Pratt has observed that astronomical evidence also indicates 6 April 1 BC as the best-fit date for Christ's birth (see "Yet Another Eclipse for Herod," *The Planetarian* **19**, 1990, 8-14 and "Passover: Was it Symbolic of His Coming?" *The Ensign* **24**, 1994, 38-45; both articles and others pertaining to this point are available at www.johnpratt.com).

[5] This term originates in and takes its meaning from the Latin verb *ostendere* which means *to show*, as in to prove or demonstrate. The adjective "ostensible" is used herein to denote "proper" or "that may be shown or obtained," usage now rare. Simultaneously it is used in the common, present sense of "alleged" or "apparent," since the proof we address is unfamiliar to most.

[6] Draper, John William, *History of the Conflict between Religion and Science,* Sixth Edition, Appleton, New York, 1875, 201-202.

[7] *The Wysiwyg Universe* by Simon Free, http://wysiwyg.stanford.edu/ does not displace the ostensible-step method because it falls short of this method in completeness; but Free's method illuminates the appropriateness and power of the ostensible-step method.

[8] The classification of trees as inanimate objects may be questioned but is a tangential issue that could divert us from the task at hand which is ambitious enough. I observe only that even rocks and mountains may be regarded as animate in their geological formation and describing any object as inanimate could be questioned. Over short time periods, however, neither trees nor rocks are self-animated compared to humans and we shall let that distinction suffice. Moreover, what is essential is *volition* and *motivation* for choice and animation. Humans are unique in possessing a fullness of these capabilities.

[9] One might regard only *good* men and women as desiring to discover and choose what is most useful and beneficial. But nearly all people are good to some degree and potentially good to great degree. Christ's gospel addresses who we can become. He offers it to sinner and saint alike, especially the former that they might become the latter. Because of Him, goodness of the highest degree is possible in spite of past mistakes. His invitation to become good is empowered by His grace and power through which the consequences of sin are removed. One's desire, intent, and volition are the important measures because they control choice and, therefore, who one is becoming. Since desire, intent, and volition change as one chooses, none (with one, rare exception being those who turn against Christ and His work after He reveals Himself to them) is excluded from the good category, neither by Christ nor this book about choosing and becoming. Although we herein condemn no person, we do condemn foolish and destructive behavior.

[10] Born, Max, *My Life, Recollections of a Nobel Laureate,* Charles Scribners & Sons, New York, 1975, 262.

[11] Dubislav, W., *Die Philosophie der Mathematik in der Gegenwart,* Junker und Dunnhaupt Verlag, Berlin, 1932, 1.

[12] Creation from nothing.

[13] Ayer, A. J., *The problem of Knowledge,* Penguin Books, Baltimore, MD, 1956, 7. Early in his career Ayer spent time in Vienna studying the approach and views of the *Vienna Circle*, a prominent and influential group in promoting *logical positivism*. The Vienna Circle was founded in 1924 by M. Schlick and included G. Bergmann, R. Carnap, H. Feigl, Ph. Franck, K. Gödel, H. Hahn, O. Neurath, and F. Waismann. The logical positivism or logical empiricism or philosophy of science

promoted by the Vienna Circle was based on and, in turn, strongly influenced three movements: (i) empiricism and positivism particularly as influenced by David Hume (1711-1776) and further expounded by John Stuart Mill (1806-1873) and Ernst Mach (1838-1916), (ii) the empirical science methodology developed by nineteenth century scientists including Ludwig Boltzmann (1844-1906), Pierre Duhem (1861-1916), Albert Einstein (1879-1955), Hermann Helmholtz (1821-1894), Mach, and Jules Henri Poincaré (1854-1912), and (iii) the symbolic logic and logical analysis of language further developed by Gottlob Frege (1848-1925), Alfred North Whitehead (1861-1947) and Bertrand Russell (1872-1970), and Ludwig Wittgenstein (1889-1951). General characteristics of the view of the Vienna Circle were (a) empiricism, i.e., the belief that all factual knowledge is related by experience through which verification of concepts is possible, and (b) scientific cooperation and unity, which led to their interest in intersubjective language and unity of science. The Vienna Circle was dissolved with the death of Schlick in 1936. Ayer became prominent as the English spokesperson writing about and promoting the views of the Vienna Circle and his own views that reflected and extended their thinking.

Philosophers and scientists had long sought a concise and coherent interpretation of experience to unify their observations and reflections. A unified view or general understanding of the observed universe was, in turn, represented by the names philosophy, natural philosophy, and, finally, science. Science was not directed towards truth but rather utility, the utility of concepts that rationalize observation and are verified by it.

Because observation admits a diversity of concepts that rationalize it, an additional criterion was adopted, namely, *Ockham's* or *Occam's Razor*, named after fourteenth-century logician and Franciscan friar William of Ockham or Occam, Surrey, England. His statement of the principle is "Entities should not be multiplied unnecessarily." Others also conceived and stated this principle differently. Plato called the principle *mathematical harmony* which he stated as "a simpler system that saves the appearances (agrees with the observations) is preferred." Aristotle's form was "Nature operates in the shortest way possible." Isaac Newton's form was "We are to admit no more causes of natural things than such as are both true and sufficient to explain their appearances." A common form used today is "Scientific concepts are not to be complicated beyond necessity." Mathematician P. A. M. Dirac posed a different form "[Research workers expressing] the fundamental laws of Nature in mathematical form should strive mainly for mathematical beauty [or aesthetics]. It often happens that the requirements of simplicity and beauty are the same, but where they clash the latter must take precedence." The common thought, excluding Dirac's statement, is the well-stated one, perhaps by Einstein, "Everything should be made as simple as possible, but not simpler." The last clause provides an Einstein-like, humorous twist. This principle is merely assumed. It is simply a "rule of thumb" that often seems to be valid, but not always. Indeed, Steven Weinberg's observation on this topic runs counter to those above: "We generally find that any complication in our theories that is not forbidden by symmetry or other fundamental principle actually occurs." (*Dreams of a Final Theory,* Vintage Books, New York, 1991, 224.)

Science can be decomposed into two efforts: (i) discovery of useful concepts and (ii) their testing or verification. Any demonstration of truth in science is contingent on the concept or criterion by which it is validated. Concepts may therefore be "scientifically true" only in a limited range, which may be quite distinct from universally-valid, absolute truth. Nevertheless, unification of all human knowledge sought in science is a useful goal which may provide insight into absolute truth even though the latter apparently lies far beyond scientific truth.

Because language consists of symbols that are not exact in representing objects, positivists looked to analysis of language in a search for unification of language to reach the ideal of unification of scientific knowledge. It was not thought proper that physics, chemistry, biology, psychology, sociology, and other disciplines were separated by tongues foreign to one another. If methods, truth criterion, and concepts were identical or similar in all science then a single pattern well described by a common language should be adopted, with dialects in individual specialties translatable to the common underlying, scientific mother-tongue. While Carnap and Neurath initially believed that physics as a language met necessary requirements, it was soon recognized that even the language of physics was too narrow. Thereupon, Carnap modified his thinking adopting a "thesis of the reducibility of scientific language to a thing-language" in which statements invoking concepts may be translated into exact descriptions of material objects. Of course this led to problems in not being able to address concepts directly nor to consider a duality of material objects and thought, as is necessary in, say, psychology and philosophy. For over a decade the Vienna Circle and its survivors emphasized logical analysis of language as the central problem of philosophy and tried to identify the causes of absurdities and misconceptions resident in conventional language, regarding conventional-language statements not as false but as senseless in any definite, material-object (science) context. But the effort resulted in the same heated, unresolved debates that had occupied those interested in these issues for millennia. R. G. H. Siu (*The Tao of Science,* The Technology Press, MIT, Cambridge, MA and John Wiley & Sons, New York, 1957) discusses these details.

A fundamental problem in the approach of the Vienna Circle is that a language cannot definitively describe itself, a logically circular exercise. To describe it, another language having a different structure must be used. For instance, the Euclidian and Newtonian systems were not improved, or fully understood, until Einstein provided another structure in which to understand and evaluate them. Without a new structure and perspective, analysis of conventional language was necessarily limited. Moreover, "improving" language considering only its ability to describe material objects would be fatal to many valuable uses of language. While science may motivate meaning only as it relates directly to a material body or phenomenon, broader thinking also values language in artistic usage able to imply meaning that transcends such a limit.

[14] Heisenberg, Werner, "Positivism, Metaphysics, and Religion," in *The World Treasury of Physics, Astronomy, and Mathematics,* Timothy Ferris (editor), Little, Brown and Company, New York, 1991, 821-827.

[15] Kenny, loc. cit., x.

[16] Baker, Kenneth, in *Philosophical Dictionary,* Walter Brugger and Kenneth Baker (editors), Gonzaga University Press, Spokane, WA, 1972, xiv-xv.

[17] Modern philosophy sometimes seems to be learning a catalog of other people's opinions with little concern for personal, independent thought. Such an approach leads to a focus on authority and precedence rather than personal reasoning and experience. The former was the pattern of the scholastics and the Aristotelian philosophers to be described in Chapter 6 and such a pattern is still followed by many. Primary concern with who thought this or that and how it relates to the thought of so and so displaces concern for inherent value and truth. In conventional study of philosophy, authority and tradition are implicitly emphasized over inherent value by the usual presentation of the subject. (In the absence of fundamental knowledge of values and an adequate truth criterion, organization of content in philosophy is largely by history and/or author, as also occurs in other fields not sufficiently understood to organize content by topic in some more fundamental structure. In contrast, treatments of physics and mathematics are highly organized by topic as the topic fits in a broad scope of physical or mathematical thought. Organizing content by author, like taking a case-study approach, reveals an absence of knowledge of a fundamental structure in, say, function of the material and implicitly emphasizes author rather than function or value or position in a hierarchy of any fundamental structure of thought and thinking.) Moreover, because philosophy lacks an adequate truth criterion it has little to say about truth. What self-respecting philosopher wants to talk about his or her ignorance? Support of authority and precedence as well as demonstration of personal learnedness, with their accompanying restrictions in one's thinking, seems to be sought in philosophy, as elsewhere, perhaps defensively in philosophy because philosophy is so discretionary.

Such tradition is apparent in comments of an unknown philosopher who kindly reviewed my preface at the request of another. Some of his or her comments follow.

> My first concern, with regard to this particular effort, is that it is not clear exactly to whom the author is writing. At one point, he seems to want to make a rather sophisticated appeal to the educated reader. However, later in the preface, it would appear that it is a much more personal piece, directed at his family and friends. This is important because if he is simply addressing a common sense audience with common

> sense arguments, which is entirely okay in my book, then his rather loose definition of terms including science, reason, logic and mathematical thinking, etc. is no problem. For example, it is not correct to define philosophy, paradigm, and system of belief as the same thing; they are actually used differently in the literature, although they do have common elements. But in a loosely defined conversation, I suppose it would be okay to equate them.
>
> Clearly this is not genuinely a philosophical piece, since at no point does the author seem to have a hold on philosophy as a tradition of thought, or a full grasp of a particular philosophical movement such as, for example, logical empiricism and the philosophy of science. There is no reference to the Vienna Circle, Wittgenstein, Carnap, Bergmann, Popper or any of the major or minor figures. There is some discussion of mathematics, but I was surprised to see it advanced as a kind of philosophy. I think that Gödel's failure to ground mathematics in the early twentieth century has long since defined the actual place that mathematics plays in science.

The present writer admits he is no philosopher in any modern, formal sense. I state herein my personal views reached via thinking and bases described, by myself and others. Citing philosophers, movements, and schools to lend authority and precedence that justify a view has not been a priority. Rather, I cite *knowledgeable sources*, especially He who I describe as the greatest philosopher in the history of humankind, for the inherent value of their insight and the authority it imparts. I thank the reviewer for his or her useful comments and I apologize for any confusion caused by my merely plain-English, common-sense use of terminology.

I recall a comment of E. T. Jaynes about the language of philosophers. He wrote

> [S]ome readers should be warned not to look for hidden subtleties of meaning which are not present. We shall, of course, explain and use all the standard technical jargon of probability and statistics – because that is our topic. But, though our concern with the nature of logical inference leads us to discuss many of the same issues, our language differs greatly from the stilted jargon of logicians and philosophers. There are no linguistic tricks, and there is no 'meta-language' gobbledygook; only plain English. We think that this will convey our message clearly enough to anyone who seriously wants to understand it. In any event, we feel sure that no further clarity would be achieved by taking the first few steps down that infinite regress that starts with: 'What do you mean by exists?' (Jaynes, E. T., *Probability Theory, The Logic of Science,* Cambridge University Press, Cambridge, 2003, xxviii.)

I also recall comments of Steven Weinberg (*Dreams of a Final Theory,* Vintage Books, New York, 1994, 168-169) on philosophy and philosophers relative to physics. He wrote "... a knowledge of philosophy does not seem to be of use to physicists – always with the exception that the work of some philosophers helps us to avoid the error of other philosophers." About work on philosophy of science he comments "Some of it I find to be written in a jargon so impenetrable that I can only think that it aimed at impressing those who confound obscurity with profundity." He summarizes with "I know of no one who has participated actively in the advance of physics in the postwar period whose research has been significantly helped by the work of philosophers. ... [a] puzzling phenomenon [is] the unreasonable ineffectiveness of philosophy."

With regard to the equivalence of the terms *philosophy*, *paradigm*, and *system of belief*, each of these terms represents a basis for a *world view* or *vision of reality*. Two such visions, their bases, and their meanings are the nominal subjects of this book and, I believe, commonly and appropriately indicated by any and each of these three terms. Moreover, according to Kenny (loc. cit.), while "it is not possible in advance to explain what philosophy is about," certainly philosophy, and scholarship as well, should be about discovering and establishing truth, the subject we address herein. Science, with its continuously applied reality test of comparison with observation, represents an honest attempt to discover truth. Philosophy (and scholarship more generally) is (are) not so direct and honest. For lack of an adequate truth criterion, studies in philosophy too rarely address the issue of truth and are generally more confusing than helpful. One should determine his or her own world view by his or her own experience and contemplation invoking invaluable help freely offered (Book III). Philosophy embraces and promotes many notions and opinions but establishes none as truth, assigning them all equally to some vague, unrestricted reservoir of philosophical possibilities. Indeed, philosophers sometimes scoff at a "naïve belief in absolute truth" because, seemingly, they cannot establish truth by their philosophy and therefore tacitly dismiss such a possibility. Like a materialist scientist or science enthusiast who dismisses all nonmaterial evidence, a skeptical philosopher rejects truth or value as such if it cannot be so established by his or her philosophy, which it generally can't be. (Actually, such rigor is quite justifiable and good, provided one is open to learning better philosophy as we shall describe in due course because that is what this book is about.) At the mention of "absolutely true understanding" in the first paragraph of the preface, the anonymous philosopher-reviewer wrote "What does this mean?" This query reminds me of the "infinite regress started with the question: What do you mean by exists?" The problem in philosophy lies not with truth, which is merely what it is, but with limitations in tools, methods, and scope of thought restricting modern philosophy. We circumvent these limitations of modern philosophy in this book.

[18] Klee, loc. cit., 237.

[19] Weinberg, Steven, 1994, loc. cit., Chapter 7 and *Facing Up,* Harvard University Press, Cambridge, MA, 2001, Chapters 12 and 13.

[20] Sokal, Alan D., and Jean Bricmont, *Fashionable Nonsense: Postmodern Intellectuals' Abuse of Science,* Picador USA, New York, 1999.

[21] Branch, Glenn, Editorial Review of *Fashionable Nonsense* at http://www.amazon.com.

[22] Quoted in Ferris, Timothy, *Coming of Age in the Milky Way,* William Morrow, New York, 1988, 285. Sir James Jeans observed in a similar vein that "Science advances in two ways, by the discovery of new facts, and by the discovery of mechanisms or systems which account for the facts already known. The outstanding landmarks in the progress of science have all been of the second kind." (Quoted in Polanyi, Michael, *Science, Faith and Society,* The University of Chicago Press, Chicago, 1946, 28.)

[23] Ayer (loc. cit., 7, 88-89) claims all evidence bearing on a problem is available but he ignores basic geometrical principles in his illustration that observation of a coin from one perspective reveals a circular shape and from another an elliptical one, implying two different shapes with only one being the "real" shape of the coin. Does that also imply only one "real" perspective for viewing a coin? Of course analogies are never perfect, but simple geometry should not be disregarded. Other philosophers are anything but casual in their effort and care. For instance, Jean-Paul Sartre's 628 pages of abstract thinking and argument entitled *Being and Nothingness, An Essay on Phenomenological Ontology* (English translation by Hazel E. Barnes, Philosophical Library, New York, 1956) is elaborate, carefully developed, and heavy reading because of its abstract level. How well Sartre in particular and philosophy in general relate to reality is another matter. Philosophy is often arbitrary, unconstrained speculation and, in this sense, casual.

[24] How can a literature professor who freely admitted lack of ability in mathematics nonetheless possess rigor similar to that of a mathematical physicist? The answer lies in the rigorous and analytical Greek poetry Lewis loved and with which he was so familiar. Lewis' mathematical ability was abominable, probably due to a psychological block dating to his bad experience in public (private) schools described in his autobiographical *Surprised by Joy* (Harcourt Brace & Company, New York, 1955).

[25] *Bible,* John 14:6.

[26] *Bible,* Philippians 4:7.

[27] *Bible,* 1 Peter 1:8.

2. The Facts and Nothing But the Facts

As a former youth Sunday-school teacher, scoutmaster, youth leader, and father of teenagers, I sometimes received the response to a question in the form of a recitation of a few facts. Such a response is, of course, often quite proper. I am an engineer and scientist by trade and have learned the importance of knowing the facts. However, on some occasions the tone of the recitation of the few facts is condescending and is meant to imply "There, we have dispatched that topic. Now can we talk about something significant?" In such a case the response is not proper because it is disrespectful. It reveals ignorance and indicates an unwillingness to learn from a parent or teacher who knows more than facts, i.e., it indicates an unbecoming pride on the part of the student.

A hierarchy of ignorance consists of the following *student categories* (a hierarchy we use throughout this book) in the order of from lesser to greater ignorance:

(1) one who doesn't know and realizes he or she doesn't know and wants to learn;
(2) one who doesn't know but thinks that he or she does and is not ready to learn;
(3) one who doesn't know and doesn't care.

The category-three student of this hierarchy is illustrated by a story. A teacher asked a class "Why are ignorance and apathy problems in learning?" Rather than call on one of the usually eager students who always participated or one of the merely non-disruptive ones, the teacher selected one from the other group hoping to draw this student and his group into the discussion. The student called on responded, "I don't know and I don't care," thus answering the question. (How one can be proud in ignorance or poverty or both may seem mysterious but it is nevertheless observed.)

Which category of student would you prefer to teach? Students in the first category are a delight to teach. The others are a challenge. With them a category shift must precede learning. Hereafter we characterize a person's attitude toward learning as a category-one-, -two-, or -three-student attitude.

How can an ignorant person think that he or she is knowledgeable? Everyone knows at least some *facts*. *Knowledge*, as we use the term, is merely knowing facts and facts-based art and science. More elusive than facts is *understanding* of them and their *meaning*. Implied by but beyond the facts are layers of understanding and meaning, like layers in an onion. Understanding and meaning contain realization of connections and relationships between facts, including recognition of which facts are important and why. We learn to interpret facts by learning something of their organization, pattern, and connection.

Facts do not change but with ability to interpret them our understanding of them and their meaning does. The facts are a language of a deeper awareness –

unspoken understanding and meaning. A person speaking of facts may really be talking about something deeper, but deeper meaning is not understood by another who knows only the facts. We often observe such a situation when an adult speaks with a young child in the latter's wonderful innocence and naïvete. And subtle meaning implied by simple facts can be obscure to adults as well. The meanings of Christ's parables were regularly lost on His disciples and others because, as was His intent, they understood the facts but not the deeper meaning represented by them.

When a person first learns the facts he or she can immediately speak and understand the "language of meaning" and may therefore believe that he or she fully understands a topic being discussed. One may be fluent in the medium of communication but, like a young child, he or she may be unaware of deeper significance and meaning represented by the facts. Ignorance can be most severe at the threshold of learning, a sentiment poetically captured by Alexander Pope:

> A little learning is a dangerous thing;
> Drink deep or taste not the Pierian spring,
> There shallow draughts intoxicate the brain,
> And drinking largely sobers us up again.

Ignorance at the threshold of learning is natural – we were all once teenagers. Such ignorance is only overcome by deeper learning, a learning of wisdom. One must move beyond facts to understanding and meaning, a transition which marks a "coming of age" in learning represented by four additional lines:

> Only shallow sipping, while intoxicated still,
> Prevents us our goal of learning ever to fulfil.
> Alas, sippers, not drinking, remain forever dull;
> As wisdom broad and deep is ne'er by sipping full.

A worse transgression, represented by my last four lines, is to remain ignorant in spite of much sipping or shallow learning, intoxicated by the many facts learned. That is, one who believes he possesses great knowledge can effectively cease to learn. As the joke goes, "You can always tell an Ivy-League man – but you can't tell him very much." A self-image of great knowledge and a ready explanation of all things in terms of facts suits such a person, as he or she supposes, to be always a teacher and never a student. Such a person, ever engaged in teaching and ignoring learning beyond new facts, fails to "come of age," remaining ignorant of wisdom: understanding of connection, significance, and meaning. While such a one may continue to learn new facts, he or she neglects to learn understanding in pattern, connection, and meaning.

Both of these conditions, too-under-learned or greatly-but-only-factually-learned, correspond to a category-two-student if one's attitude is flawed by refusing to learn because one presumes he or she already knows. Because recognition of ignorance and a desire to learn (i.e., a category-one-student attitude) are (is) necessary to learning and the category-two student holds his or her ignorance tenaciously and defiantly, imagining him- or her-self already "vested in wisdom" and unteachable, a category-two-student attitude prevents learning. For such a person, understanding and meaning remain invisible, with ignorance and attitude preventing even perception of a higher-level beyond his or her current level of awareness.

Level of awareness of understanding and meaning accessible to a person is controlled by the person's philosophy, system of belief, or paradigm. In seeking understanding and meaning one inevitably embraces some philosophy, system of belief, or paradigm by which understanding and meaning are provided. The better the paradigm, the more reliable, comprehensive, and higher the level of awareness of understanding and meaning it provides. Important questions, then, are "What paradigms are better?" and "Which is best?," questions we now begin to address focusing on science and Christianity.

Preferred Paradigm Provides Proper Picture

About thirty years ago, while living in Germany, I attended a devotional meeting of several hundred youth in which any was free to speak or testify. The meeting was the concluding event of a Friday-Saturday retreat for teenagers. I was there with another adult guest, a friend of a mission president in my "Mormon" Church. This mission president asked me to invite his friend because I lived near both his friend and the site of the retreat. My guest was a professional clergyman who had been educated for the ministry in another church. As the young men and women expressed gratitude to God for blessings they enjoyed including understanding of significance and meaning of certain facts, I was moved and uplifted in my own feeling and understanding. Their expressions of feeling and meaning "resonated" with my own. However, my guest had a different reaction. He discreetly confided to me that the comments of these youth seemed to him insincere and self-serving. We were both hearing the same comments, observing the same facts, but because our systems of belief were different we did not perceive the same understanding and meaning. What one believes often differs from what another believes and meaning of facts understood by one may be quite different from their meaning understood by another.

A chosen paradigm dictates which facts are important, one of two functions by which a paradigm controls understanding and meaning. One sees "proper" patterns and connections among the facts only when one considers (a) the "right" set of facts (b) in the "right" way. Without the right pieces and the right thinking the puzzle-picture is not correct. We implicitly adopt a picture as proper when we adopt a system of belief, philosophy, or paradigm. The facts one recognizes as important and how they are viewed are not independent of paradigm. While a philosophy helps us to recognize and order facts, it also controls which facts one regards as important and what puzzle-picture is correct.

Knowledge is based on facts (experience, observation, evidence) because knowledge is simply knowing facts. Understanding and meaning derive from one's embraced system of belief, paradigm, or philosophy by which priorities of facts and their interpretations are assigned. It is by paradigm that one associates and interprets the facts to obtain understanding and comprehend meaning. Persons embracing different paradigms perceive different understanding and meaning. As illustrated above, two people observing the same event have different experience and draw entirely different conclusions about meaning. They may later describe the facts that both observed so differently and reach such different conclusions as to meaning that a third person might question whether they were recalling the same event. The testimony of an eyewitness in a trial is not always useful in discovery of truth, especially if events caused stress and anxiety in the initial seeing or later recalling and telling of them by which, beyond differences due to paradigm, the witness's processing, association, and interpretation of the facts are distorted. Although generally transparent and invisible, such mental/emotional processes are complex and subject to distortion. Paradigm differences among jurists and jurors also lead to different understandings and meanings.

In our natural development we learn to sort and classify (filter) elements of the sensory data stream constantly received through our eyes, ears, etc. so that we are not overwhelmed by the need to steadily concentrate on interpretation of each element. This filtering process is good. By experience we learn to function effectively while processing our sensory data stream in a "background mode" that does not require our full attention until an "alarm event" occurs and causes us to attend carefully to what may be a critical or an emergency situation. If we had to continuously devote full attention to our incoming data stream it would fully occupy us and we would accomplish nothing else. We would be like the baby of age 6 or 8 months in total awe of and fully engaged in observing all the amazing events occurring around him or her. This background filtering capability is useful as it allows us to be simultaneously engaged in multiple activities.

However, as suggested by Kuhn,[1] in our quest to simply and rapidly categorize elements of the incoming data stream we sometimes miss or misread a data element or fact, especially one that does not fit our paradigm, perhaps because it may be distorted by our being under stress when we are hurried or witnessing a crime. In our natural rush to simply and rapidly categorize events we sometimes misread or miscategorize a strange or "fuzzy" signal as one that is familiar or anticipated according to our paradigm. We can even so mislead ourselves in a "seemingly deliberate" process. For instance, most hunters are familiar with "buck fever," the mental/emotional condition where a hunter is so focused on seeing a buck that he may shoot at any moving object he sees, a cow, a horse, or even a hunting partner. Another example perhaps most have experienced is momentarily seeing something for which one is intently searching. Smoot and Davidson[2] observe in their book on cosmology that in science it's all too easy to be seduced into believing you have seen an effect for which you are looking. And physicist Richard Feynman has further warned in a similar sense "… that you must not fool yourself and you are the easiest person to fool."[3] Or we may simply dismiss as unimportant a strange or fuzzy signal because it doesn't fit our paradigm!

Consequently, dependence on our paradigm for interpretation of understanding and meaning is compounded. Not only do we select and interpret the facts by means of our paradigm, we use our paradigm to categorize, store, recall, and associate the facts.

Proposition Number 1: **One's *paradigm*, *system of belief*, or *philosophy* is utilized in and essential to observing, classifying, and storing the facts and in recalling, associating, and interpreting them to obtain understanding and meaning.**

Despite a natural (learned) urge to rush to a decision in classifying a sensory fact, we should not be in such a hurry that we don't notice, that we misread, or that we discard as artifactual (because it seems to contradict our paradigm) what may be an important signal (experience or sensory fact). Occasionally, a signal or sequence of signals does not neatly fit any preconceived category of our paradigm. It may consequently seem strange and unrealistic. Such a result may indicate that the signal is garbled or rendered fuzzy by interference due to poor visibility or background noise or due to a stressed mental state. Or, it may indicate that one's range of preconceived categories, i.e., the scope of one's paradigm, is inadequate because "strange" and "unrealistic" are paradigm dependent. In this last case, when we encounter a "strange" or "unrealistic" event we are in fact encountering a great opportunity to learn at a fundamental level, the level of foundation of paradigm, an opportunity well illustrated by the following bit of history.

Learning from the Unexpected, Strange, and Nonsensical: Roentgen's Discovery of X-rays

Encountering a non-intuitive or strange fact implies that it lies outside our paradigm and therefore, if it is valid, this fact represents fundamentally new knowledge. Because it seems strange and incorrect and may even seem nonsensical, there exists a temptation to dismiss it as an aberration. But it is just when we encounter such a fact that we may have encountered a huge opportunity to learn something beyond, maybe far beyond, our present knowledge, something that will perhaps revise or even revolutionize our understanding. As a scientist I learned to relish the events that I found surprising, the unexpected, the apparently incorrect, because they often led me to something I didn't know. Such was the reaction of a German physics professor named Roentgen when he happened to observe an unexpected result.

Wilhelm Konrad Roentgen (1845-1923) obtained his education first in Holland where he received a degree in mechanical engineering and then in Switzerland where he studied physics under August Kundt at Zürich. Upon receiving a Ph.D. in 1869 Roentgen continued working with Kundt as an assistant, accompanying Kundt when he returned to Germany. Roentgen worked in several branches of physics and did competent work, but he did not distinguish himself as being among the elite physicists.

In the fall of 1895, Roentgen was in Bavaria at the University of Würzburg serving as head of the Department of Physics. Roentgen then encountered the great moment in which he rose as a physicist from a level of the merely competent to that of the elite. He was studying electron beams, called *cathode rays*, and the luminescence these rays caused upon colliding with and energizing coatings of certain chemicals on sheets of paper. On 5 November 1895, to observe faint luminescence, he enclosed the cathode-ray apparatus in blackened cardboard in a darkened room. Upon turning on the ray he noticed out of the corner of his eye a faint flash of light far outside the apparatus. On closer inspection he found the source was a glowing coating of barium platinocyanide on a paper sheet. One of his luminescing samples was glowing when the cathode rays were not energizing it! This result was completely unexpected.

Roentgen turned the cathode ray off and the sample stopped glowing. He turned it on and the sample glowed. He carried the sample into an adjacent room, shut the door and closed the blinds. The sample still glowed when the cathode ray was on and did not glow when it was off.

Roentgen surmised that some unknown radiation was being generated in the cathode-ray apparatus and exciting luminescence in the sample and that this radiation was both highly penetrating and invisible. He quickly found by experiment that the radiation could pass apparently undiminished through a stack of paper of significant thickness and even through thin metal sheets. Because the nature of this radiation was completely unknown to Roentgen, he named it X-rays, X being a common mathematical and scientific symbol for an unknown. The name has persisted even though the radiation's nature is now as well known as any other radiation. By international convention, the standard unit of X-ray radiation is named the *roentgen* and X-rays themselves are called Roentgen-strahlen in German-speaking countries.

Roentgen recognized the importance of his discovery and was anxious to publish before someone else announced the same discovery. Simultaneously, he wanted to include as much data as possible in his announcement. He confined himself to his laboratory for seven weeks, rarely leaving, to perform X-ray experiments. On 28 December 1895, he finally submitted for publication his first manuscript on X-rays including not only an account of their discovery but also measured results for all fundamental X-ray properties, such as the ionization of gases these rays cause and the absence of any influence of electric or magnetic fields on these rays.

Roentgen gave the first public lecture on his discoveries on 23 January 1896. When he finished his lecture he asked for a volunteer from the audience and Rudolf Kölliker came forward. Kölliker, appropriately, was an anatomist and physiologist and was nearing the age of 80. Roentgen took an X-ray photograph of Kölliker's hand and quickly developed and displayed it to the audience. It showed Kölliker's bones to be in beautiful condition for an octogenarian and the finely-detailed outline of a ring on one of Kölliker's fingers. The importance of this demonstration was not lost on the audience and they responded with enthusiastic applause. X-ray research immediately spread throughout Europe and America.

Roentgen's discovery led to a rash of further discoveries that caused such a thorough revision of old concepts that Roentgen's discovery is widely regarded as the beginning of a Second Scientific Revolution, following the work of Galileo and others introducing the First Scientific Revolution three centuries earlier (described in Chapter 6). Within one year of the discovery of X-rays, a thousand papers had been published on this topic.

Roentgen shared the 1896 Rumford medal with Philipp Lenard, who had discovered certain properties of the photoelectric effect (Chapter 9), and Roentgen was awarded the first Nobel Prize in physics in 1901.

What was the critical step in Roentgen's discovery? When was the moment he distinguished himself as a physicist? It was the moment he noted the unexpected, faint flash out of the corner of his eye, the sensory event that didn't fit his paradigm and set off an alarm to take note, an alarm to which he immediately responded as a category-one student (defined in the second paragraph of this chapter). Everything that followed was routine, except for the intensity of his effort, and could have been done by any physicist of normal competence. The quality by which Roentgen distinguished himself was his astuteness in recognizing something unexpected and his enlightened, category-one-student reaction to it.

Here is a lesson for us all. When we observe or learn something new, unexpected, unusual, or strange we should not dismiss it as irrelevant and should certainly not treat it as some kind of threat. We should not lock ourselves into a category-two- or -three-student attitude (also defined in the second paragraph of this chapter). We may have encountered an important opportunity to learn a fundamentally new fact and greatly expand our paradigm. We should always be willing to learn, like a category-one student, "as wisdom broad and deep is ne'er by sipping full." The greatest learning opportunities are never scheduled. Nor should they have to be. If we are wise, we note unexpected events and promptly pursue them.

Proposition Number 2: **To expand and enhance a paradigm, one must pay attention to facts which are unexpected, which seem strange, which are non-intuitive. In other words, one must seek to learn at a fundamental level.**

Lewis' Process of Transposition

Relating to differences in perception of reality, C. S. Lewis has described a process he called *Transposition*.[4] A Transposition is the translation of facts, concepts, and meaning between levels of understanding. The Transposition process is to large degree hypothetical, because understanding comes through a personal paradigm which represents an individual's scope of awareness and comprehension at a given time and is, therefore, not known or understood by another person or, perhaps, even by the same person at another time. Nevertheless, Transposition hypothetically applied between two different persons or one person at different times serves as a powerful tool by which several essential points relating to understanding and meaning may be clearly visualized.

Lewis points out that all of us recognize and react to a set of sensations and emotions (both being facts) but that while the facts may be identical, the understanding and meaning they communicate may vary between individuals. As we have already suggested, such differences naturally occur, forced by differing cultures, philosophies, or paradigms and levels of personal development. Lewis further points out that the "language" of understanding of meaning contains a limited set of sensory sensations and emotions, with richer, higher-level systems of understanding and belief consequently containing more variations of meaning in the same language elements, i.e., the same sensations and emotions. Like the English alphabet which contains five vowel characters but twenty-two vowel sounds, each sensation and emotion and combination may have multiple meanings. Translating or Transposing from a richer system of belief to a poorer one involves the same unchanged facts, but understanding and meaning are lost as some variations of meaning of facts recognized and understood in the richer system are not recognized in the poorer system.

As a simple illustration of Transposition we consider the American Christmas tradition of Santa Claus. A child receives gifts on Christmas morning left during the night by some unknown person the child's parents call Santa Claus. This mysterious event and the gifts are exciting and wonderful. An older child or adult who does not believe in Santa Claus (here is the Transposition) may also receive a gift, still exciting and wonderful, but not from an unknown source. In this case knowledge of the identity of the giver enhances the gift because in addition to its inherent value it also communicates affection of and may represent considerable effort by the giver on behalf of the receiver. The increased understanding in the latter case allows the receiver to more fully understand and appreciate the meaning of the gift.

Lewis also points out that higher, richer levels of awareness and understanding are always invisible to one at a lower-level.

> Let us now return to our original question about Spirit and Nature, God and Man. Our problem was that in what claims to be our spiritual life all the elements of our natural life recur, and, what is worse, it looks at first glance as if no other elements are present. We now see that if the spiritual is richer than the natural (as no one who believes in its existence would deny), then this is exactly what we should expect. And the skeptic's conclusion that the so-called spiritual is really derived from the natural, that it is a mirage or projection or imaginary extension of the natural, is also exactly what we should expect, for, as we have seen, this is the mistake that an observer who knew only the lower medium would be bound to make in every case of Transposition. The brutal man never can by analysis find anything but lust in love; ...; physiology never can find anything in thought except twitching of the grey matter. It is no good browbeating the critic who approaches a Transposition from below. On the evidence available to him his conclusion is the only possible one. ... Spiritual things are [only] spiritually discerned.[4]

Lewis goes on to address meaning versus materialism, a contrast in which we are particularly interested, using a compelling illustration of awareness of facts but lack of awareness of meaning.

> I have tried to stress throughout the inevitableness of the error made about every Transposition by one who approaches it from the lower medium only. The strength of such a critic lies in the words 'merely' or 'nothing but.' He sees all the facts but not the meaning. Quite truly, therefore, he claims to have seen all the facts. There *is* nothing else there, except the meaning. He is therefore, as regards the matter in hand, in the position of an animal. You will have noticed that most dogs cannot understand *pointing*. You point to a bit of food on the floor; the dog, instead of looking at the floor, sniffs at your finger. A finger is a finger to him, and that is all. His world is all fact and no meaning. And in a period when factual realism is dominant we shall find people deliberately inducing upon themselves this doglike mind. A man who has experienced love from within will deliberately go about to inspect it analytically from outside and regard the results of this analysis as truer

> than his experience. The extreme limit of this self-binding is seen in those who, like the rest of us, have consciousness, yet go about to study the human organism as if they did not know it was conscious. As long as this deliberate refusal to understand things from above, even where such understanding is possible, continues, it is idle to talk of any final victory over materialism. The critique of every experience from below, the voluntary ignoring of meaning and concentration on fact, will always have the same plausibility. There will always be evidence, and every month fresh evidence, to show that religion is only psychological, justice only self-protection, politics only economics, love only lust, and thought itself only cerebral biochemistry.[4]

Proposition Number 3: **Knowledge of objective facts provides no comprehension of deeper meaning. Only through interpretation of facts utilizing a higher understanding does one comprehend such meaning. An adopted *paradigm*, *system of belief*, or *philosophy* used to interpret facts thus strongly influences and, indeed, controls meaning.**

Material-Universe and Total-Universe Facts

Facts are the basic elements of knowledge, understanding, and meaning. The scientist uses facts in seeking scientific laws that are universally valid, ones that apply in the hands and mind of any capable user in any situation. To discover a universally valid law, the facts from which the law is deduced must be universally valid since the nature of the facts follows from the nature of the laws governing them. For this reason scientists exclusively seek *objective*, *reproducible*, material-related evidence (facts) to depersonalize scientific insights and laws. In a scientific context *objective* means existing outside and independent of mind in the sensible (material) universe and being intersubjectively observable and verifiable. *Reproducible* means repeatable with the same result by either the same or a different observer in different situations and at different times whenever necessary physical conditions are reproduced. Thus, reproducible facts are independent of observer (personality) and situation and time (culture). Scientific facts are therefore *lowest-common-denominator* facts or facts that all capable observers agree on, including capable observers of the lowest perception and awareness. The term *universal* denotes a scope of application that spans the universe. It thus implies individual-user or specific-situation independence.

Through its empirical methods, science has continually become more comprehensive in its observations and more accurate in its theories and laws. In consequence, scientists and others have accepted the belief that any desired level of accuracy and any breadth of knowledge will eventually be obtained through continuing improvements in science. This assumption has led to the belief that all phenomena may be known and described by science on the basis of scientific measurements, theories, and laws, if not at present then in the future, giving science a comprehensive, universal capability. We shall later refer to this assumption of universal, comprehensive capability of science as the *universality assumption*.

Because of the required objectivity of scientific evidence, such evidence must be limited to the *material universe* existing outside and independent of mind and being intersubjectively observable and verifiable by all capable observers. Nevertheless, science incorporates intellectual models and tools, principally mathematical ones, and uses them to characterize the material universe thus imposing on it a regularity and order that (presumably) represents and reveals its true nature.

French mathematician and mathematical physicist Jules Henri Poincaré (1854-1912) made the following statement on the contribution of mathematics in science:

> ... without this language [mathematics] most of the intimate analogies of things would have remained forever unknown to us; and we should forever have been ignorant of the internal harmony of the world, which is ... the only true objective reality.[5]

Poincaré thus describes mathematics in science as providing knowledge of pattern and organization among the facts, i.e., "the intimate analogies of things" and "the internal harmony of the world," and further describes it as "the only true objective reality," i.e., the revealed (inferred) nature of the material universe. Poincaré's statement indicates that the intent in science is deeper than merely learning facts. Of interest in science is learning what is often called the *meaning of the facts*, i.e., relationship, pattern, organization, and structure among the facts and, beyond that, fundamental truths implied by these connections. Scientific facts contain a wealth of information extracted, as Poincaré suggests, by careful deliberation of *what the facts mean*. But scientific facts are limited by the nature of science to material-universe objects and phenomena and abstract principles deduced therefrom. Consequently, meaning communicated by or deduced from these facts is limited by science and scientific thinking to material things and processes.

The *universe* is defined and generally regarded as *the totality of all things and phenomena observed or postulated*. Science addresses only a portion of this universe, the *material universe*. Although intellectual capability and (mathematical) devices are employed in assessing it, nonmaterial mind, the intellect, and reasoning as well as emotion, feeling, values, and spiritual things and influence are excluded from this universe. A materialist recognizes no reality beyond a material one and considers thought and feeling and all real being and phenomena to be fully explainable in terms of matter alone (Chapter 11). This belief is merely assumed with no proof offered. Spirit and spiritual phenomena must be attributed by a pure materialist to imagination, trickery, superstition, or ignorance. But those who have experienced spiritual influence recognize its reality and importance. Those who have not still have something fundamental to learn, as do most of us who already believe in the spiritual.

Containing but extending beyond the material universe lies the *total universe*. In addition to material-universe facts, total-universe facts also include those pertaining to the subjective and personal, the cognitive, the emotional, and the spiritual. Because these facts may be primarily subjective rather than objective, they cannot be regarded as identically intersubjectively perceivable, nor reproducible by recreating outward physical conditions, nor verifiable by all in a diverse group of even capable observers.

The descriptor "lowest-common-denominator" again refers to those facts sensed and agreed upon by all observers including those least perceptive and aware. Since nonmaterial facts appear to extend far beyond material ones in both number and diversity, the total universe seems to possess a much larger "factual dimension" than the material universe suggesting different and more diverse sensitivities are required for perceiving total-universe facts. With respect to total-universe facts, restriction to lowest-common-denominator perception is severely limiting and undesirable.

Intellectual processes such as reason, mathematical, and personal thinking do not fit exclusively into either objective or subjective because they fit in both. In the case of mathematics, a formal structure is utilized by which any capable person can learn mathematics and use it in a common, intersubjectively-verifiable manner. On the other hand, reason and personal thinking, at least that based on unique, personal experience, can only be classified as subjective, not existing outside and independent of mind and not intersubjectively verifiable. Indeed, all intellectual processes fully exist only within the mind and only aspects of them are transferable to an imagined, ideal, objective, *external universe*. This imaginary, ideal, external universe (or world) is where objective, material-universe facts of science are placed and used, but all intellectual activity is fully contained in only the total universe.

Ability to perceive and awareness of the nonmaterial universe differs from perception and awareness of the material universe. An excellent scientist quite capable of observing the most obscure details of the material universe may be unperceptive and unaware of many nonmaterial-universe facts quite apparent to another. (Generally, women perceive nonmaterial-universe facts better than men.) And such facts are likely to contain most of the meaning-important ones because of the greater diversity in facts and much greater dimension and scope of the total universe over the material universe. No material-universe meaning is comparable in depth or power of feeling to some total-universe meaning.

We must broaden our consideration beyond the material when we consider subjects or creatures possessing intelligence, emotions, and spirit. That is, we must consider the broader scope of total-universe understanding and meaning and in doing so we transcend the limits of science.[6] Sufficient intelligence, emotions, and spirit in a creature (e.g., a person) preclude its proper study by the scientific method because intelligence, emotions, and spirit impart subjectivity. While observation of such subjects (in psychology, psychiatry, medicine, sociology, political science, anthropology, etc.) might be objective, the subjects themselves are not, their actions being neither objective nor subject-to-subject reproducible in strictly following fundamental, universal law.[7] Consequently, observed behaviors of such creatures do not unambiguously reflect fundamental, universal, physical law like motions of atoms or planets seem to. Rather, if a subject is capable of and free to express individual choice, its actions reflect some unknown mixture of universal law and subjective preference of the individual, intelligent-emotional-spirit creature. Since such creatures may be similar or even identical in appearance but possess different (invisible) subjectivity, no complete subject-to-subject reproducibility in behavior, as is observed with identical atoms or similar planets, should be expected. Thus, traditional application of scientific inquiry to the study of subjects possessing and capable of expressing intelligence, emotions, and spirit should not be expected to easily discover either fundamental law or any complete meaning of observed facts. This deficiency in applicability of scientific inquiry is severe but almost uniformly unrecognized in scientific studies of subjects possessing intelligence, emotions, and spirit, as C. S. Lewis bemoaned in the latter of his two, previously-quoted comments. It is no wonder that results in such science are often inconclusive, vague, or spurious compared to observed accuracy of fundamental laws discovered and precisely defined in hard science as relating to atoms, planets, etc.[8]

Meaning and its Value

Meaning in the imaginary, ideal, external world (or universe) of science is only discerned by discovering relationships, patterns, organization, and structure among the material-universe facts and, beyond that, more fundamental connections and principles they imply. Such meaning represents *some* of the essence, significance, and understanding of import of these material-universe facts. But the most fundamental, comprehensive, and important meaning cannot be based only on material-connected, scientific facts. In the quotation of William James in the Preface, meaning depends on abstract concepts or *values*, totally absent in a system of belief based only on objective, material-connected facts. Consideration of only material things ignoring intelligence, emotions, and spirit recognizes no values. Values such as honesty, patience, beauty, kindness, and love are not material but intelligence, emotion, and spirit related, qualities ignored in the material-connected facts of science because they are not objective and universal but are subjective and individual-intelligence-emotional-spirit related. Science is by its nature value free. By design, i.e., by its required objectivity, science is also free of perception and awareness of nonmaterial-intelligence-, -emotion- and -spirit-connected facts. But only perception and awareness of values, intelligence, feelings, and the spiritual guide one to an understanding of deepest meaning. To discover this meaning one must seek beyond the merely-material-universe and science focused exclusively on describing only it.

We hereafter generally use the term “meaning” to refer to comprehensive or total-universe meaning and we sometimes take “nonmaterial meaning” to be essentially equivalent to this meaning. To be sure, science and meaning of its facts are real, useful, and even profound and do describe real significance in material-universe science. But such significance is not comprehensive in scope. Paradigms broader and deeper than science contain values and simple facts that can convey meaning beyond any indicated in science. In the two systems we examine in this book, science draws its facts and meaning exclusively from the material universe using the intellect of man while Christianity draws its facts from the total universe, especially the nonmaterial, intellectual-moral-emotional-and-spiritual universe, using the intellect of man, revealed truth, and divine providence. As already indicated, both universes are indefinitely large but the Christian universe is substantially larger. Much of the total universe, especially values, is not directly sensed by sight, hearing, taste, touch, or smell and many total-universe facts must therefore be inferred from sight-hearing-touch-taste-smell facts and, importantly and at least occasionally, from *other-(spiritual-)sense* facts as well, making the Christian universe at once more comprehensive and subtle, deeper, and far richer in the meaning it contains and conveys.

For these reasons meaning perceived by a Christian sensitive to total-universe facts is generally invisible to one focused on only the material universe or, even more so, on the imaginary, ideal, external world (or universe) representation of reality used in science. Moreover, the "same" facts observed in "the universe" communicate different meanings to different observers with information content, in principle and practice, richer to one than another. With respect to understanding of meaning, is one right and the other wrong? Both are correct in their own system. But which system is superior in providing a knowledge and meaning of reality?

We shall eventually answer this last question. For the present we will be satisfied with a few quotations from eminent American physicist E. T. Jaynes (1922-1998) who, among few others, recognized *the critical problem of meaning*. With respect to the utility and value of meaning Jaynes observed

> At the stage of development of a theory where we already have a formalism successful in one domain, and we are trying to extend it to a wider one, some [other] kind of philosophy about what the formalism "means" is absolutely essential to provide us with a [comprehensive vision and, thereby, a] sense of direction.[9]

> And perhaps that other philosophy will lead to still further generalizations, to which my own philosophy makes me blind. That is, after all, just the process by which all progress in theoretical physics has been made.[10]

That is also the process by which progress in *life* is made. Whether or not Jaynes had only the domain of science in mind, his thinking applies throughout a total-universe scope of application for which he correctly interprets the universal value of meaning, a scope I have emphasized by my square-bracketed additions to his comment.

It is therefore clear that one's understanding of meaning is critical to success because it provides the vision by which success and progress toward it are defined. Thus, "the critical problem of meaning" addresses what we desire to become, why, and how we get there. Its solution is essential if success is to be recognized and effectively sought and, for this reason, the problem of meaning illuminates the danger of incorrect interpretation of reality. Jaynes gives two material-universe-based illustrations in the form of incorrect and misleading syllogisms that fail to capture correct meaning. They are also good illustrations for the broader scope we consider.

> (i) The present *mathematical formalism* [of quantum theory] can be made to reproduce many experimental facts very accurately.
>
> ***Therefore***
>
> The *physical [Copenhagen] interpretation* which Niels Bohr tried to associate with it must be true; and it is naïve to try to circumvent it.[11] (the italics are Jaynes')

> (ii) The mathematical system of epicycles [used in describing orbits in terms of circles] can be made to reproduce the motions of the planets very accurately.
>
> ***Therefore***
>
> The theological arguments for the necessity of epicycles must be true, and it is heresy to try to circumvent them.[11]

All of these statements of Jaynes contain meaning that will be enhanced for the uninitiated reader after the science from which they originate is addressed in sufficient detail. But their importance is already evident.

In spite of its focus on material-universe facts and nothing but these facts, few, if any, would condemn science. Indeed, many, like Poincaré, applaud its practical and real foundation. Science has led to philosophical relief from oppressive dogma (Chapter 6) and provided greatly expanded knowledge of natural philosophy (Chapters 5 through 11) as well as tangible benefits of great importance in easing human afflictions and materially elevating human amenity.

But science is nonetheless a limiting philosophy because purely objective, scientific inquiry must be exclusively focused on material facts for discovering the nature of reality, a philosophy we denote *materialism*. As proposed in the above quotations of Lewis, materialism precludes any full comprehension of meaning and, therefore, is a threat to both the individual and society. This threat has been more clearly described by Owen Barfield.

Enter Science, Exit Meaning?

Owen Barfield[12] has observed that absence of a sense of (moral, emotional, and spiritual) meaning underlies much of deviant and destructive behavior. Such a result is due, in my words, to the fact that a sense of meaning provides a sense of values and consequences, furnishing one with both an understanding of and a motivation for constructive behavior. Loss of meaning within a culture, Barfield notes, therefore leads thoughtful people to a feeling of foreboding. It seems the greater the ability of humans to control the world, the less meaning we are able to perceive. Barfield notes that this dilemma follows as a direct consequence of a rather recent historical event. We shall examine and expand on Barfield's views in the following pages, beginning with the "rather recent historical event."

The inauguration of the scientific revolution some 400 years ago and its successful application in addressing a wide range of problems has had considerable impact on human thinking. Beginning at that time there arose in natural philosophy the practice of meticulous observation of positive (or definitive) data of sense-experience facts and systematic analysis and organization of them in terms of natural cause-and-effect relationships. Because objectivity is required in science, subjective perception of feelings, emotions, values, and consequences are excluded. Only lowest-common-denominator perceptions of material objects or phenomena recognized (apparently) uniformly by each of a group of observers are considered objective. While the practice originated in the natural philosophy (science), this method was promoted for pursuing all kinds of knowledge in the nineteenth century as a dogma under the name of *positive philosophy* or *positivism*. Positivism addresses the material universe utilizing science and mathematics. But stating a precise definition of positivism has proven to be difficult, with significant alterations quickly following every attempt.[13] Because it focuses exclusively on material objects and phenomena, *scientific positivism* is equivalent in its scope to *materialism*: the belief or doctrine that matter is the only reality and that everything including thought, consciousness, will, and feeling can only be understood and explained in terms of matter. Barfield described the consequence of such a belief as follows.

> The denial of ... [any] inner being to the processes of nature leads inevitably to the denial of it to man himself. For if physical objects and physical causes and effects are all that we can know, it follows that man himself can be known only to the extent that he is a physical object among physical objects. Thus, it is implicit in positivism [and materialism] that man can never know anything about his specifically human self – his own inner being – any more than he can ever really know anything about the meaning of the world of nature by which he is surrounded.[14]

Positivism includes the belief, perhaps originally propounded by the French philosopher Auguste Comte (1798-1857), that the meticulous, objective observation of the facts of material nature and the deduction of cause-and-effect relationships among them is not just a useful philosophy but the only viable one. Here the logic is elusive since the proposal of one methodology alone being viable in intellectual investigation is not legitimately established by evidence collected and evaluated only by that methodology, a classic example of circular or self-dependent argument. Thus, this belief is, in fact, a dogma. (Indeed, *positivism* and *dogmatism* are listed as equivalents in many dictionaries.) This logical inconsistency of positivism apparently escaped the notice of scientist-followers (whether through Comtist teachings or their own practice of the scientific method) intently involved with the application of the method rather than a consideration of the philosophical foundation thereof. And such details as logical inconsistency or the high ambitions of Comte, who described the anticipated impact of his principles in grand, self-serving terms, did not concern its devout believers. At the end of a course of lectures at the Palais Royal in 1849, 1850 and 1851, Comte concluded with the following claim.

> In the name of the past and of the future, the servants of humanity – both its philosophical and its practical servants – come forward to claim as their due the general direction of this world. Their object is to constitute at length a real Providence in all departments – moral, intellectual and material. Consequently they exclude once [and] for all from political supremacy all the different servants of God – Catholic, Protestant or Deist – as being at once behindhand and a cause of disturbance.[15]

Comte and his followers went on to establish a *positivist religion* in which traditional religious emblems such as sacraments and saints were replaced with scientific accomplishments. Comte's philosophy established a hierarchy of truths as follows: (1) mathematics, (2) astronomy, (3) physics, (4) chemistry, (5) biology, and (6) sociology. Each member of this series is more special (less fundamental) than the member preceding it and, because it depends on the more fundamental levels, cannot be fully understood without first understanding all the preceding levels. It follows that the crowning science of the hierarchy – sociology, which deals with the phenomena of human society – will remain longest under the influence of theological dogmas and "abstract figments" and will be the last to pass into the positive stage. Such a philosophy is, of course, antithetical to Christian belief. It is also naïve since we neither understand mathematics, astronomy, physics, chemistry, and biology nor seem to be approaching anywhere near a complete understanding of any one. Indeed, in being forced to abandon long-held certainties in science and mathematics (Chapter 10) we seem to be moving backward even though we are moving forward.

Although the formal Comtist religious movement now seems to be abandoned, materialism or scientific positivism is still embraced by many as is much Comtist dogma, particularly the premise or creed that the meticulous, objective observation of the facts of material nature and the deduction of cause-and-effect relationships among them is not merely a useful philosophy but the only possible one. The success and prestige of early science from which materialism and positivism so heavily borrow and the popular acceptance among scientists and others of the scientific method as the exclusive or most powerful source of reliable, demonstrable knowledge have encouraged acceptance of this premise or creed. Indeed, it has now been thoroughly absorbed into Western thinking to the extent that it is widely held not as dogma but rather as a fact established by science. Nothing could be further from the truth, as will be demonstrated in examining both scientific principles and practice.

Danger in Comtist and Christian Dogmas

The principal dangers of the Comtist dogma (positivism) or materialism are two, and they are related so that their effects compound one another. First, when one regards knowledge exclusively as the knowing of objective, lowest-common-denominator, material facts and, perhaps, some cause-and-effect relationships between or physical-mechanistic interpretations of them, one is ultimately led to the conclusion that *nothing* is known with certainty. This latent instability in the dogma has been more clearly exposed by a relatively recent further step in the doctrine. While the older form of positivism proclaimed that humans could *know* nothing except through physical-world facts and mechanisms deduced from sensory observation, the twentieth century version, known variously as "logical positivism," "scientific empiricism," "linguistic analysis," "analytical philosophy," and so on (see endnotes 13 and 16), claims nothing can even be legitimately *stated* when based on any other rationale. This modern thinking in the form of logical positivism, etc., illuminated in the quotations of Ayer and Heisenberg and associated commentary in Chapter 1, forces a logical conclusion and exposes the implied predicament always philosophically inherent in positivism. Namely, either it must be admitted that what we think and say is without *meaning* beyond that based on only the clearly-described, material-universe, absolute facts of positivism or positivism (materialism) must be abandoned. For if meaning is based on more than material-universe facts and phenomena, positivism or materialism is inadequate for comprehending or describing the universe. And there is little doubt that real facts and phenomena that transcend the material, such as human values and volition based thereon, are essential to full rationalization of observed facts and phenomena.

Here I must add a little background to Barfield's argument which will, hopefully, clarify the basis of his sweeping conclusion that, ultimately, nothing may be certainly known by positivism. We note from above that materialism is based on facts relating to material-universe phenomena which we perceive through our senses by meticulous observation followed by rigorous analysis of these facts. Moreover, these facts must be reproducible and objective, i.e., both person and situation independent. Under materialism, these principles are held so strongly that no other possibilities are even contemplated. But, when one adopts a truly rigorous level of evaluation or criticism, there exists no such thing as an objective fact perceived through our senses. Our senses are not objective. They are subjective, indeed, so subjective we cannot determine the level of subjectivity at which they function.

Consider the example of sight. We all recognize the color yellow because this color has from our earliest recollection been identified to us by the name yellow. While the color yellow or green or blue as perceived in one person's visual system of eyes, optical nerve, brain, and mind may have quite another sequence of appearances (colors) in another's, we all recognize the "same" colors by the common, learned names. This commonality in reading of colors is *linguistic* or *cultural* and it in no way assures that two observers "see" the same thing. Yet in positivism the observed color of an object, the observed frequency of a tone, etc. are regarded as the only absolutes. A list of physical properties of the elements generally includes the appearance of the material in its various physical states. But such properties as transparency, translucency, opaqueness, and color are subjective, not only in degree but also in quality. They are in fact culturally-conditioned, subjective facts rather than objectively perceived, absolute, material properties.

Precisely the same kind of limitations apply to our other senses. What does sugar or salt taste like or ammonia smell like? These are individual, subjective experiences that only seem to be unambiguously shared by a learned, cultural commonality, namely, language (-based thought). The actual sensations experienced by any individual are unknown to any other because they are subjective and personal and because language is not capable of direct and unambiguous communication of personal, subjective experience on any objective, absolute basis. Knowledge of an individual *or* group is ultimately based on personal, individual, subjective experience and is merely relative within objective description of that experience.

While personal perception of any fact is direct, unambiguous, and subjective, intersubjective communication of such perception is neither direct nor unambiguous. According to linguistic analysts (posivitists), direct and unambiguous communication requires incorporation of objectivity and universality into language and culture beyond just mathematics and science. However, such ideal ability is never attained even in mathematics and science, nor will it be until humans can fully read each others' minds. Nor is it desirable in language and culture.

Basis of Christian belief is often less compelling than basis of scientific belief. The historical, military-enforced spread of Christian beliefs by violating them was arrogant, hypocritical, and evil. Being called to serve God as a preacher by "a cloud formation in the sky" is not authoritative. Neither is uninspired interpretation of the Bible. Claims of spiritual guidance have led to truth-and-contention or confusion-and-contention dating from far before the time of Christ. A huge diversity in Christian belief exists today and a test of validity of belief is not commonly known, forcing many to *arbitrarily* choose a Christian paradigm or some alternative. One must be no less careful in considering Christian belief as one is in considering science.

Filtering or Coloring the Facts

Inherent uncertainty in the scientific meaning of evidence thus accompanies all objective, material-universe observation due to the personal, subjective nature of such observation and limitations in ability to fully and accurately communicate observation. This uncertainty occurs because the ideal of objectivity of observation is fundamentally mismatched with the subjective nature of observation, categorization, and analysis.

Other limitations in observation and, consequently, in scientific and Christian belief occur. One example is outright fallibility of sensory experience. Most people have thought they saw or heard something at one time or another that was not what they originally thought it was. A shading of light, a congruence of background noises, or an expectation of a certain result can cause sensory input to be misread or miscategorized.[17] And once such a process is known to occur, it can occur in undetected instances.

Expectation of a certain result can be especially consequential in observation. Paradigm, philosophy, and belief are essentially incorporated into intuition and the process of categorizing and analyzing events (facts) perceived in our sensory data stream in a *sensual-neural-cerebral-cultural-filtering system*. Severe limitation can occur at each of two distinct levels. On an *individual* level, occasional, unexpected or fuzzy signals may be miscategorized and misanalyzed, especially in a non-normal mode of distress or excitement or when an interpretation involves information (culture) that is sketchy. Often, with care, one can nonetheless functionally approach the ideal of objective, reliable facts through requirement that the facts be reproducible. However, not all experience is repeatable and some kinds of experience inherently stress or excite normal functioning so that the ideal cannot be approached. Facts we recall and recount are "colored" not only by individual mental/emotional state but also by individual philosophy including individual culture, since even within a common culture each personal philosophy and culture is individualized in its composition of many elements whether deliberately chosen or not.

At a second level, *group* miscategorization occurs not due to fuzziness of signal or sketchiness of personal culture but due to outright error in philosophy or culture embraced by the group and employed in the sensual-neural-cerebral-cultural filter. Philosophy is a controlling ingredient in any evaluation of observation because it is by philosophy that the facts are "pertinent," the argument is "cogent," and the view is "realistic," these being standards by which we include or reject evidence. Thus, error in philosophy is often self-screening and self-propagating, self-screening because an error imposes and supports its own "truth" and facts are recognized and evaluated in this "truth" and self-propagating because a continuation in holding the error to be truth prevents discovery of contrary evidence. For instance, if we hold that mass is fixed and always conserved, we must reject the equivalence of mass and energy ($E = mc^2$) discovered by Einstein (Chapter 8) by which a body is more massive when hot than cold. As physicist Hans Christian von Baeyer has noted, "At a certain level of precision the concept of mass as a fixed attribute of an object loses its meaning."[18] Or if we hold that a perfect vacuum contains nothing, we must disregard the known, spontaneous generation of particle pairs (most notably electrons and positrons) and photons (particles or quanta of light) produced by energy fluctuations in the vacuum (Chapter 9). Thus, group miscategorization is caused by a common error in philosophy or culture of a group.

However, error is error whether in an individual or group. Its net effect is indistinguishable since any such error influences the same filter system imposing the same uncertainty. But group cultural error can be more difficult to identify and correct, properties well illustrated and discussed in the next chapter.

Likewise, we recognize that individual and group culture, for instance a Christian group culture, may contain error that severely limits and invalidates belief of that group, error apparent only in belief and culture held by another group, Christian or otherwise. We address such error in Book III.

A Second Danger of Materialism

A second danger of materialism described by Barfield[12] is non-deliberate but chosen as "ignorance of meaning by simple displacement." The relationship between the physical causes of experience and its meaning is often vague (unless you are a scientist focused only on physical details, in which case physical cause becomes the full meaning of the experience - QED[19]). Investigating exclusively physical causes and effects in nature through meticulous observation and rigorous analysis of objective facts fully displaces consideration of their meaning beyond such cause and effect. With the advent and wide acceptance of science and materialism, inattention to meaning became first a habit which then led to the assumption that any meaning beyond that scientifically comprehensible was not useful and, finally, not possible. Positivists became so entrenched in their own thinking they regarded any alternative as illegitimate.

As Frank Herbert asked and answered in his classic novel *Dune*, "What senses do we lack that we cannot see and cannot hear another world around us?" and "If you rely only on your eyes, your other senses weaken."[20] If one relies only on perception by sight, hearing, touch, taste, and smell, his or her other senses never develop. When ignored, these deeper senses are never discovered, developed, and utilized. The richer levels of language and thought dealing with, say, devotion, patience, beauty, love, …, the kinds suggested above in describing Lewis' process of Transposition, the kind used in recognizing and communicating feeling and meaning, are denied and lost through ignorance and lack of interest because these senses are disregarded due to exclusive focus on objective, lowest-common-denominator, material-based facts and physical cause-and-effect relationships. Denial of meaning at any level, i.e., considering exclusively the material universe and denying any richer level of language which conveys meaning and feeling in thought, writing, and speech, denies meaning at all levels by envisioning a person and all creatures and things to each be merely "physical objects among physical objects." Thus, it is implicit in modern positivism or materialism or exclusive use of the scientific method that one can know neither about one's human self, one's inner feelings, and one's subjective, emotional reaction to one's experience, nor about one's Creator, a subject only comprehensible through "meaning-based" learning.

Medieval European thought was so constrained by the thinking attributed to Christ and to Aristotle (for reasons to be criticized later) and the effect so debilitating (as implied by the term "Dark Ages") that it is difficult to appreciate its severity now that the break from this tradition is long accomplished. But the imposed influence of the medieval Church and the Aristotelians on Middle-Age thinking was indeed profoundly constrictive and the break therefrom was wrenching. In Barfield's estimation and including of some of my own, the present situation is well described if we take the cultural constraints of the Middle Ages, imposed by tradition of the Church and Aristotelians, and substitute cultural constraints of today imposed by concurrent disestablishment of Christianity and promotion of positivism/materialism/exclusive-use-of-the-scientific-methodism belief as the two-sided dogma to be overthrown. We thus obtain an idea of what is in store in the next Revolution/Renaissance. Barfield considers it a mistake to suppose our culture is more open-minded today than medieval European cultures were. Modern media, entertainment, political, social, and even some religious leaders are generally open-minded about ideas that support materialism, but not ideas that support religious values and beliefs. And even in science only certain ideas are "correct" (Appendix A describes an "incorrect" idea).

While a "wrenching" experience breaking free of constrictive dogma does not conjure up a pretty image, the sadder image to me is the ignorance, inveterate stubbornness in resisting truth and meaning, and the intellectual backwardness imposed on one's self by a category-two-student-like belief in materialism or other flawed dogma. Placing complete faith in any unprovable belief is not wise. Inability of science to demonstrate that any of its assumptions, principles, theories, or laws is reliable will be addressed in detail in Chapters 5 and 16 and in Chapters 12 – 17 we address the same inability in much of modern Christianity due to corrupted beliefs. We consider in following chapters both why exclusive use of science (or any unprovable dogma) is unwise and why a complementary Christian paradigm is useful and, indeed, essential because it provides proof of its validity, the nature of reality, and the deepest meaning we both seek and need.

Notes and References for Chapter 2.

[1] Kuhn, Thomas S., *The Structure of Scientific Revolutions,* Second Edition, Enlarged, University of Chicago Press, Chicago, IL, 1970.

[2] Smoot, George, and Keay Davidson, *Wrinkles in Time,* Avon Books, New York, 1993.

[3] Feynman, Richard P., *Surely You're Joking, Mr. Feynman!,* Bantam, New York, 1985, 313.

[4] In a sermon entitled *Transposition* C. S. Lewis preached in the chapel at Mansfield College, Oxford, on 28 May 1944 and included in *The Weight of Glory and Other Addresses,* Walter Hooper (editor), a Touchstone Book published by Simon and Schuster, New York, 1996.

[5] Quoted in Kaplan, Wilfred, *Advanced Calculus,* Addison-Wesley, Reading, MA, 1952, frontispiece.

[6] According to *Doctrine and Covenants* 131:7-8, spiritual bodies are also composed of matter. "There is no such thing as immaterial matter. All spirit is matter, but it is more fine and pure, and can only be discerned by purer eyes; We cannot see it; but when our bodies are purified [like Adam's and Eve's were before they partook of the forbidden fruit] we shall see that it is all matter."

[7] *Doctrine and Covenants* 93:29-30, *Book of Mormon,* 2 Nephi 2:13-26.

[8] In his 1964 Messenger Lectures at Cornell University, published under the title *The Character of Physical Law* by The MIT Press, Cambridge, MA, 1965, Richard Feynman made the point on pages 158-159 that

> ... you cannot prove a vague theory wrong. ... if the process of computing the consequences is indefinite, then with a little skill any experimental results can be made to look like the expected consequences. ... It is usually said when this is pointed out, 'When you are dealing with psychological matters things can't be defined so precisely.' Yes, but then you cannot claim to know anything about it.

[9] *E. T. Jaynes: Papers on Probability, Statistics and Statistical Physics,* R. D. Rosenkrantz (editor), Kluwer Academic Publishers, Dordrecht, The Netherlands, 1983, 103. All of Jaynes' papers are available at http://bayes.uwstl.edu/etj/node1.html This comment appears in his "Delaware Lecture" in the cited book.

[10] Ibid., 112.

[11] Jaynes, E. T., "A Backward Look to the Future," http://bayes.uwstl.edu/etj/node1.html 1993, 270.

Further elucidation by Jaynes on "the critical problem of meaning" addresses a more basic need, namely, that one must carefully define his or her terms and concepts so that one contributes clarity rather than confusion. If such care is not taken, many opinions will arise and all be strongly held. The following quotation is long but I could not bear to shorten it because none of it should be left out. In this quotation Jaynes is describing the simple, elegant, and powerful conceptual basis of statistical mechanics proposed at the beginning of the twentieth century by American engineer-physicist Josiah Willard Gibbs and its confused use by others over succeeding years.

> [Gibbs' theory provided] for the first time in what has always been a rather messy subject, ... a glimpse of the formal elegance that we have in mechanics, where a single equation (Hamilton's principle) summarizes everything that needs to be said. Of all the founders of statistical mechanics, only Gibbs gives us this formal simplicity, generality, and as it turned out, a technique for practical calculation which the labors of another sixty years have not been able to improve on. The transition to quantum statistics took place so quietly and uneventfully because it consisted simply in the replacement of [an] integral ... by the corresponding discrete sum; and nothing else in the formalism was altered.
>
> In the history of science, whenever a field has reached such a stage, in which thousands of separate details can be summarized by, and deduced from, a single rule – then an extremely important synthesis has been accomplished. Furthermore, by understanding the basis of this rule it has always been possible to extend its application far beyond the original set of facts for which it was designed. And yet, this did not happen in the case of Gibbs' formal rule. With only a few exceptions, writers on statistical mechanics since Gibbs have tried to snatch away this formal elegance by grafting Gibbs' method onto the substrate of Boltzmann's ideas, for which Gibbs had no need. However, a few, including Tolman and Schrödinger, have seen Gibbs' work in a different light – as something that can stand by itself without having to lean on unproved ergodic hypotheses, intricate but arbitrarily defined cells in phase space, Z-

stars, and the like. Thus, while a detailed study will show that there are as many different opinions as to the reason for Gibbs' rules as there are writers on the subject, a more coarse-grained view shows that these writers are split into two basic camps; those who hold that the ultimate justification of Gibbs' rules must be found in ergodic theorems; and those who hold that a principle for assigning [equal] *a priori* probabilities will provide a sufficient justification. Basically, the confusion that still exists in this field arises from the fact that, while the *mathematical content* of Gibbs' rules can be set forth in a few lines, the *conceptual basis* underlying it has never been agreed upon. (The italics are Jaynes'; quoted from *E. T. Jaynes: Papers on Probability, Statistics and Statistical Physics,* loc. cit., 102.)

[12] Barfield, Owen, "The Rediscovery of Meaning," in *Adventures of the Mind, Second Series,* Richard Thruelsen and John Kobler (editors), Knopf, New York, 1961, 311-324. Other related works by the same author: *Saving the Appearances,* Hillary House, New York, 1957 and *Poetic Diction – A Study in Meaning,* McGraw-Hill, New York, 1964.

[13] While not providing a definition of positivism, Werner Heisenberg ("Positivism, Metaphysics, and Religion," in *The World Treasury of Physics, Astronomy and Mathematics*, Timothy Ferris (editor), Little, Brown and Company, New York, 1991, 826) has provided the following description. "... the meaning of 'consciousness' becomes wider and at the same time vaguer if we try to apply it outside the human realm. The positivists have a simple solution: the world must be divided into that which we can say clearly and the rest, which we had better pass over in silence. But can anyone conceive of a more pointless philosophy, seeing that what we can say clearly amounts to next to nothing? If we omitted all that is unclear, we would probably be left with completely uninteresting and trivial tautologies."

[14] Barfield, 1961, loc. cit., 312-313.

[15] See, for example, the listing under Auguste Comte in the Encyclopædia Britannica.

[16] The terms *logical positivism*, *empiricism*, *logical empiricism*, *linguistic analysis*, and *the philosophy of science* are used herein synonymously. They all refer to the belief or philosophy that the sciences (and all knowledge) may be unified and clarified by analysis of language including mathematics and the development of a suitable linguistic structure that includes "legitimate" concepts and expressions (those that can be clearly said or stated – see note 13 above) and excludes all others. Positivists have failed to provide a definition of logical positivism because of a sequence of continuing corrections that followed every attempt. In other words, they have been unable to clearly state a definition of what they believe, namely, (approximately) that only clearly stated theories and laws are legitimately described and understood. Their inability to provide a clear definition of their belief is therefore ironic. We make no attempt at a complete and correct definition of positivism here.

[17] Such psychological confusion cannot occur in materialist-psychology theories we consider in Chapter 11 in which predisposition of active-brain-materials controls all functions. In any case, these theories are presently unsuitable because of their inherent dilemmas.

[18] Von Baeyer, Hans Christian, *Taming the Atom,* Random House, New York, 1992, 160.

[19] QED is an abbreviation for the Latin phrase *quod erat demonstrandum* which has the meaning "which was to be demonstrated." QED is also and more commonly used in this book and elsewhere as an acronym for *quantum electrodynamics.*

[20] Herbert, Frank, *Dune,* Berkeley Books, New York, 1965, 40, 227.

3. Culture, Values, and Meaning

Just as the nature of one's *senses* is invisible when focusing on the facts, one's *culture* is also used uncritically in evaluating facts, despite bias and error it may contain. The reason in the former case applies again in the latter: the objects of interest are the facts and their implications, not the means for observing and interpreting them. While straining to see through a window, we don't examine the window. While straining to understand facts, we don't examine the basis of understanding, which is culture, values, and meaning or, to use again the most generally appropriate term, culture.

Culture includes the knowledge we learn dating back to a very young age. It includes common sense, which has been described as the facts and opinions learned by age 18. Personal culture, one's personal philosophy, paradigm, belief, and intuition based thereon, includes inextricable elements of one's societal culture and generally has a transparent but consequential influence on one's perception of the facts.

A scientist, mathematician, or philosopher who takes a vocation of improving knowledge and revising culture based on examination of facts has great difficulty separating essential and nonessential elements of culture. Counter to the usual process wherein culture (intuition, learning, knowledge, paradigm, belief, philosophy, convention, tradition) is used to interpret facts, the scientist, mathematician, or philosopher seeks to abandon culture and its intuition and use selected facts to establish new culture, a difficult, unnatural, and potentially dangerous task indeed. But it is more dangerous to ignore improvement in (personal) culture, values, and meaning.

Some talk of *background independent* knowledge as if it could be error-free and superior, not encumbered with the preconception, error, prejudice, and superstition we suffer in our present culture. But no reliable knowledge is background independent because (1) observation itself, to be careful, must comply with some method or set of rules or beliefs which itself imposes a background and (2) conclusions deduced from observation must utilize some method of deducing that also imposes a background.

We consider an illustration of the influence of culture. This illustration involves a treatise on mathematics written some 2300 years ago as well as more recent related results in mathematics and physics. While the account is long, it is interesting and it provides insights essential to our story.

Cultural Influence of Euclid's *Elements*

Excluding scripture, the most important and most widely used text in the history of the Western world may be the masterpiece of Euclid (ca. 325 – ca. 265 BC) known universally as Euclid's *Elements*, written about 300 BC. It is actually a collection of 13 books which deal with 465 propositions (theorems) relating to plane and solid geometry and to number theory. In it, Euclid collected and codified all the mathematics then known, all the results discovered over the previous millennia. It has been so highly regarded and universally accepted among mathematicians that a reference in a mathematical paper having the form II.16 is understood to mean the second book and 16th proposition of the *Elements*. Over the centuries, more than 2,000 editions of the *Elements* have been published, nearly an average of one per year. (That such a challenging book was so widely read in past ages may be a surprise considering the mindless level of most of today's popular literature, television, and movies. This fact might be profitably remembered when speculating about the intelligence and self-improvement effort of earlier generations compared to our own.)

Among those the *Elements* influenced was Galileo Galilei (Chapter 6) who was a medical student at the University of Pisa until he encountered the geometry of Euclid in 1583 and, with great subsequent benefit to physics, science, and philosophy, switched his field of study from medicine to mathematics. Another was Isaac Newton (Chapter 7) who was serious by nature and not given to gaiety or casual laughter. But on one occasion when Newton asked an acquaintance his opinion of a copy of Euclid's *Elements* that Newton had loaned him and received in response a question about what benefit the study of such an old book might provide, Newton laughed long and loud. Carl Sandburg mentions in his biography of Abraham Lincoln how the largely unschooled young lawyer sharpened his reasoning skills by studying the *Elements* at night, by candlelight after others had fallen asleep.

We quote from the excellent account of William Dunham.

> Euclid's great genius was not so much in creating a new mathematics as in presenting the old mathematics in a thoroughly clear, organized and logical fashion. This is no small accomplishment. ... Euclid gave us a splendid *axiomatic* development of his subject, and this is a critical distinction. He began the Elements with a few basics: 23 definitions, 5 postulates, and 5 common notions or general axioms. These were the foundations, the 'givens,' of his system. He could use them at any time he chose. From these basics, he proved his first proposition. With this behind him, he could then blend his definitions, postulates, common notions, and his first proposition into a proof of his second. And on it went.
>
> Consequently, Euclid did not just furnish proofs; he furnished them within this axiomatic framework. The advantages of such a development are significant. For one thing, it avoids circularity in reasoning. Each proposition has a clear and unambiguous string of predecessors leading back to the original axioms. Those familiar with computers could even draw a flow chart showing precisely which results went into the proof of a given theorem. This approach is far superior to 'plunging in' to prove a proposition, for in such a case it is never clear which previous results can and cannot be used. The great danger from starting in the middle, as it were, is that to prove theorem A, one might need to use result B, which, it may turn out, cannot be proved without using theorem A itself. This results in a circular argument, the logical equivalent of a snake swallowing its own tail; in mathematics it surely leads to no good.
>
> But the axiomatic approach has another benefit. Since we can clearly pick out the predecessors of any proposition, we have an immediate sense of what happens if we should alter or eliminate one of our basic postulates. If, for instance, we have proved

theorem A without ever using either postulate C or any result previously proved by means of postulate C, then we are assured that our theorem A remains valid even if postulate C is discarded. While this might seem a bit esoteric, just such an issue arose with respect to Euclid's controversial fifth postulate and led to one of the longest and most profound debates in the history of mathematics.[1]

Euclid's fifth postulate, his parallel postulate, reads: "If a straight line falling on two straight lines make the interior angles on the same side less than two right angles, the two straight lines, if produced indefinitely, meet on that side on which are the angles less than the two right angles." Such interior angle pairs on the same side are illustrated in the following drawing either by angles A and B or C and D. Only if a pair sums to two right angles (90° + 90° = 180°), in which case both pairs do, are the two straight lines parallel and the two straight lines do not intersect even when extended indefinitely. When A and B sum to less than 180°, C and D sum to more and the two lines will intersect on the right side and *vice versa*.

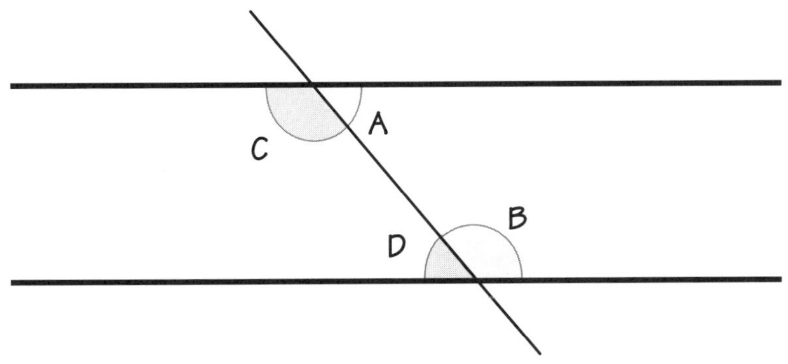

Origins of Non-Euclidian Geometry

Apparently the first mathematician to doubt elements of Euclid's theory was Euclid. For sake of discussion let us consolidate the five postulates and five common notions into a set of ten axioms. Then the geometry described by Euclid or *Euclidian geometry* is based on 23 definitions and ten axioms. But, in the clarity of hindsight, two of the axioms seem to have been troubling to Euclid. The first states that a line segment may be extended indefinitely in either direction. The second is the parallel postulate which includes the concept of extension of two straight lines indefinitely. Extension of a line or two lines indefinitely is beyond our experience. The longest straight lines observed are ones that lie on the surface of the earth, e.g., railroad tracks or a road. And in the case of both, the two parallel lines (two tracks or two edges of the road) appear to converge. Moreover, the lines are not straight in any case since they coincide with the surface of the (nominally) spherical earth.

The manner in which Euclid uses these two axioms suggests he had some concern about them. Only after he proved as many theorems as possible without it did Euclid first use the parallel axiom, the more questionable of the two. And the theorems of his geometry that utilize a line segment never supposed an infinite straight line. When necessary, he extended a straight-line segment in either direction but only as far as a proof required. We cannot conclude that Euclid doubted the validity of these two axioms but it seems he avoided using them whenever possible.

Many mathematicians through the centuries wondered about Euclid's parallel axiom, but the concern was based on its form. It had the form of a theorem rather than an axiom. A challenge of its validity was not contemplated because the basis of mathematics, and especially Euclidian geometry, was held to be fundamental truth, a belief that grew stronger with the passing of the centuries. Thus many attempted to deduce this axiom from the other axioms or to deduce a simpler alternative that contained the same concept. After two millennia, hundreds of assaults had been made, many by superb mathematicians. But all had failed to either deduce the parallel postulate from the other axioms or to find a simpler alternative. Nonetheless, powerful methods had been invented and utilized which enhanced mathematical insight and capability. To illustrate, we consider one such attempt.

Girolamo Saccheri (1667-1733), a Jesuit priest and professor of mathematics at the University of Pavia, attempted to prove the parallel postulate using the other nine axioms. Being a capable logician, Saccheri conceived a clever strategy. In essence, he argued that given a line L and a point P not on the line, one of only three possibilities could be true. (1) No line through P can be drawn parallel to L. (2) Only one line through P can be drawn parallel to L. (3) Two or more lines through P can be drawn parallel to L. Saccheri reasoned that if he could utilize in turn each of (1) and (3) together with the other nine axioms to obtain theorems contradictory to valid results then he would have proved both (1) and (3) to be absurd and (2), Euclid's parallel postulate, would be established as the only valid possibility. This process of proving a result by proving all its alternatives to be absurd or contradictory to valid results is today a frequently-used method referred to as *reductio ad absurdum*. Using (1) together with the nine other axioms Saccheri did derive contradictory results thus eliminating possibility (1). But with (3) he could prove no contradictions. *Saccheri was at the threshold of mathematical history*, but he did not step over. The alternative theorems he derived using (3) were so strange to him that he finally concluded they could not be valid and claimed the parallel postulate was thus proven. Accordingly, he authored a book entitled *Euclid Vindicated from All Defects* describing his results. His book appeared the year he died.

As talented as the many eighteenth century and earlier-era mathematicians were who investigated the problem of Euclid's fifth postulate, they confronted not only a difficult problem but also a many-centuries-old habit of thinking, the habit of regarding mathematics and geometry as based on fundamental truths. The issue remained undiminished in its appeal but unresolved through the Renaissance.

In the early nineteenth century, however, many mathematical results were being revisited with a new attitude of skepticism and rigor. This new attitude originated in the need to establish firm mathematical foundations for much of the mathematics invented in the previous century and used intensively to obtain still more marvelous, new results. The progress in eighteenth century mathematics was so great that this period is now referred to as the "heroic age" of mathematics. But with the focus of this age on creative invention and expanding limits of capability, careful foundations were not established and this age might also be called the "age of confusion." It remained for the nineteenth century mathematicians to go back and establish foundations that properly supported the earlier results. In the process they examined many assumptions and traditions of earlier ages as well and developed a broad-based, critical approach in their reexaminations unrestrained by earlier convention. It was in this atmosphere of unrestrained, skeptical reexamination of fundamentals that the problem of Euclid's fifth postulate was finally solved, by no less than three different mathematicians working independently.

Discoveries of Gauss, Lobachevski, and Bolyai

The first who discovered non-Euclidian geometry was among the few most preeminent mathematicians in history, ranking with Archimedes, Newton, and Euler. His name is Johann Friedrich Karl Gauss (1777-1855) but he went by the name Karl Friedrich Gauss. From early age Gauss had shown precocity in mathematics but, unlike others, his precocity never stopped. It is therefore no surprise that he worked on a huge range of problems, including Euclid's fifth or parallel postulate, beginning in his youth. He later adopted essentially Saccheri's strategy and, while he hesitated at the threshold, he eventually passed over, but only barely. Postulating that two or more lines can be drawn through P parallel to L and using the other nine axioms of Euclid, Gauss derived strange theorems like Saccheri had. But instead of being perplexed by the strangeness of the new theorems, Gauss reached the novel conclusion that had eluded Saccheri and other previous investigators: there exist geometries different from Euclid's but equally legitimate. Here Gauss hesitated. While he was bold enough to create non-Euclidian geometry, he was not bold enough to tell anyone beyond a few intimate friends about it. His results lay in his desk drawer for many years unread by any eyes but his own, which was his habit in many of his discoveries. He was, at the peak of his career, regarded as the greatest mathematician of his age. One comment in a letter Gauss wrote in 1829 reveals his anticipation of the controversy that would certainly be associated with announcing such a discovery and might diminish his standing among mathematicians or, at the least, cause much distraction from his future work. In this letter Gauss stated that he had discovered a new geometry alternative to Euclid's but had no plans "... to work up my very extensive researches for publication, and perhaps they will never appear in my lifetime, for I fear the howl of the Boeotians [unimaginative, crudely obtuse dullards[2]] if I speak my opinion out loud."[2] Gauss indeed remained silent about his discovery of non-Euclidian geometry until his death in 1855. His account of non-Euclidian geometry was published when it was found among his papers after his death. Judging from the fate of one of his fellow discoverers, in particular the first to publish the new results, Gauss' reticence to publish was prudent.

Nikolai Ivanovich Lobachevski (1793-1856) was born to poor Russian parents. His widowed mother managed to provide schooling for him and he was accepted into the newly established University of Kazan on merit at age 14. Because of the remarkable mathematical talent he displayed he was appointed to the faculty at age 21 and climbed through the ranks, becoming a full professor at age 23 and president of the university at age 34. His appointment to this position was fortunate because he excelled not only in mathematics but in administration as well. He twice saved the university, once by leading a successful battle against Cholera in 1830 and later by leading another battle against a great fire in 1842.

Lobachevski's approach to the parallel-postulate problem was bold. Rather than wonder if the parallel postulate was provable he investigated an alternative geometry based on the axiom that two or more lines could be drawn through P parallel to L. He was thinking about this strategy as early as 1826, for he then mentioned it in his lectures. Lobachevski published his ideas about this new geometry and their proofs in 1829, the first to do so.

But the traditional Euclidian geometry was so entrenched as truth in the narrow minds of "second-tier" mathematicians and scholars that his results were minimized and ignored. He was eventually dismissed from the university in 1848 without a reason being stated, despite all he had done.

The third discoverer of non-Euclidian geometry was Janos Bolyai (1802-1860). His father, Wolfgang, was a mathematician and a friend of Gauss. While the father had worked on the parallel postulate problem he had not solved it. But the son did. Apparently Janos was working on the same ideas as Lobachevski during the same time period. When the father published a book in 1831, he included a twenty-six page appendix written by his son that explained the same non-Euclidian geometry that Lobachevski had published nearly three years earlier unbeknownst to the Bolyais. When the older Bolyai communicated the results obtained by his son to his friend Gauss, Gauss privately revealed that he had long before obtained the same results but never published them. The younger Bolyai was taken aback by this disclosure and never worked further in this area. The circumstances of Janos' results being published merely as an appendix in another's book, the (private) disclosure that Gauss had obtained the same results, and his abandoning the field of non-Euclidian geometry may have protected Janos from a reaction similar to that which befell Lobachevski, although Lobachevski's fate seems excessively cruel and mean-spirited.

Further Discoveries of Riemann and Beltrami

Georg Friedrich Bernhard Riemann (1826-1866) was noted for his originality and innovation in his all-too-brief career as a mathematician. Riemann was born into a poor family in Hanover, Germany. His father was a Lutheran pastor, a respectable position in the community, but Riemann had one brother and four sisters so there were a lot of mouths to feed and bodies to clothe on the meager pastoral salary. It is believed that the poor health and early deaths of most of the Riemann children were due to undernourishment in their youth. Riemann's mother also died early, before the children were grown.

Riemann received his first instruction from his father. At about the age of six young Riemann began a study of arithmetic. At age ten he was taught advanced arithmetic and geometry by a professional tutor named Schulz. He entered Gymnasium in Hanover at age fourteen. Later he transferred to another Gymnasium in Lüneberg where the director, Schmalfuss, recognized Riemann's talent for mathematics, excused Riemann from the regular mathematics class, and invited him to utilize his private library. "Schmalfuss had suggested that Riemann borrow some mathematical book for private study. Riemann said that would be nice provided the book was not too easy and, at the suggestion of Schmalfuss, carried off Legendre's *Théorie des Nombres* (*Theory of Numbers*). This is a mere trifle of 859 large quarto pages, many of them crammed with very close reasoning indeed. Six days later Riemann returned the book. 'How far did you read?' Schmalfuss asked. Without replying directly, Riemann expressed his appreciation of Legendre's classic. 'That is certainly a wonderful book. I have mastered it.' And in fact he had. Some time later when he was examined he answered perfectly, although he had not seen the book for months."[3]

Thanks to Schmalfuss lending him his own books and excusing him from mathematics classes, Riemann studied other masters of mathematics and absorbed their writings, always with unbelievable quickness. He studied Euler, for one, from whom he may have gleaned a manipulative ingenuity.

At age nineteen, Riemann began studies in philology at the University of Göttingen. Riemann's family was close and his earnest desire was to please his father and help support the family by obtaining a paid position as soon as possible. To reach these two goals he would study theology. But young Riemann could not resist attending lectures on mathematics and science and he soon petitioned his father for permission to change his study to mathematics, a request his father immediately approved. Between his studies at Göttingen (first year) and Berlin (second and third years), Riemann was instructed by Stern, Jacobi, Dirichlet, Steiner, and Eisenstein. In his last three semesters at Göttingen, Riemann, by then considered a pure mathematician, attended philosophy lectures and lectures by Wilhelm Weber on experimental physics. Riemann's genius in physics was recognized by Weber, who became a good friend of and mentor to Riemann. In fact, Riemann was so fascinated by physics that he ignored his studies in mathematics while he pursued a study in mathematical physics. He spent the time he might have otherwise spent on his doctoral thesis pursuing experiments in physics. E. T. Bell[4] describes Riemann as having ability as a physical mathematician in the same class as Newton, Gauss, and Einstein because of his instinct for the mathematics that is likely to be of scientific use.

Riemann finally submitted his doctoral dissertation in mathematics at age twenty five. The dissertation entitled *Grundlagen für eine allegemeine Theorie der Functionen einer veränderlichen complexen Grösse* (Foundations for a General Theory of Functions of a Complex Variable) was read by Gauss in November 1851. Gauss responded to the faculty as follows.

> The dissertation submitted by Herr Riemann offers convincing evidence of the author's thorough and penetrating investigations in those parts of the subject treated in the dissertation, of a creative, active, truly mathematical mind, and of a gloriously fertile originality. The presentation is perspicuous and concise and, in places, beautiful. The majority of readers would have preferred a greater clarity of arrangement. The whole is a substantial, valuable work, which not only satisfies the standards demanded for doctoral dissertations, but far exceeds them.[5]

Not a bad review from one widely regarded as the preeminent mathematician of all time.

The next step was for Riemann to obtain his *Habilitation*, certification which qualified him to teach tutorial lectures to students and required for any kind of faculty appointment. To become certified he had to submit an essay and deliver a lecture on a chosen topic. However, he didn't exactly get to choose the topic. The topic of the lecture, to be presented before a faculty committee, was by convention selected by the committee from a list of three subjects submitted by the candidate. Customarily, as a courtesy to the candidate, the third topic was rarely chosen. But in this case Riemann had listed "the foundations of geometry" as his third topic, a topic Gauss had studied for some sixty years by then and a topic that Gauss undoubtedly wanted to discover how Riemann would treat with his "gloriously fertile originality." So, contrary to usual convention, the committee chose the third topic. It then remained for Riemann to prepare his essay and lecture in an area he was interested in but had not yet completed any work.

But again, other activities first got in the way. Finally he satisfied his other obligations and in a mere seven weeks completed his research on foundations of geometry. In a letter to his father he said

> I became so absorbed in my investigation of the unity of all physical laws that when the subject of the trial lecture was given me, I could not tear myself away from my research. Then, ... I fell ill. ... Having finished two weeks after Easter a piece of work I could not get out of, I began at once working on my trial lecture and finished it around Pentecost [i.e., after seven weeks]. I had some difficulty getting a date for my lecture right away ... For Gauss is seriously ill and the physicians fear that his death is imminent. Being too weak to examine me, he asked me to wait till August, hoping that he might improve, especially as I would not lecture anyhow till fall. Then he decided anyway on the Friday after Pentecost to set the lecture for the next day at eleven thirty. On Saturday [10 June 1854] I was happily through with everything.[6]

As the reader may have already guessed, this lecture was on foundations so deep and broad they encompassed both Euclidian and non-Euclidian geometry. In it Riemann generalized and revolutionized differential geometry. It prepared the way for relativity and the modern concept of spacetime. The published essay is among the great masterpieces in the history of mathematics and the lecture itself was noteworthy. Gauss' reaction was suffused with enthusiasm, a rare reaction for Gauss. Although Gauss had praised Riemann's "gloriously fertile originality," he was pleasantly surprised beyond expectation.

In 1857 Riemann was appointed an assistant professor. In 1858 he produced a mathematical-physics paper on electrodynamics. In 1859, upon the death of Dirichlet, Riemann at age thirty-three succeeded him and became the second successor to Gauss in the position of full professor at Göttingen.

During a long battle with poor health, Riemann fled periodically to Italy to escape the northern winters. Even in his poor health he was offered a professorship at the University of Pisa, which he declined. He died in Italy of consumption on 20 July 1866 at the age of 39, at the peak of his abilities. His tombstone inscription, composed by his Italian friends based on their observation of his gentle, pious spirit, ends with the words "All things work for good to them that love the Lord."

We briefly summarize the essential concepts of Riemann's differential geometry by which new views of space were established. Riemann reasoned that Euclid's second postulate, which prescribed that a straight line could be extended indefinitely, merely asserted that the end of the line would never be reached. Riemann cited the cases where curved lines, such as circles and ellipses, may have finite extent but no end. He distinguished between unboundedness and infinite extent. He ascribed unboundedness to space but claimed that an infinite extent by no means follows from this.

In other words, space may be curved, like a sphere, spheroid, etc. so that it is unbounded in any direction on one of its characteristic surfaces (sphere, spheroid, etc.) yet finite in extent. But how can one generally account for the curvature of space? By use of the differential geometry Riemann introduced in his famous lecture and essay. Mathematical details are elaborated in Appendix B.

While Gauss, Lobachevski, and Bolyai all considered only the case where two or more lines may be drawn through P parallel to L, Riemann's analysis is general and also includes the cases where only one line or no line may be drawn through P parallel to L. To illustrate this last case, consider a "straight" line drawn on the surface of a sphere (spherically curved space) for which the line takes the shape of a circle. Now imagine two separate lines both drawn on the sphere perpendicular to the circle which, by Euclid's fifth postulate stated above, constitutes a pair of parallel lines. But both of these lines intersect at both a "north and south pole" of the sphere and so the lines are not parallel according to other definitions equivalent to Euclid's for flat space. Thus, a line L may have no parallel, only one parallel, or more than one parallel through a point P not on line L. Riemann's theory includes all possibilities. A shape invented by Beltrami (introduced below) for illustration of the last case is that of a *pseudosphere*, a shape of constant, negative curvature (in two dimensions) as opposed to a sphere being a shape of constant positive curvature (in three dimensions). A pseudosphere has the shape shown in the following figure, something like that of two identical trumpets joined at their largest (outlet or exit) planes.[7]

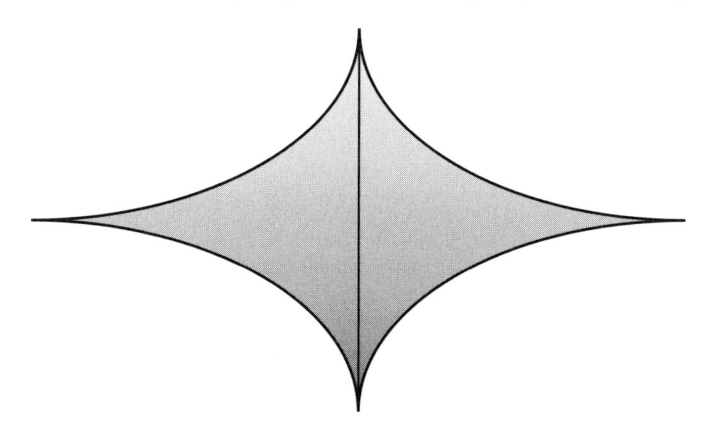

In 1868 Italian mathematician Eugenio Beltrami (1835-1900) placed an exclamation point behind the results of Gauss, Lobachevski, Bolyai, and Riemann by proving conclusively that non-Euclidian geometry was equally consistent in its logic to Euclidian geometry. In particular, he proved that if a contradiction was contained in the geometry of Gauss, Lobachevski, and Bolyai or in Riemann's geometry, then a contradiction also existed in Euclid's geometry. In other words, Euclidian and non-Euclidian geometries are logically equivalent in their consistency.

While this history of geometry is a story of human ingenuity, it simultaneously reveals human mulishness and intransigence in wrong thinking. In retrospect it is clear that there exists no inherent superiority of Euclidian geometry over its alternatives and the long history of man's inveterate persistence in insisting the former alone correctly describes reality is a witness of "the blindness of human beings, great and small. ... For thousands of years this geometry [of a spherical earth] has been right under the feet of man. Yet during all those years the greatest mathematicians never once sought to test their attack on the parallel axiom by checking with the geometry of a sphere. And as a climax to these thousands of years the great Kant built his profound philosophy on the incontrovertible truth of Euclidian geometry. Yet all this time he was living *on*, if not in, a non-Euclidian world."[8]

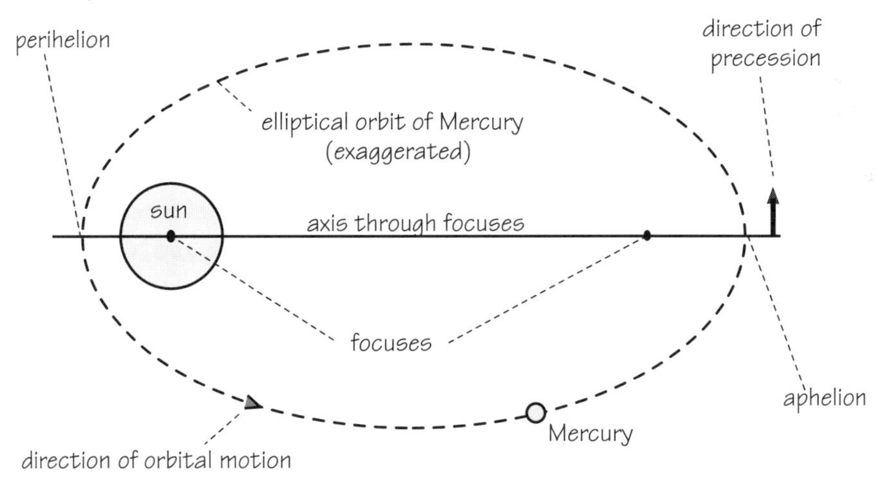

Non-Euclidian Geometry in Physics

While our account of the *mathematical* story of non-Euclidian geometry is now complete, we continue with the *physical* story. Since details are presented in Chapter 8 and Appendix B, we note here merely that Albert Einstein used Riemann's differential geometry in place of Euclidian geometry in his general theory of relativity. He eliminated gravity as a force by implicitly including its effect in the curvature of spacetime. Einstein's general theory of relativity, published in 1916, correctly predicts observed results not previously predicted or suspected and this success makes it the best, presently-available theory for recognizing connections between physical spacetime features of the universe.

For instance, the (much exaggerated) elliptical orbit of Mercury around the sun with the sun located at one of the elliptical orbit's two focuses is illustrated in the opposite figure. The smallest Mercury-sun separation is denoted the *perihelion* and the largest is the *aphelion*, both of which lie on the line drawn through the two focuses of the ellipse. It is observed that the elliptical orbit of Mercury is not stationary relative to the fixed stars because the line through the focuses slowly rotates, *advancing* slightly with each orbit of Mercury.

This rotation of the elliptical orbit or the line through the perihelion and aphelion is referred to as the *precession* of the orbit of Mercury. The total measured precession is 574 seconds of angle or arcseconds per (earth-time) century. One *arcsecond* is one sixtieth of one *arcminute* which is one sixtieth of one degree of angle so that one arcsecond = 1/3,600 of one degree. Of the total precession of 574 arcseconds per century only 43 arcseconds per century is not accounted for by Newtonian gravitational influence of the other planets (Appendix D). In rounded numbers Venus contributes an influence of 277 arcseconds per century, Jupiter 153, earth 90, Mars and the remaining planets 10, giving 531 arcseconds per century as the total planetary influence. In the mid-nineteenth-century these results were derived independently by John Couch Adams (1819-1892) in England and Joseph Le Verrier (1811-1877) in France using Newton's theory. The missing 43 arcseconds per century, called the *excess precession*, was unexplained until Einstein's theory of relativity predicted it exactly. This correct prediction of relativity and others to be described (Chapter 8) suggest the geometry of real space is better represented by non-Euclidian geometry and relativity theory than by traditional Euclidian geometry and Newtonian mechanics.

As Einstein investigated the application of his general theory of relativity, he was somewhat dismayed to find that a static, equilibrium state of the universe was not allowed by the theory. The theory predicted only a dynamic state in which the universe was either expanding or contracting. But the orthodox view of that time was that the universe was in static equilibrium. The now-well-known expansion of the universe was only to be later deduced from Einstein's theory and other evidence. To correct for this apparent shortcoming of his theory, i.e., for its inability to describe a stationary universe, Einstein published in 1917 a revision of the theory which added a constant term he called the *cosmological constant*, an *ad hoc*[9] fix to his equations to cause his theory to correspond to what he believed was reality: a stationary universe. One now wonders about the basis of the orthodox view of a stationary universe but it was generally accepted in the culture of that day. In any case, to Einstein's chagrin, the universal repulsion provided by the contrived (positive) cosmological constant was not a fix after all. It was later noticed that while the cosmological constant apparently stabilized bodies in certain configurations, the resulting force balance was *unstable*. Displacement of any of a set of bodies from their balanced configuration led to ever-increasing forces driving the bodies further from the balanced configuration. Indeed, the cosmological-constant force is used in current cosmology, again *ad hoc*, to describe continuing acceleration in expansion of the universe.

Many mathematicians and physicists investigated mathematical models (solutions) of Einstein's equations seeking implications of relativity theory. Three in particular, Dutch astronomer Willem de Sitter (1872-1934), Russian meteorologist Alexander Alexandrovich Friedmann (1888-1925), and Belgian abbé and physicist Georges-Henri Lemaître (1894-1966), first described the most important implication of the theory. The results of all three (eventually) indicated that the universe was expanding, as deduced from the original theory without addition of the *ad hoc* cosmological constant. De Sitter proposed in 1917 possible cosmological models that (eventually) predicted an expanding or an oscillating universe. He solved the relativity equations for the simple case of a matterless universe (empty spacetime) that seemed to predict a static universe. But his result was later used, by Arthur Eddington in the 1920s, with particles scattered throughout spacetime that receded from one another, indicating his model predicted an expanding universe. Friedmann provided early models that definitely showed the universe to be expanding or oscillating. Friedmann died at age 36 in 1925, before his results were appreciated, but Lemaître independently derived them in 1927. When de Sitter died in 1934, Lemaître became the senior advocate of an expanding universe and principal proponent of what is now called the "big bang" theory of cosmology. This theory regards the universe as originating from a minuscule point of extremely high energy-material density or, as Lemaître termed it in 1931, a "primeval atom." But, as always occurs in proposing a significantly new view of reality, Lemaître suffered criticism. Upon presenting calculations in 1927 at the Fifth Solvay Conference, Lemaître's work was challenged by Einstein with the comment "Your calculations are correct, but your physical insight is abominable."[10]

In 1929 Edwin Hubble began publishing data that indicated the universe was expanding with the rate of expansion (the recessional velocity) increasing with distance from earth, which supported Lemaître's primeval-atom or big-bang theory. After Einstein and de Sitter together visited Hubble in Pasadena in 1931 and Einstein realized his mistake, Einstein was generous to Lemaître in connection with the latter's early insight into the implication of general relativity. However, in a 1933 discussion in which Lemaître mentioned his primeval-atom model, Einstein interrupted him with the comment "No, not that, that suggests too much the creation."[11] Apparently Lemaître's position as an abbé caused some concern about his objectivity. But it was others who were prejudiced. Lemaître was right. Einstein's equations imply a singularity in the past.

Curiously, the greatest intellectual innovator in the history of physics, Albert Einstein, was held back by the (cultural) orthodox view that the universe was in a state of static equilibrium. Moreover, his concern about the objectivity of Lemaître apparently hid his own lack of objectivity. Usually Einstein saw past such limitations as well as anyone, but not this time. He described his cosmological-constant error as the greatest blunder of his life. That such a brilliant innovator as Einstein could be blinded to the meaning of his own theory by the orthodox view illustrates that cultural knowledge – tradition, convention, learning, and intuition or paradigm based thereon, our view of reality – has a powerful influence on our ability to acquire understanding. It indicates that new insights and new understanding of truth and meaning are difficult to obtain when we hold to our old paradigm too tenaciously, because new and improved understanding is always in conflict with the orthodox paradigm. Otherwise it is not new and improved.

This short summary of a little mathematical-physics history reveals that human understanding or culture (culture here representing knowledge and belief in general and Euclidian geometry, Newtonian physics, and a stationary universe assumption in particular) was both strongly entrenched and false. It means humans based over two millennia of mathematical and physical contemplation on belief falsely regarded as fundamental truth. It means that culture-based philosophy may be wrong and that examination of evidence, no matter how meticulous and rigorous, using inadequate (false) philosophy merely propagates error and entrenches thinking deeper therein. (Indeed, Immanuel Kant severely damaged his credibility by irreversibly attaching himself to Euclidian geometry and Newtonian physics as the only possible truths because he could conceive of no others. Morris Kline[12] describes non-Euclidian geometry as demolishing Kant's arguments.) It means that even our most highly refined intuition may hold us *off* a path toward truth and meaning because it contains an intuition based on an invalid vision of reality. It means that, although we appear to be approaching understanding of some elements of the universe, we may not yet properly understand many fundamentals. It means that we shouldn't change our category-one-student classification. Thinking that we already understand is fatal to learning and who among us has full understanding of truth and meaning? It means that "Alas, ... wisdom broad and deep is ne'er by sipping full."

Shortcomings in our knowledge may have minimal consequence in describing much of physical behavior of the universe, e.g., use of Euclidian geometry and Newtonian mechanics leads to a negligible error in many predictions. But, as will be addressed in later chapters, no error is insignificant in answering ultimate questions or defining abstract foundations of philosophy that control vision of reality and intuition. Any comprehensive philosophy capable of both correctly predicting everyday experience and correctly answering ultimate questions pertaining to ontology and meaning must rest on a strong pylon of knowledge anchored firmly in a deep, abstract-level foundation of understanding which rests securely on bedrock of truth. Reliable consideration must be based strictly on truth. Otherwise, the cumulative error inherent in extrapolating over long spans that run from this pylon to remote but important issues will be large and the resulting, intuitive view of reality hopelessly incorrect.

Values – A Prescription for Acquiring Comprehension of Meaning

In this book we use the term "meaning" in its common sense. The sentence "The car is red" contains and conveys meaning: the red color of the car. This function is useful, to be sure, but at this level "meaning" is hardly worthy of a book. We examine meaning at a deeper level. The deepest understanding of meaning occurs in the connection of personal values, feelings and other facts, and consequences.

Meaning provides guidance in answering such questions as "What behavior should I desire?" and "To where does this behavior lead?" and "What am I becoming?" We focus on meaning derived from observation of the total universe utilizing a suitable paradigm and associated perception, thought, action, and consequences. Awareness of meaning varies with adopted paradigm and values that lead to desires, expectations, and lived experience, as illustrated in the preface and in the following paragraphs.

To properly understand, evaluate, and use experience one must recognize its subjective nature. And experience is even more subjective than has so far been indicated. Experience involves more than mere sensing of external phenomena and more than rationalization of them by means of paradigm and culture. Experience, cognition, and awareness also involve *subjective sensations* and *personal reactions* resulting from observation and rationalization of external phenomena. Such reactions are also facts, highly personal and subjective ones involving both the external and internal.

For instance, a good man or woman does not merely observe a brutal act on another person. Feelings of anger, outrage, sorrow, sympathy, and desire to assist the victim spontaneously accompany the observation. (For this reason a person who observes a violent crime may make a poor witness because the meaning of the experience can upset his or her normal functioning.) While awareness of physical causes and effects may represent some understanding of objective, lowest-common-denominator facts, the deepest meaning of observed facts is generally apparent only in subjective reactions: thoughts, feelings, and emotions related to personal experience, values, and belief. Such values and belief may include conscience, justice, fairness, kindness, mercy, the brotherhood of man, and fatherhood of God.

A second observer, in addition to the good man or woman, may understand the objective facts, but only the meaning to the extent that its precursors based on values (sympathy, feeling of brotherhood, desire to assist others, etc.) and personal experience already reside in him or her. These values are essential to feeling and comprehension of meaning communicated by facts. Other values lead to comprehension of other meaning.[13] Comprehension of meaning thus occurs in response to observed facts, rational thinking, and feeling in those who possess qualities essential to comprehension of a particular meaning. Such qualities based on and cultivated by personal belief, values, anticipated consequences, volition, feelings, and experience are denoted the *precursors of comprehension of meaning* or, in short, *precursors of meaning*. Possession of these precursors provides an individual with a richer content of "language" in thought and speech that enables and promotes individual acuity and sensitivity in observation, sympathy in feeling, and generosity in attitude about the plight of a victim and the reaction of a good person to his or her plight. While meaning is triggered or communicated by facts, it is perceived through personally developed precursors individually acquired. Thus, comprehension of meaning transcends objective facts, i.e., objective facts convey meaning to one and not to another or different meaning to different persons. Especially in matters involving initially vague and elusive facts, such as belief or faith in an unseen Christ, comprehension of meaning requires cultivation.

A sense and comprehension of meaning is cultivated by adopting values and acquiring experience with them. Such lived experience provides understanding of meaning through a subjective knowing (details are discussed in Book III). Adopting Godlike values causes a person to have Godlike feelings and thoughts about his or her fellows and to be attracted by similar values and feelings in others, especially God Himself whose virtues are perfect. Exactly this principle is taught in the following passage in regard to several values.

> For intelligence cleaveth unto intelligence; wisdom receiveth wisdom; truth embraceth truth; virtue loveth virtue; light cleaveth unto light; mercy hath compassion on mercy and claimeth her own; justice continueth its course and claimeth its own; judgement goeth before the face of him who sitteth upon the throne and governeth and executeth all things.[14]

According to this passage each value in one person seeks itself in another. That is, as one perfects each value in one's self, his or her knowledge of and bonding to God and others (cleaveth, receiveth, embraceth, hath compassion on, claimeth) is enhanced in a oneness or common feeling and desire among all those who hold and practice these values. Ultimately, such persons become one in thought and purpose through their common values and the meaning to which they aspire in their lived experience. Such a oneness or unity with God represents deep significance, consequence, and meaning. No wonder Barfield associated a feeling of foreboding with absence of meaning.

Contrariwise, negative qualities lead to negative thoughts, desires, feelings, and meaning.[13] Such qualities lead not to any kind of inclusion or oneness but to their opposites: feelings of rejection, betrayal, alienation, being a victim of injustice, exclusive interest in and pity for only one's self. The term meaning without a modifier denotes the former, positive meaning, the only meaning we seek.

Comprehension of meaning is obtained cumulatively through adopted values and experience in striving to live these values. It is also obtained by divine gift in consequence of just such effort.

In other words, comprehension of meaning depends on the *values* a person holds and lives and is the *consequence* that results. Only if honesty is valued and practiced does a person become honest and feel offense when another is cheated. Only if kindness and compassion are valued and practiced does one become compassionate and feel sympathy for others. A neutral, objective, external view oblivious to or heedless of values and consequences does not lead to desired personal qualities; precursors of meaning must be deliberately adopted and cultivated. Establishing worthy values and personal qualities is essential to understanding positive meaning. Objective, neutral, universal, value-free materialism prevents understanding of total-universe meaning by simple displacement. Even honesty is not required in science (Appendix A). Rather than expand the scope of science to encompass meaning, logical positivists, analytical philosophers, or linguistic analysts have sought instead to use language to describe only the narrow domain of clearly understood science. To do otherwise would compromise objectivity, universality, and clarity. However, instead of making science trivial and infallible, a better path is to recognize that science is not trivial and it is fallible, fallible in not providing understanding of essence or meaning in any scope beyond that of an external, material universe.

Perhaps you think the comments about feeling are not pertinent to you. If you do, they aren't – yet. You may presently regard yourself as definitely not the "touchy-feely" type. You may presently be interested only in yourself or in hard facts of hard science from which you can extract hard meaning. But, when one considers only the hard facts, meaning is severely limited and shallow. Any deep meaning and true essence lies beyond knowledge of objective facts and detached reasoning. Even an understanding of hard-science meaning lies beyond hard facts, as noted by physicist Hans Christian von Baeyer:

> The atom is difficult to imagine. The vocabulary of quantum mechanics, which describes electrons with great precision, is not easily translated into the words and images of everyday life. Our lack of understanding is not on the technical level. On the contrary, the success of quantum mechanics, measured by the accuracy of the quantitative predictions it makes, is unprecedented in physical science. The fault, rather, is in the interpretation of the theoretical concepts; we understand the substance of quantum mechanics, but not its meaning. ... We know everything about the structure of the atom except its meaning.[15]

Connection and Belonging

A real-life illustration of comprehending total-universe meaning including feelings of connection and belonging is provided in an experience of Orson F. Whitney while he was serving as a missionary in Columbia, PA in late March or early April 1877. On this occasion Elder Whitney was shown in vision the Savior during His suffering in Gethsemane. He described his own reaction to seeing the Savior suffering and weeping in Gethsemane in the following words: "I was so moved at the sight that I also wept, out of pure sympathy. My whole heart went out to Him; I loved Him with all my soul, and longed to be with Him as I longed for nothing else."[16]

In mortality, with its ever pending death or emotional divorce and separation, to love is to risk, to be emotionally exposed. But avoiding love, devotion, and commitment in order to protect one's self is a worse fate. Thank God a spouse mourns the death of his or her mate and that a parent grieves any mishap involving his or her child. Insulation from such sadness is also insulation from love, devotion, commitment, and the most precious experiences of life.

In science, subjective feelings and emotions are generally ignored. Science attaches no meaning or consequence to facts beyond value-free, detached, objective, lowest-common-denominator, material ones. But without values and subjective feelings, very little significance remains.

We respond to facts by the thoughts and emotions they generate in us. Inspiring scenes or accounts of valor or accomplishment of great feats all derive their significance and meaning from values of beauty, courage, love, and associated subjective feelings. A painting is not adequately perceived or described in terms of the hues of its pigments and textures of its strokes, but rather as the connection and feeling it generates, facts (consequences) that lie beyond the material. The meaning and value of a poem is not found in its rhymes or meter but in the associations and emotions it evokes. The rhymes and meter are required in the medium the poet chooses but when feeling and meaning are communicated in good poetry, word facts are unnoticed. Because objective, material-universe science excludes any deep and powerful meaning of connection and belonging, science is meaningless in these essential things and deaf-blind-and-dumb to the most important lived experiences.

Background independent culture, besides being unrealistic, could be fatal to the full experience of living. While some difficult questions about material matters may be avoided or reduced in a culture by proper selection of a *different* background, I don't believe a fully background-independent culture would be desirable. But a different-background culture may be beneficial, such as one based on feeling, love, devotion, commitment, beauty, courage, and meaning. Selection of cultural background to alleviate material problems with little regard for feeling and meaning presents a danger of reducing concepts of living to a mere organic or material level, the only level that science recognizes. But, to solve problems in science, different-background cultures ought to be and are being tried (Chapter 9).

Awareness of "higher living" is not reached through science. Even the thrill of scientific discovery has no meaning when it is strictly objectively considered. A composer works for the enjoyment of hearing, with others, his or her beautiful music. A scientist should also work to obtain a similar feeling from his or her beautiful, no-less-creative work. Materialism, as represented by the scientific method and strictly objective, detached consideration of material facts, may represent an intellectual ideal, but one that holds little or no meaning even for the scientist and especially for those who understand deep meaning and true essence.

A wise person seeks beyond objective, neutral, lowest-common-denominator, external-world, strictly-material-universe, background-independent, human-disconnected facts and pursues meaning, especially meaning of connection and belonging. A wise person examines *paradigm* or *system of belief* or *philosophy* for potential meaning content. And he or she is willing to pay a required cost in devotion to values to discover deep meaning and obtain desired consequences. While facts are useful and must be learned, understanding of meaning requires a combination of facts, philosophy, values, effort, and devotion. Almost everyone may know the facts, but far from everyone knows the facts and understands their meaning. Only few understand and appreciate the deepest meaning of all, a meaning of an ultimate connection and belonging – knowing Christ. Be one of the few.

Such meaning is associated with the *principles of Christ's gospel*,[17] especially, the first: faith in the Lord Jesus Christ. (We have ignored the mechanics or background of Christian inquiry, although one result to be expected therefrom has been mentioned, namely, comprehension of meaning. Mechanics of inquiry are addressed in a later chapter.) Although often mentioned first, faith in Christ is not merely the chronological first in a series of principles and ordinances (faith in Christ, repentance, baptism, receiving the Holy Ghost, enduring to the end), although it often is first in this sense. More importantly, it, together with its essential counterpart:

repentance, are first in *priority*. Increasing depth of devotion to Christ, to others, to high values, all magnify one's comprehension of meaning and feeling of connection and belonging, one's unity with God.[14] If we want to improve our understanding and expand our vision of reality beyond the objective, neutral, lowest-common-denominator facts, we must instill within ourselves required values of sympathy and devotion. Jesus Christ is the most powerful object of such devotion because He is the most powerful and devoted Person in the universe (save One). Trying to follow His gospel and His example leads to expanded vision of reality, to deeper awareness of lived experience, to improved perception of meaning, to appreciation for and identification with Him, to peace that passes all understanding, and to joy. Such consequences derive from understanding of deep meaning, a topic we pursue in some detail in Book III by comparison and contrast of total-universe Christianity of Book III with material-universe science of Book II in order to better understand both.

Notes and References for Chapter 3.

[1] Dunham, William, *Journey Through Genius, The Great Theorems of Mathematics,* Wiley Science Editions, John Wiley and Sons, New York, 1990, 31-32. For additional details, see Hofstadter, Douglas R., *Gödel, Escher, Bach: an Eternal Golden Braid*, Basic Books, New York, 1979, 88-92 and ff.

[2] Dunham, William, loc. cit., 55.

[3] Quoted in Bell, E. T., *Men of Mathematics,* Simon and Schuster, New York, 1937, 487. Bell's colorful writing is noted for fanciful descriptions and imaginative accounts. This quotation may therefore be of a fanciful and imaginative nature.

[4] Ibid., 491. [5] Ibid., 495-496. [6] Ibid., 497-498.

[7] Other drawings of a pseudosphere and a discussion of this surface in connection with the non-Euclidian geometry of Gauss, Lobachevski, and Bolyai are provided by Morris Kline (*Mathematics in Western Culture,* Oxford University Press, New York, 1953, 415-421) and also by E. T. Bell (loc. cit., 303-305).

[8] Kline, Morris, loc. cit., 426-427.

[9] The Latin term *ad hoc* is translated "to this" or "for this." It is used to denote the notion of a theory or hypothesis "for this specific purpose" or "for this case only," meaning a theory or hypothesis for a special or specific case only and not for a general result.

[10] Smoot, George, and Keay Davidson, *Wrinkles in Time,* Avon Books, New York, 1993, 54.

[11] Quoted in Godart, Odan, "Contributions of Lemaître to General Relativity (1922-1934)," in *Studies in the History of General Relativity,* Jean Eisenstaedt and A. J. Knox (editors), Birkhäuser, Boston, 1992, 449.

[12] Kline, Morris, loc. cit., 251.

[13] In terms of science and mathematics, *meaning* may be thought of as a "signed quantity;" that is to say, it possesses a magnitude and also a sign, positive or negative, or a "one-dimensional direction." We consider first magnitude or quantity of meaning. Since meaning is manifest in sympathy and other feeling for an object (e.g., spouse, child, parent, friend, stranger, Lord) to which the meaning is attached, quantity of meaning relates to the magnitude and scope of feeling developed by the individual in support of the specified object(s). A person who has developed faith in Christ may therefore find deep feeling and great meaning in hearing or performing sacred music because it expresses adoration of Him, a feeling and meaning beyond that which music alone can evoke.

With respect to sign or direction of meaning we utilize the following definitions. *Good* meaning (the desired version and the one understood when no modifier is used) is taken to be true or positive; this meaning is associated with one or more of many feelings including compassion, sympathy, honesty, faith in Christ, desire to align with His way, charity, generosity, etc. *Evil* meaning is regarded as a counterfeit version of true meaning and is consequently taken to be false or negative. This version of meaning is opposite to the true version. While the counterfeit version of meaning may contain one or more of the manifestations of hate, envy, strife, pride, contempt, lust, greed, etc., its hallmark and single essential feeling is one of self-interest above all else. In the most general terms, the two directions correspond to Christ's way (following Him) or one's own way (rebellion). When the measures of desire, attitude, intention, and motivation are included, there exists no zero-meaning position, no neutral ground; we are either with Him (for others) or against Him (primarily only for one's self) on the deepest, personal level – the level of meaning.

Manifestations of meaning are therefore several. Good meaning developed in an individual is manifest when observations of facts in some real or imagined interaction lead to feelings of sympathy and support for or identification with good behavior or innocence. For example, identification with good behavior and acquired ability to so behave leads to self esteem. In contrast, when evil meaning or intent has been developed in an observer, essentially all sympathy is self directed but it may rest with a participant in an observed interaction when this participant is perceived to be acting in a rebellious or vengeful manner by which the observer feels gratified or avenged because of his own supposed unjust victimhood.

The following example illustrates several principles associated with understanding of meaning, in particular that acquiring comprehension of meaning requires more than knowledge of facts or decree of authority. To comprehend meaning, to acquire a feeling of identification with a principle, cause, or person, one must first "pay his or her dues" or expressions of devotion.

Consider the example of an educational strategy in which the objective of true learning is placed secondary to another objective: instilling self esteem. If it does not involve true learning with associated principles of desire, fairness and honesty, organization, and work, such a strategy cheats students out of both true learning and self esteem, as it fails to help the student acquire necessary tools for success, the real basis of self esteem. If a student is rewarded for lowest-common-denominator performance and success (passing grades, graduation) comes by arbitrary decree of the system, no dues are paid and no identification with positive behavior is encouraged or learned. On the contrary, identification with negative behavior is promoted.

The danger and futility of such a strategy are apparent on very little reflection. To declare a student successful in the absence of achievement ultimately serves to trivialize "success," the genuine, enduring basis for self esteem. Denying knowledge of and means for obtaining success and preventing identification of the student with achievement based on honest effort delays him or her from even understanding what self esteem is, not to mention how to obtain it. To say one individual who has exhibited neither ambition nor effort has performed equally in learning to another who has excelled through ambition and effort trivializes ambition, effort, hard-earned skills, and success. Where, then, does the student learn the basis of success and self esteem. In a welfare system? In prison? And where does the student obtain the motivation, encouragement, and tools necessary to achieve? A product of such an educational strategy may regard success to be merely a decree of a teacher or a succeeding authority figure such as a social worker or prison authority or, more likely, fellow prisoner. At each level where the lie is propagated, the motivation to learn and truly succeed continues to be displaced with unrealistic images of success that do not contribute to enduring, positive feelings of worth, individual dignity, and self esteem. The product of such a system is a victim of such a system. To truly succeed, the student must raise himself or herself above the lowest common denominator (the educational strategy) by effort and expression of desire. Only through effort does one reach a level of constructive feeling, a positive meaning first for one's self and then others. Personal effort in living personal values is the origin of self esteem because self esteem or how one feels about one's self is merely self respect. While the summit is the goal, the virtue is in the climb. Without the climb, there is no fulfillment in summitting.

Because self esteem is so essential to an individual and to a society – because respect for another requires and depends on respect for self – failure to teach useful principles leads to individual and social disaster. Failure to teach principles that lead to self esteem and meaning leads to lack of respect and destructive behavior. These are the consequences which Barfield apparently had in mind (Chapter 2) when he observed that a lack of meaning "fills thoughtful people with a sense of foreboding."

Incidently, physicist E. T. Jaynes ("A Backward Look to the Future," http://bayes.wustl.edu/etj/node1.html 1993, 274) has commented on the issue of educational strategy.

> But it must not be supposed that our problems arise only in advanced science education; they commence already in kindergarten. From the educationalists one hears constantly such phrases as: 'skills for effective living,' 'socially desirable responses,' or 'adequate social behavior.' Why is it important to be literate? Not because one will need to read with comprehension; but rather because 'personal adjustment demands some speech and reading facility.' Why is it important for a child to learn arithmetic? Not because he is going to have to know how to add and subtract numbers correctly for all the rest of his life. Of course not! It is important that he learn arithmetic because 'a sense of failure here might affect his personality development.' This is not material for standup comedians: every one of these quotations was found in course catalogs for Schools of Education. Such phrases as 'adequate knowledge' or 'rational behavior' do not occur at all. We need look no further to understand what needs to be corrected in American elementary education.

And another physicist Richard Feynman made observations on our modern educational system based on his experience as a member of the State of California Curriculum Commission charged with recommending textbooks for elementary and secondary science and mathematics instruction. (*Surely You're Joking, Mr. Feynman!,* Bantam Books, New York, 1985, 264-276.) A fair summary of his evaluation of the textbooks used and even available in these two fields is "horrible." And his description of the methods used in promotion and selection of such textbooks is not encouraging. While money is a factor, it seems that continually throwing more money at education is not an effective answer. Even more money won't solve the textbook problem when adequate textbooks aren't available. What is needed is not money but competence and, especially, education directed at clear definition and meaning of a subject rather than vague, ill-defined qualities like self-esteem that different people (educators) are satisfied to interpret differently.

[14] *Doctrine and Covenants* 88:40.

[15] Von Baeyer, Hans Christian, *Taming the Atom,* Random House, New York, 1992, 56,74.

[16] Whitney, Orson F., *Through Memory's Halls*, Zion Printing and Publishing Company, Independence, MO, 1930, 82-83. Whitney states in his introduction that this book was published "not for the general public, but for those nearest and dearest to me." A reference copy is available in the Special Collections Library, Brigham Young University, Provo, UT.

[17] *Book of Mormon,* 3 Nephi 27:13-21, *Pearl of Great Price,* Articles of Faith, (number 4, note also numbers 1-3), 60-61.

4. Inherent Subjectivity

Objectivity is correctly regarded as essential in many activities including science, matters of law, recording of history, and news reporting. But, rigorously speaking, objectivity is rarely, if ever, fully achieved. We argue in this chapter that it is a fallacy to think one can view things and processes in a completely detached and objective manner. We are never completely detached because we observe and learn by subjective experience to which we feel subjective reactions. Moreover, our truth criterion in science and much, if not all, of philosophy is mere consistency and thus relative rather than absolute. Relative to what? Relative to our experience, knowledge, and paradigm. In addition, our conclusions are always reached in some level of ignorance rather than in full and correct understanding and any conclusion or point of view adopted in the absence of objectivity and complete truth is relative, contingent *prejudice* rather than truth or even merely an objectively-reached conclusion. Philosophical *ideals* of objective, absolutely-correct observation and deduction tacitly assume human qualities that do not correspond to reality and these unattainable ideals themselves, and belief that science and judicial decisions and history and news reporting can regularly be objective and absolutely correct, lead to much confusion and error as we shall see in considering a few selected scientific, religious, and philosophical beliefs in this chapter and in more fundamental and complete consideration of them in Books II and III. And prejudice is often most severe in consideration of religion in general and Christianity in particular, the latter of which we consider in Book III.

Our inherently subjective perception is not bad, it is simply the way things are. Science requires objectivity but a superior paradigm would recognize and be based on the way things are, i.e., the truth. For this reason the following discussion of the *ideals* of human objectivity and absolutely-true observation is useful and important; for it is essential in overcoming limitations to first identify and understand them.

Subjectivity – What are the Real Length, Time Interval, and Mass?

Science herself reveals and requires inherent subjectivity in observation of scientific interest. Traditional scientific concepts and practices which seemed intuitively correct a century ago are now in question. For instance, the assumption that a body in motion follows a continuous path in space and time, a basis of analysis in classical mechanics, can no longer be regarded as unquestionable. According to David Bohm,

> … on a purely logical basis, there is no reason to choose the concept of a continuous trajectory in preference to that of a discontinuous trajectory. … eventually [as time interval Dt or considered system volume decreases] we reach intervals of time [Dt] so small that the Brownian movement [or transitions between quantized states] becomes important, and Dx/Dt ceases to approach a definite limit. … We conclude that, in a very accurate description, the concept of a continuous trajectory does not apply to the motion of real particles.[1]

While Bohm's Brownian-motion example could be contested using known theory and measured results,[2] his basic point is valid. Classical concepts such as uniform motion and smoothly varying velocity (continuous acceleration) are ideal and may often be nonphysical together with much of the analyses of classical mechanics (as opposed to that of quantum mechanics or other superior theory).

Indeed, Einstein's theory of relativity shows space and time to be relative, with length contraction and time dilation causing quantities of length and time to vary with the relative velocity of an observer. Mass of an object also varies with relative velocity of the observer. Indeed, the mass of a body by itself is an ill-defined quantity. In accurate calculations, mass of a body varies with its (ponderable) kinetic, heat, sound, and potential energy content. Length, time, and mass are the three most fundamental measures in physics; hardly any physical conclusion is possible without referencing them directly or indirectly. And yet relativity leads us to the questions: What is the real length of an object? – What is the real time interval between two events? – What is the real mass of a body? The answers depend on the relative velocity of an observer or acceleration or ponderable energy content of mass or local strength of gravity at an observed object. What appeared to be simple quantities in Newtonian mechanics (Chapter 7) are no longer simple with the discovery of relativity (Chapter 8) and quantum mechanics (Chapter 9).

Length and time interval are observed as required in science but the real length and the real time interval are *not always* those perceived by an observer. Indeed, observation itself is relative in relativity (Chapter 8). Over fifty years after Einstein published his 1905-special theory of relativity, American physicist J. Terrell noted in 1959 that, even though a body's length is contracted in the direction of relative motion of an observer according to relativity, a length contraction is not apparent even in principle by direct visual observation or fast, stop-motion imaging.[3] Unless rather elaborate precaution is taken,[3] a length-contracted object, such as a sphere length-contracted to the shape of a pancake, moving at near-light velocity will appear to have its "rest-length" as explained by the following three-step reasoning. (1) A view or image of an object at any instant is composed of the light from the object simultaneously observed or collected at that instant. (2) Because of light's finite speed, light arriving simultaneously must leave different points on a stationary or moving object at different departure times. (3) Since different departure times correspond to different locations of a moving object, light arriving simultaneously must depart from a high-speed object at significantly different object locations.

Thus, we simultaneously see different parts of a fast-moving object at different object locations. Just as looking farther into space corresponds to looking further back in time, looking at farther points on a high-speed object does also, with the earlier object being in an earlier or "upmotion" position. Because simultaneously observed light departs from a farther point on the object before it does a nearer point, with direction-of-motion separation of these points including the difference in object location between their times of departure, the trailing tip of a sphere moving at near-light speed is observed about one-sphere-radius displacement "earlier." The near half of a flattened sphere therefore appears to be nearly semi-spherical instead of flattened. (Quiz: how does the far half appear?[3]) Of course neither length-contraction flattening nor its natural, apparent compensation just described are detectable for objects moving at low speeds, motions that are the basis of our intuition. For this reason both length contraction and its natural compensation are obscure. Nevertheless, they can prevent visual, optical, electromagnetic, or other observation from revealing a true length or shape of a high-speed object.

To enhance accuracy and avoid uncertainty due to subjectivity, scientific measurements utilize a wide variety of techniques for "observing" various phenomena objectively and reproducibly. These techniques are many including, as illustrations, (1) spectroscopic methods for optical analysis of composition and measurement of relative motions of astronomical bodies and (2) imaging of particle tracks in cloud and bubble chambers to determine particle properties. Results obtained using these techniques are ideally repeated by many scientists to insure facts used are reproducible, objective, and lowest-common-denominator-perceived in both laboratory and field measurements.

Nevertheless, subjectivity always remains. For instance, even using a precise, objective, reproducible optical method, a length contraction of a fast moving object may be undetected because of the above process described by Terrell. Such subjectivity can thus result from measurement-method selection.

Even though observations made ignoring relativity may be corrected by the theory, the corrections that account for length contraction and time dilation seem strange and non-intuitive to a nonexpert. If one employs or learns of another's results employing "strange" and "non-intuitive" corrections to the facts, do the corrected facts then represent one's own vision of reality? Hardly, since one's vision of reality provides a sense of normal (as opposed to strange) and forms the basis of intuition. Though many possess a knowledge of relativity, Newtonian mechanics or something even less sophisticated persists as the common, deeply-ingrained, personal culture of most people.

Indeed, if relativity has revealed fundamental and essential subjectivity in pre-relativity facts, what will be revealed about our current knowledge by its successor theory? And the one that follows? The expected course in philosophical progress is that the simplest, most apparent patterns, organizations, and connections (theories, laws, paradigms) pertaining to the facts are first discovered and only thereafter are deeper, more abstract, and more fundamental ones discovered. Our insight improves with each succeeding vision of reality, each new vision superceding an earlier one in providing new, improved knowledge. As insight deepens, might not current knowledge of the facts again be found to be more subjective than we presently realize?

In view of the scientific requirements of objectivity, reproducibility, and rigor, how has fundamental and essential subjectivity of observation escaped human notice? Errors in traditional culture (the assumed view that Euclidian geometry and Newtonian physics are correct) long went undetected because this culture was and is very accurate in the range of normal experience. Because the accuracy and reliability of the old paradigm was compelling in describing direct experience, the need for a new paradigm was long invisible. The little need that was apparent, the few cases in which the old paradigm did not adequately connect and rationalize facts, was (were) highly obscured by success of the old paradigm in rationalizing all the other facts. The superiority of the new paradigm (e.g., relativity, quantum mechanics) was only clear after the vision of reality it provided properly connected all the facts and correctly predicted others in which the old paradigm failed. (This history is elaborated in Book II.) Thus, only after successful utilization in applications wherein the old vision failed was the new vision widely adopted by the experts and, later, commonly adopted.

Incidently, the argument that correctness of science is demonstrated by the accuracy of its predictions[4] is not conclusive. Science is comprised of laws, theories, and principles contrived to provide accurate (consistent) predictions. Thus, Newtonian theory, relativity, and quantum mechanics all provide accurate predictions while none can yet be demonstrated to be universally correct. A new, not-yet-discovered and more correct theory may always be expected to be more accurate (consistent) over a broader range of predictions. No *a-priori*-chosen scope or level of accuracy selected in advance could be used to indicate a theory is universally consistent with truth. Rather, accuracy provided by all three of these theories is impressive.

Correct Theoretical Prejudices – Getting the Right Result

The very origins of relativity and other scientific discoveries are subjective in their nature. Early in his career Einstein was an admirer of Austrian philosopher Ernst Mach, a positivist. (Mach with other positivists held that lengths, time intervals, mass, colors, etc. are objective absolutes and the only realities and that clear description must depend on these absolutes.) But Einstein, perhaps unconsciously at first, abandoned that belief in the course of discovering relativity. In a letter to his longtime friend and confidant Michele Angelo Besso he declared "Now I am fully satisfied, and I no longer doubt the correctness of the whole system [relativity], whether the observation of the eclipse succeeds or not. The sense of the thing is too evident."[5] The observation of the eclipse he refers to was anticipated to occur in Russia, where a full eclipse of the sun was soon to occur, by physicist-astronomer Erwin Finlay-Freundlich. The goal of this observation was to determine if light from distant stars passing near the sun was deflected with space itself by the sun's gravity. The experiment was prevented by Germany's 1914 declaration of war on Russia.

But subsequent observations carried out by Arthur Eddington *et al* during an eclipse in 1919 did indicate the expected deflection and provided important experimental support for general relativity. Shortly after this latter event, before any public announcement of the result, Einstein and his student Ilse Rosenthal-Schneider were discussing a criticism of his theory when Einstein showed her a cable he had just received with the first news of Eddington's results. She expressed joy to which Einstein responded, as she later recorded,[6] "But I knew that the theory is correct." When she then asked what if his prediction had not been confirmed he responded "Then I would have been sorry for the dear Lord – the theory is correct."

Einstein's lighthearted, confident response is understandable. He had just received positive news for which he had long hoped. But his confidence preceding objective evidence, however useful, broke positivist and scientific rules because his conclusion was purely subjective, based merely on his intuition or "the sense of the thing." The only constructive comment one might make about his method was that it gave results that were "dead right!" It has been proposed that Eddington's measurements could have been used to confirm or confute Einstein's theory.[7] Eddington did not think so and neither does the present writer.

Similar histories are recounted in cases of other important discoveries, another notable one being the discovery of the theory of electromagnetism by James Clerk Maxwell (1831-1879) who concluded that his theory must be correct when he combined two constants in his equations, constants giving purely electromagnetic properties of free space, to find the speed of electromagnetic-wave propagation is exactly that of light. Quantity $\varepsilon_0 = 8.8542\times10^{-12}$ F/m is the electric permittivity constant for free space and $\mu_0 = 1.2566\times10^{-6}$ H/m the magnetic permeability constant for free space, with neither property having any previous connection to any speed. But when combined as Maxwell's theory specifies, the resulting speed $c = 1/\sqrt{(\varepsilon_0\mu_0)} = 2.99\times10^8$ m/s is exactly the speed of light.

Many profound discoveries in science have not only been based on the subjective processes of sensory perception and reasoning but they have also been motivated and adopted as correct by their discoverers on the basis of intuition, "feel," or "the sense of the thing." Steven Weinberg has observed,

> I do not believe that scientific progress is always best advanced by keeping an altogether open mind. It is often necessary to forget one's doubts and to follow the consequences of one's assumptions wherever they may lead – the great thing is not to be free of theoretical prejudices, but to have the right theoretical prejudices. And always, the test of any theoretical preconception is in where it leads.[8]

Similarly, Michael Polanyi's view is that the scientist "is bound to no explicit rules and is entitled to accept or reject any evidence at his own discretion. The scientist's task is not to observe any allegedly correct procedure but to get the right results."[9] The ideal of objective observation, disinterested analysis, and the removal of personality and prejudice from science makes good theory, but personal, subjective, even passionate, and prejudiced belief has made better practice.

Another process regularly introduces subjectivity into science and inhibits the discovery of new vision. When a scientific theory or hypothesis fails, while it is recognized that it is wrong it is also recognized that there exist different levels of "wrongness." The theory may have failed merely in some nuance of thought and language rather than in a fundamental error. Thus, an attempt is generally made to salvage the failed theory by revising its language. Reflecting back on Newtonian theory, Arthur Eddington observed "In default of a better framework, it [Newtonian theory] was still used [in the absence of relativity], ... but definitions were strained to purposes for which they were never intended."[10] Revising nuances of thought and language as well as the initial composing of a theory or hypothesis are highly subjective processes based on intuition and "feel." Indeed, unless one considers all possible hypotheses, a process evidently beyond human capability, the selection of a theory is discretionary and thus inherently subjective and prejudiced in the arbitrary choice of candidates considered, a fundamental limitation in method we shall revisit.

Objectivity: Merely Common Subjectivity

We talk of objective facts but when one adopts highly rigorous thinking there are none available to us through either our senses or a scientific paradigm. The more meticulous and rigorous one becomes in considering observation, the fewer the objective facts become until, in the extreme-rigor limit, none remain.

Sir Arthur Eddington wrote a delightful account that illustrates the failure of rigor to provide explanation of physical processes. In it Eddington refers to "an endless cycle of physical terms" by which physical facts and processes are explained or understood. He refers to Einstein's law of gravitation with the tongue-in-cheek introduction that "this time I am going to expound it in a way so complete that there is not much likelihood that anyone will understand it. Never mind. We are not now seeking further light on the cause of gravitation; we are interested in seeing what would really be involved in a *complete* explanation of anything physical."[11]

> Einstein's law in its analytical form is a statement that in empty space certain quantities called *potentials* obey certain lengthy differential equations. We make a memorandum of the word 'potential' to remind us that we must later on explain what it means. We might conceive a world in which the potentials at every moment and every place had quite arbitrary values. The actual world is not so unlimited, the potentials being restricted to those values which conform to Einstein's equations. The next question is, What are potentials? They can be defined as quantities derived by quite simple mathematical calculations from certain fundamental quantities called *intervals*. (Mem. Explain 'interval.') If we know the values of the various intervals throughout the world definite rules can be given for deriving the values of the potentials. What are intervals? They are relations between pairs of events which can be measured with a *scale* or a *clock* or with both. (Mem. Explain 'scale' and 'clock.') Instructions can be given for the correct use of the scale and clock so that the interval is given by a prescribed combination of their readings. What are scales and clocks? A scale is a graduated strip of *matter* which ... (Mem. Explain 'matter.') On second thought I will leave the rest of the description as 'an exercise to the reader' since it would take rather a long time to enumerate all of the properties and niceties of behavior of the material standard which a physicist would accept as a perfect scale or clock. We pass on to the next question, What is matter? We have dismissed the metaphysical conception of substance. We might perhaps here describe the atomic and electrical structure of matter, but that leads to the microscopic aspects of the world, whereas we are here taking the macroscopic outlook. Confining ourselves to mechanics, which is the subject in which the law of gravitation arises, matter may be defined as the embodiment of three related physical quantities, *mass* (or energy), *momentum* and *stress*. What are 'mass,' 'momentum' and 'stress?' It is one of the most far-

reaching achievements of Einstein's theory that it has given an exact answer to this question. They are rather formidable looking expressions containing the *potentials* and their first and second derivatives with respect to the coordinates. What are the potentials? Why, that is just what I have been explaining to you![12]

This illustration is reminiscent of a statement by Richard Feynman to the effect that in science we have to allow something to be known, we have to start somewhere.[13] And I say that the something and the somewhere are personally chosen, whether in science or other philosophy or belief.

Eddington next explains that subjectivity is not eliminated in physics, it is merely consolidated.

> Let us first examine the definition [of "reality"] according to the purely scientific usage of the word ... The only subject presented to me for study is the content of my consciousness. ... For reasons which are generally admitted, though I should not like to have to prove they are conclusive, I grant your consciousness equal status to my own; ... Accordingly my subject of study becomes differentiated into the contents of many consciousnesses, each content constituting a *view-point*. There then arises the problem of combining the view-points, and it is through this that the *external world* [or universe] of physics arises. Much that is in any one consciousness is individual, much is apparently alterable by volition; but there is a stable element which is common to other consciousnesses. ... This common element cannot be placed in one man's consciousness rather than in another's; it must be [conceived and used] in *neutral ground – an external world.* ... The *external world* is the [objective] world that confronts [and is comprised of] that experience which *we have in common* ...[12] (italics are added.)

Subjectivity is not eliminated in physics nor can it be; it is merely consolidated into a lowest-common-denominator, external-world model representing common experience. And some forms of subjectivity or "things characteristic of or belonging to reality as perceived rather than as independent of mind"[10] may be common. Thus, physics neither does nor can nor should attempt to fully eliminate subjectivity; it should instead build an ideal, external world of common experience representing many points of view that eliminates *spurious* subjectivity, but it includes all *common* subjectivity.

Which viewpoints are spurious? Any that fail to satisfy both a homogeneous viewpoint of a group *and* fit its adopted paradigm, philosophy, or system of belief consistent with the homogeneous viewpoint. Because it is paradigm, philosophy, or system of belief which gives pertinence to the facts, cogency to the argument, and realism to the vision, these are (paradigm is) the criteria (criterion) by which evidence is judged.

The inescapable conclusion is that even the most careful scientific observations are inherently subjective for, among other reasons, choice of paradigm is subjective. This concept is not new and its deep and far-reaching implications have been considered. They were fully recognized by the Greek philosophers.[14] Nearer our time the French philosopher and mathematician René Descartes (1596-1650) concluded he existed only on the basis of subjective evidence because he regarded "objective" evidence as too questionable.[15] At the most meticulous and rigorous level of skepticism he employed in his "method of doubt," he could find no compelling objective evidence. While science has advanced much in the nearly four intervening centuries, this conclusion is still at least equally defensible.

Indeed, a most insightful physicist, E. T. Jaynes, has made the point that

> Quite generally in science, when predictions based on our present knowledge succeed, we are pleased but have not learned much. It is only when our best predictions fail that we acquire new fundamental knowledge. But all such subtleties are lost on those who do not comprehend the distinction between deduction and inference, and try to suppress all mention of human information on the grounds that it is "subjective." Well, human information is all we have, and we had better recognize that fact. ... Any science that refuses to recognize that it is based, fundamentally and inevitably, on human knowledge, is in no way made more objective by this; quite the contrary, it operates under a serious self-inflicted handicap.[16]

Implications of essential, ever-present subjectivity are not simply captured in their full scope. German mathematician and philosopher Hermann Weyl (1885-1955) wrote this summary in 1927:

> ... immediate experience is *subjective and absolute*. However hazy it may be, it is given in its very haziness thus and not otherwise. The objective world, on the other hand, with which we reckon continually in our daily lives ... this *objective* world is of necessity *relative*; it can be represented by numbers or other symbols only after a system of coordinates has been arbitrarily imposed on the world. It seems to me that this pair of opposites, subjective-absolute and objective-relative, contains one of the most fundamental epistemological insights which can be gleaned from science. Whoever desires the absolute must take the subjectivity and egocentricity into the bargain; whoever feels drawn toward the objective cannot avoid the problem of relativism.[17]

The "absolute" referred to by Weyl corresponds only remotely to the "absolute" we seek. Weyl's absolute contains the sole (egocentric) perception of the universe to which an individual has direct access. Perception is indeed absolute, whether hazy or not. But another sense of absolute, the one we pursue, is implied in the phrases "absolute and universal truth" and "correct understanding of unique reality." This absolute is neither automatically and directly perceived nor subjective and absolute in the egocentric sense. And it is *much* more difficult to realize beyond a natural, intuitive sense for reasons we now consider.

Material or Mental?

Is something only known mentally or does knowledge correspond to a real universe? All perception is mental as was argued by Bertrand Russell and others before him. We paraphrase their argument. It is generally supposed that visual observation of a physical object starts with light travelling from object to eye, changed in the eye into another signal, and into still another in the optic nerve, to finally produce an effect in the brain. Since the final effect of the observation in the brain occurs only when an object is present, as determined by experience with other senses and by induction – this process being regarded as substantially reliable by past experience and by induction – we regard the seeing of an object to be a reliable manifestation that it is physically present. However, this association is purely mental. The final effect of observation, whether by sight or another sense, occurs inside the brain as a mental event. How one chooses to interpret such mental events depends on his or her personal philosophy. Development of such a philosophy leads eventually to the possibility that distinction between mental and material is, because of these concepts, in some sense illusory and some have concluded it is always illusory. Physical objects may be called, as we please, material or mental or both or neither, with such distinction being meaningless in an absolute sense without further consideration. According to such thinking, observation of the universe, things we see or think we see and what they mean, are a matter of personal philosophy. And so is the objectivity of science.

In other words, philosophy, and by extension perception, is personal. What one sees or believes is, ultimately, what one chooses to see or believe. Sir James Jeans includes a useful and interesting comment to this effect in his book *Physics and Philosophy*.

> The preacher ... exhorted [his flock] to try to accomplish things of their own volition, to strive after virtue and righteousness, and in brief to attempt precisely those things which their Articles of Religion pronounced to be impossible. ... The plain man might be content to place himself and his thoughts unreservedly in the hands of his spiritual teachers, but others saw there was a case for investigation. It seemed to be a case for philosophy to decide and yet, if philosophy was to sit in judgement, its verdict might well seem to be a foregone conclusion. It is said that a man's philosophy is determined by his personality, or, in Fichte's words: 'Tell me what sort a man is, and I well tell you what philosophy he will choose,' and the history of human thought supplies many confirmations of the truth of this remark. As Prof. W. K. Wright has said: 'No one in the seventeenth century but a lonely excommunicated Jew like Spinoza would have snatched at the mechanistic side of Descartes and Hobbes and given it a spiritual interpretation that could afford peace and serenity to his own tortured soul. Only enthusiastic lovers of the strenuous life like Leibniz and Fichte could have found ground for unqualified optimism in the prospect of an immortal life of unceasing activity. No one but a neurotic and selfish lover of success, with a distaste for having to work for it, such as Shopenhauer, would have seen in such a prospect the justification for a philosophy of unqualified pessimism and world renunciation. The philosophy of every great thinker is the most important part of his biography.' To which we may surely add that the biography of every great thinker is the most important part of his philosophy.[18]

Yet interpretation of reality cannot be arbitrary. Objects we see either exist or not. If so, where? Can an object exist outside of mind? In science this question is answered by compiling evidence for and against the object's existence as a physical entity. If such evidence presents a consistent physical picture of a physical object we conclude on the basis of this evidence that the physical object exists. But for small particles such as electrons and photons the evidence may not be conclusive. Measurements of relative particle properties are ambiguous, some indicating a small, definite, material entity and others indicating a wave.

We might ask, Properties relative to what? The answer is, Relative to our knowledge. For we naturally see what we choose to see, assign meaning we prefer, and know what we accept as known.

Such are the vagaries of lower philosophy: Russell and other atheist-materialists questioning the material. As we later describe, Russell the logician also abandoned logic as too dubious.

Does absolute truth exist? It does, but it is not accessible by lower philosophy. Before addressing absolute truth we first complete our consideration of obstacles and pitfalls to be avoided in discovery of reality.

What is a Particle?

Failure to recognize limitations in our (direct, subjective) perception and thinking are natural. Just as one straining to see through a window doesn't examine the window, one focusing on observation and interpretation of reality using experience obtained with one's eyes and ears hardly pauses to examine the nature of his eyes and ears. The focus is instead fixed on the experience and its interpretation. Likewise one does not always consider uncertainty in conclusions already reached when utilizing such conclusions in interpreting new results. For instance, the dual particle-wave nature of light[19] and matter (Chapter 9) leads to the question: What is a particle? As a positivist might ask: How can one rigorously talk about particles and their effects without understanding (already able to clearly state) what a particle is?[13] And yet we do, thankfully, continuously think and talk without understanding; else where would discovery and enlargement of mind originate and how would they be developed and tested?

Since our earliest recollection, our sensory stimulation and thinking have been natural parts of experience. Development of both our sensory capabilities and processing powers date to a time so early in our experience that we cannot remember it. Consequently, the sensing processes are completely natural and transparent and, as we have already surmised, influenced (superficially homogenized) by culture (language). Hopefully, we perceive through our senses in a transparent and neutral way; no perceived sensory interference or bias appears to be introduced – but, compared to what? Perception can be tricky, especially when it is rooted deeply and naturally in (subjective) awareness and unconsciously influenced by paradigm and culture (also subjective in choosing and using them). The concept of a (real) particle is widely used but only poorly defined. We have already considered the observations of Smoot and Davidson, that in science it's all too easy to be seduced into believing you have seen an effect for which you are looking, and of physicist Richard Feynman, that you must not fool yourself and you are the easiest person to fool. On the basis of his intuition Einstein properly concluded relativity was correct, but others have not been so fortunate. Luminiferous aether, phlogiston, and caloric were each once universally held to be real substances; but all are now discarded. Because perception, cognizance, and awareness are deep and natural, they are beyond routine control. Paradigm and thinking may occasionally be revised to reduce subjectivity but naturally and culturally conditioned (superficially homogenized) perception, cognizance, and awareness subjectively influence our thinking to an undetermined but undoubtedly large extent.

Knowledge, paradigm, and culture are based on a subjective sensual-neural-cerebral-cultural filter between our environment and logical deductions made using our reasoning power. One might conclude that subjectivity embedded in this process causes a certain *invisible fragility* in a tenuous, difficult-to-isolate-and-envision connection between environment (facts to be observed, reality) and awareness (knowledge, paradigm, culture). It does, but in holding such a thought one may be clinging to the traditional belief that subjective experience is inferior to meticulous, rigorous, objective, reproducible, absolute, value-neutral (detached), external-world, lowest-common-denominator-facts experience. I have suggested and I now urge that the old belief is a simple, idealized model that is mismatched with reality and thus contains worse than invisible fragility. Namely, there exists no experience or rationalization thereof free of subjectivity. We must learn to view subjective observation differently. It is not inferior. It is superior because, indeed, it is all there is, embedded invisible fragility included.

I repeat this thought using different words. When one is observing and interpreting the world through one's culture, one hardly pauses to examine his or her culture. The focus is instead on the observation and interpretation. But subjectivity is inherent in awareness, knowledge, perception of reality, culture. The ideal, external-world model of physics is merely a part of apparently-commonly-experienced reality. We can easily confuse ourselves in the absence of an ideal, objective, reproducible, absolute, infallible scientific vision of reality. But a belief that this simple, ideal, old paradigm (e.g., the absolute determinism of Comte and Laplace, with the latter's yet to be described) provides a uniquely correct vision of reality is already confused. Clinging to such an unrealistic ideal is a cause of significant confusion.

Indeed, the deliberate choice made in exclusively adopting a scientific paradigm is to disregard all experience except that contained in a lowest-common-denominator-perceived, ideal, neutral, external, material universe. This choice is tantamount to placing blinders on oneself and adopting unquestioning belief in the methods and results of science alone. The previous quotation of Eddington concludes

> ... clearly if we are to assert of anything not comprised in the external world of physics, we must look beyond the physical definition. The mere questioning of the reality of the physical world [like that of Russell *et al*, as described in the previous section] implies some higher censorship than the scientific method itself can supply.[12]

Choosing an external-world paradigm leads directly to loss or absence of subjective meaning because subjective meaning does not exist in an ideal, imaginary, common, neutral, objective, material-only, external world. Subjective meaning involves the total universe and a unique, personal, "internal world," in particular, one involving personal, subjective thoughts, values, feelings, and anticipated consequences. Without consequences there exists little meaning. The final or ultimate meaning of my mortal experience, the final me produced by my choices, wholly derives from consequences. To get where one desires, one must consider and utilize these consequences and the laws by which they are governed.

In searching for absolute truth and real reality one should not seek to impose his or her preferred conditions and presuppositions. While it is common that one's vision reveals what one chooses to see, one's belief coincides with what one wants to believe, and one's knowledge is knowing what one accepts, such personal choices do not influence either reality or correct knowledge of it – the truth. To discover reality we must honestly seek it rather than seek to impose our own preferred conditions and qualities on it. The former attempt, higher philosophy, is to seek truth; the latter, lower philosophy, is fantasy or megalomania.

Many look to science as an independent, higher-philosophy arbiter of reality because of insistence of scientists that any accepted validity must be established by conformation with all objectively observed facts. Science is therefore seen as and often is an antidote to ideology not properly based in reality. But science imposes its own constraints that dictate the nature of reliable facts and any conformation thereto. And a central problem in identifying reality is deciding which facts most directly and reliably define it.

The world we directly perceive is an internal one. Understanding a directly-perceived internal world is difficult because signals received are not always clear and definite (positive), nor are they always confirmed by others, nor are some senses necessarily involved ones regularly used and therefore familiar. Nevertheless, understanding an external world is far more difficult because construction of an objective, external world requires several "layers" of consolidated descriptions, interpretations, translations, and abstractions, each a complex process susceptible to error to which a consensus agreement among scientists must be reached. Such a process may, in fact, be largely political. *aarrrghhh*!

An urgent question arises in considering methodology alternative to science in which subjective facts are accepted and utilized. Since all direct observation and its rationalization are ultimately individual and subjective and may therefore contain variations and uncertainties related to personal sensitivity, perspective, and ability to perceive and communicate subtleties in subjective experience, how are order, pattern, and structure in the facts and universal laws relating cause-and-effect relationships among them to be reliably discovered?

Order, pattern, and universality of laws should be apparent from subjective facts, however imperfectly they may be perceived, understood, or communicated. Order, pattern, and universality (i.e., universal laws) govern the facts. Connected facts thus imply their common basis in any adequate method used to examine them. Both objective and subjective facts can be subjectively compelling, which is the only "compelling" one has direct access to. Ultimately, awareness, cognition, and reason are themselves subjective. The only change finally resulting from utilization of subjective facts is a better realization of the nature of facts and method. The overall structure discovered in the universe will still possess order and universality if those are its true properties; it will still appear and behave as if it were created and governed by God if it was.

And why not? This tradition has been passed down to us purported to be of the highest importance and verity. And, if we are forced to utilize subjective data anyway, why not include the most compelling and powerful, the knowledge, values, and lived experience obtained by believing in Christ and seeking to follow Him? This experiment and the knowledge and insight it provides answer many questions regarding ultimate cause in the universe and the source of order and organization found therein. According to the Christian paradigm (Chapter 12), this experiment provides the basis for a correct vision of reality and an understanding of absolute truth. Such vision and understanding are contemplated in both Christianity and science, but not yet reached by science because, if Christ is the Author of Creation and is Omniscience and Omnipotence, He has the authority and power to tell us how to discover Him. And, when He has told us, the method is fixed and the discussion is ended. Only one question remains: How will I react to Him?

While we have raised and left unresolved many issues, we have sufficiently considered the "necessary preliminaries" so that we can begin to carefully examine scientific belief, in Book II, and Christian belief, in Book III. In the end, resolution of issues and questions must be made by you, dear reader, using, as you desire, either one of these two higher philosophies to yet be more fully described, some combination of them, or some other philosophy.

Notes and References for Chapter 4.

[1] Bohm, David, *Quantum Theory,* Prentice-Hall, New York, 1951, 148.

[2] For a review of Brownian motion theory see Chandrasekhar, S., "Stochastic Problems in Physics and Astronomy," *Reviews of Modern Physics* **15** (1), 1943, 1-89. Chandrasekhar's paper is reprinted in *Selected Papers on Noise and Stochastic Processes,* Nelson Wax (editor), Dover, New York, 1954. For a description of modern application of Brownian motion theory see Hutchins, Darrell K., and Barton E. Dahneke, "Characterization of Particles by Modulated Dynamic Light Scattering," *Journal of Chemical Physics* **100** (11), 1994, 7890-7915.

[3] Terrell, J., "Invisibility of the Lorentz contraction," *Physical Review* **116**, 1959, 1041-1045. This effect had been earlier described in Lampa, A., "Wie erscheint nach der Relativitätstheorie ein bewegter Stab einem ruhenden Beobachter," *Zeitschrift für Physik* **27**, 1924, 138-148. Also, the effect was described nearly simultaneously with Terrell by Penrose, R., "The Apparent Shape of a Relativistically Moving Sphere," *Proceedings of the Cambridge Philosophical Society* **55**, 1959, 137. In recognition of all three discoverers the effect is now called the *Lampa-Terrell-Penrose effect.* It is well illustrated on web site www.th.physik.uni-frankfurt.de/~scherer/qmd/mpegs/lampa_terrell_penrose_info.html. The "Quiz" question is answered in this illustration.

[4] Laughlin, Robert B., *A Different Universe (Reinventing Physics from the Bottom Down),* Basic Books, New York, 2005.

[5] Quoted in Clark, Ronald W., *Einstein, The Life and Times,* Avon Books, New York, 1971.

[6] Quoted in Holton, Gerald, "Mach, Einstein, and the Search for Reality," *Daedalus,* Spring, 1968, 636-673.

[7] Earman, J., and C. Glymour, "Relativity and Eclipses: The British Eclipse Expeditions of 1919 and their Predecessors," *Historical Studies in the Physical Sciences* **11** (1), 1980, 49-85. Results of this study are interpreted in a "non-science" context in Collins, Harry, and Trevor Pinch, *The Golem,* Second Edition, Cambridge University Press, Cambridge, England, 1998, 49-55. Many scientists question the preconceptions of these authors (see the warning in end-note 3 of Chapter 1).

[8] Weinberg, Steven, *The First Three Minutes,* Basic Books, New York, 1977, 1988, 119.

[9] Polanyi, Michael, *Science, Faith and Society,* The University of Chicago Press, Chicago, 1946, 40.

[10] Eddington, Arthur, *Relativity,* Eighth Annual Haldane Lecture, 26 May 1937.

[11] Eddington, Arthur, *The Nature of the Physical World,* Cambridge University Press, 1928, 261-263.

[12] Ibid., 282-286.

[13] Knowledge has to start somewhere – we have to allow something to be known, as Richard Feynman and others have stated. Aristotle declared that known facts and principles must underlie theories and even definitions (although he also correctly observed in the *Organon* that undefined terms are essential in mathematics – their definitions to be deduced from the axioms – to prevent an infinite regress in definitions). Without an axiom, assumption, or something known, on what would we build or in what terms could we think and talk. But the terms in which we think and talk control in large degree what we think and say. What we allow to be known becomes the basis of our paradigm, philosophy, and belief. As stated below in endnote 15, "starting point of knowledge [is] the entire problem of method."

A starting point in modern physics is particles. Quantum field theory (Chapter 9) has led physicists to believe that particles are local "distortions" of fields in spacetime. In string theory particles possess the mathematical behavior of a loop of string or a segment of an open surface or of a closed surface, all of which vibrate in certain patterns that agree with patterns observed in measured results. These views provide images or interpretations of what a particle is. Thus, particles are not understood but rather they are assumed or axiomatic entities in terms of which other entities and processes are described. Fritjof Capra (*The Tao of Physics,* Shambhala, Boulder, CO, 1975, 80) states

> ... classical concepts like 'elementary particle,' 'material substance' or 'isolated object' have lost their meaning; the whole universe appears as a dynamic web of inseparable energy patterns.

And Gary Zukav (*The Dancing Wu Li Masters: An Overview of the New Physics,* William Morrow, New York, 1979, 281) has noted that, based on quantum field theory and the no-longer-invisible connections in quantum mechanics implied (for example, by one of Bell's theorems and associated experiments described in Chapter 10), individual things and events

> ... are no longer separate entities. They are different *forms* of the same thing. Everything is a *manifestation.* It is not possible to answer the question, 'Manifestation of what?' because the 'what' is that which is beyond words, beyond concept, beyond form, beyond even space and time. Everything is a manifestation of what which is.

[14] See the page-6 quotation of Draper.

[15] Descartes addresses the topic of reasoning and truth in a number of treatises: *Rules for the Direction of the Mind* (1628 or 1629), *The Search after Truth* (1628 or 1641), *Discourse on the Method of Rightly Conducting the Reason* (1637), *Meditations on First Philosophy* (1641), and *The Principles of Philosophy* (1644).

In his autobiographical *Discourse*, Descartes rehearsed his education at the Jesuit College at La Flèche and the great deficiencies he perceived therein. "I have been nourished on letters since my childhood, and since I was given to believe that by their means a clear and certain knowledge could be obtained of all that is useful in life, I had an extreme desire to acquire instruction. But so soon as I had achieved the entire course of [Aristotelian] study, at the close of which one is usually received into the ranks of the learned, I entirely changed my opinion. For I found myself embarrassed with so many doubts and errors that it seemed to me that the effort to instruct myself had no effect other than the increasing discovery of my own ignorance. And yet I was studying at one of the most celebrated schools in Europe. ... And this made me take the liberty of judging all others by myself and of coming to the conclusion that there was no learning in the world such as I was formerly led to believe ...."

In his *Rules*, Descartes urged that investigation of any problem should be focused on what one can clearly see or infer with certainty, not by what others have thought. "For we shall not, for instance, become mathematicians, even if we know by heart all the proofs that others have elaborated, unless we have an intellectual talent that fits us to resolve difficulties of that kind. Neither, though we have mastered all the arguments of Plato and Aristotle, if we have not the capacity for forming a solid judgement on these matters, shall we become philosophers." Mathematics, "because of the certainty of its demonstrations and the evidence of its reasoning," was uniquely satisfying to Descartes. In particular, it was the *method* of mathematics that attracted him. He gradually decided that mathematical methods could and should be extended to other areas of thought, which he attempted to do. He came to regard methodology or methodical procedure as having the highest importance. He condemned random search or study and a trust in luck or chance as being intellectually demoralizing and sterile.

Descartes realized that experience and deduction are the basis of knowledge. Because experience involves complex objects, inferences from experience may often be in error. He regarded deduction, on the other hand, as free from error when carried out with even moderate understanding. He therefore urged that "in our search for the direct road toward truth, we should busy ourselves with no object about which we cannot attain a certitude equal to that of the demonstrations of arithmetic and geometry." We shall directly see what evidence Descartes regarded as most reliable and certain on the direct road toward truth. It is not the objective, reproducible, lowest-common-denominator facts highly esteemed by scientists of today, because they are not what they are generally believed to be.

The beginning of method is an axiomatic base, philosophical foundation, certain belief, or starting point of knowledge. Indeed, one might describe starting point of knowledge as the entire problem of method, a view that was not proposed but clearly appreciated by Descartes. Thus, in his sophisticated *Discourse on Method* Descartes begins with methodical doubt to eliminate dependence on intuition (culture) in finding a reliable starting point of knowledge. He uses methodical doubt to severely test whatever might serve as such a starting point. And numerous candidates he tested failed to survive the skeptical scrutiny of his methodical doubt. Casualties cast to the trash pile included common beliefs, traditionally accepted ideas, and directly observed facts. In the skeptical eye of methodical doubt, these may all be mere dreams or illusions. However, Descartes eventually discovered a candidate starting point that survived his methodical doubt. This candidate is doubt itself. To the doubter, the reality of his doubt is certain. And what gives rise to doubt? Thinking is the origin of doubt. But thinking requires a thinker. And so, concludes Descartes, "I think, therefore, I am."

Then thinking or personal, critical reasoning power, by Descartes' philosophy, is the ultimate certainty. Why must it be accepted as certain? Because doubt is independent, distinct, and clear and thus not subject to internal or external distortion or manipulation.

Among the philosophical starting points Descartes considered, he discarded the facts of direct observation as too questionable in their certainty while he finally adopted the *subjective* process of reasoning as a uniquely certain basis for philosophy. For a philosophical basis scientists (and much of society) currently accept lowest-common-denominator facts as the only reliable evidence and exclude subjective experience as unreliable evidence. This current practice is exactly opposite to Descartes'.

(This account of Descartes life and works is condensed from Descartes, René, *Discourse on Method and the Meditations,* F. E. Sutcliffe (translator), Penguin Books, London, 1968 and the *Encyclopædia Britannica.*)

[16] Jaynes, E. T., "Notes on Present Status and Future Prospects," http://bayes.wustl.edu/etj/node1.html 1991, 2, 5.

[17] Weyl, Hermann, *Philosophy of Mathematics and Natural Science,* Princeton University Press, Princeton, NJ, 1949, 116. This book is a revised and augmented English translation by Olaf Helmer of a chapter entitled *Philosophie der Mathematik und Naturwissenschaft* which originally appeared in German in *Handbuch der Philosophie* published by R. Oldenbourg, 1927. The quoted translation is partly Helmer's and partly Karl Popper's. (*The Logic of Scientific Discovery,* Harper and Row, New York, 1959, 111.)

[18] Jeans, James, *Physics and Philosophy,* Cambridge University Press, Cambridge, 1942, 22-23.

[19] For a brief summary of the dual nature of light see Ekspong, Gösta, *The Dual Nature of Light as Reflected in the Nobel Archive,* last revised 5 March 2004, www.nobel.se/physics/articles/ekspong/index.html.

Book II:

Material-Universe Science

Book II:

Material-Universe Science

5. A Model or Paradigm for Science

In our quest to discover absolute truth and meaning we evaluate two particular philosophies, paradigms, or systems of belief, namely, *science* and *Christianity*. Some would object that these two philosophies are more than two because they are rather two classes of philosophies each containing many philosophies. I agree and we shall recognize and address the diversity in both science and Christianity, an essential requirement because we shall select and examine a single representative model for each in a best-models-case comparison and evaluation of these two classes. This chapter is devoted to selecting and justifying a model for science. In Chapter 12 we select and justify a model for Christianity.

A careful examination and comparison of scientific and Christian belief must employ a well-defined, accurate, comprehensive model for each. We therefore seek a succinct, comprehensive, accurate statement of scientific belief as a scientific model or paradigm. Selecting this model and the parallel one for Christianity are the most critical tasks in our examination, comparison, and evaluation of science and Christianity. The criticality of these selections rests, of course, in the fact that if both chosen models are not accurate and fully representative, any comparative examination and evaluation of them will accurately portray neither science nor Christianity. Each must faithfully contain the essence of the philosophy it represents so that all comparisons and conclusions will properly represent both science and Christianity, especially since we shall ultimately compare them on the basis of essence or meaning. Discovering reality, our goal in this book, depends on the validity of our models if reality is to be discovered using either or both of these two philosophies and we must consequently take great care in these choices.

Early science was regarded as philosophy because in its early years science was distinguished by neither separate methodology nor distinct subject matter. It was eventually recognized as a distinct branch of philosophy, called *natural philosophy*, having its own methodology and focus of interest. The early practice of Plato, Aristotle, Archimedes, and others was useful in establishing natural philosophy. Francis Bacon (1561-1626) was one of the first to attempt to formalize a distinct philosophy of science. Bacon laid great stress on experiment, diverging from Aristotelian tradition (Chapter 6) in which experiment was all but ignored, and on induction, i.e., going from the specific to the general or from particular facts to universal laws.[1] Yet, the multitude of specific facts and phenomena of natural philosophy or science soon became difficult to comprehensively address since, contrary to the opinion of Bacon and others, the facts do not simply and clearly suggest the laws of science. A simpler, more focused approach is required. Simplicity and focus are provided by a *hypothesis, theory, or law* simply guessed and posed to relate observed facts and phenomena, an approach sometimes described as "conjectural realism." Consequences deduced from the hypothesis are compared to observation. Agreement supports the hypothesis, unavoidable contradiction requires the hypothesis be either modified or abandoned.[2]

Galileo (Chapter 6) strongly influenced modern science. Where others had philosophized, Galileo practiced. The success of Galileo, in science and especially in his literary descriptions of science, caused others to emulate his methods. Eventually a formal scientific method emerged which follows the pattern first used by Archimedes and refined by Galileo. Galileo's work seems modern in its methodology because Galileo more than any other individual established modern scientific methodology.

While many or most previous investigators were concerned with purpose or questions of *who* or *what* and *why*, Galileo's investigations addressed instead primarily questions of *how*. Following this tradition, scientists generally avoid *teleological* theories or explanations, i.e., theories or explanations of phenomena in terms of a design or purpose which drives or motivates the phenomena. Today's scientists seek instead fundamental laws by which phenomena may be predicted and described, so-called cause-and-effect relationships between facts. Moreover, scientists generally adopt the less demanding task of *describing* relations of facts and phenomena, as mathematical theories do, rather than *explaining* them, i.e., they describe only *how* things happen, even when utilizing cause-and-effect knowledge. Fundamental *who*, *what*, and *why* questions are evaded by scientists. "They would argue that [such a] question has been wrongly posed: we should not try to ask *what* reality is; merely, *how* does it behave."[3] While some might think cause-and-effect descriptions of *how* are explanations, they have not yet completely explained any process or thing.

Simultaneously, many matters of theological dogma are not explained. Because much religious dogma is not justified by a clear logical structure and/or facts (as perceived by humans), one may regard it as arbitrary or contingent and tentative. Elements of dogma itself or deductions therefrom may or may not be testable against natural phenomena. When such tests are possible, conflict between science and religion may occur and, indeed, such conflict is prominent in history. But laws and theories of science herself are merely tentative, as are some deductions and inferences from religious dogma and, perhaps, the dogma itself (Chapters 10 and 12 through 15). Conflict between science and religion is sometimes only apparent and it is always no more than tentative and contingent because conclusions of science and often of religion as well are no more than tentative and contingent. Conflict may also be merely apparent for reasons to be considered later.

We now consider scientific method and deduce its inherently tentative nature.

A Scientific Paradigm (Model)

Students in a high-school-science class usually learn "the scientific method," referring to the logical or philosophical method as opposed to any method of instrumentation, mathematics, or other techniques of scientific theory and practice. Alternatively, one may look up the scientific method in a good textbook, dictionary, or encyclopædia. The *logical or philosophical scientific method* consists of a series of steps equivalent to the following series we quote from William Buckman.

> The scientific method is the accurate observation of facts and the determination of order among the facts. ... The scientific method usually has at least five steps: (i) stating the problem, (ii) forming the hypothesis, (iii) observing the experiment[s], (iv) interpreting the data, and (v) drawing the [tentative] conclusion[s].[4]

In step (v) we have added the word *tentative*. We shall shortly see its necessity pertaining to adopting any hypothesis, assumption, principle, theory, or law as truth. However, a conclusion is not regarded as tentative when discarding an incorrect hypothesis because of *unavoidable* conflict with at least one established fact. Such a conclusion based on established, unavoidable conflict is definite and conclusive.

This description is not the only possible one for scientific methodology or philosophy. Indeed, some scientists today deny any formal method is needed or useful because a fixed method could restrict the creativity and imagination essential to scientific discovery. There are no requirements or limits in the discovery of scientific truth beyond the requirement that any such discovery must somehow be "justified" utilizing objective, reproducible, material-universe facts, i.e., facts others can reproduce, observe, and agree on. No specific formula for scientific discovery has or probably can be devised; nor is one sought. A scientist is free to devise his or her own methodology as best befits a need, provided any conclusions can be justified by their consistency with the known facts. A formal statement of the scientific method was not emphasized in either the training I received or gave in physical-science courses at the university level. Neither do many texts used in college- or university-level physics courses today contain any specific description of the scientific method. (Buckman's text, quoted above, is one that does.) Instead, attention is focused on discovery and use of scientific laws and principles with little or no concern for logical and philosophical structure of method. The student thereby learns of methodology that has been used in past scientific discovery with minimum restriction as to how science *should* be done which could limit his or her adaptability and creativity.

But it is essential to our purposes here to adopt a suitable statement of the scientific method in order to discover its inherent capabilities and limitations. Noting that the above-quoted method is not restrictive of either creativity or adaptability because of its general, nonrestrictive language, we adopt it as our model of the scientific method. Nevertheless, this specific statement of the method is not crucial to the conclusions we shall draw since variations contain the same essential elements and, thus, the same capabilities and limitations inherent in these elements.[5]

Variations in description of the scientific method occur in its use by different scientists. We just stated that such variations do not have significant consequence when the essential elements of the method are even just implicitly present. We now ask rhetorically, "What are these essential elements?" The essential, fundamental elements of science are two: (a) the known or observed objective, reproducible, material-universe facts from which an hypothesis must be conceived and (b) consistency with all these facts as the truth criterion in testing hypotheses to eliminate those that unavoidably contradict at least one established fact and for justification of those that don't. That is, justification of a hypothesis in science consists of absence of any established, unavoidable contradiction between it and all known facts. Element (a) is essential because consideration is limited by scientific convention to objective, reproducible, material facts to preserve purity (universality) of the scientific database. Element (b) is essential only because no alternative is known, i.e., scientific knowledge cannot be regarded as indubitable and absolute but only as consistent relative to the known facts. In the absence of a certain truth criterion for establishing absolute laws, complete consistency is the next best thing. In science we cannot judge relative to any absolute because no fact, assumption, principle, theory, law, or axiom of science has yet been established to be absolute and neither has observation of reality (Book I).[6] Moreover, establishing either consistency or inconsistency is not simple in practice since experience or data or, for that matter, theory is usually, if not always, incomplete and imperfect.[7]

The two above-listed, essential elements impart to science its fundamental nature, i.e., they provide, by themselves, the essence of the scientific method. Nevertheless, because many scientists do not yet think in these terms but are familiar with the method quoted from Buckman, we use it, understanding that it contains and represents these two fundamental elements as the essence of science.

In imparting these two essential elements to science, the above-listed scientific method is as good as any and better than most. A succinct, accurate, comprehensive, and widely recognized model for science is therefore provided by this definition of scientific method. The only possibly-superior alternative that comes to mind is the totality of all theoretical, mathematical, instrumental, ... techniques, all observations, and all results of science. While such a comprehensive model is superior in its completeness and is succinctly stated in general terms, it is not fully defined without a comprehensive description of all scientific techniques, observations, and results. And a need to learn all scientific techniques and concepts on a comprehensive list would delay and limit use of science and tend to restrict creativity and adaptability. In any case, elements (a) and (b) are always required for elimination of unsuitable hypotheses and failure to find any conflict between a hypothesis and known facts is a *de facto* justification of a surviving hypothesis. These essentials are implicit in our adopted method listed above. Without loss of generality we shall use this model for the scientific method.

I asked a European physicist how he defines the scientific method. He immediately and articulately responded with the summary that it is a repeating inductive-deductive sequence of observation and reasoning. His definition is easily reconciled with the one quoted above which is generally used in a repeating sequence or iterative manner utilizing induction in forming the hypothesis. Indeed, my European friend's response is very close to the listing in *The Dictionary of Philosophy*: "Scientific method ... is usually considered as a branch of logic; in fact, ... science in general is accounted for by the combination of deduction and induction as such."[8]

Other terms, such as "scientific inquiry," are regarded as referring to "scientific method" because no separate methodology is associated with such other terms.

Trouble in Scientific Paradise

Early conception of scientific method was influenced by Francis Bacon. He realized that science must be a trial and error process. He wrote

> We must ... completely resolve and separate Nature, not by fire [the principal tool of alchemy], certainly, but by the mind, which is a kind of divine fire. ... There will remain, all volatile opinions vanishing into smoke, the affirmative form, solid, true and well defined. Now this is quickly said, but it is only reached after many twists and turns.[9]

Bacon's view is today often held implicitly and uncritically, leading to a blind, misplaced, and undeserved faith in an absolute authority of science. While Bacon believed that error (volatile opinions) is eliminated by observation and reason, he failed to recognize an essential, tentativeness in the nature of every scientific theory or law however solid and well-defined it may be. His solid and well-defined truth is to be established by trial-and-error science. The only definitive or final result in trial-and-error science is error (unavoidable contradiction), leading to choice of another trial hypothesis. If only a few trials or hypotheses need be considered the method could work well. But the number of possible hypotheses pertaining to any significant problem is indefinitely large, in contrast to the single "affirmative form" envisioned by Bacon, and not all these hypotheses are even apparent. Here is a principal flaw in Bacon's reasoning: "there will remain [the truth]" only if it was present in the scientist's list of possibilities *and* if all others are eliminated. Bacon did recognize limitation in the method when he warned "God forbid that we should give out a dream of our imagination for a pattern of the world."[10] In fact, this latter possibility usually overpowers the desired alternative because there are never enough experimental results to fully test or even suggest all possible hypotheses. Indeed, the number of experiments required to establish any general scientific law as final and certain truth is indefinitely large, a principle we shall directly demonstrate.

From this and earlier discussion we can anticipate trouble in scientific paradise in the limitation inherently imposed by scientific method. Knowledge obtained by the scientific method is always tentative, always subject to revision. The path of history in science is littered with many laws adopted for a time and revised or discarded as new (or old) evidence was found to unavoidably contradict them. That science must be inherently tentative in its positive conclusions is demonstrated by the following reasoning.

Validity of a scientific law, theory, principle, or assumption depends on the absence of any fact that contradicts the law, theory, principle, or assumption so that consistency is preserved. That is, *consistency (between theory and observation) is the truth criterion of science* or, to state this principle another way, *contradiction in science (between theory and observation or theory and theory) is forbidden.* We will find that consistency by itself is an insufficient truth criterion. At least one additional constraint is often added. The additional constraint is frequently *Ockham's razor.*[11]

Since we continually learn new facts, it is essential to and inherent in the method that scientific hypotheses in the form of assumptions, principles, theories, and laws must be regarded as no better than tentative even after they are successfully tested against all known facts because other possibly important facts are not yet known. In the absence of a complete knowledge of all facts and all deductions therefrom (a state we shall describe by the term *omniscience*), one can only conclusively demonstrate by use of at least one established, unavoidable contradiction that an assumption, principle, theory, or law is invalid. The reverse process, proving a theory or law indubitable, is never possible while some facts or their implications even possibly remain unknown.[12] Science thereby provides definite *no* answers regarding the truth of a hypothesis or law but never a definite *yes* answer.[13]

It follows that a scientific law may, at best, be only tentatively *assumed* to be correct in the perhaps temporary absence of contradictory evidence. How long must a law be justified by assumption? Until it is disproved and discarded or until all facts and all deductions therefrom are known. Only a knowledge of all facts and all their implications, only omniscience, allows elimination of all possible contradictions.

The full scope of this limitation of science was perhaps first expressed by Austrian and British scientific logician and philosopher Sir Karl Popper (1902-1994). Drawing on the insight of Hermann Weyl quoted in Chapter 4, Popper reached the following conclusion summarizing concepts and arguments he presented in his seminal book *The Logic of Scientific Discovery*. And he stated it more strongly than I have (because he specified a longer duration for the tentative state):

> The old scientific ideal of *epistêmê* [Greek for *knowledge*] – of absolutely certain, demonstrable knowledge – has proved to be an idol. The demand for scientific objectivity makes it inevitable that every scientific statement must remain *tentative for ever.*[14] (the italics are Popper's)

More Trouble in Scientific Paradise

While I was preparing this book several friends provided inestimable help by criticizing my thinking. Of these friends, two trained in science were the least accepting of many of my points. One did not object to any individual contrast we make between science and true, definite understanding but nonetheless held the opinion that science should have a final say in establishing truth. The other was more articulate in expressing possible contrary thinking, stating that our truth criterion or characterization of proof in science as consistency or absence of disproof was *superficially* correct but there exists a *deeper* concept of proof. Namely, he said, that proof should be considered to be a high ("very high – someone has to choose how high") probability of the concept, theory, or law based on *all* the evidence. He stated that probability theory, such as that described by American physicist E. T. Jaynes,[15] is well defined and allows a quantitative comparison of different theories taking into account "everything we think we know" in establishing scientific truth. The interrelatedness of different theories, concepts, and observations is part of what should be included in such an evaluation, so that a single piece of new evidence is seldom, if ever, sufficient to disprove a theory. Even when a new piece of evidence appears to unavoidably conflict with previous scientific understanding, that evidence must be considered in a large, interconnected framework of knowledge and thought, and taking the inconsistency at simple face value can cause a ripple of unjustified doubt through concepts in which we have great confidence based on much other evidence. He concludes that new data that diverges from traditional science may require small adjustments in science or, very occasionally, revolutions in scientific thought, but most often they require a reexamination of the new data.

Of course my articulate-scientist adviser makes a valid point. I agree with him that the most important feature of new data or new theory is validity and one should not too quickly abandon principles and knowledge previously regarded as reliable in a reckless race to new understanding based on unproven data. However, confusion as well as wisdom resides in his support of such scientific tradition for three reasons. First, he speaks of "great confidence [in a scientific result] based on much other evidence." Since the only possible definitive result in a truth-or-error decision or non-comprehensive set of truth-or-error decisions in science is error, indicated by at least one unavoidable conflict with observation, what "other evidence" would that be? Consistency is common and expected, a scientific principle or law being contrived to provide this very result. Consistency is hardly remarkable. What is remarkable is either unavoidable conflict with at least one fact or universal and comprehensive agreement with all presently-known facts. We propose that these two outcomes are together the only easily recognizable and trustworthy truth criterion in science in which the first provides a definite *no* and the second a tentative *yes* or *maybe*.

Second, he speaks of interconnections and required agreement of scientific principles, theories, and observations and their potential use in establishing scientific truth. Truth cannot presently be positively established in science, only error. (And in establishing error we must utilize great care because, in the absence of established truth, determining unavoidable conflict using imperfect knowledge is difficult.) When knowledge has reached the level of omniscience and error or conflict is still absent, then truth is established as a *de facto* result in a comprehensive absence of error.

Third, he proposes *plausibility* and *probability* as a basis of scientific truth. But plausibility and probability are poor criteria for establishing plausibility and probability. Any argument for such qualities in terms of or based on such qualities themselves is circular. We can easily deceive ourselves in an internally-consistent but logically circular argument that knowledge is plausible and probable when we deliberately introduce such qualities as properties of the knowledge we are examining.

We return to the thought of Richard Feynman that in science we must allow something to be known, that we have to start somewhere. What we allow to be known, where we start, is critical because it, more than any other factor, controls where we arrive in our thinking, at least early-on. The notion of probability is comfortable; we can include many thoughts and observations, indeed, "everything we think we know," without commitment, without justification, since no single item is crucial and judgement is based on a whole rather than on any particular concept or observation.

Yet embracing notions of plausibility and probability theory themselves, despite their apparently undemanding nature and broad range of applicability, tacitly introduces an intellectual inertia that renders this strategy highly suspect (at best) when considered in the light of history of science. One may indeed choose observations, theories, principles, and syllogisms he or she regards as plausible as a starting point and utilize probability theory to establish a projected scientific truth to some selected confidence level. But this strategy fails to identify truth whenever truth is regarded as implausible, as occurs so frequently and conspicuously in the history of science. Dramatic examples are provided in following chapters but we list three illustrations here.

(i) Maxwell's 1864 theory of electromagnetism was initially rejected because of Maxwell's unconventional methods used to deduce it. Twenty-five years later, shortly following Maxwell's death, Hertz's brilliant experiments proved it correct in every detail. (ii) Continuum theories of matter and energy were nearly universally preferred (Appendix A) until they were suddenly and finally superceded by molecular and quantum theories discovered and developed by a few insightful and independent-thinking "mavericks." (iii) The universe was generally regarded as *stationary* or unchanging in time until, over a period of years, the evidence that it is expanding provided by a few "renegades" finally became convincing to most, if not all, scientists.

The most interesting new facts are those regarded as impossible according to an accepted paradigm. Only in a new (not-yet-accepted), more-correct paradigm, ever the goal in science, are these impossible facts possible. This scenario of science describes a common history of major advances wherein the impossible investigated by a single or a few gifted individuals, paddling against mainstream opinion of the Establishment, eventually becomes the plausible. It is therefore imprudent to suggest we should stake our establishment of scientific truth on a basis of plausibility and probability of a few or even many selected observations and syllogisms. We have already made that mistake too often. In science, nothing can be beyond question – everything must be tested for consistency against everything else. This strategy is required so that even incorrect starting-point knowledge may be corrected.

Science invokes objectivity or the assent of others. If science were based on subjective notions of plausibility and a few discretionary syllogisms, science could degenerate to "truth determined by popularity" in which a most-popular orthodoxy would surely be uniquely held as "legitimate thinking" by its supporters regardless of careful, insightful reasoning conceived and developed by a lone and dedicated genius like, say, Galileo, Newton, Maxwell, Planck, or Einstein. As in other activities, power politics could hold, and in isolated instances has held, its dangerous sway in science (Appendix A). However, most scientists, surely the enlightened ones, would ignore such nonsense and simply continue correctly practicing their trade.

To be reliable and apolitical, truth must be established using a fundamental and trustworthy standard or *truth criterion*. What criterion would that be? Certainly it is not found in the statements of the truth-by-decree sociologist and cultural-scholar critics of science mentioned in Chapter 1 who apparently seek merely to destroy without building. In science, the better tradition is to displace, rather than destroy, with superior construction. This tradition requires a certain openness of thought not consistent with premature establishment of final scientific truth based on everything we think we know. Final truth in science will not be established without final and complete knowledge of the material universe, and probably much more knowledge than we now possess of the nonmaterial universe as well.

That is, the truth criterion in science and much of philosophy must be comprehensive consistency with all facts and all correct implications thereof – a comprehensive consistency based ultimately on omniscience or a full and complete knowledge of the material universe. Such consistency is supposed to be sufficient to establish truth but is only possible when all facts and all their implications are known. Until truth is so established, revision will be required for both newly found understanding on some occasions and for long-accepted understanding on others. This strategy is tedious and lengthy but no suitable alternative has yet been proposed as a truth criterion for science and secular philosophy because comprehensive consistency is the only recognized, universal property of truth presently believed to be known.[16]

Some scientists are attempting to develop theory that is "background independent,"[17] that is, to develop fundamental theory that is independent of context or background, avoiding our familiar but nonetheless ignorant and highly questionable understanding of such qualities as, say, space and time. Some indefiniteness and confusion that occur at the frontiers of fundamental science (Chapters 8-11) point to ignorance of basic notions with which we are familiar and have strong preconceptions, perhaps too familiar and too preconceived to allow critical, objective evaluation. But we must always begin by allowing something to be known. We must always start somewhere. Our starting place is crucial and it should ideally be confirmed and validated by later knowledge, which it generally is unless it is discarded as inconsistent, a necessary capability giving science the power to correct error even in the information it starts from. Confirmation that starting information is correct by stronger means than mere consistency and plausibility, qualities that automatically follow in a carefully reasoned structure, is unknown in science *per se* but we shall find it in Christianity.[13]

Familiarity is not understanding and, indeed, familiarity, plausibility, and apparent consistency are often an opaque barrier to understanding. The eternal requirement for progress in science is seeing beyond the familiar and obvious, the currently plausible and consistent. Such vision is almost invariably initially provided by an insightful individual. Familiarity, plausibility, and consistency often hide both ignorance and deeper understanding by obviating further contemplation of the familiar, plausible, and consistent.

In our scientific search for truth we must not be deceived by familiarity, plausibility, and apparent consistency because these intuitive properties can obscure our most severe ignorance. And science must retain both objectivity and consistency (despite the possible danger of some group claiming a most-popular, and therefore true, orthodoxy without due regard for reality). At the present, there is no suitable known or supposed alternative means for testing truth in science. Science and philosophy desperately need a more definite and trustworthy truth criterion.

Where do We go from Here?

While variations in statement of the scientific method and in thinking of individuals about it are not fundamentally consequential provided the essential components and tentativeness of science are implied, as in our adopted statement but not in Bacon's, variations in its application and in the results it provides are sometimes consequential. Conflicting results occur in science due to different assumptions, tools, and observations or evidence preferred by different users.[18]

Although we cannot disregard these variations attributable to personal choice and individual practice, we seek a fundamental-level description of the inherent capabilities and limitations of the scientific method itself rather than a catalog of its valid results. In following chapters we describe and consider many results of science primarily to obtain a useful understanding of its substance and nature. Uncertainty in and controversy about particular results will be described for the theory of quantum mechanics to illustrate the tentative nature of all scientific results. And in Appendix A other controversy and its causes due to different preferences of different users are addressed. We seek the fundamental, inherent capabilities and limitations of science for comparison with those of Christianity. In considering the scientific method in this comparison we shall generally take a "best-case-scenario" or "pro-science but realistic" attitude about both method and application. But one should keep in mind that some scientific results are not accepted by all scientists. Indeed, perhaps relatively few scientific results are uniformly and unconditionally accepted by all scientists.[19]

An independence of mind and other observed traits of scientific colleagues and of science enthusiasts have led the present author to believe that those trained in science obtain in their scientific training a substantial predisposition in thinking, an instilled bias, and a supposed intellectual independence, in some even an arrogance, related to vestment in the robes of intellectual power, prestige, and status of a scientist (if only in the scientist's mind). Therefore, we attempt to make our points clear, stating them in what may sometimes seem to be painful detail, despite the goal of a simple, declarative style. If the reader is not a scientist or science enthusiast, the discussion may occasionally seem to extend beyond the mark – past the obvious – making it difficult to "stay tuned" to tedious detail. Please be compassionate. We are trying to make these points compelling to trained scientists and others of self-perceived high status who seem to require considerable encouragement in order to overcome instilled bias and supposed intellectual independence (sometimes arrogance) that inhibit serious consideration of them. That is, we are trying to help each reader overcome pride manifest in one's resistance to being influenced in his or her thinking. In doing so, however, we do not wish an individual to abandon his or her intellectual independence. Indeed, we are trying to help them to increase it.

To discern differences in evidence, awareness, knowledge, understanding, and, particularly, meaning in science and Christianity, we examine in following chapters our models of science and Christianity, beginning in this Book II with science. To understand the nature of science we consider accounts of scientists who made important discoveries, their discoveries, and associated implications. We mention deficiencies in science but generally give science the "benefit of the doubt" in these accounts and focus on its many successful and beneficial accomplishments. We introduce and consider fundamental Christian methodology in Book III. Capabilities and limitations of both scientific and Christian methodology are all finally stated and evaluated when we summarize both and extract their meanings in the final chapters of this book. This order is chosen so that we may utilize contrasts between science and Christianity to plumb the simple but obscure, consequential but subtle, powerful but delicate, poorly understood and not easily captured essences of both science and Christianity, especially the latter.

Notes and References for Chapter 5.

[1] Different opinions have existed over what the scientific method should include. In the infancy of science it was believed that scientific laws were directly suggested by observed facts used with

logical induction by which scientific laws were directly indicated. Some still hold this opinion. Two objections may be raised against this belief. (1) Induction, leaping from the specific to the general, is a weak logical tool. Just because something has always been observed to occur in a certain way is no proof it cannot occur differently. Induction can introduce or strengthen prejudice and preconception. (2) The comprehensive, material-universe scope of science, i.e., the many results now known, make it difficult to induce laws that are sufficiently fundamental and general and agree with all known data. An inductive approach to discovering new laws is therefore difficult and can lack the scope and efficiency provided by simply proposing (guessing) a hypothesis and deducing therefrom consequences to test against known facts. However, ignoring induction in stating the method does not exclude its use, since a guessed hypothesis or theory may always be based on induction. An induced-or-deduced-or-guessed hypothesis generally used in hard science includes all cases. In softer science the tendency to propose laws on the basis of induction, suggested and justified only by specific case studies, still remains popular.

[2] Establishing either agreement or disagreement between theory and experiment is not simple. Steven Weinberg (*Dreams of a Final Theory,* Pantheon Books, New York, 1992) has pointed out that experimental results are often repeatedly corrected until they agree with accepted theory and then, suddenly, regarded as correct. He quotes Arthur Eddington in the half tongue-in-cheek comment "One should never believe any experiment until it has been confirmed by theory." On the other hand, Weinberg also points out (page 93), that any widely applicable theory, just the kind we are seeking, is always plagued by experimental anomalies. "There is no theory that is not contradicted by experiment." While Newtonian theory otherwise explained the solar system in precise detail, it failed to explain Mercury's orbit and the orbits of Halley's and Encke's comets and the moon. While general relativity (Chapter 8) was required to fully explain Mercury's orbit, unrecog-nized influences caused discrepancies between theory and observation of the orbits of the comets and the moon. Near the sun the comets are heated and emit gas molecules from their heated side that influence their motions. And the moon, being rather large, experiences tidal forces sufficient to dissipate energy and influence its motion. Apparent experimental anomalies will always exist for broadly applicable theories. But the cause may be either failure of the theory or additional influences not considered in the theory. Establishing correctness of either theory or experiment is not simple.

[3] Penrose, Roger, *The Road to Reality,* Alfred A. Knopf, New York, 2004, 1028. Penrose's *what* and *why* questions in this section could also be properly posed as *how* questions.

[4] Buckman, William G., *College Physics, Principles and Applications,* D. Van Nostrand, New York, 1981, 2. We adopt as our scientific method Buckman's version as altered herein. Because they are not crucial we ignore many of the finer points of scientific methodology described, say, in *The Dictionary of Philosophy,* Dragobert D. Runes (editor), Citadel Press, New York, 2001, 346-348 under "methodology," wherein variations in method are indicated for different areas of science. We adopt the fundamental and essential method common to all hard physical science and mathematical physics. This choice seems appropriate because, as we shall argue, physics and mathematical physics are the foundation of all hard science but not the science found in disciplines sometimes referred to as soft or descriptive science.

[5] Popper, Karl R., *The Logic of Scientific Discovery,* Harper and Row, New York, 1959; *The Dictionary of Philosophy,* loc. cit.

[6] Indeed, some positivists (e.g., Mach, Comte) have described as absolute truths a body's color, a tone's frequency, or an object's length while others (e.g., Born, Langmuir) have insisted that absolute truth and fundamental reality are topics not properly addressed in science (or positivism). These two views are not necessarily opposed because, according to Heisenberg, they involve perceptions, the only things scientists have to work with. Any discrepancy between these views lies in whether or not perceptions are absolute, a topic considered in Book I.

[7] Our discussion is idealized here for brevity and simplicity. In the practice of science, perfect consistency is rarely, if ever, observed because real data and experience are rarely, if ever, perfect and complete. With imperfect data, judgement may be improved by use of "probability theory."

Such theory may also be useful in choosing between alternative theories nearly equally consistent with data. The probability theory we refer to is well described by E. T. Jaynes in his book *Probability Theory: The Logic of Science* (Cambridge University Press, Cambridge, 2003).

Although probability theory is useful, it cannot provide certainty in establishing either consistency or inconsistency between theory and data no matter how good a real-world theory or extensive the real-world data. There always exists uncertainty at some level in formulation of theory to explain data or in interpretation of data to test theory. (See endnote 2.) Jaynes (loc. cit.) comments on probability versus certainty in this process. (See endnote 8 of Chapter 11.) Allan Franklin has provided a substantial body of work relating to this topic with some of his titles being *The Rise and Fall of the Fifth Force: Discovery, Pursuit, and Justification in Modern Physics*; *Selectivity and Discord: Two Problems of Experiment; Are There Really Neutrinos?: An Evidential History*; *Can That Be Right?: Essays on Experiment, Evidence, and Science*; *Experiment, Right or Wrong*; *Principle of Inertia in the Middle Ages*, and *The Neglect of Experiment*. Also useful is William H. Newton-Smith's *The Rationality of Science,* Routledge & Kegan Paul, London, 1981.

[8] *The Dictionary of Philosophy*, loc. cit., under methodology, 346-347.

[9] Bacon, Francis, *Novum Organum,* Peter Urbach and John Gibson (translators and editors), Open Court, Chicago, 1994, 169.

[10] Ibid., 30.

[11] For a definition of Ockham's razor, see endnote 13 of Chapter 1.

[12] To illustrate we quote Dan Brown's (*Deception Point,* Pocket Books, New York, 2001, 348-349) dialogue between *Corky* and *Rachel*. *Corky:* The mineralogical proof here is not that the mineral content is conclusively meteoritelike, but rather that it is conclusively non-earth like. *Rachel*: Sorry, but in my business that's the kind of faulty logic that gets people killed. Saying a rock is non-earth-like doesn't prove it's a meteorite. It simple proves that it's not like anything we have ever seen on earth. *Corky:* What the ____'s the difference! *Rachel:* Nothing if you've seen every rock on earth.

[13] A conclusive disproof of a theory requires an *unavoidable* contradiction. But even an unavoidable contradiction or *no* answer regarding one theory does not prove a competing theory correct. To establish correctness of an assumption, principle, theory, or law a reliable *yes* answer is necessary. Such proof is unknown in science *per se* but we shall consider it, a reliable *yes* answer, in Book III.

[14] Popper, Karl R., loc. cit., 280. Popper's reference to scientific objectivity follows Hermann Weyl's thought, quoted in Chapter 4, distinguishing between subjective and absolute or objective and relative (merely consistent).

[15] Jaynes, E. T., loc. cit. See endnote 8 of Chapter 11 of the present book.

[16] We present a simple proof-by-definition that truth is consistent. Suppose existential elements (or elements having being in time and space) A, B, C, ... are known, where these elements are principles, concepts, objects, bodies, creatures, or any other real or postulated things. Suppose also that existential things are consistent in the sense that they have existed, do exist, or shall exist, as required of existential things. Then knowledge of elements A, B, C, ..., which are consistent, is truth because it is knowledge of things as they were, and are, and are to be, i.e., the axiom we accept as defining truth (endnote 2 of Chapter 1).

[17] For a brief but excellent treatment of such a goal, see Greene, Brian, *The Fabric of the Cosmos,* Alfred A. Knopf, New York, 2004.

[18] For insight into practical problems that arise in the ideal, seemingly-straightforward scientific method, see Weinberg, (loc. cit.). See also Collins, Harry, and Trevor Pinch (*The Golem*, Second Edition, Cambridge University Press, Cambridge, England, 1998), but see endnote 7 of Chapter 4.

[19] See Franklin, Allan, *Selectivity and Discord: Two Problems of Experiment,* University of Pittsburgh Press, Pittsburgh, PA, 2002.

6. Copernicus, Kepler, and Galileo - Scientific Revolution

Even just freshly emerging, as its early users were still making it up as they proceeded, natural philosophy or science provided a powerful tool for discovering organization, pattern, and connection among the facts. It provided results that conflicted with dogma sometimes repressively imposed by vested authority. Because the results of the new method were compelling, they contributed to the overthrow of the dogma and, to the same degree, the authority (Church) supporting it. This history is generally referred to as the "scientific revolution" and the "conflict between science and religion." We shall consider in this chapter the history of this conflict and compare science and dogma of the medieval Church. In this chapter and in Chapters 7-11 we further examine and celebrate success of the scientific method, illustrate its utility, and consider its limitations. From Book II the reader should gain some understanding of science, how it is used, and what it can and cannot do.

Aristotelian and Medieval-Church Philosophy

Science collided with the church that dominated medieval Europe, the Roman Catholic Church of that period which we refer to herein as the *medieval Church*. While the collision was evidently unintentional, it was nonetheless consequential, resulting in severe punishment of one of the first modern scientists, Galileo. But ultimately the scientific revolution, led primarily by Galileo and Kepler pursuing the theory of a deceased predecessor, Copernicus, together with a concurrent religious Reformation, caused the eventual overthrow of incorrect and repressive dogma. The Church held (functionally if not officially) that correct understanding of natural philosophy and all other matters was provided exclusively by sacred scripture and supplementary writing held to strictly agree therewith and sanctioned by priestly authority. This supplementary writing was thus regarded as additional dogma that supported, strengthened, and augmented the scriptural teachings. This supplementary dogma pertaining to natural philosophy was primarily the writings of the Greek philosopher Aristotle (384 - 322 BC), whose writings were wholly regarded by the Church as correct and authoritative.[1] Aristotle's system of philosophy was never as influential in ancient times as that of Plato, who was Aristotle's teacher. In fact, Aristotle's books were not preserved in Europe. When some of his works were retrieved from the Arabs and translated into Latin in the twelfth and thirteenth centuries, Aristotle replaced Plato as the most prominent philosopher of antiquity. Over the next four centuries Aristotle's views became accepted at nearly a divine level of authority.[1] Thereafter he became, unfairly, a symbol of wrong thinking and in the sixteenth- and seventeenth-century scientific revolution, the first casualty was Aristotelian physics.

It was held in the so-called Aristotelian tradition that the laws that govern the universe could be discovered by pure thought and that observation was not necessary. But Aristotle frequently invoked observed facts in his arguments. He argued the earth was spherical because as one moved north new stars appeared above the northern horizon while other stars disappeared below the southern horizon, a process which, he observed, would not occur on a flat earth. He further observed:

> The evidence of all the senses further corroborates this. How else would eclipses of the moon show segments as we see them? ... since it is the interposition of the earth that makes the eclipse, the form of this line will be caused by the form of the earth's surface, which is therefore spherical.[2]

Elsewhere Aristotle wrote that

> Lack of experience diminishes our power of taking a comprehensive view of the admitted facts. Hence, those who dwell in intimate association with nature and its phenomena grow more and more able to formulate, as the foundation of their theories, principles such as to admit of a wide and coherent development; while those whom devotion to abstract discussions has rendered unobservant of the facts are too ready to dogmatize on the basis of a few observations.[3]

The purported aversion of Aristotle to experience is not apparent in these writings, although it may have been present to some degree in his thinking. After all, neither procedures nor apparatus were then available for making careful, quantitative measurements and an awareness of such a possibility in the common mind did not emerge for over two millennia, and then only following an intense battle between schools of philosophy. Judging particularly from the last quotation, the complete disdain for experiment and the resulting inveterate orthodoxy adopted in "Aristotelian" philosophy seems to have emerged as a tradition in Aristotle's "followers" contrary to the teaching and practice of Aristotle himself.

When the ancient laws of natural philosophy came under consideration of competent philosophers using scientific inquiry in place of the principle of authority, the ancient laws or views were challenged. And because the Church had adopted many of Aristotle's views, a challenge of these views was also a challenge of the authority of the Church. To protect its position, the Church reacted strongly. Although it won the early battle, the outcome of the war was decided once natural philosophy embraced scientific methodology for discovering the nature of nature. The Church's tradition of authority and the ancient views on science it had adopted were no match for the new method of investigation in the hands of geniuses like Galileo Galilei and Johannes Kepler. Galileo wrote of Aristotelian philosophers in his 1590 work entitled *De motu*: "Few there are who seek to discover whether what Aristotle says is true; it is enough for them that the more texts of Aristotle they have to quote, the more learned they will be thought."[4] Galileo amplified this opinion in a letter to Kepler dated 19 August 1610, further describing Aristotelian philosophers as people who "think that philosophy is a sort of book like *The Aeneid* or *The Odyssey*, and that the truth is to be sought not in the universe, not in nature, but by comparing texts!"[5]

However, ultimate victory was far from apparent in the sixteenth century and the early battles were costly. Galileo, a faithful Catholic but the principal antagonist of the Church in the early battle, did not appear to fully recognize that an attack on Aristotelian philosophy was an attack on the medieval Church which had embraced this philosophy and was an institution that held great power. Thus, this battle, the "conflict between science and religion" or the "scientific revolution," proved costly to Galileo.

The terms "scientific revolution" and "conflict between science and religion" are regarded by some today as describing an essential incompatibility of scientific and religious paradigms. They are indeed incompatible but not for the reasons commonly believed. In this chapter we consider the history of the scientific revolution and in later chapters we consider the conflict between science and religion it reveals.

Aristotle believed, for metaphysical reasons, that the earth was the stationary center of the universe and that the sun, moon, planets, and stars moved about the earth in circular orbits. The Greek-Alexandrian astronomer Claudius Ptolemy (70-147 AD) elaborated and expanded this idea to form a (quite different) model of the universe in which, as in the Aristotelian model, the earth was the stationary center surrounded by eight concentric spherical layers that contained the circular orbits of the moon, sun, the five planets then known (Mercury, Venus, Mars, Jupiter, and Saturn), and the "fixed stars." The *geocentric* (earth-centered or "world system," as opposed to the *heliocentric* or sun-centered or solar system) theory of the sixteenth and seventeenth centuries contained a mixture of the ideas of Aristotle and Ptolemy. This world-system model had been adopted by the Church (implicitly and functionally if not officially[6]) as the scripturally correct picture of the universe. While heaven and hell were not specified in the model, there was room for them outside the outer sphere which contained the fixed stars.

Galileo was the first prominent, modern-era scientist to use scientific inquiry as we recognize it today and he applied this method in the study of forces and motions. Because of entrenched Aristotelian tradition and the ridicule and intrigue that generally accompanied any deviation therefrom, no one of prominence had bothered to *test and publicize* whether bodies of different weight fell at different speeds, as Aristotle had maintained. (However, again, the tradition may have done Aristotle an injustice even beyond attributing to him a disdain for experiment since Aristotle in his statements on falling bodies may have been referring to "terminal" velocity in water or air in which case the velocity of fall would indeed depend on size and weight.)

To challenge the powerful authority of the Aristotelians (and the Church) was to invite attack which sought to crush any opposition, especially that invoking new and original thinking. To avoid being so crushed by the system's great weight, to flourish in the face of ridicule, to reverse error and intrigue and turn powerful opposition into personal advantage would require a genius supplying a flood of novel ideas and compelling demonstrations as well as a forceful, dedicated, enduring character. Such a scientist or philosopher would have to possess not only singular strength of intellect and remarkable insight but also deep reserves of fortitude and unusual self-confidence, even to the point of vanity. He or she would also have to be very risk tolerant and even cavalier regarding convention and tradition in a day when those things were regarded as much more important than they are now. We have just described Galileo Galilei.

Galileo challenged the claim of the Aristotelian philosophers of his day that bodies of different weight fall at different speeds. He alienated himself from the philosophers at the University of Pisa by his audacious attack of their tradition-justified authority, adding insult to injury in a dramatic public setting he created. As legend maintains, before a crowd of onlookers two balls were simultaneously released from near the top of the leaning tower, one weighing one pound and the other one-hundred pounds. The heavier ball reached the ground slightly ahead of the other (as Dava Sobel observes, "to the great relief of the Pisan philosophy department"[7]), it being less susceptible to the slight effect of air resistance, as was recognized by Galileo. Galileo's adversaries claimed vindication when the heavier ball reached the ground first, as predicted by Aristotle. The event was recounted in its aftermath in a posthumous autobiographical sketch of Galileo provided by his student Vincenzio Viviani as follows:

> Aristotle says that a hundred-pound ball falling from a height of a hundred *braccia* [arm lengths] hits the ground before a one-pound ball has fallen one *braccio*. I say they arrive at the same time. You find on making the test, that the larger ball beats the smaller one by two inches. Now, behind those two inches you want to hide Aristotle's ninety-nine *braccia* and, speaking only of my tiny error, remain silent about his enormous mistake.[8]

The combination of (Aristotle, Ptolemy, and Church) authorities were united in sixteenth and seventeenth century dogma held to be in accord with scripture. But this view was not to last long once a superior one was proposed by Copernicus.

Copernicus: Dawn of a New Age

Nicholas Copernicus (1473-1543) was born at Thorn, Poland on 19 February 1473. By age ten he was orphaned and adopted by an uncle, Lucas Waczenrode, who was then a Catholic Priest but became bishop of Ermland in 1489. Under the sponsorship of his uncle, Copernicus studied humanities at the University of Cracow from 1491 to 1495. Failing to obtain a post for Copernicus as Canon of the Frauenberg Cathedral, his uncle sponsored Copernicus in further study in Church Law at the University of Bologna in 1496 to enhance his employability. At Bologna, Copernicus also studied mathematics and astronomy, the latter being an interest sparked by a previous meeting with the noted astronomer Albert Brudzewski in Cracow. His instructor in Bologna, Domenico di Novara, was a Platonist and therefore taught Copernicus that the systems due to Aristotle and Ptolemy were sufficiently complex that they violated *mathematical harmony*, a principle taught by Plato. Under mathematical harmony a simpler and thus superior system that "saved the appearances" (agreed with the observations) should always be sought, a principle generally referred to today as Ockham's razor.[9] Copernicus searched the history of thought for a mathematical basis for such a superior system in astronomy and, because he found none, Copernicus began a quest through which he would greatly impact philosophy.

In 1497 Copernicus's appointment as Canon of the Frauenberg Cathedral was obtained for him by his uncle. However, he began his appointment in 1501 by taking a leave of absence to return to Italy to study law and medicine at the University of Padua. In 1506 he returned to Ermland but spent the next six years as personal physician attending his aged and infirm uncle and studying astronomy and experimenting with diagrams of the stars (star maps). Following his uncle's death in 1512, Copernicus finally assumed his duties as Canon of the Frauenberg Cathedral. There he recited canons each day and administered temporal matters for the diocese in return for a salary which supported him in a comfortable living. Contrary to common belief, Copernicus was never a priest.

In addition to his work as a canon, Copernicus established an observatory at Frauenberg and pursued his interest in astronomy. In 1530 Copernicus provided friends with a *Commentariolus* or outline of his astronomy, worked out many years earlier. This new Copernican theory was heliocentric rather than geocentric, a solar system rather than a world system. It soon attracted wide attention, drawing favorable impressions from many including the pope. Copernicus was encouraged by Nicholas Cardinal Schoenberg to quickly publish complete details. But he was reluctant to publish, not for fear of persecution by the Church, as is commonly held, but of ridicule. He wrote, "... the scorn which I had to fear on account of the newness and absurdity of my opinion almost drove me to abandon a work already undertaken."[10] His fears were not without basis. In 1533, Martin Luther spoke of him in the following tone.

> People give ear to an upstart astrologer who strove to show that the earth revolves, and not the heavens or the firmament, the sun and the moon. Whosoever wishes to appear clever must devise some new system which of all systems, of course, is the very best. This fool wishes to reverse the entire science of astronomy; but Sacred Scripture tells us that Josue [Joshua 10:12-14] commanded the sun to stand still, and not the earth.[11]

It seems that novelty and originality are costly in every age and deviating from the norm can be expensive even when one is right. Copernicus's work *De revolutionibus orbium coelestium* was finally published in 1543, an advance copy being delivered to the author on his deathbed on 24 May 1543 just hours before he died. And even then a last intrigue was accomplished by a smaller mind that sought to sabotage his work. The man who oversaw publication of the book was a Lutheran theologian and, aware of Luther's opposition to Copernicus' theory, wrote an unsigned preface that appeared to have been written by Copernicus disclaiming belief in the system as physical and presenting it only as a hypothetical model useful for astronomical calculations. Such was not the intent of Copernicus.

In his book Copernicus proposed a solar system much simpler than the orthodox world system. In his solar system the sun was at a stationary center and the earth and planets moved in circular orbits about it. (The Greek philosopher Aristarchus (310-230 BC) had proposed a system identical to that of Copernicus, according to a description given by Archimedes (287-212 BC) in his book *The Sand-Reckoner*. But Aristarchus and his theory could not overcome the prestige and authority of Aristotle and the theory was lost.) However, because the actual planetary orbits are elliptical rather than circular, a fact later discovered by Kepler, Copernicus had to invoke eccentrics and epicycles superimposed on circular orbits to explain observed motions. Thus, much of the simplicity introduced by the new model was lost. Nevertheless, it was a great step forward.

About fifty years after Copernicus published his theory, two astronomers, Johannes Kepler (1571-1630) in Austria and Galileo Galilei (1564-1642) in Italy, began to promote the Copernican theory. The accomplishments of these two men were to provide the bridge between metaphysics and mysticism of the old system dating from the Greeks to the new science they established.

Kepler

Johannes Kepler was born on 27 December 1571 in Weil der Stadt, Württemberg, near the Black Forest in southwestern Germany. His early life was full of difficulty beginning at age three or four when he had to battle smallpox which left him with crippled hands and weakened eyes. And Kepler's difficulty did not end there. His family was contentious and disputatious. At age 26, Kepler composed astrological portraits of members of his family that described Grandma Kepler as "restless, clever, and lying, of a fiery nature, an inveterate troublemaker, violent ... And all her children have something of this."[12] Kepler described his mother, Katherine, as "small, thin, swarthy, gossiping, and quarrelsome, of a bad disposition."[10] His mother nearly suffered the same fate as her aunt who raised her: being burned at the stake for witchcraft. Arrested in 1620, she was only saved by Kepler's lengthy intervention and his noble patronage.

Kepler's childhood was a sequence of sickness, contention, beatings, and misfortunes. Because of poor health, skin ailments, wounds, and badly crippled hands it was believed he would only be fit to become a minister. The Protestant Church then needed learned clergy and were willing to educate young prospects. At age thirteen Kepler entered a theological seminary and studied Greek classics, mathematics, and music. However, Kepler carried emotional scars from his early home life that left him an emotional cripple throughout his life. At the seminary he fought with boys and teachers alike and was frequently beaten. Nevertheless, at age seventeen he moved on to the well-regarded Lutheran University at Tübingen where, though he continued to experience difficulties due to his emotional problems, he graduated with a Bachelor of Arts (BA) degree in 1588 at age twenty and joined the theological faculty. Despite his contention with other students he was regarded favorably by at least some of his teachers because of his brilliance in mathematics. In 1591 he received a master of arts degree (MA).

An event in 1594 diverted him from his intended vocation in the clergy. In that year his teachers recommended him as a substitute in an astronomy and mathematics position at the Lutheran University of Graz, in the capital of the Austrian province of Styria. One of his duties was to compose an annual calendar or almanac based on astrological forecasts. His first calendar was a success, correctly predicting both a cold spell and a Turkish invasion. At some point his substitute status evidently became permanent because his work continued and was regarded as satisfactory.

Kepler believed astrology or casting of horoscopes should not be an artificial pretense pursued solely in the interest of money. He attempted to expand astrology to a science, to find physical causes and effects that would make astrology more reliable and fundamental. As naïve as this may now sound, it was a valuable new concept that would eventually lead to incorporation of physics into astronomy and cosmology. Kepler lived in and influenced an age of transition. In his day there was no science to serve as an adequate model for astrology or anything else and Aristotelian dogma and authority ruled over observation and deduction. It was the eventual overthrow of such tradition to which Kepler's and Galileo's work would lead. (An unending task as it seems that nearly every generation must contribute to this same process of overthrowing, perhaps only on a personal level, some incorrect, authority-based tradition or other element of culture.)

Because of the mysticism and metaphysics that dominated science in his age, Kepler believed he had made an important, fundamental discovery while lecturing on astrological conjunctions of Jupiter and Saturn on 9 July 1595. A "blinding insight"[13] came to him then that geometry was the key to understanding the universe and the thinking of God. It was known from the Greeks that there existed five perfect solid (three-dimensional) shapes, the "Platonic solids." These were the *tetrahedron* (having four identical equilateral triangles as faces), the *cube* (having six identical squares as faces), the *octahedron* (having eight identical equilateral triangles as faces), the *dodecahedron* (having twelve identical pentagons as faces), and the *icosahedron* (having twenty identical equilateral triangles as faces). Kepler speculated these five perfect or Platonic solids corresponded to the number of known planets not only in their number but also in their other properties. He constructed a sequence of drawings of these shapes on a common center with a sphere inscribed inside each perfect-solid shape and a sphere also circumscribed about each one, with each inscribed sphere being the circumscribed sphere about the next-smaller shape. He then took the ratio of sphere diameters as the ratio of planetary-orbit diameters. The result fit the Copernican model within about five percent, a remarkable agreement that encouraged him to continue developing this concept as an "explanation" of the solar system cosmology. This agreement was purely fortuitous and his "blinding insight" did not explain anything and held Kepler back in his subsequent efforts to understand and describe the solar system.[14]

While Kepler's perfect-solids-solar-system concept fell within the mystical Pythagorean tradition, Kepler subsequently brought to science two distinctive considerations: (1) theories must agree with observed facts and not *vice versa*, and (2) such theories must be physical rather than mystical or metaphysical, i.e., they (we) must seek to reveal a physical cause-and-effect relationship behind observed results. These concepts are buried in the mysticism and metaphysics that Kepler included in his writing but his writing did contain the first quantitative mathematical laws that describe planetary motions. In 1596 Kepler elaborated his early ideas in his first book: *Mysterium cosmographicum* (The Cosmic Mystery). In it Kepler combined classic Greek philosophy, number mysticism, Christian theology, and elementary physics. It is a confusing mixture of his superstition, mysticism, and physical intuition.

On 28 September 1598, Catholic counter-reformation authorities ordered all Lutheran teachers to leave Graz. Kepler was suddenly required to find a new position. In 1599 Tycho Brahe (1546-1601), the foremost observational astronomer of the age, relocated and established an observatory in Benatek Castle near Prague as imperial mathematicus to and under patronage of the Holy Roman Emperor Rudolph II. Brahe needed an assistant and was aware of Kepler from his book. In December 1599 Brahe wrote Kepler inviting him to come to Benatek as his assistant, a timely opportunity for both. Kepler accepted Brahe's offer and the two spent the next eighteen months, until Brahe's death, arguing in a clash of arrogance and ego.

Brahe asked Kepler to determine the orbit of Mars from his measured data. This was no simple problem. As Brahe knew, rationalizing the highly eccentric orbit of Mars would be difficult. But Kepler, with inveterate arrogance, declared he would complete this task within eight days. After eight years he was still working on it.

In the meantime, within two days of Brahe's death, Kepler was appointed his successor but at only a small fraction of his predecessor's salary. Nevertheless, Kepler was pleased. In addition to his new position, Kepler inherited all of Brahe's careful and extensive measurements. Kepler continued his analysis of the orbit of Mars and design of instrumental optics, another area of astronomy he pioneered. Kepler was seeking not only a simple description of the shape of the orbit of Mars but also a theory that incorporated some force that caused the orbit's shape. He considered magnetism as an origin of this force but never found a suitable expression for it. Nevertheless, after fifty-one chapters including hundreds of pages of calculations he did solve the Mars-orbit-shape problem determining the orbit to be an ellipse with the sun at one of its two focuses. Kepler had earlier considered an elliptical shape but rejected it as incompatible with a magnetic force. Considering just the orbit shape without any force restriction, he now found the orbit of Mars around the sun to be quite accurately represented by an ellipse. Kepler thus proposed his *first law of planetary motion*: "The planets travel in elliptical orbits with the sun located at one focus of the ellipse."

While Kepler was unable to describe planetary orbits in terms of a force, a task Newton was to later fulfil motivated by Kepler's first law (Chapter 7), his considerations and his deadly intuition led him to his *second law of planetary motion*: "The imaginary line connecting the sun to a planet sweeps (covers) equal areas in equal times." This law accurately describes the fact that a planet's orbital motion near the sun is greater than its orbital motion far from the sun.

Kepler's two laws of planetary motion were presented amidst an already-mentioned sea of calculations in his book *Astronomia nova* (The New Astronomy) published in 1609.

In 1618 Kepler published a third book *Harmonice mundi* (Harmonies of the World) in which he addressed harmony in mathematics, music, astrology, and astronomy. In it he presented his *third law of planetary motion*: "The square of a planet's orbital period is proportional to the cubic power of its mean distance from the sun." Kepler's three laws of planetary motion were the original basis of the mathematical physics of the solar system. It was these laws, in particular the elliptical orbits of planets, that caused Newton to write his wonderful book *Principia* (Chapter 7) that compellingly and beautifully established mathematical physics and applied mathematics. Kepler more than anyone else motivated Newton's book. Thus Kepler's contributions influenced the very mainstream of science.

Kepler finished his longest work, entitled *Epitome of Copernicum Astronomy*, in 1621. For the next century it was the most important book in astronomy. In 1627 he published the *Rudolphine Tables*, named in honor of his former patron and dedicated to Tycho Brahe, which contained all Brahe's measured data for 777 stars and additional data measured by Kepler thus including measured data for a grand total of 1,005 stars. It also included tables and rules for predicting planet locations. In these data Kepler used the recently invented logarithms of John Napier, their first important application.

Johannes Kepler's grave was destroyed and his remains scattered during the thirty-years war. But his contributions remain together with the epitaph from his own pen on his gravestone:

> I measured the skies, now the shadows I measure.
> Skybound was the mind, earthbound the body rests.[14]

Galileo

Galileo Galilei was born 15 February 1564 in Pisa, Italy. Galileo was directed by his father, a mathematician, to the study of medicine and was deliberately diverted from mathematics and science. (A physician then earned thirty times what a mathematician earned.) Galileo would have made a good physician, or artist, or musician, as he was quite gifted. His father, Vincenzio Galilei, was a musician and, in particular, a musical theorist in a time when this discipline was regarded as a branch of mathematics. His father taught Galileo to sing and play the organ and other instruments and introduced him to the Pythagorean rule of musical ratios. Vincenzio made his own studies on the physics of sound and enlisted his son as an assistant in his experiments. In a resulting book, Vincenzio defended tuning an instrument in pursuit of sweetness of sound rather than strict mathematical rule and came under condemnation of a former teacher who he criticized and who prevented publication of his book, *Dialogue of Ancient and Modern Music*, in Pisa. It was only later published in Florence in 1581. In it Vincenzio states:

> It appears to me, that they who in proof of any assertion rely simply on the weight of authority, without adducing any argument in support of it, act very absurdly. I, on the contrary, wish to be allowed freely to question and freely to answer you without any sort of adulation, as well becomes those who are in search of truth.[15]

Galileo is regarded as the first modern scientist, one who utilizes experiment as well as theory, with the latter justified by the former, and accepts the truth thus revealed in spite of existing tradition and authority. But it seems Galileo learned this approach from his father.

While still a teenager in 1581, the year he began his medical studies in Pisa, he noticed a swinging chandelier in the cathedral during a service. In what was to become his characteristic quantitative style, he noted by counting his pulsebeats that the period of each swing remained fixed even though the air currents caused widely varying amplitudes in varying directions. At home after the service he set up an experiment where he used two pendulums of equal length and simultaneously swung them at different amplitudes. His observation in the cathedral was verified; the periods of the pendulum swings were the same, independent of the amplitude of the arc. Although this discovery eventually served as the basis for the pendulum clock, Galileo apparently did not recognize this possibility. Such a device based on Galileo's discovery was first demonstrated by Christiaan Huygens (1629-1695) in Holland in 1656. Instead, Galileo measured time intervals using either his pulse or the amount of water flowing through an orifice and accumulated in a small container, methods which limited the experiments he could perform and required the use of balls rolling down inclined planes, as in the experiments described below, rather than falling freely. This "chandelier incident" while significant in its eventual value is useful here in its indication of insight, style, and suggestion of things to come.

Vincenzio's plan to make a medical doctor of his son failed when the young Galilei, through accident, happened to attend a lecture on Euclidian geometry and upon further exploration of the subject discovered Archimedes and his works. He promptly convinced his reluctant father that he should study mathematics and science, a result that was fortunate for the world, for Galileo's career had a major impact.

Galileo was not satisfied by mere experimental observation, although that already was a novel approach in his day. Beyond that he sought to explain and understand his results by use of theories that correctly predicted his observations. Thus he continually attempted to conceive and perform critical experiments that would allow him to better define and test his theories. He utilized the practice of quantitative measurement and formulation of a mathematical relationship or theory that succinctly and generally described a process, a practice he adopted from Archimedes who had preceded him by some eighteen centuries and whose technique and ability he admired enormously.

Galileo's Telescope

In 1609, Galileo learned that a "magnifying tube" making use of two spectacle lenses had been invented in Holland the previous year by the optician Hans Lippershey, as a result of a chance observation of an apprentice. Galileo immediately grasped the principles involved and made an improved "looking tube." By 1610 he had constructed a refracting telescope with magnification of thirty-two diameters, utilizing a double convex objective lens and a double concave eyepiece.[16] In contrast to the earlier magnifying-tube design, in which the image was inverted, the image was erect in Galileo's telescope. Galileo eventually became the best lensmaker in Europe and sent telescopes to others, including Kepler, to test his discoveries.

Galileo turned his telescope to the heavens and observed mountains and valleys on the moon and spots on the sun. According to Aristotelian philosophy, the heavens were perfect and irregularity and disorder were only to be found on the earth. Galileo showed Aristotle and his "followers" to be wrong. To "save the appearances" a leading Aristotelian, Lodovico delle Colombe, would not accept the moon being an imperfect sphere and suggested mountains and craters that Galileo had observed were actually covered with some smooth, transparent material which gave a perfectly smooth and spherical outer surface to the moon.[17] It is claimed a foremost Aristotelian at Pisa, Giulio Libri, refused to even look through Galileo's telescope.[18]

Other astronomers observed sunspots at about the same time as Galileo and there was heated debate over priority. Galileo evidently approached this debate in his typical style and made additional enemies. Whether he was the original discoverer or not, Galileo did more than merely observe the existence of these sunspots. Galileo followed individual spots around the sun and discovered that the sun rotated about its axis every 27 days. By the same observations he also determined the orientation of the sun's axis was inclined at a non-normal angle to the plane of the earth's orbit, the changing of which with the seasons he used (incorrectly) as support for the Copernican model. These observations of the sun combined with eye infections he had suffered as a youth caused him to go blind in old age.

Galileo noted that while planets grew from tiny spots of light without use of his telescope to little spheres when using it, the stars remained mere tiny spots. Like Ptolemy[19] before him who had reached the same conclusion, Galileo deduced that the stars must be much farther away than the planets and that the universe may be indefinitely large. Galileo observed that many stars were visible using his telescope that were invisible to the naked eye and that the Milky Way itself owed its luminosity to the fact it was composed of a high concentration of stars.

Upon finding Jupiter was attended by four subsidiary bodies or moons that circled it regularly, visible only by telescope, Galileo was able within a few weeks of observation to determine the period of each. Kepler gave these moons the name of satellites and they are known today collectively as the Galilean satellites. Individually they carry the mythological names of Io, Europa, Ganymede, and Callisto. Jupiter and its satellites – small bodies circling a large one – represented a Copernican system and proved that not all astronomical bodies circled the earth, again in contradiction to Aristotelian philosophy.

Galileo's observations of Venus revealed further discrepancies with the Aristotelian-Ptolemaic-medieval-Church dogma. He observed that Venus showed entirely moon-like phases, from full to crescent, which it must according to the Copernican model. Alternatively, Venus should appear as a perpetual crescent according to the Ptolemaic model.

Galileo's observations of the phases of Venus revealed that planets shine by reflected sunlight. He then observed and correctly explained the dim glow of the night side of the moon as being due to earthshine. Earthshine showed the earth to be like the other planets, which gleamed in the sun, and removed one more difference between the earth and the heavenly bodies.

The sum of all these telescopic discoveries fully established to Galileo and many others the superiority of the Copernican theory over the Aristotelian-Ptolemaic-medieval-Church dogma. In March of 1610, two-thirds of a century after Copernicus' book was published, Galileo finally announced to the public his discoveries and made his claim regarding the Copernican theory in a booklet he called *Siderius nuncius* or Starry Messenger. Marcelo Gleiser points out in his excellent book[20] that Galileo apparently intended that the star in the Starry Messenger was himself, envisioning himself as saving philosophy and theology from error-constricted tradition. But, not surprisingly, because these results were new and challenged traditional thinking they aroused profound anger as well as great enthusiasm.

When Galileo visited Rome the following year he was greeted with mixed reactions – honor and acclaim for his accomplishments and dismay at the problems he had caused with the revelation of imperfect heavens and the invalidation of the Aristotelian view, with the implication that earth no longer occupied the stationary center of the universe. Most unsettling to many, the dogma and therefore the authority of the Church had been challenged. The delicacy of the situation was not appreciated by Galileo and opposition was exacerbated when Galileo unwisely proceeded to write a book describing his views on theological topics and the Bible, an act which many theologians regarded as presumptuous and offensive. Moreover, Galileo overreached his position, insisting that his discoveries had positively established the validity of Copernicanism, which they had not. Consistency is not proof. Merely proving the Aristotelian view to be false (inconsistency is disproof) did not prove the Copernican view to be true. And other views were possible, a fact known particularly to the astronomer-scholar priests who had verified Galileo's observations and eagerly awaited further evidence of Galileo's claims – but Galileo had provided little evidence to dismiss possible alternative views or to positively establish the Copernican one.

Nevertheless, Galileo continued to force the issue to the point where an official response was needed, exactly what Galileo desired. But the response was not. Pope Pius V was persuaded by his advisors, undoubtedly considering opinions of astronomers priests quite aware of deficiencies in Galileo's argument that Copernicanism had been positively established by his results, to declare Copernicanism a heresy and Galileo was forced into silence in 1616. Did not the scriptures speak of the sun and the moon standing still in response to the prayer of Joshua to the Lord? Clearly, among the opponents of Copernicanism and Galileo, it was the sun and moon that move and not the earth.[21]

Dialogue on Two World Systems

Pope Pius V was succeeded by Pope Gregory XV and then, two years later on 6 August 1623, Maffeo Cardinal Barberini was elected to succeed Gregory and chose the name Urban VIII. Urban had been a friend of Galileo and this gave the latter hope that perhaps he would be able again to write about his astronomical discoveries. Other developments added to his optimism. The new pope selected as his chief lieutenant a twenty-six-year-old nephew, Francesco Barberini, a recently ordained cardinal and a recent recipient of a doctoral degree from Pisa, where he studied under Benedetto Castelli and, through him, under Galileo as well. Urban chose as his Master of Pontifical Ceremonies Monsignor Virginio Cesarini, a poet who had some years earlier heard an inspirational lecture on mathematics by Galileo and taken up that topic himself. Assured of a friendly reception by his supporters, Galileo determined to visit the new pope in Rome.

In April of 1624 Galileo set out for Rome. Galileo had been encouraged to approach Urban about writing a book on astronomy because Urban was sympathetic, being himself a scholar who saw the Copernican system as a useful tool for astronomical calculations and predictions even though he did not believe it. The justification Galileo presented in seeking permission to resume his writing on astronomy was to show Protestants to the north (notably Kepler) that Catholics in general understood much more about astronomy than an essay by Ingoli (an adversary of Galileo and an apologist for the traditional Aristotelian-Ptolemaic-Church dogma) would lead them to believe. Galileo wrote

> I am thinking about treating this topic very extensively, in opposition to heretics the most influential of whom I hear accept Copernicus's opinion; I would want to show them that we Catholics continue to be certain of the old truth taught us by the sacred authors, not for lack of scientific understanding, or for not having studied as many arguments, experiments, observations, and demonstrations as they have, but rather because of the reverence we have toward the writings of our Fathers and because of our zeal in religion and faith.[22]

Galileo thus proposed examining the Copernican model as a philosophical system, recognizing the need to reject it on theological grounds. Urban was sympathetic to this view and Galileo left Rome authorized and encouraged to write his book.

With a knowledge of this background, we see the flexibility and ingenuity of the literary device Galileo employed in his book *Dialogue of Galileo Galilei, ..., Where, in the meetings of four days, there is discussion concerning the two Chief Systems of the World, Ptolemaic and Copernican, Propounding inconclusively the philosophical and physical reasons as much for one side as for the other.* In the dialogue style, Galileo could present powerful evidence and arguments for both sides without explicitly committing himself to one or the other. We also see the reason for the choice of this title, for whether Galileo personally believed the Copernican system to be superior to the Ptolemaic or not, he was required by the understanding he had proposed not to support this system and, indeed, to support the traditional one. However, Galileo failed to live up to this understanding, whether due to duplicity or enthusiasm for science no one can now say.

Excerpts from Galileo's "Dialogue on Two World Systems," the first of his two dialogue books,[23] illustrate Galileo's wonderful writing style and the power of his challenge to the vested system. In both books Galileo employs a literary device consisting of a dialogue between three characters. The first is Salviati, an expert assistant to (and spokesman for) the eminent professor (Galileo). Sagredo, the second, is an intelligent and progressive lay person who takes the role of a witty, impartial, good-natured moderator. And Simplicio, the third participant, is of a traditional Aristotelian persuasion (the adversary) and is both pompous and encumbered by the (supposed) great weight of the authority he has studied. It is clear in his rigid, text-citing responses that he is not so imaginative and quick-witted as the others. (His name is suggestively close to *sempliciotto*, meaning *simpleton*.)

I quote two excerpts, both spoken by Salviati. The first indicates why the Aristotelians were so offended by Galileo and why his first book was so controversial. In this excerpt Salviati is about to describe evidence of why the earth should be regarded as moving. But he begins with an attack on the Aristotelians to introduce doubt in their then-accepted, contrary tradition.

> I have many times wondered how these pedantic maintainers of whatever came from Aristotle's pen are not aware how great a prejudice they are to his reputation and credit and how, the more they go about to increase his authority, the more they diminish it. When I see them obstinate in their attempts to maintain those propositions which are manifestly false, and trying to persuade me that to do so is the part of a philosopher, and that Aristotle himself would do the same, it much discourages me in the belief that he has rightly philosophized about other conclusions, for if I could see them concede and change opinion in a manifest truth, I would be more willing to believe that, where they persist, they may have some solid demonstrations, by me not understood or even heard of.[24]

The second excerpt indicates Galileo's insight and simultaneous lack of insight in that one of his main arguments for a moving earth is powerful but not conclusive.

> If we consider only the immense magnitude of the starry sphere compared to the smallness of the terrestrial globe, and weigh the velocity of the motions which must, in a day and night make an entire revolution, I cannot persuade myself that there is any man who believes it more reasonable and credible that it is the celestial sphere that moves around, while the terrestrial globe stands still.[25]

In other words, there is no need to have the entire universe race around the earth in part at superluminal velocity if a simple rotation of the earth accomplishes the same result. But few were then so sophisticated as to understand Plato's principle of mathematical harmony (or Ockham's razor), ancient though it is, and mathematical harmony or Ockham's razor is neither required nor are its consequences conclusive. A demonstration that Galileo's intuition was correct is now possible by the theory of relativity (Chapter 8) by which superluminal velocity of stars required by a stationary earth is believed to be prohibited; but such results were not known in Galileo's day. Galileo's self-confidence and doggedness in the absence of positive proof caused him to make the same kind of mistake for which he condemned the Aristotelians and one for which he would pay a heavy price.

Thus, *Dialogue on Two World Systems* came to be with its 500 pages, its grand, eloquent language, and its three characters: Salviati, the Copernican (Galileo, the professor and also the Lyncean Academician, which he was, whose ideas and discoveries were invoked), Simplicio, the Aristotelian, and Sagredo, the witty, good-natured moderator. Simplicio does not appear to have a specific alter identity, but represents well the philosophers with which Galileo often contended in his long, tradition-bound quotations and discourses before being made to look the fool. The evidence and arguments for and against each system are presented in *Dialogue* with apparent impartiality and without reaching any formal conclusion. However, the overall impact of the book was a strong argument for Copernicanism, even after the book was carefully reviewed and approved with required changes by censors in Rome and Pisa.

Urban had requested of Galileo that one of his own sentiments regarding a philosophical difficulty in science be somehow included in the book, the idea that God and nature present unlimited means for causing observed effects. (This concept, which Galileo himself had penned in his earlier work *The Assayer* to the delight of

Pope Urban, is, in fact, profound and consequential in its implications regarding the scientific method, as has been indicated in Chapter 5 and will be further discussed.) Galileo, of course, complied with the request of his friend and mentor. Unfortunately, he placed the words in the mouth of Simplicio so that their impact was opposite to that intended in the request.

The book appeared in Pisa in February of 1632 and it arrived in Rome later that same year. Unusual for a scholarly work, it was published in Italian, rather than Latin, so that it could be read by all the literate population. In Rome, advisers of the pope judged the book to be insulting to him and concluded that he had been betrayed by Galileo by having Simplicio speak his philosophy. It was even claimed by some advisors that Simplicio was intended to represent the pope. The situation was undoubtedly charged with emotions of anger and a feeling of betrayal.

Galileo before the Inquisition

It appears now, far removed from the intensity of the moment but in possession of only some of the facts, that a betrayal did occur, but probably not an intentional one. Galileo was a scientist and mathematician and was clearly not political. The subtle nuances of the situation were apparently invisible to Galileo.

Galileo was vain and ambitious and politically naïve. He had a brilliant mind and a caustic wit and did not resist the temptation to make those who argued against him appear foolish. An observer in early 1616, when Galileo openly spoke about his beliefs, described Galileo's ability in the following terms.

> ... he talks frequently with fifteen or twenty guests who argue with him ... But he is so well fortified that he laughs them off; and although people are left unpersuaded because of the novelty of his opinion, still he shows up as worthless the majority of the arguments with which his opponents try to defeat him. Monday ... he was especially effective. What I enjoyed most was that before he would answer the arguments of his opponents, he would amplify them and strengthen them with new grounds which made them appear invincible, so that, when he proceeded to demolish them, he made his opponents look all the more ridiculous.[26]

As a university student Galileo had received the nickname "the wrangler" because it described his contentious style and rebellion against conformity. He often paid fines because he refused to wear conventional academic dress, not as a student but as a member of the faculty! In what may have infuriated adversaries most of all, students flocked to hear his lectures. As one might surmise from the preceding quote, he probably put on quite a show. One contemporary estimated his lecture audiences as large as (a possibly exaggerated) two thousand[1] while colleagues spoke to mostly-empty halls. But performing a successful show for students or others, including non-conventional dress, is a different world from political astuteness and the former behavior suggests the latter is neither yet imagined or appreciated.

Except when he moved from the University of Pisa to a better position at the University at Padua, in Venetian territory where considerably more intellectual freedom was enjoyed, to escape problems and to triple his salary, Galileo rarely showed any awareness of need for politically appropriate discretion. At Padua, Galileo corresponded with Kepler and discreetly admitted as early as 1597 that he had come to believe the Copernican model. His discretion was certainly encouraged by the execution of Italian philosopher-priest Giordano Bruno (1548-1600) who was burned alive at the stake after a seven-year trial by the Inquisition in Venice for his scorn of traditional religious and philosophical dogma in his assertion, begun in 1584, that stars are like our sun. (Bruno might have gotten off by recanting, but he refused. He accused his judges of being more afraid of him than he was of them. It was said that no one since the days of Socrates had worked quite so hard to secure his own execution.) With this local, contemporary example of the danger of speaking too freely against tradition, Galileo refrained for many years from expressing his opinions.

Otherwise Galileo showed no concern or awareness of any political dimension, apparently being controlled in his behavior by vanity and ambition. His style in debating and writing on his scientific views was to roll up his sleeves and leave blood on the floor. In the granting of his plea to Urban for permission to resume publishing his work in astronomy, Galileo may have viewed the situation as one in which a legitimate justification needed to be established for reasons of "face" and, accomplishing that, the stricture was removed. At the simplest level of understanding, the papal decree of 1616 that ended his writing on astronomy had been reversed by a papal decree of 1624 re-allowing it.

On the other hand, Urban had responsibility to govern all kinds of situations including those involving subtle manipulations and intrigues at the highest levels of power. He must have been aware of great potential costs of apparent lapses in judgement and the fickleness of image and winds of political fortune potentially damaging to effective rule, matters especially at risk in a high-stakes game in which a peripheral player (Galileo) is utterly unconscious of basic rules. An apparently cavalier disregard of the terms of their agreement by Galileo was certainly troubling to Urban, not only personally but also for reasons of "face." From the perspective of Urban, what was at stake or appeared to be at stake may exceed remote appraisal. And in a confrontation between these two, Galileo loses.

Whatever the transgressions, whatever the motivations, Galileo was brought before the Inquisition in Rome. The full transcript of Galileo's testimony before the Inquisition and other pertinent documentation are readily available[27] so, although not lengthy, they need not be included here. We note only that during the trial Galileo confessed to the error "of vainglorious ambition and of pure ignorance and inadvertence" at the urging of his supporter, Father Riccardi, "so as to let the affair end quietly with the least loss of face all around."[28] In his report to Cardinal Barberini, the Father Commissary concluded "The tribunal will retain its reputation and be able to use benignity with the accused."[28] Galileo was old at this time, nearly seventy. Moreover, his energy was dissipated by recent illness, a strenuous journey to Rome in winter, and emotional stress prolonged over months of procedural delays by the Inquisition. He followed the proffered advice and confessed. But the affair did not end quietly; neither was benignity used with the accused for he was sentenced on 22 June 1633 to imprisonment for heinous crimes in which condition, imprisonment under house arrest, he remained for the final eight and one-half years of his life.

Galileo's *Dialogue* was included on the next Index (of Prohibited Books), published in 1635, where it remained for two-hundred years. But the book had sold out in Italy; its impact was to gain new converts to the Copernican view. By 1635, a Latin translation prepared in Austria by Mathias Berneggar was ready for general distribution in Europe. In 1661, an English translation by Thomas Salisbury appeared.

Rolling Balls and Falling Bodies

When Galileo began studying falling bodies, virtually all scholars held the belief attributed to Aristotle that the rate of fall was proportional to the weight of the body. Galileo showed that this was an erroneous conclusion due to air resistance having a greater affect on lighter bodies, such as a feather, leaf, or snowflake, which applied in their *terminal* velocity rather than in their initial, *free-fall* velocity. Objects that were heavy and compact enough to have only small differences in fall velocity due to air resistance fell with nearly the same free-fall acceleration irrespective of their weight. Galileo conjectured that in vacuum all bodies would fall at this same rate, an experiment beyond the capabilities of his day.

The genius of Galileo was apparent in his experiments on balls rolling down an inclined plane, thus "diluting" gravity to extend time intervals to a range that he could accurately measure. The validity of this approach was far from obvious to others of his day. Galileo was the first to recognize that the motion of a body could be regarded as a sum of two or three independent components. If a force acted only in one direction, he correctly surmised its influence on a body's motion would apply only in that direction. Thus, he calculated the trajectories of projectiles by treating horizontal and vertical motions separately, the former containing no influence of weight and the latter the full influence. He then combined the results to obtain complete description of the motion of projectiles. He correctly deduced that projectiles always follow a parabolic curve and that maximum "throw" occurred for an initial inclination of forty-five degrees. He utilized his novel insight to conceive his ingenious experiments in which he diluted the effect of gravity using an inclined plane to slow down the motion of a ball and make accurate measurements possible.

By comparison of measured results for balls of different weights, Galileo showed that the early rate of fall of a body was independent of its weight. He also showed that a body moved along an inclined plane with a uniformly increasing velocity, i.e., with a constant acceleration. These observations had important implications. Aristotle held that a force was required to maintain a body's motion, even when the motion was unchanging. Medieval philosophers had surmised from this principle that the motion of planets required the eternal labors of angels pushing them along in their motion. Such arguments were even used to deduce the existence of God. In contrast, other medieval philosophers, such as the French philosopher Jean Buridan (ca. 1300-1385), taught that constant motion required no force after an initial impulse and, by that view, God needed only to start the motions of the planets and they would run forever without additional force. If an additional force were applied, taught these philosophers, the resulting motion would become ever more rapid. Galileo's experiments decided in favor of the second view, against Aristotle and those who urged his beliefs.

The achievements of Galileo and his successors, particularly Newton, in accounting for motion by forces gave rise to the thought that observed motions in the universe could be explained on the basis of pushes and pulls (forces) no more complicated in essence than the pushes and pulls of gears, levers, and screws. This mechanistic view of motion in the universe led to the branch of physics denoted *mechanics* by which the motions of bodies such as stars, planets, billiard balls, atoms, and electrons are described. However, things were not to remain as simple as first envisioned and mechanics now includes many more subtle concepts first discovered some three centuries after Galileo, to be described in later chapters.

Galileo's final book, *Discourses and Mathematical Demonstrations, Concerning Two New Sciences Pertaining to Mechanics and Local Motions*, more simply known as *Discourses on Two New Sciences*, was prepared while Galileo was imprisoned and smuggled out of Italy for publication in Leiden, free of Catholic censorship. It appeared in June of 1638 and was his most consequential work in influencing the future path of science.

An excerpt illustrates the scientific method this book promoted, thereby challenging Aristotelian tradition and the Church. In this excerpt Salviati is explaining experimental results for a ball rolling down a channel in an inclined plane.

> We rolled the ball along the channel, noting, in a manner presently to be described, the time required to make the descent. We repeated this experiment more than once in order to measure the time with an accuracy such that the deviation between two observations never exceeded one-tenth of a pulse-beat. Having performed this operation and having assured ourselves of its reliability, we now rolled the ball only one-quarter the length of the channel; and having measured the time of its descent, we found it precisely one-half of the former. Next we tried other distances, comparing the time for the whole length with that for the half, or with that for two-thirds, or three-fourths, or indeed for any fraction; in such experiments, repeated a full hundred times, we always found that the spaces traversed were to each other as the squares of the times, and this was true for all inclinations of the plane ... along which we rolled the ball.[29]

In spite of his elegant prose to the contrary, Galileo was not the most careful experimenter as he retained the traditional tendency of the Greek philosophers to theorize too quickly. Nevertheless, he had great literary skill, illustrated in this excerpt, and described his experimental method so lucidly and elegantly that he made his quantitative approach appealing and stylish. Most importantly, he emphasized measurement of material-universe facts, as opposed to speculating about theoretical, metaphysical considerations of cause, which set him apart from his contemporaries. While Aristotelian philosophers addressed metaphysical theories of ultimate cause, Galileo measured relations of time and distance and velocity. He addressed physical phenomena with questions of mechanism or cause-and-effect rather than teleology, questions of *how* rather than *why*.

These were the new and compelling contents of Galileo's last book on motion of falling bodies and much more which influenced future science generally. When a copy of this book reached Galileo's prison-home in Italy, Galileo was blind. He died, still imprisoned in his home, three and one-half years later on 8 January 1642.

Galileo's first *Dialogue* book was finally removed from the Index in 1835. On a visit to Pisa in 1965, Pope Paul VI spoke highly of Galileo. In 1992, Pope John Paul II officially reversed the Catholic Church's condemnation of Galileo and in 2000 this same pope expressed remorse for past sins of the Church.

Scientific Revolution and Religious Reformation

The scientific revolution, consisting primarily of scientific observations and speculations of Copernicus, Kepler, and Galileo that disagreed with medieval-Church dogma, was not a revolution in a military or political sense. Rather, it was an intellectual or ideological revolution consisting of the discovery of new knowledge, education, and persuasion. The experience of Galileo at the hands of the Church did not discourage other courageous individuals from resisting repressive dogma based on unjustified authority and ignorant tradition (prejudice). These others also believed results of the new, scientific paradigm were superior indicators of reality over tradition and dogma. This scientific revolution[30] coincided with and was supported by a religious reformation movement which had a similar objective. Heroic efforts on the part of a few to make scripture and its understanding available to the common person, principal goals of the Reformation, were generally met with savage reaction by the Church. This reaction itself emphasized discrepancy between the precepts taught by God in scripture and the action of Church authorities who claimed to represent Him. Many of the reformers paid for their convictions a price dearer than the one Galileo paid. Such statements are difficult for an aware and sensitive person to ignore.[31] Together, the scientific revolution, the reformation movement, and the freedom of thought they encouraged were the substance of the Renaissance, the dawn of enlightenment that followed the night of the Dark Ages of Europe. In the freedom and enlightenment that resulted, the arts, the letters, and science flourished.

Freedom and success led some, such as the French mathematical physicist Pierre Simon Laplace (1749-1827), to condemn religion and belief in God. Napoleon is supposed to have leafed through Laplace's five-volume work *Celestial Mechanics*, published over the interval from 1799 to 1825, and remarked that he saw no mention of God, to which Laplace responded "I had no need of that hypothesis."[32] But other scientists were more circumspect. Joseph Louis Lagrange (1736-1813), Laplace's contemporary and superior as a mathematician and scientist,[33] supposedly remarked upon hearing of Laplace's rejection of the hypothesis of God "Ah, but it is a beautiful hypothesis just the same. It explains so many things."[32] As the reader can surmise from these reactions to the proposition of God, the nature of the revolution and of the conflict between science and religion was defined, then and now, on a personal level.

In the Revolution/Renaissance the Church lost influence it could not hold in an honest exchange of ideas, i.e., without punishing adversaries.[31] But some, e.g., Comte and Laplace, intoxicated by the success of science, repeated the mistake, the root cause, of the original problem. They overstated the power of their new paradigm and inflated their role. They attributed to science authority it does not possess. Science was, after all, their contribution and its value was a reflection of their own. This problem is, of course, not limited to scientists but encompasses all of self-centered humans. To proud proponents of themselves, any value found in a competing system detracts from their own and the competing system therefore deserves their scorn. Among some scientists (then and now) renouncing of religion became a purifying rite required, in their own minds, for acceptance as *bona fide* scientists able to properly practice science.[34] Such an attitude strikes me as similar to joining a gang for emotional support rather than an honest quest for truth. But we are all free to make such state-ments in a way we deem best.

And we should certainly not condemn scientists for following honest inquiry using tools of reason, rigor, deductive logic, and comprehensive consistency.[35] The religions with which they were and are most familiar are corrupted (a proposition to be enlarged and justified in Book III) to the extent that they wear poorly against these tools. And medieval-Church authorities claimed that knowledge contrary to observation was divine, required that others believe without question the orthodox knowledge that priestly authority alone understood and dispensed, and displayed a discrepancy between Church goals and methods and the teachings of Christ (as in the efforts of the Church to impose its dogma by force instead of by honest reason, evidence, and persuasion). All of these practices of the medieval Church suggested its claims of heavenly authority and divine wisdom were patently false. Error and sin of members and even leaders are universal to all churches, but continuing, unremitted sin and error are not justified in Christ's Church. He will either correct such a church or, if sin persists, disown it. Practices of the medieval Church and others were inscrutable as polar opposites to the teachings of Christ: promotion of love, patience, humility, charity, faith in Christ, repentance, and baptism using honest reason, experiment, rigor, deductive logic, consistency, and individual agency or free will.

Despite now-obvious failings in medieval-Church dogma and the severe abuse dispensed in its attempted enforcement,[31] it was and is a mistake to inductively dismiss all religion as invalid because one once was. While science led to valid conclusions opposed to those of the medieval Church, the situation has since completely changed by the Reformation and by even more consequential later events to be elaborated in due course. Inductive dismissal of all religion is not justified by honest reason, rigor, deductive logic, or comprehensive consistency. "Just because something has never been observed or imagined is no reason to exclude it from consideration."[36] Among those who held or hold a narrow view and simply reject all organized religion as invalid, deceptive, or otherwise unsatisfactory, a measure of the old intolerance is repeated anew and we see that humans are still mortal. On the other hand, others, who I think of as possessing the best qualities of category-one students, neither overstate their power nor inflate their role. They simply do their job. And, as with Lagrange, success for them is not intoxicating.

Understanding the so-called conflict between science and religion is important because its implications are important. Some believe that this conflict reveals an essential deficiency in Christianity. But this conclusion is a huge conceptual leap from the conflict revealed only between the *two specific models historically involved*, namely, the scientific observations and discoveries of Copernicus, Kepler, and Galileo and, opposed thereto, the dogma of the medieval Church and Aristotelian philosophy. The vague notion that the terms "scientific revolution" and "conflict between science and religion (Christianity)" somehow represent conclusive proof of an essential deficiency in religion (Christianity) is not justified.

Notes and References for Chapter 6.

[1] Asimov, Isaac, *Asimov's Biographical Encyclopedia of Science and Technology,* Avon Books, New York, 1976.

[2] Aristotle, *De Caelo,* Book II, Cap. XIV. Quoted in F. K. Richtmyer, E. H. Kennard, and T. Lauritsen, *Introduction to Modern Physics,* McGraw-Hill Book Company, New York, 1955, 7.

[3] Aristotle, *De Generatione et Corruptione,* Book I, Cap. II. Quoted in Richtmyer, Kennard and Lauritsen, loc. cit., 7.

[4] Galilei, Galileo, *De motu,* as quoted by F. S. Taylor in *Galileo and the Freedom of Thought,* Watts, London, 1938, 39.

[5] Letter from Galileo to Kepler dated 19 August 1610 found in Galilei, Galileo, *Le Opere di Galileo Galilei,* Edizione Nazionale, Antonio Fàvaro (editor), Barbèra, Florence, 1890-1909, Volume X, 423.

[6] A concise but excellent treatment of the collision of Galileo and the Church is given by Jerome J. Langford (*Galileo, Science and the Church,* Desclee Company, New York, 1966). Besides its main focus, this short book contains much useful background information. Langford describes the confrontation as being finally forced by Galileo's relentless pushing for a decision when he had not made a conclusive case for Copernicanism, although he thought he had. On the other hand, the wall against which Galileo was pushing should have been less rigid. Quoting the decree of the Council of Trent (1545-1563), Langford points out that the prohibition against distorting scripture according to one's own conceptions contrary to the sense in which the holy mother Church holds only applies in matters of faith and morals. While Copernicanism was then thought to be in direct contradiction to scripture, its promotion did not broach matters of faith or morals. Thus, official Church policy was violated when Galileo was silenced from teaching or discussing the Copernican theory in 1616. A similar argument applies against his 1633 conviction and imprisonment and the banning of his book *Dialogue on Two World Systems.* While the Inquisition acted officially for the Church, it did not follow official Church policy.

[7] Sobel, Dava, *Galileo's Daughter,* Walker and Company, New York, 1999, 20.

[8] Galilei, Galileo, *Two New Sciences, Including Centers of Gravity and Force of Percussion* Stillman Drake (translator), Second Edition, Wall and Thompson, Toronto, 1989, 68. Whether this leaning-tower experiment is fact or fable has never been finally resolved by historians. Galileo frequently utilized "thought experiments" and this tradition may have derived from one.

[9] See endnote 13 of Chapter 1. A brief history of the principle of *Ockham's* or *Occam's razor* with illustrative applications is given by Jefferys, William H., and James O. Berger, "Ockham's Razor and Bayesian Analysis," *American Scientist* **80**, January-February 1992, 64-72.

[10] Copernicus, Nicholas, *On the Revolutions of the Heavenly Spheres,* quoted (and translated) in *Great Books of the Western World*, Britannica, Chicago, 1952, Volume XVI, 508.

[11] Luther, Martin, *Tischreden,* Walsch (editor), Volume XXII, n. p., n. d., 2260.

[12] Gleiser, Marcelo, *The Dancing Universe,* Dutton, Penguin Putnam Inc., New York, 1997, 75.

[13] Ibid., 79. [14] Ibid.

[15] Galilei, Vincenzio, *Dialogue of Ancient and Modern Music,* Florence, 1581. Quoted by Sobel, loc. cit., 17.

[16] Asimov, loc. cit., 94; Richtmyer, Kennard, and Lauritsen, loc. cit., 14.

[17] Drake (1962), loc. cit., 73. [18] Langford, loc. cit., 41.

[19] In his book *The Almagest*, the standard astronomical handbook used throughout the middle ages, Ptolemy states, in Book I, Chapter 5, "The earth in relation to the fixed stars, has no appreciable size and must be treated as a mathematical point." Quoted by C. S. Lewis in an essay entitled "Religion and Science," in *God in the Dock*, Walter Hooper (editor), William B. Eerdmans Publishing Company, Grand Rapids, MI, 1970. See also Ptolemy, Claudius, *The Almagest*, R. C. Taliaferro (translator), *Great Books of the Western World*, Britannica, Chicago, 1952, Volume XVI, 1-478.

[20] Gleiser, Marcelo, loc. cit.

[21] Several Biblical scriptures can be cited here. See Joshua 10:12-14, Psalms 18:6-7, 92:1, 103:5, Ecclesiastes 1:5.

[22] Galilei, Galileo, "Reply to Ingoli," see, for example, Maurice A. Finnocchiaro, *The Galileo Affair: A Documentary History,* University of California Press, Berkeley, 1989, 156.

[23] While the second of Galileo's two dialogue books is entitled "Discourses ...," this was an error due to the book being published remotely in Leiden where the author could not monitor the editing. "Discourses" was substituted for "Dialogue" against the intention of the author. The style and character of both Dialogue books are identical.

[24] Galilei, Galileo, *The Dialogue on the Great World Systems,* G. de Santillana (translator), Chicago University Press, Chicago, 1953, 124. See also *Dialogue Concerning the Two Chief World Systems,* Stillman Drake (translator), The University of California Press, Berkeley, 1962.

[25] *The Dialogue on the Great World Systems,* loc. cit., 128.

[26] Letter of Antonio Querengo to Alessandro D'Este, dated 20 January 1616, *Opere,* loc. cit., Volume XII, 226f.

[27] Finnocchiaro, loc. cit.; Sobel, loc. cit.; Langford, loc. cit.; *Opere*, loc. cit.

[28] Quoted from a letter dated 28 April 1633 of Father Commissary Vincenzo Maculano da Firenzuola to Francesco Cardinal Barberini, nephew of Pope Urban VIII and former student of Galileo, Stillman Drake (translator), *Galileo at Work: His Scientific Biography,* University of Chicago Press, Chicago, 1978, 349-350.

[29] Galilei, Galileo, *Dialogues Concerning Two New Sciences,* Henry Crew and Alfonso de Salvio (translators), Macmillan, New York, 1914; Dover, New York, 1954; 178-179. See also *Two New Sciences, Including Centers of Gravity and Force of Percussion,* loc. cit.

[30] While physicists would nearly uniformly cite the story of Galileo as the original and essential scientific revolution, historians and others sometimes cite other history. H. G. Wells (*The Outline of History,* Volume 2, Garden City Books, Garden City, New York, 1920-1961, 777-778) makes the following comments regarding the scientific revolution.

> In 1859 [Charles Darwin] published his *Origin of Species by Means of Natural Selection,* a powerful and permanently valuable exposition ...
>
> Many men and women [in 1920] ... remember the dismay and distress among ordinary intelligent people in the Western communities as the invincible case of the biologists and geologists against the orthodox Christian cosmogony unfolded itself. The minds of many resisted the new knowledge instinctively and irrationally. Their whole moral edifice was built upon false history; they were too old and too set to rebuild it; they felt the practical truth of their moral convictions, and this new truth seemed to them to be incompatible with that. They believed to assent to it would be to prepare a moral collapse of the world. And so they produced a moral collapse by not assenting to it. ...
>
> The Darwinian movement took formal Christianity unawares, suddenly. Formal Christianity was confronted with a clearly demonstrable error in her theological statements. The Christian theologians were neither wise enough nor mentally nimble enough to accept the new truth, modify their formulæ, and insist upon the living and undiminished vitality of the religious reality those formulæ had hitherto sufficed to express. For the discovery of man's descent from sub-human forms does not even remotely touch the teaching of the Kingdom of Heaven. Yet priests and bishops raged at Darwin; foolish attempts were made to suppress Darwinian literature and to insult and discredit the exponents of the new views. There was much wild talk of the 'antagonism' of religion and science. ...
>
> Christendom became, as a whole, sceptical. ... It was the orthodox theology that the new scientific advances had compromised, but the angry theologians declared that it was religion. ... it seemed as if, indeed, there had been a conflict between science and religion, and that in the conflict science had won. ... There was a real loss of faith after 1859.

While recognizing that "man's descent from sub-human forms does not even remotely touch the teaching of the Kingdom of Heaven," Wells observed that scientific advances had compromised orthodox theology by exposing "clearly demonstrable error" and "the invincible case of the biologists and geologists against the orthodox Christian cosmogony." However, some of Well's implicit assumptions are based on the adopted Darwinian and other theory rather than evidence. An alternative view taken in this book is that while some problems do lie at the feet of (corrupted) orthodox theology, more severe ones are due to unrecognized flaws in use of both science and religion. Many of the unresolvable problems indicated by apparent conflict between science and religion are in fact resolvable. They are due, at least in part, to inherent uncertainty, misunderstanding, and corruption in both science and orthodox Christian belief, both being topics addressed in this book. For science examples see Chapters 5 and 16 and for Christian ones see the section of Chapter 7 entitled "Newton's Bible Studies" (pages 143-147), endnotes 20 and 21 of Chapter 10, endnote 9 of Chapter 13, Chapters 14 and 15, and Appendix I.

[31] Of the many leaders of the Reformation that could be cited for their courage and heroic effort I will cite one: William Tyndale (ca. 1492-1536). He is known today for his masterful English translations of the entire New Testament from the Greek and about half of the Old Testament from the Hebrew. Translating scripture was of central importance to the Reformation. The medieval Church approved only the Latin Vulgate Bible, translated by St. Jerome in the fourth century. Even so, access to scripture was severely limited in Tyndale's time because only the educated could read Latin, with education largely controlled by the Church. Thus, contact with scripture by everyday persons was restricted and, of course, such restriction effectively limited independent consideration and alternative interpretation of scripture. The reformers therefore urged greater access to the Bible; and access to scripture by the common people was exactly as advantageous to the reform movement as it was damaging to the established Church. This inverse proportionality was not coincidental because credibility and justification were at stake for both the orthodox and reformer through appeal to scripture. Since the Vulgate text had been authorized and officially or learnedly commented on for centuries, every line mattered. New translation of scripture was consequently regarded by the reformers as illuminating and essential, to be pursued at all cost, and by the established Church as dangerous and heretical, to be prevented at all cost.

Scripture in the common vernacular became available in some European languages. For examples, a Spanish text of the Old Testament had been used by Jews on the Iberian Peninsula and a Swedish translation of the Bible was published in 1541. The Lollard Bible was prepared in the 1380s by John Wycliffe and his followers but was an English translation from the Latin Vulgate which therefore provided limited new perspective. Erasmus translated an alternative Latin New Testament from the Greek in 1516, in which he corrected the Vulgate version. Although Erasmus' work was not declared heretical, perhaps because of his high reputation as a scholar and diplomat and his faithful-Catholic status, it must have been viewed with some concern by Roman authorities, especially since he urged in his preface that the Bible be made available in the language of lay people. No adequate English translation of scripture was available at the time of William Tyndale. Providing one became Tyndale's lifelong quest and, in the end, it cost him his life. Nevertheless, provide one he did and it has proved to be most excellent.

William Tyndale was born in England on the Welsh border, probably in Gloucestershire. He studied at Oxford, beginning Easter term 1510 in Magdalen Hall, and received the MA degree in 1515. He went from Oxford to Cambridge, where Erasmus was then lecturing and famous for its scholarship in Greek and theology – two areas in which Tyndale focused and excelled.

Tyndale was ordained a Catholic priest, probably in 1521. He served for two years as domestic tutor and chaplain in the home of Sir John Walsh in Old Sodbury, Gloucestershire. On his leisure he preached in the villages and at Bristol, through which experience he came into conflict with the backward clergy of the district. He later declared his ambition to "cause the boy that driveth the plough to know more of the scriptures" than these poorly educated clergy. He was called before the Chancellor of Worcester as a suspected heretic but he received neither censure nor penance.

Tyndale regarded the Church as being corrupted, with the persecution he suffered from the clergy being a symptom. As an antidote to this corruption he planned to translate the New Testament into the vernacular so the common people could read it. To seek the help of the bishop of London, Cuthbert Tunstall, he left Gloucestershire for London in summer, 1523. When Tunstall provided no support, Tyndale obtained employment as a preacher and as chaplain in the house of Humphrey Monmouth. While living with Monmouth he worked at translation of the New Testament.

Tyndale found it impossible to publish his translation in England. Unauthorized English translations of scripture and (under threat of excommunication) merely reading an English Bible were forbidden in the Constitutions of Oxford in 1408, a reaction to Wycliffe's Lollard movement. Tyndale therefore sailed for Hamburg in May of 1524. He visited Luther in Wittenberg and settled in Cologne, where he lived with his amanuensis William Roy. During printing of his 4to edition of the New Testament, the dean at Frankfurt, John Cochläus, learned of Tyndale's effort and caused the Senate of Cologne to prohibit further printing and alerted Henry VIII and Wolsey to monitor the English ports. Tyndale's and Roy's effort survived the attempted suppression when they escaped to Worms with their sheets. There they completed and printed the 8vo edition of the New Testament in 1526. Copies of these were secreted into England but their usage was suppressed by the bishops. The archbishop of Canterbury, William Warham, actively purchased copies on the continent for the purpose of destroying them, as further described below. But some did reach their intended audience and attempts were made to seize Tyndale at Worms. Tyndale fled to Marburg and was granted refuge with Philip, Langrave of Hesse.

In England, Tunstall gave permission for humanist Thomas More (1478-1535), Lord Chancellor of England, to read Tyndale's works so that he could refute them. More then initiated a literary battle and Tyndale responded. To counter brutal attacks by More, Tyndale wrote *Obedience of a Christian Man* in 1528, which provided the two great principles of the English Reformation, namely, the authority of scripture in the Church and the supremacy of the king in the state. Tyndale also published *Parable of the Wicked Mammon* in 1528. Subsequent tracts in the battle were entitled *Dialogue* by More in 1529, *An Answer* by Tyndale in 1531, and *Confutation* by More in 1532. In 1530 Tyndale published his *Practyse of Prelates*, a strong indictment of the Roman Church and also of Henry's divorce proceedings, serving to further embitter Henry against him. One can regard Tyndale as winning the debate since More was beheaded by the king in 1535 for refusing to recognize him as head of the Church, but Tyndale did not survive the following year.

In 1529 while traveling to Hamburg, his ship was wrecked on the Dutch coast, and his recently completed translation of Deuteronomy from the Hebrew was lost.

About this same time England (Henry VIII) broke with the Catholic Church and formed the Church of England with the king (himself) as head, thus rendering impotent the pope's opposition to Henry's intended divorce from Katherine of Aragon. It is noteworthy that no lust for his future wife, Anne Boleyn, was involved as motivation for a divorce because Anne was only seven years old at the time the divorce was first rumored. "The problem with Henry VIII was not passion but succession. He knew how to satisfy passion without benefit of matrimony and already had an illegitimate son – but not one to succeed him born of the queen, and no hope of one after 1525, for although in that year Henry was but thirty-three, his wife Katherine was forty." (Bainton, Roland H., *The Reformation of the Sixteenth Century,* Beacon Press, Boston, 1952, 186.) To accomplish his goals (including his divorce), Henry and his cohorts packed and skillfully managed the Parliament beginning in 1529. One change made by Henry as head of the church was introduction of the Bible in the vernacular in the churches. Rome would probably not have objected to such a move provided the translation was orthodox and authorized. "Henry's order therefore that an English Bible be installed in all the churches would not of itself have invited papal censure. Nevertheless it is not too much to say that a genuinely scholarly translation taken directly from the Hebrew and the Greek was at that period bound to offend the Church of Rome because certain renderings of the Latin version commonly adduced in support of crucial doctrines would be expunged." (Bainton, loc. cit., 195.) Among the English only few were capable of such translation and few of those possessed zeal for both new understanding and new religion. Tyndale was prominent on both accounts.

However, recruiting Tyndale to perform the work would have contradicted royal policy. The archbishop of Canterbury, under the head of the church, had commissioned a certain Augustine Packington to buy copies of Tyndale's translation on the Continent in order that he could burn them. Packington approached Tyndale directly and announced that he represented a merchant who would buy out his stock. "Who is this merchant?" asked Tyndale. "The Bishop of London," answered Packington. "Oh, that is because he will burn them," responded Tyndale. "Yea, marry," quoth Packington. "I am the gladder," said Tyndale, "for these two benefits shall come thereof: I shall get money from him for these books and bring myself out of debt, and the whole world shall cry out on the burning of God's Word, and the overplus of the money that shall remain to me shall make me more studious to correct the said New Testament, and so newly to imprint the same once again; and I trust the second will much better like you than ever did the first. And so went the bargain: the Bishop had the books, Packington had the thanks, and Tyndale had the money." (Bainton, loc. cit., 195-196.)

Subsequently the attack was escalated from Tyndale's books to Tyndale himself. The English envoy to the Netherlands, Stephen Vaughan, claimed Henry had adopted a new attitude toward Tyndale and urged him to return to England. However, Tyndale prudently feared hostility and declined to return. His caution was wise and provided him freedom to work a few more years, his most productive. When Tyndale failed to return, Henry demanded his surrender by the emperor on the charge of spreading sedition in England and Tyndale fled Antwerp for two years. In 1533 Tyndale returned and continued the revision of his translations. In 1534 he completed and printed his greatest achievement: his 1534 revision of the New Testament.

In 1535 he was betrayed by Henry Phillips and imprisoned by imperial officers at the state prison, Vilvorde Castle, located some six miles from Brussels. In spite of the support of English merchants and an appeal of Thomas Cromwell to Archbishop Carandolet, Tyndale was tried for heresy and condemned by the Inquisition. On 6 October 1536, Tyndale was tied to a stake, strangled, and then burned together with all copies of his books that could be found. The Inquisition operated on the principle that persecution and coercion were effective "Christian" tools. One of the inquisitors of the time remarked regarding Tyndale's trial that "It is of no great matter, whether they that die on account of religion be guilty or innocent, provided we terrify the people by such examples; which generally succeeds best when persons eminent for learning, riches, nobility or high station are thus sacrificed." (quoted in Bainton, loc. cit., 224.) Winning the hearts and minds of the people after the manner Christ exemplified could not be more opposite from such an arrogant, perverted, and cruel attitude.

Miles Coverdale received the royal commission to provide the Bible in English translation for the churches in England. To complete the task in the allotted time Coverdale utilized Tyndale's translation which thereby became the standard version and a basis of the 1611 King James Bible.

In tragic irony Tyndale's translation indirectly became the predominant source of the official English Bible despite his martyrdom motivated by England (Henry VIII) for translating it.

Though in exile from his native land, Tyndale was one of the great forces in the English Reformation. His writings, based on sound scholarship and composed with great literary power, helped shape the thought of the Puritan party in England. Even more consequential were his English translations of scripture: the Books of Moses from the Hebrew and, especially, the New Testament from the Greek. These provided a scriptural basis for the Reformation in England and have had profound influence on subsequent English Bibles. Tyndale's translations are warm, happy, and certain. His origins on the Welsh border, his intelligence, excellent training, and his natural literary gifts uniquely qualified him for this work and has endeared Tyndale to those today who read and love the King James Bible and its descendents. The linguistic richness, the warmth, and the depth of feeling conveyed in this translation are due largely to William Tyndale from whom the translators drew heavily in compiling their version. About 90 percent of the King James New Testament came directly from Tyndale. Thus, far more than any other individual, William Tyndale is the translator of the English Bible we read today.

By their fruits ye shall know them.

(Sources: Encyclopædia Britannica; Foxe, John, *Foxe's Book of Martyrs;* and Bainton, loc. cit.)

[32] Quoted in Asimov, Isaac, loc. cit., 211.

[33] Bell, E. T., *Men of Mathematics,* Simon & Schuster, New York, 1937, Chapter 10.

[34] Renouncing religion as a purifying rite necessary for proper practice of science is similar to the belief that aligning with a school of thought compromises a philosopher's freedom of thought and objectivity. The concern is that one may become prejudiced in becoming knowledgeable and involved in a particular school, that one may become captured by a dogma and lose desire and ability to reason. But what should be of equal concern is that one or many or most or all may initially be prejudiced. Becoming intimately familiar with the thinking and belief of some school dispels ignorance which must act to reduce prejudice. If, on the other hand, one was previously attached to a popular dogma prejudiced against this school, desire and ability to reason may have been impaired. One who thinks freely and deeply is not captured and held prisoner by ideas or dogma, although many (who do not think freely and deeply) are so held by tradition and culture, in or out of science.

In science and Christianity no necessity for exclusivity, no mutual exclusivity, exists because, despite their *methods* being adversarial (science considering only objective facts using one truth criterion and Christianity considering all facts but with a primary emphasis on subjective ones using a different truth criterion), the two paradigms are only complementary in their *conclusions* (science is able to provide only tentative, contingent conclusions while, as we describe and justify in Book III, Christianity is able to provide certain, absolute conclusions). Thus, we refer to science and Christianity in this book variously as adversarial and as complementary because they are both.

[35] Neither should we condemn anyone for his or her religious belief because of pervasive corruption of religious tradition.

[36] I like this statement because it illustrates the unanticipated nature of fundamental discovery and the need to retain an open mind to make such discovery. It implicitly recognizes inherent weakness in logical induction. As we shall see, both scientific and religious knowledge reveal that reality is stranger than any fiction so far imagined.

7. Science and the Search for Truth: Isaac Newton

In order to obtain a clearer vision of how the scientific method and deductive analysis are used, we continue in this and the next two chapters a summary of the development of mechanics following the time of Kepler and Galileo. These chapters describe the laws of mechanics manifest in nature, the profundity of these laws, and, especially, the history of their discovery. The desired product of scientific discovery is a deep and complete knowledge of organization, pattern, and connection among the objective, reproducible, lowest-common-denominator, material-universe facts. Newly discovered organization, pattern, and connection constitute an improvement in vision or abstraction or paradigm which supersedes previous vision and allows better rationalization of the facts by providing deeper insights and further-reaching, more comprehensive knowledge of their interrelations.

In later chapters, science and mathematics are further examined and criticized in considering what we can say about fundamental structure, organization, and validity of scientific facts. Applications in mathematical physics (Chapter 10) and psychology (Chapter 11) are considered. Following the survey and critique of science in Book II, we examine Christianity in Book III by comparing it to science, whose properties shall then be familiar, in addressing profound and consequential (ultimate) questions. By such comparison we pursue the theme of this book: method and result for discovering the nature of reality. We begin with an insightful dialogue on discovery.

Salviati, Sagredo, and Simplicio on the Discovery Process

The general nature of discovery in science and in some other approaches to knowledge is well represented by the following dialogue which wonderfully illuminates the processes of abstraction and discovery and the understanding of reality they produce. This Galilean-style dialogue is taken from J. M. Jauch's book *Are Quanta Real?*

Salviati: Suppose I give you two sequences of numbers, such as

7 8 5 3 9 8 1 6 3 3 9 7 4 4 8 3 0 9 6 1 5 6 6 0 8 4 ...

and

+ 1 – 1/3 + 1/5 – 1/7 + 1/9 – 1/11 + 1/13 – 1/15 ...

If I asked you, Simplicio, what the next number of the first sequence is, what would you say?

Simplicio: I could not tell you. I think it is a random sequence and that there is no law in it.

Salviati: And for the second sequence?

Simplicio: That would be easy. It must be +1/17.

Salviati: Right. But what would you say if I told you that the first sequence is also constructed by a law and this law is in fact identical with the one you have just discovered for the second sequence.

Simplicio: This does not seem probable to me.

Salviati: But it is indeed so, since the first sequence is simply the beginning of the decimal fraction of the sum of the second. Its value is $\pi/4$.

Simplicio: You are full of such mathematical tricks, but I do not see what this has to do with abstraction and reality.

Salviati: The relationship with abstraction is easy to see. The first sequence looks random unless one has developed through a process of abstraction a kind of filter which sees a simple structure behind the apparent randomness. It is exactly in this manner that laws of nature are discovered. Nature presents us with a host of phenomena which appear mostly as chaotic randomness until we select some significant events, and abstract from their particular, irrelevant circumstances so that they become idealized. Only then can they exhibit their true structure in full splendor.

Sagredo: This is a marvelous idea! It suggests that when we try to understand nature, we should look at the phenomena as if they were messages to be understood. Except that each message appears to be random until the code takes the form of an abstraction, that is, we choose to ignore certain things as irrelevant and we thus partially select the content of the message by a free choice. These irrelevant signals form the "background noise," which will limit the accuracy of our message.

But since the code is not absolute there may be several messages in the same raw material of the data, so changing the code [theory, paradigm, philosophy, belief] will result in a message of equally deep significance in something that was merely noise before, and *conversely*: In a new code a former message may be devoid of meaning.

Thus a code presupposes a free choice among different, complementary aspects, each of which has equal claim to *reality*, if I may use this dubious word.

Some of these aspects may be completely unknown to us now but they may reveal themselves to an observer with a different system of abstractions. But tell me, Salviati, how can we then still claim that we *discover* something out there in the objective real world? Does this not mean that we are merely creating things according to our own images and that reality is only within ourselves?

Salviati: I don't think that this is necessarily so, but it is a question which requires deeper reflection.[1]

Personal Qualities and Discovery

This dialogue accurately depicts an uncertain and arbitrary nature of all scientific theory and of scientific methodology itself. Such a nature of the scientific method is apparent from our Chapter-5 deduction of inherent tentativeness in science, due to absence of any definite *yes* answer obtainable by its method, as is repeatedly apparent in the history of science. The dialogue also indicates another significant source of uncertainty and arbitrariness that precedes even a *yes* or *no* question, namely, selection of abstractions, theories, or laws to consider and test from an indefinitely large number of possibilities that could properly relate the facts.[2] (We consider both of these sources of ambiguity inherent in scientific inquiry in terms of rigorous theorems in Chapter 10 and further discuss them in Chapters 16 and 17. We illustrate the abstract nature of finding candidate theories in this and later chapters and in Appendices D and F.)

Two examples illustrate the tenuous relationship between science (theory) and what we perceive as the real universe (observation).

(1) In 1666 Isaac Newton performed several insightful and implication-rich investigations and demonstrations on the nature of light. In one, Newton made a hole in a window shade to obtain a beam of sunlight projected onto a wall 22 feet from the window. This light beam formed a circle of 2 5/8 inches diameter on the wall. Placing a glass prism in the beam near the perforated shade, Newton noted that the circle was altered to an oblong shape, still 2 5/8 inches in width but 13 1/4 inches in height, in which the colors of the rainbow were separated into horizontal bands. Others had previously used a prism to generate colors from sunlight, resulting in controversy over whether the colors came from the sunlight or from the prism. Newton therefore conceived a clever demonstration to settle the controversy. Extending the previous experiment by adding two boards each with a small hole (a "stop"), he isolated a beam of selected color, by rotating prism 1 with the boards, prism 2, and screen fixed, as illustrated in the following figure. In passing through prism 2, no beam of any selected color showed further elongation or color separation. Newton concluded that the colors were contained not in a prism but in sunlight.

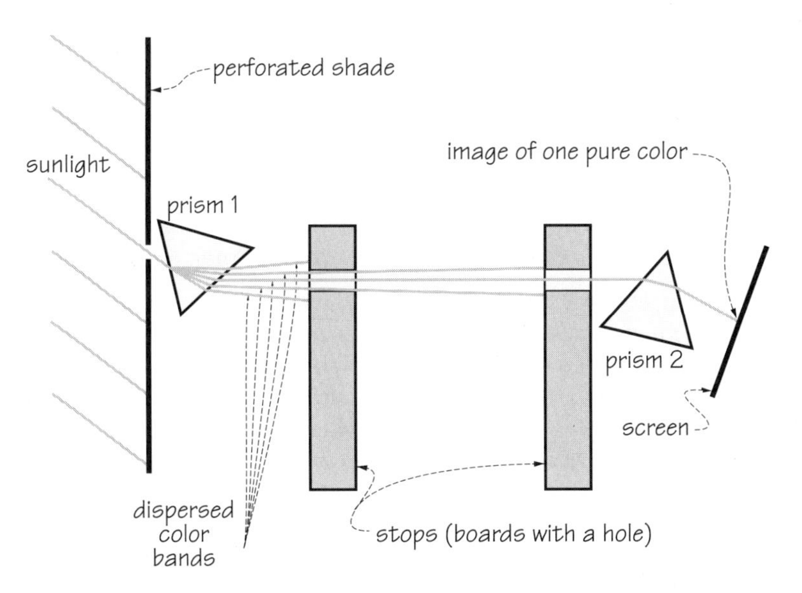

Newton's experiment isolated one pure color not divisible into multiple colors. By this demonstration Newton deduced the colors were in white light, not a prism.

Newton also performed several other experiments or demonstrations. In one he recombined the light of different colors separated by a prism by focusing the separated colors onto a small spot using a lens, as illustrated in the next figure. The color of the spot at its smallest size, i.e., at the focal point of the lens where all the colors were uniformly mixed, was white. Yet, as he moved the screen from the focal point closer to the lens the separate colors emerged from the white dot, each in its own band; and when he moved the screen from the focal point farther from the lens the separated colors again appeared, each in its own band but with the color sequence reversed. Light of all colors converged and mixed only at the focal point where the dot was white. Thus, white light is composed of many colors! A prism only separates colors already in the light.

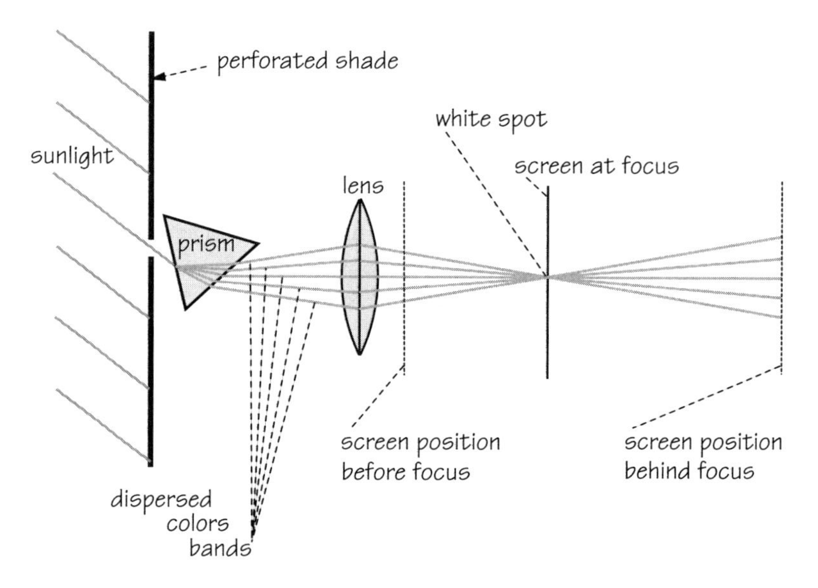

Newton's experiment split sunlight into colors and recombined them into a white spot.

Another Newton experiment was based on his realization that the retina of the eye had a minimum response time below which human vision did not temporally resolve colors but only averaged them. He therefore observed prism-separated colors through a "spoked" wheel. As the wheel rotated slowly, Newton observed a repeating sequence of separated color bands as they individually passed through each narrow gap between spokes. At faster rotation he observed only the averaged or combined color – *white.*

Newton anticipated these results because he already knew (how) such spreading of white light into colors would occur. Otherwise he could not have conceived such compelling demonstrations. He already knew what experiments to perform and what results to expect from knowledge he deduced from previous observations of blue and red threads through a prism that the *refraction* of the two colors passing through it differed. Newton's "augmentation of vision" inferred by his keen mind from a little knowledge was to recur in his study of mechanics in which he became intimately familiar with motions of bodies through internalizing hundreds of calculations using his calculus to characterize such motions, generating in himself a "feel" or intuition for proper motions of bodies. This intuition eventually provided his laws of motion, certainly a great advance in mechanics but not fully correct. Neither did his demonstrations of the properties of light provide a basic understanding of its nature, an understanding we still lack today.

Nor is there reason to believe any law inferred from an incomplete-knowledge basis will be fully correct. Because a law is chosen to agree with known observation, it always does. But observation is never comprehensive and whether the law will fully agree with later, more complete, refined, and enlightened observation can never be assured by science in advance of this observation. Thus, proposing any scientific law is arbitrary to some extent because, correctly or incorrectly, it predicts facts not yet observed.

(2) An experience of Charles H. Townes, who won the 1964 Nobel Prize in physics for his discoveries of the maser and laser, illustrates preconception and bias that occur in science. In his autobiographical *How the Laser Happened* Townes states: "Scientific principles are so general and pervasive that they continually show up as familiar friends in new territory – or with exploration in any direction."[3] And yet I. I. Rabi and P. Kusch, the former and then-current head of the physics department at Columbia University when Townes worked there and both Nobel Prize winners themselves, visited his lab and together told him "Look, you should stop the work you are doing. It isn't going to work. You know it's not going to work. We know it's not going to work. You're wasting money. Just stop."[4] He, of course, didn't.

We see "familiar friends" (scientific laws and principles) because we recognize and look for them. But different persons see their consequences differently and they therefore understand different meanings, in spite of attempted objectivity in science. Acquired knowledge is useful, but it inevitably contains preconception and bias, channeling understanding and meaning into familiar but not necessarily correct directions. One is so easily drawn to familiar understanding that familiarity is therefore a barrier to new understanding.

These two examples provide an antidote against the misconception that science and scientific thinking are fixed and routine rather than creative and imaginative. In fact, science (or religion or politics) is so demanding of creativity and so effectively promoted by creativity or charisma or reputation that more than once a creative, charismatic, or famous scientist (or ...) has led a large following to believe in nonsense largely or even strictly on the strength of his or her creativity or charisma or reputation. Ernst Mach's positivism "crusade" serves as one example. "Polywater" and "cold fusion" were the subjects of others.

Instead, a scientist should discover an abstraction (theory or law) that imposes compelling order, pattern, and connection on apparent chaos and properly relates all known observations (facts) without undue dependence on charisma, perhaps without a following, but certainly using creativity and imagination. Out of many possible candidates the scientist chooses one principle, theory, or law that may seem obscure and "unpromising" to another scientist, "unpromising" in the intuition of a present, incorrect or incomplete paradigm. And, in the absence of a *yes* answer and of a knowledge of all facts, any uniqueness of a correct law over others that also give correct predictions will not be apparent either before or after it is selected and tested. Indeed, lacking a reliable *yes* answer, it can never be established that a fully correct theory has even been considered. But a best-agreement-with-observation-up-to-now law can often be selected providing useful function if not fundamental understanding.

After their successful use, Newton's laws of motion were accepted as universally valid and, relative to previous understanding, this assessment is not much of an exaggeration. But a little over two centuries later they were found to fail in some predictions. Reliable predictions of high-speed electron motions and properties of atoms were first achieved with the development of Einstein's theory of relativity (Chapter 8) and quantum mechanics (Chapter 9). Relativistic and Newtonian predictions disagree when bodies move at high speeds or mass (gravity) significantly exceeds that found in our solar system. Newtonian mechanics and Euclidian space impose a "spacetime" that is not convenient for description of such conditions. The discovery of more suitable, alternative, non-Euclidian spaces (geometries) required over two thousand years because it ran counter to "obviously correct" tradition (Chapter 3). History thus illustrates the difficulty in even conceiving new, unfamiliar relationships among the facts and new visions of reality while one "resides" in an established culture and paradigm.

The story we recite in this and the next few chapters is one of tentative discovery of truth at an ever-deeper and more abstract level, step-by-step, eliminating one misconception after another. The story illustrates the difficulty of discovering truth by science's sole truth criterion: mere consistency. If science could provide a comprehensive, universally-correct theory, we would not need the three currently used in mechanics (Chapters 7 - 9). And beyond the *how* questions on which science focuses lie the deeper and more important *who*, *what*, and *why* questions (Book III). The history of the search for truth in mechanics recited in this and following chapters illustrates the importance of a category-one-student attitude. To continue to learn, we must realize we don't yet fully understand and, in such realization, be teachable.

That is, we ever seek new meaning even in familiar sights few or none of which we fully understand. Despite their familiarity we must not fail to recognize our ignorance. The discovery process requires seeing beyond the traditional and familiar, although both are necessarily and unavoidably used in obtaining new vision. To discover new knowledge, one must be willing and able to see with new vision beginning with a simple look not restricted by prejudice in one's tradition and culture. Such willingness and ability are not common in either science or religion (Appendix A). To the willing and able, the discovery process reveals deeper knowledge, understanding, and meaning, pertaining not only to *how* questions of science but also to ultimate *who*, *what*, and *why* questions.

The following stories of scientific discoveries and scientists who made them in this and following chapters are interesting and instructive. Understanding the dedication, courage, and independence of thought these scientists used to make their discoveries is more important than understanding the discoveries. These qualities are necessary ingredients in all important, fundamental discovery. Therefore, as we consider scientific discovery in these chapters, we also consider discovery of other kinds of knowledge, knowledge broader, deeper, and more important than science.

Young Newton

Isaac Newton was born in Woolsthorpe, Lincolnshire, England on Christmas day 1642 according to the Julian calendar still then in use but on 4 January 1643 by the Gregorian calendar used today. He was born prematurely and was tiny and frail. Notwithstanding the fact that his father, Isaac, had died at age 36 some two months previous, he provided well for his family by leaving to his wife a sixty-acre estate that included a stone manor house, several barns containing oats, barley, and malt, 234 sheep, and 46 head of cattle. Nevertheless, in 1646 when Newton was three, his mother, Hannah Ayscough-Newton, married Barnabas Smith, a wealthy, 63-year-old rector of the nearby village of North Witham. The terms agreed upon were that Hannah would move to North Witham, young Isaac would live with his grandparents in the Newton home which was to be fully refurbished, and young Isaac would inherit at age twenty-one a parcel of land purchased for that purpose at a cost of £50. As an adult, Newton was neurotic and paranoid, probably at least partly due to the emotional pain and insecurity caused by this early separation from his mother. But Hannah's affection for her son was demonstrated when she made him the principal heir of the augmented estate upon her death, leaving but little to her two daughters and one son by Smith.

Hannah returned to Woolsthorpe with Isaac's three half-siblings on the death of Smith in 1653 when Newton was ten. A year later, Newton began his formal education at King Edward Grammar School in Grantham, a village containing a few hundred families, a church, a guild hall, two inns, an apothecary, and two mills. Because Grantham, a distance of eight miles from Woolsthorpe, was too far for a daily commute, Newton boarded in Grantham with the family of apothecary William Clarke in their apartment above his business on High Street.[5] With the eighty boys who then studied in a single classroom under headmaster Henry Stokes at King's School, he received a respectable grammar-school education which, according to the convention of the day, emphasized rudiments of Latin and theology, and contained some Greek, Hebrew, and practical arithmetic.

As a student Newton's performance was initially poor. Apparently learning by rote did not appeal to Newton. Moreover, he was somewhat of a loner and evidently had no friends among the other boys, not surprising in his sudden immersion among many boys after his earlier isolation from children. To counter loneliness Newton read. He was led to an interest in science by reading *The Mysteries of Nature and Art* by John Bates, a book that contained detailed instructions for making various machines and devices. He occupied himself with designing and building working models of various devices such as windmills. He made sundials and installed them in his quarters and flew a candle-powered, hot-air-balloon-like "kite" on dark spring nights. Such activities indicated and enhanced both manual and mental dexterity, abilities he would later use to advantage in the laboratory and in development of his theories.

As a young boy Newton showed curiosity but no signs of unusual intelligence. He seemed rather slow, being placed in the lowest form of his grade and second to last therein upon entering King's School. Newton first exerted himself academically only to challenge another boy. Walking to school one morning with other boys, Newton was kicked in the stomach by one of them. Isaac's response was two-pronged. He immediately challenged the much larger bully to a fight after school in which Newton beat him through his spirit and resolution despite his smaller size. Newton then declared that he would displace his antagonist from his superior academic standing, the larger boy who kicked him being one position above Isaac in studies. In a short time Newton rose not only one position but to the very top of his class.

Newton was taken out of school by his mother in 1658 in order to help on the farm. Hannah saw little value in education; after all, Isaac's father had been successful in managing his estate despite being illiterate. But Isaac proved to be inept at farm work. Moreover, he rebelled at every attempt of his mother to train him to manage the estate. On Saturdays when he was sent to Grantham to sell produce and buy supplies, Isaac would send a servant to the market to accomplish these tasks while he would visit the Clarke apothecary where he would spend the day in a back room reading books on science and philosophy. Headmaster Stokes, upon hearing of Newton's continued resistance to follow his mother's will, appealed to her to continue Newton's education and enlisted assistance in this effort from Isaac's uncle, William Ayscough, a graduate of Trinity College of Cambridge University, and Humphrey Babington, brother of Mrs. Clarke and a fellow at Cambridge. In the fall of 1660, Isaac was back in King's School preparing for Cambridge.

Newton at Cambridge

Newton began his studies in Trinity College at Cambridge on 5 June 1661 and graduated in the spring of 1665 without particular distinction, indeed, with only a second-class Bachelor of Arts degree (BA). Nevertheless, Newton was to stay on after graduation to obtain a Master of Arts degree (MA) and a fellowship. Before that happened, however, the University was closed for two years because of a bubonic plague epidemic in England. The University reopened in early 1667. That year Humphrey Babington was promoted to senior fellow and was one of only eight men who reported directly to the Master of Trinity in selecting new fellows. Moreover, because of the epidemic no fellowship elections occurred during 1665 and 1666. Due to promotions, retirements, and deaths by plague and otherwise, nine fellowship positions were open in 1667 out of a total of some sixty. Minor fellows received a small wage (£2 per annum), a room, use of the library, and continuing inclusion in the university community. Chastity was required and on marriage a fellow forfeited his position. Each fellow took an oath that included the phrases "I will embrace the true religion of Christ with all my soul" and "I will either set theology as the object of my studies and will take holy orders when the time prescribed by these statutes arrives, or I will resign from the college."[6] A major fellow, a position to which a fellow was automatically promoted upon receipt of an MA, could hold his position for as long as he desired, provided he committed no crimes, receiving considerably higher wages, occupying an apartment of several rooms, and studying at his leisure in pursuit of any desired scholarly accomplishment, since all studies were regarded as encompassed by theology. Fellowships only opened upon the promotion, resignation, or death of a fellow and the inflated number of nine open fellowships in 1667 was therefore fortuitous for Newton. While achievement was not considered a requirement for a fellowship, a candidate was subject to three days of oral questioning and a required paper was written on a fourth day. Newton returned to Trinity on 25 March 1667 to prepare for these exams in September. On 1 October the candidates were notified of the results and the chosen fellows were sworn the next day. Newton was among the new group of minor fellows sworn.

Newton obtained an MA in March 1668 and was promoted to major fellow. One year and a half thereafter his mathematics professor, Isaac Barrow, abdicated his position in favor of Newton and, on 29 October 1669, at age 27, Newton was appointed Lucasian Professor of Mathematics at Trinity College, Cambridge. Newton's meteoric rise was unusual, to say the least, and it occurred as a consequence incidental to Barrow's plans. In effect, Newton was appointed by Barrow. Barrow had his sights on the position of Master of Trinity and thought the position of Royal Chaplain to King Charles II would be a faster route to this goal. Barrow had a two-year tenure as the initial Lucasian Professor, a chair endowed by Henry Lucas and one of only eight endowed chairs in the university. This prestigious chair put Barrow high in the hierarchy but he wanted to be higher. Within one year after resigning his professorship Barrow was appointed royal chaplain and within three years he returned to Trinity College as master.

In 1667 Barrow had shown Newton a new book entitled *Logarithmotechnia* by mathematician Nicholas Mercator. In it Mercator had employed two expansions of a binomial into infinite series useful to calculating the values of logarithms. Newton was startled to find Mercator's independent discovery of two cases of the general binomial theorem he had derived two years earlier at Woolsthorpe, so startled he disclosed to Barrow some of his own results by drafting in Latin a paper *On Analysis by Infinite Series* which he let Barrow read and even loan to one of his friends and Royal-Society mathematics colleague John Collins. Only when Collins responded with enthusiasm about his results did Newton allow Barrow to identify him as the author. "I am glad my friends paper giveth you so much satisfaction. his name is Mr Newton; a fellow of our college, & very young ... but of an extraordinary genius and proficiency in these things."[7] Collins sent information from Newton's work on to others in Scotland, France, and Italy and asked Newton for more results. He asked him how to calculate the rate of interest on an annuity and Newton sent him the answer with the stipulation that Newton's name be withheld if Collins published it "For I see not what there is desirable in publik esteeme, were I able to aquire &

maintaine it. It would perhaps increase my acquaintence, the thing which I chiefly study to decline."[8] Collins' reaction indicates young Newton's substantial mathematical ability, developed before he obtained his BA and nearly completely unknown to others. Newton's reaction suggests a preoccupation with self.

When preparing his lectures for publication, Barrow asked Newton for help, especially in his material on optics, a field in which Newton, unbeknownst to others, was then the leading authority in the world. Barrow acknowledged Newton's assistance effusively as "a Man of great Learning and Sagacity, who revised my Copy and noted such things that wanted correction."[9]

Thus, while Newton's principal accomplishments were still unknown to anyone else, Barrow had seen enough to recognize his genius. Indeed, Isaac Barrow was the only one both capable of understanding his work and privy to some of it, enough that it was clear to Barrow that Newton, young though he be, was a loyal friend and the best choice to succeed him as Lucasian Professor at Cambridge.

As a student and scholar, Newton was a voracious reader and spent hours in deep contemplation. When his interest was engaged Newton would often forget to eat and sleep, being so engrossed in single-minded concentration on a problem. And even when he remembered to eat he would often take only a few bites while standing at his desk[10] engrossed in thought or writing. Years later, after publication of his famous book the *Principia*, Scottish mathematician John Arbuthnot while visiting France met with French mathematician the Marquis de l'Hôpital. Their discussion turned to the accomplishments of Newton. Perhaps as a result, the Marquis wondered why none of the English could demonstrate what shape a body must have to pass through a fluid with least resistance and Arbuthnot told him that Newton had included the solution of this problem in his book.

> He cried out with admiration Good god what a fund of knowledge there is in that book? he then asked the Dr every particular about Sr I. even to the colour of his hair said does he eat & drink & sleep? is he like other men?[11]

In fact, the answer was no!

Newton later attributed his ability to solve difficult problems to his habit of holding them in his mind continually (apparently for hours, days, and weeks). Newton's power of concentration evidently exceeded that of others and his position at Cambridge with its absence of undesired distraction gave him unusual advantage to develop and utilize it.

While the Cambridge of his day had shortcomings, being still under the influence of the Aristotelian tradition, it did possess a first-rate library which was the one resource necessary for development of Newton's mind. By constant reading and contemplation, Newton brought himself from an ordinary level of science and mathematics to a level of master of the most up-to-date discoveries. He read the works of Galileo and René Descartes including, in what is significant because it represents the culture Newton's innovative vision was to supplant and supercede, Descartes' arguments that material bodies may only influence one another through physical contact, proscribing "action at a distance" as an influence on motion. And from the frontier of then-available knowledge, Newton moved on into uncharted territory.

The Calculus

Newton's genius as a physicist has already been illustrated by his discovery of the nature of light. His genius as a mathematician is illustrated by his already-mentioned work on infinite series. Working with infinite series or sums of an unending list of terms was regarded as anathema in Newton's time. Descartes had warned "We should never enter into arguments about the infinite."[12] But Newton nevertheless took an interest in the sum of two quantities $(a + b)$ called a *binomial*, where a and b represent any two numbers, and he obtained a useful, general solution in the form of a series for such a binomial raised to any power n, i.e., written $(a + b)^n$, where n may be either positive or negative and either integer or non-integer. His solution, practical and easily used, is written and described in endnote 13. Newton discovered his solution, now called the *binomial theorem*, during the winter of 1664-1665 and it is a fundamental tool used frequently today throughout mathematics and science. Newton noted that in the case where one of the terms a or b is smaller than the other, while the solution may still consist of a sum of an infinite number of terms, it is only necessary to include a limited number of terms to obtain any desired accuracy.[13] Newton used this theorem to solve an important problem pertaining to gravity, one we will shortly describe, and many others.

When and how did Newton discover and establish his binomial theorem? The when has already been stated (winter of 1664-1665) and it was confirmed 50 years later when Newton reminisced

> In the beginning of the year 1665 I found the Method of approximating series and the Rule for reducing any dignity [power] of any Binomial into such a series. The same year in May I found the method of Tangents of Gregory & Slusius, & in November had the direct method of fluxions ... All this was in the two plague years of 1665-1666. For in those days I was in the prime of my age for invention & minded Mathematicks and Philosophy more then at any time since.[14]

As to the how, his method was already mentioned, namely, keeping the problem continually in his mind. Moreover, Newton already had considerable knowledge of a powerful tool, his method of fluxions, by the beginning of 1665 because by the end of that year he had the "direct" (unbroken, fully connected, complete, perfected, unimpaired) method.

Before Newton had completed his BA in April 1665, he had invented a new branch of mathematics now called *the calculus* and used it to obtain novel and important results. Infinitesimal calculus allowed precise analysis of motion, calculation of parabolas and hyperbolas and ellipses and spirals as the trajectories of moving points. He thus developed a powerful mathematical technique which supplanted the algebraic methods utilized by his predecessors, including Galileo, Kepler, and Descartes. Newton's notebooks from 1664 and early 1665 show a mastery of mathematics unrivaled by anyone of his day. By itself this accomplishment made him the greatest mathematician in Europe and he was yet merely an undergraduate student, a very unique one. But it was all then unknown to others. Twenty-seven years passed before Newton finally published his results. Nevertheless, Newton wrote "papers" for himself, three major ones in 1666. One of these, known as the "tract of October 1666," fully defined Newton's method of fluxions, today called infinitesimal or differential calculus. While Newton's graduation contained no *public* distinction, he had already *privately* demonstrated unmatched greatness as a mathematician. On this point, Newton biographer R. S. Westfall has written

> The tract of October 1666 was a virtuoso performance that would have left the mathematicians of Europe breathless with admiration, envy, and awe. As it happened, only one other mathematician in Europe, Isaac Barrow, even knew that Newton existed, and it is unlikely that in 1666 Barrow had any inkling of his accomplishment. The fact that he was unknown does not alter the other fact that the young man not yet twenty-four, without benefit of formal instruction, had become the leading mathematician in Europe and the only one who really mattered. Newton himself, understood his position clearly enough. He had studied the acknowledged masters. He knew the limits they could not surpass. He had outstripped them all, and by far.[15]

After Newton's accomplishments were known, the queen of Prussia was instructed by G. W. Leibniz in Berlin that mathematics could be divided into two halves, all its accomplishments from the beginning of the world to Newton and the part contributed by Newton, with Newton's constituting the better half. This was before the unfortunate bitter and unworthy battle between the two men over the priority of invention of the calculus. While Newton probably had considerable priority, because he hadn't published his results Leibniz independently derived them. Moreover, Leibniz contributed important innovations, including his superior notation used in the calculus today. Both names are now properly associated with the calculus.

Other later praise of Newtons' calculus and his ability to use it came from Johann Bernoulli in Holland who, upon receiving from London (where Newton then resided as Warden of the Mint) an anonymous solution to a problem which Bernoulli had published as a challenge to the "Christian world," "recognized the lion [Newton] by his claw [in-depth knowledge and authority in use of the calculus]."

Musing on Gravitation

During the plague epidemic of 1665 and 1666 with the university closed, Newton retreated to his mother's farm in Woolsthorpe. He occupied himself there with reflections and calculations. It was then he envisioned the grand theory that had eluded Kepler and Galileo, a single, comprehensive theory of how the gravitational force dictates the motion of the moon and the planets: *a universal theory of gravitation.* He later recounted (in the remaining part of an already-partially-given quotation):

> I began to think of gravity extending to the orb of the Moon & ... from Kepler's rule of the periodical times of the Planets being in sesquialterate proportion of their distances from the center of their Orbs, I deduced that the forces which keep the planets in their Orbs must [vary] reciprocally as the squares of their distances from the centers about which they revolve: & thereby compared the force requisite to keep the Moon in her Orb with the force of gravity at the surface of the earth, & found them [to] answer pretty nearly.[14]

The reciprocal square of distance or separation on which the gravity force depends was *deduced* by Newton. Others, notably Robert Hooke, had used such a dependence in calculations but they were only guessing. Newton showed that only two dependencies on separation R were compatible with the stable elliptical orbits discovered by Kepler: one a reciprocal square (i.e., $\times 1/R^2$) and the other a direct multiplication (i.e., $\times R$), with the latter eliminated using a result of Kepler.

Near the end of his life, some 50 years later, Newton recalled to several people that inspiration for his solution of the gravity problem came to him when he saw an apple fall from a tree in front of his mother's house. Newton supposed that the same force controlling the falling apple near the surface of the earth also held the moon in its orbit.

To *test* this hypothesis Newton calculated the acceleration or fall of the moon, a_m, as if it were governed by the same gravitation acting on the apple, adjusting for the moon's greater separation from the center of the earth. One critical insight, obtained through his application of the calculus, was Newton's realization that the separation from the earth's center to the apple's or moon's center was the correct separation to use. Thus, using an earth radius of 4,000 miles and a center-to-center separation of $R = 240{,}000$ miles from earth to moon (both numbers being slightly rounded for simplicity), Newton obtained a ratio of 60 as the ratio of the center-to-center earth to moon separation to center-to-center earth-to-apple separation. Squaring 60 he obtained 3,600 as the expected ratio of the acceleration of the falling apple to that of the falling moon. Newton thus reasoned that if gravitational attraction of the earth provides the acceleration causing the moon's orbit to be (nearly) circular instead of a straight line, the moon should fall toward the earth at $1/3{,}600^{th}$ the acceleration at which the apple falls. Since the apple and other bodies near the earth were known to fall at $a = 32.2$ feet per second squared, it remained only for Newton to somehow determine the fall of the moon to the earth and compare it with the fall of the apple.

What follows are calculations as Newton *could* have made them. The earth-moon system is illustrated in the following figure. In any time interval t the moon would travel distance $\omega R t$ in its natural, straight-line, inertial trajectory (horizontal line) at constant tangential velocity ωR were it not influenced by earth's gravity. The term ω (Greek "omega") represents the orbital angular velocity of the moon about the earth. Because the moon follows a circular orbit at radius R (solid curve), radial deflection δ (Greek "delta") from the straight line is caused by an inward fall or acceleration a_m. Is this acceleration the one expected due to earth's gravity, i.e., does $3{,}600 \times a_m = a = 32.2$ feet per second squared? To answer this question Newton calculated $3{,}600 \times a_m$.

Referring to the figure and to endnotes 16 and 17 we write

$$R/(R+\delta) = 1/(1+\delta/R) = 1 - \delta/R = \cos\omega t = 1 - \omega^2 t^2/2,$$

provided both δ/R and ωt are small. Neither the restriction that δ/R nor ωt be small is critical since time interval t and displacement δ are small near *any* chosen initial or zero time. Moreover, radial displacement or radial moon velocity v_{mr} is zero because moon radius R is fixed.

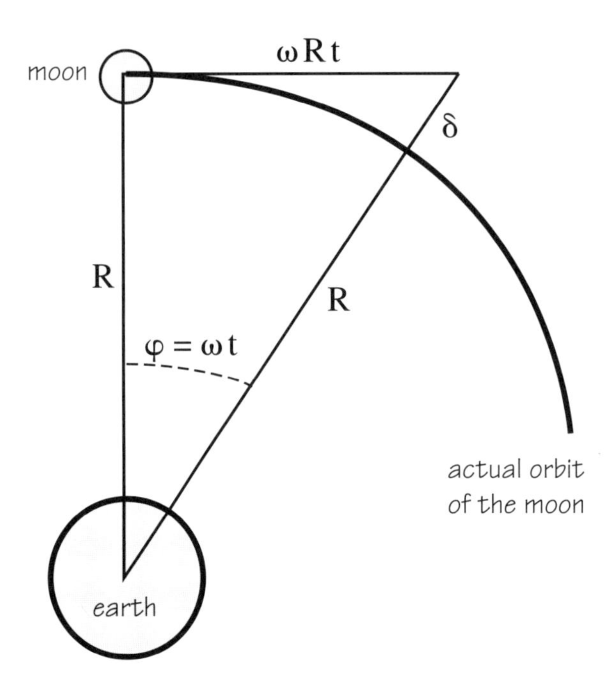

Constant tangential velocity $v_{mt} = \omega R$ and constant radial acceleration a_m must therefore occur because no distinct zero time occurs in the moon's orbital motion. Thus the moon's fall toward earth is constant and the above equations give

$$\delta = \omega^2 R t^2/2 = a_m t^2/2 \qquad \text{and} \qquad a_m = \omega^2 R.$$

The moon circles the earth circumscribing an angle of 2π radians every 27.3 days. The angular velocity of the moon is therefore $\omega = 2\pi / 27.3$ days $= 0.00000266$ radians per second or 2.66×10^{-6} radians per second while $R = 240{,}000$ miles. These values give $3{,}600 \times a_m = 3{,}600 \times \omega^2 R = 32.3$ feet per second squared, which agrees "pretty nearly" with $a = 32.2$ feet per second squared. By this kind of comparison Newton solved the problem of gravity, concluding that the earth's gravity which causes an apple to fall also causes the continuous acceleration (fall) of the moon toward the earth in its circular orbit. Newton thus concluded, by induction, that gravity is a universal law.[18]

At the time he first made the calculations in 1665-66, Newton used a radius of the earth of 3,500 miles, calculated by Galileo and nearly 500 miles too small (the currently accepted value is 3,963 miles), an error that, once it is squared, leads to a 25 percent discrepancy. He therefore set the results aside for many years. Only in 1685 as he was preparing his book *Principia* did he repeat the calculation using a more accurate earth radius of 3,950 miles, published in 1671 by French astronomer Jean Picard, to find the law to answer "pretty nearly."

Newton's Bible Studies

In later years Newton wrote his famous book, the *Principia*, refined and extended the calculus and developed analytical geometry. Although he did no further significant research in optics, his book entitled *Opticks* describing his experiments and deductions, even thirty years after his experiments, still pioneered the field. He also pursued experiments in alchemy, in which he eventually had no peer in Europe, and contemplated Biblical teachings and prophecy. His Bible research was a major effort, in which he determined that the length of a (pyramid) cubit was 25 inches, rejected the Nicene creed as contradictory to the Bible, determined a date for the crucifixion of Christ,[19] and predicted Christ's Advent at 2060 AD. Because Newton's Bible study was, like his mathematics and science, careful and exhaustive, it also deserves our attention.

Newton was a good Puritan by inclination and demeanor. But rather than an Anglican or Puritan he was an Arian in his belief. Arius, the namesake of Arianism, was a fourth-century Christian priest in Alexandria, Egypt. He taught that the Son of God was a created being, like the rest of us. Indeed as we learn from the Bible, besides being the Firstborn or First Created of all creatures, through Him all other creatures and things were created. However, the divinity of Christ is secondary to that of God the Father Who created Him.

Arianism is opposed to trinitarianism. Within the scope of our brief description, Arianism originated with Christ and the primitive church, as Newton concluded based on research to shortly be summarized. Arianism contradicted, then and now, orthodox trinitarianism held to be correct by the Roman and Anglican Churches (and virtually all Christianity). Newton had vowed to support Anglican doctrine by his signature when he received his BA, when he accepted his fellowship, and when he received his MA. Moreover, his appointment as Lucasian Professor required him to be ordained an Anglican priest within seven years. Newton delayed as long as he could and finally applied to Charles II for exemption from this requirement. He was apparently secretly supported in this request by Isaac Barrow, the former King's Chaplain and Master of Trinity College. Newton did not disclose the reason he desired exemption and only after other possible avenues closed did Newton make application to the King, delivering documents in early March 1675 on a visit to London for this purpose. In late April he received notice that exemption was granted in perpetuity for the Lucasian Professorship.

Newton was surprised his request had been granted because it broke strong, strictly-followed precedent. Moreover, the in-perpetuity nature of the royal dispensation suggested the decision was based on general considerations rather than on an individual personality and served to deflect suspicion from Newton. One sees a friendly hand behind this scene.

Meanwhile, Newton had been solidifying his thinking and began preparations to defend his position were he to so decide. He carefully investigated the Bible and early Christian belief, especially pertaining to the relationship of the Father and the Son. He posed a specific question: What does the Bible teach regarding the Holy Trinity? Newton engaged this project with his characteristic, single-minded dedication and passion, his study quickly becoming a comprehensive study of early Christian history, writing, and thought. He examined and analyzed a broad range of evidence in great depth, as indicated by the quotations to follow, and deduced his answers. He identified what he regarded as two major flaws in orthodox trinitarianism. First, trinitarianism is repeatedly contradicted in many Bible passages. As he delved further into the anomalies of conflict relating to this issue he reached an even more dramatic and consequential conclusion to be stated shortly together with evidence he considered.

Second, Newton found trinitarianism to be counter-logical. He recognized the virgin birth, turning water into wine, healing by a touch, and the resurrection were all miracles and, as such, were not understood. But to Newton these did not defy logic and there was no confusion in the Biblical descriptions of them. To Newton, One equaling Three and Three equaling One did defy logic, especially with so much contradiction between it and Biblical texts and other early writings.

Newton decided trinitarianism was an institutionalized mistake and searched for its origin. He found the origin in the radical and revolutionary decision of the Council of Nicaea in Bithynia, convened by the Roman Emperor Constantine in 325 AD beginning on 20 May and ending on 25 July.

Because of its location in Asia Minor, the West was largely unrepresented. While the objective of this council had been to bring peace and unity to the church by clarifying ambiguities in Christian doctrine, it was instead a forum for dispute between Arius and the young deacon Athanasius, later bishop of Alexandria. The council was sharply divided on the question of the true nature of God but it nevertheless decided by majority vote to ratify and certify a compromise creed proposed by the unbaptized emperor. Trinitarianism, the new Christian orthodoxy, became correct doctrine because it was *proposed by Constantine*. In it he combined the Caesarian creed and Alexandrian passwords. It is the Nicene or Athanasian creed which is the basis for orthodox Christian belief today regarding the nature of God. To counter what some considered inflated claims by Arius about the nature and station of Christ, the new creed was excessive in the other direction.

"Constantine had no understanding of the questions at issue" and was probably quite unaware his compromise creed was "virtually the proclamation of a new doctrine" leading to "an arduous path of theological work" to bring the church "into compliance with those principles enunciated at Nicaea." Instead of bringing peace and unity, the council itself was sharply divided and the dispute spilled beyond the council and continued for decades. Christian bishops in different synods cursed one another and a passionate and bloody conflict raged between followers of Arius against followers of Athanasius. Such an "artificial unity was no ratification of peace; in fact, it paved the way for a struggle which convulsed the whole empire."[20] This method of attempted pacification of the church, in effect a decree by a king focused on his worldly kingdom, was unsuccessful as is clearly intimated that it would be in the Bible. Christ, not any worldly power, established and owns Christianity. Anyone who might doubt His authority should note that the Bible teaches we are all His creatures and that He created heaven and earth as well as Christianity in its original form.

The contention and strife over the nature of God continued until church officials finally caused the Arian view to be outlawed by majority vote in 381 AD. (Yet, even in Newton's day, some preferred this belief to Christian orthodoxy.) In that year Emperor Theodosius convened the Council of Constantinople at which Arianism was officially and finally outlawed. Previously, only the pope and a few bishops among Western Christians accepted trinitarianism or Athanasianism. Today it is the orthodox view, with slight variations, among almost all Christians.

In fact, what is today called the Nicene creed is any of several descendents of earlier versions. It has been changed over the centuries following its "official" approval. St. Augustine (354-430 AD), among many later individuals, appears to have altered it. It is widely used today in Western liturgies in many forms, all generically called Nicene.

Newton had long been an avid student of the Bible with interest extending beyond merely the academic. Newton owned and read Bibles in Latin, Greek, Hebrew, French, and probably English.[21] John Locke, himself a noted scholar and celebrated philosopher, was amazed at the depth of knowledge of the Bible Newton exhibited in their discussion of the Bible and theology. In this discussion Newton told Locke "There cannot be a better service done to the truth then to purge it of things spurious."[22] Newton believed what he read in the Bible, except where his suspicion was aroused by confused or inconsistent text or description – possible spurious teachings.

Newton's study of the Bible struck directly to the heart of Christianity, questions of belief and behavior (what we called "faith and morals" in the previous chapter). He regarded such study as his duty. In belief, the subjects that captured his greatest interest were the relation of God and Christ, Father and Son, and, especially, *De Trinitate* or of the Trinity. In seeking answers he researched and wrote, multiple times, the history of Christianity. His interpretation of the Bible was literal and he was particularly fascinated with prophecy. Newton calculated many times when the Second Coming or Advent of Christ would occur, at which he believed a Restoration of original (primitive), uncorrupted Christianity would also occur. In scope, Newton studied what amounts to the history and philosophy of religious belief in and derived from early Christianity. He found and digested the writings of the "fathers" of the early church, martyrs and saints, Athanasius, Arius, Origen who wrote *Hexapla*, Eusebius of Caesarea, Epiphanius of Constantia, and dozens of others.[23] "Newton set himself the task of mastering the whole corpus of patristic literature. ... There was no single patristic writer of importance whose words he did not devour. And always, his eye was on the allied problems of the nature of Christ and the nature of God."[24] He finally focused on the confusion and controversy concentrated in the fourth century AD, centered in Nicaea and Constantinople and in Constantine and Theodosius.

The Trinity was regarded as a mystery because it was not understood. But why was it not understood? Through his studies and thinking Newton eventually reached the conclusion that the reason it was not understood was

> that a massive fraud, which began in the fourth and fifth centuries, had perverted the legacy of the early church. Central to the fraud were the Scriptures, which Newton began to believe had been corrupted to support trinitarianism. ... [His] original notes themselves testify to early doubts. ... [He wrote] "For there are three that bear record in heaven, the Father, the Word, and the Holy Ghost: and these three are one." Such is the wording of 1 John 5:7, which he read in his Bible. "It is not thus read in the Syrian Bible," Newton discovered. "[Nor] by Ignatius, Justin, Irenaeus, Tertull, Origen, Athanus, Nazianzen Didym Chrysostom, Hilarius, Augustine, Beda, and others. Perhaps Jerome is the first who reads it thus." "And without controversy great is the mystery of godliness: God was manifest in the flesh ..." Thus [reads] 1 Timothy 3:16, in the orthodox version. The word *God* is obviously critical to the usefulness of the verse to support trinitarianism. Newton found that early versions did not contain the word [God] but read only, "great is the mystery of godliness which was manifested in the flesh." "Furthermore in the fourth and fifth centuries," he noted, "this place was not cited against the Arians."
>
> The corruptions of Scripture came relatively late. The earlier corruption of doctrine, which called for the corruption of Scripture to support it, occurred in the fourth century, when the triumph of Athanasius over Arius imposed the false doctrine of the trinity on Christianity.[25]

Newton discovered many other Bible passages that contradict trinitarianism in its corrupted understanding of the relationship of the Father and the Son. He noted from Hebrews 1:8-9, which says that God set Christ on His right hand, called Him God, and told Him that because he had loved righteousness "therefore God, even thy God, hath anointed thee with the oil of gladness above thy fellows." Newton wrote a marginal note at the two words he had underlined: "Therefore the Father is God of the Son [when the Son is considered] as God."[26] In later entries Newton expanded and strengthened the implication. (In the following read "the" for "y^e^.")

> Concerning the subordination of Christ see Acts 2.33.36. Phil 2.9.10. 1 Pet 1.21. John 12.44. Rom 1.8 & 16.27. Acts 10.38 & 2.22. 1 Cor 3.23, & 15.24, 28.. & 11.3. 2 Cor. 22, 23. ...
>
> There is one God and one Mediator between God and Man ye Man Christ Jesus. 1 Tim. 2.5.
>
> The head of every man is Christ, & ye head of ye woman is ye man, & the head of Christ is God. 1 Cor. 11.3.
>
> He shall be great and shall be called ye son of ye most high. Luke 1.32.[27]

As an explicit foundation of orthodox trinitarianism in the Bible, its believers cited the already-mentioned passage 1 John 5:7 that states "For there are three that bear record in heaven, the Father, the Word, and the Holy Ghost: and these three are one." Newton noted that only the orthodox King James version of the Bible contained the last phrase.

Newton reacted strongly to these discoveries, possibly because of feelings of betrayal.

> In his reading notes and "articles" and "points" and "observations'" his "Short Schem of the True Religion" and his analysis of prophecies and revelations, he raged against the blasphemers. He called them fornicators – for he associated this special blasphemy with lust. "Seducers waxing worse and worse," he wrote, "deceiving and being deceived – such as will not endure sound doctrine but after

their own lusts heap to themselves teachers, having itching ears and turning away their ears from the truth. ..." He felt trinitarianism not just as error but as sin, and the sin was idolatry.[28]

Newton's critical reading persuaded him that the original texts had been deliberately debased in support of false doctrine – a false infernal religion.[29]

He discussed some of his theological views with John Locke, saying he placed his trust in Locke's "prudence and calmness of temper" because Newton would have been instantly dismissed from his university positions had his beliefs become known.

He may have presented some of the results of his Bible studies in his lectures (but certainly excepting his conclusion about the Nicene creed and trinitarianism), but apparently neither faculty nor student who attended could understand him, whether he lectured on mathematics, physics, alchemy, or the Bible, because the hall was usually nearly or wholly empty when he was to lecture.

Newton, Halley, and the *Principia*

Because of his knowledge of optics and his skill in building devices, Newton both knew how and had the full scope of skills necessary to build a reflecting telescope that avoided a major problem of the best ones of the day, one using a reflecting mirror rather than a refracting lens. Although it was not the motivation for his invention, he eliminated *chromatic aberration* (due to light of different colors refracting differently in passing through a prism or lens giving, in the last case, a color dependent focal length) that obscured the image of any multicolored object such as a star or planet. Indeed, Newton may then have been one of few in understanding that white light by which stars and planets are viewed contained many colors. The small reflecting telescope Newton built was only six inches long. Newton himself ground the spherical mirror that gave it a magnification of nearly 40 diameters. A refracting telescope with comparable magnification would require a length of over six feet. It was to become the most popular type of telescope in the world.

Newton must have shown it to others at Cambridge because, while information about his mathematics had been closely controlled, news of his telescope quickly spread. Members of the Royal Society asked to see it and at the end of 1671 Barrow, a member of the society, delivered it for Newton and it caused quite a sensation.

The next month, January 1672, Newton received correspondence from Henry Oldenburg, secretary of the Society. (Read Old English S^r as "Sir" and y^e as "the.")

S^r

Your Ingenuity is the occasion of this addresse by hand unknowne to you. You have been so generous, as to impart to the Philosophers here, your invention of contracting Telescopes [making telescopes smaller]. It having been considered, and examined here by some of ye most eminent in Opticall Science and practise, and applauded by them, they think it necessary to use some meanes to secure the Invention from ye Usurpation of forreiners; And therefore have taken care to represent by a scheme

> that first Specimen, sent hither by you, and to describe all ye parts of ye Instrumemnt, together wth its effect, compared wth an ordinary, but much larger, Glasse; ... But yet it was not thought fit to send this away wthout first giving you notice of it, and sending to you ye very figure and description, as it was here drawne up; y^{t} so you might adde, & alter, as you shall see cause; wch being done here wth, I shall desire your favour of returning it to me wth all convenient speed, together wth such alterations, as you shall think fit to make therein ...
>
> S^{r}
> your humble servant
> Oldenburg[30]

With the invention of his reflecting telescope Newton became known to the scientists of his day and was elected a member of the Royal Society. In particular, he became known to the astronomer Edmond Halley (1656-1742) who was to play an important role in publishing Newton's book, the *Principia*.

Robert Hooke (1635-1703), while involved in the evaluation of Newton's telescope for the Royal Society observed the interest of other members, claimed that he had in 1664 constructed a more powerful telescope just one-inch in length but did not bother to pursue it because of the plague and fire. Hooke's fanciful claim was not mentioned in the *Philosophical Transactions* article composed by Oldenburg.[31]

Halley's interest in Newton was motivated not by telescopes but by the hope that Newton could establish pattern and organization among the facts and derive an equation or law that described this pattern. An event that may be regarded as the genesis of their interaction that was to lead to Newton's book was a London-coffee-house meeting in January 1684 of three members of the Royal Society of London – Halley, Christopher Wren (1632-1723), and Hooke.

The Royal Society had been formed by a small group of men in 1662 to promote natural philosophy by collecting and circulating information thereon. These men worried that philosophy "had mired itself in its own florid eloquence. They sought 'not the Artifice of words, but a bare knowledge of things.' ... when possible this meant the language of mathematics."[32] Henry Oldenburg, a master of languages, was the Society's first secretary. He started the Society's journal, *Philosophical Transactions of the Royal Society*, in 1665, originally a news sheet which he sent by post and diplomatic couriers he knew personally. From these same diplomatic couriers he also received news.

Wren was a past president of the Royal Society, the architect of St. Paul's Cathedral, a physicist, astronomer, and geometrician. Hooke was the Society's Curator of Experiments and an able and productive physicist who contributed many discoveries.[33] Halley was only twenty-seven, a full generation behind his companions, but was already recognized for astronomical charts of the southern skies he prepared on the Island of St. Helena in the southern Atlantic in 1677. There, far from the equator, he also noted that his pendulum clock ran slower than in London, but he did not note how much slower. Halley would distinguish himself by many accomplishments including correctly predicting that the comet that now bears his name would periodically return to our view in its elongated orbit about the sun.

Wren, Hooke, and Halley discussed the possibility that an inverse-square-separation law of gravity could explain Kepler's discovery of elliptical planetary orbits as well as other laws of celestial mechanics. However, no one had yet been able to derive from known facts that gravitational attraction depended on the inverse square of the separation or to mathematically demonstrate that elliptical orbits resulted. Hooke vainly claimed that he knew a proof but preferred not to reveal it so that when others had tried and failed to find such a proof they would appreciate the value of his accomplishment. Wren "called his bluff" by offering as a reward to Hooke or Halley a valuable book if either could produce a proof before the end of two months time, a proof Wren had been unable to produce. Hooke quickly accepted the challenge, but provided no proof. Halley also tried, unsuccessfully, and thereafter continued to ponder the problem.

Halley had met Newton two years earlier when Newton had asked Halley for orbital data on the great comet observed in 1680 and he realized that Newton might solve this problem. So on an August-1684 visit to Cambridge, Halley called on Newton. Halley asked Newton what shape the orbits of the planets would take if gravity held them in their orbits by an inverse-square-separation force law? "An ellipse" answered Newton immediately. Halley, showing "joy and amazement," as Newton later recalled, inquired how Newton knew this result was correct. Newton answered that he had derived (calculated) it. Halley requested to see the derivation. Newton looked through many papers, stacks of papers were profuse in his quarters, but could not find it. He promised to send Halley a newly-written copy.

Five years earlier, when he returned to Cambridge from a one-year leave to tend his mother and then settle affairs after her death, Newton had derived the elliptical orbit. During this stay in Woolsthorpe he apparently returned to the study of universal gravitation he had long ignored. This time his interest endured longer because he was motivated by an antagonist – Robert Hooke. Hooke had earlier written Newton to engage him in scientific discussion and explained some ideas on motion under gravitational attraction. Newton had declined the invitation of further correspondence, but had shared a result he had calculated, namely the trajectory of an object dropped from a tower and thus falling toward a rotating, gravitationally-attracting earth. He described the object as falling along a path given by a spiral. To his chagrin, Newton had made an error which Hooke corrected in a reply, pointing out the path would be given by an ellipse. Although Hooke had promised to keep private any information shared, he presented Newton's erroneous result together with his own correction at a meeting of the Royal Society, making Newton look foolish and himself clever. Consequently, Newton carefully studied the problem of gravity and demonstrated that gravity force, with its inverse square dependence on separation, correctly accounted for the elliptical orbits of the planets. Then, satisfied, he set his results aside without making them known. It was this demonstration he referred to and sought during Halley's visit.

However, he now found this demonstration also contained an error. But, because of his promise to Halley, Newton corrected the error and, in November of 1684, sent Halley a paper in which *all three* of Kepler's laws of planetary motion were derived utilizing a universal gravitational force obeying an inverse square separation dependence. Halley immediately recognized the importance of Newton's accomplishment and convinced Newton to publish his methods and results relating gravity and the dynamics (mechanics) of the solar system. Newton began the writing of the *Principia* in March 1686 upon returning to his work.[34] Characteristically, this project became a passion to which all his attention was devoted. He delivered the finished manuscript to Halley in three books or parts. The first, *De Motu Corporum,* was received by the Royal Society (Halley) on 28 April 1686 and collected together material from his earlier writings. The second followed. Then Newton proposed that the third part be suppressed because of contention over groundless claims of priority by Hooke, which drove Newton to write "Philosophy is such an impertinently litigious lady that a man had as good be engaged in lawsuits as have to do with her."[35] Halley was able to dissuade Newton from this design and the third part, *De Systemate Mundi* or, as Galileo had also called it, *The System of the World* was presented to the Royal Society on 6 September 1687. The complete book, printed in midsummer 1687 (before the Society had officially received the third part), was Newton's masterpiece: *Philosophiae naturalis principia mathematica* or *Mathematical Principles of Natural Philosophy*, known universally now simply as Newton's *Principia.* Parts I and II address forces on bodies and their resulting motions. Part III addresses applications.

Like other great works, Newton's *Principia* provides deep insight, its style is confident, and the development of the content seems to the reader to be inevitable. With this work science and philosophy parted ways. Newton had removed metaphysics from physics and set a new standard of rigor and accuracy for scientific explanation and prediction.

While this 550 page masterpiece required only eighteen months to compose, it was based on intense, focused work accomplished by Newton alone spanning a period of over twenty years. Newton achieved a full unification of the mechanics of Galileo and Kepler, a problem, as noted by Michael White,[36] comparable to today's problem of unifying relativity (Chapter 8) and quantum mechanics (Chapter 9), a task yet unsuccessfully addressed although it has been considered by hundreds of theoretical physicists and mathematicians over the last eighty years.

Newton's Laws of Motion and Universal Gravitation

In the *Principia*, Newton provides three general laws that govern the motion of any body under any conditions. In these laws Newton invented and used a quantity called *mass.* Because of mass, a body possesses *inertia* – the resistance of a body to any change in its motion. Thus, Newton's *first law* states (upon translation from Latin to English): "Every body continues in its state of rest, or of uniform motion in a straight line, unless it is compelled to change that state by forces impressed on it." By this first law a force is required to set a body in motion or to change the motion of a moving body.

Newton provides in his second law the relationship between an *applied force* **F** and the changing motion of the body, represented by its *acceleration* **a**. He phrased the *second law* as follows (translated from Latin to English): "The change of motion [acceleration] is proportional to the motive [applied] force impressed; and is made in the direction of the straight line in which that force is impressed." For a body of constant mass m, the second law may be represented by the equation:

$$\mathbf{F} = m\mathbf{a}.$$

The second law involves not only a relationship of magnitudes but also of directions. In the modern notation used here, adopted since Newton's time, the boldface type indicates quantities **F** and **a** are *vectors*, quantities possessing both magnitude and direction. A vector equation, like this one, indicates both equal *magnitude* and equal *direction* as well. Newton's second law states that an applied force on a body and the resulting acceleration of the body times the mass of the body are equal in magnitude and directed along a common straight line.

To preserve balance, Newton's *third law* states (after translation): "To every action there is always opposed an equal reaction: or, the mutual actions of two bodies upon each other are always equal, and directed to contrary parts [in opposite directions]."

Applying the second law to a simple body at rest or in uniform motion (and utilizing the third law as well in the case of a complex body) one obtains the first law, which is therefore not independent of the others. However, inefficiency in exposition is compensated by conceptual introduction provided by the first law.

These fundamental laws together with Newton's law of universal gravitation provide a complete rational basis for all mechanics then known. Newton's law of universal gravitation may be stated (upon translation): "Every particle of matter attracts every other particle with a force which is directly proportional to the product of the masses of the particles and inversely proportional to the square of the distance [separation] between them." Mathematically, the law is expressed in terms of a mutual force of attraction F_{12} between body 1 and body 2, their centers-of-mass separation r_{12} and the product of their masses m_1m_2 as follows:

$$F_{12} = -G\,m_1\,m_2/r_{12}^{2}.$$

In this equation, constant G is the universal gravitational constant.[37] While every force is strictly a vector quantity, the direction of the force F_{12} is specified as being in the direction along the line connecting the centers-of-mass of the two bodies. And it is always attractive (negative). With these conditions understood, F_{12} may be treated as a *scalar*, i.e., possessing only a (negative) magnitude, with F_{12} not represented as a vector by boldface type.

Thus, in the *Principia*, Newton presented the basis for description of the entirety of mechanics observed in the solar system, including balls rolling down inclined planes, orbits of planets, the moon, Halley's comet, and the tides. The last phenomenon, the tides, arises from the mutuality of gravitation. Galileo (and others) failed to grasp the basic cause of the tides as being directly due to gravity. Galileo thought they were due to sloshing because of influence of the combined rotation and orbital motion of the earth, like water in a tank sloshing when the tank is accelerated. But Newton correctly stated that the sun not only attracts the earth and the earth not only attracts the moon, but the moon attracts the earth and the earth attracts the sun. Water has mass and experiences a portion of these attractions according to the law of gravity. And since water flows under the action of a force, the symmetrical solar and lunar tides occur as bulges in the oceans on their respective sides of the earth.

Newton calculated the shape of the earth, not a sphere but an oblate spheroid because it bulges around the equator due to centrifugal force caused by the earth's rotation. Indeed, Newton showed that the precession of the rotational axis of the earth as measured against the distant starry background was due to attraction of the sun and moon to this equatorial bulge. This slow precession – approximately one degree every 72 years – was the most mysterious of the earth's known motions, a motion that no one had previously even pretended to explain, but Newton predicted it exactly in his *Principia*.

Also observed but not understood until Newton's book properly described it was the influence of Jupiter, which contains ninety percent of the total planetary mass, on the motion of planets near it. Jupiter perturbs the orbit of Saturn sufficiently that this perturbation had been observed by astronomers who did not recognize its cause.

Newton's laws provided the key to correctly describing all motion observable in his day, whether on an extraterrestrial or a minute scale. It still provides a consistent rationalization of the motions of all bodies in our solar system with the exceptions of (1) the slight excess precession of the orbit of Mercury which is only correctly predicted by relativity and (2) the motions of atomic- and subatomic-scale systems for which quantum mechanics (including relativistic theory) is required.

Halley had Newton's *Principia* published by personally paying the costs, necessary because of the bleak economic situation of the *Royal Society*. The *Principia* appeared in July 1687 in an edition of 300 to 400 copies, 60 of which Halley sent to Newton in Cambridge with 40 of these to be placed with local booksellers. The *Principia* is difficult to read, but Halley promoted it tirelessly; writing himself a review of it which appeared in the *Philosophical Transactions of the Royal Society*.

The *Principia* was, of course, a huge success as a scholarly work, but not economically. Nevertheless, Halley recovered his money and even made a small profit. Little time was required for it to be fully accepted in the British Kingdom and Continental Europe. It has been described as the most significant work ever published, bar none, and its author has been described as the most intelligent man in history. I would differ with both assessments, particularly the latter, as I have already described my belief that Christ *is* the most intelligent of all persons.[38] But Newton's *Principia* with its invaluable set of universal laws governing motion and extensive, detailed, and exact applications that resolve ancient mysteries is a truly remarkable accomplishment demonstrating that Newton was an extraordinary genius. And beyond being a genius of highest order, Newton was the leading scholar of his age or possibly of any since in science, mathematics, alchemy, and in Bible and Christian history.

Newton's accomplishments were recognized in 1695 when he was appointed Warden of the Mint and, though he took up residence in the Tower of London, he retained his rooms, fellowship, and professorship at Cambridge. Four years later he was appointed Master of the Mint and shortly thereafter resigned his appointments at Cambridge. He was elected president of the Royal Society in 1703, a position to which he was annually reelected for the remainder of his life. He was also elected one of only eight foreign associates of the French Academy of Science. In 1705 he was knighted by Queen Ann at Cambridge and upon his death on 20 March 1727 he was buried in Westminster abbey.

Notes and References for Chapter 7.

[1] Jauch, J. M., *Are Quanta Real?,* Indiana University Press, Bloomington, IN, 1973.

[2] It is because of the large number of possible theories and laws that simple induction by itself is inadequate. And it was this difficulty in science that Urban VIII urged Galileo to include in his book (Chapter 6).

[3] Townes, Charles H., *How the Laser Happened,* Oxford University Press, Oxford, 1999, 190.

[4] Ibid., 65.

[5] Details here and hereafter are taken from Gleick, James, *Isaac Newton,* Advance Reader's Edition, Pantheon Books, New York, 2003, 13, from Westfall, Richard S., *The Life of Isaac Newton,* Canto Edition, Cambridge University Press, 1994, from White, Michael, *Isaac Newton, The Last Sorcerer,* Perseus Books, Reading, MA, 1997, and from Ferris, Timothy, *Coming of Age in the Milky Way,* William Morrow, New York, 1988, Chapter 6.

[6] Westfall, loc. cit., 62.

[7] Westfall, loc. cit., 68.

[8] Westfall, loc. cit., 77.

[9] Gleick, loc. cit., 68.

[10] Gleick, loc. cit., 120.

[11] MS 130.5 of the John Maynard Keynes Collection in King's College, Cambridge. This anecdote is taken from John Conduitt, husband of Newton's niece, who attempted a biography of Newton and collected much material. Quoted in Westfall, loc. cit., 193.

[12] Quoted in Gleick, loc. cit., 38.

[13] In modern notation the binomial theorem is written

$$(a+b)^n = a^n(1+b/a)^n = a^n + n/1!\,a^{n-1}b + n(n-1)/2!\,a^{n-2}b^2 + n(n-1)(n-2)/3!\,a^{n-3}b^3 + \ldots$$
$$= a^n\{1 + n/1!\,(b/a) + n(n-1)/2!\,(b/a)^2 + n(n-1)(n-2)/3!\,(b/a)^3 + \ldots\}$$

where for nonnegative integer m the quantity m! is called "m factorial" and is defined by $m! = m \times (m-1) \times (m-2) \times \ldots \times 2 \times 1$. For instance, if m = 4, $m! = 4 \times 3 \times 2 \times 1 = 24$. By definition, 0! = 1! = 1. When n is a positive integer, the series sum contains $n + 1$ terms. When n is non-integer or negative, the series is infinite, i.e., the list of terms to be added is unending.

Consider the example wherein $b/a = 0.02$ and $n = -1$. Newton's binomial theorem gives

$$a^n(1+b/a)^n = a^n\{1 - (b/a) + (b/a)^2 - (b/a)^3/2 + \ldots\}$$
$$= 1/a\,\{1 - 0.02 + 0.0004 - 0.000004 + \ldots\} = 0.980396\ldots/a$$

with only four terms required to provide six-digit accuracy regardless of the value of *a*. When *b*/*a* is smaller still, terms beyond the first two become increasingly negligible and only the first two terms are significant and need be considered to adequately approximate the infinite series.

[14] Westfall, loc. cit., 39.

[15] Westfall, loc. cit., 45.

[16] The cosine function of angle θ, denoted cos θ, may be defined in several ways. A common way utilizes a right triangle (any triangle containing a "right" or 90 degree angle opposite side *c*) with angle θ shown in the figure below. Quantity $\cos\theta = a/c$, the ratio of triangle-side lengths shown, $\sin\theta = b/c$, and $\tan\theta = \sin\theta / \cos\theta = b/a$. These three functions are known respectively as the cosine, sine and tangent functions. By the *Pythagorean theorem*, $a^2 + b^2 = c^2$ for any right triangle which gives $(a/c)^2 + (b/c)^2 = 1$ or $\sin^2\theta + \cos^2\theta = 1$. Angle θ is generally expressed in radians but also commonly expressed in degrees, with the conversion factor from radians to degrees being $180/\pi = 57.2958$ degrees per radian. Calculator values of sin θ, cos θ and tan θ are given for θ in degrees or radians.

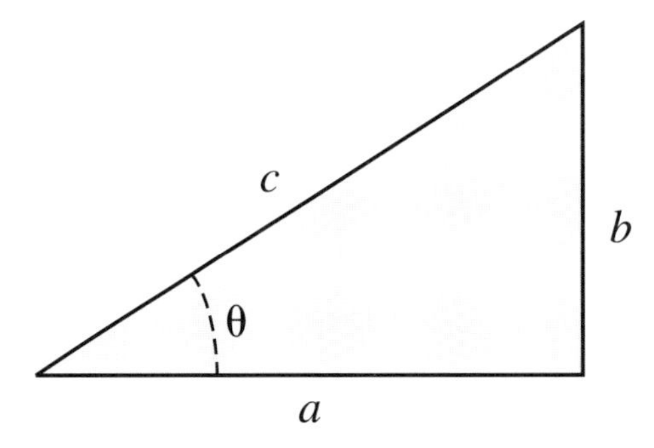

Useful *expansions* for cos θ and sin θ, with θ in radians, are

$$\cos\theta = 1 - \theta^2/2! + \theta^4/4! - \theta^6/6! + \ldots,$$

and

$$\sin\theta = \theta - \theta^3/3! + \theta^5/5! - \theta^7/7! + \ldots$$

with *n factorial* $n! = n\times(n-1)\times(n-2)\times\ldots\times3\times2\times1$ and as further described in endnote 13. When θ in radians is small compared to one, only the first term or two of the series for either cos θ or sin θ is required to obtain adequate accuracy.

[17] The following equation is obtained directly from Newton's binomial theorem (note 13).

$$1/(1+\delta/R) = (1+\delta/R)^{-1} = 1 - \delta/R + (\delta/R)^2 - (\delta/R)^3 + \ldots$$

When δ/R is much smaller than one, $1/(1+\delta/R) = 1 - \delta/R$.

[18] We present here an alternative derivation that verifies $3{,}600\times a_m$ as "pretty nearly" equal to a. The outward centrifugal force on the moon in its circular orbit about the earth at radius R and angular velocity ω is $m\,\omega^2 R$, with m the mass of the moon. For a stable orbit, this force must be balanced by an equal, inward gravitational attraction **F** and, since **F** = m**a**, $|\mathbf{a}| = \omega^2 R = v_{mt}^2/R$ must be the magnitude of the inward, radial acceleration due to gravity. In his notebook of 1664 Newton had already derived the centrifugal acceleration to be v_{mt}^2/R. Even without a knowledge of **F** = m**a** or the nature of the gravitational force, Newton may have deduced the value of $3600\times a_m$ from this result. Such hindsight is always clear after the correct answer has already been derived.

[19] See Pratt, John P., "Newton's Date for the Crucifixion," *Quarterly Journal of Royal Astronomical Society* **32**, 1991, 31-34 (available on www.johnpratt.com).

[20] This summary is paraphrased from the *Encyclopædia Britannica* and White, loc. cit., 149-153. The quotations are taken from the former source.

[21] Gleick, loc. cit., 106-107.

[22] Gleick, loc. cit., 142. *Doctrine and Covenants* 123:7-9, 11-14 addresses this same issue.

[23] Gleick, loc. cit., 106-107. Many of these other authors are listed by Westfall, loc. cit., 122.

[24] Westfall, loc. cit., 122.

[25] Westfall, loc. cit., 122. Appendix I quotes material from the Book of Mormon that indicates the same conclusion.

[26] Westfall, loc. cit., 121.

[27] Westfall, loc. cit., 121.

[28] Gleick, loc. cit., 110. In this quote Gleick quotes Westfall, Richard S., "Newton's Theological Manuscripts," in Zev Bechler (editor), *Contemporary Newtonian Research,* D. Reidel, Dordrecht, The Netherlands, 1982, 132.

[29] Gleick, loc. cit., 107. Gleick notes that "Scholars agree that no ancient Greek texts include the phrase *these three are one*."

[30] Westfall, loc. cit., 82-83.

[31] Gleick, loc. cit., 76.

[32] Gleick, loc. cit., 71.

[33] The Royal Society of London sponsored a conference on 7-9 July 2003 that marked the tercentenary of the death of Robert Hooke. The speakers covered many of Hooke's diverse scientific contributions. The 58-page keynote address by Michael Nauenberg is available at http://mike.ucsc.edu/~michael/hooke5.pdf. Other sites present brief historical summaries of the life of Hooke and his contributions. Two of these other sites are http://www. ucmp.berkeley.edu/history/hooke.html and http://www.rod.beavon.clara.net/robert _hooke.htm. The former of these two begins "No portrait survives of Robert Hooke. His name is somewhat obscure today, due in part to the enmity of his famous, influential and extremely vindictive colleague, Sir Isaac Newton. Yet Hooke was perhaps the single greatest experimental scientist of the seventeenth century." The references to Hooke cited in this chapter are taken from books on Newton, Hooke's famous, influential and vindictive colleague, drawing from Newton's opinions, writings, acts, and attitudes. But every story has at least two sides and we have not told Hooke's. It was Newton who had a propensity for conflict as demonstrated with both Hooke and Leibniz. While our comments about Hooke in this chapter truly represent the common record as told in documents by or about Newton, this common record probably needs to be corrected, perhaps substantially, to present a fair account of both men.

[34] The year 1685 was unsettling to Newton. Apparently the only thing that could penetrate Newton's famous powers of concentration was a threat to the order, stability, and intellectual freedom enjoyed at Cambridge. At the death of King Charles II in February 1685, his brother James II succeeded him as king. The unpopular James was headstrong and it was feared that he would attempt conversion of the country to Catholicism, with the Catholic monarchism of France then presenting a horrible vision of possible consequences. In 1687 James was thwarted in his

attempt to force admission of a Benedictine monk into the university as a Master of Arts without taking required oaths of allegiance and supremacy. Newton was a principal resistance leader and his effort and success led to his election to parliament in 1689 as representative of the university. He was reelected in 1701 but never played any prominent role in politics.

[35] *The Correspondence of Isaac Newton,* Volume 3, H. Turnbull (editor), Cambridge University Press, Cambridge, England, 1961, 435-437. This citation gives not only the quotation but reveals the circumstances of it. See also White, loc. cit., 218-221.

[36] White, Michael, loc. cit., 216.

[37] The value of the universal gravitational constant G is obtained today by equating the inertial and gravitational forces given by Newton's laws to obtain

$$F = m_1 a = G m_1 m_2 / r_{12}^2.$$

by which $a = m_2\, G / r_{12}^2$ after m_1 is divided out. Near the earth's surface, the acceleration of gravity $a = 9.8067$ m/sec^2 and the radius of the earth is $r_{12} = R_e = 6{,}376$ km. The mass of the earth is $m_2 = m_e = 5.980 \times 10^{24}$ kg. Thus, $G = a\, R_e^2 / m_e = 6.67 \times 10^{-11}$ m^3/kg sec^2.

Of course, neither m_e nor R_e were accurately known in the late seventeenth century. But by 1798 Sir Henry Cavendish had succeeded in accurately measuring the gravitational attraction between two small bodies of known mass and separation, from which the value of G was determined. It was, in fact, such a value of G and measured values of a and R_e that provided a value of m_e.

As is usual with a powerful new theory, previously unrecognized relationships between the facts were revealed by Newton's laws and many quantities could be calculated for the first time. In this case the quantities included the orbits of the planets and other heavenly bodies, the motions of any body of known mass subjected to known force, and the mass of the earth. And Newton's *Principia* contained much more. Quite a harvest for one theory! The measure of the harvest provides the measure of the theory and, accordingly, Newtonian theory including Newton's universal law of gravity described in the *Principia* ranks at the highest level. No other single work has revealed so much about the physical nature of the universe.

An excellent paper by C. D. Hoyle, *et al*, describing modern experimental and theoretical research on gravitation may be accessed at http://arxiv.org/abs/hep-ph/0405262. Professor Hoyle has informed me that this article is submitted for publication in *Physical Review D.*

[38] *Doctrine and Covenants* 93:36 and *Pearl of Great Price,* Abraham 3:19. The former verse reads "The glory of God is intelligence, or, in other words, light and truth."

The latter reads "And the Lord said unto me: These two facts do exist, that there are two spirits, one being more intelligent than the other; there shall be another more intelligent than they; I am the Lord thy God, I am more intelligent than they all."

8. Science and the Search for Truth: Albert Einstein

Newtonian mechanics has served mankind well for over 300 years and continues to do so as the "workhorse" theory of mechanics used in everyday calculations. It has thereby become a fundamental element of our culture. As an undergraduate, mechanical-engineering student I learned Newtonian mechanics. Only later as a graduate student did I study quantum mechanics and special relativity. In the common culture of today, Newtonian mechanics is the paradigm or philosophy or vision of reality by which we generally envision and relate motions and forces. Although superior theories of mechanics have now been discovered and are required to correct Newtonian-theory predictions in certain circumstances, predictions of the new theories are often regarded as strange, indicating that an implicit, underlying Newtonian vision of reality still dominates our popular culture. It was in contradiction to this culture based on the powerful, comprehensive Newtonian vision of reality and its associated intuition that new, abstract visions of reality had to be discovered. It is hard to exaggerate the difficulty of the task of finding new and more abstract vision in such discovery. Nevertheless, excellent examples of it are described in this chapter and the next as well as in later chapters.

These new visions or theories of mechanics appeared early in the twentieth century. The origin of one of the new paradigms, *relativity*, was a "flash of insight" perceived by a gifted innovator (Albert Einstein). The second new paradigm, *quantum mechanics*, arose from meticulous and deliberate investigation of observed and deduced facts together with testing of many hypotheses. In accord with the scientific methodology, new theories or visions of reality were guessed in both cases (if we regard Einstein's postulates as guesses) and then compared to observed facts to test the theory until, in quantum mechanics, a version consistent with observation was found.

The discoveries of these theories provide insight into discovery of improved paradigm, belief, and philosophy. Thus, we shall examine the histories of these theories and their discoverers as well as the theories themselves. As before, the objective is to learn not only about each theory and the fascinating story of its discovery, but about discovery itself. The first new theory includes special and general relativity – with the latter encompassing the former so that both may be regarded as a single, complete theory of relativity – was discovered by Albert Einstein. The second is now called quantum mechanics or quantum theory or quantum physics and its discovery was a relatively long, strenuous, combined effort of many. In this chapter we consider Albert Einstein and his theory of relativity. In the next we consider quantum mechanics.

Albert Einstein

Albert Einstein (1879-1955) was a German-Swiss-American physicist. He was born at Ulm, Germany, on 14 March 1879. His family lived in Munich during his early years so it was there he received his early education, in a Catholic grammar school despite his Jewish ancestry. Einstein did not flourish as a student. In fact, according to family legend, when Albert's father Hermann asked his son's headmaster what profession he should pursue the answer was to the effect that it didn't matter because the boy was not suited for success in anything. Einstein entered high school (Luitpold Gymnasium) in Munich in 1889, where he spent the next six years. While his experience there had strong influence on him, the impact seems to have been more psychological than intellectual. Nevertheless, it was during this period that Albert received direction in science, mathematics, and philosophy that would steer him to his life's work, direction provided not by a teacher but by a family friend: Max Talmey. Talmey was a Jewish medical student at Munich University who met the Einstein family through his brother, a practicing physician who was acquainted with the Einsteins. The younger Talmey was received warmly into the cheerful Einstein home and often visited and ate with them. He befriended young Albert and gave him books, initially about physical phenomena. When Albert showed interest in mathematics, Talmey gave him a textbook on geometry by Spieker. Talmey's midday meal visits on Thursdays soon became lesson periods where Albert would show Talmey his solutions to problems from Spieker's book. After a few months he had worked through the whole book and went on to higher mathematics in Lubsen's books, which Talmey had recommended. Albert soon outstripped his mentor in mathematical ability and a frequent topic of their discussions became philosophy instead of mathematics. Talmey recommended that Albert read Immanuel Kant, who became Albert's favorite philosopher after he read through *Critique of Pure Reason* at age 13, a book that is incomprehensible to ordinary mortals but which seemed to be clear to Albert. (A brief critical review of Kant's *Critique of Pure Reason* is provided in Appendix C.) Talmey thus gave Einstein valuable encouragement and guidance. He would need it.

Because his father's business failed, the family moved in 1894 from Munich to Milan, Italy. This left Albert alone in Munich to finish his last two years of Gymnasium living in a boardinghouse and under nominal care of a distant relative. Einstein was quite unhappy in this situation and left the Gymnasium before completing his last two years of study. Without a diploma he could not be admitted to a German university. The family's strategy therefore became for Albert to enter the Swiss Federal Institute of Technology or, in German, the Eidgenössische Technische Hochschule (ETH), which admitted students solely on the basis of entrance examinations. So, in the fall of 1895 at age sixteen and one-half, Einstein traveled to Zürich with his mother to take the ETH entrance exams. It was no surprise that Albert did poorly; he was about two years younger than the other applicants taking the exams, since he had failed to finish his last two years of Gymnasium studies, and he had not prepared by any appropriate study. He failed in all subjects except mathematics. However, his score in this field, together with the extenuating circumstances, caused the ETH principal Albin Herzog to be impressed with Albert's potential and he arranged for

Albert to be enrolled for one year of preparation at the cantonal school in Aarau, some thirty kilometers west of Zürich. Following this additional year of study, Albert retook the entrance exams in the summer of 1896 and passed. He began his tenure as a student at the ETH in October 1896.

Einstein's goal was to become a teacher of mathematical physics. Accordingly, he took courses in mathematics and the natural sciences which included physics, astrophysics, and astronomy. He also studied theory of scientific thought, Kantian philosophy, anthropology, geology of mountains, business, politics, and, under a private tutor, Goethe's works and philosophy. Not unusual for the day, his physics instructor Heinrich Weber did not cover contemporary or even recent material in his lectures. Einstein biographer Ronald W. Clark has observed that Einstein appeared on "the scene as a student at a moment when physics was about to be revolutionized but when few students were encouraged to be revolutionary."[1] However, in the case of Einstein, revolution did not need encouragement.

Einstein, like Newton before him, read and studied for himself. In his spare time he became familiar with the works of Kirchhoff, Helmholtz, Maxwell, and Hertz. Indeed, Einstein appeared something of a "Bohemian" (gypsy or hippie), albeit an ambitious one, because he preferred to spend time in his room, at the coffeehouses, and at the Zürichsee beach reading instead of listening in the lecture hall, where his friend Marcell Grossman attended the lectures and took notes which he later shared with Einstein.

Contributing to his image as a Bohemian, Einstein had an illegitimate daughter with his girlfriend (who became his first wife), Mileva Maric, an ETH student in mathematics from Hungary who was, like most others in his class, a couple of years his senior. As they were in no situation to support a daughter, they wisely placed her for adoption.

Einstein passed the exams and graduated in 1900 without distinguishing himself. In fact, upon being temporarily appointed to teach mathematics for two months at a technical school at Winterthur while the regular professor was away on army duty, he wrote in 1901 that "I have no idea who recommended me, because as far as I know not one of my teachers has a good word to say about me ..."[2] Finally, through the influence of his friend Marcel Grossman's father who intervened on Einstein's behalf with the director of the Swiss Patent Office, his personal friend Friedrich Haller, Einstein obtained an appointment on 16 June 1902 as Technical Expert (Third Class) in the Swiss Patent Office in Berne.

Einstein's 1905 Papers

Although he enjoyed his work at the patent office, regarding it as an opportunity to learn by seeing a very broad range of problems and perspectives, he was intellectually active in physics beyond what was required in his job. Thus, in 1905, he published five papers in the prestigious physics journal *Annalan der Physik* all of which became famous and consequential.[3]

One of these papers[4] explained *Brownian motion*, a process first reported in 1827 by Scottish botanist Robert Brown based on his microscopic examination of plant pollen particles in water. Watching these suspended particles, Brown noted they danced about irregularly. While Brown thought this motion was an indication of life hidden in the pollen grains, Einstein proposed the small particles were animated by brief, dynamic forces due to fluctuations in their continual bombardment by surrounding fluid molecules. Einstein developed an elegant theory and worked out its consequences to find the *mean-square-displacement* σ^2 (Greek "sigma" squared) of a molecule or particle during time interval t. Brownian motion is the basis of the *diffusion* process whereby molecules and particles experience a net transport in the direction in which their concentration decreases. However, diffusion for any specific molecule or particle is generally random and has no preferred direction, i.e., positive and negative displacements are equally likely. Consequently, the sum of the incremental displacements of a particle by diffusion in time interval t is nearly zero and its average value is zero. To obtain a useful, nonzero quantity by which to characterize Brownian motion and diffusion, each Brownian-motion displacement is squared – made positive – before summing it. The mean (average) value of this sum determined by Einstein's theory is σ^2, the *mean-square displacement* in time t,

$$\sigma^2 = 2Dt,$$

where D is the particle diffusion coefficient. Einstein also discovered that $D = kT/f$, with k the Boltzmann's constant, T the absolute fluid temperature, and f the particle-fluid friction coefficient. For a spherical particle of diameter *d* in a fluid having viscosity η (Greek "eta") $f = 3\pi\eta\, d/C_{slip}$, with C_{slip} a "slip correction factor" that is essentially unity in liquids.

These results for both σ^2 and D had immediate impact. Since the value of f depends on particle diameter *d*, particle diffusion resulting from the chaotic motions first observed by Brown and characterized by Einstein provides a means for determining particle size, including the case when the particle is a molecule. Thus, in one paper, Einstein described how motions of small suspended particles provide indirect evidence of molecular motions *and* a means for determining molecular sizes using measured diffusion coefficients $D = kT/f$. As the foremost scientific controversy of that day was the continuum versus the atomic/molecular theory of matter, Einstein's paper was important. The continuum model of matter provided no explanation of the Brownian motion and Einstein's erudite observations and elegant mathematical demonstration left the atom skeptic without a response. Because of this and other results, within five years the long-held continuum theory of matter had been essentially abandoned.

The physical richness of Einstein's theory of Brownian motion is apparent in its continuous use up to today, a century later, as the basis for powerful measurement methods.[5] Each new generation of computer, electronic, or photonic device allows a new depth of information to be harvested using Einstein's theory. And even without computers or electronics, use of Einstein's theory led to an early Nobel Prize for Jean Perrin. And this was only one of the papers he wrote in 1905, all of which had similar profundity!

In a second 1905 paper,[7] Einstein explored interactions of light and matter, especially the photoelectric effect. This was the paper cited in the award of Einstein's 1921 Nobel Prize in physics. Its content is considered in the next chapter as an important contribution in the discovery of quantum mechanics.

Two other 1905 Einstein papers described his *special relativity* theory.[7] In them he described the strange processes of time dilation, length contraction, velocity dependence of mass, and equivalence of mass and energy. In the second of these papers Einstein first stated his famous equation $E = mc^2$ relating mass m, energy E, and the velocity of light c. Because it predicts strange effects, relativity theory captured public imagination and received much attention in the press. But public awareness came predominantly after he published his *general relativity* theory in 1916, of which special relativity is a particular case, and only after Sir Arthur Eddington and his colleagues announced their experimental "confirmation" of general relativity in 1919. But we are now getting ahead of the story. To properly continue we next describe the essential elements of Einstein's relativity theory, beginning with description of some physic's terminology we will use as well as a few comments about physical-mechanics knowledge in 1905.

Special Relativity

In mathematical physics the term *coordinate frame* or *frame* denotes, say, an orthogonal (perpendicular) x-y-z *coordinate system* utilizing location coordinates on x,y,z axes relative to a coordinate-system origin ($x = y = z = 0$) fixed on some selected object or point in space. We take as implicit in the use of such a system a perhaps imaginary *observer* and *laboratory* both fixed to the system, with the observer able to determine coordinates utilizing any necessary laboratory instruments. We therefore use the terms "coordinate system" and "observer" and "laboratory" interchangeably and denote them all by S (for system). Two or more systems, each with its own origin fixed on some body or reference point, are denoted S_0, S_1, S_2, ...

One quantity besides position and velocity that must be considered in multiple frames (systems) is force. It is known from classical physics (Newtonian mechanics) that any force on a body causes it to accelerate. Special relativity is limited to force-free systems, systems which experience no acceleration. Einstein described such frames (observers) as *inertial*, meaning they move only according to their inertia: on straight lines at constant velocity. Special relativity is limited to inertial systems and observers.

Even among inertial systems, important quantities can change between coordinate systems or in observed properties of an object in motion relative to an observer. One example is the properties of waves. The frequency or "pitch" of a sound wave, such as that of a train or factory whistle or ambulance siren, heard by an observer changes with motion relative to it. Such change in the nature (frequency) of a wave emitted by an object due to change in relative velocity is called a *Doppler shift*, after Austrian physicist Christian Johann Doppler (1803-1853) who first analyzed it. The Doppler shift is familiar in common experience when passengers in a moving car pass a train or factory or ambulance while a whistle or siren is engaged and hear a shift in pitch on passing. A Doppler shift always occurs with a relative velocity between a sound source and an observer. When an observer is moving at radial velocity u_r relative to a stationary source of sound having *frequency* ν (Greek letter "nu"), the observer hears frequency ν′ (read "nu prime") instead, with

$$\nu' = \nu\,(1 \pm u_r/c_s),$$

where c_s is the speed of sound in the ambient medium (air, water, …). The plus sign applies when the relative speed is directly toward the source and the minus sign when it is directly away from the source, as derived in endnote 8.

Because of such experience with sound waves transmitted through a medium (air, water, …) in classical physics, it was believed other traveling waves such as light waves must be similarly transmitted through a supporting medium and be subject to similar distortion with change in relative velocity. But Albert Michelson and Edward Morley, in a famous experiment completed in 1887 having the object of detecting a luminiferous aether, the medium of vibration in which light was believed to propagate, found no variation of light *velocity* in two beams from a common source oriented at right angles to one another. These measurements were made in a rotating apparatus spanning a full range of direction. If, as was then supposed, light traveled as a disturbance through the (absolutely) motionless aether, one of the light beams was expected to travel faster due to motion of the earth through the aether and thus have a higher velocity than its orthogonal twin. Michelson and Morley expected their data to merely confirm a nearly universally accepted theory. Instead, they found the velocity of both light beams to be identical irrespective of the orientation of their apparatus. Light waves (and, by extension, electromagnetic radiation) were (was) thus found to behave fundamentally differently from sound waves in that velocity of light relative to an observer is always fixed at c irrespective of any relative velocity between light source and observer. Nevertheless, light can contain a Doppler shift.

In 1895 Irish physicist George Francis Fitzgerald (1851-1901) and, shortly thereafter, Dutch physicist Hendrik Antoon Lorentz (1853-1928) independently postulated that contraction in length depending on relative motion of an observer was required to preserve constant velocity of light at any relative motion of the observer. From them arose the *Lorentz-Fitzgerald correction factor*

$$\gamma = 1 / \sqrt{(1 - u_r^2/c^2)} \geq 1,$$

where γ is the Greek "gamma," √(…) denotes "the square root of (…)," u_r is the relative speed of an observed object with respect to an observer, $c = 2.99792\times10^8$ m/sec is the speed of light in vacuum, 10^8 = one-hundred million, the velocity unit is m/sec or meters per second, and symbol ≥ is read "greater than or equal to." To preserve constant speed of light, gamma is employed in the *length contraction* equation

$$L_1 = L_0 / \gamma,$$

where L_1 is the length of an object in direction u_r moving with speed u_r relative to an observer (S_1) and L_0 is its corresponding *rest length* in that same direction measured at rest relative to the observer (S_0). Since $\gamma \geq 1$, it is seen that length of an object perceived by an observer is reduced when the object is moving relative to the observer. Such length contraction occurs only in the direction of relative motion u_r. For instance, a sphere moving at sufficiently large velocity relative to an observer appears (when the pitfall discovered by Terrell and others described in Chapter 4 is avoided) to be flattened like a pancake. The sphere diameter is length contracted to the pancake thickness in only the direction of relative motion, the pancake retaining the motionless-sphere diameter in all directions orthogonal to the direction of relative motion.

Lorentz also predicted a change in the "flow of time" with relative motion, a process called *time dilation* characterized by a simple expression given below.

In addition to length contraction and time dilation, Lorentz also predicted the mass of an electron (or other body) as determined by an observer should increase with relative velocity according to

$$m_1 = m_0 \gamma,$$

where m_0 is the electron *rest mass* measured by observer S_0 when the electron is at rest relative to S_0 and m_1 is the electron mass measured at electron speed u_r relative to observer S_0. Even before 1905 analyses of the mass of high-velocity electrons supported Lorentz's prediction.[9]

Lorentz's prediction of mass increase appeared to be confirmed by experiment,[9] but what was its cause? Mass increase could not then be derived by any known theory of broad scope. At this point, in 1905, Einstein's paper on special relativity appeared providing a comprehensive, systematic theory that gave precisely these predictions of length contraction, time dilation, magnification of mass, and more. Were it not for the previous results of Lorentz and Fitzgerald and the comparison with measurement that supported Lorentz's mass-increase prediction, Einstein's paper might have been rejected as that of a crank. Einstein was then unknown and he had quoted no other authors in any substantive matter he addressed in his revolutionary paper. Einstein, apparently, was not then even aware of the Michelson-Morley experiment but independently reached their conclusion by his own reasoning. As editorial director of *Annalan der Physik*, Max Planck read the submitted manuscript to judge its suitability for publication and, after reading it, Planck realized Einstein's paper was correct and that physics had just experienced a major change.[10]

Einstein's theory of special relativity is based on two postulates. *First*, the laws of electrodynamics, optics, and mechanics are valid for all frames of reference and possess no properties corresponding to the idea of absolute rest (as in the failed luminiferous aether theory). This postulate is called the *principle of relativity*. And, *second*, that light is always propagated in empty space with a definite, fixed velocity c independent of and relative to any emitting or detecting body.

An interesting aside is that the second Einstein postulate is implied by the first, as noted by Einstein later in 1905.[7] By Maxwell's electromagnetic wave theory, the velocity of light (electromagnetic radiation) is c, a constant fixed by the electromagnetic properties ε_0 and μ_0 (see page 77) of a medium such as the vacuum. This velocity occurs in any coordinate frame in which the theory is applied, i.e., one fixed to any emitting or detecting body. According to the first of Einstein's postulates and Maxwell's equations, light must always be emitted and detected at relative velocity c irrespective of any relative velocity between an emitter and a detector because light travels at velocity c in the coordinate frame fixed to the emitter *and* at velocity c in the coordinate frame fixed to the detector. Thus, light is everywhere measured to have only velocity c but with length contraction and time dilation required between observers fixed in two frames in relative motion to reconcile the same velocity c being measured in these two frames in relative motion.

From a straightforward application of his two postulates, Einstein found strange and interesting relations between quantities measured by observers S_0 and S_1 at constant relative velocity u_r, including those proposed by Fitzgerald and Lorentz and others not yet suspected. As already indicated, to retain a fixed velocity of light in each of two frames moving with relative x-direction velocity u_r, time dilation and length contraction must occur in each frame as perceived by an observer in the other. The length contraction of Einstein's special relativity is identical to that predicted by Lorentz and Fitzgerald given above. And so was Einstein's time dilation result identical to that of Lorentz and Fitzgerald, viz,

$$\Delta t_1 = \Delta t_0 / \gamma,$$

where time interval (difference) measured by a moving clock (Δt_1, read "delta t sub one") is smaller than the corresponding time difference measured by an identical stationary clock (Δt_0, read "delta t sub naught"). That is, as perceived by an observer, time in a system "flows" slower the faster the system moves relative to the observer. Observer S_0 or S_1 always sees him- or her-self as stationary and the situation is (subscripts are) reversible. Thus, time dilation, length contraction, and magnification of mass are *reciprocal*. The Lorentz transformation, given in endnote 11 and derived in Appendix B, provides prediction of any quantity measured by S_1 from one measured by S_0 and *vice versa*.

By special relativity the mass of an object increases exactly as postulated by Lorentz. It follows that as a body approaches velocity c relative to an observer, both its γ and mass seem to the observer to become indefinitely large, precluding the possibility of a body reaching velocity c.

Einstein found that light emitted with frequency ν from a source that is approaching or receding from an observer at relative velocity u_r is frequency shifted to give an observed (Doppler-shifted) frequency ν' measured by the observer, where $\nu' = \nu\gamma(1 \pm u_r/c)$. For a receding source (take the minus sign),[12]

$$\nu' = \nu\gamma(1 - u_r/c) = \nu\sqrt{\{(1 - u_r/c)/(1 + u_r/c)\}}.$$

A signal from a receding source is reduced in frequency or *redshifted*. Since $\nu \times \lambda = c$ with c constant, if ν is reduced by a redshift then wavelength λ (Greek "lambda") is proportionately increased by the same redshift. Einstein also found that energy carried in a signal is reduced at the observer's location, retaining only the fraction

$$\gamma^2 (1 - u_r/c)^2 = (1 - u_r/c)/(1 + u_r/c)$$

of the quantity of emitted signal energy directed toward the observer. As perceived by an observer, then, an emitted signal from a receding source is redshifted in both frequency ($\nu' < \nu$) and wavelength ($\lambda' > \lambda$) and is reduced in signal energy. For a relative recessional velocity $u_r \to c$, no signal should be detectable. Therefore, an expanding universe in which u_r increases with separation implies a *visibility limit* or *event horizon* beyond which objects are not visible.

Such are the properties of redshift predicted by special relativity, or *Doppler redshift*. However, the more inclusive general relativity theory, which we address below, predicts a redshift due to an additional cause, namely, the expansion of space. With the expansion of the universe or space itself, radiation waves contained in space are also expanded, i.e., redshifted. This effect is termed *cosmological redshift*. General relativity predicts that radiation from an object receding at the speed of light will obtain a redshift of about 1.5 or a redshifted wavelength that is 150 percent the original. Over a thousand galaxies have been observed to be receding from earth "at" a redshift greater than 1.5, i.e., at recessional velocity greater than the speed of light.[12] Another general-relativity redshift process, called *gravitational redshift*, is similar in its origin. As radiation leaves a high-gravity environment, wherein space is compressed by gravity, space and the radiation wavelength expand and the radiation is thereby redshifted. We shall later describe measurements of this process.

Einstein explored the consequences of relativity and found that relativity implies radiation of energy from a body results in a loss of mass and inertia. What is the origin of radiant energy? In a brief supplement[7] published in 1905 three months after his special-relativity paper, Einstein concluded mass is equivalent to energy and Einstein's famous relation for equivalence of mass and energy emerged[13]

$$E = mc^2.$$

All of these results follow directly from the two postulates Einstein assumed in special relativity. Although strange compared to Newtonian physics, the theory successfully rationalizes not only observed results predicted by Newtonian theory, i.e., for the case $\gamma = 1$, but also real observations that are not.

One commonly cited test of time dilation and, thus, of special relativity is the observation of mu-mesons or *muons* at sea level. Muons are unstable, high-energy particles having a mass equal to that of 207 electrons and a mean lifetime before they decay of 2.197 millionths of a second. They are produced in the upper atmosphere by collisions of cosmic rays and atmospheric molecules. Their lifetime is sufficiently short so that they should fully disappear by spontaneous decay by the time they have traversed only one-twentieth of the distance to the earth's surface. Yet they are observed at sea level. This apparent paradox is simply resolved by special relativity since time interval in a muon-fixed frame Δt_1 is dilated compared to time in an earth-fixed frame Δt_0; by simple rearrangement of the opposite-page time-dilation expression $\Delta t_0 = \gamma \Delta t_1$ with γ being large for a fast moving particle.[14] Thus, while apparent decay time Δt_0 is much too long, actual decay time Δt_1 is not.

Another oft-cited illustration of time dilation is a thought experiment originally called the "clock paradox." Later, after (apparently) Langevin substituted human travelers for clocks in 1911,[3] it was called the "twin paradox." Suppose one of two twins remains behind at $x_0 = 0$ while the second boards a rocket ship and travels at velocity u_r beginning at time $t_0 = 0$ so that her position is $x_0 = u_r t_0$ after her age has increased by $t_1 = t_0/\gamma$. When u_r/c is significant, γ is significantly larger than one and, while the twin that stayed behind aged by t_0, the traveling twin aged by the smaller amount $t_1 = t_0/\gamma$. In fact, the same discrepancy in aging occurs if the rocket ship reverses velocity at the midpoint of its journey and returns to $x_0 = 0$ where the twins reunite, one relatively old and the other relatively young. This prediction of special relativity is non-intuitive as it violates Newton's assumption of absolute time and our intuition based thereon. However, it is not a paradox but merely a prediction contrary to intuition contrived to illustrate the novelty of special relativity, which it does well. But, like most analogies and many illustrations, it is flawed.[15]

The principle of relativity predates Einstein. The French mathematician and physicist Jules Henri Poincaré (1854-1912) coined the term to represent the principle that no experiment could detect an observer's uniform motion (through the luminiferous aether). The fundamental concept of relativity dates back much further, at least to Galileo who questioned whether someone sleeping on an anchored boat could later discern, upon awakening, whether the boat was drifting at a fixed velocity.[16] But Einstein was the first to incorporate all the above concepts into a consistent, systematic theory or paradigm that provides a new vision of physical reality. However, correct prediction of these novel properties by use of a systematic theory does not answer our earlier question regarding their cause. Maxwell's theory is known but not it's cause and special relativity is derived utilizing Maxwell's theory. Thus, predictability does not correspond to understanding. Nor does it reveal meaning.

Just as length contraction, time dilation, magnification of mass, and the principle of relativity had been known before Einstein's special theory of relativity, some features of his later, more comprehensive general theory of relativity were also anticipated. Poincaré was scheduled to attend the First International Congress of Mathematicians held in Zürich during Einstein's first year there at the ETH. Although he was prevented from attending, his paper was read before the Congress and it contained the statement: "Absolute space, absolute time, even Euclidian geometry, are not conditions to be imposed on mechanics; one can express the facts concerning them in terms of non-Euclidian space." While Einstein was probably not in attendance, he might nonetheless have learned of Poincaré's proposal. But even if he had, Einstein's thinking followed characteristically original directions that led him down his own novel path in general relativity to even more revolutionary results.

General Relativity

Eleven years after he published special relativity, Einstein's paper fully describing his general theory of relativity appeared[17] in 1916, although he had presented it in lectures to the Berlin Academy in November of 1915. (For this reason some authors give 1915 as the year of publication.) In general relativity, Einstein eliminated gravity as a distinct force by a novel definition of "spacetime." The term spacetime denotes the four dimensional space x,y,z,t involving three spatial-displacement coordinates x,y,z and one time-displacement coordinate t. Einstein's goal in formulating general relativity was to obtain a better, more complete basis for mechanics that reconciles the fact that inertial mass and gravitational mass are identical, a known fact but one that had no apparent explanation. This fact suggested to Einstein that gravity is an inertial effect. He thus proposed his *equivalence principle* which forms the basis of general relativity. It can be stated in several forms. One form is simply "Physics appears the same to any observer in free fall regardless of the strength of the gravitational field." Another form states "All physical experiments in a uniform gravitational field in which the acceleration of gravity is g are equivalent to experiments in a gravity-free system having acceleration g." Using this equivalence principle and a few other assumptions, Einstein deduced his general theory of relativity. In it he eliminated gravity utilizing a suitably curved (non-Euclidian) rather than flat (Euclidian) spacetime, the latter having been almost[18] universally assumed up to relativity. (For a mathematical description of curved spacetime see Appendix B.)

In a freely falling laboratory there exists no gravity force or weight. Consequently, this condition removes gravity as an explicit cause of force and instead includes it implicitly in the accelerating motion of the laboratory in curved spacetime (i.e., in the coordinate system or reference frame of the laboratory). That is, space and time are curved so as to cause the force of gravity in flat space to disappear in a body's natural motion in curved spacetime. Note that *distortion* of spacetime is not new with general relativity as it occurred already in the flat spacetime of special relativity in the form of time dilation and length contraction to preserve constant c in every reference frame. However, in special relativity no *curvature* of spacetime occurs because all of an observed spacetime is uniformly dilated or contracted according to the constant relative velocity between the observer and the observed. For two inertial frames moving with constant relative velocity, special relativity emerges as a special case of general relativity. But general relativity is not limited to inertial frames only. It applies also for frames in *relative acceleration*, a very significant generalization since acceleration is involved in any nonlinear motion, such as the orbiting of a planet around a star, and is common, the rule rather than the exception.

In flat spacetime, Newton's theory of gravitation shows gravity to depend on quantity and proximity of matter (mass). Consequently, a freely falling laboratory must fall faster or slower at different points in the laboratory. Thus, spacetime must be curved, i.e., length contraction varies with position.

Moreover, in general relativity spacetime contains energy that acts equivalently to mass, through the relation $E = mc^2$, which provides an additional source of gravitational field or curvature of spacetime, in radical departure from Newtonian theory. Einstein characterized this feature of general relativity with the following statement in his 1916 paper.

> The special theory of relativity has led to the conclusion that inert mass is nothing more or less than energy ... Thus in the general theory of relativity we must introduce a corresponding energy-tensor of matter ... For if we consider a complete system (e.g. the solar system), the total mass of the system, and therefore its total gravitating action as well, will depend on the total energy of the system, and therefore on the ponderable energy together with the gravitational energy.[19]

That is, a cold or non-spinning sun exerts less gravitational attraction than a hot or spinning one of identical "mass," with the difference being $\Delta m = \Delta E/c^2$. Thus, ponderable energy ΔE such as heat or kinetic energy of rotation contributes to the gravitational field and to the curvature of spacetime. Because spacetime curvature depends on energy as well as mass, the determination of the spacetime curvature in general relativity is much more complex than implied by Newtonian gravitation.

Ignoring unrecognized complexity due to ponderable energy, early measurements[18] seeking to directly establish curvature of space were not successful for the reason that this curvature is too slight to detect directly in the relatively weak gravity and energy density found in our solar system. It was discovered only when Einstein's theory indicated exactly what to look for and how. We shall shortly discuss experiments guided by Einstein's theory that appear to confirm curvature of spacetime.

A general-relativity solution for motion of a body under the influence of only gravity force (i.e., a freely-falling body) must satisfy two equations derived by Einstein in 1916.[17] The first equation is now called *Einstein's field equation.* Its solution gives the *Einstein potential field* which relates the local curvature of spacetime to the distribution of all curvature-causing matter and energy. This Einstein potential field enters into the second equation describing motion of the body by defining the spacetime (or gravity) environment of the body. Einstein originally called the second equation the *equation of motion* because its solution describes the motion of the body in spacetime. It is now generally called the *geodesic equation* because the motion of a freely-falling body follows a geodesic. One characteristic of a geodesic is that it defines the shortest spacetime distance between any beginning and ending points on a body's trajectory.

Karl Schwarzschild (1873-1916) was the first to obtain exact solutions of the Einstein field equation. Schwarzschild (pronounced "shwarz-shild"), a German astronomer and able mathematician, considered the influence of only a single spherical mass, such as that of an isolated particle, planet, or star. His personal circumstance at the time he began work solving Einstein's field equation is noteworthy as it was far from ideal for such demanding work. Schwarzschild was over age forty at the outbreak of World War I but nevertheless volunteered for military duty. He was eventually posted on the eastern front where he contracted pemphigus, a skin disease that was then incurable, and was released from the army. He died on 11 May 1916. Before his infirmity he kept abreast of scientific developments in Germany and continued his own scientific contemplation while serving in Russia, from which resulted the Schwarzschild solutions of Einstein's field equation. From his death bed he sent two papers to Einstein who read them in Schwarzschild's absence to the Academy of Sciences in Berlin on 16 January and 24 February 1916. In the first of the two papers, Schwarzschild described a solution or "metric" (the *Schwarzschild metric*) by which curved spacetime is described outside a spherical mass. In response to receiving this first paper, Einstein wrote to Schwarzschild in a letter dated 9 January 1916:

> I have read your paper with the utmost interest. I had not expected that one could formulate the exact solution of the problem in such a simple way. I liked very much your mathematical treatment of the subject. Next Thursday I shall present the work to the Academy with a few words of explanation.[20]

In his second paper, Schwarzschild described the complementary metric by which spacetime is described inside a spherical mass. He showed that a spherical body of material of specified mass density could only exist below a certain mass-density-dependent diameter, now called the *Schwarzschild limit*, without collapsing under the action of its own gravitational attraction into a tiny, ultra-dense body (a "singularity" or discrete point in spacetime). He further showed that an event horizon exists around such a singularity at the *Schwarzschild radius*, across which nothing including light could exit, which eventually led to naming such a body a *black hole*. The Schwarzschild radius is $\alpha = 2GM/c^2$, where G is the universal gravitational constant, M is the mass of the black hole, c is the velocity of light in vacuum, and α is the Greek "alpha." This radius is important as a horizon in both of Schwarzschild's solutions.

Incidentally, a violation of the inescapability of light or matter from a black hole was discovered by British cosmologist Stephen Hawking (1942-), another prolific physicist laboring under less than ideal conditions since Hawking has suffered from ALS since 1962. Combining results from quantum theory, thermodynamics, and relativity, Hawking showed that a small current of matter (energy) is, in effect, continually radiated from a black hole. The phenomenon is based in the uncertainty principle of quantum mechanics (to be discussed in the next chapter) which, in one of its forms, states that the product of uncertainty in energy ΔE in unit volume of space and uncertainty in time interval Δt in which energy is measured must equal or exceed constant h, i.e., $\Delta E \Delta t \geq h$, due to random fluctuations in energy (and mass) about an average value. That is, empty space is not empty, as will become clearer when we discuss the Dirac equation in the next chapter. As predicted by the uncertainty principle, particle pairs such as an electron and its antimatter counterpart, the *positron*, may spontaneously emerge from the vacuum before quickly annihilating each other and restoring the energy in the small volume to its original value. However, Hawking observed that with a strong "tidal gravitational force" (a force difference with change in radial location associated with a strong curvature of spacetime) near a black hole just beyond the event horizon, the two particles may be separated with the nearer one drawn irreversibly into the black hole and the other escaping, preventing their recombination. The energy required to produce such escaping particles is ultimately drawn from the gravitational field of the black hole so that its mass is correspondingly decreased. Thus, in effect, the escaping particles are radiated from the black hole giving it a minuscule, characteristic, black-body-radiation temperature. The process is called *Hawking radiation*. This process is related in its origin to the "particle jets" predicted by Richard Feynman and his students and later observed in collisions of high-energy particles wherein strong, attractive-force fields between separating particles (high local energy density – the more energy, the more spontaneously emerging particles) are observed to "draw" jets of particles from the vacuum as predicted by the uncertainty principle.

Willem de Sitter (1872-1934), a Dutch physicist and astronomer, realized that Einstein's relativity theory would have important astronomical implications and began a careful study of it with the interest of using the theory to evaluate astronomical evidence after reading a 1911 paper by Einstein. Shortly after the publication of general relativity, de Sitter published solutions of the equations of this theory for *a matterless universe*, an approximation he thought might be useful for some calculations because of the low average mass density of the universe (of only ≈ 10^{-27} kg/m^3). Initially, his solutions seemed to predict a static universe. However, without discrete masses to serve as reference points, motion was difficult to follow. Later addition, by Arthur Eddington and German mathematician/theoretical physicist Hermann Weyl in the early 1920s, of finely dispersed particles in the de Sitter solution gave increasing separation of particles with time, i.e., the particles were observed to follow expanding space, indicating that the universe is expanding. De Sitters solutions implied other properties of the universe as well, including an exponential *inflationary growth* of the early universe, a concept proposed by Alan H. Guth in 1980 to reconcile theory and related cosmological observations.[21] Although implied in one of de Sitter's early solutions, inflation was not at first recognized nor was it thought to be important when it was. It was Guth's work in 1980 that, although it still contained problems,[21] made a case for its existence and importance by showing how it solved even greater, more fundamental cosmological problems. It is significant that inflation was implied but unrecognized in an early solution of Einstein's field equation. Descriptions provided by complex and abstract theories can take many decades to interpret correctly, as we shall shortly see in considering the Schwarzschild metric.

Additionally, de Sitter's theory implied a body should be unobservable when its relative recessional velocity is sufficiently high. Thus, an *event horizon* must exist within an expanding universe beyond which observation is impossible. Such a horizon had already been implied by special relativity, as described above, due to a *Doppler redshift* and associated reduction in signal power of light emitted from a receding body. Redshifts are in fact found in the astronomical data and have become a tool for measuring *relative velocity* or *distance*, the two being nominally related in an expanding universe in which more distant bodies are receding at nominally higher velocities. A second type of redshift, *cosmological* or *gravitational redshift*, is implied by general relativity. These redshifts are due to decompression of space by expansion of the universe and light therein or as light emitted from a massive star moves outward and space and wavelength both expand. In gravitational redshift, increasing separation reduces gravity and space expands to eventually decompress to Euclidian flatness far from the star. Gravitational redshift has been measured and found to agree with predictions of general relativity. We shall later describe the experiment of Pound and Rebka, published in 1960, as well as other experiments which verify the gravitational redshift and other relativity predictions.

Aleksandr Aleksandrovich Friedmann (1888-1925), a Russian applied mathematician in Petrograd who specialized in hydromechanics and meteorology, derived a solution of Einstein's field equation for a distributed mass system, apparently around 1917 but not published until 1922 (a period spanning the Bolshevik revolution and the subsequent civil war).[22] He also published additional solutions in 1924.[22] He found a family of solutions rather than the unique solution for which Einstein hoped. Or, alternatively, Friedmann found a unique solution for each of many different assumed values of the (average) mass density of the universe. Friedmann found that his solutions described an *expanding* universe. In some solutions, the universe expands indefinitely; in others with higher mass and/or energy density, it expands to a certain size and then collapses back into itself due to attraction of gravity; and he also found more complicated, oscillating solutions. Friedmann reportedly sent his first solution to Einstein for his comments. Only after hearing no response for several years did he finally publish it. Unfortunately, for several years his solutions for a non-static universe were rejected as too revolutionary, Einstein himself attacking them in a published criticism he quickly had to withdraw because it was invalid.

Eventually, Georges Lemaître independently discovered these solutions in his Ph.D. thesis research at the Massachusetts Institute of Technology. The concept of the expanding universe and, ultimately, the big-bang theory of cosmology emerged from Lemaître's thinking and from astronomical observations of Edwin Hubble, assisted by Milton Humason, that confirmed the expanding state of the universe, work founded on previous results of Henrietta Leavitt and Vesto Slipher. (Humason's contributions are particularly warming. A high-school dropout after *one day*, Humason was initially employed in the construction of the Mt. Wilson observatories and stayed on as a janitor. Humason had a unique ability to manipulate the big telescopes so that his assistance was often called for when a difficult adjustment was needed. Moreover, he soon mastered the skills of observational astronomy. Perhaps to avoid embarrassment when senior staff had to call the janitor to solve problems they couldn't, Humason was promoted to the position of assistant astronomer and allowed to pursue his own work.)

Schwarzschild's Solution of the Einstein Field Equation#

A general relativity solution for motion of a body includes, first, a solution of Einstein's field equation and, second, a solution of the geodesic equation which incorporates the first solution in defining the nature of spacetime. It is easy and, in fact, essential to get very mathematical in a detailed discussion of general relativity, a temptation we shall gladly resist here. (Indeed, we do not even write either the Einstein or geodesic equation.) But Schwarzschild's solution of the Einstein field equation, *the Schwarzschild metric*, is comparatively simple and it reveals the complete nature of spacetime in the vicinity of a spherical mass. It provides considerable insight at moderate mathematical cost so we dare to consider it briefly.

Schwarzschild's solution or metric for spacetime external to a spherical body of mass M is

$$ds^2 = c^2 d\tau^2 = c^2 dt^2 (1 - \alpha/r) - dr^2 / (1 - \alpha/r) - r^2 d\Omega^2.$$

In this equation $ds = c\,d\tau$ is a differential or small incremental displacement in s or *interval* of spacetime, $d\tau$ is a differential displacement in local or *proper* time τ (tau) defined as the time interval registered on a clock travelling locally with an observer at the indicated r coordinate while *coordinate* time t is registered by another, remote ($r \to \infty$) observer and clock in flat spacetime. As elsewhere, c is the velocity of light in a vacuum and $\alpha = 2GM/c^2$ is the Schwarzschild radius with $G = 6.6726 \times 10^{-11}$ m^3/ kg/sec^2, the universal gravitational constant. Quantity dr is a differential or small displacement in the radial direction and r is the radial separation from the center of spherical mass M. Finally, $d\Omega^2 = d\theta^2 + \sin^2\theta\, d\phi^2$ is the square of a differential or small change in angle $d\Omega$ (Ω is the upper case Greek "omega") that defines direction on the surface of a sphere of radius r, everywhere orthogonal (perpendicular) to the radial direction. On this sphere ϕ (Greek "phi") represents a longitude and θ (Greek "theta") a latitude angle.

Why, one might ask, are we considering only differential spacetime geometry, i.e., merely a local metric rather than a more universal representation? The answer involves the fact that spacetime is curved. In flat, Euclidian spacetime, coordinates x,y,z,t possess directions and scales that are invariant throughout spacetime. In curved spacetime the direction or scale of a line (e.g., a geodesic) may change with a change in location. In flat spacetime we can regard a coordinate value of, say, x as a scalar (rather than a vector) because length scale and direction of that coordinate are fixed universally throughout spacetime by an adopted coordinate frame. In curved spacetime the length scale of a coordinate is not universally fixed and, in fact, direction can become elusive. To avoid the problem of complex tensor representation of quantities, spacetime is simply defined locally by a metric using small differentials with specified length scales and directions in a flat spacetime locally tangent to the curved spacetime. This practice was established by Riemann in his initial 1854 differential-geometry treatment of curved spaces (Chapter 3 and Appendix B). Thus, the Schwarzschild metric is useful even though it only applies over a limited, local extent, i.e., it is a local representation of spacetime. A more rigorous, universal representation of spacetime that utilizes the tensor calculus of general relativity tends to obscure interesting features readily apparent in this simple metric. And, as we shall demonstrate, the simple metric may be used to solve important problems in unlimited, curved spacetime. We shall now investigate some of the properties of Schwarzschild spacetime apparent from the moderately simple Schwarzschild metric.

In Schwarzschild spacetime, if mass M approaches zero ($M \to 0$) or r becomes indefinitely large or infinite ($r \to \infty$) then α/r approaches zero ($\alpha/r \to 0$) and spacetime becomes flat. When α/r is nonzero, spacetime is *curved* and the curvature is everywhere "spherically symmetric." That is, on the surface of an imaginary sphere at any fixed radius r, no change in spacetime curvature occurs since the coefficients in the Schwarzschild metric depend only on r with no dependence on t, θ or ϕ. The non-unity (curved-dimension) coefficients are $(1 - \alpha/r)c^2$ in the dt^2 term and $1/(1 - \alpha/r)$ in the dr^2 term, together giving curvature to spacetime that replaces the acceleration of gravity in flat spacetime. Thus, spacetime described by this metric is simultaneously curved (by gravity) in the t and r dimensions but is flat in the Ω or tangential on-any-fixed-sphere-surface dimension (i.e., in the θ and ϕ dimensions on a sphere of any fixed radius r).

At fixed r, θ, and ϕ, $dr = d\theta = d\phi = 0$ and no displacement or velocity occurs. But time dilation still depends on (fixed) r, i.e., the Schwarzschild metric becomes

$$d\tau^2 = dt^2\,(1 - \alpha/r), \qquad \text{giving } t = \gamma\tau, \text{ with } \gamma = 1/\sqrt{(1-\alpha/r)} \geq 1.$$

Thus, local proper time τ flows slower than coordinate time t due purely to influence of gravity, with the difference disappearing at large separation $r \rightarrow \infty$ where they flow at the same rate. The ratio of dt and $d\tau$, i.e., the non-unity factor $\gamma = \delta t/\delta\tau$, indicates the time dimension of Schwarzschild spacetime is curved, with curvature of this dimension dependent on r and diminishing to flatness ($\gamma = 1$) as $r \rightarrow \infty$.

Though Schwarzschild quickly provided an important solution to the Einstein equation, its correct interpretation was intensely debated and remained unsettled for decades. Two singularities (infinities due to division of a nonzero quantity by zero) seem to occur in the Schwarzschild metric, one in the dt^2 coefficient at $r = 0$ and a second in the dr^2 coefficient at $r = \alpha$. However, it was soon discovered that every mass M, even including a neutron or proton, has a radius greater than $\alpha = 2GM/c^2$. Thus, the first possible singularity ($r = 0$) has, as yet, no known physical significance. But the second apparent singularity does. This apparent singularity was, however, removed. The first step in its removal was taken by Lemaître[23] when he proved the condition $r = \alpha$ does not have the character of a singularity. The apparent singularity arises because the chosen coordinate system is not adequate to properly represent this spacetime. Eddington and Finkelstein in the early 1930s discovered a new coordinate representation that eliminates apparently singular behavior of Schwarzschild spacetime at $r = \alpha$. The issue was finally settled in 1961 by use of even more suitable coordinates.[24] Nevertheless, the current understanding of the Schwarzschild metric is that it contains an apparently impenetrable sphere at radius $r = \alpha$ near which light and matter appear to a distant observer to accumulate, always moving toward but never reaching or away but never escaping $r = \alpha$. Eddington referred to this sphere (in a profile view) as a "magic circle."[25]

Consider the *null radial geodesic* (i.e., the exact solution of both the Einstein and geodesic equations for the radial spacetime path of a *photon*, a particle or quanta of light, with $d\Omega = 0$) defined by

$$0 = c^2 dt^2 (1 - \alpha/r) - dr^2/(1 - \alpha/r),$$

taking as the geodesic the spacetime interval $\Delta s = c\,\Delta t = 0$ (and thus a *null* geodesic). That is, a clock attached to a photon moving radially at speed c shows zero time flow ($d\tau = 0$) and, therefore, zero interval ($ds = 0$). The photon path follows a radial trajectory in Schwarzschild spacetime either rising from or falling toward gravitational center M. Taking the square root of the above equation rearranged we obtain

$$\pm\, c\,dt = dr/(1 - \alpha/r),$$

where the + sign corresponds to a rising photon ($dr > 0$) and the – sign to a falling one ($dr < 0$). The solution of this equation is presented and discussed in endnote 26. For either sign, as $r \to \alpha$, $dr/(r - \alpha) \to \pm\infty$ (plus or minus infinity). A remote observer (in coordinate time t) sees falling and rising photons ever accumulating near, never quite reaching or leaving position $r = \alpha$, because, in both cases, an infinitely long coordinate-time interval is required for the photon to traverse an infinitesimal distance dr at $r = \alpha$. Similar conclusions apply for matter. This behavior is the cause of Eddington's "magic circle" apparent to a distant observer. However, to a local observer traveling with a photon or material body (in local proper time τ), the surface $r = \alpha$ is reached and passed without notice, indeed, without passage of local, proper time.

Consider next two spacetime points $P_1 = t,r_1,\theta,\phi$ and $P_2 = t,r_2,\theta,\phi$, i.e., no change in t, θ, or ϕ occurs between P_1 and P_2. Thus, dt and $d\Omega$ are both zero and the metric equation relates the magnitudes of ds and dr according to

$$ds = dr / \sqrt{(1 - \alpha/r)} = dr \{1 + 1/2\, \alpha/r + 3/8\, (\alpha/r)^2 + 15/48\, (\alpha/r)^3 + ... \}$$

where Newton's binomial theorem (described in endnote 13 of Chapter 7) has been used to expand $1/\sqrt{(1 - \alpha/r)}$. Integration (summation of differential lengths taking account of their variations) over spacetime interval Δs gives

$$\Delta s = (s_2 - s_1) = (r_2 - r_1) + (\alpha/2) \log_e(r_2/r_1) + 3/8\, \alpha^2 (r_2 - r_1) / (r_1 r_2) + \ldots$$

All terms on the right are positive when $r_2 > r_1$ and negative when $r_2 < r_1$. (Symbols > and < read "is greater than" and "is less than" and function $\log_e(z)$ of z, with z any positive argument or variable, is defined in endnote 27.) That is, even for pure radial motion the magnitude of spacetime interval Δs is greater than magnitude $\Delta r = r_2 - r_1$. How can this be, since we traverse exactly the radial difference $\Delta r = r_2 - r_1$ from P_1 to P_2? The answer is that the interval traversed between r_1 and r_2 in Schwarzschild spacetime is *curved* so that interval $\Delta s > \Delta r$. This result is inherent to curved spacetime defined by Riemann's differential geometry. (See Appendix B, equation [B16] which gives for the general case $ds = \pm \sqrt{(g_{22})}\, dr$ with $g_{22} \geq 1$. Therefore, the magnitude of Δs *must* exceed that of Δr when $g_{22} > 1$.) It follows that the length Δr of a radially directed rod is "length contracted" by compression of space itself by gravity.

Now let $P_1 = t,r,\Omega_1$ and $P_2 = t,r,\Omega_2$ so that in moving from P_1 to P_2 both dt and dr are zero and $ds = r\,d\Omega$. A sum of the proper sequence of differentials (integration) gives the exact result

$$\Delta s = (s_2 - s_1) = r\Delta\Omega = r(\Omega_2 - \Omega_1).$$

In this case distance between P_1 and P_2 is equal to the simple difference $r(\Omega_2 - \Omega_1)$. In other words, no curvature occurs in the Ω dimension (θ and ϕ dimensions) of Schwarzschild spacetime.

Consider an observer moving in Schwarzschild spacetime. We ask: what is the relationship between proper (local) time τ and coordinate (remote, flat) time t?

Or, how does the flow of time differ between a distant, stationary observer who experiences flat time t and the local, moving observer? To answer this question we alter the metric equation by dividing both sides of the equation by the quantity c^2dt^2. The metric equation then takes the form

$$d\tau^2/dt^2 = 1 - \alpha/r - (dr/dt)^2 / [c^2(1 - \alpha/r)] - r^2/c^2(d\Omega/dt)^2.$$

But $d\tau/dt = 1/\gamma$ by definition of γ and with $dr/dt = v_r$ the radial velocity component and $r\,d\Omega/dt = v_\Omega$ the tangential velocity component, i.e., v_Ω is a velocity component momentarily in (tangential to) the surface of a sphere of radius r. This equation may be rearranged and rewritten in terms of these quantities to take the form

$$dt/d\tau = \gamma = 1 / \sqrt{[1 - \alpha/r - v_r^2/c^2 / (1 - \alpha/r) - v_\Omega^2/c^2]}.$$

Thus, in Schwarzschild spacetime, the local *time dilation factor* $\gamma \geq 1$ depends on α/r, v_r/c, and v_Ω/c. This factor predicts *local* proper time τ is dilated and curved (in the r-dependence of γ) compared to flat, remote coordinate time t. In the absence of gravity, i.e., when $\alpha/r \to 0$, the Lorentz-Fitzgerald factor of special relativity is recovered since $v_r^2 + v_\Omega^2 = u_r^2$ in flat space. While the factor γ of special relativity applies uniformly over all spacetime depending only on relative velocity u_r, the correction factor γ of general relativity in Schwarzschild spacetime depends on radius r through the ratio α/r and on velocity components v_r and v_Ω, but differently for these two velocity components when $\alpha/r > 0$.

We mention one final discovery connected with Schwarzschild spacetime, namely, the discovery of the *Kerr metric* by New-Zealander Roy P. Kerr. This metric extends Schwarzschild's metric to include a rotating spherical mass as well as a stationary one. The utility and need for such extension are obvious as bodies in space are usually rotating. Kerr, like Schwarzschild, was a capable mathematician and utilized novel, sophisticated, mathematical methods together with symmetry concepts in his study of relativity. The First Texas Symposium on Relativistic Astrophysics was held in 1963 in Austin, Texas, to bring together astronomers, astrophysicists, and relativists who were often working on similar problems unaware of each other's interests and results. Each discipline had its own methods, journals, and meetings and there was little cross-fertilization in thinking or sharing of results. Kerr presented his new metric at this meeting to a silent, unappreciative audience who, because of the novel, advanced mathematics and approach, had little understanding of what Kerr was talking about. But a few did. One of these was Greek relativist Achilles Papapetrou who had spent much of his career seeking the kind of result he was seeing presented to an unappreciative audience. He immediately recognized the importance of this result he himself had unsuccessfully sought and the mathematical and physical breakthroughs it represented. When Papapetrou spoke, he educated the audience regarding Kerr's accomplishment. Kerr and Papapetrou personified the purpose of what turned into a regular series of "Texas Symposia," the purpose being education of scientists in different fields by one another. Gone are the days when competent astronomers need know only astronomy.

Evidence for and against Relativity

One author has made the interesting observation "that Einstein did not give a rigorous mathematical proof of general relativity and neither has anyone else."[28] General relativity is not a mathematical theorem but is rather a physical theory. As such, its only possible test (not proof) is a comparison with observed reality. And then the theory can only be tentatively regarded as valid so long as no contradiction is established. We therefore seek to *test the validity of* (a terminology used in physics in preference to *prove*) relativity by accurate comparison of its predictions to those of Newtonian mechanics and to observations of physical reality. And predictions of relativity and Newtonian mechanics must be compared to discover what tests are feasible and useful. Several such tests have been discovered.

Evidence that supports special relativity includes successful use of Einstein's expression for the equivalence of mass and energy ($E = mc^2$). This result has been utilized to consistently predict nuclear reactions including radioactive decay and diagnose various products of high-energy particle collisions. Such diagnostics have consistently provided identification of product-particle species, characterization of particle properties, and, occasionally, prediction of the masses (energies) at which new particles were later found.

Tests of general relativity also apply to special relativity, since the latter is merely a special case of the former. In other words, if general relativity is correct, so is special relativity. But the opposite statement is not necessarily true, since the general theory is based on a broader postulate (the principle of equivalence) and covers a broader range of phenomena than those considered in the special theory.

The earliest test of general relativity was a comparison of the deflection of light from distant stars as it passed near the sun. This test was demanding. A light ray grazing the sun's surface is deflected only 1.745 arcseconds according to relativity and half of that amount or 0.8725 arcseconds according to Newtonian theory (gravity). (How a massless photon may be deflected by gravity is described in endnote 13.) One arcsecond is 1/60th of one arcminute which, in turn, is 1/60th of one degree; thus one arcsecond is 1/3600th of one degree of angle. While a deflection of order one arcsecond is easily determined using an observatory where telescopes are programmed to automatically and precisely follow moving stars, such accuracy is challenging for experiments conducted "in the field" with a simple, portable apparatus. Nevertheless, such a test was successfully conducted in the field during a total eclipse on 29 May 1919 by Arthur Eddington and his colleagues.

Eddington was born in 1882 in Kendal, Cumbria, England. When his father died in 1884 his mother moved with him and his sister to the seaside town Weston-super-Mare, Somerset, where he was raised and attended school. He later studied at Owens College in Manchester (now the University of Manchester) and there established himself as an outstanding scholar. Upon graduation in 1902 he attended Cambridge University for three years and in 1907 became a Fellow of Trinity College and, simultaneously, Chief Assistant at the Royal Greenwich Observatory. In 1912, at age twenty-nine, he was promoted to Plumian Professor of Astronomy and Experimental Philosophy at Cambridge and in 1914 became director of the

Cambridge Observatories. This rapid advancement recognized his keen abilities. He was a gifted communicator and later wrote prolifically, popularizing science throughout the 1920s and 1930s.

Eddington's greatest achievements lay in two areas. He was one of the inventors of astrophysics, the study of stars by the light they emit as analyzed by laws of physics known from earthbound observations and deductions. And he was the principal, English-language popularizer of Einstein's theory of relativity to both lay person and scientist alike. Such contributions were anticipated by his friends who, at the outbreak of World War I, obtained exemption for Eddington on the basis of his value as a scientist. He was a Quaker throughout his life and would have objected to conscription, which he did in any case. In returning the letter granting him exemption, which required only his signature, Eddington added a footnote that he would have objected had he been conscripted. Curiously, the letter of exemption required him to test relativity upon conclusion of the war. His scientist-friends' arguments were evidently convincing to the conscription authorities.

In November of 1915, while England and Germany were at war, Einstein presented his completed theory to the Berlin Academy and in 1916 published it in *Annalen der Physik*. Einstein sent copies of these papers to his friends including Willem de Sitter in the neutral Netherlands who, in turn, sent copies to Eddington. De Sitter also submitted, in 1916 and 1917, three of his own papers for publication by the Royal Astronomical Society of which Eddington was secretary. As secretary Eddington carefully read and reported on these papers. De Sitter's papers included a review and applications of general relativity and, in the third paper, an application to a matterless universe that requires the universe to be expanding. Eddington's position at that time was fortunate for the Royal Astronomical Society, for English science, and for science everywhere because with his mental acuity Eddington soon became thoroughly knowledgeable in relativity and contributed much to the theory and its application, including the first important experimental test of it. Eddington in 1917 joined with several colleagues, including Sir Frank Dyson, the Astronomer Royal, to plan measurements that would provide a test of relativity. Timing was clear: a successful test like they had in mind must follow the war because all instrument makers were fully engaged in manufacturing war material and funding of an experiment would be contingent on a successful completion of the war.

The optimal date for the intended test was 29 May (of any year) because of the high density of bright stars located near the sun unique to this date. In the test, an apparent shift in location of a star, whose light travelling to earth just grazed the sun, was to be measured (photographed). As Einstein had pointed out, relativity theory predicted a small deflection (1.745 arcseconds) of a ray of light by the sun's gravity giving an apparent shift in each star's location so that measured shifts in location could be compared to unshifted locations as a test of the theory. To determine deflection of its light, stars had to be measured (photographed) when their light passed "near" the sun and not near it. Comparison of the relative star positions when their light did not pass near the sun (photographed six months earlier or later) would provide the shifts. Fortuitously, a full eclipse of the sun would occur on 29 May 1919, an event that might not recur in another thousand years. When an armistice ending the fighting was signed on 11 November 1918, final planning of the expeditions began. The measurements were to be jointly made by expeditions of two groups, one each from the Royal Greenwich Observatory and from the Cambridge Observatories, widely separated along the line of totality (line of total eclipse of the sun) to reduce the risk of failure due to bad weather. One expedition[29] led by A. C. D. Crommelin assisted by C. Davidson of the Greenwich Observatory went to Sobral in northern Brazil and the other led by Eddington assisted by E. T. Cottingham of the Cambridge Observatories traveled to the Ilse of Principe in the Gulf of Guinea off the coast of West Africa one degree north of the equator. Equipment was manufactured, assembled, tested, and personnel and equipment dispatched to Sobral and Principe.

During the 302 seconds of total eclipse in Principe, sixteen photographic plates were exposed. Because of some cloudiness a wide range of exposures was used in the hope that a few would be good. One plate was found to show fairly good images of five stars. In addition, four plates were brought back to England undeveloped because they could not be developed in the hot climate. One of these four was also found to contain adequate images of five stars. "Check-plates" made six months in advance for comparison showed good images of twelve stars, including these five, without displacement.

Meanwhile, the Sobral expedition had experienced fine weather and obtained photographs of the full number of expected stars (12) but the image definition of these stars was poor due to some cause, probably heat distortion of the *coelostat mirror*. In an observatory a telescope is mounted on a mechanism that provides automatic tracking of a star as it moves across the sky due to the earth's rotation. In Sobral and Principe, no such mechanism was available; instead, a moving coelostat mirror was used with a stationary telescope. Cloudiness at Principe or some mechanical difference perhaps prevented this mirror from heating in the sun and suddenly cooling and distorting the image during the eclipse; but with clear weather in Sobral, one of the coelostat mirrors apparently heated and some transient distortion occurred during the eclipse making the value of plates acquired using this mirror questionable.

However, a second telescope and coelostat mirror were also employed in Sobral and seven images were acquired using this apparatus. These were the last developed and analyzed because equipment had to be modified to examine these plates. Yet it was clear by then that with the enfeebled images due to cloud cover at Principe and the distorted images from the first telescope at Sobral that the fate of the whole experiment would rest with these seven plates. And despite the unwieldy length of the second Sobral telescope, its slower-speed lens necessitating longer exposures, and a better required accuracy of the clock apparatus driving the coelostat mirror, rendering it more susceptible to distortion because of the larger magnification of the image and longer exposure, the images were nearly perfect in these seven plates.

The final deflections and their probable errors were determined by Eddington *et al* as follows:

Sobral	1.98 ± 0.12 arcseconds
Principe	1.61 ± 0.30 arcseconds.

Eddington wrote "It is usual to allow a margin of safety of about twice the probable error on either side of the mean. The evidence of the Principe plates is thus just about sufficient to rule out the possibility of the "half-deflection" (predicted by Newtonian gravity in Euclidian space), and the Sobral plates exclude it with practical certainty."[30] Later analysis with another possible interpretation of the data are described by J. Earman and C. Glymour.[31]

The expeditions' results were reported at a joint meeting in London of the Royal Society and the Royal Astronomical Society on 6 November 1919. Dyson spoke first and gave a lengthy account of how the expeditions were conceived and planned and gave a detailed summary of all results. Crommelin spoke next but didn't have much to add to Dyson's detailed account but thanked a long list of officials who assisted. Eddington, the third speaker, had little to describe after these long and tedious talks, except for their scientific meaning. He gave an exciting talk about relativity theory, a subject that was far better known to him than anyone else present. Eddington described curvature of space (not unique to relativity) and bending of light in addition to that caused by curvature (caused by relativity). He concluded by showing how the expeditions' results demonstrated that space was curved and that relativity correctly predicted their observations.

Edwin Hubble and his coworkers provided other early evidence supporting general relativity in their astronomical observation of expansion of the universe. Another was correct prediction of the 43 arcseconds of angle-per-century excess precession of the observed orbit of Mercury not accounted for by Newtonian mechanics (or theory) of gravitational attraction by other planets (Appendix D). The excess precession of Mercury's orbit predicted by general relativity agrees with the measured result of 43 arcseconds per century. Kenyon[28] and Martin[32] treat details of the calculation. Both the calculation and their comparison with observed results are summarized in Appendix D.

A similar but more exaggerated process, which therefore provides a superior test, was described by Russell A. Hulse and Joseph H. Taylor[33] in their 1975 description of a binary *pulsating source of radio emissions* PSR 1913+16 which they discovered using the 305 meter diameter, single-dish, radio telescope located at Arecibo, Puerto Rico. Pulsars are stars having masses about 1.4 times that of the sun but diameters of only a few kilometers, compared to the sun diameter of 1.39 million kilometers. They are believed to be old, in the final active phase of intermediate-mass stars. Their cores have already contracted into dense neutron stars. And with their contraction both their magnetic field and rotational velocity are greatly magnified. The combination of strong magnetic field and rapid spin together with a plasma effect leads to an emission of an intense and coherent beam of radiation along the pulsar *magnetic* axis, which only rarely coincides with the *spin* axis. A favorably oriented pulsar thus illuminates the earth with its radiation beam once each pulsar revolution. Such a characteristic, a regularly-spaced sequence of pulses, is the source of their name. For instance, PSR 1937+21 has a measured pulse interval of 1.5578 milliseconds (one-thousands of a second) with a rate of change of only 10^{-19} seconds per second (one second per ten million trillion seconds).

Hulse and Taylor observed that pulses from PSR 1913+16 were separated by an average of 59 milliseconds and that the pulse separation changed by as much as 80 microseconds (80×10^{-6} seconds or 80 one-millionths of a second). Such variation is uncharacteristically irregular for a pulsar. They deduced this pulsar is one of a pair of stars orbiting one another in an orbit about 4 light-seconds across, which would therefore fit within our sun (4.64 light-seconds diameter). The other star of the pair has not been observed and might be a black hole of similar mass. The precession of the star-pair orbit of PSR 1913+16 is 4.42263(3) degrees per year. (A number with a last digit in parentheses indicates the last digit is uncertain.) Since first observed in 1974 the two-star, elliptical orbit has advanced more than 120 degrees. The observed orbital period is 7.75 hours having a measured rate of change of $-2.40(9)\times 10^{-12}$ seconds per second compared to $-2.403(2)\times 10^{-12}$ seconds per second predicted by general relativity due to *gravitational radiation.* (The minus sign indicates the orbital period is decreasing.) Although indirect, this result is the first and, thus far, only experimental evidence supporting the gravity radiation of energy predicted by general relativity. For their discoveries Hulse and Taylor received the 1993 Nobel Prize in physics.

According to general relativity a *gravitational redshift* occurs when light travels away from a gravitational source. This redshift may be described using the principle of equivalence, the previously stated postulate on which general relativity is based, by which downward "gravitational acceleration" g may be ignored in a reference frame accelerated downward with acceleration g. As upward directed light leaves a moving frame the light is redshifted to lower frequency (longer wavelength). Downward light is blueshifted. The shift for either is derived in endnote 34.

In 1960 R. V. Pound and G. A. Rebka[35] published results of their measurements of gravitational blueshift of radiation traveling down the 22.6 meters of Jefferson Tower at the physics building at Harvard. Because the relative blueshift, predicted by the equation of endnote 34, is extremely small, only about 10^{-15} (i.e., one part in one thousand trillion), a successful earthbound experiment must be extremely well conceived and executed. The experiment of Pound and Rebka was. For a radiation source, Pound and Rebka utilized the recently discovered Mössbauer-transition emission from ^{57}Fe (radioactive iron) of 14.4 keV photons. Rudolph Ludwig Mössbauer had discovered in 1958 that the relative linewidth (spread in frequency divided by frequency) of radiation of ^{57}Fe *bound in a crystal lattice* was extremely narrow, about one part in 10^{12} (i.e., one part per trillion), for which Mössbauer received the 1961 Nobel Prize in physics. Still, to measure a relative shift of 10^{-15} required accuracy improved by significantly better than 10^3 or 1,000 times that afforded by this radiation source itself. Pound and Rebka obtained this additional accuracy by repeatedly "tuning" relative velocity between radioactive source and detector to measure the slight Doppler shift that gave the strongest radiation signal from the target ^{57}Fe at nearly 2 mm per hour relative velocity. This measured Doppler shift provides a gravitational blueshift of

$$\Delta\nu/\nu = (2.57 \pm 0.26) \times 10^{-15}$$

which agrees within their given measurement error of 10 percent with the relative shift predicted by general relativity. Pound and Joseph L. Snyder improved the experiment in 1965 to obtain agreement within one percent.

Another well conceived and well executed test of general relativity was described in 1976 by E. B. Fomalont and R. A. Sramek.[36] They used a radio telescope at Green Bank, West Virginia to achieve important advantages over the Eddington *et al* experiment. During the sudden cooling that accompanies an eclipse, visible-wavelength radiation is disturbed and obscured by strong atmospheric turbulence and by transients in observational apparatus such as a coelostat mirror. Alternatively, radio frequency radiation is not affected by turbulence and, more importantly, no eclipse is required as radio-frequency radiation is outside the spectrum of radiation emitted by the sun. In the Fomalont and Sramek experiment, two radio receivers were spaced a length L = 35 km apart and raised together from the horizontal (zero) angle to angle θ (theta). Then the path-length difference of the radiation detected by the two detectors was precisely given by $L \times \cos\theta$. (For a definition of the cosine function of argument θ, cos θ, see endnote 16 of Chapter 7.) Moreover, real radio-frequency (rf) signal features sometimes occurred in signals by which the separation in phase of real feature events in the two signals yielded a measured phase difference or delay Δ (the uppercase Greek "delta" in fraction of a period) between the two signals. At wavelength $\lambda = c/\nu$, where ν is the center of the interrogated narrow-rf-band frequency, the following, equivalent relations must hold.

$$\Delta = 2\pi/\lambda \times L\cos\theta \;=\; 2\pi\nu/c \times L\cos\theta.$$

With measurement of Δ, the only unknown in either of these two equations is the angle θ, the exact quantity needed to locate a star. Thus, angle θ was accurately determined for radio-source stars when their radio emission passed both near to and far from the sun. Using radio frequencies of 2.7 and 8.1 GHz, Fomalont and Sramek found a mean deflection of the path of rf waves in the sun's gravity field of 1.760 ± 0.016 arcseconds of angle, which agrees well with the Einstein-theory prediction of 1.745 arcseconds. The precision of this result is ten times better than that of the Eddington *et al* result.

In December 1964, a paper by Irwin Shapiro entitled "Fourth Test of General Relativity" (in addition to the three initially proposed by Einstein) appeared in *Physical Review Letters*. It described how a light beam travelling near a star would be delayed compared to one travelling in flat spacetime because the curvature of spacetime in the star's gravity field would cause the spacetime path of the beam to be curved and thereby lengthened. This effect is due to curvature of spacetime predicted by exact and detailed mathematical theory, examples of which have already been described using the Schwarzschild metric. Calculations by Shapiro of the total delay, now called the *Shapiro time*, for a signal sent from and reflected back to earth by Mercury just before or after it passes behind the sun would be 250 microseconds (or millionths of a second). While such a time delay could be easily resolved using 1964 technology, detection of weak radar or radio echoes was then impossible.

By the late 1960s, improvements in signal detection first made the experiments feasible. The first measurements of the Shapiro time by 400 radar reflections from Mercury in January, May, and August of 1967 showed agreement with theory within 20 percent. Experiments in 1970 using Mariner satellites 6 and 7 orbiting Mars with radio transponders to return strong radio signals to earth improved agreement between theoretical and measured Shapiro times to within 3 percent while radar reflection data from Mercury improved to 5 percent. The next improvements came with the Viking Landers on Mars with their stable, known elevations and capability to receive and return radio signals at both S- and X-band frequencies (2.3 and 8.4 Gigahertz or billion cycles per second). Delay of signals by interference in the sun's corona caused a significant uncertainty in measured Shapiro times. While this delay was unknown, its frequency dependence was known. Use of simultaneous signals at two frequencies allows corona delay uncertainty to be nearly eliminated from the measured data. Collection of Viking-Lander data and its analysis completed in 1979 gave a measured Shapiro time in agreement within 0.1 percent of relativity theory. The first new test of relativity proposed since 1916 has provided the most accurate confirmation of relativity yet obtained.

On the other hand, some authors have questioned the validity of relativity. For instance, Wallace Kantor examined results of 60 pre-1976 experiments commonly cited as supporting *kinematics* of the motion of light as predicted by special relativity. In the few cases where he judged the results to be sufficiently accurate to allow a meaningful conclusion, he claims that the results either did not exclusively support special relativity or contradicted it. Because no widely read physics journals accept papers critical of relativity (or quantum mechanics) according to Kantor, he had to publish his findings in a book.[37] Many of his criticisms seem carefully reasoned, well supported, and justified, but he does recognize that "No established physical theory is ever displaced by demonstrations of its logical, nor even observational, dubiousness; nor should it be. What displaces theories is alternative theories."[38]

Clifford Will describes unresolved questions pertaining to gravity and relativity theory in his interesting and well written book *Was Einstein Right?*[39] But he also presents compelling evidence that supports the affirmative answer to the question posed in his title, including a full account of Shapiro time measurement.

This chapter has provided a brief account of the essence of Einstein's theory of relativity and indicates the nature of evidence for and against its validity. It indicates the novelty of relativity theory, the distinctly new view of spacetime-material reality it provides, and some rather compelling evidence of its validity so far accumulated. Indeed, the "strangeness" of the predicted results, compared to those of the Newtonian paradigm which forms the basis of our traditional culture and of our intuition, confirms the newness of the reality described by relativity. Of course the new paradigm and it's predictions are not strange when it is adopted as the correct view of reality. And, after all, it does provide the superior predictions. (The interested reader may pursue further study of relativity including technical details by referring to the excellent texts by Kenyon,[28] Martin,[32] Will,[39] and Longair[40] which all list additional texts.)

So with tentative confirmation of relativity, do we now understand gravity? Certainly we can better predict its effects, but unanswered questions remain throughout science. Janna Levin remarks that

> Probing questions expose the fact that no one had a clear, tangible understanding of gravity before Einstein. Newton wrote down a mathematical expression describing how all mass attracts all other mass, but he still had to confess that in some sense he didn't fundamentally understand what this force was. Before Einstein, we had a set of rules for describing gravitational attraction but no real sense of how these rules were enforced."[41]

And we still have no fundamental understanding of gravity but merely a set of rules for describing gravity effects in time and space. Lack of tangible understanding is illustrated by *non-mathematical descriptions* of relativistic gravity wherein curvature of spacetime is substituted for weight and bodies "fall down a curved surface" or "follow a path of least resistance."[42] But without weight why would bodies fall or which way is down and without force where is resistance? Throughout history, probing questions have always revealed deficiency in scientific understanding, a fact learned by every good scientist.

An interesting dilemma arises among scientists and nonscientists alike, the dilemma in which a new paradigm or culture, even one supposed to be superior, is rejected because it *seems* strange, non-intuitive, inconsistent, and implausible. But that is just how the new is supposed to seem! This reaction suggests how we prevent ourselves from seeing a truer view of reality when, like a category-two student, we cling to a traditional paradigm or culture, refusing to let go of the familiar and traditional.

This reaction is general to the human condition. Psychiatrist M. Scott Peck arrives at the same reaction in an altogether different and more important challenge: finding spiritual truth and meaning. He prescribes the following treatment.

> To develop a broader vision we must be willing to forsake, to kill, our narrower vision. In the short run it is more comfortable not to do this – to stay where we are, to keep using the same microcosmic map, to avoid suffering the death of cherished notions. The road of spiritual growth, however, lies in the opposite direction. We begin by disturbing what we already believe, by actively seeking the threatening and unfamiliar, by deliberately challenging the validity of what we have previously been taught and hold dear. The path to holiness lies through questioning *everything*.[43] (the italics are Peck's)

Discovering or just accepting a new vision is difficult. A new, abstract, non-intuitive vision leads to loss of intuition and understanding while one develops intuition and understanding in a new paradigm, i.e., to progress one must impose on him- or her-self temporary confusion, disorientation, and ignorance. In following chapters we shall find that Peck's diagnosis applies in adopting the theory of quantum mechanics, in science in general, and in a search for truth in personal belief and meaning. In each case, despite introducing temporary confusion and perhaps even fear if one is not confident in him- or her-self and in truth, Peck's prescription leads ultimately to improved discovery and understanding of truth.

Notes and References for Chapter 8.

[1] Clark, Ronald W., *Einstein: The Life and Times,* Avon Books, New York, 1971.

[2] From a 3 May 1901 letter from Einstein to ETH Professor Alfred Stern.

[3] We address herein four of these five papers excluding only Einstein's Doctoral Thesis he submitted in 1905 to the University of Zürich and published later that year in *Annalen der Physik.* Modern English translations of all five together with insightful commentary are provided in Stachel, John, *Einstein's Miraculous Year: Five Papers That Changed the Face of Physics,* Princeton University Press, Princeton, NJ, 1998.

[4] Einstein, A., *Annalen der Physik* **17**, 1905, 549. English translation of this article, "Investigations on the Theory of the Brownian Movement," and others by A. D. Cowper is found in Einstein, Albert, *Investigations on the Theory of the Brownian Movement,* Dover, New York, 1956.

[5] See, for example, Hutchins, Darrell K., and Barton E. Dahneke, "Characterization of particles by modulated dynamic light scattering," *Journal of Chemical Physics* **100**, 1994, 7890-7915.

[6] Einstein, A., *Annalen der Physik* **17**, 1905, 132. An English translation of this article, "On a Heuristic Viewpoint Concerning the Production and Transformation of Light," by A. B. Arons and M. B. Peppard is found in *American Journal of Physics* **33**, 1965, 357.

[7] Einstein, A., "Zur Electrodynamik bewegter Körper " (On the Electrodynamics of Moving Bodies), *Annalen der Physik* **17**, 1905, 891. A second, three-page article by Einstein followed in *Annalen der Physik* **18**, 1905, 639. Both are reprinted in *The Principle of Relativity,* A. Einstein, H. A. Lorentz, H. Weyl, and H. Minkowski, Dover, New York, 1952, 37-71. (This book is a reproduction of the English translations by W. Perrett and G. B. Jeffrey of papers by the listed authors, Methuen and Company, Ltd., 1923.)

[8] The Doppler shift is derived using the basic relationship between wave frequency ν, wavelength λ, and wave velocity c_s, namely, $\nu \times \lambda = c_s$. Since frequency detected is number of wave cycles arriving at a detector per second, which is the relative velocity of the wave with respect to the detector $c_s \pm u_r$ divided by the wavelength λ, we obtain for the case when the detector moves with speed $\pm u_r$ relative to a stationary sound source of frequency ν the apparent frequency ν' given by

$$\nu' = (c_s \pm u_r) / \lambda = \nu (c_s \pm u_r) / c_s = \nu (1 \pm u_r / c_s).$$

[9] Lorentz, H. A., "Electromagnetic phenomena in a system moving with any velocity less than that of light," *Proceedings of the Academy of Sciences of Amsterdam* (English Version) **6**, 1904. Reprinted in *The Principle of Relativity,* loc. cit., 3-34.

[10] Ferris, Timothy, *Coming of Age in the Milky Way,* William Morrow, New York, 1988, 183.

[11] To derive the Lorentz transformation let x_0 and t_0 represent x-direction displacement and time as they appear to an observer S_0 motionless in frame S_0. Let x_1 and t_1 represent these same properties as they appear to an observer S_1 motionless in frame S_1, where S_1 is moving relative to S_0 with x-direction velocity u_r. Place one of two identical clocks in each system, with the clock in S_0 reading time t_0 and the clock in S_1 reading time t_1. Synchronize them at $x_0 = x_1 = t_0 = t_1 = 0$. Special relativity requires that S_1 coordinates appear *to observer S_0* in S_0 coordinates

$$x_1 = \gamma (x_0 - u_r t_0), \qquad y_1 = y_0, \qquad z_1 = z_0, \qquad t_1 = \gamma (t_0 - u_r x_0/c^2),$$

with γ (gamma) $= 1 / \sqrt{(1 - u_r^2/c^2)}$. *Observer S_1* sees S_0 coordinates in S_1 coordinates (obtained by inverting the above equations to obtain equations for x_0, y_0, z_0, t_0)

$$x_0 = \gamma (x_1 + u_r t_1), \qquad y_0 = y_1, \qquad z_0 = z_1, \qquad t_0 = \gamma (t_1 + u_r x_1/c^2).$$

When relative velocity u_r is zero, $\gamma = 1$ and corresponding measures in both frames are nonrelativistic. These equations were first discovered by H. A. Lorentz. H. Poincaré later derived and called them the *Lorentz transformation.* They are derived in Appendix B.

[12] The relative velocity of magnitude u_r in $\nu' = \nu \gamma (1 \pm u_r/c)$ (page 162) is taken to be recessional or away from a light source with the negative sign, resulting in a redshift $\nu' < \nu$. For relative velocity toward a light source the positive sign is chosen, and a blueshift $\nu' > \nu$ results. In our expanding universe wherein increasingly distant objects are nominally receding with increasing velocity, the light frequency from these objects is generally increasingly redshifted as distance increases. However, an occasional, anomalous light source is observed moving toward earth and its light spectrum is blueshifted. In general in our expanding universe, redshift provides a measure of nominal recessional velocity and, thereby, a nominal measure of distance between earth and the light source, a relation called Hubble's law. To determine redshift a specific emission line of, say, the hydrogen spectrum having exactly known frequency at $u_r = 0$ is selected and observed. Because light always travels at fixed velocity c (in empty space or vacuum or air) and $c = \lambda \nu$, where λ is the light wavelength and ν its frequency, a shift in frequency, $\Delta\nu$, is always accompanied by an opposite shift in wavelength, $\Delta\lambda$, i.e., $\Delta\nu/\nu = - \Delta\lambda/\lambda$. The above result is the *Doppler redshift* of special relativity due to relative motion of bodies. In an expanding universe a *cosmological redshift* emerges from general relativity that predicts a redshift of light between two bodies receding due purely to expansion of space. While the Doppler redshift implies an event horizon at recession velocity < c, the cosmological redshift predicts a relative redshift increase to 1.50 (150 percent) for an object receding at c. These effects may combine to give a redshift due to both special and general relativity effects. See Lineweaver, Charles H., and Tamara M. Davis, "Misconceptions about the Big Bang," *Scientific American,* March 2005, 36-45.

[13] The kinetic energy of a body of mass m moving with velocity v is derived by calculating the work energy W required to produce the velocity v and kinetic energy KE since, by conservation of energy, W = KE. Using the definition of work W we write

$$[1] \qquad W = \int_{x=0}^{x} F\,dx = \int_{t=0}^{t} d(mv)/dt\; dx/dt\; dt = \int_{t=0}^{t} v\, d(mv)/dt\; dt = \int_{mv=0}^{mv} v\, d(mv) = KE.$$

For the simplest case of constant mass m the result is the well-known expression

$$KE = m v^2/2.$$

But in special relativity mass m depends on rest mass m_0 and relative velocity v so that $m v = m_0 \gamma v = m_0 v / \sqrt{(1 - v^2/c^2)}$. Then,

$$[2] \qquad KE = \int_{mv=0}^{mv} v\, d(mv) = m_0 \int_{v=0}^{v} v\, \{1/(1 - v^2/c^2)^{1/2} + (v^2/c^2)/(1 - v^2/c^2)^{3/2}\}\, dv$$

$$= m_0 \int_{v=0}^{v} v\, dv/(1 - v^2/c^2)^{3/2} = m_0\, c^2 \{1/(1 - v^2/c^2)^{1/2} - 1\}$$

In other words we obtain $KE = (m - m_0)\, c^2$. That is, KE may be regarded as equivalent to c^2 times the increase in mass of the moving body over that of the body at rest. This result suggests that mass $\times\, c^2$ and energy are equivalent, that a body at rest contains a rest energy $RE = m_0 c^2$, and that total energy E of a moving body is a sum of its rest and kinetic energies, namely,

$$[3] \qquad E = RE + KE = m c^2 = m_0 c^2/(1 - v^2/c^2)^{1/2} \qquad \text{or}$$

[3] $$E = m_0 c^2 + m_0 v^2/2 \{1 + 3/4\, v^2/c^2 + 5/8\, v^4/c^4 + \ldots\}.$$

An "expansion" derived by Newton, similar to ones given in endnotes 13 and 17 of Chapter 7, was used to obtain the last equation. When $v^2/c^2 << 1$ (for "<<" read "is much less than") only the first term in curly brackets is significant and

[4] $$E = RE + KE = m_0 c^2 + m_0 v^2/2.$$

This derivation of [4] follows Richtmyer, Kennard, and Lauritsen (*Introduction to Modern Physics,* Fourth Edition, McGraw-Hill, New York, 1955, 67-68) and Albert Einstein (*Relativity, The Special and General Theory,* Robert W. Lawson (translator), Wings Books, Random House, New York, 1961, 50); however, the derivation is incomplete in the latter source.

When a body is motionless ($v = 0$, $m = m_0$), only the rest energy remains. We therefore obtain at $v = 0$ Einstein's famous relation giving the equivalence of mass and energy,

[5] $$E = m_0 c^2.$$

In classical physics, energy has no distinct zero value, i.e., zero energy may be arbitrarily assigned, because only energy differences are considered in applying the principle of conservation of energy and any zero energy value cancels whenever an energy difference is calculated, such as in [1]. But in relativity a zero-velocity energy of an object is included in such a constant as the mass-equivalent energy of the object at rest. This result provides a fundamental insight uniquely obtained (up to now) by relativity.

The result [5] is apparently general in describing all mass and energy equivalence. If we consider internal kinetic energy of a body's molecules in the form of heat or sound energy or rotational or any other ponderable energy δE (where Greek "delta" denotes difference, incremental, or change in), δE has equivalent mass $\delta m = \delta E/c^2$. If a body gains or loses energy δE by radiation, its mass increase or decrease is $\delta m = \delta E/c^2$. The total-energy-equivalent mass of a body is therefore $m_0 + \delta m$. In relativity it is $m_0 + \delta m$ that influences gravity. Thus, in relativity the mass of a body and the gravity force depend on any ponderable energy in or on the body and even on other forms of energy (i.e., mass or radiation or ...) present in nearby space.

A photon is a massless particle but it carries photon energy $h\nu$, h being Planck's constant and ν being the photon frequency. Thus, equivalence of mass and energy gives a photon mass $m = E/c^2 = h\nu/c^2$ and a photon momentum $p = h\nu/c$. Photons are affected by gravity because of their equivalent mass. As a result, a large mass can "gravity focus" diverging light.

[14] Calculations of length contraction and time dilation are symmetric or reciprocal in special relativity in the sense that either system may be regarded as moving relative to the other with relative speed u_r. Using $t_1 = \gamma(t_0 - u_r x_0/c^2)$ from note 11, we take in a first case $\Delta x_0 = 0$ and obtain $\Delta t_1 = \gamma \Delta t_0$ while in a second case we take $\Delta x_1 = 0$ and obtain $\Delta t_0 = \gamma \Delta t_1$. Regardless of which system is fixed as the reference, time dilation and length contraction always apply for an observer moving relative to a system containing the time or length interval. Thus, an observer in a first system sees in a second system the identical time dilation and length contraction that an observer in the second system sees in the first.

[15] The twin paradox is a vivid illustration of time dilation in special relativity but not one easily understood because, in ignoring acceleration or some other asymmetry (Bondi, Hermann, *Relativity and Common Sense, A New Approach to Einstein,* Doubleday, Garden City, NY, 1962), reciprocity applies (relative velocity is always reciprocal). But reciprocity doesn't apply because only one twin experiences acceleration, feeling its direction and strength. Unless one considers acceleration as treated in general relativity and advanced special-relativity texts (see, for example, Pauli, W., *Theory of Relativity,* Dover, New York, 1958, 13, *inter alia*, or Bondi, loc. cit.), special relativity predicts that aging of the traveling *or* other twin is reduced *or* aging of both is reduced somewhat less. The illustration usually ends without mention of the last two possibilities. But, only one twin ages less than a stationary clock left behind in the rocket terminal. As Bondi observed, "... acceleration does matter and it is not so easy to specify just how it matters. To say that something does not matter is a

complete description; to say that something does matter requires a great deal of further elucidation." (Bondi, loc. cit., 147-148.) Considering acceleration, aging is slowed only for the traveling twin.

[16] Milonni, Peter W., *The Quantum Vacuum,* Academic Press, New York, 1994, 304. Gamow, George, *The Great Physicists from Galileo to Einstein,* Dover, New York, 1961, 173-174.

[17] Einstein, A., *Annalen der Physik* **49**, 1916, 769. Einstein's papers describing both relativity theories as well as several other related papers by Einstein and other authors are provided in English translation in *The Principle of Relativity,* loc. cit. Einstein's papers on the theory of special relativity are provided in English by Stachel, John, loc. cit.

[18] Johann Friedrich Karl Gauss, who we met earlier in our discussion of non-Euclidian geometry, questioned the flatness of space and even performed experiments wherein he attempted to measure the sum of angles between legs of a triangle defined by three mountain peaks to test the flatness of space. To the accuracy then available and perhaps even now, the curvature of space is undetectable by this experiment. With the exception of a few obscure processes in which one must exert great effort to detect an effect of relativity, such as the excess precession of the orbit of Mercury, bending and delaying of light passing near the sun, the gravitational redshift of light emitted from a massive star, and gravity focusing of light from distant sources passing near a massive intermediate body or set of bodies, observable effects in the solar system that distinctly favor general relativity over Newtonian theory are presently unknown. But Gauss' early insight and conviction, to the extent he attempted an experiment to test his non-Euclidian geometry against real space, is remarkable.

[19] *The Principle of Relativity,* loc. cit., 148.

[20] Quoted in Eisenstaedt, Jean, "The Early Interpretation of the Schwarzschild Solution," in *Einstein and the History of General Relativity,* Don Howard and John Stachel (editors), Birkhäuser, Berlin, 1989, 213.

[21] Guth, Alan H., *The Inflationary Universe,* Addison-Wesley, Reading, MA, 1997.

[22] Friedmann, A., *Zeitschrift für Physik* **10**, 1922, 377-386, **21**, 1924, 326-332. English translations of these articles are found in *Cosmological Constants: Papers in Modern Cosmology,* J. Bernstein and G. Feinberg (editors), Columbia University Press, New York, 1987, 22.

[23] However, Georges Lemaître explicitly proved in 1932, a proof already implicit in a 1925 paper by him, that the mathematical character of the Schwarzschild metric at $r = \alpha$ is non-singular.

[24] Martin, J. L., *General Relativity: A Guide to its Consequences for Gravity and Cosmology,* Ellis Horwood Limited, Chichester, West Sussex, England, 1988, Chapter 9 and 106-117.

[25] Eddington, Arthur, *Space, Time and Gravitation,* Cambridge University Press, Cambridge, 1920, 98.

[26] A single integration of the differential equation $\pm c\,dt = dr/(1 - \alpha/r)$ gives the exact solution for the *null radial geodesic*

$$\pm c\,(t - t_0) = r - r_0 + \alpha \log_e[(r - \alpha)/(r_0 - \alpha)].$$

This spacetime trajectory is for a photon moving radially at velocity c in Schwarzschild spacetime.

For a *rising photon*, the plus sign applies. Assume $r > r_0$. At $r_0 = \alpha$, $[(r - \alpha)/(r_0 - \alpha)]$ and $\log_e[(r - \alpha)/(r_0 - \alpha)] \to \infty$ and $(t - t_0) \to \infty$ even when $(r - \alpha)$ is small. Thus, a rising photon takes infinite coordinate time to rise even an infinitesimal radial distance from $r = \alpha$.

For a *falling photon*, the minus sign applies. Assume $r < r_0$. At $r = \alpha$, $[(r - \alpha)/(r_0 - \alpha)] \rightarrow 0$, $\alpha \log_e[(r - \alpha)/(r_0 - \alpha)] \rightarrow -\infty$ and $(t - t_0) \rightarrow \infty$ even when $(r_0 - \alpha)$ is small. Thus, a falling photon takes infinite coordinate time to fall an infinitesimal distance at $r = \alpha$.

Therefore, to a distant observer, light (and mass) appear to accumulate in Schwarzschild spacetime at radius $r = \alpha$.

[27] The *exponential function* of z is denoted $\exp(z) = e^z$ with the constant $e = 2.718281828...$; z may be positive or negative. Since $\exp(2.3026) = 10$, $\exp(z) = 10^{(z/2.3026)}$.

The exponential function is very common because it describes many physical processes. It arises whenever a rate of change of some quantity (chemical reactant, velocity, ...) is proportional to the amount of the quantity. Thus, when the deceleration of a particle of mass m suspended in a motionless fluid is due to particle-fluid friction and is characterized by Newton's second law $m\, dv/dt = -f v$, with f the friction coefficient which is constant at small velocities and v the particle velocity in the motionless fluid, the solution for the particle motion at time t is

$$v(t) = v(0) \exp(-ft/m).$$

z	0	±0.01	±0.02	±0.05	±0.1	±0.2
[exp(z) - 1] / z	1.00	1.005	1.010	1.025	1.052	1.107
% error	0	0.5	1.0	2.5	5.2	10.7

At small z values the exponential function of z is well approximated by $\exp(z) \cong 1 + z$ or $[\exp(z) - 1]/z \cong 1$ (see above table).

Because of its *asymptotic form* $\exp(z) = 1 + z$ when z is small, the following approximation is valid for small z and constant A. The smaller the value of z, the better the approximation.

$$F(z) = A/[\exp(z) - 1] \cong A/z.$$

This result is the "mathematical trick" Planck utilized in discovering that energy occurs only in discrete quanta (Chapter 9).

Another function, called the *logarithm function,* is a companion to the exponential function as it represents an *inverse of the exponential function.* That is,

$$\log_e(\exp(z)) = \log_e(e^z) = z,$$

where the subscript e denotes the natural or e *base* of the logarithm. Also, $\log_{10}(10^w) = w$, with the logarithm now having base 10. In general, $\log_a(a^b) = b$, with the logarithm base a.

x	1/e	1/e²	1/10	1/e³	1/e⁴	1/100	0
$\log_e(x)$	- 1	- 2	- 2.3026	- 3	- 4	- 4.6052	- ∞
$\log_{10}(x)$	- 0.43429	- 0.86859	- 1	- 1.3029	- 1.7372	- 2	- ∞

x	1	e	e²	10	e³	e⁴	100
$\log_e(x)$	0	1	2	2.3026	3	4	4.6052
$\log_{10}(x)$	0	0.43429	0.86859	1	1.3029	1.7372	2

The logarithm function has several useful properties, three of which we now describe. First, as in the opposite-bottom table, the logarithm function *compresses* data. Recall the constant (base) e = 2.718281828... Then,

$$\log_e(e^x) = \log_e(2.718281828^x) = x,$$

where x represents any number and e^x represents a corresponding positive number. The logarithm with any base q and argument 1 is zero since any base q raised to the power zero is 1, i.e., $q^0 = 1$ and $\log_q(1) = 0$.

Second, *a logarithm of a product of terms is the sum of their logarithms.* Let $w = \exp(x)\times\exp(y)\times\exp(-z) = e^x \times e^y \times e^{-z} = e^{(x + y - z)}$. Then the logarithm function gives

$$\log_e(w) = \log_e(e^{(x + y - z)}) = x + y - z = \log_e(e^x) + \log_e(e^y) + \log_e(e^{-z})$$

and the logarithm function may thus be used to *convert a product of terms into a sum of terms.*

Third, the logarithm function also *simplifies* data for the function $y = A\exp(B\,x)$ since $\log_e(y) = \log_e(A) + B\,x$ is a straight line with intercept $\log_e(A)$ and slope B in a *semilog plot* (the y-axis scale is logarithmic, the x-axis scale is linear).

When $F(t) = A\exp(-at) + B\exp(-bt)$, such as is encountered in a rate process involving two mechanisms of different rates, a "semilog plot" of F(t) (logarithmic scale) versus t (linear scale) shows a curve consisting of two straight lines connected by a smooth transition. At small times both processes are active but decay is dominated by the faster process and measured data take the form of a straight line of slope $-a$. At large times when the faster-process is complete, measured data take the form of a second straight line having slope $-b$. Thus, multiple mechanisms may be *isolated and evaluated* using the logarithm function.

[28] Kenyon, I. R., *General Relativity,* Oxford University Press, Oxford, 1990.

[29] Further details are given by Aczel, Amir D., *God's Equation,* Four Walls Eight Windows, New York, 1999, 126-127, 143.

[30] Eddington, Arthur, loc. cit., 118.

[31] Earman, J., and C. Glymour, "Relativity and Eclipses: The British Eclipse Expeditions of 1919 and their Predecessors," *Historical Studies in the Physical Sciences* **11** (1), 1980, 49-85. The preconceptions of these authors are questioned by many scientists. See endnote 7 of Chapter 4.

[32] Martin, J. L., loc. cit.

[33] Hulse, R. A., and J. H. Taylor, *Astrophysical Journal* **195**, 1975, L51-53. For a popular-level account that includes many interesting details see Will, Clifford M., *Was Einstein Right?,* Basic Books, New York, 1986, Chapter 10.

[34] The *gravitational redshift* occurs in light emitted from a gravitational source of mass M. By the principle of equivalence the shift is calculated using the downward light-emitter-fixed frame acceleration $g = dv/dt = GM/r^2$. Frame velocity as the light leaves it, Δv, is determined at the time light escapes the frame. In interval dt frame velocity increases by $dv = GM/r^2\,dt = GM/r^2\,dr/c$. The "source velocity" for upward-traveling light departing $(r \to \infty)$ the downward traveling frame is

$$\Delta v = GM/c \int_{r_0}^{\infty} dr/r^2 = GM/r_0 c,$$

where r_0 is the starting radius in the gravitational field, e.g., surface of star or planet M. It follows that the relative shift in wavelength λ (Greek "lambda") resulting from source velocity Δv is, invoking $c = \lambda\nu$ where ν (Greek "nu") is frequency,

$$\Delta\lambda = \lambda - \lambda_0 = (c + \Delta v)/\nu_0 - c/\nu_0 = \Delta v/\nu_0 = GM/(r_0 c \nu_0) = GM\lambda_0/(r_0 c^2),$$

with $\Delta\lambda$ ("delta lambda") a wavelength shift and λ_0 ("lambda sub-naught") or ν_0 ("nu sub-naught") an original wavelength or frequency. Thus,

$$\Delta\lambda/\lambda_0 = GM/(r_0 c^2).$$

To an observer, gravitational wavelength shift for outward-traveling light from a star is always positive, toward longer λ or toward the red end of the color spectrum. Light moving toward an observer on M is blueshifted. Since $c = \lambda \times \nu$, it follows that $\Delta\lambda/\lambda = -\Delta\nu/\nu$ and the relative wavelength shift applies with opposite sign for relative frequency shift, toward red in both cases.

When light rises only from r_0 to r_1 or falls from r_1 to r_0 the same calculation applies except that r_0 and r_1 become the limits of integration in the above integral equation. Integration with new upper limit r_1 gives

$$\Delta\lambda / \lambda_0 = -\Delta\nu / \nu_0 \cong G M/c^2 \ (r_1 - r_0)/r_0 r_1.$$

An alternative derivation of this result invokes conservation of system energy E = constant, light or photon energy $E' = h\nu$, equivalence of photon mass and photon energy $m = E'/c^2 = h\nu/c^2$ (see endnote 13 above), and gravitational potential energy of a photon $-GMh\nu/(r c^2)$. Combining these principles/quantities we write, using subscripts 0 and 1 to denote smaller and larger radii, $E_0 = h\nu_0 - GMh\nu_0/(r_0 c^2) = E_1 = h\nu_1 - GMh\nu_1/(r_1 c^2)$ from which

$$\Delta\lambda/\lambda_0 = -\Delta\nu/\nu_0 = -(\nu_1 - \nu_0)/\nu_0 \cong GM/c^2 (r_1 - r_0)/r_0 r_1.$$

[35] Pound, R. V., and Rebka, G. A., *Physical Review Letters* **4**, 1960, 337-341.

[36] Fomalont, E. B., and R. A. Sramek, *Physical Review Letters* **36**, 1976, 1475-1478.

[37] Kantor, Wallace, *Relativistic Propagation of Light,* Coronado Press, Lawrence, KN, 1976.

[38] Kantor, loc. cit., ix.

[39] Will, Clifford M., loc. cit.

[40] Longair, M. S., *Theoretical Concepts in Physics,* Cambridge University Press, Cambridge, 1984.

[41] Levin, Janna, *How the Universe got its Spots,* Anchor Books, New York, 2002, 45. This book is both charming and useful.

[42] Ibid., 47. In illustrating relativity Levin describes the moon *falling* due to the earth's mass (gravity), mixing two intuitions. The present writer commits the same transgression in Chapter 9 (and probably elsewhere as well) mixing intuitions in describing electron orbits, as if electrons were discrete particles in deterministic orbits instead of quantum-theory probability distributions filling their so-called "orbitals." It is difficult to describe a paradigm from outside its own intuition; yet, that is the only way a paradigm may be reliably described, i.e., free of circular logic and self reference.

[43] Peck, M. Scott, *The Road Less Traveled, A New Psychology of Love, Traditional Values and Spiritual Growth,* Simon and Schuster, New York, 1978, 193-194.

9. Science and the Search for Truth: Quantum Mechanics

We have completed summaries of two theories of mechanics: Newtonian mechanics and relativity. In this chapter we turn our attention to the scientists and their discoveries that led to a third: quantum mechanics or quantum theory or quantum physics, a theory of a much different character that consequently suggests much different visions of reality. The novelty of the quantum theory and the contrast of its visions of reality with previous culture and convention caused its discovery to be difficult, only possible through non-intuitive, indirect implications of observed results suggesting new relationships between facts, both new facts and old. These new relationships or principles or laws provide the new visions of quantum physics.

We begin with Hertz's investigation of Maxwell's electromagnetic theory and Hertz's discovery of the photoelectric effect unexpectedly discovered in this investigation.

Hertz and the Discovery of the Photoelectric Effect

Heinrich Rudolf Hertz (1857-1894) first pursued a study of engineering but switched to physics and studied under Hermann Helmholtz and Gustav Kirchhoff at the University of Berlin. In 1880 Hertz received his Ph.D. *magna cum laude* in physics. He is honored today as the namesake of a basic unit (the unit of frequency, or one cycle per second, is called a Hertz, abbreviated Hz) in recognition of his seminal contributions to electromagnetics even though his entire career lasted a mere twelve years after he left Berlin. Hertz went from Berlin to Karlsruhe where he took a faculty position and began his work there by seeking a worthy problem. Helmholtz suggested to his former student that he work in the area of electromagnetics because of a prize being offered by the Berlin Academy of Sciences. Physics of electromagnetics was just emerging as theoretical and experimental disciplines.

The recently deceased Scottish physicist James Clerk Maxwell (1831-1879) had developed a comprehensive theory of electromagnetics. He presented it before the Royal Society in 1864 as a paper entitled *A Dynamic Theory of the Electromagnetic Field.* This classic paper has been equaled by few other single papers in physics, if any, in its eventual impact. This impact is founded in two properties of his theory. (1) The scope of the theory is huge. It embraces not only electric and magnetic fields but also optics, radioactive emissions, and technologies based on infrared, radio, radar, X-ray, and microwave radiation as well as electric power production and use. (2) It was a new type of theory. Michael Faraday and others requested Maxwell to express it in plain language instead of a set of four coupled (interdependent) differential equations, but it couldn't (and still can't) be done. Oliver Heaviside (1850-1925) succeeded in reducing the set to just two complex equations, but that is as "simple" as it gets. (The relativistic Maxwell's theory takes the form of two coupled equations containing a single rank-2 tensor, more sophisticated mathematically but also simpler, like Heaviside's set, in containing only two equations.) While early physical theories were generally based on *physical mechanisms*, Newton's second law of motion and his theory of gravitation and Coulomb's law of attraction/repulsion of unlike/like charges were strictly mathematics based; and Maxwell's theory was even more-so based on *abstract mathematical expressions.* These expressions provide an exact, comprehensive, definitive *description* of electromagnetic phenomena but provide no physical *understanding* in even a qualitative mechanical or material model by which a mechanism can be visualized physically. Maxwell's theory took physics to a new level of mathematical abstraction. And its mathematical foundation is the most fundamental level known so that it cannot be reduced to any simpler alternative view. However, it is implied in the more basic and more complex and more recent quantum electrodynamics we shall discuss below.

Following his seminal work investigating Maxwell's theory we are about to consider, Hertz was asked to explain the theory. He responded "To the question, 'What is Maxwell's theory?' I know of no shorter or more definite answer than the following: Maxwell's theory is Maxwell's system of equations." To this day, light and other electromagnetic radiation are only poorly understood in a classical-physics sense, being represented alternatively by a wave and a corpuscular (particle) model as best suits the application. This practice gave rise to an early joke that on odd days of the month light was a wave and on even it was a particle. No wonder the Berlin Academy sought to encourage better understanding of electromagnetics.

In fact, like any highly original theory, Maxwell's theory had not been well received and was only one among several candidates describing electromagnetics, including one due to Riemann (now lost). It was only one of several candidates, that is, until Hertz completed and published the results of his experiments in 1888 which verified Maxwell's theory down to the smallest details.[1]

To investigate electromagnetic radiation, Hertz followed a strategy suggested by Maxwell himself. He set up a circuit containing an inductance L and a capacitance C, the latter taking the form of two metal spheres separated by an air gap. Such an LC circuit sustains an oscillating signal that, once initiated, continues nearly unchanging in time, slowly decaying by energy loss in repeating sparks across the capacitor air gap. Once Hertz initiated a current in this circuit it spontaneously oscillated, producing a spark in the air gap near each oscillation peak. Hertz mounted the circuit on a cylindrical-paraboloid reflector with the center between the electrodes at the focal point of the reflector to obtain a directed beam of parallel, planar, electromagnetic waves. According to Maxwell's theory, a regular sequence of oscillations (sparks) should produce radiation of electromagnetic waves. To detect and measure such radiation Hertz used the complementary concept that, were such waves produced, they would in turn produce current in a second, "antenna" circuit. Thus, Hertz utilized a second antenna circuit containing an adjustable air gap between two smaller metal spheres of small separation. When electromagnetic waves excited the antenna circuit, he reasoned, he would observe sparks in the small gap, with only stronger signals giving sparks at larger gaps. By use of this portable-antenna-probe device he determined the amplitude-versus-location nature of the standing electromagnetic waves emitted from his first circuit.

Hertz first determined the wavelength of the radiated waves by placing a reflecting (metal) sheet some distance from and perpendicular to his LC-emitter circuit. He determined that a standing wave was present by repeatedly probing the field along the axis between the emitter and the reflecting sheet. By this means he found the separations at which the signal was maximum. By Maxwell's theory the distance between maxima in this standing wave was one-half the wavelength of the radiation. He knew the frequency ν (Greek "nu") of the emitted waves (sparks) and could control it by tuning the LC-emitter circuit, which he did to obtain good signals. Knowing both the wavelength λ (Greek "lambda") and the frequency ν, he could calculate the velocity of propagation of the wave $v = \nu \times \lambda$. He thereby obtained $v = c$, the velocity of light, the same velocity predicted twenty years earlier by Maxwell. (Quantities ε_0 and μ_0, described on page 77, are essentially the same in air and in vacuum.) Hertz demonstrated in a series of experiments[1] that these waves showed all the other properties of light as well: polarization, reflection, and refraction. In other words, light and electromagnetic radiation are the same thing, with light being distinguished only as the special case of electromagnetic radiation having wavelength in the range visible to the human eye (between 0.4 and 0.7 millionths of a meter).

The point of present interest is somewhat tangential to this full account. Hertz astutely observed and documented during his studies an important, incidental observation, an observation that would prove important in the discovery of quantum mechanics. Hertz noted that the sparks between the metal spheres in his antenna circuit occurred more readily when they were illuminated with ultraviolet light from the sparks in his LC-emitter circuit. Enclosing the antenna-circuit spheres in a black box or merely placing a glass sheet between the emitter and antenna sparks, to stop the ultraviolet light, suppressed or retarded the latter sparks. This was the first recorded observation of the *photoelectric effect*: emission of electrons from matter caused by light. Hertz was unable to pursue any study of this effect, due to his untimely death at age 36 caused by massive food poisoning, but Philipp Lenard, Albert Einstein, and Robert Millikan continued the effort. Einstein succeeded in fully predicting the nature of the photoelectric effect by reason alone in one of his 1905 papers we have not yet but soon shall consider.

Planck's Theory of Black-Body Radiation

The next major step in the discovery of quantum mechanics, and the most significant and profound one, was made by German physicist Max Planck (1858-1947). Like Hertz, Planck studied physics under Helmholtz and Kirchhoff in Berlin. He received his doctorate in 1879, one year previous to Hertz, upon completion of his doctoral thesis on the subject of thermodynamics.

He was appointed to the faculty at Munich from where, after five years, he moved to Kiel University. In 1889, on the death of Kirchhoff, he was appointed to replace his old teacher. One problem Kirchhoff had studied and undoubtedly described to his students was the radiation of heat between bodies. Kirchhoff had discovered a law that bears his name stating that the ratio of emissive to absorptive radiative "power" of a body was independent of the nature of the body. Perhaps in honor of his predecessor, Planck took up the study of heat radiation himself in 1894. He sought to discover a complete theory that described the energy distribution over frequency in the heat radiated from a *black body*. The term "black body" denotes a body which has no spectral characteristics that result in enhanced emission or absorption of the energy at one or more particular frequencies, causing special structure in the emitted or absorbed energy distribution. Black bodies thus exhibit a universal, smooth-curve, energy distribution over frequency in their radiant energy emission that depends only on their temperature. By 1894, due to the work of Maxwell and Hertz, it was known that heat radiation took the form of electromagnetic waves or light (as evidence, a body is observed to visibly glow more brightly as it becomes hotter, beginning at a deep red and progressing through the colors of the rainbow to a purplish hue). While the form of the blackbody energy distribution function was known from experimental measurements, neither a theory nor a mechanism that caused the form of the measured curve was known. The classical-physics Rayleigh-Jeans law, published in 1900,[2] provided a theory valid for part of the frequency range but it diverges at large ν, giving rise to the so-called "ultraviolet catastrophe." In that same year Planck provided a theory that fully described the nature of the radiation-energy-distribution curve, the theory he had sought, but, as often happens in science and philosophy, the theory raised questions even more profound than the original problem it addressed because the theory sharply contradicted accepted culture (science).

In studying blackbody radiation, Plank assumed a black body to be composed of simple dipole (harmonic) oscillators, in behavior like two bodies of opposite charge connected by a stiff spring and a model amenable to analysis. How is one assured that such a simple model properly represents real materials? By *Kirchhoff's law*: any real or hypothetical black body *in thermal equilibrium* must emit and absorb radiant energy at the black body rate whatever its composition and whatever the blackbody radiation spectrum. (As has since been demonstrated by quantum electrodynamics theory, the radiation field in the vacuum itself is exactly described by a harmonic oscillator model.[3]) The dipole model was of particular interest because excitation (motion or energy) of the dipole causes a radiation of energy characterized by Maxwell's laws. This evidently seemed to Planck a means of relating thermal energy in a body to radiant heat emitted therefrom, a strategy that proved eminently successful.

Planck was systematic in his approach and addressed the overall problem by solving a series of problems that formed constituent parts of the whole, i.e., using the reductionism typical of classical science. After strenuous investigation he finally obtained in 1899 a simple but general result for the desired *spectral energy density* $u(\nu)$ of black-body radiation emitted from an oscillating dipole

$$u(\nu)\,d\nu = 8\pi\nu^2/c^3\,E\,d\nu,$$

where $u(\nu)d\nu$ is radiant energy per unit volume of space contained in the frequency interval between ν and $\nu+d\nu$, ν (Greek "nu") is a selected frequency value, $d\nu$ is a small increment in ν, c is the velocity of light, and E is average energy of the dipole oscillator. (We follow the notation of M. S. Longair.[4]) The simplicity of this result should not mislead one regarding either the effort required to obtain it or its importance.

The average energy E of a dipole oscillator or any other model is predicted by classical thermodynamics to be ½ kT for each degree of freedom that can store energy, with k being Boltzmann's constant and T the absolute temperature of the radiating body (dipole oscillator). A one-dimensional dipole oscillator has two degrees of freedom in which energy can be stored, one being dipole stretching motion manifesting kinetic energy and a second being dipole (spring) stretching manifesting potential energy. For simplicity, as allowed by Kirchhoff's law, the dipoles are assumed to be constrained so that dipole center-of-mass and rotational motions may be ignored. Thus, average dipole energy according to classical thermodynamics is $E = kT$.

Planck next utilized a law which had recently been discovered by German physicist Wilhelm Wien (1864-1928) in 1896. This law empirically combines Wien's earlier (1894) theoretical displacement law with all the data on blackbody radiation available in 1896. The result, denoted *Wien's law*, thus represented well all the experimental data then existing. Wien's law is written

$$u(\nu)\, d\nu \;=\; 8\pi\alpha\, \nu^3/c^3 \exp(-\,\beta\nu/T)\, d\nu,$$

where α (Greek "alpha") and β (Greek "beta") are constants and T is the temperature of the radiating body. The function exp(z), called the *exponential function* of argument z, is described in endnote 27 of Chapter 8. Comparison of the two equations for $u(\nu)$ gives the average oscillator energy

$$E \;=\; \alpha\nu \exp(-\,\beta\nu/T).$$

This energy clearly does not correspond to the classical thermodynamic value $E = kT$. Something unusual is occurring in the blackbody radiation, Planck must have thought. But what?

In February of 1900, Lummer and Pringsheim had reported measured results showing conclusively that Wien's law failed at small values of ν/T. Rubens and Kurlbaum reported similar results in October. These measurements showed that $u(\nu)$ was proportional to T at small ν/T, the result expected from classical thermodynamics by which $E = kT$. As a courtesy, Planck's friend Rubens sent their results to Planck before they were published and Planck was thereby in early possession of this data.

Planck then sought a form of the law that agreed with these new data while retaining the old result where it was valid. The form Planck ultimately adopted was derived (in effect – Planck[5] used a more obscure, entropy-based derivation and we include several incremental results here in one step) by replacing

$$E \;=\; \alpha\nu \exp(-\,\beta\nu/T)$$

with

$$E \;=\; h\nu/[\exp(h\nu/kT) - 1],$$

a standard mathematical trick[6] which gave agreement with the data of Lummer and Pringsheim and of Rubens and Kurlbaum at small ν/T and also with Wien's law at large ν/T. Thus, Planck found the constants $\alpha = h$ and $\beta = h/k$, where h is now called *Planck's constant* and k is *Boltzmann's constant*. (Both of these constants are fundamentally important, acknowledging singular contributions of their two namesakes.) *Planck's law* for the spectral energy density of blackbody radiation thus took the final form

$$u(\nu) = [8\pi h\nu^3/c^3] / [\exp(h\nu/kT) - 1].$$

This expression eliminates the ultraviolet catastrophe of the Rayleigh-Jeans classical-physics law since for both $\nu \rightarrow 0$ and $\nu \rightarrow \infty$, $u(\nu) \rightarrow 0$ (for "$\rightarrow$" read "approaches"). This law not only predicts these correct limits, it also correctly describes all the data relating to the spectral energy density of blackbody radiation, both that known in 1900 and that since discovered – including that of the omnidirectional, background cosmic radiation ubiquitous in space due, apparently, to a big-bang origin of the universe.

This account is already an exciting bit of history showing keen insight by Planck enabled by his years of intense effort to obtain these original results. And we have not yet reached the more profound part of Planck's discovery, the discovery of quantum physics, the answer to the above "But what?" question.

Planck presented his result at a meeting on 19 October 1900. It was received as a valuable result that provided an excellent fit of experimental black-body-radiation data over the full range of both frequency and wavelength (one is equivalent to the other since $c/\nu = \lambda$.). But, as is not unusual with revolutionary results, its importance was not appreciated for several years. Only when it was finally realized that classical physics (both the Rayleigh-Jeans law and the equipartition of energy principle) was in fundamental disagreement with Planck's law, was the significance of Planck's derivation in revealing and correcting a fundamental failure in classical physics finally realized.

A few details of Planck's derivation indicate the revolutionary concept he introduced. In his analysis Planck denoted dipole-oscillator energy as $\epsilon = nh\nu$, with $n = 1,2,3,4, \ldots$ and ϵ the Greek "epsilon," notation Planck used in his original papers[5] and still used today. According to classical physics $n = 1$ and ϵ and ν are continuous variables that can take any positive values or zero; i.e., dipole motion and extension (stretch) variables were regarded as continuous having no restricted or forbidden values. Contrary to this classical belief, Planck's analysis allowed only discrete energy levels to be populated. It is only discrete levels in Planck's theory that give his result its correct form.[7] It was not an uncommon theoretical tool in deriving a law like Planck's law to initially regard ϵ as taking only discrete values. Then, after a relatively simple result corresponding to a limited set of ϵ values was obtained, the restriction would be relaxed by regarding ϵ as a value in an infinite set of finely separated energy values, in effect continuously varying down to and including the value zero. But in the case of Planck's law, this restriction could not be relaxed. When ϵ is continuous, the energy density $u(\nu)$ takes the wrong form.[7]

Planck's law consequently contradicts classical physics. While it provided a simple and elegant description of the observed spectral energy distribution in blackbody radiation, it presented a dilemma. Either it was correct, in which case $\epsilon = nh\nu$ could not be continuous and classical physics is contradicted, or it is false and classical physics is not contradicted. But it wasn't false because it gave the correct results for $u(\nu)$ and classical physics is contradicted anyway by the same data. Planck's proposed condition, that energy ϵ is discrete or quantized instead of continuous, may be thought of heuristically[8] as a consequence of the above-mentioned theoretical tool in which energy-level spacings were to be uniformly diminished to zero as the lowest-level energy diminished to zero. With no reduction to zero of the latter allowed,[7] the separation $h\nu$ of allowed energy states $\epsilon = nh\nu$ must remain finite and the energy levels must therefore be *discrete* or *quantized.* Planck's law thus presented the enigma that *energy is quantized* as opposed to the classical picture of continuously varying energy.[9] This enigma was the first important "road sign" leading to quantum mechanics, and it was eventually recognized as a "large billboard."

Planck's methods have been criticized in hindsight. One criticism is his incorrect use of the statistical physics of Boltzmann.[4] He was saved from error in this instance because he had apparently worked backwards in part of his derivation and his statistical physics contained compensating errors. A second criticism was the logical inconsistency in using classical physics to derive a quantum-physics result (as if he had any choice). Here he was simply lucky and got the correct result. Luck is always important when you are blazing a new trail and nothing had ever been newer than this. He was beginning to see a vision far deeper and broader than any even remotely otherwise suggested in the culture of his day.

Because it was so revolutionary and posed such a disturbing enigma, Planck's result and its implications were not accepted for many years. It took even Planck some ten years to finally accept its implications as he continued to struggle toward a physical understanding. But though he didn't fully understand the new quantum physics, he did understand the significance of his discoveries. In his 1918 Nobel Prize address he stated "The greater [its] difficulties ... the more significant it finally will show itself to be for the broadening and deepening of our whole knowledge in physics." In Planck's struggle to understand quantum physics he would have been consoled to hear Niels Bohr, who won the Nobel Prize in physics for proposing the first quantum theory of the (hydrogen) atom, later say that "anyone who claims that quantum mechanics is clear doesn't really understand it" and some sixty years later to hear Richard Feynman, another Nobel-Prize-winning physicist, say

> There was a time when the newspapers said that only twelve men understood the theory of relativity. I do not believe that there ever was such a time. There might have been a time when only one man did because he was the only guy who caught on, before he wrote his paper. But after people read the paper a lot of people understood the theory of relativity in one way or another, certainly more than twelve. On the other hand I think I can safely say that nobody understands quantum mechanics.[10]

Planck received the 1918 Nobel Prize in physics for this work and the most prestigious system of research institutes in Germany today bears his name.

Einstein and the Photoelectric Effect

Of Einstein's five 1905 papers mentioned above, one we have not yet examined addresses the quantum nature of light. It is often described as being on the photoelectric effect but it addresses a wide range of applications and provides the first glimmering of understanding of not only the mechanism of the photoelectric effect but also of Planck's theory of blackbody radiation and other phenomena.

In this paper Einstein addresses processes where *light interacting with a material* behaves as if it were *corpuscular* and *quantized*, a discrete particle of energy $\epsilon = h\nu$ now called a *photon*. Einstein discussed several examples: fluorescence, the black-body-radiation spectrum, the photoelectric effect, and photoionization of gases by ultraviolet light. He described in some detail several known experimental results in terms of his model, supporting his concepts. Although little was then known experimentally about the photoelectric effect, his treatment of this process was the most complete of all the examples he considered and he made bold predictions which were later fully substantiated by measurement. (For this reason the paper is generally associated with the photoelectric effect, but its implications are general.)

Hertz had discovered the photoelectric effect, which is the process wherein electrons are emitted from (atoms or molecules of) a solid when irradiated with light of a suitable frequency. Lenard next discovered that the energies of the emitted electrons are independent of the intensity of the incident radiation. Einstein utilized his concept of light quanta to predict these properties and much more. Einstein reasoned that absorption of a photon's energy by an atom or molecule may impart sufficient energy to cause an electron to escape. If the intensity is increased, more light quanta or photon energies may be absorbed and more electrons emitted, no more than one per atom, but the energy of the emitted electrons would not be affected because the energy provided only occurs in discrete amounts $\epsilon = h\nu$, where ν is the frequency of an incident photon and h is Planck's constant. Einstein thus proposed that the maximum kinetic energy a photo-electric-emitted electron can possess, denoted by E_k, would be described by

$$E_k = h\nu - W,$$

where $W > 0$ is now called the *work function* and is the energy required to remove an electron from a solid-state atom or molecule and from near the surface of the solid itself and $h\nu$ is the photon energy absorbed and available for use in freeing the electron. Then, if a metal sample is illuminated by light of frequency ν near an electrode maintained at a retarding (negative) potential difference V relative to that of the sample, electrons emitted by the sample will reach the electrode if and only if $E_k \geq -eV$, where e is the positive proton charge and $-e$ the negative electron charge. Measured values of the *threshold voltage* V, i.e., the value of V where arrival of electrons at the electrode first disappears with increasing magnitude of (negative) V and first appears with decreasing magnitude of V, should then be related to ν and W according to

$$-V = h\nu/e - W/e.$$

Einstein provided the above pair of equations and pointed out that a plot of $-V$ versus ν should take the form of a straight line with slope h/e (a poorly known value in 1905) and intercept W/e (a fully unknown and previously unrecognized value). These were bold predictions as nothing was then known about the frequency dependence of photoelectric emission. But Einstein's predictions were exactly confirmed in later experiments by American physicist Robert Andrews Millikan (1868-1953). In fact, Millikan was awarded the Nobel Prize in physics in 1923 for his measurements of the electron charge and the photoelectric effect wherein he confirmed Einstein's theory.

In later papers, Einstein expanded his concept of energy occurring in only discrete quanta. He authored a paper giving an improved interpretation of Planck's law and the blackbody radiation based on this concept. He authored another on the specific heat of solids, predicting specific heat would diminish to zero as temperature approached zero. This result was particularly interesting to German physical chemist Hermann Nernst (1864-1941) who had undertaken the measurement of specific heats at low temperatures and found experimentally the result predicted by Einstein's theory and, thereby, another contradiction with classical physics. Nernst's research led to the *third law of thermodynamics*, that change in entropy S with change in temperature T approaches zero as temperature approaches zero, i.e., $dS/dT \rightarrow 0$ as $T \rightarrow 0$, thus precluding a body reaching absolute zero temperature. For his discovery Nernst was awarded the 1920 Nobel Prize in chemistry.

These theoretical and experimental results provided compelling evidence that classical physics failed to properly describe certain observed phenomena. Instead, these phenomena were described by a new physics involving the discrete energy quanta proposed by Planck and Einstein.

Bohr's Atom, Matter Waves, and Quantum Mechanics[part #]

Niels Bohr (1885-1962) discovered the first successful quantum model of the hydrogen atom in 1913, for which he received the 1922 Nobel Prize in physics. Bohr combined the atomic model of Ernest Rutherford, an electrically neutral object consisting of a small, positively-charged nucleus surrounded by at least one negatively-charged, orbiting electron, and the energy quantum of Planck.

In marrying these two concepts Bohr adopted the rule that only discrete energy levels occurred for electron orbits around an atomic nucleus. Bohr also added the outward centrifugal force $m_e v^2/r$ and the inward attractive (Coulomb's law) force $-e^2/r^2$ on a single electron having negative charge $-e$ circling a proton having positive charge e in stable equilibrium to obtain a zero net-force sum, i.e., a stable hydrogen atom. Bohr thus obtained via Newtonian mechanics

$$m_e v^2/r - e^2/r^2 = 0 \qquad \text{or} \qquad v = e/\sqrt{(m_e r)},$$

where m_e is the electron mass, v the electron velocity, and r the radius of its (circular) orbit. Bohr then stipulated that the product of electron velocity, mass, and circumference (= *action*) around one full orbit ($2\pi r_n$) must be an integral multiple of h in order to agree with his assumption of Planck's discrete energy levels. Bohr thus obtained for the radius of the nth orbit, given by r_n with n = 1,2,3,4,... being the orbit number defining the orbital *quantum state* of the atom,

$$nh = v_n \times m_e \times 2\pi r_n = e/\sqrt{(m_e r_n)} \times m_e \times 2\pi r_n \quad \text{or} \quad r_n = n^2h^2/(4\pi^2e^2m_e).$$

Bohr next calculated the energy of the atom with the electron at $r = r_n$ by summing the kinetic K and potential P energies to obtain

$$E_n = K_n + P_n = \tfrac{1}{2} m_e e^2/(m_e r_n) - e^2/r_n = -\tfrac{1}{2} e^2/r_n = -2\pi^2 e^4 m_e/(n^2h^2).$$

Bohr's result thus gives $E_n = -h\nu_n = -hc/\lambda_n = -2\pi^2e^4m_e/(n^2h^2)$ since $c = \nu_n \times \lambda_n$, and $1/\lambda_n = R/n^2$, where the *Rydberg constant* R is $R = 2\pi^2e^4m_e/(h^3c) = 109{,}737\ cm^{-1}$. Of course, what is invariably observed in absorption or emission of light is a quantum jump between quantum states j = 1,2,3,4,... and k = 1,2,3,4, ... in which an observed energy difference is, by the above results,

$$\Delta E_{jk} = -hcR(1/j^2 - 1/k^2) = -h\nu_{jk} = -hc/\lambda_{jk}$$

for which the absorbed ($k < j$) or emitted ($j < k$) light quantum (photon) has frequency ν_{jk} or wavelength λ_{jk} that agrees with measured absorption and emission spectra of atomic hydrogen, i.e.,

$$1/\lambda_{jk} = R\,(1/j^2 - 1/k^2) = 109{,}737\ cm^{-1}\,(1/j^2 - 1/k^2).$$

It does exactly, supporting the correctness of Bohr's result.

While the Bohr theory successfully rationalized (predicted) discrete spectral absorption and emission lines of atomic hydrogen, it was regarded as unacceptable because it was based on classical physics and, according to Maxwell's equations, the orbiting electrons should radiate energy and fall into the nucleus. This problem was only later "explained" by de Broglie and Schrödinger with the proposal that an electron is not an orbiting particle but a standing "probability wave" or *orbital* around the atomic nucleus. Moreover, Bohr's method was successful only for the hydrogen atom.

Louis de Broglie (1892-1987) extended quantum theory to describe *matter waves.* De Broglie served with the French Army during World War I in radio communications. After the war he returned to university study to learn science. (He had previously studied medieval history at the Sorbonne.) He completed his studies in 1924, receiving a doctoral degree for a thesis on quantum theory. By this time, the dual particle-wave nature of light and other radiation was generally recognized, although it was by no means understood. (It still isn't.) But up till then, no one had ventured that *matter* also might have a dual nature. De Broglie in his doctoral thesis was the first to propose such a theory.

To obtain the de Broglie wavelength for an electron, we may use two expressions already given above in describing Bohr's theory, namely,

$$r_n = n^2h^2/(4\pi^2e^2m_e) \qquad \text{and} \qquad e^2 = m_e v^2 r_n.$$

Combining these two equations to eliminate e^2 gives $2\pi r_n = nh/(m_e v)$ or, since the circumference $2\pi r_n$ of the nth electron orbit must contain exactly n wavelengths, $n\lambda_e = nh/(m_e v)$ and the electron wavelength $\lambda_e = h/(m_e v)$. De Broglie proposed that *any particle of mass* m *moving with velocity* v *has wavelength*

$$\lambda = h/(mv).$$

Because of the smallness of Planck's constant h (= 6.6252×10^{-34} kg m^2/sec), the wavelength for any large body and even for a proton was then too small to detect. However, the wavelength for a fast-moving electron was in the X-ray-wavelength range and was detectable. C. J. Davisson and G. P. Thomson independently detected it in 1927, for which feat they shared the 1937 Nobel Prize in physics.

Matter waves might not have survived as a topic of much interest even that long except for a fortuitous event. Erwin Schrödinger (1887-1961), an Austrian physics professor at Zürich, read of the matter waves postulated by de Broglie in a footnote in one of Einstein's papers. While de Broglie never developed a precise theory for such waves, Schrödinger found one and published his results in 1926. He reasoned that the model of the atom postulated by Niels Bohr might be improved if one obtained a *wave theory of matter to define electron orbitals as standing matter waves* around an atom's nucleus. Schrödinger thus discovered a wave equation[11] that defines *wave function* $\psi_n(x,y,z,t)$ (ψ is the Greek "psi" and n represents an orbital quantum number 1,2,3,4,...) that describes the wavelike nature of electrons (and other particles), now called the Schrödinger equation. Each ψ_n wave function is a particular solution of Schrödinger's equation and each provides one possible orbital state. A general solution, ψ, consisting of a "weighted sum"[12] of all the ψ_n wave functions, simultaneously predicts all orbital states[12] or orbital property values even though only one exists in any measurement of an atom. The atomic model based on solutions of this equation contains electrons in orbitals or standing waves that contain an integral number of wavelengths (equal to the orbital quantum number n) in a complete circumference of the nucleus. The ability of quantum mechanics to predict discreteness, allowed and forbidden states, transitions, and an array of quantized properties in material systems are all evident in solutions of the Schrödinger equation. However, Schrödinger was not the first to provide such predictions and there was some question as to what the ψ_n-wave functions represented. Max Born and Pascual Jordan proposed that for solution ψ_n, $<|\psi_n|^2>/<|\psi|^2>$ is the local probability density of the particle being in its nth quantum state, a definition still used ($<|\psi_n|^2>$ denotes an average absolute value or real part of $\psi_n^{\,2}$). Further details are described in endnote 12.

Schrödinger's theory,[13] published beginning in March 1926, had been anticipated in a paper by German physicist Werner Heisenberg[14] and a follow-up to this paper by his physicist colleagues Max Born and Pascual Jordan,[15] both papers appearing in 1925. The two theories describe conclusions reached by two different paths, conclusions only later shown to be equivalent. Heisenberg, Born, and Jordan constructed a theory in which allowed (observed) states were represented by sets of specific values. Instead of modeling a system in terms of some picture by which wavelengths are envisioned and calculated, the model considers specific values used directly to determine desired properties without a physically artificial wavelength picture. The model employs matrices, which contain rows and columns of wavelength-related data and the Heisenberg-Born-Jordan method thus acquired the name "matrix mechanics." But Heisenberg's first paper, of which he was the sole author, did not mention matrices. It was Born, for whom Heisenberg and Jordan then worked, who read his paper and recognized that the operations described by Heisenberg represented multiplication of matrices. In the resulting paper written by Max Born and Pascual Jordan in Göttingen – while Heisenberg was on leave in Cambridge – entitled *Zur Quantenmechanik*, Born and Jordan coined the term "quantum mechanics" (in German, "quantenmechanik"), utilized matrices to describe the operations, and quantized the electromagnetic field using matrices. They sent a copy to Heisenberg, who was pleased with their extension of his work, and the three agreed to jointly author a third paper, which they did. Yet later textbooks usually mention "Heisenberg's" *matrix mechanics* and "Dirac's" *field quantization*, both innovations due to Born and Jordan. It is also curious that Heisenberg alone was honored with the 1932 Nobel Prize in Physics,[16] although his uncertainty principle (see below) published in 1927 was itself a singular contribution.

As with Maxwell's electromagnetic theory, particle (quantum) mechanics is based on a *foundation of abstract mathematics* rather than a physical mechanism. "Understanding" of physical phenomena and properties, like the dual wave-particle nature of light and matter, is therefore necessarily founded on abstract mathematical equations and their interpretations instead of on physical processes. While such an approach does not provide a satisfying *physical understanding and explanation* in a clear, classical sense, it is nevertheless justified on the simple basis that it provides *correct descriptions and predictions*, i.e., consistency.

Heisenberg also discovered a subtle but important principle that bears his name: the *Heisenberg uncertainty principle* mentioned above. According to this principle it is impossible to determine simultaneously the exact position x and x-direction momentum p_x ($p_x = mu$ is the product of mass m and x-direction velocity u) of a particle. The determination of position within uncertainty Δx and momentum within uncertainty Δp_x must always satisfy this uncertainty principle: $\Delta x \, \Delta p_x \geq h$, where h is Planck's constant. Such expressions apply for spatial directions x, y, and z. Uncertainty must also occur in other quantities such as in $\Delta E \Delta t \geq h$, where ΔE is uncertainty in energy and Δt in time. This principle is fundamental, i.e., it does not result from other known principles. It is also profound in its implications. While Laplace and others believed in absolute determinism by which the universe was wholly deterministic, that specification of the velocities and positions of all particles in the universe at any instant in time would impose a fixed behavior on the universe at all other times before or after, Heisenberg's uncertainty principle proscribes this possibility. By Heisenberg's principle, "initial" conditions can never be sufficient for exact determinism significantly earlier or later.

The wave theory of Schrödinger and the matrix mechanics of Heisenberg *et al* are fundamentally different in their approaches. Nevertheless, Schrödinger[17] and C. Eckart[18] independently proved in 1926 that the information content of one was equivalent to that of the other and that quantum theory had been born as fraternal twins. Because of its close resemblance to classical wave theories of physics and Bohr's atomic theory with their similarities to conventional, physical-model-based approaches, Schrödinger's method was initially preferred,[19] but both methods have been and are widely used.

Many worked to improve and extend the new theory. Paul Adrien Maurice Dirac (1902-1984) provided considerable insight and greatly extended the utility of the new theory, particularly into the relativistic realm in which particle (electron) velocities approached that of light.[20] Dirac, a graduate electrical engineer who (fortunately) couldn't find a job and stayed in academe to became a mathematical physicist and eventually fill Newton's former position as Lucasian Professor at Cambridge, combined Einstein's relativity theory and quantum mechanics in his relativistic "Dirac equation." Using his new equation in a theoretical exploration of electron properties and their mathematical basis, he predicted the existence of antimatter. An earlier quantum-mechanics equation, called the Klein-Gordon equation because it was independently discovered in 1926 by Oscar Klein (who we shall meet again) and Walter Gordon, did include relativistic effects. This equation provided solutions for particles (electrons) in negative energy states as well as positive ones, but the former were not essential and were ignored as unphysical. They were regarded as unreasonable because they would allow electrons to jump down an unending sequence of ever-lower-energy states, radiating energy with each jump, thus providing a source of infinite energy. And the Klein-Gordon equation is, in fact, invalid for electrons as it applies only for "spinless" particles such as mesons, like the muons, short for mu-mesons, we discussed in Chapter 8.

The Dirac equation predicts an essential (while the negative energy electron states could be ignored in Klein-Gordon-equation solutions, they cannot be in Dirac-equation solutions), unending sequence of *negative* as well as positive energy states, i.e., its solutions for the possible energies of an electron give both positive and negative energy sequences. Negative energy is a problem. By Einstein's relation $E = mc^2$ a negative energy requires a negative mass, a property which was unknown and regarded as absurd. Nevertheless, Dirac made a bold conceptual leap. He proposed the negative energy levels corresponded to positively charged particles, namely, protons, even though the mass was that of an electron, only $1/1836^{th}$ times as massive. This conclusion was not predicted by his equation. Perhaps Dirac was hoping to find a solution for protons as well as electrons and thereby resolve the entire atomic system. German mathematician Hermann Weyl advised Dirac from Göttingen that the particles could not be protons and saving his theory would require a new type of particle having the same mass as an electron but an opposite charge.

Dirac eventually adopted, in 1929, a new picture of the vacuum (space itself) as containing a "sea" of negative energy electrons, with one electron in each required negative-energy state. Yet we don't notice the sea of omnipresent electrons just as we don't notice the air we breathe. Electrons near the surface of this sea can not "fall in" because all negative-energy states are already filled. But, as Dirac stated, "There is, then, the possibility that holes may appear in the sea."[21] Such transient holes could be caused by collisions of photons with the negative-energy electrons imparting to the latter enough energy for them to achieve a positive-energy state and rise above the "sea level" leaving behind a momentary hole in the negative-energy electron sea. Such an *electron hole* would appear to be a particle having the electron mass and an opposite charge. In short, Dirac predicted the *positron* to be an electron hole in a sea of electrons. And such a hole correctly corresponds to the negative mass and energy predicted by both the Einstein relation and the Dirac equation. Combination of an electron and positron (the annihilation of matter by antimatter) to produce nothing except energy is readily understood in this model as a positive-energy electron falling into a vacant, lower-energy electron hole in an otherwise invisible sea of electrons.

In 1932 the fleeting existence of positrons was established when they were observed by American physicist Carl Anderson (1905-1991) by analysis of curved tracks of cosmic-ray-generated particles in a *cloud chamber*. Here, a brief digression to describe a cloud chamber and its origin will be useful.

C. T. R. (Charles Thomson Rees) Wilson (1869-1959), a young Scottish physicist on a scholarship at Cambridge working with J. J. Thomson in the Cavendish Laboratory, was fascinated with cloud formation and proposed to study this process. Thomson agreed to let him make clouds in the Cavendish and Wilson began in 1896 the project that would last until 1912 and for which Wilson would receive the Nobel Prize in physics in 1927. Wilson constructed a glass chamber with a piston so that the enclosed gas could be rapidly expanded and, thereby, cooled. With sufficient water vapor in the chamber, the cooling induced condensation of many microscopic water droplets, i.e., a cloud. In an initial condensation, ions and dust particles present in the chamber served as "condensation nuclei" causing the cloud to form at relatively low expansion. After these droplets settled, subsequent expansion required for cloud formation was greater because condensation nuclei (ions and dust particles) were absent. Irradiation of the expansion chamber with X-rays (just two months after Roentgen announced their discovery) again reduced the expansion required for cloud formation. The cause of this phenomenon became clear within one year when J. J. Thomson published his discovery of the electron.[22] It was thus learned that missing or extra electrons, i.e., ions generated, say, by X-rays, served as condensation nuclei. And it was also learned that ions were produced in air by small, fast-moving particles when Wilson placed a small amount of uranium in the chamber, expanded it and photographed the visible tracks emanating from the uranium, visible due to condensation of droplets on the ions formed by collisions of high-speed, radioactive-decay particles with air molecules. Wilson thus demonstrated use of his chamber for observation of fast-particle tracks (with the fast particles being radioactive-decay particles in this first case and, later, cosmic-rays and their collision products). When ions and nuclei were cleared and the chamber was expanded to a level just below that required for spontaneous cloud formation, the tracks of high-speed particles were made readily visible by the water droplets that formed only on ions generated along the path of fast moving particles. This method for observing particle tracks was widely and successfully used for many decades and variations of it are still used.

Anderson was able to determine curvature of particle tracks in a cloud chamber by use of a thin lead-foil "window" through which the particles passed, causing their velocity to be reduced. The charge-and-momentum-dependent curvature of the tracks was magnified by slowing the particles, allowing Anderson to deduce the charge-to-mass ratio of the particles from the measured curvature in the known magnetic field. Despite slowing of the particles in passing through the window, they still carried sufficient energy to ionize gas molecules along their path so that a track on both sides of the window was marked by a visible path of water droplets.

Anderson's thin-lead-foil window had another purpose. Convergence of two particle tracks may result from different causes. Two particles may be *simultaneously* formed in a single event, e.g., the formation of high-energy particles when a cosmic ray shatters an atom or molecule in a cloud chamber. Or, two particles may be *sequentially* formed in two events, e.g., secondary electron emission may occur after collision of, say, an electron and an atom. In both cases the tracks appear to emerge from a common source but their correct interpretation depends on whether they formed simultaneously or sequentially. For instance, a track of a positive and of a negative curvature could be caused by two electrons moving in opposite directions or by an electron and a positron moving in the same direction. The development of the water-droplet tracks is too slow to determine simultaneity or direction. But a lead-foil window in which track curvature is observed on *both* sides reveals direction of motion because the particle's momentum is attenuated and the curvature of its track increased after passing through the window. In fact, Anderson used curvature to infer the ratio of particle momentum after and before attenuation and this ratio to infer particle mass. In this manner he established that an occasional pair of collision-product particles of opposite curvature both had the mass of an electron and the tracks were those of an electron and a "positive electron" or positron, instead of two electrons.

De Broglie received the Nobel Prize in physics in 1929, Heisenberg was awarded the same Prize in 1932, Schrödinger and Dirac shared the 1933 Prize and Anderson shared the 1936 Prize. The rapid recognition in view of the high originality of the results recognizes the importance of these discoveries.

As with relativity, quantum mechanics led to strange predictions. Yet quantum mechanics is now established as the best theory for describing phenomena involving small particles. Indeed, it is regarded as the most fundamental theory of physics. So we may ask again, why are the results of a superior vision of reality regarded as strange compared to those of an inferior paradigm, the one which forms the basis of our popular culture and intuition. The answer is clear, our popular culture and intuition are not correct despite their apparent consistency and plausibility.

Quantum Electrodynamics

The term electrodynamics refers to processes having to do with electron or charged particle or photon motions in electric or magnetic fields. A successful theory of quantum electrodynamics (QED) must describe motions and phenomena of electrons and photons (particles of light). "How nice." you may think. But it's more than nice because solving such problems would explain *all fundamental physical phenomena* with the exceptions of gravity and certain kinds of radioactivity. For examples, chemical reactions and the stability of materials are predicted by such solutions because chemical bonds are determined by electronic configurations in atoms and molecules. Indeed, all chemical, physical, and optical properties of materials (or empty space for that matter) are characterized by such solutions. Consequently, all biochemical and biological properties are controlled by laws described by a valid QED theory. A correct quantum mechanical description of electrons and photons is thus more than an academic curiosity, it is essential for describing nature on a broadly valid, fundamental basis.

The Schrödinger equation does not properly describe the mechanics of electrons and photons. A major problem with this equation is that electrons and photons move at or near the speed of light and relativistic effects must be incorporated into laws that properly describe such motion, effects beyond the scope of Schrödinger theory. The Klein-Gordon and the Dirac equations include relativity effects but only the latter is valid for electrons. For twenty years the Dirac equation properly described the known energy spectra of electronic transitions in atoms including fine splitting and hyperfine splitting of energy levels until, in 1947, a small *Lamb shift* in hydrogen atoms was accurately measured. This measurement by W. E. Lamb and his graduate student R. C. Retherford,[23] for which Lamb was awarded the 1955 Nobel Prize in physics, revealed that interactions occurred that were not properly described by any then-existing theory. A new theory was required, a theory capable of describing the quantum vacuum with its spontaneous generations and annihilations of electron-positron pairs with consequent fluctuation of electric field intensity in the quantum vacuum that influences an electron bound in a hydrogen atom. The concept of a fluctuating field had been successfully invoked by Einstein[24] in 1917 to predict absorption, (stimulated) emission, and scattering of radiation. Without it Robert Oppenheimer's 1930 calculation[25] of the interaction of an electron with a quantized field yielded meaningless results in which electron energy (mass) was infinite and all spectral lines were infinitely shifted. Victor Weisskopf proposed[26] in 1934 that zero-point energy fluctuations are required for spontaneous emission to occur but lead to drastic disagreements with other results. Vision through the fog began to improve with T. A. Welton's 1948-identification[27] of the cause of the 1947-measured Lamb shift as fluctuations in the quantum-vacuum electric field inducing rapid and highly erratic electron motions about the nominal electron position so that the electronic point charge is well approximated by a charge density smeared over a small sphere of nearly 1 pcm (= 1 pico-centimeter = 10^{-12} cm) radius. The lowest orbital-state energy (as observed by an energy difference between the ground-electron-orbital state and a higher-orbital state, with shift of higher-orbital-state energies becoming increasingly insignificant because of the smallness of the 1 pc sphere compared to higher-state-orbital radii) of the atom caused by a smeared-sphere rather than a point charge is thereby reduced by the Lamb shift. To fully dispel the fog, a *QED* theory utilizing new insights and methods was needed.

New theoretical approaches that solved the spherical-smeared charge and other problems were simultaneously and independently discovered by three investigators. One of the three was Julian Schwinger. Schwinger was born in New York City on 16 March 1918. A child prodigy, he entered New York City College at age fourteen, transferred to Columbia University and graduated at age eighteen and received a Ph.D. at age 21. After studying with Oppenheimer at the University of California at Berkeley he joined the physics faculty at Harvard in 1945 and became a full professor there in 1947, one of very few to achieve this rank while still in his twenties. Schwinger was an able mathematician and used this ability in developing a formal, mathematically-intense QED theory that used a process called "renormalization" to remove infinities encountered in QED to obtain a workable theory.

Sin-itiro Tomonaga (1906-1979), another of the three, was born in Tokyo on 31 March 1906 and graduated from Kyoto University in 1929. He studied in Germany with Heisenberg and then returned to obtain his doctorate from Kyoto University in 1939. He taught at Tokyo University until after World War II when he worked out his QED theory. Because of the war his working conditions must have been sparse. Tomonaga's contributions are described in a memorial lecture delivered by Julian Schwinger.[28]

Richard Feynman, the other of the three, was born in New York on 11 May 1918 and grew up on Long Island. He graduated from MIT in 1939 and received a Ph.D. in physics from Princeton University in 1942. During World War II he worked on the atomic bomb project in New Mexico and was present at the test-explosion of the first such bomb at Alamogordo. Following the war he joined the faculty at Cornell University in 1945 and subsequently went to the California Institute of Technology in 1950. In the late 1940s, Feynman worked out his QED theory. Feynman had a gift for seeing physics in a comprehensive vision that incorporated all levels from the fundamental to the practical. Feynman's approach to a QED theory is the more novel, simpler, and more intuitive in its application compared to the other two alternatives, and has become the most widely used. It provides a different approach to quantum mechanics, one which may eventually prove to be more fundamental.

These three physicists shared the 1965 Nobel Prize in physics for their accomplishments. While the new QED theories utilized quantum field theory introduced by Born and Jordan and by Dirac, they utilized a new form more amenable to calculations and new definitions of masses and charges that were more realistic. Most importantly, they properly addressed the continuous creation and annihilation of particles, the quantum vacuum fluctuations, and the myriad possibilities thus introduced in even simple problems.

In Feynman's approach, the only one we consider further, a few basic actions are envisioned: (1) a photon may transform from point-to-point (state-to-state), (2) an electron may transform from point-to-point (state-to-state), (3) an electron may absorb or emit a photon, and (4) a photon may decompose into an electron-positron pair, two separate particles that later recombine with each other or with other partners. The transformation of an electron or a photon between two states may thus occur in any number of ways, i.e., along any number of "paths" or histories. Either type of particle may transform between two points either (a) not encountering another particle or (b) encountering one or more particles or decomposing into two particles, in either case influencing the path or history of the electron or photon and moderating its energy. Thus, transformation of a particle between two states may occur without interaction in case (a) or along any of many different paths in case (b) in which an encounter or decomposition influences a particle in its transformation between the two states. And also in case (b), particle interactions may occur in any number or sort, including interactions with particles generated temporarily by decompositions of photons. The total probability that an electron or photon will transform between two specified states is obtained in this theory as a vector sum of the probabilities that the electron or photon will follow each possible path or history between two states, or the "sum of paths" probability. While an infinite number of possible paths and encounters is possible, the simplest paths with the smallest numbers of encounters have the highest probabilities, with probability falling sharply with complexity of path and number of encounters so that not all combinations need be considered. Feynman's theory is thus called a *sum of paths* or *path integral* theory.

Feynman provided rules by which the probability of any path or path element may be determined. In each case the probability depends on both a magnitude and a phase, so that wavelike interference effects are properly included in the model. Indeed, paths symmetrical about an intermediate path, the path of least or stationary action,[29] act to symmetrically interfere and cancel one another because of phase differences. Each path element is represented by an arrow or vector having a magnitude (square root of the probability for the path element) and direction (phase). A vector addition of all the path-element vectors gives a single, overall path vector with the square of its magnitude being the probability the particle will transform by that specific path or history between the two specified states. The sum of probabilities for all possible paths provides the probability of observing the transformation of the electron or photon between the two specified states by any possible path.

Feynman introduced diagramming of particle paths by which all the common paths and the various particles involved are efficiently represented and envisioned. These *Feynman diagrams* show position transformation as horizontal displacement and time transformation as vertical displacement. Electron transformations are shown as straight lines with arrows while photon transformations are shown as wavy lines which can bifurcate and recombine in a wavy, ellipse-shaped segment in a straight (wavy) line, representing a decomposition and recombination. A series of such diagrams allows one to quickly represent the paths and particles to be considered in a sum-of-paths solution. An excellent, popular-level description of these diagrams and the complete method is presented in Feynman's book entitled *QED*.[30]

By this conceptually simple process, Feynman's sum-of-paths method predicts the probability of any electron or photon transformation in state. The model shows that the probable orbitals of electrons bound to an atomic nucleus are controlled by photons transforming between the electron and the nucleus and *vice versa*, with the photons conveying the attractive electronic force between the positive nucleus and the negative electron. Most notably, *in Feynman's approach the uncertainty principle disappears* because it arises in the Heisenberg-Schrödinger and other theories due to conceptual inadequacy of at least one quantity, such as Newtonian time, used in those models.[31] Feynman's method is also used to determine probable transformations of subnuclear or fundamental particles such as quarks, but the accuracy as yet obtained in such calculations is comparatively poor, containing as much as a ten percent or so error.

QED is the most accurate theory ever devised in science providing ten- and even twelve-digit agreement with measured values.

Quantum field theory addresses not only electrons and photons but also other particles such as protons, neutrons, gravitons, subnuclear, and fundamental particles. Quantized field influence is imposed by "messenger particles," such as gravitons for the gravity force field, using concepts of quantum field theory introduced by Born and Jordan[15] and by Dirac.[20] Indeed, in quantum field theory *particles are regarded as quanta of fields* rather than discrete material entities while the universe, composed of material bodies, is a matter field. Particles are initially described in terms of this matter field. A second application of quantum formalism (second quantization) characterizes the particles and the universe as quanta of mass-energy. In quantum field theory these quantized quantum fields are all that exist in the universe. While these field theories rationalize the dilemma of action at a distance, they highlight the question of what a particle or field is.[32]

A Theory of Everything?

Here we make an ambitious attempt to summarize the progress in relativity and quantum mechanics over the last 50 years or so in a few paragraphs. The weight of the task is considerably lightened by the availability of popular-level books by Brian Greene[33] and David Lindley[34] which do the job beautifully, the former providing a wonderfully readable, detailed yet popular-level account of superstring theory and related topics and the latter some useful scope and perspective. With reference to and recommendation of these sources for more comprehensive treatment, especially the former, we can be rather sparse here in both topics treated and level of treatment. Indeed we will restrict our discussion to only a cursory treatment of a few interesting concepts, many of which are elaborated in greater detail by Greene.

Joint progress in both relativity and quantum mechanics is being intensively pursued because a fundamental discrepancy remains between these two theories: relativity is not quantized. As a comprehensive consideration of nature requires both theories, such a fundamental discrepancy suggests the possibility that one or both theories is incomplete or wrong, a point Einstein repeatedly urged about quantum mechanics. Recent research is therefore concerned with unification of these two theories and much more. The goal is a Grand Unified Theory (GUT) or a Theory of Everything (TOE).

A GUT or TOE must unify relativity and quantum theory. Such a TOE should not only rationalize observed results, like the properties of fundamental particles generated in high-energy colliders, but also predict the specific properties of these particles. Such a theory would form a basis for describing all matter and all forces, thus providing a basis for describing all materials and processes. But, I hasten to add, "a basis for" and "an accomplishment of" are two different things. (As Laughlin and Pines,[35] citing P. W. Anderson, have pointed out, a "Theory of Everything is not even remotely a theory of every thing.") Many current questions in both applied and fundamental science involve systems consisting of many components. Such systems are complex and chaotic in their behavior, a few examples being fluid turbulence and meteorology, population dynamics, and public health. Improved descriptions of the atomic nucleus, its components, and their forces of interaction will not help in solving these kinds of problems, so the GUT and the TOE fall a little short of the scope implied by their names when taken out of context. Also, some scientists have questioned the arbitrary choice of particles and forces as the ultimate basis of physical description. But a GUT or TOE remains an important and ambitious goal for obtaining more fundamental, more broadly valid scientific knowledge.

One GUT approach was thought to be quantum field theory. Steven Weinberg summarized the scope of quantum field theory in 1977 – two years before he received the Nobel Prize in physics – in the following comment.

> The inhabitants of the universe [are] conceived to be a set of fields – an electron field, an electromagnetic field, ... this point of view ... forms the central dogma of quantum field theory: the essential reality is a set of fields, subject to the rules of special relativity and quantum mechanics; all else is derived as a consequence of the quantum dynamics of these fields.[36]

We illustrate the role of messenger particles in quantum field theory, by which quantum fields are implemented, in Appendix E by a specific example – the electrostatic repulsion between two protons. Because the field theory causing the repulsion must be quantized, the force must occur in discrete elements or quanta. In other words, the force must be composed of or carried by discrete particles. What are these particles? For electromagnetic forces they are photons. For gravity they are supposed to be gravitons. However, gravitons have not yet been observed. (One possible theory of gravity, utilizing direct action of discrete particles as a mechanism, is described in Appendix D.) In both of these cases the photon or graviton particles represent fields or a manifestation thereof. The *standard model* by which subatomic particles are now best described is a quantum field theory. However, little progress over the last three decades or so has caused interest to now focus on the newest version of quantum mechanics, called superstring theory, that we shall next discuss.

Can a GUT or a TOE in fact be discovered? This question remains to be answered and any answer provided by science will be tentative and subject to revision. But the goal is being pursued primarily by means of superstring theory. Principal and interesting features of superstring theory are summarized in the following paragraphs.

String theory derives its name from being based on fundamental particles having the properties of vibrating strings (or vibrating loops thereof or vibrating membranes or vibrating three-dimensional bodies; all are thought of as membranes or *branes* of specified dimension: point particles are zero-branes, strings are one-branes, surfaces are two-branes, three-dimensional objects are three-branes, and p-dimensional objects are p-branes – and, yes, physicists have a sense of humor). This approach grew out of an observation of Gabriel Veneziano of CERN that certain high-energy particles exhibit a sequence of properties predicted by the mathematical description of vibrating strings, later extended to vibrating membranes, etc. The proposed strings or loops of string, etc., are believed to be very small, so small they cannot currently be distinguished from or detected as anything other than local, single-point particles (zero-branes). But the more the mathematical model of these string particles is refined, the more the model appears capable of providing a comprehensive quantum-mechanics theory of fundamental particles – a GUT or TOE.

One strikingly novel feature of string theories is that they invoke many more spatial dimensions than the conventional three which correspond to the universe we observe. The most general string theory invokes ten spatial dimensions and one time dimension, giving an eleven-dimensional spacetime. Of course this is preposterous because everybody knows that the universe contains only three spatial dimensions. However, novel, revolutionary theories are supposed to be preposterous, as they always have been, so this reaction to the theory is not discouraging. When we are bound by convention, we are limited to conventional understanding. And, since conventional understanding is not adequate, we are forced to cut the bindings of convention and seek revolutionary theories. An early interpretation of the theory supposed that only three of the ten spatial dimensions are *extended* with the remaining seven tightly *curled* so as to be undetectable to any sensing method we might employ. And yet the curls of these dimensions are large compared to the much smaller strings so that the latter can vibrate in all ten dimensions. Another, later interpretation of why we sense only three spatial dimensions will shortly be described.

A precedent for such extra spatial dimensions is found in the work of the Polish mathematician Theodor Franz Eduard Kaluza (1885-1945) who proposed in 1919 one extra, non-extended (and therefore invisible) spatial dimension. When Kaluza extended the general relativity equations to four spatial dimensions, he found extra equations beyond those contained in the normal theory based in three-dimensional space. And upon examination of these extra equations he found they were exactly the Maxwell electromagnetic field equations. By the act of extending by one the dimensions of space, Kaluza had unified relativity and electromagnetic theory with the consequence that the gravity and electromagnetic forces, the only ones then known and then thought to be unrelated, were fully described in a single, unified theory.

Oskar Klein (1894-1977), a Swedish mathematician and physicist, refined the Kaluza theory in 1926. Nevertheless, the refined Kaluza-Klein theory was found to be in severe conflict with measured data and interest in it waned. However, after discovery of two additional fundamental forces, the strong and weak nuclear forces, it was thought additional dimensions included in a Kaluza-Klein theory might account for the additional forces and interest in the theory revived. Late 1970s results gave additional equations resembling those for the strong and weak forces, but problems remained. In the words of Greene

> It gradually became clear that bits and pieces of a unified theory were surfacing, but that a crucial element capable of tying them all together in a quantum-mechanically consistent manner was missing. In 1984 this missing piece – string theory – dramatically entered the story and took center stage.
>
> ... a sign of ... incompatibility between general relativity and quantum mechanics in a point-particle framework is that calculations result in infinite probabilities. ... string theory cures these infinities. But ... a residual, somewhat more subtle problem still remains. ... string theory physicists found that certain calculations yielded negative probabilities, which are also outside of the acceptable range.
>
> ... The negative probabilities arose from a *mismatch* between what the theory required and what reality seemed to impose: The calculations showed that if strings could vibrate in *nine* independent spatial directions, all the negative probabilities would cancel out.[37]

In 1995, five apparently unrelated and competing superstring theories in nine spatial dimensions were consolidated in a single stroke by American physicist Edward Witten into a comprehensive-ten-spatial-dimensions theory. Witten recognized connections no one else had seen or suspected. The mathematical demands of Witten's "master" theory – now called *M-theory* and denoting all kinds of string theories – are formidable and will take years to surmount. Thus any semi-conclusive test of the validity of the approach lies in the future. But the potential for unifying all forces in a single, comprehensive, relativistic, quantum-mechanical theory that correctly predicts the properties of all fundamental forces and particles – a GUT or TOE – is exciting. Borrowing from Greene,[38] let's take a quick look at some details to get an idea of the scope now being pursued in M-theory and another theory for characterizing spacetime called *loop quantum gravity theory.*

M-theory was initially conceived and has been developed to explain the myriad particles and their properties known from high-energy-physics experiments with cosmic particles and colliders. Physicists have made considerable progress toward this goal and generalized M-theory now includes gravity and relativity (through invisible graviton branes attached to or communicating with two bodies as a means of transmission of force between them). Goals in developing M-theory now include making it *background independent*, meaning that no assumed characters of time and space are adopted *a priori* as a background for the theory but rather the natures of time and space are derived as part of the theory from more basic elements of the theory. What elements are more basic than time and space? The answer to this question is not yet known, but an illustrative concept is provided by the strings themselves which may weave together to form a "fabric of space and time." Early results suggest an interesting interpretation. If we do live in an eleven-brane spacetime, we nonetheless sense only a three-dimensional space and four-dimensional spacetime because electromagnetic phenomena (as well as the strong and weak nuclear forces, in other words three of the four known fundamental forces) are confined to three-brane space. Only gravity may transcend the three spatial dimensions we sense. Since we don't sense by gravity but we see, hear, feel, taste, smell, and, apparently, think at least partially through electromagnetic processes mediated by photons, which mediate all electromagnetic atomic and molecular interactions, *by this interpretation we sense and perceive only three spatial dimensions and one time dimension of the proposed eleven-dimensional spacetime we occupy.* The prospect of discovering more fundamental natures of time and space is exciting because the basic concepts of space and time are familiar but only vaguely understood. Until they are better understood, no correct origin or deep physical meaning can be assigned to them or much else. "Our understanding [of space and time is] the arena ... of experiential reality. After centuries of thought, we still can only portray space and time as the most familiar of strangers."[39] Indeed, our familiarity with space and time obscures the fact that we don't understand them.

Loop quantum gravity theory originated in the mid 1980s to explain gravity. It is based in general relativity and gravity as its main focuses. It is a top-down theory that begins with the largest issues (gravity, general relativity) and is then refined to include quantum mechanics and details such as particle properties. M-theory is an opposite, bottom-up theory starting with quantum mechanics. (In fact, the successful inclusion of gravity in string theory was unintentional and fortuitous.) Loop quantum gravity theory is remarkable because it is a background-independent framework except for its adoption of general relativity. However, deducing the natures of space and time and even the successful features of general relativity from an abstract spaceless and timeless framework is complex and has not yet been successfully accomplished for any ordinary space and time. The abstractness of the theory is apparent in the question "Loops of what?" having no simple, non-mathematical answer; but a rough answer is "Elementary loops of space."[40] Except for background independence, progress in loop quantum gravity lags that in M-theory.

These approaches to a GUT/TOE do not ideally follow the scientific method (Chapter 5) in one important sense. In its ideal use, the scientific method assumes as little as possible while it discovers a theory that correctly predicts as much as possible. In the scientific method, a principle or theory is proposed (in steps 1 and 2), its consequences are deduced, tested against the facts, and the principle or theory is then adopted, revised, or discarded according to its agreement with reality (steps 3 through 5). As Karl Popper has noted, successful theories that are fundamental and incorporate few or no observed facts in their formulation can be adopted with greater confidence because these more general theories necessarily predict and test against a broader scope of observed facts. For instance, the minimal, fundamental principles adopted by Einstein in his theories of relativity provide many correct and novel results and useful insights. The contingency of relativity depends only on the contingency of its few basic principles. Quantum mechanics, in comparison, incorporates many essential, fundamental observations into the theory to give, in comparison to Einstein's theories, mere consistency and interpolation of details contingent upon all its incorporated observations. Lack of fundamental insight and greater contingency in quantum mechanics were the bases for Einstein's belief that quantum mechanics was incomplete and limited in its utility and depth of insight. The weakness of "up-front-loading" of facts in a contrived theory is especially apparent when two or more competing theories cannot be distinguished by an appeal to measurement, as occurs with the Schrödinger,[13] Heisenberg-Born-Jordan,[14, 15] and Bohm[41] versions of quantum mechanics. Unless theories predict different facts accessible to observation they must be regarded as equivalent and indistinguishable, like the Schrödinger, Heisenberg-Born-Jordan, and Bohm theories should be. This concern is important in seeking a TOE that contains as few as possible "up-front-loaded" observations, restrictions, and contingencies.

By the same token, a soft theory containing adjustable parameters is difficult to justify if agreement with observation is provided simply by selecting the value of these parameters. The *standard model* of high-energy-particle physics consists of *quantum chromodynamics*[42] to deal with the strong nuclear force and *electroweak theory* to deal with the weak nuclear force and with the electromagnetic forces and it contains many preconceptions and assumptions. (The gravity force is not important in describing high-energy particles.) In addition, the standard model contains 19 free parameters adjusted so that it fits measured data. Although this model is an important contribution to scientific knowledge, rationalizing the large menu of high-energy particles from which all matter is composed, it is clear that we do not yet possess a hard-science understanding of high-energy physics in particular and our understanding of physics in general is neither comprehensive nor fundamental.

In science, the fewer known facts deliberately incorporated into a theory, the better the test of the theory may be. Such incorporation forces consistency with known facts, perhaps by use of free parameters, mathematical constructs, and physical definitions contrived for this purpose. Such a strategy reduces evidence to test the theory against, renders the theory soft, contingent on built-in facts, and may limit its scope to a superficial level of interpolation of details. These dangers are present in the TOE versions currently being developed. In M-theory an eleven-dimensional spacetime is adopted to eliminate negative and infinite probabilities and point-like particles are replaced with strings or membranes or ... having desired mathematical properties. Forced consistency deliberately built into the foundation of a theory is contrived. The theory may then contain no truth deeper than the built-in facts on which it is contingent, i.e., the facts with which we start or the background we adopt. Einstein and many physicists would describe such a theory as incompletely founded, even though, like quantum mechanics, it predicts correct answers and no alternative is presently evident.

While a contingent TOE may be useful and necessary in exploration of the fundamental natures of space, time, and matter, contrived agreement does not provide understanding. Nor does it reveal meaning.

Notes and References for Chapter 9.

[1] Hertz, H., *Electric Waves,* Macmillan and Company, London, 1893.

[2] The Rayleigh-Jeans law provides the classical-physics distribution of radiant energy per unit volume of space over frequency ν or wavelength λ according to

$$u(\nu)\,d\nu = 8\pi kT\nu^2/c^3\,d\nu \qquad \text{or} \qquad u(\lambda)\,d\lambda = 8\pi kT/\lambda^2 c\,d\lambda,$$

where $u(\nu)\,d\nu$ is the energy per unit volume contained in radiation having frequency between ν and $\nu+d\nu$, k is Boltzmann's constant, T is the absolute temperature of the radiating body, and c =

$\nu \times \lambda$ (by which the two forms above are equivalent) is the velocity of light in vacuum. At small λ or large ν, both $u(\lambda)$ and $u(\nu)$ "diverge" (become indefinitely large) contrary to observation. This property of the law is referred to as the "ultraviolet catastrophe," i.e., this law and classical physics fail at small λ and large ν. The law is correct at large λ or small ν. Rayleigh derived this law in *Philosophical Magazine* **49**, 1900, 539-540. See Longair, M. S., *Theoretical Concepts in Physics,* Cambridge University Press, Cambridge, 1984, 206-212 and it is also derived in Allis, W. P., and M. A. Herlin, *Thermodynamics and Statistical Mechanics,* McGraw-Hill Book Company, New York, 1952, 199-214.

Normal energy flux between ν and $\nu+d\nu$ is the radiant energy passing unit surface area normal to the radiation per unit time, given by $c \times u(\nu)\, d\nu$. Conversion of $|\nu^2/c^2\, d\nu|$ to $|1/\lambda^2 \times c / \lambda^2\, d\lambda| = c/\lambda^4\, d\lambda$ gives the normal radiant energy flux between λ and $\lambda+d\lambda$ of

$$c \times u(\lambda)\, d\lambda = 8\pi\, kT c^2\, d\lambda / \lambda^4.$$

[3] Milonni, Peter W., *The Quantum Vacuum,* Academic Press, New York, 1994, Chapter 2.

[4] Longair, M. S., loc. cit.

[5] Planck, Max, *The Theory of Heat Radiation,* Dover, New York, 1959. For Planck's descriptions of his "First" and "Second" Theories, see *Annalen der Physik* **4**, 1901, 553 and **37**, 1912, 642.

[6] See endnote 27 of Chapter 8.

[7] When $h \to 0$, $\exp(h\nu/kT) - 1 = h\nu/kT$, Planck's law $u(\nu) = [8\pi h\nu^3/c^3] / [\exp(h\nu/kT) - 1]$ becomes the Rayleigh-Jeans law (endnote 2) $u(\nu) = 8\pi kT\, \nu^2/c^3$ and $\epsilon = n h\nu$, even with $n = 1, 2, 3, 4, \ldots$, becomes continuous. Only when energy occurs in discrete quanta $h\nu$ with h small but finite is the form of Planck's law required. Conversely, the form of Planck's law demands that energy transfer occurs only in discrete quanta. Thus, Planck's result was the origin of quantum physics.

[8] The adjective *heuristic* derives from the Greek *heuriskein* which means to invent or discover. The term "heuristic" or "heuristically" denotes serving to guide, discover, reveal, or helping to learn.

[9] If $\epsilon = nh\nu = 0$, then the system must be at its minimum potential and kinetic energies. That is, the system elements have fixed position and fixed velocity. Such a condition violates the Heisenberg uncertainty principle. Some physicists would even state that "$\epsilon = 0$ is *forbidden* by the uncertainty principle" taking this principle to exclude the possibility $\epsilon = 0$.

[10] Feynman, Richard, *The Character of Physical Law,* The MIT Press, Cambridge, MA, 1965.

[11] De Broglie had postulated that wave mechanics should bear the same relationship to classical mechanics as wave optics does to geometrical optics. Using this analogy Schrödinger discovered his wave equation in which the "index of refraction" depends on energy.

[12] To understand the concept of state we consider first the state of a system in classical physics. A number of property values is required to fully define the condition or state of a system. For example, a system containing N spherically symmetric atoms is fully defined on a *microscopic level* if three velocity components and three location coordinates are given for each of N unexcited atoms. With these values the *microscopic state* of the system is fully characterized. Other values may be used in place of some of these. For an atom of known mass, momentum is equivalent to velocity.

If the following description of quantum mechanics seems complex and irrational, that is only because quantum mechanics itself possesses these properties as indicated in the following summary comment of physicist E. T. Jaynes with which we begin; we quote from his "A Backward Look to the Future" (1993, 269-270 http://bayes.wustl.edu/etj/node1.html).

> In relativity theory one deduces the computational algorithm from the general principles. In quantum theory, the logic is the opposite; one chooses the principle to fit the empirically successful algorithm. But after all, how can one build rationally from a theory whose basic principles are in this condition: Present quantum theory uses relativistic wave equations, but tries to solve them with propagators that – quite aside from the divergencies [or infinities that arise] – violate relativity by failing to vanish outside the light cone [the region of spacetime about a point accessible to signals traveling at up to the velocity of light], and run backward in time! What can this possibly mean? On a more elementary level, present quantum theory claims on the one hand that local microevents [Chapter 10] have no physical causes, only probability laws; but at the same time admits (from the EPR paradox [Chapter 10]) instantaneous action at a distance. Today we have in full flower the blatant, spooky contradictions that Einstein foresaw and warned us about 60 years ago, and there is no way to reason logically from them. This mysticism *must* be replaced by a physical interpretation that restores the possibility of thinking rationally about the world.

Accordingly, while the algorithms of QED theory are extremely accurate, the physical basis and its meaning are unknown. Physicists tend to ignore the latter and focus on the former and such human preference is not limited to issues in science but is also found in philosophy and religion.

In quantum mechanics the concept of state is similar, with the property values provided by the wave function ψ_n for each particle or by a generic wave function ψ_n that applies for every particle. Wave functions ψ_n for different n values contain property values that define the state of a particle having quantum number n, such as an electron in an atom or an atom in a molecule or container. A complete specification of the state of a quantum system is provided by the wave function(s) for the system and *all* their integer *quantum numbers*. These ψ_n specify all system properties. The orbital quantum number n for an electron in an atom is used as a prototype for all quantum numbers. Example properties specified by a quantum number are spin components and electron orbital state or orbital energy. Since different quantum properties are generally independent of one another, the relative probability of a certain combination of, say, orbital and spin quantum states is given by the product of each probability or by the square of the product of the local orbital and spin wave functions $|\psi_{nj}|^2 = |\psi_n|^2 \times |\psi_j|^2$. A product of several wave functions, one for each property value each having its own quantum number designating the value of that property, thus fully specifies the relative probability of the state of each particle of a quantum system. A sum of all relative probabilities is used to calculate the probability of observing any state, e.g., {probability of state n} = $P(n) = C_n |\psi_n|^2 / |\psi|^2$, with $|\psi|^2 = \Sigma_n\ C_n\ |\psi_n|^2$. When desired, this sum is "weighted" by coefficient C_n to efficiently include multiple occurrences of identical energy levels (not states).

A "weighted sum" is simply a sum of components in which the nth component is multiplied (or weighted) by a coefficient C_n determined according to some rule. When perfect gas atoms do not interact and a single set of ψ_n solutions applies to all atoms and when total system energy dictates the N_1, N_2, N_3, ... set, then the C_n are given by this set of N_i numbers.

Consider an electron with orbital quantum number n having wave-function solution of, say, the Dirac equation $\psi_n(x,y,z,t)$. The probability that the electron is in a particular quantum state n_0 is obtained as follows. One finds relative probability of each state n, or each value $|\psi_n|^2$, with n=1,2,3,4,... The *probability density* $\rho_{n_0j}(x,y,z,t)$ in x,y,z,t-spacetime for an electron in quantum state n_0 and other quantum state(s) j, ... representing, say, spin components (j_1, j_2, j_3) at specified spacetime location is given by

$$\rho_{n_0j}(x,y,z,t) = |\psi_{n_0j}(x,y,z,,t)|^2 / \Sigma_n \Sigma_j |\psi_{nj}(x,y,z,t)|^2,$$

with $|\psi_{nj}|^2 = |\psi_n|^2 \times |\psi_j|^2$. Then the probability of finding the electron in joint quantum state n_0j between x,y,z,t and x+dx,y+dy,z+dz,t+dt is $\rho_{n_0j}(x,y,z,t)\,dx\,dy\,dz\,dt$. Since probability of a state involving independent property values (independent quantum numbers) is normalized (divided) by a sum of products of squared wave functions, additional squared terms must be included for each additional property considered, with more than two properties requiring quantum numbers and sums beyond the two shown in the double sum above. Summation over all quantum numbers is required. Every quantum number appearing in the wave function solution thus influences the probability density of an electron or electron-state property.

Wave functions are generally *complex*, i.e., of the *complex number* form $a + b\mathrm{i}$, where a and b are *real numbers*, $b\mathrm{i}$ is an *imaginary number*, and $\mathrm{i} = \sqrt{(-1)}$ is the *imaginary index*, because the wave equation itself contains the imaginary index. To obtain a real magnitude of a complex number, i.e., a number devoid of imaginary index $\mathrm{i} = \sqrt{(-1)}$, one utilizes the real magnitude squared of a complex number defined as the product $\psi^*\psi$, where ψ^* is the *complex conjugate* of ψ obtained by reversing the sign of the imaginary part of the complex number ψ (if $\psi = a + b\mathrm{i}$ then $\psi^* = a - b\mathrm{i}$ so that $\psi^*\psi = |\psi|^2 = a^2 + b^2$). This product is represented in any one of several ways: $\psi^*\psi = |\psi|^2 = \langle|\psi|^2\rangle$, with the angular brackets $\langle..\rangle$ representing an average value. After Born, we take the real value $\psi^*\psi$ to be proportional to particle probability density.

Generally, quantity $|\psi_n|^2$ decreases as quantum number n becomes large when n is associated with an energy level, but it does not decrease monotonically. Nevertheless, a desired accuracy may always be obtained using a finite number of n terms in a sum over n, even when the actual number of terms is infinite. In solutions for some properties, such as spin, only a few terms occur, e.g., an electron has only two spin states: “up” and “down.”

[13] Schrödinger, Erwin, *Annalen der Physik* **79**, 1926, 361-376, **79**, 1926, 489-527, **80**, 1926, 437-490, **81**, 1926, 109-139. Schrödinger, Erwin, *Collected Papers,* Blackie, London, 1927 contains English translations.

[14] Heisenberg, Werner, *Zeitschrift fûr Physik* **33**, 1925, 879.

[15] Born, Max, and Pascual Jordan, *Zeitschrift für Physik* **34**, 1925, 858.

[16] Heisenberg corresponded with Born on 25 November 1933 after it was announced that Heisenberg alone would received the 1932 Nobel Prize in Physics, writing

> If I have not written you for such a long time, and have not thanked you for your congratulations, it was partly because of my rather bad conscience with respect to you. The fact that I am to receive the Nobel Prize alone, for work done in Göttingen in collaboration – you, Jordan and I – this fact depresses me and I hardly know what to write to you. I am, of course, glad that our common efforts are now appreciated, and I enjoy the recollection of the beautiful time of collaboration. I also believe that all good physicists know how great was your and Jordan’s contribution to the structure of quantum mechanics – and this remains unchanged by a wrong decision from outside. Yet I myself can do nothing but thank you again for all the fine collaboration, and feel a little ashamed. (Born, Max, *My Life,* Charles Scribner’s Sons, New York, 1978, 220.)

[17] Schrödinger, E., *Annalen der Physik* **79**, 1926, 734.

[18] Eckart, C., *Physical Review* **28**, 1926, 711.

[19] Beller, Mara, *Quantum Dialogue,* The University of Chicago Press, Chicago, 1999.

[20] Dirac, P. A. M., *Proceedings of the Royal Society* (London) **A117**, 1928, 610.

[21] Quoted in Crease, Robert P., and Charles C. Mann, *The Second Creation,* Macmillan, New York, 1986.

[22] Thomson, J. J., *Philosophical Magazine* **44**, 1897, 293.

[23] Lamb, W. E., and R. C. Retherford, *Physical Review* **72**, 1947, 241.

[24] Einstein, Albert, *Physikalische Zeitschrift* **18**, 1917, 121.

[25] Oppenheimer, J. R., *Physical Review* **35**, 1930, 461.

[26] Weisskopf, V. F., *Zeitschrift für Physik* **90**, 1934, 817.

[27] Following Lamb's announcement of the Lamb shift in 1947, T. A. Welton provided this description of its origin (*Physical Review* **74**, 1948, 1157). Welton's description clearly indicates that a new QED capable of describing an electrodynamic vacuum was required.

[28] Schwinger, Julian, *Two Shakers of Physics: Memorial Lecture for Sin-itiro Tomonaga,* delivered 8 July 1980 at the Nishina Memorial Foundation, Tokyo. This lecture appeared in Laurie M. Brown and Lillian Hoddeson (editors), *The Birth of Particle Physics,* Cambridge University Press and has also been reprinted in Timothy Ferris (editor), *Physics, Astronomy, and Mathematics,* Little, Brown and Company, Boston, 1991. Tomonaga's series of 12 lectures on spin was published in Japanese in 1974 and has recently been translated into English as *The Story of Spin,* University of Chicago Press, Chicago, 1997. In these, Tomonaga shows his mastery of quantum mechanics and its history.

[29] This intermediate path is called the "path of least or stationary action." For an excellent description of it see Townsend, John S., *A Modern Approach to Quantum Mechanics,* University Science Books, Sausalito, CA, 2000, Chapter 8.

[30] Feynman, Richard, *QED,* Princeton University Press, Princeton, NJ, 1985. This book is a 150-page account of the four inaugural Alix G. Mautner Memorial Lectures presented at UCLA in 1983 and is an excellent, popular-level overview of Feynman's "sum of paths" QED theory.

[31] In his book *QED,* loc. cit., 55-56, Feynman describes the uncertainty principle as historically necessary in understanding quantum principles in terms of old fashioned ideas, e.g., that light travels in a straight line. Feynman claims that by eliminating the old fashioned ideas in using sum-of-paths theory, no need exists for an uncertainty principle. But absolute determinism is still proscribed in quantum mechanics as currently understood because its solutions are probabilistic rather than deterministic, i.e., alternative QED paths from any one to any other state are always possible. Nevertheless, uncertainty must still exist because of the many different possibilities that could be included in a sum-of-histories solution, not all of which ever are.

[32] See endnote 13 of Chapter 4.

[33] Greene, Brian, *The Elegant Universe,* Vintage Books, New York, 2000. See also Greene's later and equally marvelous book, *The Fabric of the Cosmos, Space, Time, and the Texture of Reality,* Alfred A. Knopf, New York, 2004.

[34] Lindley, David, *The End of Physics,* Basic Books, New York, 1993, 219-221; see also for additional background, Lindley, David, *Where Does the Weirdness Go?,* Basic Books, New York, 1996.

[35] Laughlin, R. B., and David Pines, "The Theory of Everything," *Proceedings of the National Academy of Sciences of the United States of America* **97**, 2000, 28-31.

[36] Weinberg, S., "The Search for Unity: Notes for a History of Quantum Field Theory," *Daedalus* **106**, 1977, 17.

[37] Greene, Brian, 2000, loc. cit., 201-202. [38] Greene, Brian, 2004, loc. cit. [39] Ibid., 489-490.

[40] Ibid., 492. [41] Bohm, David, *Physical Review* **85**, 1952, 166-179, 180-193.

[42] *Quantum chromodynamics* is the name of a quantum theory of *quarks* and the eight *gluon* fields by which they interact. The nuclear particles (protons and neutrons) and similar particles (six hyperons in all) are made from quarks and gluons, with gluons the fields or messenger particles for the strong nuclear force. Since the several types of quarks each comes in three "colors," their theory involves colors and carries the name quantum chromodynamics.

10. Faith and Its Essential Role in Science

Archimedes (287 - 212 BC), the greatest mathematician and engineer-physicist of antiquity, once stated "Give me a place to stand on, and I can move the world." While he was referring to mechanics and the systems of levers, pulleys, screws, and gears with which he was expert, the same sentiment applies in philosophy.[1] In the case of philosophy, the "place to stand on" is the foundation, the thing one allows to be known, upon which one builds his or her philosophy or vision of reality. The deeper and broader and truer the foundation, the more reliable and definitive the philosophy and the vision of reality it implies.

Thus, we must choose carefully our standing place. Of course this choice is the challenge. From among the candidate places we could select, including belief in Christ, the scientific method, or a combination of the two, none can be *a priori*[2] demonstrated to be superior. Only after we choose a paradigm does a consistent and broad vision of reality begin to emerge. Indeed, the preferred evidence and the resulting vision of reality are imposed by the choice of paradigm! But truth of a paradigm cannot be established without an adequate truth criterion. Without such a truth criterion *any belief is based on faith.*

Reliance on faith instead of facts may seem too vague, indefinite, and nebulous to some. However, no one has any alternative but to rely on faith because no matter what one believes it is always a discretionary choice founded initially and ultimately on personal preference and/or faith. Believing objective, reproducible, rigorous science provides useful and reliable knowledge is an act of faith. Faith is required in any belief since humans cannot demonstrate any indubitable truth. The question is not whether to rely on faith but rather in what to place faith. In this chapter we examine the reliance on faith required in science.

Proof in Science and Mathematics

Science is based on experience. Science is therefore empirical, developed by rationalizing and abstractly connecting observed facts and deductions they imply. Resulting theories and laws are utilized with mathematics to discover connections and patterns among the facts and to infer additional facts and deeper organization.

But experience and its interpretations are fallible and intuition is not rigorous. To be as certain as possible about scientific and mathematical matters, and other matters in logic and philosophy as well, formal methods of proof are used. The methods are careful, deliberate, and rigorously based on objective and disinterested consideration of the facts. Charisma is desired in a political candidate (by the candidate's supporters) but establishing truth in science and mathematics must be, as far as possible, unbiased and universal, based on facts and substance rather than power of personality of a proponent of a particular view. Thus, proof in science and mathematics, were it possible, would be invaluable in consolidating knowledge into a reliable, universally-applicable system.

In science, mathematics, logic, and philosophy, demonstration of validity, establishment of truth, or proof of a law or hypothesis may take an unlimited number of forms with the only limitations being in imagination and insight. Nevertheless, two general forms of proof are prominent. The first form, prominent in mathematics, is a demonstration that A is sufficient for B, where A represents some axiomatic base, accepted convention, or other philosophical foundation and B represents a statement, principle, theory, law, or condition of interest. In this form, B is proven in the sense that if A is demonstrated to be sufficient for B to be true, then, given the truth of A (by assumption or convention), the truth of B is proved. Many mathematical theorems rest on proofs of this type or one of its variations, such as proving A is sufficient for "not B" (the opposite of B) to be false in an "excluded middle" system, i.e., the system of Aristotelian logic in which one of only two logical states of B, true or false, is possible.

The second common form of proof is the one utilized in science. In fact, in science the term proof is not used because the real basis of science is not proof but consistency or absence of disproof. A term preferred in science in place of "proof of postulate B" would be "test of validity of theory B," with the specific evidence of the test which supports (fails to contradict) the postulate or theory included, preferably in the form of novel predictions demonstrated to be correct and at variance with previous belief and understanding. Laws of physics, including Newton's theory of gravitation and his laws of motion, Einstein's relativity theory, and quantum mechanics, rest on demonstrations of this type. While no axiomatic base or accepted convention A is specified, one is still required in the form of accepted scientific principles and conventions used in the postulated theory and in the methods testing it.

In either case, proof is not an accurate descriptor. For a process in which the sufficiency of A is invoked to deduce the truth of B, "proof" certainly cannot be used in an absolute sense because we don't prove A and we therefore don't prove B. This fact is, of course, well known to mathematicians and is the origin of numerous quips. One states "A proof tells us where to concentrate our doubts." Another is "Logic is the art of going wrong with confidence." Morris Kline summarizes the process of mathematical invention as creation "by acts of insight and intuition. Logic then sanctions the conquests of intuition. It is the hygiene that mathematics practices to keep its ideas healthy and strong. ... [But] the whole structure rests fundamentally on uncertain ground, the intuitions of man."[3] And the inherent inability to finally prove any scientific law is implicit in the scientific method in that any result may only be tentatively accepted until disproved, i.e., until one unavoidable, inconsistent or contrary fact is established. While disproof may be conclusive, assumption or faith is essential in the use of tentative scientific theories. Max Planck, perhaps as a result of his long struggle to understand quantum physics, observed that "over the gates of the temple of science are written the words: Ye must have faith."[4]

The Gödel and Löwenheim-Skolem Theorems

Even in theoretical mathematics, rigor and proof are elusive as is illustrated by some interesting history we now summarize.[5] Once the results of Gauss, Bolyai, Lobachevski, Riemann, and Beltrami had supplanted the centuries-held certainty of Euclidian geometry (Chapter 3), search for a new mathematical certainty began. Superior systems of axioms for geometry were established by German mathematician David Hilbert (1862-1943) and others. Still others used the symbolic logic introduced by English logician George Boole (1815-1864) in an attempt to establish axioms that provided a rigorous basis for all mathematics. In the period from 1910 to 1913, Bertrand Russell (1872-1970) and Alfred North Whitehead (1861-1947) published a monumental, three-volume work entitled *Principia Mathematica* dealing with logic, set theory, and number theory. The object of this work was to establish a *consistent* and *complete* system by which definitive mathematical results could be logically derived without contradictions, to eliminate the various paradoxes that had resulted in less careful approaches. A *complete system* means a system containing a sufficient basis for the derivation of all mathematics while a *consistent system* or *consistent set* of methods means that some part of the system or set of methods cannot be used to prove a certain result while another part of the system or set of methods is used to disprove the same result or to prove a contradictory result. The utility of establishing, say, that a system is complete would justify it use in addressing all mathematics.

In their system Whitehead and Russell prohibit self-reference to avoid circularity of argument. Paradoxes can result from self-reference, as illustrated by the following example. Suppose we adopt as true the axiom "All rules have exceptions." This axiom is itself a rule and it must therefore have an exception. But if it does then it contradicts itself by implying a rule without an exception. This statement denies itself by referring to itself and thus leads to a paradox based in self-reference. The best-known paradox of this type is called the "liar's paradox," which Aristotle and many later logicians have discussed. A standard version is "This sentence is false." Another is "I am lying." If the statement is true, then it is false. If it is false, then it is true.

But beyond eliminating circular logic due to self-reference, mathe-maticians were not certain that any methods including those in *Principia Mathematica* were complete or even that they were consistent. Answers to the questions of completeness and consistency and their proofs were broadly pursued until 1931 when Austrian logician Kurt Gödel (1906-1978), at age twenty-five, resolved the matter by proving two important results in a single paper: "On Formally Undecidable Propositions of *Principia Mathematica* and Related Systems."[6] Gödel cleverly mapped symbolic logic onto arithmetic space (integer numbers) and was able to write logical statements and sequences thereof as single integers. By this device he addressed the problem in a "symbolic-logic arithmetic space" in a direct and comprehensive manner and proved a powerful theorem and a corollary to it. While the problem is less directly and comprehensively addressed in language, language nevertheless provides the gist of Gödel's proof, indicated in the following box.

Gödel wrote an arithmetical assertion H, represented by a "Gödel number," that stated "This sentence is not provable." If H is provable, then what it asserts is not true. Alternatively, if H is not provable, what it asserts is true. The statement is true if and only if it is not provable. But assertion H must be valid because of its legitimate, symbolic-logic synthesis in "Gödel-number space." H is not a contradiction but a true statement that is undecidable and unprovable. Since H is undecidable and unprovable, it follows that if the system is consistent it must be incomplete.

Gödel thus proved his incompleteness theorem: *for any consistent set of axioms, statements always exist in a system based on those axioms which can be proved neither true nor false.* Even when an axiomatic base of a system is altered so that alternative or additional selected statements can be proved true or false, then other statements can be formulated which can be proved neither true nor false. And so on. In other words, the totality of mathematics cannot be based on any single set of axioms – *any* set of axioms is *incomplete* (not able to decide all questions). No set of axioms is complete. All mathematical systems unavoidably contain statements or paradoxes which can never be resolved in that system.

Gödel then utilized his incompleteness theorem to prove a corollary: *proving the consistency of a mathematical system by use of the system is impossible.* The gist of Gödel's proof of this corollary is indicated in the following box.

To prove this corollary to his theorem Gödel constructed the arithmetical assertion G that states, in words, "Arithmetic is consistent." He then proved this integer assertion G implies the former integer assertion H, defined in the previous box. But the former (H) is undecidable. Thus, we conclude, G must also be undecidable.

This corollary pertaining to arithmetic is both consequential and comprehensive. Because of earlier proofs[7] it was known that the mathematical consistency of geometry, the calculus, and other areas of mathematics including applied mathematics (i.e., analysis consisting of ordinary and partial differential equations, the calculus of variations, differential geometry, infinite series, the calculus of functions of a complex variable, potential theory, etc.) is established with and only with the consistency of arithmetic.

Gödel thus conclusively ended the quest to prove both completeness and consistency of the system described in *Principia Mathematica* or any other system by demonstrating that (1) any consistent system, if such a system can indeed be found, must contain propositions that cannot be proven even if true and (2) consistency of a system can never be proven using the system. Gödel's results show no fixed (finite) system, regardless of its scope and complexity, can adequately represent the complexity, organization, connection, and pattern contained in the whole integers: $1, 2, 3, 4, \ldots$ When one adds zero, negative integers, rational non-integers, irrational, imaginary, and complex numbers to the integers, to accommodate the calculations of analysis, it is clear that no system of axioms should naïvely be considered to be both consistent and sufficiently comprehensive for all desired proofs. To obtain a desired proof a mathematical system itself, and any vision of reality it represents, must be appropriately selected or invented.

To further frustrate mathematicians and logicians, another result was even more devastating to the traditional axiomatic method of creating mathematical and logical systems, such as the ones addressed by Whitehead and Russell in their *Principia Mathematica*. Beginning in 1915, Leopold Löwenheim (ca. 1878-1940) discovered new flaws in logic and mathematics. Thoralf Skolem (1887-1963) simplified and finalized Löwenheim's work in several papers published over thirteen-years beginning in 1920. A noteworthy result called the *Löwenheim-Skolem theorem* thus emerged. While Gödel's incompleteness theorem reveals that a set of axioms is never sufficient to prove all possible assertions or theorems in a mathematical system, the Löwenheim-Skolem theorem states that *a set of axioms must support and define many different mathematical systems*, e.g., different interpretations or models in science. Whereas the Löwenheim-Skolem theorem goes beyond Gödel's theorem, the two are related. The former requires radically different interpretations or models based on a given set of axioms because a meaningful statement in one interpretation is undecidable, as required by Gödel's theorem, and may thus be replaced by an alternative, undecidable but meaningful statement in a second interpretation, and so on. However detailed and exhaustive a set of axioms may be, it is insufficient to completely establish any mathematical system or model in mathematical physics; any axiomatic system (model) is never unique, with radically different alternatives equally defined and supported by and consistent with its axioms or with extensive measured data.

In the clarity of hindsight it is now recognized that these theorems lie at the basis of the centuries-long confusion relating to Euclid's fifth or parallel postulate. Without this fifth postulate, Euclid's remaining axioms permit many alternative and essentially different but equally valid geometries. Even with Euclid's parallel postulate many alternative geometries are still permitted. In Euclid's time and throughout most of the following centuries, a unique, realistic system of geometry that coincided with physical space was not sought because, until relativity, Euclid's geometry with his parallel postulate was believed to be this system. Other perceived properties of reality were also invoked to constrain mathematics to be uniquely real. But such a goal now appears to be unachievable.

Inherent Uncertainty in Mathematics

With the proofs that no mathematical system can be used to prove itself either consistent or complete and no unique system or model may be deduced from any set of axioms, with radically different alternatives always expected, discovery and demonstration of universal or absolute truth or a unique and exact description of reality in the form of a set of logicomathematical axioms (theories, laws, principles, statements, assumptions, data) is precluded. While logic and mathematics may be profitably employed to discover truth, any conclusive demonstration by them that a logicomathematical system corresponds to a unique reality is impossible because the system must correspond equally to many "models of reality."

As might be imagined, these proofs and their implications had profound impact. In several retrospective comments Bertrand Russell evaluated logic and the logical approach he developed with Alfred North Whitehead in *Principia Mathematica.* In his *Portraits from Memory* (1958), Russell described thoughts reminiscent of those of Descartes:[8]

> I wanted certainty in the kind of way in which people want religious faith. I thought that certainty is more likely to be found in mathematics than elsewhere. But I discovered that many mathematical demonstrations, which my teachers expected me to accept, were full of fallacies, and that, if certainty were indeed discoverable in mathematics, it would be in a new field of mathematics, with more solid foundations than those that had hitherto been thought secure. But as the work proceeded ... and after some twenty years of very arduous toil, I came to the conclusion that there was nothing more that I could do in the way of making mathematical knowledge indubitable.

At the beginning of his effort in writing *Principia Mathematica* with Whitehead, Russell thought that the axioms of logic were truths. By his 1937 *Principles of Mathematics*, six years after Gödel's paper appeared, he had abandoned this belief and thus a belief in the *a priori* truth of mathematics, since it is based on logic. In *My Philosophical Development* (1959) Russell wrote "The splendid certainty which I had always hoped to find in mathematics was lost in a bewildering maze ... It is truly a complicated conceptual labyrinth." In a different context but in this same spirit Russell commented, not tongue in cheek, that "mathematics is the subject in which we never know what we are talking about nor whether what we are saying is true."[9] The influence of Gödel and of Löwenheim and Skolem is apparent in these sentiments.

Two contrary views have succeeded these results that, considered together, illustrate Löwenheim-Skolem. Beginning especially in the last century, most mathematicians no longer limit themselves by any concern about reality but instead study unrestricted, purely hypothetical systems. In science, reality is, in principle, uniquely fixed by direct and indirect observation of it. In science and applied mathematics used therein, any invented, external-world reality must be consistent with the actually observed or implied one. This constraint is essential to science and applied mathematics as it allows testing against reality as a guiding discipline. But, according to one school of thought, most mathematicians in recent decades have neither studied nor been interested in science. While pure mathematics is interesting (otherwise one wouldn't do it), such work is regarded by this school as isolated and sterile with respect to practical applications with the consequence that most of it will be useless for such purposes. Such concerns were expressed by both John von Neuman and Morris Kline. The former wrote,

> As a mathematical discipline travels far from its empirical source, or still worse, if it is a second or third generation only indirectly inspired by ideas coming from 'reality,' it is beset with very grave dangers. It becomes more and more purely aestheticizing, more and more purely *l'art pour l'art*. This need not be bad, if the field is surrounded by correlated subjects which still have close empirical connections, or if the discipline is under the influence of men with an exceptionally well-developed taste. But there is a grave danger that the subject will develop along the line of least resistance, that the stream, so far from its source, will separate into a multitude of insignificant branches, and that the discipline will become a disorganized mass of details and complexities. In other words, at a great distance from its empirical source, or after much abstract inbreeding, a mathematical subject is in danger of degeneration.[10]

And the latter wrote,

> In the halls of mathematics today, one dare not ask for meaning and purpose. Mathematics must not be tainted by reality. The ivy has grown so thick that the researchers within can no longer see the world outside. These sequestered minds are content in their own isolation. ...
>
> Mathematical theories have enabled us to know something of nature, to embrace in comprehensive intelligible accounts varieties of seemingly diverse phenomena. Mathematical theories have revealed whatever order and plan man has found in nature and have given us mastery or partial mastery over vast domains.
>
> But most mathematicians have abandoned their traditions and heritage. The pregnant messages that nature sends to the senses now fall on closed eyes and inattentive ears. Mathematicians are living on the reputation earned by their predecessors and still expect the acclaim and support that the older work warranted. ... On the whole mathematics is now turned inward; it feeds on itself; and it is extremely unlikely, if one may judge by what happened in the past, that most of the modern mathematical research will ever contribute to the advancement of science; mathematics may be doomed to grope in darkness. Mathematics is now an almost entirely self-contained enterprise. Moving in directions determined by its own criteria of relevance and excellence, it is even proud of its independence from outside problems, motivations, and inspirations. It no longer has unity and purpose.[11]

Applied mathematics that conforms with reality and is useful to science is still pursued by a few mathematicians, Kline estimated ten percent.[12] And applied mathematics needed in science will still be invented, if necessary by scientists and engineers. Historical precedent for this process exists: many of the Greeks including Archimedes as well as Bessel, Cauchy, Euler, Fourier, Gauss, Hamilton, Heaviside,[13] Jacobi, Lagrange, Laplace, Legendre, Newton, Riemann, and many others, most now properly regarded as eminent mathematicians, were either physicists (e.g., Newton, Gauss, Laplace) or engineers (e.g., Archimedes, Cauchy, Fourier) or distinguished themselves in these areas as well as in mathematics. Many powerful methods of mathematics were invented only because they were necessary for applied work.

Twentieth century British mathematician G. H. Hardy (1877-1947), perhaps in defense against criticism, boasted that none of his results had any practical value. "I have never done anything 'useful.' No discovery of mine has made, or is likely to make, directly or indirectly, for good or ill, the least difference to the amenity of the world. ... Judged by all practical standards, the value of my mathematical life is nil."[14]

But some results of Hardy and other "pure" mathematicians will be useful and we can't anticipate which results. Thus, a second school of thought, contrary to the one described above, believes that many, if not all, results of even pure mathematics will eventually be useful. Thinking of this school is well represented by several thoughts of physicist Steven Weinberg.

> It is precisely in the application of pure mathematics to physics that the effectiveness of aesthetic judgements is most amazing. It has become commonplace that mathematicians are driven in their work by the wish to construct formalisms that are conceptually beautiful. ... And yet mathematical structures that confessedly are developed ... [in pursuit of] a sort of beauty are often found later to be extraordinarily valuable by the physicist. ...
>
> When Einstein started to develop general relativity, he realized that one way of expressing his ideas about the symmetry that relates different frames of reference was to ascribe gravitation to the curvature of spacetime. ... He asked a friend, Marcel Grossman, whether there existed any mathematical theory of curved spaces ... Grossman gave Einstein the good news that there did in fact exist such a mathematical formalism, the one developed by Riemann and others, and taught him this mathematics, which Einstein then incorporated into general relativity. The mathematics was there waiting for Einstein to make use of...
>
> An even stranger example is provided by the history of internal symmetry principles. In physics internal symmetry principles typically impose a kind of family structure on the menu of possible particles. ...
>
> Around 1960 physicists studying this question [family structure on the menu of possible particles] began to turn for help to the literature of mathematics. It came to them as a delightful surprise that mathematicians had in a sense already cataloged all possible symmetries. The complete set of transformations that leaves anything unchanged, whether a specific object or the laws of nature, forms a mathematical structure known as a *group*, and the general mathematics of symmetry transformations is known as *group theory*. ...
>
> In 1960 [Murray] Gell-Mann and Israeli physicist Yuval Ne'eman independently found that one of these simple ... groups ... was just right to impose a family structure on the crowd of elementary particles much like what had been found experimentally. Gell-Mann borrowed a term from Buddhism and called this symmetry principle the eightfold way ...
>
> Yet this group theory that turned out to be so relevant to physics had been invented by mathematicians for reasons that were strictly internal to mathematics. Group theory was initiated in the early nineteenth century by Evariste Galois, in his proof that there are no general formulas for the solution of certain algebraic equations (equations that contain fifth or higher powers of the unknown quantity). ...
>
> Physicists generally find the ability of mathematicians to anticipate the mathematics needed in the theories of physics quite uncanny.[15] (italics are the original author's)

The contrary views of these two schools suggest an uncertainty in the nature of mathematics and its uses reminiscent of Gödel and Löwenheim-Skolem. Even a general direction of mathematical research useful to science cannot be anticipated, perhaps because none is unique and many are equally suitable.

What does a proven absence of complete and consistent mathematical and logical basis supporting a chosen system mean? By the theorems of Gödel and Löwenheim-Skolem it means that the tentative nature of science in describing reality is also inherent in mathematics, the language of science, down to its very basis. It means that even in logic and mathematics, a unique and correct model (of reality) based on some logicomathematical axiomatic foundation is precluded because any such basis must support many alternative, radically different interpretations.[16] Since modern science consists of mathematics-and-logic-based theories, quantum mechanics being one example, it means essential uncertainty and lack of absolute provability occur in science not only in the inherent uncertainty and tentative nature of the scientific method, but also in the uncertainty and tentative nature of the logic and mathematics utilized in science. It means that any set of mathematical axioms invoked to define a unique scientific reality must fail because it actually defines many, highly diverse realities. It means comprehension of truth or vision of reality can never be demonstrated to be absolute or universal by a scientific or logico-mathematical paradigm. It means that acceptance of truth based solely on mathematical-logical-scientific results always requires substantial assumption or faith. It means that discovery *and* demonstration of absolute truth, if they are possible, must be obtained through some other methodology. These points will all be well illustrated in considering interpretations of quantum mechanics and Bell's theorem.

The deficiencies in logic and mathematics were, of course, recognized by the best mathematicians. German mathematician Felix Klein (1849-1925) estimated that "Mathematics has been advanced most by those who are distinguished more for intuition than for rigorous methods of proof."[17] After all, as in science, the real challenge in creative, exploratory work is not "how to prove," but "what to prove." Once the "what" is identified, mere competence suffices. Yet, some

> contemporary mathematicians [and scientists] are aware of the uncertainties in the foundations but prefer to take an aloof attitude toward what they characterize as philosophical questions. ... They prefer to be suckled in a creed outworn. ... They speak of proof in some universally accepted sense even though there is no such animal, and write and publish as if the uncertainties were non-existent.[18]

Proposition Number 4: **While logic and mathematics may be used to investigate truth by conclusive elimination of incorrect assumptions and theories, no demonstration that a logicomathematical axiomatic system absolutely or uniquely represents observed reality is possible because any set of logicomathematical axioms must support many diverse models. In science and mathematics no method is known for discovering, specifying, or demonstrating the true nature of the universe. Discovery and demonstration of such truth, if possible, requires a different paradigm.**

Inherent Uncertainty in Science

While pure mathematics may be pursued without consideration of reality, science is a study of material reality. To utilize the scientific method is to guess, hypothesize, assume, or synthesize at least one principle, theory, or law and then test whether it and its consequences are consistent with observed reality. And any success in such an effort leads directly to a network of interconnected ideas that is science.

A deep scientific knowledge of reality requires deeply correct laws, postulates, and assumptions as a basis and correct deduction of their consequences. And no uniqueness can be expected in a valid model as multiple models may always be inferred from any set of axioms or assumptions or data. That is, by the Löwenheim-Skolem theorem no unique paradigm derives from a set of logicomathematical axioms regardless of its scope; instead, the set equally justifies many paradigms. Any claim that a paradigm based on logicomathematical axioms is unique must be considered with great skepticism.

While knowledge of reality is the objective of science, reality presents a dilemma to science: in order to discover the nature of reality we must first know the nature of reality – in order to conceive tests and questions that are significant and necessary to discovering reality. Where does initial knowledge of reality originate? It must be *guessed.*

Inherent uncertainty in scientific laws and the essential role of guessing in science were emphasized by physicist Richard Feynman in the John Danz Lectures at the University of Washington in April of 1963 but only published in 1998. The following is a quotation from Feynman's first lecture of the three-lecture series:

> In all of this I have left out something very important. I said that observation is the judge of the truth of an idea. But where does the idea come from? …
>
> It was thought in the Middle Ages that people simply make observations, and the observations themselves suggest the laws. But it does not work that way. It takes much more imagination than that. So the next thing we have to talk about is where the new ideas come from. Actually, it does not make any difference, as long as they come. We have a way of checking whether an idea is correct or not that has nothing to do with where it came from. We simply test it against observation. So in science we are not interested in where an idea comes from. …
>
> It is surprising that people do not believe that there is imagination in science. It is a very interesting kind of imagination, unlike that of the artist. The great difficulty is in trying to imagine something that you have never seen, that is consistent in every detail with what has already been seen, and that is different from what has been thought of; furthermore, it must be definite and not a vague proposition. That is indeed difficult. …
>
> I now come to an important point. The old laws may be wrong. How can an observation be incorrect? If it has been carefully checked, how can it be wrong? Why are physicists always having to change the laws? The answer is, first, that the laws are not the observations and, second, that the experiments are always inaccurate. The laws are guessed laws, extrapolations, not something that the observations insist upon. They are just good guesses …
>
> Scientists, therefore, are used to dealing with doubt and uncertainty. All scientific knowledge is uncertain. …
>
> So what we call scientific knowledge today is a body of statements of varying degrees of certainty. Some of them are most unsure; some of them are nearly sure; but none is absolutely certain. Scientists are used to this. We know that it is consistent to be able to live and not know. Some people say, "How can you *live* without knowing?" I do not know what they mean. I always live without knowing. That is easy. How you get to know is what I want to know.[19]

To all this concern about rigor, consistency, completeness, and guessing the right law, the utilitarian skeptic would ask "So we can't prove something is absolutely true, what's the problem? Science is empirical anyway; we need do no more than observe results and codify them to obtain adequate knowledge." The problem is that to use known facts to discover unknown facts or, for that matter, to properly codify empirical results, we must infer a fundamental principle or law which is more general than the specific known facts from which the law is inferred. And the deeper, the more fundamental and general the law or principle, the more abstract its nature and the less intuitive and more elusive is its discovery. While deep principles are valid over broad ranges of application, they are difficult to discover because they are deeply buried in the facts. If reality were simple, insights would be neither deep nor obscure. But reality is not simple; rather, it is often, perhaps generally, surprising because our shallow, culture-based intuition is not deeply accurate. Using only empirical results, which the skeptic correctly suggests are ultimately all we have in science (besides philosophy), is tedious and tentative for discovering deep, abstract principles. Until a principle is discovered (or guessed) we don't know what questions to ask or what experiments to perform.

Nevertheless, we seek always to discover truth at a fundamental and abstract level. It is discovery on this level by which progress in science is measured. Usually a breakthrough in science comes not by new facts but rather by new interpretation of well-known facts, which often reveals previously unknown connections and facts as well. Such were the natures of the great discoveries of Newton and Einstein. And such is the nature of thermodynamics.

Thermodynamics: Prototype of a Good Theory

An excellent example in science (and, by extension, other philosophy) of a powerful philosophical structure is provided by *thermodynamics*, the axiomatic study of heat and heat related processes. Thermodynamics is generally regarded by scientists as the final test on any question on which it can be brought to bear, for good reasons. Thermodynamics is a mature science, one that has been studied intensively for centuries and refined to the point where it rests on fundamental, abstract axioms or thermodynamic laws. By use of thermodynamics, observed events have been understood and previously unobserved events have been correctly predicted. Such prediction of unexpected results is a highly demanding test of the power and utility of a philosophical structure: if the structure tells us things we don't already know, i.e., things that are not deliberately built into the structure, then it is powerful. We seek to discover such structures. We seek to use observed facts to deduce a philosophical structure that applies beyond them and is therefore capable of telling us what we don't already know. Thermodynamics thus illustrates the desired capability of a powerful philosophical system.

Discovery of the principles and laws of thermodynamics has occurred because of two principal reasons. First, thermodynamics is focused on a relatively narrow range of processes of common utility, processes relating to thermal and mechanical properties of materials and thus to processes such as heating, cooling, forging, boring, forming, casting, compressing, expanding, friction, mixing, combusting, *et cetera*. Flow of electricity through conductors involves generation of heat and electrical processes are therefore addressed in thermodynamics. Chemical reactions involve production or consumption of heat and these processes are also thus included. Wide usage of many of these processes date to antiquity and they have all been thoroughly studied in modern times in an intensive effort spanning several centuries. Through this effort the fundamental principles and laws of thermodynamics governing such processes have been discovered by some of the greatest scientific intellects, especially during the nineteenth and twentieth centuries, which is the second principal reason for the development of such a powerful and successful theory. These intellects include Boltzmann, Carnot, Clausius, Debye, Einstein, Gibbs, Helmholtz, Kelvin, Maxwell, and many others.

The first law of thermodynamics is simply a statement of conservation of energy in an explicit and complete form in which heat energy is included as a separate kind of energy together with work energy and internal (kinetic and various kinds of potential) energy: mechanical, electrical, chemical, etc. The second law of thermodynamics may be stated in several equivalent forms, a simple one being that heat will flow only from hot to cold which, although it seems rather obvious, is a law that allows powerful insights. In 1824 French engineer Sadi Carnot (1796-1832) discovered the optimum efficiency of a heat engine: the maximum fraction of available heat energy that can be converted into useful work. He deduced the best efficiency any heat-engine device could obtain in drawing heat from a hot reservoir at absolute temperature T_h and discharging unusable heat to a lowest-temperature cold reservoir available at T_c. Carnot's simple but profound result for optimum efficiency is $\varepsilon = 1 - T_c/T_h$. This simple result is a powerful tool for characterizing and testing processes and devices. For example, a prototype heat engine may be tested and, if it is found to have efficiency very close to the optimum value given by Carnot's expression, further development to improve efficiency is not justified.

In the early 1850s, German physicist Rudolph Clausius (1822-1888), Scottish physicist-engineer William Thomson (Lord Kelvin, 1824-1907), and Scottish engineer William Rankine (1820-1872) jointly discovered a property which Clausius finally named *entropy* in 1865. Entropy S is a thermodynamic-state property defined by $\Delta S = \Delta Q/T + I$, where ΔS is change in system entropy between two *equilibrium* states and I is the always-non-negative energy irretrievably lost as unusable heat through *irreversible*, non-ideal processes such as friction, viscous dissipation, or transfer of heat from higher to lower temperature. We therefore write $\Delta S \geq \Delta Q/T$ with equality (=) applying, rather than greater than (>), only when change occurs by *reversible* or *ideal* processes for which $I = 0$ and the system passes strictly through equilibrium states. ΔQ is heat transferred to the system and T is absolute temperature of its source. Because of nonnegative I, Clausius stated in 1865, "The energy of the world is constant; the entropy of the world is increasing." The latter half of this statement would be wrong if world meant earth, as we shall presently demonstrate. But in the times of Galileo, Newton, and Clausius the term "world" often meant universe. A subtle, elusive nature of entropy is apparent from its above exact but tenuous definition. The concept of entropy is both powerful and subtle, the latter often to the point of obscurity. This obscurity is apparent in the abstruse definition of entropy and in its common and continuing misuse.[20] Its nature and power are apparent in the sketch of thermodynamics and kinetic theory we include as Appendix F.

Subtle and deep implications have emerged from careful applications of thermodynamics and thermodynamics has correctly predicted and characterized previously unknown states, process pathways, and transition rates. It thus illustrates the desired function of a good philosophical structure in that the organization and pattern it reveals among the facts, inferred from observed facts, is sufficiently deep to reveal additional, previously-unobserved facts. It also thereby suggests inherent tentativeness in scientific inquiry in that a database used to infer hypotheses is always incomplete, demonstrated whenever previously unknown facts are correctly predicted.

One might wonder why powerful sets of laws similar to thermodynamics laws have not been obtained in other scientific disciplines. Understanding of more complex subjects like biology and evolution,[21] sociology, psychology, reasoning, and cognition, has proved to be elusive. An understanding of humans is particularly elusive because, not surprisingly, the objective, reproducible, lowest-common-denominator, material-related facts of hard science are not the whole story with humans (independent agents). Such facts are insufficient to describe human behavior so they are insufficient for understanding it. Such behavior is influenced by subjective, nonmaterial-related factors as well as by objective, material-related facts. Which acts of a person or group, then, are strictly objective, entirely material-related-facts motivated and fully reproducible and always predictable among all persons? None. What person (or group of persons) can serve as a universally-valid representative of "humanity?" None. How does behavior of an individual person relate to behavior of humanity? Not simply. We touch on these issues in the next chapter.

While the forgoing chapters correctly indicate science has provided wonderfully useful results, they also demonstrate that science can prove no guess true, no principle certain, no law universal. We use science to find tentative principles, tentative laws, and tentatively established "scientific truth" but, in utilizing any of these, assumption of or faith in their validity is an essential ingredient of science.

A Philosophy without Faith?

If a person claims that his or her philosophy contains no element of assumption or faith, that it stands wholly on reliable, regularly observed phenomena, they either have a high risk tolerance or their philosophy is trivial compared to one that is more comprehensive in the knowledge it encompasses. One acquaintance told me his philosophy of nature was "everything in nature tends to green." He meant that in nature plants grow wherever open space exists. While this philosophy is simple and "catchy," it is quite limited in its power to take us beyond or even close to the limit of our current knowledge. For that purpose, a deep, profound foundation is required in any significant philosophical structure. Adopting a philosophy on the accuracy of what it predicts is a good test if the scope of the test is broad. When testing a philosophy, we should always retain a broad vision. Nature does not grow many green plants in a dry desert and even fewer on the moon or the sun or in outer space.

Also, it is useful to remember that mortals cannot predict any event indubitably. Please take a half-minute or so to consider and complete in your mind the following two-part thought-assignment.

(1) Select in your mind a prediction you regard as having a high level of reliability.
(2) Determine what assumptions, if any, your prediction depends on.

If your prediction can stand without support of any assumption, an assumption in which faith must be placed, no faith is required and you have discovered an immutable, universal, absolute prediction. Congratulations – you are the first mortal to have ever accomplished this feat! If, on the other hand, your prediction requires that an assumption or two be valid, it is normal in this regard and belief in it requires faith in the validity of your assumption(s). Thus, without faith, no predictions can be made, no knowledge of cause-and-effect relationships among the facts can be claimed.

From a practical point of view, neither assumptions in science nor the tentative laws that result do not have to be exactly correct to provide improved results. New assumptions or laws need only agree with reality over a broader and deeper range for science to provide improved, more broadly applicable results. Science based on imperfect assumptions has provided many benefits and who can argue with success. For this reason many scientists regard "reality research" as a distraction from useful work. Such an attitude has some justification.

But science without philosophy is sterile. Science reveals the true nature of reality as deeply and broadly as its assumptions correspond to reality, ignoring for the moment the uncertainty in science due to its inherent flaws. Depth of truthfulness of a foundation dictates range of validity of deductions made therefrom. Since understanding derives from the more fundamental and since the basis of science is unknown, scientific understanding is shallow. If a fundamental basis for understanding can be discovered (Book III) it will allow deep insights and broadly applicable deductions. Shallow understanding of the material universe precludes a realistic intuition and makes science a difficult, trial-and-error process. A realistic intuition based on deeper understanding may allow intuitive formulation or deduction of laws instead of guessing. (Guessing of not-yet-observed-or-imagined principles and laws is currently necessary because their discovery is not systematic or programmable. Significant leaps forward occasionally occur with the discovery by guessing of a deep, new abstraction and its new insights.) Without knowledge of a fundamental basis, science provides no universal-, absolute-level understanding, no ultimate-question answers, and no essence or meaning. And without philosophy we don't even realize it.

Limitations in science due to its inherent flaws impose a tentative nature to any theory or law, a lack of unique correctness to any model, and an unrealistic scientific intuition. These consequences of method are all well illustrated in examination of quantum mechanics – the most fundamental of modern physical theories. Of particular interest are the interpretations or meanings that have been attached to the theory. None of these interpretations has been established experimentally; neither has any yet been philosophically established as superior or eliminated as inferior. As should be expected from the Löwenheim-Skolem theorem, multiple, radically-different models are supported by the common set of axioms of (the mathematical theory of) quantum mechanics and the diversity among them is indeed great despite a complete absence of predicted differences in measured results. Consistency with observed results is not sufficient to establish truth or uniqueness or meaning of a paradigm.

A complete interpretation represents the deepest level of understanding. A comprehension of the full meaning of a subject therefore indicates a mastery of it. Conversely, failure to comprehend meaning of a subject indicates its essence is not yet understood. Quantum mechanics has uncannily provided correct predictions for all tested phenomena at the quantum level. In the vision of our current scientific paradigm, it does not give incorrect predictions. Apparently, all recognized, tested properties of reality are correctly built into quantum mechanics, not as known physical mechanisms but as a mathematical construct fully consistent with observed reality. Yet the meaning of quantum mechanics is not understood and it is not known whether such deficiency in understanding, perception, preconception, or reasoning ability arises from the theory itself, our general scientific paradigm, or derives from some other cause. Our ignorance is apparent in examination of the broadly diverse interpretations of quantum mechanics, each with an equal claim to being valid. The constraint that predictions be realistic (consistent with observation) does not indicate a preferred interpretation because, as we shall see, we are probing reality sufficiently deeply in quantum mechanics that reality itself remains unknown at this level.

Interpretations of Quantum Mechanics

Various interpretations of quantum mechanics have been proposed over the years by several investigators, including many of the luminaries who contributed greatly to its development. Bell[22] summarizes six different interpretations, Polkinghorne[23] discusses four, Herbert[24] describes eight as does Cramer[25] and Gribbin[26] describes "an overview of the handful or so [seven] of main contenders," with substantial overlap existing within these numbers. New approaches have also been proposed[27] but we limit discussion here to nine interpretations of quantum mechanics, including the 1952 theory of David Bohm and the Cramer-transaction-theory interpretation. These interpretations indicate the diversity represented and the seemingly bizarre reality an interpretation often (usually) represents. But, as we must ask ourselves, bizarre compared to what?

Most interpretations of quantum mechanics or quantum theory or quantum physics (these terms are generally equivalent) attempt to deal with fundamental problems in reconciling quantum mechanics with Newtonian mechanics or relativity, where quantum theory applies to small systems, Newtonian theory applies to large systems, and relativity applies to both but is not quantized. But where is the border between large and small or where does a transition occur? When I was a student attending my first lecture on quantum mechanics, my instructor analyzed the motion of a free electron utilizing Newton's second law. I raised my hand and challenged (in my endearing style) his use of a classical law to describe motion of an electron. I was expecting to learn a new mechanics for describing electron motions. He was taken back by the challenge of a novice and, of course, he was correct to adequate approximation.[28] In such free-particle approximations classical laws can be applied even to electrons in situations where their energy is (almost) not quantized, i.e., where they are unconfined or free. Thus, based solely on an object's or system's size, no distinct boundary exists between the regimes of quantum and classical physics. But it is nominally true that quantum systems are small and classical (Newtonian) systems are large.

As already indicated, quantum mechanics provides a general, wave-function solution describing a quantum system, where the wave function is a sum of many particular wave-function solutions and thus simultaneously describes all possible states or sets of values of the various attributes of the system, one state or set of values for each particular wave function. (Because the two quantum theories are equivalent, we only discuss the wave mechanics version due, originally, to de Broglie and Schrödinger.) Of the many possible values of some selected attribute, one of only these is always observed in a measurement. Yet, according to the theory, all are simultaneously possible until the measurement occurs. The measurement process is thus referred to as *collapsing the wave function* since the many possibilities in the complete wave function are only then reduced to a single, definite result represented by a particular wave function. Collapse of the wave function does not arise in the mathematics of quantum mechanics. It is, as it were, a correction of the mathematics by hand once a specific state is determined. Consequently, the mathematical theory of quantum mechanics imposes no process or prescription for collapsing the wave function. One simply observes that upon successful measurement the wave function is collapsed. When does the collapse occur and how is the specific state selected? These questions represents the so-called *measurement problem* in quantum mechanics.

Quantum property measurements are only realized utilizing classical-regime (large) instruments since quantum-regime properties are not directly observable. Thus, any quantum system being measured may be regarded as containing a small quantum component as part of a much larger system. And, of course, the larger part of the system generally influences the behavior of a tiny quantum component.

With these concepts in mind we consider summaries of nine different interpretations of quantum mechanics. Each addresses the measurement problem and some address other problems as well.

(1) The *Copenhagen interpretation* is so named because it was championed by Niels Bohr and his students and colleagues at the physics research institute in Copenhagen that Bohr directed. Werner Heisenberg, Wolfgang Pauli, P. A. M. Dirac, and Max Born were collaborators in this interpretation. While its authors provided no succinct, authoritative statement of this interpretation,[23] or even a coherent, consistent use of it,[29] the former void being one Cramer[25] has attempted to fill, Bohr *et al* maintained that no underlying reality exists in the sense that no quantum particle possesses a definite or real attribute before it is measured. Citing the measurement problem, Copenhagenists claim that the particle is in no distinct state before measurement, precluding existence of an underlying reality. Moreover, the measured attribute is fixed not only by the quantum system but also by the measuring device which must be regarded as part of the overall system. An elusive or indefinite or unreal quality of a quantum system's attributes thus follows from dependence of

the attributes on what measurement method and apparatus are chosen to determine them. One of Bohr's most commonly used phrases was "the entire measurement system determines an attribute."

Measurement or observation receives a peculiar priority in quantum mechanics over underlying reality of a quantum system because realism is a property never directly considered in the theory. Attributes in early quantum theory were conceived and defined only in terms of being *observables*, with no further consideration of an underlying reality.[30] Thus, in the Copenhagen interpretation, reality is regarded as observer created merely by a selection of what is to be measured or observed and how, with no underlying reality actually otherwise existing. By this view many believe that quantum particles only exist to the extent they are observed. Some restrict this view to quantum-level systems but others apply it generally to all objects and phenomena. To such a one, a tree falling in the forest makes no sound without an observer present to hear it. Indeed, without the observer watching, the forest is not really there.

(2) In the *undivided-whole interpretation*, reality is regarded as an undivided whole. This concept arises from the process of *phase entanglement* whereby, roughly speaking, two quantum systems having once interacted retain a mutual influence due to previous wave function "entanglement," even after separation, that effects any subsequent attribute observed in either system. That is, systems having had their configuration spaces once coordinated somehow mutually influence one another thereafter, irrespective of their separation. By this interpretation, any simple measurement may involve the entire universe since all matter and energy apparently originated from a single, minuscule volume.

Phase entanglement was first recognized and emphasized by Erwin Schrödinger. He discovered via theoretical calculations that phase entanglement led to subsequent mutual influence between two, once-joined systems after they were separated and that the influence was instantaneous. Schrödinger regarded this property of quantum mechanics as its principal distinguishing feature.

(3) The *many-worlds interpretation* was invented to remove the measurement process, the so-called collapse of the wave function, from its peculiar, preeminent position in influencing or controlling reality. In his 1957 Ph.D. thesis, Hugh Everett III proposed the many-worlds interpretation of reality wherein for each possible attribute value of each quantum particle undergoing some process the universe is cloned into multiple copies of itself. Each copy is identical except for a difference in the attribute value resulting from the process. And each possible value is thus represented by its own, newly-created universe. With each quantum process for each particle in each star in the universe, this continual branching generates an inconceivably large number of parallel universes. However, no communication occurs between them so no universe is aware of the presence of any other. The singular act of measuring, observing, or selecting a quantum attribute is thereby removed as a primary cause of or influence on reality. For this reason, this model is occasionally used by cosmologists in spite of the seemingly bizarre reality it imposes with the need to create an indefinitely large number of whole universes in order to create one reality (plus all its alternative realities).

(4) In the *quantum-logic interpretation* of reality, invented in 1936 by mathematicians John von Neuman and Garrett Birkoff, quantum processes are strange not because they involve strange objects and attributes but because they are controlled by a logical process foreign to our everyday experience. The inventors of this interpretation showed that because of the wave nature of quantum objects, they and their attributes must combine differently – according to a different logic – from the way ordinary objects with ordinary attributes combine. The study of quantum logic has almost exclusively involved investigations exploring novel features of a mathematical nature instead of features that pertain to practical, physical interest and the interpretation has therefore not yet provided any physical understanding of reality.

(5) In what might be called a *local realism interpretation* of quantum mechanics, quantum objects are regarded to be real objects having real properties even before their measurement or when unobserved and subject only to local interactions and not to influence from afar. "Realists" thus believe atoms are real objects with real position and momentum attributes. This view was regarded as hopelessly naïve and misdirected by such luminaries as Werner Heisenberg who claimed "The ontology of materialism rested upon the illusion that the kind of existence, the direct 'actuality' of the world around us, can be extrapolated into the atomic range. This extrapolation is impossible, however."[31] In addition, John von Neuman showed that ordinary objects cannot duplicate the attributes observed in quantum systems because the latter are represented by wave functions. He proved that a locally-real interpretation is impossible if quantum mechanics is correct, a result known as "von Neuman's proof." The Copenhagenist view was thus supported by this proof and local realism so battered by it that physicists ignored this view for over two decades before active interest was again taken in it in the 1950s due to David Bohm's work (number 8). Incidentally, non-local realism is possible as shown by von Neuman and later by John Bell (see below).

(6) The *consciousness-created reality interpretation* resulted from John von Neuman's thinking and his monumental work on quantum theory. Von Neuman wrote the "bible" of quantum theory published in 1932: *Mathematische Grundlagen der Quantunmechanik.*[32] In his interpretation, von Neuman, like Bohr, was concerned with the measurement problem. However, unlike Bohr, von Neuman treats both the quantum system and the measuring device as many integrated quantum elements, with each element contributing to the integrated system's wave function. Thus, the process of measurement by which the wave function is collapsed to determine a quantum attribute involves a number of elements between the object and the observer which are all fundamentally similar. Where in such a "logic chain" is the peculiar step that causes the wave function to collapse? Von Neuman decided on the basis of logic that the only peculiar step, the only privileged transition, occurs when the observation passes from the brain to the mind of the observer. (It is noteworthy that von Neuman distinguishes between the material brain and the mind.) The peculiar step is thus the registration of the value of the attribute in the *mind* of the observer. Until then, nothing is fixed because the multiple possibilities carried in the wave function at every level up to a collapse allows multiple attribute values. The attribute

value is finally fixed, the wave function is collapsed, and reality is created in the mind of the observer. Consequently, without an observer, neither fixation of attribute value nor reality occurs, as reality is consciousness created.

Two interpretations, observer-created and consciousness-created reality, may seem to be quite similar and they are in certain respects. However, in other respects they are quite different. In the first, reality is created by the observer in merely deciding what attributes of a quantum system to measure and how to measure them, thereby determining what attributes will be observed. In principle, no measurement is required to establish reality because it is fixed by the *intended* measurement. And remote, automated, machine-performed observation is adequate to establish such a reality. In the second, reality is consciousness created in the decision or realization or awareness in the mind of what the attribute value is. In other words, by the latter interpretation the reality of an attribute is only established in the mind of an observer. While the observation may be automated and recorded or merely intended and reality thereby established by the former interpretation, reality is not established in the latter interpretation until a measurement is made and an observer reads the result into his or her mind. However, by both interpretations the reality of nearly all the universe is never established. Rather, its attributes remain in some sort of unreal, ill-defined, simultaneous mixture of definite attribute values, with one only becoming distinct and real when it is either observed or consciously observed. In one case, the tree falling in the forest makes no sound unless an observer intends to or an observer or recorder does hear it. In the other, an observer must hear the event or recording to make the event real.

(7) The *duplex-world interpretation* was the brainchild of Werner Heisenberg, who insisted that atoms and quantum systems are not real but exist only as a set of possibilities until a measurement is performed. Until attributes are measured they remain only possibilities. Thus, the world or reality possesses two types of or duplex attributes: real or measured attributes and unreal or merely possible attributes. Because so few attributes are explicitly measured and most of the universe is always unmeasured, it remains mostly unreal or merely a set of possible attributes, unfixed and indefinite until a measurement occurs. By this interpretation as well as previous ones, a definite, underlying reality does not exist for most of the universe most of the time.

(8) The *hidden variable theory and interpretation* of reality invokes a different approach to quantum systems. It originated in the matter waves of de Broglie and took definite form with the theory and interpretation provided by David Bohm in 1952.[33] While von Neuman had proved that real objects could not reproduce known behavior of quantum systems, Bohm nevertheless proceeded to invent a theory of real objects that could. In his proof, von Neuman assumed locality while Bohm's theory assumes non-locality. Thus, these real objects are endowed with peculiar properties. They interact with and are guided in their behavior by an invisible, ubiquitous *quantum potential* manifest as a *pilot wave*. Particle properties by which such influence occurs are unknown and thus hidden. The interaction between pilot wave and particle(s) is instantaneous. Utilizing real objects possessing such properties, Bohm's theory reproduces all features generated by traditional, nonrelativistic (Schrödinger-Born) quantum theory.

Critics of Bohm's theory were quick to point out that such particles that can instantly change attributes because of a small "signal" originating from an arbitrarily large distance are not ordinary. But in quantum systems it should be clear by now that nothing is "ordinary" – the concept of ordinary being, of course, subjective because it depends on one's choice of interpretation (paradigm). Although Bohm's theory is consistent with all the quantum facts and thus represents a legitimate view of reality, Copenhagenists deny it on the grounds that (a) objects are not generally believed to be in communication with the entire remainder of the universe and (b) especially when such communication is instantaneous and therefore faster than light. As we shall shortly see, at least one of these objections and perhaps both contradict implications of recent measurements.

(9) The *transactional interpretation* was proposed by John Cramer in 1980.[25,34] It is based on a classical-physics theory of John Wheeler and Richard Feynman[35] and its QED descendent.[36] Cramer calls his interpretation an emitter-absorber transaction model for the following photon-physics reason.

Because of the form of the wave equation of classical or quantum mechanics, two symmetric solutions are always possible. In one, called the *retarded* wave solution, the solution moves forward in time. In the second, called the *advanced* wave solution, the solution moves backward in time. The two waveform solutions develop symmetrically but with opposite amplitudes and move through time in opposite directions. Such time-symmetric solutions are common in physics, but usually the solution moving backward in time is simply discarded as unphysical.

In the case of an electromagnetic wave or photon traveling at the speed of light, the Lorentz-Fitzgerald factor $\gamma = \infty$. Thus, while time moves forward on a stationary clock, no time elapses for a wave or photon itself traveling either forward or backward in time. The two solutions (the retarded and advanced wavefunctions) seem to move instantaneously with either wave or photon experiencing no aging and one traveling backward in time is thus argued to be physical. By this process an emitter (or absorber) site (electron) sends out a signal into all space and excites a response in the absorber (or emitter) electron which then sends its own signal into all space. The two signals, one advanced and one retarded, thus seem to transact only a direct transfer by exactly subtracting (canceling each other out) except on the direct (least- or stationary-action) path between the emitter and absorber over which the two signals add. It thus appears that a quantum transfer of light, energy, momentum, ... has occurred directly between the emitter and absorber sites with no signal or influence sent elsewhere. Most interestingly, this transaction between sites may be applied to various problems in such a way that the measurement problem is automatically solved. It provides solutions that agree with relativity (the Copenhagen interpretation is based only on Newtonian spacetime) and resolves all paradoxes of quantum mechanics, like particle-wave duality and various mysterious interference effects that result. The idea of a photon moving backwards in time is the novel feature of this interpretation and the fact that the moving photon experiences no change in time (or age) is thought to make this feature physical, i.e., to agree with observation of other processes where time corresponds to change in age. It is perhaps no stranger than locally dilated time in relativity which is believed to be physical.

The transactional interpretation can be broadly applied and the method is powerful. A complete description exceeds the scope of our brief summary. Descriptions that convey the full scope and power of this interpretation are provided in the technical paper by Cramer[25] and a popular-level book by Gribbin.[26]

This completes the summaries of nine interpretations of quantum theory. While details given are sparse, they are sufficient to indicate most are bizarre in at least one regard compared to reality inferred from our experience and culture. Nevertheless, all are consistent with known facts and with quantum theory.

Interpretation of Interpretations

Since quantum mechanics is a mathematical theory, one might object that its interpretation in words is inadequate. Of course it is unless one comprehends the meaning of the theory, which meaning is not yet apparent. Mathematics is also inadequate when essence or meaning is unknown. Nevertheless, the high divergence of the different interpretations is clearly apparent in the words used to describe them.

Which interpretation, if any, is correct? Which theory behind the theory is best? These questions cannot presently be answered on the basis of science. However, I cannot resist making a few observations.

I first make the obvious but nonetheless important observation that a hidden-variable theory and interpretation are clearly compatible with the belief that the universe was organized and is governed by a Powerful Intelligence. Comparison of Bohm's hidden-variable, pilot-wave theory, which implies non-local influence, and a passage from the Doctrine and Covenants[37] is particularly intriguing. Other interpretations are also compatible with the belief that the universe was organized and is governed by a Powerful Intelligence.

Bohr maintained "There is no quantum world. There is only an abstract quantum mechanical description. It is wrong to think that the task of physics is to find out how nature is. Physics concerns what we can say about nature."[38] What can we say about nature except to describe how nature is or how we observe it to be? Here, Bohr is adopting as fundamental reality quantum-mechanics theory and its predictions. But quantum mechanics must be regarded as a theory that reveals how nature is, else what is its pertinence? The issue in the long, unresolved debate between Bohr and Einstein was whether quantum mechanics was fully accurate and complete and just how one may distinguish between the imagined quantum world of Copenhagenism and the real world made up, ultimately, of quantum elements. In contrast to Bohr, Einstein believed quantum mechanics was incomplete and maintained "Reality is the real business of physics."[39] The contrast between these two views recalls a statement of C. S. Lewis, "What we learn from experience depends on the kind of philosophy we bring to experience."[40] As Bohr adopted quantum theory as his view of reality, he saw nothing beyond it. If quantum theory defines the scope of reality, what is not revealed by quantum theory cannot be known. Einstein, on the other hand, sought a more complete but yet undetermined view of reality and the power of his argument was limited because it was necessarily vague. Either position was and is a belief based on faith.

Any position adopted in ignorance of the *real* quantum world is based on faith in some belief or prejudice. One author associates the strong, blinding faith in Copenhagenism of some with an intolerance for politically-incorrect nonbelievers.

> Much in the spirit of Bohr, some physicists believe that searching for ... an explanation of how a single, definite outcome arises is misguided. These physicists argue that quantum mechanics ... is a sharply formulated theory whose predictions account for the behavior of laboratory measuring devices. And according to this view, *that* is the goal of science. To seek an explanation of *what's really going on*, to strive for understanding of *how a particular outcome came to be*, to hunt for a level *of reality beyond detector readings and computer printouts* betrays an unreasonable intellectual greediness.[41] (the italics are the original author's)

Of course it is good to be strong in one's belief if one is correct. But one had better be right in adopting intellectual intransigence. Even so, intolerance is never wise; it derives from pride and leads to scorn and contention by which only the proud (that you don't want on your side) are converted or confirmed in their belief. Persons using such small-minded persuasion would force others to believe as they do if they could.

In 1927 Heisenberg wrote

> ... it is possible to ask whether there is still concealed behind the statistical [indeterminate] universe of perception a 'true' universe [reality] in which the law of causality [determinism] would be valid. But such speculations seem to us to be without value and meaningless, for physics must confine itself to the description of the relationships between perceptions.[42]

In this statement Heisenberg concedes the battle declaring reality and truth to be without value, meaningless, and inaccessible. Such an attitude leaves only the sterile, lower-philosophy, language-game science addressed in Chapter 1, devoid of significant conclusions and investigating power or even faith to seek reality and truth or to admit they exist. But suppose we use the "relationships between perceptions" to seek the true nature of reality. The moment we attempt to do so, we raise our philosophy from lower to higher.

Because I believe that science is or should be a pursuit of truth – the description and explanation of reality – adoption of Copenhagenism, positivism, or some other limiting view that denies truth and reality exist seem to me to be a dereliction of scientific duty. The view of Copenhagenists and some others strikes me as oxymoronic when they say, in effect, "Our view of underlying reality is that there is no underlying reality." Why should no reality be claimed as reality? This is a logical paradox. Such sterile thinking simultaneously provides no advantage and is severely incapacitating.

I regard as absurd the claim that quantum mechanics (of the 1920s and 1930s) defines the scope of reality. Other equally valid but highly divergent theories must exist according to Löwenheim-Skolem. Bohr's belief reminds me of Kant's argument that Newtonian theory and Euclidian geometry must describe reality because he could conceive of no alternatives. While Laplace embraced absolute determinism, Copenhagenists adopt the opposite extreme denying any underlying reality on the basis of their belief that "such speculation seems to us to be without value or meaning."

The "tight logical circularity" of their reasoning is notable. Kant and Laplace had more basis for their beliefs, naïve though they now seem.

Of course, in any matter of faith a broad diversity of opinion can occur. Nobel Prize winning physicist Murray Gell-Mann was of the opinion expressed in 1976 that "Niels Bohr brainwashed a whole generation of physicists into believing the [quantum reality] problem had been solved."[43] And E. T. Jaynes commented

> The mathematical rules of present Quantum Theory ... are highly successful and clearly contain a great deal of very fundamental truth. But nobody knows what they mean; they are in part expressions of laws of Nature, in part expressions of principles of human inference, and we have not yet learned how to disentangle them. The positivist Copenhagen philosophy has prevented solution of the problem by denying that there is any distinction between reality and our knowledge of reality.[44]
>
> Our students are indoctrinated about the great pragmatic success of the quantum formalism – with the conclusion that the Copenhagen interpretation of that formalism must be correct. This is the logic of [that flawed] Quantum Syllogism:
>
> The present *mathematical formalism* can be made to reproduce many experimental facts very accurately.
>
> **Therefore**
>
> The *physical interpretation* which Niels Bohr tried to associate with it must be true; and it is naive to try to circumvent it.
>
> I am convinced, as were Einstein and Schrödinger, that the major obstacle that has prevented any real progress in our understanding of Nature since 1927, is the Copenhagen Interpretation of Quantum Theory. This theory is now 65 years old, it has long since ceased to be productive, and it is time for its retirement (along with mine). ...
>
> Today we have in full flower the blatant, spooky contradictions that Einstein foresaw and warned us about 60 years ago, and there is no way to reason logically from them. This mysticism *must* be replaced by a physical interpretation that restores the possibility of thinking rationally about the world.[45]

While Copenhagenism is commonly held to be the predominant belief among physicists, it is also appropriate to say, after Polkinghorne, that "Your average quantum mechanic is about as philosophically minded as your average garage mechanic."[46] It is no wonder that little interest in philosophy occurs among physicists. The nature of the Copenhagen interpretation and its promotion both seem strange. Why promote a reality that consists of no reality? That those who promoted this view did not recognize its implication is barely imaginable – these men were brilliant. But they were also emotionally involved through their ambition and vital interest in promoting their own results.[28] In the functions of a paradigm it (i) integrates knowledge into a definite, comprehensive world view (desirable), but (ii) a definite, comprehensive world view obscures and excludes others (paradigm paralysis, undesirable).

Generally an abstract, underlying view provides a broad range of knowledge and predictive power. However, when the view denies existence of reality or its accessibility it is profoundly limiting. In the long exchange between Einstein and Bohr over interpretation of quantum mechanics, it is widely held that Bohr won the debate based on the belief that his interpretation is the most popular. But this belief may merely reflect indifference to philosophy on the part of physicists. It seems to me that Bohm[33] and Cramer[25] have presented better theories behind the theory or better interpretations of material-universe quantum mechanics. When I read Bohr's state-ments describing Copenhagen orthodoxy, like the one quoted on page 239, I find their meaning elusive, as should be expected of a statement absent an underlying reality.

A physicist's aversion to sticky philosophical questions is natural. By the rules of quantum mechanics one may calculate useful results that are amazingly accurate and reliable, to ten or even twelve digits. Most physicists therefore turn their attention to applications rather than "venturing into the swamps of incomprehensibility and doubt that beset those who venture into the meaning of quantum mechanics."[47]

However, recent evidence has provided new insight on interpretation of quantum mechanics, evidence that demands quantum theory be non-local, consistent particularly with Bohm's interpretation and the above cited one in the Doctrine and Covenants.[37] To gain some understanding of this evidence, its implications, and their significance, we consider a 1935 paper written by Einstein and two of his colleagues.

EPR

In 1935 Albert Einstein, Boris Podolsky, and Nathan Rosen[48] described a paradox intended to reveal that quantum mechanics is incomplete and unable to fully describe reality. This paper as well as its three authors are now universally referred to as EPR. EPR began by noting that a complete theory must contain a descriptor or variable quantity corresponding to each element of reality that is not fixed. (Otherwise the theory is incapable of describing all the various possible states of reality.) EPR proposed *a minimal condition for the reality of a physical quantity* is describing it with certainty. But quantum mechanics forbids exact, simultaneous knowledge of both of certain pairs of quantities so that knowledge of one of such a pair precludes knowledge of the other. Thus, EPR claimed that either (1) the description of reality given in quantum mechanics by a wave function is incomplete or (2) certain pairs of quantities cannot have simultaneous reality.

EPR thus posed a paradox to those who believed quantum mechanics is complete *and* the universe is real. It was not a paradox to EPR because, while they believed the universe is real, they believed quantum mechanics is incomplete and wrote their paper to make that very point as part of the long-running Einstein-Bohr debate. Bohr quickly answered but it is EPR that is well remembered today because its implications are clear, striking, deep, and, as it turns out, testable by experiment.

In 1951, David Bohm[49] extended EPR's illustration of the paradox in a *Gedankenexperiment* or thought experiment that we refer to as EPRB. Similar experiments, some strictly thought experiments with others realizable in the laboratory, have succeeded this original and are included in a generic class of EPRB experiments.

In an example EPRB experiment, pairs of *singlet-state protons* are emitted by decomposition of an atom or molecule having zero spin in which the decomposition mechanism introduces no angular momentum or spin. Each singlet-state proton of such a pair travels along a common axis in direction opposite to that of its proton-pair counterpart (satisfying conservation of momentum). Because they are emitted from a zero-spin source with no addition of angular momentum, the spins of the two protons must be antiparallel, i.e., they must sum to zero (for conservation of angular momentum). Consequently, components of the spins of the proton pair *along any chosen axis* must exactly cancel. Thus, when a spin component of one of such a proton pair is measured at location C and found to be up (or down), then the spin of the other proton of the pair at location D, along the axis in the other direction from the source, must be down (or up). This result must hold for arbitrary separation of C and D, provided no interaction influences the spin of either proton in its flight from their common source to C or D.

According to various interpretations of quantum mechanics, an attribute such as a spin component in a selected direction is not definite until it is measured and the wave function is collapsed. Yet, if one measures the spin component of one proton at C, the spin component of its counterpart at D is *immediately* established, even though no measurement at D has occurred. What has caused a collapse of the wave function at D? Does some kind of communication connect C and D? For any finite separation of C and D such communication, being immediate, must be superluminal in apparent violation of special relativity. To EPR there existed no paradox in this experiment because they believed quantum mechanics to be incomplete. But to others who believe that quantum mechanics is a complete description of reality, this thought experiment involving only well-known processes presented a paradox.

A remarkable theorem conceived and proved by an Irish physicist named Bell brings these issues into a clearer focus by providing better understanding of the implications contained in the enigma posed by EPRB. It also allows experimental investigation of this enigma.

Bell's Theorem[part #]

John Stewart Bell (1928-1990) contributed to knowledge of physics through a number of investigations of "quantum philosophy." Twenty-two of Bell's journal articles on quantum philosophy have been collected into a monograph entitled *Speakable and unspeakable in quantum mechanics*.[50] In this book Bell makes a telling criticism of Copenhagenism, delightfully understated as follows.

> While imagining that I understand the position of Einstein, as regards the EPR correlations, I have little understanding of his principal opponent, Bohr. Yet most contemporary theorists have the impression that Bohr got the better of Einstein in the argument and are under the impression that they themselves share Bohr's view.[51]

Indeed, Mara Beller observes that "There is a widespread myth that Bohr enjoyed a triumph over Einstein in their dialogue on EPR. Yet none of Bohr's answers are satisfactory [being] fatally flawed."[52]

All but two of the articles in Bell's book are highly technical, at least in part, and directed at readers with extensive mathematical preparation. However, extended discussions in several of these papers require only a minimal level of mathematical ability and are useful because of Bell's insight and lucid writing style. Other authors[53] have described the essential implications of Bell's theorem wholly or largely on a popular level, as I will do here – although I include a few key formulas and description of an experiment for enhanced understanding of those mathematically and scientifically inclined. As elsewhere, detailed consideration of the formulas and experiment is not required.

Bell identified the point of discrepancy between classical and quantum physics. Moreover, he discovered his theorem by which both could be tested against measured results to determine which, if either, was incorrect. Bell's theorem was originally a single theorem but Bell and others have derived additional ones and the term "Bell's theorem" now represents a class of theorems just as EPRB represents a class of experiments. A Bell's theorem deals with events that are related or *correlated.* Such correlated events are illustrated in EPRB experiments in which directions of spin in spin-correlated pairs of protons or polarization in polarization-correlated pairs of photons are measured at separate locations C and D. The latter experiment involves photons in place of protons, typically two photons nearly simultaneously ejected in a *two-photon cascade-emission process.* Such dual photon emissions commonly occur, for instance in a mercury vapor lamp wherein a mercury atom is excited in an electric discharge and the excited electron rapidly decays twice to lower energy orbitals in a two-photon cascade emission, emitting one photon of blue wavelength and another of green. While the direction of polarization of any one such photon is random, equally likely to be in any direction, the polarization direction of each photon of a pair is identical. The two polarization directions are thus correlated. Since polarization component of a photon may be measured, this EPRB experiment is equivalent to and more convenient than one involving protons.

Bell's theorem applies when a component of proton spin or photon polarization of each of a correlated pair is simultaneously measured for many pairs. Since a particle may be disturbed in such a measurement, multiple spin or polarization components of a single proton or photon cannot generally be measured. However, polarization of a pair of polarization-correlated photons can each be measured and, because any polarization component of one is exactly that of the other, two polarization components are established for each photon by measuring only one for each. This possibility leads to a question: "How does probability of correlation of photon polarization depend on the angle between the directions of measured polarization components?" This question is addressed by Bell's theorem and it is intriguing because classical and quantum physics predict different results, the experiment can be performed to test the predictions and determine which physics, classical or quantum, is (are) incorrect, and the results imply a previously unknown nature of nature, as we shall see. We illustrate usage of one such theorem, the predictions with which results will agree or conflict, the comparisons, and an implication about the nature of nature.

(A reader not interested in experimental details can skip to the beginning of the paragraph containing Equation [1] on page 246.)

An EPRB experiment is illustrated in the following figure. Mercury (Hg) or calcium (Ca) atoms are heated in an "Oven Source" to form a vapor of rapidly moving Hg or Ca atoms. A small effusion of these atoms exits through a pinhole and, after passing through a second pinhole or "Atomic Beam Collimator," forms a narrow, high-speed atomic "Beam of Hg or Ca Atoms" in a vacuum environment. These isolated, atoms are intercepted by a "Beam of quanta of excitation energy" composed of photons, electrons, or other suitable carriers of a discrete quantity of energy to excite individual beam atoms to a specific energy, driving one of the atom's electrons to a selected energy level or orbital. (An orbital in quantum theory replaces a deterministic orbit in classical physics.) From this orbital the atomic electron quickly decays back to its stable, lowest-energy state in a two-step process, momentarily pausing at a nearly-stable intermediate level orbital. Such a two-photon cascade-emission process emits, nearly simultaneously, pairs of photons traveling in opposite (correlated) directions and having identical (correlated) direction of polarization.

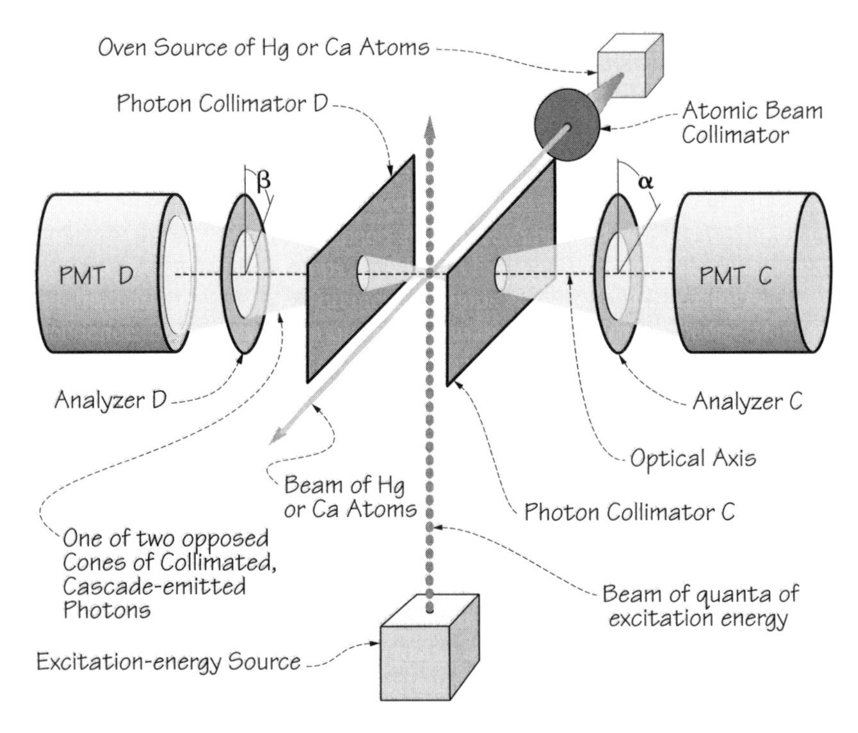

A calculable fraction of one of the photons of each correlated pair passes through the small hole in "Photon Collimator C" while (ideally) the counterpart-twin fraction passes through the hole in "Photon Collimator D." The photons of each fraction then encounters an analyzer (polarizer) set at a selected angle. "Analyzer C" is set to angle α (alpha) and "Analyzer D" to angle β (beta). By counting the photons that reach each photo-multipliertube (PMT) photon detector, the total count rates at "PMT C" and "PMT D" are measured as is the rate of *nearly simultaneous* counts at both PMT detectors for each selected set of angles α,β.

While the polarization angle of both of a pair of photons generated by a two-photon-cascade emission is identical, the direction of polarization of any pair is randomly distributed and equally likely to be in any direction normal to the "Optical Axis." Thus, when directions α and β are parallel ($\alpha = \beta$), all correlated pairs counted should be nearly simultaneously detected at C and D; and when α and β are "crossed" ($|\alpha - \beta| = 90° = \pi/2$ radians), no correlated counts should (ideally) be observed. At these extremes, both quantum mechanics and Bell's theorem agree with experiment. It is at intermediate angular differences that disagreement is predicted and Bell's theorem becomes important.

To illustrate Bell's theorem we describe an experiment that uses the above-illustrated apparatus. Suppose photons of correlated pairs pass through their respective collimating holes and arrive at Analyzer C or D. These analyzers each stop some fraction of the photons. But, because angle of polarization is random, the average fraction stopped in either analyzer is the same and independent of both α and β. (While this equality is assumed it is verified by measurement.) For Analyzer C and D oriented in directions α and β, we define the rate of joint or nearly simultaneous penetrations or a pair of correlated photons as $R(\alpha,\beta) = R(\theta)$, where $\theta = |\alpha - \beta|$, θ (theta) thus being the magnitude of the angular displacement of direction α from direction β since the $|(\ldots)|$ notation indicates the absolute value or positive magnitude of $(\ldots)$. Moreover, we assume the ratio $R(\theta)/R_{CD}$ or ratio of rate of joint penetration of both of a correlated pair divided by the total rate of correlated pairs depends only on θ.

Furthermore, we assume rates of penetration $R(\alpha)$ and $R(\beta)$ are independent of α and β because of the random distribution in polarization orientation. Joint penetration of a pair is indicated by nearly simultaneous penetration of both photon twins each through its respective analyzer. We assume that such joint penetration depends only on θ. These last assumptions are also experimentally verified.

While $R(\theta)$ is the rate of joint or nearly coincident detections, i.e., the rate correlated pairs are detected by PMT C and D with Analyzer D set at angle $\pm\,\theta$ from Analyzer C, we determine R_{CD} as the measured $R(\theta)$ *with both analyzers removed.* Thus, R_{CD} is the total rate of correlated photons nearly simultaneously arriving at analyzers C and D, i.e., the rate of correlated pairs in the experiment.

For this experiment the (ideal-case) Bell's theorem predicts for signal S (subscripted "BT") the Bell's inequality (derived by Clauser and Horne[54] and in Appendix G for the mathematically inclined)

$$[1] \qquad S_{BT} = R(\pi/8)\,/\,R_{CD} - R(3\pi/8)\,/\,R_{CD} \leq \tfrac{1}{4} = 0.250000\ldots.$$

(While the symbol = reads "is equal to," the symbol ≤ reads "is less than or equal to." In [1] two values of θ are indicated: $\theta = \pi/8$ and $\theta = 3\pi/8$ radians.) To obtain a measured value of S_{BT}, only four quantities must be experimentally determined: $R(\pi/8)$, $R(3\pi/8)$ and R_{CD} (twice). R_{CD} is measured twice, once with each $R(\theta)$ measurement, to insure a correct value of R_{CD} is used in each ratio $R(\theta)/R_{CD}$.

In contrast, quantum theory provides an ideal-case S value (subscripted "QT")

$$[2] \qquad S_{QT} = R(\pi/8)\,/\,R_{CD} - R(3\pi/8)\,/\,R_{CD} = \sqrt{(2)}/4 = 0.353553\ldots$$

In a non-ideal (real) case, both values are slightly-to-greatly reduced[55] due to non-perfect analyzer transmissions, non-perfect PMT detection of photons, asymmetric alignment of collimator holes, etc.

In case you haven't noticed, our illustration of Bell's theorem just became *very* interesting because the results [1] and [2] are *mutually exclusive*, i.e., at least one must be incorrect. Either Bell's theorem or quantum mechanics is incorrect or both are incorrect. If Bell's theorem is incorrect, at least one assumption on which it is based must be false so that establishing Bell's theorem to be invalid may (and does) reveal something previously unknown about the nature of reality.

Whether quantum theory or Bell's theorem is incorrect, if not both, must be settled by experiment. Early results for S obtained in several experiments utilizing three different forms of Bell's theorem for cascade-photon experiments are listed in the following table. Columns 1 and 2 contain ideal-system values, Column 3 values are corrected to the real cases for which the measured values of Column 4 apply.

Bell's Theorem S_{BT}	Quantum Theory* S_{QT}	Quantum Theory# S_{QT}	Measured Value of S	Reference
$S \leq 0.250$	$S = 0.3536$	0.301 ± 0.007	0.300 ± 0.008	56
$S \leq 0.250$	$S = 0.3536$	0.266	0.216 ± 0.013	57
$S \leq 0.250$	$S = 0.3536$	0.2841	0.2885 ± 0.0093	58
$S \leq 0.250$	$S = 0.3536$	0.294 ± 0.007	0.296 ± 0.014	59
$-2 \leq S \leq 2$	$S = 2.8284$	2.70 ± 0.050	2.697 ± 0.015	60
$-1 \leq S \leq 1$	---	0.112	0.101 ± 0.020	61
Key : * ideal case # corrected case				

Of these six early investigations summarized in the above table, five confirm the quantum mechanics prediction and violate Bell's theorem. Only one, that listed in the second row, prevents consensus agreement. Clauser and Shimony[55] discuss the relative merits of these investigations and suggest a possible systematic error in the second-row results. Overall, the evidence is sufficient to show almost certainly that the measured S agrees with predictions of quantum mechanics and violates Bell's theorem. Therefore, almost certainly, Bell's theorem is incorrect.

Later extensions of this experiment in different variations[62] testing photon correlations over increasing distances (up to 11 km by Nicolas Gisin *et al*[62] at the University of Geneva in 1997), with brighter sources, and employing rapid switching to preclude communication between detectors at signal velocities $\leq$ c, all confirm the conclusion that Bell's theorem is incorrect.

One specific implication these results "demand," according to I. Duck and E. C. G. Sudarshan,[63] is the adoption of the Heisenberg-Born-Jordan wave-calculation-approach in quantum mechanics but considering the method and wave function it provides to be no more than an *information theoretic device*. The comfortable, semiclassical interpretation of Schrödinger's wave mechanics as representing some kind of direct physical property is "misleading." This fact was, of course, well known to Heisenberg, Born, Jordan, Schrödinger, Dirac, and many others. Usually only beginning students of quantum mechanics need such a reminder. Feynman's "sum of paths" QED method avoids the temptation entirely.

Of greater interest are the general implications of the "failure" of Bell's theorem. Bell's theorem is general and depends on neither quantum mechanics nor the specific nature of an experiment. Consequently, the inescapable conclusion is that at least one of the assumptions upon which Bell's theorem rests must be false. Which assumptions are suspect seems clear because all other assumptions can be experimentally verified and because the mathematics Bell employed is general and straightforward. Bell identified two suspect assumptions used in deriving his theorem: (1) the universe is real and therefore involves additional (hidden) variables in its complete description and (2) only local interactions affect a physical result. The latter is the so-called *locality assumption*: that an event at D is not influenced by an event at C, where C and D may be separated by arbitrarily large distance. Because Bell's theorem is not satisfied, at least one of these two assumptions must be incorrect. After Bell, if we assume a real universe, i.e., if we assume a reality exists in which all properties are definite even when they are not being measured or observed and in which a hidden-variable theory might properly describe reality, disagreement with Bell's theorem indicates *the locality assumption is invalid.* According to current interpretation, only locality is false with hidden variables possible if not preferred.[65] That is, failure of Bell's theorem does not preclude quantum particles from having definite properties in hidden variables, as in Bohm's theory. Even definite properties forbidden by the uncertainty principle are no longer excluded. Only locality is excluded, and Bohm's theory is not local. Originally, Bell's theorem stated that in a real universe either quantum mechanics is incorrect or physics is non-local. With the experimental verification of quantum mechanical predictions, Bell's theorem requires that *quantum physics must be non-local.*

We again quote Bell succinctly describing the implication of the class of theorems he discovered, given the evident correctness of quantum mechanics.

> Let us summarize ... the logic that leads to the impasse. The [EPRB] correlations are such that the result of the experiment on one side [C] immediately foretells that on the other [D], whenever the analyzers happen to be parallel. If we do not accept the intervention on one side as a causal influence on the other, we seem obliged to admit that the results on both sides are determined in advance anyway, independently of the intervention on the other side, by signals from the source and by the local [analyzer] setting. But this has implications for nonparallel settings which conflict with those of quantum mechanics. So we *cannot* dismiss intervention on one side as a causal influence on the other.[65]

In other words, we cannot dismiss non-local quantum interactions. And, since all systems are composed of quantum elements, non-local interaction may be general. One problem with non-local interaction, because it represents influence or action from an arbitrarily large distance, is that it leads to contradictions with what physicists regard as fundamental law. A contradiction between non-local interaction and relativity occurs when separated, interacting bodies show "mutual instantaneous awareness" or "superluminal-velocity signaling," the latter capable of communicating even *backwards in time*. We recall that Newton's law of universal gravitation (i.e., $F = - GMm/r^2$) describing mutual attraction at a distance has this form, a mutual *instantaneous* awareness implied by the mathematical form of the law (Appendix D). Because such awareness violates relativity (by which superluminal communication is believed to be forbidden), Newton's law of gravity is regarded as incorrect in this property. To satisfy relativity, physicists have generally preferred to regard physical reality as local. Rather than deny locality, many physicists would rather deny reality,[66] which some do in any case as has already been mentioned. But it has been shown for a real or non-real universe that non-locality is intrinsic to quantum phenomena.[67] To save relativity, the common caveat now is to assert that superluminal communication is prohibited. And superluminal communication is only required if the universe must *respond* to a situation after-the-fact. If, in contrast, the universe responds to a before-the-fact, previously-emitted pilot-wave-type signal that guides physical behavior, no superluminal communication is required.

Steven Weinberg[68] proposed that a weak non-linearity occurs in the equations of quantum mechanics and Joseph Polchinski[69] analyzed the effect of such a non-linearity, concluding that it would allow an "EPR telephone" by which one could communicate with the past. Experiments have not yet found Weinberg's proposed effect but only low-energy atomic transitions have been examined and the effect, being weak, may require high energy transitions to be detectable. If it exists, the Copenhagen interpretation based on "observer knowledge" will be devastated. In any case, because of current, unanswered questions, some now regard the interpretation that relativity prohibits faster-than-light communication as uncertain.[70]

Non-local theories in physics have not been seriously pursued (Bohm's hidden-variable quantum theory is a notable exception) because of a profound problem non-local reality introduces, namely, how does one take account of all influences when some of such influences may originate anywhere in the universe? One possible answer – like the Bohm pilot-wave theory. Another similar but deeper answer is found in the previously mentioned passage in the Doctrine and Covenants.[37] But, it has been difficult enough to properly take account of all local influences. (Conversely, perhaps difficulty has been introduced by the assumption of locality.)

Moreover, all cause-and-effect relationships that have previously been investigated have failed to reveal any non-locality. The discovery that physics is non-local has profound implications as it would appear to lead to great complication in discovering and testing scientific theories. Any number of influences might be exerted from arbitrarily far away through presently unknown mechanisms. The theoretical and experimental results that indicate a non-local reality thus bring into question all physics that we presently think we understand. The possibility of miracles can no longer be denied on the basis of known physical laws and cause-and-effect relationships. (In fact, it never could be.) In a non-local universe we must presume that many possible causes have been neither considered nor imagined.

But if no experimental result has ever contradicted either explicit or tacit assumption of locality in physics, how do we see such a contradiction now? The answer to this question is that no evidence that *directly* contradicts local reality has ever been observed.[71] In contrast, EPRB and Bell's theorem allow, for the first time, a subtle, *indirect* test of the locality assumption. And, if our present understanding of quantum mechanics is correct, the test is conclusive. Using quantum mechanics as a sufficiency condition, EPRB, Bell, and others[54-62] have proven the universe is non-local, at least at the quantum level.

We therefore conclude that any deep level of underlying reality, if one in fact exists, remains mysterious as far as we have yet been able to imagine, investigate, and demonstrate through physics in particular and science in general.

Proposition Number 5: **Physics in particular and science in general have not established any unique underlying reality by which material phenomena can be understood at a fundamental level. Recent results indicate that a basic axiom of physics (locality) is inconsistent with quantum processes. Much understanding of physics previously thought to be consistent is now in question.**

A science-based search for reality, interpretation, or meaning has not been efficacious. Von Baeyer concludes his book on the atom with the comment "In physics, as in human affairs, the deepest truths cannot be seen – they must be felt."[72] In other words, science, by itself, is insufficient for understanding even scientific knowledge because it is insufficient for understanding meaning. One writer has characterized the futility of a scientific search for an understanding of reality in poetic terms:

> Reality is the most alluring of all courtesans, for she makes herself what you would have her at the moment; but she is no rock on which to anchor your soul, for her substance is of the stuff of shadows; she has no existence outside your dreams and is often no more than the reflection of your own thoughts shining upon the face of nature.[73]

Crisis?

Does this emerging realization of fundamental and far-reaching ignorance in scientific understanding and meaning represent a crisis? Some who have based their paradigm on the objectivity, rigor, and exactness of science may rethink their position as evidence accumulates and long-standing scientific "certainties," such as the assumption that the universe is local, must be abandoned. But most probably they will not switch paradigms because of emerging knowledge. After all, the abandonment of scientific certainty is driven by scientific discovery and new theory to replace the old will eventually be proposed by scientists.[74] The initial attraction to and choice of science as one's principal paradigm typically occurs before a person uses it to form a comprehensive view of reality. Why, then, should a changing view of reality affect his or her paradigm preference? When one initially adopts a paradigm because of a romantic notion, the romantic notion is likely to remain even as the paradigm collapses; the appeal of the notion, for whatever reason, precedes the choice. Or one may have simply acquiesced to a paradigm passively inherited and just as passively not consider a change. Materialism has been increasingly promoted over recent generations and passive acceptance of it in Western society is now common.

Among passive materialists a crisis may arise, but only if they start actively thinking for themselves – and that is hardly a crisis. For those who do think about ultimate questions and philosophy, those who are or become agents actively searching for truth, a new Renaissance may be emerging wherein the developing evidence may cause materialism to be questioned and even displaced by some alternative paradigm(s). What it (they) will be I cannot say, but I hope the new-sought focus is meaning. And I hope the seeker accepts the invitation of Omniscience to receive His guidance (Book III). Without such guidance there is no knowledge of truth.

What can happen when one doesn't have faith, even just in science? (Remember we are examining in this chapter the essential role of faith in science.) German physicist Max Born stated in his Nobel Lecture that "I believe that ideas such as absolute certitude, absolute exactness, final truth, etc. are figments of the imagination which should not be admissible in any field of science."[75] American Nobel-Prize-winning chemist Irving Langmuir (1881-1957) wrote in 1950

> Beginning with Einstein's relativity theory and Planck's quantum theory ... the scientist has ceased to believe that words or concepts can have any absolute meaning. He is not often concerned with questions of existence; he does not know what is the meaning of the question, "Does an atom really exist?" ... Furthermore, we can not be sure just what we mean by the word "exist." Such questions are largely metaphysical [relating to abstract philosophy, especially ontology, epistemology, and religion] and in general do not interest the modern scientist.[76]

Born's and Langmuir's views advocate an elusiveness or impossibility of absolute certainty, final truth, and demonstration of existence itself that is held, in one form or another, by many scientists and nonscientists alike having a philosophy based on materialism. This view, like that based on logical positivism, is a "defeatist" view. Just because no one can at present correctly answer a question is no reason to regard the question as unanswerable, not useful, inadmissible, or illegitimate and then to restrict language and thinking (logical positivism) to have the function of suppressing the question. Such an attitude is supported by statements like those of both Born and Langmuir (above) and Ayer (in Chapter 1). Or, what is worse because it obviates learning, materialists ignorantly and persistently asserting they understand matters while failing to recognize materialism's severe defects.

But such attitudes are inconsistent with a range of more sophisticated views embraced by many of today's scientists. A category-one student or an agent in search of truth, like many scientists are, does not adopt an artificially restrictive philosophy for long. Rather than avoiding unanswered questions pertaining to ultimate issues like existence, truth, meaning, and the absolute, a person in search of truth eagerly pursues them. As suggested in this chapter, answers to these questions are not sought merely to gratify esoteric interest, they are now central to progress in science or any paradigm. Recognition that a lack of answers to such fundamental questions now limits science has only begun to be widely recognized, but it has begun. Regarding these questions as illegitimate because they are beyond the scope of present knowledge is tantamount to outlawing progress and rendering futile the whole point and exercise of science and philosophy, the situation described by Barfield as a "latent instability." But his term fails, it seems to me, to capture the full implication of this attitude.

The attitude of one who avoids a question because it (just the question) lies beyond the scope of his or her paradigm and is therefore deemed not useful reminds me of a category-two or -three student who would rather fight than switch or who doesn't care one way or the other about anything he or she doesn't already "know." When a category-one student or an agent in search of truth encounters a question of fundamental importance, one that lies beyond the scope of his or her paradigm, that person looks for another paradigm to supplement or replace his or her current one. If one is content to ignore questions like "Is there an underlying reality?" and "What is its nature?" he or she does not fit philosophically in even honest materialism because science is a search for truth, a quest to discover reality, an examination of the ontology and nature of existence. An honest search for truth, just the search itself, presupposes, assumes, and invokes faith that truth exists and can be established. And without a desire and intent to discover truth, what is science or a scientist about? Perhaps a scientist is content to examine merely superficial matters, ones that present no challenge to paradigm. But this is merely practicing science without substantial purpose. Nevertheless, many (perhaps most?) scientists are satisfied to pursue science at only this level.

In contrast, to an agent earnestly searching for truth, fundamental matters matter. A paradigm is merely a tool for understanding reality, not reality itself. If one cannot establish or demonstrate or prove an answer to an important question by one paradigm, another should be sought. One must avoid the danger of becoming comfortably paralyzed in a paradigm rather than using it as a tool to discover truth, which is the real goal of an agent in search thereof and the purpose of a paradigm.

Without formal establishment or demonstration of truth, one's judgements and opinions are based on mere prejudice, i.e., positions or attitudes adopted without sufficient knowledge or just grounds. Thus, if we are to think and act based on sufficient knowledge and understanding (i.e., truth) rather than prejudice, the challenge we face is to seek, find, and adopt a paradigm capable of providing formal demonstration of truth. Science has not been found to possess such capability and, indeed, many scientists in the past have acted to inhibit such an attempt by adopting a positivist or strictly materialist philosophy or by just accepting limitations of science as limitations of human knowledge.

The failure of science to discover and demonstrate absolute truth and the nature of reality does not mean such understanding is beyond human reach. The other paradigm we are considering in this book, Christianity, makes the claim that by it one can obtain such insight. And the evidence in support of this claim is conclusive, if one will receive it. But true Christianity is difficult for mortal man to receive. In mortality, the "question of paradigm" confronts every individual of every generation and few are the individuals, especially among the rich in goods and education and status, who successfully find a fully adequate answer. Among mortals, especially the rich, educated, and powerful, being humble and teachable, like a little child (Chapter 12), is difficult.

Because establishing truth for one's self is crucial, "crisis" is an appropriate description of the present general lack of interest in finding a paradigm that empowers one to establish the true nature of reality. While Barfield predicted an inevitable self-destruction of positivism in its multiple forms due to its latent instability, there are many who will live and die by a paradigm once they have chosen it, with little or no further thought about it. In a wide-angle retrospection, a crisis now exists because this exact crisis has confronted every generation. This crisis, a fundamental ignorance of reality, is inherent to the initial natural or mortal condition. And relatively few are the individuals who overcome it. In this sense the crisis is not an instability at all; rather, it is the normal condition, the rule rather than the exception.

The crisis concerns what one *will* seek, either truth and meaning or something less (comfort, image, status and power among humans, worldly riches or the ever-elusive goal of world-based security and happiness). In the absence of faith in Christ there is no understanding of the absolute, no security or status or power that endures, and no lasting happiness or joy. Because choice of an adequate paradigm is crucial, *crisis is neither now nor has it been too dramatic a descriptor of the need of each individual to seek an adequate paradigm.*

And part of the crisis is that there will be no sensational collapse of a "tower of error" before the multitudes because of its latent flaws until after it is too late to change one's paradigm. To discover error one must first establish truth – just the opposite of the scientific method in both order and attainability. And this exercise is personal and individual, as we shall see.

No paradigm should be abandoned because it is old, just as none should be adopted because it is new. New and better are not always synonymous. A personal paradigm is essentially what it was when it was adopted. The essence or meaning of the paradigm doesn't change. Materialism fundamentally remains materialism and Christian faith remains a trust and confidence in Christ. But *a person* can grow in his or her understanding and desire and thereby outgrow a paradigm. Never-theless, an old paradigm should not be casually discarded nor a new one haphazardly adopted. Important questions should be asked, e.g., is a new paradigm better suited for the seeking of greater goals and aspiring to higher ideals? I think it is exactly with respect to such a search that Christ taught "if ye continue in my word, then are ye my disciples indeed; And ye shall know the truth, and the truth shall make you free."[77]

Of what do we need to be free? Well, for starters, ignorance and prejudice, vanity, pride, greed, lust, deficiency in love, fixation on self and the world, and a dearth of understanding of meaning – in short one needs to be free of the mastery of the world (one's natural self) over one's spiritual self. But also, more obscurely but equally important, our thinking needs to be free from domination by Satan, an invisible and blinding influence of the unseen enemy whose agents would guide us in any wrong way.[78] There is a battle invisible to unseeing eyes focused on only the material universe. Each of us is participating in this battle, on one side or the other. To be victorious we need to be informed, strengthened, armed with and guided by a powerful paradigm. We need to be strengthened by an omniscient, omnipotent Champion always ready to assist because of His devotion to us. This battle, this powerful paradigm, and this Champion are the principal focuses of Book III.

Notes and References for Chapter 10.

[1] French philosopher René Descartes compared himself to Archimedes in this thought, in that if he could discover something indubitable he would build on it a whole system of science. In contrast to the ancient Greeks and others, Descartes did not look externally for such a basis, but internally. He found for his "standing place" doubt or thought itself. (See endnotes 13 and 15 of Chapter 4.)

[2] The Latin term *a priori* is translated "from the former." It is used to denote the notions of "presumptive: without or before examination" or "prior to experience" or "in advance of proof" or "based on theory instead of experience."

[3] Kline, Morris, *Mathematics in Western Culture,* Oxford University Press, New York, 1953, 408.

[4] Planck, Max, *Where is Science Going?,* Ox Bow Press, Woodbridge, CN, 1981, 214. Michael Polanyi duplicated this thought with the comment "But the ultimate justification of my scientific convictions lies always in myself. At some point I can only answer, 'For I believe so.' " (Polanyi, Michael, *Science, Faith and Society,* The University of Chicago Press, Chicago, 1947, 9.)

[5] For further details see Gödel, Kurt, *On Formally Undecidable Propositions of Principia Mathematica and Related Systems,* B. Meltzer (translator), Dover, New York, 1992; Nagel, Ernest, and James R. Newman, *Gödel's Proof,* New York University Press, New York, 1958; Kline, Morris, *Mathematics, The Loss of Certainty,* Oxford University Press, New York, 1980; Hofstadter, Douglas R., *Gödel, Escher, Bach: an Eternal Golden Braid,* Basic Books, New York, 1979; and Asimov, Isaac, *Isaac Asimov's Biographical Encyclopedia of Science and Technology,* Avon Books, New York, 1964.

[6] Gödel, Kurt, "Über formal unentscheidbare Sätze der Principia Mathematica und verwandter Systeme I," *Monatschefte für Mathematik und Physik* **38**, 1931, 173. Available in English with an extensive introduction by R. B. Braithwaite in Gödel, Kurt, *On Formally Undecidable Propositions of Principia Mathematica and Related Systems,* Basic Books, New York, 1962; Dover reprint, loc. cit.

[7] Kline, Morris, 1980, loc. cit.

[8] See endnote 15 of Chapter 4.

[9] Quoted from Kline, Morris, 1980, loc. cit., 228.

[10] Von Neuman, John, "The Mathematician," in *The World of Mathematics,* James R. Newman (editor), Simon & Schuster, New York, 1956, volume 4, 2063.

[11] Kline, Morris, 1980, loc. cit., 303-304.

[12] Kline, Morris, 1980, loc. cit., 303.

[13] Oliver Heaviside was an interesting character whose colorful, disparaging statements about pure mathematics and pure mathematicians offset a reciprocal bias among the latter. Heaviside had no formal education and his professional career consisted of six years as a telegraph operator after which, because of increasing deafness, he retired to live in his parents' home and took up electromagnetic theory as an avocation, eventually writing a three-volume work entitled *Electromagnetic Theory.* He predicted the increase in mass of a charged particle moving at large velocity and the upper-atmospheric ionosphere, known as the Kennelly-Heaviside layer, independently codiscovered by A. E. Kennelly and Heaviside. To the disdain of physicists and mathematicians, Heaviside used outlandish methods and notation totally unjustifiable to the "logic choppers," his term for pure mathematicians. To antagonize the purists he would make statements like "Ha, the series diverges; now we can do something with it." Then he would proceed to describe some novel result. Heaviside's methods have since been rigorously justified and have indicated new directions in mathematics. To nettle purists, in the spirit of Heaviside, applied mathematicians have observed that pure mathematicians are able to find a difficulty with any solution while applied mathematicians find a solution to any difficulty. (This couplet is taken from Kline, 1980, loc. cit., 301.)

[14] Hardy, Godfrey H., *A Mathematician's Apology,* Cambridge University Press, Cambridge, 1967.

[15] Weinberg, Steven, *Dreams of a Final Theory,* Vintage Books, New York, 1994, 154-157.

[16] The path leading to the general conclusion reached here may be obscure. If any (logicomathematical) system leads to many diverse representations of reality then, conversely, observation of reality as a starting point cannot imply a unique (logicomathematical) system except in the unlikely event that only one leads to that reality. The problem in discovering, describing, and demonstrating truth is then specifying the system that best defines it because such truth is probably equally represented by many diverse systems. This principle, it seems to me, extends beyond the range of logicomathematical thinking to include all strictly-objective thinking and description. More than material facts are required to establish the nature of reality.

[17] Morris Kline (1980, loc. cit., 96) describes Felix Klein as "one of the truly great mathematicians of recent times." Klein was chairmen of mathematics at the University of Göttingen. He was accomplished in and made contributions to mathematical physics as well as mathematics. In physics he was Boltzmann's debating partner in scientific debates against Friedrich Wilhelm Ostwald and Ernst Mach who advocated building science (thermodynamic theory) on energetics alone, ignoring entropy. And in mathematics Klein extended topography (using group theory) as Riemann had extended geometry. Klein succeeded Gauss and Riemann and others as the most prominent mathematician at Göttingen when it was a world center in both mathematics and mathematical physics. Immediately following Klein's tenure, quantum mechanics was invented at Göttingen by Werner Heisenberg, Max Born, and Pascual Jordan.

[18] Kline, Morris, 1980, loc. cit., 334.

[19] Feynman, Richard P., *The Meaning of It All,* Addison-Wesley, Reading MA, 1998.

[20] For instance, the second law of thermodynamics implies that in any *isolated* system an eventual "heat or entropy death" must occur, representing a maximum in entropy and a minimum in specification of order and organization among the system elements, e.g., atoms and molecules. I have seen the entropy concept or word misused in articles written by scientists, psychiatrists, marriage counselors, creationists, and theologians. A commonly mistaken notion is that creation or evolution is unphysical because it represents spontaneous organization (reduction of entropy). While the universe as a whole is isolated, the earth and many other systems are *not*. We demonstrate in Chapter 11 that entropy of the earth is continually decreasing. Some regard this fact as an enigma. "The laws of thermodynamics seem to dictate ... that nature should inexorably degenerate toward a state of greater disorder, greater entropy. Yet all around us we see magnificent structures – galaxies, cells, ecosystems, human beings – that have somehow managed to assemble themselves. This enigma bedevils all of science today." as Steven Strogatz has described it (*SYNC: The Emerging Science of Spontaneous Order,* Hyperion, New York, 2003, 1). Unfortunately, the laws of thermodynamics have often been incorrectly understood and interpreted (Appendix F).

[21] Regarding psychology, sociology, etc., see the comment of Richard Feynman on page 51.

Although Charles Darwin was a genius, the biological sciences are still awaiting their Isaac Newton and Albert Einstein. In Newton's *Principia* many mysteries pertaining to the earth, the moon, and the solar system were rigorously explained for the first time with predictions that agreed with observation in compelling exactness. Newton obtained these predictions from his proposed laws of motion and gravity using the calculus which Newton invented and, indeed, which was required for such exact calculations. One example is the lunar and solar tides, first explained in the *Principia*. Others are exact calculations of the planetary orbits including the perturbing influence of interplanetary gravitational attraction between Jupiter and its neighbors. These perturbations had actually been observed but remained unexplained until Newton's *Principia.*

Darwin's *Origin of Species* is a useful book, but it is not in the same class as Newton's *Principia*. In fact Darwin didn't provide the information advertised in his title and neither has later scientific effort. The law of natural selection is vague. Commonality between creatures is not necessarily due to direct ancestry but may simply have occurred by independent, randomly-developed similarity. Origin of species is not fully articulated by the concept of random, indeterminate natural selection. Many possible pathways from many possible species could have occurred. Survival of the fittest does not explain origin of species or initial conditions. It "explains" neither progeny nor ancestry. It is like regarding molecular randomness as the origin of the laws of thermodynamics. Thermodynamic laws derive from randomness, true enough, but only utilizing additional principles and constraints. Natural selection is evidently a correct principle, but what other principles apply? Possible constraints should be tested. Evolution may correctly describe some processes but it, by itself, is too vague.

A sharp contrast exists between Newton's and Darwin's methods. Darwin proposes a fundamental, universal, random, undefined, *generic* process – natural selection or survival of the fittest – and the far weaker logical induction, rather than deduction, to reach conclusions. For instance, Darwin discusses in detail various species of pigeons and then generalizes. Such leaps based on induction are, to the present author, simply not compelling in comparison to the rigorous, hard science Newton invented, utilized, and demonstrated by his exact predictions. Without such predictions where are compelling comparisons with observation? I refer to Feynman's above-referenced comment those who cite relative difficulty as preventive. Astronomy was also difficult before Newton.

Rare is the modern biologist who considers natural selection carefully, if not hard-science rigorously, but one is Kenneth R. Miller (*Finding Darwin's God,* Cliff Street Books, an Imprint of Harper Collins Publishers, New York, 1999). Miller supports and uses natural selection and, of course, observation should support this principle because that was its origin. But we cannot claim, even if observational evidence becomes quite universal and compelling, that we have established creation's basis as natural selection. Belivers searching for natural-selection-paradigm evidence ignore or dismiss other evidence as a matter of course. Claiming natural selection is creation's basis ignores and excludes alternatives to natural-selection paradigms when other possibilities may be superior. We use science to decide whether a theory or principle agrees with observation but not to decide whether another theory or principle not yet imagined or tested agrees better with observation. It is therefore naïve to say upon examination of one (or a few) paradigm(s) that "evolution is no longer just a theory, it is now established fact." Believers reject other creation paradigms because they believe natural selection best rationalizes their selected evidence. But they ignore other evidence. Testing a paradigm by use of the paradigm is logically circular; this approach tilts a level playing field and forces the outcome. These scientists presumptuously think others ought to accept their conclusions based on their paradigm and its evidence because it is all so compelling to them. In this attitude such scientists dismiss out-of-hand other paradigms (Miller, loc. cit., Chapter 6; Weinberg, Steven, *Facing Up,* Harvard University Press, 2001, 240-242). Another paradigm with its evidence *and meaning* can be equally legitimate and superior. Miller avoids common pitfalls and considers his topic from both scientific and believing-Christian views.

To many, evolutionary theory carries an implicit message of atheism (see endnote 9 of Chapter 13). Both *intent* and *reaction* have led to debate between so-called "creationists" and "evolutionists." Of course God could utilize evolution in creation. Evolution implies neither materialism nor atheism because these *assumptions* are additional and independent. Evolution implies evolution. But that is not to say it implies universal, unconstrained, random, natural selection ignoring initial conditions, environment, and spiritual influence over material processes (Appendix L and Chapter 11). All such influences can constrain natural selection and control any creatures produced.

The essence of the debate between creationists and evolutionists is well represented by two Jaynesian-style syllogisms that capture the bases of the two sides in creation-evolution debates.

> The Bible contains the word of God and must be regarded as the purest and deepest truth available to humans.
>
> *Therefore,*
>
> the *interpretation* of Bible passages by creationists must be correct.

> Scientific truth must be consistent with all objective observation, often satisfies Ockham's razor, and follows principles of symmetry and aesthetics.
>
> *Therefore,*
>
> all life descended from a single-cell lifeform by process of natural selection.

The debate appears to the present author to be misdirected for the following reasons. First, both sides are addressing the issues within a scientific paradigm. The medieval Church and the Aristotelians paid little heed to paradigm until they found they had trapped themselves in many false claims unjustified by their paradigm. Paradigm implicitly defines range of concepts, scope

Comparison of Texts from the *Bible* and the *Book of Moses*

Genesis	Moses
Genesis 2:1. THUS the heavens and the earth were finished, and all the host of them.	Moses 3:1. THUS the heaven and the earth were finished, and all the host of them.
2. And on the seventh day God ended his work which he had made; and he rested on the seventh day from all his work which he had made.	2. And on the seventh day I, God, ended my work, and all things which I had made; and I rested on the seventh day from all my work, and all things which I had made were finished, and I, God, saw that they were good;
3. And God blessed the seventh day, and sanctified it: because that in it he had rested from all his work which God created and made.	3. And I, God, blessed the seventh day, and sanctified it; because that in it I had rested from all my work which I, God, had created and made.
4. These are the generations of the heavens and of the earth when they were created, in the day that the LORD God made the earth and the heavens,	4. And now, behold, I say unto you, that these are the generations of the heaven and of the earth, when they were created, in the day that I, the Lord God, made the heaven and the earth,
5. And every plant of the field before it was in the earth, and every herb of the field before it grew: for the LORD God had not caused it to rain upon the earth, and there was not a man to till the ground.	5. And every plant of the field before it was in the earth, and every herb of the field before it grew. For I, the Lord God, created all things, of which I have spoken, spiritually, before they were naturally upon the face of the earth. For I, the Lord God, had not caused it to rain upon the face of the earth. And I, the Lord God, had created all the children of men; and not yet a man to till the ground; for in heaven created I them; and there was not yet flesh upon the earth, neither in the water, neither in the air;
6. But there went up a mist from the earth, and watered the whole face of the ground.	6. But I, the Lord God, spake, and there went up a mist from the earth, and watered the whole face of the ground.
7. And the LORD God formed man of the dust of the ground, and breathed into his nostrels the breath of life; and man became a living soul.	7. And I, the Lord God, formed man from the dust of the ground, and breathed into his nostrils the breath of life; and man became a living soul, the first flesh upon the earth, the first man also; nevertheless, all things were before created; but spiritually were they created and made according to my word.
8. And the LORD God planted a garden eastward in Eden; and there he put the man whom he had formed.	8. And I, the Lord God, planted a garden eastward in Eden, and there I put the man whom I had formed.
9. And out of the ground made the LORD God to grow every tree that is pleasant to the sight, and good for food; the tree of life also in the midst of the garden, and the tree of knowledge of good and evil.	9. And out of the ground made I, the Lord God, to grow every tree, naturally, that is pleasant to the sight of man; and man could behold it. And it became also a living soul. For it was spiritual in the day that I creared it; for it remaineth in the sphere in which I, God, created it, yea, even all things which I prepared for the use of man; and man saw that it was good for food. And I, the Lord God, planted the tree of life also in the midst of the garden, and also the tree of knowledge of good and evil.

of evidence, and meaning of vocabulary. What existence or function is assigned to "spirit" within materialistic science? None, inherent in the language and thought used in a materialistic-science discussion. Second, establishing *how* the world obtained its present state, the topic addressed by science, does not address the separate, more important questions of *who* or *what* caused it to happen and *why*, the focus of religious paradigms. No matter what *how* answers are eventually established, answers to *who*, *what*, and *why* provide both more complete and more important information not necessarily closely related to *how*-question answers. Limiting consideration to *how*, science is blind to purpose and meaning of life. A strictly scientific context renders "life" common and purposeless. Even secular humanism does better.

As to creation of the earth and its age, Biblical description gives some details but certainly not a clear, comprehensive picture. The conclusion of some that "creation," as they *interpret* its description in the Bible, and "evolution" are fundamentally in conflict and mutually exclusive is not compelling because the common interpretation of the Biblical description is not correct, as indicated by the following evidence. The creation story in the Bible describes *two creations*, a fact long recognized by some Bible scholars. That two creations are described in the Bible is confirmed in the Book of Moses of the *Pearl of Great Price*, a few verses of which are listed in the preceding table parallel to verses from the Book of Genesis of the *Bible*. These verses describe the end of the first creation and the beginning of the second, with the first creation inaugurating our *first estate* as God's spirit children in heaven and the second inaugurating our *second estate* as God's mortal children on earth. The two creations are more fully described in the Book of Moses. In Moses, revealed through Joseph Smith for the purpose of restoring information removed from the Bible, description of a six-day *spiritual creation of things in heaven* clarifies the account in Genesis 1 through Genesis 2:3. A second creation, parallel to the account beginning in Genesis 2:4, describes a *natural* or *physical creation of things on earth*. The description of the second creation, no duration of which is specified, is more sparsely described but clearly presents a different sequence than the first creation.

The restored version in Moses teaches two creations: a spiritual one in heaven followed by a natural or physical one on earth. *No "days" or periods of time in either Genesis or Moses are specified for the natural creation.* In both, a special place or Garden is designated. No activity outside this Garden is described until after Adam and Eve are cast out of the Garden; neither is any length of time identified with their tenure in the Garden. We can even *speculate* that just as time flows more slowly in heaven than in the natural earth, with one heavenly day being as an earthly millennium (*Bible*, 2 Peter 3:8; *Pearl of Great Price*, Abraham 3:4; 5:13), time may have flowed more slowly in paradise (the Garden of Eden) than in the rest of the earth. Indeed, the nature of time is not well understood. (*Bible,* Revelation 10:6, *Doctrine and Covenants* 88:110, 130:4. The middle one of these citations reads "there shall be time no longer; and Satan ... shall not be loosed for the space of a thousand years." There is (are) evidently some aspect(s) of time we do not yet understand.) Note that the preceding discussion is not in terms of a materialistic-science paradigm.

Combining this vision with science, the fossil record evidently accumulated over epochs outside the Garden of Eden, with no death in the Garden during the parallel period (perhaps of much shorter duration). The condemning of Adam and Eve to death and their ejection from the Garden were apparently equivalent, both resulting from their new, *mortal state* consequent to (literal) partaking of the forbidden fruit. In this combined vision, human evolution doesn't occur until after the fossil-record period, even though humans were created first (Appendix L). It therefore precludes much evolutionary change in the human genome from creation of Adam to today, a period of perhaps a billion years over which the rest of the animal and other kingdoms have apparently evolved.

In light of this vision, young-earth creationists are "shooting themselves in the foot" in arguing against a long history of the earth. They believe that earth's age is no more than 13,000 years or so corresponding to the Biblical account that the six plus one days of creation were each as 1,000 years "in the earth," as supported by scripture, and that the earth has now existed 6,000 years since Adam and Eve left the Garden. But this interpretation of Genesis 1 and 2 and Exodus 20:11 ignores the two creations described with the first occurring in heaven, not on earth. The persistent, perfunctory, peremptory pertinacity of protagonists who promote either this model or universal evolution is reminiscent of the rigid position taken by the medieval Church based on misunderstanding of scripture. Premature adoption of a dogma is unwise. Rigid attachment to medieval Church and Aristotelian dogma prevented discovery of truth and destroyed credibility and authority. Nevertheless, many on both sides resist and fight against truth because their attachment to error is so dear.

While survival of the fittest has actually been observed in significant mutations of living species, which confirms the reality of evolution within a species, evolution between species has not been observed *in vivo* and remains a theory (and a viable one; see, for example, Miller, loc. cit.) that must be regarded as tentative on the basis that science itself is merely tentative. However, humans are nearly completely excluded from past evolution in the vision we have described because their evolution could only have occurred over a short period (Appendix L).

Whatever the mechanism of human creation, I believe we are God's creatures both spiritually and physically. In a "Mormon" paradigm, in which family relationships have high eternal importance, the idea that mothers and fathers in an ancestral chain are cut off preceding the "first man and woman" is repugnant. In any case, the critical question is not *how*, but *Who*? And *why*?

If one is concerned about the apparent conflict between science (materialism) and religion (Christianity), the best course is to discover truth directly by means of the ostensible-step method offered and received through the doctrine of Christ described in Book III. By this method one ignores speculation and discovers fundamental truth, the *Who* and *why* in the existence and station of Christ. Questions of *how* can also be considered, but they are not then so critical.

We can add some reliable information that supports our earlier discussion about the "Garden of Eden period" and the paradisiacal state that applied in this environment ending for Adam and Eve when they were expelled from the Garden for partaking of the forbidden fruit. Who would venture to guess how long our noble and obedient first parents lived in childlike innocence in the Garden of Eden before violating a commandment of God? Adam in his premortal life was known as the Archangel Michael and led, under Christ, the followers of God (us who have been, are, and will be mortals) in driving out of heaven Satan and those who followed him in rebellion against God (*Bible,* Revelation 12:7-9, Jude 1:9). And Michael will lead, under Christ, the followers of God in another future battle in which Satan and his followers will be finally cast away into outer darkness (see *Doctrine and Covenants* 27:11, 29:26, 88:112-115, 107:54). With no death in the paradisiacal Garden of Eden (Appendix L), Adam and Eve could have lived there for epochs before the history of mortal or natural humans on the earth began. As we already speculated, their tenure in the Garden may have been of much shorter duration if time flows more slowly in the paradisiacal state. Meanwhile, the rest of the earth into which Adam and Eve were expelled apparently existed in a different state as indicated by the fossil record. Carnivores such as Tyrannosaurus Rex probably did not exist in an absence of death. And, without death in the Garden, from where except outside the Garden where death existed could the Lord have made "coats of skins" for Adam and Eve (*Bible,* Genesis 3:21, *Pearl of Great Price,* Moses 4:27) before they were cast out? Apostle James E. Talmage delivered an address on 9 August 1931 at the request of the presidency of the Church of Jesus Christ of Latter-day Saints. Talmage, holder of a Ph.D. in geology, entitled his address *The Earth and Man* (reprinted in Evenson, William E., and Duane E. Jeffery, *Mormonism and Evolution,* Greg Kofford Books, Salt Lake City, 2005) and he recognized therein the great antiquity of the earth and of life and death upon it, beginning long before humans arrived (in the mortal state). Talmage's talk was apparently invited and published to counter a contrary opinion then being dogmatically promoted. (See Roberts, B. H., *The Truth, The Way, The Life, An Elementary Treatise on Theology,* BYU Studies, Provo, Utah, 1996, 681-720,729-734.)

[22] Bell, J. S., *Speakable and unspeakable in quantum mechanics,* Cambridge U. P., 1993, 181-195.

[23] Polkinghorne, J. C., *The Quantum World,* Princeton University Press, 1984, especially 78-82.

[24] Herbert, N., *Quantum Reality,* Anchor Books, New York, 1985, 1987, Chapters 9 and 10.

[25] Cramer, John G., "The transactional interpretation of quantum mechanics," *Reviews of Modern Physics* **58**, 1986, 647-687. See also http://www.npl.washington.edu/npl/int_rep/qm_nl.html.

[26] Gribbin, John, *Schrödinger's Kittens and the Search for Reality,* Little, Brown and Company, Boston, 1995, Chapters 4-6.

[27] *Quantum Implications,* B. J. Hiley and F. David Peat (editors), Routledge and Kegan Paul Ltd., London, 1987. This book contains thirty essays by authors generally either originators of or pioneers in a new approach or perspective perhaps usable in quantum theory.

[28] My teacher was correct to adequate approximation. Quantum mechanics predicts that a free particle has quantized properties, the wave function being in this case a narrow "wave packet" moving with the particle and defining its possible properties. Because possible properties are quantized but closely spaced for a free particle, they closely approximate a Newtonian one.

[29] Beller, Mara, *Quantum Dialogue,* The University of Chicago Press, Chicago, 1999.

[30] Bell, J. S., loc. cit., 40.

[31] Heisenberg, Werner, *Physics and Philosophy,* Harper and Row, New York, 1958, 145.

[32] Von Neuman, John, *Mathematische Grundlagen der Quantunmechanik,* Springer-Verlag, Berlin, 1932. An English translation was published by Princeton University Press in 1955.

[33] Bohm, David, *Physical Review* **85**, 1952, 166, 180 (two articles).

[34] Cramer, John G., *Physical Review D* **22**, 1980, 362.

[35] Wheeler, J. A., and R. P. Feynman, *Reviews of Modern Physics* **17**, 1945, p. 157, **21**, 1949, 425.

[36] Hoyle, F., and J. V. Narlikar, Ann. Phys. (N. Y.) **54**, 1969, 207; **62**, 1971, 44; Davies, P. C. W., Proc. Cambridge Philos. Soc. **68**, 1970, 751, J. Phys. A **4**, 1971, 836; **5**, 1972, 1025. These articles develop the QED version of Wheeler-Feynman theory.

[37] *Doctrine and Covenants* 88:6,11-13 reads "He [Christ] that ascended up on high, as also he descended below all things, in that he comprehended all things, that he might be in all and through all things, the light of truth; ... And the light which shineth, which giveth you light, is through him who enlighteneth your eyes, which is the same light that quickeneth your understanding; Which light proceedeth forth from the presence of God to fill the immensity of space – *The light which is in all things, which giveth life to all things, which is the law by which all things are governed,* even the power of God who sitteth upon his throne, who is in the bosom of eternity, who is in the midst of all things." (italics added)

The text continues "Now, verily I say unto you, that through the redemption which is made for you is brought to pass the resurrection from the dead. And the spirit and the body are the soul of man. And the resurrection from the dead is the redemption of the soul. And the redemption of the soul is through him that quickeneth all things, in whose bosom it is decreed that the poor and the meek of the earth shall inherit it. ... they shall return again to their own place [house, philosophy, paradigm], to enjoy that which they are willing to receive, ... For what doth it profit a man if a gift is bestowed upon him, and he receive not the gift? Behold, he rejoices not in that which is given unto him, neither rejoices in him the giver of the gift. And again, verily I say unto you, that which is governed by law is also preserved by law and perfected and sanctified by the same. That which breaketh a law, and abideth not by law, but seeketh to become a law unto itself, and willeth to abide in sin, and altogether abideth in sin, cannot be sanctified by law, neither by mercy, justice, nor judgement. Therefore, they must remain filthy still."

"All kingdoms have a law given; And there are many kingdoms; for there is no space in the which there is no kingdom; and there is no kingdom in which there is no space, either a greater or a lesser kingdom. And unto every kingdom is given a law; and unto every law there are certain bounds also and conditions. All beings who abide not in those conditions are not justified. For intelligence cleaveth unto intelligence; wisdom receiveth wisdom; truth embraceth truth; virtue loveth virtue; light cleaveth unto light; mercy hath compassion on mercy and claimeth her own; justice continueth its course and claimeth its own; judgement goeth before the face of him who sitteth upon the throne and governeth and executeth all things. He comprehendeth all things, and all things are before him, and all things are round about him; and he is above all things, and in all things, and is through all things, and is round about all things; and all things are by him, and of him, even God, forever and ever. And again, verily I say unto you, he hath given a law unto all things, by which they move in their times and their seasons; And their courses are fixed, even the courses of the heavens and the earth, which comprehend the earth and all the planets." (*Doctrine and Covenants* 88:14-17,32-42.)

[38] Bell, J. S., loc. cit., attributes this quote to Max Jammer, *The Philosophy of Quantum Mechanics,* John Wiley, New York, 1974, 204, quoting A. Petersen, *Bulletin of the Atomic Scientist* **19**, 1963, 12.

[39] Einstein, Albert, quoted by N. Herbert, loc. cit., 188. Steven Weinberg reinforces Einstein's thinking with his statement that "... the laws of physics as we understand them now are nothing but a description of reality." (*Facing Up,* loc. cit., 136).

[40] Lewis, C. S., *Miracles, a Preliminary Study,* The Macmillan Company, New York, 1947, 7.

[41] Greene, Brian, *The Fabric of the Cosmos,* Alfred A. Knopf, New York, 2004, 213.

[42] Heisenberg, W., *Zeitschrift für Physik* **43**, 1927, 172.

[43] Gell-Mann, Murray, *The Nature of the Physical Universe,* John Wiley, New York, 1976, 29.

[44] *E. T. Jaynes: Papers on Probability, Statistics and Statistical Physics,* R. D. Rosenkrantz (editor), Kluwer Academic Publishers, Dordrecht, The Netherlands, 1983, 87. All of Jaynes' papers are available at http://bayes.uwstl.edu/etj/node1.html but this comment appears only in his book in the introduction to his "Delaware Lecture.".

[45] Jaynes, E. T., "A Backward Look to the Future," 1993, 269-270, http://bayes.uwstl.edu/etj/node1.html.

[46] Polkinghorne, J. C., loc. cit., 33.

[47] Von Baeyer, Hans Christian, *Taming the Atom,* Random House, New York, 1992, 143.

[48] Einstein, A., B. Podolsky, and N. Rosen, *Physical Review* **46**, 1935, 777-780.

[49] Bohm, David, *Quantum Theory,* Prentice-Hall, Englewood Cliffs, NJ, 1951, 614-615.

[50] Bell, J. S., loc. cit. [51] Ibid., 155. [52] Beller, Mara, loc. cit., 151.

[53] Polkinghorne, loc. cit.; Herbert, loc. cit.; Gribbin, loc. cit., Zukav, Gary, *The Dancing Wu Li Masters,* Bantam Books, New York, 1979, Lindley, David, *Where Does the Weirdness Go?,* Basic Books, New York, 1996, Nadeau, Robert, and Menas Kafatos, *The Non-local Universe,* Oxford University Press, New York, 1999.

[54] Clauser, J. F., and M. A. Horne, *Physical Review D* **10**, 1974, 526-535.

[55] Clauser, John F., and Abner Shimony, *Reports in Progress in Physics* **41**, 1978, 1881-1927.

[56] Freedman, S. J., and J. F. Clauser, *Physical Review Letters* **28**, 1972, 938-941.

[57] Holt, R. A., and F. M. Pipkin, as quoted in Clauser and Shimony, loc. cit., 1909-1911.

[58] Clauser, J. F., *Physical Review Letters* **36**, 1976, 1223-1226.

[59] Fry, E. S., and R. C. Thompson, *Physical Review Letters* **37**, 1976, 465-468.

[60] Aspect, Alain, Philippe Graingier, and Gérard Roger, *Physical Review Letters* **49**, 1982, 91-94.

[61] Aspect, Alain, Jean Dalibard, and Gérard Roger, *Physical Review Letters* **49**, 1982, 1804-1807.

[62] See: *Physics Today* **51**, Issue 12, 1998, 9 and in *Physical Review Letters* **81**, 1998, see articles by (1) Buttler, W. T., R. J. Hughes, P. G. Kwiat, S. K. Lamoreaux, G. G. Luther, G. L. Morgan, J. E. Nordholt, C. G. Peterson, and C. M. Simmons, 3283, (2) Tittel, W., J. Brendel, H. Zbinden, and N. Gisin, 3563, (3) Weihs, G., T. Jennewein, C. Simon, H. Weinfurter, and A. Zeilinger, 5039.

[63] Duck, Ian, and E. C. G. Sudarshan, *100 Years of Planck's Quantum,* World Scientific, Singapore, 2000, 463.

[64] Greene, loc. cit., 99-123 and note 5, 501-502.

[65] Bell, J. S., loc. cit., 149.

[66] Herbert, N., loc. cit., 230, 234-235.

[67] See, for example, Ballentine, Leslie E., *Quantum Mechanics: A Modern Development,* World Scientific, Singapore, 1998.

[68] Weinberg, Steven, *Physical Review Letters* **62**, 1989, 485.

[69] Polchinski, Joseph, *Physical Review Letters* **66**, 1991, 397.

[70] Greene, loc. cit., 115-120.

[71] All the fundamental forces – gravity, electromagnetic, weak- and strong-nuclear forces – are possible exceptions to what was believed to be an absence of non-local forces known to science. All operate through an intervening vacuum, a property that frustrated Newton's attempt to understand gravity. These forces have been artificially "localized" by invention of a mathematical construct called the "potential field" regarded as a local property. But supposition of locality is arbitrary. These forces still operate from a distance with no demonstrated mechanism, at least in the case of gravity. Use of a mathematical construct, namely, the field, can hardly provide any mechanistic understanding as this construct is merely a mathematical device contrived to give correct predictions. Indeed, that is the kind of theory particle physicists now seek. Janna Levin has observed (*How the Universe got its Spots,* Anchor Books, New York, 2002, 31) "Sometimes it is a great advantage to bury your mind in the formalism of the equations because we often understand math when plain English isn't useful. We don't often worry about the real meaning of a concept such as 'field.' "

My criticism does not apply to general relativity. General relativity could not have been contrived to agree with previously-unknown phenomena. But knowledge is not understanding. What would provide more complete understanding of these forces would be discovery of a physical mechanism by which they operate. Such a physical mechanism would provide an explanation of their action in terms of fundamental principles or laws, not merely a picture of some simple mechanical apparatus that Weinberg calls the "old, naïve mechanical worldview." Quantum field theory provides such a mechanism by use of "graviton messenger particles" (fields). String theory utilizes more elaborate mathematical objects (or fields) having p-dimensional membrane-like properties. But these inventions, useful as they are, are mathematical contrivances devoid of physical understanding. This criticism is harsh but pertinent to our consideration of what we truly know and what is adopted, assumed, or believed on a basis of faith.

[72] Von Baeyer, Hans Christian, loc. cit., 222.

[73] Quoted by Kline, Morris, 1980, loc. cit., 342.

[74] However, recognizing symptoms and identifying root cause of a problem are two different things. And fixing the root cause is another. Inherent limitations in value-free, objective-evidence-only science preclude discovery of the meaning we address. In fact, it is encouraging that symptoms have been recognized and attributed by a few, like von Baeyer, to what I believe is their actual cause. But it remains highly unlikely that science will provide any improved ability to discover meaning. Among materialists, justification of science as the only legitimate approach is likely to be more broadly embraced, especially with some expanded truth criterion that includes, say, simplicity (Ockham's razor), symmetry, and aesthetics as well as consistency with observation. Meaning must ultimately occur in mind and science, with its focus on objectivity or out-of-mind objects and processes, doesn't see the most important evidence. With this break from scientific orthodoxy, materialists may all the more energetically declare that meaning, with its subjective values and evidence, is unscientific, unnecessary, and illegitimate.

[75] Born, Max, *My Life,* Charles Scribner's Sons, New York, 1978, 298.

[76] Langmuir, Irving, *Phenomena, Atoms and Molecules,* Philosophical Library, New York, 1950, 3.

[77] *Bible,* John 8:31-32.

[78] See Chapter 14.

11. Psychology, Free Will, and Agency

In this final chapter of Book II we further prepare to answer the central question addressed in this book: *what, if any, certain test of truth is possible*? We soon shall, but only after necessary preliminary topics are properly addressed. In this chapter we consider two such preliminary topics, namely, *psychology* and *free will.*

How are these topics connected to the test of truth sought in this book? Some claim that a test involving subjective evidence is not conclusive, that psychogenesis can cause one to reach a false conclusion. We therefore include a brief account of materialist psychology, sufficient to indicate that neither such a psychogenic-reaction claim nor few, if any, other conclusions are well supported by materialist models of psychology. In particular, we consider the mind-body problem, a problem that, between materialists and Christians, only exists for materialists since the coexistence of a material brain and a spiritual mind is, in principle, not a problem for Christians who believe the universe contains both matter and spirit.

Free will is of interest because without it there is no meaningful human test or decision of any kind. Understanding the nature of free will or agency is necessary to utilizing it well. The uncertainty principle confounded Laplace's absolute determinism by which free will was thought to be precluded. Feynman's theory of quantum electrodynamics contains no such uncertainty principle *per se* but still contains its effect in the multiplicity of paths it contemplates or, more particularly, those it doesn't. And quantum mechanics generally provides probabilistic, not definitive, predictions, equally proscribing absolute determinism. Nevertheless, quantum theory suggests some level of determinism just as a Theory of Everything (TOE) will impose some level of determinism. We consider interesting beliefs on free will and determinism in the perspective of (a) materialist psychology and (b) physics, with the latter represented by the thoughts of Wolfgang Pauli and K. V. Laurikainen.

While examinations of materialist psychology and of free will or agency involve concepts already considered, we consider an important one first fully articulated by Wolfgang Pauli. Its full articulation allows us to better envision the nature and significance of agency. And, indeed, this concept also enhances our insight into the nature and significance of science.

Psychology and Psychiatry

Psychology and psychiatry are not hard science. Yet, many consider them to be science. Because of this notion we examine elements of psychology pertinent to our comparison of science and Christianity. In particular, we consider elements of psychology pertaining to discovery and justification of truth.

We begin by considering a basic question. How can nonmaterial-related qualities like impressions, feelings, emotions, and the "unconscious self" be treated in science, since science is a system conceived to treat observable, reproducible, material-related facts? Surprise! – impressions, feelings, emotions, and the unconscious self are the exact qualities we necessarily deal with in hard science, ultimately, for we only perceive through impressions (such as seeing and hearing), feelings and emotions (such as the touch of an object or comfort felt when a result fits our paradigm), and the unconscious self and cognizance (by which we partially evaluate and judge information). These are the "window" through which we perceive and examine, the window we usually ignore because we are focused instead on the object(s) being examined. Impressions used in hard science are usually familiar (seeing, hearing, touching, tasting, or smelling a material object or process), reproducible (in repeated observations of one and many observers in many situations), and universal (leading in practice or in belief to an anticipated understanding of all things). Significantly, impressions treated in psychology and psychiatry are generally not as familiar, not material-related (cannot be seen, heard, touched, …), not objective, not always reproducible, and certainly not universal. These properties give psychology and psychiatry a vague and ill-defined basis compared to that of hard science. Social science is even more vague because of the many psychologies and psychological interactions involved. A major difference between behavioral science and hard science is suggested by the case-study approach the former utilizes. Case studies are necessary in the absence of knowledge of general, fundamental laws. Logical induction is used (perhaps implicitly) with such case studies in place of logical deduction used with rigorous, quantitative, general-law treatments of reproducible, material-facts evidence.

Consequently, I regard psychology and psychiatry in particular and behavioral science in general as *art* rather than *science*. But, I hasten to add, my judgement is not devoid of appreciation of the value of this art in the hands of an artist. If you haven't noticed, I've consistently brutalized even the hardest science as utterly insufficient for establishing truth because it is always tentative and contingent. Classifying psychology, psychiatry, and behavioral science as art does not carry a negative insinuation. But in all areas of art, level of artistic ability varies with intangible, difficult-to-quantify capability of the artist. While science by its nature is objective or material-related, reproducible, quantitative, and universal, art by its nature is subjective or nonmaterial-related, qualitative, and individual.

Deciding issues in Christianity is generally more art-like than science-like because such decisions involve impressions and feelings not closely associated with material facts. In seeking truth such impressions and feelings are usually dismissed by the materialist skeptic who thinks "Aha, the stated conditions required in a test together with desire for a positive result induce a sympathetic, psychogenic affinity for the effect being sought and cause one to believe that he or she has experienced it." In the Bible dreams, visions, voices, and their interpretations are often vehicles of divine revelation. Psychologists and psychiatrists frequently regard dreams, visions, voices, thoughts, and feelings as revealing a vast "unconscious self," some, in the past, believing it contains knowledge inherited from our ancestors through a genetic, biomolecular code.[1] Both questions and answers relating to such matters seem quite nebulous compared to hard-science laws and facts.

The question of whether experience-like, unconscious-self knowledge can have psychogenic origin is certainly legitimate. But, even a hard-science version of the arts of psychology, psychiatry, and other behavioral science utilizing only well defined quantities and concepts, were one available, could never provide a certain answer to such a question. As previously stated, questions pertaining to values and meaning lie beyond the domain of objective, material-based, value-free, lowest-common-denominator-facts science. When one looks closely, as we do herein, one discovers that the scope of the philosophy, paradigm, or system of belief encompassed by neutral, objective science alone, i.e., materialism, provides no basis for a claim of any knowledge or power to conclusively prove any answer correct. Indeed, objective, neutral, external, value-free science in the form of logical positivism does not even recognize the validity of such *questions* – a consequence and symptom of weakness in such philosophy. Answers also lie beyond the scope of psychology and psychiatry because they attempt to utilize the scientific method to some extent and cannot claim more than tentative and contingent knowledge or any power to *demonstrate* truth. It is true they, like science, can often be used to discover truth, but not to conclusively establish it as such. While skepticism and agnosticism can be quite honest, philosophically-legitimate, and useful positions, the condescending skepticism of an arrogant materialist-atheist is ironic in its revelation of ignorance.

The objective, external, material world (universe) created by scientists in their construction of a scientific paradigm, a world that they invisibly monitor without perturbing by any causative action or participation therein, precludes any knowledge of the human person beyond his or her existence as a mere material object. And, as we shall shortly see, this limited, remote approach is exactly the one taken by a materialist in very soft behavioral science and, to some degree, in his or her philosophy in general. Such a limited approach is required in any purely objective methodology since participation is subjective. But such an approach ignores the most significant qualities of a person which are subjective rather than objective. Indeed, as we argued in Book I, all persons are limited to subjective perception and reasoning, unavoidably contaminated with personal and cultural preconceptions, so that no person possesses any fully objective capability. Study of human behavior by strictly objective methodology leads only to superficial knowledge and fantasy when one uses its results to consider a human as anything beyond a merely material object. It is not the dreams, visions, and feelings often associated with religious experience and attacked as fantasies by materialists that are, in fact, the fantasies. Rather, the fantasies are the objective scientific study and the pretense that it provides knowledge of a human person. It does not because objective science ignores the essence of the subject, namely, a person's subjective nature and participation in the universe in developing and using knowledge, skills, character, strength, values, understanding, devotion, a feeling of meaning, the complete "self," and volition through his or her unique, real, "lived, participative experience," the kind of lived experience described in examples of understanding of meaning given in the Preface and Chapter 18.

In recognizing these limitations of objective science in the study of subjective beings one immediately sees the futility in using objective science to understand a human person, consisting of his or her material self, unconscious self, knowledge, understanding, and values learned by participation, feelings of devotion derived therefrom, and comprehension of meaning and volition to which these lead. Except for the first, these components are excluded from materialism or objective science. How, then, can science provide any understanding of the complete human? It cannot. It can provide only the most superficial-level knowledge, knowledge of a person as a material object. The very approach of objective-science psychology and psychiatry and other behavioral science is disabling. Any power these disciplines truly possess resides in their practice as art rather than science.

Biblical Insights into the Unconscious Self

That rational power and awareness are provided by one's spirit is suggested in several Biblical passages.[2] Christ conversed with "unclean spirits" who controlled a possessed body, were aware of who He was, and reasoned with Him.[2] These unclean spirits always immediately recognized the Son of God. A pre-earth existence is categorically denied in now-orthodox Christianity because of the latter's assumption of *ex nihilo* creation (creation out of nothing). But the Bible nowhere supports *ex nihilo* creation. To the contrary, Moses described a spiritual creation followed by a natural or physical one, implying a pre-earth existence.[3] By Abraham's account, God *organized* and *formed* the heavens and the earth.[4] Thus, a possible origin of the unconscious self and cognizance, alternative to inheriting a genetic, biomolecular code, is unique, personal, pre-earth experience dimly remembered by each individual with the knowledge, understanding, and values we then acquired constituting our "unconscious self" and "cognizance." Such a pre-earth existence is consistently indicated in scripture[2-5] and possession of another's body by an unclean spirit is frequently described in the Bible. No scientific test seems able to distinguish between different possible origins of the unconscious self. To decide this matter with certainty requires proof from beyond science.

In my own experience, the result of the Christian test (described in Book III) is uniquely powerful and compelling. Nevertheless, one can believe it to be merely a random or a sympathetic, self-induced, psychogenic effect. Neither belief can be regarded as reliable for at least two reasons. First, a random psychological effect caused by any random process such as random predisposition or fluctuation in active-brain-material, perhaps at the neuron, molecular, or sub-molecular level, can hardly be regarded as reliable because if brain function is random and unreliable one cannot trust any theory, analysis, or conclusion obtained by use of his or her brain. We must reject this result or give up reasoning. Second, we may ask whether a sympathetic, self-induced effect drawing on our unconscious-self knowledge can eclipse all of one's conscious experience, and by far? Can we envision beyond our conscious knowledge? And, most importantly, without the influence of God can one experience peace that passeth all understanding and indescribable joy?[6] Some in psychology-psychiatry and in Christianity may answer yes to some of these questions. And, indeed, dimly-remembered, pre-earth experience[5] is undoubtedly much richer than consciously-remembered experience. But science and Christianity can and often do assign different origins or causes to cognizance and the unconscious self with the effect that the two interpretations are highly-divergent and mutually exclusive. But any origin or cause assigned by use of science is merely tentative.

We are agents free to choose what we believe. If one will not see or hear certain kinds of facts, he or she will not – regardless of his or her reason. But, it is meaningless that from his or her exclusively materialist perspective the Empiricist character of Edward O. Wilson observes that "No statistical proofs exist that prayer reduces illness and mortality, except perhaps through a psychogenic enhancement of the immune system; if it were otherwise the whole world would pray continuously."[7] It is perhaps more accurate to say a good part of the world does pray continuously than to say it does not. As to statistical "proofs," such a "proof" requires a control,[8] say, a continuously praying world, to which non-praying and partially-praying worlds may be compared by some form of "relative hypothesis testing," the fundamental function and capability of statistics. What and where is this control, this "otherwise?" The "otherwise" in this case appears to exist only in the materialist-paradigm-controlled mind of the Empiricist, an image based on the tentative, contingent knowledge that defines his or her view of reality. One does not easily see another vision of reality when it contradicts one's own, strongly-held paradigm because a paradigm imposes both a view of reality and the acceptable kind and range of evidence, sometimes proscribing evidence by which this view, if incorrect, might be corrected. These beliefs (in paradigm and evidence) force conclusions that seem so consistent, reasonable, and inevitable that they blind one to alternative views, a fact true for many materialists, atheists, agnostics, Christians, and other people of faith alike. In particular, the *low-meaning paradigm of materialism* fills a vacuum in perception and reasoning in the absence of any higher-level view of reality in which meaning and feeling are held to be significant. Prayer helps and miracles occur among those who have faith in Christ and see beyond the apparent dominance of a material reality that is the focus of science. I have observed and experienced them.

The Empiricist also states that "a 1996 survey of American scientists (to take one respectable segment of society) revealed ... only 46 percent expressed a desire for immortality, and most of those only moderately so; 64 percent claimed no desire at all."[7] (The latter quantity should perhaps read 54 percent.) Fortunately, "someone" with a lot more knowledge has already settled the issue, no matter what materialists with their highly-educated, deeply-insightful (proud?) view focused only on the material world now think they understand and desire. The issue of immortality is not understood in objective, worldly terms – Christ's kingdom is not of this world – because faith in Christ and other values necessary to comprehension of meaning, particularly mutual devotion with Christ, are required to understand it. In fact, when God's plan of life for us was originally described to us as angels, or "morning stars" and "sons [and daughters] of God," during our pre-earth life, we all agreed to the plan and fought a war in heaven to defend and realize it,[5] concepts we shall presently pursue in detail. Indeed, we sang and shouted for joy at the plan.[9] But we then knew more about values and personal growth and meaning and joy and God and mutual devotion with Him. Each of us was the "someone" who already settled the issue for him- or her-self.

In contrast to science and to the arts of psychology, psychiatry, and other behavioral study, the Christian paradigm is capable of and specializes in definite and certain answers to questions, particularly ultimate ones. Through this paradigm the value of Christ's life and the meaning of His devotion to His Father and to us are offered as the light of the world. This is "the light that shineth in darkness [the world]; and the darkness [the world by worldly understanding] comprehendeth it not,"[10] the light He commands His followers to display to the world,[11] Himself.[12] The essence of Christ's life and the light that shines forth in His example are His devotion to His Father and to us. Its meaning is apparent in the peace of God which passeth all understanding and the indescribable joy He will give those who diligently seek Him. This light, peace, and joy are meaning and guidance, invisible to science but found by and in the lives of Christians, like those we consider in Chapter 18. They are the deepest meaning one can obtain, if one will receive them. They are knowing Christ, truth, peace, and joy. Failing to actively seek and obtain them now, while we best can, will be the cause of later torment that we didn't.

Materialist Visions of Mind and Body

Many variations of materialist psychology have been invented. Following Jon Mills[13] we list a number of materialist theories pertaining to psychology and explore their general character. These theories include identity theories,[14] functionalism,[15] supervenience,[16] eliminativism,[17] representationalism,[18] and anomalous monism.[19] We shall attempt no detailed description or treatment of this spectrum. Instead, after Mills,[13] we shall delineate the general nature of materialist psychology utilizing two tools generally assumed in this discipline. These two tools are *physical reductionism* and *naturalism*. We apply them to the brain to address mental function. While use of only these two tools does not capture all details of the above listed spectrum, it provides a materialist vision of human mental capability.

Physical reductionism involves separating a system into its individual components with respect to both substance and function and then employing the functions of the divided components as a source of knowledge of the functioning of the whole. It employs the following materialist assumptions, particularly when it is applied to the brain. (a) Mental states are differentiated and controlled by different physical states of the brain; biological-neurochemical-physiological materials, structures, and processes together with evolutionary driving forces are the total substance and function of the brain and all mental activity; (b) the brain consists of a material, energy, and information-processing system wherein function derives from active materials whose properties cause brain function; (c) mental state and activity follow from the physical properties of the active brain materials, structures, and physical preconditions that, if understood and known, would allow prediction of mental activity.

Naturalism contains the following beliefs: (a) all knowledge derives from physical conditions and material cause-and-effect relationships known through empirical observation and analysis; (b) naturalism supports positivism in the sense that truth consists only of observed and measured facts and rational methods applied thereto; (c) it denies supernatural, religious, spiritual, and metaphysical objects and processes; (d) it assumes that all phenomena may be explained (presently or eventually) by use of scientific methodology; and (e) it is biased against teleological, anthropomorphic, and animistic causes and theories.

These two conceptual tools dictate that no mind exists above and beyond material brain (or physical body). Contrary to this belief and to rationalize capabilities many regard to be real, Descartes proposed that the human consists of both material and "thinking substance," a Cartesian[20] dualism that has been invoked in various philosophies and refuted in others like those invoking naturalism and physical reductionism. Hence, the views of reductionism and naturalism deny Cartesian dualism wherein both material and super-material "thinking substance" (spirit) coexist and the mind is composed of or utilizes in its function a super-material substance.

If materialism is to be regarded as realistic and useful in addressing the philosophy of mind, it must provide a consistent view of reality by which its assertions are reasonable and may be used without immediately introducing further and deeper questions. A consistent and reasonable theory should provide some justification of its assertions in its consistent and reasonable applications, even if they are not conclusive. To evaluate materialism we examine consequences of the above assertions (naturalism and physical reductionism) to discover if they and their implications seem reasonable and consistent. They often don't, leading to dilemma instead of justification. Mills[13] has addressed exactly this topic in greater detail than we do here. We include, in the form of the aforementioned dilemmas, several that Mills presents as well as several based on our own thinking and on thinking provided by others.

One concept we utilize, authored by physicist Wolfgang Pauli in a letter to Niels Bohr dated 15 February 1955, is "the ideal of the detached observer."

> To me it seems quite adequate to call the conceptual description of nature in classical physics, which Einstein wants to keep so emphatically, *the ideal of the detached observer*. In drastic words the spectator must, according to this ideal, appear in fully discrete manner as a hidden spectator. He can never appear as an actor. Nature is hereby left alone in its predetermined course of events, without regard to the manner in which the phenomena are observed.[21] (italics added)

In physics and other science an observer is regarded as unobtrusive, observing the universe but never influencing it. This leads to the idealized, objective, reproducible, external, material world (universe) of physics in particular and of science in general. This objective, ideal world necessarily excludes human participation. Yet, humans do participate in the universe and the idealized, external world of science artificially ignores their active, subjective, human nature – recognizing only their role as unobtrusive, nonparticipating, objective, idealized-external-world observers.

In following descriptions of recent but not up-to-date psychological thought, multiple visions of mind and body are rather strongly asserted. A scientist accustomed to hard science may be "jarred" by the combination of breadth and strength of an assertion and weakness of evidence supporting it. While breadth and strength of these visions are summarized and quoted in the style and spirit of the authors' writings, descriptions of their bases is, at best, highly abbreviated. The original works cited should be consulted for full descriptions. But these descriptions generally lack the deductive and compelling kind of treatment used in hard science and mathematics.

Dilemmas in Materialist Psychology

(i) When one asks an atheist how he or she knows some fact or claim to be correct, his or her justification is inevitably based on science. But, as we have previously noted, science provides no ability to conclusively certify any scientific law, theory, or principle. The materialist in general and the naturalist in particular do not possess a criterion for truth, only for consistency. This is the ages-old problem recognized by the ancient Greek philosophers and given its proper due by them.[22] However, absence of a truth criterion is often unrecognized or ignored in science or materialism, evidently because many materialists (and others) deny or ignore the need for a conclusive test of truth to justify their assertions or of the complete lack of such a test in science. They seem so preoccupied with their own understanding of the material universe they do not consider that their tentative and contingent science-based view may not correspond to truth or that an alternative view may be superior.

(ii) A basic tool the materialist tacitly believes to be powerful is objective and rigorous observation and analysis. Based on these tools science is regarded as capable of (eventually) providing universal understanding of all phenomena. However, objective observation requires a material object or an object outside of mind which may be independently sensed and examined by many who then reach a common conclusion about the nature of the object. (The definition of *objective* invokes such requirements.) Psychology and psychiatry deal with objects that are at least partially and often wholly in the mind. Multiple observers can examine such objects and even reach a consensus in general terminology (definitions) commonly learned from common case studies. But the objects are not accessible to objective observation or examination. Psychology and psychiatry are art rather than science.

Indeed, when one regards observation and analysis rigorously, fully objective observation and analysis of even material objects is probability beyond human capability (Book I). A person possesses neither capabilities for fully objective observation nor can he or she analyze observed facts in a fully objective manner. Even the most basic observations and analyses are paradigm dependent and paradigm, in the absence of any *a priori* truth criterion, is subjectively chosen and held.

(iii) Many facts are language- and culture-formulable entities. The truth of and in facts will always be semantics or language and culture dependent. Indeed, it is by alteration of language that the logical positivist or linguistic analyst wants to make science infallible. But such an ambition is probably non-realizable because of the huge problem it presents in accomplishing it for all cultures. Who wants to eliminate confusion in science by "dumbing down" their language and culture?

In the view of Ludwig Wittgenstein, the debate over truth claims becomes a language game.[23] Every language has its own vocabulary and rules and any may be utilized to express some fact *in a social or cultural context*. All language practice is culturally dependent and no language captures any fundamental structure of reality. Reason obtains only in the context of paradigm (culture). "The ideal language," "inductive logic," and "the empiricist criterion of significance" are "fantasies of the positivist."[24] Within human philosophy the only truth one can recognize is that *defined* by one's culture (paradigm).[13] It follows that different cultures may hold different truths, a fact confirmed by observation. When one addresses the issue of and seeks absolute truth, as we do in this book, one learns that a Source beyond a human one must be approached to obtain it and it must be done in the manner He has prescribed. No other prescription will suffice and no other effective one is offered or contemplated for providing conclusive proof.

(iv) Materialist views of mind are fraught with difficulty. What the materialist cannot explain is the ability of a person to think self-selected thoughts in any sequence he or she desires. In materialism, mental activity exists in the brain in the form of physical activity of atomic and subatomic particles, e.g., electrons. In materialism, thoughts are controlled by physical predisposition of active brain material, not by nonmaterial mind. According to materialism, consciousness does not exist.[13] And without consciousness there exists neither comprehension of meaning discovered by "lived experience," reason, and feeling nor any agency. Yet we intentionally think, we willfully act, we are aware of much that transpires around us and of the implications of our observations as if we were conscious; and we acquire real experience by which we reason, feel, and comprehend meaning. That is because mind must exist above and beyond materialist brain for persons to be aware of what occurs around them and, to some extent, what will occur in the future. Such awareness exceeds expected mental activity according to a materialist-brain model in which a mental process depends only on physical predisposition of active brain materials.

(v) One recurring theme of the materialist is that "If one cannot observe and measure it, it does not exist." "Materialism fallaciously believes that if events are realized physically, then their tenets are proved. At the very least, materialists are obliged to take an agnostic position with regard to an ontology of consciousness. Just because one cannot directly observe or measure conscious phenomena, this does not mean that neurophysiology is all there is. ... this is a naturalistic or reductive fallacy."[13] Even if one can measure activity correlated with mental processes, that does not mean that a cause-and-effect relationship is established. The mind-body problem is deep and complex relative to human knowledge. Although a mind may be physically located in the brain, it is not localized there. Rather, it is free to wander where and when it (a person-owner) will. Observed psychological facts will not equate to understanding until our knowledge of deep and complex psychological issues is tremendously improved and understanding may not occur even then. At present we don't fully understand even the simplest phenomena of mind on the basis of science. Understanding of emotion, volition, and meaning are now beyond science.

(vi) According to the materialist, the human being is the product of biology and environment. Yet we all appear to have functionally-similar biology. And many multiples of similar persons experience similar and even nearly identical environments. How, then, does the diversity seen in human beings arise in cases of common heredity and environment? One possible explanation is that the unconscious self (in its nonmaterial form) or pre-earth experience, denied or ignored by materialists, gives full and unique personality to each individual, often even when mortal biologies and environments are identical.

(vii) Reductionism and naturalism invoke unknown causal explanations as well as unspecified physical preconditions necessary to mental activity that preclude free will. This concept is equivalent to one we have expressed in different terms, i.e., determinism precludes free will. Materialists believe that humans possess no more mental power beyond material function of a material brain than any other physical object or system. Consciousness and action are not directed by mind but rather by quantum mechanics (in the next sections we pursue this topic). Free will as a mental capability is thereby precluded. We do not possess the ability to choose, according to materialism, and consequently we are not free. Rather, our thoughts and actions are constrained by physical conditions that cause particular sequences of thoughts and actions. In this context we can appreciate the conclusion of Descartes that his method of doubt indicated free and independent thinking and that he therefore existed as a free and independent person.

Freedom involves at least two levels: freedom to think or to will and freedom to act. Mills regards agency as being "telic, purposeful, and self directed via choices and deliberation in judgements constituting self-conscious activity. Therefore, thoughts, volitional intentions, and behaviors are the activities of the will: freedom is ultimately defined as the ability to choose or *be* [or become] otherwise. ... agency, free will, intentionality, and final causality (e.g., choosing the grounds for the sake of which to behave) is problematic for the materialist, for physical matter is caused rather than being freely causal."[13]

The animal acts, the human wills to act, and Christians and some others will to will. While materialists tend to define freedom in terms of action, what is more important and more significantly human is volition or will to act. Volition precedes and controls action and is consequently the more fundamental and important of the two.[25] Actions are easily dealt with in materialism but not volition or any material-predisposition cause of psychogenesis. For the materialist, desire and choice are not free but are imposed by physical predisposition in the form of material states. That one can think or do "otherwise," apparently whatever one desires, transcends the reductionism/naturalism theories of human mental function.

(viii) With regard to the assumption of physical reductionism, by which substance and function of an object may be fully represented by substance and function of its component parts, Philip Anderson and Daniel Stein[26] considered dissipative structures and systems in thermodynamic equilibrium. They found that for complex physical systems, properties due to self-organization spontaneously emerge that are apparently unrelated to any constituent part of the system. Such behavior, now denoted by the term *emergence* – the concept that order and function spontaneously arise in complex systems containing many interacting parts – is believed to be a broadly encountered phenomenon in complex systems.[27]

Mark Buchanan has proposed that a better definition of reductionism would be "a system that can be fully understood in terms of its parts *and the interactions between them*."[28] He has also noted that "Network architecture is a property not of parts but of the whole."[28] Indeed, the very scope and focus of physics is evolving dramatically. Recent studies in sociology, neurology, cell biology, communication networks, and other such subjects have been led or participated in by physicists. Physics as a search for cause-and-effect relationships that explain *how* material phenomena occur is being superceded by a study of order encountered in material systems and its effects in explaining function on a *how* level. Physicists Robert Laughlin and David Pines, in a paper entitled *The Theory of Everything*, state that

> The central task of theoretical physics in our time is no longer to write down the ultimate equations but rather to catalogue and understand emergent behavior in its many guises including, potentially, life itself. We call this physics of the next century the study of complex adaptive matter ... we are now witnessing a transition from the science of the past, so intimately linked to reductionism, to the study of complex adaptive matter ... with its hope for providing a jumping-off point for new discoveries, new concepts, and new wisdom.[29]

(ix) Beyond issues of reductionism and adaptation or emergence, the scientific view of the world (universe) has evolved such that matter no longer occupies a central role. Questions like "What is a particle?" are no longer answerable like they once seemed to be. What was once regarded as matter, e.g., particles, is now tentatively regarded as energy, fields, waves, strings, p-branes, probability density, or even holes. That is, our improved understanding is confusing. To be sure, our questions are improving and that must precede finding correct answers; but we can't yet be certain we have *any*. This situation leaves traditional materialism and objective science without foundation. Materialist theories, once regarded, by at least some, as rigorous and indubitable because of their solid foundation of careful, reproducible observation of the material world, are now supplanted by theories founded on mathematics, aesthetics, symmetry, or other more-abstract bases. Some materialists have been left behind in the accelerating pace of change and they still cling to their old habit of indubitable thinking unaware that scientific perception of the world has changed.

- - - - -

The above dilemmas suggest conceptions of brain and mental capability in materialism are simplistic and fallacious and lead to inconsistency and dilemma in comparisons with observation (and reason). Recognizing that reductionism as used in the past is inadequate and misleading, especially in highly linked, complex systems like the brain, materialism presently suggests no mechanism or justification that psychogenic knowledge or "proof" is based on desire and belief. Indeed, independent desire and belief are rejected in materialist psychology. Claiming that Christian faith is a psychogenic response to desire and belief may be motivated by desire and belief.

Seeing an image for which we are searching can be caused, at least fleetingly, by recognition of known features identical or merely similar to some in the expected image. Experiencing a previously unknown epiphany is something else indeed.

Materialist psychology proscribes independent or deliberate thought. According to materialist psychology, you did not choose to read this book but are doing so because predisposition of material states in your brain "made you do it."[30] Neither did I choose to write it nor is its composition due to independent or deliberate thinking. Indeed, why need we a book or you or me at all in view of the role of predisposition? If brain function is wholly, internally, materially predisposed, no reality outside of it is required or pertinent.

What remains to be discovered by some scientists and others is that objective science alone (materialism) is inadequate for study of the human person, e.g., the mind-body problem.

Determinism versus Free Will

We now approach the mind-body problem and the problem of free will from a perspective different from the materialist-psychology perspective examined above, namely, from a more fundamental and rigorous perspective of hard-physics science.

In science many have come to believe that physical laws control and determine all phenomena. Others instead advocate that physical laws emerge from all phenomena or the collective milieu. Nobel Prize winning physicist Robert B. Laughlin describes the latter belief as follows.

> The transition to the Age of Emergence brings to an end the myth of the absolute power of mathematics. This myth is still entrenched in our culture, unfortunately, a fact revealed routinely in the press and popular publications promoting the search for ultimate laws as the only scientific activity worth pursuing, notwithstanding massive and overwhelming experimental evidence that exactly the opposite is the case. ... Law instead follows from collective behavior, as do things that flow from it, such as logic and mathematics. The reason our minds can anticipate and master what the physical world does is not because we are geniuses but because nature facilitates understanding by organizing itself and generating law.[31]

Laughlin and like-minded colleagues have adopted a new scientific vision and, as a result, further diversified science. That is, science has become more confusing to scientist and nonscientists alike. Unfortunately, the new view does not eliminate the scientific method or its fundamental flaws and inherent limitations.

The former belief is illustrated in Chapter 9 in addressing a TOE (theory of everything) by which, at least in principle, all phenomena may be described and predicted. Were a universe controlled by such a TOE it might be absolutely deterministic, i.e., all events might be irreversibly fixed by fundamental law. In deterministic thinking, once the universe is started it simply runs thereafter, automatically and invariantly in its predestined course. Such a view of the universe is a natural inductive extension of scientific law that has been used to predict and describe external-world physical phenomena. But in a fully deterministic reality in which behavior is imposed, where is free will or agency?

As you may already anticipate from previously discussed failure of either science or philosophy to establish the nature or existence of reality, science has not demonstrated that the universe, including humans, is fully deterministic and it is unlikely ever to do so because science is inherently incapable of establishing conclusive truth of any theory, law, or principle, especially – as Hawking has pointed out (Chapter 14) – if its not already programmed into a deterministic universe. While science focuses on objective observation, humans are fundamentally subjective, participative, and disruptive. We argue scientifically that the universe is likely *not* deterministic or, at least, we now have no basis for claiming that it is because absolute determinism could be proscribed by any one of (at least) the following four reasons.

(1) According to present scientific knowledge, *atomic and subatomic phenomena are not fully deterministic because they are instead probabilistic*. Consequently, we think phenomena are *almost* always correctly predicted on a whole, large-system basis when they involve a large number of small systems and quantum

mechanics and quantum statistical mechanics provide (a) what *possible* states these small systems may obtain and (b) in what proportions the small systems are *probably* distributed over these possible states. But, the state of any single microscopic component is not established when the whole, large-system state is only statistically established. Such a "leak in the dike of determinism" has been utilized by scientists in arguing against absolute determinism and for free will.

(2) Another cause that may preclude absolute determinism is *complex, nonlinear phenomena (sometimes denoted chaotic phenomena).* This cause may render the behavior of complex systems fundamentally unpredictable, at least by us. An interesting view of the impact of complexity or chaos on the utility of science is the following one of Ian Malcolm (a fictional character of Michael Crichton).

> All this attempt at control ... We are talking about Western attitudes that are five hundred years old. ... The basic idea of science – that there was a new way to look at reality, that it was objective, that it did not depend on your beliefs or your nationality, that it was *rational* – that idea was fresh and exciting back then.
>
> But now science is the belief system that is hundreds of years old. And, like the medieval system before it, science is starting not to fit the world anymore. Science has attained so much power that its practical limits begin to be apparent. ... Science can make a nuclear reactor, but it cannot tell us not to build it. Science can make pesticide, but it cannot tell us not to use it. And our world starts to seem polluted in fundamental ways – air, and water, and land – because of ungovernable science. ...
>
> At the same time, the greatest intellectual justification of science has vanished. Ever since Newton and Descartes, science has explicitly offered us the vision of total control. Science has claimed the power to eventually control everything, through its understanding of natural laws. But in the twentieth century, that claim has been shattered beyond repair. First, Heisenberg's uncertainty principle set limits on what we could know about the subatomic world. Oh well, we say. None of us lives in a subatomic world. It doesn't make any practical difference as we go through our lives. Then Gödel's theorem set similar limits to mathematics, the formal language of science. Mathematicians used to think that their language had some special inherent trueness that derived from the laws of logic. Now we know that what we call 'reason' is just an arbitrary game. It's not special, in the way we thought it was.
>
> And now chaos theory proves that unpredictability is built into our daily lives. It is as mundane as the rainstorm we cannot predict. And so the grand vision of science, hundreds of years old – the dream of total control – has died, in our century. ...
>
> We are witnessing the end of the scientific era. Science, like other outmoded systems, is destroying itself. As it gains in power, it proves itself incapable of handling the power. ... And that will force everyone to ask the same question – What should I do with my power? – which is the very question science says it cannot answer.[32] (the italics are Crichton's)

(3) A third cause that may preclude absolute determinism joins the mix with this book, namely, human disruption or *scrambling of the local universe by agents exercising free will.* Although, as we shall shortly see, free will has long been considered as a basic property of humans in the universe, "scrambling theory," in essence that free will of independent agents is a fundamental causative process in the universe, may be new in at least some of its aspects. Exercise of agency by a person alters (scrambles) deterministic phenomena occurring in the universe precluding

absolute determinism. The conventional view in science is that objective, non-participative observation is used to discover an idealized "external world of science" from which the laws that govern the universe may be envisioned, extracted, and used. But humans actively participate in the universe. We ignite forest fires, produce and release halocarbons, and detonate nuclear bombs all of which are causative of subsequent, not-always-predictable effects. On a cultural level many also believe in Christ and share their belief with others. Such belief influences a person's volition and, thereby, through his or her activity causes effects in both the material- and nonmaterial-universe. A person does not detachedly hide behind a curtain and observe, as supposed in an ideal, material, external world of science. He or she participates in natural (physical), mental, social, and spiritual, i.e., total-universe, phenomena. External-world science applies only in an ideal, external world.

(4) If physical law and associated organization such as logic and mathematics emerge from all phenomena, the collective milieu, and if we humans possess agency and our independent acts are part of the collective milieu from which physical law emerges, then physical law does not preclude agency but derives, in part, from it. Agency does not exclude universal physical law, but individual and collective human behavior, because of agency and enemy influence, may be irrational and disruptive.

Incidently, it is difficult to argue against determinism without an answer to an ultimate question. The determinist only has to maintain that universal law causes everything to happen the way it does, no matter what the process or event. But scrambling theory is also difficult to dismiss. Events may be subtly and invisibly caused or influenced by an earlier act, especially in a non-local universe.

Beyond a scientific quest to learn *how* things occur lie deeper questions of *who*, *what*, and *why*. If free will and independent behavior do not exist, we are mere intellectual and physical automatons following imposed law, beings whose acquired knowledge and even existence have little or no meaning. While such a possibility would be of little consequence to the scientific quest of seeking answers to *how* questions, so long as we got answers like materialist psychologists seek in their mindless theories (i.e., theories in which existence of mind is rejected), it would be of great consequence in answering questions of *who*, *what*, and *why* and especially of *meaning*.

Thus, some physicists have addressed the issue of free will from a viewpoint that transcends physics. Edwin T. Jaynes is one[33] with two others being John Stewart Bell and Wolfgang Pauli (who considered not only physics but also his dreams), all three of whom we have already met. Finnish physicist K. V. Laurikainen (1916-1997) is a fourth. Quantum mechanics is regarded as the most fundamental theory of science and the last three cite indeterminacy of atomic-level processes in quantum mechanics being probabilistic rather than deterministic as a break from absolute determinism. Bell's and Pauli's thoughts on free will are described in their papers and letters; Bell's are found in his earlier-cited book *Speakable and unspeakable in quantum mechanics* and Pauli's are discussed in Laurikainen's book *Beyond the Atom: The Philosophical Thought of Wolfgang Pauli.*[34] But our primary focus here is Laurikainen's views incorporating some views of others, especially Pauli.

Laurikainen described his views in a number of papers, one being a 1990 paper *Quantum Theory and the Problem of Free Will*[35] having the following summary.

> The statistical laws of quantum mechanics give rise to a new conception of causality, and, *a fortiori*,[36] to a new ontological view, as Wolfgang Pauli ... pointed out. What is characteristic of this new conception of reality is a *freedom* to choose between different alternatives in individual phenomena. Thus the "material world" is presupposed to have also "psychic aspects" such as *free will* which influences phenomena in the "material world." If this freedom is considered ... basic ..., [the] possibility [exists] for reintroducing *teleology* and the idea of *continuous creation* into the scientific view of the world.[35]

To introduce two alternative views, Laurikainen describes a debate by correspondence on the nature or interpretation of science between Göttfried Wilhelm Leibniz and Samuel Clarke, a philosopher and theologian who was perhaps Isaac Newton's most distinguished student. In November 1715 Leibniz replied to a question asked of Clarke by the princess of Wales which included the now-famous challenge:

> Sir Isaac Newton, and his followers, have also a very odd opinion concerning the work of God. According to their doctrine, God Almighty wants to wind up his watch from time to time: otherwise it would cease to move. He had not, it seems, sufficient foresight to make it a perpetual motion.[37]

What followed was an exchange of five letters each – a total of ten letters – between Leibniz and Clarke, the latter a dedicated Newtonian writing for the princess. Each letter became longer as the refutations addressed more detail. The death of Leibniz in November 1716 ended the correspondence.

Leibniz took the position of a determinist, considering the world to be controlled by absolutely causal law. In his view, God never needs to interfere because everything takes place according to God's plan by which everything is predestined.

Newton's philosophy, presented by Clarke, was not deterministic. He believed God providentially intercedes but that humans have free will and this is a major factor in the determination of history. Newton believed that God Himself cannot foresee the future because of human-free-will choices. Nevertheless, according to Clarke (Newton), God shepherds important events.

This debate highlights two fundamental views on causality. In one, predestination or determinism completely controls every outcome. In the other, humans together with providential influence of God control their own destiny through their free will. While the language of this debate was religious, the fundamental concepts are those of the two principal scientific schools on the issue of free will today.

Today these two views are considered in the probabilistic and statistical concepts of quantum mechanics and statistical mechanics. In these theories various possible states of a (sub)system are each completely defined but none are explicitly predicted. That is, quantum mechanics exactly describes the system properties for all possible states of a quantum system and whenever a measurement is made a system is found to be in one of the predicted states, i.e., the "wave function collapses" or a "reduction of state" occurs to one of the predicted states. How the wave function of the system "collapses" or the system "reduces" to a particular state and how this state is selected remain "mysterious" or, as Laurikainen prefers, "irrational." But two schools of thought, those of determinism and free will, have each adopted their own view.

One school believes that any particular "collapsed" state is selected by pure chance. Incorporating pure chance into quantum and statistical mechanics, the universe is governed by deterministic laws *and* pure chance. The introduction of pure chance has had significant impact in philosophy as indicated by such statements as "people are no longer accustomed to searching for unifying principles in science"[35] and "the belief in a coherent wholeness of the world has disappeared."[35] Laurikainen describes the advent of this pure-chance plus determinism theory as representing an extremely critical juncture in science. Pure chance, while it leads to uncertainty in any specific case, provides an increasingly accurate but never infallible prediction the greater the number of identical systems or processes involved. And identical molecules occur in great numbers in all observable systems. Laurikainen's concern is that because of an apparently complete description of all basic processes provided by the combination of pure chance and determinism "the most fundamental and most important questions of existence will completely disappear from our mental horizon."[35]

The belief of the other school is that while the "reduction in state" or "collapse of the wave function" is a fundamentally irrational (mysterious) process which cannot be predicted by any known theory, it is *not* properly represented by pure chance but by freedom or "actualization," the ability to fix a choice or to determine a selected alternative. The situation is described by Laurikainen in the summary statement: "laws of nature allow free choices between different alternatives."[35]

This statement begs the question: Who or what makes the choice? Those of the first school would answer pure chance. Those of the second, according to Laurikainen, invoke the (teleological) providential influence of God or regard the universe as consisting of matter and spirit in which the material world is governed by strict causality while the spiritual world is independent of causal laws and the combination of the two introduces the *psychophysical problem.* Suppose, reasons Laurikainen, "we consider causality to be statistical rather than deterministic. Then the material world (or phenomenal world) remains open to 'influences' on the statistics which do not belong to this world." "One can see freedom of expression of the spiritual element of the world. It appears as free choices which ... give direction to processes…"[35]

"Do elementary particles have the capacity of 'willing' something?"[35] In the philosophy of materialism they do not because the existence of intelligence or spirit in matter is denied by postulation. But considering alternatives to materialism "we run against very profound questions."[35]

In a materialistic, deterministic view of the universe, a *teleological* or purpose-driven interpretation of reality may seem to be precluded but, as we shall see, it is not. In a non-teleological view the universe is merely a fixed material system apparently constrained to certain behavior by law that does not spontaneously strive toward some purpose or goal. But, in principle, a spiritual component of the universe and freedom of choice among alternative states allow expression of teleology.

"The solution presupposed in the evolutionary theories of today can be called a *religion of chance.* It is so cleverly hidden under the carpet of scientific argumentation that one does not see the basic decision which determines the direction of the investigation. In fact, the argumentation is based on one definite belief: that in reality there is nothing like free choices which could steer the progress of phenomena."[35]

In theory of evolution each step involves a choice, "and there is no scientific motivation for excluding teleology from these choices."[35]

Ontological implications, implications relating to existence or being, of quantum mechanics are of high interest, evident in the various interpretations of quantum mechanics summarized and discussed in the previous chapter. But quantum theory provides no unique interpretation of existence or reality, with different possibilities being preferred by different scientists.

Laurikainen concludes "The world cannot be fully described by purely rational [deterministic] theories. Therefore it is not right that logical requirements are used for atheistic propaganda and for strengthening materialistic beliefs. Science has not any right [basis] to deprive people of the faith on the meaningfulness of existence ..."[35]

It seems to me that modern scripture directly implies a solution to Laurikainen's psychophysical problem. Moses taught that all things were created by God spiritually before they were created materially.[38] God taught that He commanded and the elements obeyed,[39] which implies that the elements are physical, spiritual, and intelligent.[40] Why did they obey? Because obedience leads to joy.[41] Thus, God directs the universe through voluntary obedience. This organization is the basis of the physical laws we observe, the explanation of the emergence of ultimate collective behavior. It is also the basis of exceptions to physical laws we call miracles.

Discovering Deity

Natural processes may be regarded as teleological or directed toward a purpose. Who or what motivates such processes? The Motivator is either an Intelligent Designer in the person of God or a *de facto* designer in mindless nature, with the net result being the same, i.e., the universe is what it is. By the second law of thermodynamics the entropy of the earth system, including its reservoirs of life, continually decreases – yes, I said decreases. Since decrease in entropy corresponds to increase in order and organization, earth material is continually ordered and organized in a continuing creation of life and life supporting resources. Many authors have incorrectly interpreted this law to justify an opposite conclusion.[42] But the correct conclusion is simply demonstrated using the law by which entropy of a *non-isolated* system (earth) changes with the transfer of heat (a process which renders the earth non-isolated): $\Delta S = Q/T$, where ΔS is the change in entropy of the earth system, Q is the quantity of heat transferred to the system, and T is the absolute temperature of the heat source or of the heat itself.[43] The earth receives from the sun and radiates to outer space average radiant heat Q per day. (Otherwise average earth temperature would not be nearly constant.) Consequently, the net change of the earth's entropy per day is given by

$$\Delta S = Q/T_s - Q/T_e = Q\,(T_e - T_s)/T_e T_s,$$

where T_s and T_e are the absolute temperatures of the sun and earth surfaces. Because the sun is hotter than the earth, $T_e - T_s$ is negative and the entropy of the earth is continually decreasing. This concept is not new but it was imperfectly understood by Ludwig Boltzmann at the end of the nineteenth-century. Boltzmann, a believer in Darwin's evolution, then wrote (with my additions in square brackets)

> The overall struggle for existence of living beings is therefore not a struggle for raw materials – the raw materials of all organisms are available in excess in the air, water, and ground – nor for energy, which in the form of heat is plentiful in every body, but rather a struggle for [elimination of] entropy, which becomes available in the flow of energy from the hot sun to the cold earth [and then to colder space].[44]

In promoting order and organization on the earth, the second law of thermodynamics together with heat transfer may be regarded as teleological, i.e., as following a design or purpose. This result presents something of a teleological dilemma because the second law of thermodynamics is derived from the assumptions that molecules are governed by known laws of motion and pure chance.[45] Thus, the deterministic and random natures of the underlying processes, consisting of deterministic mechanics and random chance, mask the teleological nature of the overall process resulting from these underlying ones. We might have expected such a result because God has revealed how He may be discovered and known[46] and it is not by science.

The issue of free will versus determinism has a resolution in a belief in Christ and simple reason on the level of *who*, *what*, and *why*.[47] If a mortal truly possesses independence or agency and the challenge of life is to find and follow truth, each mortal must be free to choose on the basis of faith (which is the only available basis anyway) without compelling physical or intellectual constriction in his or her choices, i.e., by compelling force or *a priori* knowledge. In other words, conclusive knowledge of absolute truth is to be obtained only in the way its Author has declared. An Intelligent Designer who planned the continuing creation of life on earth would therefore accomplish His purpose leaving no compelling material (scientific) evidence of His "trail." The choice to believe in Christ is to be freely embraced as a volitive act which is only thereafter ostensibly confirmed. Indeed, unique access to ostensible understanding is provided for this most important kind of knowledge, available by the Christian test prescribed in the next chapter. While the requirements of this test may strike one as too demanding (demeaning?) for intelligent, responsible (proud?) adults, a similar leap of faith is also required in science with the difference that no confirmation of truth, no *yes* answer, is either promised or contemplated in science. The test of life is not exercise of faith, which is universally required, but whether or not one chooses to place faith in Christ counter to real opposition, with no middle position available (Appendix I).

Agents Free to Find, Follow, and Create Truth

Neither agency nor its consequences and meaning are yet even remotely understood by means of science. Lack of understanding is largely imposed by the view of physics described by Pauli as "the ideal of the detached observer" in which an observer cannot influence what he or she observes of the possibly predestined course of nature. Such a role provides no meaning for the observer who, like undisturbed nature, is predestined in his or her lack of any participation beyond unobtrusive observation, precluding any significance except observing and discovering the facts of undisturbed nature. When one is attempting to discover the facts and laws of an external-world nature, such a role may be desirable. But if one wants also to understand and comprehend people and meaning, the role of the detached observer must be expanded to that of the involved observer able to view, participate, and influence, i.e., one must consider the real universe.

My view of the natures of agency and determinism is probably different than Laurikainen's, but I cannot be sure. I certainly reach it by a different route of simple reasoning, one principal leg of which is that reality is not fully described by objective facts and, therefore, by science alone. My scrambling-theory view is simply that the power to observe, participate, influence, and reason resides in every normal adult. When one *acts*, the deterministic, material universe or "nature" simply *reacts*. Within only one person's sphere of influence, that person, together with natural law, controls the universe. In a sphere influenced by many, the actions of the many and natural law control the universe. The material universe usually or exclusively reacts through natural law. Were we only hidden, unobtrusive observers, the course of events in the material universe might indeed be predetermined. But humans are not merely hidden observers. Natural law cannot control a person's thinking and acting if that person is independent or autonomous, as I believe each normal adult is: an agent endowed with intelligence and choice. One's agency does not consist of atomic-level uncertainty (so far as I can tell – here is the difficulty in relating my view to Laurikainen's) but rather it resides in one's ability to perform deliberate, volitional acts of will in mind and body. And by one's choices in these deliberate acts one influences the course of events in the universe and creates his or her own future state or truth, i.e., each writing our own end of truth either aligned with or opposed to Christ (with no middle ground; Appendix I). Through acts supporting values, like faith in Christ and charity or Christ-like love for humankind, one discovers meaning – the interactions of one with others in the total universe is manifest, say, in the understanding, comprehension of meaning, and feelings one acquires. Such "lived experience" is infinitely beyond what a hidden observer not interacting with or influencing the universe experiences. Such a materialist view is intentionally lacking in subjective feeling and values and meaning. Without agency and its wise expression there is no joy.

Likewise God is an Agent with choice and His thoughts and actions are only controlled by Him. The material universe can only react to Him through law or light that governs it.[48] When Christ turned water into wine, what was the consequence? The wine sat in its stone containers subject to laws of gravity and chemistry and was eventually enjoyed by the guests at the wedding feast because it tasted like other good wine.[49] When Christ walked on water, what was the consequence? It or something supported Him, of course, but the water otherwise behaved as regular water, as demonstrated in Peter's failed attempt to join Him.[50] Christ or His Father imposed a local, temporary change of the water or of natural law of some kind to which the universe simply reacted. Indeed, the power of God is the law by which all things are governed.[48] When He is not imposing an irregular (miraculous) process, regular law applies and natural reaction, but only reaction, of the universe to His acts necessarily follows not only miracles but all obtrusive and deliberate acts of God and of any independent agent. And by His obtrusive and deliberate acts God guides and responds to our own, as we seek His guidance and influence in (by) our lives. He has promised us such assistance if we will but receive it (Chapter 12). In the words of scripture,

> All truth is independent in that sphere in which God has placed it, to act for itself, as all intelligence also; otherwise there is no existence. Behold, here is the agency of man, and here is the condemnation of man; because that which was from the beginning [Christ] is plainly manifest unto them [if they will receive it], and they receive not the light.[51]

As stated, by choice each individual establishes the way things will be for him or her in the future – that is, by intelligence and agency one writes one's own future truth. Without independence (agency) there is no present freedom or self-established future, no autonomous truth beyond God. Do you think God, who made us agents free to think, choose, and act, will decide who we will be? Our agency is either opportunity or condemnation. If we fail to utilize it well, if we don't seek to follow and establish truth, we condemn ourselves to endless torment in ever wondering what might have been. Those who utilize well their opportunity to discover and follow truth find eternal fullness of joy (Book III). For that which was from the beginning (Christ) is plainly manifest to all who seek to find, follow, and establish truth.

While the test of mortality is difficult, the difficulty does not reside in recognizing which of these two alternatives is most desirable.

A Holistic View

We have reached the end of Book II, our summary of science. We sought in Book II a knowledge of reality by establishing connections over an inclusive scope of objective facts and scientific method. But progress in science and all fields depends on a more comprehensive range of facts and a more powerful method providing an improved view of reality, as others have expressed. Wolfgang Pauli stated

> When the layman says 'reality' he usually thinks that he is speaking about something which is self-evidently known; while to me it appears to be specifically the most important and extremely difficult task of our time to work on the elaboration of a new idea of reality. This is also what I mean when I emphasize that science and religion *must* have something to do with one another.[52] (the italics are Pauli's)

Improved science, philosophy, and religion will rely on expanded knowledge or, without it, progress will be halted. The present view of reality in science is tentative and incomplete as are diverse views described by other philosophy and many denominations of Christianity and other religions. In every unsuccessful search for truth an adequate truth criterion, a reliable *yes* answer, is lacking.

Use of science in its usual manner requires faith in its usual assumptions. Similar requirements apply in philosophy and religion. Yet E. T. Jaynes observed that "Throughout the history of science, it has been doubt, and not faith, that first points the way to new advances."[53] Jaynes continues,

> [But] to anyone who has new ideas of a currently unconventional kind ... *Do not allow yourself to be discouraged or deflected from your course by negative criticisms ...* unless they exhibit some clear and specific error of reasoning or conflict with experiment. Unless they can do this, your critics are almost certainly wrong, but to reply by trying to show exactly where and why they are wrong would not convince your critics and would only keep you from the far more important, constructive things that you might have

> accomplished in the same time. Let others deal with them; if you allow your enemies to direct your work, then they have won after all.
>
> Although the arguments of your critics are almost certainly wrong, they will retain just enough plausibility in the minds of some to maintain a place for them in the realm of controversy; that is just a fact of life that you must accept as the price of doing creative work [independent thinking]. Take comfort in the historical record, which shows that no creative person [independent thinker] has ever been able to escape this; the more fundamental the new idea, the more bitter the controversy it will stir up. Newton, Darwin, Boltzmann, Pasteur, Einstein, Wegener [and Peter, Paul, John, Joseph, Christ] were all embroiled in [controversy]. Newton wrote in 1676: '*I see a man must either resolve to put out nothing new, or become a slave to defend it.*' ... We revere the names of James Clerk Maxwell and J. Willard Gibbs [and Jesus Christ]; yet their work was never fully appreciated in their lifetimes, and even today it is still ... under attack by persons who, after a Century [or twen-ty], have not yet comprehended their message.[54]

The earlier-quoted prescription of M. Scott Peck (page 183) indicates that this human malady of resisting improved understanding is general, including independent searching for spiritual truth and meaning. To better one's self in a non-passive, contrary universe is to meet resistance, whether in seeking new knowledge in science or answers to ultimate questions relating to spiritual meaning.

All dimensions of reality help define and are important to understanding it, to borrow a thought from EPR. Each dimension is necessary for specifying and appraising reality. Science and the objective are therefore useful in understanding reality, but can be a barrier. The behavioral arts are useful, but can be barriers. Scriptural knowledge may be deep and broadly applicable, but (supposed) scriptural knowledge can also be a barrier. One's limitations in understanding generally lie partly in his or her limits of knowledge, partly in (self) imposed barriers and preconceptions including incorrect traditions, and partly in inadequate philosophy or paradigm. An unrestricted scope of thinking, thinking beyond the barriers, especially in the matter of faith in Christ and associated desire and intent, will lead to new insight and understanding of truth. To the extent one is diligent and persistent, ignoring negative criticism and resistance in an honest quest for truth by methodology we describe in Book III, personal knowledge will be ever-expanding in truth and therefore in utility and importance.

Understanding of reality must contain elements of science, religion, philosophy, the behavioral arts, i.e., a full spectrum of knowledge. Truth is found in all these categories and can be discerned by the power of God (the Holy Ghost).[55] In truth they are all complementary, not adversarial.[56] Understanding of reality is holistic, drawing on and building understanding of all things. The glory of God is intelligence.[57]

The only essential and reliable source of knowledge of absolute reality or universal truth is God because He alone understands it absolutely and is capable of communicating both it and its meaning to us. And He has expressed the desire to so enlighten those who will receive Him. Yet the world, even Christianity for the most part, is lost in erroneous tradition, has forgotten or refuses to hearken to His word, has rejected and changed His laws, altered His church, and ignored or rejected His power and guidance. Unfortunately, human need for truth is not generally matched by faith in the Source of Truth, and by desire, effort, and intent in seeking it. But God hears and responds to those who seek Him, as we consider next in Book III.

Notes and References for Chapter 11.

[1] Early thoughts on memory or knowledge as a biomolecular material are reviewed by Collins, Harry, and Trevor Pinch, *The Golem,* Second Edition, Cambridge University Press, Cambridge, England, 1998, 5-25. See endnote 7 of Chapter 4 and endnote 3 of Chapter 1.

[2] Life-giving function of a spirit is indicated in *Bible,* Genesis 2:7; a spirit's premortal origin is indicated in Hebrews 12:9. Mark 3:11,15,22-30, 5:1-20, 7:24-30, 9:14-29 all depict unlawful possession of a body by unclean spirits that have memory, awareness, reasoning power, volition ...

[3] See endnote 21 of Chapter 10.

[4] *Pearl of Great Price,* Abraham 4:1 reads "And then the Lord said: Let us go down. And they went down at the beginning, and they, that is the Gods, *organized* and *formed* the heavens and the earth." (italics added) The term "created" in Genesis 1:1 takes the sense of "shaped, fashioned, organized, or formed." It is incorrect to infer that nothing existed before the heavens and earth were created.

[5] Many scriptures refer to events that occurred in a pre-earth life we experienced in heaven. These include *Bible,* Job 38:7-8, Isaiah 14:12-16, Luke 10:18, John 9:2, 14:26-27, Revelation 5, 12:7, *Book of Mormon,* 2 Nephi 2:17, Alma 13:3, *Doctrine and Covenants* 29:36, 76:25, *Pearl of Great Price,* Moses 4:3, Abraham 3:22, 4:26, 5:2.

[6] *Doctrine and Covenants* 6:23 reads: "Did I not speak peace to your mind concerning the matter? What greater witness can you have than from God?" Different Christians have experienced a variety of experiences that have led to various beliefs. We assert that knowledge revealed by God never contradicts other knowledge revealed by God. The knowledge most complete in guidance should predominate in answering questions on which it bears. Knowledge is always revealed with a purpose, such as to answer a question. Guidance is most illuminating taking cognizance of both question and answer; an answer to one question doesn't necessarily apply to a different one. Confusion in Biblical teachings arise in Paul's seemingly clear answers to unknown questions.

[7] Wilson, Edward O., *Consilience, The Unity of Knowledge,* A. A. Knopf, New York, 1998, 268-269.

[8] Statistics is tricky because (as compellingly argued by Jaynes, E. T., *Probability Theory,* Cambridge University Press, 2003) much if not most of statistics and its applications are confused *ad hockeries* (Ibid., 143). In hypothesis testing, one has not even asked a definite, well-posed question until alternative hypotheses have been specified (Ibid., 136). Indeed, Bayes' theorem stipulates that "unless observed facts are absolutely impossible on Hypothesis H_0, it is meaningless to ask how much those facts tend 'in themselves' to confirm or refute H_0." (Ibid.) Jaynes points out that in the warfare of recent times between science and religion, science advocates invoked "physical probability" seeking to strengthen the objectivity of their argument against those invoking only a "state of knowledge." Jaynes continues, "Yet to assert as fact something which cannot be either proved or disproved by observation of facts is the opposite of objectivity; it is to assert something that one could not possibly know to be true." (Ibid., 324-325) For this reason science, using probability theory, neither can make nor undermine conclusions about subjective matters.

Moreover, any observation by which the probability of a physical fact is asserted is subject to physical analysis dependent on initial conditions. For, once we understand a mechanism behind an observation, the result depends only on the initial conditions and the question is transformed into what are the probabilities of the initial conditions. In asking what the physical probability of an observation is, we have entered an infinite regress. (Ibid., 324) In stating that "objective evidence supporting [religion] is not strong" the Empiricist implies that his or her objective-probability evidence is strong (Wilson, loc. cit.). His or her assumption could not be more wrong.

Jaynes also observes that "new data that we insist on analyzing in terms of old ideas ... *cannot lead us out of the old ideas.* However many data we record and analyze, we may just keep repeating the same old errors, missing the same crucially important things that the experiment was competent to find. That is what ignoring prior information [or preconception] can do to us." (Ibid., xxvi)

[9] *Bible,* Job 38:4-7. [10] *Bible,* John 1:5.

[11] *Bible,* Matthew 5:16; Mark 4:22; Luke 8:17; *Book of Mormon,* 3 Nephi 12:16.

[12] *Book of Mormon,* 3 Nephi 18:24.

[13] Mills, Jon, "Five Dangers of Materialism," *Genetic, Social, and General Psychology Monographs* **128**, 2002, 5-27.

[14] Armstrong, D. M., *A Materialist Theory of Mind,* Routledge, Kegan and Paul, London, 1968; Lewis, D., "An Argument for the Identity Theory," *Journal of Philosophy* **63**, 1966, 17-25; Place, U. T., "Is Consciousness a Brain Process?" *The British Journal of Psychology* **47**, 1956, 42-51.

[15] Levin, M. E., *Metaphysics and the Mind-Body Problem,* Clarendon Press, Oxford, England, 1979; Putnam, H., "Psychological Predicates," in *Art, Mind, and Religion,* W. H. Capitan and D. D. Merrill (editors), University of Pittsburgh Press, Pittsburgh, 1967; Smart, J. J. C., "Sensations and Brain Processes," in *The Philosophy of Mind,* V. C. Chappell (editor), Prentice-Hall, Englewood Cliffs, 1962; Sober, E., "Putting the Function back into Functionalism," *Synthese* **64** (2), 1985, 165-193.

[16] Teller, P., "A Poor Man's Guide to Supervenience and Determination," *Southern Journal of Philosophy* **22** Supplement, 1983, 147.

[17] Churchland, P. M., "Eliminative Materialism and the Propositional Attitudes," *The Journal of Philosophy* **78**, 1981, 67-90; Stich, S. P., "What is a Theory of Mental Representation?" in *The Mind-Body Problem,* R. Warner and T. Szubka (editors), Blackwell, Oxford, England, 1994.

[18] Dretske, F., *Explaining Behavior: Reasons in a World of Causes,* MIT Press, Cambridge, MA, 1988; Dretske, F., *Naturalizing the Mind,* Bradford Books/MIT Press, Cambridge, MA, 1995; Fodor, J., *Psychosomatics: The Problem of Meaning in the Philosophy of Mind,* Bradford Books/ MIT Press, Cambridge, MA, 1987; Fodor, J., *In Critical Condition: Polemical Essays on Cognitive Science and the Philosophy of Mind,* Bradford Books/MIT Press, Cambridge, MA, 1998.

[19] Davidson, D., *Essays on Actions and Events,* Clarendon Press, Oxford, England, 1980.

[20] Descartes' Latin name is Cartesius. Thus, the coordinate system he invented in analytical geometry is called the Cartesian coordinate system and his concept of dualism is called Cartesian dualism.

[21] Quoted by Laurikainen, Kalervo Vihtori, "Wolfgang Pauli and the Copenhagen Interpretation," *Symposium on the Foundations of Modern Physics*, Pekka Lahti and Peter Mittelstaedt (editors), World Scientific, Singapore, 1985, 273-287. Also quoted at greater length by the same author in *Beyond the Atom: The Philosophical Thought of Wolfgang Pauli*, Springer-Verlag, Berlin, 1988, 60. Pauli's letter in which he authored this statement is found in the *Pauli Letter Collection* at CERN, Geneva, number 0014.51. This quote, directed to classical physics, also applies to modern physics.

[22] See the page-6 quotation of Draper.

[23] See *The Dictionary of Philosophy,* Dagobert D. Runes (editor), Citadel Press, New York, 2001, 596-597; www.utm.edu/research/iep; and Post, J. F., *Metaphysics,* Paragon, New York, 1991.

[24] Putnam, H., "Why Reason can't be Naturalized," in *Human Knowledge,* P. K. Moser and A. Vandernat (editors), Oxford University Press, Oxford, England, 1983, 355-365.

[25] *Bible,* Matthew 15:11, Mark 7:15,20,23, Hebrews 3:10, 4:12, James 3:6.

[26] Anderson, P. W., and D. L. Stein, "Broken Symmetry, Emergent Properties, Dissipative Structures, Life: Are They Related?" in *Self-Organizing Systems: The Emergence of Order,* F. E. Yates (editor), Plenum Press, New York, 1987.

[27] See Gleick, James, *Chaos: Making a New Science,* Penguin Books, New York, 1987; Waldrop, M. Mitchell, *Complexity,* Touchstone, New York, 1992; Strogatz, Steven, *SYNC: The Emerging Science of Spontaneous Order,* Hyperion, New York, 2003.

[28] Buchanan, Mark, *nexus,* W. W. Norton, New York, 2002, 185.

[29] Laughlin, Robert, and David Pines, "The Theory of Everything," *Proceedings of the National Academy of Science of the United States of America* **97**, 2000, 28-31. Laughlin, Robert B., *A Different Universe,* Basic Books, New York, 2005.

[30] What a boon to defense lawyers to learn "material predisposition of one's brain makes one do it." But what a bane to freedom and the law, both enabled by and based on personal responsibility.

[31] Laughlin, Robert B., *A Different Universe,* Basic Books, New York, 2005, 209.

[32] Ian Malcolm is a fictional character of Michael Crichton (in *Jurassic Park,* Ballantine Books, New York, 1990, 312-313). While Crichton addressed biological science in this insightful commentary, I altered his last paragraph by omissions (...) so that it applies generally to all science, which it does.

[33] Jaynes, Edwin T., "How Does the Brain Do Plausible Reasoning?" in *Maximum-Entropy and Bayesian Methods in Science and Engineering* (Volume 1), G. J. Erickson and C. R. Smith (editors), Kluwer Academic Publishers, Dordrecht, The Netherlands, 1988, 1-24.

[34] Laurikainen, K. V., *Beyond the Atom: The Philosophical Thought of Wolfgang Pauli,* loc. cit.

[35] Laurikainen, K. V., "Quantum Theory and the Problem of Free Will," in *Symposium on the Foundations of Modern Physics 1990,* Pekka Lahti and Peter Mittelstaedt (editors), World Scientific, Singapore, 1991, 213-225. Professor Laurikainen's results are necessarily vague but his independence and originality of thought are those of an agent in search of truth or a category-one student.

[36] The New Latin term *a fortiori* denotes "with greater reason" or "with more convincing force."

[37] Quoted in Westfall, Richard S., *The Life of Isaac Newton,* Canto Edition, Cambridge University Press, Cambridge, 1994, 294.

[38] *Pearl of Great Price,* Moses 3:1,7.

[39] Ibid, Abraham 4:3,7,9-12,18,21-24-25.

[40] *Doctrine and Covenants,* 88:36-40,42-50, 93:33, *Pearl of Great Price,* Moses 7:48-49.

[41] *Doctrine and Covenants,* 88:25-26 (16-26).

[42] See endnote 20 of Chapter 10.

[43] The energy spectrum of heat radiated from a star or planet is sufficiently close to heat radiated from a black body that the temperature of the radiating body is always implied by the radiant energy distribution over frequency $u(\nu)$ described by Planck's law in Chapter 9. While star or planet or atmosphere composition may introduce spectral emission or absorption bands in the energy distribution, it will elsewhere be easily recognized as will its temperature.

[44] Quoted in Lindley, David, *Boltzmann's Atom,* The Free Press, New York, 2001, 225.

[45] Tolman, Richard C., *The Principles of Statistical Mechanics,* Oxford University Press, 1938, see especially 558-564.

[46] *Bible,* Matthew 7:21-23, 25:8-13, Luke 13:24-30, John 1:10, 8:17-19, 10:14-15, 14:6-9, 17:3, 25, 1 Corinthians 8:3, 2 Timothy 2:19, Titus 1:16, 1 John 3:1, 6, 4:7-8, 2 John 1:9-10.

[47] The sense in which the term *why* is used in science is discussed by Steven Weinberg (*Dreams of a Final Theory,* Random House, New York, 1992, Chapter 2). Our use of this term includes this scientific usage and more – involving ultimate questions and their absolute-, universal-truth answers.

[48] See endnote 37 of Chapter 10.

[49] *Book of Mormon,* Alma 30:44.

[50] *Bible,* Matthew 14:22-33.

[51] *Bible,* John 2:9-10.

[52] Quoted in Laurikainen, K. V., *Beyond the Atom,* loc. cit., 227-228.

[53] Jaynes, E. T., "Is QED Necessary," http://bayes.wustl.edu/etj/node1.html 1966, 21.

[54] Jaynes, E. T., "A Backward Look to the Future," ibid., 1993, 273.

[55] *Book of Mormon,* Moroni 10:5 "by the power of the Holy Ghost ye may know the truth of all things."

[56] See endnote 34 of Chapter 6.

[57] *Doctrine and Covenants* 93:36.

Book III:

Total-Universe Christianity

Book III:

Total-Universe Christianity

12. A Model or Paradigm for Christianity

In our quest for absolute truth and meaning we evaluate the efficacy of two classes of philosophies, paradigms, or systems of belief, namely, *science* and *Christianity*. To evaluate these we select and examine a paradigm or model for each class. We have already selected one for science in Chapter 5 and examined it in Book II. This chapter is devoted to selecting and justifying a model for Christianity, for which many models are strongly held to be valid by many different groups. Although only one model for Christianity is explicitly considered in this book, its examination is rich in implications. Properties of this model identified as crucial may be compared to properties of other systems (models) to determine relative capability of the latter. Hence, this book provides not only an explicit comparison of the two models treated herein, one each for science and Christianity, but also standards against which others may be compared and judged. The ostensible-step methodology of the Christian model introduced in this chapter can provide knowledge and implications that are both general and conclusive.

We herein regard as Christians all who believe in Christ as the Son of God and seek to follow His commandments, a definition deliberately vague in its absence of details in order to be inclusive. However, beyond these first two principles of faith in Christ and repentance, a postponed obedience with regret for the postponement, other Christian principles, ordinances, and practices are also important and these must also be addressed in a careful evaluation. In writing this book I have stated what I believe and know. The full power of Christianity is frequently diminished by confusion and error in understanding of even its most basic principles, evidenced by the diversity in belief among Christians on many issues. The Christianity we consider and compare to science is not so diminished. Likewise, science is often romanticized to the point where its power is misunderstood and misrepresented, by interested nonscientists, by science enthusiasts, and even by professional scientists, error we avoid. Any reliable comparison of these subjects must employ such care.

A careful examination and comparison of scientific and Christian belief must employ a well-defined, accurate, comprehensive model for Christianity, a challenge because of the extensive diversity of belief within Christianity. We therefore seek a succinct, comprehensive, accurate, and authoritative statement of Christian belief, parallel to the one we chose for science. Selecting these two models is the most critical task of our examination, comparison, and evaluation of these two paradigms. The criticality of these selections rests, as stated in Chapter 5, in the fact that if both chosen models are not accurate and fully representative, any examination and evaluation of them will accurately represent neither science nor Christianity. Each must faithfully contain the essence of the philosophy it represents so that all comparisons and conclusions will properly represent both science and Christianity, especially since we ultimately compare them on the basis of essence or meaning. Discovering reality, a stated goal of this book, depends on the inherent utility and power of the paradigms we consider and the fidelity of our models for them, if reality is to be found in either or both, and we must consequently take great care in these choices.

In Book III we utilize comparison with science as a means of describing Christianity. Critical subtleties of Christianity are, in a straightforward description without such comparison, beyond the ken of many. Comparison of Christianity and material-based, relatively-simple science eases assimilation of abstract subtleties and their significance in an otherwise difficult-to-grasp topic. It is also useful in recognizing subtleties in science and thus we continue our discussion of science in Book III.

The Greatest Philosopher

One philosopher we have not yet considered as such, except in passing comment, far exceeds any previously considered and, indeed, all others in understanding of truth. He is both the most rigorous and authoritative philosopher of any age, the most exact, comprehensive in insight, scope of vision, and discernment of meaning. Moreover, this philosopher eclipses all scientists as well. Though "untrained" in science and mathematics, it is difficult, nonetheless, to classify Him as a nonscientist. He preceded all modern schools of scientific thought, yet He could turn water into wine, walk on water, recall the dead back to life, and it was He, in a premortal condition, "who made the Heavens and all the hosts thereof, and by whom all things were made which live, and move, and have a being."[1] Not surprisingly, as is apparent in the accounts of those who knew Him recorded in scripture,[2] He was the most intelligent being who ever walked the face of the earth. His treatments of issues and their interconnections reveal keen philosophical ability and deep insight. His teachings, while they may appear simple on first encounter, require intense, continuing study because they are deep and rich in meaning and, He claims, they are unsurpassed in their revelation of absolute truth – the way things really are. Indeed, it is by application of His teachings that one acquires appreciation and feeling for deepest meaning. According to His claim, and mine and many others, He is the Son of God, the predicted Messiah, the Savior of the world. And He, especially, we must quote in this book. We shall consider the words He spoke, as related by those who were with Him, and also the words His disciples spoke for Him, especially John, Peter, Paul, Nephi, and Moroni, five of my favorites because the deeper meaning (the "meat") of Christ's teachings was not lost on them.

If Christ indeed represents truth in the sense He declared in saying "no man cometh unto the Father [to eternal life with its everlasting fullness of joy] but by me,"[3] no other philosopher can approach Him in authority and ability to declare truth. And, to substantiate His claim, He performed mighty miracles and even resurrected Himself from death.[4] Even without miracles, His ability to neutralize and reverse political-intrigue attacks back onto its confounded perpetrators is unmatched in human history.[5] Nor can any other philosopher approach Him in wisdom, power, fidelity or integrity, grace, or importance.

Christ spoke of building our house on a foundation of rock that will not fail when the floods come, rather than on a foundation of sand that will wash away.[6] This metaphor is dear to anyone who has struggled to construct a rigorous logical structure that is accurate and broadly applicable. Such a structure must be founded on a reliable base that is both deep and broad – a rock. Christ's *philosophy*, *system of belief*, or *paradigm* is a powerful, elegant, logical structure. But how are we to succinctly, accurately, comprehensively, and authoritatively state it? Such a statement is not found in the Bible, which is a principal reason for so many different Christian denominations, each having its own interpretation of Christianity. Indeed, we shall later discuss the fact that important teachings prominently and repeatedly mentioned in the Bible are neither adequately stated nor described therein. One example is the "gospel of Christ."[7] Another is the "doctrine of Christ."[8]

Candidate Christian Paradigms (Models)

In choosing models of science and Christianity, the greater challenge comes in choosing a model fully representative of Christianity. I estimate that throughout the world some 100,000 different Christian denominations have existed in recent times because of wide failure to successfully meet this very challenge. This estimate depends on the minimum number of adherents required for a denomination to be recognized but, since we are utilizing only an estimate, we ignore such details here. It is sufficient to recognize that the number of different interpretations of Christianity is huge, each providing a *possible* model or paradigm of true Christian belief and practice. Otherwise a denomination wouldn't exist separately from others, except where the founding person or group was of an independent turn of mind and/or a schism occurred because of a political difference, personality clash, personal ambition, royal prerogative, or other reason. This huge number of possible choices for a model of Christianity makes the choice difficult and controversial. Since we are seeking a specific model, no generic choice, such as Lewis' "mere Christianity,"[9] would serve well, no matter how attractive it may be.

Some possible candidates for a model are easily eliminated because no succinct, accurate, comprehensive, authoritative statement of them exists. Nor is this accidental. In cases where a schism based on an independent turn of mind or personal ambition of a founder, a personality clash, a political intrigue, a royal decree, or some other such reason was the cause of formation of a new "Christian" denomination, the true history of its formation may not be fully revealed. Rather, such history may have been closely held and a more acceptable reason stated for "public consumption." After all, true religion is based on lofty ideals and eternal principles and not on personal opinion, individual ambition, or royal prerogative. I hasten to add that lofty motivation for formation of new denominations has often occurred. For instance, one Baptist denomination formed as a result of intolerance by the Puritans who had fled England to escape rigid stricture. Yet the Puritans, in turn, imposed a stricture regarded as too rigid by some members of their American colony. Those members broke from the group because of intolerance of their honestly-held conviction. And, of course, the Reformation movement was generally, but not exclusively, motivated by a desire to abandon corrupted traditions and practices and return to Christian principles taught in the Bible.

Parallel to the Chapter-5-mentioned, comprehensive methodology of science involving the totality of all scientific methods and results, one possible model of Christianity would be the totality of Christian principles and practices taught in the Bible and in religious tradition. But, as with science, such a comprehensive model is too indefinite for our purposes, lacking any succinct, accurate, comprehensive, and authoritative statement of it. After all, it is precisely the variations in strongly-held opinions about the various interpretations of the totality of Christian principles and practices taught in the Bible and/or in different traditions that is the basis for the huge number of different Christian beliefs and practices. In fact, few models are suitable for our purpose and, in any case, no model will be universally accepted. What we can do is select one that is reasonable and satisfies our requirements of being succinct, accurate, comprehensive, and authoritative. By reasonable I mean that the choice must be justified by citing both broad and specific support in Biblical and other scriptural teachings as well as those of other ancient writings, utilizing both reason and rigor in interpreting them.

The Best Christian Paradigm (Model)

The best succinct, accurate, comprehensive, and authoritative model of Christian belief and practice I have found is called *the doctrine of Christ*. While no longer found therein, it is referred to in the Bible in ways that indicate this doctrine was a specific doctrine, rather than a generic class, regarded at the highest priority.[8] In urging the Hebrews to greater spiritual effort, so they would not need to repeatedly be re-instructed in fundamentals, Paul reviews again the fundamentals for attaining perfection or the doctrine of Christ as (a) faith in God, (b) repentance, (c) baptism, (d) laying on of hands (to give the gift of the Holy Ghost), (e) resurrection, and (d) eternal judgement. Paul urges them to continue in their practice of these principles and teaches that to learn, follow, and be fully blessed by them and then turn altogether away from the knowledge received is the unforgivable sin.[10] Christ Himself mentions *the* important benefit of His ("My") doctrine; that is, by doing the will of God – this doctrine – one receives knowledge from God that Jesus is the Christ who was sent by God.[11] John's account of the teachings of Christ is consistently the most insightful in the Bible. It would certainly have contained the doctrine of Christ and if-and-when a sufficiently ancient manuscript of John's account is found I expect it will contain the doctrine of Christ preceding John 7:15. Indeed, John is emphatic about the importance of the doctrine of Christ. He warns Christians against deception and designates this doctrine as the way one may know the Father and the Son[12] and recognize a minister who would deceive. John wrote

> Whosoever transgresseth, and abideth not in the doctrine of Christ, hath not [knowledge of] God, [while] he that abideth in the doctrine of Christ, he hath [knowledge of] both the Father and the Son. If there come any unto you, and bring not this doctrine, receive him not into your house, neither bid him God speed: for he that biddeth him God speed is [a] partaker of his evil deeds.[12]

These passages together with others[12] indicate the doctrine of Christ was regarded to be at the highest level of importance by those who best understood Christ's teachings, including Christ, Paul, and John.

While no longer found in the Bible,[13] the doctrine of Christ is clearly stated in the Book of Mormon[14] and is referred to by name and function in other scriptural passages.[15] Were the Book of Mormon a counterfeit, as has been proposed, agreement between the Bible and the Book of Mormon would not consistently occur on such subtle and obscure points. All major teachings would agree in any careful forgery, to be sure, because of their prominence. But discrepancies would inevitably occur in subtle and obscure points. Anyone who has written an extensive work knows it is difficult to obtain mere *internal* consistency on all subtle and obscure points. Thus, it is just such references as the ones cited in John, Hebrews, and 2 John that indicate the authenticity of *both* the Bible and the Book of Mormon and provide essential guidance, because the teaching is in this case an important, fundamental one only obscurely referred to in our present Bible. To fully see its import and direct connection to Christ's central message, invitation, and warning, one should read the Bible references given in endnote 12.

Because the doctrine of Christ is not stated in the Bible, it is not generally recognized that there exists a succinct, accurate, comprehensive, authoritative statement of Christian belief and practice. We shall shortly quote the doctrine of Christ from the Book of Mormon and, thereafter, show that each point of the doctrine corresponds to Christ's teachings in the Bible and to Christ's, Paul's, and John's specific references to it mentioned above. The doctrine of Christ clearly stated *by Christ Himself* in the Book of Mormon is the succinct, accurate, comprehensive, and authoritative statement we seek providing a brief yet wonderfully comprehensive and illuminating model of Christian belief and practice. Though the principles and ordinances taught in this doctrine are taught elsewhere as well, the association and context it provides in collecting them together into *the* central Christian doctrine gives deep insight. This set of principles is greater than the sum of its component parts because it invites all to perform a systematic and rigorous test of this doctrine, a test of Christ, and a test of His Father, a possibility suggested but not clearly and fully taught elsewhere.[12]

Ignorance of the Book of Mormon, past hearing or reading or even promoting of prejudicial, hearsay information against it should not be cause for concern, nor should humor that makes light of it, such as Mark Twain's assessment of the Book of Mormon as "chloroform in print." We shall examine reasons why ignorance of, disregard for, and opposition to it are expected, like stamps of authenticity, if the Book of Mormon is genuine. More important is a principle we have already mentioned: that arbitrary exclusion of evidence because of personal preference based on preconception, ignorance, or prejudice can be fatal to the discovery of truth. If we are seeking truth or simply encounter it by chance, these very processes indicate we have not yet established what it is and that we are therefore not yet certain of its nature. If we don't know its nature we shouldn't discard without honest examination a possibility as failing to meet premature, ill-defined expectations. In doing so we might ignorantly discard the very truth for which we should be searching and need.

Use of the succinct and authoritative Christian model taken from the Book of Mormon and justified below by comparison of its teachings with those of the Bible and other sources is both a useful application and an excellent illustration of this principle. In the absence of any comparably clear, succinct, and authoritative model in the Bible, the doctrine of Christ is the best available and we are constrained to use it or compromise our examination.

Furthermore, we seek in the present book a reliable test of truth regardless of its source. Such a test or truth criterion is essential to the discovery of truth, a test the ancient Greek philosophers correctly recognized was missing in their philosophy. Science seeks to provide such a test for matters relating to reproducible, objective, material-related facts and scientists claim the origin of a scientific theory or law is unimportant since its scientific validity, full consistency with observation, can be established whatever its source. But while full consistency is necessary, it is an inadequate truth criterion and a superior test with a more powerful truth criterion that is definitive and broadly applicable would be far more useful. That such a test exists and is freely offered to all, will be new to many and is a primary message of this book. We shall compare the consistency test of science and the test described as the doctrine of Christ, and mention a variation of it found in the Book of Mormon that provides a means for conclusively establishing the validity and verity of that doctrine and book. In fact, of the two methods we examine, we have already shown that even full consistency in scientific inquiry is not capable of establishing truth to *any* level approaching certainty and we shall show in following chapters that "Christian inquiry," based on the doctrine of Christ, is capable of establishing fundamental, absolute truth with *rigorous certainty* if one is willing to believe in God.

Some Background on the Doctrine of Christ

Before we quote the doctrine of Christ, we consider some background information since the source of a doctrine can be useful in determining its value and validity. This doctrine came to mortals in one of only a few ways it could have, seeing it is no longer contained in the Bible and no ancient manuscripts containing it have yet been found (besides the Book of Mormon). It came by direct revelation from God to the people of the Book of Mormon (which comes to us by revelation) wherein it was carefully recorded, not once but twice by two prophets at two different times.

The Book of Mormon is an account of primarily one of three ancient peoples who immigrated to what is now called America, this one people emigrating from Jerusalem in 600 BC. These people were descendants of Joseph, a son of Jacob (Israel). They came to and eventually established themselves in a new land (North, Central, and South America). The authors of the Book of Mormon were among a group called the Nephites because they were followers of Nephi (rhymes with "knee-high") and brought with them the Old Testament up to the time of their departure in 600 BC, the first year of the reign of King Zedekiah, the last king of Judah, and during the time of the prophet Jeremiah, and they were generally devout in their observance of the Mosaic Law. In fact they were so devout they came to understand its full meaning while the Jews in Palestine, even by the time of Christ, had not. For nearly six centuries before Christ was born, the Nephites correctly worshipped Jesus Christ by name, as both the predicted Messiah and the God of the Old Testament, as is illustrated in part by the following quotation from Nephi written about 550 BC.

> And, notwithstanding we believe in Christ, we keep the law of Moses, and look forward with steadfastness unto Christ, until the law shall be fulfilled. For, for this end was the law given; wherefore the law hath become dead unto us, and we are made alive in Christ because of our faith; yet we keep the law because of the commandments. And we talk of Christ, we rejoice in Christ, we preach of Christ, we prophesy of Christ, and we write according to our prophecies, that our children may know to what source they may look for a remission of their sins.[16]

Through their prophets the Nephites understood who Christ was and why He was to come. They knew the circumstances of His birth and when it occurred. They knew that He would be crucified because of His people's assent thereto and when He was. Teachings of prophets among the Jews in the Middle East were recorded in the Bible and among the Nephites in America in the Book of Mormon.[17] The principal event in both records was the coming of Christ to His people, the house or family of Israel. In Palestine, Christ was born and raised among the Jews, served the last three years of His life as a minister, prophet, and Messiah to them, and was crucified. Following His death and resurrection in Jerusalem, Christ visited His followers in America, as He had predicted in the Bible,[18] because these were also His people of the house of Israel.

At Christ's death, great destruction devastated America. Indeed, this was the sign of His death long-prophesied to the Nephites. The more wicked of the people were killed in this destruction by terrible earthquakes, collapsing structures, fires, and flooding or burial of areas that sunk. Most of the Nephites had become wicked and in such a state it is no blessing to see God before repenting, since one cannot repent on the basis of faith after one has seen and knows. After three days of darkness and silence, except for sounds of mourning among the survivors, Christ appeared to them.

Darkness and a violent earthquake that rent the rocks were also recorded in the Bible as occurring in the whole land or country or region of Palestine, causing the veil in the temple to be rent from top to bottom.[19] But some modern historians and other sophisticates condescendingly explain such things away without offering any explanation.

> It was inevitable that simple believers should have tried to enhance the stark terrors of this tragedy [of Christ's death] by foolish stories of physical disturbances … We are told that a great darkness fell upon the earth, and that the veil of the temple was rent in twain; but if, indeed, these things occurred, they produced not the slightest effect upon the minds of the people in Jerusalem at that time. It is difficult to believe that the order of nature indulged in any such meaningless comments.[20]

One wonders how modern scholars know what was in the minds of the people in Jerusalem at that time. Matthew states "Now when the centurion, and those that were with him, watching Jesus, saw the earthquake, and those things that were done, they feared greatly, saying. Truly this was the Son of God."[19] And also "And the graves were opened; and many bodies of the saints which slept arose, and came out of the graves after his resurrection, and went into the holy city, and appeared unto many."[19] The Bible, in fact, thus states that these events had profound influence on the minds of many, Christian and non-Christian alike. So-called meaningless indulgence of nature has no meaning only when one refuses to acknowledge the Author and Creator of nature. And in refusing Him, other evidence is also dismissed as "foolish stories" of "simple believers." Such assumption is not supported by any evidence provided and is fraught with preconception and prejudice. It is therefore unnecessary, unjustified, and infinitely more risky than merely being proven wrong in one's preconception and prejudice about less important matters. But such is the nature of human pride and vanity that wisdom or its appearance must be pursued and even pretended when such an image (or idol) is the scholar's highest aspiration.

In America the darkness "dispersed" on the morning of the fourth day. This day Christ appeared to the remaining Nephites, preceded by a thrice-repeated announcement by a voice out of heaven, not a harsh voice nor a loud voice but a small voice that pierced them "that they did hear to the center, insomuch that there was no part of their frame that it did not cause to quake; yea, it did pierce them to the very soul, and did cause their hearts to burn."[21] They finally understood the voice on the last repeat. It said "Behold, my Beloved Son, in whom I am well pleased, in whom I have glorified my name – hear ye him."[21] Christ then appeared, descending to them out of heaven in the sight of all. They thought He was an angel until He identified Himself as Jesus Christ "whom the prophets testified shall come into the world" and showed them the wounds in His hands, feet, and side. He commanded all those originally present (2,500 men, women, and children[22]) to

> Arise and come forth unto me, that ye may thrust your hands into my side, and also that ye may feel the prints of the nails in my hands and in my feet, that ye may know that I am the God of Israel, and the God of the whole earth, and have been slain for the sins of the world.[23]

The Doctrine of Christ

Following this dramatic and miraculous appearance the *first thing* Christ taught all these people, over a visit of several-days, was His doctrine. It is succinct, accurate, complete, and authoritative because He, the resurrected Christ, proclaimed it Himself as one of the highest-priority teachings to His people, exactly the sort of statement we are seeking as a definitive Christian model. We now quote and analyze the *doctrine of Christ*. Then we demonstrate in detail that the principles contained in it are identical to those taught by Christ and His prophets in the Bible.

> Behold, verily, verily, I say unto you, I will declare unto you *my doctrine*. And this is *my doctrine*, and it is *the doctrine which the Father hath given unto me*; and I bear record of the Father, and the Father beareth record of me, and the Holy Ghost beareth record of the Father and me; and I bear record that the Father commandeth all men, everywhere, to repent and believe in me. And whoso believeth in me, and is baptized, the same shall be saved; and they are they who shall inherit the kingdom of God. And whoso believeth not in me, and is not baptized, shall be damned. Verily,

> verily, I say unto you, that this is *my doctrine*, and I bear record of it from the Father; and whoso believeth in me believeth in the Father also; and unto him will the Father bear record of me, for he will visit him with fire and with the Holy Ghost. And thus will the Father bear record of me, and the Holy Ghost will bear record unto him of the Father and me; for the Father, and I, and the Holy Ghost are one. And again I say unto you, ye must repent, and become as a little child, and be baptized in my name, or ye can in nowise receive these things. And again I say unto you, ye must repent, and be baptized in my name, and become as a little child, or ye can in nowise inherit the kingdom of God. Verily, verily, I say unto you, that this is *my doctrine*, and whoso buildeth upon this buildeth upon my rock, and the gates of hell shall not prevail against them. And whoso shall declare more or less than this, and establish it for *my doctrine*, the same cometh of evil, and is not built upon my rock; but he buildeth upon a sandy foundation, and the gates of hell stand open to receive such when the floods come and the winds beat upon them.[24] (italics added)

The term "doctrine" implies a teaching, instruction, or principle or a collection thereof accepted by a body of believers or adherents to a philosophy or school of thought. It is synonymous with "dogma" only when it is further implied that the accepted doctrine is true and beyond dispute. According to the Book of Mormon, the doctrine of Christ is identified *by Him* as the body of teachings, instructions, or principles accepted and authorized by Christ and His Father. Christ emphasizes that the instructions given are to be uniquely regarded as His doctrine by referring to them as "my doctrine" no fewer than five times (italicized) within the above quoted ten verses and, moreover, He disclaims as His doctrine[25] any that contains more or less than that stated, although continuing direction from Him is implied in the instruction to remain as a little child and in receiving the Holy Ghost.[26] In addition, He also describes the doctrine as originating with the Father, from whom He received it. Clearly then, if the Book of Mormon is valid (the validity of the Book of Mormon is addressed hereafter from time-to-time as it is pertinent to different topics treated), the above one-paragraph-length declaration of instructions exclusively identified by Christ as "my doctrine" and as being singularly important, despite its brevity, truly is. It represents a complete set of instructions He has given as His doctrine, "whoso shall declare more or less than this, and establish it for *my doctrine*, the same cometh of evil, and is not built upon my rock;" By following the imperative of this doctrine to "receive these things," one obtains the "record" from the Father by fire and the Holy Ghost which provides knowledge of God the Father and God the Son, continuing guidance, and salvation. This single-paragraph description thus provides an excellent and unique Christian model to be regarded as profound and deserving of careful examination, to which we proceed.[27]

The doctrine of Christ begins, ends, and is "punctuated" once within with the expression "verily, verily," meaning "truly, truly." This expression is used to call the hearer's or reader's attention to an important statement, one that is to be regarded as both true and noteworthy. Following an introductory "verily, verily," Christ declares that He is about to teach His doctrine. At the closing "verily, verily" He indicates that He has finished teaching His doctrine. Christ utilizes an intermediate "verily, verily" to again emphasize that He is teaching His doctrine, that it is issued by and He received it from God the Father, the highest known authority, that the

Father will bear record of Christ by "fire and the Holy Ghost" to one who receives or believes in and follows Christ, and that the Holy Ghost will bear record or testify to him or her of both the Father and the Son.

Authority is generally an undesired basis for adopting a philosophy when its accuracy and scope are not established except by claim of the same authority. The danger of error or corruption is real, as is well illustrated in human history. Given human nature and history, reticence to blindly accept authority is prudent.

However, Christ does not propose blind acceptance, even on the authority of His Father. He cites His Father as the origin and His Father's authority as the basis of His doctrine, but He also invites experiment, observation, and analysis by which the doctrine is to be tested. He promises one who embraces this philosophy a witness of its truthfulness "by fire and the Holy Ghost," by which gift the origin and basis as well as the truth and meaning of the philosophical system are communicated and validated.[28] This confirmation, referred to by John as "having [knowledge of] both the Father and the Son,"[12] is the desired, independent, external, ostensible-step proof that the basis of the doctrine (the existence of the Father and the Son) corresponds to reality. It is an external confirmation that this system of belief is valid beyond being merely consistent. It is the manifestation of power and authority by which the doctrine and its Author are to be recognized and received. The declaration of the authority on which this system is based is clear and the authority cited is unsurpassed, but the validity of the system and the authority itself are established to the experimenter by the power of God, the Holy Ghost, through application of the prescribed test: repentance and belief in Christ as the Son of God followed by baptism and receipt of the Holy Ghost, etc. We are invited to test Christ's doctrine and, indeed, Christianity itself to discover their truth and meaning, utilizing our God-given gifts of observation, rational analysis, and, ultimately, individual agency or choice.

Christ's expression of deference to the Father is the first lesson of His doctrine. And while He invokes the authority of the Father as the foundation of His doctrine, He describes the Trinity as one, in purpose and power,[29] indicating that He can speak and act for this Body. His deference to the Father and His inclusion of the Holy Ghost in His revelation of the functions of the Members of the Trinity in Christianity are important in defining the philosophical basis of Christianity. Christ teaches that the Father holds the higher station, that the Father is the source of doctrine and authority, and that Christ and the Holy Ghost possess stature below that of the Father. Both God the Father and God the Son know answers to questions we don't even know, or know how, to ask. But one cannot question His doctrine in good faith and refuse to test it, to exercise due diligence, to receive His power offered therein. His power offered in the doctrine of Christ, which gives a knowledge of the Father and the Son, is the "rock" or foundation on which He admonishes us to build our belief and philosophy[30] as, by virtue of its source, it contains a vision of truth and meaning "broader than the universe and deeper than time."[31]

Christ includes in His doctrine specific instructions and requirements (repentance, belief in Christ on the command of the Father, and baptism), eternal judgement in the form of either benefits obtained by following these instructions (receiving a witness of Christ and His Father by fire and the Holy Ghost, salvation or inheritance of the kingdom of God) or consequence imposed for choosing not to do so (damnation). He can't say it more clearly. And the instructions are emphasized and enlarged: become as a little child and be baptized, be baptized and become as a little child. Note the continuing need to be as a little child: "submissive, meek, humble, patient, full of love, willing to submit to all things which the Lord seeth fit to inflict upon him, even as a child doth submit to his father."[32] Similar instruction is given in the Bible wherein Christ states "Whosoever shall not receive the kingdom of God as a little child, he shall not enter therein."[33] and "Verily I say unto you, except ye be converted, and become as little children, ye shall not enter into the kingdom of heaven"[34] In these two verses we see the same order in (1) receiving the kingdom as a little child and (2) being converted and becoming as little children. But Biblical statements nowhere contain the clarification of what desired qualities little children possess like the above-quoted Book-of-Mormon statement does.

In His closure, Christ indicates the full doctrine has been included and assures the hearer that the authority supporting this doctrine will never be displaced or superceded, that it is eternally and universally valid, i.e., that the authority of the Father will never fail. Christ condemns the teaching of any other doctrine or philosophy or element thereof as "His doctrine," thus elevating this doctrine, system of belief, or philosophy to a singular, exclusive position at the highest possible priority.

Scope and Power of the Doctrine of Christ

There is no philosophical flaw in this doctrine. Who can question the validity of a doctrine that invokes both the highest known Authority – Who is held to be both omniscient and omnipotent – *and* promises a demonstration of power to confirm His Authority. It was precisely this witness, the power of God, that Christ utilized to heal the sick, give sight to the blind, and raise the dead, that manifest His identity during His earthly ministry.[35] And to many, Peter among them, a manifestation of the power of God was received from the Father confirming that Jesus was the Christ, the Son of the Living God.[36] This identical manifestation of power by fire and the Holy Ghost is offered by Christ to any earnest inquirer who would learn the truth of the doctrine of Christ and of the authority of its Author by embracing or testing His doctrine, a doctrine which promises much but requires little.[37] Of course there are the *cognoscenti* who question and maintain they know better – the lawyers, scribes, and Pharisees of our day. Understanding and motivation of such are, in my opinion, highly flawed, as I describe in later chapters. The doctrine of Christ is simple, powerful, comprehensive, elegant, gracious, and irrefutable, except when one refuses to test it. The test is personal and subjective, quite different from a scientific test. But, as we shall see in Chapters 16 and 17, this nature of the test endows Christianity with a power and certainty infinitely superior to science. The authority of this doctrine is established by its test.[28] So tested, no other philosophy can challenge or approach it in scope, power, authority, and importance. It transcends intuition and the limits of the material universe and addresses truth and meaning on a fundamental, absolute, eternal level, invoking the power, authority, virtue, and grace of God. This doctrine provides a vision of reality, a Christian vision, that one accepts upon embracing it. It is, therefore, a call to service, a call to battle against the enemy, and not for the faint hearted or "ditherer" (qualities which it transforms), all points to be amplified later.

One might ask: "How is such a simple concise doctrine powerful and comprehensive?" "Where is the scope of the commission or call to action?" Or one might comment, "It's a nice sentiment, as far as it goes, but it doesn't address substantive matters, being only the elemental precepts of a faith, and it is consequently partial and incomplete." If you find yourself so confused or doubtful, look to God for direction; trust and follow Him. There is more here than first meets the eye; the meaning is deep.

When Nicodemus, a ruler of the Jews, came to Christ for instruction, the lesson[38] was brief and its meaning seemed mysterious and elusive. Nicodemus didn't know what to make of it. But, unbeknownst to the hearer at that time and many who read about it now, Christ's instruction to Nicodemus was similarly comprehensive and powerful. Christ spoke of being born of the water (baptism) and of the Spirit (receiving the Holy Ghost) in order to see the kingdom of God (to be saved). Nicodemus was schooled in details, facts he understood, even highly symbolic facts (facts which represent still other facts) which allowed him to rule based on his knowledge and the authority it imparted. But Christ rules. His doctrine is that we act according to His knowledge and His authority (become and remain as a little child). Thus, to teach Nicodemus and the rest of us this principle, He responded "Marvel not that I said unto thee, Ye must be born again. The wind bloweth where it listeth, and thou hearest the sound thereof, but canst not tell from whence it cometh, and whither it goeth: so is every one that is born of the Spirit."[39]

Lessons Taught on the Day of Pentecost

On the day of Pentecost, Christ completed His instruction to Nicodemus and the rest of us.[40] Beginning on that day, those who had been born of water, about an hundred and twenty in number,[41] were also born of fire and the Holy Ghost. "And when the day of Pentecost was fully come, they were all with one accord in one place. And suddenly there came a sound from heaven as of a rushing mighty wind, and it filled all the house where they were sitting."[40] They knew not in terms of worldly facts when or from whence the "wind" would come or whither it would blow or guide them, but they were committed to Christ and, like little children, ready to follow.

> And they were all filled with the Holy Ghost, and began to speak with other tongues, as the Spirit gave them utterance. ... Now when this was noised abroad, the multitude came together, and were confounded, because that every man heard them speak in his own language. And they were all amazed and marvelled, saying one to another, Behold, are not all these which speak Galilaeans? And how hear we every man in our own tongue, wherein we were born? Parthians, and Medes, and Elamites, and the dwellers in Mesopotamia, and in Judaea, and Cappadocia, in Pontus, and Asia, Phrygia, and Pamphylia, in Egypt, and in the parts of Libya about Cyrene, and strangers of Rome, Jews and proselytes, Cretes and Arabians, we do hear them speak in our tongues the wonderful works of God. ... What meaneth this?[40]

Then stood Peter with (as one of) the eleven and declared what it meaneth. Peter recited the recent events in Jerusalem regarding the predicted Messiah sent from the Father and His rejection and crucifixion by His people. After this recitation he said, "Therefore, let all the house of Israel know assuredly, that *God hath made this same Jesus*, whom ye have crucified, *both Lord and Christ*."[42] Because the Spirit gave utterance, Peter's words were powerful and the people were "pricked in their heart" and asked "men and brethren, what shall we do?" The alarm and humility in this plea manifests *their belief in Peter's words and their remorse* for their support of or failure to object to the crucifixion of Christ.

What followed is nearly unique in the New Testament. Christ's charge to Peter was "feed my sheep."[43] Here, in one of two instances alone in the entire post-crucifixion New Testament, we are told exactly what a large group of people (several thousand) heard Peter declare in his preaching – that Jesus is the Christ – as well as their reaction. They felt the guiding influence of the Holy Ghost (were "pricked in their hearts") and expressed belief and willingness to follow Him ("men and brethren, what shall we do?"). Like little children they were ready to be led. The instruction given by Peter in such an instance would therefore reveal the essence and heart of Christian belief and practice. What food did Peter feed these sheep?

"Then Peter said unto them, *Repent*, and *be baptized* every one of you in the name of Jesus Christ for the remission of sins, and ye shall *receive the gift of the Holy Ghost*."[44] This is the gift which Christ spoke of to Nicodemus. This is the gift promised in the doctrine of Christ. This is the gift these 120 Christians had received. Many who heard them and Peter also became willing followers, those who spoke and those who heard, like little children in their belief, faith, and trust and the Spirit guided and empowered them to the effect that many were blessed that day. "… and the same day were added unto them about three thousand souls."[45]

Peter taught this doctrine because this is the doctrine he had learned from his Master who he now represented and from the Holy Ghost. On one occasion when Christ taught the Jews in the temple,

> And the Jews marvelled, saying, How knoweth this man letters, having never learned? Jesus answered them, and said, *My doctrine* is not mine, but his that sent me. If any man will do his will, he shall know of the doctrine, whether it be of God, or whether I speak of myself.[28] (italics added)

This passage and Peter's sermon contain elements of the doctrine Christ taught to His Book-of-Mormon followers, namely, repentance, faith in Christ, baptism, receiving the Holy Ghost, the doctrine's name, its source, and that a witness of its truth follows when one receives the doctrine. Peter also included another principle of the doctrine of Christ, teaching that God hath made Jesus both Lord and Christ. Receipt of the Holy Ghost implies "having [a knowledge of]" or a witness of the Father and the Son, for the function of the Holy Ghost is to testify of God the Father and God the Son and to lead all those who will to follow Them, which is exactly what occurred under the influence of the Holy Ghost on the day of Pentecost.

When we embrace the doctrine of Christ, the exact elements of which we find in Peter's discourse (italicized), we declare belief and trust in Christ and willingness to follow Him, to do things His way, as a little child follows a parent. He, in turn, promises to guide and strengthen us in our effort through influence of the Spirit. Nephi, an early Book-of-Mormon prophet, also declared the doctrine of Christ about 550 BC.[46] He concluded with the following instruction. "For behold, … if ye will enter in by the way [baptism], and receive the Holy Ghost, it will show unto you all things what ye should do. Behold, this is the doctrine of Christ, …"[47] Thus, a Christian seeks to follow Christ without knowing when His influence, like the wind, will come or where it will lead. Christ leads, Christians follow. And when we follow, marvelous things happen to the effect that we are blessed. Such was the instruction to Christ's followers in the Book of Mormon; such was the instruction to Nicodemus and the early Christians in the Bible; and such is the instruction to us today.[48]

In Christ's day, as in ours, the fundamental principles of devotion and obedience to God were not held at the highest priority by every person vested in human power and authority. During the time of Christ, the high priest as the political and spiritual head of the Jews was inappropriatcly appointed and deposed at pleasure by Herod and the Romans.[49] While Nicodemus, a ruler as a member of the Sanhedrin, may have sought knowledge to protect and enhance his privileged status, his later-demonstrated devotion to Christ indicates otherwise.[50] Nevertheless, corruption was then rife, as it is now. The world was and still is the world. Christ spoke against selfish interest in His day, as He has in ours. When 14-year-old Joseph Smith, Jr., offered his humble prayer in 1820 (Appendix H) requesting guidance regarding which Christian church to join, he was instructed by the Author of Christianity Himself to beware of those vested in the power and privilege of the world who do not seek first to follow Him, for they deny "the power of God," the very principle that was and is so essential to Christian discipleship, i.e., being led by the Holy Ghost.[30] Why does natural man deny the power of God? Because the power of God attacks darkness and evil. Because it does not tolerate pride or power of man over man. Because it condemns those who refuse to repent and believe and instead seek their own glory or pursue some worldly idol.[51]

Incidentally, at least part of another sermon by Peter was heard by thousands and is recorded together with the reactions of many who heard it in the next two chapters of Acts. This sermon was delivered in the temple after Peter and John healed a well-known, lame beggar at the temple gate and a large, amazed crowd of thousands recognized the miraculously healed beggar leaping and exultant. The crowd of thousands gathered around these three in great curiosity. Although the account of this sermon ends with the arrest of Peter and John, the reaction of many who heard it is included.

> And they ["the priests, and the captain of the temple, and the Sadducees"] laid hands on them [Peter and John], and put them in hold unto the next day: for it was now eventide. Howbeit many of them which heard the word believed; and the number of the men was about five thousand.[52]

The recorded content of this sermon is also invaluable since it was delivered by Peter under inspiration from God. Indeed, its content is at least as valuable in what it tells us today as it was in what it told its original hearers. The question of when Christ would return, an event referred to as His second coming or Advent, was of great interest among believers then,[53] as it is among believers today. In his sermon Peter declared the station of Christ and answered this question to some extent for both his hearers and for later generations saying,

> Repent ye therefore, and be converted, that your sins may be blotted out, when the times of refreshing shall come from the presence of the Lord [under His direction]; And he shall send [knowledge of] Jesus Christ, which before was preached to you ["whom ye have crucified"[54]]; whom the heaven must receive until the times of restitution of all things, which God has spoken by the mouth of all his holy prophets since the world began.[55]

We are now living in the times of restitution of knowledge of Christ and His gospel and authority and Church and of all things ever taught by His prophets, as we shall argue in Chapters 14 and 15. While His Advent could not have occurred before now, according to Peter's declaration, it now can happen and is imminent.[56]

Where does the doctrine of Christ lead us? Exactly where He wants us to go. Thus the continuing need to be as a little child. Where does He want us to go? Not necessarily where we might think or hope. Probably not to greatness in the eyes of the world. The world adores the world. The death of Mother Theresa was eclipsed in the eyes of the world (the press) by the concurrent deaths of Princess Diana and her boyfriend! And John F. Kennedy is still more prominent in the public eye (the press) than C. S. Lewis who passed away on the same day, 22 November 1963. Christ leads us out of the world, intellectually and spiritually, to where we can be useful to Him in accomplishing His purposes. And His purposes are to bless and save us, the other children of His and our Father in Heaven, all of us, that is, who will receive Him.

If true, no other belief or philosophy can match the doctrine of Christ in its scope and power. It does not leave one without direction following acceptance of a few elementary principles of faith. On the contrary, it leads one to the most brilliant, revolutionary, creative, magnanimous, and miraculous acts of all, the acts which Christ Himself did and which He would have us do, to which He guides and empowers us individually by the Holy Ghost – and for which the brilliance, novelty, creativity, and magnanimity are His as well as ours. He has the power, authority, and wisdom. He leads, we follow. This is the genius and power of His doctrine. It also suggests the central question we face in our philosophical battle of life. Should I lead or follow Him? The extended question is "Should I seek to glorify myself or Him?"

The Beginning of Truth

Genuine truth is, by its nature, universal, eternal, and part of a comprehensive whole and, consequently, it can only be fully understood, including its connections and implications, on such a level, i.e., with assistance from a power that is universal, eternal, and comprehensive, a power that understands, declares, introduces, or imposes it. Who or what are the candidates for this causal power? God, nature, ... And what is the evidence supporting the candidates? Christ taught that (1) He was commissioned by His Father,[57] (2) He created all things,[58] (3) He commanded and the elements obeyed,[59] and (4) by His Spirit He gives light and truth to every person that comes into the world.[60] In His doctrine, in Moroni's promise, and elsewhere, Christ teaches that we can receive a witness of the verity of His role and station if we seek it with faith in and intent to follow Him. We can't find the important answers until we discover and ask the important questions. The important questions that one should address along the way, sooner rather than later, are "Who and What are truth?"

Fundamental truth transcends facts. Truth contains not only *how* but also *why*, not only *what* but also *who*, not only *effect* but also *cause*, not only *knowledge* but also *meaning*. When Pontius Pilate asked Christ "What is truth?" Christ chose not to answer him. He, of course, could have. The evening before, during His last supper with His apostles, Christ taught "I am the way, the truth and the life; no man cometh unto the Father but by me."[3] The question He answered then was not "What is truth?" but "Who is truth?" and the answer refers to one of His many titles, in whole or in part, and to His assignment as the Son of God and Savior of humankind.[61] In this assignment we see the connection between the Who and the What of truth.

To answer the question, "What is truth?" we recall that God the Father said to Moses "For as I, the Lord God, liveth, even so my words cannot return void, for as they go forth out of my mouth they must be fulfilled."[62] God the Son said "truth is knowledge of things as they are, and as they were, and as they are to come."[63] Therefore, these two concepts are related – knowledge of the declarations of God is equivalent to knowledge of things as they were, and are, and will be, which is knowledge of truth. Truth thus includes knowledge of that which has been declared by God: that which has been, is, and is to be. The source of knowledge of the declarations of God the Father is God the Son. Only knowledge and meaning declared or personally communicated by God the Son may be regarded as universal and absolute truth.

Pertaining to individual, personal salvation, the origin or *beginning of truth* is not abstract thought or limitless, independent, nondenominational, uncommitted concept; rather, He has a name and a title: Jesus Christ, the Son of God.

The End of Truth

What shall happen to the creatures, men and women, Christ created? What is the end of truth? Definition of that part of truth has been granted to each person in the gift of agency. While Christ and His Father have provided a standard (including the doctrine of Christ) by which humans shall be judged, His Father has granted agency to each person.[64] Each person can receive and follow truth and "live" or reject truth and "die." The meanings of "live" and "die" are spiritual or eternal, as addressed later. Each person accepts or rejects truth through his or her agency and, in the end, each person determines for him- or her-self the way things will be, the *end of truth*. While Christ established the way, the truth, and the life, it is each person who chooses to follow or not follow His way. Thus, the "who" of truth is not only Christ, but you and me as well. We were each empowered to create our own past, present, and future truth and each of us has done well in the past (before birth, as will be described).

The requirements of Christ's doctrine, the writing of a *desirable* truth for one's self as one's own end of truth, will be difficult when one has too much pride or not enough faith in Christ. It is difficult for a proud human to accept the idea that he or she is not the final judge, the preeminent intelligence in the universe, the exclusive discoverer and broker of truth. But each individual "writes" his or her own truth, we could say his or her own ticket, by either humbly following Christ or not. While the role of a Christian is not often heroic in the world-focused vision of proud humans, it is nonetheless a heroic role that can provide much goodness to self and others. A proud human may struggle with the question "How can truth be universal, comprehensive, infinite, and eternal and yet be known and, in its basis and beginning, personified by One Individual?" This question reveals incomplete understanding of the station of Christ and insufficient faith in Him. But we grow in faith in Christ as we sincerely, earnestly, and humbly seek to better follow and know Him.

And an ignorance of Christ's station suggests an ignorance of our own. The role of each individual is potentially great. Christ promised His followers: "He that believeth on me, the works that I do shall he do also; and greater works than these shall he do; because I go unto my Father."[65] The truth we can represent through our agency and by our choices is important to us and to Them and to many others. How many? Who? Each person must discover answers to these questions, but, to start, each should consider his or her own family. So, learn and follow truth by diligently seeking knowledge of Christ. By seeking to follow Him, the basis and foundation of truth, we do that which He did in following His Father and we become creators of our own beneficial truth, we establish our own desirable destiny, we determine the way we are to be, what we become.

Reality in science may be described as truth with the relatively shallow comment "truth is knowledge of how things are." But Christian insight sees much deeper as represented by the comment "truth shows me how I may become, according to my and His desire, and how I can help others."

Proposition Number 6: **Repentance and faith in Jesus Christ are the first two principles of His doctrine with baptism and receipt of the gift of the Holy Ghost (confirmation) two required ordinances that follow. According to the doctrine of Christ, these principles and ordinances and continued desire to follow Christ provide salvation and are the basis of a true vision of reality.**

Observations of commitment in thought and emotion of Christians in their particular faiths and of others in other faiths have led the present author to believe that those trained in a faith obtain a substantial predisposition in thinking, an instilled bias, and sometimes a supposed intellectual independence or even arrogance related to vestment in the robes of spiritual knowledge, prestige, status, and inclusion in a unique orthodoxy of correct thinking (if only in the mind of the individual or group). Therefore, we attempt to make our points clear, stating them in what may sometimes seem to be painful detail, despite the goal of a simple, declarative style. If the reader is not a Christian or religious person, our discussion may occasionally seem to extend beyond the mark – past the obvious – making it difficult to "stay tuned" to tedious detail. Please be compassionate. We are trying to make these points compelling to trained Christians and others of self-perceived high status who seem to require considerable encouragement in order to overcome instilled bias and a supposed intellectual independence (sometimes arrogance) that inhibit serious consideration of them. That is, we are trying to help each reader overcome pride manifest in his or her resistance to being influenced in his or her thinking. In doing so, however, the object is never to destroy a reader's faith in God or intellectual independence but to help the reader construct superior knowledge and belief by which both faith in God and intellectual independence are tremendously strengthened.

Notes and References for Chapter 12.

[1] *Bible,* John 1:1-5,14, Hebrews 1:2,10, 2:10, *Doctrine and Covenants* 45:1. The quoted passage is the last.

[2] *Pearl of Great Price,* Abraham 3:19.

[3] *Bible,* John 14:6.

[4] *Bible,* John 2:19-22.

[5] The leading council of the Jews sent spies and plotted to trap Christ in an error, real or apparent, to confound and discredit Him in the eyes of the Jews. But all to no avail because His seemingly spontaneous and effortless answers invariably confounded and discredited them instead. History has seen no equal to His ability to recognize and counter such political intrigue. The results were as predictable as a Roadrunner cartoon. See, for example, the twentieth chapter of Luke wherein three carefully contrived plots of the Jews to discredit Christ are deflected back onto the perpetrators. The first of these was all the more painful because the plot choreography had the chief priests, scribes, and elders all present front and center (verse 1), I suppose in their splendid robes and ostentatious accessories, to intimidate Christ and impress upon the people their rank and authority. They demanded Christ tell them by what authority He "doest these things." (verse 2) He responded, "I will also ask you one thing; and answer me: The baptism of John, was it from heaven or of men?" They huddled in private deliberation and decided if they answered yes He would ask them why they didn't believe John and if they said no the people would stone them. Thus, this official party, whose steward-ship and authority it was to make pronouncements on exactly such matters as this one, "answered that they could not tell whence it was." This public admission was painful for the esteemed doctors of the law and rulers of the people because they were supposed to possess great knowledge of the law; and to have to publicly admit "we cannot tell" was disgraceful. Then said Christ, "Neither tell I you by what authority I do these things." I suppose that many faces were then very red, but the fireworks and pain were only beginning. Jesus then told the parable of the vineyard with all the rulers standing there before the people as exhibit A. While the Jewish rulers only partially understood, "the chief priests and the scribes the same hour sought to lay hands on him; and they feared the people: for they perceived that he had spoken this parable against them." (verse 19) Thus they withdrew "and sent forth spies, which should feign themselves just men, that they might take hold of his words, that so they might deliver him to the power and authority of the governor [to execute by crucifixion]." One of their spies then asked a politically and emotionally loaded question: "Is it lawful for us to give tribute unto Caesar, or no?" (verse 22) Christ asked them, "Shew me a penny. Whose image and superscription hath it? They answered and said, Caesar's. And He said unto them, Render therefore unto Caesar the things which be Caesar's, and unto God the things which be God's. And they could not take hold of his words before the people; and they marvelled at his answer, and held their peace." (verses 24-26) Then entered the Sadducees, who denied the resurrection. After a long description about seven brothers who each, in turn, married the same wife and died, a situation contrived under mosaic law to make the answer difficult, they asked "Therefore in the resurrection whose wife of them is she." Jesus dismissed their contrived complexity with a simple answer and then continued with His own attack on their ignorance that went to the heart of their disbelief. He stated, "Now that the dead are raised, even Moses showed at the bush when he called the Lord the God of Abraham, and the God of Isaac, and the God of Jacob. For he is not a God of the dead, but of the living: for all live unto him." (verses 37-38) "And after that they durst not ask him any question at all." (verse 40)

[6] *Bible,* Matthew 7:24-27.

[7] The term "gospel" or "gospel of Christ" or "gospel of the kingdom" etc. is used exactly one-hundred times in the New Testament. Some examples are Matthew 24:14, 26:13, Mark 1:1, 1:14, 13:10, 16:15, Luke 4:18, 9:6, Acts 8:25, 15:7, Romans 1:16, 15:19, 1 Corinthians 1:17, 15:1, 2 Corinthians 4:3, 11:4, ... 1 Peter 4:6, Revelation 14:6. But the gospel is not completely described in the Bible because it and many other "plain and precious things" have been removed from the Bible by wicked men. (*Book of Mormon,* 1 Nephi 13:19-37; Appendix I.) However, enough of the gospel of Christ remains in the Bible to indicate it's general content, beauty, and importance.

[8] *Bible* Matthew 7:28, 22:33, Mark 1:22, Luke 4:32, John 7:16-17 (Jesus cites "my doctrine"), 1 Timothy 6:1, Hebrews 6:1, 2 John 9. (Five of these eight citations refer generally to doctrine taught by Christ and three specifically to "the doctrine of Christ." The three that specifically address "the doctrine of Christ" are John 7:14-17, Hebrews 6:1-6, and 2 John 9-11. See Appendix K.)

[9] Lewis, C. S., *Mere Christianity,* Collier Books, Macmillan Publishing Company, New York, 1943.

[10] *Bible,* Hebrews 6:1-6. In the first three of these six verses Paul admonishes the members of Christ's Church or saints to "go on unto perfection," building on and "[not] leaving the [fundamental] principles of the doctrine of Christ, not laying again the foundation of repentance from dead works, and of faith toward God. Of the doctrine of baptisms, and laying on of hands [for the gift of the Holy Ghost], and of resurrection of the dead, and of eternal judgement [salvation]." These fundamental principles are exactly those stated by Christ in this precise order in the doctrine of Christ recorded in the Book of Mormon. The added word "not" in this quotation is from the Bible translation of Joseph Smith. (*Joseph Smith's "New Translation" of the Bible,* Herald Publishing House, Independence, MO, 1970, 500.) Such reversal or change in meaning through error in present Bible texts caused by incorrect transcription or translation occurs elsewhere in the Bible. A few examples follow. In Matthew 10:10 and Luke 9:3 Jesus forbids the apostles to take anything with them, not even a "staff," while in Mark 6:8 we read that Jesus forbids them to take anything except a "staff only." We read in Matthew 8:28-34 that Jesus heals two demonaics of the Gadarenes or Gerasenes while in Mark 5:1-20 and Luke 8:26-39 we read that He heals only one. In Matthew 20:29-34 we read that Jesus, near Jericho, gives sight to two blind men while we read in Mark 10:46-52 and Luke 18:35-43 that only one received sight. Other examples could also be cited.

The importance of the doctrine of Christ is indicated by Paul in verses 4-6. (See also *Doctrine and Covenants* 76:25-49.) In these verses Paul warns that full, personal knowledge of God obtained by this doctrine must be honored and held sacred. Deliberate violation of this doctrine, knowledge and demonstrated devotion that is willfully betrayed, is unforgivable.

Whether or not the added "not" is included in this passage, Paul refers to this doctrine by name and cites as its principles exactly those cited in, and in identical order to, the Book-of-Mormon version, providing evidence that supports both books. Neither Joseph Smith nor anyone else (below Christ) was or is smart enough to get every detail right throughout the whole Book of Mormon, were it not simply genuine. But the principal evidence that supports its validity is not facts gleaned through scholarly criticism (understood and appreciated only by the learned few) but other evidence, namely, a personal witness from the Holy Ghost, described and attained by the doctrine of Christ as emphasized by Christ in John 7:15-17 (easily appreciated by all). This fundamentally important element of Christianity, the doctrine of Christ, is mentioned but no longer defined or described in John's text or elsewhere in the Bible; apparently it was removed by writing it out of the Bible (Appendices I and K; what would be more disconcerting to those falsely assuming exclusive power to interpret the word of God than a Godgiven promise to each individual to receive true guidance directly from God?).

[11] *Bible,* John 7:16-17: "Jesus answered them, and said, 'My doctrine is not mine, but his that sent me. If any man will do his will, he shall know of the doctrine, whether it be of God, or whether I speak of myself.' "

[12] *Bible,* 2 John 9-11. In verse 9 John teaches that "Whosoever transgresseth, and abideth not in the doctrine of Christ, hath not [knowledge of and guidance by] God. He that abideth in the doctrine of Christ, he hath [knowledge of and guidance by] both the Father and the Son." In verse 10 John admonishes rejecting any who come "unto you, and bring not this doctrine." Clearly, John teaches that *the doctrine of Christ* is fundamental and essential to Christianity, sufficiently so to provide a test of whether a Christian is teaching true and essential doctrine regarding the Father and the Son. Why? Because knowing the Father and the Son and Them knowing us are fundamental and essential to Christianity. (See *Bible,* Matthew 7:21-23, 25:1-13, Luke 13:24-30, John 1:10-13, 7:14-18, 8:19, 10:1-18 [note especially verses 14 and 15], 17:3,25-26, 1 Corinthians 8:3, 2 Timothy 2:19, 1 John 4:7-8.)

While much information remains in the Bible about the *gospel of Christ,* practically none remains about the fundamental and essential *doctrine of Christ* (Appendices I and K). But the full *doctrine of Christ,* as well as His gospel, are stated by Christ Himself in the Book of Mormon.

[13] Appendix I.

[14] The Bible mentions but contains no statements of important Christian doctrines, such as "the gospel of Christ" and "the doctrine of Christ." Why? While the next endnote gives an important and reliable answer, we speculate here about additional influences.

Even before Christ's death, He and His church, primarily the former, were attacked at every opportunity by the lawyers, scribes, and Pharisees motivated by the highest governing council of the nation, the corrupt Sanhedrin. [This conclusion is based on their acts and on the statement of Christ (*Bible,* Matthew 15:1-14)]. His death was finally contrived by these apostate Jewish leaders to suppress the threat of Him and His followers capturing the affection and allegiance of the people, depriving the Jewish leaders of recognition, authority, and wealth. And persecution of His church remained intense after His death. Peter and John were imprisoned, tried, and threatened for publicly healing a lame beggar at the temple gate in the name of Christ and preaching Christ to thousands in the temple. Stephen was stoned to death for proclaiming that Christ the Messiah was murdered by the Jews. Saul was sent to Damascus to capture Christians and return them to Jerusalem for trial. The new church was necessarily an underground movement in Palestine. To be sure, documentation of beliefs and practices of the church were faithfully recorded, despite persecution, for diligence and devotion to their Lord in such matters is a noble tradition of faithful Jews. But today, little earlier than fourth and fifth century Greek New-Testament parts have, up to now, been discovered. And much of the New Testament contains incomplete accounts in epistles directed to particular groups addressing specific but undefined problems. Paul's prescriptions are recorded but not the maladies he addressed (another reason for so many different beliefs and practices within Christianity today). The biggest question pertaining to authenticity of our present Bible is "How careful and accurate were the many translations and transcriptions required over the first 14 centuries of its history, the period before it was printed?" The answer is, "not very" (Appendix I).

In contrast, the Nephites who recorded the Book of Mormon were numerous, faithful Christians dating in their belief to centuries before Christ. And they lived in a land where the government was often Christian friendly. Their Christian documents could therefore be more deliberately and carefully recorded and preserved. Christ personally visited the Book-of-Mormon people following His resurrection, taught all the principal teachings He taught to the Jews, and they were all carefully recorded. Most importantly, upon its completion the Book of Mormon escaped any contamination by being hidden by a prophet-steward and remaining undiscovered for 14 centuries until it was passed on to, translated, and published by another prophet-steward. This history, together with that given in the next endnote, explains why the doctrines contained in the Book of Mormon are authentic and definitive and provide fuller description of important Christian belief and practice that correct, supplement, and illuminate principles taught in the Bible.

[15] *Book of Mormon,* 3 Nephi 11:31-40; see also *Bible,* Matthew 7:28, 22:33, Mark 1:22, 27, Luke 4:32, John 7:16-17, 18:19-21, Titus 2:10, Hebrews 6:1, 2 John 1:9-11, *Book of Mormon,* 2 Nephi Chapters 31 and 32, Ether 4:18, *Doctrine and Covenants* 10:67-70. The Book of Mormon states that many "plain and precious parts of the gospel of the Lamb" would be "written out" of the Bible

(see Appendix I). But though these plain and precious things have been removed, evidence of them remains. The Bible contains several references to the doctrine of Christ or "My doctrine" even though it no longer contains any explicit statement or complete description of it. The Bible includes doctrine taught by Christ's apostles, which they learned from Him, which provides the principles of the doctrine of Christ, in complete agreement with the doctrine Christ taught in the Book of Mormon (3 Nephi 11:31-40). Christ's concluding comments in His sermon on the mount (Matthew 7) are reminiscent of His concluding comments in the declaration of His doctrine in the Book of Mormon. And in both cases He promises divine guidance to each person who sincerely seeks truth and He urges all to build their house on His rock (this guidance) rather than on sand (any other guidance or none at all). An early New-Testament illustration of this process was provided by Peter when he declared "Thou art the Christ, the Son of the living God." to which Christ responded, "Blessed art thou, Simon Bar-jona: for flesh and blood hath not revealed it unto thee, but my Father which is in heaven. ... and upon this rock I will build my church; and the gates of hell shall not prevail against it." (Matthew 16:16-18; see also John 7:15-17 and endnote 21 of Chapter 14.)

[16] *Book of Mormon,* 2 Nephi 25:24-26.

[17] The Old-Testament Prophet Ezekiel (*Bible,* Ezekiel 37:15-22) foretold of a "stick of Judah" and a "stick of Joseph" that would be joined into one in God's hand to unite the children of Israel (those who will receive salvation) into one nation (family, group, or church). Ezekiel refers to these "sticks" as written records, like scrolls wrapped around sticks, i.e., books, or, perhaps, the wooden writing tablets common in Babylon in Ezekiel's time. According to Ezekiel the record written on these sticks was, in the first instance, to be "for Judah and for the children of Israel his companions" and, in the second, "for Joseph, the stick of Ephraim, and for all the house of Israel his companions." The role of Joseph (up to and) in the last days as the favored son of Jacob who received the birthright (priesthood line) in the great blessing given him by his father Jacob (Genesis 49:22-26) and passed on by Jacob to Joseph's son Ephraim (Genesis 48:15-16) is not understood without knowledge of the stick of Joseph. Bible scholars have long interpreted the record written for Judah (the Jews) to be the Bible, as it is the record of the Jews, but no candidate for the stick of Joseph or Ephraim (Joseph's son favored in the blessing his grandfather Jacob gave him over his older brother Manasseh – see Genesis 48) has been widely recognized or accepted. By far the best and perhaps the only candidate satisfying all six elements prophesied in Joseph's blessing is the Book of Mormon, but it is clear that a severe political problem exists in accepting this Book in the implication it carries supporting, favoring, and authenticating the unique claims of the church which publishes it. However, Moroni, in the concluding chapter of the Book of Mormon offers a powerful promise by which the truth of this Book may be established to any person through faith in Christ, study, prayer, and intent to practice. While politics trumps faith and honest scholarship in the world, the power of God, when one has sufficient faith in Him to seek it, will eventually rule supreme over the limited capabilities of humans and fallible judgements of the world.

[18] *Bible,* John 10:14,16 reads, "I am the good shepherd, and know my sheep, and am known of mine. ... And other sheep I have, which are not of this fold: them also I must bring, and they shall hear my voice; and there shall be one fold, and one shepherd."

Christ had more to say regarding this matter in *Book of Mormon,* 3 Nephi 15:16-24 "This much did the Father command me, that I should tell unto them: That other sheep I have which are not of this fold; them also I must bring, and there shall be one fold and one shepherd. And now, because of stiffneckedness and unbelief they understood not my word; therefore I was commanded to say no more of the Father concerning this thing unto them. But, verily, I say unto you that the Father hath commanded me, and I tell it unto you, that ye were separated from among them because of their iniquity; therefore it is because of their iniquity that they know not of you. And verily, I say unto you again that the other tribes hath the Father separated from them; and it is because of their iniquity that they know not of them. And verily I say unto you that ye are they of whom I said: Other sheep I have which are not of this fold; them also I must bring, and they shall hear my voice; and there shall be one fold and one shepherd. And they understood me not, for they supposed it had been the Gentiles; for they understood not that the Gentiles should be converted through their preaching.

And they understood me not that I said they shall hear my voice; and they understood me not that the Gentiles should not at any time hear my voice – *that I should not manifest myself unto them save it were by the Holy Ghost.* But behold, ye have both heard my voice, and seen me; and ye are my sheep, and ye are numbered among those whom the Father hath given me." (italics added)

[19] *Bible,* Matthew 27:45, 50-54, Mark 15:33, 38-39, Luke 23:44-48.

[20] Wells, H. G., *The Outline of History,* Volume 1, Garden City Books, Garden City, New York, 1961, 428-429.

[21] *Book of Mormon,* 3 Nephi 11:3,7.

[22] Ibid., 3 Nephi 17:25.

[23] Ibid., 3 Nephi 11:14.

[24] Ibid., 3 Nephi 11:31-40.

[25] This is not the only doctrine He taught but it is the only doctrine He designated and set apart as "my doctrine," including no doctrine more or less than what He explicitly declared it to contain.

[26] *Book of Mormon,* 2 Nephi 32:5-6.

[27] The scientific method is limited to consideration of observed, objective facts and their implications and, as a result (illustrated by the Löwenheim-Skolem theorem described in Chapter 10), it can never establish unique truth or a definitive *yes* answer. On the other hand, the doctrine of Christ is unlimited, allowing a full range of guidance and definitive *yes* answer that uniquely defines reality and provides a complete basis for understanding of truth.

[28] *Bible,* John 7:15-17.

[29] This reference to the Trinity as one is not to be taken in the traditional trinitarian- or Nicene- or Athanasian-creed sense of "three in one and one in three ..." Rather it alludes to the oneness in desire, intent, purpose, and power among the Father, the Son, and the Holy Ghost as described by Christ and sought by Him for the faithful amongst all people in His great intercessory prayer. (*Bible,* John 17:21.)

[30] *Bible,* Matthew 16:13-18. The rock on which we are to build is *knowledge that Jesus is the Christ* received by the power of God, the Holy Ghost, the Source of ostensible-step knowledge, the Source of Peter's knowledge that Christ certified as the foundation of His church. Peter had heard the voice of God on the Mount of Transfiguration declaring Christ as His Son, but he describes the witness of the Holy Ghost as "a more sure word." (*Bible,* 2 Peter 1:18-19.)

[31] The term "the Rock of Heaven [meaning Christ], which is broad as eternity" was used by the Lord speaking to the Old-Testament prophet Enoch (*Pearl of Great Price,* Moses 7:53). By my own metaphor, "the rock broader than the universe and deeper than time," I also refer to Christ and His knowledge and power that transcend the spatial-temporal, material universe (spacetime and its material contents).

[32] *Book of Mormon,* Mosiah 3:19.

[33] *Bible,* Mark 10:14, (Luke 18:17).

[34] *Bible,* Matthew 18:3, see also 19:14.

[35] *Bible,* Isaiah 9:6, 42:6-7, Luke 4:18, John 3:2, 10:25, 36-38, 11:43-45, 14:10-11, 20:30-31.

[36] *Bible,* Matthew 16:13-17, 2:1-2, Luke 2:9-10, 25-32, 36-38, 3:15-18.

[37] The term "little" here is relative. Christ sacrificed *all* and on behalf of each individual suffered incomprehensible pain sufficient to remove from each of us all guilt for our thoughtless, disobedient, and selfish acts. In comparison, what Christ asks of us is small. He asks us to follow after Him, to give our lives to His direction (through the Holy Ghost) as He gave His to the Father's. He wants our hearts and minds rather than only our actions; but giving the former provides the latter as well. He, in turn, strengthens and guides us. The gracious, magnanimous, exciting prospect in this exchange is the magnification of our personal qualities, abilities, and powers He provides as we seek to do His work. And as we focus our heart and soul on His way and His work they become ours, we draw close to and become like Him. In consequence of the help, the burden is easy. In light of the reward, the effort is little, within the reach of all willing to try.

[38] *Bible,* John 3:1-21. [39] *Bible,* John 3:8 (and the whole chapter.)

[40] *Bible,* Acts, Chapter 2. *Wind* in verse 2 appears in John 3:8. [41] *Bible,* Acts 1:15.

[42] *Bible,* Acts 2:36. [43] *Bible,* John 21:15-17. [44] *Bible,* Acts 2:38.

[45] *Bible,* Acts 2:41. [46] *Book of Mormon,* 2 Nephi, Chapters 31 and 32.

[47] *Book of Mormon,* 2 Nephi 32:5-6. [48] *Doctrine and Covenants* 10:67-70.

[49] Bible Dictionary appended to the *Holy Bible, containing the Old and New Testaments, Authorized King James Version,* published by the Church of Jesus Christ of Latter-day Saints, Salt Lake City, 1979. See listing under "High Priest." Under the law of Moses "the office [of high priest] was hereditary and came through the firstborn among the family of Aaron, Aaron himself being the first high priest." It was therefore a lifetime calling, nominally providing only one high priest per generation. "During the Maccabaean period the high priest was also the political head of the nation. After the Maccabaean rule was overthrown, high priests were inappropriately appointed by Herod and the Romans. The office was filled with 28 different men between 37 BC and 68 AD. Since the latter year the office has ceased to exist among the Jews, but they were in apostasy long before that time." For additional details see Ricciotti, Giuseppe, *The Life of Christ,* Bruce Publishing, Milwaukee, 1947, 48.

[50] Besides the mention of Nicodemus visiting Christ by night described in John 3:1-13, Nicodemus is mentioned by John in two other places. As related in John 7:45-52, when officers were sent by the rulers to apprehend Jesus and returned empty handed with the comment that "never [has a] man spake like this man," their allegiance was challenged with the retort "Are ye also deceived?" This was followed by the rhetorical question meant to provide obvious and conclusive evidence that Christ's ministry was of no import "Have any of the rulers or of the Pharisees believed on him? But this people who knoweth not the law are cursed." At what must have been some risk to his standing in the Sanhedrin and his vestment of power and status among his people in the face of the attitude so declared by the other rulers, Nicodemus responded with his own rhetorical question "Doth our law judge any man, before it hear him, and know what he doeth?" suggesting that, whatever the motive and whatever the threat, condemnation of Jesus was not justified based on hearsay evidence. Later, as related in John 19:39-40, this Nicodemus brought a mixture of myrrh and aloes, about an hundred-pound weight (worth a considerable sum of money), which spices were used to embalm the body of Jesus. These three instances wherein Nicodemus is mentioned in the gospel according to John, taken together, indicate belief and devotion.

[51] *Bible,* John 3:18-21. [52] *Bible,* Acts 4:3-4. [53] *Bible,* Acts 1:6-8.

[54] From the Joseph Smith Translation of the Bible as quoted in *The Holy Bible, King James Version,* The Church of Jesus Christ of Latter-day Saints, Salt Lake City, 1979, 1370, footnote 20b.

[55] *Bible,* Acts 3:19-21.

[56] The tacit assumption made here is that the restored church that Peter refers to is, as it claims, The Church of Jesus Christ of Latter-day Saints (Mormons) organized in 1830. The prophecy of Peter places severe requirements on any church making such a claim, including the requirement of science or comprehensive consistency with all material evidence. Peter's prophecy describes a restitution of all things spoken by *all God's holy prophets since the world began.* A church fulfilling this prophecy must be able to explain the meaning of all essential Bible teachings as well as provide much knowledge beyond Biblical scripture, since scripture is the writing of prophets or the record of their words and acts and since some scripture is known to have been lost or corrupted (Appendix I). Such information should and does fill volumes beyond what the Bible contains. Here is a crucial test of a church claiming to be Christ's restored original, namely, whether it can provide valid explanations of obscure principles and doctrine mentioned in the Bible or, equivalently, what it teaches beyond that known from the Bible. Missionaries from such a restored church would eagerly seek to explain such knowledge to all willing to receive it. The Book of Mormon itself is powerful. Occasionally even an adversary reads the Book of Mormon with intent to disprove it, only to be convinced it is genuine by its marvelous teachings, wonderfully-Christian spirit, and the power of God available to a sincere reader through Moroni's promise.

[57] *Bible,* Matthew 3:16-17, Mark 1:10-11, Luke 3:21-22, John 1:1,14, Revelation 5:5-30, *Pearl of Great Price,* Moses 1:30-38.

[58] *Bible,* John 1:1-3,10,14, *Doctrine and Covenants* 29:31-32, 45:1.

[59] *Pearl of Great Price,* Abraham 4, especially verses 7, 9-12, 17-18, 21, 25, 31.

[60] *Bible,* Isaiah 2:5, 45:7, 60:19, John 1:4-5, 3:19, 8:12, Ephesians 5:14, James 1:17, 1 John 1:5-7, *Doctrine and Covenants* 84:45-46, 88:11.

[61] In the *Doctrine and Covenants* 93:28,29-30,36 truth and intelligence are each treated as independent and free to act for itself, as in an individual possessing agency. "... otherwise there is no existence [roughly as Descartes surmised]." And "He that keepeth [God's] commandments receiveth truth and light, until he is glorified in truth and knoweth all things." "The glory of God is intelligence, or, in other words, light and truth."

[62] *Pearl of Great Price,* Moses 4:30. Whether Moses spoke with God the Father or God the Son empowered with "divine investiture" speaking for the Father is immaterial since the statement originates with God the Father and carries the weight of His authority.

[63] *Doctrine and Covenants* 93:24.

[64] *Pearl of Great Price,* Moses 4:3.

[65] *Bible,* John 14:12, *Book of Mormon,* 3 Nephi 27:21.

13. Escaping Paradigm Paralysis

The title of this chapter implies that one may be paralyzed by or captured in a paradigm. That is exactly what can occur, but even a deficient paradigm can not act to endlessly trap an astute user.

Because science considers only the material universe while Christianity considers the total universe, science may be regarded as a subset of Christianity. That is, between these two philosophies only Christianity considers the full scope of evidence. This does not imply that all Christians are accomplished scientists because they are not. But some are. And among them one would often find, if one were to ask, that the believing-Christian-scientist's science was secondary in priority to his or her Christianity. And, indeed, that the Christian considers total-universe evidence while the materialist considers only material-universe evidence, as required by objectivity, imposes critical consequences (described in Chapters 2 and 16).

Since the scope of Christianity includes science, in principle if not in practice, and since we have already examined science, we can draw on science in our examination of Christianity. In particular, we shall examine Christianity by contrasting it with science, especially the limitations of science, to provide clearer vision of and improved insight into both. Using such comparison the abstract properties of Christianity are more easily perceived and assimilated and so are those of science. In the rather stark contrasts that result, advantages of Christianity become especially clear, the principal one being avoidance of inherent, fatal pitfalls in science in Christian pursuit of an unrestricted understanding of reality.

A pure materialist neither seeks nor recognizes any meaning or associated feeling beyond the objective, material-universe facts and the patterns and connections he or she perceives therein. Total-universe facts containing meaning and feeling are contemplated and addressed in Christianity. When a materialist encounters the Christian belief founded on meaning and feeling, he or she must regard it on the basis of materialism as superstition, tradition-bound ignorance, self delusion, or some other flawed belief. Spiritual matters hold no priority for a materialist whose paradigm denies and ignores all but material-universe facts. A materialist is thus paralyzed by and captured in his or her paradigm, in not seeing beyond materialism. Conversely, the Christian believes the "gospel of Christ is hid to them that are lost: In whom the god of this world [Satan] hath blinded the minds of them which believe not [in Christ]."[1] Spiritual things are "hid from the wise and the prudent [as they suppose], and [God] hast revealed them to babes."[2] Thus, childlike Christians seek further light, knowledge, and meaning from God through fire and the Holy Ghost. Yet, Christians too may be paralyzed in a flawed paradigm.

Partially Informed Christians

One may be captured in an incorrect tradition, attitude, or paradigm of a particular Christian or other religious denomination or sect when one is unaware of or unwilling to consider broad and deep evidence, including the ostensible step urged by Christ in His doctrine. Or, despite awareness but because of desire to please family or community more than Christ, one may choose to remain in a limited paradigm. The brilliant mathematician Ian Malcolm in Michael Crichton's fictional novel *The Lost World*, in his usual pessimistic view, asks and answers (truly enough with my one suggested alteration in square brackets)

> What makes you think human beings are sentient and aware? There's no evidence for it. Human beings never [too rarely] think for themselves, they find it too uncomfortable. For the most part, members of our species simply repeat what they are told – and become upset if they are exposed to any different view. The characteristic human trait is not awareness but conformity, and the characteristic result is religious warfare. Other animals fight for territory or food; but, uniquely in the animal kingdom, human beings fight for 'beliefs.' The reason is that beliefs guide behavior ... But at a time when our behavior may well lead us to extinction, I see no reason to assume we have any awareness at all. We are stubborn, self-destructive conformists. Any other view of our species is just a self-congratulatory delusion. Next question.[3]

A "partially informed Christian"[4] can be as blinded and captured in ignorance as a materialist can be when such a Christian incorrectly believes he or she has already embraced the full scope of Christian knowledge and experience. In terms of Lewis' process of Transposition, one looks for no higher level of meaning when one believes he or she is already at the highest level. Christianity itself, including its myriad, corrupted forms wherein faith in Christ and belief in the power of God are limited or denied, is its own worst hindrance. We have not accidentally come to this state. This condition has been conceived and motivated by the enemy (see Appendix I).

Of course all are limited in capability and/or paradigm. Every person can look higher and try harder to achieve childlike humility, sagacious wisdom, and saintly charity. But both possibility and need to find and follow the way, the truth, and the life are masked by paradigm-limited vision of partially-informed Christians.

Partially Informed Scientists

A paradigm is simultaneously limiting and empowering. Science has provided great insights into pattern and connection among the objective facts, as we have seen. Yet it leads only to tentative, often changing (up to now) knowledge rather than definitive understanding of reality, as we have also seen. Because of inherent limitation in the scientific method, even though false conclusions may be disproved by establishing at least one contrary fact, no proof of any theory or law, no conclusive *yes* answer, may be established by science. Because science only works to sometimes eliminate false guesses and because the number of possible guesses is indefinitely large, the materialist is "ever learning and never able to come to the knowledge of the truth,"[5] a perilous paradigm of the last days (now) Paul warned us against. Materialism is indeed paralysis – a bottomless trap in which failure is masked by small successes obtained along the way to tentative knowledge. Clever is the enemy who conceived and choreographed acceptance of materialism with widespread authority and prestige in modern, "sophisticated" society. So accepted, materialism with human pride and historical failures of corrupted Christianity (Chapters 14 and 15) is utilized by the enemy to generate among many a feeling of scorn toward and dismissal of Christianity because of its required simple belief in Christ compared to man's (supposed) great, self-achieved knowledge of science and mathematics. But *great is as great results and prospects provides.*[6] Materialism doesn't provide any great results or prospects comparable to those of the doctrine of Christ. A scientist not informed on this point, a partially informed scientist, is crippled in his or her search for truth.

An illustration may here be helpful. A prominent physicist posed the question "... if we believe in a theory because it agrees with observation, and it agrees with observation because it is true (which is not always the case), then isn't it just a harmless abbreviation to say that we believe in it because it is true?"[7] The sticking point is his "which is not always the case." Observations are limited. This same physicist remarks, "It is true that quantum mechanics does apply 'always and everywhere.'"[7] But we have not yet observed always and everywhere, so how can we know?

In its function, a paradigm provides a consistent, broad view of reality with many details and connections therein recognized or implied. This function of a paradigm is desired and the very reason one is useful. But if the paradigm is not accurate or is incomplete, it provides a distorted or restricted view of reality. One might think such a distorted view is easily recognized as one utilizes the paradigm in observing reality. But distortion is not easily recognized because of circular reasoning inherent in a paradigm – valid evidence supports the paradigm and the paradigm provides criteria that defines valid evidence – as will be examined for materialism (Chapter 16). This same concept also applies in Christianity. Christians of different belief cite different Bible passages as "important" in supporting their particular views.

Although paradigm-based investigations may be regarded as important, results of such investigations are often quite predictable because conclusions are generally established at the point a paradigm is adopted. Apparently not everyone reads and understands their C. S. Lewis. ("What we learn from experience depends on the kind of philosophy we bring to experience."[8]) Yet significant insight is obtained by resolving conflicts and limitations of science and applied mathematics most clearly evident at their frontiers, frontiers where the deepest questions appear, where knowledge is scant, where no conclusions are yet universally or even widely accepted, and where we encounter the limit(s) of validity of the paradigm. Work focused on resolving ignorance and confusion at these frontiers[9] in determining correct implications of the scientific paradigm is therefore fruitful. Likewise in Christianity, the deepest questions often appear at the edge of knowledge. It is generally at a frontier that one discovers new territory (new knowledge) and where territory (paradigm) is expanded.

For every paradigm there exists frontiers of knowledge. For science, an expansive frontier joins the material universe with an inner, intellectual, emotional, spiritual universe. Ignoring this inner universe leaves one lacking important information with little or no awareness of knowledge of a most critical kind. Where such deliberate ignorance exists, so does a severe paradigm paralysis.

Perspicacious Probing of Paradigm

Studies based on a single, adopted paradigm often follow a single, foreordained path – a consequence of the function of a paradigm and its internal reasoning. Deep and penetrating studies, like Newton's *Principia* and others considered in Book II, do not simply follow an existing paradigm. Such studies propose and justify a new paradigm or an essential new component by which an old paradigm is expanded. Or they examine at a fundamental level the validity and limitations of a paradigm (as we do here for two). Even when one has already, perhaps tentatively, adopted a paradigm, independent, critical thinking is prudent because no paradigm is universally accepted. According to "other people," many people are simply wrong in their adopted paradigm. One or both groups may remain captured in their paradigm because of a lack of independent, critical thinking. After all, a paradigm simultaneously enlarges and constrains one's view.

As is clear from Chapter 10, many paradigms exist that are consistent with a considered set of facts. This conclusion applies for all paradigms, not only ones based on logicomathematics for which the Löwenheim-Skolem theorem applies, because the number of paradigms consistent with a specified set of assumptions, axioms, and other facts is limited only by one's imagination. That a paradigm provides a consistent interpretation of the facts is not sufficient to establish its truth, which is why one or more additional conditions such as Ockham's razor,[10] aesthetics, or symmetry are often invoked as convenient but arbitrary constraints. Irrespective of such augmentation of a truth criterion, the mendacity in a study attempting to prove a paradigm by use of the paradigm lies in that because a paradigm and its evidence are always consistent and use of a paradigm to test itself is circular, consistency between a paradigm and its evidence or consistency of a paradigm with itself are inevitable. Even a false paradigm based on consistency can never contradict itself. To establish truth of a paradigm, definitive, independent evidence originating *outside* any circular reasoning must be established by *external proof* that "breaks" any circular reasoning or self-dependence or internal flaw in reasoning and supersedes mere consistency as a truth criterion. No other approach can reliably establish truth.

A study that merely lists page after page of detailed consequences that, obscure though they may be, are already assumed or implied in the adopted paradigm is not as deep, insightful, and profound as one describing a successful new paradigm. While the present study does not attempt to propose a new paradigm, its principal object is to delineate the exact method and scope of evidence (facts) utilized in a Christian and a scientific paradigm, how the method and evidence of each one are internally interdependent, how differences in the two sets of method and evidence dictate differences in knowledge, understanding, and meaning, how external proof is required to conclusively validate either paradigm, and how for one of these paradigms such external proof is available for the receiving.

Short of the powerful ostensible-step methodology we urge for establishing truth, science or materialism at least provides a means for eliminating many false conclusions and paradigms. While science cannot establish truth with certainty, it can eliminate incorrect hypotheses, theories, or laws which cause a "paradigm reality" to conflict with an "observed reality" to eliminate false notions. But this capability falls far short of establishing certain truth – complete agreement with reality cannot be established until the nature of reality is known by *yes* as well as *no* answers, and *yes* answers fall beyond the present scope of science.

Scientific Theory and Vision of Reality

In hard, deductive science, fundamental questions inevitably arise about all theories and paradigms, such as the theories of Newton, Einstein, Planck, and the many contributors to quantum mechanics we have met. Newton's *Principia* was written because of one such question and it placed mechanics on a fundamental, broad, and powerful basis that, for the first time, provided definite answers to many scientific questions and made Newton famous. But Newton was acutely aware that his theories left other fundamental questions unanswered and he was candid and forthcoming in recognizing these deficiencies. A principal unanswered question that long concerned Newton was the means by which the force of gravity makes itself felt across a large expanse of empty space. This type of force is the so-called *action at a distance* against which Descartes had cautioned. About it Newton wrote

> That gravity should be innate inherent and essential to matter so that one body may act upon another at a distance through a vacuum without the mediation of any thing else by and through which their action or force may be conveyed from one another is to me so great an absurdity that I believe no man who has in philosophical matters any competent faculty of thinking can ever fall into it.[11]

Although Newton proposed his mathematical theory of gravity and used it brilliantly with his calculus to accurately describe the solar system and many things therein, he didn't understand or try to explain the theory itself. He felt his new theory, paradigm, or vision of reality was strange, non-intuitive, and unexplainable. But Newton's theory was so successful and comprehensive it eventually became the basis of our now-conventional culture, the philosophical difficulty of not understanding action at a distance being simply ignored, at least by most, and Newton's mathematical law of gravity simply accepted. Such acceptance of initially-strange elements of a new paradigm is inevitable because our paradigm must agree with our "observed reality." Some have proposed mathematical field theories as "explaining" gravity and other actions at a distance. But theses "explanations" are mere *mathematical descriptions* which provide no *physical understanding*. Appreciating this difference between description or prediction and explanation or understanding is of critical importance to true understanding, as will be illustrated using a physical mechanism of gravity to shortly be described. Have we fooled ourselves into thinking that by Newton's mathematical *description* we *understand* gravity? We have been warned against such illusions in the earlier-quoted statements of Smoot and Davidson and of Feynman. "Locking in" on low-level knowledge (description) as adequate and complete can inhibit or prevent discovery of high-level understanding (explanation).

Newton and others long struggled with the strange, non-intuitive implications of Newton's new theory, principally with how a force of gravity can be exerted over a vast expanse of empty space. Such a struggle is a hallmark of all powerful, new paradigms, especially mathematical-based ones that merely predict and describe rather than explain, because our intuition is invariably based in the old paradigm. Another hallmark is the eventual acceptance of new, implied concepts and qualities originally regarded as strange, non-intuitive, and unexplainable.

We recognize a huge gap remains between describing or predicting something and understanding, interpreting, or explaining it. Describing represents mere knowledge of facts while explaining requires deeper knowledge of underlying principles, facts, and their connections and patterns that provide higher, more deeply-founded understanding. If only a mathematical theory that describes or predicts some phenomena is known, in what terms can a physical understanding go deeper than or even just as deep as mere description? And beyond understanding lies the highest realization of all: meaning. Without understanding and its interpretation of essence, value, and significance there exists no comprehension of meaning.

Newton recognized and candidly bemoaned in the above quote and in other writings[12] as late as 1706 that his theory of gravity addressed only the level of description or knowledge. However, many now seem to regard physical description as explanation and material knowledge as understanding and, to them, meaning is invisible. We propose and examine in this chapter the thought that such an illusion is symptomatic of a lack of true understanding and an absence of critical thinking. When one thinks describing or predicting is equal to explaining or understanding, a wiser person questions whether such a one understands anything at all. The nature and desirability of true understanding as well as barriers that prevent its discovery and how these barriers may be overcome are addressed later in this chapter and a uniquely reliable method for obtaining true understanding is advocated.

Materialists hold the belief that reality is only revealed by scientific-type inquiry and the resulting theories it produces. While the business of physics is the discovery of reality, some may legitimately question equating the terms "reality" and "theory" because such association denotes too comprehensive and reliable a sense to mere theory. However, "personal vision of reality" and "theory" coincide for the case of one holding theory or paradigm to represent maximum possible understanding and his or her full conviction. And one seeking to find reality exclusively through science considers or perceives no other possibilities because others are deliberately ignored as misguided and impertinent.

Alternatively, one can believe or entertain scientific theories and simultaneously hold other belief as well, other belief that strongly moderates or even controls that person's view of reality. For scientists who are believing Christians, subscription to a particular theory does not exert much influence on their vision of "ultimate reality," the reality consistent with their answers to ultimate questions. Their vision is dominated by the principles which Christ taught while their science defines only the limited realm of objective, reproducible, lowest-common-denominator, material-universe facts.

In the absence of other belief, for one engaged in discovering reality exclusively through science, scientific theories may represent one's entire vision of reality, even for a nonscientist enthusiast who doesn't understand much science. Such a person may hold that his or her belief, based "solidly" on rigorous consideration of only objective, reproducible, lowest-common-denominator facts, is superior to that of a Christian, whose notions seem vague at best compared to objective, lowest-common-denominator facts and the supposed rigor of science. But, as already argued, the scientific method and lowest-common-denominator facts provide no better than tentative conclusions confined to a narrow venue, namely, pertaining only to reproducibly seen, heard, touched, smelled, or tasted experience[13] and deductions made from a lowest-common-denominator-*consensus* interpretation of such experience. In seeking answers to ultimate questions, what can be discovered using only this venue is severely restrictive and hopelessly inadequate compared to what the doctrine of Christ claims to provide.

Too Tightly Tethered to Technical Tasks

While scientific and mathematical discoveries may be inspired, they are limited by their venue. Deliberately ignoring everything but the objective, reproducible, lowest-common-denominator, material facts, and thereby severely restricting one's view, precludes proper consideration of subjective matters – the emotional self, subjective perception, cognizance, man's religious yearning, faith in Christ, comprehension of meaning, and mystically obtained certainty. Such matters are personal and individual-experience influenced and they therefore lie beyond the scope of science, which may be considered the body of *objective knowledge* which, in fact, is the body of *subjective knowledge* common to all "adequately trained" or "expert" observers (a concept treated in Book I and Appendix A).

Nevertheless, ability to collect data, evaluate information, order and associate facts, and draw conclusions by logical deduction are useful tools in any study or investigation. In use of these tools the scientist, mathematician, and philosopher excel. Thus, scientists are at no disadvantage in matters involving the subjective and abstract once such matters are assigned due value; indeed, abilities hard won in science, mathematics, and philosophy are greatly beneficial.

But while a scientist may have developed useful capabilities, he or she may be disadvantaged by the "convention of the trade" in matters of breadth of vision, recognition of the value of subjective facts, patience in ignorance, humility and willingness to be guided by others, and, above all, faith in Christ. Of course some scientists are not deficient in any of these qualities. But scientists are vulnerable to narrowness of vision because love of science, like love of any other thing, can become consuming. And science is one of the leading alternatives commonly adopted in place of religion because it is also a higher philosophy by which one seeks a correct vision of reality. Even, and maybe especially, those who do not understand much science may be attracted from religious belief to science, perhaps because of personal belief about conflict between science and religion, perhaps because of ubiquitous materialistic bias, or perhaps because of some romantic notion. Another leading alternative to religious belief is simple indifference; but the category-three students of Chapter 2, the ones who simply don't care, are the most difficult to reach so I address primarily category-one and -two students herein. Nevertheless, if any "category-three" reads this book, I make the simple plea not to waste the opportunity to find and follow knowledge, understanding, and meaning. This opportunity is more precious than we currently understand. Between those who will inherit the highest level of salvation – eternal life – and those who will inherit salvation at a lower level, both are described as "honorable men [and women]" while the latter are differentiated as having been "blinded by the craftiness of men [and women]" while the former were valiant in finding and following truth.[14]

Among scientists the alluring, "siren-song"[15] call of science is strong for the following reasons. Scientists are generally well educated, by both formal education and by the rigor of their trade. Most scientists become quite self reliant and independent in certain aspects of their thinking and capable in developing and presenting their ideas before large groups, often presenting papers at meetings describing and defending their results and writing scientific journal articles and books for the same purposes. Independence, affluence, implicit and explicit recognition of success, occasionally even acclamation, formidable professional and personal skills, and personal satisfaction all lead to comfort and gratification, all based only on consensus acceptance of objective, reproducible, lowest-common-denominator facts. For many if not most scientists, science seems to provide a clear sense of reality, validated by uniform belief among similarly-educated, homogeneously-minded peers. The issues ignored in science are easily swept under the communal scientific rug because they fall outside the scope of science and make many uncomfortable in addressing them. Except for the rare believer willing to express personal faith or the rare atheist willing to express an opposing belief or a disdain for such faith, a belief or disdain he or she incorrectly believes is science-supported, the topic of God or religion is rarely broached among scientists.

This world of the scientist can indeed be a comfortable and gratifying one, especially with respect to isolation from any paradigm challenge, the isolation of a category-two-student attitude. There would have to be strong reason to do something risky, something that might threaten the *status quo*, like allowing a perfectly good paradigm to be questioned.

And there is a strong reason. There exists a better student category, a better paradigm, a more trustworthy path, a deeper and more satisfying understanding, a broader vision that sees beyond a material-universe-limited scope, a clearer comprehension of reality. This better paradigm leads to increased knowledge, self-discipline, personal growth, understanding, comprehension of meaning, and joy.

To contrast scientific and Christian views, paradigms which are *not* mutually exclusive in spite of these contrasts, consider the following three pairs of vignettes:

(1) "Any good scientific research raises more questions than it answers" summarized the professor to the group of graduate students touring his laboratory. "Ever learning, and never able to come to the knowledge of the truth"[5] preached the pastor to his flock.

(2) "If it can't be quantified, it can't be understood" concluded the distinguished "41st Annual Downawell Quantum Particle Lecture Series" honoree at Poison Ivy University.[16] "Now faith is the substance of things hoped for, the evidence of things not seen"[17] earnestly confided one friend to another during their luncheon conversation.

(3) "These results will revolutionize man's thinking in cosmology and the origins of the universe" enthused the NASA publicist, referring to the sensational, weightless data from the space shuttle experiment measuring reproduction of fruit flies. "Thomas saith unto him, Lord, we know not whither thou goest; and how can we know the way? Jesus saith unto him, I am the way, the truth, and the life: no man cometh unto the Father but by me."[18]

Of course the above pairs are contrived to provide a little humor, but only on the "scientific" side. A little truth is also thrown in. In fact, a lot of truth is thrown in. Two points of view, two paradigms, are contrasted, a Christian one and a scientific one or a very loose approximation thereto, especially in the third pair, but not unlike that encountered in commercialized or politicized, look-at-wonderful-me science.

Reader Quiz: answer in your mind the following three questions. In making a candid comparison of science and your religion, would you be strongly sympathetic to one or both views? If you were to identify one paradigm between these two as your primary or controlling one, which would you choose? Would you prefer not to reveal the other view?

I am posing these questions because I am attempting to call to your attention your knee-jerk sympathy, your intellectual identification, your preferred paradigm, your conception of reality. There exists an urgency in these questions because there exists an urgency in discovering your answers and whether better ones exist.

An absolutely best answer to such questions exists and may be discovered and demonstrated to be absolutely correct by one willing to receive the answer with intent to follow where it leads. This answer is available and certain by the doctrine of Christ. The current, normal, everyday routine has a limited term, personally and universally according to the Christian paradigm, and the time for addressing such questions is now rather than later according to this paradigm. Later, neither the opportunity to find and align with the best answer nor even the question will exist. The answer will be imposed; the opportunity to voluntarily align with an answer as a confession of faith in Christ will be lost. We will already have declared our allegiance.

Paradigm Paralysis

We now enlarge on the already introduced concept that material-universe science is inadequate for conclusively addressing total-universe phenomena and, in fact, even material-universe phenomena. This inadequacy is a symptom of faulty reasoning inherent in rigorous, objective, universal science. In Book I and Chapters 10 and 11 we addressed the objectivity of science. Objectivity is illusory because when one limits consideration to only strictly-rigorously-objective facts, no facts remain. Nor do complete human personalities ever appear in the imaginary, ideal, deterministic, external universe of science because of irrational disruption or subjective scrambling of objective facts they cause – precluding scientific study of humans beyond their existence as mere physical objects. We must therefore address the universality of science, i.e., the universality assumption, the belief that science has power to eventually provide to any person capable in science a knowledge and description of all things based on (eventually) known scientific laws. (Eager and ambitious scientists do not want themselves or their contributions, real and potential, to be regarded as limited; nor should they limit their scope and depth of inquiry.)

It is believed that to make science universal – capable in the hands of any able user of addressing all things – we must limit consideration to only objective, reproducible phenomena to protect the database and resulting paradigm from spurious evidence that may not be universally valid, such as evidence from strong personalities, institutions, or traditions that may attempt to dictate a reality they envision. Examples of spurious evidence are dogma of the Aristotelians and of the medieval Church and that of their modern counterparts, those who strongly hold and wish to impose on others intellectual, political, religious, social, scientific, or other belief. Consequently, in science we disregard or deny at the outset any phenomena and evidence that does not satisfy objectivity and reproducibility requirements, eliminating all nonmaterial (in-mind only) evidence.

However, all evidence is subjective to some extent. Temporarily ignoring this problem, we further note that some otherwise legitimate evidence is not reproducible, like observation of rare or unique events (miracles, flying saucers, ...). Disregarding such events to protect universality of science prevents its universality.

To make science capable of addressing all things we must *limit the definition of all things* to only those things considered by science. How is this limitation of science to be regarded? We can either (1) recognize a limited, non-universal scope and power of science or (2) dismiss "unscientific" phenomena by scientifically explaining them away or claiming their observation was invalid on the grounds that because they aren't explainable by science they are impossible and the observation must be invalid, an illusion, an imagined fantasy, a trick, or hallucination. Among some, unacceptable results are indeed denied or explained away using well-known (and even unknown!) phenomena, even when the explanation must be stretched beyond credulity (see Appendix A). While science appears to be a powerful and broadly applicable method, it is severely limited by its internal reasoning – valid science is based on limited evidence and only such limited evidence is scientifically valid. Science deliberately ignores important or potentially important phenomena at the cost of universality, which cost is unmentioned and probably unrecognized by many scientists. The rigid materialist is knowingly or unknowingly paralyzed in his or her paradigm, recognizing no possibility that faith in Christ or an associated ostensible step can provide any real and useful guidance. To fix deficiency in science the logical positivist or linguistic analyst seeks to redefine "how anything at all is to be described." But denying ignorance doesn't lessen its effect.

A theory, paradigm, philosophy, system of belief, culture, or view of reality provides a means for rationalizing the facts we perceive and organizing knowledge of the universe we observe. Simultaneously it limits our view, constrains our understanding, and hides meaning contrary to that supported by the adopted paradigm or philosophy. We have suggested how one may be paralyzed in the paradigm of materialism by "valid" sensing of only things and events allowed in the paradigm and nothing more. If the paradigm is a merely empirical view of reality that contains no deep understanding and provides no more than a quantitatively accurate catalog of individual, lowest-common-denominator facts and some of their connections, it contains knowledge but not much understanding and no meaning. And when one views the facts utilizing this paradigm it obscures any different vision and causes rejection of alternative paradigms, even one more comprehensive that better connects and organizes the facts. One is distracted from the latter vision by recognition of the connections and consistency provided in the former; one tends to ignore facts that his or her paradigm and intuition based thereon does not validate, or *vice versa.* Just as one does not normally re-examine a familiar person but merely recognizes him or her, one does not re-evaluate a paradigm upon encountering familiar facts but merely recognizes them in the vision of his or her paradigm. As in passing through a crowd of strangers one does not usually dwell on unfamiliar faces, one also does not recognize facts that don't fit his or her paradigm's vision. By this function a paradigm is both a boon and a bane – a boon because many events can be quickly recognized and evaluated in "background mode" and a bane because an adopted paradigm blinds one to any alternative, perhaps superior view of the facts, the effect we call paradigm paralysis, whose consequences are further considered in Chapter 16.

Because any adopted paradigm, philosophy or culture defines what is "normal and reasonable," it also defines what is "strange and unreasonable." The adjectives "strange," "unusual," "inconsistent" and "unreasonable" on the one hand or "usual," "likely," "consistent", "reasonable," "obvious" and "certain" on the other are, therefore, always tacitly paradigm dependent and should be regarded with careful skepticism. Justification by the common teenager plea "all my friends are doing it" is superficial. What should instead be addressed is the broader-and-deeper question: "Do I hold or should I adopt the same paradigm as my friends?"

It seems to be part of human nature that the more tentative the knowledge and understanding justifying one's adopted paradigm, the greater the perceived threat in any criticism, however accurate it may be, and the more fierce the tenacity with which one holds and defends his or her paradigm – in a category-two-student-like attitude. In contrast, a category-one-student attitude leads one to seek better knowledge and truer understanding, to expand breadth of vision, and to welcome critical thinking and improved methods for discovering knowledge and understanding.

Bohr and Einstein were adversaries in a long-running debate over the nature of quantum mechanics, a debate involving opposing beliefs of what physics is about. To Bohr, the fact that quantum mechanics provided answers that worked was the preeminent consideration. To Einstein, the fact that it was an *ad hoc*, strictly contrived, utilitarian theory with no discerned underlying basis by which it could be understood and tested was limiting. Regarding such a theory Einstein might have asked: "Where is the insight, the guidance, the understanding?" But, to be fair, one must admit that quantum mechanics has never yet failed to give a correct answer. It is a mathematical theory so intimately and fully connected to the measured data, i.e., so empirical, that different versions or theories of quantum mechanics cannot be discriminated by an appeal to experiment, i.e., no unique underlying reality emerges from quantum mechanics.[19] Quantum mechanics "merely" reliably describes or predicts correct results when other theories, like Newtonian mechanics, badly fail.

Neither Bohr nor Einstein was against quantum mechanics; they differed "only" on its interpretation or meaning or on its lack thereof. One might then be driven to say, out of frustration, "The difference between the Bohr and Einstein views is not important. Quantum mechanics is still quantum mechanics with its uncanny ability to provide correct answers. The rest is mere philosophy."

But without understanding founded on some demonstrable basis, it is difficult to decide which philosophy or paradigm is best to adopt. Without understanding founded on a secure, demonstrated basis we may find ourselves in the hapless situation in which we are fiercely defending our paradigm against any alternative, especially the most superior one because it is the most threatening.[20] This situation is, of course, fatal to new learning and progress. We must mind our philosophy.

An emotional reaction, in the absence of a demonstrated basis for a paradigm, appears to be at least occasionally the root of antagonism a few materialists hold toward religion. To these materialists, certainty in and devotion to religion by others is contemptuously attributed to ignorance.

More commonly, scientists and other intelligent observers view the panorama of history and see widespread abuse of people in the name of institutionalized religion. This fact, with the scientist's habit of seeking conclusions consistent with all observation, leads naturally to the conclusion that such religion is bad.[21] Based on too-simple but natural induction, religion motivates in some materialists and others a resentful scorn and out-of-hand dismissal, the kind of scorn and dismissal displayed by the proud Laplace who had no need of the hypothesis of God. In Laplace, pure arrogance was a factor.[22] Indeed, pride is the universal basis of contempt, scorn, and resentment, including resentment of religious belief. But such a reaction is emotional rather than reasoned. We must mind our philosophy.

Such a reaction also occurs in Christians holding one view toward those holding another. Frederic William Farrar (1831-1903) in his *The Life of Christ*, one of the seminal English-language treatments of this subject first issued in 1874 and printed 26 times in its first two years, describes a reaction of Jewish leaders to Christ.

> But there is no ignorance so deep as the ignorance that will not know; no blindness so incurable as the blindness that will not see. And the dogmatism of a narrow and stolid prejudice which believes itself to be theological [or scientific or ...] learning is, of all others, the most ignorant and the most blind.[23]

The applicability of this indictment is broad. It is usually knowledgeable people with good intentions that would lead others to catastrophe, for such people think they understand on the basis of their knowledge; but catastrophe looms when they really don't.[24] For instance, a prominent physicist has written "I am all in favor of a dialogue between science and religion, but not a constructive dialogue. One of the great achievements of science has been, if not to make it impossible for intelligent people to be religious, then at least to make it possible for them not to be religious. We should not retreat from this accomplishment."[21] This same physicist later asks "But if we believe in a theory because it agrees with observation, and it agrees with observation because it is true (which is not always the case), then isn't it just a harmless abbreviation to say that we believe in it because it is true?"[21] The answer to this question is a tentative and contingent *yes* – not good enough. If one isolates him- or her-self in a narrow paradigm it is difficult, if not impossible, to broaden one's awareness, the general goal of constructive dialogue. We must mind our philosophy and, to be reliable, it must rest on a basis of *demonstrated* truth and understanding. Otherwise it is merely prejudice and someone else's karma will run over our dogma.

In Lewis' Transposition process one may anticipate a move from a richer-level system to a less-rich one with full awareness of what will be lost. But in seeking to go the other way it is impossible to imagine what is to be gained in the richer system when necessary experience and vision are not yet acquired. Until one somehow obtains understanding and meaning at the higher level, the richer understanding is invisible and one is blinded to its existence and value by the lower-level paradigm in which he or she already knows the facts, their connections, and has a working intuition. What more could there be? To the eventual detriment of his credibility, Immanuel Kant subscribed to Euclidian geometry and Newtonian physics as the true descriptions of the universe because he could envision no others.

Euclidian geometry and Newtonian mechanics (ignoring acceleration) are a simple limiting case of special relativity, the limiting case where the Lorentz-Fitzgerald factor $\gamma = 1$. Newtonian mechanics (without acceleration) is easily recovered (in effect) from relativity by setting $\gamma = 1$. The opposite derivation, obtaining relativity from Newtonian mechanics, required a genius using revolutionary insight. An additional observation or axiom was required, like the Michelson-Morley result or the postulate that c is constant or the use of Maxwell's electromagnetic theory – with the use of electromagnetic theory to refine mechanics the novel insight. In Newtonian mechanics the very existence and function of the factor γ are invisible because they lie outside the vision of reality provided by Euclidian geometry and Newtonian mechanics. Discovery of a new paradigm that provides a more correct and comprehensive vision of reality is difficult because the new always contradicts the old, otherwise it is not new. And yet the old is never totally wrong and usually nearly right. Thus, a strongly-held, never-critically-considered paradigm is blinding to deeper understanding, interpretation, and meaning. We must mind our philosophy.

Personal qualities also enhance or retard discovery of improved vision. Change requires desire and courage. Abandoning ideas in which we are comfortable is difficult. We may be rebelling against ideas of respected peers and, in some cases, our own former "declaration of allegiance."

The requirements of faith, independence, imagination, perseverance, and courage needed in discovery of truth and improvement of paradigm are now characterized in a Galilean-style dialogue. Vision and faith in the possibility of discovering truth through an improved paradigm are essential, for a person must see the benefit of finding truth and have hope in success to persevere in the search.

Salviati: The major problem in envisioning the fundamental nature of reality is that the reliability of many assumptions and laws that seem intuitively correct in one's current paradigm is inevitably challenged in extending scientific knowledge to ever deeper levels.

Simplicio: I don't think so at all. We just have to think about a problem more carefully in order to incrementally build on our present knowledge. Little increments will eventually get us to any desired level and for such increments traditional knowledge and assumptions are quite adequate.

Salviati: Not so, Simplicio. A philosophical system or paradigm is fundamentally limiting in the view it imposes. Trying to see independent of it is difficult and confirmation of knowledge in science is mere consistency between the observed and expected or, rather, failing to find disagreement between observation and one's scientific paradigm or some deduction therefrom. Therefore, it is paradigm that limits understanding. And the only path beyond a limiting paradigm is a new paradigm.

Sagredo: Then basic breakthroughs in science and revolutions in understanding must come with adoption of new paradigms. Casting away an old, incor rect view and adopting in its place a more accurate one would be the only way to escape inherent error imposed by an old paradigm. But such a revision would be difficult because a paradigm is deep and comprehensive.

Salviati: Because it is deep and comprehensive, mere definition of a paradigm is a difficult task. We generally try to define a paradigm by a set of assumptions or axioms. But any workable paradigm capable of providing a comprehensive view must contain many assumptions and preconceptions beyond a stated basis and all must be correct for the paradigm to be fully valid. Much of a paradigm is transparent or invisible making its specification difficult. Moreover, an axiomatic base always supports many diverse paradigms making even comprehensive consistency insufficient for establishing unique truth.

Conversely, any set of observed facts probably implies multiple, diverse axiomatic systems each having equal logical legitimacy and each equally consistent with the facts. The usual scientific justification by consistency with observation is quite inadequate for justifying any unique paradigm!

Specifying the nature of reality in the form of a paradigm contains inherent uncertainty no matter what approach we take, with many pitfalls all associated directly with specifying a paradigm. And, of course, probability theory is no help when multiple paradigms are equally consistent with the data.

Simplicio: I am not so eager to abandon the traditional beliefs of our intellectual fathers. Their insights and reason have brought us far and can take us further still if we will faithfully study and follow them, as I have sought to do throughout my career.

Salviati: Your dedication is admirable, Simplicio, but there will come a point when your progress requires revision of past belief even though it be universally held among your intellectual colleagues. While our predecessors have contributed greatly to our knowledge, our continuing study eventually discovers error in the paths they followed. Improving an undefined paradigm is difficult. A new paradigm must be adopted and tested by trial and error without knowledge of where the old one is wrong or even exactly what it is.

Sagredo: The adoring crowd does not celebrate one's departure on such a journey nor do the wise and powerful foresee a successful return of that traveler. Rather, most regard such a seeker of fundamental truth as both a fool and a troublemaker. Only few would embark on such a quest.

Salviati: It is wisdom won on a lonely journey that leads to discovery of fundamental truth – for though much remains undiscovered in familiar sights along well-trod paths, familiar sights are quickly recognized in one's old paradigm which obscures any further-seeing vision. Yet truth and its new paradigm returned by the rare and lonely traveler are regarded as foolishness by those unwilling to make such a journey. They are left behind, paralyzed in their paradigm, in both the departure and the return.

Even after hard-won discovery, truth and its new paradigm often remain unrecognized and unappreciated. Vanity and vested interest seem to be behind such reticence to accept new ideas. E. T. Jaynes has observed,

> In any field, the Establishment is not seeking the truth, because it is composed of those who, having found part of it yesterday, believe that they are in possession of all of it today. Progress requires the introduction, not just of new mathematics which is always tolerated by the Establishment, but [of] new conceptual ideas which are *necessarily* different from those held by the Establishment (for, if the ideas of the Establishment were sufficient to lead to further progress, that progress would have been made).[25]

Kuhn[26] characterizes major advances in science as revolutions because those holding the traditional view must be ideologically engaged and their view overthrown once an improved view is discovered, because the old view is never completely wrong. The new view or paradigm is superior and should be preferred if it is broader in its application and more correct and insightful in the knowledge it provides.

Max Planck, himself a rare and lonely traveler in quest of truth, proposed a characterization different from Kuhn's. Planck said "A new scientific truth does not triumph by convincing its opponents and making them see the light, but rather because its opponents eventually die, and a new generation grows up that is familiar with it."[27]

In either case a dramatic event, war or death of a generation, is required to cause adoption of a new paradigm. Such change does not occur easily. Courage and devotion to truth are required to personally discover and follow the right way.

A pair of quotations from Marcelo Gleiser is here pertinent and useful.

> Change, for better or worse, always demands courage. Letting go of old, treasured ideas and the feeling of confidence they bring is hard to do. But as we look at the work of Galileo, Kepler, Newton, Faraday, Maxwell, Boltzmann, and many others we have encountered so far, it becomes clear that one of the most important characteristics of great scientists is freedom of thought. This independence brings with it flexibility that allows them, with the help from that elusive trait called genius, to find new and unexpected links where others see only dead ends. But finding new links is not enough; to chart new territory, scientists must also have the courage to let go of old, established notions. They must believe in their ideas.[28]

Discovery requires a willingness and a desire to explore and experiment. While prejudice and dogmatism are cousins to ignorance, exploration and honest inquiry are brothers to enlightenment. "… if we don't stretch our limits we can't enlarge our boundaries, and risk is curiosity's best friend."[28]

Description versus Explanation

In proposing his theory of gravity, as well as his laws of motion, Newton broke from the traditional ideal of science then established. Instead of basing understanding on a simple *physical* (or religious) *mechanism*, Newton's universal theory of gravitation was based on an *abstract mathematical equation* providing no mechanistic understanding or physical interpretation. While this deficiency in physical interpretation was then disturbing to Newton, as indicated by his statement quoted earlier in this chapter, later theories such as Maxwell's theory of electromagnetism and quantum mechanics go much further in the abstractness of their purely mathematical bases. Abstract-mathematical-based physical theories are no longer disturbing because we have simply grown accustomed to such theories.

But discovering abstract mathematical theories that describe reality and understanding their meaning are two different matters. Such theories are often referred to as *explaining* various processes or phenomena. But they provide, after all is said, mere *descriptions or predictions and connections* of observed results and they do not explain much of anything at or near a fundamental level. In its common meaning, explanation refers an event or phenomenon to the laws governing it. Understanding or explaining lies beyond description because fundamental, underlying concepts, laws, or mechanisms are required in explanation and not in description. Only when these fundamentals are known can a process or theory be understood, interpreted, and explained in terms of underlying concepts, mechanisms, or laws which are more fundamental than the process or theory itself. This distinction between description and understanding was recognized at least as early as Aristotle.[29] When a theory or law consists solely of a mathematical model that merely describes or predicts, it provides no physical understanding at any deeper or even that same level; such theory can provide understanding only at shallower levels. At its most fundamental level, any theory not based on a physical mechanism that provides a basic understanding of the theory, and thereby a clear deduction (derivation) of it, represents not understanding but mere knowledge. While we essentially agree with Weinberg's observations[30] that "after Einstein there was no place in serious physics research for the old naïve mechanical world" and that "naïve [mechanical] mechanism seems safely dead," we also recognize that mechanism in a broader and deeper sense is necessary to understanding. Modern physicists certainly recognize the difference between knowledge and understanding and seek understanding, although they must often be temporarily satisfied with knowledge.

To illustrate the utility of a mechanism we consider a theory of (mechanism for) Newtonian gravity, a theory in which a physical mechanism is invoked to derive and understand Newton's mathematical theory. This physical mechanism thus provides an understanding and explanation of Newton's mathematical theory at a fundamental level of physical knowledge. Without a physical mechanism from which the mathematical description is deduced, the mathematical law is the most fundamental knowledge possessed and cannot be understood or explained in terms of any more basic concept(s). But with knowledge of a physical mechanism of gravity, i.e., its fundamental cause, the mathematical description is readily derived, understood, and explained in terms of fundamental physical concepts. The heuristic mechanism we now describe leads directly to the mathematical law and several conclusions more fundamental than any provided by Newton's theory.

A Hypothetical Gravity Mechanism

Consider the following model or mechanism for Newtonian gravity. Imagine, first, that empty space contains a huge number of very small, uncharged, high-velocity particles (radiation) moving in all directions such that the number passing through any unit area in a unit of time (i.e., the number "flux") is equal irrespective of the location and orientation of the unit area and is of the order of, say, many billions per unit area per second. In other words, the flux of these particles is both isotropic (independent of location and direction) and huge. Now, secondly, suppose that we introduce a single, spherical body (star, planet, or particle) of matter into the empty space. Suppose, further, that the small, high-velocity particles interact only weakly with the matter (protons, neutrons, and electrons) of the spherical body because the former are small, rapidly moving, and uncharged. A physicist would describe such particles as having a small collision cross section. Nevertheless, despite their small collision cross section, a small fraction is scattered from their incident trajectories due to short-range repulsive interaction between matter and the small particles, i.e., due to an occasional nearly-direct or head-on collision with a proton, neutron, or electron. And with the scattering comes a momentum transfer rate or gravitational force acting on each mass element of the spherical body.

Like particle number flux, particle-momentum flux[31] is isotropic. Because of scattering, the momentum flux incident upon a mass element of the sphere depends on "shielding" of the mass element from the radiation by other matter. Thus, the surface layer of the sphere will experience a net inward force because incident momentum flux from outside the sphere is not attenuated by shielding like that incident from the inside direction. Neither the whole sphere nor a spherical element centered at the sphere center experiences a net force other than radial compression because of symmetry. Any layer intermediate between the center and the surface also experiences a net inward-radial force or compression because of difference in incident momentum flux from the inner and outer directions due to shielding.

Third, to characterize this force we consider two particles of matter, one of mass M and the other of mass m, separated by center-to-center distance r in space otherwise empty except for the small, high-velocity-particle radiation. The presence of two particles partly destroys radial symmetry. Besides a compressive force due to symmetric, intra-body shielding just described, asymmetric, inter-body shielding also occurs causing a net attractive force on each body having the mathematical form

$$F = -G\,M m/r^2$$

where G is a constant. This equation, Newton's law of gravity, is derived in Appendix D where related theory is described and implications of this mechanism are considered.

Neutrinos – A Digression

Essential to our hypothetical gravity mechanism is an isotropic, background flux of unknown particles that cause gravity. These small, uncharged, low-mass, high-velocity particles are neutrino-like and may be residual from the big-bang origin of the universe. Neutrinos were first detected in 1956 by Frederick Reines and Clyde L. Cowan, Jr. who discovered their emission from the Savannah River reactor. In 1965 Reines and coworkers detected neutrinos from space in a sensitive detector located deep in a gold mine in South Africa. After Cowan's death, Reines received the Nobel Prize in physics for their discovery. Because neutrinos are known to be emitted from the sun and other stars it is a small leap to imagine emission of similar particles throughout the small, hot, energetic universe in early big-bang cosmology. Neutrinos are expected to penetrate stars and planets at nearly undiminished momentum. It has been estimated a trillion miles (about 1/6 light-year) of lead is required to stop a neutrino. Steven Weinberg "upped the ante" stating high-energy beta-particle-decay neutrinos can penetrate light years of lead and they are therefore enormously difficult to detect.[32] Bethe and Bacher estimate a neutrino travels an average path of 1,000 light years in a condensed substance before it is captured by a proton in an inverse β-radioactive-decay process, with approximate capture cross section of 10^{-44} cm^2.[33] Halliday and Resnick estimate a mean path length in water to collision of a neutrino with a proton is 3,000 light years.[34] An alternative measure of penetrating power of neutrinos is comparison of traverse times for a neutrino and a photon to reach the earth from the sun's center. The neutrino requires about 8 minutes and the photon about 10 million years, because photons suffer many collisions ascending to the sun's surface. Hence, quite a time difference occurs between neutrino and photon observation of stars.[35] Because of penetrating power of neutrinos they are preferably observed deep underground where other particles do not penetrate.

Two classes of methods have been used to detect neutrinos. *Cerenkov-radiation methods* detect emission of light as a particle passes through a substance at velocity greater than light in the substance (but not greater than light in a vacuum, believed to be an absolute upper limit on velocity). Such light emission was discovered in 1934 by Russian physicist Pavel Cerenkov (pronounced cher-en-koff) who shared the 1958 Nobel Prize in physics for his effort. Cerenkov radiation is analogous to a shock wave or "wake of sound" caused by an object moving through a medium faster than the speed of sound in the medium. An object moving faster than light in the medium causes a "wake of light" or Cerenkov radiation. In Cerenkov counting, a large container of clear fluid (e.g., water) is continuously observed by hundreds of photon detectors to detect Cerenkov light emissions. The method can provide both neutrino time-of-arrival and direction.

In the 1980s two Cerenkov-counting detectors were built to detect neutrinos. Both had huge detection pools or containers of water located in mines, one in Ohio (the Irvine-Michigan-Brookhaven project) and the other in Japan (the Kamiokonde project). In 1987 both of these observatories detected neutrinos from a supernova explosion in the Large Magellanic Cloud visible only from the southern hemisphere. That means, in both cases, the neutrinos passed through the earth to reach the detectors.

The Kamiokonde high-energy-neutrino observatory is located in a zinc mine 50 km north of Takayama, Japan. Its detector holds 2,142 metric tons of ultra-pure water and contains 948 photon detectors of 50 cm sensitive diameter that cover 20 percent of the container's inside surface area. Kamiokonde neutrino detection as early as January 1987 has been reported. Long-term measurements by this observatory have detected about half the expected solar neutrinos. Additional details are provided by Allan Franklin[36] who also provides references to original scientific-journal articles.

Nuclear-reaction methods is a second class of methods for detecting neutrinos. These methods utilize at least one nuclear reaction requiring a neutrino so each reaction product indicates a neutrino count. These methods provide neither neutrino arrival time nor direction. They simply count neutrinos by counting reactions they cause (at known efficiency). Three experiments have utilized reaction methods.

(1) Raymond Davis, Jr., began neutrino count rate or flux measurements in 1967 using a chlorine-containing cleaning fluid detector located 1478 meters underground in a Homestake gold mine in South Dakota, work for which Davis received the 2002 Nobel Prize in physics. In his Nobel lecture,[37] Davis quantifies neutrino flux by saying a fingernail (1 cm^2) is penetrated by 100 billion or 10^{11} neutrinos per second. Though this number is large, it is the flux predicted for solar production of neutrinos by nuclear, hydrogen-fusion reactions in the sun. (That leaves little isotropic-background neutrino flux for a gravity mechanism, a point we address below.) Davis' measurements utilized a tank of 100,000 gallons of cleaning fluid (perchloroethylene). A neutrino striking a ^{37}Cl chlorine atom, with the superscripted prefix number denoting isotope atomic weight, sometimes caused it to transform to a ^{37}Ar radioactive argon atom which was released from the perchloroethylene and rose in helium bubbled through the fluid into the top five percent of the tank volume always filled with circulating helium. The ^{37}Ar was extracted in helium, separated, and counted. The overall process was 94 percent efficient in isolating and detecting argon atoms. Including all factors, a detection rate of 4 to 11 ^{37}Ar atoms per day was expected. After 30 years of taking data and refining method, Davis concluded that the average count rate implies a high-energy-neutrino flux of 2.55 solar neutrino units (SNU), about one-third the expected value.

The discrepancy between prediction and measurement was resolved when it was realized, as suggested in 1969 and again in 1978, that neutrinos oscillate (transform) between three neutrino types, only one of which is detected by Davis' method. A theory for such oscillations was published in 1985. According to this quantum-mechanics theory, a neutrino oscillates between its three types – the electron, the muon, and the tau neutrino – only if it has nonzero mass. Using the new oscillation theory Davis showed his data and data measured by others agree with the predicted solar neutrino flux.[37]

(2) Another type of reaction detector for low-energy neutrinos utilizes the gallium-to-germanium reaction $\nu_e + {}^{71}Ga \rightarrow e^- + {}^{71}Ge$. That is, an *electron neutrino* ν_e captured by a gallium atom ^{71}Ga causes it to emit an electron e^- and transform into a germanium atom ^{71}Ge. A joint Soviet-American Gallium Experiment (SAGE) provided its first data in 1991 using a 30 ton liquid gallium detector in a 4 km tunnel into Mount Andrychi in the North Caucasus Mountains. Germanium produced by neutrino capture during typical exposure times of 3 to 4 weeks was separated from the gallium and counted by its radioactivity which for ^{71}Ge has a half-life of 11.4 days. The data imply a low-energy-neutrino flux of 71 SNU, about half the predicted solar flux of 132 SNU. Davis shows this result and the one yet to be described both agree with his and the Kamiokonde results and with solar neutrino flux theory.[37]

(3) Concurrent with SAGE another gallium-neutrino-detector experiment called GALLEX was conducted in Italy. In GALLEX the detector differed from that used in SAGE, the GALLEX detector being a 30.3 tons of gallium chloride ($GaCl_3$) in

aqueous (water) solution in two tanks placed in a tunnel under a mountain near Gran Sasso, equivalent in protection from cosmic ray particles to being submerged under 3 km of water. Of the 30.3 tons of gallium chloride solution, 12 tons were the ^{71}Ga isotope sensitive to low-energy neutrinos. The same reaction ($\nu_e + {}^{71}Ga \rightarrow e^- + {}^{71}Ge$) occurred with the product Ge atoms quickly forming germanium tetrachloride ($GeCl_4$) which, being volatile, was removed by bubbling inert gas through the solution. The measured results again imply a low-energy-neutrino flux of 71 SNU. Franklin[36] provides further details about these experiments.

How can these measured neutrino fluxes be rationalized with a background flux perhaps residual from the big bang that we invoke as the basis of a gravity theory? They can't be because the full flux is apparently accounted for as solar neutrinos which would provide a repulsive solar-gravity force according to our proposed mechanism. One possible solution to the dilemma is, as usual, to propose a new particle not yet detected but present at a momentum flux that overwhelms the effect of the solar-neutrino flux. We call this new particle the *gravitrino* because it is expected to have penetrating power similar to the neutrino and function similar to the *graviton*. Does such a particle exist? We don't know, but we utilize it in our heuristic theory. Because of astronomical observations that spinning galaxies hold together presumably by gravity, astronomers believe that some dark (unobserved) matter is required with this matter estimated to constitute 90 percent of the mass of the universe. So lots of yet unobserved matter may exist in the universe.

Our hypothetical gravity theory illustrates well the function and utility of a physical mechanism. As an example, the mechanism is realistic enough to be a good one and it or some variation may eventually prove to be more than an example.

Hypothetical Gravity Mechanism – Continued

By the proposed mechanism of momentum-flux scattering, every body present in the universe continuously projects in every direction a measure of its presence and mass in the form of a slight outward-directed diminishment in the "background" gravitrino-momentum flux, which in its consequences, corresponds exactly to a "gravitational potential." This slight diminishment in outward gravitrino-momentum flux would cause a mutual, attractive, gravitational force between any body and every other body in the universe to obey Newton's law, i.e., the equation on page 329. However, the gravity force between sun and earth would be repulsive if the sun is the principal source of gravitrinos in the solar system, which it cannot be. Where is the residual neutrino-like radiation from the big bang?[38] Like residual photon radiation, it is dilute and cool and yet gravitrino-particle radiation in the universe may be invoked as a background-radiation-cause of gravity.[39]

This mechanism provides Newton's mathematical theory of gravity and it provides deeper physical insight by which associated phenomena may be physically understood and explained. It implies processes that describe the origin of and are therefore more fundamental than Newton's equation which merely predicts the result or describes the effect of the mechanism. The "momentum-flux mechanism" of gravity provides a classical-physics basis for understanding Newton's law of gravity in terms of an isotropic, gravitrino-momentum flux ubiquitous in the universe. Without a correct mechanism, Newton's law (or relativity) is not understood but merely known. But with a correct mechanism the physical basis of gravity and some striking features related thereto are understood and predicted, as *heuristically illustrated* by the simple gravitrino-momentum-flux mechanism of gravity that follows.

The momentum-flux mechanism of gravity *implies*, either correctly or incorrectly, the following insights about the nature of gravity. (1) Gravity is a fundamental force equivalent to an inertial force associated with acceleration. (2) The mass values in gravity and inertia are therefore identical because gravity is an inertial effect. (3) The range of the gravitational force is limited to the order of an average or "mean-free-path" length between collisions of the gravitrino particles or radiation causing the gravitational force and other matter. (4) Quantum graviton "messenger" particles that have never yet been observed may be the gravitrino particles invoked in momentum-flux theory. (5) The gravitational force between two bodies is not instantaneous (as Newton's law indicates) but requires for its establishment or change the time for the radiation or particles to traverse some distance (Appendix D). (6) Cosmological inflation of the early universe resulted from a delay in onset of gravity until the universe became sufficiently diluted (expanded) to be transparent to gravitrinos and momentum-flux gravity "turned on." Previously, during the first millionth of a second or so duration of inflation, the gravitrinos may have contributed to inflationary pressure. (7) In violation of general relativity, gravity constant G diminishes in time with expansion of the universe and decrease in background gravitrino density and momentum flux. (8) Different measured values of the Hubble constant H = R/V, the proportionality constant in an equation relating recessional velocity V and separation R, is obtained from measured recessional velocities and separations of stars from the earth. Differences in measured values of H is due to an otherwise undetected, slow diminishing of the gravitational constant G in time. It may also be caused by differences in initial velocities of bodies (Appendix D). By the former effect gravity would have a larger cumulative effect on farther (faster) stars, since faster (farther) bodies receded when G was larger than its current value. Recent supernova data suggest an accelerating expansion of space if it is assumed that G is constant in time. Looking at distant galaxies receding at implied speeds up to 95.6 percent of the speed of light corresponds to looking far back in time, by which data the expansion of the universe might only appear to be accelerating assuming constant G.[40] (9) A gravity induced energy "radiation" from a pair of bodies orbiting one another is predicted by momentum-flux-gravity theory (Appendix D), but a radiation of energy having the wrong sign.

Several known results are not predicted by this gravity mechanism, examples being gravitational radiation of energy as observed by Hulse and Taylor,[41] the gravitational redshift, and the bending of light rays (space) by gravity. In other words, the new theory does not predict apparently-confirmed predictions of general relativity, so it is only a heuristic mechanism in its present form. But some variation of this mechanism may one day provide a viable gravity mechanism. It does provide insights that nicely rationalize a few supposed properties of big-bang theory and astronomical measurements, qualitatively if not quantitatively.

In any case, the features listed above *illustrate* the insight and understanding a physical mechanism can provide. Whether or not our mechanism is valid, this point is well illustrated by our hypothetical theory. This point is that a difference occurs between describing and explaining Newton's law of gravity and other scientific observations and laws. A physical mechanism allows one to go beyond mere description and obtain more fundamental insights in terms of underlying processes. It is only in terms of underlying processes that understanding and explanation are possible and supercede mere description and prediction. That is, up to the present and excluding artificial mathematical constructs, scientific knowledge and description of phenomena are superceded by understanding and explanation only when a physical mechanism for the process is provided.

Knowledge versus Understanding

When a theory consists of only an abstract mathematical basis for or from which no underlying processes or mechanisms are apparent, when the theory itself is the most fundamental thing known, it cannot be understood, interpreted, or explained in any terms other than itself. For instance, we recall the earlier quoted comment of Heinrich Hertz: "To the question, 'What is Maxwell's theory?' I know of no shorter or more definite answer than the following: Maxwell's theory is Maxwell's system of equations."

Maxwell's theory is now implied by QED theory. While Maxwell's theory is thus understood in terms of QED theory, QED theory only describes or predicts observed results. It thus provides no deeper concepts necessary for understanding or explaining either QED theory or the observations. One can only say the observed facts are predicted by the theory and the theory is supported by the observed facts (following the spirit of Hertz's comment). The same capability to predict events is provided by empirical knowledge of sufficient scope, without theory. Thus, any theory that provides no deeper, underlying understanding than describing the observed facts is, in one important sense, functionally equivalent to no more than empirical data. A theoretical mathematical expression may be broadly applicable due to its abstract nature, which is indeed a useful feature and fulfils an important goal in science. But with respect to fundamental understanding, description is like empirical data in function and provides only knowledge rather than understanding.

One sometimes hears statements like, say, "Such and such must occur because of the Pauli exclusion principle." This principle was proposed by Austrian physicist Wolfgang Pauli (1900-1958) in 1925 for which he was awarded the 1945 Nobel Prize in physics.[42] Pauli was unquestionably a genius of high order. When Einstein was unable to write on relativity in 1919 as he had promised Arnold Sommerfeld, the editor of the German *Encyclopädie der mathematischen Wissenschaften* (*Encyclopædia of Mathematical Science*), Pauli, at age 19 and already studying for his doctorate in mathematical physics (which he received at age 21) and only three years after Einstein's paper had introduced general relativity, was asked by Sommerfeld, his Ph.D. advisor or "Doktorvater," to write on relativity in place of Einstein. Pauli did a wonderful job completing a whole *volume* on this one subject, a work that was praised by many including Einstein.[43] Pauli's volume appeared in 1921, the same year he completed his doctoral thesis showing that Bohr's model of the *atom* fails for the ionized hydrogen *molecule*.[44] In 1930 Pauli proposed the existence of a small particle he called a "neutron" in order to preserve conservation of energy, momentum, and spin in nuclear (radioactive) beta-decay reactions in which a beta particle (an electron) and a previously unobserved and unsuspected "neutron" are emitted. Pauli's "neutron" was later renamed the "neutrino" by Italian-American physicist Enrico Fermi to distinguish it from what we now call the neutron.

Pauli's exclusion principle, a worthy result but one arbitrarily chosen here for the purpose of illustration, asserts that no two electrons in an atom may have the same set of quantum numbers, the set that describes the exact state of an atomic electron. To state this principle Pauli had to introduce a new quantum number, one defining *electron spin*. Electrons were then known, from the Stern-Gerlach experiment,[45] to occur in two spin states, either "up" or "down." Otherwise two electrons possessing the same orbital quantum numbers would both indistinctly occupy a single state. By Pauli's principle only two electrons, having opposite spin and therefore distinct quantum states, may inhabit the lowest-energy orbital about a nucleus, only two may inhabit the second lowest-energy orbital, and so on. This principle is consistent with the observation that electrons fill the orbitals about a nucleus in a specific order with electrons forbidden to simultaneously occupy an already occupied orbital and spin state. It thereby rationalizes the characteristically uniform properties of groups of chemical elements and Mendelèev's periodic table. Full consistency with all known facts is regarded in science as verification. Invoking knowledge of the Pauli exclusion principle provides some understanding at a level shallower than the principle itself but, as profound as it is, not at its most fundamental level because at this level it is like a merely empirical result consistent with observation but expressing no known, fundamental, underlying processes or principles (to our level of consideration here, i.e., ignoring deeper implications of electron spins and their quantum numbers) by which deeper understanding is illuminated. Such an "explanation" at its deepest level thus simply describes empirical-like qualities or observed-like facts. The answer provided by such knowledge to "the next question," pertaining to the same level or any deeper one, must therefore be "I don't know." revealing limitation in understanding. While scientific *knowledge* extends to the deepest describable or predicted level, scientific *understanding* extends no deeper than at least one level short of that one.

A lack of actual or true or universal or absolute understanding in science, by which lack pertinent questions remained unanswerable, bothered Newton. It also bothers those who want to truly understand at a fundamental level and fail to find meaning in mere knowledge of empirical facts. Let us therefore adopt here a restricted sense of the term "understanding" that embodies the deepest, most profound quality in its entire range of usage. We denote deep, complete, universal, absolute understanding by the italicized *understanding*. In so doing we are, of course, going beyond the normal usage of "understanding" in science and in general. But that is our objective in this book. We are seeking herein to go beyond knowledge and even understanding to discover and comprehend meaning.

Thus, we use the italicized *understanding* to denote knowledge pertaining to which the response "I don't know" need not be employed in at least one sequence of increasingly deeper questions, because *understanding* is based on fundamental, absolute truth so recognized. Absolute scientific *understanding*, were it known, would take us a far and rarely-visited distance forward – it is an uncommon mortal acquisition; only a few, like Moses (quoted below), have obtained and described it.

The desired "abstract-level empiricism" of science provides a useful indication of regularity, pattern, and connection among the facts and allows an organized vision and cataloging of knowledge. For these purposes abstraction is extremely useful. Indeed, if one regards broad knowledge in science as knowledge of regularity, pattern, and connection among the facts, abstract empiricism truly represents broad scientific knowledge. But such scientific knowledge is merely a start toward *understanding* as it is merely tentative knowledge rather than absolute and not necessarily deep. No product of science has ever provided true *understanding* of any fact because scientific inquiry cannot provide certain or absolute explanation or even description. While science can make no claim to provide *understanding* because of its inherent limitations, some seem to believe it can. It can't, for the reasons we have discussed. In contrast, the doctrine of Christ is a method that claims to provide *understanding*, a claim we shall shortly examine.

Even highly educated scientists (like me – my denigration that follows is first person plural) never truly understand on the basis of science and we therefore can't explain any particulars in any certain or fundamental sense despite our futile attempts in which we generally overwhelm a poor, nonexpert listener with obscurity. Yet we scientists are so blinded by our knowledge and the seemingly compelling power of our paradigm that we do not recognize that our inability to explain to a nonexpert manifests an absence of understanding. Of course a fellow expert "understands" immediately and this reassures us in our paradigm. But the fact remains that by science we merely predict and describe rather than explain and merely know rather than understand. Our predicament is well described by adapting Galileo's observation of Chapter 6 regarding his nemeses, the Aristotelians, by substituting "science" for "Aristotle" and taking one or two other liberties. We then obtain the following statement which may depict well us devout scientists – you judge.

> I have many times wondered how these pedantic maintainers of whatever came from science are not aware how great a prejudice they are to science's reputation and credit and how, the more they go about to increase science's authority, the more they diminish it. When I see them obstinate in maintaining they truly understand those propositions which are manifestly not truly understood, and trying to persuade me that to do so is the part of a scientist-philosopher, and that all scientists would do the same, it much discourages me in the belief that scientists have rightly philosophized about any conclusions, for if I could see them concede they do not truly understand in a manifest lack of true understanding, I would be more willing to believe that, where they persist, they may have some true understanding, by me not understood or even heard of.

In contrast to acquiring *understanding*, as we have supposed, we scientists have learned merely by rote.[46] Familiarity has served as a substitute for understanding and only a few critical thinkers, like Hermann Weyl, Karl Popper, Owen Barfield, C.

S. Lewis, K. V. Laurikainen, E. T. Jaynes, and Hans Christian von Baeyer, have been astute enough to recognize and correctly describe our sad situation. Objective, reproducible, lowest-common-denominator facts and the usual scientific knowledge built upon them have not led to certain knowledge or *understanding*. They have distracted us from the effort, dulled our desire for true learning, and substituted in its place common, homogeneous thinking at a superficial level of tentative knowledge. We have sold our agent-in-search-of-truth birthright for a mess of objective pottage. We are category-two students with an *attitude*, and don't even recognize it.

Escaping Paradigm Paralysis

What is to be done? To begin, we must first recognize that *understanding* of anything requires an absolutely true answer to an ultimate question, like "What is the true nature of reality?" The answer must be based on at least one element of absolute truth so recognized and identified (demonstrated, established, or justified). *Understanding* is beyond the scope of tentative knowledge of the facts (science) because it must invoke a fundamental, universal, *absolute* basis rather than a merely tentative and relative (consistent) one. Without such an absolute basis, further questions of every sequence lead eventually to "I don't know," indicating that *understanding* has once again eluded us.

Science does not establish indubitable conclusions, merely tentative ones. (Now we are beginning to truly understand.) The absolute truth of laws required to provide certain answers to ultimate questions lies beyond the scope of scientific inquiry, not due to lack of desire or effort by scientists but due to the inherent deficiencies in and limited scope of methodology and philosophy of science.

This first as well as other considerations are summarized in the following three conclusions about science. (1) Science deals with inferring organization, pattern, and connection among the facts and tentative theories and laws deduced or guessed using them. (2) Knowledge of apparent cause-and-effect relationships among the facts is represented by these theories and laws so that phenomena may usually be precisely, albeit tentatively, described and predicted. But, discovering only tentative results provides no absolute understanding. And it is by no means clear that either all pertinent facts or candidate laws and theories have been recognized and considered. Some cause or effect facts may be entirely unperceived. (3) If *understanding* entails knowledge in the sense that at least one ever deeper sequence of questions can be fully answered, some *absolute* basis must be contained in that *understanding* and it must be so recognized and justified. Science cannot provide *understanding* because its base of information contains only observations of objective, neutral, external, … relative facts and tentative theories and laws consistently relating them.

By the definition of *understanding* and by this reasoning we are led to the conclusion that science neither does nor can provide *understanding*. It provides merely tentative knowledge of and about the facts, or more correctly, of the "objective" facts we perceive, regard as important, and bring to scientific inquiry.

With such a restrictive definition of *understanding*, can it actually be obtained? If so, how? Keep reading.

An independent agent may abandon a paradigm at any time. Such an agent in search of truth will indeed adopt or at least test a different paradigm when it becomes apparent or seems possible that the new paradigm will better lead him or her to a reliable knowledge of truth. In so doing, he or she escapes paradigm paralysis imposed by his or her old system of belief.

As it is useful in exactly this process of finding a reliable knowledge of truth, we shall soon examine the remarkable doctrine of Christ. But first we consider the nature of the truth we seek.

Who, *What*, and *Why* versus *How*

Both the power of examination of empirical, lowest-common-denominator facts (science) in finding simple cause-and-effect relationships and up-to-now failure of this approach to provide deep, comprehensive connection among these facts are simultaneously suggested in a desire once expressed by Albert Einstein.

> I want to know how God created this world. I am not interested in this or that phenomenon, in the spectrum of this or that element. I want to know His thoughts, the rest are details.[47]

Let's go further than Einstein did. Beyond the limited domain of science and tentative connections of lowest-common-denominator facts,[48] let's ask not only *how* but also *who*, *what*, and *why*. The *how* are details. This expanded question recognizes Barfield's valuable point described in Chapter 2. He proposes, in my words, that single-minded pursuit of a tentative knowledge of cause and effect among lowest-common-denominator facts is not adequate to discover meaning and, indeed, actually prevents the seeking and finding of it. The meticulous preoccupation with the *how* in all its complex details precludes discovery of the *who*, *what*, and *why*. That is, it precludes discovery and even seeking of *understanding* and comprehension of meaning.

If one understands a *who*, *what*, and *why* basis of something, a pretty comprehensive vision is generally understood even in the absence of a knowledge of *how*. On the other hand, if one has some scattered knowledge of *how*, but little or no understanding of *who*, *what*, and *why*, the overall picture is incomplete; scope and direction are missing and understanding is far from comprehensive. For this reason, detailed knowledge of *how* – or, what is worse, mere familiarity with some aspects of *how*, however intimate – in the absence of understanding leads to isolated, piecewise, fragmented, unconnected knowledge and restricted vision. Understanding of important connections, comprehensive pattern and organization among, and meaning of the facts at any deep level are missing because they are contained in understanding of *who*, *what*, and *why* rather than *how*.

But where do we find an understanding of *who*, *what*, and *why*? We don't find it through scientific analysis of lowest-common-denominator facts. In introducing a four-lecture description of quantum electrodynamics, Richard Feynman stated

> The next reason that you might think you do not understand what I am telling you is, while I am describing to you *how* Nature works, you won't understand *why* Nature works that way. But you see, nobody understands that. I can't explain why Nature behaves in this peculiar way.[49]

Feynman also referred to the dual interpretation in quantum mechanics of an electron as a particle and a wave as "the only mystery" and continued "we cannot make it go away by explaining how it works."[50]

While science provides no understanding of *who*, *what*, and *why*, answers to such questions may be obtained by the doctrine of Christ, by fire and the Holy Ghost.

Who, *What*, and *Why* by Fire and the Holy Ghost

A profound observation and, by all appearances, a description of personal experience in knowing God's thoughts – the above quoted desire of Einstein and the object of our expanded version of Einstein's question – was made in 1896 by Joseph F. Smith (1838-1918), sixth president of the Church of Jesus Christ of Latter-day Saints.

> We may see a great many things with our natural sight, but that may be deceived. We may hear with our ears, but they may be deceived. Our natural senses are susceptible to deception. ... But ... when the Almighty reveals Himself unto man, He does it by the power of the Holy Ghost, and not through the natural eye or the natural ear. He speaks to man as if He were speaking to him independent of his body [independent of sight, hearing, touch, taste, or smell]; He speaks to the spirit. ... if God speaks to you and bears record of His truth by the power of the Holy Ghost, ... *you will know as God knows*.[51] (italics added)

Smith continued by addressing what we call herein comprehension of meaning:

> ... Who can tell the joy and the satisfaction that comes to the soul of man who has received this witness from Almighty God? No man can utter it. ... There are no words of man that can speak it. It can only be felt. ... Unspeakable is the joy that a man feels who has received this testimony from the Holy Ghost.[51]

The current successor to Smith, Gordon B. Hinckley, referred to this same Source of knowledge in speaking of the Book of Mormon: "Reasonable people may sincerely question its origin; but those who have read it prayerfully have come to know by a power beyond their natural senses that it is true, that it contains the word of God,..."[52]

Others have also testified of this power. Joseph Smith, Jr., and Sidney Rigdon described the power and feeling conveyed by the Holy Ghost as exceeding those of any other experience.

> ... great and marvelous are the works of the Lord, and the mysteries of his kingdom which he showed unto us, which surpass all understanding in glory, and in might, and in dominion; Which he commanded us we should not write ... Neither is man capable to make them known, for they are only to be seen and understood by the power of the Holy Spirit, which God bestows on those who love him, and purify themselves before him; To whom he grants this privilege of seeing and knowing for themselves; That through the power and manifestation of the Spirit, while in the flesh, they may be able to bear his presence in the world of glory.[53]

Moses' experience, referred to above, illustrates the depth of understanding and scope of comprehension of meaning obtainable from God. This great Old-Testament prophet described in his writings (revealed afresh through Joseph Smith to restore removed material) the following experience.

> And calling upon the name of God, he [Moses] beheld his glory again, for it was upon him; and he heard a voice, ... as the voice was still speaking, Moses cast his eyes and beheld the earth, yea, even all of it; and there was not a particle of it which he did not behold, discerning it by the spirit of God [the Holy Ghost]. And he beheld also the inhabitants thereof, and there was not a soul which he beheld not; and he discerned them by the Spirit of God; and their numbers were great, even numberless as the sand upon the sea shore. ...
>
> Moses called upon God, saying: Tell me, I pray thee, *why* these things are so, and by *what* thou madest them? And behold, the glory of the Lord was upon Moses, so that Moses stood in the presence of God, and talked with him face to face. And the Lord God said unto Moses: For mine own purpose have I made these things. Here is wisdom and it remaineth in me. And by the word of my power, have I created them, which is mine Only Begotten Son, who is full of grace and truth. And worlds without number have I created; and I also created them for mine own purpose; and by the Son I created them, which is mine Only Begotten. ... But only an account of this earth, and the inhabitants thereof, give I unto you.
>
> And ... Moses spake unto the Lord, saying: Be merciful unto thy servant, O God, and tell me concerning this earth, and the inhabitants thereof, ... And the Lord God spake unto Moses, saying: ... there is no end to my works, neither to my words. For behold, this is my work and my glory – to bring to pass the immortality and eternal life of man.
>
> And now, Moses, my son, I will speak unto thee concerning this earth upon which thou standest; and thou shalt write the things which I shall speak.
>
> And in a day when the children of men shall esteem my words as naught and take many of them from the book which thou shalt write, behold, I will raise up another like unto thee; and they shall be had again among the children of men – among as many as shall believe.[54] (italics added)

Moses already knew the answer to *Who?* He sought answers to *what* and *why* questions. These three are the primary questions one must ask to know God or to understand reality, which is our primary assignment as agents in search of truth.[55] The answers to these types of questions, which many besides Moses have also received,[56] reveal universal connections and deep, true comprehension of meaning, of *Who*, *what*, and *why*. The *how* are details.

To further illuminate the meaning contained in answers to these questions and the power and value of the doctrine of Christ, I quote another Old-Testament prophet, namely, Enoch, the great-grandfather of Noah. There are many interesting facts contained in this quote, including the fact that principles contained in the doctrine of Christ – the plan of salvation – have been taught and eventually lost in all previous ages (dispensations) beginning with that of Adam.[57] I include it because it reveals these facts and again identifies the source of *understanding*.

> And as Enoch spake forth the words of God, the people trembled, and could not stand in his presence. And he said unto them: Because that Adam fell, we are; and by his fall came death; and we are made partakers of misery and woe. Behold Satan hath come among the children of men, and tempteth them to worship him; and men have become carnal, sensual, and devilish, and are shut out from the presence of God.
>
> But God hath made known unto our fathers that all men must repent. And he called upon our father Adam by his own voice, saying: I am God; I made the world, and men

> before they were in the flesh. And he also said unto him: If thou wilt turn unto me, and hearken unto my voice, and believe, and repent of all thy transgressions, and be baptized, even in water, in the name of mine Only Begotten Son, who is full of grace and truth, which is Jesus Christ, the only name which shall be given under heaven, whereby salvation shall come unto the children of men, ye shall receive the gift of the Holy Ghost, asking all things in his [Christ's] name, and whatsoever ye shall ask, it shall be given you.
>
> And our father Adam spake unto the Lord, and said: Why is it that men must repent and be baptized in water? And the Lord said unto Adam: Behold I have forgiven thee thy transgression in the Garden of Eden. Hence came the saying abroad among the people, that the Son of God hath atoned for original guilt, wherein the sins of the parents cannot be answered upon the heads of the children, for they are whole from the foundation of the world [a council in heaven where we accepted God's plan of salvation – see following chapters].
>
> And the Lord spake unto Adam, saying: Inasmuch as thy children are conceived in sin [i.e., in the mortal condition, "shut out from the presence of God," which condition is the eternal consequence of unremitted sin], even so when they begin to grow up, sin conceiveth in their hearts, and they taste the bitter, that they may know to prize the good. And it is given unto them to know good from evil; wherefore they are agents unto themselves, and I have given unto you another law and commandment. Wherefore teach it unto your children, that all men, everywhere, must repent, or they can in nowise inherit the kingdom of God, for no unclean thing can dwell there, or dwell in his presence; for, in the language of Adam, Man of Holiness is his name, and the name of his Only Begotten is the Son of Man, even Jesus Christ, a righteous Judge, who shall come in the meridian of time.
>
> Therefore I give unto you a commandment, to teach these things freely unto your children, saying: That by reason of transgression cometh the fall, which fall bringeth death, and inasmuch as ye were born into the world by water, and blood, and the spirit, which I have made [in a pre-earth creation in heaven (see endnote 21, Chapter 10)], and so became of dust a living soul, even so ye must be born again into the kingdom of heaven, of water, and of the Spirit, and be cleansed by blood, even the blood of mine Only Begotten; that ye might be sanctified from all sin, and enjoy the words of eternal life in this world, and eternal life in the world to come, even immortal glory;
>
> For by the water [baptism] ye keep the commandment; by the Spirit [the Holy Ghost] ye are justified, and by the blood [of Christ] ye are sanctified; Therefore it [the Holy Ghost] is given to abide in you; the record of heaven; the Comforter; the peaceable things of immortal glory; the truth of all things; that which quickeneth all things, which maketh alive all things; that which knoweth all things, and hath all power according to wisdom, mercy, truth, justice, and judgement. And now, behold, I say unto you: This is the *plan of salvation* unto all men, through the blood of mine Only Begotten, who shall come in the meridian of time.[58] (italics added)

To those who have had even a small measure of experience with the Holy Ghost, lowest-common-denominator facts and tentative knowledge have lost their luster. The focus on the facts is replaced with one on the joy, on the peaceable things, that which quickeneth and maketh alive, and knoweth all things. Once one tastes this power, understanding, and feeling, nothing else matters, and yet, everything matters more. I would love to explain my own personal experiences of this type in tedious detail. On the few occasions I have had one, I savored the joy for days. But there simply are no words. "Neither is man capable to make them known, for they are only to be ... understood by the power of the Holy Spirit, ..." The attempted description would trivialize the experience. It is *understanding*, meaning, and feeling at a high, rich level and I cannot translate it to a lower level, to mere words or lowest-common-denominator facts. To understand it one must experience it for one's self.

And my assessment of this kind of experience is not unique. Eliza R. Snow recounted her experience at the dedicatory service of the Kirtland Temple, which had been built at great sacrifice by the saints, in the words "no mortal language [can] describe the heavenly manifestations of that memorable day." Those present experienced the "sweet spirit of love and union, ... a sense of divine presence," and "each heart was filled with joy inexpressible."[59] Paul's words were well chosen when he called it "... the peace of God, which passeth all understanding ..."[60]

And such experiences are not intended only for the few. Paul instructed the Galatians that "the fruit of the Spirit is love, joy, peace, ..."[61] He reminded the "church of the Thessalonians" that they "became followers of us, and of the Lord, having received the word in much affliction, with joy in the Holy Ghost."[62] In connection with the doctrine of Christ, Paul urges the Hebrews to become "enlightened" and to "taste the heavenly gift."[63] In his first epistle general to all members of the original Christian Church, Peter addressed them as those "Whom having not seen [Jesus Christ], ye love; in whom, though now ye see him not, yet believing, ye rejoice with joy unspeakable and full of glory."[64] Upon instructing His apostles Christ said "These things have I spoken unto you, that my joy might remain in you, and that your joy might be full."[65] Without the Holy Ghost, Christianity retains little of its personal impact and power. In response to the simple prayer of Joseph Smith requesting direction on which church to join, the instruction given by Christ Himself to Smith, and to us, cited several fatal flaws common to the Christian churches of that day, one of which flaws was and is denying the power of God as manifest by the Holy Ghost (Appendix H).

When you tire of the *how* questions and want to graduate to the *who*, *what*, and *why*, when you want to find deep understanding and comprehension of meaning, embrace the doctrine of Christ. It promises endowment of absolute knowledge, *understanding*, and comprehension of meaning. It provides connection with Omniscience, "that which knoweth all things, and hath all power according to wisdom, mercy, truth, justice, and judgement." While I relate in Chapter 15 some of my own experience, I will express here one consequence of my own personal experience with joy. And that is that I know for myself that my Redeemer lives. I know by the certain witness of fire and the Holy Ghost Who has revealed it to me.[66]

Instead of describing my experience in terms of commonly understood facts, which I am unable to do, I illustrate in Chapter 18 the powerful effect this kind of experience had on several who came to understand joy and meaning, that is, to personal knowledge of Christ by fire and the Holy Ghost. By the light of their lives we may see the power of the doctrine of Christ. "Wherefore by their fruits ye shall know them."[67]

To those not yet experienced with inexpressible joy, the experience may sound strange, non-intuitive, unbelievable, or even preposterous. These reactions are characteristic of an encounter with knowledge and understanding that lie beyond one's present paradigm. These reactions hallmark first exposure to a powerful, new paradigm. These reactions therefore suggest one has encountered an opportunity to learn something fundamentally new. If the doctrine of Christ is powerful, as is claimed here, then these are the expected reactions one should have on early encounters with it. For such a one, not yet experienced in this paradigm, it is a richer system, one whose meaning is deeper and, at first, beyond comprehension. But the comprehension of meaning and the joy come with desire, intent, effort, and faith – paying one's dues. Try it, you'll like it. Until you do, you simply won't understand.

Proposition Number 7: **While science addresses and provides useful but tentative answers to *how* questions relating to objective, reproducible, lowest-common-denominator, material facts, it neither answers nor even contemplates ultimate *who*, *what*, and *why* questions relating to existence, to God, and to meaning. Compared to answers to *who*, *what*, and *why* questions, answers to *how* questions seem incomplete and unsatisfying, preoccupied with tedious detail and lacking comprehensive vision and any feeling of certain, universal connection and joy.**

Einstein's general theory of relativity encountered early and continuing opposition in Germany based not on science but on race! Einstein was Jewish. A present-day physicist has noted.

> Any new theory of nature [like the Christian one described herein] must stand the test of many theoretical and experimental checks. But there were other doubts about general relativity, nonscientific doubts of a scurrilous nature that were expressed by individuals who called themselves scientists [including two who had received the Nobel Prize in physics]. ... The rise of anti-Semitism in Germany between the world wars had its counterpart in scientific circles. ... The vast majority of non-Jewish German scientists did not share this view, however, and despite the Nazi takeover in Germany and the subsequent dismissal and emigration of many Jewish physicists (including Einstein), the anti-relativity program became little more than a footnote in the history of science [reflecting negatively not on German-Jewish scientists but on those who persecuted them]. ... Fortunately, most physicists were not swayed by these kinds of considerations, and instead focused their attention on experimentation, not race, as the judge of scientific theory.[68]

This same physicist, Clifford Will, describes a prominent, senior physicist approached by a young, unknown physicist for advice about a new idea that would destroy the prominent physicist's own published theoretical work. At first skeptical, the prominent physicist studied the idea and became convinced his young colleague was correct. To his credit he then supported experiments enabling the younger physicist's theory to be tested even though the results would ultimately contradict and invalidate his own, upon which his reputation was largely established.[68]

Those who regard themselves as open to testing and evidence rather than prejudiced should be willing to consider and test the ostensible-step or doctrine-of-Christ method and not simply dismiss it out of hand because of prejudice. Even if one is very busy with little extra time, this issue is too important to simply dismiss. Christ is busy too; yet He and His Father and the Holy Ghost make us Their top priority, available on call 24/7.[69] Don't you, dear reader, have a little time for Them?

Notes and References for Chapter 13.

[1] *Bible,* 2 Corinthians 4:3-4.

[2] *Bible,* Matthew 11:25, Luke 10:21.

[3] Crichton, Michael, *The Lost World,* Ballantine Books, New York, 1995, 7.

[4] Of course humans are only partially informed, this condition being inherent to the mortal state. With the term "partially informed Christian" I refer especially to those Christians yet under the influence of corrupted beliefs. Of good men and women of all beliefs the Lord said in 1839 "... there are many yet on the earth among all sects, parties, and denominations, who are blinded by the subtle craftiness of men, whereby they lie in wait to deceive, and who are only kept from the truth because they know not where to find it ..." (*Doctrine and Covenants* 123:12.)

[5] *Bible,* 2 Timothy 3:7.

[6] This expression is adapted from J. R. R. Tolkien's *Lord of the Rings* Trilogy (Part Two: *The Two Towers,* Ballantine Books, New York, 1965, 366) wherein Samwise Gamgee states "But *handsome is as handsome does* we say."

[7] Weinberg, Steven, *Facing Up,* Harvard University Press, Cambridge, MA, 2001, 269-270, 156-157.

[8] Lewis, C. S., *Miracles, A Preliminary Study,* Macmillan, New York, 1947, 7.

[9] And conflict is generally more intense and longer lived at frontiers in the merely descriptive sciences because they are more vague, indeterminate, and arbitrary. One example is the unfortunate controversy between "creationists" and "evolutionists," unfortunate because it only obliquely addresses a basic issue. A basic issue is atheism versus belief in God, not whether evolution occurs or contradicts the Bible, not even whether evolution occurred in sufficient strength to produce humans. Does evolution occur? Yes. But even an answer to whether it is strong enough to produce humans does not answer remaining questions like "Does evolution imply atheism?" While a vocal few claim it does, many, if not most, scientists who believe in some level of evolution also believe in God. Over reaction of both those on the religious side as well as of the vocal few materialists has contributed to the controversy. An *apparent* contradiction with the Bible is threatening if one believes the Bible to be the literally correct. And I do with the exceptions that Biblical text (1) often being symbolic is sometimes difficult to understand and (2) has been corrupted, mostly by removal of information (Appendix I). With restoration of knowledge, understanding of Biblical passages is more perfect and the fossil record and theory of evolution are no longer threatening. Evolution does not account for a paradisiacal garden in which no death occurred (endnote 21 of Chapter 10 and Appendix L).

At the base of the conflict is the notion that exists among both lay persons and clergy that evolution and atheism are somehow inseparably associated, possibly due to overreaction of religious leaders to the claims of a few vocal adherents to Godless evolution, possibly exacerbated by weakness in religious dogma thereby exposed. Such a notion is not readily dispelled by scientists in their scientific talks and articles in scientific journals because the topic of God lies beyond the range of scientific discussion. And thus the perceived threat remains. The problem is exacerbated by articles in popular-level newspapers and magazines, publications in which editorial policy and/or comments could distinguish between evolution and atheism if they so chose. But they don't so choose because such comments do not appear. Writing of a materialist-evolutionary persuasion with no reference to any other possibility appeared in *U. S. NEWS and World Report* (29 July 2002, 43). "When scientists introduced the world to humankind's earliest known ancestor two weeks ago, they showed us more than a mere museum piece. Peering at the 7 million-year-old skull is almost like seeing a reflection of our earlier selves. And yet that fossil represents only a recent chapter in a grander story, beginning with the first single-celled life that arose and began evolving some 3.8 billion years ago. Now, as the science of evolution moves beyond guesswork, we are learning something even more remarkable: how that tale unfolded. Scientists are uncovering the step-by-step changes in form and function that ultimately produced humanity and the diversity of life surrounding us. By now, scientists say, evolution is no longer 'just a theory.' It's an everyday phenomenon, a fundamental fact of biology as real as hunger and as unavoidable as death."

But evolution in particular and science in general have not and never will move beyond guesswork because guesswork is fundamental to the nature of scientific inquiry. The assumption (guess) that the 7 million-year-old Toumai skull is human was quickly challenged (see Senut, Brigitte, Milford H. Wolpoff, and Martin Pickford in *Nature*, 10 October 2002). Any principle, theory, or law in science is initially guessed and never more than tentatively confirmed. This is far from pure guesswork but still guesswork. Statements like the above-quoted one exhibit a category-two-student attitude, possessed of a vain, Laplace-like ignorance and arrogance.

Ignorance on both sides leads to claims of a few advocates of Godless evolution, on the one side, perfunctorily reported as fact by most of the news media, which claims invite responses arguing against atheism *and* evolution on the other, suggesting in the minds of some that any support of or claims favorable to evolution, however generic and innocent, support Godless evolution. Such a misdirected debate, about evolution rather than atheism, immediately raises two questions. First, since God lies beyond the range of scientific discussion, what responsible scientist would support *Godless* evolution? To a scientist, evolution should merely be evolution as suggested by the evidence. Such evidence provides no reason that a natural, survival-of-the-fittest cause was not intended by God in creation of nature, the means by which He created humans, although other considerations (our aforementioned premortal existence as spirit children of God with mortality a continuation of this existence; see also endnote 21 of Chapter 10) exclude evolution by chance in creation of humans. But evolution does occur and arguing against evolution in a scientific style without scientific evidence is not wise, misses the point, and encourages the opposition. Second, ill-considered outbursts against a neutral, generic theory may be due to desire to distract from or justify deficient knowledge or belief. Both entrenched positions are distractions in a search for truth.

[10] The principle known as Ockham's or Occam's razor is defined in endnote 13 of Chapter 1. See also endnote 9 of Chapter 6.

[11] Cohen, I. Bernard (editor), *Isaac Newton's Papers and Letters on Natural Philosophy,* Harvard University Press, Cambridge, MA, 1958, 7. In quantum mechanics, light particles called photons are now believed to communicate action at a distance for the electromagnetic force (Appendix E) and hypothetical particles called gravitons are believed to communicate the gravitational force. While photons have been observed, gravitons are yet hypothetical because none has been observed.

[12] White, Michael, *Isaac Newton, the Last Sorcerer*, Perseus Books, Reading, MA, 1997, see, *inter alia,* 350.

[13] While science supposedly deals with objective, material (out-of-mind) facts, with positivism regarding these as the only absolutes, none of the seeing, hearing, touching, smelling, or tasting sensations occurs out of mind nor can any such sensation be absolutely described.

[14] *Doctrine and Covenants* 76:71-80.

[15] One of the tests of Odysseus on his long journey home from Troy was to pass "the island of the Sirens twain." To sailors that passed, the Sirens "raised their clear-toned song: 'Hither, come hither, ... that thou mayest listen to the voice of us twain. For none hath ever driven by this way in his black ship, till he hath heard from our lips the voice sweet as the honeycomb, and hath had joy thereof and gone on his way the wiser. For lo, we know all things, ... yea, and we know all that shall hereafter be upon the fruitful earth.' " (Homer, *The Odyssey,* S. H. Butcher and A. Lang (translators), The Modern Library [Random House], New York, 1950, 186.) The siren song was alluring, intoxicating, and irresistible to any who heard it. Sailors were drawn to a counterfeit power, a prospect of temporary joy, a false knowledge of all things of both now and what shall be hereafter. Is this not the siren song of science or religion in the minds of some? Is it not alluring, intoxicating, and irresistible to some in pursuit of recognition and honor of men, i.e., worldly idols?

[16] Richard Feynman gave the 1964 Messenger Lectures at Cornell University (the 41st series); see endnote 8 of Chapter 2.

[17] *Bible,* Hebrews 11:1.

[18] *Bible,* John 14:5-6.

[19] The Schrödinger-Born theory and the de Broglie-Bohm theory cannot be distinguished by appeal to experiment. However, a theory of everything (TOE) would contain a scope of application that is expected to allow more complete experimental tests of the theory, unless too many additional (empirically suggested) mathematical constructs are added. Because of its scope, a TOE may not be simply contrived by use of a few mathematical constructs to agree with all known results. A TOE is expected to be more comprehensive and to therefore provide predictions beyond known results built into the theory. While some scientists believe that a theory of everything or grand unified theory is not far beyond our current knowledge, others are not so optimistic. Optimistic outlooks like the former opinion have often been held in history, e.g., when Dirac introduced his famous equation and he and others used it to discover a broad range of electron behaviors and related effects. But in the past, deeper knowledge has always revealed deeper questions. To be sure, awareness of deeper questions is progress, but it also presents the challenge of finding deeper answers. In quantum mechanics the challenge has been to understand and incorporate into a unified theory the four fundamental forces: the gravity, electromagnetic, strong, and weak forces. These deeper questions have led to answers in the form of a multiplicity of new particles including pions and muons, taus, muon-, electron-, and tau-neutrinos, and various quarks. Quantum chromodynamics, for example, is a synthesis of field theories in which the three quark "colors" play an important role. Then there are the questions of spin and charge and symmetry rules, not to mention the remaining mystery of the wave-particle duality of both matter and light. In super-string theory, purely mathematical constructs called strings are envisioned to extend in ten spatial dimensions. It will be interesting to see if these concepts are sufficient for a unified theory or if new mathematical constructs are required. Invoking new constructs or, perhaps, those already invoked is equivalent to discovering deeper questions which will require answers. If we take history as a guide, new and deeper questions will emerge.

[20] This concept is implied in Gamaliel's advice to the Sanhedrin: "But if it be of God ye cannot overthrow it; lest haply [by misfortune] ye be found even to fight against God." (*Bible,* Acts 5:39.)

Nephi also broached this concept when he wrote "Yea, wo be unto him that hearkeneth unto the precepts of men, and denieth the power of God, and the gift of the Holy Ghost. Yea, wo be unto him that saith: We have received, and we need no more! And in fine, wo unto all those who tremble, and are angry because of the truth of God! For behold, he that is built upon the rock receiveth it with gladness; and he that is built upon a sandy foundation trembleth [and is angry and defensive] lest he shall fall." (*Book of Mormon,* 2 Nephi 28:26-28.)

[21] Like Steven Weinberg's views (loc. cit., 240-242, 270). I regard Weinberg's scientific views as informed and insightful and his willingness to state his views beyond science as honest and courageous. We differ in our conclusions because I know more about religion than he does. He has induced a general conclusion that does not hold up against the (subjective) evidence I possess.

[22] E. T. Bell in his excellent book *Men of Mathematics* (Simon & Schuster, New York, 1937) entitles Chapter 11, on Laplace, "From Peasant to Snob." In this chapter he describes the nature of Laplace's personality as well as his mathematical achievements.

[23] Farrar, Frederic William, *The Life of Christ,* A. L. Burt, New York, n. d., 296. To fully appreciate Farrar's accomplishments in his excellent writing one must be familiar with his personal history. Writing an extensive work like *The Life of Christ* requires much time in both research and writing. Had he remained a Fellow of Trinity College, Cambridge, he would have had ample time and much more immediate access to plentiful resources for these demanding tasks. But Farrar left his prestigious position for one in which he might have more direct, positive influence on young English men as an educator, administrator, and cleric in English Public Schools. He was appointed first at Marlborough as assistant master, then later at Harrow in a similar position but with expanded duties and, finally, he returned to Marlborough as master. His duties required his effort from 7:00 am to 9:00 pm each day. This left few hours for his research and writing. The level of excellence attained by Farrar in his books, especially *The Life of Christ*, is eloquent testimony to his singular abilities and diligence as a writer and a Christian. One only has to read this book to realize that Farrar was indeed a faithful Christian and able scholar. Later appointments culminating in the Deanery at Canterbury also attest

to the Christian qualities he exemplified, his superior capabilities, and his dedication. One example that was much appreciated and noted was his ever-present courtesy to all, young and old alike.

[24] "And if the blind lead the blind, both shall fall into the ditch." *Bible,* Matthew 15:14.

[25] Jaynes, E. T., "A Backward Look to the Future," http://bayes.wustl.edu/etj/node1.html 1993, 273.

[26] Kuhn, Thomas S., *The Structure of Scientific Revolutions,* Second Edition, Enlarged, University of Chicago Press, 1970, Chapters 9 and 10.

[27] Quoted by Kline, Morris, *Mathematics, The Loss of Certainty,* Oxford University Press, New York, 1980, 88.

[28] Gleiser, Marcelo, *The Dancing Universe,* Dutton, Penguin Putnam, New York, 1997, 193, 278.

[29] See endnote 13 of Chapter 4.

[30] Weinberg, Steven, *Dreams of a Final Theory,* Vintage Books, New York, 1994, 171-173.

[31] Particle number flux is number of particles passing unit area per unit time = particle number density × particle velocity ÷ 6. Division by 6 arises from a cube which has six surfaces facing in six possible directions, approximately the fraction of particles moving toward a unit area at any orientation. (Division by 4 instead of 6 is exact when the arithmetic mean velocity is used.) Particle momentum flux is the total quantity of particle-momentum passing unit area per unit time = particle number density × particle velocity × particle momentum ÷ 6, where particle momentum is particle mass × particle velocity. When particle number density, velocity, and mass are assumed to be isotropic, both particle number flux and momentum flux are isotropic.

[32] Weinberg, Steven, *The Discovery of Sub-Atomic Particles,* Revised Edition, Cambridge University Press, Cambridge, 2003, 147.

[33] Bethe, H. A., and R. F. Bacher ("Nuclear Physics," *Reviews of Modern Physics* **8**, 1936, 82-229) estimated 10^{16} km or 1,000 light years as average distance a neutrino travels in a condensed (solid or liquid) substance before capture in an inverse β-decay process. Allan Franklin (*Are there really Neutrinos? An Evidential History,* Perseus Books, Cambridge, MA, 2001, 166) uses this estimate and the capture cross section involved, calculated by Bethe and Bacher, about 10^{-44} cm^2 or 10^{-20} barns.

[34] Halliday, David, and Robert Resnick, *Fundamentals of Physics,* Second Edition, John Wiley & Sons, New York, 1981, 895.

[35] Observation of star interiors and surfaces by neutrino and photon emissions may one day be useful. The two methods reveal what is happening at two places and at two times separated by the time required for photons to reach the star's surface.

[36] Franklin, Allan, loc. cit., Chapters 5, 7, and 8.

[37] Davis, Raymond, Jr., *A Half-century with Solar Neutrinos,* Nobel Lecture, www.nobel.se

[38] Steven Weinberg (*The First Three Minutes,* Basic Books, New York, 1988, 177-178) estimates the energy density of neutrinos and antineutrinos u_ν relative to the energy density of photons u_γ residual from the big bang, obtaining the ratio $u_\nu/u_\gamma = 0.4542$. Since equivalent mass density is just energy density divided by the square of the speed of light, this same ratio also applies for the respective equivalent mass densities. To obtain the number density of photons one uses the Planck's-law energy distribution at 2.79 K that relates equivalent mass per photon $h\nu / c^2$ to their energy density in each energy stratum and sums the number densities for all strata. But the number density of neutrinos residual from the big bang is unknown because the neutrino mass m_ν has not yet been determined. Even though the total equivalent mass density of neutrinos and antineutrinos is known, their number density $u_\nu / (c^2 m_\nu)$ is not.

[39] High-energy particles including neutrinos are discussed by Weinberg, 2003, loc. cit. Other useful sources on neutrinos are Gribbin, John, *The Case of the Missing Neutrinos,* Fromm International, New York, 1998, and Franklin, loc. cit.

[40] Recessional velocities greater than the velocity of light are possible due to expansion of the universe because the expansion velocity component does not count against the Einstein limit c according to Lineweaver, Charles H., and Tamara M. Davis, "Misconceptions about the Big Bang," *Scientific American,* March 2005, 36-45.

[41] Hulse, R. A., and J. H. Taylor, *Astrophysical Journal* **195**, 1975, L51-53.

[42] Pauli, W., *Zeitschrift für Physik* **31**, 1925, 765. For a history of spin that includes the contributions of Pauli and many others, see Tomonaga, Sin-itiro, *The Story of Spin,* University of Chicago Press, Chicago, 1997.

[43] Pauli's "Relativitätstheorie" appeared as volume 19 of *Encyklopädie der matematischen Wissenschaften,* B. G. Teibner, Leipzig, 1921. In 1958 Pergamon Press published an English translation by G. Field with the title *Theory of Relativity*, now available as a reprint from Dover Publications.

[44] This account is paraphrased from Laurikainen, Kalervo V., *Beyond the Atom: The Philosophical Thought of Wolfgang Pauli,* Springer-Verlag, Berlin, 1988, 9.

[45] Stern, Otto, and Walther Gerlach, *Zeitschrift für Physik* **8**, 1922, 110, **9**, 1922, 349. Their experiment used silver atoms having 47 electrons, 46 of which balance one another. Net spin measured was therefore due to the single, unbalanced electron. See Halliday and Resnick, loc. cit., 827-832.

[46] Learning science by rote is briefly discussed by Robert B. Laughlin (*A Different Universe (Reinventing Physics from the Bottom Down),* Basic Books, New York, 2005, 28-32) and by Richard Feynman (in Gleick, James, *Genius,* Vintage Books, New York, 1992, 283-285). Neither discussion includes American university physics students *per se*, but the difference is in degree, not in kind.

[47] Quoted in Ferris, Timothy, *Coming of Age in the Milky Way,* William Morrow, New York, 1988, 177. To be fair I must also point out that Einstein was quite aware of the limited power of physics to provide understanding of value, meaning, and other subjective entities. When asked whether science was exhausted, Einstein reportedly responded "Possibly, but what's the use of describing a Beethoven symphony in terms of air-pressure waves?" (Quoted in John Horgan, *The End of Science,* Broadway Books, New York, 1996, 172.)

[48] We look beyond the limited domain of science and tentative knowledge of lowest-common-denominator facts in search of a more complete vision of reality when we expand the database to include all facts, not just the reproducible, objective, lowest-common-denominator ones on which universal laws of science are to be based. The database is larger and more complete – we haven't discarded anything while we have added new facts. But a barrier, a materialistic bias, contained in much of current culture inhibits the equal inclusion of these other facts. With this extended database I am not talking about traditional science but rather about an expanded personal paradigm which may include science and other tools as well. While science is *ideally* based on objective, universally accepted facts so that it is universally applicable, a personal paradigm or belief is neither objective nor universal. *Practically*, neither is science; and because one is an agent, one's own paradigm is always personally selected subject to no rules beyond those the agent chooses. Thus, one may include subjective facts and personal experience as part of the basis of personal paradigm and belief. Here, again, we may have to look beyond the constraining influence of culture to select the fundamentals of a reliable personal paradigm or belief, one that provides an accurate vision of reality. In such a belief why shouldn't one consider as legitimate the facts which are known only to oneself if, in fact, he or she knows them? What difference does it make if a fact is subjectively known, if it is known? Why should universally accepted facts be exclusively utilized in developing a personal paradigm, philosophy, or belief? Why should any valid evidence be excluded from one's database? Are we of a herd that must follow the common instinct? Are we restrained to homogeneous thinking and thereby forced to follow commonly accepted convention?

Or are we independent agents capable of original thought and demonstration of courage and devotion in our search for truth? If the latter, how can we dismiss a potentially invaluable source of information without at least examining and testing it?

[49] Feynman, Richard, *QED,* Princeton University Press, Princeton, NJ, 1985, 10. Other Feynman comments on *why* are recorded in Gleick, James, *Genius, The Life and Science of Richard Feynman,* Vintage Books, New York, 1992, 364-375.

[50] Quoted in Hans Christian von Baeyer, *Taming the Atom,* Random House, New York, 1992, 48.

[51] Smith, Joseph F., quoted in the *Deseret News: Semi-Weekly,* 17 November 1896.

[52] Hinckley, Gordon B., *Ensign,* Volume 34, Number 2, February 2004, 6.

[53] *Doctrine and Covenants* 76:114-118.

[54] *Pearl of Great Price,* Moses 1:25-41.

[55] *Bible,* John 17:3, 8:19, 10:14-38, Matthew 7:21-23, John 14:6-7, 15:20-23, 1:10-12.

[56] *Book of Mormon,* Ether 3: 25-26, 12:19-20. The first citation reads in part "[God] showed unto the brother of Jared all the inhabitants of the earth which had been, and also all that would be; and he withheld them not from his sight, even unto the ends of the earth." The second citation reads in part "And there were many whose faith was so exceedingly strong, even before Christ came, who could not be kept from within the veil, but truly saw with their eyes the things which they had beheld with an eye of faith, and they were glad. ... one of these was the brother of Jared;" Moroni, final author of the Book of Mormon, revealed his source of insight in writing so powerfully to us, namely, "Jesus Christ hath shown you unto me, and I know your doing." (*Book of Mormon,* Mormon 8:35)

[57] In the Bible (Hebrews 4:1-2) Paul indicates the Israelites during their 40 years of wandering on the Sinai Peninsula were taught the gospel of Christ but had insufficient faith in Him to receive it.

[58] *Pearl of Great Price,* Moses 6:47-62.

[59] Snow, Eliza R., *Eliza R. Snow: An Immortal – Selected Writings of Eliza R. Snow,* compiled by Nicholas G. Morgan, Nicholas G. Morgan Sr. Foundation, Salt Lake City, UT, 1957, 58, 62.

[60] *Bible,* Philippians 4:7.

[61] *Bible,* Galatians 5:22.

[62] *Bible,* Thessalonians 1:1,6.

[63] *Bible,* Hebrews 6:1-6.

[64] *Bible,* 1 Peter 1:8.

[65] *Bible,* John 15:11.

[66] At the risk of seeming to be reactionary I will defend my "testimony" before it is even attacked. Actually, my intent is not to defend myself but to enlarge the view of those who would dismiss personal testimony as unimportant. I make four points about the importance of personal testimony, i.e., the establishment of truth for one's self by receipt of fire and the Holy Ghost.

First, if one does not establish truth for him- or her-self, how will one be certain he or she has discovered it? To be certain, truth must be established by ostensible proof, validated by personal testimony from the Holy Ghost. There is no other reliable way.

Second, when Peter declared his personal testimony of Christ, Christ's response was to sanction it as originating from God and to declare that upon this rock (of personal revelation) He would build His church. (*Bible,* Matthew 16:13-20.) If personal revelation is the foundation of Christ's church, does He not intend that it be used in support of Him and His followers and those who might become His followers? He does and many have been blessed through others declaring or bearing record or confessing or witnessing or testifying of knowledge received from the Holy Ghost.

On the day of Pentecost when the Holy Ghost was given to the saints (all 120 of them) many others heard their spoken testimonies, especially the testimony of Peter, and were "pricked in their heart." Consequently, these hearers asked Peter and the rest of the apostles "what shall we do?" (*Bible,* Acts 2.) Because of the witness of the Holy Ghost who testifies of truth, 3,000 "that gladly received his [Peter's] word" were baptized and added to the church that day. The role of the Holy Ghost is to testify of truth, to impart testimony. Two terms used to describe Him are the Comforter and the Record of Heaven (*Pearl of Great Price,* Moses 6:61) because He bears record of the Father and the Son. But how can the Holy Ghost witness to peoples hearts that they have heard truth if truth is not declared? The "world" mocks truth because the "world" (Satan) seeks to mislead and destroy.

Third, rejecting, trivializing, or mocking of testimony of Christ indicates ignorance of Him and the role He has designated for testimony. It was by testimony of prophets that individuals and nations were and are warned. It is by testimony of believers that family and friends hear of Christ and, if they will receive it, feel the power of the Holy Ghost confirming truth. Testimony or personal revelation is the ostensible proof by which truth and meaning are established. Those focused on the world will not receive such testimony until they change their focus (paradigm). Such persons will not hear because they are focused on material facts and worldly idols. They are thus unconscious to deeper meaning – they neither see nor seek understanding beyond some level of understanding they have already reached. Materialist-atheists, for example, cannot appreciate a *full* knowledge of truth because such a level – an understanding of meaning – is beyond their experience and, like a category-two student, they doubt and reject. They possess no certain knowledge because the material facts and knowledge of the world do not lead to any certain conclusion (Chapters 5 and 10). To see, one must be willing. To understand, one must be both willing and seeking to learn with real intent. No ignorance is deeper and more blinding than the mistaken conviction that one already understands by knowledge of mere facts. Understanding of meaning requires spiritual vision, vision imparted to a willing recipient by the Holy Ghost when truth is encountered – spiritual things are spiritually discerned. When this state is reached, testimony of truth is recognized and "gladly received."

Fourth, we live in enemy territory. Pernicious forces are trying to push us in any wrong direction. For humans, one common wrong direction involves ambition and pride. Among many political leaders, media reporters, and intellectual activists – to mention only three groups, the following observation is not limited only to them – resides a desire to appear learned and wise. This appearance is sometimes difficult within the constraint of nearly homogeneous materialistic and liberal-agenda thinking, but is nevertheless sought with great energy and creativity among our "independent minded" and "deep thinking" media reporters, political leaders, and intellectuals. Thus, a school of thought and behavior has arisen similar to scholasticism and medieval Aristotelianism, wherein pursuit of ambition and recognition among like-minded peers and the public is based more on uniformity of "proper" thinking than on discovery of truth. To such a group, independent thought and action among the masses are anathema; to them uncritical conformity (of others) should supercede substance; to them appearance ("spin, smoke, and mirrors") is more important than reality. Members of such a school who fight against discovery of truth are the equivalents in today's society of the medieval Aristotelians and the scribes and Pharisees of the time of Christ. But from among them many have and yet will discover truth and raise themselves to an understanding of meaning with Christ's help and the help of another through personal testimony, either spoken or "merely" lived. All of us have been given exactly this opportunity and assignment in mortality as agents in search of truth. The assignment involves not only our personal finding and following of truth but also assisting others in their search and journey.

Christ, who those with faith and testimony seek to follow, was ever diligent to the assignment He had received in "teaching, preaching, traveling, doing works of mercy, bearing patiently with fretful impatience of the stiff-necked and ignorant, enduring without a murmur the incessant and selfish pressure of the multitude ... so many coming and going as to leave no leisure even to eat." (Farrar, loc. cit., 169.) We who are commissioned with a testimony of truth must also seek to help others.

[67] *Bible,* Matthew 7:16,20, Luke 6:44, *Book of Mormon,* 3 Nephi 14:16,20.

[68] Will, Clifford M., *Was Einstein Right?,* Basic Books, New York, 1986, 78-79, 140.

[69] Evidence of (1) dedication, (2) busyness, and (3) our position in the priorities of the Father and the Son follows. (1) Last paragraph of endnote 63. (2) God declared unto Moses "And worlds without number have I created; and I also created them for mine own purpose; and by the Son [Christ] I created them, which is mine Only Begotten." (3) God further declared "And as one earth shall pass away, and the heavens thereof even so shall another come; and there is no end to my works, neither to my words. For behold, this is my work and my glory – to bring to pass the immortality and eternal life of man." (*Pearl of Great Price,* Moses 1: 33, 38-39)

14. Each of Us Versus the Universe

The *us* in the title of this chapter is humankind. The *each of us* is every individual person. Ultimately, we do not face the universe as a group. Each person perceives and engages the universe primarily as an individual. And the universe is enemy territory. We are currently engaged in a life-and-death struggle – a war – completely invisible to many and only vaguely sensed by others. We are agents battling to find and follow truth. Whether we realize it or not, that is our commission. And the enemy each of us must individually face is great in number and powerful in subtle influence. Sounds farfetched and scary? Scary? – yes, but no more than we can handle. Farfetched? – maybe you won't think so after you read this chapter and the next.

The war is between seekers of truth and goodness on the one side and, on the other, the enemy, Satan and those who intentionally follow him and those who simply acquiesce to his domination by remaining indifferent. The battle is ideological, involving philosophy, belief, faith, desire, intent, and volition. The battle is about paradigm, for it is by paradigm that we aspire, choose, and act. And choice of paradigm is not accidental but deliberate in either our choice or indifference. Freedom of choice or agency has been given to each individual; it is the only possession any of us truly owns - one's self. The battle thus concerns what each of us will do with his or her one possession, what paradigm we will choose and live in exercising our freedom. For each it is as a parable of the one talent. One cannot escape the battle by any strategy, even indifference. One either chooses to fight the battle on the side of good or is dominated by Satan. If we choose good and are valiant in the battle we receive eternal life (different from immortality which all of us shall receive). If we capitulate we don't.

The image of war is a familiar Christian one, illustrated by the hymns "Onward Christian Soldiers," "We are All Enlisted," and "Battle Hymn of the Republic." The war presents the choice of whether or not to take the side of Christ, the perfect embodiment of truth and goodness, and become His disciple, follow His example, seek to do His will, i.e., give to Him our one and only possession: our independence. This war image is realistic as will shortly be indicated by scriptural evidence and by reason. The enemy and the battle are real according to the Christian paradigm and the outcome on a personal level is very much in question. The end of truth must personally be established (written) by each individual for him- or her-self with the most beneficial truth written by one's own valor in the battle.

While terminology may differ, other Christian writers have made similar statements. My favorite, C. S. Lewis, stated

> People often think of Christian morality as a kind of bargain in which God says, 'If you keep a lot of rules I'll reward you, and if you don't I'll do the other thing.' I do not think this is the best way of looking at it. I would much rather say that every time you make a choice you are turning the central part of you, the part of you that chooses, into something a little different from what it was before. And taking your life as a whole, with all your innumerable choices, all your life long you are slowly turning this central thing into either a heavenly creature or into a hellish creature: either a creature that is in harmony with God, and with other creatures, and with itself, or else into one that is in a state of war and hatred with God, and with its fellow-creatures, and with itself. To be the one kind of creature is heaven: that is, joy and peace and knowledge and power. To be the other means madness, horror, idiocy, rage, impotence, and eternal loneliness. Each of us at each moment is progressing to the one state or the other.[1]

Thus, Lewis also sees each of us figuratively writing our own end of truth. He recognizes that the heavenly creature must possess a mutual devotion with Christ ("in harmony with God," in contrast to "a state of war and hatred with God"). The struggle against the universe to obtain this nature is the battle. As we shall see in this and later chapters, acquiring the nature of a heavenly creature in becoming one with Christ in preparation for the heavenly consummation of this process is the very purposes of our mortal-experience "battle service."

Rather than a collective Christian battle, the situation is one of personal battle wherein each individual faces the unseen enemy. The battle is therefore many battles and the outcome of each individual's battle depends ultimately on the individual rather than Christianity or any group as a whole, although good people of all persuasions can and do provide help and strength to others and Christian teachings provide both truth and lead to required saving ordinances. Collective Christianity was only at risk in the battle Christ Himself fought and won during His perfect mortality. Now, Omniscience and Omnipotence is beyond challenge of the enemy, a result foreseen based upon His personal qualities to be indicated in Chapter 15. What is still at risk is the fate of each of the rest of us, His creatures. As soldiers in the battle each individual experiences the ideological battlefield (mortal life) and adopts his or her attitude and response (paradigm). No neutral position exists; either we are for or against Him. A supposed mere observer loses by acquiescing to domination by Satan. This battle is the challenge and opportunity of life. It is the ultimate issue each individual faces, the matter our adopted paradigm and personal determination and vigor are required to successfully address if we are to win. Choice of paradigm is critical. By it we write our own story of truth. Indeed, it becomes our truth.

We examine the battleground situation and the strategy, intelligence, tactics, and weapons available in Christianity as commonly understood by most Christians (represented by Lewis' "mere Christianity") and as taught in the Bible and other scripture. The perspective taken in this account and much of the intelligence utilized originates in this other scripture supported by the Bible, as an informed reader will recognize in the agreement of many of our conclusions and those of Lewis in his perceptive writing based on his study of the Bible, his practice of Christian faith, and his reasoning.

We end this chapter considering a criticism of religion, useful because it illustrates blindness a paradigm can impose through narrow and erroneous thinking.

While the style of presentation in Book II, the "science chapters," has been somewhat tentative due to the fact that science is itself only tentative, the style of presentation in this chapter and in Book III is more definite because the facts and their meaning are more definitely known to me.[2] Also, scriptural citations are frequently given because, while secular books such as *The Aeneid* or *The Odyssey* contain much cultural value, truth and meaning are gleaned primarily from scripture.

Defeating the Universe by Learning and Living Truth

Stephen Hawking, the current successor to Isaac Newton as Lucasian Professor at Cambridge University, describes the following paradox in his popular summary of cosmology *A Brief History of Time*.

> Now, if you believe the universe is not arbitrary, but is governed by definite laws, you ultimately have to combine the partial theories into a complete unified theory that will describe everything in the universe. But there is a fundamental paradox in the search for such a complete unified theory. The ideas about scientific theories outlined above assume we are rational beings who are free to observe the universe as we want and to draw logical deductions from what we see. In such a scheme it is reasonable to suppose that we might progress ever closer toward the laws that govern our universe. Yet if there really is a complete unified theory, it would also presumably determine our actions. And so the theory itself would determine the outcome of our search for it! And why should it determine that we come to the right conclusions from the evidence? Might it not equally well determine that we draw the wrong conclusion? Or no conclusion at all?[3]

Thus, discovering basic truth about the universe may require defeating the universe! Rather than being passive, the universe may be and in fact is active in influencing our thinking and behavior. While the universe, containing you and me, is not fully deterministic as Hawking perhaps assumes, it does contain a real force (the enemy) that attempts to steer our thinking, belief, and behavior in any wrong direction, away from essential truth. To think and behave as one desires contrary to the enemy's desire therefore involves a battle against the universe. To win such a battle, no possible unreliability can be allowed in one's answers to certain ultimate questions, which we shall soon address, whether due to known or not yet imagined causes! *Understanding* is required, i.e., *understanding* that supports at least one sequence of ever-deeper questions down to a fundamental, absolute truth so recognized. Else we are vulnerable to diversion from a correct path or way and an accurate understanding of reality.

This description of our current state is not casually chosen. Man is currently living in space temporarily occupied by the enemy, once again using Lewis' apt description. While the true owner will shortly return and reclaim ownership, humans must meanwhile survive steamroller-force tactics of an unseen enemy to confuse and mislead, tactics wherein philosophies containing subtle mixtures of truth and error exist in an overwhelming number of variations (Appendix I). Thus, the strategy of the enemy is subtlety with the steamroller force is in the number of variations in philosophies or systems of belief he has inspired, motivated, and directed, all of which contain truth and virtue mixed with error meant to imprison people therein.

Perhaps an illustration would be useful. In reviewing a recent movie filled with kindness, abstinence, honesty, wholesome activity, and Christian values, journalists disparagingly described it as "sappy," "cornball," and "it plays like a propaganda film sponsored by Jerry Falwell and the religious right."[4] These comments were written in an ignorant wisdom. Their apparent intent is the usual mocking cynicism, the belief that human conduct is motivated wholly by self-interest, a belief a few reporters use as a substitute for wisdom. The mocking cynicism is directed at those who support traditional values and conservative attitudes. Value-free materialists and other atheists apparently imagine they "see through" a transparent façade of traditional values of Christianity. "But," as C. S. Lewis has written,

> you cannot go on 'explaining away' for ever: you will find that you have explained explanation itself away. ... If you see through everything, then everything is transparent. But a transparent world is an invisible world. To 'see through' all things is the same as not to see.[5]

Skeptics willfully blind to goodness do not readily find goodness and generosity because their paradigms are largely devoid of these things and such things are therefore imaginary and artificial rather than real to them. Ironically, it is those joined together in self-interest accusing and mocking others for their own fault. The near homogeneity of this collective, mindless bias against traditional mores and values so predominant among some outspoken "independent-thinking guardians of the public mind" (journalists) and many Hollywood producers is not remarkable since it is organized and choreographed by the enemy. Perhaps such journalists and producers (and intellectuals) envision themselves as champions freeing a suppressed people from restrictive inhibitions (while seeking personal fame and fortune – herein lies the irony) or perhaps they possess no altruism and simply destroy without building, offering in place of traditional values only materialism, humanism, preoccupation with worldly idols, or nothing at all. Christian values have an important function – they inhibit us from doing bad things. Mocking cynicism, materialism, or lack of any belief cannot replace their function. In view of potential impact of journalists and movie producers, one may correctly believe that an unseen enemy is drawing their allegiance in its own perverse direction, which enemy some of them obediently follow for lack of understanding or spiritual resolve to resist. Propaganda consists of ideas, facts, or allegations spread deliberately to further one's cause or to damage an opposing cause. Propaganda and misinformation are especially essential in an ideological war wherein they, with truth and education, are the principal weapons. Sources of propaganda are consequently primary targets in the war we are examining. And either promoting of propaganda, misinformation, ignorance, and evil on the one side or truth and goodness on the other, reveals one's allegiance in the war.

The doctrine of Christ is the most effective intelligence and strategy by which one may resist the enemy's intense propaganda campaign. And, beyond personal survival, it is the only strategy by which one can fully join with Christ in helping others defeat the enemy and receive eternal life.

God revealed to Moses an event that occurred in heaven before humans were placed on the earth that illuminates the nature of the battle now being fought.

> Wherefore, because that Satan rebelled against me, and sought to destroy the agency of man which I, the Lord God, had given him, and also that I should give unto him mine own power; by the power of mine Only Begotten, I caused that he should be cast down [to the earth[6]]; And he became Satan, yea, even the devil, the father of all lies, *to deceive and to blind men, and to lead them captive at his will, even as many as would not hearken unto my voice.*[7] (italics added)

Thus, the agency of man is a God-given gift and this agency contains a choice: whether a person will follow God or not. If not, if one refuses to hearken to the voice of God, he or she will be led captive at the will of Satan. This synopsis, however brief, captures the essence of the battle – by choice we either willingly follow God or are deceived, blinded, and led captive by Satan. There are no neutral observers.

Moses was not the only prophet to write about these things, important as they are. Additional insight regarding the nature of the battle – particularly regarding our hearkening unto the voice of God – is given by Paul.

> ... I came to you, ... not with excellency of speech or of wisdom, declaring unto you the testimony of God. ... And my speech and my preaching was not with enticing words of man's wisdom, but *in demonstration of the Spirit and of power: That your faith should not stand in the wisdom of men, but in the power of God.* ... Now we have received not the spirit of the world, but the spirit which is of God; *that we might know the things that are freely given to us of God.* Which things also we speak, not in the words which man's wisdom teacheth, but which the Holy Ghost teacheth; comparing spiritual things with spiritual. *But the natural man receiveth not the things of the Spirit of God: for they are foolishness unto him: neither can he know them, because they are spiritually discerned.*[8] (italics added)

The insight and faith Paul urges are based not on the thinking of natural man but on the power of God, on "fire and the Holy Ghost," "that we might know the things that are freely given to us of God." As we should expect, Paul's admonition is reminiscent of the doctrine of Christ, urging us to seek wisdom through the power of God, the Spirit of God, or the Holy Ghost; all of these terms mean the same thing in this case. And a similar message is implied by God in addressing Moses because God's "voice" includes all communication from Him. How do we hearken unto the voice of God? Paul says by seeking faith that stands not "in the wisdom of men, but in the power of God [fire and the Holy Ghost]." The implication is not that human wisdom is bad – to the contrary, human wisdom is useful and desirable – but the wisdom that stands in the power of God is infinitely more useful and important.

How do we receive wisdom through the power of God? In 124 BC, a Book-of-Mormon prophet-king Benjamin while addressing his people who had each made a covenant to follow Christ's teachings, known in detail for centuries among these faithful people, provided an essential insight. He said (with my italics added),

> And now, because of the covenant which ye have made ye shall be called the children of Christ, ... for ... your hearts are changed through faith on his name; ... whosoever doeth this shall be found at the right hand of God, for he shall know the name by which he is called; for he shall be called by the name of Christ. And ... whosoever shall not take upon him the name of Christ must be called by some other name; therefore, he findeth himself on the left hand of God. ... *For how knoweth a man the master whom he has not served, and who is a stranger unto him, and is far from the thoughts and intents of his heart?*[9]

All of these prophets, Moses, Paul, and Benjamin, taught basic elements essential to the doctrine of Christ and thus give useful guidance about how one may acquire wisdom by it. They indicate, in turn, that (1) the wisdom and strength of natural humans are not sufficient to resist the power of Satan, (2) to resist Satan, human wisdom must be magnified by spiritual wisdom and strength received through the power of God, and (3) this wisdom and strength are received by obeying Him, by serving the Master, and thereby coming to know Him "that we might know the things that are freely given to us of God."

The concepts described in this book indicate that discovery of absolute truth, or absolute demonstration of truth, by the scientific method or natural human ability is impossible because tentative knowledge is not demonstrated truth. In other words, science or human philosophy provides no adequate truth criterion or method by which truth may be reliably established. That is one reason human wisdom and strength are insufficient to withstand domination by Satan. The insufficiency of science, namely, its inherent inability to reliably establish truth, has already been and will yet be further examined. We focus now on a superior wisdom obtained through the power of God or the Holy Ghost, wisdom required for resisting domination by Satan, required to prevent captivity by his will. Science is further considered in comparisons and in summaries of science and Christianity in Chapters 16 and 17 to provide better understanding of both and of meaning.

Knowledge with and without Help from Omniscience

The single element missing in the scientific method, the element whose absence is fatal to obtaining absolute understanding, is an absolute *yes* answer, i.e., an adequate truth criterion. Therefore, any progress in science must occur by an incremental series of *no* answers, with each *no* answer requiring a revision of knowledge, i.e., a new guess. And a *no* answer may appear at any time in the form of a single, established fact in essential contradiction to a guessed theory or law. That is, the absence of a *no* answer may not be regarded as a *yes* answer. Even when a guess is correct, it is only tentatively established to be free of contradiction. A guess becomes knowledge only after all facts are determined, i.e., after omniscience is obtained, and we no longer need to guess. It was this conclusion – that empiricism and reason are forever inconclusive – that caused the Greek philosophers to lament their inability to establish truth.[10]

In effect, the scientific method recognizes that omniscience required for final or absolute establishment of any conclusion is not resident in humans. And the method, by itself, does not include Omniscience. By the scientific method we may adopt and practice a law as we continue to learn, even for just an interim period, only as a matter of assumption or faith that it is correct. If we can never regard a law as absolutely proven, then assumption and faith therein are eternal requirements for its use. Assumption and Godless faith are, however, insufficient to win the above-described battle to defeat a non-passive universe. More powerful armament, *understanding* and motivation in feelings of love, peace, and joy, are needed.

These concepts reveal the value and advantage provided by the power of God or Holy Ghost promised in the doctrine of Christ to anyone who will receive it. First and foremost, rather than a limited, tentative philosophy, it represents a comprehensive philosophy including "things not of this world," i.e., capable of and, indeed, focussed on answering ultimate questions – to "know the things that are freely given to us of God." It deals not only with ultimate facts but also with their meaning, not only with *how* but also with *who*, *what*, and *why*. Given the difficult task of discovering truth on any kind of fundamental, abstract level, it is a great advantage to be told what the truth is by Someone who is certain to know. Omniscience and certain *yes* as well as *no* answers are allowed in and are essential to the doctrine of Christ. Indeed, the only way we can include "consideration of facts not yet observed or imagined," as is required to obtain *understanding* and to "defeat the universe," is to take counsel from Someone to whom all facts are known. Steps one and two of the scientific method address an indefinitely large number of possibilities, not all of which have yet been imagined by humans – we not only don't know the right answers, we don't even know the right questions. Help obtained using the doctrine of Christ puts us infinitely ahead.

Science and the doctrine of Christ may therefore be contrasted, with regard to ultimate issues, using comparative terms like helpless versus empowered, or hopelessly ignorant versus enlightened. In the doctrine of Christ we are offered the truth by a Kind Friend; we need then only receive and apply it, which are one and the same process and comprise the test of the doctrine. Then, when our Friend who gave it to us also provides the promised proof, we begin to understand fundamental truth that securely defines reality and enables us to use a powerful philosophy to greatly expand our understanding of the true nature of the universe. The doctrine of Christ (DOC) may thus be regarded as a sort of ultimate theory of the total universe (UTTU), a theory not focused merely on material facts and processes but encompassing a much broader scope, broad enough to empower One to walk on water, give sight to the blind, raise the dead to life including one day you and me, and create worlds and creatures. And, it's not theory because it's revealed knowledge (INTBIRK). (These acronyms are invoked purely to make Christianity competitive with science. Don't bother to remember them though; we do not use them again.) We only receive this knowledge a little at a time as we prepare and qualify ourselves to receive it, precept by precept and grace by grace. But the understanding we thereby attain is based on absolute truth, so established, together with deep meaning. In contrast, science provides merely tentative knowledge of reproducible, external, value-neutral, lowest-common-denominator, material facts and a few tentative, "long-leap" guesses of only material-based truth. Value of the doctrine of Christ as a fundamental Christian doctrine is indicated in Appendix K. Further details about the scope of insight obtainable through the doctrine of Christ are included in endnote 11.

However, in spite of these sharp and fundamental-level contrasts between methods, it is clear that science and Christianity have much in common, more so than one perhaps realized at the outset. Adherents of both methods seek truth and adherents of both methods invoke faith. In both methods we adopt a hypothesis, law, or principle based on faith and learn of its verity through application of it. Principal differences, and these are significant, lie in the means we utilize for finding truth or the object of our faith. If we embrace the scientific method exclusively, then we seek truth through human power and we place our faith in humans. Humans become the champions and heroes of the exercise. If we embrace the doctrine of Christ, we look to Christ for truth and for salvation; He is the Rock on whom we build and it is Christ who we regard as the Real Champion of humanity.

The Real Champion

While the scientific method ideally utilizes careful, unbiased examination of material facts for the discovery of pattern and organization therein, the method is focused on only objective, reproducible, lowest-common-denominator, material facts. Comprehensive understanding at a deep, abstract level is so remote from such facts that it is probably unattainable by this method and, indeed, certainly *understanding* cannot be acquired through science by which any law is merely tentative. The issues we are addressing in this book are too important to casually decide based on incomplete, tentative knowledge, that is, to base in some degree on prejudice. To obtain *understanding* we must invoke a method superior to science.

One alternative method is to attach ourselves to a Champion who understands truth, life, cause, and meaning and who is willing to share such understanding in guiding us. If a person must struggle to merely discover a few facts and simple connections and pattern therein, how can he or she attain *understanding*? In fact, in view of the occurrence of miracles, what fact does anyone understand? Without the help of a Friend, a human can't understand essential things, like the way, the truth, and the life.

If one wishes to believe in something in the absence of absolute truth (or absolutely demonstrable truth), one has a single choice with no possible alternative, namely, assumption or faith. No matter in what or in whom we choose to believe, without *understanding* our choice is ultimately a "leap of faith" and a prejudice. The situation is ironic. Some, who fight against faith in general and religion in particular, seem completely unaware – like Simplicio, the prototype category-two student – that whatever their paradigm, system of belief, or philosophy, it is adopted as an act of faith. (Or is the absence of mention of faith simply an honest oversight?) At best, if one has adopted his or her philosophy intelligently, recognizing its limitations and dependent structure (as B depends on A in the mathematical proofs addressed in Chapter 10), one may have deliberately chosen a philosophy based on faith in some notion or axiom to which one is partial; but faith is always required.

The inverse of this principle also applies: one may exclude a notion or axiom because of a dislike for it. But arbitrary exclusion of a fact or axiom is dangerous. For instance, a bias on the part of Einstein was revealed in the earlier-quoted 1933 conversation between Einstein and Lemaître in which the latter mentioned his primeval-atom model and Einstein interrupted him with the comment "No, not that, that suggests too much the creation." While Einstein wanted to avoid in the theory anything that appeared close to a creation, Lemaître was right and

Einstein wrong. Einstein's equations imply a singularity in the past. Arbitrary exclusion of any notion, fact, concept, principle, or axiom is dangerous.

An essential, fundamental-level ingredient of a philosophy is a *principal*, *hero*, or *champion* in the philosophy. This explicit or implicit champion can, in some philosophies, provide reliable guidance and otherwise empower a holder of the philosophy. In other philosophies the principal or champion is not so powerful. Thus, an implicit act in adopting a philosophy is the embracing of a champion who or which is the principal or source of insight and power in that philosophy and, often tacitly, placing faith and trust in Him, him, her, them, me, us, or it. Categorizing a philosophy by its champion(s) thus becomes a means of comparing and evaluating different philosophies. For this purpose, useful questions in examining a philosophy are (1) "Who or what is the champion?" (2) "What power does the champion hold according to the philosophy?" and (3) "To what end does the champion participate in the philosophy (who serves, is served, leads, follows, etc.)?"

Some philosophies are *ad hoc* conglomerations of different concepts and principles picked up along the way of life. In fact, all personal philosophies contain and should contain elements of this type. It is good to see virtue and capability and to try to emulate these qualities. But a contrived, *ad hoc* philosophy can carry a danger in extreme cases where it becomes so complex that its foundation is obscured and neither the reliance on faith nor the object(s) of the faith is (are) apparent. Such *ad hoc* philosophy sometimes seems to me to be reactionary in that more attention is paid to avoiding or attacking (i.e., reacting to) perceived weak points of other philosophy than to an honest quest for truth or a devout expression of faith and trust. For some, a faith-free or faithless philosophy seems to be the paramount goal. (Guess who the champions are in such philosophies? Fallible humans.) But the need for faith cannot be avoided by mortals, since we cannot yet of ourselves demonstrate the truth of any notion, axiom, or "sufficiency foundation" and, consequently, of any deduction made therefrom. Assumption or faith is essential to any conclusion reached by human reason, which makes assumption or faith an essential element in any philosophy one chooses, especially one contrived to avoid the "weak and useless opiate of the masses," i.e., religion. In such philosophies, Satan dominates.

Therefore, I make the following general claim.

Proposition Number 8: **Embracing *any* paradigm, system of belief, or philosophy involves an essential "leap of faith."**

When we make a leap of faith we vote, so to speak, with our leap. What we choose to believe is what we choose to stand for. Make it count. Don't just be against (reactionary to) some group or philosophy. Avoid "herd instinct" and "party faithful" mentality (mere desire for acceptance by others) as motivation. Seek the truth sincerely, diligently, and independently with a willingness to be influenced and guided only by One who is capable and wants the best for you. Pick a worthy Champion. Stand for Someone you can believe in, for Someone who is uplifting, Someone who is gracious, magnanimous, and beneficent, Someone who will allow you and others who join you in "the cause" to reach the highest pinnacle of your potentials, Someone who will be faithful to you if you are faithful to Him, Someone who will bring you an eternal fullness of joy. Is there really such a Someone, such a cause, philosophy, system of belief, paradigm? Although it sounds too good to be true the answer is yes. The Real Champion is Jesus Christ, the Son of God, who because of His love for us chose to suffer as the Savior of the World. Without Christ there is neither *understanding* nor a resurrection nor an eternal fullness of joy.[12]

A Strong Philosophy versus a Weak Philosophy

Our interpretation of reality depends on our paradigm, belief, or philosophy. This connection between what we see and our paradigm by which we see was evidently on the mind of German astronomer Johannes Kepler when he quipped "Eyesight should learn from reason."[13] Kepler's quip represents a scientist's wistful longing for reasoning that correctly anticipates vision, reasoning suggested in Lewis' oft-quoted thought: "What we learn from experience depends on the kind of philosophy we bring to experience."[14] Correct reasoning and the vision it implies depend on correctness of paradigm. Especially in a matter as deep and elusive, delicate and powerful as meaning, paradigm, belief, or philosophy exerts a controlling or forcing influence on how we reason and what we "see." At every level, from the facts or evidential basis, to reasoned deductions, to intuition, the vision of reality we see is the vision of reality we have chosen to see, imposed by the paradigm, system of belief, or philosophy we have adopted.

That a philosophy forces a vision of reality may induce pause on the part of one considering embracing or continuing to embrace Christianity or some other paradigm. Such a one might say "I do not wish to adopt a philosophy that imposes all conclusions. I prefer a less conclusive, more open approach in which I can consider the facts, case by case, and reach my conclusions in an unrestricted, unbiased way. A way where a full latitude of my logic and my reason and my analysis are allowed and encouraged and a way in which what I decide is the best is so accepted. A way where my scope of action and my breadth of vision are not limited by narrow views on issues like faith, morality, and salvation."

Even the most liberal and nonrestrictive philosophy forces a conclusion, maybe only in justification of one's choice of that philosophy, but nonetheless a conclusion required to retain it, which colors one's view of the facts. Keep in mind a rule of thumb: "The more liberal and permissive (indefinite) a philosophy, the less definite and powerful its effect." A permissive philosophy, like the one described in the previous paragraph, requires minimal commitment and negligible, if any, restriction in behavior. A disciple of such an "enlightened" philosophy commits only to follow himself. Where is the guidance? Where is the power? In the other extreme, the most powerful philosophy is the one whose influence is most restrictive in behavior, most definite in its requirements of application, most comprehensive in the scope and vision of its prescription. Required in the Christian philosophy is commitment to strictly follow Omniscience and Omnipotence. Here is guidance and power. And in our following of the philosophy (or Him) we become like the Followed. Here is meaning.

Does a strong philosophy rob us of independence or agency? My answer to this question is no, because subscription to any philosophy is voluntary. We are agents free to think and act how we will. One can abandon a philosophy, even a strong one, at any time because one is an independent agent. The stronger and more powerful a philosophy, the better it may provide its desired function. Like a hard-science theory, the view provided by a strong philosophy is definite. In contrast, like a soft-science theory, a view provided by a weak philosophy is flexible and relative, adaptable to the conditions at hand. What the Christian philosophy both requires and provides as an opportunity is the giving away of our independence as a voluntarily gift. And it is not freely given if it can't be taken back. An enduring act of such giving is the ultimate expression of trust, allegiance, and devotion. For agency is the only possession we truly own because it is the only thing God, our Creator, has given us, His creatures, living in His creation.[4]

But in choosing a strong philosophy we had better be right. The questions of Christ's existence and Godhood are therefore paramount. Was Christ a crackpot megalomaniac or the Son of God, imposter or Savior? He has left no middle ground as possible. While He was a great teacher and prophet, His essential message was inextricably centered in His proclaimed station as the Son of God and His divine mission as Savior of the world. His teachings, prophecies, and miracles cannot be separated from this claim. The former were provided as evidence of the latter. We must either accept Him completely, or not at all.

What is the evidence? Is the two-thousand-year-old testimony of a few witnesses enough? After all, the Bible was subject to many translations and transcriptions and is clearly erroneous or confusing to some degree. No book, in the hands of humans, has introduced more confusion and contention than the Bible, resulting partly from our mortal natures but also from errors of omission[15] in the Bible and, consequently, because no other book has led to such strongly-held faith and belief in so many different interpretations. But even with its omissions and its many interpretations, the Bible provides true and powerful witnesses of many that Jesus is the Christ. One can also fairly say that no book has introduced more peace and truth and wisdom than the Bible. Other scriptures, notably the Book of Mormon, the Pearl of Great Price, and the Doctrine and Covenants, serve this same purpose. The combined witnesses of several ancient and modern cultures as recorded in the scriptural record serve to bring the paramount question "Who is Christ?" to our attention. But how does one obtain a reliable answer to this question?

What distinguishes Christ the Son of God from merely a great teacher and from other claimants who would have us believe they are *the* champion? It is evidence of His Godly attributes: knowledge, power, omniscience, omnipotence, love, and desire, intent, and ability to save. The Christ described in scripture projects power, grace, authority, beneficence, devotion, and intent to save His followers as well as legendary intelligence and wisdom.[16] Moreover, He has given much more to us than He asks us to give to Him. These are the qualities that make Him worthy of our love and worship. These are the qualities we seek in a God to Whom we would freely and gladly give up our independence (with Him then giving us back more than we gave). These are the qualities we are invited to examine and test in the doctrine of Christ.

Christ's doctrine is the test of His validity. It was the test of His validity in ancient times, for the people He taught in earlier ages, to whom He prophesied, and before whom He performed miracles. It is the test of His validity today, and He still can and will teach, prophesy, and perform miracles for the benefit of those who seek to follow Him. Simply observing a miracle did or does not confer comprehension of meaning. Many Jewish rulers observed His miracles but the Pharisees ascribed them to Beelzebub[17] and regularly challenged His authority in spite of its manifestation in the marvelous miracles He performed.

Then and now, only by faith in Christ is *understanding* received through the power of God. The doctrine of Christ is simultaneously a test of our faith, our worthiness to be included among those He identifies as His followers. The paramount questions regarding the station of Christ and regarding our relationship to Him are answered by Him, in His way, according to His doctrine. He extends the promise contained in His doctrine, an invitation to know Him, to become enlightened by tasting the heavenly gift.[18] We need only embrace and test it to receive an ostensible-step answer regarding the station of Christ and to be included by Him among His followers.

Beyond Belief

I have faith in Christ. However, I do not regard this as a bias (remember, I am utterly unbiased) because bias or prejudice is founded in ignorance and my faith in Christ is no longer merely a belief because its truth has been confirmed to me. I am a rocket scientist (really; well, by training anyway) who was baptized over 50 years ago and I've kept my eyes and ears open and my mind in gear for much of the intervening time, and I have tried to be devoted to Him who is devoted to us all. He has given me, through the power of God as He promised, personal assurance that He lives and is the Son of God and Savior of humankind. I am speaking here of spiritual things which are only discerned by a gift of the Spirit. I am speaking of higher-level understanding of facts and comprehension of meaning which are only apparent to those who have come to a higher level. And I have, by the grace of God and the help of many. And so can anyone by the doctrine of Christ. By the doctrine of Christ and the belief in Him it requires and builds, one may reach beyond rudimentary faith in Christ at the level of mere belief to a higher, magnified level of knowledge and trust.

While an individual might be biased or prejudiced due to ignorance, argument is never biased. Although I am a father and grandfather, I am not presenting views to be accepted by my family on my authority. I invoked authority over my children for a period when they were young, but that period is over. Argument is presented for consideration and response. It is usually presented from a particular point of view or philosophy, and it may, therefore, be incomplete. But argument as a *process* is never biased. Indeed, we use argument and evidence to overcome bias, to find the correct way. In this sense Socrates exhorted us to "follow the argument wherever it leads man." And I am arguing by presenting evidence and describing a methodology by which one can reach his or her own *reliable* conclusion.

But beyond argument and facts lies the power of God, the sure, ostensible witness of the Holy Ghost, the proof proffered in the doctrine of Christ, absolute meaning. When God speaks clearly and directly, the argument is over. And it is from Him I have learned for myself that Jesus was sent by the Father, that He is the Christ, the Son of God, our Savior, our Rock, that He lives, and loves us all. Moreover, as a corollary, I have also learned that His (and our) arch enemy has temporary power to influence the thoughts and actions of men and women and many are seduced into bad desire and worse action by this foe – a fallen angel who once held great authority but now has no purpose other than to vindictively destroy us and thereby mock God.[19] Such knowledge, in both cases but especially the former, is part of the needed "armour" required to successfully defeat the universe and win a true understanding of reality. By such knowledge we choose the correct path in spite of pervasive, contrary influence of the universe.

It is personal knowledge by the sure witness of the Holy Ghost, the power of God, which I am urging. Anything less, while it may provide an engaging and entertaining exercise and a fulfilling occupation, while it may lead us to consider virtue and value and the eternal state of man, while it may focus our attention on ultimate questions pertaining to the meaning of creation and our existence, anything less is inconclusive. The bottom line is that while human reason may suggest, only the power of God can convince and prove on an absolute level and provide a definite, reliable *yes* answer. While conclusions reached by humans may be tentatively regarded as correct, only truth revealed by God is certain. Thus, I argue that He and His power are the only sure foundation, the only reliable Rock, the only absolute truth criterion or comprehensive sufficiency condition on which to build a reliable philosophy and resist domination by an evil influence that would destroy us.

Proposition Number 9: **Of all the various faiths, paradigms, systems of belief, and philosophies, one stands above all others in the assurance offered of its truth and the benefits promised to all who will receive it; its champion is Christ and the system is His doctrine.**

Once we accept Christ and demonstrate sufficient faith in Him by baptism, as specified in His doctrine, we receive a witness by "fire and the Holy Ghost" of things for which belief-level faith was initially required. By this witness we obtain *understanding* of something we previously knew only by faith. I quote the Book-of-Mormon-prophet Moroni who refers to an earlier prophet named Ether:

> ... Ether did prophesy great and marvelous things unto the people, which they did not believe, because they saw them not. And now, I, Moroni, would speak somewhat concerning these things; I would show unto the world that faith is things which are hoped for and not seen; wherefore, dispute not because ye see not, for *ye receive no witness until after the trial of your faith.*[20] (italics added)

Faith is required first, before knowledge is given. When one is ready (as determined by God) knowledge is given by God for the purpose of guiding him or her, providing a foundation upon which knowledge of truth and goodness rests. This foundation is the knowledge that God exists and that His name is Jesus Christ.

To receive such knowledge we must first believe that Jesus is the Christ and that He was sent by His Father, because it is required, and only then do we recognize the source, proper use, and meaning of the ostensible proof given. Only then do we appreciate its value. For these reasons and perhaps others, the sure witness comes only as a confirmation of true belief. In the words of Christ, as recorded in the Bible and the Book of Mormon, we must become and remain "as a little child" in our faith in Him.

The need for faith and humility as a precondition for receiving powerful knowledge is clear from the example of Satan, a fallen angel who knows all about God but is ambitious rather than humble and uses his superior knowledge for his own selfish and evil purposes.[21] Even if one destroys only one's self, such destruction is beyond human capacity to measure. To God, the worth of a human soul is great. Were we not bought and paid for with a price? How great was that price? We cannot say. It is another quantity beyond human capacity to measure; but at least we can equate the two quantities now both mentioned which are beyond human measure, namely, the unplumbed depth of suffering of Christ and the price by which He bought our salvation through His infinite atonement.

God requires faith before He reveals Himself to us. Until our faith is tried and tested, and thereby established to some minimal degree, we are not ready to receive knowledge of God and the great power for good or evil it imparts. Lack of faith in one who has received knowledge by the power of God is a much worse condition than lack of faith in one who hasn't.[18] God wants to guide us and lead us to do His work in blessing man. We must place Him and His work above ourselves to qualify for His blessing, for His blessing is given to His followers so that they may bless others. In so doing we follow His example, His way, His life. It is by losing one's life in His service that one finds it.

The idolatrous attitude of the detached, neutral, objective, wise sage content to observe at a distance without commitment (and therefore having no understanding whatsoever of the spiritual and its meaning) is not compatible with the inclusive, devoted, compassionate, service-to-others attitude required in the gospel of Christ. Such an uncommitted one is dominated and led by Satan and those who follow him. Christ's followers are or aspire to be humble, believing, attending, supporting, caring, loving, contributing, scripture-reading, preaching, witnessing proponents of Him and His faith who are ready to follow wherever He directs. A detached, neutral, objective, uncommitted, nondenominational, far-above-the-common-understanding aspiration is not conducive to selfless service but rather to selfish interest and pride and, unaware, follows Satan rather than Christ. Until we grow beyond an inflated, self-centered, heroic image of ourselves and accept Christ as the Central Figure, *the Hero* (as He accepts the Father and instructs us to accept the Father), we are not ready to follow Him as a little child and we remain subject to domination by Satan.

The preconditions of faith and repentance implicitly groom us in correct priorities, priorities which allow us to recognize and appreciate the value and power of absolute, personal knowledge of truth regarding Him and His Father and desire to avoid its abuse.

While we move beyond faith in receiving knowledge in place of belief, rather than eliminating faith in Him who is the Giver of the gift, the gift of knowledge serves to increase our faith in the higher form of trust in the Giver and in His qualities we don't yet understand and in His ability to guide and save us. As we come to better know Him and His station and to better understand His power and nature and His devotion, especially to those who would follow Him, our belief in Him progresses and matures from simple belief to knowledge, hope, trust, confidence, and, finally, charity (the love of Christ) toward others.

Moroni places conditions in his promise of an ostensible witness from the Holy Ghost or power of God assuring the truthfulness of the Book of Mormon and the divinity of Christ of which it testifies. These conditions are[22] (1) desire and effort (one must carefully read, ponder, and pray about the Book to receive a witness of its truthfulness regarding its teachings of the Savior), (2) sincerity, (3) faith in Christ, and (4) real intent. The last one may be conceptually new to some, although Moroni is not unique in using this concept or terminology since Nephi used both nearly a millennium earlier[23] and Benjamin used similar terminology a half-millennium earlier.[9] It means that to qualify for guidance we must have the intention to follow that guidance. It relates to sincerity, but it goes beyond sincerity. If God tells us something that implies action, it is not enough to sincerely believe, we must act if we are to please Him, if our intent is real. For example, the token of God's great covenant with Abraham's family was circumcision and Abraham fulfilled his part by being circumcised with his son and every male of Abraham's house *the selfsame day*.[24] Such real intent exemplified by Abraham indicates the nature of and cultivates the faith and the resolve therein one must attain to receive God's guidance. By real intent we raise (humble) ourselves from an idolatrous, inflated, self-centered attitude of a detached, neutral, objective, uncommitted, nondenominational, above-the-common-understanding, heroic sage to that of a Christian: a humble believer who truly desires and intends to follow Christ like a little child.

Unlike our use of the scientific method involving meticulous observation, rigorous study, and careful analysis together with a guess or two as to what a true law might be[25] (and the appeal of the notion that one possesses power to make a correct deduction), the compelling evidence that Christ exists and holds great power is not obtained by personal intellectual or physical power, although these qualities are used in the process in study, lived experience, and thought. It is a spiritual gift given personally by the certain witness of the Holy Ghost, as promised in the doctrine of Christ, when we recognize and appeal to God in sincere effort to receive this power. Indeed, our need to recognize and call on His power and His desire to bless us therewith are great lessons of the gift. This gift causes the individual to experience nothing less than a paradigm shift. The hunger to know and the wondering are displaced by the savoring of a deep, peaceful joy in Him. Hunger to know is replaced by yearning to please Him who has the power and desire to extend such love that gives such joy. Values, goals, and aspirations are suddenly changed from being motivated by self to being Him and His centered. Once one tastes this joy, nothing is the same. The feeling of joy in knowing Christ is the certain evidence and power of the doctrine of Christ, but how can one describe it? It transcends material facts and objective understanding. To know it one must experience it.

Proposition Number 10: **The doctrine of Christ leads one to appeal to the power of God above his or her own power. Only through the power of God may one reach beyond the limits of tentative, mortal knowledge to a level of absolute truth, understanding of meaning, and indescribable joy.**

A Critical Analysis of Religion

Intelligent, educated individuals are sometimes quick to categorically dismiss all religion because of some real or perceived imperfection therein. But within religion there exists a myriad of beliefs on practically any topic one may choose, distributed throughout many thousands of different systems of belief. It should therefore be difficult if not impossible to disprove religion in general, unless one attacks some fundamental notion common to all beliefs, provided such a commonly-held notion, in fact, exists. Even restricting consideration to Christianity, the situation is not much changed. How, then, do educated, otherwise perspicacious persons capable of critical thinking make sweeping claims regarding Christianity in general, claims which are not supported by careful analysis or even minimal understanding of the nature of the evidence? It seems debilitating blind spots in knowledge of the spiritual are common, like those that cause a materialist's failure to comprehend meaning. These blind spots are due to paradigm and such blindness may be compounded by induction wherein disappointment with one or a few denominations leads a person to conclude all are deficient. One scholar has observed, "... on balance the moral influence of religion has been awful."[26] But induction is an unreliable basis for a general conclusion.

Certainly there exists religion and, opposed thereto in practically any direction one chooses to look, religion. Those who would contest "science" and "religion" often ignore the greater diversity and competition between "religion" and "religion." Some fundamental, essential, and consequential aspects of the latter competition in Christianity are discussed in Chapter 15. We briefly consider here the former competition represented by the attack of the critical, science-like, only-objective-evidence-allowed analysis of religion. Of course, when any claim in such an attack is sweeping, it is highly vulnerable because only one exception need be shown to repudiate it. Often many can be, as we now illustrate.

In a beautifully written, sweeping argument against religion, Edward O. Wilson invokes the following image as seen by his Empiricist figure. (He also presents a contrary view through another voice.)

> I'll begin by freely acknowledging that religion has an overwhelming attraction for the human mind, and that religious conviction is largely beneficent. Religion rises from the innermost coils of the human spirit. It nourishes love, devotion, and, above all, hope. People hunger for the assurance it offers. I can think of nothing more emotionally compelling than the Christian doctrine that God incarnated himself in testimony of the sacredness of all human life, even of the slave, and that he died and rose again in promise of eternal life for everyone.
>
> But religious belief has another, destructive side, equaling the worst excesses of materialism. An estimated one hundred thousand belief systems have existed in

history, and many have fostered ethnic and tribal wars. Each of the three great Western religions in particular expanded at one time or another in symbiosis with military aggression. Islam, which means 'submission,' was imposed by force of arms on large portions of the Middle East, Mediterranean perimeter, and southern Asia. Christianity dominated the new world as much by colonial expansion as by spiritual grace. It benefited by a historical accident: Europe, having been blocked to the East by the Muslim Arabs, turned west to occupy the Americas, whereupon the cross accompanied the sword in one campaign of enslavement and genocide after another.

The Christian rulers had an instructive example to follow in the early history of Judaism. If we are to believe the Old Testament, the Israelites were ordered by God to wipe the promised land clean of heathen. ...

I bring up these historical facts not to cast aspersions on present-day faiths but rather to cast light on their material origins and those of the ethical systems they sponsor. All great civilizations were spread by conquest, and among their chief beneficiaries were the religions validating them. No doubt membership in state-sponsored religions has always been deeply satisfying in many psychological dimensions, and spiritual wisdom has evolved to moderate the more barbaric tenets obeyed in the days of conquest. But every major religion today is a winner in the Darwinian struggle waged among cultures, and none ever flourished by tolerating its rivals. The swiftest road to success has always been sponsorship by a conquering state. ...

The most dangerous of devotions, in my opinion, is the one endemic to Christianity: *I was not born to be of this world*. With a second life waiting, suffering can be endured – especially in other people. The natural environment can be used up. Enemies of the faith can be savaged and suicidal martyrdom praised.

Is it all an illusion? Well, I hesitate to call it that or, worse, a noble lie, the harsh phrase sometimes used by skeptics, but one has to admit that the objective evidence supporting it is not strong. No statistical proofs exist that prayer reduces illness and mortality, except perhaps through a psychogenic enhancement of the immune system; if it were otherwise the whole world would pray continuously. When two armies blessed by priests clash, one still loses. And when the martyr's righteous forebrain is exploded by the executioner's bullet and his mind disintegrates, what then? Can we safely assume that all those millions of neural circuits will be reconstituted in an immaterial state, so that the conscious mind carries on?[27]

Close, but no Cigar!

This critical analysis of religion is sweeping, insightful, and correct, except for a "few details." But the few incorrect details are critical and their corrections happen to change everything. Moreover, in the end the champion or hero of the above paradigm promoted by the Empiricist is proud, self-centered, fallible humanity. But this analysis does provide valuable insight. Therefore, before we consider where the analysis is wrong, let's first consider where it is right.

The destructive side of religion cited by Wilson's Empiricist cannot be denied by anyone familiar with history. Invoking the name of God in committing enslavement and genocide does not moderate the effect of the acts. Mutual validation of two corrupt authorities, military and religious, combining to rule over others by whatever means still results in enslavement and mass destruction, an experience no less severe than if only one had imposed these conditions. Greed and lust for power and wealth are unchanged in their function and effect whatever the name of the institution practicing them or the reasons cited therefor. The desire of natural humans to obtain power and wealth and to retain them by any means is all-too-well illustrated in human history, too often in the name of religion. Wilson's Empiricist is correct in condemning such goals and methods and pointing out arrogance, hypocrisy, and evil of religious institutions that embrace these goals and methods. We do not argue against the fact that the moral influence of much religion has been awful.

But the Empiricist's analysis fails to consider critical evidence. He seems to assume, tacitly, that religion must survive from one age to another and is thus locked in some kind of natural, Darwinian struggle for existence. Religions come and go, often with no apparent continuity or direct ancestry. True religion is not an institution of humans, but of God. As such, it has no need of Darwinian survival. Neither does false religion, which is inspired, motivated, and directed by the enemy.

In contrast to the inductive analysis of the Empiricist, consider the following inductive and deductive analyses that lead to an opposite conclusion.

In Biblical history, God frequently called prophets to restore lost truth. A few rulers of both the Northern and Southern Kingdoms (Israel and Judah) of the Old Testament misled their people to follow idols such as Baal and "grove worship" with its associated enticements rather than to worship the One, True God of Abraham, Isaac, and Jacob. Isaiah condemned the people because they had "changed the ordinance, broken the everlasting covenant"[28] and predicted that "darkness shall cover the earth."[29] Amos foretold of "a famine in the land, not a famine of bread, nor a thirst for water, but of hearing the words of the Lord."[30] Because humans contaminated and perverted religion and murdered true believers, e.g., killing early prophets, crucifying Christ and all but one of His apostles, and killing many early Christians, loss of true religion is a recurring historical theme dating to the beginning of the human race. By the time the Roman Emperor Constantine adopted "Christianity" as the state-sponsored religion in 312 AD, it was far removed from the original Christian religion and but one of many derivatives conniving to grow at the expense of others, as foreseen by the apostles and prophets, the result of "grievous wolves" entering into the church.[31] Paul describes a "falling away" to occur before the second coming of Christ, motivated by the son of perdition, "Who opposeth and exalteth himself above ... God."[32] Peter foresaw "times of refreshing" and a "restitution of all things"[33] to precede the second coming of Christ, the term "restitution" implying first possessing, then losing, then reacquiring something. John's test against deception,[34] valid anciently and now, is that the doctrine of Christ – an adequate truth criterion – is known to true believers, to those who know Christ. This doctrine is not contained in our current Bible but is known today from the Book of Mormon, knowledge that required and that is a restitution. The prophetic message is always a call to repent, to believe in the true God, to worship Him alone, and to receive forgiveness. Survival of true religion is not a natural, Darwinian process. While evil may flourish for a day, the return of good is always possible. God has power to give, to take away, and to restore, as He has repeatedly done through prophets in past ages.

The grand historical view proposed by Wilson's Empiricist ignores the most essential facts in one of the major world religions he describes. This religion is Christianity and the facts are that Christ was miraculously born of a virgin mother in the most humble of conditions, in a stable, undertook a ministry to which He was appointed by His Father in which He taught the people, healed the sick, raised the dead, organized a church and chose and ordained priesthood leaders therein, lived a life of perfect obedience to His Father's will, bore an unspeakable burden in Gethsemane on behalf of all others, gave up His life on a cross, and then resurrected Himself for the benefit of us all. These are the founding acts and origin of a major world religion, of "mere Christianity." One familiar with them would hardly describe them as symbiotic with military conquest or as "a winner in the Darwinian struggle waged among cultures," or as flourishing by not tolerating its rivals, or as a swift road to success by sponsorship of a conquering state. Christ's impact on humankind was not encouraged or supported by either the Jewish or Roman rulers; indeed, they combined to crucify Him. Nevertheless, His life and His acts as recorded in the Bible remain a guide and inspiration to millions throughout the world, irrespective of any formal religious affiliation. Religions of humans come and go, but the inspiring life and death and resurrection of Christ and the promise they hold for us remain a guide to all generations. They can motivate earnest desire to seek His truth and to attempt to follow His way. Never mind numerical or geographical extent or one's institutional affiliation, to seek to follow Christ, including praying to God in the name of Christ for guidance, is true religion because such sincere seeking eventually leads to truth.

As mentioned, Christ died and the apostles and prophets and many members of the early Christian Church were killed. The Christian Church was subsequently corrupted (Chapter 15 and Appendix I). H. G. Wells remarks that the council of Nicaea "marks the definite entry upon the stage of human affairs of the Christian Church and Christianity as it is generally understood in the world today."[35] A pedigree of true Christianity runs to Christ, not Constantine. Christ and His early followers knew His intent but the world today does not, nor did the council of Nicaea in 325 AD presided over by the unbaptized emperor Constantine, who sat on a golden throne in the center of the council but could not understand the deliberations because he did not speak Greek. He did however understand some of the proceedings, such as when elderly Arius stood to address the council and was struck in the face by Nicholas of Myra. Nevertheless, Constantine proposed and ratified the Nicene or trinitarian creed and Christianity suddenly diverged further from what its Author had taught. It was a corrupted church in its various forms (Appendix I) that combined with armies and sought sponsorship of conquering states to spread and empower itself, to provide awful moral influence, contrary to the example and teachings of Christ. This condition led to moral bankruptcy of religious institutions, to a famine of hearing the words of the Lord, and to the Dark Ages of Europe. Apostasy has its substantial cost.

A Foundation of Sand

Objective evidence neither supports nor denies true religion, contrary to what the Empiricist supposes. True religion is primarily based on subjective evidence.

This detail is another critical one missed by the Empiricist. Scientific and religious paradigms focus on different evidential realms. One evidential realm is implicitly preferred with the deliberate and subjective adoption of either system of belief, philosophy, or paradigm: science or Christianity. That "objective evidence supporting it [religion] is not strong" is not surprising since religion is based on a paradigm that focuses primarily on other evidence. To a materialist, subjective evidence supporting science or religion is also not strong because the scientific method ignores subjective evidence. Neither statement is condemning in view of the separate, primary-evidence realms of science and religion. Citing a lack of objective evidence supporting religion indicates a lack of understanding of the nature of *both* systems. Moreover, the Empiricist seems to tacitly adopt a romantic, Laplace-like assumption that the scientific method can provide definite answers to ultimate questions. The scientific method has yet to establish *any* definite, hard-science interpretation of a mere lowest-common-denominator-facts reality. Clinging to classical notions of scientific objectivity and definiteness contrary to the tentativeness and confusion encountered in modern physics, due ultimately to inherent but unrecognized limitations in the scientific method itself, also indicates lack of understanding of the scientific method by Wilson's Empiricist.

As Barfield noted (Chapter 2) and as a consequence of a chosen belief through which only a narrow evidential realm is considered, exclusive focus on meticulous examination of the *objective facts and physical cause-and-effect relationships* produces a corresponding inattention to *meaning*. The meaning we address is based on values. Materialism is value free. Consequently, a materialist does not comprehend meaning. Denial of meaning at any level denies meaning at all levels. For instance, meaning is denied by denying the spiritual and emotional components of humans and the richer levels of language which convey value-based meaning and feeling in thought and speech. Thus, it is implicit in materialism or exclusive use of strictly objective science that a materialist cannot understand the human self, the inner feelings, the subjective, emotional reaction to experience, or to the Creator of humanity. The substance of religion is not recognized by and, indeed, is invisible to a materialist who sees only material facts and objective experience and allows no meaning beyond them. Spiritual things must be spiritually discerned.

The inherent limitations in any paradigm are fixed by the paradigm itself. In science, no certain proof is possible that *any* scientific hypothesis is true because of the nature of the paradigm. In contrast, the doctrine of Christ imposes no such limitation. Indeed, it *focuses* on the important capability it alone claims to provide: the ability to discover and establish as genuine by an ostensible-step proof the most fundamental and far-reaching truth of the universe, the ostensible step being a witness by fire and the Holy Ghost that Christ is the predicted Messiah. Thereafter guidance continues to one who remains humble, like a little child. Omniscience Himself operates by this method to reveal beneficial guidance to those who sincerely seek it. To receive such guidance and basis of knowledge is to build on a philosophical foundation of rock; refusal to receive it is to build on a foundation of sand.

As should by now be clear, even the careful use of what were once regarded as powerful tools such as rigor and logical deduction have brought us no certain laws. In view of the elusive notions of rigor and objectivity and the collapse of certainty in logic and mathematics, summarized in Chapter 10, and the inherent inability of science to discover and establish truth, isn't it time to try a new approach?

True religion, the doctrine of Christ, requires an inner leap of faith, a profession of belief in and a commitment to an unseen God. It involves meaning beyond facts which is only revealed after the trial of faith by the evidence which follows belief. Finding and following the doctrine of Christ are required to win the individual, ideological battle against an unseen enemy in a non-passive, contrary universe. The negative qualities of religion cited by Wilson's Empiricist and others of like persuasion as evidence against religion are qualities found in perverted religion, religion invented by humans losing the battle and worshiping worldly idols of power, wealth, and acclamation of others, inspired by the evil one to mislead and entrap. These idols of worship are evidence that true religion has been corrupted.

To find truth we must look beyond "traditional" religion that has embraced human inventions and instead seek guidance from God. We must look for absolute truth from God through One He has appointed, truth that includes knowledge of the nature and purposes of God (rather than conceptions of Constantine, his council, and the like). We must seek and submit ourselves, like little children, to the power of God to find it. And we must relish rather than ignore or reject the invaluable, intimate, subjective guidance from God whispered directly to an individual's spirit located deep within a person's self.

Proposition Number 11: **Perverted religion is a human product inspired by the enemy and may be recognized by the principles and methods it utilizes contrary to the teachings of Christ. These principles and methods include *active* ones like force, coercion, privilege and power of human over human, deceit, vanity, and pride as well as *passive* ones like distraction through indifference and preoccupation with "higher priority" objectives. Perverted religion, including Godless materialism, is designed and promoted by the enemy to prevent one from finding and following the power of God (i.e., divine guidance) that Christ offers in His doctrine, an offer frequently repeated in scripture.**

Guidance from God

The possibility of restoration of true religion is another critical detail missed in the analysis of Wilson's Empiricist. While Christianity was corrupted, was used by evil and greedy persons to accomplish selfish goals, was imposed by symbiosis with military colonialism to degrade cultures and nations, was utilized by the enemy to spread confusion, ignorance, and evil, pure Christianity should not be condemned for these transgressions. These transgressions were instead the works of humans.

To natural humans, success is recognition, acclamation, influence, power, wealth, gratification of pride. But a system seeking such qualities is a system not concerned with the status and condition of its followers beyond the success such followers bring to the system. Unhealthy desire (lust) for wealth, recognition, influence, and power does not lead to beneficence. A system benefits that which the system was conceived and designed to benefit. If a system is concerned primarily with its own Darwinian survival, it serves primarily itself for the benefit of itself.

If, on the other hand, a system is sponsored by One holding true power (omnipotence), it is not concerned with power. If its owner and champion is Eternal, it is not concerned with Darwinian survival. It may cease to exist in world history from time to time, but it can reappear as suddenly as it disappeared, according to the will and purpose of its Owner. Such a system and its Champion do not seek unrighteous influence, power, and wealth. They have no need for such worldly idols and find lust for them repugnant. And, in any case, what creature could contest a claim of ownership of all things by the Creator of all things, Who happens to be omniscient and omnipotent? True Christianity and its Champion lead humans to think above and aspire beyond the images and idols of the natural mortal, fixated on influence, power, and wealth of the world.

While true religion may suddenly disappear or reappear, it does not do so without prophetic and scriptural announcement to "whom it may concern." Paul describes a condition of apostasy in the last days. In particular, he cites the condition of "Ever learning, and never able to come to the knowledge of the truth,"[36] terminology that reminds us of materialism, the exclusive use of the scientific method with its strictly objective evidence and merely tentative conclusions. Life is inherently a personal and subjective experience involving, only if one will, the power of God. Critical thinking should lead one to utilize rather than discard the natural, subjective view obtained from deep within one's self, instead of a forced, unnatural objective view from a detached distance. We really can't see from a detached distance, no matter how hard we try. Neither are one's eyes attached there nor is one's brain located there. Since meaning comes from within, restricting our view to an external one denies comprehension of meaning. And, in any case, our awareness and intelligence – our mind – is attached to our spirit rather than our physical body. When we die, awareness does not cease for even an instant. There is no escaping the subjectivity of personal existence. By restricting our view to be distant and objective we lose useful perspective and ignore the most valuable source of information. Our relationship with God is personal and intimate rather than remote. He does not speak to us from a detached, objective distance. He whispers to our spirit.

Paul refers to (human) institutions or religions of our time as "Having a form of Godliness, but denying the power thereof: from such turn away."[37] This instruction was exactly that repeated to the boy Joseph Smith in 1820 when he sought direction from God about which church to join and was answered directly in an appearance to him of both God the Father and His Son. The Former introduced the Author of Christianity Himself, with whom Joseph spoke (Appendix H). I agree with the Empiricist that the history of religion has a destructive side, but I do not deny the power of God to correct His repentant followers and I do not, therefore, find the destructive side in human history to be fatal. The power of God to restore, to correct, to forgive, to redeem, to grant eternal life supersedes any result of a Darwinian struggle. More consequential than a Darwinian struggle is the pride wherein humans refuse to acknowledge the power of God and insists on saving themselves, on being their own champion, and not allowing another, even God, to know more than they do. The power of God, who created the millions of neural circuits contained in the human brain, is adequate for reassembling them no matter how they may be destroyed. They are already permanently imprinted by Him in our spirit body which is the indestructible prototype of our physical body and which contains the mind. Proud humans are ever so intoxicated by a little, recently-obtained knowledge (i.e., their heroism) that they fail to recognize that Someone Else knew it all a long time ago and knows answers to questions humans can't even ask. Indeed, these same persons don't "get it." Reconstruction of a brain exploded by a bullet is no more difficult than one burnt to ashes, eaten and digested by an animal, or simply buried and decomposed to "dust." Because such a task is beyond the materialist, he or she is skeptical that it can be done. But God possesses knowledge and power far beyond what we can imagine. Resurrection is a miracle accomplished by the power of God. The higher level of faith is trust in the omniscience, power, and intentions of God. It follows the beginning level where commitment is made to believe in Him. In this trust the martyr is willing to serve Christ at the cost of a bullet exploding his brain (not his mind). We all die. The question is for what do we live and die? Dying is not fatal. But refusal to believe in Christ is utterly fatal, not to receiving immortality which all receive but to receiving eternal life with its everlasting fullness of joy.

Contrary to the pattern described by the Empiricist, a major Christian religion is emerging, beginning in the last two centuries (i.e., beginning in the "last" or "latter" days). This religion is emerging totally independent of and, indeed, despite worldly power. I am referring to the Church of Jesus Christ of Latter-day Saints, otherwise known by its nickname, the "Mormons." One might say, in accord with Wilson's Empiricist, that this religion is a winner in a "Darwinian struggle in a war waged among cultures," if one knew exactly what this phrase means. If it means overcoming natural processes (the universe) in order to survive, then I agree. If it refers to humans being in enemy territory and successfully engaging followers of evil in a life-or-death ideological battle, then I agree. The usually law-abiding "Mormons" have survived an extermination order by the governor of the State of Missouri, where the church membership then largely resided. Their leader, Joseph Smith, Jr., was assassinated by a mob while he was in jail under pledge of protection by the governor of the State of Illinois,[38] to which state they had fled from Missouri. They were expelled, again, from Illinois by mob violence and threat thereof largely without protection of law or recompense for property. In the former case Smith appealed to the President of the United States who responded "Your cause is just, but I can do nothing for you."[39]

To escape persecution the Mormons finally settled in a nearly uninhabited, high-desert region on the western slopes of the Rocky Mountains. In so doing they neither waged war nor committed genocide. The arduous journey to the unsettled West by a distressed people was itself a remarkable feat. Now, approaching two centuries later with a membership of over ten million, this system of belief is being embraced by converts throughout the world. It is a major religion not because of numbers, although the numbers may eventually come, but because of its impact on individual members, because of its power to influence good people to become better, to abandon natural, mortal pride, and receive the power of God.

Examining the history and nature of the "Mormon" system of belief, one finds no symbiotic effect with any worldly organization. Rather, this system has survived and flourished, like the original Christian Church initially did for its first century, in spite of worldly governments and evil influence bent on destroying it, as if one supernatural power were fighting it and another, more powerful one were guiding and prospering it. I and others regard this church to be the kingdom of God to be set up in the latter days, this time never to be destroyed but to supercede and supplant all other kingdoms. This kingdom is the stone seen in the dream of King Nebuchadnezzar interpreted by the Old-Testament prophet Daniel to reveal "what shall be in the latter days."[40]

> And in the days of these kings shall the God of heaven set up a kingdom, which shall never be destroyed: and the kingdom shall not be left to other people, but it shall break in pieces and consume all these [earlier] kingdoms, and it shall stand forever. Forasmuch as thou sawest that the stone was cut out of the mountain without [human] hands, and that it brake in pieces the iron, the brass, the clay, the silver, and the gold; the great God hath made known to the king what shall come to pass hereafter: and the dream is certain and the interpretation thereof sure.[40]

This prophecy is interpreted by Catholics and Protestants to fit their paradigms, in both cases to make the organization by Christ of His kingdom (or church) correspond to the "latter days." But what are the "latter days?" Validity of Catholic and Protestant interpretations is severely limited or precluded by the break between Eastern and Western Catholicism in 1054 AD and further dissolution of the Western Catholics by the Reformation beginning in the sixteenth century. The Bible puts as much as nearly two millennia[41] between a first setting up of Christ's kingdom and its restoration or restitution to precede His second coming, as noted. According to modern-day scripture,[42] Christ originally set up His church in the "meridian of time."[43] The Mormon paradigm then differs from those of Catholics and Protestants because the meridian of time is its middle, e.g., its noon or midday, not its end.

Nothing is lost and restored simultaneously. If a people value something enough for it to be restored, then it is too valued to be lost. The two first-mentioned paradigms, the Catholic and Protestant ones, preclude a fulfillment of important prophecies in the Bible, some of which are quoted above, pertaining to an apostasy[27-34] or falling away of the Christian Church to be followed in the latter days by a "restitution of all things" before the second coming of Christ.[33-34] (Indeed, this is one of the signs given to indicate the approach of His second coming[33-34,36] – after a restitution of all things; and "restitution" implies the consecutive states wherein something is first possessed, then lost, and then restored.) Interpreting Christ's birth to have occurred in the meridian of time and His second coming or Advent to be in the latter days provides a simple, straightforward interpretation of history and Biblical prophecy devoid of contrived distortions of either. For the latter-day setting up of a kingdom, the restored-original Christian Church, is to occur "in the days of these kings," i.e., in the days of the kingdoms descended from the Roman empire – represented by iron and clay as kingdoms which do not cling together (see Daniel 2:36-43, the eight verses preceding the above quotation). The days of these kingdoms, the time when they were all established seems to have occurred in the early nineteenth century (which involved France leaving then returning to the ranks of kingdoms). This restored kingdom represented by Daniel as the stone "cut out of the mountain without [human] hands," which requires its restoration independent of other churches all influenced by humans (page 384), shall never be destroyed. And the dream is certain and the interpretation thereof sure.

Notes and References for Chapter 14.

[1] Lewis, C. S., *Mere Christianity,* Simon and Schuster, A Touchstone Book, New York, 1952, 87.

[2] On the one hand I have urged the category-one-student attitude, recognizing ignorance in one's self and being eager to learn, even becoming as a little child, humble and teachable. On the other hand I have claimed that absolute knowledge may be obtained by fire and the Holy Ghost through the doctrine of Christ. This may appear to pose a logical dilemma, for why should one possessing absolute knowledge, when he or she realizes its absolute nature, remain teachable? Is he or she to abandon the absolute truth learned for other knowledge? Such a one should be a teacher rather than a student, a leader rather than a follower.

The resolution of the dilemma is that we should remain as little children *before God*, not humans. While one may possess absolute knowledge, his or her absolute knowledge may not be comprehensive in scope – thus the need to remain as a little child *before God* and teachable *by Him*, directly and through those He utilizes. The principal source of truth is God, and we should ever seek to learn from Him by faithfully following the Source of absolute truth. When one has obtained absolute truth by fire and the Holy Ghost, this evidence is inviolate and nonnegotiable. It will not be supplanted by further truth from anyone, including God. Any useful paradigm must be based on and follow this knowledge. But the need always remains to follow the Source of absolute truth as an expression of allegiance, trust, and devotion to Him and to obtain additional truth. The reception of truth from God does not diminish the need and desire to be humble before and teachable by God; rather, it increases them. (See also endnote 63 of Chapter 13.)

[3] Hawking, Stephen, *A Brief History of Time,* Bantam, New York, 1988, 12.

[4] Quoted from Michelle Malkin's column which appeared in the *Democrat and Chronicle,* Rochester, NY on 9 February 2002.

[5] Lewis, C. S., *The Abolition of Man,* Collier Books, New York, 1962, 91.

[6] *Bible,* Revelation 12:9.

[7] *Pearl of Great Price,* Moses 4:3-4. Also, in *Doctrine and Covenants* 46:7-9 Christ instructs members of His church, restored barely eleven months earlier, as follows.

> But ye are commanded in all things to ask of God, who giveth liberally; and that which the Spirit testifies unto you even so I would that ye should do in all holiness of heart, walking uprightly before me, considering the end of your salvation, doing all things with prayer and thanksgiving, that ye may not be seduced by evil spirits, or doctrines of devils, or the commandments of men; for some are of men and others of devils.
>
> Wherefore, beware lest ye are deceived; and that ye may not be deceived seek ye earnestly the best gifts, always remembering for what they are given; For verily I say unto you, they are given for the benefit of those who love me and keep all my commandments, and him that seeketh so to do; that all may be benefited that seek or that ask of me, that ask and not for a sign that they may consume it upon their lusts.

[8] *Bible,* 1 Corinthians 2:1, 4-5, 12-14.

[9] *Book of Mormon,* Mosiah 5:5, 7, 9-10, 13.

[10] See the page-6 quotation of Draper.

[11] *Doctrine and Covenants* 76:5-10 reads

> For thus saith the Lord – I, the Lord, am merciful to those who fear me, and delight to honor those who serve me in righteousness and truth unto the end. Great shall be their reward and eternal shall be their glory. And to them will I reveal all mysteries, yea, all the hidden mysteries of my kingdom from days of old, and for ages to come, will I make known unto them the good pleasure of my will concerning all things pertaining to my kingdom. Yea, even the wonders of eternity shall they know, and things to come will I show them, even the things of many generations. And their wisdom shall be great, and their understanding reach to heaven; and before them the wisdom of the wise shall perish, and the understanding of the prudent shall come to naught. For by my Spirit will I enlighten them, and by my power will I make known unto them the secrets of my will – yea, even those things which eye has not seen, nor ear heard, nor yet entered into the heart of man.

Doctrine and Covenants 6:21-23 contains an answer to a question posed by Oliver Cowdery.

> Behold, I am Jesus Christ, the Son of God. I am the same that came unto mine own, and mine own received me not. I am the light which shineth in darkness, and the darkness comprehendeth it not. Verily, verily, I say unto you, if you desire a further witness, cast your mind upon the night that you cried unto me in your heart, that you might know concerning the truth of these things [Joseph Smith's appointment as a prophet of God]. Did I not speak peace to your mind concerning the matter? What greater witness can you have than from God?

[12] *Bible,* Psalms 16:11, John 1:12, 10:10; *Book of Mormon,* 3 Nephi 28:10; *Doctrine and Covenants* 93:32-34.

[13] Quoted in Ferris, Timothy, *Coming of Age in the Milky Way,* William Morrow, New York, 1988, 205.

[14] Lewis, C. S., *Miracles, a Preliminary Study,* The Macmillan Company, New York, 1947, 7.

[15] *Book of Mormon,* 1 Nephi 13:26 (see Appendix I).

[16] See endnote 5 of Chapter 12.

[17] *Bible,* Matthew 12:24, Luke 11:15.

[18] *Bible,* Hebrews 6:1-6.

[19] That Satan held authority in the presence of God (*Doctrine and Covenants* 76:25) and that he was a charismatic leader during our pre-earth life is evident in his leading one-third of the host of heaven (premortal spirit-children of God, or angels, denoted "stars") into open rebellion (war) against God. (*Bible,* Revelation 12:1-9, *Doctrine and Covenants* 29:36-39, 76:25-26, *Pearl of Great Price,* Moses 4:1-4, Abraham 3:27-28.) He is described as Lucifer, a son of the morning, indicating he was one of the elder siblings among the spirit children of God. (*Doctrine and Covenants* 76:26-27.) Satan is a formal Hebrew name that denotes *adversary*. Devil means *liar* or *slanderer*. Satan is described as "a liar from the beginning." (*Doctrine and Covenants* 93:25) Satan has temporarily made himself the god of this world and has successfully caused many to worship him instead of the true God. He has thereby won the adoration and worship of those whose hearts and minds are set upon the world. Satan has founded his own church, the church of the devil, "a church which is most abominable above all other churches." (*Bible,* 1 Corinthians 10:20, Revelation 2:9, *Book of Mormon,* 1 Nephi 13:4-6 – see Appendix I) As John described the

members of this apostate church, "They worshiped the dragon [devil]." (*Bible,* Revelation 13:4.) In warning against the influence of this church Paul mentions "false apostles, deceitful workers" and says "Satan himself is transformed into an angel of light. Therefore it is no great thing if his ministers also be transformed as the ministers of righteousness; whose end shall be according to their works." (*Bible,* 2 Corinthians 11:13-15) The Book-of-Mormon-prophet Nephi (*Book of Mormon,* 2 Nephi 9:8-9) provides, in a soliloquy, a similar description but one that goes substantially further. He describes what must have been our fate without the redemption provided by the atonement and death of Christ.

> O the wisdom of God, his mercy and grace! For behold, if the flesh should rise no more our spirits must become subject to that angel who fell from before the presence of the Eternal God, and became the devil, to rise no more. And our spirits must have become like unto him, and we become devils, angels to a devil, to be shut out from the presence of our God, and to remain with the father of lies, in misery, like unto himself; yea, to that being who beguiled our first parents, who transformeth himself nigh unto an angel of light, and stirreth up the children of men unto secret combinations [societies] of murder and all manner of secret works of darkness.

Mormon (as quoted by his son, Moroni, *Book of Mormon,* Moroni 7:5-20) taught how to distinguish agents and doctrine of Christ's church from those of the devil's.

> [A] bitter fountain cannot bring forth good water; neither can a good fountain bring forth bitter water; wherefore, a man being a servant of the devil cannot follow Christ; and if he follow Christ he cannot be a servant of the devil. ... For behold, the Spirit of Christ is given to every man that he may know good from evil; wherefore, I show unto you the way to judge; for everything which inviteth to do good, and to persuade to believe in Christ, is sent forth by the power and gift of Christ; wherefore ye may know with a perfect knowledge it is of God. But whatsoever thing persuadeth men to do evil, and believe not in Christ, and deny him, and serve not God, then ye may know with a perfect knowledge it is of the devil; for after this manner does the devil work, for he persuadeth no man to do good, no, not one; neither do his angels; neither do they who subject themselves unto him.

[20] *Book of Mormon,* Ether 12:6.

[21] Satan and his angels have superior knowledge because they remember our premortal history, all that was learned there, while we mortals have forgotten everything. Indeed, Satan was a leader among the angels of God (us). He used this knowledge to beguile Eve and he uses it to deceive those of us who regard not the "voice" of God. Pertaining to his knowledge and power, *Doctrine and Covenants* 93:38-39 states "Every spirit of man was innocent in the beginning; and God having redeemed man from the fall, men became again, in their infant state, innocent before God. And that wicked one cometh and taketh away light and truth, through disobedience, from the children of men, and because of the tradition of their fathers." That is, Satan has corrupted religious traditions by removing light and truth from them. Consequently, we must search for light and truth and, if we are valiant, find and follow them.

[22] *Book of Mormon,* Moroni 10:4-7. Unfortunately, only the first two of these verses are usually quoted with verse 5 stating "And by the power of the Holy Ghost ye may know the truth of all things." But verse 7 reveals the truth of all things to be conveyed by the Holy Ghost or the power of God, namely, that Christ *is.* Verse 7 and *Doctrine and Covenants* 76:22 are similar, the latter stating "And now, after the many testimonies which have been given of him [Christ], this is the testimony, last of all, which we [Joseph Smith and Sidney Rigdon] give of him: That he lives!" To be, to exist, to live are equivalent, all implied by His name *I Am.*

The testimony of Peter as recorded in the Bible in Matthew 16:13-18 is similar in its origin: "When Jesus came into the coasts of Caesarea Philippi, he asked his disciples, saying,

Whom do men say that I the Son of man am? And they said, Some say that thou art John the Baptist: some, Elias: and others, Jeremias, or one of the prophets. He saith unto them, But whom say ye that I am? And Simon Peter answered and said, Thou art the Christ, the Son of the living God. And Jesus answered and said unto him, Blessed art thou, Simon Bar-jona: for flesh and blood hath not revealed it unto thee, but my Father which is in heaven. And I say also unto thee, That thou art Peter [Petros], and upon this rock [petra] I will build my church; and the gates of hell shall not prevail against it."

This rock referred to by Christ as the foundation of His church is personal revelation by which the Holy Ghost or power of God reveals that Jesus *is* the Son of the living God. The power of God the Father had just been identified by Christ as the source of Peter's knowledge. This same source of truth, viz., the power of God, is identified by Moroni (verses 5 and 7) and by Joseph and Sidney in *Doctrine and Covenants* 76:113-116. And this same truth from this same source, God, is described in the *doctrine of Christ* as the rock upon which we must build our own house so that the gates of hell shall not prevail against us.

Regarding a similar play-on-words reference to Peter as a rock, Frederic W. Farrar on page 78 of his wonderful book *The Life of Christ* (A. L. Burt, New York, n. d.) indicates the meaning to be that Simon the son of the dove (Peter's father's name was Jona which means dove) shall hereafter be as the rock in which the dove hides or resides. The Holy Ghost is represented in the Bible as a dove. I therefore regard this statement to be a promise that the Holy Ghost would reside in Peter – a promise that was fulfilled (see, for examples, Acts 2, 3, 5, 10). With respect to the present, apparent play-on-words Farrar (270) makes no comment although he comments extensively on both Peter's confession and Jesus' response, with some of the latter following. "Never did the lips of Jesus utter more memorable words. It was His own testimony of Himself. [This comment reflects Farrar's belief in the Nicene creed.] It was the promise that they who can acknowledge it are blessed. It was the revealed fact that they only *can* acknowledge it who are led thereto by the Spirit of God. It told mankind forever that not by earthly criticisms, but only by heavenly grace, can the full knowledge of that truth be obtained. It was the laying of the corner-stone of the CHURCH OF CHRIST, and the earliest [Biblical] occasion on which was uttered that memorable word [Christ], thereafter to be so intimately blended with the history of the world. It was the promise that that Church founded upon the rock of inspired confession should remain unconquered by all the powers of hell. ..." But through corruption the church abandoned this foundation of individual and collective guidance by the power of God and fell (see Chapter 15 and Appendix I).

[23] *Book of Mormon,* 2 Nephi 31:13.

[24] *Bible,* Genesis 17:10, 23.

[25] The essential role of guessing in science was emphasized by physicist Richard P. Feynman in *The Meaning of It All,* Addison-Wesley, Reading MA, 1998. See the quotation from this reference on page 228 of the present book.

[26] Weinberg, Steven, *Facing Up,* Harvard University Press, Cambridge, MA, 2001, 241.

[27] Wilson, Edward O., *Consilience, The Unity of Knowledge,* Alfred A. Knopf, New York, 1999, 266-268.

[28] *Bible,* Isaiah 24:5-6.

[29] *Bible,* Isaiah 60:2-3.

[30] *Bible,* Amos 8:11.

[31] *Bible,* Acts 20:28-30.

[32] *Bible,* 2 Thessalonians 2:1-4.

[33] *Bible,* Acts 3:19-21.

[34] *Bible,* 2 John 7-11.

[35] Wells, H. G., *The Outline of History,* Volume 1, Garden City Books, Garden City, NY, 1961, 438 (see 436-440).

[36] *Bible,* 2 Timothy 3.

[37] *Bible,* 2 Timothy 3:5.

[38] For a detailed, scholarly account of some of the history of this event see Oaks, Dallin H., and Marvin S. Hill, *Carthage Conspiracy, The Trial of the Accused Assassins of Joseph Smith,* University of Illinois Press, Urbana, IL, 1976.

[39] Joseph Smith had an interview with Martin Van Buren, President of the United States, on 29 November 1839. The following account of this interview is quoted from Smith's journal.

> During my stay I had an interview with Martin Van Buren, the President, who treated me very insolently, and it was with great reluctance he listened to our message, which, when he had heard, he said: "Gentlemen, your cause is just, but I can do nothing for you;" and "If I take up for you I shall lose the vote of Missouri." His whole course went to show that he was an office-seeker, that self-aggrandizement was his ruling passion, and that justice and righteousness were no part of his composition. I found him such a man as I could not conscientiously support at the head of our noble Republic.

Quoted from *History of The Church of Jesus Christ of Latter-day Saints,* Second Edition Revised, The Church of Jesus Christ of Latter-day Saints, Deseret Book Company, Salt Lake City, UT, 1960, Volume IV, 80.

[40] *Bible,* Daniel 2:28,44-45.

[41] *Bible,* Revelation. The Book of Revelation provides a panoramic view of human history. In Chapters 4 and 5 it describes John's vision of events in a premortal, heavenly existence to begin the account and it ends in Chapters 21 and 22 with the bride (the church) receiving her elevated position at the dwelling place of God. Along the way many events are symbolically represented so that identifying their times is difficult. But if we can interpret just a few of these events and decipher at least some of the chronology of Revelation, then perhaps we can determine the time that Daniel's prophecy refers to, i.e., when the "latter days" occur. And, we need not distinguish between the *last days* (*Bible,* Genesis 49:1) and the *latter days* despite Peter's reference (*Bible,* Acts 2:14-21) that appears to describe the prophecy of Joel (*Bible,* Joel 2:28-32) regarding the last days as fulfilled on the day of Pentecost. Peter's citation is one of similarity, placing this event with other signs not yet fulfilled (verses 19-21). The Angel Moroni declared to Joseph Smith in 1823 that Joel's prophecy "was not yet fulfilled, but was soon to be." (*Pearl of great Price*, Joseph Smith – History, 41.)

In the Bible's Book of Revelation 6 and 7 the opening of each seal represents a period of a thousand years (*Doctrine and Covenants* 77:7). The opening of the first four seals, or the first four-thousand years, was already history at the time of John's vision, i.e., the Book of Revelation. Only the sixth and seventh seals plus most of the thousand years of the fifth seal were future history. In eleven verses (Rev. 6:1-11), John summarizes the history corresponding to the first five seals. He describes the opening of the sixth seal in 23 verses (Rev. 6:12 to 7:17). John's description of the opening of the seventh seal occupies well over 200 verses (Rev. 8:1 -). We consider in detail the symbolism associated with the opening of the sixth and seventh seals with particular interest in identifying the times of these events, i.e., when they occurred or will occur. Because interpreting symbolism involves some uncertainty, our interpretation should be regarded as speculation to some unknown extent. If you don't like my interpretation try one of your own. But you must make it consistent with all Bible prophecies and all known facts.

Here I mention a useful and interesting interpretation of Revelation 6-8 provided by Anthony E. Larson (*And the Moon shall turn to Blood,* Zedek Books, Orem, Utah, 1983) based on theories of Immanuel Velikovsky (*Worlds in Collision,* Doubleday, Garden City, New York, 1950). While the Velikovsky-Larson interpretation is detailed and compelling, it considers primarily physical-cause-and-effect meaning. But scripture often addresses several levels, the deepest one not generally in terms of material-cause-and-effect laws but in the most spiritual and meaningful terms – addressing the level of understanding we seek.

We begin with the symbolism of a great earthquake (Rev. 6:12). I believe it represents some event of "earth-shaking" importance, not necessarily a literal earthquake, related to other symbols in this and the next verse, namely, *the sun becoming black as sackcloth of hair* and *the moon becoming as blood* (see also Acts 2:18-20); and *the stars of heaven falling into the earth*. Symbolically and actually, natural light from the stars, moon, and even the sun is faint compared to the light that emanates from God. This is indicated in Revelation itself. John describes the holy city (Jerusalem) in its celestialized state in the following terms (Rev. 21:23, see also verse 25 and 22:5). "And the city *had no need of the sun, neither of the moon, to shine in it: for the glory of God did lighten it, and the Lamb is the light thereof*." Elsewhere the same author writes of Christ coming into the world not to condemn the world but to save it. But those that believe not are condemned because "... men loved darkness rather than light, because their deeds were evil. For every one that doeth evil hateth the light, neither cometh to the light, lest his deeds should be reproved." (*Bible*, John 3:16-21)

That powerful light emanates from God the Father and God the Son is also indicated in Joseph Smith – History (Appendix H) "... just at this moment of great alarm, I saw a pillar of light exactly over my head, *above the brightness of the sun*, which descended gradually until it fell upon me. ... When the light rested upon me I saw *two Personages, whose brightness and glory defy all description*, ..." In about 600 BC the Book-of-Mormon prophet Lehi saw Christ in vision descending out of heaven, followed by twelve others, and Lehi "beheld that his luster was above that of the sun at noon-day." (*Book of Mormon*, 1 Nephi 1:9) Paul, on the road to Damascus, saw at midday "a light from heaven, above the brightness of the sun." (*Bible*, Acts 26:13)

Thus, I propose the event of earth-shaking importance was God the Father and God the Son revealing themselves to humans whereby their light, speaking spiritually, exceeds the light of the sun. In Biblical symbolism (Gaskill, Alonzo L., *The Lost Language of Symbolism*, Deseret Book, Salt Lake City, 2003) the valiant among us – celestial souls, those who obtain eternal life – are able to bear the light and come to it. But the world will perceive not the light because of the blanket (sin). The moon, representing honorable but not valiant persons – terrestrial souls, misled into sin and disbelief of truth – those not able to dwell in the full light, becomes as blood. Blood represents impurity and guilt, sacrifice for sin and redemption, or both. These souls fail to perceive and follow the light but they will be redeemed to a terrestrial level, able to bear some light. And stars – representing wicked or telestial souls unable to bear light – fall unto the earth (hide from God, as if they are covered or gone). Those who love the world and its god (Satan) fight against and hide from the light. One event that could have been represented by these symbols was the birth and ministry of Christ among His people. (*Bible*, John 1:4-5, 3:16-21.) The events they actually represent began in 1820 (Appendix H). These events are the Restoration of the kingdom prophesied by Daniel because this kingdom established earlier by Christ was destroyed by crafty and wicked mortals (Appendix I and references 27-33, 35). Christ established His kingdom again in the "latter days," beginning in 1820, and this kingdom shall never be destroyed but shall consume all other kingdoms and stand forever.

What is the meaning of men of all classes hiding in dens and rocks and desiring to be covered by mountains and rocks (*Bible*, Revelation 6:15-17)? Such hiding is a hiding from the Lord or the Light of God or His restored gospel. Speaking of Christ, Isaiah predicted "He is despised and rejected of men; a man of sorrows, and acquainted with grief; *and we hid as it were our faces from him*; he was despised, and we esteemed him not." (*Bible*, Isaiah 53:3, italics added.) The Book-of-Mormon prophet Alma described in about 82 BC our eventual appearance before God in these words: "For our words will condemn us, yea, all our works will condemn us; we shall not be found spotless; and our thoughts will also condemn us; and in this awful state we shall not dare to look up to our God; and we would fain be glad if we could command the rocks and the mountains to fall upon us to hide us from his presence." (*Book of Mormon*, Alma 12:14.) Hiding from Light represents an *absence of worthiness and faith in Christ* among telestial-level people of all classes (kings, great men, rich men, chief captains, mighty men, every bondman, and every free man) who love the world rather than God. Some would point out that these concepts pertain to the second coming of Christ. I agree. Such hiding also occurred and will occur, literally and figuratively, at the coming of Christ or His gospel among humans whenever and however He reveals Himself and His gospel to mortals. When the Gadarenes and Gergesenes learned that Christ was in their land performing miracles they implored Him to leave. (*Bible,* Matthew 8:34, Mark 5:17.) Many of the Jews were finally more forceful in rejecting Him but, let us remember, some accepted Him. And the Jews remain, with all Israel and those who follow Christ, His covenant people one day to be recovered and redeemed.

"... the human mind has a singular capacity for rejecting that which it cannot comprehend – for ignoring and forgetting all that does not fall within the range of its previous conceptions." (Farrar, Frederic W., loc. cit., 273.) When one loves the world or is deceived by its craftiness, knowledge of heaven is threatening and unwelcome. To be counted among the valiant, we must reject the world and seek and receive instead the light and life of the world – Christ. The gospel of Christ has been offered to people of many ages or dispensations, the term dispensation referring to this very process. Often the prophet bringing the gospel message was killed, as Christ was. The final dispensation before He returns is now ending. The gospel of Christ in its fullness has again been brought to the world by Christ through a prophet of God and offered to all men and women who will receive it. As in earlier dispensations, the prophet through whom God revealed His will and His word in our time [Joseph Smith] was murdered by the world. The description of "hiding from the light" represents the usual reaction of "the world," or those who love the world more than God, to His revealing of Himself. Rejection of His light and hating it is the reaction of the world led by its present ruler, Satan. However, at the "great and terrible day" of His second coming when He will reveal Himself to all flesh, no one will be able to hide. It will be a great day for the righteous, one that the followers of Christ of all ages are anticipating with joy, and a terrible day for those who love the world and its temporary god.

The symbolism of Revelation 7 and 8:1 represents this great and terrible day of the seventh seal, being delayed while missionaries gather the tribes of Israel (representing all the willing) out of the world. We read in Rev. 7:2-3, "And I saw another angel ascending from the east" (Elias – *Doctrine and Covenants* 77:9) ... "Saying, Hurt not the earth, ... till we have sealed the servants of our God in their foreheads." After the willing are gathered the world as it is now known will end. Christ will appear to the whole world in power and glory, as if a scroll covering heaven "departs" or is opened and an event often called "the rapture" simultaneously occurs (Rev. 6:14, *Doctrine and Covenants* 88:95-98). How long is this great event delayed into the seventh seal? "And when he had opened the seventh seal there was silence in heaven about the space of half an hour." (Rev. 8:1; see also *Doctrine and Covenants* 88:95.) If a thousand years is one day, a half-hour is twenty-one years. There is some uncertainty contained both in the *about* and in when the sixth period ends, i.e., whether the thousand year periods are exact or approximate. They appear to be exact with the sixth period ended in the year 2000. Then Christ will appear in *about* 2021 ± 11 years (or ± half the smallest division mentioned: one-half hour). No man knows the exact hour but His Advent is close. While I may not live to see it, I expect at least some of my children will.

I conclude that we are now living in the latter days (as well as the last days) and observing the stone cut out of the mountain without hands (of man) and rolling forth to fill the earth, to establish a kingdom that will never again be destroyed, a kingdom that Christ Himself leads. The gospel of Christ has been restored and is being preached "in all the world" one last time (*Bible,* Matthew 24:14, Mark 13:10) and the willing are thereby being gathered out of the world in preparation for the great and dreadful day of the Lord, which is imminent. Now is the time, dear reader, to consider these things and align yourself on the side of truth and goodness in writing your own story of truth. You will be opposed by the world but if you are valiant you will do it anyway.

Christ said of some who were valiant, "If the world hate you, ye know that it hated me before it hated you. If ye were of the world, the world would love his own: but because ye are not of the world, but I have chosen you out of the world, therefore the world hateth you." (*Bible,* John 15:18-19.) In the world ye shall have tribulation: but be of good cheer; I have overcome the world. (*Bible,* John 16:33.)

[42] See, for example, *Pearl of Great Price,* Moses 6:47-62.

[43] Physicist John P. Pratt convincingly places the meridian of time in 1 BC (year 0) using the Enoch calendar (see "Celestial Witnesses of the Meridian of Time," *Meridian Magazine,* 10 July 2002; the article is available on www.johnpratt.com). This date and the manner by which it is identified is, in its significance and the implicit, exciting confirmation it implies, reminiscent of the message described in Carl Sagan's fictional novel *Contact* (Pocket Books, New York, 1985, 367-372, 430-431) from a Higher Caretaker Intelligence found in an isolated pattern of zeroes and ones buried deeply, beginning at about digit number 10^{20}, in the decimal representation of pi: the ratio of the circumference to the diameter of a circle.

15. Right, Wrong, and Other Absolutes

We seek in this book to compare, contrast, and, if possible, harmonize and consolidate the views of science and Christianity. Despite the common notion that they are adversarial, and they are, science and religion are also only complementary in their conclusions, a relationship that follows from their different methodologies and different primary-evidence realms.[1] Both are higher philosophies used in seeking truth and, if we are careful to embrace only truth, no conflict between the two methods should be expected. For truth does not conflict with truth; rather, truth embraces truth.

We have nearly completed a critical examination of science and discovered that our current scientific knowledge neither imposes nor even suggests the nature of a unique, underlying reality and that the definiteness science and mathematics seemed to mandate a century ago no longer exists, certainly not at any fundamental level. Indeed, as we have seen, some scientists claim on the basis of science that *no* underlying reality exists. We have also seen that science is sometimes naïvely invoked as evidence or even proof against religion. When one understands the complementary and only complementary relationship between science and religion, such evidence against religion is not compelling and, instead, raises a question regarding the wisdom of one urging scientific evidence against religion. It is materialism rather than our model of Christianity that suffers under rigorous inspection.

On the other hand, the mixture of various religions encountered in society today and throughout human history is well described, in the overall view, as an abundance of strongly-held confusion. For this reason we must be careful in contemplating religion. Too much of religious belief and thinking is simply wrong, despite the strength with which it is held. Indeed, religion as a whole – and even Christianity taken altogether – is more confused than science. And because people generally do not address their religious convictions in the same way they address other issues, with many feeling uncomfortable at a mere broaching of this topic, honest discussion is often avoided. However, we shall do well to incorporate the honesty, care, and caution of scientific inquiry, if not the method, in our consideration of religion, carefully evaluating the basis of each belief and critically examining the consistency of any claim with the scriptural record and reliable historical accounts as our guides. And beyond this, to know for certain (for instance, to validate the scriptural record itself), we must receive the help offered by the One who truly knows.

We consider one model of Christian philosophy in contrast to one scientific model to gain improved understanding of both classes. Because of diversity in each, our treatment of science and Christianity, focused on these two models, is not comprehensive. Yet throughout the scope of concepts we have considered so far our models provide consistent rationalizations by both science and religion of many issues, such as the age of the earth. A systematic and critical examination of our Christian model on its own terms yet remains to be done. And as such an examination of science on its own terms was enlightening and essential to the task we have undertaken, so is such an examination of Christianity. We neither need nor desire to isolate and criticize any individual faith. Instead we consider three generic categories of Christian belief that include most Christians, which we describe as *claimed original*, *claimed reformed*, and *claimed restored*. The first category includes Roman, Greek, Orthodox (Eastern), and Anglo Catholics who believe their churches are directly descended from the original Christian Church without significant alteration. It also includes "Old Catholics" who broke from the Roman church in 1870 when Pope Pius IX promulgated the doctrine of papal infallibility. The second includes Protestant or Reformed churches which broke from the Catholics believing the latter were corrupted and attempted to reform their beliefs to coincide with Biblical teaching. This group also includes those who found it convenient to break from the Catholics for some other reason. Indeed, some use the term Protestant to include all non-Catholic Christians. We use the terms orthodox or traditional to represent widely- and long-held Catholic and Protestant beliefs. The third category is a relatively new one that includes the "Mormons," some offshoots from them, and a few other "restorationist" groups, e.g., the Catholic Apostolic Church. Retorationist groups believe essential elements of the original Church were lost and have tried to restore them. Mormons claim that God Himself has restored lost principles, practices, and authority directly through modern-day and past-age servants. The terms "Catholics," "Protestants" and "Mormons" represent these three generic categories. The first term may seem contradictory since it refers to many churches. The second term refers to reformations influenced by the first. Those of the last category are more *independent* of the others. All embrace the Bible and claim connection to original Christianity.

As stated, we attack no single church. All groups contain a spectrum of people and one finds good and bad in all churches. Indeed, each person has his or her own good and bad experiences, both being part of mortality and why we *all* need a Savior, and we can therefore find whatever we look for. The intent here is not self-justification in an "us versus them" competition but rather an honest consideration of God and me (each individual). What does He want me to do? What guidance does He provide? Christianity is practiced on this level. In search of answers to such questions we consider Christian history, scripture, and reason in which we shall discover fundamental flaws in beliefs and practices of orthodox or traditional Christianity, not in a single church but rather in nearly all of Christianity together. If you would prefer not to read such criticism you should skip to the next chapter when you reach the section entitled "Christian Catastrophe."

To attempt a rigorous, objective, strictly science-like analysis of Christianity would be to repeat a common mistake. While science deals with objective, reproducible, lowest-common-denominator, material-universe facts that everyone is supposed to agree on, religion deals with personal meaning and feeling – with joy – individually experienced and unknown to the inexperienced. To discover its meaning we must examine Christianity on its own terms and concepts, not those of science. Nevertheless, meaning and feeling are acquired and governed in accordance with law, making this law the most important among all law. When we finally leave this "brief and frail existence," what will we keep? We will keep our memories including the knowledge and wisdom gleaned from study and experience and also the joy: the joy in mutual devotion between spouses, the joy in mutual devotion within family, the joy in mutual devotion among friends and all people, and, above all, the joy in mutual devotion with our Savior and Champion.

To discover the fundamental concepts and terms in which Christianity is best considered, we ask "What is the basis of Christianity as a philosophy, system of belief, or paradigm?" It is, first and foremost, faith in Christ and, consequently, in His doctrine, the very model we have been considering, the one already shown to coincide with both Biblical and Book-of-Mormon precepts and principles. How can a basis of "mere" faith in Christ be compared to rigorous evidence, testing, and deduction used in science? It can't be – that's the problem. To compare Christianity and science we must look deeper than scientific results and seek some quality(ies) of science and Christianity expressible in comparable terms, i.e., we can seek to use Christianity like we use new theory in science to discover useful deductions, questions, experiments, and comparisons that can be scientifically tested. Seeking such comparable qualities is not a trivial task, but it is an illuminating one.

In this chapter we examine a few selected beliefs of Christianity. We seek to discover which, if any, of our three categories of Christianity follow the doctrine of Christ, the Bible-and-Book-of-Mormon-consistent model of Christianity we have adopted. By use of reason as well as scriptural and historical evidence for all substantive conclusions we strive to avoid misconception. As already indicated, rigor is not excluded from examination of religion, only exclusive use of objectivity is. Especially important and, indeed, required for any *conclusive* verdict is the evidence of "fire and the Holy Ghost" which the reader him- or her-self must individually seek. Only such a definite and conclusive confirmation provides sure direction and properly indicates where true Christianity would take us, i.e., the way we should follow.

The examination we consider could fill volumes but we have neither space nor appetite for a huge project. Instead, we treat a few selected principles. But these principles represent fundamental issues and they are hopefully treated in sufficient detail to avoid miscommunication and confusion, especially necessary in these matters in which contrary paradigms and enemy influence push our thinking in many wrong directions. Though the issues considered are few, they are critical. To those who hold the paradigm I do, careful examination of these few, critical issues is sufficient to indicate two conclusions. (1) *Much Christian tradition is erroneous.* (2) *One Christian denomination alone has been uniquely established in a way consistent with Biblical principles and prophecy by which erroneous tradition could be fully avoided and the true beliefs and practices of the original Christian Church reacquired.* Others holding other paradigms may not find the evidence compelling and may not be led to these same conclusions. Those who hold different conclusions may be correct *relative* to their own paradigm but only one, at most, of contrary, mutually exclusive views may be *absolutely* correct. The absolute test of truth in Christianity is fire and the Holy Ghost, the power of God, guidance from One familiar with the absolute and able and willing to help us. As Christ urges, we must look to Him for reliable guidance.

God and the Absolute

We begin with some concepts and definitions to establish basis of belief and scope of vision.

An absolute or universal does not depend on context or reference frame. An absolute stands independent and immutable. An absolute is totally reliable and can be depended upon under any situation or condition. We take as an axiom that God the Father is absolute and, indeed, that God is *The* Absolute so far as human knowledge extends. God is the Creator[2] and Foundation[3] of the universe. By Foundation or Foundation of Existence we refer to the influence or light or power by which God governs and sustains the universe,[3] in a way not yet understood by humans.

Without an Absolute (God) there is no progress or improvement. As C. S. Lewis reasoned,

> If things can improve [beyond what they naturally are], this means that there must be some absolute standard of good above and outside the cosmic process [deterministic nature or natural evolution] to which that process can approximate. There is no sense in talking of 'becoming better' if better means simply 'what we are becoming' – it is like congratulating yourself on reaching your destination and defining destination as 'the place you have reached.'[4]

Without an absolute, everything is relative and nothing is fixed or definite or reliable. If physical laws just happened, what is to prevent their just unhappening? Without God or The Absolute there is no omniscience, no omnipotence, no right, no wrong, no good, no bad, no salvation, no condemnation, no eternal life, and no everlasting punishment. Without God neither a person nor anything else in the universe would or could exist.[3] And it seems we do exist, as Descartes concluded. Yet science cannot establish a natural creation in the past when science cannot establish a natural reality or existence now. (Who can prove a birth occurred if no child is identified?)

Failure of science to establish a definite reality or existence reveals an utter lack of capability in science to answer ultimate questions. And stepping *down* from science, both *secularism* (rejection of any religious faith or worship) and *humanism* (a view that does not consider belief in deity vital to religion), which deny or reject any importance of The Absolute, are even more fatally flawed. It appears that many who promote these beliefs are subtle and devious in dismissing God and God's law in favor of a "gospel of tolerance." That is, many who promote secularism and humanism don't honestly present themselves as atheists, but that is effectively their stance whether they realize it or not. (If their god is not vital, then their god is not God.) They are a "poor man's" positivism (atheism) in the sense that a materialist pursues knowledge and invokes reason – he or she is generally honest and vigorous in his or her approach. Some secularists and humanists don't mention (or realize?) their fundamental position, a practice I would describe as deception or ignorance, but instead promote simpleminded, slogan-mentality, "feel-good" themes like those that arose in the 1960s in rebellion-from-anything-traditional for the sake of rebellion. The absence of value in such paradigms for discovering truth is apparent since there is no intent to discover truth but simply to pursue a moral or social program promoting humanitarianism, worship of humanity and human values, tolerance or preventing conflict by taking no stand, but denying the existence of God and the divinity of Christ. More than occasionally we even find Christian clergy supporting some of these themes (beyond the tolerance God expects us all to practice), indicating a broad and deep confusion in modern Christianity. To find truth we must vigorously seek it with real intent, utilizing a careful, responsible approach. Simply and simplemindedly following one's thinking or feeling to make truth what one thinks it ought to be, a "poor man's" logical positivism, is unwise, dangerous, and potentially fatal. To expect another to accept such wishful supposition as truth is presumptuous and irresponsible and if another does it's equally irresponsible. "And if the blind lead the blind, both shall fall into the ditch."[5]

Because God is absolute, God's ways are not relative but absolute. In His Creator's relationship with His human creatures, His laws, covenants, and ordinances are universally applicable and absolute, inviolable, and immutable if we would win the benefits of honoring them and avoid negative consequences of violating them. God said to Moses "For as I, the Lord God, liveth, even so my words cannot return void, for as they go forth out of my mouth they must be fulfilled."[6]

God didn't create one portion of the material universe under one set of physical laws and another under a different set. God's creation operates under God's laws. Order, regularity, and organization are found throughout His creation.[7] Therefore, an act is right or wrong according to whether it complies with His way or not, irrespective of who committed the act, or when, or where, or why. (However, God does not *condemn* a person who violates His law either ignorantly due to no lack of diligence on his or her part or in order to follow a perceived spirit of the law rather than its letter in his or her good-faith judgement.[8] God wants our hearts, not merely our automatic, knee-jerk reactions. But, at the same time, He requires us to find and follow His way.)

God the Father, has endowed God the Son, or Jesus Christ, with His power. Because of this endowment of power, God the Son represents God the Father and They, together with God the Holy Ghost, are One in power and purpose while being three, distinct, individual Beings.[9] The title God may thus be used in reference to any one of this Trinity as They are one in purpose and power. As the Father's agent, God the Son has spoken to or communicated with man directly and through prophets and His instructions and statements properly recorded as scripture are His words that "must be fulfilled."[10] Jehovah is God the Son, the God of both the Old and New Testaments.[11] The Bible is scripture and is God's word (in so far as it has been correctly transcribed and translated). Other scripture has also been provided by God, namely, the Book of Mormon, Doctrine and Covenants, and Pearl of Great Price. Through scripture God has revealed many important principles pertaining to the way, the truth, and the life as well as many other principles some of which will shortly be addressed. Galileo's criticism of the Aristotelians as merely searching texts to find truth was justified, as only limited truth pertaining to material phenomena was to be found in the writings of the Aristotelians and even in the writings of Aristotle himself. Galileo realized that material truths were to be discovered by measuring material processes. But God and His prophets occupy a far higher station than Aristotle and his followers. The teachings of God and His prophets found in scripture do merit careful study. Spiritual truths are also discovered and measured, but by personal and diverse processes involving desire, intent, experience, and feelings. Pertaining to spiritual truth, scripture is invaluable for indicating and testing truth. And so we cite scripture for support of claims made and for directing the reader to further information. Such citations are not proof of the truth, but they are necessary precursors to proof. The Holy Ghost can bear witness of truth, the ostensible step, if we seek truth. But not until we have sought truth, are pondering it earnestly and prayerfully in our minds, and have the intent to follow truth is its truthfulness confirmed.

God the Son was sent by God the Father to atone for the sins of man, to provide the possibility that *all effect* of our violations of His absolute laws may be fully removed, and to show us the way this may be done. Salvation consists of two processes, each involving its own salvation. The *first salvation* is denoted *immortality*; it is a permanent resurrection from death, the reuniting of the perfected body and the spirit to again form the soul, never again to be separated by death. Immortality is provided as *a free gift* to all who live or have lived. Free gift means nothing further, beyond our premortal devotion, is required on our part,[12] that it is given by Christ through His grace and our earlier devotion. The *second salvation* is denoted *eternal life*,[13] the term "eternal" referring to quality rather than duration[14] – for *Eternal* is one of the names of God.[15] *We must qualify ourselves for eternal life as our reward following this life by our adopted values, devotion to God, and works that build faith in Christ.*[16] While the grace of Christ is still essential in this salvation, our devotion and faith built and manifest by our works are also required. Thus, the full salvation provided by Christ's atonement is twofold: (1) immortality and (2) eternal life. Failure to recognize this dual nature of salvation has led to much confusion, with one advocate quoting a scripture referring to one salvation and another quoting a second scripture referring to the other, both thinking they are talking about a single, generic salvation.

To assist man in acquiring the second salvation (the first being already guaranteed[12] because of our devotion to Christ during our "first estate" or pre-earth life and the grace of Christ), Christ instituted a church with members (saints), officers (priesthood holders), ordinances, principles, doctrine, laws, and covenants. His church and these qualities of it are absolutely established because they are creations of an absolute God. It is not for man to say what is right and wrong or how Christ's church should be organized. These decisions are the purview of God and He has not abdicated His ownership of them, nor can He once He has declared Himself.[6] In following the word of God there is little maneuverability, flexibility, or compromise.

However, because we mortals are not absolute in knowledge or ability but rather are fallible, there is need in human interactions for tolerance and acceptance of individual agency (when one's actions do not infringe on the agency of another). God has given freedom of choice or agency to each person. Should we do less (when others are not harmed)? Were such not given, mortal life would lose its purpose and meaning, which are the education, growth, and progress of each individual as an agent in search of truth. Interfering with individual agency by use of compulsion or deceit is fundamentally foreign to both Christianity and, even more fundamentally, God's plan of life under which we are experiencing mortality. While He and His plan are perfect, we mortals (or pre-mortals) are (were) not. Thus, in the world we find wickedness, suffering, ignorance and confusion, and a huge number of religious groups, most contending with others and many maintaining it alone holds the truth. The liberal groups not contending to save human souls refrain because of ignorance and lack of desire. Through these qualities they have allowed themselves to be dominated by another group we also would find, if we could detect them, namely, enemy agents still in condition of rebellion. Even among Christians the confusion, conflict, and domination based on different beliefs and levels of interest and desire are extensive. Nevertheless, devout Christians share a common belief that is powerful, that Jesus is the Christ – the Son of God and Savior of the world. While devout Christians may differ in some beliefs, they unite in this most important one.

In the following sections we consider the above mentioned principles pertaining especially to God the Son and His church, citing scripture and historical writings and utilizing reason and logical deduction to discover important implications. Our justification of claims made in this chapter is based primarily on the Bible because it is most universally accepted among Christians. However, other scripture is more complete and far clearer (Appendix I contains important Book-of-Mormon passages that explain why teachings in the present Bible are sometimes indirect, obscure, and missing) so we often consider them as well.

Christian Catastrophe

While good people and many correct teachings are found today in all Christian denominations,[17] nearly all Christian denominations are severely corrupted. The tradition, the canon, the organization, the practice, the authority of churches that purport to be directly descended from (Catholics) or reformed to recover (Protestants) beliefs and practices of the original Christian Church all cause these churches and, indeed, indicate them to be corrupted. The basis for this sweeping condemnation is manifold, but we consider here only a simple but compelling example. When one compares nearly all modern Christian denominations to the original Christian Church described in the Bible, many essential elements are different. What elements are essential? Any that Christ specified. Who could have authorized a change? Only One Person would have authority to make such a change and a church which claimed to have been so authorized by that Authority must be a church that claims to have received revelation from God through a prophet speaking for Him. For only prophets speak for God. Few churches today claim to be led by Christ Himself through living apostles and prophets. The one that most prominently does is The Church of Jesus Christ of Latter-day Saints. It follows, then, that this difference and many others that exist between most of today's Christian denominations and the original Christian Church described in the Bible indicate contamination, unless such a difference has been authorized by Christ through prophetic dispensation.

But if God did instruct humans through a prophet to change His teachings, where is the claim that "Thus saith the Lord God ..." and where is the scripture describing it? Isn't this the pattern – that when God speaks through His prophets scripture is created?[18] Christ said "I spake openly to the world; I ever taught in the synagogue, and in the temple, whither the Jews always resort; and in secret have I said nothing."[19] God is not intending to guide and save only some. The Bible is not to be privately revised. Where are the apostles and prophets who authorized in the name of Christ the changing of Christ's church from its description in the Bible – or else where are the apostles and prophets in the church today, their absence being itself a major change? For one reason or the other these officers are essential.[20]

A dilemma is presented by 95 verses in the New Testament that mention the gospel (ευαγγελιου) or gospel of Christ (ευαγγελιου του Χριστου) but in which, alone or together, no clear description of this gospel is provided. Yet in one of these passages the Apostle Paul indicates an essential, absolute character of this gospel.

> I marvel that ye are so soon removed from him that called you into the *gospel of Christ* unto another *gospel*: Which is not another; but there be some that trouble you, and would pervert the *gospel of Christ*. But though we, or an angel from heaven, preach any other *gospel* unto you than that which we have preached unto you, let him be accursed.[21] (italics added)

How would this gospel be perverted? What exactly is the gospel of Christ? Without knowing exactly what the gospel of Christ is, how can we recognize any other? It is no wonder that Christianity is confused with incomplete information regarding fundamental, essential, and absolute matters such as the *gospel* and *doctrine of Christ*, (διδαχη του Χριστου or αρχησ του Χριστου) both familiar terms in the Bible but not clearly understood from it – for the former, not beyond a generic "good news" interpretation with a few specifics implied and, for the latter, even less. Fortunately, both the gospel and doctrine of Christ are explicitly declared by their Author in the Book of Mormon.[22] And, indeed, the importance of the Restoration of a knowledge of the gospel of Christ is implied in the prophecy of Christ in both Matthew and Mark that this gospel must first be preached to all nations before He comes again.[23]

This example of fundamental, essential, and absolute knowledge mentioned but no longer provided in the Bible is suggestive of other essential and absolute but missing knowledge and unfulfilled purpose, knowledge and purpose familiar by name or title but only poorly understood, knowledge and purpose in which familiarity by title has displaced understanding by substance so that such lack of understanding is unrecognized. Paul indicates another such instance of exactly this character pertaining to our present topic: apostles and prophets.

> And he [Christ] gave some, apostles; and some, prophets; and some, evangelists; and some, pastors and teachers; For the perfecting of the saints, for the work of the ministry, for the edifying of the body of Christ: Till we all come in the unity of the faith, and of the knowledge of the Son of God, unto a perfect man, unto the measure of the stature of the fulness of Christ: That we henceforth be no more children, tossed to and fro, and carried about with every wind of doctrine, by the sleight of men, and cunning craftiness, whereby they lie in wait to deceive;[24]

Christians have not come to a unity of the faith. Rather, as parts of a whole, we are cast to and fro by every wind of doctrine and craftiness of cunning men (and their evil sponsor). Thus, we Christians are not yet perfected "unto the measure of the stature of the fullness of Christ" and, consequently, neither is the work of the ministry done nor the body of Christ (membership of His church) edified. It follows that His giving of apostles, prophets, evangelists, pastors, and teachers in His church has not yet fulfilled His purpose and these officers remain essential to and absolutely required in His church.

Neither Christ nor His apostles and prophets authorized the changes in Christianity we see today. As was foretold by both Christ and the apostles,[25] Christ and His apostles were killed by wicked men because of their virtue. More exactly, the apostles were killed because of the virtue of Christ who they represented, just as Christ was crucified, as He foretold, by wicked men because of His virtue, or the virtue of His Father who He represented. And the killing and the wickedness and the rejection of God ended the Biblical record and eventually plunged the Christian world into a centuries-long night of darkness and apostasy, exactly as foretold by prophets dating back into Old Testament times.

This contamination or falling away, predicted by these very apostles and prophets before they were killed, is recorded in many places in the New Testament.[26] And historical records confirm that such contamination occurred. Dating especially to the second and third centuries AD, the organization and practices established by Christ as well as many of His teachings were changed and apostasy began in earnest wherein men deliberately changed the institution and teachings of God to satisfy their own desires and ambitions.[27] In many places, with several cited in previous chapters, the Bible foretells of an apostasy or falling away.[28] The Bible also predicts a refreshing from heaven and a restitution of all things.[29] Before something can be restored or refreshed it must first be possessed and then be lost or taken away. Then and only then can it be restored or refreshed. Prediction of a restitution necessarily implies both a loss of what is or was possessed followed by a restoration thereof.

There was, of course, plenty of opportunity for contamination to occur. To begin with, the martyrdom of the apostles and prophets left a leadership vacuum at the critical, top level through which Christ administered His church. Yet, with respect to the importance of apostles in Christ's church one might say "While the office and function of an apostle might have been institutionally essential, it doesn't seem important on a personal level. It is quite unlikely I will ever be an apostle or that I will ever know one. I will probably never even have a meaningful conversation with one. Therefore, on a personal level, what difference does it make how an apostle is remote from me. Remoteness is remoteness, whether contemporaneous due to social and geographical separation or historical due to temporal separation." I would have to agree with such a statement, except for two reasons why I can't.

What is personally important are the principles and practices Christ taught and admonished us to follow, especially those found in the doctrine of Christ. Today we have thousands of Christian denominations with nearly as many interpretations of these principles and how they should be practiced, but with no doctrine of Christ.

In case you don't yet see the problem with historical remoteness, let me cite a specific example. Central to Christian faith is a belief in Christ. But this requires some understanding of His nature – else who shall we believe in? Christ's nature is revealed in the Bible. Following His crucifixion and resurrection, He revealed Himself to the remaining eleven apostles, so they would personally know Christ as a resurrected being and be powerful witnesses to His resurrection and able to fully teach others through their preaching and writing. The latter is how we know of Christ today. Thus, on one occasion while the eleven were meeting together

> And as they thus spake, Jesus himself stood in the midst of them, and saith unto them, Peace be unto you. But they were terrified and affrighted, and supposed that they had seen a spirit. And he said unto them, Why are ye troubled? And why do thoughts arise in your hearts? Behold my hands and my feet, that it is I myself: handle me, and see; for a spirit hath not flesh and bones, as ye see me have.[30]

Jesus clearly taught His apostles that His resurrected body consisted of flesh and bones. And they in turn taught others. Yet in 325 AD at the council of Nicaea, the Nicene or Athanasian creed was adopted that represents God as being quite different, so much different that it causes difficulty in comprehension of and belief in Him, which is one of the first personal requirements of Christianity. Apostles and others remote in time have taught us – in the Bible – but the Christian world has almost united in rejecting their teaching and following instead contrary creeds. Contemporary apostles, those found in The Church of Jesus Christ of Latter-day Saints, reinforce the teachings of the ancient apostles and enable those who believe to better understand and apply the doctrine of Christ and thereby obtain the power of God.

The second reason dismissing importance of apostles is unwise involves the definition of a "meaningful conversation." Did the beggar lame from birth have a meaningful exchange with Peter and John,[31] however brief? Did Stephen, one of the seven appointed by the apostles, communicate meaning to the Sanhedrin?[32] Did the Ethiopian eunuch have a meaningful conversation with Philip, another of the seven?[32] These accounts have great contemporary meaning for they help us recognize Christ's church.

Apostles and prophets are an essential part of the Church of Christ because He placed them there and empowered them to guide members of His church according to His direction to be given through them. But how could apostles and other missing elements of the church be restored if truth and authority had been lost and even sincere, searching people were unable to recognize correct teaching and practice, such as the true nature of God and the role of apostles in His church? Loss of such knowledge as a result of contamination was a self-propagating problem that could not finally be eliminated without His direct intervention. And, beyond the immediate issue of knowledge, another is more critical, namely, who would have authority to act for God in guiding and directing His church? God intervened in two stages: first a God-inspired *Reformation* and then a God-directed *Restoration*.

The need for a Reformation was apparent to those who became Protestant leaders in the reformation movement. This movement was widely successful because it was clear to many that Christianity had been corrupted. While the ninety-five theses Martin Luther nailed to the church door in Wittenberg on 31 October 1517 condemning the Catholics for the sale of indulgences could serve to illustrate this point, I use instead quotations from two other important figures, an ancient historian and a more modern reformer. The account of the ancient writer indicates that apostasy had begun and was already far progressed early in the second century. The second writer supports the view of the first and indicates its disastrous consequence.

The ancient writer I quote is Eusebius of Caesarea (Eusebius Pamphilus (265-340 AD), born in Caesarea, educated at the school of Pamphilus, ordained bishop of Caesarea in 313, one of the prominent post-Biblical historians of Christianity). Eusebius wrote in the early fourth century but in the two cases I include he quotes the earlier writer Hegesippus who lived during and wrote about the first quarter of the second century. The first quotation speaks in general terms regarding the beginnings of the falling away or apostasy and the second also, but more specifically.

> The same author [Hegesippus] relating the events of the time, also says, that the Church continued until then as a pure and uncorrupt virgin; whilst if there were any at all that attempted to pervert the sound doctrine of the saving gospel, they were yet skulking in dark retreats; but when the sacred choir of apostles became extinct, and the generation of those that had been privileged to hear their inspired wisdom had passed away, then also the combinations of impious error arose by the fraud and delusions of false teachers. These also, as there were none of the apostles left, henceforth attempted, without shame to preach their false doctrine against the gospel of truth. Such is the statement of Hegesippus.[33]

> The same author [Hegesippus] also treats of the beginning of the heresies that arose about this time, in the following words: 'But after James the Just had suffered martyrdom, as our Lord had for the same reason, Simeon, the son of Cleophas, our Lord's uncle, was appointed the second bishop (of Jerusalem) whom all proposed as the cousin of our Lord. Hence they called the Church as yet a virgin, for it was not yet corrupted by vain discourses. Thebuthis made a beginning, secretly to corrupt it on account of his not being made bishop. He was one of those seven sects among the Jewish people. Of these also was Simeon, whence sprang the sect of Simonians; also Cleobius, from whence came the Cleobians; also Dositheus, the founder of the Dositheans. From these also sprang the Gortheonians, from Gorthoeus; and also Masbotheans from Masbothoeus. Hence also the Meandrians, and Marcionists, and Carpocratians and Valentinians, and Basilidians, and the Saturnillians, every one introducing his own peculiar opinions, one differing from the other. From these sprung the false Christs and the false prophets and false apostles, who divided the unity of the Church by the introduction of corrupt doctrines against God and against His Christ.'[34]

The more modern writer I quote is John Wesley (1703-1791), a prominent Protestant leader.

> It does not appear that these extraordinary gifts of the Holy Spirit were common in the church for more than two or three centuries. We seldom hear of them after the fatal period when the Emperor Constantine called himself a Christian, and from a vain imagination of promoting the Christian cause thereby heaped riches and power and honor upon Christians in general, but in particular upon the Christian clergy. From this time they almost totally ceased, very few instances of the kind being found. The cause of this was not, as had been supposed, because there was no more occasion for them, because all the world was become Christians. This is a miserable mistake; not a twentieth part of it was then nominally Christians. The real cause of it was that the love of many, almost all Christians, so-called, was waxed cold. The Christians had no more of the spirit of Christ than the other heathens. The Son of Man, when He came to examine His Church, could hardly find faith upon the earth. This was the real cause why the extraordinary gifts of the Holy Ghost were no longer to be found in the Christian church – because the Christians were turned heathens again, and only had a dead form left.[35]

In both cases, these writings indicate fulfillment of the Biblical predictions by the apostles and prophets pertaining to contamination and apostasy of the early Christian Church. Many other writings of similar nature support this conclusion.[27] Moreover, this contamination was clearly evident in the attitude and behavior of the medieval Church toward Galileo and reformers such as William Tyndale.[36] Tyndale was in effect martyred by Henry VIII and his medieval-Church cohorts in an intrigue which utilized Continental Inquisition authority. And even the attitude of Martin Luther toward Nicholas Copernicus (as quoted in Chapter 6) showed no tolerance. What was needed were the true teachings of Christ taught with the power and authority of God, like Jesus, Peter, Paul, Stephen, Philip and other authorized servants taught.

Proposition Number 12: **Truths, virtues, and gifts received in the original Christian Church were lost due to an apostasy and many of today's orthodox Christian traditions are corrupted.**

Reformation and Restoration

Before faithful men and women could again receive the light and truth they formerly possessed, i.e., before a restitution of all things, they had to first be prepared. Lost truth had to be restored, yet much truth had not been irretrievably lost. It was contained in the Bible but was obscured by incorrect tradition. Moreover, the Bible was unavailable to the common person. To prepare for the receiving of the full truth, we first had to learn the truth already available in the Bible. The principal purposes of the Reformation were making scripture available to the common person and educating him or her regarding its correct interpretation.[36] And the Reformation was a preparation for a restitution of remaining things irretrievably lost.

Why not just give the whole thing over again? Because God respects His servants of all ages, some of whom paid the highest price to record their knowledge and testimony. And He uses the testimonies of many nations and of different times as a witness that He is God and is unchanging. These principles were taught by Him speaking through the Book-of-Mormon prophet Nephi, about 550 BC, referring to the time the Book of Mormon would become available (1830 to present):

> ... many of the Gentiles shall say: A Bible! A Bible! We have got a Bible, and there cannot be any more Bible. But thus saith the Lord God: O fools, they shall have a Bible; and it shall proceed forth from the Jews, mine ancient covenant people. And what thank they the Jews for the Bible which they receive from them? Yea, what do the Gentiles mean? Do they remember the travails, and the labors, and the pains of the Jews, and their diligence unto me, in bringing forth salvation unto the Gentiles? O ye Gentiles, have ye remembered the Jews, mine ancient covenant people? Nay; but ye have cursed them, and have hated them, and have not sought to recover them. But behold, I will return all these things upon your own heads; for I the Lord have not forgotten my people.
>
> Thou fool, that shall say: A Bible, we have got a Bible, and we need no more Bible. Have ye obtained a Bible save it were by the Jews? Know ye not that there are more nations than one? Know ye not that I, the Lord your God, have created all men, and that I remember those who are upon the isles of the sea; and that I rule in

the heavens above and in the earth beneath; and I bring forth my word unto the children of men, yea, even upon all the nations of the earth?

Wherefore murmur ye, because ye shall receive more of my word? Know ye not that the testimony of two nations is a witness unto you that I am God, that I remember one nation like unto another? Wherefore, I speak the same words unto one nation like unto another. And when the two nations shall run together the testimony of the two nations shall run together also. And I do this that I may prove unto many that I am the same yesterday, today, and forever; and that I speak forth my words according to mine own pleasure. And because that I have spoken one word ye need not suppose that I cannot speak another; for my work is not yet finished; neither shall it be until the end of man, neither from that time henceforth and forever.

Wherefore, because that ye have a Bible ye need not suppose that it contains all my words; neither need ye suppose that I have not caused more to be written. ... For behold, I shall speak unto the Jews and they shall write it; and I shall speak unto the Nephites and they shall write it; and I shall also speak unto the other tribes of the house of Israel, which I have led away, and they shall write it; and I shall also speak unto all nations of the earth and they shall write it. And it shall come to pass that the Jews shall have the words of the Nephites, and the Nephites shall have the words of the Jews; and the Nephites and the Jews shall have the words of the lost tribes of Israel; and the lost tribes of Israel shall have the words of the Nephites and the Jews. ...

And it shall come to pass that my people, which are of the house of Israel, shall be gathered home unto the lands of their possessions; and my word also shall be gathered in one. And I will show unto them that fight against my word and against my people, who are of the house of Israel, that I am God, and that I covenanted with Abraham that I would remember his seed forever.[37]

Despite heroic, unselfish effort by many reformers, some of whom, like William Tyndale, paid the dearest cost in their effort, a fundamental limit existed in the truth that was available, a limit that could not be passed without direct, divine intervention. The available body of authoritative knowledge and correct practice had, long ago by the time of the Reformation, been severely corrupted. Obvious problems in both the record and in practice could be fixed. But what about problems not so obvious? If contamination of belief occurred, and it surely did as illustrated above regarding apostles and the nature and teachings of Christ, what was the extent thereof? After all, the requirement in Christianity is to believe in and follow Christ. That requirement involves understanding what He wants us to do and how He wants us to do it.[38] There is no approximating or compromising in the absolute. (Even in the principles of grace and mercy, the Judge has imposed rules that He Himself must follow.)

Even more limiting, the priesthood authority, which allowed man to represent God in performance of essential, saving ordinances such as baptism, was eventually lost after the martyrdom of the apostles and prophets who were the sole earthly source of such authority following Christ's death. Death of the first of the initial twelve was compensated by appointment of one to replace him, i.e., Matthias was appointed to replace Judas called Iscariot.[39] Later, Paul and James, the brother of the Lord, also became apostles.[20] But the apostles were all eventually killed without being replaced, except for John who went "under cover." How were essential ordinances such as baptism to be performed without authority from Christ to perform these ordinances? Indeed, how was the gospel even to be preached?[38]

The Reformation led man to the level of faith, enlightenment, understanding, desire, and tolerance where a Restoration could follow. A Restoration had been prophesied in the Bible and was the only means of replacing completely lost knowledge and priesthood authority to perform essential ordinances. We have benefited greatly from the heroic efforts of the reformers, but eliminating obvious falsehood was not enough. To follow Christ in His way we have to again receive His word and His authority, pure, uncontaminated, and absolute. And so, following the reformation period, the predicted Restoration occurred, mostly during the period between 1820 and 1844. This period coincides with the life of Joseph Smith, Jr., the first modern-day apostle and prophet, between age 14, when he received his first divine direction (Appendix H), and his death on 27 June 1844 at age 38. By commandment of its Author as indicated by the introductory phrase "Thus saith the Lord ...,"[40] the restored church was named The Church of Jesus Christ of Latter-day Saints. Also by command of the Lord, a full quorum of apostles and prophets was called and ordained, with Joseph Smith and two other apostles and prophets designated as a presidency over the church, as Peter, James, and John were designated in the ancient church. In Chapter 18 we shall relate the history of one of the apostles and prophets called and ordained in this Quorum of Twelve Apostles. The early events of the Restoration are related in an autobiographical account entitled *Joseph Smith – History* found in the Pearl of Great Price with some of this account quoted in Appendix H. Later Restoration events are described in the Doctrine and Covenants. Greater detail is provided in the seven-volume *History of The Church of Jesus Christ of Latter-day Saints*. We draw from all these sources.

The intention of God in restoring His true gospel was for man to have the opportunity to hear it, receive it, and benefit from it. Smith thus defined the scope of the Restoration effort in a letter dated 1 March 1842 to John Wentworth, editor and proprietor of the *Chicago Democrat*, as follows.

> Our missionaries are going forth to different nations, and ... the Standard of Truth has been erected; no unhallowed hand can stop the work from progressing; persecutions may rage, mobs may combine, armies may assemble, calumny may defame, but the truth of God will go forth boldly, nobly, and independent, till it has penetrated every continent, visited every clime, swept every country, and sounded in every ear, till the purposes of God shall be accomplished, and the Great Jehovah [Jesus Christ] shall say the work is done.[41]

Preface to the *Doctrine and Covenants*

Were the Absolute God to speak to man in our day, what would He say? We can speculate that He would mention certain things, some of which would depend on the particular faith we espouse and the priorities we hold. But who can anticipate the Absolute? Who can speak for God? In this matter it is best to listen to what God Himself has said in our time. The following quotation is taken from Section 1 of the Doctrine and Covenants. This Section was revealed to the Prophet Joseph Smith on 1 November 1831 as a preface to the Doctrine and Covenants, a book of revelations received almost entirely by Smith, which contains commandments and instructions pertaining to the principles and practices to be followed by members of Christ's Church. However, Section 1 is addressed generally to all people of the earth.

> Hearken, O ye people of my church, saith the voice of him who dwells on high, and whose eyes are upon all men; yea, verily I say: Hearken ye people from afar; and ye that are upon the islands of the sea, listen together. For verily the voice of the Lord is unto all men, and there is none to escape; and there is no eye that shall not see, neither ear that shall not hear, neither heart that shall not be penetrated.
>
> And the rebellious shall be pierced with much sorrow; for their iniquities shall be spoken upon the housetops, and their secret acts shall be revealed. And the voice of warning shall be unto all people, by the mouths of my disciples, whom I have chosen in these last days. And they shall go forth and none shall stay them, for I the Lord have commanded them. ...
>
> Wherefore the voice of the Lord is unto the ends of the earth, that all that will hear may hear: Prepare ye, prepare ye for that which is to come, for the Lord is nigh; and the anger of the Lord is kindled, and his sword is bathed in heaven, and it shall fall upon the inhabitants of the earth. And the arm of the Lord shall be revealed; and the day cometh that they who will not hear the voice of the Lord, neither the voice of his servants, neither give heed to the words of the prophets and apostles, shall be cut off from among the people;
>
> For they have strayed from mine ordinances, and have broken mine everlasting covenant; They seek not the Lord to establish his righteousness, but every man walketh in his own way, and after the image of his own god, whose image is in the likeness of the world, and whose substance is that of an idol, which waxeth old and shall perish in Babylon [the world], even Babylon the great, which shall fall.
>
> Wherefore, I the Lord, knowing the calamity which should come upon the inhabitants of the earth, called upon my servant Joseph Smith, Jun., and spake unto him from heaven, and gave him commandments;
>
> And also gave commandments to others, that they should proclaim these things unto the world; and all this that it might be fulfilled, which was written by the prophets – The weak things of the world shall come forth and break down the mighty and strong ones, that man should not counsel his fellow man, neither trust in the arm of flesh –
>
> But that every man might speak in the name of God the Lord, even the Savior of the world; That faith also might increase in the earth; That mine everlasting covenant might be established; That the fullness of my gospel might be proclaimed by the weak and the simple unto the ends of the world, and before kings and rulers.
>
> Behold, I am God and have spoken it; these commandments are of me, and were given unto my servants in their weakness, after the manner of their language, that they might come to understanding. ...
>
> And also those to whom these commandments were given, might have power to lay the foundation of this church, and bring it out of obscurity and out of darkness, the only true and living church upon the face of the whole earth, with which I the Lord, am pleased, speaking unto the church collectively and not individually –
>
> For I the Lord cannot look upon sin with the least degree of allowance; Nevertheless, he that repents and does the commandments of the Lord shall be forgiven; And he that repents not, from him shall be taken even the light which he has received; for my Spirit shall not always strive with man, saith the Lord of Hosts.
>
> And again, verily I say unto you, O inhabitants of the earth: I the Lord am willing to make these things known unto all flesh; For I am no respecter of persons, and will that all men shall know that the day speedily cometh; the hour is not yet but is nigh at hand, when peace shall be taken from the earth, and the devil shall have power over his own dominion.

> And also the Lord shall have power over his saints, and shall reign in their midst, and shall come down in judgement upon Idumea, or the world.
>
> Search these commandments, for they are true and faithful, and the prophecies and promises which are in them shall all be fulfilled.
>
> What I the Lord have spoken, I have spoken, and I excuse not myself; and though the heavens and the earth pass away, my word shall not pass away, but shall all be fulfilled, whether by mine own voice or by the voice of my servants, it is the same.
>
> For behold, and lo, the Lord is God, and the Spirit beareth record, and the record is true, and the truth abideth forever and ever. Amen.

I have only three comments to make about this powerful revelation from God because, of course, it stands on its own. First, it is comprehensive in scope. It addresses "all people," irrespective of their geographical location or historical era. The temporal universality of His warning and invitation is not immediately obvious but becomes obvious as one reads the remainder of the Doctrine and Covenants and discovers the work of Restoration and salvation is on behalf of both the living and the dead, the people of all historical eras. While the principles of the dead having an opportunity to hear and accept the gospel and of the performing of essential ordinances on their behalf were well-known in the original Christian Church, they were lost with other teachings and practices in the above-described apostasy. John taught that "the dead shall hear the voice of the Son of God" and "all that are in the graves shall hear his voice."[42] and Peter taught that "the gospel [was] preached also to them that are dead, that they might be judged according to men in the flesh, but live according to God in the spirit."[43] That vicarious ordinance work for the dead was well-known to early Christians is indicated in Paul's first letter to the Corinthians. The Christians at Corinth were struggling with the concept of resurrection and life after death. To assist them, Paul cited a familiar practice to help them better assimilate the principle with which they were struggling, saying, "Else what shall they do which are baptized for the dead, if the dead rise not at all? Why are they then baptized for the dead?"[44]

Restored knowledge in the Doctrine and Covenants provides *understanding* of these principles.

> Thus was the gospel preached to those who had died in their sins, without a knowledge of the truth, or in transgressions, having rejected the prophets. These were taught faith in God, repentance from sin, vicarious baptism for the remission of sins, the gift of the Holy Ghost by the laying on of hands, and all other principles of the gospel that were necessary for them to know in order to qualify themselves that they might be judged according to men in the flesh, but live according to God in the spirit. And so it was made known among the dead, both small and great, the unrighteous as well as the faithful, that redemption had been wrought through the sacrifice of the Son of God upon the cross. ... The dead who repent will be redeemed, through obedience to the ordinances of the house [temple] of God, and after they have paid the penalty of their transgressions, and are washed clean, shall receive a reward according to their works, for they are heirs of salvation.[45]

Second, one might wonder why the Lord uses the "weak things of the world" rather than the "mighty and strong ones." This principle is not new. Paul taught "... God hath chosen the foolish things of the world to confound the wise; and God hath chosen the weak things of the world to confound the things which are mighty."[46] The weak learn not to depend on their own strength, but are more willing, like little children, to seek and receive the strength of God and to do things in His way. Confession of weakness and humility in deference to God is pleasing unto Him. In so doing we recognize His omniscience and omnipotence. Who is not ignorant and weak compared to God? He gives knowledge and strength to those who honor Him. Moreover, if God does His work through the mighty and strong of the earth, some could question by whose strength and might the work is accomplished. The Restoration was not accomplished by an eminent faculty of a prestigious seminary, it was accomplished by God using, initially, a poor, uneducated, humble, fourteen-year-old boy, a boy who merited absolutely no distinction in the eyes of the world. Men of similar qualifications, though all older, were also later called into the task. The pattern is reminiscent of the process He used in establishing the original church. God is able to look past the outward appearance and into the heart of the spirit.[47] And God has power to accomplish His purposes. In the Restoration of His truth, no question may be maintained as to the source of the power by which it was accomplished.

Third, as in the Bible[48] and the Book of Mormon,[49] God repeats in the above quoted preface to the Doctrine and Covenants His offer to reveal Himself and make His will known to any individual who will seek and receive it. We see a consistent pattern throughout the scriptures, a pattern in which man is commanded to follow God in faith, but not in ignorance. This offer of divine help provides the formal demonstration of truth we seek, the ostensible step that breaks circular reasoning internal to some system of belief by use of an independent proof from outside the system. This offer of help extended in His doctrine, in Section 1 of the Doctrine and Covenants, and in the Bible is also central to His initial instruction to Joseph Smith which emphasized precisely this point. In response to Joseph's question about which church he should join, the question that motivated Smith to seek guidance through prayer, God responded that he was to join none of them, for "they draw near to me with their lips, but their hearts are far from me, they teach for doctrines the commandments of men, having a form of godliness, but *they deny the power thereof [the power of God]*."[50] It is precisely this power of God Moroni refers to when he urges us "And ye may know that he [Christ] is, by the power of the Holy Ghost; wherefore I would exhort you that ye deny not the power of God; …"[51] Indeed, Moroni describes the requirement to deny not the power of God as essential to being cleansed by the blood of Christ in order to receive eternal life.

> And again, if ye by the grace of God are perfect in Christ, and deny not his power, then are ye sanctified in Christ by the grace of God, through the shedding of the blood of Christ, which is in the covenant of the Father unto the remission of your sins, that ye become holy, without spot.[52]

If we refuse God's invitation to receive truth and knowledge of Him and to receive His salvation, if we reject Christ and ostensible proof that follows belief in Him, we deny the power of God. Humbly seeking and receiving truth is rare among the rich, powerful, and learned. They suppose their wealth or power or wisdom, the glories of the world, is sufficient. Each such case illustrates Christ's prediction that "It is easier for a camel to go through the eye of a needle, than for a rich [or powerful or learned] man to enter into the kingdom of God."[53] It is clear from the scriptures that to please God we must humbly seek and receive, rather than deny, His guiding power. In the terminology we use herein, each person who would be saved must receive Christ in the form of a personal knowledge of Him, a demonstration of truth by the power of God, the ostensible step. As He stated to Peter, "Upon this rock [personal guidance by the power of God] I will build my Church."[54]

What, Exactly, was Restored in the Restoration?

According to a Mormon paradigm, the missing cannon has been replaced and extended. Error has been corrected. The availability of the power of God to guide each individual is being taught. Priesthood authority, the power given to man to act for God in administering His saving ordinances (baptism, gift of the Holy Ghost, sacrament of the Lord's supper, other saving ordinances received in a holy temple), has been restored as has knowledge of these ordinances. God has instructed mankind again in His gospel, in His everlasting covenant, in the organization of His church, and in His purposes. The power of God has been offered in the Book of Mormon and the Doctrine and Covenants to demonstrate the truth of these principles.

Perhaps a simple list does not convey the import. Humans have long been used to doing things their way and appreciation for God's way is an acquired taste, acquired by trying to do things His way. Let me illustrate significance by amplifying the meaning of one of these items, namely, baptism.

While *faith in Christ* and *repentance* are principles that may be practiced initially either within or independent of institutional affiliation, baptism and the gift of the Holy Ghost are ordinances which, to be valid, must be practiced in the proper, prescribed way. In the Bible, in the doctrine of Christ, and in all scripture, we are instructed that baptism is necessary to please Him and to receive salvation. In His doctrine (quoted in Chapter 12 in its entirety), Christ teaches

> And again I say unto you, ye must repent, and become as a little child, and be baptized in my name, or ye can nowise receive these things. And again I say unto you, ye must repent, and be baptized in my name, and become as a little child, or ye can in nowise inherit the kingdom of God. Verily, verily, I say unto you, that this is my doctrine, and whoso buildeth upon this buildeth upon my rock, and the gates of hell shall not prevail against them.[55]

"I agree with that," you may think, "and that's why I came forward in my congregation and publicly declared my faith in Christ and my willingness to follow His commandments; that's why I was baptized." Your motivation may be pure, God may be pleased with your sincere desire to follow Him, He may bless you for your intent, but He requires us to follow His way to fully please Him. Was the person who baptized you authorized by God to perform this ordinance? Did he hold proper priesthood authority in the sight of God? Most, if not all, Protestant churches believe such authority is obtained from the Bible. What alternative would they have, since they rejected the Catholics' claim that such authority had been passed down from Peter?

But justification of Protestant tradition is equally lacking in a demonstration of truth. For instance, Farrar, in his *The Life of Christ*, tells of Christ's being in

Jerusalem during the Feast of Dedication shortly before He died. He was there, in His temple, to teach the multitudes as He was during other Feasts because the people gathered in Jerusalem at those times. There is no justification in the Bible that supports the following philosophical leap that Farrar makes regarding this incident.

> Our Lord's presence at such a festival sanctions the right of each Church to ordain its own rites and ceremonies, and shows that He looked with no disapproval on the joyous enthusiasm of national patriotism.[56]

Christ associated with publicans and sinners because many of them recognized their sins and were willing to hear and obey Him, because they needed and appreciated the grace and mercy He extended. It does not follow that He associated with them because He sanctioned and looked with no disapproval on their behavior as sinners. Neither does it follow that Christ's presence at the Feast of Dedication indicates His sanction for any "Christian" church to ordain its own rites and ceremonies.

There is, of course, better (but still inadequate) support found in the Bible for such a Protestant view. John the Beloved told the Savior that he and the other apostles met a man casting out devils in the name of Christ and forbade him because he was not one of them. The Savior responded, "Forbid him not: for he that is not against us is for us."[57] This text seems to generally license any that will practice Christian principles and ordinances in the name of Christ. But a second text just as generally moderates this first one. "He that is not with me is against me; and he that gathereth not with me scattereth abroad."[58] Therefore, to claim any so-called Christian practice of, say, baptism is justified by the Bible is no more accurate than to claim it is not justified by the Bible. Who would build on this rock? Indeed, Christ Himself – the Example and the Way – did not presume to teach or establish His church until He had been called and authorized by His Father to do so.[59] "And no man taketh this honor unto himself, but he that is called of God, as was Aaron." While Aaron was called by God through the Prophet Moses, Christ was called directly by God Himself.[59]

Nevertheless, each church can certainly choose to sanction its own rites and ceremonies. But then the church is not His. In the Church of Jesus Christ, the rites and ceremonies are practiced in the way He ordained because it is His Church.

Violations of precisely this principle caused both Joshua[60] and Isaiah to condemn the people to whom "… the Lord said, Forasmuch as this people draw near me with their mouth, and with their lips do honour me, but have removed their heart far from me, and their fear toward me is taught by the precept of men:"[61] Wherein did they offend the Lord? They had "… transgressed the laws, changed the ordinance, [and] broken the everlasting covenant."[62]

During His mortal ministry the Son of God similarly condemned such practice among the Jews.

> This people draweth nigh unto me with their mouth, and honoureth me with their lips; but their heart is far from me. But in vain do they worship me, teaching for doctrines the commandments of men.[63]

And this same condemnation was spoken anew in our day by the Lord Himself, in the above quoted preface to the Doctrine and Covenants, because the inhabitants of the earth again

> ... have strayed from mine ordinances, and have broken mine everlasting covenant; They seek not the Lord to establish his righteousness, but every man walketh in his own way, and after the image of his own god, whose image is in the likeness of the world, and whose substance is that of an idol, which waxeth old and shall perish in Babylon [the world], even Babylon the great, which shall fall.[64]

In his novel *The Covenant*, James A. Michener quotes a prayer of a South African Voortrekker following the terrible battle at Blood River against the Zulu, attributing victory of the Voortrekkers to God and the covenant He had offered them which He had honored, the covenant that led them to later adopt Apartheid. Michener points out that "What the Voortrekkers failed to realize in their moment of victory was that they had offered the covenant to God, not He to them. Any group of people anywhere in the world was free to propose a covenant on whatever terms they pleased, but this did not obligate God to accept that covenant, and especially not if their unilateral terms contravened His basic teachings to the detriment of another race whom He loved equally."[65] Nor does a people have latitude to alter the commandments of God, for which Christ condemned the Jews: "Thus have ye made the commandments of God of none effect by your tradition."[66]

Contrary to the wishful but above-condemned practice of arbitrary choice of rites and ceremonies by a "Christian" church, there exists an explicit account in the Bible indicating only proper practice of baptism is condoned in His church. Paul asked certain disciples ("the men were about twelve"[67]) in the church at Ephesus if they had received the Holy Ghost since they believed. They responded, "We have not so much as heard whether there be any Holy Ghost. And he said unto them, Unto what then were ye baptized? And they said unto John's baptism."[68] Now John, meaning John the Baptist, was a great prophet, as declared by the Savior Himself.[69] It was he who baptized Christ in the Jordan River. Nevertheless, John was not an authorized minister in Christ's church, organized after the baptism of Christ.[70] The Biblical record informs us of John's humble, childlike reaction to the superceding of his work by that of Christ, "He must increase, but I must decrease."[71] Here we see the greatness of John. John was an authorized servant of God, and a great one, but not a minister in Christ's church. It was the apostles and prophets who baptized those joining Christ's church, not John.[72] John the Baptist had authority to baptize unto remission of sins, to prepare the way for the higher gospel Christ would bring. While the authority John held exceeded by far any obtained today in a seminary, theological college, divinity school, or human-invented church, John's baptism did not establish membership in Christ's church. For that purpose Christ chose and ordained officers in His church. Thus, when Paul discovered what baptism these disciples at Ephesus had received,

> Then said Paul, John verily baptized with the baptism of repentance, saying unto the people, that they should believe on him which should come after him, that is, on Christ Jesus. When they heard this they were baptized in the name of the Lord Jesus. And when Paul had laid his hands upon them, the Holy Ghost came upon them; and they spake with tongues, and prophesied.[73]

The instruction is clear. When Paul discovered that the disciples in Ephesus had not been properly baptized and taught them this fact, the disciples simply received baptism from Paul according to the proper way. Then Paul gave them the Holy

Ghost. Both acts require authority of God, authority specifically given to properly ordained ministers to perform such ordinances in His church.

Why, you might ask, is that so essential? My answer is because this is the way He has instructed us; this is His way. We recognize His station, we worship Him, we follow His commandment and join His church, we seek to do things His way. Two themes recur in this last sentence: we, we, we, ... and His, Him, His, ... These themes indicate the choice. The restoration of priesthood authority has great significance because He restored it. Only through the authority He has instituted in our day by a Restoration and by our humble submission thereto, like a little child, in receiving ordinances such as baptism performed by this authority do we do things in the way that fully pleases Him. Other restored powers and knowledge have similar significance.

Various opinions about the practice of baptism, each strongly held by different groups, raise many questions. Is authority beyond that of the Bible required? Is the method to be one of sprinkling, pouring, or immersion? Should infants be baptized before they reach any age of understanding or accountability? What happens to individuals who never have an opportunity to be baptized?

To choose between truth and prejudice on these questions and others a formal demonstration of truth is needed. Methods capable of establishing certain truth are advocated in this book. Without at least one of them none of the above questions can be conclusively answered. We shall shortly pursue this matter of formal demonstration of truth. But first we consider a brief summary of items that are claimed to be restored through Joseph Smith by action of either God Himself or heavenly messengers endowed with God's power and sent by Him. The direction by God in the Restoration of each of these items is essential. He is the Owner of His church and the Sole Source of authority and Judge of Truth in it and any restitution of His church, like its earlier establishments, must originate and be directed by Him. Several of the most important claims pertaining to the restoration of the original Christian Church follow.

Joseph Smith was prepared to be a servant and prophet of God when, in response to his humble prayer asking simply which church he should join, both God the Father and God the Son appeared to and instructed him. God the Father first addressed Smith by name and then introduced "His Beloved Son" who completed all instruction. (See Appendix H.)

Over the course of twenty-four years, Smith, who had received little formal education as a member of a poor, indigenous, farming family, was further taught and groomed by God and other heavenly tutors as well. One of his principal teachers was Moroni, the prophet who had spent the last 37 years of his life completing the Book of Mormon, which was eventually committed into Joseph's hands for translation.

In restoring the pure teachings of God to replace or correct missing or corrupted teachings in the Bible, Smith provided a revised translation of the Bible called the "Inspired Version." He also received and published three "new" books of scripture, namely, the Book of Mormon, the Doctrine and Covenants, and the Pearl of Great Price, some of which he translated. This additional scripture totals 878 pages. Is this enough to provide a "restitution of all things which God hath spoken by the mouth of all his holy prophets since the world began."[29] If not it is a good start, with few minor additions (in number of pages) since added up to the present time.

Numerous holders of priesthood authority from earlier ages were sent by God to confer the same on Smith and his fellow servants in the work. These heavenly messengers who restored lost authority to act for God included John the Baptist, Peter, James, and John, Moses, Elias, and Elijah. In each case they were identified to Joseph as prophets of God in the scriptural record. John the Baptist was the forerunner of Christ who preached in the wilderness and baptized the Savior Himself. He restored the priesthood which authorizes its holder to baptize,[74] but (then) only unto a remission of sins.[73] Peter, James, and John were the chief apostles in the church Christ Himself organized, of whom He said "ye have not chosen me, but I have chosen you and ordained you."[75] They were sent by God to two (Joseph Smith and Oliver Cowdery) He had chosen in our time, to ordain them to the apostolic authority required to reestablish and administer Christ's church, which they did. Moses, who led Israel out of bondage, restored to them priesthood power to gather Israel. Elias was and is the great Prophet Noah, who built the ark, and the Angel Gabriel as well (see below). He gave Joseph and Oliver the power of Elias. Elijah gave them sealing powers that whatsoever they sealed on earth by this authority would also be sealed in heaven.[76]

These events might seem strange and unprecedented but a similar event occurred on the Mount of Transfiguration when Moses and Elias appeared to Christ, Peter, James, and John.[77] Elias is the Greek form of the Hebrew name Elijah. In the New Testament the name Elias sometimes refers to Elijah and sometimes refers generically to a *forerunner* or a *restorer*.[78] Noah or Elias or Gabriel was both[78] as was Elijah, John the Baptist, and Joseph and Oliver. John's role as a forerunner or an Elias was foretold to his father Zacharias by the Angel Gabriel[79] (Noah, the first Elias) and John's fulfillment of this role is told in the New Testament and continued in the Doctrine and Covenants. He restored priesthood authority on 15 May 1829.[80] A visitation of Elijah as an Elias was foretold by the Prophet Malachi in the last two verses of the Old Testament, a prophecy that was fulfilled both during the life of Christ on the Mount of Transfiguration[81] and on 3 April 1836 in the Kirtland (Ohio) Temple.[76] The Doctrine and Covenants describes the roles of Joseph and Oliver.

How can ministers in today's churches preach, evangelize, and baptize when they claim no authority, no commission from heaven, beyond the Bible? The traditions of most churches of today are corrupted. Truth and authority had to be restored, as taught in the Bible, and they have been. Those who recognize the station of God, His omnipotence and omniscience, are anxious to do things His way. His approval is the only approval that matters and our desire to obtain it is the most important desire.

The Mormons claim the Savior has said their (His) church is "... the only true and living church upon the face of the whole earth, with which I, the Lord, am pleased, ..."[82] "Intolerant" you may think. "Self serving and arrogant" you may say. But not if the Lord Himself, who is the Owner of Christianity and both Omniscience and Omnipotence, said it. There is little flexibility or room for maneuvering when God speaks because only one approval matters and only one desire is most important. God is absolute. And He has also said in the same revelation "I the Lord am willing to make these things known unto all flesh; For I am no respecter of persons..."[83] This promised knowledge is the formal demonstration of truth we seek. Its origin is the sole source from which we can receive reliable answers to ultimate questions or to discover which answers are truth and which are merely prejudice. As the saying goes, dear reader, the ball is in your court. And the tennis match is singles, One on one.

Proposition Number 13: **The pure and complete gospel of Christ has been restored to the earth and is available to whoever will receive it; the promise of God to reveal its truthfulness directly to one who will receive it has been repeated.**

With the above claim that the Lord regards only one church as true and living, one might wonder what claim is made about how the Lord regards the many members of false and dead churches or of no church at all. At the point when the saints were suffering great persecution from Missouri mobs and Joseph Smith was incarcerated in a Missouri jail, Smith indicated the Lord's regard for such non-Mormon persons.

> It is an imperative duty that we owe to God, to angels, with whom we shall be brought to stand, and also to ourselves, to our wives and children, who have been made to bow down with grief, sorrow and care, under the most damning hand of murder, tyranny, and oppression, supported and urged on and upheld by the influence of that spirit [Satan] *which hath so strongly riveted the creeds of the fathers, who have inherited lies, upon the hearts of the children,* and filled the world with confusion, and has been growing stronger and stronger, and is now the very mainspring of all corruption, and the whole earth groans under the weight of its iniquity.[84] It is an iron yoke, it is a strong band; they are the very handcuffs, and chains, and shackles, and fetters of hell. Therefore it is an imperative duty that we owe, not only to our own wives and children, but to ... all the rising generation, and to all the pure in heart – *For there are many yet on the earth among all sects, parties, and denominations, who are blinded by the subtle craftiness of men, whereby they lie in wait to deceive, and who are only kept from the truth because they know not where to find it* – Therefore, that we should waste and wear out our lives in bringing to light all the hidden things of darkness, wherein we know them; and they are truly manifest from heaven – These should be attended to with great earnestness.[85] (italics added)

The Lord the Mormons follow does not abandon those seeking the truth irrespective of their religious background and they, the Mormons, are admonished not to either. Rather, Smith exhorts Mormons to "waste and wear out our lives" disclosing evil and deception and warning others about it. For there are many who will believe truth once they discover where and how to find it. On a personal level, among those I regard as my friends are Catholics, Protestants, Mormons, Jews, Muslims, Hindus, agnostics, atheists, and others. Their sincerity and generosity as friends endear them to me and I would not trade for any one of them. My hope to help them know truth is part of my motivation for writing this book.

Wouldn't the Enemy try to Thwart a Restoration?

The above quotation, indicating evil and corruption are directed by Satan himself, is remarkable as a response to the desperate situation of the Mormons. Rather than addressing justice or retribution against wicked enemies or even relief from suffering, Smith admonishes a broader, more circumspect, spiritual view of a long-term battle against a universal enemy for the benefit of all people. He thus recognizes a continuing ideological war between good and evil, a war we now begin to examine.

I have previously quoted C. S. Lewis' comment to the effect that we are living in enemy (Satan's) territory and that the rightful owner (Christ) will shortly return. Of course the term enemy territory can imply a war. We now consider supporting evidence for Lewis' claim, which I also make, because it has great pertinence to the issues we are considering and the finding of truth regarding them.

In addition to several statements in the Bible to the effect that the world is the dominion and kingdom of Satan and Christ's statement that His kingdom is not of this world,[86] we will consider three types of corroborating evidence that support the "enemy-territory" concept and illuminate its significance.

First, we learn from the Bible and modern scripture that the earth and all of us who have lived on it were involved in two creations. In the first, we and all things that exist were created spiritually. In our initial created state we were not corporeal but spiritual. We dwelt in heaven in the presence of God who is our Spiritual Father. Some of us progressed in devotion and obedience to God while others rebelled, led by Lucifer or Satan, a fallen angel. But that is my second evidence. While a fuller understanding of our premortal life required a Restoration, Bible scholars have long recognized that the account in Genesis describes two creations. The first creation account ends in Genesis 2:1-5, which states

> Thus the heavens and the earth were finished, and all the host of them. And on the seventh day God ended his work which he had made; and he rested on the seventh day from all his work which he had made. And God blessed the seventh day, and sanctified it: because that in it he had rested from all his work which God created and made.
>
> These are the generations of the heavens and of the earth when they were created, in the day that the LORD God made the earth and the heavens, And every plant of the field *before it was in the earth*, and every herb of the field *before it grew*: for the LORD God had not caused it to rain upon the earth, *and there was not a man to till the ground*. (italics added)

This account describes the end of a first, premortal creation, a spiritual creation in heaven, our "first estate."[87] Thus plants were created before they were in the earth and herbs before they grew and man before he was found on earth. Even the earth was created spiritually before it was created physically and will eventually be transfigured to a celestial state.[88]

A second creation, a corporeal or physical creation of man, beasts, and fowls, etc. is next indicated in Genesis 2:6-7,19:

> But there went up a mist from the earth, and watered the whole face of the ground. And the LORD God formed man *of the dust of the ground*, and breathed into his nostrils the breath of life; *and the man became a living soul. … And out of the ground* the LORD God formed every beast of the field, and every fowl of the air. (italics added)

A living soul consists of a living physical body occupied by its "breath of life" or spirit-owner.[89] Not until the physical body is created and the spirit is placed therein does a person become a living soul and, thus, human souls did not exist before the second or physical creation. The Book of Moses of the Pearl of Great Price explicitly describes two creations, a spiritual one followed by a physical one. (Moses' original writings were revealed again to restore information no longer found in the Bible. See endnote 21 of Chapter 10 and Appendix I.) While the material of the first creation was spiritual, that of the second was physical – water and the dust or ground (elements) of the physical earth. While the first creation occupied six periods or "days" followed by a "day" of rest, generally regarded as 1,000-year periods, no specific periods are mentioned for the second creation.

The indication of two creations in Genesis, supported and clarified in the Book of Moses, are our first evidence for the enemy-territory concept. And the point we draw from this evidence is that each person existed in heaven as a unique, individual, spirit personality (angel) before he or she was born on the earth as a mortal. Beginning in heaven we possessed God-given agency or freedom of choice and each of us chose a side in an ideological war that divided the host of heaven.[90] We who have become mortals chose to follow the plan of God rather than follow Satan in rebellion against God. Else we would not have been allowed to come to the earth as embodied spirits (souls), i.e., to the "second estate"[87] in God's plan. One can then say that the gift of immortality or resurrection from death given by Christ to *all* mortals is not completely freely given after all; we have all already paid a part for it in our allegiance and devotion to God in our first estate. Those who rebelled in this estate receive no body and can never posses a soul.[89]

Second, we read in the Bible about something we experienced during our premortal life but can't now remember, the previously-mentioned war in heaven.

> And there was war in heaven: Michael and his angels fought against the dragon; and the dragon fought and his angels, and prevailed not; neither was their place found any more in heaven. And the great dragon was cast out, that old serpent, called the Devil, and Satan, which deceiveth the whole world: he was cast out into the earth, and his angels were cast out with him.[91]

How many were cast out? One-third of the host of heaven.[92] I estimate that at least one-hundred billion people have lived on the earth since its creation (details are provided in Appendix J). Moreover, if the second coming of Christ occurs within this or the next generation or so, the total population of the earth from the creation to the Advent of Christ and the beginning of the "millennium" will remain near this number. This provides an estimate of one-hundred-fifty billion spirits in heaven during the war there, one-third of whom (fifty billion) were cast out of heaven into the earth. Thus, using these approximate numbers, the population of the earth today is fifty-six billion, six billion of whom are corporeal, embodied spirits (souls) who fought on the side of Christ under Michael in the war in heaven and fifty billion of whom are non-corporeal, nominally-invisible, fallen-angel spirits, who fought on the side of Satan. And the war is not over; it is continuing here on the earth. Satan was not finally defeated, he was merely cast out of heaven into the earth. The battle for the hearts and minds of men and women continues. Paul admonishes us to

> Put on the whole armour of God, that ye may be able to stand against the wiles of the devil. For we wrestle not against flesh and blood, but against [devil-inspired] principalities, against powers, against the rulers of the darkness of this world, against spiritual wickedness in high places.[93]

Why need we "armour?" We live in enemy territory and are joined in battle with him.

Third, we consider an important related subject, namely, the capability of these spirits to influence us. The evidence I cite here is distributed in the first few chapters of the Book of Mark in the New Testament. Mark's narrative describes several occasions when evil spirits in possession of some other spirit's body recognized the Christ and acknowledged Him.[94] Without exception, Jesus silenced and cast the devils out. Jesus also authorized His twelve apostles and the seventy to cast out devils "And they cast out many devils, …"[95] We make two points from this evidence. (1) The devils remember what we have forgotten; they recognized Christ and knew His name and station in the Father's plan to which He was appointed during our first estate. They remember the war fought over this plan, the war in which they rebelled against God, the war in which they and we are still antagonists. (2) They have power only in certain instances[96] to occupy our bodies; and, much short of that power but universally for all but little children, they have power to influence our thoughts and actions. Therefore, even though we can't normally see them, they influence and tempt us. Being invisible, their strategy is generally one of subtlety and stealth. There are some who deny they exist, which strengthens their strategy of subtlety and stealth causing us to wonder if they exist instead of pondering how to resist their influence. But they are real and have power to influence and mislead. We are living in enemy-occupied territory amongst an invisible, numerically superior enemy who can covertly study us. This enemy desires our destruction by seeking, above all else, to prevent us from recognizing and following the way, the truth, and the life.

I have proposed that the enemy is trying to thwart our finding of truth by obscuring it. This enemy fully recognizes it will be defeated (bound, imprisoned, cast into "outer darkness") after the coming of Christ and the end of the world. In the meantime, out of hatred and bitterness toward God, who would not tolerate their selfish, evil intent and rebellion, and us, who helped cast them out of heaven, they seek to destroy us for the sake of vengeance and mockery of God. Their strategy is to blatantly get many to believe incorrect thoughts and commit evil deeds, at which they are quite successful among the weak and ignorant with respect to the spiritual. Among the spiritually stronger and more astute they are subtle, confusing by means of a huge variety of mixtures of truth and error. Christ would not tolerate the devils witnessing to His identity because of their practice of combining truth and error in order to deceive.[97] Where has this practice of devils led? Over human history, a multitude of different religious systems have been invented. I expect this multitude includes some 100,000 Christian religions. Followers of all of these Christian religions claim to believe in teachings of Christ but hardly two of these religions agree on exactly what those teachings are (otherwise they wouldn't be separate religions, except where schisms were caused by personality clashes or power struggles between ambitious, competing individuals and groups).

A typical Christian must consequently draw solace from his or her faith in Christ and striving to follow His way, receiving comfort and joy from God to whom sincere reverence and service is rendered. But this Christian usually pays little heed to the unsettling elements found in his or her religion, because this aspect of his or her faith does not bring comfort. Unfortunately, this usually-ignored aspect, the error mixed with the truth, holds the individual back from more good, stronger belief, and fuller joy. In the case the predicted Restoration has occurred, as I claim, reluctance to recognize error prevents one from finding absolute truth and Absolute God. Many are seeking the truth but know not where or how to find it. It is by one's valor in this battle – overcoming the deception of fallen-angel servants of the devil and of humans misled by them and instead choosing to seek, find, and follow Christ's way – that a person comes to know and follow Christ and obtains eternal life. For this truly is a valorous deed realizing that Satan "hath so strongly riveted the creeds of the fathers, who have inherited lies, upon the hearts of the children."[85]

How many of us will prove valiant and obtain eternal life? While the Great Judge alone will answer this question, it is important to remember that *all* of us mortals were noble compatriots as we fought against Satan and his angels in our first estate. And many are ready to embrace the truth and continue in this service once they discover where and how to find it.

Opposition is Required

We see from their function that world conditions that now exist are what we would expect Satan and his followers to create, to thwart the seeking, finding, and following of truth. Poverty, ignorance, prejudice, hunger, disease, greed, crime, insecurity, unrest, oppression, war, tribalism, nationalism, racism, classism, cynicism, ideological contention, and the blatant appeal to our mortal appetites and egos for acceptance, flattery, wealth (or merely enough to eat), power, and glandular gratification and the obfuscation of truth by a myriad of mixtures of truth and error all provide chaos and substantial obstacles to finding and following truth. And each person encounters many of these obstacles to finding and following the best way. We might also expect undisguised, vehement attacks against those directly involved in the restoration of truth and overt attacks on those who have allied or are about to ally themselves with truth. Such alliance with truth represents a defeat of the enemy in the face of which subtlety and stealth are often abandoned to overtly cause doubt, anxiety, temptation, and other distractions, for those about to embrace truth. We might also expect righteous servants of God to continue to further His work in blessing His children in spite of danger. We might expect popular prejudice to oppose the Restoration wherever it is taught. We might expect the most valiant among us to culminate their "war service" in forfeiting their lives, as has occurred in past ages and in the present one with reformers, prophets, and saints. We might expect the public mood and the influence of well-meaning family, friends, and clergy to be exerted to "protect us" from those who would teach us and provide saving ordinances. The pattern is clear. We are in enemy-occupied territory. While this situation may correctly be regarded as dangerous, it suits the purposes of God, as we shall see.

The good news is that the influence of Satan and his fallen-angel devils is part of God's plan. We can overcome them if we seek God's help.[98] We need to overcome them. Mortality is intended to be a period of personal growth wherein virtues are developed. Without opposition where is choice? Without adversity where is strength? Without fear where is courage? Without a battle where is valor? As the Book-of-Mormon prophet Lehi declared

> For it must needs be, that there is an opposition in all things. If not so … righteousness could not be brought to pass, neither wickedness, neither holiness nor misery, neither good nor bad [because without choice we would be mere automatons living preprogrammed lives devoid of challenge or growth]. … And to bring about his eternal purposes in the end of man, after he had created our first parents, and the beasts of the field and the fowls of the air, and in fine, all things which are created, it must needs be that there was an opposition; even the forbidden fruit in opposition to the tree of life; the one being sweet and the other bitter. Wherefore, the Lord God gave to man that he should act for himself. Wherefore, man could not act for himself save it should be that he was enticed by the one or the other. … And I, Lehi, according to the things which I have read, must needs suppose that an angel of God, according to that which is written, had fallen from heaven; wherefore, he became a devil, having sought that which was evil before God. And because he had fallen from heaven, and had become miserable forever, he sought also the misery of all mankind. Wherefore, he said unto Eve, yea, even that old serpent, who is the devil, who is the father of all lies, wherefore, he said: Partake of the forbidden fruit, and ye shall not die, but ye shall be as God, knowing good and evil. And after Adam and Eve had partaken of the forbidden fruit they were driven out of the garden of Eden, … But behold, all things have been done in the wisdom of him who knoweth all things. Adam fell that men might be; and men are, that they might have joy.[99]

My own Experience as a Christian

I chose to be baptized into the "Mormon faith" at age nine entirely because of the good influence of my mother who was a member of that faith. I learned much but didn't pay much heed to my knowledge until I married and found myself in the situation where I was establishing habits, traditions, and patterns of behavior that would influence not only me, but also my wife and children and grandchildren. That fact caught my attention. Thus, at age 23, I seriously began my quest for truth by reading the Book of Mormon.

I now describe the previously mentioned *mechanics of inquiry* which I used and the *demonstration of truth* which I received. I knew of the promise made by Moroni in the final chapter of the Book of Mormon, that one could know by the power of God of its truthfulness by reading and studying it and asking God if it is true. Obtaining that knowledge became my goal. Reading an hour or two each evening I completed the book for the first time, asking God in silent, kneeling prayer, before and after each reading, for an indication or witness of its truthfulness – which is to say I asked for a witness of the divinity of Christ of whom the book testifies and of the Bible of which it speaks and of the verity of the many principles and people described in the Book and of the truth of the prophetic calling by God of Joseph Smith through whom the book was revealed. The conditions stated by the Prophet Moroni in connection with his promise are that the supplicant must be sincere in his or her desire, must have faith in Christ, and must be seeking with real intent (to act on truth revealed). I didn't know if I met those conditions, but I wanted to know and I demonstrated my desire through consistent study and prayer, church attendance, paying my tithes and offerings, and attempted piety. However, I was not and still am not perfect by any stretch of the imagination. But I was (and am) trying, apparently to a sufficient degree that the Lord was not displeased with me. I believe the Lord is more concerned with the direction in which we are trying to go rather than with exactly where we are. He has instituted repentance, baptism, and forgiveness and He has the power and desire to perfect us if we follow His way, no matter where we are.

Studying the Book of Mormon and asking God to reveal its truthfulness was and is an excellent strategy for finding truth, for two reasons. This book is a powerful account of a faithful people containing many wonderful truths. It provides broad, fundamental knowledge and useful guidance. When the question of the Book's truthfulness is answered, one knows of the divinity of Christ of which it testifies, of the truth of the many principles it teaches, of the validity of the Bible as the word of God which it endorses, and of the station of Joseph Smith as a prophet and seer of God in restoring His church in our time. There is no question of which church one should join when one learns for him- or her-self that the Book of Mormon is genuine. If one asks with real intent and receives a positive answer, he or she will join the church which provides and follows this book. I urge this process for your benefit, dear reader, not my own or that of the church institution *per se*. The church is the Christ and His followers. They are dedicated to helping individuals and families find and follow truth, the work of gathering and blessing all those willing to follow Christ and become part of His church. I hope this book helps you in this process.

While a sincere and devout person may ask regarding the divinity of Christ or another important principle and expect to eventually receive an answer through the Holy Spirit, other important questions remain unanswered, important questions one doesn't know to ask and guidance is therefore not complete. Yet, to defeat the universe, we must seek and follow guidance which is sufficient and demonstrated to be true. God will help us, but we are agents free to choose. He expects us to take the initiative, to take charge of our lives, to use the freedom He has granted us – as independent agents searching for truth. That's why my study of the Book of Mormon and a desire for divine guidance regarding its truthfulness was so fortuitous, because the demonstration of truth implied clear and direct answers to many important questions, answers that follow immediately from the answer to my first question.[100]

And the second and equally important reason why studying and praying about the Book of Mormon is an excellent strategy for discovering truth is that this strategy is recommended by a wise man, the powerful Book-of-Mormon prophet-author Moroni, who because of his devotion to God was granted authority to make the wonderful promise he makes in the closing chapter of the book.

You might think that the claims I have described, of angels, prophets, and new books of scripture in our day, are too fantastic to believe. Why should a person believe claims so far removed from ordinary experience? Of course a person shouldn't without careful examination. But such unusual claims, so far out of the ordinary, should certainly catch one's attention and be worthy of examination. Out of the ordinary is what one should be looking for. Only something crazy or fundamentally new is this far out of the ordinary. But while these things are out of "man's ordinary," they are not crazy. Angels, prophets, and new scripture are not out of the ordinary for God when He does a great work. He has alerted us in the Bible[101] to watch for such a work; I have quoted or cited some of the verses and there are others. Christ has offered a clear and certain test and a promise through His prophet Moroni of a demonstration of truth. Do you trust Christ?

Did I get the promised answer in this test – to my study and prayer asking for a witness from God of the truthfulness of the Book of Mormon? Yes. Was it a definite and certain demonstration? Yes. And it was repeated the next day, unsolicited, in a different situation in such a manner that I learned things about myself and my priorities that I had not realized but needed to learn.

Have I received other guidance from Him in the forty intervening years that continues to guide and strengthen me in the way He wants me to go? Yes – on many occasions. Thoughts have been put into my mind and words into my mouth. I have witnessed, participated in, and even been Christ's spokesperson[102] when He performed miracles in blessing His children. I have come to know that He lives and loves us, His children, and that He is pleased when we seek to learn of Him with real intent. I have found to be true the promise in the Book of Mormon "… and signs shall follow them that believe in my name."[103]

How strong is my conviction and desire? I hope strong enough to please Him and to allow me to endure to the end of my life as a faithful servant and witness of Christ. Most importantly to me, I want for myself and my dear ones the joy in Christ coincident to being in His presence and feeling His power and love. He has allowed me to taste it by being in His presence, although I could not see Him, and compared to this joy, nothing else is important. Obtaining such fullness of joy for my loved ones and myself, which comes only through devotion to Christ, is now the principal objective of my life.

More I cannot tell you. I can tell you only words and facts while the real message is in the meaning and the feeling, in the demonstration of truth, in the certain witness of the power of God, in the indescribable joy in Christ. You have to take it from here yourself. But if you desire to learn for yourself, sincerely, having faith in Christ and real intent, I am confident your experience will be similar to mine and that of many others. Try it and see. God has power by which He can reveal truth and lead us – through the sure action of His Spirit communicating meaning directly to ours. In such communication, a misreading of the facts does not occur because meaning and feeling as well as facts are communicated. The power of this kind of experience is unmatched by any other I have had. After each such experience I have spent my idle moments for days recalling the experience and savoring the joy. The power of the experience was well described by Peter who heard the voice of God on the Mount of Transfiguration but described the Holy Ghost as "a more sure word."[104] The peace I received through such experiences passes understanding and the love of Christ I felt passes knowledge, using the terminology of Paul,[105] and herein lies the need for you to take it from here.

The Heavenly Order

There exists a certain "style" or "order" in heavenly relationships that defines our relationship with God and other heavenly beings. When we experience a contact in this style, with a heavenly or heavenly-type person, it evokes desire to respond in kind. The existence and nature of this style is revealed in many places in the scriptural record, but most clearly in a few places where the personality and behavior of God are revealed. One of these is found in the Book of Revelation, where John saw a vision in Heaven of both God the Father and God the Son when the Latter was chosen by the Former to be the Savior of humankind.

> And immediately I [John] was in the spirit: and behold, a throne was set in heaven, and one [God the Father] sat on the throne. ... And I saw in the right hand of him that sat on the throne a book [the revealed will and works of God, His plan, the general history of the earth] written within and on the backside, and sealed with seven seals [representing seven one-thousand-year periods[106] of the history of mortals on the earth]. And I saw a strong angel [an angel holding authority] proclaiming with a loud voice, Who is worthy to open the book [to carry out God's will] and to loose the seals thereof [to oversee and administer the history of the earth and humankind]? And no man in heaven, nor in the earth, neither under the earth, was able to open the book, neither to look thereon. And I wept much, because no man was found worthy to open and to read the book [do the will of God the Father – the weeping indicates the meaning and feeling and not merely facts were revealed to John].
>
> And one of the elders saith unto me, Weep not: behold, the Lion of the tribe of Juda, the Root of David [Christ], hath prevailed to open the book, and to loose the seven seals thereof. [Christ accepted the assignment to carry out His Father's will and play the principal role therein.] And I beheld, and lo, in the midst of the throne ... stood a Lamb ... And he came forth and took the book out of the right hand of him that sat upon the throne. And when he had taken the book, ... they [we] sung a new song, saying, thou art worthy to take the book, and to open the seals thereof: for thou wast slain, and hast redeemed us to God by thy blood out of every kindred, and tongue, and people, and nation; And hast made us unto our God kings and priests: and we shall reign on the earth. And I beheld, and heard the voice of many angels round about the throne and the beasts and the elders: ... Saying with a loud voice, Worthy is the Lamb that was slain [all is past tense before God, who sees the end from the beginning; but we mortals would have used future tense here] to receive power, and riches, and wisdom, and strength, and honour, and glory, and blessing. And every creature which is in heaven, and on the earth, and under the earth, and such as are in the sea, and all that are in them [all of us], heard I saying, Blessing and honour, and glory, and power, be unto him that sitteth upon the throne, and unto the Lamb for ever and ever.[107]

I read these verses to mean that when God the Father made known to us his plan and the need for a Savior contained therein, it was clear that none of us, God's creatures, could perform the key role – none was even worthy to consider it (to look on the book). To John, the *meaning* of the situation, not merely the facts, conveyed poignant feeling, perhaps sorrow, anxiety, or desperation, causing him to weep much. And others also perceived the same feeling and meaning. God the Son looked over us, His desperate creatures (for He as well as the Father is the Creator, He having performed the work at the command and commission of His Father[108]), we being so anxious for the plan to succeed. But, alas!, we saw no candidate capable of taking the key role. And He also recognized, in His greater understanding, that indeed none among us was capable. He realized that it would take a God to fulfil this assignment.

Of all of us children of God the Father, only He was perhaps capable. So, in compassion for and devotion to us, His creatures and junior spiritual siblings,[109] He volunteered to take the key role – to propitiate our sins. The act was by no means a "done deal." Christ Himself relates that fact.[110] In the Garden of Gethsemane He asked "O my Father, if it be possible, let this cup pass from me: nevertheless not as I will, but as thou wilt."[111] He feared[112] He might shrink from the magnitude of the awful, unknown burden of suffering, an awful burden of the full guilt for all our sins that, once accepted, He could escape only by either letting go of life and dying or by bearing the full-burden load of the atonement until it was finished. But despite terrible pain and anguish, He did not let go and die but suffered fully for each one of us and took upon Himself our guilt, the guilt of all one-hundred billion of us. We have no experience or feeling by which we can comprehend the depth of agony of Christ's suffering for us in Gethsemane[110] and later on the cross. It was immense, too far beyond our comprehension to imagine, only describable as infinite. He suffered so that we would not have to. The meaning of this act was clear to God's creatures (including us) in John's vision. His power, grace, and devotion to them (us) caused the universal reaction of adoration described in Chapter 5 of Revelation quoted above.

We have already jumped ahead in the story, from premortal life to mortality, from heaven to the Garden of Gethsemane at Passover, 33 AD. Christ has just suffered for us at a level so far beyond mortal comprehension, as already indicated, that it is only describable as an infinite atonement.[113] But His task is not yet finished. To finish His task He must also allow His blood to be shed in His long-predicted crucifixion. The officers sent by the chief priest and led by Judas arrive with torches and weapons to arrest Christ.

> Jesus therefore, knowing all things that should come upon him, went forth, and said unto them, Whom seek ye? They answered him, Jesus of Nazareth. Jesus saith unto them. I am he. ... As soon as he had said unto them, I am he, they went backward, and fell to the ground. [Who was in charge here? Christ was as He had received the book from His Father. He could have walked out of the garden if He had wished to, as he had previously walked away from mobs seeking his life.[114]] Then asked he them again, Whom seek ye? And they said, Jesus of Nazareth. Jesus answered, I have told you that I am he: if therefore ye seek me, let these go their way. [In other words, you can stand up now and take me, but only me.]"[115]

While giving up Himself, Christ thus preserved His apostles to lead His church and provide the record of the New Testament. It was the apostles who were present with Jesus in His public and private moments throughout His ministry. We read of the events recorded in the New Testament mostly because they told of them. What they didn't write about the Savior themselves was written by others, e.g., St. Luke, based on their eyewitness accounts of early events and based on events they themselves later experienced.

However, despairing for the safety of his Lord, Peter drew and used his sword cutting off the right ear of Malchus, the servant of the high priest. Christ healed Malchus with a touch. "Then said Jesus unto Peter, Put up thy sword into the sheath: the cup which my Father hath given me, shall I not drink it?"[116] Christ was intently focused on doing His Father's will and on our salvation, with no focus on or thought about Himself. Here is the basis of the observation of John that "perfect love casteth out fear."[117]

Christ was brought to and questioned first by Annas, then brought to and questioned by Annas' son-in-law and successor, the current high priest Caiaphas, and finally brought before and tried by the Sanhedrin.

> Now the chief priests, and elders, and all the council, sought false witness against Jesus, to put him to death. But found none: yea, though many false witnesses came, yet found they none. … And the high priest arose, and said unto him, Answerest thou nothing? What is it which these witness against thee? But Jesus held his peace. And the high priest answered and said unto him, I adjure thee by the living God, that thou tell us whether thou be the Christ, the Son of God.[118]

Here, again, Christ might have been freed if He had merely remained silent; His accusers had established no valid evidence against Him. But to be freed was not His mission. Christ was saving our souls, not His. His answer was direct. "And Jesus said, 'I am.' …"[119] (The trial had broken down under its own weight of corruption and, again, who kept the process going? Who was in charge?)

So Christ willingly suffered and died, sacrificing His perfect life that we might live again. In Gethsemane He took upon Himself the guilt and suffering for our sins that He might have power to forgive them. And He will, if we seek to keep His word and thereby come to follow and know Him. He always had the desire and He now has the power. *If we seek to follow Him He will pay our debt, forgive our sins, and take away our guilt* – He has already fully paid for them – but He can do this *only if we voluntarily follow Him.* His creatures who knew Him in heaven recognized His love and grace in advance and described them in past tense, because they knew Him. His devotion to us was known and has been fully confirmed. Here is the basis of another observation of John, "We love him, because he first loved us."[120]

In Christ we see manifest the magnanimity and love which is characteristic of heaven, because these are the qualities of God the Father and God the Son who rule in heaven. These qualities were apparent to all who resided in heaven, even to those who tried to take unrighteous advantage of them by rebelling. Thus, they who resided in heaven and knew God eagerly declared His qualities as recorded by John, quoted above, and they are apparent to all who read the accounts in the gospels of His arrest, trial, and crucifixion and comprehend their meaning.

An additional insight into the nature of heavenly beings is contained in a promise in the Doctrine and Covenants addressed to Joseph Smith, Jr. He was told by the Lord that on condition of faithfulness "… thy dominion shall be an everlasting dominion, and without compulsory means it shall flow unto thee forever and ever."[121] And, in the same book, Christ says "What I say unto one I say unto all."[122]

Thus, heaven is governed by principles of love, respect, magnanimity, and devotion. God does not compel. He doesn't rule heaven by force. He draws men to Him by love and they become devoted to Him because of His devotion to them. "We love him, because he first loved us."[120] The heavenly order, the nature of heavenly relationships, may therefore be described as *reciprocal* or *mutual devotion.*

Christ's devotion is not in question. It has been amply demonstrated. Only the reciprocal part is yet to be demonstrated by each person, the answer to the question

"Am I devoted to Him?" We each need to express to Him our response to this question, to write our own end of truth. He would have us answer this question by seeking to find and follow His way: the way, the truth, and the life. He would have us find success and joy. There is more at stake in this process than can be realized or expressed by a mere mortal. So just do it. If not beginning now, when?

Proposition Number 14: **Christ has demonstrated His devotion to each of us. We can respond to His devotion by showing our devotion to Him. He would have us do so by finding and following His way that we might obtain success and joy.**

Further Implications of the "Enemy Territory" Concept

That we now dwell in enemy territory during war is a concept that carries certain implications, some of which have already been explored. We now explore a few more.

One implication we consider is that we are being "battle tested." While we were all successfully battle tested during our premortal existence in an ideological war in heaven, the present test is *more severe* and therefore *more demanding and revealing* of the depth of our devotion to God and of the need and opportunity to build the strength of our devotion to Him. In the earlier test, the nature of God the Father and our relationship to Him were known to us by personal, remembered experience. Now, by design, we no more than occasionally and only vaguely and fleetingly remember these. Such memories are no more or less than a momentary longing for an earlier existence that we sometimes encounter when we witness beauty and feel a melancholy yearning for a faintly-remembered past and presently-lost associations.[123] If we remain faithful in our devotion to our Father in the severe conditions of our present test, and it is part of the plan that severe conditions be experienced by all, we will have greatly refined our personal qualities and demonstrated to ourselves and to Him that we have made ourselves capable of practicing the order of heaven. This final test is both the challenge and the opportunity of mortal life.

Another implication is that we have been trained for our current duty. What ruler would send his troops into action without adequate training? Perhaps a ruthless one, but our Ruler is not ruthless but loving and beneficent. Consequently, we were trained for our current duty. As part of our training we received instruction and guidance before we came to earth and they can be called to our remembrance by earnest appeal to God.[100] Our training also included our participation in the ideological war in heaven, which is now continuing on the earth. Our current duty posting in this continuing war was accepted by each individual on a voluntary basis, for this is the order of heaven. The location, circumstance, and time of our birth was proposed to us by our Commanding Officer and accepted by us as voluntary duty. And when we volunteered, we knew the plan and the ultimate outcome of the war. What was and is to be determined is the valor with which we perform our individual duty. Indeed, this is the great purpose of the war, to give us opportunity to learn and demonstrate our faithfulness in our "second estate," as we did in our "first."

But aren't location, circumstance, and era inherited in the birth of an individual critical? Since the doctrine of Christ describes certain principles and ordinances as required for salvation and absolutely necessary, don't we have to live in a location, circumstance, and time wherein following these principles and ordinances is possible? How could an uneducated aborigine of a remote area who never heard of Jesus Christ have faith in Him or experience remorse for violations of laws he or she had never heard of or comply with unknown ordinances (baptism, confirmation and gift of the Holy Ghost)? Such a one couldn't. As could no one, properly and completely, during long ages when the full truth and authority required to preach these principles and administer these ordinances were not found on the earth. Complete education, guidance, and opportunity do not come to many until their post-mortal-life existence in a "spirit world"[124] following death. In this condition we will recall only mortal experience so that, with regard to knowledge and faith, it is a continuation of mortality. And the paradigms we adopt now in mortality, which shape our attitudes and thinking, will remain intact in our minds then. For each individual the chance to receive necessary education, guidance, and opportunity will come, if not here then there. But to receive blessings one must desire them according to his or her adopted paradigm. When opportunity comes, sincere prayer offered with real intent, perhaps encouraged by missionaries and ministers whether in life or in the spirit world, will bring divine guidance to direct each supplicant in these principles. Salvation will be offered to all – whether on earth or in the spirit world, it is the same.[125] For God is "no respecter of persons." These facts were known to us when we accepted the duty He proposed.

However, we shouldn't think that if we reject our chance to learn and receive guidance here that we will receive another there. A rejection of truth, here or there, imposes a heavy burden. How heavy? While we don't know, we do know it is important to seek, examine, establish, and follow truth. Such seeking, examining, establishing, and following is our commission as agents searching for truth and should be motivated by our paradigm. Indeed, this is the essence of the battle – first to find and follow truth ourselves and then to help others do the same. If we don't seek to perform our duty here, we may not be able to do it there, for our choices form our character, forge our strength, and mold our paradigm.[126]

In the broad view, both the burden and opportunity comes to all and to all the instruction and guidance offered is equal, as they must be since God loves all His children. Despite differences in location, circumstance, and era of birth, all of us who are "of age"[127] must overcome the same obstacles, must resist similar enemy onslaughts, must endure here and in the spirit world in the battle for which we all previously received guidance, instruction, and training and in which we all receive the same offer of help. The question of primary importance is: Will we receive the offered help when we learn of it? This question is central to surviving our enemy-territory duty and helping others to survive. Faith in Christ, sincerity, and real intent required by the doctrine of Christ and by Moroni's promise lead naturally to repentance, baptism, and sure knowledge by "fire and the Holy Ghost." Receiving this process like a little child is the way, the truth, the life. An agent in search of truth will seek this process. A category-one student will receive it and receiving it is an expression of devotion to Him who is devoted to us.

We knew well His devotion to us and we were devoted to Him in our premortal existence. We volunteered to continue serving Him here because of this mutual devotion. Some knowledge of it can be restored or revealed according to our faith in Him. Are you ready, dear reader, to acquire this knowledge? Or perhaps you already have. In either case, are you ready to follow where such knowledge leads? In Chapter 18 we shall learn of the experiences of some who were ready and who did follow. The character, devotion, and strength forged by their lives of faith and effort provide a guide and an inspiration for us. We consider their accomplishments in completing our comparison of science and Christianity and perfecting our understanding of their meanings, which we do in the remaining four chapters.

Notes and References for Chapter 15.

[1] See endnote 34 of Chapter 6.

[2] *Bible,* Genesis 1:1, John 1:1-3.

[3] *Bible,* Genesis 1:1-5, John 1:4-14, *Doctrine and Covenants* 88:7-13.

[4] Lewis, C. S., *God in the Dock,* Walter Hooper (editor), William B. Eerdmans Publishing Company, Grand Rapids, MI, 1970, 21.

[5] *Bible,* Matthew 15:14.

[6] *Pearl of Great Price,* Moses 4:30. Again, Christ speaking by divine investiture.

[7] *Doctrine and Covenants* 132:8.

[8] *Book of Mormon,* 2 Nephi 9:20-53 reads in part

> ... where there is no law given there is no punishment; and where there is no punishment there is no condemnation; and where there is no condemnation the mercies of the Holy One of Israel [Christ] have claim upon them, because of the atonement; for they are delivered by the power of him. ... But wo unto him that has the law given, yea, that has all the commandments of God, like unto us, and that transgresseth them, and that wasteth the days of his probation, for awful is his state. O that cunning plan of the evil one! O the vainness, and the frailties, and the foolishness of men! When they are learned they think they are wise, and they hearken not unto the counsel of God, for they set it aside, supposing they know of themselves, wherefore, their wisdom is foolishness and it profiteth them not. And they shall perish.
>
> But to be learned is good if they hearken unto the counsels of God.
>
> But woe unto the rich, who are rich as to the things of the world. For because they are rich they despise the poor, and they persecute the meek, and their hearts are upon their treasures; wherefore, their treasure is their god. And behold, their treasure shall perish with them also. ...
>
> And whoso knocketh, to him will he open; and the wise, and the learned, and they that are rich, who are puffed up because of their learning, and their wisdom, and their riches – yea, they are they whom he [Christ] despiseth; and save they shall cast these things away, and consider themselves fools before God, and come down in the depths of humility, he will not open unto them. But the things of the wise and the prudent shall be hid from them forever – yea, that happiness which is prepared for the saints.

[9] The concept of a Trinity of Three Separate, Individual Gods is opposed to the single "Three in One and One in Three ..." God described in the now-orthodox Nicene or trinitarian creed. The former is, however, well supported over the latter in the Bible and, especially, in other scripture. Results of the research of Isaac Newton causing him to reject trinitarianism is described in Chapter 7 in the section entitled "Newton's Bible Studies."

[10] See, for examples, *Bible,* Amos 3:7, *Doctrine and Covenants* 1:38, *Pearl of Great Price,* Moses 4:30.

[11] Jehovah is the proper or covenant name of God the Son. This name denotes the "Unchangeable One" or "the eternal I Am" (Exodus 6:3, Psalms 83:18, Isaiah 12:2, 26:4). The Jews never spoke it and, following this tradition, it is replaced in the King James Bible by "the LORD" or "GOD." Jehovah is the premortal Christ as indicated by the following passages: *Bible,* Exodus 3:14, 6:3, Micah 5:2, Matthew 23:37, Luke 13:34, John 1:1-5,14, 8:58, 1 Peter 1:19-20, Revelation 4 and 5, *Book of Mormon,* 1 Nephi 21:6, 22:12, Moroni 10:34, *Doctrine and Covenants* 38:1, 45:7-9, 109:68.

[12] E.g., *Bible,* 1 Corinthians 15:21-22. "For since by man [Adam] came death, by man [Christ] came also the resurrection of the dead. For as in Adam all die, even so in Christ *shall all be made alive*." (italics added)

[13] See, for examples, *Bible,* Matthew 19:16-22, *Doctrine and Covenants* 88:4 and *Pearl of Great Price,* Moses 1:39.

[14] *Doctrine and Covenants* 88:4.

[15] *Doctrine and Covenants* 19.

[16] For examples: *Bible,* James 2:17-26. "... faith, if it hath not works, is dead, being alone. Yea, a man may say, Thou hast faith, and I have works: shew me thy faith without thy works, and I will shew thee my faith by my works. ... by works a man is justified, and not by faith only." Matthew 10:32-39. "Whosoever therefore shall confess me before men, him will I confess also before my Father which is in heaven. But whosoever shall deny me before men, him will I also deny before my Father which is in heaven. ... And he that taketh not his cross and followeth after me, is not worthy of me. He that findeth his life shall lose it; and he that loseth his life for my sake shall find it." John 5:28-29 "... for the hour is coming, in the which all that are in the graves shall hear his voice, And shall come forth; they that have done good, unto the resurrection of life; and they that have done evil, unto the resurrection of damnation." See also *Doctrine and Covenants* 76. Grace is an essential element in both of two salvations (*Bible,* Romans 3:20-24).

Our "born again" Christian friends who ask if we are saved reveal their ignorance in their question. Certainly Christ is the Savior of *all* persons (*Bible,* 1 Corinthians 15:21-22, etc.). But He is also the Judge of the world (*Bible,* Isaiah 51, John 5:22, Revelation 11:15-18). Would one deny Christ His appointed duty? The enigma of promised salvation *and* judgement is resolved if and only if there is more than one salvation. Thus, Christs's statement (John 10:10): "I am come that they may have life [a first salvation, free to all], and that they may have it more abundantly [a second salvation, received only by the obedient]." The latter salvation is reached by the straight and narrow way, the one few find because most are misled by foolish men and women, acting under influence of devils, through a wide gate and along a broad way that leadeth to destruction (Matthew 7:13-14).

[17] *Doctrine and Covenants* 123:12.

[18] An example of an apostle and prophet making an administrative decision for the church under guidance of revelation is described in *Bible,* Acts 10-11. In these chapters Peter sees a vision (three times) of unclean beasts which he is commanded to kill and eat. He wonders about the meaning of the vision and subsequently understands through additional inspiration given to Cornelius that the vision means the gospel is to be taken to the Gentiles as well as the Jews, the latter previously being the exclusive "target group." Peter concludes "Can any man forbid water [baptism], that these should not be baptized, which have received the Holy Ghost as well as we?" (*Bible,* Acts 10:47.) And, giving a full account of his experience to his fellow Christians upon their challenge that he had violated their practice of preaching only to Jews, Peter concluded "Forasmuch then as God gave them the like gift as he did unto us, who believed on the Lord Jesus Christ; what was I, that I could withstand God? When they heard these things, they held their peace, and glorified God, saying, Then hath God also to the Gentiles granted repentance unto

life." (Acts 11:17-18.) This change in practice of the church was revealed by God to Peter, the chief apostle, communicated to and accepted by members of the church, and recorded in scripture for all to read.

[19] *Bible,* John 18:20.

[20] Paul (*Bible,* Ephesians 2:19-20) refers to the members of the church (saints) being "built upon the foundation of the apostles and prophets, Jesus Christ himself being the chief cornerstone." But much confusion exists in Christianity today about many things including the role or calling of apostles and prophets. One might cite the description in Acts 1:21-26 of the qualifications of Matthias and Joseph called Bar-sabas in which they were both described as having "companied with us [the other apostles] all the time that the Lord Jesus went in and out among us." And one might then ask: "Who could meet such qualifications today?" But these qualifications were not required; they were merely stated as those of the two candidates being considered to replace Judas Iscariot. The apostles prayed for the Lord to show them who He had chosen (Acts 1:24). He chose Matthias. James, the Lord's brother and probable author of the Epistle of James, was later appointed an apostle (Galatians 1:19). Paul, an apostle later appointed by the Lord, did not have such qualifications. Indeed, he knew not Christ and fought against Him during that same period. But an old saw says "Who the Lord calls, the Lord qualifies." None of the original apostles were initially qualified by any training or ability. Initially, they were simple and uneducated. They rose to the great height of their office only when they received "fire and the Holy Ghost" beginning on the day of Pentecost. Paul was qualified as a witness of Jesus Christ by his personal experience on the road to Damascus and by "fire and the Holy Ghost." And in our own day, others have been called and qualified by the power of God or "fire and the Holy Ghost" (see *Pearl of Great Price,* Joseph Smith – History; partially quoted in Appendix H). With respect to the apostles the Lord said "Ye have not chosen me, but I have chosen you, and ordained you, ..." (*Bible,* John 15:16.) Paul said, "... no man taketh this honour [of holding the priesthood] unto himself, but he that is called of God, as was Aaron." (Hebrews 5:4.) Aaron was called of God through the Prophet Moses by commandment of the Lord (Exodus 4:10-16). The essential ingredient, then and now, is being chosen and called by the Lord. He has power to satisfy all other considerations and He presides over His church.

[21] *Bible,* Galatians 1:6-8.

[22] *Book of Mormon,* 3 Nephi 27:13-21, 11:31-40.

[23] *Bible,* Matthew 24:14, Mark 13:10.

[24] *Bible,* Ephesians 4:11-14.

[25] *Bible,* John 21:18-19, 2 Peter 1:14, 1 Corinthians 13:11-12, John 13:26, 15:18-21, 17:14, Matthew 10:38-39, Luke 9:23-26, Mark 8:34-38, Matthew 16:24-26, Luke 14:33, Acts 9:16, 12:2, 20:23-24, 21:13.

[26] *Bible,* 2 Thessalonians 2:2-5, 2 Timothy 4:1-4, 2 Peter 2:1-3.

[27] Talmage, James E., *The Great Apostasy,* Deseret News Press, Salt Lake City, 1964.

[28] Christ prophesied of conditions and events that shall precede His second coming, such as "many shall come in my name, saying, I am Christ; and shall deceive many" and "many false prophets shall rise, and shall deceive many" *suggest* an apostasy has occurred. But that an apostasy has occurred is *implied* by: "this gospel of the kingdom shall be preached to all the world for a witness unto all nations; and then shall the end come." What is remarkable about a two-thousand-year-old gospel being preached before the end comes? Is this prophecy not fulfilled throughout the whole two-thousand years by missionaries and preachers of many Christian denominations? It is not. "This gospel" was lost through apostasy as Paul predicted (*Bible,* 2 Thessalonians 2:1-4) to be restored in the latter days, as Daniel (*Bible,* Daniel 2:28,44-45), Peter (*Bible,* Acts 3:19-24), and others prophesied.

[29] See, e.g., *Bible,* Acts 3:19-21. [30] *Bible,* Luke 24:36-37.

[31] *Bible,* Acts 3:1-8. [32] *Bible,* Acts 6-8.

[33] Eusebius, *Ecclesiastical History,* Book III, Chapter 32. Quoted in Talmage, loc. cit., 45-46.

[34] Eusebius, *Ecclesiastical History,* Book IV, Chapter 22. Quoted in Talmage, loc. cit., 93.

[35] Wesley, John, *John Wesley's Works,* Volume VII, 89:26-27. Quoted in Talmage, loc. cit., 161-162.

[36] See endnote 31 of Chapter 6. [37] *Book of Mormon,* 2 Nephi 29:3-14.

[38] *Bible,* Romans 10:9-15. [39] *Bible,* Acts 1:26. [40] *Doctrine and Covenants* 115:1,4.

[41] *History of The Church of Jesus Christ of Latter-day Saints,* Second Edition Revised, The Church of Jesus Christ of Latter-day Saints, Deseret Book Company, Salt Lake City, 1960, Volume IV, 540. The original "Wentworth letter" is displayed in the Yale University library.

[42] *Bible,* John 5:25-29. [43] *Bible,* 1 Peter 4:6. [44] *Bible,* 1 Corinthians 15:29.

[45] *Doctrine and Covenants* 138:32-35, 58-59. [46] *Bible,* 1 Corinthians 1:27.

[47] Thus, Samuel was designated to be a prophet while still a boy (*Bible,* 1 Samuel 3), David was identified by the Lord to the Prophet Samuel and ordained King of Israel while an unknown boy (1 Samuel 16:6-13), and Jeremiah was ordained a prophet unto the nations before he was even born (Jeremiah 1:5), i.e., during his premortal life.

[48] *Bible,* James 1:4-5 and elsewhere.

[49] *Book of Mormon,* 3 Nephi 11:32, 35, Moroni 10:4-7, 2 Nephi 32:5, and elsewhere.

[50] *Pearl of Great Price,* Joseph Smith – History 19. [51] *Book of Mormon,* Moroni 10:7.

[52] *Book of Mormon,* Moroni 10:33. [53] *Bible,* Matthew 19:24, Mark 10:25, Luke 18:25.

[54] *Bible*, Matthew 16:13-18. [55] *Book of Mormon,* 3 Nephi 11:37-39.

[56] Farrar, Frederic W., *The Life of Christ,* A. L. Burt, New York, n. d., 344.

[57] *Bible,* Luke 9:50 and Mark 9:40. [58] *Bible,* Matthew 12:30.

[59] *Bible,* Matthew 3:17, Mark 1:11, Luke 3:22, Hebrews 5:1-10. [60] *Bible,* Joshua 23:15-16.

[61] *Bible,* Isaiah 29:13. This verse is actually an introductory one or a prelude (Forasmuch ...) to the one following wherein Isaiah prophesied "Therefore, behold, I will proceed to do a marvelous work among this people, even a marvelous work and a wonder: for the wisdom of their wise men shall perish, and the understanding of their prudent men shall be hid. ... And in that day shall the deaf hear the words of the book, and the eyes of the blind shall see out of obscurity, and out of darkness. The meek also shall increase their joy in the LORD, and the poor among men shall rejoice in the Holy One of Israel." (Isaiah 29:14,18-19.) Isaiah goes into greater detail about the

blind and about prisoners (especially in chapters 40-42). In particular, Isaiah, speaking for the LORD, says, "And I will bring the blind by a way that they knew not; I will lead them in paths that they have not known: I will make darkness light before them, and crooked things straight. These things will I do unto them, and not forsake them." (Isaiah 42:16.)

Of course the Holy One of Israel is Christ. But what book is referred to that shall give hearing to the deaf and sight to the blind, that will give joy to the meek and cause the poor to rejoice? And what is the "way that [we] knew not" that Isaiah warns us to watch for and the "paths that [we] have not known?" This marvelous work and a wonder by which the wisdom of the wise shall perish and the understanding of the prudent shall be hid must be something strange and new (just the kind of thing we should be watching for anyway).

The identity of the book and of the marvelous work and a wonder – by which the deaf shall hear and the blind see and the meek and poor (in spirit) shall receive joy – was clearly indicated by fulfillment of a prophecy Isaiah made in the preceding two verses (29:11-12). Therein he prophesied "And the vision of all is become unto you as the words of a book that is sealed, which men deliver to one that is learned, saying, Read this, I pray thee: and he saith, I cannot; for it is sealed. And the book is delivered to him that is not learned, saying, Read this, I pray thee; and he saith, I am not learned." Nevertheless, the unlearned one translated the book.

On 22 September 1827 Joseph Smith received the Book-of-Mormon plates, along with the Urim and Thummim and Breastplate, from the Angel Moroni. The Book-of-Mormon plates were bound by metal rings on one side and a portion of them was sealed by a metal band or bands. Smith was instructed that the sealed portion was to remain sealed. Owing to severe persecution and many attempts to steal the plates from him, he could make no adequate effort of translation. He decided to relocate from his father's farm near Palmyra, NY, to the home of his wife's father in Susquehanna County, PA. "While preparing to start, – being very poor, and the persecution so heavy upon us that there was no probability that we would ever be otherwise, – in the midst of our afflictions we found a friend in a gentleman by the name of Martin Harris, who came to us and gave me fifty dollars to assist us on our journey. ... By this timely aid was I enabled to reach the place of my destination in Pennsylvania; and immediately after my arrival there I commenced copying the characters off the plates. ... Some time in this month of February [1828], the aforementioned Mr. Martin Harris came to our place, got the characters which I had drawn off the plates, and started with them to the city of New York. For what took place relative to him and the characters, I refer to his own account of the circumstances, as he related them to me after his return, which was as follows:"

> I went to the city of New York, and presented the characters which had been translated, with the translation thereof, to Professor Charles Anthon, a gentleman celebrated for his literary attainments. Professor Anthon stated that the translation was correct, more so than any he had before seen translated from the Egyptian. I then showed him those which were not yet translated, and he said that they were Egyptian, Chaldaic, Assyric, and Arabic; and he said they were true characters. He gave me a certificate, certifying to the people of Palmyra that they were true characters, and that the translation of such of them as had been translated was also correct. I took the certificate and put it into my pocket, and was just leaving the house, when Mr. Anthon called me back, and asked me how the young man found out that there were gold plates in the place where he found them. I answered that an angel of God had revealed it unto him.
>
> He then said to me, "Let me see that certificate." I accordingly took it out of my pocket and gave it to him, when he took it and tore it to pieces, saying, that there was no such thing as ministering of angels, and that if I would bring the plates to him he would translate them. I informed him that part of the plates were sealed, and that I was forbidden to bring them. He replied, "I cannot read a sealed book." I left him and went to Dr. Mitchell, who sanctioned what Professor Anthon had said respecting both the characters and the translation. (Smith, Joseph, Jr., *History of the Church of Jesus Christ of Latter-day Saints,* Second Edition Revised, Deseret Book Company, Salt Lake City, Utah, 1967, Volume 1, 18-20. See also *Pearl of Great Price,* Joseph Smith – History 59-65.)

(Charles Anthon was, at the time of Martin Harris' visit, an adjunct professor of Greek and Latin at Columbia College, now Columbia University. His career at Columbia was to last 47 years. In addition to Greek and Latin he also knew French, German, Hebrew, and Babylonian and was among the leading classical scholars of his day. His library included books containing the latest discoveries pertaining to Egyptian and early work of Champollion. Samuel Latham Mitchell was Vice President of Rutgers Medical College. He served in the New York State Legislature, the United States House of Representatives, and Senate. In addition, he was noted for work as a linguist, historian, ichthyologist, botanist, editor, geologist, chemist, physician, and surgeon.)

This account describes a literal fulfillment of Isaiah's prophecy, by which Smith and Harris were, when they later realized this fact, utterly amazed. It provides insight into the importance of the claimed Restoration and validates it, for any genuine Restoration must make claims of exactly this kind. In the restored Christian Church, the one the Mormons claim their church to be, all Biblical prophecies must be fulfilled. Fulfillment of all Biblical prophecy will entail salvation being brought (offered) first to all Israel (except the Jews) and all people of the world and, finally, to the Jews. (The first shall be last and the last shall be first.)

The Restoration and events that followed have not been hidden in a corner, but they have not been widely broadcast either. The truth and meaning of these events can be established by divine demonstration, the method of ostensible proof urged in this book and spoken of by Isaiah. It requires an earnest study of and prayerful inquiry about the Book of Mormon. Is this book, the one the Mormons claim Isaiah mentions, the one that (with the Bible) gives hearing to the deaf and seeing to the blind and serves as a guide to the meek and poor in spirit to lead them by a way they knew not? This would indeed be a marvelous work and a wonder. Each person must discover this question and decide if he or she wants to also discover its answer. The process is simple and not a problem. The problem is the "paradigm challenge" in coming to this process with and honest desire to know and a real intent to find and follow truth.

Many Christians are quite familiar with the Bible but generally less familiar with ancient prophecies it contains, some of which we have considered in this chapter, because orthodox Christianity does not understand and misinterprets or largely ignores many of them. But if one has faith in Christ and trusts what He said, then one should expect all His prophecies made by Him or His servants, "it is the same," to be fulfilled. Fulfillment of ancient prophecies will guide Christ's followers to Him and His work while those of the world (i.e., those having their hearts set on worldly things) ignore such things. Marvelous fulfillment of magnificent prophecy is occurring now, under our very noses as it were, and those of the world ignore them and recognize nothing.

[62] *Bible,* Isaiah 24:5. [63] *Bible,* Matthew 15:8-9; see also Mark 7:6-13.

[64] *Doctrine and Covenants* 1:15-16.

[65] Michener, James A., *The Covenant,* Random House, New York, 1980, 487.

[66] *Bible,* Matthew 15:6. [67] *Bible,* Acts 19:7.

[68] *Bible,* John 1:26-27,32-34, Acts 19:1-3. [69] *Bible,* John 3:30.

[70] *Bible,* Matthew 11:7-11, John 5:35. [71] *Bible,* Matthew 11:11. [72] *Bible,* John 4:2.

[73] *Bible,* Acts 19:4-6. As a mortal, John the Baptist was never a member of Christ's Church. His mission was to go before and prepare the way as a forerunner of the Savior. He baptized unto repentance but not for admission into the Church of Jesus Christ, the latter act being one he had not been authorized to perform. Indeed, the Church of Jesus Christ was established only after John was imprisoned. Thus, when Paul learned that members of the Church at Ephesus had been baptized only unto John's baptism and had, therefore, not been given the gift of the Holy Ghost, he baptized them properly and gave them this gift.

When Joseph Smith and his scribe Oliver Cowdery were translating the Book of Mormon they were so moved by its instructions about the need for baptism they retired to a quiet spot in the woods next to the Susquehanna River near Harmony, PA, on 15 May 1829 and petitioned the Lord for the blessing of being baptized. In response, a heavenly messenger appeared to them and identified himself as John, the same who had baptized Jesus. He gave them priesthood authority and commanded them to baptize one another and instructed them how to do it. But as the Church of Jesus Christ had not yet been reestablished, this, too, was a baptism unto repentance only and not one giving admission into Christ's Church. A few weeks later, Joseph and Oliver were visited by Peter, James, and John, the three principal apostles in the Church at the time of Christ, and these three conferred the apostolic authority on Joseph and Oliver. These two were thus empowered to again establish the Church of Jesus Christ and baptize members into it, to give the gift of the Holy Ghost, to confer on others the authority to do the same, and to authorize the preaching and practice of the gospel of Christ. The Church of Jesus Christ of Latter-day Saints was organized on 6 April 1830 at the home of Peter Whitmer, Sr., in Fayette, NY. The six original members of the Church (or saints as they are called) were Oliver Cowdery, Joseph Smith, Jr., Hyrum Smith, Peter Whitmer, Jr., Samuel H. Smith, and David Whitmer. Some of these had been baptized previously; but all were baptized on the day of the organization of the Church to obtain membership in it. (*History of the Church of Jesus Christ of Latter-day Saints,* Second Edition Revised, The Church of Jesus Christ of Latter-day Saints, Deseret Book Company, Salt Lake City, UT, 1967, Volume I, 39-41, 76, 79-80.)

[74] *Pearl of Great Price,* Joseph Smith – History 69-70.

[75] *Bible,* John 15:16.

[76] *Doctrine and Covenants* 110.

[77] *Bible,* Matthew 17:1-13, Mark 9:2-13, Luke 9:28-36.

[78] See *Elias* in the Bible Dictionary appended to the *Holy Bible, Authorized King James Version,* The Church of Jesus Christ of Latter-day Saints, Salt Lake City, 1979. W. Cleon Skousen (*The Fourth Thousand Years,* Bookcraft, Salt Lake City, 1966, 332-333) has listed modern-day sources that indicate Elias and the Angel Gabriel are the Prophet Noah.

[79] *Bible,* Luke 1:11-17.

[80] *Doctrine and Covenants* 13, *Pearl of Great Price,* Joseph Smith – History 38.

[81] *Bible,* Malachi 4:5-6, *Doctrine and Covenants* 2, 110, *Pearl of Great Price,* Joseph Smith – History 38.

[82] *Doctrine and Covenants* 1:30.

[83] *Ibid.,* 1:34.

[84] *Pearl of Great Price,* Moses 7:48-49.

[85] *Doctrine and Covenants* 123:7-9,11-14.

[86] *Bible,* John 18:36. See also endnote 3 of Chapter 16.

[87] *Bible,* Jude 1:6, *Pearl of Great Price,* Abraham 3:24-28. The former passage gives some sense of the meaning of "first estate" while the latter gives a more complete sense of both "first estate" and "second estate." See also endnote 21 of Chapter 10.

[88] *Bible,* Isaiah 65:17, Revelation 21, 22, *Pearl of Great Price,* Moses 3:5, *Doctrine and Covenants* 63:20-21, 77:1, 88:1-26, 123:7, 130:6-9.

[89] *Doctrine and Covenants* 88:15.

[90] Christ's disciples asked if the man born blind had sinned or his parents, causing him to be born blind. (*Bible,* John 9:2.) When would he have sinned before he was born? That Christ corrected not this question implies that He taught premortal life.

[91] *Bible,* Revelation 12:7-9, Jude 1:6-8. See also *Doctrine and Covenants* 76:25-27 and *Pearl of Great Price,* Moses 4:3-4.

[92] *Bible,* Revelation 12:3-4, *Doctrine and Covenants* 29:36-39. [93] *Bible,* Ephesians 6:11-12.

[94] *Bible,* Mark 1:34, 3:11-12, 5:1-15. [95] *Bible,* Mark 6:13.

[96] Ritchie, George G., with Elizabeth Sherrill, *Return from Tomorrow,* Spire Books, Fleming H. Revell Company, Old Tappan, NJ, 1978, 59-61; Peck, M. Scott, *People of the Lie,* Simon and Schuster, New York, 1983.

[97] *Bible,* Mark 1:34, 3:11-12. [98] See endnote 7 of Chapter 14.

[99] *Book of Mormon,* 2 Nephi 2:11, 15-19, 24-25.

[100] *Book of Mormon,* Moroni 10:4-7, *Bible,* John 16:13-14. See also John 14:26 in which Christ promises that the Comforter or Holy Ghost "shall teach you all things, and bring all things to your remembrance, whatsoever I have said unto you." The full meaning of this promise is only recognized when we understand that we followed Christ in a premortal life and then learned from Him things that we do not now remember.

[101] See citations of Chapter 14 referring to an apostasy and refreshing or restitution or restoration, especially references 28-34, 36.

[102] *Doctrine and Covenants* 1:20. [103] *Book of Mormon,* Ether 4:18.

[104] *Bible,* 2 Peter 1:18-21. [105] *Bible,* Philippians 4:7 and Ephesians 3:19.

[106] *Doctrine and Covenants* 77:7. [107] *Bible,* Revelation 4:2, 5:1-12, 1 Peter 1:19-20.

[108] *Bible,* John 1:3, *Pearl of Great Price,* Moses 1:33, *Doctrine and Covenants* 45:1.

[109] *Bible,* Colossians 1:13-18, Hebrews 1:6, *Doctrine and Covenants* 93:21-22. [110] *Ibid.,* 19.

[111] *Bible,* Matthew 26:39. [112] *Doctrine and Covenants* 19:18.

[113] *Book of Mormon,* Alma 34:8-16. [114] *Bible,* Luke 4:30, John 8:59.

[115] *Bible,* John 18:4-8. [116] *Bible,* John 18:11. [117] *Bible,* 1 John 4:18.

[118] *Bible,* Matthew 26:59-63. [119] *Bible,* Mark 14:62. [120] *Bible,* I John 4:19.

[121] *Doctrine and Covenants* 121:46. [122] Ibid. 93:49.

[123] C. S. Lewis (*The Weight of Glory,* Walter Hooper (editor), Simon and Schuster, New York, 1996, 30-31) wrote of a

> ... desire for our own far-off country, which we find in ourselves even now. ... the secret which hurts so much that you take your revenge on it by calling it names like Nostalgia and Romanticism and Adolescence; the secret also which pierces with such sweetness that when, in very intimate conversation, the mention of it is imminent, we grow awkward and effect to laugh at ourselves; the secret we cannot hide and cannot tell, though we desire to do both. We cannot tell it because it is a desire for something that has never actually appeared in our experience. We cannot hide it because our experience is constantly suggesting it ... Our commonest experience is to call it beauty and behave as if that had settled the matter. ... But this is all a cheat. ... The books or the music in which we thought the beauty was located will betray us if we trust to them; it was not *in* them, it only came

> *through* them, and what came through them was longing. ... they are the scent of a flower we have not found, the echo of a tune we have not heard, news from a country we have not yet visited [and remembered].

[124] The term "spirit world," "spirit prison," and related terms are used in the Bible in Isaiah 24:22, 42:7, 49:9, 61:1, Luke 4:18, John 5:25 and 1 Peter 3:19, 4:6. To the one thief next to Him on the cross Jesus promised he would be with Him that day in "paradise." (Luke 23:43.) But where or what is paradise? Three and one-half days later when Mary encountered the Risen Christ outside the sepulchre He said "Touch me not; for I have not yet ascended unto my Father: but go to my brethren, and say unto them, I ascend unto my Father, and your Father; and to my God, and your God." (John 20:17.) Thus, paradise is not the dwelling place of God. Indeed, the Bible rendering of Luke 23:43 is not correctly translated from the Greek; it should more correctly read "Today shalt thou be with me in the world of spirits." (See *Bible Dictionary,* loc. cit.)

Modern scripture refers more consistently and definitively to the spirit world and the states of spirits after death. We read "... they who are the spirits of men kept in prison, whom the Son visited, and preached the gospel unto them, that they might be judged according to men in the flesh;" (*Doctrine and Covenants* 76:73.) Also, referring to the states of the dead and the fulfillment of the prophecies of Peter (*Bible,* 1 Peter 3:18-20, 4:6), "And there were gathered together in one place an innumerable company of the spirits of the just, who had been faithful in the testimony of Jesus while they lived in mortality; And who had offered sacrifice in the similitude of the great sacrifice of the Son of God, and had suffered tribulation in their Redeemer's name. All these had departed the mortal life, firm in the hope of a glorious resurrection, through the grace of God the Father and his Only Begotten Son, Jesus Christ. ... They were assembled awaiting the advent of the Son of God into the spirit world, to declare their redemption from the bands of death. ... While this vast multitude waited and conversed, rejoicing in the hour of their deliverance from the chains of death, the Son of God appeared, declaring liberty to the captives who had been faithful; And there he preached to them the everlasting gospel, the doctrine of the resurrection and the redemption of mankind from the fall, and from individual sins on condition of repentance. But unto the wicked he [Christ] did not [personally] go, and among the ungodly and the unrepentant who had defiled themselves while in the flesh, his voice was not raised; Neither did the rebellious who rejected the testimonies and the warnings of the ancient prophets behold his presence, nor look upon his face. Where these were, darkness reigned, but among the righteous there was peace; ... the Lord went not in person among the wicked and the disobedient who had rejected the truth, to teach them; But behold, from among the righteous, he organized his forces and appointed messengers, clothed with power and authority, and commissioned them to go forth and carry the light of the gospel to them that were in darkness, even to all the spirits of men; and thus was the gospel preached to the dead." (*Doctrine and Covenants* 138:12-14, 18-22, 29-30.)

[125] This insight provides new depth of understanding of the parable of the laborers (*Bible,* Matthew 20:1-16).

[126] *Book of Mormon,* Alma 34:32-34.

[127] *Book of Mormon,* Moroni 8:8-24, Mosiah 3:16. The former citation reads: "Listen to the words of Christ, your Redeemer, your Lord and your God. Behold, I came into the world not to call the righteous but sinners to repentance; the whole need no physician, but they that are sick; wherefore little children are whole, for they are not capable of committing sin; wherefore the curse of Adam is taken from them in me, that it hath no power over them; ... wherefore, ..., I know that it is solemn mockery before God, that ye should baptize little children. ... this thing shall ye teach – repentance and baptism unto those who are accountable and capable of committing sin; yea, teach parents that they must repent and be baptized, and humble themselves as their little children, and they shall all be saved with their little children. And their little children need no repentance, neither baptism. ... But little children are alive in Christ, even from the foundation of the world; if not so, God is a partial God, and also a changeable God, and a respecter of persons; for how many little children have died without baptism!"

16. Follow The Light

In this chapter and the next we address capabilities and limitations of science and Christianity at a fundamental, philosophical level. Careful consideration of these paradigms provides, through contrasts, a clearer understanding of the subtle natures of both. With this understanding of their subtleties we summarize and illustrate their limitations in this chapter and their meanings in the next.

In the world of facts and science, or in the facts of the external world of science, the knowledge envisioned is that of cause-and-effect relationships and deeper, more general organization of facts underlying these relationships. Discovery of cause-and-effect facts and knowledge of cause and effect and other organization allows description and prediction of events and processes. Discovery of cause and effect and deeper organization provides tentative understanding of truth – knowledge of the way things were, are, and shall be – based on consistency among the objective, reproducible, material-universe facts. Scientific knowledge is widely believed to be all-inclusive of the material universe and expected by many to (eventually) be able to explain all material-universe facts. But a limitation of science usually forgotten is its restricted scope, viz., science considers only objective, reproducible, material facts.

How is this scope limiting? We stated earlier that a basis for discovering reality must contain an *adequate range* of *accurate facts*. The need for the best possible accuracy is apparent. Indeed, some scientists regard accuracy as justifying science (page 76). But what *range* or *scope* of facts is adequate? This question is an important one, especially in connection with others: "What facts do people perceive and what facts do they fail to perceive?" The Eskimo language contains thirteen different words for "snow" and Finnish contains a comparable number, a substance represented by a single noun in most other languages. The Eskimo and the Finn see "snow facts" that others don't. It is probably valid to conclude from this and other evidence that many people fail to perceive and consider important facts, especially deliberately-excluded ones, and such failure can severely limit knowledge. Thus, spiritual things are invisible to a materialist and an atheist refuses to acknowledge miracles or benefit of personal belief in God. Consequences of such limitation are apparent when we deduce meaning of science and its tentative theories and laws. These consequences are severe, being sufficient to prevent the obtaining of *understanding* through science.

We begin a comparison of the limitations of science and Christianity by reviewing the evidence considered (allowed) in each. We then state several fundamental limitations in scientific methodology, all mentioned earlier and all but one based on the problem the ancient Greeks recognized in philosophy not restricted to science, namely, lack of an adequate truth criterion.

We have discovered no inherent limitation in our model of Christianity, although several common in Christian belief and practice according to other models have been enumerated in previous chapters. Establishing fundamental truth by the Christian paradigm is a powerful capability, all the more notable because this capability occurs at a depth of inquiry where alternative philosophy, including science, encounters debilitating limitation.

After limitations we address the question posed earlier – Does essential conflict occur between science and Christianity? Then we consider implications.

Because meaning that a paradigm can contain and convey is limited by scope of evidence, a paradigm's scope of evidence determines breadth and depth of meaning accessible by the paradigm. Scope of evidence of a paradigm is similar to range of awareness of a person. A paradigm having broader scope of evidence can therefore convey fuller awareness, greater feeling, and deeper meaning.

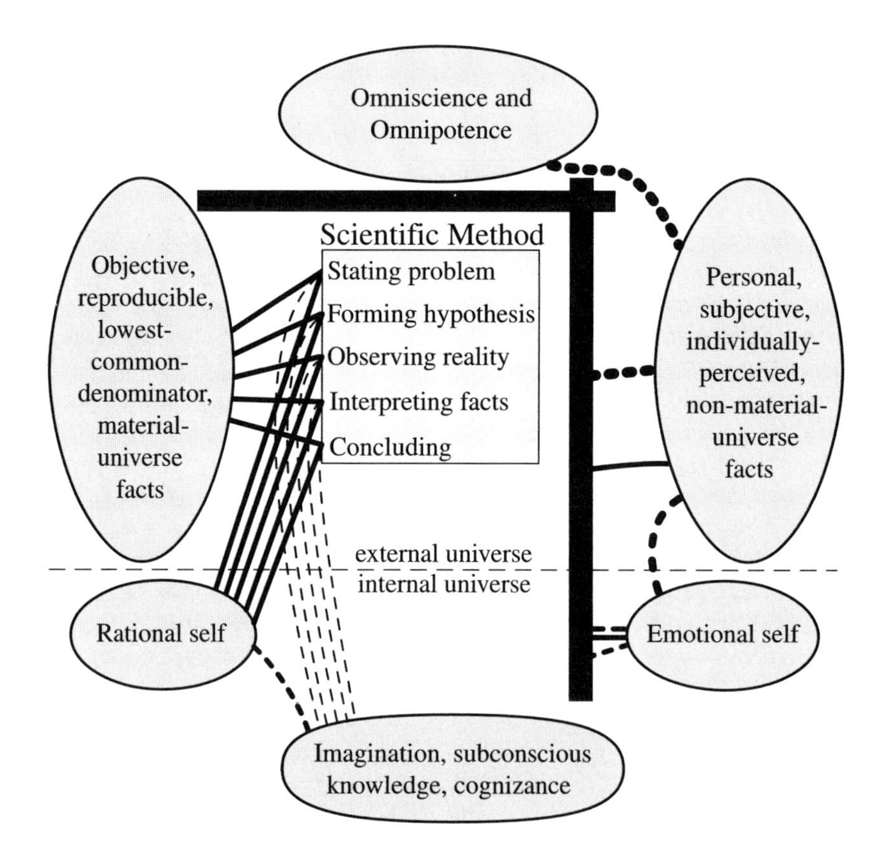

Scientific Evidence

The scope of scientific evidence is represented in the above graphic. Six possible sources of evidence are shown as shaded ellipses. These sources are (a) the observed, material universe, (b) the rational (reasoning) self, (c) the emotional (feeling) self, (d) imagination, subconscious knowledge, and cognizance, (e) the observed, nonmaterial universe, and (f) God (Omniscience and Omnipotence). A seventh influence in our non-passive universe, that of the enemy, is omitted for simplicity. That science does not contemplate and, in fact, deliberately ignores four of these seven sources is represented by self-imposed, opaque barriers screening them.

The graphic also shows steps of scientific inquiry and connections that represent from where we obtain evidence in science. Solid lines represent deliberate, rational connections between science and a source of evidence. Dashed lines represent connections that may not be rational or deliberate or even conscious.

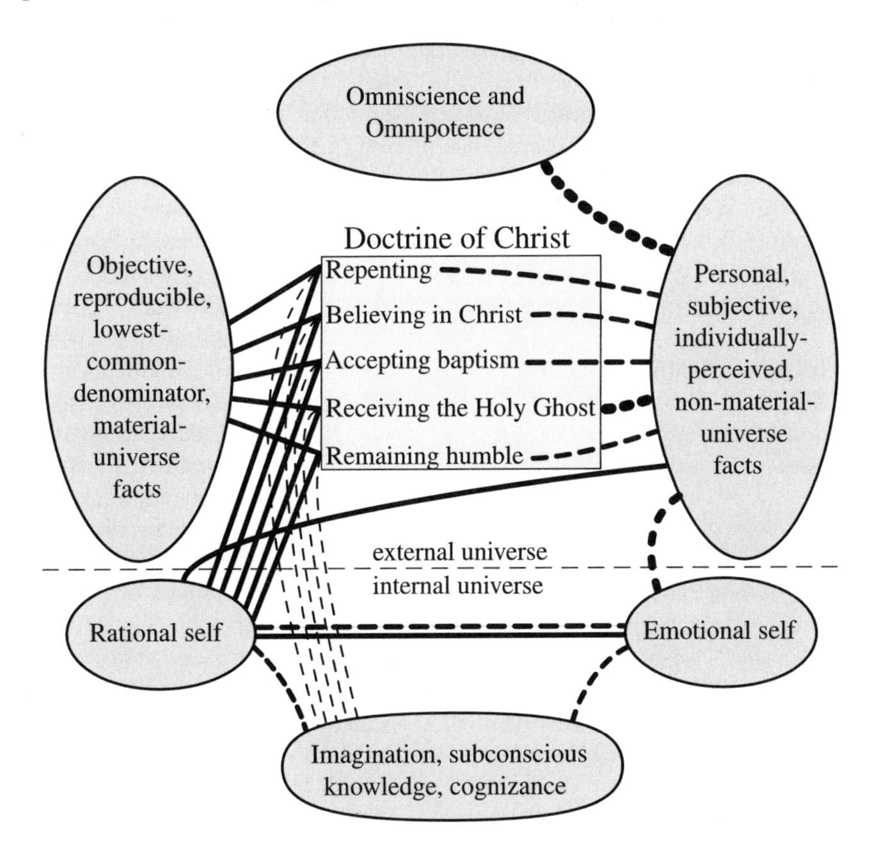

Christian Evidence

A second graphic (above) again shows the same six of the seven sources of evidence of which all are recognized and utilized in Christianity. As before, solid-line connections between elements of Christian inquiry and a source of evidence are those utilized in deliberate, rational or reasoning, and conscious processes while dashed lines indicate usage of a source of evidence that may not be through a deliberate, rational, or conscious process. The thickest, dotted line represents access to not only the most fundamental evidence but also to its associated understanding and meaning. This dotted line indicates that the transfer process involves both God's deliberate and rational as well as our non-deliberate and non-rational processes. Thickness of solid, dashed, or dotted lines, represents relative importance of a source of information. In Christianity no intentional, self-imposed barriers screen any source of evidence, although lack of belief, pride, personal unworthiness or lack of obedience, or inadequate intent can cause fully opaque screening. When a person satisfies all requirements of the doctrine of Christ, screening is eliminated and transfer of evidence is uninhibited. All these sources of evidence are not uniformly recognized throughout Christianity, but they are taught in the Bible and the Christian model we have adopted focuses on guidance from God. And as we shall see, one source, the one connected by the thick, dotted line, is essential to experiencing the considerable power of Christianity.

While the scientific method requires formulating a question and guessing a theory or law as its possible answer, the doctrine of Christ requires no such formulating or guessing. In the doctrine of Christ the laws to be tested or questions to be answered are provided (Does God the Father exist? Is Christ the Son of God? Are the Bible and the Book of Mormon genuine scripture?) as well as a full description of all requirements necessary for a successful and conclusive test by one willing to "see" beyond him- or her-self and the material universe.

An Inadequate Truth Criterion

Let us compare science (physics) and religion (Christianity) to determine whether some essential conflict occurs between them. We address the slightly broadened questions: "Does essential conflict occur between science and Christianity and, if so, does it indicate an essential flaw in one or both?" (Acceptance of validity of neither science nor religion is adopted *a priori* in our comparison.) This question is terribly broad and to find a definitive answer we limit the scope of inquiry to prevent overreaching in any conclusion. We therefore utilize our specific models for "science" and "Christianity" that are representative but minimal (do not overreach) and compare these for conflict. One might object that such a comparison is not general. I agree that it is not, but such a comparison is sufficient to refute the previously-mentioned, widely-held, sweepingly-broad notion that some essential, fundamental conflict occurs. In limiting consideration to specific models this notion is still proven false if no essential conflict is found. If no conflict occurs between these two particular models, conflict is not general and therefore not essential and fundamental. Indeed, if our comparison is sufficiently fundamental it may reveal that no-essential-conflict occurs between science and all Christianity or even between science and religion in general. In these last cases the religion must either contain the essential elements of the doctrine of Christ or the science must be shown to be incapable of causing an essential, fundamental conflict with any other system of belief.

The models we examine are summarized by listing their essential elements in the following table. Neither model contains elaboration (which might introduce nonessential conflict) beyond its most fundamental elements.

Elements of the Scientific Method	Elements of the Doctrine of Christ
1. formulate a problem.*	1. repent.*
2. state (guess) an hypothesis or law.	2. believe in Christ.
3. observe objective, reproducible, material-universe facts, i.e., collect evidence.	3. become as a little child (humble and teachable by God) and be baptized.
4. organize and interpret the facts and deduce patterns and connections.	4. receive fire and the Holy Ghost as ostensible-step proof that Christ is.
5. draw a tentative conclusion about consistency between the hypothesis or law and the evidence.	5. become (remain) as a little child, continue to receive direction and guidance, eventually receive salvation.
Key : * a sufficient knowledge for this step is assumed.	

An argument that essential conflict exists between *conclusions* obtained by the two methods is impossible to support because of the following four fundamental, inherent limitations of science.

\- - - - -

(1) As was demonstrated in Chapter 5, a conclusion in science that some theory, law, or principle is valid is always no better than tentative. And what conflict may be regarded as *essential* on the basis of merely *tentative* knowledge? Even if conclusions of science and Christianity conflict, no such difference can be regarded as an "essential conflict" because scientific theories, laws, and principles are not conclusive and essential but merely tentative and contingent. Such a basis cannot support any conclusion except a tentative, conditional one, just the kind of conclusion we, like the ancient Greeks, are trying to avoid. This inherent, fundamental limitation of science is sufficiently broad and compelling to eliminate essential conflict between science and Christianity-at-large and religion-in-general except where some principle or property of religious dogma involves material-based facts or specified relationships of a mathematical nature that can be *disproved* by science or mathematics, as medieval-Church dogma was.

On the other hand, many religions including Christian ones are no more definite or certain than science in their conclusions so that, although essential conflict with science is eliminated, uncertainty and confusion in these religions is inherent due to the same cause: lack of an adequate truth criterion.

\- - - - -

(2) In Chapter 10 we described Gödel's theorem and the Löwenheim-Skolem theorem. The latter theorem *requires* that any logicomathematical-based theory, law, or paradigm must be represented by many, divergent, alternative theories, laws, or paradigms all equally consistent with the axioms and facts that are their common basis. That is, no logicomathematical-based theory, law, or paradigm can be regarded as uniquely valid because equally-legitimate, highly-divergent alternatives are always possible and expected. While proof of this theorem restricts its rigorous application

to logicomathematical-based systems, this restriction is not drastically limiting since modern scientific theories and laws have such bases, e.g., Newtonian and quantum mechanics and relativity. And I assert the principle, but not the proof, applies for systems having other bases as well since many systems consistent with a given basis can always be imagined.[1] Consequently, unique consistency with the facts should never be expected of a scientific system. Thus we assert, with Löwenheim-Skolem proof for some cases, that *consistency is an inadequate truth criterion.* Many, highly-divergent systems are equally consistent with the same facts and all must be correct according to the traditional truth criterion of science (not invoking Ockham's razor or some other additional, arbitrary constraint). As a result, illustrated in Chapter 10 for quantum mechanics, specification of a unique mathematical and scientific system that defines the fundamental nature of reality is confusing, frustrating, and impossible. Lack of an adequate truth criterion and the existence of many different but equivalent systems inhibit progress in science because science cannot conclusively establish the truth of any unique system, now or ever, except perhaps when omniscience is obtained.

- - - - -

(3) A fundamental problem arises in science with its "ever-growing lists of candidate" theories, laws, and principles. The number of possible candidate laws is indefinitely large and no person or group is likely to ever imagine them all; over time, the list of candidates grows as more are conceived and recognized. But limitations in time, resources, and interest restrict careful testing to a limited number of candidates.

An essential question therefore arises. How are the most promising candidates to be selected and tested? Failing to select and test a correct candidate can absolutely stop progress for decades or centuries by not displacing or eliminating misdirected thinking and effort. Progress can continue only when the correct candidate is finally tested and tentatively adopted, providing tentative insight necessary to further tentative progress. An example presented in Chapter 3 describes how failure to discover and adopt non-Euclidian geometry limited progress for two millennia.

Unfortunately, there exists no scientific principle(s) by which one can be assured that a best candidate is contained on any list because science provides no adequate truth criterion. Scientific inquiry naïvely assumes a good theory or law may be guessed and focuses on the testing and refinement of it. But a substantial difficulty lies, first, in guessing good candidate theories or laws and, second, in guessing which, if any, should be tested. How is successful guessing to be accomplished? Guessing by its nature is a process of chance or luck (or knack). Is rigorous, objective science to depend on a lucky guess? A best-candidate theory is not necessarily correct and neither is one carefully selected by probability logic (in both cases partially consistent with everything we think we know), for many different candidates must agree with the same facts and syllogisms. And neither is one necessarily valid when selected using Ockham's razor as an additional constraint.

In view of an indefinite number of candidates, limited resources for testing, and human proclivity to be interested in and choose what scientists believe are the most likely or promising ones (i.e., scientific fashion), only these are tested. But, on what basis is a candidate theory or law to be regarded as likely or promising? The only natural basis for scientific judgement is one's current paradigm and the intuition it provides. This current paradigm was successfully tested against many facts and that leads one to expect it is at least near the truth. In other words, a person tends to assume that a new paradigm likely to be correct is similar to a previous one that isn't. Without such an assumption, candidate laws must be arbitrarily selected and tested with no indication, either in advance or later, that any is correct since only false (inconsistent) candidates or *no* answers are sometimes conclusive in science. But in choosing a candidate similar to an earlier, "nearly correct" one we are invoking a certain *logical circularity or self reference*. No known, *a priori* principle indicates a true law should be similar to a previous, "nearly correct" one. Indeed, the Löwenheim-Skolem theorem supports an opposite conclusion. Nor does any known principle imply that any selected sequence of testing is superior to an arbitrary one. That a candidate is established to be wrong generally provides no fundamental insight as to how wrong it is or, usually, even why it is wrong. For this reason no fundamental scientific theory or law is systematically discovered – it must simply be guessed.

That no specific method for scientific discovery exists was indicated by Richard Feynman in his 1965 Nobel-Prize Lecture when he stated

> I think equation guessing might be the best method to proceed to obtain the laws for the part of physics which is presently unknown. Yet, ... I think the problem is not to find the *best* or most efficient method to proceed to a discovery, but to find any method at all.[2] (the italics are Feynman's)

Lack of an adequate method or of an adequate truth criterion is not merely philosophical. It is a severe, inherent, essential, fundamental, and insurmountable flaw in science and most, if not all, philosophy as they are presently known and used.

While (2) and (3) follow directly from (1), a fourth limitation of science is independent of (1), (2), and (3) because even an adequate truth criterion would not necessarily remove this limitation.

- - - - -

(4) Science cannot establish truth or a correct description of reality because it is fatally circular in its reasoning due to a cause already indicated but not yet analyzed. We now describe and analyze this cause and justify this claim.

Any philosophy, system of belief, or paradigm may be non-fatally flawed. In principle, a flaw can be corrected using observed evidence. For this reason many believe that science, even containing many errors and even error in its starting information, is capable of eventually discovering and establishing truth.

The realm or domain of a philosophy, system of belief, or paradigm is comprehensive only if it regards all evidence presented by reality. If it does, then any error in paradigm may eventually be corrected by revision of the paradigm as motivated and guided by evidence. But, if a paradigm's realm is not comprehensive the paradigm can forever remain incorrect and incomplete because of its failure to consider important evidence of influence on the paradigm reality to which the paradigm is blind. Possible corrections of errors in such a paradigm remain invisible when evidence that could reveal the presence and nature of errors and guide their corrections is not considered in the paradigm. Such a paradigm is fatally flawed.

By a paradigm we accept evidence as valid or reject it as invalid. This function of a paradigm, defining the evidence it considers, is its most fundamental one. It controls scope or range of truth that can be "reached" in or *awareness* of the paradigm. Science begins, even previous to the scientific method listed in the above table, by limiting consideration to objective, reproducible, lowest-common-denominator, value-neutral, material-universe facts. Subjective or nonmaterial-universe evidence is deliberately excluded in science, as illustrated in the first of the above pair of graphics. Science necessarily contemplates only the material universe as represented and used in an ideal, imaginary, artificial "external world." And even objective, material facts are disallowed if they are not regularly reproduced whenever outward physical conditions that cause them are reproduced. That is, even valid, objective, material evidence is disallowed in science if it is rare and not reproduced by reproducing external, material facts.

Science (but not necessarily scientists) and materialism assume that the material universe contains the full scope of reliable evidence presented by reality and that the scientific paradigm thus considers all reliable evidence. But no justification supporting this assumption is provided. It is a necessary expedient adopted to preserve purity (reliability) of the scientific database from possible contamination by nonobjective, prejudiced claims. Then, materialists believe the universe is wholly material because that is what they assume. This belief is therefore an arbitrary definition, dogma, or fundamental element of a creed as well as an assumption. Materialists must reject nonmaterial-universe evidence as unreal and unnecessary or abandon their paradigm, i.e., admit the evidence they consider is not sufficient and their paradigm is fatally flawed because it ignores evidence possibly essential to correction of error in their paradigm. Such a flaw is the most fundamental and fatal kind, a flaw at the most basic level of a paradigm. If science must consider important nonmaterial-universe evidence to understand the material universe and physical cause-and-effect phenomena, science and materialism cannot be "self-correcting," as many have supposed, and are instead circular-logic traps wherein evidence is incomplete and the paradigm, by self-constriction, is forever unaware of evidence by which a paradigm flaw may be recognized and corrected.

And subjective, nonmaterial-universe facts *are* required to understand material-universe cause-and-effect phenomena. Material-universe evidence itself is subjective, as indicated in Book I and Chapters 10 and 11. Repeating a thought of Chapters 2 and 11, some objective, material-universe facts and phenomena and their cause-and-effect relationships transcend the material universe because subjective, human values and volition based thereon influence and control human behavior and, consequently, many material-universe facts and processes. Laws and theories pertaining to such facts are therefore incomplete or wholly undiscovered when it is assumed they are based exclusively on the material universe.

- - - - -

Christian belief does consider subjective, nonmaterial-universe evidence as well as objective, material evidence, i.e., Christianity holds a total-universe-range of awareness. But subjective, nonmaterial facts generally hold higher priority in religion than objective, material facts. In Christianity, recognition of meaning depends on value-based discernment and feeling. And the most valuable and certain knowledge of all, knowing Christ, is received personally and subjectively by "fire and the Holy

Ghost." Consequently, while a Christian can, in principle, fully understand both materialism and Christianity, a materialist cannot understand Christianity or Christian meaning because evidence of these and their truth criterion, feeling and subjectively knowing, inherently lie outside the awareness of science or materialism.

Proposition Number 15: **Even without an adequate truth criterion, unavoidable conflict between the elaborate, rigid dogma of the medieval Church and observation and deduction of Galileo and others disproved the dogma. A conflict between science and religion (i.e., that dogma) and a scientific revolution thus arose. Some hold the notion that this conflict reveals an essential flaw in religion but no such flaw or conflict is evident in a careful comparison of the scientific method and the doctrine of Christ. Instead, severe flaws are found to be inherent in only the scientific method.**

An Adequate Truth Criterion

Even though both philosophies, paradigms, or systems of belief (both models we consider) are intended to give a correct account of the facts, an accurate vision of reality, and a true description of the universe, a comparison of the two shows scientific and Christian belief to be very different in nature, application, and the facts and knowledge they consider or of which they are aware. In fact, they are so different that, on a superficial level, no essential conflict is found between the two paradigms. Neither are they mutually exclusive. The two philosophies focus on different primary- or preferred-evidence realms, science on objective, material-universe facts and Christianity on subjective, nonmaterial-universe facts. While the elaborate dogma of the medieval Church provided plenty of material-fact details that could be tested and conclusively disproved by science, the doctrine of Christ does not. Christ's response to Pilate's question was "My kingdom is not of this world."[3] While Christianity is cognizant of the material universe, its awareness is focused primarily on other elements of the total universe. Nevertheless, as one author has observed,

> It was not merely a moral and social revolution that Jesus proclaimed; it is clear from a score of indications that his teaching had a political bent of the plainest sort. It is true that he said his kingdom was not of this world, that it was in the hearts of men and not upon the throne; but it is equally clear that wherever and in what measure his kingdom was set up in the hearts of men, the outer world would be in that measure revolutionized and made new.[4]

And this same author continues,

> In view of what he plainly said, is it any wonder that all who were rich and prosperous felt a horror of strange things, a swimming of their world at his teaching? Perhaps the priests and the rulers and the rich men understood him better than his followers. ... In the white blaze of this kingdom of his there was to be no property, no privilege, no pride and precedence; ... Is it any wonder that the priests realized that between this man and themselves there was no choice but that he or priestcraft should perish? ... Is it any wonder that to this day this Galilean is too much for our small hearts?[5]

While the doctrine of Christ largely ignores material facts and leaves any detailed treatment of these to another paradigm such as science, Christianity does influence and cause material facts, as the forgoing quotations suggest. Therefore, on a deeper than superficial level, the material universe is not fully understood when subjective evidence is ignored. A person may use either science or Christianity or both together to seek a vision of reality. But to understand the total universe or even the material one, subjective evidence must be considered, for humans are not inert, unobtrusive observers but subjective causes of material and other facts in the universe.

Important differences between science and Christianity are centered in necessary exclusion from science of claims of influence by Omniscience and Omnipotence and essential inclusion of these in Christianity as divine power discretely guiding an individual, as taught in the doctrine of Christ. That is, receiving ostensible knowledge of Christ by "fire and the Holy Ghost" is what the Christian seeks[6] as personal, subjective knowledge of absolute truth and continuing guidance thereafter.[7]

It should by now be clear that science is incapable of establishing truth in the form of a theory or law or system thereof for lack of an adequate truth criterion. Nonetheless, science has power to disprove false theories, laws, and concepts. I do not emphasize the former point in a "best-case-scenario" account of science in the next chapter, preferring that the reader reach his or her own conclusions. Nor do I emphasize (a) contrast between materialist-atheist dogma inevitably based on "indubitable" scientific knowledge and the actual tentative nature of scientific knowledge or (b) the frequent companionship of priestcraft and corrupted Christianity.

Knowledge must start somewhere; something must be allowed to be known.[8] This claim begs the questions "Where does knowledge start?" or "What should one allow to be known?" Choice of one's answer leads directly to science, to Christian belief, or to some other paradigm, any of which may thereby be initially or subsequently selected. That is, questions one chooses utilizing knowledge one chooses lead to a preferred philosophy. The complex nature of this process due to many simultaneous choices is avoided in the doctrine of Christ by its suggestion of initial belief and the associated question regarding its validity. Not only does the doctrine of Christ remove confusion by suggesting both initial belief and its important question, it claims that its Author has both power and desire to conclusively answer this question and confirm verity and viability of the philosophy, if one trusts God. In contrast, science can be paralysis in a fatally flawed paradigm, but only trust in humans, primarily one's self,[9] is required.

In science, consistency is the principal truth criterion. While consistency is necessary, it is insufficient to establish absolute truth, as the ancient Greeks realized[10] and as we have demonstrated. All ancient, still-active philosophies are, by now, consistent in their own concepts and terms, even those fatally flawed. But consistency provides no better than relative knowledge. Only in comparing the scientific method to the doctrine of Christ are logical flaws of science so notable, because the doctrine of Christ is unique in most, if not all, philosophy in (i) being free of logical flaws, (ii) addressing a complete domain of evidence, and (iii) using a viable, absolute-truth criterion.[11] Christian inquiry via the doctrine of Christ simultaneously contemplates Christ and invokes God's offer of help to provide a conclusive, external, absolutely-true *yes* or *no* answer regarding Christ and, therefore, ultimate cause and the nature of reality. A *yes* answer, in its intense feelings of peace and joy and personal, subjective knowing of Christ, is the ostensible-proof truth criterion of the Christian paradigm, the doctrine of Christ, in stark contrast to no adequate truth criterion in science and all lower, if not all other, philosophy.

Only when evidence and method are held to be absolute may logical deductions and understanding based thereon also be held as absolute. But even if objective, factual evidence is regarded as universally valid and absolutely true by a materialist, it is not necessarily so held by a Christian because of incompleteness of experience and discrete acts of God, e.g., miracles, not considered. Likewise, even if revelation of knowledge by fire and the Holy Ghost is held as absolute truth by a Christian, it is not so regarded by a materialist who rejects such evidence as personal, subjective, not reproducible, and not material-based. Neither kind of evidence is *generally* regarded as absolute. Both systems are self-consistent (ignoring the logical flaws of science already mentioned) and both or some combination of the two are philosophically sound (continuing to ignore limitations in science). While science requires a belief that consistency, perhaps with Ockham's razor and/or other additional constraints, is a sufficient truth criterion, Christianity requires a belief and trust that absolute truth may be established to an individual by the power of God.

Both science (materialism) and Christianity are higher philosophy as they acknowledge that universal truth exists and seek to discover it. But positivism which denies absolute truth (while denoting material facts as absolute!) is not. Because Christianity encompasses a broader awareness and a meaning-richer scope than science, a Christian may focus on higher elements whose essence and significance are invisible to a materialist, exclusively focused on material facts, who denies that higher elements and associated meaning exist or contain value. Consequently, Christianity provides rich, absolutely-certain feelings and *subjectively* communicated conclusions while materialism rigorously addresses questions but only on a relative and tentative material level wherein material facts are *objectively* established. In the language of religion, such ultimate bases are founded on choice or faith, either in the material and one's self or in God.

A microcosm of such opposing views of reality is provided by the exchange between the Apostle Paul and the Roman Governor Festus. Festus, to whom Paul's account of his conversion on the road to Damascus seemed unrealistic, accused Paul in the words: "... much learning doth make thee mad" to which Paul affirmed the reality of his experience and his view by responding "I am not mad."[12]

Vision of Absolute-level Terrain

To some, the conflict between the scientific discoveries of Galileo and the Aristotelian-Ptolemaic-medieval-Church dogma support the notion that religion is false. Such a conclusion arises from the reasonable-at-first-glance view that a disagreement between two visions indicates that at least one of the two visions is incorrect. And such a conclusion must hold if a conflict occurs in a matter which is definitely and commonly understood in a single system or in both of two systems. But remember, methodology including evidence differs between the two models we consider. For this reason, matters are not commonly understood in the two systems.

The evidence of a paradigm must fit the paradigm. A scientist may think he or she, like Galileo, has found a contradiction in Christian dogma, but the supposed contradiction is almost invariably between the method and evidence of science and a conclusion or belief of Christianity based on larger scopes of method and evidence. In any case, what kind of contradiction is proven by merely tentative and contingent science? Just the questionable, inadequate kind we are seeking to avoid herein. And, because value-based meaning is invisible to science, the materialist using only his or her science is unable to perceive and comprehend the primary evidence in Christianity and its function, utility, and power in the Christian paradigm.

Any conflict between science and Christianity is between methodologies. The perceived realities or scopes of awareness of the two systems diverge as a matter of methodology – as a choice of what kinds of facts to accept and questions to consider in a preconceived nature of reality. A follower of one system reaches different conclusions utilizing different evidence and testing than a follower of the other and neither can provide convincing proof to the other of the superiority or inferiority of either system as a consequence of the different preconceptions. Indeed, they can barely communicate any complex concepts for lack of a common-primary-facts basis.

Conflict between science and religion thus originates in the ultimate basis of personal taste, choice, or expression of personal priority because choice of paradigm dictates the evidence preferred. Some would describe such an ultimate basis as absolute – in Weyl's egocentric sense (Chapter 4) it is. But not in the sense we seek – in the sense of "universal and absolute truth" or "conclusively demonstrated to universally apply."

Paradigm, philosophy, or system of belief is embraced by individual agency or choice. Because paradigm gives pertinence to the facts, cogency to the argument, realism to the vision, and power to the meaning, one's choice of paradigm closes a logical circle that includes chosen preconceptions that support one another.

On a relative level, in contrast to an absolute level, different conclusions do not necessarily result from one set of evidence or one philosophy being right and another wrong. Festus was correct according to his vision of reality while Paul had truly seen a light and heard a voice according to his. Were both right? Each conclusion is justified in its own system, and yet an apparent contradiction remains.

To determine which is right we must appeal to absolute truth and real reality to break logical circularity. While two genuinely (as opposed to apparently) conflicting conclusions may each be justified relative to its own logically circular system, only one at most may be correct in an absolutely correct system, in real reality. How does one discover and identify absolute truth? Or, more generally, how does one select an absolutely correct paradigm, an absolutely valid philosophy, an absolutely true system of belief? Here I will provide one hint. To discover absolute truth one must appeal to The Absolute or to Omniscience Himself. Only such a One who operates on an absolute level has a vision of that terrain.

A careful examination of the universe utilizing a limited methodology – science that allows only tentative, contingent, relative, circular-logic-supported conclusions about arbitrarily-guessed theories and selected facts pertaining to how questions – addresses issues on only a tentative, contingent, relative level. It can not take us to absolutely demonstrated truth regarding a *who*, *what*, *why* or any other kind of question. Without guidance by Omniscience the discovery of absolute truth is endlessly uncertain and hopelessly futile. Paul found absolute truth because he received it from One who understands it. Christ invites each of us to do the same.

Inadequate Illumination in Induction

A prominent mathematician-philosopher[13] rejected Christianity because, among other claims he objected to, the Bible predicts that some living at the time of Christ would remain alive until Christ comes again.[14] John the Beloved was one given this promise and others were also.[15] Yet everyone knows that a man lives no longer than a hundred-or-so years. This mathematician-philosopher atheist was not alone in rejecting Biblical prophecy; even some theologians also reject it.[16] But what principle of common sense or of science supports rejection of the predicted long life of John? Here we see a self-imposed blindness in the attitude of some, a failure to recognize a different-paradigm possibility: the miraculous.

The usually not even expressed argument against John living so long is based on induction. The principle of induction, i.e., going directly from the specific to the general, assumes a simple consistency that has long been associated with science. It was thought by Bacon and others that mere accumulation of knowledge led to scientific understanding through ever more general and obvious laws inferred by induction. A simple example of induction is provided by observation of swans. When only white swans are observed it becomes clear by induction that all swans are white. But, of course, we know this conclusion is incorrect because we know some swans are black. A careful scientist who doesn't trust induction would prefer to say only that the swans observed were white on the observed side(s).

Induction as it is now used in hard science is more carefully illustrated as follows: if 1,000 or 10,000, or many more identical atoms of a certain species all show the same behavior, then it is supposed by induction that another such atom will also. Yet, even this more carefully-stated principle of induction sometimes fails. One could describe all helium atoms as identical. In many properties they are and behavior related to these properties appears to be uniform. But one property differs. Helium atoms occur in two *isotopes*. One has atomic weight of about three and is called helium-3 (two protons, one neutron, and two electrons). The other has atomic weight of about four and is called helium-4 (two protons, two neutrons, and two electrons). Both species are recognized as helium atoms because of their mostly common properties. Yet, behaviors of the different isotopes are sometimes different. When sufficiently cooled, helium gas condenses into liquid helium, a process first accomplished in 1908 by Dutch physics professor Heike Kamerlingh-Onnes (1853-1926) at Leiden. For liquefying helium, the last gas to be liquefied, Kamerlingh-Onnes received the 1912 Rumford medal from the Royal Society of London and the 1913 Nobel Prize in physics. At the low temperatures accessible using liquid helium as a coolant, he discovered, in 1911, superconductivity of low-temperature metals (itself a novel process not suggested by induction[17]) with Mercury the first superconducting metal measured.

Thereafter it was discovered that liquid helium exists in two types, helium I and II.[18] Helium I is liquid helium that forms below 4.26 K (i.e., 4.26 degrees Kelvin above absolute zero temperature[19]). Helium II is a different form of liquid helium that occurs below 2.2 K and has properties radically different from those of any other known material including helium I. Helium II conducts heat eight-hundred-times better than *solid* copper. It is a *superfluid* possessing little viscosity, about one-thousandth that of hydrogen *gas* at normal temperature and hydrogen is the least viscous of all *gases*. Once a superfluid is caused to flow around a loop and then left undisturbed it will long continue such flow. And in a container of another configuration helium II superfluid spontaneously forms and maintains a flow of superfluid rising upward from its level inside a closed duct (e.g., a vertical test tube) and falling down the outside into a pool of helium II at lower level.[18] In contrast, helium I is not a superfluid and has properties best described as "usual" for liquids. Russian physicist Lev Davidovich Landau (1908-1968) developed a quantum-mechanical description of liquid helium II in 1941 and improved it in 1947. In the 1950s he studied the helium-3 isotope and predicted it has quite unexpected properties at very low temperatures compared to those of helium-4 and other substances. For these studies Landau received the Nobel Prize in physics in 1962. This history suggests how induction may unexpectedly fail due to a subtle difference that causes no noticeable distinction before an unexpected one is encountered.

While *mathematical* induction may provide a conclusive proof in mathematics when the basis for the proof is fully defined and sure, *logical* induction never provides a conclusive proof in physics. Just because something has never been observed or imagined is no reason to exclude it from consideration.[20]

If we choose to believe in miracles we can simply say that induction fails when a miracle occurs. It seems a more common cause of failure of induction is, rather than a miracle, some subtle, obscure, otherwise unnoticed difference, like the difference between helium-3 and -4 atoms, that eventually imposes an obvious one. Denying the possibility of miracles precludes, so it would seem, the possibility that the Apostle John could have lived anomalously long, contrary to induction. And denial of the possibility of miracles is often tacitly or overtly adopted with the scientific method. (It is here notable that some materialists, unable to conclusively establish any universal laws by means of their own philosophy, presume nevertheless to establish absolute conclusions by force of personality and even presume to prohibit conclusions embraced in other philosophies!) Indeed, by assumption, miracles are dismissed out of hand in science (but not necessarily by scientists) because not being *reproducible* by recreation of outward physical conditions they fail to qualify as valid scientific facts. And induction, by its nature, contains a similar deficiency. For among a group of nonidentical objects, such as a group of men, who can say what unnoticed, obscure difference might exist or what effect it might have? Using the scientific method a problem of an anomalously long life may be properly stated and many possible hypotheses formulated corresponding to the scriptural account. Then we must collect and examine the evidence and search for a contradiction with some observed or deduced fact in order to reach a tentative conclusion. While I have not learned of any sighting of John the Beloved, that doesn't mean one has not happened

– I don't know the identity of every person I see. That John hasn't been observed is readily explained if he assumed a state of anonymity. In any case, absence of a sighting cannot be regarded as conclusive, contradictory evidence. And neither is the fact that modern man is not known to live so long contradictory, because John may be unique. Without contradictory evidence, what is the basis for rejection of the hypothesis? There is none according to the scientific method. (Rigor may be applied on both sides of an argument, not just on one side which pretends to exclusively invoke rigor.)

Then perhaps someone has brought a preconception or personal bias to their use of the scientific method. Perhaps someone has adopted a category-two student attitude. We are cautioned against exactly this pitfall in considering miracles in C. S. Lewis' oft-quoted comment: "What we learn from experience depends on the kind of philosophy we bring to experience." If we believe induction cannot fail and we therefore do not believe in miracles, we shall surely discover none. The experience or evidence or realm of reality we discover depends on and is controlled by the philosophy we adopt. Surely no unreasonable fact should be admitted as reliable evidence. But "reasonable" is determined by choice of philosophy.

In belief, personal choice has, of course, controlling influence. One believes or does not on the basis of his or her choice. Scientific evidence and theory or a personal spiritual experience may be cited, but the ultimate cause of belief or disbelief is deliberate choice because it is by choice that we allow and accept the evidence. In the case of John's long life, the choice is apparently to believe or not to believe in a miracle. That translates directly into the choice to believe or not to believe in He who performs miracles. This choice is equivalent to the one eventually encountered in pursuing answers to most, if not all, ultimate questions.

And one must be careful in examining evidence not to dismiss important understanding due to paradigm paralysis. If we are locked into a narrow view that restricts awareness, such as a purely scientific one, we see only the evidence allowed by that view and fail to properly consider any other vision of reality. Herein lies the danger of the category-two-student attitude whether it belongs to the scientist who understands all the facts but not the meaning or the devout Christian or other person of faith who has a narrow, restricted view. To obtain a broadly-valid view one must become aware of and seek the highest, richest levels of *understanding*, those of absolute truth and meaning imparted by fire and the Holy Ghost. Denying that such a high level exists or refusing the invitation to use it traps one in a lower, limiting paradigm.

Pilgrimages in Search of Truth

Science does not perceive the spiritual because scientists choose to ignore and dismiss such things (in their science – their personal belief is another matter). That does not mean these things do not exist or are unimportant. Even a materialist should not be so foolish as to deny the existence of God, thereby going beyond any tentative conclusion justified by science and, in effect, assuming omniscience and thus pretending to be the Person being denied.[21] Honest application of the scientific method does not lead to megalomania. On the contrary, if one is aware, he or she is continually reminded in this method of the tentative nature of any scientific theory or law. Science and atheism are not connected by any direct intellectual relationship except a pretended one; they are instead polar opposites despite what atheists would have us believe. The qualities that seem to me to be closely connected to atheism are ignorance and pride, the former in not understanding limitations of scientific method or human knowledge in general and the latter in the category-two-student vanity of presuming that one is knowledgeable.

Hermann Weyl, one of the greatest mathematicians of the twentieth century,[22] has lauded the experimental scientist for "his struggle to wrest *interpretable facts* from an unyielding Nature who knows so well how to meet our theories with a decisive *No* – or an inaudible *Yes*."[23] Weyl is exactly correct with respect to only *no* answers being audible in science (Chapter 5). But I think he stopped short of indicating an equally important point. That is, the difficulty with *yes* answers does not lie with "unyielding Nature," which is merely what it is. The difficulty lies with philosophy which, in the instance of science and in other cases, cannot provide more than tentative theories and laws. In science tentative theories and laws are all there is, a limitation fundamentally inherent to this philosophy. And because that fact doesn't support the certain, conclusive affectation of the materialist-atheist, he or she fails to mention (or recognize?) such limitation. But neither sticking one's head in sand nor clinging to a romantic notion makes the limitation go away. This limitation remains forever or until one becomes omniscient, whichever occurs first.

In contrast to atheism, Christianity is connected to intelligence and understanding in a unique relationship described by the doctrine of Christ. This doctrine alone provides continuing access to Omniscience, to absolute truth, to certain, audible *yes* as well as *no* answers. And this doctrine alone provides comprehension of deepest meaning and associated feeling.

Science and Christianity employ different methodologies, but both seek to discover truth. If pure science and pure religion are pilgrimages in search of truth, there should be no conflict between them. Indeed, elements of the scientific method are recommended in scripture[24] and have been used to great advantage in pursuing religious questions as well as questions in science. Conflict may exist within truth for it is true that conflict does exist. Conflict may exist between parties supporting different or apparently different truths. But conflict does not occur between elements of truth. By definition,[25] truth is knowledge of the way things were and are and are to be, i.e., knowledge of the real reality. Either something is or it is not; there is no conflict here once we determine that which is.[26]

A common mistake of materialists is to bring their objective, lowest-common-denominator, material-universe-only evidence to an examination of religion. But a religious paradigm is not based on this evidence; Christianity is based on meaning that transcends objective facts. Materialists, then, usually don't perceive and consider a religious paradigm because they don't get beyond their own. To test validity beyond the scientific realm, to understand a different vision of reality, significant revision of science is required, described in the next section in a derivation of the doctrine of Christ from the scientific method. This revision so fundamentally changes the scope of evidence and methodology that a nearly complete independence exists between the scientific method and the doctrine of Christ. But while Christianity with its total-universe evidence includes science, science with only material-universe evidence does not include Christianity. A scientist need not believe in Christ to practice science; but he or she can believe and still practice equally well. A Christian does not have to be a scientist; but he or she can be. A materialist-atheist cannot be a Christian until he or she abandons materialism/atheism.

Scientific method and Christian faith are sufficiently different that these two paradigms may generally be utilized independently of one another. Utilizing both provides useful, complementary benefits beyond that obtained utilizing either one alone. The "purifying rite" of renouncing religion[27] in order to properly practice science indicates a lack of understanding of the two philosophies. In particular, it indicates an ignorance of inherent limitations of science and of a complementary capability of Christianity to transcend these limitations in the discovery of truth and meaning. An exclusive focus on the meticulous, rigorous, scientific examination of only objective, external, lowest-common-denominator, material facts leads to a denial of meaning and an ignorance of awareness of real reality because important facts, the most meaningful ones, fall outside the domain-of-data of science. Science can't take us to meaning because the scientific paradigm is unaware of its realm. Nor do some materialists want to see that the actual "tentative and contingent" nature of science and the supposed "rigorous and conclusive" nature they believe it has are mutually exclusive.

We can't see when we won't look, like one of the foremost Aristotelians at Pisa, Giulio Libri, who wouldn't look through Galileo's telescope because he was afraid of what he might see. A scientist says "seeing is believing;" a Christian says "we must believe before we can see." Both are correct. So do both.

That is, Christianity with its total-universe facts and scope contains, as a subset of itself, all the facts and the full scope of science. Consequently, science does not conflict with Christianity. But claims of materialists that the material is all there is and that complete understanding of the material universe will eventually provide a complete understanding of reality are naïve because reality extends far beyond the material.

We have sought some kind of scientific test of Christianity (page 385) and instead found a Christian test of science (materialism). Namely, that by the doctrine of Christ one may establish for one's self that the universe extends beyond the material and that the material does not encompass all reality as the materialist supposes.

A Modified Scientific Method

It is useful to derive the doctrine of Christ from the scientific method. The object here is not to justify either science or the doctrine of Christ but to clarify methodological differences between them. The derivation requires three steps, all of which involve *additions* to the scientific method while no subtractions occur.

(a) In the scientific method a law or theory is disproved and discarded if it is found to contradict the evidence. No strict statement is made in the method itself regarding the scope of the evidence but it is the general practice that the evidence utilized in scientific inquiry consists of and only of all objective, reproducible, lowest-common-denominator, material facts. If we included other evidence we would hear a call of "foul" from scientists. But, suppose we ignore such a call and include other evidence anyway, namely, personal, subjective experience, in addition to objective, lowest-common-denominator facts. The resulting modified scientific method may then be *personally* used to disprove (discard) a law or theory if it is contradictory to the evidence consisting of objective, reproducible facts *and* subjective experience. With this change, a fundamental methodological conflict between science and religion is removed, as is limitation in material-universe-only scope. One may then use this modified scientific method with total-universe evidence to understand total-universe reality.

(b) However, this modified scientific method is still very far from the doctrine of Christ. What is still missing? Only Omniscience, only everything. In addition to definite *no* answers leading to discarding a false candidate law or principle, to establish absolute truth and real reality, to select the correct candidate law, we must obtain absolute *yes* answers, answers impossible to obtain by the scientific method. Until we obtain absolute-level *yes* answers, the only adequate truth criterion, any candidate law or conclusion remains at best tentative and uncertain. Moreover, without help we may never even consider a correct law or conclusion as a candidate; we certainly can never imagine all possibilities, as Urban VIII recognized (Chapter 6). Only when we develop a trust in and seek to be led by Omniscience, only when One who operates on an absolute level and is familiar with that terrain provides definite guidance, only then may we be certain that absolute truth and real reality are reliably established to us. And the most important and meaningful absolute truth and real-reality fact we learn, promised by fire and by the Holy Ghost, is that Jesus is the Christ, the Son of God and Savior of the world. Because neither Omniscience nor omniscience is contemplated in the scientific method, we have fully superceded that method when we recognize subjective facts and appeal to Omniscience as matters of methodology.

(c) While we have nearly derived the doctrine of Christ from the scientific method, a few "minor" requirements remain. In order to access Omniscience, in order to receive fire and the Holy Ghost, we must abide by stated requirements. What are they? Repentance, belief in Christ, becoming like a little child – humble and teachable – and submitting to baptism. Upon meeting these requirements the promised gift is received. While these details may seem minor, they are not. They hold great significance and meaning. They are His way. They strengthen and prepare us in ways not visible at the outset. They condition us to trust God and to understand meaning. Yet, simple though they are, they can be great obstacles.

Obstacles to Accepting the Doctrine of Christ

Even ignoring possible conflict between science and religion, significant obstacles to embracing the doctrine of Christ exist. The scientific method is not restrictive of personal qualities or behavior in the user. The user is free to apply science whenever and in whatever manner he or she chooses, to be his or her own person, or even to aspire to be *the* person.[9] In contrast, the doctrine of Christ imposes personal-behavioral standards: repentance (obedience), belief in Christ, becoming humble and teachable like a little child, and accepting baptism. Are these difficult? No, except for the part about the little child. And, except for the repentance. And, except for the "I'm an intelligent adult very able to think for myself and you can't tell me what to believe!" Humbly following the requirements causes deep and important conditioning in attitude and priority. Just as basic training of a soldier is designed to instill new attitudes and priorities in place of old, undesirable ones, faith in Christ and repentance similarly instill new attitudes and priorities. In this gentle but powerful version of "boot camp," we see our past behavior in new light, feel remorse for past sin, sense a growing appreciation of, need for, and devotion to Christ, and we are influenced by them. He also sees our effort and strengthens us in the right way of our new paradigm. Faith in Christ and repentance are dues we must pay to obtain understanding of meaning. They bring the question of Christ front and center in our awareness. Only in this condition will we receive and properly recognize an answer.

Another potential obstacle is the requirement that one abandon personal rule or personal "rule by reason." Rule by reason still applies, of course, but (initially) it is His reason and His rule that controls beyond the immediate question of "staying in." In the role of subject rather than ruler, the acolyte is no longer the lord of the castle, the discoverer of truth, the dispenser of knowledge, *the* person, but rather the humble follower of the Real Source of Truth, the Real Person. While this position is an accurate depiction of our actual mortal state according to the Christian view, except that each person must define and write his or her own truth, the natural person[9] finds it difficult to accept the "humble servant" part in place of the "ruler" part. Any person who does not embrace the doctrine of Christ retains to him- or her-self all decisions about what is true and what is not true and who is in charge, the desired position of a prideful mortal, but a mortal ignorant of truth required for making the best decisions and choices.[28] If a person accepts the humble servant part and voluntarily gives away his or her independence, the greatest and only gift one has to give, profound conditioning occurs and a deep devotion to Christ is instilled as he or she obtains understanding of meaning.

A third potential obstacle may prove equally fatal to accepting the doctrine of Christ. This is the believing in Christ part – freely and unconditionally believing and trusting in Christ. Such trust and belief includes believing the prophecies of Christ and His prophets, believing Christ has the intent and power to fulfill them, and believing such prophecies and their fulfillments are signs of Christ's work intended to guide His faithful followers to Him. To condemn such events without a careful test, perhaps claiming they are of Beelzebub,[29] is to reject the power of God.[30]

By the time a skeptical scientist utilizing only the scientific method reaches any view in common with the doctrine of Christ, all the battles and their results will be old news! Indeed, his or her belated, after-the-fact acceptance will require the battles and their outcomes as a lowest-common-denominator-factual basis for tentatively (begrudgingly?) intellectually entertaining the possibility that Christ really exists and holds power. The potential consequence of such delay is dramatically described by C. S. Lewis.

> Why is God landing in this enemy occupied world in disguise and starting a sort of secret society to undermine the devil? Why is He not landing in force, invading it? Is it that He is not strong enough? Well, Christians think He is going to land in force; we do not know when. But we can guess why He is delaying. He wants to give us the chance of joining His side freely. ... God will invade. But I wonder whether people who ask God to interfere openly and directly in our world quite realize what it will be like when He does. When that happens, it is the end of the world. When the author walks on to the stage the play is over. God is going to invade, all right; but what is the good of saying you are on His side then, when you see the whole natural universe melting away like a dream and something else – something it never entered your head to conceive – comes crashing in; something so beautiful to some of us and so terrible to others that none of us will have any choice left? For this time it will be God without disguise; something so overwhelming that it will strike either irresistible love or irresistible horror into every creature. It will be too late then to choose your side. There is no use saying you choose to lie down when it has become impossible to stand up. That will not be the time for choosing: it will be the time we discover which side we really have chosen, whether we realized it before or not. Now, today, this moment, is our chance to choose the right side. God is holding back to give us that chance. It will not last forever. We must take it or leave it.[31]

In summary, potential obstacles to accepting the doctrine of Christ are pride, ignorance and confusion caused predominantly by the enemy, and pride.

A Meaning-rich Paradigm

A paradigm imposes its foundation of facts, domain of data, realm of reality, area of awareness, vision of verity, and manifestation of meaning. Therefore, to expand understanding of meaning one must adopt a paradigm that recognizes rich meaning, a meaning-rich paradigm. What criterion do we use to determine that a paradigm is meaning-rich? This question is fundamentally important because while learning more facts provides some incremental increase in knowledge, improving one's paradigm can increase understanding of meaning of all facts already known as well as any new facts learned. Physicist Sir James Jeans observed, "Science advances in two ways, by the discovery of new facts, and by the discovery of mechanisms or systems which account for the facts already known. The outstanding landmarks in the progress of science have all been of the second kind."[32] The outstanding advances in philosophy similarly occur with discovery of a superior system.

Broadening scope of both evidence and correct belief enhances richness of paradigm. Life is not intended to be neutral, uncommitted, nondenominational, and value or consequence free. We are not supposed to be independent, detached agents objectively monitoring the truth at a distance without participating or feeling and finally jumping into the battle of life only when no issue or meaning or truth remains to be determined. In addition to observation of the external, life is meant to be a personal, internal experience in which we choose issues to engage as well as our side and level of engagement. Objectivity and detached observation strictly at a neutral, value-free distance (the conventional, "correct" posture of a philosopher) comprise one paradigm choice as a value-free, nonparticipating, detached, uncommitted, indifferent, objective observer of only an imaginary, artificial, external world. More powerful paradigm choices with respect to discovery of meaning contain alignment, commitment, participation, and devotion. In any case, in the full range of choices there exists, ultimately, no neutral ground; in the view of the One who will judge, objectivity or neutrality is not available.[33] The right choice is the one that leads to truth, deepest comprehension of meaning, and strongest feeling of devotion toward God and all people. As we build our devotion to Christ and are willing to be led by Him, indeed as we are seeking to be led by Him, we will be. He has the power, has expressed the desire, and has extended the invitation. We find the best paradigm, the correct vision of reality, by finding and following Him and His way.

Because this paradigm aligns us with one side in a battle and may pull us to the very front between enemies is no reason to fear it. The front is where the valiant are found. Because a paradigm forces a vision of reality is no reason to avoid embracing one. Choice of paradigm is a means of seeing reality, a means of self declaration, a means of aligning with ideological fellows, a means of generating within ourselves the most important consequence of the mortal experience – the most powerful meaning, manifest in a love for Him who first loved us. With no challenge, what use are courage, valor, and devotion? The choice to believe in Christ is given highest priority in the doctrine of Christ and the highest reward is promised to those who choose Him and His way. Do we think to gain the reward without the cost?

It is sobering that choice of a paradigm forces a view of reality. We had better be right. So be right. Choose a philosophy with a promise that its verity will be ostensibly confirmed. Choose one built on an immovable Rock that is broad and deep, a Rock which cannot be subverted by any agent or force in the universe, a Rock that will forever support those who choose to build upon it. Choose to believe in such a Rock by following invaluable and irrefutable guidance from Him. And, at the last day of the mortal world, at the last moment as His people (the Jews in Jerusalem) are being overrun but can still be saved, He will appear to them and He alone will defeat the enemy and his hordes and vindicate our faith in Him.

Because the choice is so critical, according to Christ's own doctrine, as clarified (I hope) by our considerations here, He has not left us without a light to lead us through the darkness. This light is His life, His example, His love for each individual, the care He extends to us as we respond to Him, the deep comprehension of meaning and personal guidance He offers, the power of God. This light is His doctrine. As we embrace Him, He sustains and enlarges us and confirms the correctness of our chosen paradigm, philosophy, or system of belief. Follow The Light.

And we ever improve in this paradigm by increasing our depth of feeling for Him through effort and devotion in following His example. This path is the way, narrow but straight, by which we recognize true reality, acquire deep understanding of truth and meaning, obtain a feeling of connection, belonging, love for others, and peace, joy, and personal, subjective knowing of Christ which, altogether, are the ostensible proof.

Notes and References for Chapter 16.

[1] This thought has been shared to varying extent by many. In discussing Thomas Kuhn's views on scientific judgement, which he was not the first to embrace, and the role of aesthetics therein, Steven Weinberg stated "Any set of data can be fit by many different theories." (*Facing Up,* Harvard University Press, Cambridge, MA, 2001, 202).

[2] Feynman, Richard P., Nobel Lecture, 11 December 1965, *Nobel Lectures. Physics 1963-1970,* Elsevier, Amsterdam, 1972. Or see http://nobelprize.org/physics/laureates/1965/feynman-lecture.html for the full text.

[3] *Bible,* John 18:36. A similar concept is conveyed in *Doctrine and Covenants* 29:34-35 in which the Lord states

> Wherefore, verily I say unto you that all things unto me are spiritual [eternal], and not at any time have I given unto you [Joseph Smith, Jr.] a law which was temporal [temporary]; neither any man, nor the children of men; neither Adam, your father, whom I created. Behold, I gave unto him that he should be an agent unto himself; and I gave unto him commandment, but no temporal commandment gave I unto him, for my commandments are spiritual; they are not natural nor temporal, neither carnal nor sensual.

While every commandment has its natural or physical aspect, it also has a spiritual aspect pertaining to obedience and devotion. This latter aspect is the important one to us and the Lord as it affects our development of spiritual awareness and fidelity. While the physical world and our natural selves dominate our perception and awareness (until we refine our spiritual sensitivity), this condition is merely a temporary, albeit powerful, distraction to allow us to discover, develop, and test spiritual strength. Without opposition there is neither temptation nor choice. Without temptation and choice there is no growth in strength and devotion. Thus, Satan is allowed temporary dominion in the world. In the eternal world, one's spiritual self (fully unleashed – to dominate over the physical) will control desire and behavior. Thus the need to develop spiritual strength over physical distraction. Christ's interest is in the eventual us, the spiritual rather than the natural, the everlasting rather than the temporary.

[4] Wells, H. G., *The Outline of History,* Volume 1, Garden City Books, Garden City, New York, 1961, 424.

[5] Ibid., 425-426.

[6] While the scientific method may be viewed as a tedious, tentative, fact-by-fact unraveling of the truth of the universe, the doctrine of Christ may be regarded as jumping immediately to the bottom line, the axiomatic base, the philosophical foundation, the power of God, or "fire and the Holy Ghost." Only from this base and the access it provides to Omniscience and Omnipotence may absolutely correct understanding of facts and their meaning be established.

[7] *Book of Mormon,* 2 Nephi 32:5.

[8] See endnote 13 of Chapter 4.

[9] See endnote 3 following the Preface.

[10] See the page-6 quotation of Draper.

[11] See endnote 2 of Chapter 14.

[12] *Bible,* Acts 26:24-25.

[13] Russell, Bertrand, *Why I am not a Christian,* Simon and Schuster, New York, 1957, 16. This book contains a collection of essays and talks by Russell, all of which are well written and useful. Nevertheless, lack of ability to perceive meaning based on Christian principles limited Russell's awareness, such meaning being invisible to an atheist/materialist.

[14] *Bible,* Luke 9:27.

[15] *Bible,* John 21:21-23, *Book of Mormon,* 3 Nephi 28:7-10 (see quotations in the following endnote).

[16] See, for instance, Farrar, Frederic William, *The Life of Christ,* A. L. Burt, New York, n. d., 523-524. "Pointing to him [John], he [Peter] asked, 'Lord, and what shall he do?' The answer checked the spirit of idle curiosity – 'If I will that he tarry till I come, what is that to thee? Follow thou me.' Peter dared ask no more, and the answer – which was intentionally vague – led to the wide misapprehension prevalent in the early church, that John was not to die until Jesus came."

Protestants flirt with logical danger and loss of credibility when they casually reject clear statements in the Bible, like Farrar does here, because the Bible is their only possible source of authority and justification of belief.

The Book of Mormon fully illuminates Christ's prophecy that, as the early church members correctly believed, John would indeed live until the Advent of the Savior. *Book of Mormon,* 3 Nephi 28:1-10 reads

> And it came to pass when Jesus had said these words, he spake unto his [twelve, Book-of-Mormon] disciples, one by one, saying unto them: What is it that ye desire of me, after that I am gone to the Father? And they all spake, save it were three, saying: We desire that after we have lived unto the age of man, that our ministry, wherein thou has called us, may have an end, that we may speedily come unto thee in thy kingdom. And he said unto them: Blessed are ye because ye desired this thing of me; therefore, after that ye are seventy and two years old ye shall come unto me in my kingdom; and with me ye shall find rest. And when he had spoken unto them, he turned himself unto the three, and said unto them: What will ye that I should do unto you, when I am gone unto the Father? And they sorrowed in their hearts, for they durst not speak unto him the thing which they desired. And he said unto them: Behold, I know your thoughts, and ye have desired the thing which John, my beloved, who was with me in my ministry, before that I was lifted up by the Jews, desired of me. Therefore, more blessed are ye, for ye shall never taste of death; but ye shall live to behold all the doings of the Father unto the children of men, even until all things shall be fulfilled according to the will of the Father, when I shall come in my glory with the powers of heaven. And ye shall never endure the pains of death; but when I shall come in my glory ye shall be changed in the twinkling of an eye from mortality to immortality; and then shall ye be blessed in the kingdom of my Father. And again, ye shall not have pain while ye shall dwell in the flesh, neither sorrow save it be for the sins of the world; and all this will I do because of the thing which ye have desired of me, for ye have desired that ye might bring the souls of men unto me, while the world shall stand. And for this cause ye shall have fulness of joy; ...

[17] That superconductivity was completely unexpected is indicated by Kamerlingh-Onnes' reaction. He thought a short circuit had occurred in his apparatus and spent considerable time looking for it before he finally concluded he had discovered a new process: superconductivity.

[18] Lane, Cecil T., *Superfluid Physics,* McGraw-Hill, New York, 1962; Wilks, J., *An Introduction to Liquid Helium,* Oxford University Press, Oxford, 1970.

[19] A temperature *difference* in degrees Kelvin (K) is identical to the same numerical temperature *difference* in degrees Celsius (C). In this regard the K and C temperature scales are identical. The important difference between these two scales is in their respective *zero points*. Pure water freezes at 0 C and 273.2 K. At any temperature the C scale reads 273.2 degrees below the K scale. Thus, 0 K, the absolute zero temperature or lowest temperature attainable, is – 273.2 C.

[20] This statement illustrates the unanticipated nature of all fundamental discoveries and the need to retain an open mind to accept or receive them. As we have already seen and will yet further see, both science and true Christianity reveal reality to be stranger than any fiction so far imagined, with such fiction including popular scientific and orthodox Christian beliefs.

[21] This thought was expressed by Jon Mills in his article "Five Dangers of Materialism" (*Genetic, Social, and General Psychology Monographs* **128** (1), 2002, 5-27) in which he states,

> Cognitive science today is content with explaining consciousness as experimental changes in [material] brain states which can be observed, measured, and quantifiably verified. Observation is one thing, but to make the generalized claim: 'That is all there is!' is epistemically problematic. This positivist account presupposes a 'God's eye' view of reality and thus makes a sweeping metaphysical judgement.

[22] My own assessment and that of Kline, Morris, *Mathematics: The Loss of Certainty,* Oxford University Press, Oxford, 1980, 6. See also, Jaynes, E. T., *Probability Theory,* Cambridge University Press, Cambridge, 2003, 672-674.

[23] Weyl, Hermann, *Gruppentheorie und Quantenmechanik,* Second Edition, S. Hirzel, Leipzig, 1931, 2. English translation by H. P. Robertson, *The Theory of Groups and Quantum Mechanics,* Dover, New York, 1931, xx.

[24] Some examples include *Bible,* John 7:17, James 1:4-5, *Book of Mormon,* Alma 32:27-43, Moroni 10:4-7, and *Doctrine and Covenants* 1:34-39.

[25] *Doctrine and Covenants* 93:24.

[26] Endnote 21 of Chapter 14.

[27] Endnote 34 of Chapter 6.

[28] Science and Christianity differ in method and evidence, illustrated in endnote 3 following the Preface. These differences are often an obstacle to becoming a Christian for a proud scientist or philosopher or ... who desires to independently discover truth. But knowledge without God is merely tentative, providing no understanding of truth or meaning, finally giving the scientist or philosopher or ... nothing to boast of. Nevertheless, each individual writes his or her own future truth. To make it most beneficial we need to follow Christ.

[29] *Bible,* Matthew 12:24, Luke 11:15.

[30] Moroni, to whom God had showed us and our time, wrote in the last two verses of the Book of Mormon,

> ... if ye by the grace of God are perfect in Christ, and *deny not his power*, then are ye sanctified in Christ by the grace of God, through the shedding of the blood of Christ, which is the covenant of the Father unto the remission of your sins, that ye become holy, without spot.
>
> And now I bid unto all farewell. I soon go to rest in the paradise of God, until my spirit and body shall again reunite, and I am brought forth triumphant through the air, to meet you before the pleasing bar of the great Jehovah, the Eternal Judge of both quick and dead. Amen. (italics added)

[31] Lewis, C. S., *Mere Christianity,* Simon & Schuster, New York, 1952, 65-66.

[32] Quoted in Polanyi, Michael, *Science, Faith and Society,* University of Chicago Press, Chicago, 1946, 28.

[33] *Bible,* Revelation 3:15-16. "I know thy works, that thou art neither cold nor hot: I would thou wert cold or hot. So then because thou art lukewarm, and neither cold nor hot, I will spue thee out of my mouth."

Book of Mormon, 1 Nephi 14:10. Nephi's angel-instructor said unto him, "Behold there are save two churches only; the one is the church of the Lamb of God, and the other is the church of the devil; wherefore, whoso belongeth not to the church of the Lamb of God belongeth to that great church, which is the mother of abominations; and she is the whore of all the earth."

17. Meaning

We have examined and compared a scientific and a Christian system of belief, either or both of which may be used in an attempt to understand reality and its description, the truth. We have sought to determine if one or both may be used to understand reality and truth at a deep level of meaning. We have discovered that science leads to many visions of reality, not one, and we recognize that many visions of reality occur in different models of Christianity as well, some variations of which we have considered. Two tasks remain in the comparison of our two models: deduction of (1) which of the two provides the most reliable and superior vision of reality and truth and (2) what meaning this vision contains and reveals.

In Christianity, multiple visions of reality have arisen from different interpretations of the Bible and/or different thinking and motivation among various individuals and groups. Different interpretation, different thinking, and different motivation prevent any consensus agreement. But such agreement would contain little value in any case if it is based on fallible human thinking. Only God is absolute and infallible. And in Christianity one seeks to find and follow an absolute and infallible God. This God condemns a multiplicity of visions. He said "I and my Father are one,"[1] He prayed "That they [us Christians and prospective Christians] all may be one; as thou, Father, art in me, and I in thee, that they also may be one in us: that the world may believe that thou hast sent me. And the glory which thou gavest me I have given them; that they may be one even as we are one: I in them, and thou in me, that they may be made perfect in one;"[2] and He indicated "there is but one God, the Father, of whom are all things, and we in him; and one Lord Jesus Christ, by whom are all things, and we by him."[3] "There is one body, and one Spirit, … One Lord, one faith, one baptism,"[4] "they shall hear my voice and there shall be one fold, and one shepherd,"[5] "I am the [one] way, the [one] truth, and the [one] life: no man cometh unto the Father, but by me [alone],"[6] and "stand fast in one spirit, with one mind striving together …."[7] And the list continues.[8] The Christian mandate for unity with God is clear and so is the source of its unique, correct vision – the doctrine of Christ.

We have repeatedly indicated the need to identify a correct vision of reality, especially in Book II and the previous chapter for a scientific vision and in Book III and the previous paragraph for a Christian one. However, *we can relax any distinction with respect to scientific or Christian or other view of reality because reality, by its definition as the totality of all real and postulated things and events, is comprehensive, universal, and unique. Any means for discovering and establishing the nature of reality and its description – the truth – is universally useful to Christian, scientist, and all others alike.* As expressed earlier, one doesn't care about the source of a fact, principle, theory, law, or vision provided its truth can be established. The doctrine of

Christ is uniquely powerful and valuable as a certain, ostensible-step methodology for doing exactly that.

Proposition Number 16: **Reality, by its definition as the totality of all real things and events, is comprehensive, universal, and unique. Any means for discovering and establishing the nature of reality and its description – the truth – is universally useful to Christian, scientist, and all others alike. Within science and Christianity the only known means for conclusively establishing absolute truth is the power of God – the only adequate truth criterion – accessible by the doctrine of Christ.**

In this chapter and the next two we conclude our comparative examination of science and Christianity by considering meaning in each as expressed particularly in total-universe, Christian terms, since these are far richer and more powerful in conveying meaning than those of objective, value-free, material-universe science. And the richer the content in meaning, the deeper and more fundamental the revealed nature of reality. Only through understanding of meaning does one realize the importance of unity with God and the means and purpose of salvation, the consummation of the Christian life. Similarly, questions of veracity of, say, the Bible and the Book of Mormon are settled by the same ostensible-step test by which one's understanding of both the fundamental nature of reality and its meaning are obtained.

We have reached the bottom line. Drawing on our earlier observations, arguments, and deductions we can finally answer the questions of what views of reality are provided by science and by Christianity and what each *means* in its essence and significance. However, describing meaning in words is not fully efficacious so we conclude our description of meaning in the next chapter utilizing more than mere words – we consider real, lived-experiences of real people. In the final chapter we address truth and meaning and, as in the first chapter, where it can take us and why we want to get there.

Scope of Consideration

The science in this book has focused on physics and especially on mechanics. Nevertheless, our considerations apply to hard science quite generally and inclusively. Physics and mechanics were chosen as the basis of presentation of science because physics in general and mechanics in particular are the foundations of all hard science. It is electron configurations that are the basis of interatomic and intermolecular forces and these control molecular structure and chemical bonds. The very existence of chemical compounds (all materials) as well as their appearances and almost all their other properties are governed by mechanics of atomic and molecular electrons and by mechanics of subatomic, nuclear particles. Mechanics of electrons and other subatomic particles, configurations of atoms in molecules, and their motions are all analyzed and described by mechanics to provide reaction mechanisms or pathways by which material- or chemical-species are created and destroyed by nuclear, atomic, and molecular reactions and by which relative abundances of materials occur. In short, all chemistry depends ultimately on physical mechanics. Even thermodynamic principles are deduced in statistical mechanics and thereby originate in mechanics.

Likewise, fundamental biology is governed by mechanics. Structure and function of biological molecules and cells are governed by physics and chemistry. Diffusion of neutral and ionic species through gases, liquids, and solids are known and described by mechanics. The bond angle(s) in a molecule – the angle(s) at which three (or more) atoms join in their preferred, stable, molecular configuration – is (are) determined by mechanics, it (they) being the angle(s) giving a minimum electromagnetic energy of the molecule subject to certain constraints also based on mechanics. Bond angles and the resulting angular dependence of stable atomic configurations in molecules and crystals determine crystal habit and morphology of materials including biochemical molecules and materials such as intertwined, helical RNA and DNA molecules by which genetic information is encoded and replicated and such as folding of large proteins and other complex biomolecules by which they self-package themselves into reliably recognized and fully functional units. Mechanics thus describes and controls biological life processes.

Sociology, psychology, and other disciplines are referred to as sciences, the behavioral and certain medical sciences, because they are believed to utilize the scientific method. But these disciplines are not uniquely related to mechanics and, indeed, the scientific method based only on objective facts cannot properly be applied to objects (subjects) whose behaviors (the observed facts) are not objective. One atom is presumed to behave like another identical to it (i.e., behavior of identical objects is object neutral or universal) but one mouse, rat, dog, monkey, or person has no fully identical counterpart. While the *observation process* might be objective, the *observed facts* are not, precluding their being regarded as observer- and observed-neutral and universally representative. Indeed, the idealized scientific method with its invisible observers of an external world considers neither subjective human (or animal) nature nor human (or animal) scrambling of the universe.

Since we here use the term science to denote disciplines reliably based on the scientific method utilized with strictly objective facts (giving the benefit of the doubt that such facts exist), i.e., hard science, it follows that physics in general and mechanics in particular are the foundations of all hard science and, as we consider science herein, behavioral sciences are art instead of science. The foregoing discussion of physics and mechanics presented in this book thus applies directly and generally to all hard and descriptive science, but not art.

The other, parallel focus of this book is Christianity. A Christian was defined in Chapter 12 as one who believes Christ is the Son of God and seeks to follow His commandments. The doctrine of Christ, in full accord with Biblical teaching and emphasized by name and function in the Bible but no longer stated therein, was adopted as a statement of the Christian paradigm or model. This paradigm addresses the total universe, including all science and art, and implies it can provide power to establish truth.

Although succinct, this Christian model provides deep and far-reaching vision and guidance in thinking and behavior a Christian should strive to achieve. And, in the course of such effort, the Christian receives ostensible proof that he or she is on the best path. This knowledge and its associated peace and joy provide an absolute truth criterion and a universally correct vision of reality. This vision provides knowledge both in terms of *who*, *what*, and *why* and, to lesser extent, *how*. For if this model is correct, then all scripture associated with the model (Bible, Book of Mormon, Doctrine and Covenants, and Pearl of Great Price) is genuine and contains invaluable truth. And it contains absolutely correct physical and spiritual understanding of the unique reality underlying quantum mechanics, non-local physics, and everything else. The knowledge, understanding, and meaning accessible by the Christian paradigm is not accessible by any other philosophy. Science does not even contemplate God. Nor does positivism consider the absolute and universal.

Our models of science and Christianity possess quite different properties and therefore differ in their abilities to deduce meaning, essence, significance, and truth, as we shall now summarize.

Summary of Properties of Science and Christianity

We first list many previously noted and some not yet noted philosophical properties of science.

(i) Science is widely utilized to discover and understand reality. The data it employs are the objective, reproducible, material-universe, lowest-common-denominator facts. Consideration is deliberately and necessarily limited to these facts because the scientific results sought are to be universally applicable, not person (observer), object (observed), or situation dependent. While the intention of this convention is to render science universally applicable, it also severely limits its scope with respect to meaning, significance, essence, and truth. For scientific facts and the relative (objective, neutral, external, ...) connections, patterns, and organizations apparent among them comprise the total vision of science which consequently does not include values, meaning, or feeling which are therefore beyond any "awareness of science." This limited scope prevents reliable demonstration of truth by exclusive use of science.

(ii) Although advocates of science generally regard it to be certain and powerful because of its rigorous, objective method, when one takes a careful look, as we have, neither the facts it employs nor the conclusions it generates are rigorous and objective. When facts are critically examined and only those that survive strict application of rigor and objectivity are retained, there remain few or no facts. Failure of classical notions of definiteness in the nature of observation and deduction as revealed in relativity and quantum mechanics indicates and contributes to subjectivity. And the unrealistic *ideal* of the unobtrusive, invisible observer utilized to discover an artificial "external world" in which science exists and is used precludes science from being realistic in view of human activity and scrambling theory.

(iii) In proposing a scientific hypothesis, i.e., a scientific theory or law, fundamental axioms or principles must be assumed. These assumptions are adopted *a priori*, i.e., their validity is not demonstrated in advance. They are justified on the basis that they are consistent and reasonable according to experience as understood in the *eventual* paradigm of which the axioms and principles or assumptions are a part. That is, the paradigm itself, including evidence in question, serves as the criterion by which evidence is accepted or rejected. Such practice tacitly introduces self-dependence or circular reasoning into science and the results cannot therefore be regarded as rigorously established from objective evidence, particularly because the truth criterion of consistency is automatic rather than selective in such practice. Consistency is a required quality of truth but not a sufficient one, especially when it is contrived. As a truth criterion, consistency cannot insure that any result or conclusion is more than relatively and tentatively correct. Such a truth criterion cannot support claims that results are rigorously or absolutely or universally correct.

(iv) Science has little value when used to address ultimate questions, like the following one: Does an underlying reality exist? To this question many, on the basis of quantum mechanics, answer *no*. (How any answer can have significance in the absence of an underlying reality no one has explained.) And others answer *yes* because such a reality must be the foundation of the apparent order, pattern, and regularity we observe. But even among those who say yes, many different "visions of reality" and "versions of truth" are held as correct.

(v) Currently accepted scientific laws are generally consistent with observed details but there remain fundamental inconsistencies[9] between quantum mechanics, relativity, and Newtonian mechanics and associated observations. Such inconsistencies indicate present scientific laws are not consistent or complete. Correct prediction by thermodynamics, relativity, and quantum mechanics of later-observed facts demonstrates the past scientific database of observed facts from which laws were deduced was certainly incomplete and predicts the current database is also incomplete. How incomplete? We don't know. How biased? We don't know.

(vi) Such flaws may be overlooked in applications of science within a self-consistent paradigm that agrees with known facts over even a limited range of facts and thus provides a useful tool in this range, even when rigor, objectivity, and logical purity are not strictly achieved, only consistency. However, thus limited, knowledge may not be regarded as reliable in dealing with ultimate questions that consider matters extending far beyond the limited range and, indeed, beyond the objective, reproducible, material-universe, lowest-common-denominator-facts, idealized-artificial-external-world realm of science.

(vii) Scientific theory and measurement now imply that a fundamental, *a priori* assumption regularly made in physics – the *locality* assumption: that all influences are strictly local – is not valid for quantum processes. (But non-locality has long been used in arbitrary mathematical constructs called fields merely defined as "local properties."[10]) What is not yet known are the extent and consequences of non-locality, whether it is real and widespread or a symptom of incorrect preconception.

(viii) Recent demonstration of non-locality in quantum systems suggests that something fundamentally limiting in the nature of science might be used to illuminate the nature of the universe, like insight tests of Bell's theorem provide but lacking Bell's rigorous mathematics. Two fundamental propositions of materialism are that (1) reality is fully perceived and defined by objective, reproducible, material-universe, lowest-common-denominator facts and (2) material reality can be completely described and understood by use of these facts. These propositions impose a severe restriction on evidence that is believed to be necessary to protect purity of the scientific database. But, as noted in the previous chapter, proscription of evidence may preclude discovery of truth by allowing a misdirected search for it. For if evidence proscribed in science influences material facts, then necessary corrections of scientific paradigm will be invisible. Ignoring such evidence *prevents* discovery of truth by preventing refinement of method required to describe and understand it.

One type of test for discovering such inadequacy in science is comparison of deductions from material facts alone to deductions from material facts plus at least one subjective or nonmaterial fact. Where divergence occurs, testing against observation could reveal which deductions are most reliable. Of course, one such test involves the phenomena of miracles, which are generally ignored in science because science is incapable of explaining them. Is this a shortcoming of observation or of science? Existence of an Omnipotent God readily explains miracles and a lot more.

(ix) A dilemma emerges in science in inadequacy of its truth criterion – consistency – used to identify truth. A consistency test, even supplemented by arbitrary, additional constraints like Ockham's razor, aesthetics, and symmetry, only positively identifies inconsistency or error by providing a *no* answer. Unavoidable inconsistency can eliminate invalid candidates but still fail to establish truth. Unless a truth criterion provides a definite *yes* answer, demonstration of truth is impossible and a *yes* answer is unavailable by the consistency test of science, with or without additional constraints.

(x) Science contains another unavoidable dilemma: how can science with its method of isolation of truth by eliminating "non-truth" or inconsistency lead to inconsistency? Indeed, one Chapter-5 statement of the truth criterion of science is "contradiction in science is forbidden." That science does presently lead to contradiction is evident in the non-locality of quantum physics, implied by Bell's theorem and associated measurements. Non-locality, with its apparently instantaneous, mutual awareness of separated objects, conflicts with the present interpretation of relativity in that instantaneous or superluminal communication is believed impossible.

(xi) Moreover, if the universe is not real, another dilemma is an oxymoronic "unreal reality" in which measured or proposed facts cannot be reliably conceived, observed, assimilated, or used given no underlying basis or reality. In what reliable terms and principles would we be able to think, talk, and live? If the atmosphere is only real when it is sensed, we had better not all fall asleep at once or we all asphyxiate.

Such dilemmas in science and philosophy have been recognized by deep-thinking physicists, mathematicians, and scholars, such as physicists Newton, Einstein, Planck, Pauli, Bell, Laurikainen, and von Baeyer, mathematicians Weyl and Kline, and scholars Popper, Lewis, and Barfield, as their earlier-quoted comments indicate. Statements *and miracles* of Christ demonstrate that He was and is far beyond all others (save One) in awareness of total-universe reality.

Solving a problem requires identifying and eliminating its cause. What cause do we assign to the dilemma of residual inconsistency or conflict in science, conflict derived by a method based only on elimination of conflict? One possible cause is an insufficient utilization of scientific inquiry up to now so that ignorance and apparent conflict have not yet been eliminated. Given enough time, one could argue, science will eventually eliminate ignorance and conflict. However, a more likely cause is discrepancy between an "external material universe" discovered by unobtrusive, nonparticipating observers *imagined* in science and the real universe and its *real* observers. That is, external-material-universe reality and its unobtrusive, non-perturbing, objective observation imagined in science do not correspond to the real universe containing essential material *and nonmaterial* dimensions, subjective, participating observation, God, and Satan. *Fundamental discrepancies* between the imagined, external, passive universe of science and a real but different one and their divergence would lead to inherent conflict in a methodology based on conflict removal. And because of the severe, inherent limitations of science already described, including its failure to consider nonmaterial causes of material facts (human volition and independent action), conflict will forever remain between the nature of reality incorrectly imagined and assumed in present science and observed and deduced reality. We must mind our philosophy.

Inability of science to establish a definite, material-universe reality or any fundamental nature of such a reality, were it to exist, are predictable symptoms that a fundamental mismatch occurs between inadequate preconceptions, assumptions, and observations of science on the one hand and observation of reality on the other. While rigorous, objective science is the study of an external-world reality, it has yet to establish that an underlying reality actually exists for even this imaginary, external world. Descartes was thus prescient in his attempt to establish a vision of reality based not on neutral, external, material-universe evidence but on subjective, internal, nonmaterial-universe evidence. And such subjective evidence takes us from science to metaphysics and religion and to our other paradigm, namely, Christianity, based on superior assumptions and method because they can be verified by a *yes* answer.

To find a reliable system or paradigm and the correct vision of reality it provides, circular or otherwise flawed reasoning must be avoided, a complete scope of evidence must be considered, and some reliable, external, absolute test or confirmation must be utilized to insure the adopted system is correct. Otherwise we humans could adopt, and in fact have adopted, many thousands of different systems of belief, philosophies, and paradigms, including science and Christianity in all their various forms, all strongly held but nearly all flawed because of circular reasoning.[11] Conclusive confirmation of an hypothesis or law by rigorous, objective comparison with even a flexible, imaginary, external-world reality (science) has – as yet – been unobtainable. Nor can a paradigm be used to verify itself, an example of circular reasoning of the worst sort. Lack of an adequate truth criterion in science does not eliminate the requirement of an adequate truth criterion but it does eliminate science as a means for establishing truth. What is required to establish truth is a rigorous, reliable, external (to the tester) reality test that provides definite and absolute *yes* answers, with a *yes* answer having definitive value far beyond an inconsistency-based *no* answer. Without such an adequate truth criterion, any conclusion must be regarded as tentative and arbitrary. Without a *yes* answer their is no certain test of truth. A *yes* answer is available in principle and practice by the doctrine of Christ in the form of a personal, subjective-but-externally-originating, ostensible-proof communication by "fire and the Holy Ghost."[12]

But isn't a system or philosophy that includes subjective evidence weak and non-universal compared to the ideal (as opposed to the practice) of rigorous, objective, external-world science? No. A system utilizing subjective evidence is non-universal according to scientific orthodoxy but it is more universal if it includes all evidence. And, *a priori*, it is no weaker than science because (1) most, if not all, evidence is ultimately subjective and (2) initial choice and justification of a philosophy are strictly internal and subjective processes. The appeal of rigor and objectivity does not derive from the facts but rather from one's attraction to notions of rigor and objectivity. Any broad view of reality is obtained only through an adopted paradigm so that neither concept of reality nor intuition based thereon emerges until after a paradigm is adopted. Rigor, objectivity, and science seem to provide a unique, well-defined, comprehensive view of reality until one looks closely, as we have, and discovers that many diverse views are always equally justified by science and any view based solely on science is no better than tentative. Because of these fundamental deficiencies, science fails to fulfil the notions of rigor and objectivity and is incapable of conclusively demonstrating that any law or theory is correct. Moreover, the scientific "ideal of the detached observer" precludes realism by ignoring human behavior and participation as contemplated in, say, scrambling theory. This deficiency of science is particularly evident in materialist psychology (Chapter 11) wherein thinking, awareness, and volition are denied in humans beyond material-based processes in merely physical objects.

We conclude that science is incapable of establishing truth and turn to the alternative in our comparison – Christianity.

Our model of Christianity claims to provide internally-manifest, subjective evidence received from an absolute, external Source and may thus be claimed to be external evidence in an external-but-subjective reality test. Such an amazing possibility could only have been instituted by Someone of great power and authority. In contemplating the total universe and all its available evidence, Christianity provides a richer system, a more complete and comprehensive scope of evidence, vision, meaning, essence, significance, and an adequate truth criterion. This truth criterion depends on values of faith and trust in Christ together with repentance, the first principles of His doctrine commanded by the Father. Without this faith and trust, no confidence in the ostensible-step proof follows. Faith in Christ is therefore the "something allowed to be known," the "place where one can start in building knowledge."[13] This faith-in-Christ-based system is not apparent in or implied by any lowest-common-denominator knowledge of objective, material-universe facts exclusively considered in science. This condition is reminiscent of the position Einstein took on the incompleteness and apparent lack of meaning of quantum mechanics in his long-running debate with Bohr, a debate that is revealing, especially as punctuated with insights of Hans Christian von Baeyer, like

> … the success of quantum mechanics, measured by the accuracy of the quantitative predictions it makes, is unprecedented in physical science. The fault, rather, is in the interpretation of the theoretical concepts; we understand the substance of quantum mechanics, but not its meaning. … We know everything about the structure of the atom except its meaning.[14]

And Einstein's position versus Bohr's recalls Lewis' Transposition process. Transposition between levels of awareness is repeatedly suggested in the history of science, as it is again in this quotation,[15] "Transposition in which old, lower-level laws and results are obvious and implicit in a new, higher vision, but in the old, lower vision the new, higher-level laws, results, and meaning are invisible."[16]

In Christianity, all the methodological problems found in science are resolved. Its vision is total-universe and thus unrestricted. It provides definite, non-tentative knowledge through *yes* answers claimed to be absolutely-true. It contemplates and reveals deep meaning, especially through enhanced understanding of values. And it provides a comprehensive, *Who-what-why-how* description of underlying reality.

> He [Christ] that ascended up on high, as also he descended below all things, in that he comprehended all things, that he might be in all and through all things, the light of truth; ... And the light which shineth, which giveth you light, is through him who enlighteneth your eyes, which is the same light that quickeneth your understanding; Which light proceedeth forth from the presence of God to fill the immensity of space – *The light which is in all things, which giveth life to all things, which is the law by which all things are governed*, even the power of God who sitteth upon his throne, who is in the bosom of eternity, who is in the midst of all things.[17] (italics added)

This is a possible explanation for *emergence*[18] – the origin of (seemingly spontaneous) organization that governs behavior of complex systems – and all physical law.

And yet some confidently promote that science alone is exact and absolute, that its requirements of rigor, objectivity, reproducibility, and dependence on only external-world, lowest-common-denominator-material facts and human ability, instead of faith in Christ and the power of God, enable only science to eventually find correct answers to all questions. It would seem that only a stolidly stubborn and inveterately prejudiced person would maintain such orthodoxy when familiar with the deficiencies of science we have considered. Individuals who really understand science and other matters are well aware of what science can and cannot do. It is individuals with less understanding, even though they frequently have great knowledge of scientific facts and theories, who regard science with a category-two-student attitude and believe romantic notions about it. Perhaps part of the basis of such belief is prejudice against religion and refusal to believe in Christ and His power.

Many, like Bertrand Russell, did believe they had discovered serious flaws in Christianity.[19] They regard these perceived flaws as false or inconsistent statements in the Bible or in religious creeds. We have already examined the latter and indeed found orthodox Christianity to be severely flawed. With respect to the former we expect failure to understand "from below" the higher Christian philosophy. A pure materialist cannot understand the meaning we address. This meaning is not perceived because the (understood) letter killeth that to which the (not understood) spirit giveth light. In the positivist's exclusion of anything not clearly stated (despite his or her inability to clearly state what positivism is) or the materialists rejection of the nonmaterial, anything unstatable in clear, absolute facts or in terms of the material is dismissed. Examination of Christian accounts in doctrine from below fails to discover meaning and seems to indicate inconsistency. Only to one who understands from above (i.e., someone who has paid his or her dues and obtained enhanced understanding of values, precursors of meaning) is correct interpretation of many Bible statements and meaning apparent. To the materialist who rejects divine power and miracles and even to Christians who deny the power of God, many Bible statements are "obscure by design" and resulting criticisms of Bible statements and Christianity are founded more on attitude and ignorance than on study and knowledge. We must mind our philosophy.

We have to start somewhere; we have to allow something to be known.[13] But where does a starting point take us? Science without omniscience is no more than tentative, and omniscience is not contemplated in science. Only Christianity provides a confirming demonstration of its assumed Starting Point, of The Power in which we place faith and trust, Christ. Ostensible proof, peace and joy, provided by God transcend and supercede scientific inquiry devoid of any proof.

Nevertheless, we recognize in the following best-case-scenario evaluation that science has provided many valuable and interesting results. These results derive from empirical, incomplete, and merely tentative knowledge that is nevertheless beneficial. A law not demonstrated to be absolutely correct *may* nonetheless be so. In any case, laws deduced from reliable "basis" facts and from associated assumptions may agree sufficiently closely with many facts that they apply with sufficient consistency and accuracy within the scope of these facts and assumptions to provide a tool that, though limited, is useful and even powerful.

Meaning in Science

What can we then say about meaning, essence, and significance in science? First, we propose what cannot represent meaning in science. Meaning in science or materialism cannot be represented by its use in establishing indubitable, absolute, or universal truth or conclusively defining real reality since science methodology itself provides no ability to discover (a user must guess any law) and less ability to define and prove (any scientific theory or law is merely tentative). Meaning in science or materialism could be regarded as its rigor and objectivity that many believe are required to discover reality, but these properties appear to be no more than romantic notions making science an idol which its followers only pretend has the power and meaning they believe in. In fact, science is forever "rigorously tentative."

Nor can meaning in science include an ability to address ultimate questions in which it must fail because it scrupulously avoids all evidence but a narrow range of objective, reproducible, value-neutral, external-world, lowest-common-denominator, material facts. Because science limits itself to these facts, meaning in science is limited to a value-free, material domain and science is systematically devoid of all "higher-level" meaning we address, excluded by a meticulous, blinding focus on only objective, lowest-common-denominator facts. Accordingly, objective, value- and feeling-free, external-world-only science excludes the complete human person including personal values, volition, and subjective meaning and feeling. As we regard values and their practices and consequences as the basis of meaning, ignoring values is ignoring the meaning we address and volition based thereon so that neither are contained in, conveyed by, or accessible to science. The very elements that control "higher" human perception and aspiration are excluded from science because they are subjective, internal, and personal. Only objective, value-neutral facts perceived at a lowest-common-denominator human ability fall within the scope of science.

But, in a best-case view, science must have important meaning as attested by knowledge and benefits it has provided humankind. The stories of perseverance and discovery by such men as Galileo, Newton, Planck, Einstein, etc., personify imagination, dedication, boldness, effort, and achievement at high levels. These stories are inspiring examples of character traits and personal qualities (values) worthy of emulation. Let us therefore consider three meanings of science to be (1) benefits it provides mankind, (2) various worthy, human qualities often exemplified in its practice, and (3) personal satisfaction its successful practice provides. The saving of a life by use of a miracle drug has great meaning to the family of the saved person. The determination to study and achieve derived from an inspiring scientist-example has great meaning to the student who resolves to live a useful and productive life and to those who later benefit. And personal satisfaction derived from success can be great.

However, benefit number one may be countered by negative products of science, such as might be expressed by World War II residents of Hiroshima and Nagasaki. As to the second benefit, meaning itself must originate at a value-aware level higher than science from which meanings of "worthy human qualities," "useful," "productive," and "benefit" derive, as these concepts depend on personal, subjective values. And, regarding the third benefit, personal satisfaction from scientific success is relatively slight and fleeting compared to eternal, inexpressible joy for one's self and others obtained in the consummation of a genuinely Christian life.

These observations suggest a neutrality and even a negative influence of science, with the negative influence probably brought to science rather than inherent in it. We have already considered one such negative influence – preoccupation with rigor and objectivity in intense pursuit of scientific success (or merely a politically-correct attitude) that fully distracts one from any consideration of meaning. When one's full attention and purpose are exclusively focused on science, one's fallible self or fallible humans are adopted as *the* champion. Exclusive devotion to science, however productive and beneficent the science, is fatal because such devotion to a human-made champion displaces devotion to the True Champion and true beneficence. Distraction by science, like distraction by other idols, can cause failure to even perceive Christ. It can also blind one to the fact that each individual is engaged in a life-or-death battle against a non-passive, contrary universe.

While devotion to the True Champion is reciprocal, devotion to science is strictly unilateral. Materialism is a dumb idol elevated by its worshippers to the image of a god, but a god without power or feeling. Both Faust's Mephistopheles and the real Satan possess cunning, power, and misery they desire to share and should not be bargained with. They cannot provide anything of lasting value. If one bargains with the devil, one loses. Generally (I hope) one following a false god does not do so deliberately. And yet we are agents free to think and choose for ourselves. It should be clear that only the True Champion will express devotion by exercising power on eternal behalf of those who follow His way, i.e., beneficence is the intended use and purpose of His power. Exclusive focus on science represents capitulation in the battle to understand and defeat the universe. Refusing to hearken to the voice of God is forfeiting victory to the enemy.[20]

Ironically, the concept of worship of science and scientists and of Godless materialism falls outside the realm of value-free, external-world, objective science, as does worship of business or the law or … in each of these fields, and cannot be addressed by science. Indeed, any meaning, positive or negative, must be brought to science by its practitioners, as Laplace and Lagrange did. Meaning is not objectively indicated or motivated by science itself. But success, recognition, acceptance, acclamation, or simply the desire for them can be intoxicating. One should not permit such temptation and subtle forces promoting them to distract him or her from higher understanding. One must resist such forces which are intended to divert our attention from a correct view of reality; they are carefully designed and optimally applied in a continuing effort by the enemy to cause our everlasting destruction for no important reason, merely to wreak vengeance on us and thereby mock God. To resist these forces we must seek understanding of real reality, discover the battle and its true nature, and join in it following the doctrine of Christ. We must be devoted to the One who is devoted to us instead of a fallible, mindless idol whose worship is promoted by subtle, insidious forces attempting only to distract and destroy. We must mind our philosophy.

Even when we ignore the potentially disastrous pitfall of materialism and consider only the beneficial effects of science, the promise of science is limited because it is a *neutral tool* that must be humanly motivated and directed. To illustrate this nature of science let's optimistically envision the full scope of strictly positive, beneficial meaning in neutral science by determining where such a vision leads.

Well, surely science leads to improved life for a population that accepts and supports it, doesn't it? Compared to earlier generations, we possess today better knowledge of nutrition, protection against disease and suffering, longer life, greater productivity in agriculture, and improved capability in weather prediction and flood control so that hunger, want, disease, and suffering can be eliminated. We enjoy many conveniences that make life easier and more comfortable and improved communication, transportation, and entertainment technology that allow more diverse activity. Our high achievements in technology are employed to protect us against natural disasters, disease, and terrorism. All of these benefits derive from science.

How clear and sharp is this view as an image of reality? It is myopic. Although benefits of science are real and significant, we see persistent, troubling symptoms in economically and scientifically advanced countries such as the United States, symptoms that apparently measure as bad or worse than in other countries not scientifically or economically advanced. These symptoms include obesity with its related diseases, suicide, birth of children to unwed mothers, poverty and hunger in the midst of plenty, extensive alcoholism, drug abuse, and crime, terrorism and fear thereof, collapse of marriages and traditional families, failure of parents to love, nurture, and guide their children, killing of innocent students in their schools and still more innocent unborn children in their mothers' wombs, acceptance by society and even support of immoral practices and perverted sexual behavior, and disestablishment of Christian values and belief. Freedom from work and responsibility, increased leisure time, and longer life are not useful when a person doesn't know how to profit from them. I am not advocating euthanasia or regulation of activity but rather the discovery of meaning. Such discovery is not encouraged by science; on the contrary, it is discouraged by its preoccupation with meticulous attention to objective, value-free, external-world facts. And one frightening symptom toward which such scientific effort is heading is scientific creation of life by, say, cloning. This symptom is frightening because man has not the vision nor intent nor power to properly support life. Let God alone instill the breath of life (spirit) in the body and create living souls.[21] And let Him, in their finding and following of truth, provide guidance and help and save them in His kingdom with a fullness of joy. Scientific knowledge is not helping us understand these important principles and values. Indeed, for many it serves as a hindrance to true understanding.

Do such symptoms reveal a negative meaning of science? I say no. Science itself is not bad, it is potentially good. Science is a neutral tool which may be used for either good or bad. Neutral, value-free, objective science provides no good (generous) or bad (self-centered) motivation. But psychiatrist M. Scott Peck has written:

> There are profound reasons to suspect that traditional value-free science is no longer serving the needs of mankind – to suspect that science no longer can or should ignore issues of values. ... When we lived at the mercy of beasts in the forest, flood and drought, famine and infectious disease, our survival depended upon our race to control such vast external forces. We had neither time nor need for much introspection. But as we have tamed these external threats with our traditionally value-free science and its resultant technology, internal dangers have arisen with proportional rapidity. The major threats to our survival no longer stem from nature without but from our own human nature within. It is our carelessness, our hostilities, our selfishness and pride and willful ignorance that endanger the world. Unless we can now tame and transmute the potential for evil in the human soul, we shall be lost.[22]

Objective, value-free science has not effectively dealt with the human-nature problems mentioned by Peck, nor can it. As science advances, these problems seem to worsen. Where, then, shall we look for proper motivation, regulation, and direction of science, for drawing exclusively on its (our) good potential, for giving it (us) a strictly positive meaning? Such direction does not spontaneously occur because the universe is not passive. On the contrary, evil agents constantly act to pervert motivation, regulation, and direction. C. S. Lewis in his *Mere Christianity* summarized our situation thusly:

> Christians, then, believe that an evil power has made himself for the present the Prince of this World. ...
>
> God created things which had free will. That means creatures which can go either wrong or right. ... If God thinks this state of war in the universe a price worth paying for free will – that is, for making a live world in which creatures can do real good or harm and something of real importance can happen, instead of a toy world which only moves when He pulls the strings – then we may take it it is worth paying.
>
> How did the dark power go wrong? Here, no doubt, we ask a question to which human beings cannot give an answer with any certainty. A reasonable (and traditional) guess, based on our own experience of going wrong, can, however, be offered. The moment you have a self at all, there is a possibility of putting yourself first – wanting to be the centre – wanting to be God, in fact. That was the sin of Satan: and that was the sin he taught the human race. Some people think the fall of man had something to do with sex, but that is a mistake. What Satan put into the heads of our remote ancestors was the idea

> they could "be like gods" – could … invent some sort of happiness for themselves outside of God, apart from God. … God cannot give us a happiness and peace apart from Himself, because it is not there. There is no such thing.
>
> That is the key to history. Terrific energy is expended – civilisations are built up – excellent institutions devised; but each time something goes wrong. Some fatal flaw always brings the selfish and cruel people to the top and it all slides back into misery and ruin. … That is what Satan has done [and is doing] to us humans.[23]

Under enemy influence, some have been diverted from good and used science or business or the law or … to seek selfish goals. For instance, materialism and positivism are perversions of science. Materialism has led to denial of the nonmaterial, invisible, and spiritual. But spiritual influence, the Bible, and God were general beliefs of the scientists who invented the science later perverted by materialists. Galileo was a devout Catholic in spite of his history. Newton believed the Bible and in God and seriously studied these topics. Lagrange was respectful but Laplace wasn't. Darwin described God as the Creative Force behind evolution (however he became agnostic late in his life). Einstein was sensitive to religious belief and spoke of "the dear Lord" reverently. Lemaître and Eddington were religious. Feynman was agnostic but reticent to speak out – he had to be pressed to make a public comment on religion or God[24] contrary to his usually freely expressed and colorful comments in which he otherwise rarely hesitated to engage controversy. In contrast, positivism was invented to gratify pride and ambition or, at the least, those seem to have been be its common functions.

Because of its success in providing early benefits over *external* forces (wild beasts, flood, famine, sickness, hunger), individuals and nations have looked to materialistic science for advancement and salvation from problems related to *internal* forces, as if such problems originate in objective, neutral, value-free facts in a passive universe. They do not and objective, neutral, value-free, external-world science does not provide direction, motivation, or power capable of solving these kinds of problems. Indeed, science and misplaced faith in it contribute to these problems.[25] While effort in science is generally well intentioned, science has distracted us from more important problems and more powerful solutions through which comprehension of meaning is obtained and used in better addressing these problems. Preoccupation with meticulous observation and rigorous analysis of science have distracted us from pursuing meaning. And it is comprehension of meaning above and beyond any knowledge contemplated in science that now lies at the root of understanding and solving basic problems of destructive behavior and human suffering and, indeed, of science herself.

To use science well and to provide it with significant purpose, higher-level meaning must be invoked from higher-level knowledge and belief and utilized by scientists to motivate and direct science, i.e., for the scientist or businessman or lawyer or … to direct him- or her-self. The battle must be recognized and the enemy engaged utilizing all useful tools, including science where it is useful.

But no positive meaning can be assigned as inherent in a neutral tool. And the very concepts of positive and negative motivation and use are anchored in meaning that lies above and beyond science. Values and the ability they impart to guide and direct are brought to neutral, value-free science by its users and sponsors, from other understanding and belief. Science has no meaning of the kind we are addressing.

I thus propose that *science or materialism contains no meaning* since such meaning as we are addressing is derived from personal values and ultimate questions and answers that transcend objective facts. Science is a universal, objective, external-world, value-neutral tool that is meaning neutral.

Proposition Number 17: **Science based solely on objective, material-universe, lowest-common-denominator, value-free facts reliably provides neither truth nor meaning and it is therefore incapable of characterizing reality. Fundamental truth, values, and associated meaning utilized in science must be brought to it from higher understanding and belief.**

Absence or deficiency in comprehension of meaning occurs in many, Christians and others alike. Because truth and the deep meaning we address – the inexpressible peace and joy – are established by the power of God, meaning is experienced by an individual only to the extent he or she is willing to obey the principles of faith in Christ, repentance, real intent to follow guidance received (like a little child), and the ordinance of baptism, as stated in the doctrine of Christ. Liberal Christians who avoid belief that is restrictive in behavior are not inclined to believe and obey. Until they are willing, they deny God's power and fail to discover truth and meaning.

Humankind, under the influence of forces the enemy imposes to distract and debase, can become equally distracted and debased with or without science if we do not resist these forces. To truly raise our station requires more than knowledge of lowest-common-denominator facts, more than discovery of simple cause-and-effect relationships therein, more than discoveries and inventions that make life easier and extend its duration. It requires realization that a battle is raging. It requires understanding of the forces arrayed to distract and degrade and knowledge of how to "armour" ourselves against them by hearkening to the voice of God.[20] It requires following a virtuous Champion with true power, a Champion who can and will accomplish for us the parts in such a battle that are beyond our capability and who will motivate, strengthen, succor, guide, and inspire us if we will follow Him. Science does not lead us to such a Champion because science considers only evidence that is objective and value-free and this Champion is not discovered by such evidence. He is only discovered by subjective, sincere, personal desire to know Him and personal intent and effort to seek and follow Him.

But preoccupation with science and its objective evidence and the endless search for tentative knowledge of pattern within lowest-common-denominator facts can wholly distract us from any other effort. In this capacity science, in its broad, passive acceptance as wisdom by ignorant people, has become one of the signs given by Paul that we are in the last days,[26] i.e., it has become a powerful tool of the enemy by which individuals and societies think they are "ever learning but [are] never able to come to a knowledge of the truth."[27]

We must seek truth, meaning, and directionthrough a philosophy higher than science, one truly rigorous and comprehensive. We shouldn't sell our agent-in-search-of-truth birthright for a mess of objective pottage and unknowingly become category-two-students with an *attitude*. We must mind our philosophy.

Meaning in the Doctrine of Christ

The doctrine of Christ teaches that with the help of God one may discover and establish absolute truth for him- or her-self. Christian philosophy thereby sets itself apart from other philosophy by the absolutely true *understanding* it alone claims to provide. In this paradigm, absolute *yes* as well as *no* answers are accessible, as is required to discover and establish absolute truth. The purpose of this doctrine is to guide the willing, every such one, to the way, the truth, and the life.

The need for objective, disinterested consideration is sometimes emphasized in evaluating a paradigm and its evidence in order to avoid undue influence of prejudice, personality, authority, dogma, or individual and group sentiment. Because authority is not a preferred basis for a philosophy given the demonstrated nature of humans and agents that would influence human behavior, the need to test a paradigm independently of biased influence is essential to its proper evaluation. In the context of the scientific method, objective, disinterested, and independent mean that various individuals can observe a material object or process in various situations and get the same out-of-mind result, which they can describe in terms of facts similarly recognized by others.

But a subjective and interested test used in Christianity is more valid. And it is more independent. Independence in scientific method means individual-person and situation independent, with individual-person independence implying that many investigators test and judge that facts are lowest-common-denominator valid. But each of us is first an individual person, ultimately independent and unique in thoughts, experience, feelings, acquired precursors of meaning, and relationship with God. Herd instinct, following the crowd, relying only on facts a group will accept, facts that emerge from disinterested, objective testing requiring ratification by a lowest-common-denominator consensus, can hold us back, if we let them, from receiving true understanding, personal proof, and meaning. If one of a group hasn't understood elusive meaning, this person probably won't recognize or comprehend it no matter how many times he or she merely inquires regarding the facts. To a person focused only on objective, material-based facts, meaning is invisible. But an individual Christian who correctly follows the doctrine of Christ will receive absolute knowledge and meaning and learn the true nature and meaning of reality.

Why should we regard valid experience as only that which corresponds to a lowest common denominator? A subjective proof is quite reliable and adequate to a person who has indeed received a genuine proof. When Joseph Smith was ridiculed by others after he described his vision (Appendix H), he still knew he had truly seen a vision and he realized that God also knew. So he was true to what he had been taught despite ridicule and abuse. Even when one cannot describe evidence or proof in objective, disinterested, commonly recognized, lowest-common-denominator terms, in terms of out-of-mind, material facts commonly understood by others, because subjective evidence goes beyond these limits, evidence is still evidence and proof is still proof. If God has spoken to you personally in one of His many ways, you will know, if you were prepared, for that was His purpose. One can be fully confident in only such knowledge. We should seek such a highest, uncommon denominator. Such in-mind, values-and-feelings-based, subjective, beyond-the-understanding-of-most knowledge is the kind we should most intently seek because it carries the deepest meaning.

And once one discovers that Christ has power to provide unique understanding of truth and meaning through the power of God, he or she can learn our true current situation – we are in the midst of a raging battle with the enemy.

Faith in Christ is the first and most important principle (value or precursor of meaning) in knowing The Champion that has the desire and power to assist us in this battle wherein an enemy we cannot even see outnumbers and surrounds us, one motivated to destroy us because of frustrated, evil ambition, injured pride, vengeance, and hatred of God from whom it (they) knowingly rebelled and of us who helped cast them from heaven. This enemy inspires and guides human deceit and craftiness to mislead and destroy, craftiness and confusion apparent in the huge number of Christian and other religious denominations and ideologies now found in the world.

Rather than being left to cringe in fear of destruction by this enemy, we are called to rally around the Leader we formerly followed. The rallying cry is one to faith in His goodness and in His power. And other personal steps important to the outcome of this battle follow this first one. However, this first one, acceptance of our True Champion, is the critical and defining choice. This choice is deliberate and voluntary, not one of compulsion, but not a choice to be casually embraced. It initially requires personal belief and desire, a nature of the choice that should not be regarded as distinctive because it is also the nature of all alternatives. One difference in choosing the True Champion over other choices is that in doing so we exert ourselves against a non-passive, contrary universe and, after we do, we receive a demonstration of truth that follows and confirms our initial faith. Such proof is not claimed in science or most, if not all, other philosophy, which other philosophy is therefore inconclusive. Without such proof and the continuing guidance that follows, Christianity is equally flawed in uncertainty and corruption of truth manifest by the multitude of divergent Christian beliefs and past institutional sins. But the offered proof, once obtained, is a clear signal that removes logical circularity, a proof from outside of internal reasoning and from outside circular methodology and evidence. Such guidance or answer to an ultimate question, an answer from Omniscience, makes the doctrine of Christ uniquely valuable in providing absolute knowledge of Christ and of reality. Only Omniscience possesses absolute understanding and power necessary to provide absolute *yes* or *no* answers and real *understanding* of truth. Here is the first of several meanings found in the doctrine of Christ. (1) This doctrine provides a philosophy not limited by erroneous assumption or reasoning but founded instead on absolute knowledge of Christ and reality, the reality of Christ, through the power of God to all who choose to receive it.

A further revelation accompanies such proof or personal communication from Omniscience in my own experience and in that of others already described. Such communication is accompanied by a feeling of inexpressible joy Paul associates with the doctrine of Christ and refers to as being "enlightened" and "tasting the heavenly gift."[28] Continuation of this joy becomes a quest of one who experiences it. That such joy is possible is an epiphany and that such joy in its fullness is permanently obtained through enduring devotion to Christ defines the quest. This joy may simply be a manifestation of devotion of the most powerful Individual (save One) in the universe, but I consider joy and devotion separately. Thus, (2) an epiphany of joy is obtained through the doctrine of Christ.

The devotion of Christ to each of us also holds great meaning. I do not fully understand this meaning (beyond confirmation of my faith in Christ, the joy I have tasted, and other things which I *understand*). Omniscience and Omnipotence are beyond my remembered acquaintance. But I do understand that once we begin to perceive His devotion to us (by reading scripture) it motivates a reciprocal devotion in us and a desire to please Him, to improve ourselves, as Christ commands in His sermon on the mount "Be ye therefore perfect, even as your Father which is in heaven is perfect."[29] Of course we cannot accomplish such a lofty objective without considerable help. On whom then does the burden of the task fall? Well surely it falls partly on us, for we must strive to obey and do all we can. But it falls also on Another who holds much more ability and power than we and consequently will do much of the work in guiding, encouraging, and empowering us. Ultimately, the power of the atonement must be invoked for a mortal to obtain this perfection and Christ alone holds this power. A promise that He will help us is therefore implicit in the command. Then, another meaning of the doctrine of Christ is (3) Christ will help us achieve qualities and capabilities far beyond our natural ones.

(If you don't think it is beyond your mortal capacity to be perfect you haven't yet tried. The attempt leads one to ask Christ: "How did You do it?" The alcoholic, in denial of his addiction, claims he can quit at any time. Only when he tries does he finally recognize his bondage. Likewise, the sinner, any of us[30] for sin is ubiquitous in its many appealing forms, may think he or she can quit sinning at any time. Only when one tries does one finally discover his or her bondage. Only then does one truly begin to experience temptation; for to experience temptation, the attraction of and desire for sin must be resisted. Christ alone, the Sinless One, fully resisted and therefore could fully experience temptation. We mortals are, usually or at least sometimes in our lives, weaklings in temptation and in bondage to sin, a state that only the wise recognize; others prefer to remain passively ignorant. Only in trying to follow Him and escape this bondage do we discover His mighty, unequalled accomplishment in living a sinless life and thereby better know and appreciate His devotion and power.)

So who is served in this philosophy called Christianity? All who choose to embrace it. Who serves? Mostly our Champion, Christ, The Greatest of All (save One), but, in following Him, we must all serve Him, one another, and all humankind. As a natural response to His devotion, once we come to recognize it, we seek to serve Him and others. And it is required. For nothing cultivates mutual devotion like mutual devotion. "We love Him, because He first loved us."[31] (4) Mutual devotion, the order of heaven, is a fourth meaning found in the doctrine of Christ, mutual devotion between Christ and us and our own devotion to one another.

Where is one led in following Christ? What is the meaning and consequence of such desire? To summarize, following Christ leads to (1) absolute *understanding* of reality through direct, personal knowledge of Christ, the Son of God, the Creator and Controller of the universe, and the promised Messiah and Savior of mankind. It leads to (2) an epiphany of inexpressible joy, a continuation of which becomes a principal desire and objective. It leads to (3) guidance and growth in which personal qualities and capabilities are expanded and refined. And it leads to (4) mutual devotion with Christ and a devotion to all others (i.e., charity or the love of Christ).

The Christian paradigm is indeed powerful. But note that the beneficence is not directed toward a nation or community or culture, as is generally promoted in justifications of science and human institutions. It is specifically directed toward the individual – the one. Life is, after all, a personal experience. The experiment called life is largely individual and the rewards obtained are largely individual, although they both intensively involve others. The product of the experiment is a refined, capable, devoted individual, (we cannot be held back by others if we won't be) or two: a married couple, or more: a family, or more still: a nation, e.g., the City of Enoch – we can help one another. Not many details are provided about the culture of the City of Enoch, one of the great cultures of history, but it is known that its citizens were of one heart and one mind with Christ and there was no poor among them.[32] Their level of righteousness was so high they were translated to heaven. While the benefit of Christianity comes initially to the one, it then flows in the form of the light of Christ from the one to his or her society.[33]

Refinement, capability, and devotion are qualities of the Light and Example we are instructed to emulate. The magnificent qualities of Christ are his personal qualities of intelligence, integrity, wisdom, love, charity, grace, humility, devotion, and power. The omniscience and omnipotence came only after the others, after He had fully demonstrated His allegiance and devotion to His Father.[34] And for us the greater endowment will follow a demonstration of our allegiance and devotion to Him, by which devotion we write our own truth. Nations are indeed blessed by Christianity, according to the Abrahamic covenant,[35] but they are blessed individual by individual and family by family. God does not save national institutions, cultures, or groups *per se*. He saves individual souls, one by one, as they will receive salvation by receiving Him. How many does He desire to save? All of us. These facts are apparent from the rules for achieving salvation given in the doctrine of Christ, which is addressed to each individual. Thus, a final, consummative meaning of the doctrine of Christ, one incorporating all the others and the one that eventually provides the deepest feelings of love, fulfilled yearning, and confidence in belonging. It is the individual receiving (5) a bright and more excellent hope[36] of eternal life in the kingdom of God by receiving and following Christ, the True Champion of humankind.

This last meaning, the abstract concept of not-yet-experienced salvation, is impossible to fully anticipate. But as C. S. Lewis so beautifully noted

> The proper rewards are not simply tacked on to the activity for which they are given, but are the activity itself in consummation. ... Those who have attained everlasting life [a.k.a. eternal life] in the vision of God doubtless know very well that it is no mere bribe, but the very consummation of their earthly discipleship; but we who have not yet attained it cannot know this in the same way, and cannot even begin to know it at all except by continuing to obey and finding the first reward of our obedience in our increasing power to desire the ultimate reward. ... But probably this will not, for most of us, happen in a day; poetry replaces grammar, gospel replaces law, longing transforms obedience, as gradually as the tide lifts a grounded ship.[37]

Proposition Number 18: **Meaning of the doctrine of Christ may be summarized in the following five gifts received by a devoted Christian: (1) an absolute knowledge of Christ and of reality; (2) an epiphany of joy; (3) growth beyond the natural in personal qualities and capabilities; (4) mutual devotion with Christ and a devotion to all humankind; and finally, (5) a more excellent hope for eternal life in the Kingdom of God where an everlasting fullness of joy is realized.**

Of course Lewis is correct that we can't yet fully understand the state of "salvation" because we haven't yet experienced it. But my limited experience with Divinity leads me to believe that salvation will contain feelings of inclusion, belonging, devotion, and an everlasting epiphany of joy. Feelings of inclusion and belonging are called *justification* in scripture.

A cause and meaning of personal joy I have recognized while contemplating this chapter was taught by Book-of-Mormon-prophet-king Benjamin about 124 BC. Because of the belief, desire, and intent of his people when he taught them of Christ,

> ... the spirit of the Lord came upon them and they were filled with joy, having received a remission of their sins, and having peace of conscience, because of the exceeding faith which they had in Jesus Christ who should come, according to the words which king Benjamin had spoken to them.[38]

Feelings of cleanliness, peace of conscience, and worthiness are called *sanctification* in scripture. Thus, the fullness of personal joy we contemplate requires justification and sanctification. By His grace, our faith in Him, and our desire and effort, Christ intercedes with His power of the atonement and cleanses us of all sin, thereby making us one with Him and His Father in purity as well as in desire and intent. He makes us feel and be worthy to abide in Their presence. Such experience on earth is a preview of salvation, a brief taste of the eternal condition to be enjoyed by the valiant, the consummation of the Christian desire, effort, and hope, the beneficial end of truth that one has written for him- or her-self. If one feels this joy he or she has passed through the gate and is on or being directed to the straight and narrow path. I would that we all pass through the gate and follow the path – narrow but straight – and obtain the joy.

Lest you think "Is that all? Is there no more to Christianity than this?" let us close this chapter on meaning considering a final thought. The described gifts are meaningful, but to appreciate them one has to understand the meaning, to acquire a powerful, delicate, and sensitive basis for appreciation of it. If one doesn't yet understand meaning, he or she may have the reaction stated in the above pair of questions. (Is that all? ...) When one does understand meaning, when one has tasted "the heavenly gift," the prospects are exciting and even thrilling. Why? Because of the joy. The Kingdom of Heaven is far above the level we can imagine through any unassisted earthly experience. But understanding of meaning gives one some ability to pierce the fog and gain some idea of what it will be like. If your reaction to the meaning of Christianity just summarized is a casual "la te da" or one of the above questions, then, dear reader, you are in the fortunate position in which you can obtain much understanding of meaning from Him who gives this gift based on proper desire and intent. All you have to do is receive Christ's ever-extended invitation stated in His doctrine or in Moroni's promise in the last chapter of the Book of Mormon or elsewhere.

Personal joy and understanding of meaning come only through exercise of personal faith in Christ with required desire, effort, and intent. The understanding is in the expanded realization of values, the subjective knowing of Christ, the joy, the gifts of expanded capabilities, the mutual devotion, and the hope. Meaning, by its nature including realization of values in thinking and feeling, is not fully captured by a simple exchange of thoughts. It must be felt as well. Deep meaning is happiness, satisfaction, peace, and joy. These are the terms (peace and joy) used to describe meaning by those most knowledgeable: Peter, John, Paul, and Christ. These qualities of meaning are personal ones you, dear reader, must individually experience. Peace, joy, and salvation come through knowing Christ, a process between you and Him.

To obtain truth we have to want it and we have to demonstrate (largely to ourselves) that we do. Such demonstration is by embracing the stated rules in the doctrine of Christ, or those Moroni gave with his promise in the final chapter of the Book of Mormon.[39] These rules are not difficult, but they impose sufficiently different behavior to draw us out of our normal-routine attitude, to catch our attention, to lead us to anticipate that we are about to experience something unusual, to cause us to focus our thinking and desire on Christ. When we do, something special happens. We have a wonderful experience and we realize Someone with great power and love is guiding us, telling us what He wants us to do and how valuable it is, for us. This scenario is implied in the Bible, in the Book of Mormon, and in the doctrine of Christ. To receive knowledge of Christ we must be ready; if we aren't, it doesn't come because we won't receive it. We must first prepare and demonstrate to Him and ourselves that we are ready, that we are strong in desire and intent and faith, that we will receive and follow His guidance. Then it comes, and we *understand.* Then and only then are the thoughts and experiences described in this book finally fully clear and meaningful.

Notes and References for Chapter 17.

[1] *Bible,* John 10:30. [2] *Bible,* John 17:21-23. [3] *Bible,* 1 Corinthians 8:6. [4] *Bible,* Ephesians 4:4-5.

[5] *Bible,* John 10:16. [6] *Bible,* John 14:6. [7] *Bible,* Philippians 1:27.

[8] Christ declared: "I say unto you, be one; and if ye are not one ye are not mine." (*Doctrine and Covenants* 38:27.) "And there shall be no disputations among you, as there have hitherto been; ... For verily, verily I say unto you, he that hath the spirit of contention is not of me, but is of the devil who is the father of contention, and he stirreth up the hearts of men to contend with anger, one with another." (*Book of Mormon,* 3 Nephi 11:28-29.) And, pertaining to the City of Enoch, Moses recorded: "And the Lord called his people ZION, because they were of one heart and one mind, and dwelt in righteousness, and there was no poor among them." (*Pearl of Great Price,* Moses 7:18.)

[9] One example is the small but finite quantum-mechanics probability, based on the uncertainty principle, that a body will "tunnel through" a potential barrier (e.g., another body) and simply appear on the other side without ever occupying an intermediate position despite the event being impossible according to Newtonian mechanics. Such an event has never yet been observed for a large body because it has a vanishingly small probability of occurrence, but it remains a prediction of a theory which has uncannily never been found wrong and a prediction for atom-sized particles that correctly describes alpha-emission radioactivity that appears to follow exactly this process.

[10] However, some kind of explanation of phenomena in terms of local interactions may eventually occur. That a gravity field depends on the mass of an object is apparent, but it is not apparent that

the field is wholly a property of the object. In the model described in Appendix D the field depends on both the mass of an object and the flux of particles or radiation irradiating it.

[11] One objection a proud, independent-thinking scientist, philosopher, or ... might make to the doctrine of Christ is "It is too simple, too fixed, too constraining. A definite answer is promised but only to a given question." Actually there is great latitude in the doctrine for personal accomplishments and contributions of inventive, creative, brilliant kinds. But rather than seeking to rise above other followers of this doctrine, one should seek to raise all together by invention, creation, and brilliance. All that follow it serve Christ and one another. And, as humans don't even know what questions to ask, let alone what answers to propose, I ask: would an ambitious one of us aspire even to rise above God? This was the fatal mistake of Satan and his followers. What a selfish person or Satan or his followers has not yet discovered in their drive to distinguish themselves for themselves and obtain glory above others, is that it is fun, exciting, and rewarding to put others first, as Christ Himself instructed and did (see Preface). Only following Him in serving others leads to true joy and lasting happiness. The idols of the world (fame and recognition, power, wealth, etc.) do not provide lasting benefit. As Christ said, "He that findeth his life shall lose it: and he that loseth his life for my sake shall find it." (*Bible,* Matthew 10:39.) And, "For what is a man advantaged, if he gain the whole world, and lose himself, or be cast away?" (*Bible,* Luke 9:25.) Nevertheless, personal intelligence and personal relationship with Christ and others derive from personal effort.

[12] See, for examples, *Book of Mormon,* Moroni 10:5, *Doctrine and Covenants* 88:63, *Pearl of Great Price,* Moses 1:27-29 and my own experience described herein.

[13] See endnote 13 of Chapter 4.

[14] Von Baeyer, Hans Christian, *Taming the Atom,* Random House, New York, 1992, 56,74.

[15] The previous history of science here referred to is briefly summarized as follows. Galileo's measured results were valid, but Newton's laws fully predicted them and greatly extended knowledge of mechanics, allowing a broad and intuitive grasp. Newton's laws were supplanted by the theory of relativity, which, in effect, becomes equivalent to Newton's laws in a limiting case. Special relativity extends Newtonian mechanics to a broader range of application and, when the Lorentz-Fitzgerald factor is unity, the case that corresponds to essentially all our direct experience, special relativity effectively reduces to Newtonian mechanics. General relativity extends range of application substantially further and reduces to special relativity when no acceleration between bodies occurs or when gravity is small, again the condition that corresponds to our direct experience. And quantum mechanics extends range of application in other directions but also effectively reduces to Newtonian mechanics when bodies are sufficiently large or unconfined (in free motion), in agreement with essentially all our earlier direct experience.

[16] Relativistically varying quantities, i.e., quantities that vary with relative velocity or gravitational field strength, have not always been so perceived and, as previously discussed, are not trivially observed and measured properly. Without adequate strategy and procedure, subjective error may occur in such measurements. Quantum mechanical properties are only probabilistic in their nature and the state of a quantum system can therefore never be regarded as fully and definitely predicted by the theory. Moreover, as we have seen, subjective interpretations of quantum theory (Chapter 10) lead to different meanings of some quantities, even properly measured ones.

[17] *Doctrine and Covenants* 88:6, 11-13. See endnote 37 of Chapter 10.

[18] For insight into *emergence*, see Anderson, Philip W., "More is Different," *Science* **177**, 1972, 393, and Laughlin, Robert B., *A Different Universe,* Basic Books, New York, 2005.

[19] Russell, Bertrand, *Why I am not a Christian,* Simon and Schuster, New York, 1957.

[20] "Wherefore, because that Satan rebelled against me, and sought to destroy the agency of man,

which I, the Lord God, had given him, ... by the power of mine Only Begotten, I caused that he should be cast down; And *he became Satan, yea, even the devil, the father of all lies, to deceive and to blind men [and women], and to lead them captive at his will, even as many as would not hearken unto my voice*." (*Pearl of Great Price,* Moses 4:3-4, italics added.)

[21] *Bible,* Genesis 2:7, *Pearl of Great Price,* Moses 3:7. What spirit occupies a body created unnaturally?

[22] Peck, M. Scott, *People of the Lie,* Simon and Schuster, New York, 1983, 262-263.

[23] Lewis, C. S., *Mere Christianity,* Simon and Schuster, New York, 1996, 52-54.

[24] For an example see Gleick, James, *Genius, The Life and Science of Richard Feynman,* Vintage Books, New York, 1992, 372.

[25] Science and scientists *per se* are usually reactive in their work. That is, they generally address merely how *observed* phenomena occur. By this function they do not lead, they follow. However, in the original discoveries of Newton, Planck, Einstein, and many others, there exist notable exceptions to this generalization wherein predictions of theory *anticipated* observation.

Science provides little background that distinctly qualifies a scientist to lead. But neither does other professional training. Values from outside science and other professional training are brought to life and to leadership. Can a scientist be trusted to lead? Yes, if he or she is a good and capable person. So can a good and capable lawyer or business or other person.

Many politicians have highly refined skills. Unfortunately, these skills are often focused on getting elected and less attention is given by handlers and voters to whether the candidate is basically a good person, as history has tragically shown. Lawyer-politicians often found in politics seem to have less useful backgrounds if they are willing to abandon them for politics, harboring ambition for public office and its associated posturing and campaigning. Veteran politicians even seem to believe their own campaign speeches in which evidence of past usefulness in "public service" seems to me to be contrived rather than real. The public is sometimes more abused by its "public servants" than benefited. Let's be honest. The offices, with their trappings of power, recognition, and proximity to money, attract the wrong people; people not usefully employed are undoubtedly the poorest candidates, but when one is employed doing something he or she believes is useful, one is not attracted to political opportunities (like flies gathering to a dead horse). As the old saw goes, "When you want something done well, ask somebody busy to do it." The best qualifications of a leader are fundamental goodness, generosity, humility, and capability. In what other directions should we desire to be led?

I cannot say that scientists would make good candidates. They wouldn't if they had the usual desire to do science instead of anything else. As Steven Weinberg has observed,

> Most scientists would rather do their own research than govern anyone. I have known a number of academic physics departments in which faculty members actively compete for the privilege of *not* being department chairman. Anyway, I haven't seen any signs that scientists would be better than anyone else in running the country. (*Facing Up,* Harvard University Press, Cambridge, MA, 2001, 254)

To provide good candidates, drafting of good, usefully occupied persons probably would have produced better results than we have recently seen if such drafting were done by groups truly concerned about community, state, and nation. Political parties, run as they are by politicians and political hangers-on, are too strongly attracted to electability, self-propagation, and the fleeting power that political success seems to bring to seek mere goodness and capability in a candidate. Instead of promoting heartfelt belief, a "political boss" may seek to avoid risk (in low name recognition or ...) in order not to lose. But the real, long-term risk resides in an elected official lacking basic goodness and driven by personal ambition and willing to adopt an inappropriate agenda in its pursuit. This greatest risk is trusting leadership and power to unworthy people posturing and pretending rather than honestly addressing real problems.

In America we deserve what we get because we do it to ourselves. The minimal effort of merely voting is not enough. By the time the general citizenry votes, many important issues are already decided. We must exert our influence in selecting good-person candidates rather than simply reacting to what someone else decides. Not only an elite few should decide what is best for the future of America. Reading position papers of candidates is useful but insufficient as they are designed to instill priority and capture public approval of the candidate's selected causes, often in place of what should be of highest priority. Many Americans seem to lack a clear idea of goodness. A better approach is, therefore, to read the Bible and the Book of Mormon and other good literature to remind ourselves of principles of goodness and leadership. Candidates often direct their appeals to special interests because so many Americans are predictable in their ignorance or indifference and a majority of votes from a relative few can win elections. Shallow, instantly-gratifying, poll-popular platforms can also win elections, but they usually fail to help in the most basic issue: what is good for America and Americans. Principled candidates will probably not regularly emerge from a major party because the major parties are more concerned with electability and, consequently, risk aversion and business as usual. John Adams once observed that "If worthless men are sometimes at the head of affairs, it is, I believe, because worthless men are at the tail and the middle." (McCullough, David, *John Adams,* Simon & Schuster, New York, 2001, 591)

Goodness is especially needed when a people reject goodness in favor of evil, the present condition of many Americans (and Europeans). The strength of America lies in the goodness of Americans. And the goodness of Americans is indicated by the goodness of the leaders Americans elect. The problem is not just getting good candidates but, first and foremost, being a good electorate. The former problem may be addressed by concerned, well-meaning groups who draft and promote candidates that share high principles in important matters. The latter problem is a matter all Americans must individually address. It is a problem of awareness and desire.

Of course diverse opinions will emerge in elections and debates will be heated. But these qualities are exactly what we should seek. Our elections have too-long ignored important issues and focused instead on poll-directed, narrow-region targeted promotions featuring negative campaigning – bashing opponents irrespective of truth. That a candidate bashes indicates that he or she doesn't deserve to win. *Trickery and deceit in an election are a preview of trickery and deceit in an office.* There are always important, substantive matters for candidates to address. Americans have tolerated inane debates, deceit, and trickery in place of substance. We must demand better. Until we do, we shall receive the same drivel and downward spiral in performance of our leaders (electorate).

Regular Americans need to take control of our country back from the money, power, cynicism, and indifference (e.g., the deciding votes persuaded by shallow, opponent-bashing, content-empty TV commercials). We need to withhold power from the vain ambition and greed that would wield it for the sake of narrow, short-term interests. Are not most Americans concerned about the future welfare of our country, about what our children and grandchildren will inherit from us? "For we wrestle not against flesh and blood, but against principalities, against powers, against the rulers of the darkness of this world, against spiritual wickedness in high places." (*Bible,* Ephesians 6:12.) Our ancestors bought the freedom and prosperity we now enjoy with blood, sweat, and tears. We betray them and our own descendants if we fail to keep our country free, prosperous, and *good*, the last goal controlling all others, by electing worthy and capable candidates. Let's end the nonsense currently paraded before us as campaigning by demanding something better, by demanding goodness and capability.

[26] *Bible,* 2 Timothy 3:1.   [27] *Bible,* 2 Timothy 3:7.   [28] *Bible,* Hebrews 6:4.

[29] *Bible,* Matthew 5:48.   [30] *Bible,* Ecclesiastes 7:20, 1 John 1:8.   [31] *Bible,* 1 John 4:19.

[32] *Pearl of Great Price,* Moses Chapters 6 and 7, especially 7:18 (quoted in endnote 8).

[33] *Book of Mormon,* 3 Nephi 18:24.   [34] *Doctrine and Covenants* 88:6(-17).

[35] *Bible,* Genesis 26:3-5.   [36] *Book of Mormon,* 2 Nephi 31:20, Ether 12:32.

[37] Lewis, C. S., *The Weight of Glory,* Walter Hooper (editor), Simon and Schuster, New York, 1975, 26-27.

[38] *Book of Mormon,* Mosiah 4:3.   [39] Moroni's promise is quoted in endnote 24 of Chapter 19.

18. Manifestation of Meaning

To better comprehend the meaning, essence, and significance we address in this book, fully understood only through the doctrine of Christ, we examine the lives of a few individuals who followed this doctrine. Through identification with these individuals we consider meaning and the influence it has on those who understand it at a level beyond what words can communicate. Of course case studies can do no more than illustrate. And that is exactly our intent. We seek to understand what can happen in the life of an individual who follows the doctrine of Christ.

In examining the lives of these individuals we shall see the objective, neutral, external facts. But we look beyond these to what the facts communicate to one having an understanding of meaning. For the sake of understanding these histories, we assume such an understanding of meaning. That is, utilizing narration of a guide (this book) we regard the facts from a high level of understanding, realizing meaning and associated feelings as well as facts. Such an adopted perspective allows one to appreciate deep nuances in meaning and feeling as if these experiences were happening to one's self or to a loved one. Reading this chapter thus involves some level of *playacting* in which the reader attempts to feel emotions that accompany unshakable faith, complete trust, and full intent to demonstrate unconditional devotion to Christ, no matter what. The subjects of these biographies have received personal assurance by fire and the Holy Ghost that their belief is absolutely correct, they have experienced joy, several of their personal qualities have been magnified, and they feel a mutual devotion with Christ and His other followers, and a devotion to all humankind. To discern meaning in the following biographical sketches we must see beyond natural vision, for "the natural man receiveth not the things of the Spirit of God: for they are foolishness unto him: neither can he know them, because they are spiritually discerned."[1] Through personal identification the reader can best perceive and most deeply understand meaning and its influence, as if he or she were experiencing these histories.

The lives of the individuals we consider converge in a common story, but I tell their individual stories in turns. Although these stories begin two centuries ago in a setting much different from our own in some ways, obvious parallels apply. The battle of life transcends time. Consider, then, what these biographical sketches tell us about developing a heavenly style, the costs, the benefits, and the meaning. We all live, we all die. What is to be determined by each is for what goal and purpose he or she lives and dies.

Two questions seem to me to be particularly important. Does following Christ by seeking membership in the Church of Jesus Christ of Latter-day Saints inspire devotion to God and to others? Is it worth the required effort? I propose that in joining this church one correctly receives baptism, the gift of the Holy Ghost, and the promise of salvation with Christ (joy) precisely in the manner practiced in the original church – under direction of Christ through living apostles and prophets and others empowered to act for Him. Thereafter, the Holy Ghost or power of God is a personal Guide as one seeks to follow Christ, just as it guided the early Christian saints (members) for the first two centuries or so. Can we obtain and maintain a high level of devotion to Christ, or a heavenly style, by following His direction? How else could we? He only is the way, the truth, and the life; no man cometh unto the Father but by Him.

Therefore, principal questions are "Did the individuals in these stories follow Christ?" and "What was the result?" Did they exhibit qualities expected in members of a restored-original Christian Church? By their fruits ye shall know them and the Master they serve. (Incidentally, these biographies and this book are intended to benefit the reader. The Church of Jesus Christ of Latter-day Saints will do just fine, thank you. It is you, dear reader, who I hope will gain from the thoughts presented. And if you do, so do we all.)

I now simply tell the stories and you can extract such meaning as you are able, according to your precursors of meaning, desire, and intent.

David W. Patten

The first of several persons I would have you meet is David W. Patten, born in Theresa, New York, to parents Benoni Patten and Edith (Abigail) Cole on 14 November 1799. While western New York was a frontier during his youth, Patten left home while still a boy and went to southeastern Michigan, even more of a frontier region. Whether Patten traveled and initially settled with relatives or friends is not known. He homesteaded a spot in the woods near Dundee, Monroe County, located at the western tip of Lake Erie. There he and Phoebe Ann Babcock were married in 1828.

Patten was of a religious turn of mind and studied and pondered the Bible. He received a remarkable promise when he was twenty-one. It began with a manifestation of the Holy Ghost in which he was commanded to humble himself and repent of his sins and because of his efforts to comply he received dreams and visions while he slept. In one he learned that Christ's own true church would be reestablished during his lifetime, an event he thereafter looked forward to with joyous anticipation.[2] While awaiting this event he attended Methodist meetings.

At age thirty Patten saw for the first time a copy of the Book of Mormon, but only long enough to read the inspired preface and the testimony of the eleven witnesses. From this time he prayed continually for faith and a more perfect knowledge. In May of 1832, he received a letter from his brother John, of Fairplay, Indiana, informing him of the Restoration of the Gospel. He arose in the meeting that day, Sunday, and told those present that he had at last got word of the Church of Christ.

Conversion

Leaving Phoebe at home, David mounted his old grey mare the next morning and started alone through the woods for his brother's home, some 300 miles in distance, through country that was in those days little more than wilderness. There were roads, but they came from the east, in the main, and David was traveling south. So he traveled the 300 miles through woods, over hills, and across unbridged streams and rivers, all to converse with his brother about religion. Upon hearing about the new religion he was convinced it was true and was baptized by his brother.

David was ordained an elder on 17 June 1832. He was then described as being six feet one inch in height and stoutly built, weighing over two hundred pounds, but not fleshy, and of a dark complexion with piercing black eyes. Abraham O. Smoot further described him as having a jovial disposition. Patten immediately began service as a missionary for the Church upon returning to Michigan and soon discovered that the Lord had blessed him with the gift of healing. Regarding this gift he wrote:

> The Lord did work with me wonderfully, in signs and wonders following them that believed in the fullness of the Gospel of Jesus Christ, insomuch that the deaf were made to hear, the blind to see, and the lame were made whole. Fevers, palsies, crooked and withered limbs, and in fact all manner of diseases common to the country, were healed by the power of God, that was manifested through His servants.[3]

Note in the preceding quotation who Patten casts as the Hero in these experiences.

> Among those visited by him was a blind woman, the wife of Ezra Strong. After the usual testimony and questions respecting her faith in the Gospel, David rubbed and anointed her eyes, when immediately she was restored to sight;[4]

By the fall of 1833, somewhat over a year after he had joined the Church, David had completed three missions and was living in Kirtland, Ohio. In December he was asked by Joseph Smith to join with William Pratt in delivering papers bearing comfort, the recently revealed Section 101 of the Doctrine and Covenants, to distressed members of the church in Missouri.

The two of them accepted the task and thereupon faced a journey of 600 miles in the dead of winter, mostly on foot because of their poverty. Such was their generous natures that they thought more of the condition of their suffering fellows than of their own comfort.

In June of 1834, David and other church leaders were meeting with leaders of a Missouri mob who were persecuting church members, trying to resolve differences.

> At the close of the conference, on account of some remark of his, one of the mobocrats drew a bowie knife on David, swearing;
>
> 'You d___ d Mormon, I'll cut your d___ d throat.'
>
> David responded, 'My friend, do nothing rash.'
>
> (To which the mobocrat replied as he fled,) 'For God's sake don't shoot.'
>
> David's composure and gentle reply threw the man into a state of alarm. It was beyond him to conceive of such unruffled behavior unless his antagonist relied for his security on concealed weapons. But David was wholly unarmed, except with the affection which knows no fear.[5]

On 15 February 1835 David W. Patten was ordained an apostle. In his ordination the following blessing was requested upon him: "O God, give this, Thy servant, a knowledge of Thy will; may he be like one of old, who bore testimony of Jesus; may he be a new man from this day forth."[6] In seniority in the initial quorum of twelve apostles ordained in this dispensation he followed only Thomas B. Marsh. Brigham Young followed him. In addition, Joseph Smith and two counselors were apostles serving as the presidency of the church, according to direction they had received from its Owner (Christ). After joining with his brethren of the Twelve in missionary service traveling through New York, Canada, Vermont, and Maine, Patten traveled to Tennessee, the location of his next mission assignment.

During his mission in Tennessee another incident showed Patten's utter fearlessness.

> While preaching in the house of Father Fry, in Benton County, Tennessee, David was interrupted by a Mr. Rose, who asked him to raise the dead. David administered to the man a stinging rebuke for his wickedness, when Mr. Rose in great anger left the house. After [the] meeting, however, he returned, bringing with him a crowd of armed men, who stood in sullen array about the dooryard.
>
> Probably for the reason that he did not wish the family to be disturbed by them, David went out, cane in hand, to learn of their intentions. He was greeted with the brandishing of weapons and dire threats of vengeance; but with the utmost coolness he bared his chest to the mob, and told them to shoot. The same fear seemed to fall upon them that possessed the mobocrat in Missouri, for they fled the premises as if in fear of their lives.[7]

Albert J. and Catherine Petty

Albert J. Petty was born 10 August 1795 in Bourbon County, Kentucky. His father Ralph, born 20 December 1767, was a prominent Baptist Minister. Because of his willingness and ability, Ralph preached in Baptist churches throughout the area. When he died on 26 July 1851, Ralph's history as a Baptist Minister for 46 years was engraved on his tombstone because he had regarded this activity as his most important. Albert and other family members often accompanied their father when he visited a congregation and preached, so the children grew up with a good knowledge of the Bible and an intimate Christian example.

Catherine Petty, said to be no relation to Albert, was born 13 February 1803 in Dover, Stewart County, Tennessee. Albert and Catherine were married on 2 June 1829.

In the early 1830s, while Joseph Smith was organizing the restored Church of Jesus Christ in New York, Ohio, and Missouri, Albert operated a wheelwright and gunsmith shop in Benton County, Tennessee. He was also in charge of the local precinct jail, a part-time position since it only occasionally contained one or two prisoners. One day in 1835 the sheriff, accompanied by a heavily armed posse, brought two men to Albert which he instructed Albert to retain in jail and see that they didn't escape. According to Petty family history,[8] the prisoners were well mannered and refined so Albert brought them to his home to eat dinner with his family. There the two men told the family about a modern day prophet through whom God had restored His pure gospel and true church, including priesthood authority enabling man to act for God in performing necessary saving ordinances. Albert learned that such "perverted" teaching had been the offense for which they were incarcerated. Well, Albert knew something about preaching. Albert had heard his father preach year after year and he knew that preaching the gospel of Christ in the manner one understood it was not a crime; that's exactly what his father had done. So Albert listened as these two men presented to him and his wife a Book of Mormon and described the restoration of Christ's church on the earth. The two missionaries, were Elders David W. Patten and Warren Parrish.

Here I quote from the journal of Wilford Woodruff, a missionary companion of Patten, Parrish, and A. O. Smoot. Square brackets [...] indicate my addition.

> While Patten and Parrish were staying at Seth Utley's house in Benton County, Tenn., on 19 June 1835, about forty men, armed with deadly weapons, led by sheriff Robert C. Petty, a colonel, a major and other officers, besides a Methodist priest with a gun on his shoulder, surrounded the house. The sheriff informed the brethren that he had a States' warrant for D. W. Patten, W. Parrish and A. O. Smoot (who was then out of the county), issued on complaint of Matthew Williams, the Methodist priest, who swore that these brethren had put forth the following false and pretended prophecy: 'That Christ would come the second time, before this generation passed away, and that four individuals should receive the Holy Ghost within twenty-four hours.' [The gift of the Holy Ghost is promised to all who properly receive baptism (see Chapter 12). No mention was made as to exactly what law had been broken in giving a prophecy, if one was in fact given, or how its false and pretended nature had been established.] After examination, Patten and Parrish were bound over to appear on 22 June, under $2,000 bonds. Albert Petty and Seth Utley were the signers of said bond.
>
> Early on the 22nd, Patten and Parrish had their trial. The mob gathered to the number of one hundred, all fully armed. They took from Elder Patten his walking stick and a penknife, and went through with a mock trial; but would not let the defendants produce any witnesses; and without suffering them to say a word in defense, the judge pronounced them guilty of the charges preferred.
>
> Brother Patten, being filled with the Holy Ghost, arose to his feet, and by the power of God bound them fast to their seats while he addressed them for 20 minutes. He rebuked them sharply for their wickedness and unjust proceedings in persecuting two humble servants of God in their assigned duty to preach His word and warned them of the curse of God that awaited them if they did not repent. Brother Parrish afterwards said, 'My hair stood up straight on my head, for I expected to be killed.' When Patten closed, the judge addressed him, saying, 'You must be armed with concealed weapons or you would not treat an armed court as you have this.' Patten replied, 'I am armed with weapons you know not of, and my weapons are the Holy Priesthood and the power of God. God is my friend, and he permits you to exercise all the power you have, and he bestows on me all the power I have.'
>
> The court finally concluded to let the brethren go, if they would pay the cost of court and leave the county in ten days. The sheriff advised the brethren to accept these propositions, as it was the only means of escaping the violence of the mob. The saints in that vicinity paid the cost. Elders Patten and Parrish left and went to

> Brother Seth Utley's house. They had not been gone long when the mob began to quarrel among themselves and were mad because they had let the prisoners go. They soon mounted their horses and started after them with all possible speed. The news of this movement reached the brethren and they immediately mounted their mules and went into the woods. By a circuitous route they reached the house of Albert Petty, put up their mules, went to bed and slept. They had not been long asleep when some heavenly messenger came to Bro. Patten and told him to arise and leave that place, for the mob was after them and would soon be at that house. Elder Patten awoke Parrish and told him to arise and dress himself, as the mob would soon be upon them. They arose, saddled their animals and started for Henry County in the night. They had not been gone long before the house was surrounded by a mob, who demanded Patten and Parrish. Brother Petty informed them that they were not there, but the mob searched the house and remained till daybreak, when they found the tracks of the brethren's animals, which they followed to the line of the next county, when they gave up their chase.[9]

The bitterness of other ministers toward the humble "Latter-day Saint" missionaries had a familiar ring to it. It caused Albert and Catherine to wonder if there wasn't some truth to the new doctrine these elders were preaching. During the next few weeks they considered and accepted the restored gospel, were baptized, and received the gift of the Holy Ghost to become members of the Church of Jesus Christ of Latter-day Saints. Albert Petty and his family were eight of the first twenty converts to the "Mormon Church" from the South.

When they converted to their new church, the Albert Petty family left behind life as they knew it: prosperity, comfort, respect in the community. And what did they trade for this life? They, along with other early members, won trial, hardship, grief, toil, persecution, and sadness. However, they also won a new "family," strengthened faith in Christ, truth, the promise of salvation, and joy. Most importantly, they used their opportunity in hearing and accepting the restored gospel of Christ to express their devotion to God, in the style or order of heaven. Their endurance in this expression of devotion, along with that of the other saints, was nothing short of remarkable.

Far West

Albert, Catherine and their children left their home in the south to join their new "brethren and sisters" (the saints) headquartered in Far West, Missouri, as was the custom of the Mormons in that day. The departing group was encamped after their first day's travel in Graves County, Kentucky, where Wilford Woodruff met with them for the last time in the south. I quote again from his journal.

> When we had pitched our tents and taken supper I assembled this small camp of Israel at Brother Petty's tent to address them for the last time in the south. When they were gathered together I arose to speak to them upon the subject of their journey. The rain was descending in torrents so that we were soon wet through even within a good tent. Yet my soul was full of emotion and inspired with feelings of no ordinary character. I endeavored to lay before them the worth and value of the cause

> in which they were engaged and that they were the first in fulfilling the Prophets who spake of the south keeping not back, and that it would be recorded in the archives of heaven to be read in the day of eternity that they were the first fruits of the South who spread their tents for Zion.[10]

It took the group of new converts about two months to travel the 500 to 600 zigzag miles along what roads they could find to their destination of Far West, Missouri, at that time near the western frontier of American civilization.

Upon joining the other saints in Far West in 1835, Albert and Catherine placed their family in the middle of events of the church where they remained from that time on. They were among the saints expelled from Missouri without compensation for property by vicious mob action and by official decree of the governor who issued the infamous "extermination order" against the Mormon residents of the State. Some among Albert's and Catherine's friends paid the ultimate price for their faith. Because of unconstrained violence against them by their lawless Missouri neighbors in the form of murder, burning of homes and crops, and ravishing of women, Albert's and Catherine's family and the other saints left Far West in winter of 1838 and spring of 1839 and traveled east across nearly the length of the state of Missouri and across the Mississippi River to the new headquarters-to-be of the church: Nauvoo, Illinois.

Across the Mississippi River in Illinois the saints had acquired mosquito-infested marshland near the Village of Commerce that consisted of six houses. The low, swampy land near the river caused much suffering from malaria during the initial year or so before the swamp was completely drained. Nevertheless, within a year and a half, two thousand new homes were built, as well as schools, churches, and businesses, and the new community was named Nauvoo. During the Nauvoo period, Albert served as a missionary and was sent to Tennessee for this purpose. While Albert served his mission, Catherine and their children lived in Stewart, Tennessee, probably with Catherine's relatives. By 1841 they were back in Nauvoo.

Martyrdom of a Prophet

Albert and Catherine were residents of Nauvoo when Joseph Smith was martyred on 27 June 1844 by a mob in nearby Carthage, Illinois, the seat of Hancock County, a distance of 18 miles from Nauvoo. Smith had been summoned to Carthage to meet with Thomas Ford, the Governor of Illinois, who had demanded Smith, the Mayor of Nauvoo, and the entire City Council stand trial for destruction of the Nauvoo Expositor printing press and property in Nauvoo. This newspaper had been dedicated to vilification and slander of the saints. Thus the City Council had ordered its closure and destruction, an order carried out by the City Marshal and others. Except for damage to property, the enforced closure was probably legal.[11]

In hindsight, and as anticipated by some at the time, Ford's handling of the situation appeared to be contrived for the political and economic advantage of opponents of the saints and the subsequent events served those purposes well. However, the Governor had pledged his faith and that of the State to protect the defendants while they underwent a legal and fair trial. This occasion was far from the first in which the enemy had utilized wicked men making false accusations to attack Smith. In fact, Smith and his brother Hyrum considered the possibility of fleeing to the West to establish a safe place for the saints, a plan they had been considering for some time to escape unwarranted attack and one the entire body of the saints would be forced to adopt in less than two years. In preparation, the Smiths and a few intimate friends crossed the Mississippi River one evening and were standing on its west bank the next morning debating what to do. Joseph asked his older brother Hyrum what they should do. Hyrum responded, "Let us go back and give ourselves up, and see the thing out." Joseph said, "If you go back I will go with you, but we shall be butchered."[12]

In compliance with the summons, Smith and the entire City Council left for Carthage on the morning of 24 June 1844. En route, about four miles from Nauvoo, they were met by a Captain Dunn and sixty mounted militia on their way to Nauvoo. Dunn presented Smith with a written order from Governor Ford demanding the surrender of all state arms in possession of the Nauvoo Legion. Smith immediately countersigned the order commenting that it would help assure peace. Because the Nauvoo Legion was a formidable force (Nauvoo had a population of twenty thousand at that time, three times the population of Chicago), Dunn requested Smith, a General of the Nauvoo Legion, accompany them to Nauvoo and assist with the order, which he did to the great relief of Dunn and his soldiers. Upon completion of this task, the group again departed Nauvoo in company with Captain Dunn and his men. As he was about to mount his horse for the journey, Smith uttered his famous prophetic declaration to the men with him, including Captain Dunn,

> I am going like a lamb to the slaughter, but I am calm as a summer's morning. I have a conscience void of offense toward God and toward all men. If they take my life I shall die an innocent man, and my blood shall cry from the ground for vengeance, and it shall be said of me, 'He was murdered in cold blood!'[13]

Early in the morning of Thursday, 25 June, Smith and others of his party surrendered to Constable David Bettisworth. By 8:00 am Bettisworth served the two Smiths on writs of individual charges of treason, charges quite different from and more serious than the ones they were ordered to Carthage to face. Governor Ford appeared about 8:30 am, ordered assembled the troops gathered at Carthage as protection against a possible attack by Mormons, and stood on a table to address them. The troops, 1200 to 1300 in number, consisted of the Carthage Greys among which were many sworn enemies of the Mormons, military from McDonough County, and, later, an uninvited contingent from Warsaw which also contained many self-declared enemies of the Mormons. Ford's comments to these men were of an inflammatory tone, having the effect of increasing the feelings of excitement and indignation against the Mormon leaders. He supported the rumors and charges against the Mormon leaders which had caused them to be incarcerated in Carthage in his custody. He claimed that the Smiths and other Mormon leaders were dangerous men and guilty of charges to be brought against them; "still," he added, "they were in the hands of the law, which must have its course."[14] After speaking to the troops for half an hour, Ford brought out the Smiths and paraded before the troops with them, as he had promised he would the previous night in response to their unruly demands. Governor Ford introduced his prisoners as General Joseph Smith (of the Nauvoo Legion) and General Hyrum Smith to which the Carthage Greys declared they "would introduce themselves to the d____d Mormons in a different style."[15]

Smith *et al* were visited in their hotel room in late afternoon by a group including some officers of the Illinois militia. In conversation he asked for an honest opinion regarding his appearance, whether it would indicate he was the desperate character his enemies made him out to be. They responded that his "appearance would indicate the very contrary." But, they continued, "we cannot see what is in your heart, neither can we tell what are your intentions." Joseph responded with a startling, prophetic reply:

> Very true, gentlemen, you cannot see what is in my heart, and you are therefore unable to judge me or my intentions; but I can see what is in your hearts, and I will tell you what I see. I can see that you thirst for blood, and nothing but my blood will satisfy you. It is not for crime of any description that I and my brethren are thus continually persecuted and harassed by our enemies, but there are other motives, and some of them I have expressed, so far as relates to myself; and inasmuch as you and the people thirst for blood, I will prophesy, in the name of the Lord, that you shall witness scenes of blood and sorrow to your entire satisfaction. Your souls shall be perfectly satiated with blood, and many of you who are now present shall have an opportunity to face the canon's mouth from sources you think not of; and those people that desire this great evil upon me and my brethren, shall be filled with regret and sorrow because of the scenes of desolation and distress that await them. They shall seek for peace, and shall not be able to find it. Gentlemen, you will find what I have told you to be true.[16]

This prophecy was fulfilled when two regiments – the first and second – from western Illinois were practically annihilated in the battle of Buena Vista on 23 February 1847 when they met numerically superior forces under General Santa Anna in the war with Mexico. Also, 13 to 17 years later during the civil war, Illinois troops suffered proportional casualties far in excess of those of any other northern state.[17]

That evening at eight the two Smiths and eight others were illegally jailed according to the following sequence of events. Constable Bettisworth appeared at their hotel room and insisted they go to jail on the charge of treason. The two Smiths demanded a copy of the mittimus (warrant), as required by law, but they were refused. Lawyers representing the group insisted they were entitled to appear before a justice of the peace for examination before they could be jailed. The constable then produced a mittimus issued by Justice Robert F. Smith, the captain of the Mormon-hating Carthage Greys, declaring that they had appeared before him and commanding the constable to incarcerate the defendants in jail, "there to remain until discharged by due course of law."[18] This perjury on the part of Justice Smith, a sworn Mormon enemy, was, of course, highly illegal as the lawyers defending Smith complained, but to no avail. As the Smiths were staying in the hotel room next to Governor Ford's, Ford was quite aware of everything that was occurring. Ford knew the proceeding was illegal; he had been an associate-justice of the state supreme court. At one point, seeming to encourage Bettisworth in his intention to jail the Smiths over the objections of the Smith lawyers, he told Bettisworth that he could not interrupt a civil officer in the course of his duty.[19] And when Justice Smith himself came to Ford for advice, perhaps because both his mittimus and the committal were illegal, Ford advised "You have the Carthage Greys at your command."[19]

The following day, 26 June, the prisoners spent in jail. Because of the dire threats expressed freely by many of the troops, it was apparent to the Smiths and their associates that the troops and others of the mobbers intended to murder the Smiths. These concerns were communicated to Governor Ford, but he stated the opinion that it was bluster and the danger was not real. Instead of concern for the prisoners who had surrendered under his pledge of protection, Ford concerned himself with plans to visit Nauvoo with a show of military force to intimidate the Mormons in searching for rumored criminals and illegal materials, namely, counterfeit money and a printing press for making it. In these plans he decided to take the most Mormon-friendly troops with him and leave the jail and prisoners under the guard of the Carthage Greys, the ones making the fiercest threats against the prisoners. It will probably never be proven by mortal man that Ford was or was not an accomplice in the plans to kill the Smiths. If he wasn't by intention, he was by function. The best that could be said about him was his judgement was extremely poor.

Midmorning on 27 June Dan Jones was sent by the Prophet with a message for Governor Ford. As he crossed the street to enter the hotel he heard a leader say to a group: "Our troops will be discharged this morning in obedience to orders, and for a sham we will leave town; but when the Governor and the McDonough troops have left for Nauvoo this afternoon, we will return and kill those men if we have to tear the jail down."[20] Jones forcefully related this information to the Governor, but either Ford did not regard it as significant or he was an accomplice in the plot.

When Ford and the McDonough troops were ready to leave for Nauvoo, Ford dismissed the other troops. They formed a disbanded mob and retired to the rear shouting loudly that they were going only a short distance out of town and then they would return and kill the Smiths.[21] Dan Jones happened to be passing the Governor at that moment and again called his attention to the threats, which Ford must have heard. But Ford ignored them and rode off with his troops to Nauvoo.[21]

The exact scenario that had been threatened so often, including threats within the hearing and sight of the Governor, occurred in the late afternoon of that day. Joseph Smith was shot and, mortally wounded, either jumped or fell out of an upstairs jail window (accounts differ in this particular). He may have been trying to save others in the room since more were shooting at him outside and below the window than in the jail. Hyrum Smith was shot dead in the room, Willard Richards was nicked in an ear, hid under a bed, and survived while John Taylor was shot several times and severely wounded. Taylor may well have died had his pocket-watch not stopped a bullet from inflicting another severe wound. To protect Richards, Taylor hid him under a bed but further violence was prevented when someone shouted "The Mormons are coming!" and the mob scattered.

The mob (and the enemy who it served) had obtained their desire. Joseph Smith, the American prophet, was killed at the age of 38 together with his brother Hyrum. However, not before Joseph had completed the work assigned to him by God, a work which continues forward today with ever increasing urgency and meaning. In fact, Smith's death was required as a part of the work God had given him. "For," as Paul states, "where a testament is, there must also of necessity be the death of the testifier."[22]

The death of the Smiths was a great shock to those who had known and held them in high esteem. And the murder of Joseph and Hyrum did not end the attacks on the saints. Rather, it caused them to intensify. Violence and threat thereof soon became so great the saints determined they had to leave their homes again.

From Nauvoo through Iowa to Nebraska

Albert, Catherine, and their children were among the saints driven out of Nauvoo by threat of mob action, again with little or no compensation for property left behind. In the cold winter of 1846, 1600 rode in wagons or walked away from Nauvoo beginning on 4th of February. By February's end the exodus crossed the frozen Mississippi River on the ice, a rare possibility in that location. Even as they left, many were not adequately clothed or not well, and they had to cross the entire State of Iowa before they could stop – some 500 trackless miles over rolling hills thickly covered with brush and trees, through swamplands, and across many streams, all in the cold winter with many lacking adequate food, clothes, or supplies. Albert, Catherine and the others struggled through the journey. Disease and death visited many families. When John Ralph Petty, age 9 years and ten months, died at Winter Quarters, Nebraska, a year later on 6 February 1847, Albert and Catherine had lost four of their nine children. Some families were entirely wiped out. In the course of eleven years since they had joined the church, the Pettys had made five long journeys, two forced under unfavorable circumstances, amounting to more than 2,000 miles of travel, mostly through wilderness. And they were to shortly lose another child to sickness, no doubt caused by meager housing and poor diet in harsh conditions. When scurvy broke out among the saints in Winter Quarters, there were insufficient potatoes and other remedies to treat the sick.

What could have made them stay on this difficult path they had chosen? Might it have been devotion to their Lord? That, apparently, would have been their answer, because stay on it they did.

When 1667 saints left Winter Quarters on the westward trek of over 1,000 miles to the Salt Lake Valley in 1847, Albert and Catherine stayed behind with most of the saints. Albert was a blacksmith and wheelwright and he was needed at the point of departure to build wagons and assist the saints coming through on their journey to the west, coming through by the thousands over the next several years as new members from the Eastern United States moved west and from Western Europe immigrated to be with their fellow members of their new religion.

On to a Brief Stay in the Salt Lake Valley

In spring and early summer of 1848, three companies left Winter Quarters for the west. The first contained 1220 persons and was directed by Brigham Young. All of those directing companies were members of the presidency of the church who had returned from the Salt Lake Valley for that purpose. The first company departed on 26 May 1848 and arrived in Salt Lake City on 21 September 1848. The second was directed by Heber C. Kimball and contained 662 persons. It both departed and arrived three days after the first on 29 May and 24 September. The third was directed by Willard Richards and contained 526 persons. The Willard Richards company departed on 30 June and arrived on 9 October. Albert and Catherine and their children were in the Heber C. Kimball company.

When they arrived in the Salt Lake Valley, Albert was 53, Catherine was 45, and their five surviving children were 17, 15, 7, 4 and 3 months, with the youngest having been born en route; the company traveled 20 miles the day the Petty boy was born. They had established five homes in five different states or territories. They had traveled thousands of miles, much of it through wild country under great hardship. Perhaps they were looking for a chance to catch their breath and rest, to establish a home and to enjoy living there. Well that's exactly what they were working for, but only for one year and two weeks. In the October conference of 1849, they learned from a sermon delivered by Brigham Young that they were among a group assigned to settle the Sanpete area, now Sanpete County with Manti, Utah, its seat and principal city. Because it was late in the year, the challenge was to arrive and establish residence before the winter cold and snow. They would be supplied that first winter with food from the more established headquarters of the church in the Salt Lake Valley.

Settling the Wild Country of Sanpete

The challenge just to arrive in the Sanpete Valley and establish residence was formidable. There were no roads or bridges in any of the 140 miles to Sanpete. At that time the southernmost settlement was a fort containing a garrison of 50 soldiers on the Provo River, some 50 miles south of Salt Lake City. Moreover, Manti is some 1,500 feet higher than Salt Lake City, a point we will consider again. But the group of 224 males and 100 females, true to the assignment of their leader, left Salt Lake City on 28 October 1849. They built roads and bridged streams at great effort to arrive at their appointed destination before winter. The greatest difficulty was a road up the Salt Creek Canyon to a 6,200-feet-high divide. From there they soon entered the beautiful Sanpete Valley on 22 November, after twenty-five days of strenuous travel.

The season of the year did not leave time for relaxation. Winter was nearly upon them and they needed shelter from the cold. There exists a prominent ridge in Manti, on which the beautiful Manti Temple now stands. To obtain shelter from the wind and cold, some of the pioneers dug caves in the south side of this ridge in which to escape the cold that first winter. However, when they moved in and warmed themselves with fires in their new domiciles, the co-resident rattlesnakes were awakened. During the first night of their encounter with their new neighbors some three hundred rattlesnakes were destroyed, without anyone being harmed by the snakes.

When Brigham Young assigned Albert's and Catherine's group to settle the Sanpete Valley, he didn't anticipate there was such a significant difference in altitude and, of course, he didn't appreciate the consequence of it, namely, that Sanpete and Manti would receive a great deal more snowfall than they had seen in the Salt Lake Valley, particularly in the high area at the head of the Salt Creek Canyon. Although the colonizers had built a crude road with a bridge over any significant stream, they were cut off from their supply of food for themselves and their stock by the heavy snowfall. Disaster was averted only by superhuman effort on the part of men who packed in supplies on their backs through the deep snow!

After this first winter, the residents of Sanpete planted crops and built more adequate and comfortable homes and became fully self-sufficient. Albert, following his earlier tradition of official service, besides being jailer in Tennessee he had been elected Justice of the Peace in Far West, was elected to the Territorial Legislature where he served with many prominent men of that time, including his friend Wilford Woodruff. He also later served as Mayor of Manti.

The Dixie Cotton Mission: the Final Segment of Albert's and Catherine's Mortal Journey

During the civil war cotton became a very valuable commodity in the union. There were plenty of worthy causes for which money was needed, such as assisting new members in their immigration to be with the body of the saints in Utah and its surrounding communities. Brigham Young therefore sent farmers experienced in the growing of cotton to settle Utah's "Dixie," the southern area of the State noted today for its rugged, high-desert topography and great beauty. Southern Utah is a well kept secret with regard to concentration of natural beauty; it contains no less than *five* large national parks. In Utah's Dixie the climate was right for cotton. But could farmers produce the crop in sufficient quantity in such rough, unsettled country? Settlers, in addition to growing cotton, would also have to establish their homes starting, again, from nothing. Brigham Young thought they could. At the General Conference held 7 October 1861, Brigham Young extended an official call to the "Dixie Cotton Mission" by reading over the pulpit the names of those assigned and by letter to Apostle Orson Hyde in Sanpete County. Young's advisors estimated good, tillable acreage at between 4,000 and 5,000 acres. They needed men to plant and grow the crop and to build viable communities there. Because Albert was from and had farmed in Tennessee, he knew how to grow cotton. At ages 67 and 59, Albert and Catherine and their family were again assigned to travel into wilderness and establish a new home there. The older boys were sent ahead that fall to select and prepare a homestead. The rest of the family spent the winter accumulating supplies and settling affairs and departed in the spring.

This challenge was different from the cold, muddy trek across Iowa or any of the earlier journeys. One observer, George A. Smith, wrote about one stretch "I thought it was the most desperate piece of road that I ever traveled in my life, the whole ground being covered for miles with stones, volcanic rock, cobbleheads and so forth, and in places, deep sand ..."[23]

From Charles B. Petty's book, *The Albert Petty Family*, we read

> The pioneer road was usually poor in the springtime on account of the frost coming out of the ground and running water from the melting snows, causing it to be muddy in places. A suitable dry campground where there was feed and water for the livestock, and wood for the campfires, was sometimes hard to find. Women and children usually slept in the wagon on top of the load under the protection of the canvas wagon cover, while the men slept on the ground. Pioneers were often delayed in their travels by storms, bad roads, poor feed for the animals, a broken down wagon, sickness, etc. Then there was Sunday, the Sabbath of the Lord when both man and beast must rest. However, in spite of these conditions they usually made twelve to fifteen miles per day.[24]
>
> At Sandy it was sand and rocks, or all sand, as the road led through cactus, prickly pears, oose, and sand burrs, much to the discomfort of those barefooted. Everyone who was able, walked and the small children were carried. Here again a delay was caused by having to "double up" [teams of oxen to pull one wagon at a time], where the road led up a sandy slope. With the extra oxen all hitched, and men at each wheel, the head driver walking by the side of the beasts would crack his whip and shout, "Heave, Heave!" As all responded with one accord the wagon wheels started to turn and, the ships of the desert, moved slowly forward a few rods. At the sound of "Whoa," from the driver, all would stop, puff and pant, and get ready for another pull.[25]

So was the travel of 67-year-old Albert and 59-year-old Catherine to their new mission assignment. The Dixie Cotton Mission did not result in much cotton production and, had the effort been productive, adequate transportation to the Northeastern United States market would have been needed. But Albert and the others did build viable settlements and the commerce necessary thereto. Albert established a blacksmith and gunsmith shop that provided valuable service to the community. He later built and ran a gristmill which served a broad region. He and his family founded Springdale, Utah, where they enjoyed their final years together. Albert died at Springdale on 19 July 1869 at age 73. Catherine died eight years later in Sterling, Utah, near her earlier home of Manti, on 1 August 1877.

Perspective

So what did Albert, Catherine and their family accomplish in a life of hardship, toil, and grief. They accomplished expression of devotion to Christ and His other followers. And nothing permits fuller expression of devotion than hardship, toil, and grief. When we see ourselves bearing hardship, toil, and grief, we notice. It catches our attention and impresses us. We send ourselves a message regarding our priorities, not only who or what we put first, but how far first, a message that has the power to influence our values and attitudes down to knee-jerk-reaction level. Nothing cultivates devotion like devotion.

And Somebody Else is also watching whenever we express devotion to Him, the most devoted Somebody of all. He took upon Himself more hardship, toil, and grief than can be imagined by the human mind. He did it as an expression of His devotion to His Father and to us. And nothing cultivates devotion like devotion. We are bought with a price. We are paid for a by cost which is beyond mortal measure. The scale of the atonement is infinite, beyond the ability of man to measure or comprehend. To Him, we have great value. He paid a great cost for us because of His devotion to us.

So, I say to you, my child, or grandchild (, or friend), cultivate your devotion to Christ like our beloved Albert and Catherine did. Albert and Catherine are my third great grandparents and your fourth or fifth great grandparents and they have left an honorable name and legacy of faith in Christ for you to follow. Their lives express great meaning.

I say live well and die well. We don't know when death will occur beyond knowing the Lord is in charge and death will only occur when He allows. But, because we don't know when it will occur, take care to be ready. Unless guided otherwise by the Holy Ghost, don't avoid or hide your identity as a Christian, even when it is unpopular or dangerous. We cannot know the influence our expression of faith in and devotion to Christ may have. We all live and die. The more remarkable issue is what we desire and strive for in our life and death.

The Prophet Moroni addressed this very issue in the Book of Mormon, to which he dedicated the last 37 years of his life, completing it even though he could show it to no living soul during his lifetime. In fact, he wrote the book for the descendents of those who had destroyed his people and for the rest of us who live today. Beginning in 385 AD and until the Book of Mormon was completed in 421, the remnant of his people, the Nephites, were being hunted and executed by their enemies, the Lamanites. If captured, a Nephite could only save himself by denying the Christ. He wrote

> Now I, Moroni, after having made an end of abridging the account of the people of Jared [the Book of Ether in the Book of Mormon], I had supposed not to have written more, but I have not as yet perished; and I make not myself known to the Lamanites lest they should destroy me. For behold, their wars are exceedingly fierce among themselves; and because of their hatred they put to death every Nephite that will not deny the Christ. And I, Moroni, will not deny the Christ; wherefore, I wander whithersoever I can for the safety of mine own life.[26]

And what did David W. Patten accomplish in his life of effort and hardship and suffering and grief? He also expressed his devotion to Christ and His other children. And nothing permits fuller expression of devotion than effort, hardship, suffering, and grief.

Among members of the Church in Missouri, David was known as "Captain Fearnot" because of his fearless defense of the saints, illustrated again in the following account.

On 24 October 1838 the rumor reached Far West that a mob had taken prisoners near Crooked River, Missouri. As mentioned earlier, these lawless Missouri mobbers felt it proper to answer the Mormon beliefs, with which they disagreed, with murder, burning, and ravishing of women. Such acts caused much concern for any possible prisoners captured by the mob. Thus, David led a group of 75 volunteers who departed the community about midnight to seek release of the prisoners. It was later learned there were no prisoners; the rumor of prisoners may have been initiated by th quantum mechanicse enemy to insure a response and the opportunity to accomplish more violence and murder against the Mormons. The mob was strategically positioned and waiting. Near Crooked River, a shot was fired and the "battle of Crooked River" was engaged. Unfortunately for the Mormons, they were silhouetted by the approaching dawn and one of them was shot dead in the initial exchange of gunfire. Crying the words "God and Liberty," Patten rushed forward and led a charge. The mob fled in confusion but as David led the charge down the river bank a mobber, hiding momentarily behind a tree before fleeing to the river, stepped out and shot him in the abdomen. David W. Patten died in his wife's arms at age 38 at 10:00 pm on 25 October 1838. His last words, to his wife Phoebe, were "Whatever you do else, O do not deny the faith."[27]

Legacy

In a letter dated 6 February 1900 the fifth President of the Church of Jesus Christ of Latter-day Saints, Lorenzo Snow (1814-1901), related this personal experience.

> All the circumstances of my first and last meeting with Apostle David W. Patten are as clear to my mind as if it were an occurrence of but yesterday, and yet it took place some sixty-four years ago. He appeared to me then to be a remarkable man, and that impression has remained with me ever since.
>
> We traveled together on horseback from my father's home, at Mantua, Ohio, to Kirtland, a distance of perhaps twenty-five miles, he on his return from some missionary labor, I to commence a course of studies at Oberlin College.
>
> On the way our conversation fell upon religion and philosophy, and being young and having enjoyed some scholastic advantages, I was at first disposed to treat his opinions lightly, especially so as they were not always clothed in grammatical language; but as he proceeded in his earnest and humble way to open up before my mind the plan of salvation, I seemed unable to resist the knowledge that he was a man of God and that his testimony was true. I felt pricked in my heart.
>
> This he evidently perceived, for almost the last thing he said to me after bearing his testimony, was that I should go to the Lord before retiring at night and ask Him myself. This I did with the result that from the day I met that great Apostle, all my aspirations have been enlarged and heightened immeasurably. This was the turning point in my life.
>
> What impressed me most was his absolute sincerity, his earnestness and his spiritual power; and I believe I cannot do better in this connection than to commend a careful study of his life to the honest in heart everywhere.[28]

David W. Patten lived the doctrine of Christ and became a power in His hand for the blessing of His children. His faith in Christ endowed him with generosity, love, fearlessness, and energy in the service of God and man or, in other words, devotion to Christ. And nothing cultivates devotion like devotion. God Himself said of David W. Patten, in a revelation given to Joseph Smith on 19 January 1841 and recorded as Section 124 of the Doctrine and Covenants, starting in verse 18,

> … it is my will that my servant Lyman Wight should continue in preaching for Zion, in the spirit of meekness, confessing me before the world; and I will bear him up as on eagles' wings; and he shall beget glory and honor to himself and unto my name. That when he shall finish his work I may receive him unto myself, even as I did my servant David W. Patten, who is with me at this time, …

And in verse 130 of the same Section,

> David W. Patten I have taken unto myself; behold, his priesthood no man taketh from him; but, verily I say unto you, another may be appointed into the same calling.

Truth and Meaning

We all live, we all die, but for what purpose? I would that you, family and friend alike, and I might live an expression of devotion to Christ, like Albert and Catherine Petty, Joseph and Hyrum Smith, and David and Phoebe Patten did. And I would that we all obtain the same judgement from the same Great Judge. In fact, we will all obtain exactly the judgement that we have written for ourselves – our own end of truth – written by each person in the purpose for and paradigm in which he or she has lived. Make both purpose and paradigm worthy of your life and death. Generate devotion to Christ and endless fullness of joy, the greatest truth and deepest meaning of all.

Where did devotion to Christ lead David W. Patten, the one whose story is most fully known? It lead to knowing and being found acceptable by Christ so that David was "taken unto Him" where he will experience an everlasting fullness of joy. And I have no doubt that Joseph and Hyrum are also so accepted and that Albert and Catherine will be found there as well. For God the Father is well pleased with those with whom God the Son is well pleased. Christ is our advocate with the Father[29] and the Great Judge by whom all who would enter the gate of heaven must pass because "the keeper of the gate is the Holy One of Israel, and he employeth no servant there."[30] Our devotion to Christ as well as much help from Him leads to our becoming *like* Him.[31] It leads to dwelling in His and His Father's presence. It leads to inexpressible, everlasting joy.

What are the rules for obtaining joy? The full set of rules is given simply and succinctly in the doctrine of Christ, for anything "more or less than this … cometh of evil and is not built upon my rock …"[32] Although there are other ordinances to which one is eventually led by the Holy Ghost and authorized servants of God, there is no extensive "check list," no requirement to do things comprehensive in number or great in magnitude. We must simply develop a devotion to Christ and His

Father by following the way, the truth, and the light. Indeed, we do best to forget about ourselves and focus instead on Them and Theirs. *Our* list and *our* story can be a distraction if they cause us to be concerned too much about *ourselves*. Christ, our Example, lived His life for others. In so doing, He forgot about Himself. Christ leads, we follow. And, if we do, He does for us all the necessary rest beyond what we can do because of our mutual devotion with Him. As Moroni counseled, "Deny not the power of God."[33]

What about all the other doctrines in the scriptures? What other doctrine should we be concerned about? The doctrine of Christ alone is uniquely identified and set apart by Him as His own. An "extensive checklist mentality" and the idea it sometimes implicitly carries, that one is saving him- or her-self, distracts from a focus on the Savior we all depend upon and who has shown and will show us the way. The single, primary objective is to follow Him. Getting caught in a checklist mentality prevented nearly a whole nation from recognizing Christ when He lived among them as a man, despite their noble history of long periods of devotion to Him as Jehovah, the God of the Old Testament.[34] We must be devoted to and follow Him without distraction. The principles of His doctrine teach precisely this singular objective in becoming and remaining like a little child (humble, teachable, guidable) after receiving the Holy Ghost or power of God which thereafter guides us as we seek to do what He wants us to do.[35] Even though we know not from whence "the wind" cometh or whither it taketh us, we can do no better than to follow God.

But shouldn't a Christian try to accomplish many things? Yes, the many things God guides and empowers the Christian to do. But shouldn't a Christian try to be a good example? Yes, of course. However, a personal, ambitious list of goals may originate in pride rather than pious discipleship or divine guidance. One accomplishment is sufficient to please Christ if that is what He wants an individual to accomplish. But, in fact, He wants each individual to do more, to be willing to give all he or she is able to give,[36] for His and for the individual's sake, for nothing cultivates devotion like devotion. The more one exerts him- or her-self in following Christ, the greater his or her growth in devotion to Christ. He counsels us to be anxiously engaged in good causes on our own volition for this purpose.[37]

The steeper the path, the harder the climb, but the higher the summit. Is this metaphor not consistent with the history, ancient and modern, of devoted Christians willingly suffering hardship or persecution or death because of their faith in and devotion to Christ? Is this metaphor not consistent with His expression of devotion to us, unmatched and unmatchable? And history and the scriptures[38] suggest that He will allow each of us to express our faith in and devotion to Him by bearing our own cross to our own Golgotha, ever giving us the opportunity to extend the depth of our devotion with Him. Indeed, He will lead us, if we will, to greatly expand and enlarge our mutual devotion with Him. Is that bad? Yes, from a worldly perspective, but not from an eternal one. Following Christ leads to devotion, joy, belonging, meaning. The stories in the scriptures and elsewhere of Jonah, Job, Stephen, Peter, Paul, …, even Christ, have personal meaning and application because nothing cultivates devotion like devotion.

Notes and References for Chapter 18.

[1] *Bible,* 1 Corinthians 2:14.

[2] Wilson, Lycurgus A., *Life of David W. Patten,* Deseret News Press, Salt Lake City, 1904, 2.

[3] Ibid., 16. [4] Ibid., 29.

[5] Ibid., 47. The "affection which knows no fear" refers to *Bible,* 1 John 4:18 and *Book of Mormon,* Moroni 8:16.

[6] Ibid., 33. [7] Ibid., 67.

[8] *Wilford Woodruff's Daily Journal,* Mathias F. Cowley (editor), Bookcraft, Salt Lake City, 1964, 20.

[9] Ibid., 59-60. [10] Ibid.

[11] The question of legality of the destruction of the Nauvoo Expositor was treated by Oaks, Dallin H., *The Suppression of the Nauvoo Expositor,* Utah Law Review **9** (Winter 1965), 862-903. Oaks concludes his lengthy, detailed study citing 220 references with the following conclusion found on page 903. "Aside from damages for unnecessary destruction of the press, for which the Nauvoo authorities were unquestionably liable, the remaining action of the council, including its interpretation of the constitutional guarantee of a free press, can be supported by references to the law of their day." General historical information is provided by Oaks, Dallin H., and Marvin S. Hill, *Carthage Conspiracy,* University of Illinois Press, Urbana, 1975, especially 14-16.

[12] *History of The Church of Jesus Christ of Latter-day Saints,* Second Edition, The Church of Jesus Christ of Latter-day Saints, Salt Lake City, UT, 1965, Volume VI, 549-550.

[13] Ibid., 555. [14] Ibid., 562-563. [15] Ibid., 564. [16] Ibid., 566.

[17] Smith, Henry A., *The Day They Martyred The Prophet,* Bookcraft, Salt Lake City, 1963, 115.

[18] The false mittimus is quoted in its entirety in *History of The Church of Jesus Christ of Latter-day Saints,* loc. cit., 569-570. Francis M. Higbee named as a material witness in this mittimus was one of a group discussing the Smiths the day previous to his testimony, and not too secretly. Someone of the group was overheard to say "there was nothing against these men; the law could not reach them but powder and ball would, and they should not go out of Carthage alive." (Ibid., 566.) This threat and many others were relayed to Governor Ford, but to no avail. His actions strongly suggest his complicity in a plot to murder the Smiths. At least the crude Governor of Missouri had been direct about his wicked intention in issuing the infamous extermination order against the Mormons.

[19] Ibid., 570. [20] Ibid., 602-603.

[21] Ibid., 603-604. [22] *Bible,* Hebrews 9:16.

[23] Petty, Charles B., *The Albert Petty Family,* Deseret News Press, Salt Lake City, 1954-55, 117.

[24] Ibid., 116. [25] Ibid., 118. [26] *Book of Mormon,* Moroni 1:1-3.

[27] Paraphrased from Wilson, loc. cit.

[28] Quoted in Wilson, loc. cit..

[29] *Bible,* Isaiah 3:13, 51:22, Matthew 10:32-33, *Book of Mormon,* 2 Nephi 2:9, 8:22, Jacob 3:1, Mosiah 14:12, Moroni 7:28, *Doctrine and Covenants* 29:5, 32:3, 38:4, 45:3, 62:1, 110:4.

[30] *Book of Mormon,* 2 Nephi 9:41.

[31] *Doctrine and Covenants* 88:40.

[32] *Book of Mormon,* 3 Nephi 11:40.

[33] *Book of Mormon,* Moroni 10:7.

[34] That Jehovah is the Christ is indicated in the following passages: *Bible,* Isaiah 26:3, 19,21, John 1:1-5,14, *Doctrine and Covenants* 38:1-4, 45:1-12, 110:1-10 (for additional references see endnote 11 of Chapter 15). The title *Jehovah* is generally rendered *LORD* in the King James Bible. The meaning of His title was clear to the people of Palestine during Christ's mortal ministry. Christ was charged with blasphemy by the Sanhedrin and crucified because He declared that He truly was Jehovah – the great I Am, the Son of God, the Christ. But one problem remains with their conclusion about His blasphemy. He really is Jehovah (*Bible,* Matthew 3:17, Mark 1:11, Luke 3:22, Hebrews 5:5).

[35] *Book of Mormon,* 2 Nephi 32:5.

[36] *Bible,* Matthew 10:38-39.

[37] *Doctrine and Covenants* 58:27.

[38] *Bible,* Matthew 10:32-39.

19. Retrospection

We conclude our comparative examination of science and Christianity with a look back, a survey of the story, a retrospection. This looking back is a metaphor representing the eventual view of one's life obtained at its end, from which perspective a final judgement of one's mortal effort can and will be made. But even now a judgement of the reader by the reader, in the form of the reader's response to a question, indirectly assesses the value contained in his or her life up to now in the truth and meaning found and followed and, perhaps, help provided to others seeking to find and follow the beneficial way. Such a retrospection allows one to see, rather well, how he or she is doing and to make any desired or necessary mid-course correction.

Looking Back – A Summary of Principles Considered in this Book

We are cautioned in scripture by the image of "fire and brimstone" or "lake of fire and brimstone"[1] as an inheritance of those who disregard and do not seek salvation or realization of meaning. These terms are figurative, dramatically descriptive, meant to catch attention. They do, but because of disbelief of many they are often regarded as mere fable, myth, or superstition. Such unbelief naïvely dismisses valuable insight into the range of possible future conditions of humans. We read in the Book of Mormon that the term "lake of fire and brimstone" has a specific meaning, namely, "endless torment."[2] The future of us mortals thus holds at its two extremes an everlasting fullness of joy or an endless torment.

We have already discussed the joy. What will be the cause and nature of an endless torment? Those who willfully reject Christ and His teachings or simply don't care because they are interested in other things (also willful; we are talking about category two- and three-student attitudes, dereliction of agent-in-search-of-truth duty, so the rejection is willful in both cases) will fail to receive an eternal fullness of joy. Realization that a state of joy is irreversibly and forever lost is its own punishment. Endless torment may then be the everlasting realization that for lack of sufficient devotion one has lost joy by excluding him- or her-self from the inner circle of our original home and family. This lack is caused by willful rejection of Christ during a brief period of mortal life – due simply to pride, ignorance, pride, fear of others, pride, pursuit of worldly idols of comfort, wealth, and power, and pride. Lack of devotion will be most painful in the realization, apparent all along if one seeks truth, of the great devotion the Father and the Son held and hold for each of us.

I have heard some express the wishful opinion that we don't have to worry. They believe that because of God's goodness and love He will provide no less than the best for all His children. He has done exactly that – the best opportunity for personal growth and development. We are now maturing. What we become we must decide. No one else can write our own end of truth because we are now and are to forever be independent agents. We have more to look forward to than an eternal, glorious day-care center. God did not create us to forever remain dependent under His continuing supervision and care. He has greater things in mind for us, things that

> no tongue can speak, neither can there be written by any man, neither can the hearts of men conceive so great and marvelous things as we both saw and heard Jesus speak; and no one can conceive of the joy which filled our souls at the time we heard him pray for us unto the Father.[3]

Christ would have us become independent and capable adults devoted to Him and His Father, adults They can trust with Their power and authority. Without mutual devotion, endowment of power is unwise in view of the havoc and grief Satan has caused even without the power of God he selfishly sought. For the purposes of developing and demonstrating devotion to Christ in response to His devotion to us we have now left home and are on earth, on our own, establishing our paradigms and abilities. The responsibility and station God will one day assign us or we will one day assume will be commensurate with who we become, what end of truth we write for ourselves. It will be one's personal abilities and attitude (one's paradigm) that enables him or her to independently serve and rule (under God) in His kingdom, according to the level of capability and devotion to which each has raised him- or her-self, with considerable, indispensable help from Christ. For this purpose God has given us agency that has meaning, that allows personal growth and development or stagnation or even backsliding and despondency. If we do not follow Christ we fight against Him and we are on the side we fought against in winning our chance to be here now. This is backsliding. The despondency resides in endless torment if one writes that end of truth for him- or her-self.

We are not experiencing a meaningless mortal existence wherein what we do has no significance or consequence. Rather, each person has the freedom and capacity to do real good or real evil, to follow Christ or be misled and dominated by Satan. And with the opportunity to do good there is opportunity for personal growth and development. With the opportunity to pursue evil there exists power to stop, close up, confine, or restrain. Thus a dammed river or a damned person is contained. Those who choose evil and remain fixed in it are stopped and isolated.

Beneficial growth and development, ability and desire to do good in our choices and effort, are the intended products of our mortal experience. Any physical injury, deficiency, and death itself will be undone in the resurrection. Yet, all personal growth in honesty, intelligence, strength of character, and devotion to family, friends, humanity, and God will remain. All such qualities will remain part of us in the influence they hold in our paradigm. Development of our own, unique paradigm is the challenge and opportunity of mortality. Because our paradigm influences and controls our personal attitudes, desires, ambitions, and values, it is the basis of our behavior. It is who we are. To those who think God should be Santa Claus, providing free gifts with no underlying purpose, I would observe that it is not God's but the paradigm of each of *us* that needs to be and is being developed and refined. It is not God but us having the opportunity to develop under His care, if we will receive it, and being tested in a non-passive, contrary universe. Each person thereby writes his or her own future story or truth, the way things are to be for that person.

To obtain a fullness of joy and eternal association with Christ and His Father, which joy and association are inseparably connected, one must believe in Christ and follow His doctrine. Only in this way do we develop and express the mutual devotion which is the order of heaven. He is unconditionally devoted to us. He alone has taken upon Himself our guilt and suffering, so that we can escape them if we but follow Him. Only He has both the power and desire to redeem us from our sins and thereby enable us to return to our heavenly home.

> Man by himself is priced;
> for 30 pieces of silver Judas sold himself, not Christ.
> Christ by Himself our freedom bought,
> paying dearly to save each soul a heavy fraught.
> Following Christ is salvation's measure;
> forever binding us in joy to Father and Son its treasure.[4]

Christ requires merely our honest, energetic, valiant attempt to follow Him. Automatically there results in each person who does so, who valiantly tries to follow Him, a broken heart and contrite spirit.[5] Not despite but because of this condition of sorrow for sin and recognition of our absolute need for His help, Christ will provide a glorious salvation and joy. He has been concerned with our glorification from the beginning. That is why my Chapter-12 question – Should I seek to glorify myself or Him? – is so pertinent. Nothing strengthens mutual devotion like mutual devotion (i.e., the expression or heartfelt demonstration of mutual devotion).

We have considered that finding and following the doctrine of Christ is our commission as agents in search of truth. Finding and following this doctrine allow one to establish a true vision of reality and to realize a glorious, self-selected, and personal-effort-established truth, thanks to the grace of Christ. As we sincerely try to follow this commission and as we ask for His help, He will assist us in our search for truth, tell us when we have found it, and guide us to Himself along His way. Only these principles allow us to know Christ, the Rock on which we should build our house, and, thereby, escape domination by the enemy.

Two topics have been systematically addressed in this book: scientific method and the doctrine of Christ. It appears that throughout science, Christianity, and much, if not all, philosophy, the doctrine of Christ is the only methodology capable of conclusively establishing absolute truth, a quest dating back to at least the early Greek philosophers. No wonder Christ describes His doctrine as a rock and assigns it high priority; and no wonder the enemy tries to prevent the finding and following of it by using so many philosophies including Christian and scientific ones to hide true Christianity. The essential component of Christ's method is a direct, personal connection with Omniscience, which we are each invited to establish by the doctrine of Christ. Without this connection there exists neither a knowledge of absolute truth nor anything approaching full comprehension of deep meaning. Without assistance from outside, without an external "reality constraint," one's logic and reasoning are inevitably insufficient for conclusively establishing truth. We have considered the danger in logic, philosophy, and paradigm, that they can be very wrong without one realizing it. The multiplicity of strongly-held Christian and other religious views is a reminder of this danger. To be certain a belief is absolutely correct requires a reliable, external, ostensible confirmation and Omniscience and Omnipotence is capable, reliable, and willing. He has invited us to approach Him.

Reliable understanding of truth and comprehension of meaning lead to knowledge of everything needed to find and follow "the way." Truth and meaning (joy) are indicators that the way leads to a fullness of joy. For joy is manifest in both the struggle and its reward, in both the earthly discipleship and its heavenly consummation. But the Lord has cautioned that a temporary joy may mislead.[6]

The way does not include interesting but nonessential minutia in answers to endless *how* questions, but it does include at least one essential, conclusive answer to an ultimate *who*, *what*, or *why* question. And from the Source of one *who*, *what*, or *why* answer, more answers are available in continuing guidance by the Holy Ghost promised by Christ in His gospel and His doctrine.[7] The rest is details.

We have considered the value of understanding and following truth and of comprehension of meaning and associated feeling. Genuine truth and value are only fully understood through comprehension of their meaning. Albert and Catherine Petty found such understanding by their effort and devotion, as did David W. Patten.

The understanding I am describing in this book provides vision and direction and participation in fulfillment of *the* ancient promise[8] given to Abraham, Isaac, and Jacob (Israel). The type or foreshadow or preview of its fulfillment in our time occurred long ago in salvation from famine of the family or nation of Israel. This original salvation through Joseph of old who was sold into Egypt by his brothers was a symbol of the future salvation which that Joseph himself had foreseen.[9] That the temporal salvation of Israel provided by Joseph of old is a type of the spiritual salvation now offered in our time is suggested in the great blessing Joseph received from his father Jacob (Israel), a blessing that exceeded those given to all his brethren including the one given to Judah which indicated that Christ would descend from him.[10] All these blessings foretell especially what will occur in the *last days*.[11] While the ancient type of the event to come involved a physical famine of food, its fulfillment is a story of salvation of a nation/family (Israel and all who desire to be included) from a famine of hearing the words of the Lord, as foretold by Amos.[12] It is from lack of vision and absence of direction of this nation/family in a spiritual famine of God's word that the Lord's servant, a descendant of this ancient Joseph,[13] was called and ordained in our time to initiate and guide us in this last dispensation of the gospel to provide salvation to all who will receive it, in strict fulfillment of ancient prophecy and in exact accordance with promises made of old.[14]

> What I the Lord have spoken, I have spoken, and I excuse not myself; and though the heavens and the earth shall pass away, my word shall not pass away, but shall all be fulfilled, whether by mine own voice or by the voice of my servants, it is the same.[15]

Joseph Smith was instructed and empowered by Christ and many of His chosen servants from past ages[16] to lead this dispensation. As a devoted follower of Christ and a modern-day prophet and seer, he received, followed, and taught the doctrine of Christ to reach a level of faith at which, like many ancient servants of God, he knowingly went to his death "as calm as a summer's morning, having a conscience void of offense toward God and toward all men." Through this Joseph, Christ has reestablished the knowledge and means by which any who will can receive His gospel, obey His commandments, and obtain His salvation. Nothing cultivates devotion like devotion.

Reaching a high level of devotion is, for each person, a great personal victory in man's ages-old yet new-to-every-generation battle with the enemy, the finding and following of truth that sets one free from the bondage of deceit, ignorance, sin, and domination by Satan.

To obtain understanding of truth, victory, freedom, and enduring joy one must find and follow the doctrine of Christ, incorporating it into his or her own paradigm, philosophy, or system of belief – because only by this doctrine is true reality and understanding of meaning discovered and established. This understanding reveals Christ and His devotion to us, knowledge that raises and expands our vision and frees us from material-dominated thinking to comprehension of meaning and inexpressible joy. This joy is the ostensible-step proof. It confirms that baptism into His restored-original church is the narrow gate that few among the rich in possessions, education, and power, i.e., the potentially prideful, find. Finding this gate is an essential step that many never even contemplate or seek, whether because of ignorance or pride or lack of interest and desire or craftiness of men. After baptism one must continue to follow Him and do His work through the remainder of the war, i.e., throughout his or her mortal and spirit-world life. But, having found and received His way through obedience to His truth, we are helped to endure in it by the power of God, the gift of the Holy Ghost, continually building our devotion to Christ. Our Champion does the rest.

What is the Conclusion?

As "The Preacher" (Ecclesiastes) admonished, "Let us hear the conclusion of the whole matter."[17] We have considered and evaluated the meaning of science and Christianity, examining many concepts of each. Now, at the end of our story, we shall reach a conclusion.

You, dear reader, must shortly compose your own answer to a question, useful because your answer indicates to you how you have understood this book, how you have valued the scientific and Christian principles described in it, and what priorities you place upon them. It therefore indicates to you the priorities you have adopted in your present paradigm. Are these priorities worthy of your life and death? Do they lead to meaning, to great deeds, and to joy? Or are they primarily adopted for pursuit of worldly idols? Your answer to the following question suggests, indirectly, your answers to these other questions.

Before you consider the question it may first be useful to consider a response of the valiant Lady Éowyn of J. R. R. Tolkien's epic saga *The Lord of the Rings*. To noble Lord Aragorn's question, "What do you fear, lady?" she responded "A cage. To stay behind bars, until use and old age accept them, and all chance of doing great deeds is gone beyond recall or desire."[18] One's paradigm can be bars and cage in the limitation it imposes. It can prevent or enable freedom and the doing of great deeds. These are exactly the issues we address. Damnation is to be stopped, to be prevented from progressing, from performing great deeds. Salvation is continued growth in virtue, power, freedom, joy, and the opportunity to accomplish ever-greater deeds for ever-greater purposes. One may be damned now and forever by his or her paradigm if it is fatally flawed, if it allows one only to continually learn but never leads to knowledge of truth, if it denies the power of God. Or one may be saved, enabled, and liberated from a prison of confinement and restriction by finding and following truth.

As your own candid answer to the following question will reveal to you alone important information about yourself, each reader should now honestly answer the following question. Here is the question. Please answer it before reading further.

What do you regard as the few most important, profound, consequential, powerful, and meaningful concepts described in this book?

An indication of your present priorities is almost certainly implied by your answer. To help you extract this indication I tell you my answer and its bases. While your answer is private, I tell you what concepts I find most profound, consequential, powerful, and, therefore, most meaningful (author's prerogative).

(1) We are spirit children of God and as His children He has given us a capacity to become like Him. That is what Fathers do. Since He is our literal spiritual Father, our direct inheritance from Him is primarily spiritual rather than physical. If we wish to discover our inheritance from Him we must seek it through spiritual means, following the designated representative of the Father.

(2) Christ is the designated representative of the Father. He has taken upon Himself (volunteered) and been authorized (chosen) by His Father in the major role that enables us, according to Christ's own command, to become "perfect, even as your Father which is in heaven is perfect."[19] In this role Christ was miraculously born of a virgin mother, sired by God Himself,[20] thus inheriting both a mortal and an immortal nature essential to His mission. (For this cause He is known as the Firstborn of the Father in the Spirit and the Only Begotten of the Father in the flesh.) In this role He willingly suffered inconceivable pain and grief in Gethsemane and died on a cross, rejected and abused by all but a few of His people. In this role He resurrected Himself and will resurrect all of us, His fellow mortals. In this role He called Joseph Smith as His prophet and seer in out time through whom He restored His Church and its necessary teachings and practices so that all the families of the earth may be blessed (the Abrahamic covenant). In this role He loves each person and hopes each of us will love Him, will embrace the Bible and Book of Mormon, receive His doctrine, and the order of heaven by which we may receive fire and the Holy Ghost (the only adequate truth criterion) and inherit a fullness of joy. It was these feelings Christ sincerely holds for us that qualified Him to be chosen, to be the Light and the Example. For God the Father also holds these same feelings for us. How else would the Son faithfully represent the Father to His children?[21]

(3) We chose to participate in this process of becoming perfect. In this process we do not merely act out a predestined history of the universe. Rather, we seek truth, we choose, we act, we will, and the universe responds. Each person is the most important determining force in his or her local, contrary universe. What we do and cause establishes the way things will be for us – our future truth. While Christ wrote the beginning of truth by establishing the way, each of us is the author of his or her own end of truth. For each person the end truth – the future state of that person between the extremes of everlasting joy or endless torment – depends on finding the beginning of truth (Christ) and then writing his or her own end of truth either following Him by obeying His commandments and knowing Him through His doctrine (tasting the heavenly gift) or rejecting Him. In the end, their is no middle ground.

Concepts of science do not make my list, not because they are lacking in either profundity or value but because the above listed ones are more profound and valuable and contain greater meaning. Indeed, it was for these listed concepts and their meaning, and these alone, that the world and the universe were created.[22] These principles are God's truth; the rest is details.

However, many scientific details and inferences from them are profound and I will at least list one. We considered in Chapter 9 one concept that I regard as most profound. We recall it by stating it again:

> Only gravity may transcend the three spatial dimensions we sense. Since we don't sense by gravity but we see, hear, feel, taste, smell, and, apparently, think at least partially through electromagnetic processes mediated by photons, which mediate all atomic and molecular interactions, *by this interpretation we can sense and perceive only three spatial dimensions and one time dimension of the proposed eleven-dimensional spacetime we occupy.*

This theory implies that other, undetected realms of existence may be superimposed on and cohabitant in our own. The spirit world may concurrently occupy the space we live in. As thus illustrated, at least for the present author, even the most profound scientific concepts derive their meaning from their relationship with knowledge and meaning from Christian belief, the only certain basis for *understanding* of reality.

How should one interpret his or her answer? I make two suggestions. First, if no concept beyond the objective and material is included, one's interest is focused primarily, perhaps exclusively, on the mere temporal. The real danger here is being dominated by the enemy who would have us ever excitedly learning but never able to come to a knowledge of the truth. We must mind our philosophy.

Second, one must not only discover truth, one must write his or her own end of truth. Our focus and our aspiration are our guide and our inspiration. Let them be beneficial truth, for the truth one writes for one's self inevitably influences the truth written by others near and dear. Our Silent Coauthor has written an essential, most-beneficial beginning of our future truth and He would have each of us write the most beneficial end of truth for ourselves and help others do the same. We can write such truth, but only if we know Him and receive His help. This is where we want to be.

While many Christian denominations contain truth and promote faith in Christ and obedience to His laws, salvation also requires that baptism and confirmation be received in His way, by His authorized servants holding His priesthood authority in His church. These few listed concepts largely comprise the so-called *plan of salvation* not fully understood or taught outside His restored church, although C. S. Lewis came amazingly close through his devout study and practice of the (original-Greek) Bible.

The truth and value of this plan are testable, if one dares to be sufficiently valiant to test them. And here is the test: sincerely, faithfully, and humbly pray for guidance with real intent to follow it and see what happens. Don't simply recite someone else's prayer, express your own thanks and desires in your own words – establish your own personal connection with Omniscience. Be persistent, to indicate to God the priority you hold for Him. Be specific in your questions and requests. Studying both the Bible and the Book of Mormon is invaluable to this test, especially the latter. Only one church is consistent with *all* the principles and prophecies described in the Bible, all prophecies spoken by God or His servants have been or must be fulfilled. The Book of Mormon or "Stick of Joseph" itself represents fulfillment of several of these prophecies[23] and it has been made available by Christ through the restored-original Church of Jesus Christ.

These are important matters. Both the Bible and Book of Mormon contain truth and describe divine power and offer divine assistance. But the Book of Mormon is unique among books in its origin, purity of truth, and the unmistakable direction it provides because of the many questions implicitly answered when this book is established to be exactly what it represents itself to be. Its truthfulness may be certainly established by the power of God using the test described by Moroni in its final chapter.[24] A similar test is described in the doctrine of Christ and, in either case, the power of God is the key to establishing truth, a capability not available in science or taught in Christian denominations that "deny the power of God." Moroni's test consists of reading the Book of Mormon, asking God with sincerity and faith in Christ if it is truth, and listening for and to an answer with the intent to follow where it leads. An answer may come in innumerable ways. Don't ignore either feelings or "fortuitous coincidences." If you have faith in Christ, expect a miracle. Also expect opposition from the world, for it is temporarily the kingdom of the enemy. The test is conditioned on faith in Christ, willingness and effort to obey Him, humility like a little child (to take instruction and direction), and real intent (to follow guidance received, wherever He leads). Without these qualities the guidance is neither appreciated nor useful and, rejected, is a liability instead of a blessing. For one not yet having these qualities, guidance is therefore withheld.[25] This process alone provides, via a personally-addressed response from God to the individual inquirer, a certain, wonderful witness of truth accompanied by deep feelings of peace and joy.

Truth of the plan of salvation may be partially established by another test, namely, dying. But either passively waiting for or aggressively pursuing this test precludes critical mortal preparation required for obtaining eternal life, that preparation being discovery and adoption of an effective paradigm (including the doctrine of Christ) that will serve one well both here-and-now and there-and-then and obedience to Christ's commandments for generation of devotion to Him. An agent in search of truth wants to discover truth early by valiant, independent effort rather than late by feeble, passive absence of effort or the wrong effort. Changing our paradigm after death will be more difficult because one's paradigm is based on both physical and spiritual experience, especially spiritual experience. Compassion, commitment, and discipline are learned through action, much of which requires a physical body and a physical environment. In developing devotion, how can we place ourselves at risk on behalf of another if there is no risk? Or give physical exertion or prized material goods to another when we possess neither a physical body to exert nor material goods to give? And without a physical body what need would another have for such risk, exertion, or goods? Important opportunities, possessions, and needs by which priorities, values, and devotion may be established and schooled are not available without a physical body in a physical world. Now is the time for personal development.[26]

Moreover, not all questions are answered by dying. If we don't believe in Christ now, we won't believe in Him after we die, at least not for some time. How could we suddenly believe in Christ if our paradigm – the sum of our habits, beliefs, values, attitudes, and priorities including all our biases, preconceptions, and prejudices – is unchanged at death? After death we will know that our spirits continue living and our knowledge and thought continue undiminished and uninterrupted. But simple knowledge does not establish Christ as King in our hearts. Satan and his angels have known the station of Christ and much more from the beginning and regard this knowledge as unimportant in their selfish, rebellious, perverted, and evil paradigms. We must mind our philosophy.

To obtain the best result we must find and follow truth while we have full capacity to do so and to benefit most therefrom. Such opportunity exists now, during our mortal life while we are physical beings in a physical world subject to material needs, appetites, desires, risks, and death. Failure to act now may preclude later action because our will to act (character) is weakened when we don't and our ability to change is diminished. Life is a series of choices few of which are inconsequential in their cumulative effect.

We began in Chapter 1 describing each person as an agent in search of truth, of where we are in this search, and of where we want to eventually be. Now, in this last chapter, we consider these things with greater awareness of their powerful meanings. Test the doctrine of Christ; find, follow, and write the best future truth for yourself by obedience to Christ and help others do the same. Discover the deepest meaning of all – the devotion of the Son of God to you. Be valiant in finding and following truth and in resisting the enemy in his non-passive, contrary universe in which we now, for a brief moment, live. And, last of all, obtain joy, now and forever, for the final state we achieve is a consummation and fulfillment of our present pursuit of devotion to Him who was first devoted to us.

I am a Mortal

In the early 1960s when repeated blockades of land access to Berlin caused much anxiety to its residents and the Western world in general, President John F. Kennedy brought support and comfort to "Berliners" and others in a speech delivered in Berlin wherein he forcefully stated "Ich bin ein Berliner." The feeling created between himself and a huge crowd of over 300,000 by this declaration was powerful, clearly apparent even to a later TV newscast viewer (me). By this statement Kennedy promised the people of Berlin that the might and will of America would be fully invoked to sustain them; in making that pledge he won their affection. (From 1969 to 1972 our oldest children attended primary school in West Germany. The one prominent picture in a well-appointed lobby of their school was of John F. Kennedy.)

The favor was returned in the aftermath of the 11 September 2001 terrorist attack on the United States when some three thousand innocent victims including many rescuers were killed in the destruction of the World Trade Center towers in New York City, part of the Pentagon in Washington, D. C., and four airliners with their passengers and crews. In the period immediately following, sorrow, confusion, and anxiety suffused America. It was then that good people of Berlin, of Europe, and of the world in one way or another declared "We are Americans." These sympathizers through their expressions of support offered their might and will, and in some cases national resources, to succor Americans in their grief and join them in fighting evil. Similar sympathies were expressed on behalf of the Spanish people after a terrorist bombing killed and wounded hundreds of her innocent citizens. These powerful statements buoyed the spirit of Americans and Spaniards.

Another expression of support, however, exceeds in power and scope all others. It was and is the offer of the greatest and most powerful Person in the universe (save One) to succor and save a lost and fallen people. It was expressed by One hanging on a cross when He said "Father, into thy hands I commend my spirit."[27] By this statement the Author of Life,[28] Who had and has absolute power over life and death, died. In so doing He declared *I am a mortal.* And when He took up His life again, He saved from death not only Himself but *all* His fellow mortals as well. Because of His grace, courage, and devotion, immortality is a free gift to all mortals.[29]

And the meaning is deep. Through His power over death He will save all mortals from endless death, freely giving *immortality* to every mortal that lives, has lived, or will live. And for another noble purpose He took upon Himself the unspeakable burden of all sin, wickedness, and suffering – all these that ever occurred or ever will occur, either in our present world or in the world of spirits to come – with the statement "O my Father, if it be possible, let this cup pass from me: nevertheless not as I will, but as thou wilt."[30] It is significant and revealing that just preceding this prayer, when the hour of His greatest need was come, in His great intercessory prayer[31] Christ prayed more for us than for Himself. By His magnanimous, willing acceptance of the terrible, unknown burden of guilt and punishment for our sins and His incomprehensible bearing of them, He took our burdens upon Himself. The yoke Christ would have us wear is easy and the burden He would have us bear is light, because He has already worn the heavy yoke and borne the massive burden. In paying our debts Christ became for all who approach Him "with a broken heart and a contrite spirit" our advocate with the Father to grant unto us not only immortality but also *eternal life*, which is salvation with its everlasting fullness of joy in the presence of and association with both God the Father and God the Son. This state is the only one in which a fullness of joy is received. It is the state reached only by following the doctrine of Christ to approach and know Him, the doctrine uniquely identified and set apart by its Author for this very purpose, for this is the salvation referred to therein. It is the state He lovingly urges each of us to seek. It is the state of which He spoke when He said: "I am come that they might have life [immortality, free to all mortals], and that they might have it more abundantly [eternal life, obtained through the doctrine of Christ]."[32] We can plead to the Father for this life and He will not hear us. But He hears the pleading of His Son, our Advocate with the Father if we follow Him.[33]

The Prophet Joseph Smith taught that "All are within the reach of pardoning mercy, who have not committed the unpardonable sin,[34] which hath no forgiveness, neither in this world, nor in the world to come … [this great reach of pardoning mercy comes through] the greatness of divine compassion and benevolence …"[35] What of the Jews of the time of Christ? They insisted, contrary to the offer and attempts of Pilate,[36] on the release of Bar-abbas and the crucifixion of Christ with the shouts "We have no king but Caesar."[37] and "His blood be upon us, and upon our children."[38] If they don't already, those Jews will one day regret those indiscretions. Although the Great Judge alone must decide, their action was certainly not the unpardonable sin.[34] They hadn't learned by the power of God that Christ is the Son of God and their Messiah, for enlightenment by tasting the heavenly gift through fire and the Holy Ghost is the ostensible proof to the individual seeking to find and follow His way according to the doctrine of Christ.[39] But we had best have real intent when we ask for such knowledge. While this knowledge is meant to be and is a blessing, a certain exposure comes with it since, as Paul teaches by linking the unpardonable sin and the doctrine of Christ,[39] only for one who so knows Christ and thereafter willfully, knowingly, and deliberately rejects and fights against Him, betraying His demonstrated devotion and figuratively assenting to His shame and crucifixion anew and thereby shedding His innocent blood, is the sin unpardonable.[39] While the cost of abusing knowledge of Christ is high, the valiant are not discouraged. They recognize instead the cost of not knowing Christ, which is higher, and they will not betray Him.[40] Without strength, courage, valor, and devotion, the greatest reward is neither sought nor obtained.

You may wonder, dear reader, if you can do it. You already have, once before. Of course the circumstances were different from what they are now. Even so, one-third were lost having full knowledge of God. But that one-third did not include you, dear reader; and you can do it again if you will. The enemy seeks to discourage you. He will try to influence you to think you are unworthy and should not even try. But the power and grace of Christ and His atonement are infinite. "All are within the reach of pardoning mercy, who have not committed the unpardonable sin."

Or Satan may carefully lead you to think you are already saved and need nothing further. He may amplify concern that if you pursue ostensible truth and its ostensible proof you will be ridiculed and rejected by well-meaning friends, associates, and even family and clergy who think they know better. Only Christ has the power to redeem and to grant eternal life, and He states in His doctrine that He will save only those who find and follow His way.[41] Otherwise there is no eternal-life or salvation at the highest level, the more abundant life. He loves sinners who are humble and recognize their need for His help. He also loves the proud and haughty

– after they humble themselves and recognize their need for Him. Although family and friends may fight you at first and perhaps throughout their lifetimes, they will eventually understand and thank you. Be a leader by showing your family, friends, and associates the way to Christ. And save yourself in the process. There is no timetable, but I recommend you not procrastinate for no person knows what tomorrow brings.

We conclude our I-am-a-mortal story and define-universe book with four Bible passages spoken or written by Paul, Christ, and Isaiah (speaking Messianically or for Christ), quotations that summarize the heart and meaning of our story.

> Know this also, that in the last days perilous times shall come. For men shall be lovers of their own selves, covetous, boastful, proud, blasphemers, disobedient to parents, unthankful, unholy, without natural affection, trucebreakers, false accusers, incontinent, fierce, despisers of those that are good, traitors, heady, highminded, lovers of pleasures more than lovers of God; having a form of Godliness, but *denying the power thereof*: from such turn away.[42] (italics added)

> Therefore whosoever heareth these sayings of mine, and doeth them, I will liken him unto a wise man, which built his house upon a rock: and the rain descended, and the floods came, and the wind blew, and beat upon that house; and it fell not: for it was founded upon a rock. And everyone that heareth these sayings of mine, and doeth them not, shall be likened unto a foolish man, which built his house upon the sand: and the rain descended, and the floods came, and the winds blew, and beat upon that house; and it fell: and great was the fall of it.[43]

> These things I have spoken to you, that in me ye might have peace. In the world ye shall have tribulation: but be of good cheer; I have overcome the world.[44]

> And I will bring the blind by a way that they knew not; I will lead them in paths that they had not known: I will make darkness light before them, and crooked things straight. These things will I do unto them, and not forsake them.[45]

Final Notes

I have yet to give the second reason mentioned in the second paragraph of Chapter 1 for forbidding teenagers to read this book. It is, of course, that forbidding teenagers to do something is usually the most effective way to get them to do it. (If you have read this far it worked, even if you are not a teenager.) My reading of a book of this nature as a teenager would have been very useful. That's why I wrote it, why I wanted you to read it, and why I forbade it. I hope you have and will find it useful, dear reader, especially if you are my child, grandchild, niece, nephew, other family, or friend – teenager or adult.

Now a final note addressed to my family: my wife and all our descendents and their spouses and our nieces and nephews and cousins and ... Like our Albert and Catherine and like our friends David and Phoebe, Joseph and Hyrum, we should seek the way, the truth, the life. Like them, we should find the best paradigm and live according to it, with a love for all humans and a devotion to Christ that casteth out fear of man, nature, and even death. Nothing cultivates devotion like devotion. Devotion to Christ and His Father is the order of heaven. It alone is the appropriate response to Their devotion to us, despite us being Their mere creatures and despite Their high and glorious state and magnificent nature compared to our low state and mortal nature. Devotion to Them alone leads to true happiness now and everlasting fullness of joy in the presence of both our Savior and His and our Father. Because of Their devotion to us, They would share all that They have and are with us if only we reciprocate Their devotion.[46] And if I make it there, and it is my intent to do so, I want you there too. Each of you.

Like our Albert and Catherine and like Joseph and David, we also, with the help of Christ, can win the battles and the war. I'll be cheering for you every step of the way, even when you can't see me.[47] Be valiant. I love you always.

Poppa

Notes and References for Chapter 19.

[1] *Bible,* Genesis 19:24, Ezekiel 38:22, Luke 17:29, Revelation 14:10, 19:20; 20:10,14; 21:8.

[2] *Book of Mormon,* 2 Nephi 9:19,26.

[3] *Book of Mormon*, 3 Nephi 17:17, see also *Bible,* 1 Corinthians 2:9.

[4] I have heard the first two lines of this poem but I do not know the author. The last four lines I have added to complete the story.

[5] *Book of Mormon,* 2 Nephi 2:7, 3 Nephi 9:20, 12:19, Moroni 6:2, *Doctrine and Covenants* 20:37, 56:17-18, 97:8. Contrast the attitude of a broken heart and a contrite spirit with an attitude of haughty, prideful contempt.

[6] *Book of Mormon,* 3 Nephi 27:10-11.

[7] Christ states His gospel in Ibid., verses 13-21. See also Ibid., 2 Nephi 32:5-6.

[8] *Bible,* Genesis 12:1-3, 17:2-21, 22:15-18, 26:1-5, 27:26-29, 28:13-15, 32:24-29, 49:1-27, Exodus 19:3-6, Deuteronomy 14:1-2, Isaiah 49:5-26, Jeremiah 3:14, 31:31-37, Hosea 2:18-23, Acts 3:25, 7:2-53, *Book of Mormon,* 1 Nephi 19:15-17, 2 Nephi 10:7-19, 29:14, *Doctrine and Covenants* 84:33-42 and 124:58.

[9] *Bible,* Genesis Chapters 37, 39-48, *Book of Mormon,* 2 Nephi 3, 4:1-2.

[10] Judah's blessing is described in *Bible,* Genesis 49:8-12. While the present Bible text of verse 11 is obscure, its fulfillment is told in Matthew 21:2-5 and the concept is even more clearly described in Zechariah 9:9. Thus, (1) the Messiah was to come through the lineage of Judah. Two other blessings God gave Judah through Jacob were (2) his descendants would be brave warriors (verse 9) and (3) the tribe of Judah would retain political control until the Messiah came (verse 10). This last prophecy was fulfilled under Roman rule because, while Rome had conquered Palestine, Judah still ruled Israel under Rome until 70 AD when they lost all control.

In contrast to Judah's three promises, Joseph's blessing contained six specified in *Bible,* Genesis 49:22-26. (1) Joseph's posterity would be like a "fruitful bough by a well; whose branches run over the wall." In other words, Joseph's posterity would not be confined even by oceans. They would eventually extend "unto the utmost bound of the everlasting hills" (the mountain chain that extends from Alaska through Central America and to southern South America, called the Rocky Mountains and the Andes). (2) Joseph's posterity would experience violence and war but would be courageous soldiers who, in the end, would be victorious (watch Joseph!). (3) The blessings of heaven (sunshine and moisture) would make their inheritance productive. (4) The blessings of the great deep, the oceans, would be with Joseph's posterity. Lehi and his family and other descendents of Joseph in the Book of Mormon reached the American Continents by traveling halfway around the world over the oceans. (5) Joseph received the promise of "blessings of the breast and of the womb." That is, Joseph's posterity would be fertile, strong, and numerous. They are found around the world in many, perhaps all, nationalities. (6) Joseph received the birthright blessing. This was the coveted blessing each patriarch passed on to his most worthy son. By this blessing Joseph received the written record kept by the patriarchal line dating back to Adam, to which Joseph himself contributed great prophecies. Joseph's prophecies and many others are not found in our present Bible in which Moses wrote the first five books. But some of Joseph's prophecies are found in the "inspired version of the Bible" and in the Book of Mormon because Lehi had the record of the patriarchal line, included in the brass plates he brought to America. Some of these prophecies are thereby quoted and referred to in the Book of Mormon.

One of Joseph's prophecies (*Inspired Version of the Bible,* Genesis 50:25), pertaining to after the gathering of Israel from Egypt to the promised land, states "And it shall come to pass that they shall be scattered again; and a branch shall be broken off, and shall be carried into a far country; nevertheless they shall be remembered in the covenants of the Lord, when the Messiah cometh; for he shall be made manifest unto them in the latter days, in the Spirit of power; and shall bring them out of darkness into light; out of hidden darkness, and out of captivity unto freedom." (See also *Book of Mormon,* 2 Nephi 3:5.) The last-quoted phrases are reminiscent of the prophecies of Isaiah, like the one to be quoted later in this chapter cited in endnote 45.

Joseph's sons Ephraim and Manasseh were also blessed by Jacob (*Bible,* Genesis 48:15-22). Jacob blesses them (verse 19), especially Ephraim, that "his seed shall become a multitude of nations." "In thee" (verse 20) may instead be translated "Through thee" and the Septuagint renders "bless" (of this same verse) as "be blessed." We thus find in the blessings of Joseph's sons and Jacob's grandsons a repeat of the covenant given by God to Abraham "And I will make of thee a great nation," in which thy posterity shall become numerous as the sands of the sea shore or the stars of heaven, "and in thee shall all families of the earth be blessed." (*Bible,* Genesis 12:2-3)

Before he left the Israelites, Moses blessed each of the twelve tribes, following Jacob's original language rather closely except for his blessing of Joseph (*Bible,* Deuteronomy 33:13-17). In the case of Joseph's blessing he uses some of the same language of Jacob but he provides additional information. In particular, Moses refers to "his land," suggesting a different land for Joseph across the "deep." He also states that Joseph "shall push the people together to the ends of the earth" with his horns "like the horns of unicorns." In Biblical symbolism, horns represent power and strength, sometimes with outpouring of the Holy Ghost or the power of God (Gaskill, Alonzo L., *The Lost Language of Symbolism,* Deseret Book, Salt Lake City, 2003, 49-50). The Church of Jesus Christ of Latter-day Saints, its restored priesthood power and missionary effort, and publication of the Book of Mormon in many languages all represent a worldwide demonstration of power drawing (pushing) faithful believers in Christ together in fulfillment of the promises given to Joseph, Ephraim, and Manasseh.

[11] *Bible,* Genesis 49:1. However, "in" could be rendered "up to and in" since many of the 12 blessings were long-fulfilled even before the time of Christ. In any case the blessings do tell what will befall Jacob's sons in the last days.

[12] *Bible,* Amos 8:11.

[13] *Book of Mormon,* 2 Nephi 3, 4:1-2.

[14] *Bible,* Genesis 49:22-26, Isaiah 11:11-16; 18:3, 24:3, 29:11-19, 42:16, 54:1-3, Ezekiel 37:15-20, Daniel 2:28,44-45, Malachi 4:5-6, John 10:14-16, 2 Thessalonians 2:3, Acts 3:19-21, 19:1-7, 1 Corinthians 15:29, 1 Peter 3:18-20, 4:6, 2 Peter 2:1.

[15] *Doctrine and Covenants* 1:38; see also *Bible,* Isaiah 55:11.

[16] *Bible,* Matthew 17:9-13, *Doctrine and Covenants* 7, 76, 110.

[17] *Bible,* Ecclesiastes or, The Preacher 12:13.

[18] Tolkien, J. R. R., *The Lord of the Rings: Part Three: The Return of the King,* Ballantine Books, New York, 1965, 62.

[19] *Bible,* Matthew 5:48.

[20] *Bible,* Luke 1:26-37, *Book of Mormon,* Alma 7:10.

[21] *Bible,* John 14:7-9.

[22] *Pearl of Great Price,* Moses 1:33,39, Abraham 3:22-26.

[23] Teachings and prophecies in the Bible that relate to the Book of Mormon include the following (among others not listed) *Bible,* Genesis 49:1,22-26, Isaiah 29:11-14,18-19 (see endnote 61 of Chapter 15), 42:16, Ezekiel 37:15-20, Matthew 24:3,14, Mark 13:4,10, John 7:14-17, 10:14-16, Hebrews 6:1-6, 2 John 1:9-11.

[24] *Book of Mormon,* Moroni 10:4-5, 7 Moroni's promise reads "And when ye shall receive these things (knowledge through reading the Book of Mormon), I would exhort you that ye would ask God, the Eternal Father, in the name of Christ, if these things are not true; and if ye shall ask with a sincere heart, with real intent, having faith in Christ, he will manifest the truth of it unto you, by the power of the Holy Ghost. And by the power of the Holy Ghost ye may know the truth of all things. ... And ye may know the he [Christ] is, by the power of the Holy Ghost."

While the wording "if these things are *not* true;" seems awkward by today's convention, it is the convention of the Biblical language in which the Book of Mormon was written (see, for example, *Bible,* Malachi 3:10 – "if I will *not* open you the windows of heaven, and pour you out a blessing"). Would an uneducated frontier laborer (Joseph Smith, Jr.) have noticed such a detail? Possibly, in this case, but not in the cases of all the many other subtleties more obscure and wholly unknown in the Western world until after the Book of Mormon was published. Examination of literary structures, wordprint analyses of the prophets who wrote the book (of which no wordprint corresponds to Joseph Smith's, the translator), and distinct terminology and proper names it uses have only recently been carefully studied and this scholarly work taken together forms a compelling body of evidence that the Book of Mormon is genuine. (See, for example, Givens, Terryl L., *By the Hand of Mormon,* Oxford University Press, Oxford, 2002.) However, the importance of this scholarly evidence is less conclusive than the more powerful proof, the method for discovering truth described in the doctrine of Christ. This ostensible-step proof is additionally and similarly described by the Prophet Moroni (see above quotation in this endnote and the next endnote) in the final pages of the book. Until one performs one of these tests, no answer is certain and no issue is conclusively settled.

[25] *Book of Mormon,* Moroni 10:3. "... if it be wisdom in God that ye should read [the Book of Mormon]..." This clause refers to receiving a witness of the truth in reading the Book of Mormon, according to Moroni's promise, but the principle is more general. The general principle is that if we are not ready in desire and intent, we receive no witness by fire and the Holy Ghost to spare us additional accountability. How do we discover if we are ready? By applying Moroni's promise to receive the witness. If we are not ready and therefore receive no witness, we make adjustments in personal behavior and attitude, more carefully follow the requirements given by Moroni in his promise – thus strengthening ourselves – and do it over again taking greater care to satisfy them.

[26] However, aside from temporary separation from loved ones, death is not so tragic as we generally suppose, leading to questions of how a loving God could allow "such a tragedy" to

occur? Between birth and judgement we experience two realms, earth and spirit world. What we don't accomplish in the first, we can accomplish in the second, provided we have established and continue to hold a good paradigm and good habits. While necessary ordinances must be performed on earth, such as baptism, confirmation, and eternal marriage, these can be done by others on behalf of the dead and will be the principal work of the "millennium" in fulfilling God's covenant with Abraham, Isaac, and Jacob and their descendents. This knowledge allows understanding of Jesus' statement (*Bible,* Matthew 22:30, Mark 12:25) that in the resurrection they neither marry nor are given in marriage. Eternal marriage, the only kind that endures beyond death, is an earthly ordinance. (*Doctrine and Covenants* 132:15-27, 45-48.)

[27] *Bible,* Luke 23:46, Matthew 27:50, Mark 15:37.

[28] *Bible,* John 1:1-3.

[29] *Bible,* 1 Corinthians 15:21-22.

[30] *Bible,* Matthew 26:39,42, Mark 14:36,39, Luke 22:42.

[31] *Bible,* John 17.

[32] *Bible,* John 10:10.

[33] *Bible,* Isaiah 3:13, 51:22, 53:12, Matthew 10:32-33, *Book of Mormon,* 2 Nephi 2:9, Mosiah 15:8, Moroni 7:28, *Doctrine and Covenants* 29:5, 38:4.

[34] "For it is impossible for those who were once enlightened, and have tasted of the heavenly gift, and were made partakers of the Holy Ghost (by following the principles and ordinances of the doctrine of Christ), and have tasted the good word of God, and the powers of the world to come, if they shall fall away, to renew them again unto repentance; seeing they crucify to themselves the Son of God afresh, and put him to an open shame." (*Bible,* Hebrews 6:4-6; see also *Doctrine and Covenants* 76:25-49.)

[35] *Teachings of the Prophet Joseph Smith,* Deseret Book Company, Salt Lake City, 1961.

[36] *Bible,* Acts 3:13-18.

[37] *Bible,* John 19:15.

[38] *Bible,* Matthew 27:25.

[39] *Bible,* Hebrews 6:1-6.

[40] *Book of Mormon,* Moroni 1:3 begins "And I, Moroni, will not deny the Christ." Each of us, like Moroni, must decide who he or she will be and what he or she will do. If we just let what happens happen in our non-passive, contrary universe, it won't be what we will want.

[41] See also *Bible,* John 3:16-21, James 2:17-26, Mark 16:14-20.

[42] *Bible,* Matthew 7:24-27.

[43] *Bible,* 2 Timothy 3:1-5.

[44] *Bible,* John 16:33.

[45] *Bible,* Isaiah 42:16; see also 17-23. Luke 4:18 refers to Isaiah 61:1-2 but is connected to these passages as well.

[46] *Bible,* Romans 8:16-17, *Doctrine and Covenants* 76:50-70, 132:20-24.

[47] *Doctrine and Covenants* 38:11-12 states "For all flesh is corrupted before me; and the powers of darkness prevail upon the earth, among the children of men, in the presence of all the hosts of heaven – Which causeth silence to reign, and all eternity is pained, and the angels are waiting the great command to reap down the earth, to gather the tares that they may be burned; and, behold, the enemy is combined." This passage indicates that the hosts of heaven are observing our activity on earth (perhaps from a realm within seven of the ten proposed spatial dimensions we don't now sense). When darkness prevails, silence reigns; when light prevails, I suppose an attitude of cheering occurs. Even when I can't interfere or you can't see me, I'll be watching and cheering for you.

Appendices

Appendices

Appendix A

An Examination of *Use* of the Scientific Method

To be realistic a critical examination of scientific and of Christian belief must consider one particular limitation common to both. That is, beyond any limitations or flaws in either the scientific method or Christian inquiry themselves, humans are limited in their ability and nature in applying either. Newton, in Chapter 7, and we, in Chapter 15, compared a few beliefs found in current Christianity to those described in the Bible and historical records. These comparisons indicate that belief and practice of most Christian denominations differ from that described in the Bible despite the fact that the Bible is the authority traditionally claimed by these denominations. What influence or limitation leads to this inconsistency? And what leads to inconsistency in the practice of science?

Indeed, how can inconsistency occur in science given that consistency is its essential truth criterion and its strict requirements of objectivity, reproducibility, and rigor? The answer is science is utilized by humans, creatures that are not very objective, reproducible, or rigorous and influenced by preconception, bias, and culture even when they strive to be objective and free of prejudice. In view of this nature of humans, any philosophical tool in their hands is flawed. Tradition, culture, paradigm, and, consequently, what many seek and accept can lead to inconsistency in both religion and science. In this appendix we illustrate this effect for the case of science. But the illustration covers a broader range of application that includes religion.

The susceptibility of science or another tool to error because of the limited, imperfect nature of humans in a non-passive, contrary universe is well illustrated by scientific inquiry into topics amenable to scientific treatment. Especially when a topic is new, ill-defined, and controversial, no entrenched tradition rationalizing the new topic has yet developed. A topic with "new" status is a scientific specialty at the beginning and most fragile stage of its development, the stage where results are not yet compelling and multiple, contrary opinions are strongly held. This is the stage in which scientific (political) battles are intense. Kuhn's "revolutions" may be only the last part of such wars, after the new science or theory is sufficiently established to mobilize large forces on both (all) sides. After a revolution, once scientific development of a field is mature, little controversy remains and, for better or worse, the mature science is accepted as compelling, correct tradition. (Of course, a new rebellion may begin with the emergence of new facts or theory.) Thus, a new theory and scientific inquiry itself are most open and vulnerable at the early stage when results are not yet widely accepted with at least two contrary opinions popular, with ideological war occurring between at least two camps. Ideally, any error will be recognized and corrected by the consistency-with-observation test, settling the war. But during battle, conditions are seldom ideal. And interpretation of experience is always influenced by paradigm so that error in paradigm is not always detected. Indeed, E. T. Jaynes (*Probability Theory, The Logic of Science,* Cambridge University Press, 2003, xxvi) observed that "new data that we insist on analyzing in terms of old ideas (that is, old models [or theories or data] which are not questioned) cannot lead us out of the old ideas."

A similar problem occurs in a religious paradigm when followers of some denomination are divided between at least two contrary beliefs on some issue. An examination of history of scientific theories thus also illuminates the process of adoption of new religious truth.

Surviving and becoming part of a common culture presumably indicates a new theory or belief is more correct *in the common paradigm* than its alternative(s). I say "usually" because one might ask "How many of our present scientific theories or religious traditions are fundamentally correct?" A responsible answer is, especially in religion, "Probably not all." A skeptical answer is, "Possibly not any."

But even in a non-skeptical view, historical instances demonstrate that new theories later demonstrated to be more correct were suppressed because scientists who judged them didn't understand them or rejected them for another reason. One example is Maxwell's electromagnetics theory which was condemned by leading scientists and thereafter languished for twenty-five years until Hertz's experiments found it to be correct in every detail (Chapter 9). Another example occurred in an early investigation in the kinetic theory of gases. As Garber, Brush, and Everitt summarize,

> Any kinetic theory of gases, even after the acceptance of the wave theory of heat, faced a formidable array of data to explain and the equally formidable barrier of the traditional coupling of the nature of heat and matter to explicate or explain away. ... Before 1857 kinetic theories of gases had been proposed, but by theorists whose works stand in isolation against a background of indifference and outright hostility.[1]

In 1845 British engineer John James Waterston submitted from Bombay, where he was employed teaching navigation and gunnery to naval cadets for the East India Company, a manuscript for publication in *Philosophical Transactions* of the Royal Society. It described his profound and truly innovative work in kinetic theory of gases including discovery of the connections between gas temperature and both pressure and average gas-molecule velocity, results published twelve years later by Rudolph Clausius for which Clausius was lauded. Waterston's paper even contained estimates of gas-molecule sizes as well as hints of many other useful ideas later developed. Waterston received no response regarding his submission. But it finally appeared in the Royal Society's *Philosophical Transactions* in 1892 nearly fifty years later and nine years after the death in obscurity of Waterston at age 72. It had been filed away, rejected for publication by two dismissive "expert" referees. One referee described it as "nonsense, unfit even for reading before the Society,"[1] and the other as exhibiting "much skill and many remarkable accordances with the general facts ... but the original principle is ... by no means a satisfactory basis for a mathematical theory."[1] The "original principle" was the atomic theory of matter. Behind these criticisms lay a deep bias against atomic theory which persisted through the century until it was finally and dramatically overthrown in the early 1900s. Thus, this valuable paper sat unpublished in the Royal Society archives until it was finally discovered there by Lord Rayleigh in 1891, then secretary of the Royal Society, who immediately had it published along with his own brief account of the history of the paper, as the first article in the first 1892 issue. Waterston's paper anticipated many important results for which other scientists had later been credited and "omission to publish it at the time," wrote Rayleigh, "probably retarded the subject by ten or fifteen years"[1] besides being tragic in denying Waterston recognition he rightfully should have received.

Limitations in Scientific Inquiry

To assess limitations in scientific and Christian inquiry due to "paradigm inertia" or tradition, we examine the influence of tradition or culture on scientific inquiry in a test case. The parallel between science and religion, already noted, allows us to consider both while drawing our illustration solely from science. Because the early stage of a new specialty is most critical in scientific belief, we choose a test case in this stage. What test case would be useful? One characteristic of such a case is that its subject is regarded as highly controversial or even heretical because thinking about it is diverse and may run counter to currently accepted belief, as Waterston's theory did. (No electromagnetic theory existed at the time Maxwell proposed his theory. It was rejected not for itself but because of the novel method Maxwell used in deducing it.) Such a new theory or belief and those espousing it would consequently be regarded with scorn by many of those bonded strongly to established tradition or alternative theory.

Many candidate subjects have recently fit these requirements including claims of out-of-body experiences, cold fusion, polywater, and the historical chronology proposed by Immanuel Velikovsky. (In fact, when one considers every criticism seriously, no scientific belief may be regarded as certain, as also follows from logical flaws in scientific methodology itself.) We choose the topic of unidentified flying objects (UFOs) and take as our test case *the question of the existence of UFOs*. Few issues were more skeptically regarded, controversial, and emotionally charged a few decades ago by scientists and nonscientists alike. A little temporal separation allows us to now take a more detached and objective look.[2]

We shall therefore examine *the reaction of scientists* to the UFO question. In scientific inquiry care must be taken to sort fact from fantasy among circulating observations, beliefs, and opinions, i.e., to establish a reliable basis of facts. We do not attempt to establish UFO facts herein for the reason that we shall not attempt any conclusion about UFOs, nor is any required to make our point. Our point is only to illustrate that *limitation of scientific inquiry is imposed by humans' less-than-perfect-use of the method*. This limitation is apparent in reactions of some who investigated UFOs and others who sabotaged such effort.

In examining effective use of scientific inquiry it is useful to recall the discussion of Chapter 2 of three student categories and their different attitudes toward learning. Category-one students seek to learn because while they may be knowledgeable they realize they still have much to learn; category-two students won't learn because they think they already know; and category-three students don't learn because they simply don't care.

Before beginning we review essential qualities of scientific methodology so that we can readily recognize both good science and its opposite.

Philosophy Required in Scientific Inquiry

Objectivity or absence of bias and preconception is required in scientific inquiry. For this very reason only objective, lowest-common-denominator, reproducible facts are used in science. Observation, analysis, evaluation, and deduction must all be lowest-common-denominator objective and reproducible. Any scientific inquiry is compromised if any element is not objectively performed (performed without bias or preconception) such that the objectivity and universality of the result may be compromised. This limitation has been recognized by thinkers in many ages. Thus the caution of Aristotle: "Those who wish to succeed must ask the right preliminary questions." And just this point is compellingly urged by C. S. Lewis regarding evaluation of miracles. We quote here two paragraphs from Lewis' book *Miracles*, with the word "miracles" or words "the miraculous" replaced by "*UFO phenomena*" or "*a UFO phenomenon*."

> Every event which might claim to be *a UFO phenomenon* is, in the last resort, something presented to our senses, something seen, heard, touched, smelled or tasted. And our senses are not infallible. If anything extraordinary seems to have happened, we can always say that we have been the victims of an illusion. If we hold a philosophy which excludes *UFO phenomena*, this is what we always shall say. What we learn from experience depends on the philosophy we bring to experience. It is therefore useless to appeal to experience before we have settled, as well as we can, the philosophical question.
>
> If immediate experience cannot prove or disprove *UFO phenomena*, still less can history do so. Many people think one can decide whether *a UFO phenomenon* occurred in the past by examining the evidence "according to the ordinary rules of historical inquiry." But the ordinary rules cannot be worked until we have decided whether *UFO phenomena* are possible, and if so, how probable they are. For if they are impossible, then no amount of historical evidence will convince us. If they are possible but immensely improbable, then only mathematically demonstrative evidence will convince us: and since history never provides that degree of evidence for any event, history can never convince us that *a UFO phenomenon* occurred. If, on the other hand, *UFO phenomena* are not intrinsically improbable, then the existing evidence will be sufficient to convince us that quite a number of *UFO phenomena* have occurred. The result of our historical inquiries thus depends on the philosophical views which we have been holding before we even began to look at the evidence. The philosophical question must therefore come first.[3]

Objectivity is an essential philosophical position when an issue is to be treated without preconception, bias, or prejudice. No evidence may then be dismissed out of hand – the value of evidence must be determined by objective observation, analysis, and evaluation. But humans are not objective in observation, analysis, and evaluation.

Here is an inherent limitation in scientific inquiry employed by humans – inherent subjectivity or bias – that will become glaringly obvious as we proceed. One problem arises when evidence is rejected because it doesn't agree with a fixed, preconceived scientific paradigm which is supposed to be consistent with all previously known evidence. But not all evidence is previously known. New evidence is not only possible, it should be sought. This problem of prejudice lies not in the method but rather in its use. But, simultaneously, it lies in the method because the method is always used by real (rather than ideal, detached-observer) humans.

A Common Attitude among Scientists regarding UFOs

Without objectivity and, in particular, without recognition of the possibility that new events may occur that lie beyond scientists' present ability to predict, unpredictable events are sometimes simply dismissed out of hand (indicative of a non-category-one-student attitude). To some, only observations of things already understood or only results predicted by laws already known are acceptable. Otherwise, evidence must be rejected because it conflicts with accepted paradigms. But science, and philosophy in general, are not a destination but a journey to a distant goal – understanding of universal truth. Thus, a category-two-student attitude, or paradigm paralysis, leads to sterility because it is fatal to learning anything new. It is reminiscent of the positivist attitude (see endnotes 13 and 16 of Chapter 2). And just such an attitude has been brought to science by many in the case of UFO evidence.

> During an evening reception of several hundred astronomers at Victoria, British Columbia, in the summer of 1968, word spread that just outside the hall strangely maneuvering lights – UFOs – had been spotted. The news was met by casual banter and the giggling sound that often accompanies an embarrassing situation. Not one astronomer ventured outside in the summer night to see for himself.[4]

Indeed, the reaction of some highly regarded scientists when confronted with accounts of UFO sightings has resembled a modern witch-hunt, with the observer the object of the hunt. Sometimes such a scientist has even proudly declared that he or she has not bothered to even examine evidence, supposedly thereby implying the evidence is unworthy of examination. However, arrogantly dismissing evidence out of hand indicates prejudice and dogmatism, the antithesis of science and of an agent in search of truth. Despite a contrary intention, such behavior reveals more about the scientist than it does about the evidence.

Of course a scientist should not be too harshly condemned for being merely human. The information about UFOs, especially that found in the popular press, was highly sensationalized. While little would seem to be at stake in establishing merely if a flying object is or is not identifiable, it appears that some scientists reacted to the general sensationalizing of the phenomena by avoiding it. A few individuals made fantastic, self-serving claims about UFO experiences resulting in "flying saucer cults" based on their claimed experiences in which the leader of a cult was typically so recognized by virtue of a singular experience, which was often not so singular after all being conveniently followed by other similar claims which keep the claimant on front pages of cooperative newspapers and at the head of a growing cult. Adequate evidence for evaluating such a case should include mental capacity, stability, credibility, and possible motivations for making a false claim, evidence that newspaper reporters rarely bother to acquire. Many scientists chose to express their distaste for such a mess by avoiding any involvement, as if it were the plague, including not even considering merely whether a flying object was or was not identifiable.

While some UFO sighting claimants fail to pass reasonable requirements of mental capacity, stability, and credibility, others do and their claims are coherent and consistent, with a sighting often reported by several, clearly responsible, stable, and capable witnesses. Although non-repeatable by their nature, such accounts have come from all over the world, often from persons because of a sense of duty expecting and sometimes experiencing ridicule for their effort from officials and the press.

One careful analysis[5] of UFO reports by only multiple, responsible, often independent observers indicates that, while undeniably describing events quite novel according to present understanding, clear and consistent patterns emerge containing elements common to almost all these reports. Such patterns could be useful in scientific inquiry if they regularly occur in experience that is not reproducible in a conventional sense. Indeed, in some fields such as anthropology, evolutionary biology, and political science, information in the form of consistent patterns is the kind sought. But a careful scientific inquiry into UFO phenomena of sufficient scope, duration, and motivation has never been performed.

The single, large-scale investigation of UFO phenomena was severely flawed as scientific inquiry by the attitude and motivation of its personnel, apparently due to a pervasive attitude among scientists and the public (the common culture). Evidence of an absence of the requisite philosophy for scientific inquiry in this investigation and, particularly, in its later evaluation by scientists will be described. This unique, large-scale investigation was an official inquiry into UFOs performed by the United States Air Force and was assigned the code name Project Blue Book for most of its lifetime.

Project Blue Book

The U. S. Air Force acted as steward and investigator of reports on UFO phenomena for twenty-two years. The original investigation was initiated in September 1947 and code-named Project Sign. The effort was renamed Project Grudge on 11 February 1949 and Project Blue Book in the summer of 1951. The investigation retained this code-name until it was terminated in December of 1969. Apparently the mission statement for this project included simply the generic task of logging and evaluating or explaining UFO phenomena reports from any observers. The mission was one of national defense, rather than science, and was therefore focused on whether such sightings suggested an aggressive or dangerous intent of some unknown enemy. UFO sightings have not seemed to indicate such an intent. Perhaps for this reason, all sightings, both ones reported by crackpots and ones reported by multiple, responsible witnesses, to cite the two extremes, came to be regarded in a single light.

The officers who headed Project Blue Book and its predecessors were underlings in the military hierarchy, either captains or majors. Between 1952 and 1969 the project heads were, in order, Captains Ruppelt, Hardin, Gregory, and Majors Friend and Quintanilla. The rank of a project head is an indication of the perceived importance of the project and the relatively low ranks of the Blue Book heads indicated that the Air Force did not regard this project as important. Career officers at this level typically anticipate two things with greatest interest: promotion and early retirement. Because of these interests, especially the first, such officers generally defer to their superiors in any difference in opinion, even when their superiors know little about a project or the nature of its data. And superior officers, accustomed to such deferential treatment, are not always careful about their pronouncements. For these reasons it seems that the predominant attitude within the project was established not by those working in it or even heading it, but by remote superiors in the pentagon having little knowledge of the evidence but who were instead insiders at the top of a rigid-military-thinking hierarchy which established official Air Force policy by unspoken fiat.

The location of the project was Wright-Patterson Air Force Base in Dayton, Ohio. Consequently, when the Air Force hired a civilian consultant astronomer to help analyze (explain) UFO reports, they chose J. Allen Hynek (1910-1986) a professional astronomer then acting as the director of the McMillin Observatory at Ohio State University and later the Chairman of the Department of Astronomy and Director of the Lindheimer Astronomical Research Center at Northwestern University. Hynek describes his selection as a "natural choice" because he was "the closest professional astronomer at hand." Despite Hynek's modesty, the choice was fortunate. Not only were Hynek's credentials impressive, anyone who reads his remarkable book, *The UFO Experience, A Scientific Inquiry,*[5] will quickly recognize his excellent facility in scientific inquiry as well as his gift for clear and careful writing. These qualities are too rarely found in UFO literature and Hynek's book is invaluable in assessing the problem we are considering. We use it as our primary source of information.

Hynek's twenty-two-year tenure as scientific consultant in this project gave him unique insight and complete access to the data, some of which he personally collected and evaluated. While the data were advertised by the Air Force as being unclassified, they were housed in a classified area so that no one had access without proper clearance. Hynek, as a civilian Air Force employee, had the necessary clearance.

As early as the Project Grudge period, the subject of UFO phenomena began to be treated with subtle ridicule by the Pentagon.[6] With the highest-authority levels setting this tone, those involved throughout the whole effort took on a skeptical attitude. Successful UFO investigations were regarded as those which found explanations in some natural process for a purported UFO sighting. Marsh gas was a common one used throughout the 1960s, an explanation first proposed by Hynek for sightings over a swampy area but later used widely by the Air Force and one for which Hynek consequently suffered some ridicule in the press. When a purported UFO sighting could not be explained in terms of some natural process, the investigation was regarded as a failure. This attitude led to convoluted wording and constrained logic like that contained in the following report by an Air Force captain.

> The unquestioned reliability of the observer, together with the clear visibility existing at the time of the sighting, indicate that the objects were observed. The probable cause of such sightings opens itself only to conjecture and leaves no logical explanation based on the facts at hand.[7]

Might not one logical explanation based on the facts at hand be that the observer actually observed some unidentified flying objects. It seems that "the facts at hand" covered only "known" natural phenomena and no others were allowed. From the viewpoint of scientific inquiry, the culture that pervaded the project doomed any scientific benefit it might provide from nearly the beginning. For how can one come to see any object whose existence he regards to be impossible. He must regard it as an illusion. All the easier when he himself did not see it but only had to log it as such in the project record. Nevertheless, in spite of this *de facto* philosophical predisposition, there eventually existed 12,000 reports of UFO sightings among which twenty percent were categorized as "unidentified."

Moreover, from a scientific point of view, the significant reports are the ones that remained unexplained after a competent investigation was concluded. These were the reports that potentially had something new to tell us. But these were the ones regarded as failures and simply filed away and forgotten. Except that Hynek did not forget them. He gleaned more than 60 such reports for which he was not able to find a consistent, logical explanation and which were most reliable by reasons, in practically each case, of multiple, often independent witnesses of high credibility, including flight controllers, pilots, radar operators, policemen, scientists, engineers, and just common everyday people with families and responsible jobs. It is interesting to compare Hynek's book to the officially commissioned report of the Condon Committee that resulted in the termination of the Blue Book effort, which we will do. But before we come to this comparison, more information about the Air Force attitude and data will be useful.

Hynek characterized the Air Force attitude in terms like "official apathy" and "ridicule gauntlet." After years of investigation, no meaningful results of any scientific use were ever obtained. Why? Hynek's answer is "in very large measure simply because no one in authority ... conducted any investigation worthy of the name. What investigations were carried out (and I overheard many phone conversations during my regular visits to Blue Book) and what questions were asked were almost always aimed at establishing a misperception, and the questions were so directed. ... Investigations were predicated on the assumption that all UFO sightings were either misperceptions or the products of unstable minds. Such official failings are tragic in the extreme ..."[8] Some specific examples follow.

An Air Force lieutenant-colonel reported independent, simultaneous observations by radar and multiple visual observers in New Mexico on 4 November 1957:

> The opinion of the preparing officer is that this object may possibly have been an unidentified aircraft, possibly confused by the runways at Kirtland Air Force Base. The reasons for this opinion are:

1. The observers are considered competent and reliable sources and in the opinion of this interviewer actually saw an object they could not identify.
2. The object was tracked on radarscope by a competent operator.
3. The object does not meet identification criteria for any other phenomena.[9]

With respect to this report, Hynek makes the following observation:

> That is, the observers were reliable, the radar operator was competent, and the object couldn't be identified: therefore, it was an *airplane*. In the face of such reasoning one might well ask whether it would ever be possible to discover the existence of new empirical phenomena in any area of human experience.[9]

Hynek introduces another case as follows:

> One case ... stands on the record as an example of the ludicrous manner in which Project Blue Book sometimes went about investigating a case. A more lucid example of the disregard of evidence unfavorable to a preconceived explanation could hardly be found. Were such a blatant disregard of evidence to occur in a court of law, it would be considered an outrageous travesty of legal procedures. The astounding disregard and distortion of reported facts, failure to listen to witnesses, and obdurate and adamant closemindedness can be explained either as incompetence of the most gross variety or as a deliberate attempt to present a semblance of incompetence for ulterior purposes.[10]

This case involved an initial sighting of a UFO on 16 April 1966 by two Sheriff's deputies, Dale F. Spaur and Wilbur Neff, of Portage County, Ohio. A woman in neighboring Summit County called in a report about 4:45 am of a brightly lighted object "as big as a house" flying over her neighborhood. The deputies were directed by radio to investigate. When the deputies saw the object and reported in, they were instructed to follow and observe it, which they did for some 70 miles. About 40 miles into the chase they were joined by Officer Wayne Huston in his police cruiser near East Palestine, Ohio. Huston had been monitoring the radio conversation between the first pair of deputies and their headquarters. Thereafter both cars pursued the UFO, at 80 to 85 mph and sometimes at speeds up to 105 mph. A fourth observer, Police Officer Frank Panzenella of Conway, Pennsylvania, who was already watching the UFO, was joined by this group some 20 miles into Pennsylvania, where all four observers watched the UFO eventually shoot straight up into the air and disappear. Written reports from all four witnesses provided many details about the UFO and its behavior. According to Hynek,

> Major Quintanilla, then head of Project Blue Book, attempted to establish the interpretation that all four officers, who were sequentially and independently involved, had first seen a satellite (even though no satellite was visible at that time over Ohio) and somehow had transferred their attention to Venus (which was seen by the observers while the object was in sight). The original "investigation" was perfunctory; the initial inquiry, made of only one witness, Spaur, was a two and one-half minute phone call, which, according to Spaur, began with the words, "Tell me about this mirage you saw." The second interview, also by phone, lasted only one and one-half minutes. According to a signed statement by Spaur, Quintanilla apparently wanted Spaur to say he had seen the UFO for only a few minutes; when he told that it had been in sight almost continuously while the observers chased it from Ohio into Pennsylvania, a distance of some 60 miles, he quickly terminated the discussion.

Quintanilla's method was simple: disregard any evidence that was counter to his hypothesis. Less than five minutes of phone interview sufficed for Blue Book to come to a "solution" of the case; ...

This case now appears in Blue Book statistics as an observation of Venus even though the object *and* Venus were reported to have been seen.

... this incident ... is representative of my experience with Blue Book over many years as consultant. What I considered obvious cases of misinterpretation and unreliable reporting Blue Book would take some pains to establish for the record; cases such as this, which were open to question and contained the possibility that something "genuinely new and empirical" might be contained in it, were treated with little or no interest.

... two issues are interwoven in this entire matter: one is the question of the reality of the reported UFO phenomena; the other is the matter of scientific methodology and scientific integrity. Regardless of how the first issue is resolved in time, the record will show that once again in the long history of science prejudice, emotion, and "temporal provincialism" marred, in the case of UFO research, the otherwise largely exemplary march of science and intellectual adventure.[11]

Hynek summarizes his twenty-two year experience within Blue Book in a theorem and a corollary. The Blue Book Theorem and corollary are:

For any given reported UFO case, if taken by itself and without respect and regard to correlations with other UFO cases in this and other countries, it is always possible to adduce a possible even though farfetched natural explanation, if one operates solely on the hypothesis that all UFO reports, by the very nature of things, must result from purely well known and accepted causes.[12]

In popular language this theorem states "It can't be; therefore, it isn't." The corollary is

It is impossible for Blue Book to evaluate a UFO report as anything other than a misidentification, a hoax, or a hallucination. (In those relatively few cases where even this procedure met with difficulty, the report was evaluated as "Unidentified" but with no indication that the theorem had been outraged.)[12]

Some accused Project Blue Book of being a cover-up operation. Hynek dismissed this thought with the following comment.

All my association with Blue Book showed clearly that the project rarely exhibited any scientific interest in the UFO problem. They certainly did not address themselves to what should have been considered the central problem of the UFO phenomenon: is there an as yet unknown physical or psychological or even paranormal process that gives rise to those UFO reports that survive severe screening and still remain truly puzzling?

Such lack of interest belies any charge of "cover-up;" they just didn't care.[13]

In this book we call that approach a category-three-student attitude, one in which learning is impossible.

The Condon Committee Report

On 6 October 1966 the fate of Project Blue Book was placed in the hands of a scientific committee charged with the responsibility of reviewing the work of the Project and recommending on the basis of objective science whether continuation of the effort was justified. A formal contract began on this day between the University of Colorado and the U. S. Air Force. Dr. Edward U. Condon was the director of the committee. Condon was an accomplished physicist of considerable renown.

The investigative tone the committee would adopt was quickly established. Since Condon was busy he did not oversee committee activities himself. Rather, a project administrator, Mr. Robert Low, was appointed to this task. Within the first two weeks of the project, Low had already outlined the format of the final report, including the probable chapter headings and space dedicated to each chapter. The implication of Low's early disposition regarding the tone and substance of the final report suggested his attitude toward the project was already fixed.

Indeed, Low was active before the committee was even established laying the "proper" conceptual groundwork in anticipation that the University would obtain the contract. In an infamous memo written by Low on 9 August 1966, some three months before the project even began, Low stated his view of the posture the committee should take *in their final report*.

> The trick would be, I think, to describe the project so that, to the public, it would appear a totally objective study but, to the scientific community, would present the image of a group of nonbelievers trying their best to be objective but having an almost zero expectation of finding a saucer.[14]

Of course Low was only an assistant expressing an attitude that he perceived his boss, Condon, would approve. But two members of the committee were dismissed apparently because they disclosed the content of this memo and Condon's administrative assistant eventually resigned because of the ethical and political quagmire that had been created.[15]

And what was Condon's predisposition on the material he was charged to objectively evaluate? Barely three months into the eighteen month term of the study, Condon spoke to a group on 26 January 1967 in Corning, NY. The *Star-Gazette* of Elmira, NY, of that date reported the following quotation of Condon. "It is my inclination right now to recommend that the government get out of this business. My attitude right now is that there's nothing to it … but I'm not supposed to reach a conclusion for another year. Maybe it (the UFO problem) would be a worthwhile study for those groups interested in meteorological phenomena." While Condon's attitude here is that there is "nothing to it" and that it really belonged in the domain of meteorological phenomena (as if meteorological phenomena were nothing?), he shortly thereafter requested an additional 259,146 1967 dollars to continue the work.

That same year Condon spoke at the National Bureau of Standards in Washington. Condon later admitted, as substantiated by reports of those in attendance, that almost his entire talk was directed to three crackpot cases with which he had *not* been involved. A scientist should not adopt ridicule as a method or argument. Ridicule is hardly objective. Rather, it is adopted because of pride and results in a feeling of contempt.

While Blue Book at the time of the Condon Committee had some 25,000 UFO reports on file, the committee examined only 90 and made their definitive conclusions based on these examinations. And even so, the committee was not able to adequately explain a quarter of the reports they did examine.

Hynek regards two statements of the Committee's final report[16] as illuminating.

> Careful consideration of the record as it is available to us leads us to conclude that further extensive study of UFOs probably cannot be justified in the expectation that science will be advanced thereby.[17]

No expectation that science would be advanced was ever contemplated in the founding and operation of the project. The project was pointed in another direction. Is it fair to criticize the project for not accomplishing something that had never been intended?

> Therefore we think that all of the agencies of the federal government, and the private foundations as well, ought to be willing to consider UFO research proposals along with others submitted to them on an open-minded, unprejudiced basis. While we do not think at present that anything worthwhile is likely to come of such research, each individual case ought to be carefully considered on its own merits.[16]

A masterful statement of insincerity that attempts to accomplish Mr. Low's desire to play to all sides at once in attempting to appease both public and scientific community bias.

In some sections of the report, selected UFO cases are dealt with directly. Thus, statements like the following are encountered in the body of the report. "In conclusion, although conventional or natural explanations certainly cannot be ruled out, the probability of such seems low in this case, and the probability that at least one genuine UFO was involved appears to be fairly high." "This must remain as one of the most puzzling radar cases on record, and no conclusion is possible at this time." "It does appear that this sighting defies explanation by conventional means." "Three unexplained sightings which have been gleaned from a great mass of reports are a challenge to the analyst." "This unusual sighting should therefore be assigned to the category of *some almost certainly natural phenomenon which is so rare that it apparently has never been reported before or since*." (italics added)

I'm not making these up, folks! These are actual quotations from the final report of the Condon Committee. One wonders what other unusual results never observed before or since (but almost certainly natural) might be described in the other 24,910 reports the committee didn't consider. And yet in their sweeping conclusions no unexplainable reports were acknowledged.

Hynek points out that the committee may have made strategic errors, depending on what their objective was, in that (a) the subject matter they studied was incorrectly defined and, moreover, (b) they studied the wrong problem.

Condon *et al* defined a UFO as "something that puzzled a given observer." Thus, a "Condon UFO" was not subject to any screening process to eliminate cases that would otherwise remain unexplained after screening by experts. The natures of these two types of UFO reports differ remarkably. As a result of looking at unscreened reports, the committee focused on proposing natural explanations for the reported phenomena. And yet the committee could not explain more than 25 percent of the cases they examined. In other words, by a more careful definition of a UFO report, the committee only examined twenty or so, instead of the 90 they considered as valid reports by their less-careful criterion. And it is the reports that cannot be simply explained that are the potentially useful ones. Only these present an opportunity to learn something new, rather than merely to validate "our expertise" and "our extensive knowledge."

In a second unfortunate decision, the committee chose to address only the question of whether a UFO report indicated the earth was being visited by extraterrestrial intelligence (ETI). They thus jumped to a conclusion that UFO is equal to ETI. While the questions of the reality of UFOs and some of their common characteristics might have been successfully addressed, although bias and preconception on these questions seem to have compromised even this possibility, how can one address the ETI question? When we are struggling to just determine if these unidentified objects are real or imagined hardly seems the time to jump to questions of who is driving them, where they come from, and what they want. When the former question cannot be answered to the satisfaction of the committee, how could the latter one? Yet these are the questions they focused on! This abandonment of reason may not be so unjustified as it first appears because in the public mind the UFO phenomenon was regarded as synonymous with "little green men." While the approach was scientifically unjustified, it was justified politically and from public relations and marketing perspectives. But the committee was chosen to perform a scientific evaluation.

In the scientific method, one generally tests a hypothesis or proposed law. The hypothesis usually declares some cause-and-effect relationship: if ... then ... And to test the hypothesis, the then ... must be testable. If the then ... cannot be shown to be true or false, how can one test the law? In short, one cannot. In selecting their ETI question the Condon Committee *imposed* the tone and conclusion of their report. What could possibly be said about the ETI hypothesis on the basis of controversial or outright denied sightings of unidentified objects? Exactly nothing. It doesn't take an expensive committee over a year to reach that conclusion. They selected a task whose accomplishment was hopeless. Had they instead selected a reasonable task, like determining whether some UFO reports seem to indicate phenomena that are not presently explainable by known scientific laws, their deliberation and report could have been useful. Instead, the opportunity and the money were squandered while the committee floundered with the impossible task it had chosen. Their experts were at a loss to explain many of the observations reported in only the few cases examined. It is unfortunate that the strategy was so poorly chosen that they accomplished nothing useful.

Nevertheless, Condon obtained for his effort the seal of approval of the National Academy of Sciences. On the date the Condon Committee Report was released to the public, on 9 January 1969, the Academy released a supporting document that stated

> a) In our opinion the scope of the study was adequate to its purpose: a scientific study of the UFO phenomena.
> b) We think the methodology and approach were well chosen, in accordance with accepted standards of scientific investigation.

We have already indicated that the hypothesis the committee chose to test was impossible to prove without capturing one of the UFOs of questioned existence and forcing an occupant, if any, to "talk." In this regard the methodology was severely flawed, despite the seal of approval of the National Academy of Sciences. The seal thus indicates that either the report was not flawed and the National Academy of Sciences was responsible or the report was flawed and the National Academy of Sciences was irresponsible. You have already read some of the evidence relating to the quality of the report. You can decide about the National Academy of Politics, err uh, Sciences.

In addition, the methodology of the committee is otherwise flawed. Page 9 of the Condon Report contains a definition of a UFO, as follows. "An unidentified flying object is here defined as the stimulus for a report made by one or more individuals of something seen in the sky (or an object thought to be capable of flight but seen when landed on earth) which the observer could not identify as having an ordinary natural origin, and which seemed to him sufficiently puzzling that he undertook to make a report of it ..." Hynek observes: "The problem then becomes that of learning to recognize the various kinds of stimuli that give rise to UFO reports."

What kind of objective method assumes the answer before an investigation even starts. The assumption clearly made here is that UFOs are never real and their reports are motivated solely by stimuli that cause misperceptions. With this definition a UFO is not considered, only the stimuli that cannot be explained. Some observers are not puzzled by what they clearly saw. They can describe it in detail and realize it was a UFO. The puzzle occurs when an investigator does not accept the report and tries to maneuver the reporter into telling a different story. In such a situation, both the one giving the report and the one receiving it are confused, the former by the inveterate stubbornness in the latter's defiant ignorance and the latter in the formers audacity to describe something the interviewer cannot readily explain in terms of his or her preconceived bias according to which the report could not possibly describe any real event.

To save the appearances in such a situation, fancy dancing is required as in language such as "learning to recognize the various kinds of stimuli ..." Any accountability here is deeply buried. First one has to learn. Then one has to recognize. Recognize what? Various kinds of stimuli. How many kinds? What is their nature? Are they physical, emotional, psychological, ...? Weren't we originally talking about UFOs? Why did we lose interest in them? When were they reduced to secondary importance below reports thereof and the stimuli that motivated them? No possibility of a conclusion like "There was a flying object and it was unidentified" was allowed in the conceptual realm the committee carefully constructed.

Note that it cannot be left to the observer to explain what he saw, to conclude an object was a UFO, to define the problem his observation raised. Such matters can only be settled by proper screening, learning, recognition, and identification of various kinds of stimuli by those deemed capable because this is the only allowed methodology by the Condon Committee and the only process recognized by the

Condon definition. And, coincidentally, members of the Committee were the only ones capable of applying it. Any observer or other unqualified person, such as the authors and investigators of the 24,910 reports not considered by the Condon Committee and, for that matter, the ninety which were, who had deviated from this methodology was peripheralized by definition as incapable.

And, of course, no previous report or its investigation had adopted such an ill-conceived problem and unworkable methodology. All other observations and investigations were automatically disqualified.

The apparent beginning assumption of the Condon Committee that a stimulus for a report must be in the category of a misperception is a violation of objectivity, fairness in general, and of scientific inquiry in particular. It also leads to a deeper problem. How can the observation of natural stimuli be used to test the hypothesis of extraterrestrial intelligence. Either the data chosen for the study must be relevant to the hypothesis being tested or the hypothesis being tested must somehow connect to the data being considered. These conditions are equivalent and uniformly violated by the Condon Committee investigation and report. The data and the hypothesis (supposedly) being tested were completely unrelated. Only by their own rules of evidence and method could any conclusion be pretended.

And, for a conclusion to be regarded as valid, its author must be regarded as capable, a requirement the Condon Committee was careful to implicitly define as befitting only their own selves. This is not science, this is power politics and super salesmanship.

Hynek indirectly comments on the Condon Committee effort with strong but appropriate language. "The relevance of science in daily life has in our times been seriously questioned. Supercilious attitudes, pontifical *ex cathedra* statements, and demands that authority be worshipped just because a scientists said so – these things do not help. … in science one never knows where the inquiry will lead … a primary aim of science is to satisfy human curiosity, to probe the unknown, and to open new paths for intellectual adventure."[18] Such exciting possibilities were ignored in the Condon Committee investigation.

Conclusions

One who presumes to understand a matter and requires others to adopt his or her view by use of force (such as power politics) or deception (such as super salesmanship), suppressing honest inquiry, and preventing others their free choice in the matter, exhibits arrogance and despotism. Such qualities are or should be foreign to scientific inquiry. Scientific methodology must be based only on honest inquiry and be free of subjective reactions, like prideful scorn associated with ridicule. As we have seen, scientists are very mortal. The case we have examined is extreme with deficiencies that are starkly apparent. More generally, deficiencies are not so extreme and not so visible but they are, nevertheless, often present.

An important, broadly applicable point is apparent: that a method or system is only so useful in the hands of humans as the fidelity and care with which they apply and utilize the method or system. This principle applies especially when a system contains inherent flaws, as the scientific method does even in competent, honest, and careful hands. Although this principle serves as a danger flag pointing out that bad persons can abuse even good systems, it also suggests that good persons have used and can use even poor systems well to accomplish good things. Many examples of this result in science, with its inherent flaws, are described in Book II.

The value of any product of a system ultimately depends on both the system and the competence and integrity of the person(s) using it. Science or religion can be good or bad beyond virtues and faults of a system itself. It is important to recognize limitations and faults in a system and more important still to recognize that any benefits derived from the system are dependent on the skill, care and integrity, and "agenda" of those applying it. To be forewarned is to be forearmed.

Notes and References for Appendix A

[1] Garber, Elizabeth, Stephen G. Brush, and C. W. F. Everitt (editors), *Maxwell on Molecules and Gases,* The MIT Press, Cambridge, MA, 1986, 3. Lindley, David, *Boltzmann's Atom,* The Free Press, New York, 2001, 1-3, 19-20.

[2] The craze is gone but UFO sightings continue. On 5 March 2004 Mexican Air Force pilots filmed, in infra red, eleven UFOs three of which also appeared on their plane's radar.

[3] Lewis, C. S., *Miracles, A Preliminary Study,* Macmillan, New York, 1967, 7-8.

[4] Hynek, J. Allen, *The UFO Experience, A Scientific Inquiry,* Henry Regnery Company, Chicago, 1972, 6.

[5] Hynek, J. Allen, loc. cit. [6] Ibid., 2, 170-171. [7] Ibid., 16.

[8] Ibid., 67-68. [9] Ibid., 76. [10] Ibid., 98-99.

[11] Ibid., 103, 106-107. [12] Ibid., 70, 171, 181. [13] Ibid., 186.

[14] Ibid., 211. [15] Ibid., 243-250.

[16] Condon, Edward U., *Scientific Study of Unidentified Flying Objects,* Bantam Books, New York, 1969. This report is a rambling 937-page document that presents sweeping conclusions that are not supported by 25 percent of the evidence examined.

[17] Hynek, J. Allen, loc. cit., 193. [18] Ibid., 207.

Appendix B

Summaries of Equations for Length in (1) Euclidian Geometry, (2) Special Relativity, (3) Riemann's Differential Geometry, and (4) General Relativity#

Part 1: Length in Euclidian Geometry

The Pythagorean theorem in two-dimensional, Euclidian space applies to any right triangle of side lengths *a*, *b*, and *c*, with *c* the longest side opposite the right (i.e., 90 degree) angle. Such a right triangle is shown in the following figure with vertices P_1, P_2, and P_3. The Pythagorean theorem states that $a^2 + b^2 = c^2$.

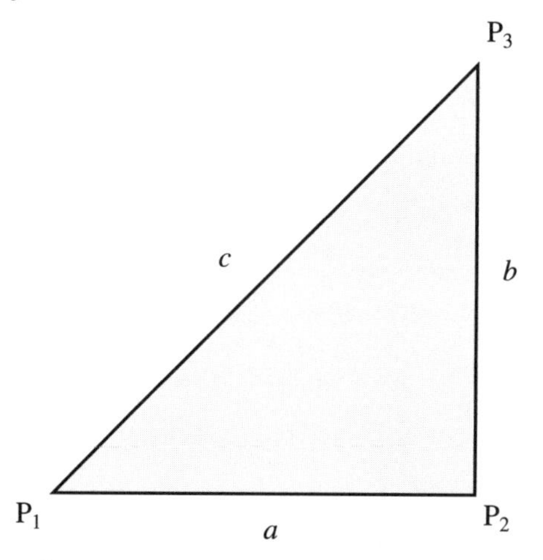

Without loss of generality, let $P_1 = x,y$; $P_2 = x+\Delta x,y$; $P_3 = x+\Delta x,y+\Delta y$. Then, side *a* is parallel to the x axis and has length Δx, side *b* is parallel to the y axis and has length Δy and, by the Pythagorean theorem, side *c* must have length

[B1] $$c = \sqrt{\{a^2 + b^2\}} = \sqrt{\{\Delta x^2 + \Delta y^2\}}$$

where the symbol $\sqrt{\{\ldots\}}$ denotes the square root of the quantity in brackets {...}.

This result is simply extended to three-dimensional Euclidian space (by applying the Pythagorean theorem twice) to give the length *d* of the line between $P_4 = x,y,z$ and $P_5 = x+\Delta x,y+\Delta y,z+\Delta z$.

[B2] $$d = \sqrt{\{\Delta x^2 + \Delta y^2 + \Delta z^2\}}.$$

This length is correct irrespective of the location of P_4 or P_5 because Euclidian space is flat. That is, an object, such as a line, may be translated and rotated in Euclidian space without changing either the size or shape of the object.

Now consider a flat, f>our-dimensional spacetime in which distance is represented in terms of generalized coordinates x_1, x_2, x_3, and x_4 where, for example, $x_1 = \Delta x$, $x_2 = \Delta y$, $x_3 = \Delta z$ and $x_4 = ic\Delta t$, where $i = \sqrt{(-1)}$ is the *imaginary index*, c is the velocity of light in vacuum, and t is time. It follows that $x_4^2 = - c^2t^2$. Thus, the distance d between two points in Euclidian (Minkowski) spacetime is

$$[B3] \quad d = \sqrt{\{\Delta x^2 + \Delta y^2 + \Delta z^2 - c^2\Delta t^2\}} = \sqrt{\{x_1^2 + x_2^2 + x_3^2 + x_4^2\}} = \sqrt{\{\sum_{j=1}^{j=4} x_j^2\}}.$$

In this expression the notation Σ (upper case Greek "sigma") with an index (j) value below and above indicates the argument (x_j^2) behind the "summation operator Σ" is summed for each value of index j from its lowest value (below) to its highest value (above).

Part 2: Length in Special Relativity

In the spacetime of relativity introduced by Albert Einstein and, later, Hermann Minkowski, a spacetime distance or *interval* Δs (designated *d* above) between two points involves a time coordinate difference Δt and three spatial coordinate differences Δx, Δy, Δz. To picture the behavior of an object in spacetime, Minkowski invoked the so-called *Minkowski* or *spacetime diagram* with displacement in space (x) represented as a horizontal displacement while displacement in time (t) is represented as a vertical displacement. Such a spacetime diagram is illustrated in the following figure.

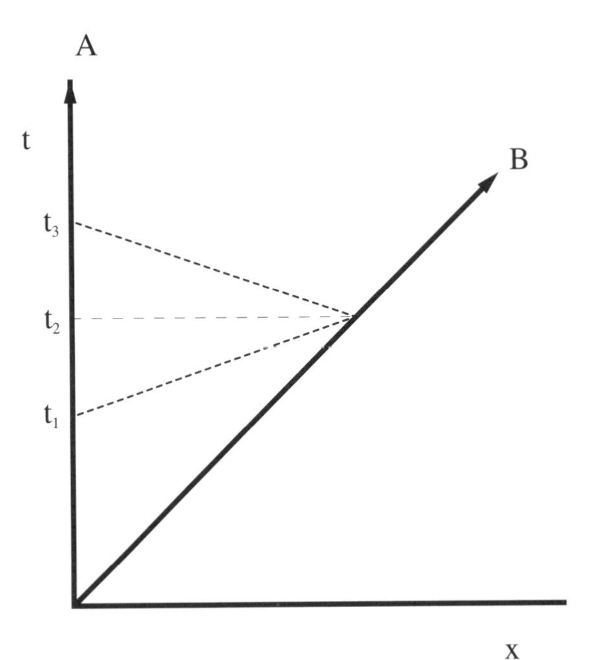

In this diagram we see two *worldlines* defining the motion of two observers: A and B. Observer A is stationary in space and thus remains at $x = 0$. Observer B is moving with x-direction velocity u_B.

Also shown as dashed lines are worldlines for an electromagnetic (light or radar) signal pulse traveling with velocity c. The signal is emitted by observer A from $x = 0$ at (her) time t_1. It intercepts observer B at (his) time t_2 and is reflected (or repeated) back to observer A at $x = 0$ at (her) time t_3. Observers A and B move with constant velocity $u_r = u_B - u_A$ relative to one another, i.e., they are *inertial* (neither having any acceleration). This is the situation treated in special relativity.

The equations for the two worldlines A and B are:

[B4] $$x_A(t) = u_A\, t \qquad \text{and} \qquad x_B(t) = u_B\, t,$$

where, without loss of generality, we choose $u_A = 0$. Since only x_B and u_B are nonzero, we hereafter let $x = x_B$ and $u_r = u_B$, the displacement and velocity of B relative to A.

We now utilize an analysis introduced by Hermann Bondi (*Relativity and Common Sense, A New Approach to Einstein,* Doubleday and Company, Garden City, NY, 1962). At time $t = t_2 = (t_1 + t_3)/2$, the x displacement of B with respect to A is given by the so-called *radar formulas*

[B5] $$x = c(t_3 - t_1)/2 = u_r\,(t_3 + t_1)/2.$$

From these two formulas we obtain

[B6] $$t_3 = t_1(c + u_r)/(c - u_r) = t_1 K^2.$$

The equation $K^2 = (c + u_r)/(c - u_r)$ defines the *Bondi K-factor*. It can be shown that $t_n = t_{n-1} K$, $t_{n+1} = t_n K$ and that $t_{n\pm m} = t_n K^{\pm m}$. (The symbol ± is read "plus or minus.") Using these *Bondi relations* we shall show that time and length are *local* properties.

Consider two identical clocks, one carried by observer A and one by observer B. Stationary clock A provides the *coordinate time* t while clock B provides the *proper time* τ (= Greek "tau"). While it might seem natural that these two identical clocks may be synchronized to give identical times thereafter, such an assumption is incorrect as we shall now demonstrate.

In the opposite spacetime diagram, three times, t_1, t_2 and t_3, are indicated. We recognize that the number of these times can be indefinitely extended to represent the series of instants at which repeatedly reflected (or repeated) signal pulses are detected by observers A and B. We thus obtain a series of time values, t_n with n = 1,2,3,4,…, some of which are measured by clock A and some by clock B. The t_n values measured by clock A (coordinate times) are those for which n is odd (n = 1,3,5,7,…) while those measured by clock B (proper times) correspond to even values of n (n = 2,4,6,8,…). All times, both the unmixed and mixed clock signals, obey the *Bondi relations* $t_n = t_{n-1} K$, $t_{n+1} = t_n K$ and $t_{n\pm m} = t_n K^{\pm m}$.

Consider first only the coordinate times of clock A: t_n with n = 1,3,5,7,... For these times the radar formulas give

$$\text{[B7]} \qquad t_n = (t_{n+2} + t_{n-2})/2 = t_n (K^2 + 1/K^2)/2 = t_n,$$

because, using the above defined K, $K^2 + 1/K^2 = 2$. In other words, no distortion or *dilation* of time occurs among the coordinate time (clock A) values, i.e., clock-A times are self-consistent in interpolation.

Likewise, when we consider only the proper times of clock B: t_n with n = 2,4,6,8,..., the identical results and conclusion are reached.

However, considering mixed times we obtain

$$\text{[B8]} \qquad t_n = (t_{n+1} + t_{n-1})/2 = \tau_n (K + 1/K)/2 = \gamma\tau_n,$$

with γ (Greek "gamma") a constant. That is, $K + 1/K = \gamma \neq 1$ and $\tau_n \neq t_n$ ($\neq$ is read "not equal to"). In other words, his clock-B proper time τ_n value is not properly interpolated as an average of her two surrounding clock-A coordinate times. Representing her clock-A coordinate time as t and his clock-B proper time as τ it follows that

$$\text{[B9]} \qquad t = \gamma\tau, \qquad \text{with } \gamma = (K + 1/K)/2 = 1/\sqrt{(1 - u_r^2/c^2)} \geq 1.$$

(Symbol $\geq$ is read "greater than or equal to.") Constant γ is exactly the *Lorentz-Fitzgerald correction factor* of special relativity and it reveals that the coordinate time t always runs equal to (when $u_r = 0$) or faster than (when $u_r \neq 0$) the proper time τ. In other words, two clocks (his and hers) in relative motion can never remain synchronized because they run at different rates; their times "flow" differently by the factor γ of [B9].

It was this time dilation result that caused early critics to reject relativity. For them, the concept that flow of time is relative depending on relative velocity between clocks was too strange to accept – it varied too radically from the traditional Newtonian theory of an absolute, universal time that flowed uniformly throughout the universe and to which any clock would remain synchronized. But the above derivation of $t = \gamma\tau$ is quite consistent and its predictions are supported by measured results (see Chapter 8).

Now that we are aware that fundamental changes occur between Newtonian theory and special relativity, let's consider exactly what is different and how. We utilize a new spacetime diagram (opposite page).

In this spacetime diagram we again have two observers, A and B, and we also have worldline C on which a body is located at point P at a particular instant. Observer A uses the radar formulas as does observer B to determine the spacetime location of P, with subscript A, for instance, now denoting "as observed by A,"

$$\text{[B10a]} \qquad x_A = c(t_4 - t_1)/2 \qquad\qquad x_B = c(t_3 - t_2)/2$$

$$\text{[B10b]} \qquad t_A = (t_4 + t_1)/2 \qquad\qquad t_B = (t_3 + t_2)/2,$$

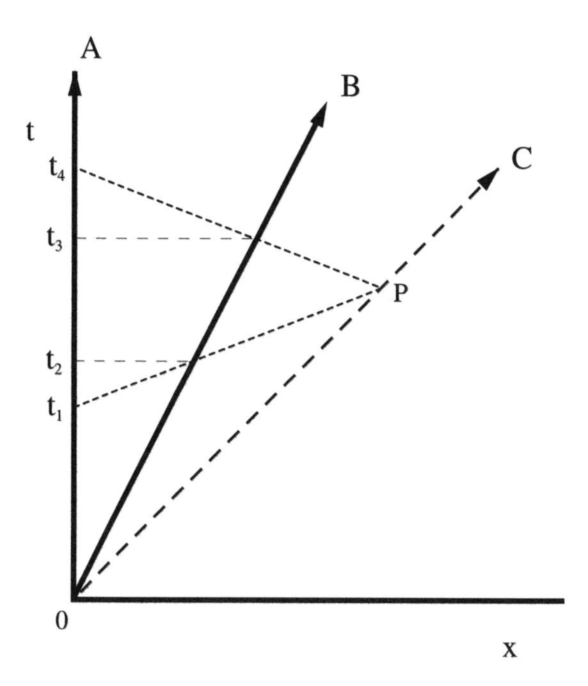

where t_1 and t_4 are coordinate times (her clock A) and t_2 and t_3 are proper times (his clock B). These four equations combined with the Bondi relations provide six equations by which the five quantities t_1, t_2, t_3, t_4 and K are eliminated leaving the single independent equation

[B11] $$c^2 t_A^{\,2} - x_A^{\,2} = c^2 t_B^{\,2} - x_B^{\,2} = s^2.$$

This remarkable result indicates that any inertial observer whose worldline passes through O must observe the same value s^2 for spacetime location P. The only relationship between observers A and B specified was their relative, uniform velocity u_r and this quantity doesn't appear in the result [B11]. Since the two left-hand sides of [B11] depend only on values observed by A or B, respectively, the right-hand-side result must be valid for any inertial observer passing through O. Thus, we write the general result

[B12] $$c^2 t^2 - x^2 = s^2.$$

Quantity $s^2 = c^2 d\tau^2$ must have the same value for any inertial observer whose worldline passes through point O, with point O defined by $t = x\ (= y = z) = 0$, that is, where her and his clocks and displacement rulers are synchronized at $x = y = z = ct = 0$. Quantity s is called the *spacetime interval* $s = c\tau$ between O and P with τ the local proper time or the time registered on a clock carried by an observer C traversing the worldline from O to P.

Expanding the above result to three-dimensional space we obtain for the interval measured by any inertial observer whose worldline passes through O

[B13] $$s^2 = c^2 \tau^2 = c^2 t^2 - x^2 - y^2 - z^2.$$

While [B13] is general and universal for the flat (Euclidian) spacetimes we consider in special relativity, i.e., for all inertial observers having worldline passing through O, it will take many different forms in spacetimes of different curvatures in general relativity, as we shall see.

Because interval s is common to all inertial observers whose worldline passes through O, a transformation must exist between the values observed by observers A and B moving with relative velocity u_r (in the x direction). Utilizing the above equations [B10] together with the Bondi relations to eliminate t_1, t_2, t_3, t_4 and solving for t_B and x_B we obtain

[B14a] $$t_B = \gamma\{t_A - u_r x_A/c^2\},$$

[B14b] $$x_B = \gamma\{x_A - u_r t_A\}, \qquad y_B = y_A, \qquad z_B = z_A.$$

These equations represent the *Lorentz transformation* in which the relative velocity u_r is specified to be in the x direction. By solving them for t_A, x_A, y_A and z_A we obtain the inverse transformation

[B15a] $$t_A = \gamma\{t_B + u_r x_B/c^2\},$$

[B15b] $$x_A = \gamma\{x_B + u_r t_B\}, \qquad y_A = y_B, \qquad z_A = z_B.$$

These transformations [B14] and [B15] imply *time dilation* and *length contraction* described in Chapter 8.

Part 3: Length in Riemann's Differential Geometry

With the background of Part 1 describing the familiar, intuitive, Euclidian geometry and of Part 2 describing the less intuitive spacetime of special relativity, we now summarize Riemann's differential geometry for any (non-intuitive) space and explore its utility.

Riemann's geometry is a breathtakingly-powerful general description of any geometry. It applies to both Euclidian and non-Euclidian spaces. Riemann reasoned that Euclid's second postulate, which prescribes that a straight line can be extended indefinitely, merely asserts that the end of the line would never be reached. Riemann noted cases wherein closed lines, such as circles, may have finite extent but no end. He distinguished between unboundedness and infinite extent. He ascribed unboundedness to space but claimed that an infinite extent by no means follows.

In other words, space may be curved, like a sphere for instance, so that it is unbounded in any direction but yet finite in extent. How does one account for curvature of space? By use of the differential geometry Riemann introduced in his now-famous 1854 lecture (Habilitatsionsvortrag) and composition (Habilitatsionschrift) to demonstrate his qualification to teach students (accounts of which were given in Chapter 3).

Riemann was accomplished in physics as well as mathematics and through this combination he came to the conclusion that elementary laws pertaining to points in space needed to be generalized by comprehensive mathematical technique to extend the elementary laws from their scope of application at individual points to the whole plenum (volume of space). Although he had not yet worked specifically on this problem this objective arises from other work that seems to have been in his mind.

Riemann was familiar with Gauss' definition of curvature and with the new, non-Euclidian geometry of Gauss, Lobachevski, and Bolyai. In the short time of a few weeks Riemann revised and generalized curvature-of-space theory comprehensively applicable to all space geometries. Like the best mathematicians and scientists, Riemann was a generalist who always sought abstraction and generality over the particular and specific. Riemann sought a metric (or measure or length) by which any surface or volume could be described regardless of the local geometry and, in fact, even for cases when geometry changed in its nature over space or time from, say, flat-space Euclidian to curved-space non-Euclidian. We follow loosely the path Riemann took in deriving his metric.

Recalling the spacetime of Einstein and Minkowski, we consider four-coordinate space x_1, x_2, x_3, x_4. Specifying any set of these four coordinates specifies a definite point in spacetime relative to a selected origin. How are such individual points in spacetime of different geometries related? What is the distance between two points in any spacetime geometry? We now answer the latter question.

Advantages of the "x_j notation" (introduced in part 1 above) are real but subtle. We point out two. First, using this notation a theoretical space can be expanded or contracted to any number of dimensions using coordinates x_j, where j = 1,2,…,n and n is the selected dimension or number-of-coordinates of the space, four in the present case. Thus theorems can be expressed and proved in general, not only for a space of specified dimension. Second, sums and products containing many terms are simply denoted by a single term. For example, consider the sum of products, due to Riemann, represented by the following single-term expression (in the middle between the equal signs).

[B16] $$d^2 = \sum_{j=1}^{j=4}\sum_{k=1}^{k=j}\{g_{jk}\, x_j\, x_k\} = g_{11}\, x_1^{\,2} + g_{22}\, x_2^{\,2} + g_{33}\, x_3^{\,2} + g_{44}\, x_4^{\,2} + g_{12}\, x_1\, x_2 + g_{13}\, x_1\, x_3 + g_{14}\, x_1 + g_{23}\, x_2\, x_3 + g_{24}\, x_2\, x_4 + g_{34}\, x_3\, x_4$$

As before, summation operator Σ ("sigma") with an index (j or k) value below and above indicates that the operator's argument (in this case the product of three terms: $g_{jk}\, x_j\, x_k$) is summed for each value of the index from lowest (below) to highest (above).

A second Σ operator with a second index is "nested" behind the first indicating the summation is performed for all k values for each j value. Riemann's theory is symmetric. That is, $g_{jk}\, x_j\, x_k = g_{kj}\, x_k\, x_j$ and some terms are redundant and excluded. To exclude redundant terms, the right or inner summation operator includes only the terms for which $1 \le k \le j$ (read "one is less than or equal to k is less than or equal to j") so that only ten terms are included, as shown after the second equal sign in [B16] which includes all terms $1 \le j \le 4$ from the left or outer summation as well. In general, for any n-dimensional space, the number of unique terms in such a double sum is n(n+1)/2. Note how efficiently the middle expression is written (and thought) compared to the equivalent, right-hand expression.

This expression for d^2 is the answer to the above question about the "length" or interval between two points in a spacetime that includes any geometrical space and is fundamental to Riemann's general, differential geometry. Suppose *d* is a small interval between two points in four-dimensional spacetime. The above expression for interval *d* (squared) holds for any geometry of the space whatever, with the coefficients g_{jk} specifying local *curvature* of spacetime in the jk plane. Conversely, from specified curvatures of spacetime for all its orthogonal planes, the local geometry of spacetime is determined. Equation [B16] thus relates interval *d* and quantities Δx, Δy, Δz and Δt in *any* four-dimensional spacetime. When all such displacements are small, the g_{jk} are adequately represented as local constants.

We can express these same concepts in other words. Each element Δx, Δy, Δz, and Δt may be regarded as a vector, possessing both a magnitude (length) and a direction. In flat spacetime a direction specified by a set of dx_j/dx_k (the traditional "direction cosines") is everywhere fixed. In curved spacetime such directions may change with location or time. At and near specified locations one may take spacetime to be locally flat, tangent to curved spacetime, and spacetime is then well approximated as flat for small increments Δx, Δy, Δz, and Δt. For this reason the geometry of curved spaces is described using small increments or differentials of the variables and is thus called a differential geometry.

If *d* is a differential interval element, a large interval may be determined by summing (integrating) a sequence of small-d differentials. Only by such a sum, called an integration, is an exact result obtained because only such a process takes proper account of g_{jk} variations with location. Such summation (integration) is used, say, to determine the trajectories of bodies in spacetime.

Solving for a body's free-fall trajectory in general relativity may utilize the principle that every trajectory element lies on a geodesic which is a curve representing the shortest spacetime interval between any starting and any ending points on the trajectory. That is, on a geodesic interval *d* is a minimum with respect to variation in coordinates Δx, Δy, Δz and icΔt. This property may be used to discover the solution of the geodesic equation, i.e., the geodesic.

Taking the square root of [B16], we write for local spacetime interval *d*

[B17] $$d = \sqrt{\{\sum_{j=1}^{j=4} \sum_{k=1}^{k=j} \{g_{jk}\, x_j\, x_k\}\}},$$

where coefficients g_{jk} are, in general, location dependent and where the *d*, x_j and x_k are therefore small. When spacetime is Euclidian (flat), $g_{jk} = 1$ when $j = k$ and 0 when $j \neq k$ and the result [B17] becomes exactly [B3]. When spacetime is non-Euclidian (curved) the g_{jk}-coefficients may be non-unity for $j = k$ and nonzero for $j \neq k$ with functions for the g_{jk}-coefficients defining the nature of spacetime.

As an illustration of curved space(time), consider the case where the *spherical spacetime coordinates* are

$$x_1 = r, \quad x_2 = \theta \text{ (Greek "theta")}, \quad x_3 = \varphi \text{ (Greek "phi")}, \quad \text{and} \quad x_4 = ict.$$

Let all $g_{jk} = 0$ when $j \neq k$ and let

$$g_{rr} = -1/(1 - \alpha/r), \quad g_{\theta\theta} = 1, \quad g_{\varphi\varphi} = 1, \quad \text{and} \quad g_{tt} = (1 - \alpha/r).$$

(These properties apply for Schwarzschild spacetime.) We determine the differential spacetime interval Δs between points r_1,θ,φ,ict_1 and r_2,θ,φ,ict_2, i.e., between two points which differ in no more than their r and t coordinate values, where $r_2 = r_1 + \Delta r$ and $t_2 = t_1 + \Delta t$. Then by [B17] the spacetime interval between these points is given by

$$\text{[B18]} \qquad i\,\Delta s \;=\; i\,c\,\Delta\tau \;=\; \sqrt{\{g_{rr}\,\Delta r^2 \;+\; g_{tt}\,\Delta t^2\}}, \qquad \text{or}$$

$$\Delta s \;=\; \sqrt{\{\Delta r^2/(1 - \alpha/r) \;-\; (1 - \alpha/r)\,c^2\Delta t^2\}}.$$

Note that in curved Schwarzschild spacetime even when $\Delta t = 0$ a purely radial spacetime interval has length $\Delta s = c\Delta\tau = \Delta r/\sqrt{(1 - \alpha/r)}$, which distance is greater than the radial distance Δr because of curvature of space.

Part 4: Length in General Relativity

Einstein's basic goal in his general theory of relativity was to replace gravity with suitable curvature of spacetime. To do so Einstein specified by the Einstein field equation the properties of spacetime that eliminate gravity. This condition is specified by the Einstein field equation

$$\text{[B19]} \qquad R_{\mu\nu} \;-\; g_{\mu\nu}\,R/2 \;=\; -\,8\pi G\,T_{\mu\nu},$$

$R_{\mu\nu}$ is the Ricci tensor, R is its trace, $g_{\mu\nu}$ is the metric tensor defining the geometry of space, G is Newton's universal gravitational constant, $T_{\mu\nu}$ is a tensor containing mass, momentum, and energy properties, and 8π is a constant. This equation is valid for all geometries including transitions between spaces of different geometries. That is, this equation is independent of spatial geometry and is therefore invariant in any transformation between geometries. This property was the one that eluded Einstein for many of the years he spent developing general relativity until November 1915. The generality of this equation allows powerful capability. If one can specify $T_{\mu\nu}$ to account for the gravitational influence of matter, momentum, and energy, solution of this equation gives the full influence of relativistic gravity (including mass-equivalent energy) in the metric tensor $g_{\mu\nu}$ used in solving the geodesic equation or equation of motion of a body in spacetime.

In general relativity, events are still characterized by points and trajectories in spacetime but the connections between events (cause-and-effect relations) are simultaneously simplified by the absence of gravity as an explicit influence and complicated by the curvature of spacetime and mass-equivalence of energy. To one accustomed to traditional Newtonian mechanics, implicit complexity introduced by curvature of spacetime and associated need to write and solve a tensor equation with its implicit complexity adds more complication than any simplification by removal of gravity. However, only general relativity provides correct answers when mass is large or energy-equivalent mass must be considered to properly characterize spacetime, as by the Schwarzschild metric with $\alpha = 2GM/c^2$:

[B20] $$ds = c\,d\tau = \sqrt{\{(1-\alpha/r)c^2dt^2 - dr^2/(1-\alpha/r) - r^2 d\theta^2 - r^2\cos^2\theta\, d\varphi^2\}}.$$

Comparison of [B17] and [B20] gives curvatures $g_{tt} = (1-\alpha/r)$, $g_{rr} = -1/(1-\alpha/r)$, $g_{\theta\theta} = 1$, $g_{\varphi\varphi} = 1$, and $g_{jk} = 0$ when $j \neq k$.

Appendix C

The Metaphysics of Immanuel Kant

A Review of *Critik der reinen Vernunft* (*Critique of Pure Reason*), Second Edition, 1787.

Rachel Dahneke

(used without permission because Rachel just left it lying around the house – in her room, actually)

Immanuel Kant, a professor at the University of Königsberg, states in his *Critique of Pure Reason*, "... by critique of pure reason ... I mean the critique of our power to reason as such, in regard to all cognition after which reason may strive independently of all experience. Hence I mean by it the decision as to whether a metaphysics as such is possible or impossible." The goal of Kant's critique is to know if metaphysics, or [the study of] the ultimate structure of reality, as a science is possible.

Traditionally, philosophers have thought of only two types of judgements: synthetic and analytic. Analytic judgements are explicatory and according to Leibniz are truths of reason. Synthetic judgements are known after an appropriate experience and these are truths of fact to Leibniz. These judgements are validated *a priori* or *a posteriori*. *A priori* validation is necessary and universal; therefore, such judgements have traditionally been placed with analytic judgements. For example, all uncles are male is an analytic *a priori* judgement. Analytic because the definition of uncle means that such a person is a male. It is *a priori* because an uncle being male is necessary and unchanging. Also, it is *a priori* because one does not have to experience all uncles to know that they are male. Such an analytic *a priori* judgement is known as *de dicto*, or by definition. Synthetic judgements are known *a posteriori*, or after experience. For example, this composition is printed on white paper. One would have to see this composition to know its paper was white. Synthetic *a posteriori* judgements are also contingent [depending on evidence], for most paper is white but some is of other colors. It is important that analytic *a priori* and synthetic *a posteriori* judgements are understood because these definitions provide the basis for finding whether metaphysics [as a science] is possible.

Kant derives that in order for metaphysics to be a science, it must be derived from synthetic *a priori* judgements. Synthetic because if metaphysics is analytic, the answers to metaphysical questions would already be known without any disagreement between philosophers; and *a priori* because the basics of the universe need to be necessary and unchanging. This is counterintuitive according to traditional thought, but Kant answers three important questions that prove his underlying theme of synthetic *a priori* judgements to be possible. First, "How is pure mathematics possible?" then, "How is pure natural science possible?" and lastly, "How is metaphysics as a natural predisposition possible?" Kant, according to how [he believes] the mind works, shows that these two sciences consist of synthetic *a priori* judgements and that metaphysics is a natural predisposition. These conclusions make it more likely that metaphysics can exist as a science.

The first step for Kant is to see if pure mathematics is possible. In doing this, Kant uses transcendental philosophy where he defines the preconditions of obtaining knowledge. The precondition of knowledge is that there must be regularity in the world, so the mind is able to understand. The mind understands the world with two faculties: the faculty of sensibility and the faculty of understanding. Interaction between these faculties gives rise to knowledge.

Mathematics, or arithmetic and geometry, corresponds with the faculty of sensibility. The faculty of sensibility, also referred to as transcendental aesthetic, is then separated into two subdivisions: material and formal. The material subdivision of the faculty of sensibility receives impressions and the formal subdivision is the capability of the mind to structure perceptions in time and space. Objects in themselves do not have the properties of time and space; rather, sensibility imposes these intuitions of time and space on perceptions. All objects of experience are situated in time and space and give rise to synthetic *a priori* judgements. These pure intuitions of time and space must be applied or certain communication would be void. For example, Jane could not tell Sally she was standing by a mailbox about an hour ago with John jump-roping four feet away. Naturally, when discussing time, sequence is introduced with events happening one after the other. Sequence derives arithmetic. The intuition of space, or objects relative to each other simultaneously, gives rise to geometry. Mathematics, or arithmetic and geometry, are synthetic *a priori.* Synthetic because it is not true by definition, i.e., it increases our knowledge. And *a priori* because it precedes or is independent of experience, deriving from pure intuitions of space and time; therefore, arithmetic and geometry are necessarily true and universal. Mathematics may also be regarded as synthetic because it is experienced. For example, in adding ten-digit numbers one does not immediately know the sum of the numbers because the sum has to be synthesized by [properly] adding the constituent digits. Mathematics is necessary and universal [*a priori*], for everyone experiences such a summation equation in the same way, yet synthetic because one has to synthesize the equation [answer]. Mathematics, as thus proven by Kant, is derived from synthetic *a priori* judgements.

After addressing pure mathematics, Kant asks "How is pure natural science possible?" Natural science is known from the mind's faculty for understanding, or transcendental logic. In this faculty there are twelve pure concepts, or "the original pure concepts of synthesis that the understanding contains *a priori*." The mind uses understanding, judgement, and inference to develop these concepts. The understanding, of the faculty of understanding, structures intuitions into concepts. The judgement, then, creates knowledge by comparing concepts. Lastly, inference explains ideas or judgements further and is verified with experience. For example, if Moe really likes pizza, and Moe is going out to eat, he is most likely going to eat pizza. Inference applies to what is known and develops it further. This makes physics possible. Physics is a science explained by cause and effect [or as we would say in this book, physics is the discovery and application of cause-and-effect and other relationships among the facts]. Of the twelve pure concepts of the faculty of understanding, causality is one. Causality is invoked in [discovering and using] cause and effect in physics making it possible as a science due to synthetic *a priori* judgements; physics is synthetic because the laws and theories of physics are justified by experience rather than *de dicto* and *a priori* because they are assumed to be necessary, unchanging, and universal.

After proving that two sciences [mathematics and physics] exist as synthetic *a priori* judgements, Kant then examines how metaphysics as a natural predisposition is possible. Philosophers throughout time have been trying to prove the existence of transcendental ideas; therefore, it is because of inference that metaphysics is a natural predisposition. Understanding produces concepts in the mind, which are then judged. The mind is not structured to stop there. The mind cannot help but ask metaphysical questions because of inference, thus making it [metaphysics] a natural predisposition.

These [results] lead to Kant's final question: "Is metaphysics as a science possible?" It would most likely be so with two sciences proven synthetic *a priori* judgements; yet metaphysics as a science is not possible. Kant proved that there are sciences, such as mathematics and physics, but one can never experience transcendental ideas as a whole to verify inferences. One cannot experience God as a whole, or the world as a whole. A conclusion can be drawn on these ideas, yet validity is uncertain because experience cannot verify premises. Kant then concludes that Spinoza, Leibniz, and other philosophers are under the dialectic illusion. For example, one philosopher can claim God exists and the other God does not exist, but neither [claim] can be proven through reason alone. These philosophers try to draw conclusions that go beyond experience. Metaphysics, according to Kant, is not a science because it can never be [fully] verified through experience.

In conclusion, Kant proved synthetic *a priori* judgements. This refutes the rationalist and the empiricist because it shows that knowledge does not begin with experience and is not derived from experience. Because metaphysics is not possible as a science, transcendental ideas cannot be found through reason. With this conclusion, philosophers can make judgements about God, the world, and the soul, but the conclusions are dialectic illusions for these ideas cannot be proven through experience.

How Concepts in this Book Conflict with Kant's Philosophy

Kant places knowledge above understanding, opposite to the order we assign these entities in this book. Herein we regard facts as the basis of knowledge (knowledge is the knowing of facts); understanding extends beyond knowledge of facts by also including knowledge of the relations, patterns, connections, and organization found within or implied by the facts.

Kant regards the "sciences" of mathematics and physics as verified by experience yet he concludes that transcendental ideas cannot be validated by experience because God or the world cannot be experienced as a whole. But then neither can we regard these two sciences as validated by experience because one cannot experience experience as a whole. Since proof in science is really absence of disproof, a reliable proof of any theory requires all possible contradictions to be eliminated as impossible, including those not yet recognized. Such capability requires experiencing experience as a whole or, in other words, it requires omniscience. Because unassisted humans are incapable of such absolute or universal knowledge we can conclude, contrary to Kant but using his reasoning, if metaphysics is not possible as a science because it can't be validated by experience, then neither are mathematics or physics or other science possible as sciences, as Kant uses the term.

Appendix D

Near-Newtonian Gravity and Retardation of Gravity[#]

Introduction

A classical analysis of gravity effects is often useful because relativity theory is more rigorous and exact! This enigma highlights two important points. First, the mathematics of relativity is sufficiently complex so that subtle physical processes, though properly characterized in a complex mathematical solution, can long remain obscure before they are finally recognized and understood, as illustrated by the history of magic-circles of Chapter 8. Second, classical theory, in contrast, often provides less exact but more easily understood predictions. This latter point is repeatedly illustrated in history. Gravitational redshift of light was suggested by classical-gravity theory, with black holes or "dark stars" predicted by John Michell (1724-1793), Woodwardian Professor of Geology at Cambridge University and the first seismologist, in his paper read by Henry Cavendish to the Royal Society and causing quite a stir on 27 November 1783. This concept was, apparently independently, described by French mathematical physicist Pierre Simon Laplace (1749-1827) in 1796 in his book *Exposition du système du monde*, in which his name for dark stars was *corps obscurs* or invisible bodies. Both authors invoked the same mechanism: for an object to escape the gravity of a star or planet the object's velocity must exceed an *escape velocity* that becomes greater than the speed of light for sufficiently massive bodies.

Guided by Laplace's proposal of the influence of gravity on light, Bavarian astronomer Johann Georg von Soldner (1776-1833) wondered if gravity would deflect light passing near a star or planet. In 1803, preceding modern relativity theory by a century, Soldner published the correct prediction based on Newtonian theory that a light ray would be deflected in skimming the surface of the sun by 0.875 arcseconds, half the deflection later predicted by relativity theory with its compound effect of curvature of space and dilation of time.

In the nineteenth century, 531 of the total observed 574 arcseconds-per-century precession of the orbit of Mercury (Chapter 3) were correctly predicted using Newtonian mechanics in many-planet orbit calculations by John Couch Adams (1819-1892) in England and Joseph Le Verrier (1811-1877) in France.

A statistical-quantum-mechanics theory of gravity, somewhat like that used in Appendix E but invoking gravitons as the messenger particles, is presently envisioned to be the next-generation theory of gravity as part of a theory of everything. A repulsive force is intuitively associated with small, momentum-carrying particles shuttling back and forth between two bodies while an attractive force is not, the latter perhaps utilizing quantum antiparticles of negative mass (holes in a background of particles in the vacuum), with the massless photon being its own antiparticle for repulsive and attractive electrostatic forces. But gravitons or gravity waves supporting a quantum theory of gravity have not yet been observed. Therefore, alternatives, such as a universe non-local in gravity (Chapter 10 addresses quantum non-locality and provides an idea of non-locality in general), should not yet be dismissed, a thought we visit again at the end of this appendix.

In this appendix we use classical physics to explore possible properties of gravity. We first describe a classical two-body theory of planetary orbits and extend it to include general relativistic gravity. We next describe a simple mechanism that explains properties of Newtonian gravity, deriving Newton's equation for gravitational attraction between two bodies via this classical-physics mechanism. The derivation is simple but the mechanism, as with others utilizing classical physics, predicts results that conflict with relativity. Nevertheless, the theory provides excellent illustrations of two principles. (1) A physical mechanism provides understanding of a physical phenomenon and allows it to be explained in terms of fundamental concepts. (2) Because a valid physical mechanism must lead to a theory in comprehensive agreement with all known facts, discovery of such a theory is difficult.

Finally, we predict a *retardation* or delay of gravity force and explore its consequences. Such retardation is a general effect that occurs for many adopted theories of gravity.

Part 1: Mechanics of Planetary Orbits

We address two-body, *planetary-orbit mechanics* to provide an understanding of planetary orbits and the influence of gravity on them. Observed moon, planetary, and binary star motions to which predictions may be compared provide useful tests of gravity theories.

For an orbiting planet, star, or galaxy, energy dissipation that acts to reduce orbital radius is not significant over a short term. The earth falls toward the sun about 1 cm per year, due predominantly and approximately equally to friction (interception of interplanetary matter including solar wind generated by emission of 300,000 tons per second of solar matter in nominally radial motion) and energy dissipation by tidal action,[1] while the lunar orbital radius increases about 3.8 cm per year.[2] Electromagnetic interactions do not significantly dissipate orbital energy or momentum. Such orbital motion may be regarded as "conservative," meaning that the total orbital energy (kinetic energy plus potential energy) and angular momentum are each constant or conserved. Orbits in two-body systems may be fully characterized by use of these two constant quantities plus a law of gravity. Following Martin[3] and Longair[4] we now describe such an analysis.

Constant total energy E in a conservative two-body system is

[D1.1] $$E = \mu/2\,[(dr/dt)^2 + r^2\,(d\theta/dt)^2] + V(r).$$

Angular velocity is $\omega = d\theta/dt$, the angular velocity (Greek "omega") of either body is around their common center of mass, tangential velocity is $r\,\omega$, reduced mass

(Greek "mu" =) $\mu = Mm/(M + m)$, M and m are the masses of the bodies, and r is the instantaneous center-of-mass to center-of-mass orbital radius or separation. The orbital radius usually varies slightly in time because all planetary orbits are slightly elliptical, ranging from Venus with a variation in orbital radius of 0.0023 percent to Pluto with a variation of 3.2 percent. Mercury has the second largest variation in orbital radius at 2.14 percent. Note that when $M >> m$, $\mu = m$, i.e., m rotates about M.

The quantity in square brackets in [D1.1] is the total relative velocity of the bodies squared, given by the sum of the squares of their relative radial and relative tangential velocity components. One-half the total velocity squared multiplied by the reduced mass is the kinetic energy internal to the two-body system, or for motion relative to the center-of-mass. We ignore center-of-mass motion as it has no influence on orbital motion. The last term, V(r), is the potential energy which depends on the chosen law of gravity. This quantity is defined by its relationships with the radial gravity force F, viz.,

$$F(r) = -\,dV/dr \qquad \text{and} \qquad V(r) = -\int_r^{\infty} dr\, F(r).$$

Since the near-Newtonian gravity law (Part 2) gives the same force as Newton's gravity law, they both predict the same potential, namely,

$$V(r) = -\,GMm/r. \qquad \text{[D1.2]}$$

Constant angular momentum J of the system,

$$J = \mu r^2 d\theta/dt, \qquad \text{[D1.3]}$$

provides the value of $\omega = d\theta/dt = J/\mu r^2$. Substituting this value of $d\theta/dt$ into [D1.1], using the chain rule by which $dr/dt = dr/d\theta \times d\theta/dt = J/\mu r^2 \times dr/d\theta$, and rearranging we obtain

$$1/r^4\,(dr/d\theta)^2 = 2\mu E/J^2 - 2\mu V(r)/J^2 - 1/r^2. \qquad \text{[D1.4]}$$

We further simplify by making the substitution $u = 1/r$, as is customary in solving orbit problems. With this substitution [D1.4] simplifies to

$$(du/d\theta)^2 = 2\mu E/J^2 - 2\mu V(u)/J^2 - u^2, \qquad \text{[D1.5]}$$

where $V(u) = -\,GMmu$. Solution of [D1.5] with this V(u) provides the Newtonian orbit of bodies M and m around their center of mass, the two-body solution we seek.

To further simplify, let the right-hand side of [D1.5] be rewritten as

$$2\mu E/J^2 + 2\mu GMmu/J^2 - u^2 = au^3 - u^2 + bu + c,$$

with constants *a*, *b*, and *c* chosen to satisfy this equation. By equating coefficients of terms having like power of u,

[D1.6] $a_N = 0$ $b_N = 2\mu GMm/J^2$ $c_N = 2\mu E/J^2$

with the subscripted N indicating the coefficients apply for Newtonian gravity. These coefficients also apply for near-Newtonian theory that we consider in the next section.

An equation of identical form also results using general relativity.[3, 4] In both cases,

[D1.7] $$(du/d\theta)^2 = a u^3 - u^2 + b u + c$$

where either the N-subscripted coefficients of [D1.6] are used to obtain a Newtonian-theory orbit or the R-subscripted coefficients of [D1.8] are used to obtain a general-relativity-theory orbit.[3, 4]

[D1.8] $a_R = 2GM/c^2$ $b_R = 2\mu GMm/J^2$ $c_R = \text{constant}$[3, 4]

Solution of [D1.7] thus provides the orbit for Newtonian gravity, for near-Newtonian gravity, and for relativity, depending on the coefficients chosen.

The variables of [D1.7] may be separated by collecting all quantities that depend only on one variable and perhaps a constant on one side of an equation and all that depend on another variable and perhaps another constant on the other side. By this method we obtain

[D1.9] $$d\theta = \pm\, du/\sqrt{(a u^3 - u^2 + b u + c)}.$$

The plus or minus sign follows from taking the square root of [D1.7], since $x^2 = (\pm x)^2$, x representing any value. The physical significance of each sign is clear. A body in an elliptical (or any non-circular) orbit moves in and out between its maximum and minimum radii. For inward motion (decreasing r, increasing u) the plus sign applies and for outward motion (increasing r, decreasing u) the minus sign applies.

It remains only to integrate [D1.9] to obtain an exact, two-body orbit of, say, a planet around the sun. As u varies from its minimum-to-maximum-to-minimum values, the solution provides the full angular period $\Delta\theta$ (Greek "delta theta") required for a planet to complete one of its repeating radial periods. If angular period $\Delta\theta$ is exactly 2π, then the orbit is *reentrant* and always retraces itself exactly, i.e., relative to the fixed stars. If $\Delta\theta > 2\pi$, then the orbit advances with each orbital cycle, i.e., orbital precession occurs as described for Mercury in the introduction to this appendix and as illustrated in Chapter 3.

However, integration of [D1.9] is not straightforward because of *singularities* in the integrand, i.e., values of u where the denominator becomes zero causing the integral to "blow up." These singularities occur at both the minimum and maximum radii, as expected, since these are the points where dr/dt (and $dr/d\theta$ as well as du/dt) and $du/d\theta$ are zero. To avoid a blowup problem in integration, we make another substitution of variable and characterize the orbit in terms of another quantity.

To change the form of the denominator of [D1.9], we rewrite quantity[3, 4]

$$a\mathrm{u}^3 - \mathrm{u}^2 + b\mathrm{u} + c = (\mathrm{u}-\mathrm{u}_1)(\mathrm{u}_2-\mathrm{u})(A\mathrm{u}+B)$$

where u_1 and u_2 are the minimum and maximum values of u, at which the singularities occur in [D1.9]. Selecting constants $A\,(=-a)$ and $B\,(=1-a(u_1+u_2))$ and expanding the last factor of [D1.9] ignoring higher than first-order terms in a to obtain $[1-a(u+u_1+u_2)]^{-1/2} \cong [1+a/2\,(u+u_1+u_2)]$ (see endnote 13 of Chapter 7), we write,

[D1.10] $$\Delta\theta/2 = \int_{u_1}^{u_2} du\,[1+a/2\,(u+u_1+u_2)]\,/\sqrt{[(u-u_1)(u_2-u)]}.$$

The remaining half of $\Delta\theta$ is given by a second integral, between u_2 and u_1, as the planet completes a full cycle of its radial motion. But we haven't fully removed the blowup problem because singularities remain at the endpoints $u = u_1$ and u_2.

To finally remove all singularities we substitute $u = (u_1 + u_2 q^2)/(1+q^2)$ so that

[D1.11] $$\Delta\theta = 2\int_0^\infty dq\,\{2/(1+q^2) + a\,[((2u_1+u_2)+(u_1+2u_2)q^2)/(1+q^2)^2]\}.$$

Parameter q now characterizes separation of the two bodies. As q varies from $-\infty$ to 0 to $+\infty$, u varies from perihelion u_2 (maximum u) to aphelion u_1 (minimum u) and back to u_2, i.e., the orbital motion completes one full period in its repeating radial motion as θ completes the corresponding angular period $\Delta\theta$. Integration over q gives

[D1.12] $$\Delta\theta = 2\pi + 3\pi a\,(u_1+u_2)/2.$$

In Newtonian and near-Newtonian theory, a is zero by [D1.6] and all orbits are reentrant. In relativity, $a = a_R = 2GM/c^2$ by [D1.8] and each orbital cycle exceeds 2π. This precession is called *excess precession* predicted in a two-body orbital analysis only by relativity, i.e., not including precession due to attraction by other planets as determined by a many-body analysis. For Mercury the excess precession is 43 arcseconds per century, in agreement with observation (see introduction). Thus, Newtonian and near-Newtonian theory predict no excess precession of planetary orbits by [D1.12], only precession through attractions of other planets in a many-body solution. Mercury is the only planet in our solar system having excess precession large enough to be accurately measured. Venus, the next closest planet to the sun, has an orbit so nearly circular that its perihelion and aphelion are difficult to detect. Earth, the next closest, has a total precession of only 5.0 ± 1.2 arcseconds per century mostly due to influence of Jupiter. Beyond Mercury excess precession is small because it is proportional to $u_{average} \cong 1/r_{average}$.

Now that we have some understanding of the influence of a gravity law on orbital motion, we next describe the near-Newtonian theory of gravity and consider other gravity-effect influences on orbits.

Part 2: Near-Newtonian Theory of Gravity

To better understand gravity we describe a possible mechanism for it. This mechanism is nearly Newtonian in the sense that it assumes Newtonian mechanics and Euclidian space and gives Newtonian gravity. We therefore call it *near-Newtonian theory of gravity.* This theory assumes an answer to Newton's question about how gravity force is exerted over long expanses of apparently empty space.

In near-Newtonian theory the gravity force on a body is an inertial force caused by the simple, well-known process of momentum exchange, with the total exchange rate of momentum, **dp**/dt, being the gravity force. That **dp**/dt is a force follows directly from Newton's second law in its generalized form

$$\text{[D2.1]} \quad \mathbf{F} = \Sigma_j m_j \mathbf{a}_j = \Sigma_j m_j d\mathbf{v}_j/dt = \Sigma_i d(m_j \mathbf{v}_j)/dt = \Sigma_j d\mathbf{p}_j/dt = d\mathbf{p}/dt.$$

The summation operator Σ (upper case Greek "sigma") indicates a vector sum over index j to include all momentum carrying particles and bodies (j = 1,2,3,4,...) having mass m_j, velocity $\mathbf{v}_j$, and imparting nominal momentum $m_j\mathbf{v}_j$ to any body that captures, reflects, or deflects them. For simplicity we neglect a factor that provides the exact average particle momentum imparted to the body in a specified direction because this factor will ultimately be absorbed in an empirical constant. Since **dp**/dt is the total rate of momentum change imparted to a body, we have shown that total force **F** acting on a body intercepted by particles is equal to total rate of momentum exchange **dp**/dt to the body from the particles. In near-Newtonian gravity theory we named the small momentum-carrying particles gravitrinos in Chapter 13.

Assume an ubiquitous, isotropic radiation of gravitrinos moving through space in every direction and carrying momentum but interacting only weakly with matter. Because gravitrinos, like neutrinos, interact only weakly with matter, their mean-free-path length is enormous, probably many billions of light years. The mean-free-path is important as it implies a length scale or range of gravitational force in the theory to be described.

The presence of a body (matter) slightly attenuates gravitrino radiation by elastic or slightly inelastic (non-conservative) scattering (and perhaps nuclear reactions in very rare direct-hit-captures). By such scattering of gravitrinos some of their momentum and energy are imparted to a body and act to compress and heat it. Compression is normally associated with gravity but not heating once the body's material fully resists further compression. For non-conservative or inelastic scattering of gravitrinos, heating will always occur; for conservative or elastic scattering, it may occur. The present mechanism thus suggests *thermally thick* bodies, like solid planets, may have hot interiors like the earth.

Imagine a spherical body and gravitrinos alone in the universe. The sphere would experience no net force beyond inward compression because of symmetrical scattering of gravitrinos. Scattering of gravitrinos from any selected direction into another selected direction is exactly compensated by scattering of gravitrinos from the opposite of the first selected direction into the opposite of the second. But mass elements of the body would experience a net force toward the body's center of mass due to unbalanced scattering.

This result is most easily pictured by considering two bodies in the universe which experience a mutual attractive force caused by scattering of momentum, as illustrated in the following model.

Let gravitrino momentum flux (momentum of all gravitrinos passing through unit area per second) be represented by j. As the gravitrinos pass incremental distance dx through matter of mass density ρ (Greek "rho") their momentum flux is reduced by increment dj due to scattering, as defined by material constant σ (Greek "sigma") called the *momentum-scattering-cross section* expressed in scattering-cross section area per unit mass, per atom, per nucleus, or per nucleon (i.e., a proton or neutron), giving (see endnote 27 of Chapter 8)

[D2.2] $$dj = -\sigma \rho \, dx \, j \quad \text{which has solution} \quad j(x) = j_0 \exp(-\sigma \rho x).$$

Since material is composed of protons, neutrons, and electrons in nearly fixed proportions, σ for gravitrino collisions may, on a mass basis, have a single, universal value. Quantity j_0 is the incident gravitrino momentum flux, at depth $x = 0$, $j(x)$ is the gravitrino momentum flux at depth x into the scattering body, and the so-called *exponential function* of a quantity, say z, is exp(z), defined in endnote 27 of Chapter 8. In [D2.2] we have ignored a "geometry factor" because, again, it will eventually be absorbed into an empirical constant. After passing to depth L into material of mass density ρ the loss or deficiency in momentum flux Δj transferred to the scattering body is given by

[D2.3] $$\Delta j = j(L) - j_0 = j_0[\exp(-\sigma\rho L) - 1]$$

$$= j_0[1 - \sigma\rho L + (\sigma\rho L)^2/2 - \ldots - 1] \cong -\sigma\rho L j_0,$$

(Δ is the upper case Greek "delta" and symbol ≅ reads "is approximately equal to.") Because scattering cross section σ must be extremely small for gravitrinos, truncation of the series expansion after the first-order term in σ, as shown in [D2.3], is generally adequate. (See endnote 27 of Chapter 8.)

Consider an isolated sphere of radius r_0, mass density ρ_m and mass $m = 4/3 \, \pi \rho_m r_0^3$. For uniform, isotropic, gravitrino momentum flux j_0 the incident momentum rate on the sphere is $4\pi r_0^2 j_0$. A momentum-flux deficiency occurs "behind" the sphere due to scattering by the sphere matter. At radius r from the sphere center this deficiency is $4\pi r_0^2 \Delta j / 4\pi r^2$. That is, due to the presence of the sphere an outward-radial-directed deficiency in momentum flux $(r_0^2/r^2)\Delta j$ must extend in every outward radial direction from every body and it gives exactly Newton's equation for gravitational attraction, as we shall see. Based on this physical mechanism instead of an abstract mathematical equation, near-Newtonian theory is more deeply and intuitively understood, providing considerable physical insight into gravity as it is defined by this model.

To easily utilize the above result for Δj we make simplifications justified by integral-calculus calculations not included here. These simplifications introduce an already-mentioned "geometry factor" which we may ignore because it is finally absorbed into an empirical constant. Assume projected area of the sphere of mass m is $S_m = \pi r_0^2$ and nominal thickness $L_m = m/(S_m \rho_m)$. Then, at radius r from the sphere we obtain outward *momentum flux deficiency*

$$\text{[D2.4]} \qquad \Delta j = -\sigma \rho_m L_m S_m j_0/(\pi r^2) = -\sigma m j_0/(\pi r^2).$$

Now consider the influence of this deficiency Δj on a second sphere of mass M. Along the line through the centers-of-mass of the two spheres m and M the momentum-flux radiation striking the "inner" face of the second body of mass M is deficient by the amount Δj compared to that striking its "outer" face. A net inward-directed excess Δj of momentum flux thereby "illuminates" body M along the direction of the centers-of-mass line. Consequently, an attractive force F occurs on M directed toward the center-of-mass of m. This attractive force on M is, to adequate approximation,

$$\text{[D2.5]} \qquad F = \sigma \rho_M L_M S_M \Delta j = -\sigma^2 M m j_0/(\pi r^2) = -GMm/r^2,$$

where the previously mentioned empirical constant $G = \sigma^2 j_0/\pi = 6.675 \times 10^{-11}$ m^3/kg /sec^2, $m = \rho_m L_m S_m$ and $M = \rho_M L_M S_M$. By symmetry (exchanging M and m), it is clear that the identical attractive force also acts on m. We have thus used momentum exchange from isotropic radiation of gravitrinos acting on two bodies to derive Newton's universal law of gravity [D2.5] and discovered a possible physical meaning of the universal gravitational constant G.

Part 3: A Possible Test of Near-Newtonian Theory

Because momentum flux j_0 is only slightly diminished in passing through matter, the above first approximations [D2.3] and [D2.5] are probably quite accurate. But a more accurate approximation of [D2.3] might be noticeably better in rare cases. If so, the following derivation can be employed to test the theory and obtain a value of coefficient σ for near-Newtonian-gravity theory.

Consider a body M *gravitationally thick* so that the first-order-in-σ approximation [D2.3] is not adequate. An adequate result for this case must include higher-order terms. We therefore write

$$\text{[D3.1]} \qquad \Delta j = j_0[\exp(-\sigma \rho_m L_m) - 1]$$
$$= -(\sigma m/\pi r^2) j_0 [1 - (\sigma \rho_m L_m)/2 + (\sigma \rho_m L_m)^2/6 - \ldots].$$

When $(\sigma \rho_m L_m) << 1$, i.e., for a *gravitationally thin* body, the first-order approximation [D2.4] is recovered.

If one or both bodies are thick the doubly extended but truncated expression

$$[D3.2] \quad F = -GMm/r^2\{1 - \sigma/2[\rho_M L_M + \rho_m L_m] + \sigma^2/6[(\rho_M L_M)^2 + (\rho_m L_m)^2] - \ldots\}$$
$$= -GMm/r^2\,\delta$$

should be used where δ (lower case Greek "delta") defined by [D3.2] is the *thick-body correction factor*.

When, if ever, is gravitrino scattering sufficiently strong to make a body gravitationally thick? Since σ is unknown we must be content with an estimate. For the sun, $M = 1.99\times10^{30}$ kg while its average radius is 6.96×10^8 meters giving $\rho_M = 1410$ kg/m^3, $L_M = 9.27\times10^8$ m and $\rho_M L_M/2 = 6.54\times10^{11}$ kg/m^2. For the sun to be thin, $\sigma \leq 1.53\times10^{-13}$ m^2/kg (giving $\sigma\rho_M L_M/2 \leq 0.1$, i.e., near the upper limit of being negligible compared to one). The normal unit of measure for nuclear-collision cross sections is 1 *barn* = 1×10^{-28} m^2. The above restriction on σ for the sun (mostly hydrogen ions or protons) to be thin is, in barns, $\sigma \leq 5.08\times10^{-13}$ barns/proton. Such a scattering cross section is small, but not for a neutrino-like particle. As quoted in Chapter 13, neutrinos can penetrate light years of lead and 3,000 light years (2.83×10^{21} cm) of water. Using the latter number and ignoring any difference in gravitrino scattering by neutrons and protons we obtain $\sigma \approx 1\times10^{-21}$ barns per nucleon << 5.08 $\times10^{-13}$ barns/proton. For neutrino-like gravitrino scattering, the sun is very thin indeed.

Neutron stars and black holes, on the other hand, may be gravitationally thick. Neutron stars have a huge mass density and may therefore scatter or even stop a significant fraction of gravitrinos over a moderate neutron star diameter. In its collapse to a neutron-star state, a star radius decreases dramatically from r_s to r_n and the mass density of the neutron star is magnified over its former value by the factor $(r_s/r_n)^3$ while nominal thickness is reduced by (r_n/r_s) and the nominal cross section by $(r_n/r_s)^2$. Mass $M = \rho_M L_M S_M$ is unchanged in this transition but gravitational thickness $\sigma\rho_M L_M$ is increased by the very large factor $(r_s/r_n)^2$. Black holes may simply absorb all gravitrinos if they are gravitationally opaque, causing $\Delta j = j_0$ and a greatly magnified gravity. In both cases little empirical knowledge is available and our knowledge of physics becomes unsure in either of these extreme conditions. Nevertheless, comparison of [D3.2] and [D2.5] using suitable data may indicate whether gravitational thickness is actually encountered and has the predicted influence on gravity.

Part 4: Retardation of Gravity: Influence on Orbital Motion

We now consider an interesting implication rendered visible by near-Newtonian theory but not restricted to this mechanism of gravity. We first propose a *tangential drag* on a body in orbit that derives from friction. We then consider another tangential gravity effect due to *retardation of gravity*. Then we calculate the influence of these effects on the orbit of a planet or galaxy around a star or another galaxy and discuss possible implications of the results.

Einstein showed that in relativity a sum (or difference) Δv of two velocities is determined by the expression

[D4.1] $$\Delta v = (v_1 + v_2) / (1 + v_1 v_2/c^2)$$

where Δv is the sum of velocities, such as the relative velocity of a second body approaching a first moving body (a velocity difference), v_1 and v_2 are the velocities of the two bodies, and c is the velocity of light in vacuum. As required by relativity, when the speed of either body is c, then the velocity sum is also c, i.e., c is the upper limit of any velocity sum or difference. We demonstrate that [D4.1] satisfies this upper-limit requirement by setting either v_1 or v_2 equal to c and the other equal to ± v. Then,

$$\Delta v = (c \pm v) / (1 \pm v/c) = c\,(c \pm v) / (c \pm v) = c.$$

We also note that [D4.1] satisfies another limit requirement when $v_1/c << 1$ and $v_2/c << 1$, namely,

$$\Delta v = v_1 + v_2.$$

We may therefore apply the velocity sum expression [D4.1] in calculating momentum exchange from gravitrinos to which we assign velocity $c_0 = (1 - \varepsilon)c$ as the average velocity, with ε (Greek "epsilon") being some small fraction. Consider a first body m moving in a circular orbit with angular velocity ω (Greek "omega") around a second body M. The analysis thus applies to a planet circling a star and a galaxy circling another galaxy. If r is the radius of the orbit, the velocity difference between a planet having orbital velocity ωr and the gravitrinos is

$$\Delta v = [(1 - \varepsilon)c \pm \omega r] / [1 \pm (1 - \varepsilon)\omega r/c],$$

where plus or minus (±) indicates the velocity difference between the planet and the gravitrinos along the line of orbital motion of the planet, in the plus case for gravitrinos passing through the leading surface of the moving planet or in the minus case for those passing through its trailing surface. If plus is used in one term, it must also be used in the other and similarly for minus.

Because $\omega r/c$ is generally small, we may approximate the denominator with a truncated expansion: $[1 \pm (1 - \varepsilon)\omega r/c]^{-1} = [1 \pm (\varepsilon - 1)\omega r/c]$ which gives

$$\Delta v = (1 - \varepsilon)c \pm \varepsilon\,(2 - \varepsilon)\,\omega r.$$

We ignore center-of-mass motion of the star-planet system claiming, without proof, that such motion has little or no effect on long-term relative motion and less short-term effect. When $c_0 = c$, $\varepsilon = 0$ and $\Delta v = c$.

The momentum flux of the gravitrinos is given by the product of three quantities: the average gravitrino relative velocity squared, the gravitrino number density, and the gravitrino mass, none of which are known. The relative momentum flux entering the leading and trailing surfaces of the planet may differ slightly because the relative velocities differ. Since momentum flux is proportional to v^2, the momentum flux corrected for orbiting-planet velocity is $j_0\,[c_0 \pm \varepsilon(2-\varepsilon)\omega r]^2 / c_0^{\,2}$ and

$$[D4.2] \qquad F_{td} = j_0\sigma m\,[(1-\varepsilon)c - \varepsilon(2-\varepsilon)\omega r]^2 / [(1-\varepsilon)^2c^2] - j_0\sigma m\,[(1-\varepsilon)c + \varepsilon(2-\varepsilon)\omega r]^2 / [(1-\varepsilon)^2c^2] = -8\,j_0\sigma m\varepsilon\,\omega r/c_0.$$

In the last equation we have used $\varepsilon(2-\varepsilon) = 2\varepsilon$, valid when ε is small compared to one, and $c_0 = (1-\varepsilon)c$. This negative tangential force is a *drag force* resisting tangential motion ωr, as indicated by subscripts "t" for tangential and "d" for drag. Note that F_{td} contains the factor $\omega r/c_0$, which is an angle.

We next deduce a tangential force opposed to tangential drag due to *retardation of gravity.* But first we consider the term "retardation" as it is used in atomic and molecular physics. Attraction of nearby atoms and molecules to one another is enhanced at close range by cooperative motion of electrons in each so as to minimize system energy. Electron clouds (probability distributions) about a pair of atoms or molecules at small separation are strongly correlated in their movements and form attractive, oscillating dipoles and higher-order multipoles. As the atoms separate, the time required for interaction (due to the finite speed of light with which photons and the electromagnetic field propagates) becomes sufficiently large that electron displacements are large during the field traverse time, correlation is diminished, and attractive interaction is attenuated. This reduced attractive force is called a *retarded* force, retarded by time delay in communication between electron clouds in separated atoms reducing their correlation in motion.

If gravitational force requires a finite time to establish itself, a tangential retardation effect must occur in gravitational attraction between two bodies or two galaxies orbiting one another. Arising from the finite time required for the attractive force between bodies to be established, gravitational force experienced at any moment must correspond to the system configuration at an earlier time. The following figure containing a star and a planet gives an exaggerated illustration of gravity retardation. The star represents either a star or galaxy of mass M and the planet represents a planet, a second star, or a second galaxy of mass m. These entities are referred to as M and m.

At time $t = 0$ the direction of the center-to-center line from star-to-planet is the vertical line of length r and the total attractive force, as prescribed by Newton's theory, has magnitude

$$[D4.3] \qquad F = -\,GMm/r^2.$$

Suppose establishing gravity force requires time delay $\langle t \rangle$, where $\langle t \rangle$ is a propagation time of gravitrinos or gravitons or gravity waves. When the force is established it is aligned with an earlier center-to-center direction, as illustrated by vector **F**, i.e., **F** is a non-central force because the planet *displaced* by distance $\omega r\langle t \rangle$

during time <t>, as shown. We assume that in time interval <t>, m moves in a circular arc though angle $\varphi = \omega\langle t\rangle$, with φ (Greek "phi") the angular displacement in time <t> and ω (Greek "omega") the orbital angular velocity of m about M.

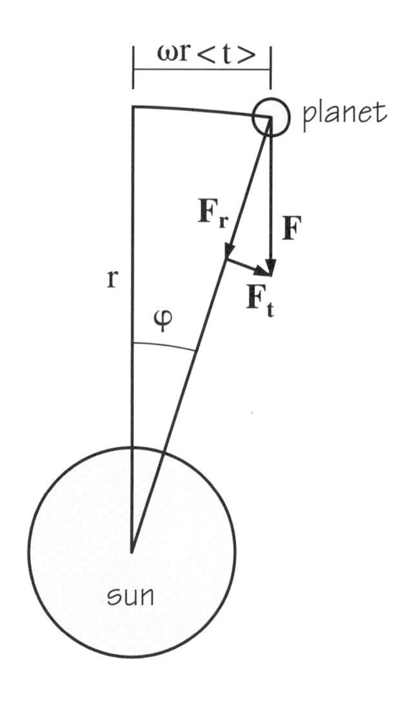

A gravitational field about M, caused by radial-outward momentum-flux deficiency Δj, is exactly or nearly stationary, since interception of M by gravitrinos is continuous. However, the lag time to establish this gravitational field fully and exactly out to radius r is $\langle t\rangle = r/c_0$. If the gravity field of M is stationary, the average retardation delay is time of penetration of momentum-flux difference Δj through half of m, viz., $\langle t\rangle = r_p/c_0$ where r_p is the radius of body m, the planet, star, or galaxy, i.e., the gravitational-force-weighted-average time required for gravitrinos to pass through m. In either case a *retardation angle* $\varphi = \omega\times\langle t\rangle$ results, like the angle factor that appears in F_{td}.

At the small φ values we consider, $\sin\varphi = \varphi - \varphi^3/6 + \ldots \cong \varphi$ and $\cos\varphi = 1 - \varphi^2/2 + \ldots \cong 1$. To first-order in φ in both cases, which is assumed to be adequate, the time-dependent-direction of *retarded force* **F** in the figure applies, as shown. This force **F** is not central (radial) but may be decomposed into a radial component $F_r = F \cos\varphi \cong F$ and a tangential component $F_t = F\sin\varphi \cong F\varphi$, as shown, where $F = |\mathbf{F}|$ given by [D4.3] represents attractive-force magnitude.

The radius and angular velocity of the M-m system may be slowly changing but always satisfies the force balance

[D4.4] $$m\omega^2 r = G\,Mm/r^2 \quad \text{giving} \quad \omega = \pm\sqrt{(GM/r^3)}.$$

That is, we assume a circular orbit with a slowly-changing radius r. Because of retardation, the slightly non-central attraction causes a *continuous tangential retardation force* F_{tr} opposed to drag force F_{td}, and both influence the angular motion of m about M. Consequently, neither angular momentum nor energy is conserved in this model of orbital motion. The tangential retardation force has magnitude

[D4.5] $$F_{tr} = G\,Mm/r^2\,\omega r_p/c_0.$$

The total tangential force $F_t = F_{td} + F_{tr}$ causes *torque* $F_t\times r$ equal to rate of change of orbital angular momentum (Newton's second law for circular motion)

[D4.6] $dJ/dt = d(I\omega)/dt = m d(\omega r^2)/dt = m\sqrt{(GM)}\, 1/(2\sqrt{r})\, dr/dt = F_t \times r$,

with $J = I\omega$ the orbital angular momentum of m around M, $I = mr^2$ the moment of inertia of m about M, and $d\omega/dt$ the orbital angular acceleration. The set of equations [D4.4-6] provides a complete basis for analysis of evolution of average motion invoking conservation of neither energy nor angular momentum.

Because both r and ω depend on time t, to solve for either we eliminate the other from the equation to be solved. This strategy utilizes [D4.4] to, for example, eliminate ω in [D4.6] and obtain

[D4.7] $m\sqrt{(GM)}\, dr/dt = 2 F_t r^{3/2} = 2m\sqrt{(GM)}\, \{-8 j_0 \sigma \varepsilon r/c_0 + GM\langle t\rangle/r^2\}$.

Further simplification gives the simple differential equation for r(t)

[D4.8] $dr/dt = \{-16 j_0 \sigma \varepsilon r/c_0 + 2\, GM\langle t\rangle/r^2\}$.

We consider two cases in solving for r(t). In both cases an implicit retardation time $\langle t\rangle = r/c_0$ appears in F_{td} while two retardation times are used in F_{tr}, $\langle t\rangle = r_p/c_0$ and r/c_0.

(i) In the first case $\langle t\rangle = r_p/c_0$ and

[D4.9] $dr/dt = -\gamma_1 r + \gamma_2/r^2$,

where $\gamma_1 = 16 j_0 \sigma\, \varepsilon/c_0$ and $\gamma_2 = 2GM r_p/c_0$ are constants (γ is the Greek "gamma"). Separating variables we obtain

[D4.10] $3\gamma_1 r^2\, dr / (\gamma_1 r^3 - \gamma_2) = -3\gamma_1\, dt$.

Integration and simplification gives

[D4.11a] $r(t)/r_o = \{\exp(-3\gamma_1 t) + (\gamma_2/\gamma_1 r_o^3)\,[1 - \exp(-3\gamma_1 t)]\}^{1/3}$.

This solution shows that when $\gamma_2/(\gamma_1 r_0^3)$ is negligible, the solution simplifies to $r/r_0 \cong \exp(-\gamma_1 t)$ by which the orbital radius of m continually decreases. However, as $t \to \infty$, r approaches a stable radius $r = (\gamma_2/\gamma_1)^{1/3}$ at which drag and retardation forces just balance one another in their opposite influences.

For stability, when orbital radius decreases, orbital angular velocity must increase. The angular velocity $\omega(t)$ is obtained from [D4.9] using [D4.4], an exercise we leave to the interested reader.

If $c_0 = c$, ε and $\gamma_1 \to 0$ and [D4.9] becomes $r^2 dr = \gamma_2 dt$ which has the solution

[D4.11b] $r(t)/r_o = \{1 + (3\gamma_2/r_o^3)\, t\}^{1/3}$ with $\gamma_2 = 2GM r_p/c_0$.

(ii) In the second case $<t> = r/c_0$, we assume the gravity force must be one-way communicated over the entire separation r by gravitons, gravitrinos, or gravity waves travelling at speed c_0. In this case [D4.8] becomes

[D4.12] $$dr/dt = -\gamma_1 r + \gamma_3/r,$$

where γ_1 is defined above and $\gamma_3 = 2GM/c_0$. Again we separate variables to obtain

[D4.13] $$2\gamma_1 r\, dr/(\gamma_1 r^2 - \gamma_3) = -2\gamma_1 dt$$

for which integration and simplification give

[D4.14a] $$r(t)/r_o = \{\exp(-2\gamma_1 t) + (\gamma_3/\gamma_1 r_o^2)[1 - \exp(-2\gamma_1 t)]\}^{1/2}.$$

We again see continual decrease over time in radius to a stable radius $r = (\gamma_3/\gamma_1)^{1/2}$, different from that of the first case.

The positive sign before γ_2 in [D4.9] and γ_3 in [D4.12] indicates the tangential retardation force *adds energy* from gravitrinos to the two-body system. The negative sign before γ_1 in both equations indicates gravitrino or other drag *removes energy* from the two-body system. Or one could say that in the rotation of two bodies about one another, retardation of gravity causes addition of energy to the system while drag causes dissipation of system energy.

If $c_0 = c$, ε and $\gamma_1 \rightarrow 0$ and [D4.12] becomes $r\,dr = \gamma_3 dt$ which has the solution

[D4.14b] $$r(t)/r_o = \{1 + (2\gamma_3/r_o^2)t\}^{1/2} \quad \text{with} \quad \gamma_3 = 2GM/c_0.$$

Solutions [D4.11b] and [D4.14b] both predict continuing increase in system radius, orbital period, energy, and angular momentum. However, even if ε and γ_1 are zero, other drag mechanisms such as tidal motion of fluids or solids may influence motion of m and solutions [D4.11] or [D4.14] still apply but with another γ_1.

What differences in motion are predicted for intergalactic M-m systems compared to intragalactic ones? Might some effect cause near-body relative motion to differ from far-body relative motion?

Possible differences between near and far body influences on motion may be differences in drag force. If $c_0 - c$, then the ε of [D4.2] is zero. Near field drag on earth is then primarily due to sun-moon-planet attractions, tidal action, or interception of momentum-carrying interplanetary gas, dust, and other matter in space, all of which dissipate earth's orbital energy. For intergalactic motion such dissipation mechanisms may all be negligible. If $\gamma_1 \cong 0$ for distant, orbiting galaxies, a gravity-retardation force drives accelerating separation of them; if γ_1 exceeds γ_2 or γ_3, an opposite net effect occurs on near and far bodies.

Part 5: Retardation of Gravity: Influence on Radial Motion

Consider now purely radial motion of a body or group of mass m moving with relative radial velocity v_r away from another body or group of mass M. Radius r represents the actual, instantaneous separation of the centers-of-mass of the two bodies or groups. The mechanics of such a two-body system may be elucidated utilizing the principle of conservation of energy.

Internal kinetic energy of the system at time t is $KE = \mu v_r^2/2$ with (Greek "mu" =) μ the reduced mass (see page 544). Kinetic energy due to center-of-mass motion of the system M+m is not included in internal kinetic energy. For simplicity we take $M >> m$, so that $\mu \cong m$, and we take at time t_0 and separation r_0 $KE_0 = m v_{r0}^2/2$. At other time t and separation r, kinetic energy is $KE = m v_r^2/2$. Corresponding Newtonian gravitational potential energies are $PE_0 = -GMm/r_0$ and $PE = -GMm/r = PE_0 r_0/r$. By conservation of energy, the total energy at time t_0 and at any other time t is $E_0 = KE_0 + PE_0$ and we characterize the motion of body or group m relative to body or group M at times t and t_0 with the expression

[D5.1] $$KE + PE = KE_0 + PE_0 \qquad \text{or}$$

$$KE/KE_0 = 1 + PE_0/KE_0 - PE_0/KE_0 \, r_0/r.$$

In this expression we introduce *energy parameter* $\alpha = |PE_0|/KE_0$ (with α the Greek "alpha"). Energy parameter α characterizes relative system motion according to

[D5.2] $$v_r/v_{r0} = \sqrt{(1 - \alpha + \alpha r_0/r)}$$

relating relative radial velocity v_r and separation r at time t to initial radial velocity v_{r0}, radius r_0, and energy parameter α all at time t_0. Expressions for radius as a function of *time* are given in endnote 5.

Plots of v_r/v_{r0} versus r/r_0 are shown in Figure D1 for several values of energy parameter α. The energy parameter controls the nature of the curve. When $\alpha > 1$, the system is "closed," i.e., the two bodies or groups are forever gravitationally bound together. As seen in the curves when $\alpha > 1$, an initial outward relative velocity falls to zero at location $r/r_0 = \alpha/(\alpha - 1)$, after which the gravitational attraction reverses the motion and brings the two bodies together. When $\alpha \leq 1$ the system is "open," i.e. the two bodies move apart to infinite separation. When $\alpha = 1$ the internal system kinetic energy KE_0 is fully depleted when $r \rightarrow \infty$ at which limit $KE = mv_r^2/2$ and $PE = -GMm/r$ both approach zero.

Six curves appear in Figure D1 corresponding to energy parameter values, beginning with the horizontal line and going clockwise, α = 0, 0.5, 1.0, 1.2, 1.5, 2. The last three curves ($\alpha > 1$) are closed.

We now introduce retardation of gravity considering the case when a local gravity interaction must be one-way communicated at speed c_0 over the *full separation* r, i.e., gravity transmission requires a time delay $\langle t \rangle = r/c_0$. Two-way communication requires twice this time delay. We determine separation dynamics of bodies for $\langle t \rangle$

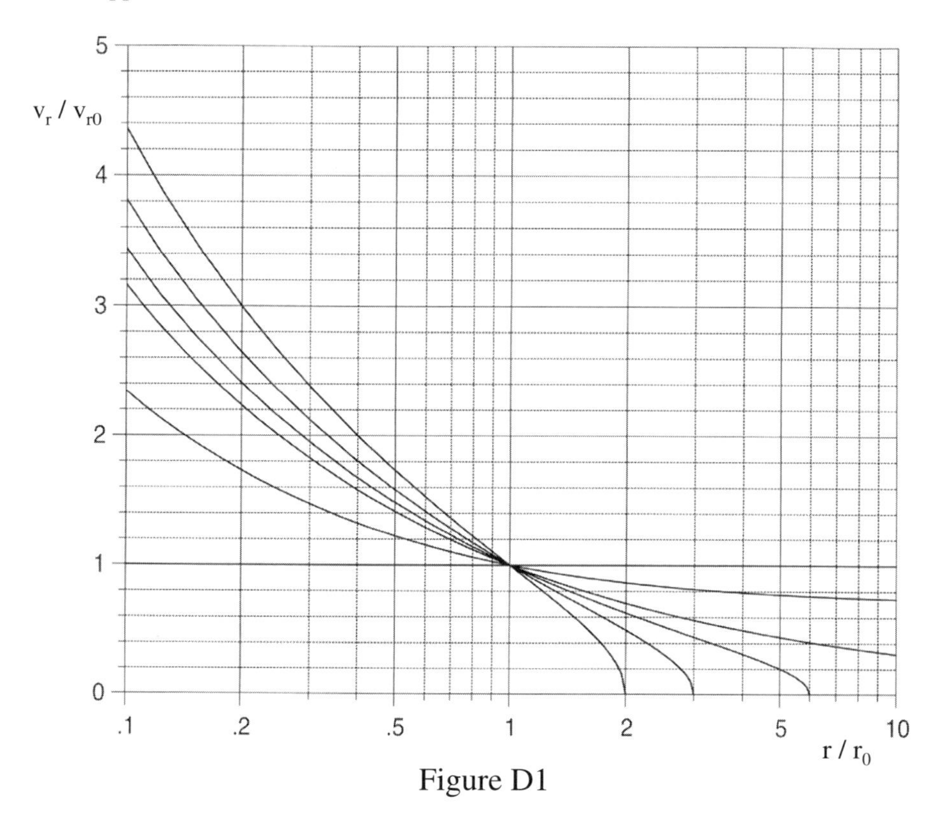

Figure D1

$= r/c_0$ ignoring other cases such as $\langle t \rangle = r_p/c_0$ which are simple extensions. Then an *effective separation* or *radius* r_e smaller than r for outward radial motion replaces r in the gravity expression to give a retarded PE and in [D5.2] we replace r with r_e to obtain

[D5.3] $$v_r/v_{r0} = \sqrt{(1 - \alpha + \alpha r_0/r_e)}$$

If one knows effective radius r_e in terms of actual radius r, one can calculate correct velocity ratio v_r/v_{r0} versus actual separation r/r_0 by use of r_e/r_0. The effective radius r_e is the real-time quantity

[D5.4] $$r_e(t) = r(t - \langle t \rangle) = r(t - r/c_0).$$

We now determine $r_e(t)/r_0$ by two methods.

(1) By a Taylor's series expansion,

[D5.5] $$r_e(t)/r_0 = r(t)/r_0 - \langle t \rangle/r_0\,(dr/dt)_t + \langle t \rangle^2/2r_0\,(d^2r/dt^2)_t - \langle t \rangle^3/6r_0\,(d^3r/dt^3)_t + \langle t \rangle^4/24r_0\,(d^4r/dt^4)_t - \ldots$$

where the subscripted t on each derivative indicates it is evaluated at t. The derivatives are obtained from dr/dt in

[D5.6a] $dr/dt = v_{r0}\sqrt{(1 - \alpha + \alpha r_0/r)}$ so that

[D5.6b] $d^2r/dt^2 = -\alpha/2\, v_{r0}^2/r_0\, (r_0/r)^2$

[D5.6c] $d^3r/dt^3 = \alpha v_{r0}^3/r_0^2\, (r_0/r)^3 \sqrt{(1 - \alpha + \alpha r_0/r)}$

[D5.6d] $d^4r/dt^4 = -3\alpha v_{r0}^5/r_0^3\, (r_0/r)^4 (1 - \alpha + \alpha r_0/r) - \alpha^2/48\, v_{r0}^4/r_0^3\, (r_0/r)^5$

and so on. The expansion through the fourth derivative term is accurate when δ_0 or r_0/r is sufficiently small. The resulting expression for r_e/r_0, in which $\delta_0 = v_{r0}/c_0$, is

[D5.7] $$r_e/r_0 = r/r_0[1 - \delta_0\sqrt{(1 - \alpha + \alpha r_0/r)}] - \alpha/4\delta_0^2 - \alpha/6\, \delta_0^3\sqrt{(1 - \alpha + \alpha r_0/r)}$$
$$- \alpha/8\, \delta_0^4 (1 - \alpha + \alpha r_0/r) - \alpha^2\delta_0^4/48\, (r_0/r) - \ldots$$

We see in Figure D2 curves with dots calculated using equation [D5.7] with $\alpha = 1$ and, from the left, $\delta_0 = 0, 0.2, 0.4, 0.6, 0.8, 1$.

(2) For $\alpha = 1$, $dr/dt = v_{r0}\sqrt{(r_0/r)}$ or $\sqrt{(r/r_0)}\, d(r/r_0) = v_{r0}/r_0\, dt = d\tau$, where *dimensionless time* (Greek "tau" =) $\tau = v_{r0}t/r_0$. This equation has solution, with $\tau = \tau_0$ corresponding to $r = r_0$,

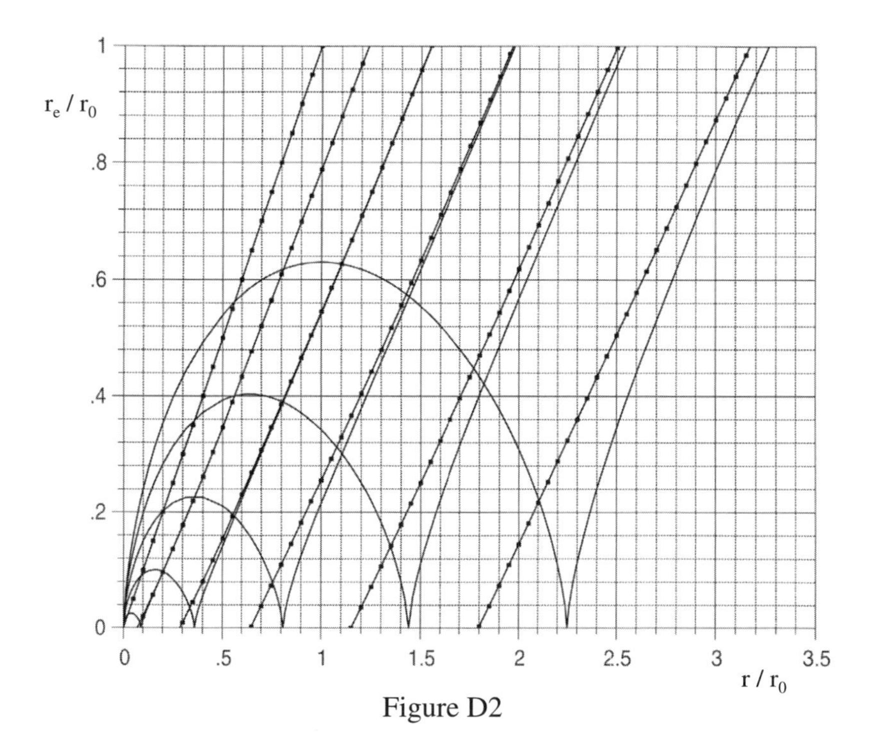

Figure D2

[D5.8] $\tau - \tau_0 = 2/3\,[(r/r_0)^{3/2} - 1]$ or $r/r_0 = [3/2\,(\tau - \tau_0) + 1]^{2/3}$.

Dimensionless retardation time $<\tau> = v_{r0} <t>/r_0 = v_{r0}/c_0\, r/r_0 = \delta_0\, r/r_0$, ("delta-sub-naught" =) $\delta_0 = v_{r0}/c_0$, and

[D5.9] $r_e/r_0 = [3/2\,(\tau - \tau_0 - \delta_0 r/r_0) + 1]^{2/3} = (r/r_0)^{3/2} - 3/2\,\delta_0\, r/r_0$.

Curves in Figure D2 calculated by [D5.9] are shown without dots (except where the two r_e/r_0 curves of [D5.7] and [D5.9] coincide).

An interesting feature of the last set of curves is their zero value when $r/r_0 = 9\delta_0^2/4$. These zeroes are mathematically real in the sense that outward radial velocity behaves as if the separation were r_e rather than actual separation r. But they and the associated nonzero values in $0 < r/r_0 < 9\,\delta_0^2/4$ are artificial in the sense that if motion is interrupted at $r/r_0 = 9\,\delta_0^2/4$ then r_e is quickly enlarged to r, represented by the connection with the leftmost curve having $\delta_0 = 0$. While the zeroes are reminiscent of the magic circles of Chapter 8, retarded-Newtonian-gravity theory with its absolute time and flat, Euclidian space does not allow magic circles to be real.

In Figure D2 the r_e/r_0 curves for $\delta_0 > 0$ lie below the Newtonian r/r_0 curve (the leftmost one) as expected for outward radial motion, i.e., the effective gravitational radius, $r_e(t) = r(t - <t>)$, is the actual radius at an earlier time which is smaller for outward radial motion. But even when $c_0 = c$ and $\delta_0 = 1$ (right curve), a body never fully "outruns gravity." It only partially and temporarily outruns gravity to the extent that gravitational attraction is altered, as indicated in the corrected conservation-of-energy equation [D5.3].

Figures D3 and D4, both calculated for the case of $\alpha = 1$, illustrate retarded-gravity effect on radial velocity according to the conservation-of-energy equation [D5.3]. That is, actual radial velocity versus actual radial separation, v_r/v_{r0} versus r/r_0, is shown in Figure D3 taking proper account of gravity retardation.

In Figure D3 we see that v_r/v_{r0} varies with δ_0. When $\delta_0 = 0$ (bottom curve), motion is slow (nonexistent) compared to c_0 and the Newtonian result obtains. As δ_0 increases, (from the bottom, $\delta_0 = 0, 0.2, 0.4, 0.6, 0.8, 1$) initial outward radial motion and motion scale v_{r0} is not negligible compared to c_0 and *actual velocities are shifted upward at early times* by gravity retardation. This shift must occur according to conservation of energy [D5.3], i.e., since potential energy is reduced or more negative, the kinetic energy must be increased to a more positive value to preserve constant total energy E_0.

The r_0 scale of Figure D3 is not an early, "big-bang radius" of the universe but a radius between two chosen bodies or groups at a selected time t_0. Many bodies may be considered with comparisons made looking farther out into space (further back in time to before t_0).

Figure D4 corresponds to Figure D3 with, from the left, $\delta_0 = 0, 0.2, 0.4, 0.6, 0.8, 1$, the only difference between them being a transformation of variable from r/r_0 to τ (Greek "tau") by [D5.8]. Thus, at dimensionless time $\tau = \tau_0 = 0$, $r/r_0 = v_r/v_{r0} = 1$ for Newtonian motion (for $\delta_0 = 0$, the leftmost curve).

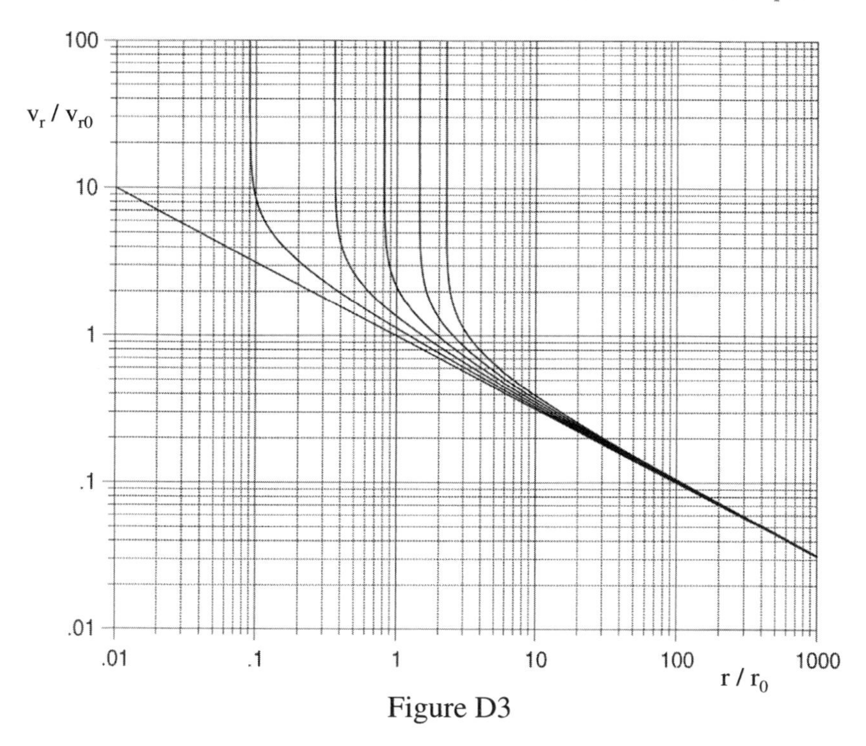

Figure D3

The case $\alpha = 1$ is not typical because curves for r_e/r_0 all converge when $r/r_0 > 1000$, as required by [D5.2] and [D5.3]. Curves for r_e/r_0 do not converge to a common value when $\alpha \neq 1$, even when r/r_0 is large. Nevertheless, values of v_r/v_{r0} converge to a common α-value curve for all δ_0 when r_e/r_0 or r/r_0 is sufficiently large because, by [D5.2], [D5.3], or [D5.9], v_r/v_{r0} no longer depends on δ_0 in this limit.

We note from Figures D3 and D4 that, if retardation of gravity occurs, when one looks sufficiently far into space (back in time) Newtonian theory may be quite wrong in its predictions with actual outward-radial-velocity prediction, utilizing retardation of gravity at $r/r_0 \leq 10$, often substantially larger than predicted by Newtonian theory or a Hubble's-law calculation. Simultaneously, predictions of radial separation or time difference may be much too large based on Newtonian theory [D5.2] and a specified v_r/v_{r0}, as shown in Figure D1, compared to separations predicted by [D5.3] and [D5.9], as shown in Figures D3 and D4. In interpreting observations, such discrepancies might cause one to conclude that expansion of the universe is accelerating when it is not in a conventional, continuing sense. Without use of retardation of gravity and its additional degree of freedom $\delta_0 = v_{r0}/c_0$, one might naturally regard an observed increase in relative outward velocity with radial separation being larger than that predicted by Newtonian theory (with which relativity theory is generally compatible in weak gravity and slow motion) as an accelerating expansion of the universe, attributable to, say, a positive cosmological constant λ. The cosmological constant is simply the energy density of empty space.

It could, in principle, be zero, positive, or negative and, if not zero, large or small. Since positive energy density causes accelerating expansion of space recent data suggest it is positive but of small magnitude. Steven Weinberg summarizes some recent thinking about λ.[6] Retardation of gravity provides another possibility to consider as a cause of real or apparent accelerating expansion of the universe.

Looking out into space (back in time) to understand evolution of structure and organization in the universe, one should observe at $\tau - \tau_0 \geq 10$, according to Newtonian-retarded-gravity theory with $\alpha < 1$, distant stars receding at nearly their

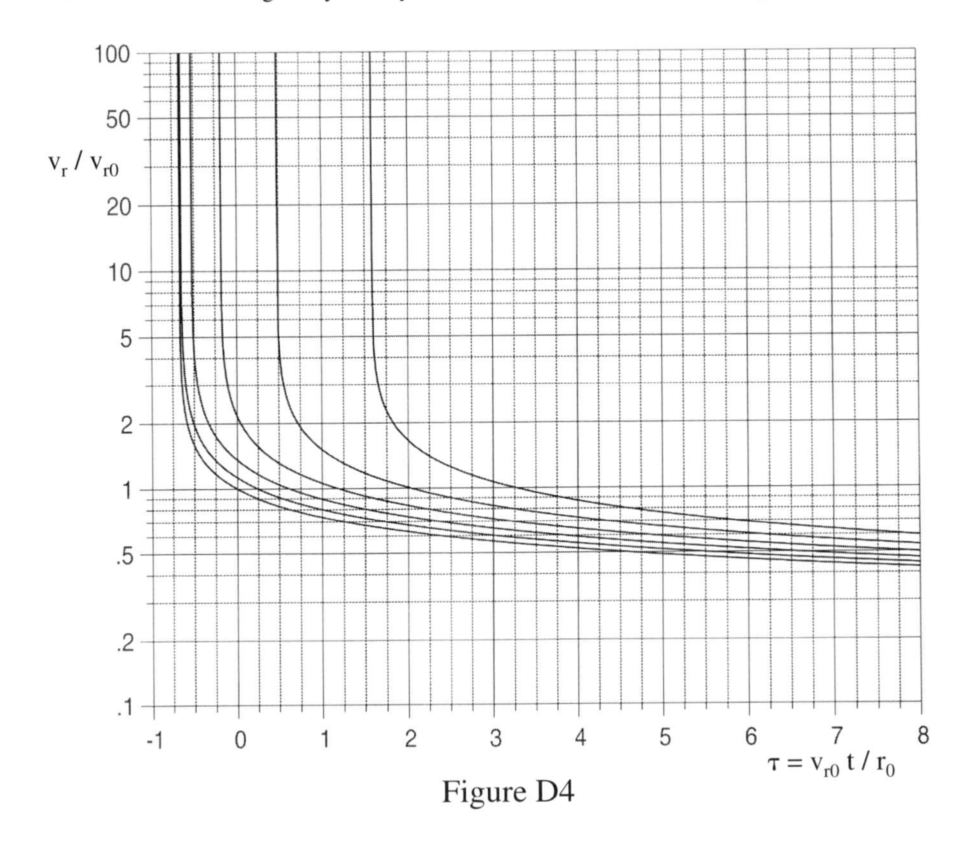

Figure D4

asymptotic velocities. But at smaller separations (smaller $\tau - \tau_0$) recessional velocity can increase on many position-versus-time paths, with examples shown in Figure D4. As δ_0 increases one can regard a body as "outrunning gravity" to the extent that effective separation is increased from r to r_e. These predictions may help explain why Hubble's law is only approximate. (Theory already explains this nature of Hubble's law.[7]) Different "δ_0 paths" with a multitude of α values, might lead an astronomer to believe the universe is ever-accelerating and chaotic. But chaos may perhaps be reduced and accelerating expansion eliminated by the present theory. The theory together with observation may even indicate direction of expansion from a big-bang center of the universe, contrary to current cosmological belief.[7]

In further pursuing retardation of gravity, retarded-gravity mechanics should be addressed in relativity to discover if similar effects to Newtonian-retarded-gravity theory are predicted in a relativistic analysis. If so, retarded-gravity prediction and observation may be compared in attempting to settle important questions.

What important questions might be settled? In relativity, instantaneous communication is believed to be forbidden.[8] However, instantaneous communication does occur in a non-local universe (Chapter 10 describes the universe as non-local in quantum-physics phenomena). With non-local, instantaneous communication, no gravity retardation is allowed because $<t> = 0$. Therefore, it is expected that retardation of gravity will only be observed in a local universe, one for which gravity waves or gravitons traveling at the speed of light or less are postulated. If gravity retardation exists, the universe is local in gravity. If it does not, the universe is non-local in gravity. The question of locality of gravity, and other questions we have mentioned or implied, are deep and their answers are elusive. But many implications may follow from their answers. Here, in the question of retarded gravity, may lie illumination if not answers. Answering gravity questions may help fulfill a vision well expressed by one astrophysicist who observed that in our science "… we are [seeking to answer] deep philosophical questions with physical measurements."[9]

Assuming the universe is local in gravity (or ignoring the question), theorists believe disturbances in spacetime generate gravity waves. Seeking to detect such gravity waves or graviton particles has been an unrealized objective in experimental physics for 50 years. The task is difficult and continuing work may indeed result in achieving this goal. Or, perhaps gravity waves haven't been detected because the universe is non-local in gravity and they don't exist. Perhaps, instead, guiding pilot waves originate from a Governing Intelligence[10] that directs cosmological motions and anticipates the future so that no communication time appears to be required and gravity appears to be non-local.

E. T. Jaynes once made the comment, "Show me a field where theoreticians have been fumbling about for forty years without producing any really significant advance; and I will show you a field where the thinking is aimed in the wrong direction."[11]

Finally, I offer an observation in connection with the basis of Newton's laws, gravity, and cosmological inflation. We note that momentum exchange in elastic or adiabatic collisions of light-speed particles does not occur when no velocity change occurs, as is often predicted by Einstein's summation of velocities relation (equation [D4.1]). But acceleration change may occur in such collisions.[4] If acceleration change of light-speed particles is the origin of gravity, inertia, and Newton's second law, then inflation of the early universe before it became transparent to light-speed messenger particles, before gravity and inertia turned on, follows. Unfortunately, my relativity knowledge is too limited for me to pursue this concept but I hope someone else will.

Note: In the above examples we assumed that gravity must propagate over the full separation r. If, instead, it must propagate over only the diameter of a body, the more remarkable conclusion is that the gravity force is nearly instantaneous, almost as Newton represented it.

Notes and References for Appendix D

[1] John P. Pratt, private communication.

[2] funphysics.jpl.nasa.gov/technical/grp/lunar-laser.html

[3] Martin, J. L., *General Relativity: A Guide to its Consequences for Gravity and Cosmology,* Ellis Horwood Limited, Chichester, West Sussex, England, 1988, 54-61.

[4] Longair, M. S., *Theoretical Concepts in Physics,* Cambridge University Press, Cambridge, 1984, Chapter 14.

[5] Newtonian theory with (Greek "tau" =) τ = dimensionless time = $v_{r0}\, t / r_0$ gives three solutions.

For $\alpha = 1$,

$$\tau - \tau_0 = v_{r0}\, t / r_0 = 2/3\, [(r / r_0)^{3/2} - 1] \quad \text{or} \quad r / r_0 = [3/2\, (\tau - \tau_0) + 1]^{2/3}$$

$$\text{or} \quad v_r / v_{r0} = [3/2\, (\tau - \tau_0) + 1]^{-1/3}.$$

For $\alpha < 1$,

$$\tau - \tau_0 = 1 / (1 - \alpha) \left\{ \sqrt{[(1 - \alpha)\, r^2 / r_0^2 + \alpha\, r / r_0]} - 1 + \alpha / (2 \sqrt{[1 - \alpha]}) \times \log_e(Z_1) \right\}$$

where $Z_1 = ([\sqrt{((1 - \alpha)\, r/r_0 + \alpha)} - \sqrt{((1 - \alpha)\, r/r_0)}] / [\sqrt{((1 - \alpha)\, r/r_0 + \alpha)} + \sqrt{((1 - \alpha)\, r/r_0)}]\,) \,/$

$$([1 - \sqrt{(1 - \alpha)}] / [1 + \sqrt{(1 - \alpha)}])$$

with function $\log_e(z)$ described in endnote 27 of Chapter 8.

For $\alpha > 1$,

$$\tau - \tau_0 = 1 / (\alpha - 1) \left\{ 1 - \sqrt{[(1 - \alpha)\, r^2 / r_0^2 + \alpha\, r / r_0]} - \alpha / \sqrt{(\alpha - 1)} \times (Z_2) \right\}$$

where

$$Z_2 = \arctan [\sqrt{((1 - \alpha)\, r/r_0 + \alpha)} / \sqrt{((\alpha - 1)\, r/r_0)}] - \arctan [\, 1 / \sqrt{(\alpha - 1)}] ,$$

valid for $1 \le r / r_0 \le \alpha / (\alpha - 1)$. The arctan(u) or arctangent function of u is *reciprocal* or *inverse* to the tangent function. If $u = \tan \theta = \sin \theta / \cos \theta$, where the sin and cosine functions are defined in endnote 16 of Chapter 7, then $\arctan(u) = \theta$, with angle θ in radians.

[6] Weinberg, Steven, *Dreams of a Final Theory,* Vintage Press, New York, 1992, 223-227, *Facing Up,* Harvard University Press, Cambridge, MA, 2001, 237.

[7] Lineweaver, Charles H., and Tamara M. Davis, *Scientific American,* March 2005, 36-45.

[8] Many texts could be cited here. I choose one that has educated several generations of physics students: Richtmyer, F. K., E. H. Kennard, and T. Lauritsen, *Introduction to Modern Physics,* Fifth Edition, McGraw-Hill, New York, 1955, 58. The earlier editions were published in 1928, 1934, 1942, and 1947.

[9] This statement is Saul Perlmutter's, as quoted by Aczel, Amir D., *God's Equation,* Four Walls Eight Windows, New York, 1999, 1.

[10] *Doctrine and Covenants* 88: 11-13. This passage is quoted on page 459.

[11] Jaynes, E. T., "Notes on Present Status and Future Prospects," http://bayes.wustl.edu/etj/node1.html 1991, 11.

Appendix E

Quantum Field Theory of Electrostatic Proton-Proton Repulsion#

Interactions between bodies in quantum field theory invoke invisible, discrete *messenger particles* that each carry a *quantum of force* between the bodies. Two examples of such messenger particles or quanta of force are photons, which carry quanta of electromagnetic forces, and gravitons, which carry quanta of the gravitational force. The latter particle is hypothetical because it has not yet been observed, but it is widely held to be real. These quanta of force resolve the dilemma of Descartes and Newton of how *action at a distance* is affected.

In the case of the mutual electrostatic repulsion force between two protons, *virtual photons* serve as the messenger particles which transfer tiny quanta of force between the two protons. Since they are virtual, as opposed to real, such action at a distance seems mysterious. But, according to quantum field theory, it is through the photon messenger particles that a normal momentum-transfer process occurs thereby exerting the mutual force in accord with Newton's second law or its relativistic equivalent.

We present here a heuristic account of the origin of this force and derive its dependence on separation r of the protons. The account is taken from Frisch and Thorndike (Frisch, David H., and Alan M. Thorndike, *Elementary Particles,* D. Van Nostrand Company, New York, 1964, 95-98.). The theory is incomplete in this derivation since the constant appearing in the equation is not derived; its derivation requires a level of statistical mechanics beyond the scope of this book and the model is merely heuristic in any case. But the correct separation dependence of the electrostatic force is determined and the action of force quanta of quantum field theory is illustrated. These are the objectives in this illustration.

The photons involved in the electrostatic force are called virtual photons because they are not observed; their lifetime is so short and fleeting that they never "wink on." They barely emerge out of the vacuum before they disappear again, and thus they are virtual rather than real photons which can be seen. The origin and nature of these virtual photons is predicted by the uncertainty principle. One form of this principle states that uncertainty in energy ΔE and time interval Δt in which the energy is determined are related by

[E1] $$\Delta t = h/(2\pi\Delta E) = \hbar/\Delta E,$$

where $h = 6.625 \times 10^{-24}$ Joule sec is Planck's constant and $\hbar = h/2\pi$.

The energy of a photon having frequency ν is $\epsilon = h\nu$. When the photon is virtual, so rapidly created and destroyed that its existence is not established, the uncertainty in its energy is $\Delta E = \epsilon = h\nu$. Consequently, the photon's lifetime before it vanishes back into the vacuum is $\Delta t = 1/(2\pi\nu)$. A photon always travels at the speed of light $c = \lambda \times \nu$ so that the distance a photon travels in time interval Δt is

$$\text{[E2]} \qquad c\,\Delta t = c/(2\pi\nu) = \lambda/2\pi = \lambda.$$

This distance is the nominal path length a virtual photon travels during its brief lifetime.

A proton continuously generates virtual photons or electromagnetic signals. Both the distance they travel and the momentum they carry are given in terms of their wavelength λ by known expressions. The nominal distance they travel before disappearing, or their range of influence, is λ and the momentum they carry, as determined from de Broglie's relation, is $p = h/\lambda$. We utilize these properties to derive the dependence on separation r that the repulsive force between protons must follow.

The number of photons generated by a proton each second having wavelength between λ and $\lambda+d\lambda$ is given by the Rayleigh-Jeans black-body-radiation distribution law (see endnote 2 and 7 of Chapter 9) and is proportional to $d\lambda/\lambda^4$. We assume the number of virtual photons generated follows this law. We use this law instead of Plank's more accurate but more complex law because both are adequate at large λ and the Rayleigh-Jeans law is simpler.

The force transmitted by the virtual photons or messenger particles, according to Newton's second law, is simply the rate of transfer of momentum by these messenger particles (see Part 1 of Appendix D). We suppose the protons are separated by distance r and recognize that only quanta having wavelength λ exceeding $2\pi r$ will transmit force because virtual photons of lesser wavelength will vanish into the vacuum before reaching the other proton. The force will therefore include the sum or integral of the discrete force quanta over all wavelengths between $\lambda = 2\pi r$ and $\lambda = \infty$ (infinity).

At any wavelength $\lambda > 2\pi r$ the transmitted force is a product of four quantities: (1) the momentum carried per photon or h/λ, (2) the probability a virtual photon is emitted from a first proton, proportional to λ, (3) the probability a photon striking the second proton is absorbed, also proportional to λ, and (4) the number of photons generated per second with wavelength between λ and $\lambda+d\lambda$, proportional to $d\lambda/\lambda^4$ (see endnote 2 of Chapter 9). Thus, integrating this force over $\lambda \geq 2\pi r$ gives for the electrostatic force F(r)

$$\text{[E3]} \qquad F(r) \propto \int_{2\pi r}^{\infty} d\lambda\; 1/\lambda \times \lambda \times \lambda/\lambda^4 = \int_{2\pi r}^{\infty} d\lambda/\lambda^3 \propto 1/r^2,$$

where the symbol "$\propto$" reads "is proportional to."

We have utilized quanta of force or messenger particles of quantum field theory to derive the inverse second power dependence on separation for the repulsive electrostatic force. Since the photon is its own antiparticle, separation dependence of the attractive force is similarly derived. This derivation utilizes a concept or mechanism of quantum field theory in which electrostatic or other action at a distance may be viewed as *direct contact* of messenger particles carrying quanta of force.

Appendix F

Thermodynamics, Statistical Mechanics, and Kinetic Theory#

1. Thermodynamic Laws, Systems, and Entropy

In Chapter 10 we described the first law of classical or macroscopic thermodynamics as the conservation of energy in a system in which heat Q is recognized as a form of energy. In its most general form the *first law of thermodynamics* is written

$$Q = \Delta E + m_{in}\times E_{in} - m_{out}\times E_{out} - W,$$

where Q is heat addition to the system, ΔE is energy increase of the system, m_{in} and m_{out} are masses added to and extracted from the system, E_{in} and E_{out} are the energy contents per unit mass of the added and extracted masses, and W is work energy extracted from the *thermodynamic system.* This form of the law applies for an *open system* in which mass, heat, energy, and work may all be exchanged. For a *closed system,* no mass exchange occurs and the law applies but with $m_{in} = m_{out} = 0$. For an *isolated system*, no mass or heat or energy or work exchange occurs. However, energy may be internally converted into heat for which process $\Delta E = \Delta E_i + Q_i = 0$.

We also mentioned in Chapter 10 that Rudolf Clausius *et al* discovered an equilibrium-state property of materials that he eventually named *entropy*. Change in entropy of a system due to heat Q transferred to the system is $\Delta S = Q/T + I$, where T is the absolute temperature of the heat (source) and I is the irreversibility of the process due to, say, friction or electrical resistance or .... In ideal processes $I = 0$ and $\Delta S = Q/T$, the only classical-thermodynamics type of process in which entropy change is exactly defined. For a real process wherein $I \geq 0$ we write $\Delta S \geq Q/T$.

Clausius stated the *second law of thermodynamics* as follows: "No spontaneous process in an isolated system causes system entropy to decrease." This law has been stated in other forms and we soon consider a famous one due to L. Boltzmann.

The universe exemplifies an *isolated system*, i.e., no transfer of energy, work, heat, or matter to or from the system. In such systems, evolution toward maximum entropy proceeds by internal processes by which, in the vicissitudes of spontaneous energy fluctuations even in the vacuum, some energy is inexorably converted to heat, a form of energy from which there is never a full or reversible return to any other. This universal, at-least-partially mono-directional process is relentless in its effect: isolated systems ever evolve toward their only possible stationary or equilibrium state, referred to as a "heat-death," in which system entropy is maximized and all system energy is unusable heat.[1] Clausius' (and Boltzmann's) statement conveys the relentless nature of entropy production in spontaneous generation and exchange of heat.

Entropy extended the scope of thermodynamics, especially beginning in the 1870s when Austrian physicist Ludwig Boltzmann (1844-1906) began developing powerful statistical mechanics thereby extending James Clerk Maxwell's introduction of statistical methods to physics in his 1859 and 1864 kinetic theories of gases.

Traditional classical thermodynamics considers *macroscopic* characterization of systems by their *bulk* properties, such as system volume V, pressure P, and energy E. But in statistical mechanics we seek deeper understanding at a more fundamental, *microscopic* level in characterization of systems by *atomic* (or even subatomic) properties, such as atom velocities. Moreover, we seek a methodology in statistical mechanics useful for small numbers of atoms and for nonequilibrium systems, possibilities not contemplated in traditional, macroscopic thermodynamics.

2. Entropy in Statistical Mechanics

Throughout Boltzmann's life most scientists held a preconception against the atomic theory of matter (illustrated by J. J. Waterston's experience described in Appendix A). Continuum theories of matter and energy were favored as superior to atomic theories. Moreover, since Newton's mechanics are fully reversible in time, i.e., any solution for forward flowing (positive) time applies equally for backward flowing (negative) time, physicists objected to the concept of a thermodynamic property, entropy, that only increases in time until it reaches a stationary, maximum value. How could such a process be consistent with the fully reversible mechanics of the atoms involved? To justify the atomic-molecular theory of matter and the existence of an entropy-like property in time-reversible mechanics, Boltzmann sought and discovered a property of a gas he called H that continually decreases in time until it reaches a stationary, minimum value. *Boltzmann's H-theorem* states that the time-rate-of-change of H is less than or equal to zero, i.e., $dH/dt \leq 0$, with H defined by[2] $H = \Sigma_j p_j \log_e(p_j)$. In this sum, index j indicates a *system state*. The sum includes all states accessible to the system, corresponding to many *microscopic configurations* or *microscopic states* or *microstates* consistent with its bulk-properties state (i.e., everything we know about the system). Each such microstate is assumed to be equally probable. The probability p_j that the system is in its jth discrete microstate is regarded as equal to the fraction of an *ensemble* – a huge number of (imaginary) identical replications of a prototype system – in microstate j or the fraction of time the prototype system is in microstate j.

In quantum statistical mechanics all possible exchanges of identical atoms are counted as a single configuration (page 573), such exchanges being conceptually beyond any capability to detect. In addition, when system energy does not vary with position of an atom in system volume V, many geometric configurations form different but bulk-property-equivalent states. The number of possible microstates of a system is usually much larger than the number of atoms in the system.[3]

By its above definition and because probability p_j must satisfy $0 \leq p_j \leq 1$ and $p_j \log_e(p_j) = 0$ when p_j is zero or one and is otherwise negative, H is always negative. Boltzmann's H and entropy S for a dilute (or perfect) gas are related by

$$S = -kH = -k \Sigma_j p_j \log_e(p_j) \geq 0,$$

with k the Boltzmann's constant. Boltzmann's version of the second law, derived from his reversible-mechanics analysis of the evolving state of perfect-gas atoms, is that isolated-system entropy only increases until it reaches a maximum value, i.e.,

$$dS/dt \geq 0.$$

In 1902, American engineer-physicist-chemist Josiah Willard Gibbs (1839-1903) entered the statistical-mechanics story.[4] He introduced the powerful concept of the ensemble as a superior foundation of statistical mechanics (see endnote 11 of Chapter 2) and utilized it to correct and extend Boltzmann's results. While Boltzmann ignored interactions, Gibbs included them. Thus, Boltzmann's results apply only for a perfect gas while Gibbs' sometimes identical expressions, such as the one for entropy of a system, are derived from the superior conceptual basis that allows their application to real gases, liquids, and solids in which strong molecular interactions occur.[5]

To illustrate the nature of entropy and the value of Gibbs' approach, consider a closed thermodynamic system containing a solution in which a crystal (with strong atomic bonding) is forming. In a closed system, heat and energy but not matter may transfer into or out of the system. A crystal represents a highly ordered state with the crystal atoms purified and fixed in a regular structure. Before crystallization, solute atoms are neither purified nor fixed (distinguishable) but are mixed and randomly drifting about in the solution. When crystal growth is slow and system temperature remains nearly fixed, the crystallization is essentially reversible. Nevertheless, *system entropy decreases in such spontaneous crystallization*, a claim justified in endnote 6.

What happened? Isn't entropy supposed to increase in spontaneous processes? Have we encountered an enigma? A reader might say "We were led to believe (by the reader's induction) that a spontaneous process should always give a positive ΔS, either when heat is indirectly generated by inefficiency (irreversibility) in use of energy or generated directly from energy. But ΔS is negative in our crystallization-of-solute-atoms illustration! What kind of swindle is going on here?"

No one is being swindled because the system is not isolated. For the closed system in our illustration no net internal-heat increase occurs. Heat slowly generated by crystallization *in* the system is slowly transferred *out of* the system so that system entropy decreases. But entropy of the universe inevitably increases by more than system entropy decreases because, for outward heat flow, the system-boundary temperature T_b is slightly smaller than internal system temperature T and environmental (universe) entropy increase $\Delta S_e = Q/T_b > |Q/T| = |\Delta S|$. In applying thermodynamics, and especially the second law, it is essential to take account of system type as well as processes. Otherwise one quickly finds him- or her-self in deep tapioca (pudding).

Our crystallization example illustrates a general principle: *entropy change represents change in information required to fully specify a system state.* Specifying a system of atoms fixed in a regular crystal structure requires less information than atoms randomly drifting in solution. In general, uncertainty in system state increases with heating ($Q = T\Delta S > 0$) and *vice versa* with cooling. Heating extends the range of accessible "configurations" and requires more information to specify the system. Cooling reduces accessible configurations, ultimately to a single, ground state. But with increase of energy content of matter or space, energy content of other matter or space decreases, so a general implication of heating or cooling is not obvious except within an isolated system such as the universe. In communication and information theory an *information entropy* identical to Boltzmann's entropy emerges and provides identical function in specifying an information-system state.[7] Entropy, then, is a measure of information required to specify a system state or information more generally.

Using entropy, consequences of exchange or conversion of heat and other related processes in systems may be characterized in illuminating ways. Clausius' and Boltzmann's versions of the second law for isolated systems and their variations for other systems introduce subtle but powerful means for analyzing thermodynamic processes and predicting if and when they will occur naturally and spontaneously.

The nature of thermodynamics and entropy and common pitfalls in their use are further indicated or implied in the microscopic-scale theories and mathematical tools provided by statistical-mechanics or -thermodynamics we next consider.

3. Characteristic Properties and Equilibrium Distributions

We have already described three types of thermodynamic systems. (1) In an isolated system (no transfer of energy or matter), increase in system entropy dS occurs when incremental heat $dQ_i = |dE_i| \cong TdS$ is internally generated at absolute temperature T at cost of internal system energy dE_i. (2) In a closed system (energy or work but not matter may enter or leave the system), heat may be generated in or transferred into or out of the system causing system entropy change $\Delta S \cong Q/T$. (3) In an open system, entropy may additionally be changed by transfer of matter into or out of the system. The most common cause of confusion and error connected with entropy occurs in use of correct principles or expressions but for a wrong system type. Therefore, in our sketch of thermodynamics we utilize *a principle valid for all systems* and already suggested by the second law: *the stationary, equilibrium, or most-probable state occurs at a maximum of the system's information entropy subject to constraints characteristic of each type of system.*[8] Maximization of system entropy or "Maxent" subject to these characteristic constraints results in a *characteristic property* for each type of system. This characteristic property is minimum at equilibrium, providing a useful criterion for the equilibrium or most-probable state.

Characteristic properties for various system types, determined by maximization of system entropy subject to the appropriate constraints, are listed in the following Table.[8,9] For isolated systems of volume V, containing N atoms and fixed system energy E, the characteristic property is $-S$ so that equilibrium corresponds to maximum S. For closed systems at fixed volume V, containing N atoms at absolute

System Type	Traditional Name in Statistical Mechanics	Fixed Properties	Characteristic Function (Partition Function)	Characteristic Property
Isolated	Microcanonical	N, V, E	$Z = \Omega$ (see text)	$-S = -k\log_e(Z)$
Closed	Canonical	N, V, T	$Z = \Sigma_j \exp(-\beta E_j)$	$F = -kT\log_e(Z)$
Open	Grand Canonical	μ, V, T	$Z = \Sigma_i\Sigma_j \exp(\beta[n_j\mu - E_i])$	$-PV = -kT\log_e(Z)$
Open	Isothermal-Isobaric	N, P, T	$Z = \Sigma_i\Sigma_j \exp(-\beta[PV_j + E_i])$	$G = -kT\log_e(Z)$

system temperature T, the characteristic property is the *Helmholtz free energy* defined as $F = E - TS$ so that equilibrium corresponds to a minimum F. For open systems at fixed V, T, and *chemical potential* μ (Greek "mu" = $\mu = G/N$) the characteristic property is $-PV$, with P the pressure, so that equilibrium corresponds to a maximum PV. For open systems at fixed N, P, and T, the characteristic property is the *Gibbs free energy* defined by $G = E + PV - TS$ so that equilibrium corresponds to a minimum G.

Let distribution $\boldsymbol{p} = \{p_1, p_2, p_3, \ldots, p_j, \ldots\}$ be defined as the *probability distribution* of a system over its possible discrete *quantum states* denoted by quantum number $j = 1, 2, 3, \ldots, j, \ldots$ for which each state has discrete system energy $\boldsymbol{E} = \{E_1, E_2, E_3, \ldots, E_j, \ldots\}$. Specification of *vectors* (i.e., quantities containing multiple values or elements) $\boldsymbol{p}$ and $\boldsymbol{E}$ statistically specifies the *microscopic state* of a system, i.e., a complete description of its statistical distribution over exact properties on a microscopic, and therefore also macroscopic, level of detail. In contrast, specifying only bulk properties such as N, V, and E or T specifies only the *macroscopic state* of the system, i.e., its state fully defined on only a bulk or macroscopic level of detail.

To derive an equilibrium distribution vector $\boldsymbol{p}$ we employ the above-stated "Maxent" principle that at equilibrium a system's Boltzmann or information entropy is a maximum subject to imposed constraints (or, equivalently, the characteristic system property is minimum). We derive distribution $\boldsymbol{p}$ for both isolated and closed systems as illustrations of statistical-mechanics methodology for all systems.

In the following illustrations we utilize important contributions of Boltzmann, Gibbs, American physicist Edwin T. Jaynes (1922–1998), and many others.[8] While Boltzmann and Gibbs lived in the age of classical physics, we use the more correct quantum physics in our illustrations but include classical-physics results when valid. In the interest of simplicity and brevity, we must ignore many interesting details.

4. Equilibrium or Most-probable Distribution for the Isolated System

The isolated system has characteristic property $-S$ so its most probable state occurs at maximum S (equivalent to minimum $-S$) subject to fixed N, V, and E. This agrees with the statements of Clausius and Boltzmann that maximum S corresponds to the stationary, equilibrium condition or $dS/dt \geq 0$. Thus, we seek the distribution $\boldsymbol{p}$ that maximizes system entropy, subject to specified N, V, and E.

For an isolated system with N, V, and E fixed, many (imagined) macroscopically-identical replications of the system (Gibbs' ensemble of the system) contain many different microscopic *configurations* or *states*, each having the same macroscopic state, i.e., identical macroscopic or bulk properties. Each microstate, being equally consistent with the known bulk properties, is regarded as equally probable, a fundamental assumption in statistical mechanics called *the assumption of equal a priori probabilities*. Let Ω (upper case Greek "omega") be the *number of microstates* giving N, V, and E. Thus, Ω is a measure of the degree of ignorance of the system's microstate. That is, the probability of observing any one microstate is $\boldsymbol{p} = \{p_1 = p_2 = \ldots = p_j = 1/\Omega\}$ and the information entropy of the ensemble is

$$S = -k \Sigma_{j=1}^{\Omega} p_j \, \mathrm{loge}(p_j) = -k \Sigma_{j=1}^{\Omega} (1/\Omega) \log_e(1/\Omega) = k \log_e(\Omega).$$

But an ensemble is, equivalently, a single system at many different times. Thus, an *ensemble average of a system property is a time average of the property*[10] and Ω is the *measured* system entropy. When $\Omega = 1$, the system microstate is fully known and S = 0. When S is large, Ω is much larger, the system distributes over Ω microstates, and its microstate is poorly known. That is, entropy of an isolated system, having known bulk properties N, V, and E, can be regarded as a measure of uncertainty in its microstate.

Equation $S = k\log_e(\Omega)$ is *Boltzmann's principle*, so named by Albert Einstein even though it was first written by Max Planck in 1906. This equation was carved on Boltzmann's headstone in the Central Cemetery in Vienna.

5. Equilibrium or Most-probable Distribution for the Closed System

Consider now an ensemble of macroscopically identical closed systems at fixed N, V, and T. System-j energy E_j may vary between different accessible E_j values at different times, because energy fluctuations of mean variance σ_E^2 in a system occur. (We shall shortly write an expression for σ_E^2.) A description of system-quantum-state distribution ***p*** must include dependence on T and E_j, with $E = \langle E\rangle = \Sigma_j p_j E_j$ the average or "expectation value" of the prototype system energy. We maximize the information entropy of the ensemble subject to this energy constraint ($E = \Sigma_j p_j E_j$) and "normalization" ($\Sigma_j p_j = 1$) to find the most-probable distribution ***p*** for the ensemble of systems over their accessible states consistent with the known bulk properties of the prototype system (everything we actually know about the system). We find the Maxent condition using Lagrange's method of undetermined multipliers.[11] In Lagrange's method we form a sum Λ (upper case Greek "lambda") containing the quantity to be maximized (information entropy) and the constraints to be applied, each multiplied by a Lagrange multiplier λ_i (lower case Greek "lambda" sub i).

$$\Lambda = -k\,\Sigma_j\, p_j \log_e(p_j) + \lambda_1\,\{\Sigma_j\, p_j - 1\} + \lambda_2\,\{\Sigma_j\, p_j E_j - \langle E\rangle\}.$$

By Lagrange's method, the Maxent or most-probable distribution ***p*** occurs when

$$\partial\Lambda/\partial p_j = 0 \quad \text{for all j} \qquad \text{and} \qquad \partial\Lambda/\partial\lambda_i = 0 \quad \text{for } i = 1 \text{ and } 2.$$

Distribution ***p*** must therefore satisfy

$$-k\,\{\log_e(p_j) + 1\} + \lambda_1 + \lambda_2 E_j = 0 \qquad \text{or} \qquad p_j = \exp(-\alpha - \beta E_j),$$

with new constants *alpha* = $\alpha = 1 - \lambda_1/k$ and *beta* = $\beta = -\lambda_2/k$. The first constraint requires that $\exp(-\alpha)\,\Sigma_j \exp(-\beta E_j) = 1$ from which $\exp(\alpha) = Z = \Sigma_j \exp(-\beta E_j)$ and the maximally-probable (equilibrium) distribution ***p*** is, for every state j,

$$\text{[F1]} \qquad p_j = \exp(-\beta E_j)\,/\,Z.$$

The value of β is determined using the energy constraint $\Sigma_j p_j E_j = \langle E\rangle$ together with entropy $S = -k\Sigma_j p_j \log_e(p_j)$ and Helmholtz free energy $F = E - TS$. We write

$$F = E - TS = \Sigma_j\, E_j \exp(-\beta E_j)/Z + kT/Z\, \Sigma_j \exp(-\beta E_j)\,\{\log_e[\exp(-\beta E_j)] - \log_e(Z)\}$$

$$= \langle E\rangle - \beta kT\langle E\rangle - kT\log_e(Z).$$

But F and E are independent thermodynamic properties; the result holds if and only if

$$\beta = 1/kT \qquad \text{and} \qquad F = -kT \log_e(Z).$$

The most-probable or equilibrium distribution ***p*** for a closed system is, for every j,

$$p_j = \exp(-E_j/kT)\,/\,Z, \qquad \text{with} \qquad Z = \Sigma_j \exp(-E_j/kT).$$

Z is called the *partition function.* It describes the partitioning of ensemble systems over their accessible energy states. When the system is one molecule, Z describes the partitioning of ensemble molecules over their accessible energy levels. Z may be evaluated by replacing summation with integration using the equality (page 202) $dx\,dp_x\,dy\,dp_y\,dz\,dp_z = h^3$ to obtain the μ-space ("mu"-space is single-molecule space) element $h^3 = dx\,dy\,dz\,dp_x dp_y dp_z$ with state-j energy

$$E_j = E_{j\,\text{translation}} + E_{j\,\text{internal}} + 1/N\,\Sigma_{k\geq j}\,\Sigma_{m\geq n}\,\Sigma_n\,\varphi_{mnjk}(r_{mn}), \quad \text{with} \quad \varphi_{nnjj}(r_{nn}) = 0.$$

$E_{j\,\text{translation}} = (p_x^{\,2} + p_y^{\,2} + p_z^{\,2})/2m$, $E_{j\,\text{internal}}$ is energy contained in rotation, vibration, and electronic excitation of a molecule, and $\varphi_{mnjk}(r_{mn})$ is the atomic interaction potential energy for atom pair j-k, in which atom-n in molecule j is separated from atom-m in molecule k by r_{mn}, with m and n = 1,2,3,4,... For dilute, noble-gas atoms, $E_{j\,\text{internal}} = 0$ for absolute temperature $T < 10{,}000$ K and φ_{mnjk} is negligible. For a single such atom

$$Z_1 = h^{-3} \int_{\text{over volume V}} dx \int dy \int dz \int_{-\infty}^{\infty} dp_x \int_{-\infty}^{\infty} dp_y \int_{-\infty}^{\infty} dp_z \exp\{-\beta(p_x^{\,2} + p_y^{\,2} + p_z^{\,2})/2m\} = V\,(2\pi m kT/h^2)^{3/2}.$$

When φ_{mnjk} is negligible, the N gas atoms of the system behave independently (except during brief collisions) in system volume V so that the partition function is $Z = Z_1^{\,N}$ or

$$Z = \Sigma_j \exp(-E_j/kT) = \{(2\pi m kT/h^2)^{3/2}\,V\}^N / N!.$$

N! (N factorial) is introduced to obtain the correct quantum statistics in the classical limit, i.e., to correct for N! exchanges of N identical atoms giving the same quantum microstate. For interacting molecules (non-negligible φ_{mnjk}), Z is more complicated.

Partition function Z fully characterizes the equilibrium-system state, i.e.,

$$P = 1/\beta\,\partial\log_e(Z)/\partial V, \quad E = -\partial\log_e(Z)/\partial\beta, \quad F = -kT\log_e(Z),$$
$$S = -\beta^2\,\partial[k/\beta\,\log_e(Z)]/\partial\beta, \quad \text{and} \quad C_v = k\beta^2\,\partial^2[\log_e(Z)]/\partial\beta^2 = k\beta^2\,\sigma_E^{\,2},$$

with P the system pressure, C_v its specific heat at constant system volume V, and $\sigma_E^{\,2} = \langle(E - \langle E\rangle)^2\rangle = \langle E^2\rangle - \langle E\rangle^2$ the *mean variance in fluctuations of system energy E.*

Mixing of discrete and continuous variables in the preceding derivation and a following one is not consequential for the usual case when N is large.

The above distribution ***p*** is justified only for the equilibrium state because we have invoked a thermodynamic relation to evaluate β. While thermodynamics strictly applies only to stationary, equilibrium systems, we suppose that the Maxent or maximum-entropy-at-most-probable-distribution principle may be used to determine most-likely, stationary distributions over accessible states for stationary, nonequilibrium systems as well. Adopting this principle to define a most-likely distribution in non-equilibrium systems, wherein deviations or fluctuations from equilibrium may be neither rare nor relatively small, provides probability distributions over even rarely-populated microscopic states.[12] Characterization of nonequilibrium systems allows characterization of nonequilibrium processes and provides most-probable *transition pathways* over an energy or other barrier inhibiting formation of a new equilibrium state as it becomes more stable than a previously more-stable one. Common transport processes and most-probable process pathways and even rate constants for transition processes have been and can be determined from such distributions, capabilities beyond the scope of equilibrium thermodynamics. Example processes so characterized by statistical mechanics include transport of heat, momentum, and mass, phase-change nucleation kinetics, such as formation of droplets or crystals in vapors, liquids, or solids, and chemical reactions.[12]

6. Velocity Distribution of Gas Particles in a Temperature Gradient

We illustrate the utility of statistical mechanics by deducing a microscopic, statistical, *nonequilibrium velocity distribution of gas particles*, that is, of atoms, molecules, and particles suspended in a gas. Nonequilibrium systems lie beyond the scope of thermodynamics. In his 1859 and 1864 kinetic theories of gases, James Clerk Maxwell deduced the equilibrium velocity distribution of gas atoms and molecules. While his methods are simple and elegant, they only apply for gases in equilibrium. But nonequilibrium gases can be in a stationary state characterized by a stationary distribution. Using Maxent with quantum and classical statistical mechanics we deduce velocity distributions for one-component gas particles and for all species in a multicomponent mixture in a stationary temperature gradient.

Consider a closed system containing N particles of dilute or perfect gas in volume $V = A \times L$, with A the uniform, x-y-plane cross-sectional area of the system of z-direction length L lying between $z = z_0 = 0$ and $z = z_1 = L$. We impose a z-direction temperature gradient so that gas temperature near plane $z' = z$, i.e., for small $[z' - z]$, is $T(z') = T_z(1 + [z' - z]\gamma_T/T_z)$, with γ_T (= Greek "gamma" sub T) = dT/dz the imposed temperature gradient at z. We assume gas pressure to be $P = n(z)kT(z)$ with n(z) the local *number density* of all gas particles at altitude z, T(z) the temperature at the same plane, and k the Boltzmann's constant. For mechanical stability we require uniform pressure P (an isobaric system). We illustrate notation in the relations

$$n_z T_z = n(z)T(z) = n_{z'} T_{z'} \quad \text{and, with } z' \text{ near } z, \quad n_{z'} = n(z') = n_z/(1 + [z' - z]\gamma_T/T_z).$$

The *probability* any selected gas particle is between planes z and z+dz is

$$p(z)\,dz = n_z A\,dz/N = PV/NkT_z\,dz/z_1 = \langle T\rangle/T_z\,dz/z_1.$$

The *probability density* p(z) is probability per unit altitude z (or, in other cases, per unit change in another property, e.g., a molecular velocity component).

Let $\langle\varepsilon_{\varphi Tz}\rangle$ (Greek "epsilon" sub "phi" Tz) be total kinetic energy of species-φ gas particles at z due to random, thermal motions u,v,w, and *systematic motion* $V_{\varphi z}$

$$\langle\varepsilon_{\varphi Tz}\rangle = \langle\varepsilon_{\varphi z'}\rangle T_z/T_{z'} + m_\varphi V_{\varphi z}^2/2 = 3/2\,kT_{z'}T_z/T_{z'} + m_\varphi V_{\varphi z}^2/2 = 3/2\,kT_z + m_\varphi V_{\varphi z}^2/2$$

where index φ = 1,2,3,... indicates the gas-particle species in a mixture. Then gas kinetic energy due to random thermal motions $<\varepsilon_{\varphi z}>$ is proportional to local gas temperature. This assumption defines local, nonequilibrium-gas temperature.[13]

We impose three constraints at every altitude z on each species of gas particles. (i) The sum of probabilities of system state j over all possible j-states equals one,

[F2a] $$\Sigma_j\, p_{\varphi j} = 1.$$

(ii) Total kinetic energy of a particle due to random, thermal motions u,v,w and to systematic motion $V_{\varphi z}$ averaged over all possible j-states is

[F2b] $$\Sigma_j\, p_{\varphi j}\, \varepsilon_{\varphi j} = <\varepsilon_{\varphi Tz}> = 3/2\, kT_z + m_\varphi V_{\varphi z}{}^2/2.$$

(iii) Number flux of all gas particles in the γ_T direction (the z-direction) is constant

[F2c] $$j_{z\,net} = \Sigma_\varphi\, j_{\varphi z\,net} = n_z\, \Sigma_\varphi\, \zeta_{\varphi z} <w_{\varphi z}> = n_z\, \Sigma_\varphi\, \zeta_{\varphi z}\, \Sigma_j\, p_{\varphi j}\, w_{\varphi j} = \text{constant}$$

with local number density of all gas particles n_z and local *number fraction* of species-φ particles $\zeta_{\varphi z}$. [F2c] prevents local accumulation or depletion of gas particles, required in an isobaric, stationary-temperature-field gas. In closed, stagnant-gas systems, $j_{z\,net} = 0$. In writing [F2b] and [F2c] we include systematic velocity $V_{\varphi z}$ in $\varepsilon_{\varphi z}$ and in $\boldsymbol{p}_\varphi$.

In [F2a-c], summation over a single quantum number, subscript j, represents sums over all quantum numbers or integration over three-dimensional velocity space.[14] In its classical form our result shall explicitly contain the three velocity components.

The following derivation is, for clarity, described for one and two species but it applies to mixtures of any number of species. We seek the *most probable quantum-state distributions* $\boldsymbol{p}_\varphi$ and $\boldsymbol{p}_\eta$ (η = Greek "eta"), where $\boldsymbol{p}_\varphi = \{p_{\varphi 1}, p_{\varphi 2}, p_{\varphi 3}, \ldots\}$ with $p_{\varphi 1}$ the probability of φ-gas-particle energy state $\varepsilon_{\varphi 1}$, $p_{\varphi 2}$ the probability of φ-gas-particle energy state $\varepsilon_{\varphi 2}$, *etc.* Ensemble systems are φ and η gas particles (in μ-space) of energies $\varepsilon_{\varphi j}$ and $\varepsilon_{\eta i}$. The strategy is to maximize information entropy subject to constraints [F2].[15] Mixed-species information entropy[14] in Lagrange's method gives

$$\Lambda = -k\Sigma_i\Sigma_j(p_{\eta i}p_{\varphi j})\log_e(p_{\eta i}p_{\varphi j}) + \{\lambda_{\eta 1}(\Sigma_i p_{\eta i} - 1) + \lambda_{\varphi 1}(\Sigma_j p_{\varphi j} - 1) + \lambda_{\eta 2}(\Sigma_i p_{\eta i}\varepsilon_{\eta i} - <\varepsilon_{\eta z}>)$$
$$+ \lambda_{\varphi 2}(\Sigma_j p_{\varphi j}\varepsilon_{\varphi j} - <\varepsilon_{\varphi z}>) + \lambda_{\eta 3}(n_z\Sigma_i p_{\eta i} w_{\eta i} - j_{\eta z\,net}) + \lambda_{\varphi 3}(n_z\Sigma_j p_{\varphi j} w_{\varphi j} - j_{\varphi z\,net})\}$$
$$= -k\Sigma_i\, p_{\eta i}\log_e(p_{\eta i}) - k\Sigma_j\, p_{\varphi j}\log_e(p_{\varphi j}) + \{\lambda_{\eta 1}(\Sigma_i p_{\eta i} - 1) + \lambda_{\varphi 1}(\Sigma_j p_{\varphi j} - 1) + \ldots\}$$

which is maximized to maximize information entropy by selecting values of elements of vector $\boldsymbol{p}_\varphi$ and of the three Lagrangian multipliers $\lambda_{\varphi 1}$, $\lambda_{\varphi 2}$, and $\lambda_{\varphi 3}$ so that

$$\partial\Lambda/\partial p_{\varphi j} = 0 \text{ for } j = 1,2,3,4,5,6,\ldots \qquad \text{and} \qquad \partial\Lambda/\partial\lambda_{\varphi j} = 0 \text{ for } j = 1,2,3,$$

with like expressions for $p_{\eta i}$, to obtain (for both $p_{\varphi j}$ and $p_{\eta i}$ but showing only $p_{\varphi j}$ results)

[F3] $$\log_e(p_{\varphi j}) = -\alpha - \beta_z\varepsilon_{\varphi j} - \gamma_\varphi w_{\varphi j} \quad \text{or} \quad p_{\varphi j} = \exp(-\alpha - \beta_z\varepsilon_{\varphi j} - \gamma_\varphi w_{\varphi j}),$$

[F3a] $$\Sigma_j\, p_{\varphi j} = \exp(-\alpha)\,\Sigma_j \exp(-\beta_z\varepsilon_{\varphi j} - \gamma_\varphi w_{\varphi j}) = 1,$$

[F3b] $$\Sigma_j\, p_{\varphi j}\,\varepsilon_{\varphi j} = \exp(-\alpha)\,\Sigma_j\,\varepsilon_{\varphi j}\exp(-\beta_z\varepsilon_{\varphi j} - \gamma_\varphi w_{\varphi j}) = 3/2\, kT_z + m_\varphi V_{\varphi z}{}^2/2,$$

[F3c] $$\Sigma_j\, p_{\varphi j}\, w_{\varphi j} = <w_{\varphi z}> = \exp(-\alpha)\,\Sigma_j\, w_{\varphi j}\exp(-\beta_z\varepsilon_{\varphi j} - \gamma_\varphi w_{\varphi j}) = j_{\varphi z\,net}/n_{\varphi z}.$$

To evaluate α_z, β_z, γ_φ, and $V_{\varphi z}$ we transform from quantized energy $\varepsilon_{\varphi j}$ to continuous energy $\varepsilon_{\varphi z} = m_\varphi(u^2 + v^2 + w^2 + V_{\varphi z}{}^2)/2$. Sums in [F3] become integrals of the form

$$e^{-\alpha_z}\int du\int dv\int dw\; g\; e^{[-\beta_z m_\varphi(u^2+v^2+w^2+V_{\varphi z}{}^2)/2\;-\;\gamma_\varphi w]} = e^{-\alpha_z}\int du\int dv\int dw\; g\; e^{[-\beta_z m_\varphi/2\,(u^2+v^2+(w+V_{\varphi z})^2)]}$$

with $g = 1$, $\varepsilon_{\varphi z}$, or w and $\gamma_\varphi = \gamma_{\varphi z} = \beta_z m_\varphi V_{\varphi z}$.

To solve these integrals we use a truncated Taylor's series: $p(u,v,w;V) = p(u,v,w;0) + V(\partial p/\partial V)_{V=0} = \{1 - \beta_z m_\varphi V w\}\, p(u,v,w;0)$. This approximation has been demonstrated[16] both theoretically and experimentally to be excellent if $V \lesssim \langle c_z\rangle/3$, which V generally is. Via [F3a] (i.e., $g = 1$), integration over u,v,w from $-\infty$ to $+\infty$ gives

$$Z_z = \exp(\alpha_z) = \int du\int dv\int dw\,\{1 - \beta_z m_\varphi V_{\varphi z} w\}\, e^{[-\beta_z m_\varphi/2\,(u^2+v^2+w^2)]} = (2\pi/\beta_z m_\varphi)^{3/2}.$$

We determine β_z using [F3b] (i.e., $g = \varepsilon$). Let $\varepsilon_{\varphi z} = m_\varphi(u^2 + v^2 + w^2 + V_{\varphi z}{}^2)/2$, where $V_{\varphi z}$ is a possible systematic, z-direction velocity of species-φ particles. Then,

$$\langle\varepsilon_{\varphi z}\rangle = m_\varphi/2Z_z \int_{-\infty}^{\infty}du\int_{-\infty}^{\infty}dv\int_{-\infty}^{\infty}dw\,\{u^2 + v^2 + w^2 + V_{\varphi z}{}^2\}\{1 - \beta_z m_\varphi V_{\varphi z} w\}e^{[-\beta_z m_\varphi(u^2+v^2+w^2)/2]}$$

$$= 3/2\beta_z + m_\varphi V_{\varphi z}{}^2/2 = \langle\varepsilon_{\varphi Tz}\rangle = 3kT_z/2 + m_\varphi V_{\varphi z}{}^2/2$$

so that $\beta_z = 1/kT_z$ and $V_{\varphi z}$, if it is not zero, is a systematic velocity associated with γ_T.

A one-way *flux* of g is the quantity of g passing unit area of an imaginary *control surface* (in plane z) per unit time, where g is particle number, mass, momentum, energy, or other quantity. Net flux is the difference between two opposing fluxes.

Z-direction flux components and net flux of g due to species-φ particles are

[F4]

$$j_{\varphi gz\pm} = n_{\varphi z\pm\lambda}/Z_{z\pm\lambda}\int_{-\infty}^{\infty}du\int_{-\infty}^{\infty}dv\int_{0\,(-\infty)}^{\infty\,(0)}dw\; w\,g\,\{1 - \beta_z m_\varphi V_{\varphi z} w\}\; e^{[-\beta_{z\pm\lambda} m_\varphi(u^2+v^2+w^2)/2]}$$

$$j_{\varphi gz\,\mathrm{net}} = n_{\varphi z-\lambda}\langle wg\rangle_{\varphi z-\lambda}/2 - n_{\varphi z+\lambda}\langle wg\rangle_{z+\lambda}/2 - n_{\varphi z}\,\beta_z m_\varphi V_{\varphi z}\langle w^2 g\rangle_z.$$

We now determine $p_{\varphi j}$ for a one-component and a two-component gas.

Case 1: the One-component Gas.

In a pure, one-component gas, average net velocity (i.e., $g = 1$) is

[F4a-1] $$j_{z\,\mathrm{net}}/n_z = \langle w_z\rangle = \langle c_z\rangle\lambda_z\gamma_T/4T_z - V_z.$$

In a closed system $\langle w_z\rangle = 0$ and distribution $\boldsymbol{p}_1 = \boldsymbol{p}$ in a temperature gradient implies two offsetting velocities in $\langle w_z\rangle$: an implicit *thermal-diffusion velocity* given by the first term on the right-hand side of [F4a-1] and a balancing *counterflow velocity* $w_{z\,\mathrm{cntr}} = -V_z$. Both derive from γ_T and, since they are opposed and balanced, neither is readily detectable in a single-species gas. When $j_{z\,\mathrm{net}} = 0$,

[F4b-1] $$w_{z\,\mathrm{cntr}} = -V_z = -\langle c_z\rangle\lambda_z\gamma_T/4T_z.$$

For a closed, stagnant, pure-gas, isobaric or stationary system ($j_{z\,\mathrm{net}} = 0$) with $\gamma_T \neq 0$ to be possible, local counterflow velocity $w_{z\,\mathrm{cntr}}$ must balance thermal diffusion.

The probability p_j of state j of a gas particle at altitude z is therefore

[F5-1a] $$p_j(\varepsilon_j;z,\gamma_T) = \exp\{-\beta_z\varepsilon_{Tj}\} / Z_z.$$

In its classical-physics form, the microscopic, probability density $\boldsymbol{p}$ is

[F5-1b] $$p(u,v,w;z,\gamma_T) = (\beta_z m/2\pi)^{3/2}\,\{1 + \beta_z m\, w_{z\,cntr} w\}\,\exp\{-\beta_z m(u^2 + v^2 + w^2)/2\}.$$

Even though [F5] is stationary, particles are not equilibrated at any altitude – thus the thermal diffusion and balancing counterflow of [F4a-1]. But stationary probability density $p(u,v,w;z,\gamma_T)$ gives the most-probable distribution for nonequilibrium just as Maxwell's result gives the most-probable distribution for equilibrium. And in both cases $p(u,v,w;z,\gamma_T)\times du\,dv\,dw$ is the fraction of all particles at z having velocity components between u and u+du, between v and v+dv, and between w and w+dw. When $\gamma_T = 0$, $w_{z\,cntr} = 0$, T is uniform, particles are uniformly equilibrated, and Maxwell's distribution – written directly from [F1] – is recovered.

Case 2: the Two-component or Binary Gas Mixture.

In a closed, binary-gas system, average-net-mixture velocity (i.e., $g = 1$) is

[F4a-2] $$j_{z\,net}/n_z = -[\langle c_{1z}\rangle\lambda_{1z}/2 - \langle c_{2z}\rangle\lambda_{2z}/2]\,\gamma_{\zeta 1} + [\zeta_{1z}\langle c_{1z}\rangle\lambda_{1z}/2 + \zeta_{2z}\langle c_{2z}\rangle\lambda_{2z}/2]\,\gamma_T/2T_z - \zeta_{1z}V_{1z} - \zeta_{2z}V_{2z} = 0$$

with $\zeta_{\varphi z}$ the number fraction of species-φ particles at z, $\langle c_{\varphi z}\rangle$ their mean velocity, and $\lambda_{\varphi z}$ their mean-free-path length. In binary mixtures, $\zeta_{1z} + \zeta_{2z} = 1$ and $d\zeta_{1z}/dz + d\zeta_{2z}/dz = \gamma_{\zeta 1} + \gamma_{\zeta 2} = 0$. From [F4a-2], with $D_{\varphi z} = \langle c_{\varphi z}\rangle\lambda_{\varphi z}/2$ and $\varepsilon_\varphi = m_\varphi(u_\varphi^{\,2} + v_\varphi^{\,2} + w_\varphi^{\,2})/2$,

[F4b-2] $$\zeta_{1z}w_{1z\,cntr} + \zeta_{2z}w_{2z\,cntr} = [D_{1z} - D_{2z}]\,\gamma_{\zeta 1} - [\zeta_{1z}D_{1z} + \zeta_{2z}D_{2z}]\,\gamma_T/2T_z,$$

and

[F5-2a] $$p_1(u_1,v_1,w_1;z,\gamma_T) = (\beta_z m_1/2\pi)^{3/2}\,\{1 + \beta_z m_1 w_{1z\,cntr} w_1\}\,\exp\{-\beta_z\varepsilon_1\},$$

[F5-2b] $$p_2(u_2,v_2,w_2;z,\gamma_T) = (\beta_z m_2/2\pi)^{3/2}\,\{1 + \beta_z m_2 w_{2z\,cntr} w_2\}\,\exp\{-\beta_z\varepsilon_2\}.$$

In cases 1 and 2 the velocity distribution for each gas-particle species is [F5]. This result is correct for all species in any mixture. Constraint [F2c] gives binary-system condition [F4b-2]. That condition, $\zeta_{1z} + \zeta_{2z} = 1$, and the stationary conditions $j_{1z\,net} = j_{2z\,net} = 0$ require $\zeta_{1z}w_{1z\,cntr} = [D_{1z} - D_{2z}]\,\gamma_{\zeta 1} - [\zeta_{1z}D_{1z} - \zeta_{2z}D_{2z}]\,\gamma_T/2T_z$ and $w_{2z\,cntr} = -D_{2z}\gamma_T/T_z$ in stagnant, binary mixtures. These binary-system equations describe *thermal diffusion* (the Soret effect) and *diffusion thermo* (the Dufour effect), the latter being the inverse of thermal diffusion, i.e., a γ_T (heat flow) due to a γ_ζ (diffusion).

Distribution [F5] provides the flux of any quantity g. For *purely translational energy* of gas particles, $g = \langle\varepsilon_{\varphi z}\rangle$. Molecules also carry internal energy of vibration and rotation and sufficiently hot atoms and molecules carry electronic excitation energy. (To make [F5] a general distribution over internal-energy states as well, internal energy is added to translational energy, as on page 573.) But internal energy of, e.g., noble-gas atoms below 10,000 K, predominantly in their ground electronic state, is fixed as atoms carry neither vibrational nor rotational energy. Total molecular energy is calculated by one of three equivalent assumptions: (1) a quasi-equilibrium process, (2) equipartition of energy, or (3) the correction factor due to A. Eucken.[17] Eucken wrote for thermal conductivity of gas φ, $\kappa_{\varphi z} = (9c_{p\varphi}/c_{v\varphi} - 5)\,\eta_{\varphi z}c_{v\varphi}/4$.[17]

After Maxwell we use the *mean-free-path length* $\lambda_{\varphi z}$ (Greek "lambda" sub φz [Greek "phi" z]) as the average distance-from-last-"re-equilibration." Dynamic viscosity η_φ (Greek "eta") of species-φ gas gives the frequently-used $\lambda_{\varphi z} = \eta_\varphi/(0.499\rho_{\varphi z} \langle c_{\varphi z}\rangle)$ with gas mass density $\rho_{\varphi z}$ (= Greek "rho" sub φz) = $n_{\varphi z} m_\varphi$ and mean speed of mass-m_φ atom, molecule, or particle $\langle c_{\varphi z}\rangle = \sqrt{(8kT_z/\pi m_\varphi)}$ in the gas at temperature T_z.

Maxwell's distribution provides useful comparisons. At $\gamma_T = 0$ number flux is

[F6] $$j_{z\pm} = n_z \int_{-\infty}^{\infty} du \int_{-\infty}^{\infty} dv \int_{0(-\infty)}^{\infty(0)} dw\, p_{Max}(u,v,w)\, w = +(-)\, n_z\langle c_z\rangle/4.$$

A crucial property of equilibrium expression [F6] is that $j_{z\,net} = j_{z+} + j_{z-} = 0$.

Using Maxwell's distribution with $\gamma_T \neq 0$ and the $n_{z\pm\lambda}$ and $\langle c_{z\pm\lambda}\rangle$ described below on this page gives upward or downward flux at z (upward flux being positive)

[F7a] $$j_{z\pm} = \pm n_{z\mp\lambda}\langle c_{z\mp\lambda}\rangle/4 = \pm n_z\langle c_z\rangle/4\,\{1 \pm \lambda_z\gamma_T/2T_z\}.$$

[F6] and the first term of [F7a] are *molecular effusion*, the origin of *molecular diffusion*. The second term of [F7a] is *thermal effusion* which is additive and is itself *thermal diffusion*, a net flux driven by γ_T. [F7a] predicts nonzero flux $j_{z\,net}$ in a closed, stationary system; $j_{z\,net}$ properly vanishes when we use [F5] in place of the Maxwell distribution, i.e., when we add $n_z w_{z\,cntr}$, $-w_{z\,cntr}$ *being* the thermal-diffusion velocity.

Thermal-diffusion flux depends on control-surface orientation relative to γ_T since $p(u,v,w;z,\gamma_T)$ is defined for γ_T parallel to the z axis. If we specify a control surface inclined at angle θ (Greek "theta") from γ_T (because control-surface "direction" is specified by the perpendicular to it) the net [F7a]-type number flux is

[F7b] $$j_{net}(z,\theta) = j_{z\theta+} + j_{z\theta-} = n_z\langle c_z\rangle \cos\theta\, \lambda_z\gamma_T/4T_z.$$

We now illustrate kinetic theory with a few applications of distribution [F5].

7. Simple Kinetic Theory of Gas Transport Processes

We determine the *transport coefficients* in gases, namely, (a) thermal conductivity κ ("kappa") that characterizes heat or energy transfer rate, (b) viscosity η ("eta") that characterizes momentum transfer rate, and (c) diffusivity $\mathcal{D}$ (script D) and thermal-diffusion diffusivity $\mathcal{D}^T$ ($\mathcal{D}$ superscript T) that characterize particle number (or mass) transfer rate. Since thermal diffusion was confirmed in 1916, no mechanism or theory, simple or elaborate, has successfully characterized it.[18] We shall provide both.

We use temperature notation $T(z\pm\lambda) = T_{z\pm\lambda} = T_z(1 \pm \lambda\gamma_T/T_z)$. In calculating number flux at z we use *number density* and *average speed* of gas particles at their last "collision" before crossing plane z, i.e., at $z \pm \lambda_z$. Expressions $n_{\varphi z\pm\lambda} = n_{\varphi z} \times(1 \mp \lambda_{\varphi z}\gamma_T/T_z)$ and $\langle c_{\varphi z\pm\lambda}\rangle = \langle c_{\varphi z}\rangle(1 \pm \lambda_{\varphi z}\gamma_T/2T_z)$ shall often be used, where $\gamma_T = dT/dz$ at z. Number flux components at z are denoted, e.g., $j_{\varphi\pm}(z) = j_{\varphi z\pm}$.

(a) *Energy transfer* or *heat flux* q_z due to translational energy of atoms and molecules in a pure, stationary gas is given by the sum of the opposing components

$$q_{z+} = n_{z-\lambda} \int_{-\infty}^{\infty} du \int_{-\infty}^{\infty} dv \int_{0}^{\infty} dw\, p(u,v,w;z,\gamma_T)\, w\, m\,(u^2 + v^2 + w^2)/2$$

$$= n_z \langle c_z \rangle kT_z/2\ \{1 - \lambda_z\gamma_T/2T_z + 5w_{cntr}/2\langle c_z \rangle\}$$

$$q_{z-} = n_{z+\lambda} \int_{-\infty}^{\infty} du \int_{-\infty}^{\infty} dv \int_{-\infty}^{0} dw\ p(u,v,w;z,\gamma_T)\ w\ m\ (u^2 + v^2 + w^2)/2$$

$$= -n_z \langle c_z \rangle kT_z/2\ \{1 + \lambda_z\gamma_T/2T_z - 5w_{cntr}/2\langle c_z \rangle\}.$$

With $w_{cntr} = -\langle c_z \rangle \lambda_z \gamma_T/4T_z$ and κ_z (Greek "kappa" sub z) the *thermal-conductivity* or *heat-transfer coefficient*, net heat transfer $q_{z\,net} = q_{z+} + q_{z-}$ is

[F8] $$q_{z\,net} = -\kappa_z \gamma_T,$$

$$\kappa_z = 9/8\ n_z \langle c_z \rangle \lambda_z k, \qquad \text{and} \qquad \lambda_{\kappa z} = 8\kappa_z/(9 n_z \langle c_z \rangle k).$$

For atomic gases ($c_p/c_v = 5/3$) Eucken's formula[17] correctly gives dimensionless Prandtl number $= \eta c_p/\kappa = 0.67$. [F8] and $\lambda_{\eta z} = \eta_z/(0.499\rho_z \langle c_z \rangle)$ (page 578) give $\lambda_{\eta z}/\lambda_{\kappa z} = 3/5$.

(b) *X-direction shear stress* (shear force per unit area) occurs in a fluid undergoing x-direction shear. X-direction shear stress at a plane normal to the z axis, denoted τ_{xz} (Greek "tau" sub xz), is a force per unit area due to net x-direction-momentum flux carried by z-direction gas-particle motions across the x-y plane at z. We consider *laminar flow*, i.e., local, x-direction velocity is $U_{z\pm\lambda} = U_z\{1 \pm \lambda\gamma_U/U_z\}$ in which the shear rate is $\gamma_U = dU/dz$ at z. We retain a temperature gradient to determine its effect, if any. Components of total z-direction transfer rate of x-direction momentum are, with $mn_z = \rho_z$ (Greek "rho" sub z) the mass density of the gas at z,

$$\tau_{xz+} = n_{z-\lambda} \int_{-\infty}^{\infty} du \int_{-\infty}^{\infty} dv \int_{0}^{\infty} dw\ p(u,v,w;z,\gamma_T)\ w\ mU_z(1 - \lambda\gamma_U/U_z)$$

$$= 1/4\ \rho_z \langle c_z \rangle U_z(1 - \lambda_z\gamma_U/U_z + \lambda_z\gamma_T/2T_z + 2w_{cntr}(1+\delta)/\langle c_z \rangle)$$

$$\tau_{xz-} = n_{z+\lambda} \int_{-\infty}^{\infty} du \int_{-\infty}^{\infty} dv \int_{-\infty}^{0} dw\ p(u,v,w;z,\gamma_T)\ w\ mU_z(1 + \lambda\gamma_U/U_z)$$

$$= -1/4\ \rho_z \langle c_z \rangle U_z(1 + \lambda_z\gamma_U/U_z - \lambda_z\gamma_T/2T_z - 2w_{cntr}(1-\delta)/\langle c_z \rangle),$$

δ is terms that cancel and $\tau_{xz\,net} = \tau_{xz+} + \tau_{xz-}$ gives gas viscosity η_z (Greek "eta" sub z)

[F9] $$\tau_{xz\,net} = -\eta_z \gamma_U,$$

$$\eta_z = \rho_z \langle c_z \rangle \lambda_z/2\ \{1 - U_z\gamma_T/2T_z\gamma_U - 2U_z w_{cntr}/\langle c_z \rangle \lambda_z \gamma_U\} \quad \text{and} \quad \lambda_{\eta z} = 2\eta_z/(\rho_z \langle c_z \rangle).$$

In a pure gas our curly-bracketed factor in η_z is unity.

The result [F9] agrees with measured data for laminar flow in *Newtonian fluids*, defined as those fluids consistent with [F9] which all but a few liquids are, and this $\lambda_{\eta z}$ result compares well with $\lambda_{\eta z}$ calculated for rigid spheres given above.

Spontaneous laminar-to-turbulent flow transitions were reported in 1883 by Osborne Reynolds[19] who discovered a *critical Reynolds number* $Re_c = \rho \langle U \rangle d/\eta = 2{,}300$ in circular ducts exists above which flows eventually became turbulent (with d the circular duct diameter and $\langle U \rangle$ the volumetric flow divided by $\pi d^2/4$). Smoothing of duct-inlet flow raises Re_c to at least 40,000. Turbulence first appears after an "entrance length" as large as order $1000 \times d$. No present theory predicts these phenomena. Our analysis suggests influence of a temperature gradient is negligible, but the assumptions (no net flux in a stationary temperature field) do not exactly match the process. After a sufficient entrance length, viscous heating might cause quantity $U_z \gamma_T / 2T_z \gamma_U$ to reach a value at which $\eta_z \rightarrow 0$. Vanishing of η_z is certainly a possible mechanism for onset of turbulence in duct flows and in clear-air-turbulence cells. "Smoothness" of flow or scale of instabilities also seems to be involved. The problem needs to be addressed in more detail, taking more space than is available here.

(c) *Diffusion and thermal diffusion* in a *binary mixture* are the final transport topics we address. While [F5] correctly characterizes both thermal conductivity and viscosity, its greater transport-theory value is describing thermal diffusion and diffusion thermo in gases and *thermophoresis* and *diffusiophoresis* of particles in gases.

In a binary-gas or a particle-in-gas mixture (i.e., $\varphi = 1$ or 2), both concentration and temperature gradients may exist, i.e., we may consider either or both of molecular diffusion and thermal diffusion. We consider the general case of both.

In a consequential correction of the traditional method, we isolate variation in concentration from variation in temperature by using for local species-φ number density $n_{\varphi z}$ the product $n_z \zeta_{\varphi z}$ with n_z the total number density $n_z = n_{1z} + n_{2z}$ containing the complete temperature dependence and number fraction (Greek "zeta" sub φz) $\zeta_{\varphi z} = n_{\varphi z} / n_z$ containing the complete concentration dependence for each species.

By [F5-2] the net-number-flux components are, with $\varphi = 1$ or 2,

$$j_{\varphi z\,net} = n_{\varphi z-\lambda} \int_{-\infty}^{\infty} du \int_{-\infty}^{\infty} dv \int_{0}^{\infty} dw\, p_{\varphi z-\lambda}\, w \;+\; n_{\varphi z+\lambda} \int_{-\infty}^{\infty} du \int_{-\infty}^{\infty} dv \int_{-\infty}^{0} dw\, p_{\varphi z+\lambda}\, w,$$

[F10a] $$j_{1z\,net} = -\,n_z \mathcal{D}_{1z} \gamma_{\zeta 1} + n_z \zeta_{1z} \mathcal{D}_{1z}{}^{T} \gamma_T / T_z = -\,n_z \mathcal{D}_{2z} \gamma_{\zeta 1} + n_z \zeta_{2z} \mathcal{D}_{2z} \gamma_T / 2T_z,$$

[F10b] $$j_{2z\,net} = -\,n_z \mathcal{D}_{2z} \gamma_{\zeta 2} + n_z \zeta_{2z} \mathcal{D}_{2z}{}^{T} \gamma_T / T_z = -\,n_z \mathcal{D}_{2z} \gamma_{\zeta 2} - n_z \zeta_{2z} \mathcal{D}_{2z} \gamma_T / 2T_z.$$

Because $\gamma_{\zeta 1}$ $(= -\gamma_{\zeta 2})$ and γ_T are independent, the two molecular-diffusion terms must cancel one another as must the two thermal-diffusion terms to give $j_{z\,net} = 0$. The *in effect* values that result are $\mathcal{D}_{1z} = \mathcal{D}_{2z}$ and $\zeta_{1z} \mathcal{D}_{1z}{}^{T} = -\zeta_{2z} \mathcal{D}_{2z}{}^{T}$, with $\mathcal{D}_{2z}{}^{T} = -\mathcal{D}_{2z}/2$. While $j_{z\,net} = 0$ and $\mathcal{D}_{1z} = \mathcal{D}_{2z}$ were recognized in earlier analyses, without the above-mentioned correction these analyses were hobbled by incorrect equations.[20] Counterflows determined on page 577 are incorporated in [F10a-b] as the basis of the *in effect* values. Microscopic-level, nonequilibrium statistical mechanics thus provides correct governing equations [F10a-b], the transport coefficients $\mathcal{D}_{\varphi z}$ and $\mathcal{D}_{\varphi z}{}^{T}$, and deeper understanding of diffusion, thermal diffusion, and diffusion thermo.

For instance, coupling of $\gamma_{\zeta\varphi}$ and γ_T is most evident in the stationary condition: [F10a-b] with $j_{1z\,net} = j_{2z\,net} = 0$. In this condition, change $\Delta(\gamma_{\zeta 1}/\zeta_{2z}) = -\Delta(\gamma_{\zeta 2}/\zeta_{2z})$ is accompanied by change $\Delta(\gamma_T / 2T_z)$, which is the diffusion-thermo effect.

For molecules or particles having friction coefficient f_z (page 160) in a gas,

[F11] $$\mathcal{D}_{\varphi\zeta z} = [\langle c_{\varphi z} \rangle \lambda_{\varphi\zeta z}/2] = kT_z / f_{\varphi\zeta z} \qquad \text{and} \qquad \lambda_{\varphi\zeta z} = 2\mathcal{D}_{\varphi\zeta z} / \langle c_{\varphi z} \rangle,$$

with subscript $\varphi\zeta z$ denoting species φ (= 1 or 2) in medium ζ (see [F12]) at location z. Condensation-/deposition-rate use of $\lambda_{\varphi\zeta z}$ is described by Dahneke.[21] In a binary mix,

[F12] $D_{1\zeta z} = D_{2\zeta z} = [D_{21z}\zeta_{1z} + D_{22z}\zeta_{2z}]$, $\zeta_{1z} D_{1\zeta z}{}^{T} = -\,\zeta_{2z} D_{2\zeta z}{}^{T} = \zeta_{2z}[D_{21z}\zeta_{1z} + D_{22z}\zeta_{2z}]/2.$

Mathematical results [F10] are interpreted in terms of the process physics. In closed, isobaric, binary, stagnant-gas mixtures, *fully free* transport is precluded by $j_{z\,net} = 0$; free diffusion occurs for only one species, the one having *limiting* diffusivity $D_{2z} < D_{1z}$, i.e., D_{2z} alone appears in [F10a-b]. Stronger thermal diffusion of species 1 preempts that of species 2 but motion of 1 is controlled by motion of 2 and by $w_{1z\,cntr}$.

The thermal-diffusion-molecule or thermophoretic-particle *velocity* of the species-2 particles is written directly from the pertinent term of [F10b]

[F13] $$w_{2z}{}^{T} = D_{2z}{}^{T}\gamma_T/T_z = -\,D_{2z}\gamma_T/2T_z = -\,k\gamma_T/2f_{2z},$$

with k the Boltzmann's constant. Note that as $\zeta_{2z} \to 0$, $w_{1z}{}^{T} = -\,\zeta_{2z} w_{2z}{}^{T}/\zeta_{1z} \to 0$. [F13] agrees within a few percent of the few measured data[22] to which it has been compared, but broader testing is needed.

In the stationary state, a closed, binary system satisfies $j_{1z\,net} = j_{2z\,net} = 0$ as well as $j_{1z\,net} + j_{2z\,net} = 0$, $n_z D_{2z}$ divides out of [F10a-b], which then have solutions

[F14] $$\zeta_{1z} = 1 - (1 - \zeta_{10})/\sqrt{(T_z/T_0)} \qquad \text{and} \qquad \zeta_{2z} = \zeta_{20}/\sqrt{(T_z/T_0)}.$$

[F14] are *universal stationary solutions* valid for any different-mobility-species pair.

We obtain T_z/T_0 for real gases using the stationary-state requirement $q = -\kappa\gamma_T = \text{constant}$ or $\gamma_T = \kappa_0\gamma_{T0}/\kappa$. We take $\kappa = \kappa(T) = \kappa_0 + \gamma_\kappa \Delta T_z$ with $\Delta T_z = T_z - T_0$, $\gamma_\kappa = d\kappa/dT$ and κ_0 fitted constants that provide excellent approximations for κ and γ_T over a substantial range of T, illustrated in Figure F1. Solving $\kappa\gamma_T = \text{constant}$ gives

[F15] $$T_z/T_0 = (\sqrt{(1 + Bz/z_1)} + C)/(1 + C).$$

gas	κ_0	γ_κ	$A = \kappa_0/\gamma_\kappa\Delta T_1$	$B = (2A+1)/A^2$	$C = T_0/A\Delta T_1 - 1$
Nitrogen	2.3998	.0064025	1.2494	2.2414	− 0.2711
Helium	14.012	.031881	1.4650	1.8311	− 0.3784
Argon	1.6402	.0043825	1.2475	2.2458	− 0.2700

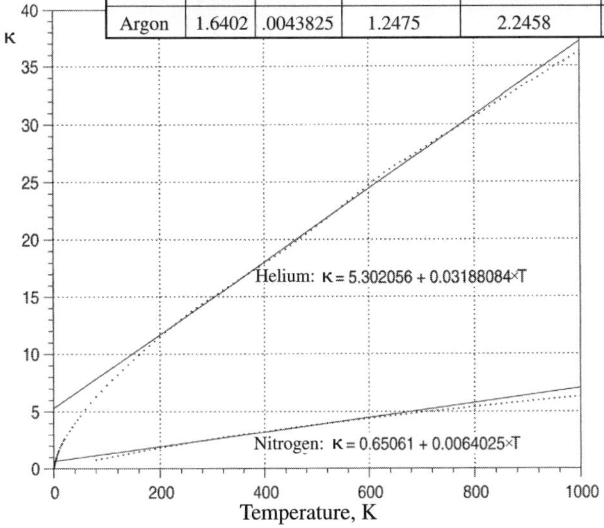

Fitted values of κ_0 and γ_κ, giving the lines in Figure F1, are listed for three gases in the above table (for $T_0 = 273.2$ K and $\Delta T_1 = 300$ K) with values of A, B, and C.

Figure F1. Thermal conductivity (watts/m/K) versus temperature.

Figure F2 shows binary-mixture, stationary solutions ζ_{1z} and ζ_{2z} versus z/z_1 obtained via [F14] and [F15] for several ζ_{10} and corresponding ζ_{20}. Nitrogen is the species-1 gas (we assume $\kappa_z = \kappa_{1z}$), $T_0 = 273.2$ K, and $\Delta T_1 = 300$ K. Although not shown in Figure F2, species-2 particles can be purged from a hot gas region or flow.

For example, consider a flow of gas or vapor containing low-level concentrations of impurities in a duct and through a heated, porous-plate "filter" in the duct with selectable velocity w_{face} at the filter face, where $\gamma_T/T_z = [\gamma_T/T_z]_{face}$. Species-2 (impurity) gas particles obtain net velocity $w_{1z} + w_{2z}{}^T$ at z and all species of particles with diffusivity $D_2 < D_1$ obtain velocity $w_{1z} - D_{2z}\gamma_T/2T_z$ and can be concentrated and held in the flow upstream of the filter face as long as $w_{face} < D_{2z}[\gamma_T/2T_z]_{face}$.

The *thermal diffusion ratio* k_T,[18, 20, 23(a)] long a popular "measure of thermal diffusion" based on stationary-state condition $\gamma_{\zeta 2} = k_{T2}\gamma_T/T_z$ and $k_{T2} = -D_{2z}{}^T/D_{2z}$, does not provide the information previously thought.[18, 20, 23(a)] These equations are supposed to characterize the *two-bulb experiment*[23] wherein one of two connected bulbs is held at temperature T_z and the other at T_0. Measured stationary-state bulb-number-fraction differences $\Delta\zeta_2 = \zeta_{2z} - \zeta_{20}$ give $k_{T2} = \Delta\zeta_2/\log_e(T_z/T_0)$ values. At some intermediate temperature it has been supposed $D_{2z}{}^T = -k_{T2}D_{2z}$. However, by the present theory the stationary equation on which the analysis should be based is [F10b] at the stationary condition: $\gamma_{\zeta 2} = k_{T2}\zeta_{2z}\gamma_T/T_z$ and $k_{T2} = -D_{2z}{}^T/D_{2z} = 1/2$.

Error and confusion in thermal diffusion date to and have propagated from its early investigations in "exact" or "rigorous" kinetic theory. Hence, thermal diffusion is the worst-predicted process of that theory. We have corrected the error in past analyses[18, 20, 23(a)] by using quantities n_z and $\zeta_{\varphi z}$ in our equations.

We conclude our analysis of thermal diffusion by describing its *mechanism*. The natural direction of thermal diffusion is that of γ_T (see [F4a-1]), the thermal-diffusion flux being balanced by a counterflow in a stagnant, one-component gas. In binary mixtures ($D_1 > D_2$), thermal diffusion of less-mobile species-2 particles is preempted by that of species-1 particles having stronger thermal diffusion. That is, while species-1 particles thermally diffuse in the direction of γ_T, species-2 particles are simply counterflowed in the opposite direction, as [F10] indicates. All transport is restricted by the limiting D_{2z}. Species 1 thus concentrates in the hot region and 2 in the cold. In mixtures of more species, each species in turn tends to concentrate in its own region, each being in turn the most-mobile of the remaining species.

8. Thermophoresis and Diffusiophoresis

Finally, we consider *phoretic velocities* of particles suspended in gas (i.e., an aerosol). Thermophoretic velocity due to γ_T is defined by [F10] and [F13]. Diffusiophoretic velocity due to γ_ζ is also defined by [F10], which couples the two velocities.

For small suspended particles, *Knudsen number* = Kn = $\lambda/a >> 1$, with *a* the spherical-particle radius or characteristic half-length for another shape and λ the mean-free-path length of the suspending gas molecules. Flow about such particles is called *free-molecule flow*. L. Waldmann[24] predicted phoretic motions of spheres in such flow. Temperature, velocity, and concentration jumps[21] occur at particle surfaces at lower Kn. Brock and Jacobsen,[25] among others,[24] considered $w_2{}^T$ for $0 \leq \text{Kn} \leq 1$.

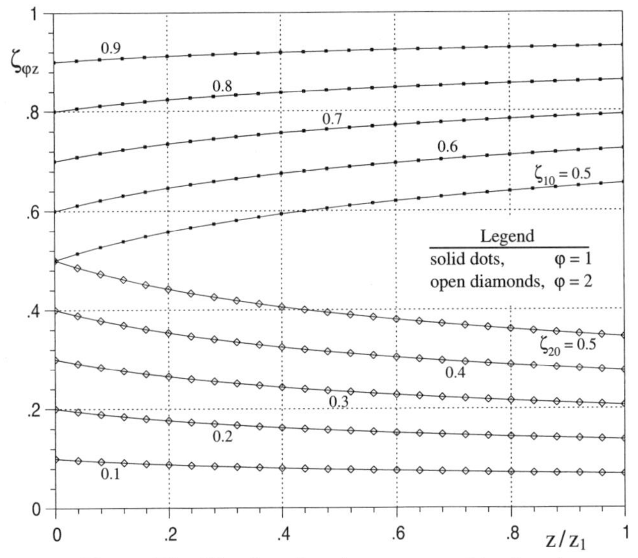

Figure F2. Number fraction versus altitude z/z_1.

Thermophoretic velocity of species-2 particles *at any Kn* (if f_{2z} dependence on Kn is included) is given by [F13]. As shown by the minus sign in [F13], this velocity is negative or opposite the direction of γ_T (the positive z-axis direction).

Until now we have ignored influence of a particle on local temperature gradient, but the data collected by Waldmann and Schmitt[24] suggest that $w_{2\,cntr}$ and $w_{2z}{}^T$ depend on actual, local γ_T. Carslaw and Jaeger[26] determined the temperature gradient γ_{Tz} across a sphere at z having Kn = 0 and thermal conductivity κ_p in a gas of thermal conductivity κ_g and temperature gradient $\gamma_{T\infty}$ at z but far from the particle,

[F16] $$\gamma_{Tz}/\gamma_{T\infty} = 1 + C_\kappa(Kn_\kappa)\times(1 - \kappa_p/\kappa_g)/(2 + \kappa_p/\kappa_g)$$

where $C_\kappa(Kn_\kappa)$ (added here to the Carslaw-Jaeger result) is 1 at $Kn_\kappa = 0$. Dahneke[21] wrote correction factor $C_\kappa(Kn_\kappa)$ by analogy. For a spherical particle of radius *a*,

[F17] $$C_\kappa(Kn_\kappa) = (Kn_\kappa + 1)/[2Kn_\kappa\times(Kn_\kappa + 1)/\alpha + 1] \quad \text{with} \quad Kn_\kappa = \lambda_\kappa/a,$$

λ_κ is given in equations [F8], and $\alpha \approx 1$ is the *thermal accommodation coefficient* or average fraction of thermal-energy difference transferred per molecular collision. At large Kn_κ, $C_\kappa(Kn_\kappa) = \alpha/2Kn_\kappa \to 0$ and thermophoresis is independent of κ_p/κ_g.

Solving [F4b-2] using $\gamma_{T\infty}$ and γ_{Tz} for species 1 and 2 gives, in place of [F13],

[F18] $$w_{2z}{}^T = -k\gamma_{Tz}/2f_{2z} = -k\{1 + C_\kappa(Kn_\kappa)\times(1 - \kappa_p/\kappa_g)/(2 + \kappa_p/\kappa_g)\}\,\gamma_{T\infty}/2f_{2z}.$$

Notes and References for Appendix F.

[1] How the second-law-predicted heat death of the universe will eventually occur has been described by Fred Adams and Greg Laughlin in their popular-level book *The Five Ages of the Universe* (The Free Press, New York, 1999). However, one should not lose sleep over the eventual demise of the universe. Our sun's brightness will not begin to diminish perceptively for another six billion years. Events described in Book III will precede and supercede that event, are more urgent, and imminent.

[2] Boltzmann's original H-theorem expression is modernized here using quantum theory concepts. For a description of the *logarithm function*, see endnote 27 of Chapter 8.

[3] The number of distinct quantum states of a system containing N identical atoms includes $N!/\Pi_j n_j!$ indistinguishable exchanges of the $N = \Sigma_j n_j$ atoms divided into distinguishable groups of n_j atoms at energy levels E_j, with j = 1,2,3,..., where symbols Π_j and Σ_j (upper case Greek "pi" sub j and "sigma" sub j) indicate, respectively, the product and sum over all j values and "n factorial" = $n! = n\times(n-1)\times(n-2)\times\ldots\times2\times1$ with $0! = 1$. This number of possible states of a system is usually much larger than its number of atoms; only when all or most atoms have one energy E_j are the two numbers comparable. But even when all or most atoms have identical energy E_j, differences in atom locations give a similarly high number of different, distinguishable states all having essentially identical E_j. (For further details see Tolman, Richard C., *The Principles of Statistical Mechanics,* Oxford University Press, Oxford, England, 1938, Chapter 13 and Hirschfelder, J. O., C. F. Curtiss, and R. B. Bird, *Molecular Theory of Gases and Liquids,* John Wiley, New York, 1954, Chapter 2.)

[4] Gibbs, J. Willard, *Elementary Principles in Statistical Mechanics,* Yale University Press, New Haven, CT, 1902; reprinted by Dover Publications, Inc., New York, 1960.

[5] See Jaynes, E. T., "Gibbs' vs Boltzmann's Entropies," *American Journal of Physics* **33**, 1965, 391-398. This same author is quoted pertinently in endnote 11 of Chapter 2. The former paper is found with other salient articles in *E. T. Jaynes: Papers on Probability, Statistics and Statistical Physics,* R. D. Rosenkrantz (editor), Kluwer Academic Publishers, Dordrecht, The Netherlands, 1983. All Jaynes' papers are available at http://bayes@wustl.edu/etj/node1.html.

[6] We demonstrate entropy decrease in slow crystallization in a closed system by use of the characteristic property for such systems (Helmholtz free energy $F = E - TS$, Section 3), which is minimum at equilibrium. Then for slow, quasi-equilibrium crystallization, $\Delta F = \{E_2 - TS_2\} - \{E_1 - TS_1\} = \Delta E - T\Delta S = 0$. It follows that for slow, quasi-equilibrium crystallization, $\Delta E = T\Delta S$.

In crystal formation from solute atoms, each molecule added to the crystal gives up a *latent heat of crystallization* q. Without work extraction from a closed system the first law of thermodynamics is $Q = \Delta E$, where ΔE is increase in system energy and heat Q is heat transferred to the system. (Positive or negative ΔE and Q represent energy and heat received by or released from the system.) Thus, crystallization of N molecules gives $\Delta E = Q = -Nq$ so that $\Delta S = Q/T = -Nq/T < 0$. That is, as N molecules slowly crystallize they slowly release into the system latent energy of crystallization Nq which is subsequently released to the environment. The net effect is system energy decrease in the form of heat released from the system. Since system-boundary temperature T_b is slightly lower than internal system temperature T, increase in entropy of the environment (universe) $\Delta S_e = Q/T_b$ slightly exceeds system entropy decrease $\Delta S = Q/T$.

[7] See, for example, Shannon, Claude E., *A Mathematical Theory of Communication,* University of Illinois Press, Urbana, IL, 1949.

[8] System type and its traditional designation in statistical mechanics are given in the first two columns of the Table on page 570. The third column indicates properties of the system regarded as fixed, known, or required for specification of system state, with N, V, E, T, μ, and P being, respectively, number of system molecules, system volume, system energy, absolute temperature, *chemical potential*, and pressure. The *partition function* Z is shown in column 4 for each system type and column 5 shows the *characteristic property* that characterizes system state, i.e., the property minimized at equilibrium. Isolated systems evolve spontaneously toward minimum negative entropy or maximum S. Closed systems evolve spontaneously toward minimum *Helmholtz free energy* $F = E - TS$. Open systems evolve toward either minimum $-PV$ or minimum *Gibbs free energy* $G = E + PV - TS$, depending on the type of open system. Like entropy for the isolated system, each of these properties characterizes system state for the indicated system type. The chemical potential is defined as $\mu = G/N$ so that specifying either one of μ or G also specifies the other if N is known. Spontaneous evolution of system types are characterized by $d(-S)/dt \le 0$, $dF/dt \le 0$, $d(-PV)/dt \le 0$, and $dG/dt \le 0$, with the equilibrium state defined by the minimum

condition at which the characteristic property is constant. A useful concept for all system types is that minimum characteristic property $-S$, F, $-PV$, or G defines maximum system entropy or level of ignorance in specification of the system's microscopic state given its known macroscopic properties, i.e., everything actually known about the system. The *Maxent principle* derives from the work of Boltzmann, Gibbs, R. T. Cox, Claude Shannon, and, especially, E. T. Jaynes (loc. cit.).

[9] This table is adapted from Lloyd L. Lee *(Molecular Thermodynamics of Nonideal Fluids,* Butterworths, Boston, 1988, 34) who provides several examples of the Maxent method.

[10] Why an ensemble average? Two *equivalent* ensembles may be used. The first is many replications of a prototype system. The second is a single prototype system observed at many times. The latter corresponds to an actual system evolving in time. The most-probable state in the ensemble of macroscopically identical systems is the most probable state of the single system evolving in time. When probability of a particular or set of microstates dominates, it dominates both averages.

[11] See, e.g., Taylor, Angus E., *Advanced Calculus,* Ginn and Company, Boston, 1955, 198-201.

[12] Consider a system containing a molecular species that may cluster, such as H_2O (water) or Ar (Argon). Let distribution vector $\boldsymbol{p} = \{p_1, p_2, ..., p_j, ...\}$ define the distribution in number of clusters per unit volume containing j molecules in the cluster, with $j = 1, 2, 3, ..., j, ...$ The questions we pose are (1) does clustering occur? and, if so, (2) what is the distribution $\boldsymbol{p}$ of cluster sizes? and (3) what is the rate of formation of clusters that survive and grow?

Associated with each cluster size is a molecular Helmholtz free energy (endnote 6) per molecule f_j, with subscript j because cluster free energy per molecule is cluster-size dependent. Hence, f_1 is the free energy of a free, isolated molecule, f_2 is the free energy per molecule for a clustered pair, etc. The free energy difference that occurs when j molecules cluster together is therefore $\Delta F_j = j(f_j - f_1)$. Cluster-size dependence of ΔF_j is adequately approximated by use of *surface free energy* or *surface tension* γ (Greek "gamma"). Spherical clusters of radius r(j) contain $j = 4/3\pi r^3/v$ molecules of bulk molecular volume v and contribute surface free energy $\Delta F_S = 4\pi r^2\gamma$ per cluster. Excess free energy associated with a cluster of size r over that of a cluster-free system is $\Delta F(r) = -4/3\pi r^3/v\ \delta F + 4\pi r^2\gamma$, where δF ("delta" F) is increase in system free energy caused by removal of a single molecule from the center of a large cluster (bulk state) to the isolated (vapor) state. The mathematical form of this expression requires a maximum in ΔF or a surface-free-energy barrier at radius $r_{max} = 2v\gamma/\delta F$ of height $\Delta F_{max} = 16\pi\, v^2\gamma^3/(3\delta F^2)$. Beyond this maximum a cluster is stable and grows spontaneously and rapidly. Similar expressions apply for other cluster shapes (crystals). Since F is the characteristic function for a closed system, we write

$$p_j(r)\ /\ p_1 = \exp(-\beta\Delta F(r)) \qquad \text{and} \qquad p_{crit} = p_1 \exp(-\beta\Delta F_{max}) \qquad \text{with } \beta = 1/kT,$$

where p_{crit} is the number concentration of *critical-size clusters*, i.e., clusters at size corresponding to the maximum of the free-energy barrier. To determine number concentration distribution $\boldsymbol{p}$ explicitly, the constraint $N = \Sigma_j\, p_j$ is used with N as the upper j-limit of the sum, N being the total number of clustering-species molecules per unit volume. But, in practice, a lower limit may be used since relatively few large clusters occur before nucleation of the new phase.

These expressions answer the first two questions posed above and we now turn to the third: what rate of nucleation of stable nuclei of a new phase will occur? We make the reasonable assumption that growth occurs predominantly in one-molecule increments because p_1 is generally larger than all other cluster populations and single molecules transport through the medium at higher speeds. (This assumption may be checked and corrected, if necessary, by including growth due to larger cluster assimilations by critical-size clusters.) The net growth rate of stable clusters is

$$I_{crit} = (dp/dt)_{crit} = [p_1\,\eta\, R_{1crit} - R_{crit-}]\ p_1 \exp(-\beta\Delta F_{max})$$

where p_1 is the concentration of single-molecules, $p_1 R_{1crit} p_{crit}$ is the rate of collisions per unit volume of single- and critical-size clusters, η (Greek "eta") is a sticking efficiency or fraction of colliding molecules that stick (η appears to be nearly unity), and $R_{crit-}p_{crit}$ is the rate per unit volume at which critical-size clusters spontaneously shrink by loss of one or more molecules. We have not specified the medium to be solid, liquid, or gas, although transport kinetics that control R_{1crit} as well as R_{crit-}, γ, and η strongly depend on both the clustering and the medium materials.

In production of small droplets from a vapor of the clustering species we estimate the rate of formation of stable, critical-size clusters by estimating R_{1crit}, R_{crit-} and η. A suitable estimate for η is unity; we take $R_{crit-} \cong p_1 \eta R_{1crit}/2$ as an approximate rate constant, i.e., about half the droplets at the maximum of a smooth free-energy barrier will pass over the barrier and half will not. Effusional flux of vapor molecules at number concentration p_1 in a gas (Equation [F6]) is $p_1\langle c\rangle/4$, where $\langle c\rangle = \sqrt{(8kT/\pi m_1)}$ with m_1 the molecular mass of the clustering species and T the absolute temperature. This flux multiplied by the effective cluster surface area gives the critical cluster growth rate $p_1 R_{1crit}$ which, multiplied by the concentration of critical size clusters $p_1 \exp(-\beta\Delta F_{max})$, gives the stable-droplet formation rate per unit volume I_{crit+},

$$I_{crit+} \cong 2\pi v^2\gamma^2/\delta F^2 \sqrt{(8kT/\pi m)}\, p_1^2 \exp(-16\beta\pi/3\ v^2\gamma^3/\delta F^2).$$

Dahneke (in *Theory of Dispersed Multiphase Flow,* Richard E. Meyer (editor), Academic Press, New York, 1983, 97-133) provides expressions for droplet growth rates in gases and vapors.

Chemical kinetics illustrations are given by Eyring, H., and E. M. Eyring, *Modern Chemical Kinetics,* Reinhold, New York, 1963.

[13] (a) Hirschfelder, J. O., *et al*, loc. cit., 455. (b) Chapman, Sydney, and T. G. Cowling, *The Mathematical Theory of Non-uniform Gases,* Cambridge University Press, 1960, 37. (c) Reed, Thomas M., and Keith E. Gubbins, *Applied Statistical Mechanics,* Butterworth-Heinemann Reprint, Boston, 1973, 354. (d) Jeans, Sir James, *An Introduction to the Kinetic Theory of Gases,* Cambridge University Press, Cambridge, 1962, 28.

[14] Hill, Terrell L., *Introduction to Statistical Thermodynamics,* Addison-Wesley, Reading, MA, 1960.

[15] Maximizing information entropy (Maxent principle) subject to macroscopic constraints imposes on a system only what is *actually known* about the system. It leads directly to characteristic properties for equilibrium systems of various sorts. Macroscopic constraints and Maxent together with known equilibrium-thermodynamic relations define a characteristic thermodynamic property for each type of system. For nonequilibrium systems, thermodynamics does not apply so that (1) the Lagrange multipliers cannot be determined by use of thermodynamics and (2) no characteristic thermodynamic property of a nonequilibrium system emerges from the analysis. Otherwise Maxent treatments of equilibrium and steady-state, nonequilibrium systems are identical.

[16] Dahneke, B., *Aerosol Science* **4**, 1973, 147-161.

[17] Eucken, A., *Physik. Zeitschrift* **14**, 1913, 324; reference 19, 237ff.

[18] Chapman, Sydney, and T. G. Cowling, loc.cit., 142-144, 252ff, 399-404.

[19] Reynolds, Osborne, *Transactions of the Royal Society (London)* **174**, 1883, 935-982.

[20] $D_{1z} = D_{2z}$ and $D_{1z}^T = -D_{2z}^T$ are standard results, the latter wrong (see [F12]). Hirschfelder, *et al*, loc. cit., 518ff, Bird, R. B., W. E. Stewart, and E. N. Lightfoot, *Transport Phenomena,* Wiley, New York, 1960, 502, 568. Error can occur in use of γ_{ni} since $\gamma_{ni} = \partial n_i/\partial z \neq dn_i/dz = \gamma_{ni} + (\partial n_i/\partial T)\gamma_T$.

[21] Dahneke, 1983, loc. cit.

[22] Talbot, L., *Rarefied Gas Dynamics,* Sam S. Fisher (editor), AIAA, New York, 1980, 467-488.

[23] (a) Grew, K. E., and T. L. Ibbs, *Thermal Diffusion in Gases,* Cambridge University Press, 1952. (b) Bird, R. B., *et al*, loc. cit., 568, 574-575.

[24] Waldmann, L., *Zeitschrift für Naturforschung* **14a**, 1959, 376. See also Waldmann, L., and K. H. Schmitt, in *Aerosol Science,* C. N. Davies (editor), Academic Press, New York, 1966, 137-162.

[25] Jacobsen, S., and J. Brock, *Journal of Colloid and Interface Science* **20**, 1965, 544.

[26] Carslaw, H. S., and J. C. Jaeger, *Conduction of Heat in Solids,* Oxford University Press, 1959, 426.

Appendix G

Derivation of a Simple Bell's Theorem#

Part 1: Definitions.

Consider the EPRB apparatus pictured in Chapter 10 and reproduced below. We denote by angles α and β the displacement of Analyzer C and Analyzer D from their vertical (reference) orientation. We denote by angle θ the absolute value of the difference between α and β, viz., $\theta = |\alpha - \beta|$.

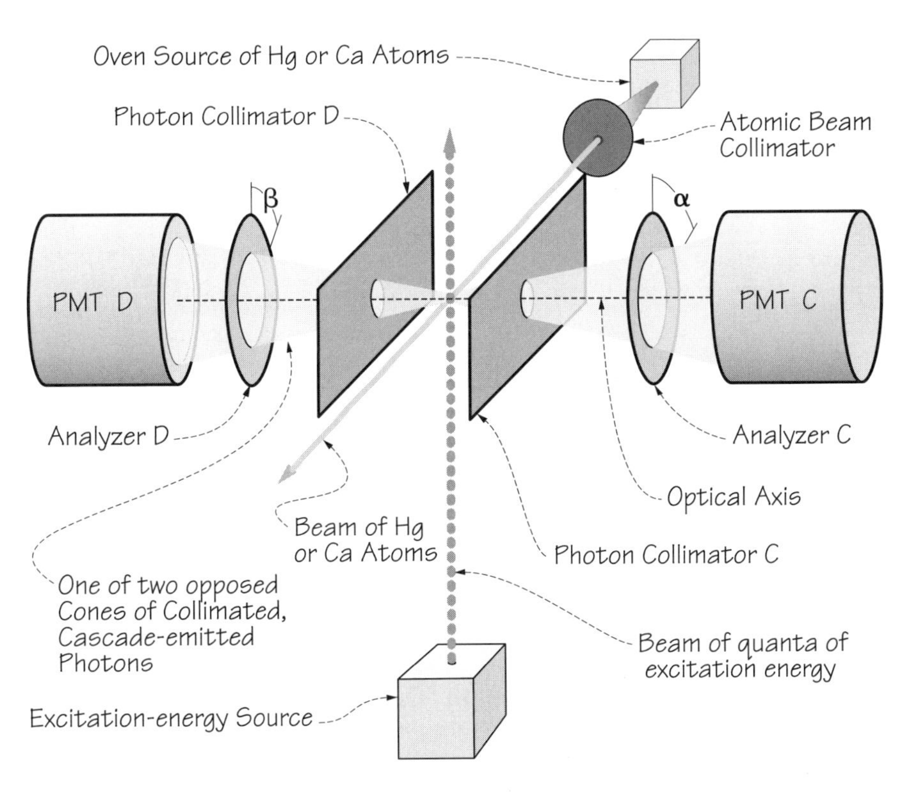

For steady-state operation let N_{CD} represent the total number of correlated (nearly simultaneous) photon pairs arriving at Analyzers C and D in time t. Then

$$R_{CD} = N_{CD}/t$$

is the total rate of correlated photon pairs. Note that R_{CD}, but only R_{CD}, is measured with both analyzers removed. Let $N_C(\alpha)$ represent the number of photons detected by PMT C in time t. Then

$$R_C(\alpha) = N_C(\alpha)/t$$

is the rate of detection of photons by PMT C. Let $N_D(\beta)$ represent the number of photons detected by PMT D in time t. Then

$$R_D(\beta) = N_D(\beta)/t$$

is the rate of detection of photons at PMT D. Let $N(\alpha,\beta)$ represent the number of correlated photons detected nearly simultaneously at both detectors C and D in time t. Then

$$R(\alpha,\beta) = N(\alpha,\beta)/t$$

is the rate of detection of correlated (nearly simultaneous) photons at both PMT C and D.

Part 2: Probabilities and Counting Rates.

Let $p_C(\alpha)$ be the probability that one of a correlated pair of protons is detected at PMT C. Let $p_D(\beta)$ be the probability that the other of the correlated pair of photons is detected at PMT D. Let $p(\alpha,\beta)$ be the probability that both photons of a correlated pair are detected nearly simultaneously at detectors PMT C and D. Then, for sufficiently large numbers of counts, these probabilities may be written as

$$p_C(\alpha) = R_C(\alpha)/R_{CD}, \qquad p_D(\beta) = R_D(\beta)/R_{CD}, \qquad p(\alpha,\beta) = R(\alpha,\beta)/R_{CD}.$$

Alternatively, we may write $p_C(\lambda,\alpha)$, $p_D(\lambda,\beta)$ and $p(\lambda,\alpha,\beta)$ as the probabilities of observing a photon at C or D or nearly simultaneously at C and D for a specified value of the *state variable* λ. This undefined state variable represents a *set of variables* required for discriminating different states of the system. In other words, we use variables λ to represent a real system in the sense of EPR, i.e., the set λ represents however many variables are necessary to fully specify any distinct system state. (Associated with each variable is an integration over that variable, represented by a single integral operator in the following equations.) Thus, after Bell, we include undefined variable set λ to make the so-called *reality assumption* in the EPR sense.

We also make a second assumption: that an event at C does not influence an event at D. This is the so-called *locality assumption*. In consequence of it, $p_C(\lambda,\alpha)$ and $p_D(\lambda,\beta)$ must be independent so that

$$p(\lambda,\alpha,\beta) = p_C(\lambda,\alpha) \times p_D(\lambda,\beta).$$

(The alternative expression for independence, i.e., $p(\alpha,\beta) = p_C(\alpha) \times p_D(\beta)$, is not valid because it is too strong.)

Moreover, we let $\rho(\lambda)$ represent the normalized probability density over λ for an ensemble of the system. We can then write for the ensemble probabilities in conventional statistical-physics style

$$p_C(\alpha) = \int p_C(\lambda,\alpha)\, \rho(\lambda)\, d\lambda$$

$$p_D(\beta) = \int p_D(\lambda,\beta)\, \rho(\lambda)\, d\lambda$$

$$p(\alpha,\beta) = \int p(\lambda,\alpha,\beta)\, \rho(\lambda)\, d\lambda$$

where the integrations are carried out over the complete λ space. This set of equations has the form of a hidden-variable theory, like the one derived by David Bohm (Chapter 10). Such a theory is not tenable in view of measured results (Chapter 10) when locality is assumed. But when locality is not assumed, a hidden-variable theory is possible with λ representing the hidden variable(s). In other words, reality may not be both local and real in the sense of EPR.

Part 3: A Simple Bell's Theorem.

To derive a Bell's theorem we use a lemma proved by Clauser and Horne (Clauser, J. F., and M. A. Horne, *Physical Review D* **10**, 1974, 526-535). This lemma involves real variables x, x′, y, y′, X and Y and it states that if $0 \le x, x' \le X, 0 \le y, y' \le Y$ then

$$-XY \le xy - xy' + x'y + x'y' - Yy' - Xy \le 0.$$

(While the symbol = reads "is equal to," the symbol ≤ reads "is less than or equal to.") Using this lemma with $X = Y = 1$, $x = p_C(\lambda,\alpha)$, $y = p_D(\lambda,\beta)$, etc. with $p(\lambda,\alpha,\beta) = p_C(\lambda,\alpha) \times p_D(\lambda,\beta)$ gives

$$-1 \le p(\lambda,\alpha,\beta) - p(\lambda,\alpha,\beta') + p(\lambda,\alpha',\beta) + p(\lambda,\alpha',\beta') - p_C(\lambda,\alpha') - p_D(\lambda,\beta) \le 0.$$

Multiplying through by $\rho(\lambda)$ and integrating over all λ space, as above, gives the result

$$-1 \le p(\alpha,\beta) - p(\alpha,\beta') + p(\alpha',\beta) + p(\alpha',\beta') - p_C(\alpha') - p_D(\beta) \le 0.$$

This result is a Bell's theorem, but one not yet simplified nor optimized for convenience and effectiveness. To simplify it we multiply the probabilities by count rate R_{CD} to obtain count rates in place of probabilities, as in Part 2. We assume sufficient counts occur so that the resulting rates are valid and obtain

$$-R_{CD} \le R(\alpha,\beta) - R(\alpha,\beta') + R(\alpha',\beta) + R(\alpha',\beta') - R_C(\alpha') - R_D(\beta) \le 0.$$

This result is a Bell's theorem inequality for the system we are considering. It is further simplified by making a few additional assumptions concerning symmetry. These assumptions do not impact validity or generality of application because they can be experimentally tested and verified.

Since polarization direction of correlated pairs of photons is random, we write

$$p_C(\alpha) = p_C = p_D(\beta) = p_D, \quad R_C(\alpha) = R_C = R_D(\beta) = R_D,$$

$$p(\alpha,\beta) = p(\theta), \quad \text{and} \quad R(\alpha,\beta) = R(\theta).$$

In 1972, S. J. Freedman discovered an additional useful property of these results. (Freedman, S. J., and J. F. Clauser, *Physical Review Letters* **28**, 1972, 938-941.) The maximum "upper limit violation" of the ideal quantum-theory result (given in Chapter 10) over the ideal Bell's-theorem limit occurs at angle $\theta = \pi/8$ radians. The maximum "lower limit violation" occurs at $\theta = 3\pi/8$. Thus, we choose these values $\theta = \pi/8$ and $3\pi/8$ to optimize a test of Bell's theorem. As Freedman noted, choosing the values of α, β, α', β' so that the two most preferred values of θ are

$$\theta = |\alpha - \beta| = |\alpha' - \beta| = |\alpha' - \beta'| = |\alpha - \beta'|/3 = \pi/8$$

$$\theta = |\alpha - \beta| = |\alpha' - \beta| = |\alpha' - \beta'| = |\alpha - \beta'|/3 = 3\pi/8$$

yields substantial simplification and optimization. Since the θ-dependence of an analyzer is periodic with period π radians, the transmissions at $\theta = 9\pi/8 = \pi + \pi/8$ and at $\theta = \pi/8$ are identical because a periodic function with period π is unchanged whenever $\theta \to \theta \pm \pi$. Freedman noted that when $\theta = 3\pi/8$, $3\theta = 9\pi/8 = \pi/8$ (equivalently). Thus, dividing through by $-R_{CD}$, the Bell's theorem inequality becomes for the cases $\theta = \pi/8$ and $3\pi/8$

$$0 \le [3\,R(\pi/8) - R(3\pi/8) - R_C - R_D] / R_{CD} \le 1$$

$$0 \le [3\,R(3\pi/8) - R(\pi/8) - R_C - R_D] / R_{CD} \le 1.$$

Subtracting the latter inequality from the former eliminates R_C and R_D but retains the 1 on the right of the $\le$ symbol to give

$$4\,R(\pi/8) / R_{CD} - 4\,R(3\pi/8) / R_{CD} \le 1.$$

Dividing this equation through by 4 gives the fully simplified and optimized Bell's theorem used in Chapter 10:

$$S_{BT} = R(\pi/8) / R_{CD} - R(3\pi/8) / R_{CD} \le 1/4 = 0.250000\ldots.$$

Since $R(\pi/8)$, $R(3\pi/8)$, and R_{CD} can all be measured, S_{BT} can be experimentally determined. If the experimental $S_{BT} > 1/4$ then Bell's theorem is violated and at least one of the two assumptions utilized in deriving the S_{BT} result (the *reality* and *locality* assumptions) must be invalid. As described in Chapter 10, experimental S_{BT} values are $> 1/4$. The conclusion is that either (1) if the universe is real in the EPR sense then the locality assumption is invalid or (2) if the locality assumption is valid then the universe is not real in the EPR sense. But it has been shown (see, for example, Ballentine, Leslie E., *Quantum Mechanics: A Modern Development,* World Scientific, Singapore, 1998) that quantum processes are intrinsically non-local whether the universe is real or non-real. The requirement in conclusion (1) may be relaxed.

Thus, at least at the quantum-physics level, the universe is non-local.

Appendix H

Excerpts from the 1838 "First Vision" Account of Joseph Smith, Jr.

Quoted from *Joseph Smith – History* found in the *Pearl of Great Price,* published by The Church of Jesus Christ of Latter-day Saints, Salt Lake City, Utah, 1981, 47-51.
Comments in square brackets [...] have been added by the present author.

"In this history I shall present the various events in relation to this Church, in truth and righteousness, as they have transpired, or as they at present exist, being now (1838) the eighth year since the organization of the said Church [i.e., The Church of Jesus Christ of Latter-day Saints].

"I was born in the year of our Lord one thousand eight hundred and five, on the twenty-third day of December, in the town of Sharon, Windsor county, State of Vermont. ... My father, Joseph Smith, Sr., left the State of Vermont, and moved to Palmyra, Ontario (now Wayne) county, in the State of New York, when I was in my tenth year, or thereabouts. In about four years after my father's arrival in Palmyra, he moved with his family into Manchester in the same county of Ontario –

"Some time in the second year after our removal to Manchester, there was in the place where we lived an unusual excitement on the subject of religion. It commenced with the Methodists, but soon became general among all the sects in that region of the country. Indeed, the whole district of country seemed affected by it, and great multitudes united themselves to the different religious parties, which created no small stir and division amongst the people, some crying, "Lo, here!" and others, "Lo, there!" Some were contending for the Methodist faith, some for the Presbyterian, and some for the Baptist.

"For, notwithstanding the great love which the converts to these different faiths expressed at the time of their conversion, and the great zeal manifested by the respective clergy, who were active in getting up and promoting this extraordinary scene of religious feeling, in order to have everybody converted, as they were pleased to call it, let them join whatever sect they pleased; yet when the converts began to file off, some to one party and some to another, it was seen that the seemingly good feelings of both the priests and the converts were more pretended than real; for a scene of great confusion and bad feeling ensued – priest contending against priest, and convert against convert; so that all their good feelings one for another, if they ever had any, were entirely lost in a strife of words and a contest about opinions.

"I was at this time in my fifteenth year. My father's family was proselyted to the Presbyterian faith, and four of them joined that church, namely, my mother, Lucy; my brothers Hyrum and Samuel Harrison; and my sister Sophronia.

"During this time of great excitement my mind was called up to serious reflection and great uneasiness; but though my feelings were deep and often poignant, still I kept myself aloof from all these parties, though I attended their several meetings as often as occasion would permit. In process of time my mind became somewhat partial to the Methodist sect, and I felt some desire to be united with them; but so great were the confusion and strife among the different denominations, that it was impossible for a person young as I was, and so unacquainted with men and things, to come to any certain conclusion who was right and who was wrong.

"My mind at times was greatly excited, the cry and tumult were so great and incessant. The Presbyterians were most decided against the Baptists and Methodists, and used all the powers of both reason and sophistry to prove their errors, or, at least, to make the people think they were in error. On the other hand, the Baptists and Methodists in their turn were equally zealous in endeavoring to establish their own tenets and disprove all others.

"While I was laboring under the extreme difficulties caused by the contests of these parties of religionists, I was one day reading the Epistle of James, first chapter and fifth verse, which reads: *If any of you lack wisdom, let him ask of God, that giveth to all men liberally, and upbraideth not; and it shall be given him.*

"Never did any passage of scripture come with more power to the heart of man than this did at this time to mine. It seemed to enter with great force into every feeling of my heart. I reflected on it again and again, knowing that if any person needed wisdom from God, I did; for how to act I did not know, and unless I could get more wisdom than I then had, I would never know; for the teachers of religion of the different sects understood the same passages of scripture so differently as to destroy all confidence in settling the question by an appeal to the Bible.

"At length I came to the conclusion that I must either remain in darkness and confusion, or else I must do as James directs, that is, ask of God. I at length came to the determination to "ask of God," concluding that if he gave wisdom to them that lacked wisdom, and would give liberally, and not upbraid, I might venture.

"So, in accordance with this, my determination to ask of God, I retired to the woods to make the attempt. It was on the morning of a beautiful, clear day, early in the spring of eighteen hundred and twenty. It was the first time in my life that I had made such an attempt, for amidst all my anxieties I had never as yet made the attempt to pray vocally.

"After I had retired to the place where I had previously designed to go, having looked around me, and finding myself alone, I kneeled down and began to offer up the desires of my heart to God. I had scarcely done so, when immediately I was seized upon by some power which entirely overcame me, and had such an astonishing influence over me as to bind my tongue so that I could not speak. Thick darkness gathered around me, and it seemed to me for a time as if I were doomed to sudden destruction.

"But, exerting all my powers to call upon God to deliver me out of the power of this enemy which had seized upon me, and at the very moment when I was ready to sink into despair and abandon myself to destruction – not to an imaginary ruin, but to the power of some actual being from the unseen world, who had such marvelous power as I had never before felt in any being – just at this moment of great alarm, I saw a pillar of light exactly over my head, above the brightness of the sun, which descended gradually until it fell upon me.

"It no sooner appeared than I found myself delivered from the enemy which held me bound. When the light rested upon me I saw two Personages, whose brightness and glory defy all description, standing above me in the air. One of them spake unto me, calling me by name and said, pointing to the other – *This is My Beloved Son. Hear Him!*

"My object in going to inquire of the Lord was to know which of all the sects was right, that I might know which to join. No sooner, therefore, did I get possession of myself, so as to be able to speak, than I asked the Personages who stood above me in the light, which of all the sects was right (for at this time it had never entered into my heart that all were wrong) – and which I should join.

"I was answered that I must join none of them, for they were all wrong; and the Personage who addressed me said that all their creeds were an abomination in his sight; that those professors were all corrupt; that: "they draw near to me with their lips, but their hearts are far from me, they teach for doctrines the commandments of men, having a form of godliness, but they deny the power thereof [the power of God]."

"He again forbade me to join with any of them; and many other things did he say unto me, which I cannot write at this time. When I came to myself again, I found myself lying on my back, looking up into heaven. When the light had departed, I had no strength; but soon recovering in some degree, I went home. And as I leaned up to the fireplace, mother inquired what the matter was. I replied, "Never mind, all is well – I am well enough off." I then said to my mother, "I have learned for myself that Presbyterianism is not true." It seems as though the adversary was aware, at a very early period of my life, that I was destined to prove a disturber and an annoyer of his kingdom; else why should the powers of darkness combine against me? Why the opposition and persecution that arose against me, almost in my infancy?

"Some few days after I had this vision, I happened to be in company with one of the Methodist preachers, who was very active in the before mentioned religious excitement; and, conversing with him on the subject of religion, I took occasion to give him an account of the vision which I had had. I was greatly surprised at his behavior; he treated my communication not only lightly, but with great contempt, saying it was all of the devil, that there were no such things as visions or revelations in these days; that all such things had ceased with the apostles, and that there would never be any more of them. [This is one of many ways "the world" denies the power of God.]

"I soon found, however, that my telling the story had excited a great deal of prejudice against me among professors of religion, and was the cause of great persecution, which continued to increase; and though I was an obscure boy, only between fourteen and fifteen years of age, and my circumstances in life such as to make a boy of no consequence in the world, yet men of high standing would take notice sufficient to excite the public mind against me, and create a bitter persecution; and this was common among all the sects – all united to persecute me.

"It caused me serious reflection then, and often has since, how very strange it was that an obscure boy, of a little over fourteen years of age, and one, too, who was doomed to the necessity of obtaining a scanty maintenance by his daily labor, should be thought a character of sufficient importance to attract the attention of the great ones of the most popular sects of the day, and in a manner to create in them a spirit of the most bitter persecution and reviling. But strange or not, so it was, and it was often the cause of great sorrow to myself.

"However, it was nevertheless a fact that I had beheld a vision. I have thought since, that I felt much like Paul, when he made his defense before King Agrippa, and related the account of the vision he had when he saw a light, and heard a voice; but still there were but few who believed him; some said he was dishonest, others said he was mad; and he was ridiculed and reviled. But all this did not destroy the reality of his vision. He had seen a vision, he knew he had, and all the persecution under heaven could not make it otherwise; and though they should persecute him unto death, yet he knew, and would know to his latest breath, that he had both seen a light and heard a voice speaking unto him, and all the world could not make him think or believe otherwise.

"So it was with me. I had actually seen a light, and in the midst of that light I saw two Personages, and they did in reality speak to me; and though I was hated and persecuted for saying that I had seen a vision, yet it was true; and while they were persecuting me, reviling me, and speaking all manner of evil against me falsely for so saying, I was led to say in my heart: Why persecute me for telling the truth? I have actually seen a vision; and who am I that I can withstand God, or why does the world think to make me deny what I have actually seen? For I had seen a vision; I knew it, and I knew that God knew it, and I could not deny it, neither dared I do it; at least I knew that by so doing I would offend God, and come under condemnation.

"I had now got my mind satisfied so far as the sectarian world was concerned – that it was not my duty to join with any of them, but to continue as I was until further directed. I had found the testimony of James to be true – that a man who lacked wisdom might ask of God, and obtain, and not be upbraided."

Interpretation

One could describe the experience of Joseph Smith and the ostensible-step method urged in this book as mystical (as its meaning is implied by our special definition of the related term *mysticism* on page xviii), that is, of, relating to, or resulting from an individual's direct communion with God or ultimate reality. (But such description is quite unlike mysticism as the term is usually used which contains little or no agency or rationalism.) However, I prefer another description, not contrary to a mystical one with strong components of agency and rationalism, based on the well-known interchange between Peter and Christ.

> [Jesus] asked his disciples "Whom do men say that I the Son of Man am?" And they answered, "Some say that thou art John the Baptist: some Elias; and others, Jeremias, or one of the prophets."
>
> [Then Christ asked], "But whom say ye that I am?" And Simon Peter answered and said, "Thou art the Christ, the Son of the living God."

> And Jesus answered and said unto him, "Blessed art thou, Simon Bar-jona: for flesh and blood hath not revealed it unto thee, but my Father which is in heaven. And I say unto thee, That thou art Peter, and upon this rock I will build my church; and the gates of hell shall not prevail against it."[1a]

The rock upon which true Christianity is built, the sure foundation that the wise build on that will not fall in winds and floods (*Bible,* Matthew 7:21-23), is direct revelation by the power of God or the Holy Ghost regarding the station of Christ and correct Christian belief, promised in the doctrine of Christ and elsewhere. This rock is personal guidance about the love of God, what one can do in response, and in so doing become one of "the elect," an issue that was utterly confusing to the reformers.

Thus, while I regard the experience of Smith and my own experience as mystical (in our special use of this term), I regard them more as genuinely, fundamentally, and essentially Christian. And Joseph Smith's experience described above is not about him more than it is about Christ and us, for Christ called and commissioned Smith as His servant through whom He would lead and teach all others of our time. Smith's experience exemplifies what each of us should obtain as our own sure foundation of knowledge. The experience of another will probably be more modest than Smith's, but no less personal and convincing and valuable. And we should be satisfied with nothing less than sure, direct guidance from God. He has the power and He has repeatedly invited us to approach Him, to knock on the door.

Some reject and even attack Smith's experience as too different from the normal, too divergent from Bible teachings (which it is not; the experiences Christ gave Smith strictly, literally, and dramatically fulfill many Bible prophecies the followers of Christ have waited millennia to see fulfilled and the work Christ started in our time through Smith will eventually fullfil *all* Bible prophecies; it only diverges from incorrect interpretations of Bible teachings which, unfortunately, are often the orthodox Christian belief of today). The detractors of Smith criticize his experience and teaching as personal and anecdotal rather than orthodox and Biblical. The Bible *is* descriptions of personal, anecdotal, and unorthodox experiences of the prophets who wrote it or passed down in legacy for later prophets to write. It seems some who attack Smith (and Christ) are threatened viewing the work of God as current and near. They seem more comfortable looking back across a far distance of many centuries with their orthodox interpretation of the Bible as a remote, rigid system. We have seen exactly this reaction before in the Jews at the time of Christ. But marvelous new scripture including the Book of Mormon has been and will yet be received (see Appendix I) and old prophecies and modern ones have been and are now being fulfilled (see endnote 61 of Chapter 15). Looking at a remote God across centuries is not so restrictive and threatening as dealing with Him here, now, and personally. Distance is ever preferred by those misled by Satan who fight Christ and His prophets whenever they live, as history has repeatedly shown. But only personal and direct connection to Christ provides salvation and joy.

Christianity is about Christ, what He has done and will yet do, and about us, what He wants us to do and what we will do for us. In our time, Joseph Smith figures centrally in our knowledge of these matters. Among all mortals Joseph is second only to Christ in importance of contribution to all men and women, but an infinitely distant second. Christ alone accepted the terrible yoke and bore the unspeakable burden in order that our yoke may be easy and our burden light. It is by the name of Christ that His followers shall be called in the last day (*Book of Mormon,* 3 Nephi 27:5 [3-8]). Yet, it is true the servant can tell us about the Master better than any other (except His Father or Christ Himself or the Holy Ghost); we must heed Peter, John, Paul, Nephi, Moroni, Joseph and all the prophets who spoke and speak for Christ. Christ is the Author of our salvation. Christ is our Light, our Example, and our Advocate with the Father.[1] He, first, foremost, and alone, represents and speaks for His Father, as taught in all scripture.[2] He also responds to those sincerely seeking Him.

If your belief in God or Christ is based on tradition and orthodoxy that Satan has influenced, it may, with its foundation, slowly wash away or collapse dramatically. The rare and lonely traveler in search of absolute and universal truth fully finds it only when he or she invokes Moroni's promise in the final chapter of the Book of Mormon and follows the doctrine of Christ. Personal knowing of Christ, His station, and His work is available to each person seeking to receive truth. This truth is the rock on which Christ's church is built. Beyond finding the way for one's self, through Christ's doctrine and its promised knowledge of Him as well as continuing personal guidance, there is much work to be done in the blessing of men and women of all times, living and dead. Indeed, the blessing of "all the families of the earth" promised in the Abrahamic covenant is only beginning. This work is directed by Christ through His servants who direct His church today, as in the original Church of Jesus Christ. Joseph, to inaugurate this dispensation, was commanded to translate the Book of Mormon and other works and to establish Christ's church again on the earth, acting under the direction and with the power of God. The value of Christ's guidance through Joseph Smith is learned by prayerfully reading the Book of Mormon and personally receiving a witness of its veracity through the power of God. While the focus is Christ, we can fully know Christ today only through Joseph's contributions.

The hardest principles are those that contain the new and, especially, the profound. It's easy to accept the same old thing but it only takes us on the same old path and not to new understanding and greater profundity of meaning. Truth and its new paradigm discovered along a new path by the rare and lonely traveler are regarded as foolishness by those unwilling to try it. Those unwilling, those who won't, are left behind, paralyzed in their paradigms, long after the return of the willing.

[1] (a) *Bible,* Matthew 16:13-18. Christ declares that Peter's knowledge of Christ's station is God-given and that "upon this rock [personal revelation of the truth of Christ's station from God to an individual sincerely seeking it with faith in Christ and real intent] I will build my church."

(b) *Book of Mormon,* 3 Nephi 27:13-21. Christ states *His gospel* in which the first seven of a total of nine verses attribute the power and beneficence of His gospel to His Father.

(c) *The Pearl of Great Price,* Moses 4:2. God states "But, behold, my Beloved Son, which was my Beloved and Chosen from the beginning, said unto me – Father, thy will be done, and the glory be thine forever." The concept of giving our agency and all glory to God is not without the perfect and selfless example Christ provided in His own life and death.

[2] *Doctrine and Covenants* 93:8-9. "Therefore, in the beginning the Word was, for he was the Word, even the messenger of salvation – The light and the Redeemer of the world; the Spirit of truth, who came into the world, because the world was made by him, and in him was the life of men and the light of men."

Appendix I

Book of Mormon Passages that indicate the Bible, Traditional Christianity, and other Religions are Corrupted

The following account is quoted from the thirteenth and fourteenth chapters of 1 Nephi of the Book of Mormon. *It describes a vision of the future and instruction by an angel received by Nephi about 594 BC.*

And it came to pass that the angel spake unto me, saying: Look! And I looked and beheld many nations and kingdoms. And the angel said unto me: What beholdest thou? And I said: I behold many nations and kingdoms. And he said unto me: These are the nations and kingdoms of the Gentiles.

And it came to pass that I saw among the nations of the Gentiles the formation of a great church. And the angel said unto me: Behold the formation of a church which is most abominable above all other churches, which slayeth the saints of God, yea, and tortureth them and bindeth them down, and yoketh them with a yoke of iron, and bringeth them down into captivity. And it came to pass that I beheld this great and abominable church; and I saw the devil that he was the founder of it. And I also saw gold, and silver, and silks, and scarlets, and fine-twined linen, and all manner of precious clothing; and I saw many harlots.

And the angel spake unto me, saying: Behold the gold, and the silver, and the silks, and the scarlets, and the fine-twined linen, and the precious clothing, and the harlots, are the desires of this great and abominable church. And also for the praise of the world do they destroy the saints of God, and bring them down into captivity.

And it came to pass that I looked and beheld many waters; and they divided the Gentiles from the seed of my brethren. [Nephi had already been shown that his own seed, the Nephites, would be destroyed because of wickedness; they were, at about 385 AD. Thus, pertaining to history following the fourth century he and the angel speak of the seed of his brethren or of his father.] And it came to pass that the angel said unto me: Behold the wrath of God is upon the seed of thy brethren. And I looked and beheld a man among the Gentiles, who was separated from the seed of my brethren by the many waters [Christopher Columbus]; and I beheld the Spirit of God, that it came down and wrought upon the man; and he went forth upon the many waters, even unto the seed of my brethren, who were in the promised land [North and South America].

And it came to pass that I beheld many multitudes of the Gentiles upon the land of promise; and I beheld the wrath of God, that it was upon the seed of my brethren; and they were scattered before the Gentiles and were smitten. And I beheld the Spirit of the Lord, that it was upon the Gentiles, and they did prosper and obtain the land for their inheritance; and I beheld that they were white, and exceedingly fair and beautiful, like unto my people before they were slain.

And it came to pass that I, Nephi, beheld that the Gentiles who had gone forth out of captivity did humble themselves before the Lord; and the power of the Lord was with them. And I beheld that their mother Gentiles [the English and others] were gathered together upon the waters, and upon the land also, to battle against them.

And I beheld that the power of God was with them, and also that the wrath of God was upon all those that were gathered together against them to battle. And I, Nephi, beheld that the Gentiles that had gone out of captivity were delivered by the power of God out of the hands of all other nations.

And it came to pass that I, Nephi, beheld that they did prosper in the land; and I beheld a book [the Bible], and it was carried forth among them. And the angel said unto me: Knowest thou the meaning of the book? And I said unto him: I know not. And he said: Behold it proceedeth out of the mouth of a Jew. And I, Nephi, beheld it; and he said unto me: The book that thou beholdest is a record of the Jews, which contains the covenants of the Lord, which he hath made unto the house of Israel; and it also containeth many of the prophecies of the holy prophets; and it is a record like unto the engravings which are upon the plates of brass, save there are not so many [in the Bible]; nevertheless, they contain the covenants of the Lord, which he hath made unto the house of Israel; wherefore, they are of great worth unto the Gentiles.

And the angel of the Lord said unto me: Thou hast beheld that the book proceeded forth from the mouth of a Jew; and when it proceeded forth from the mouth of a Jew it contained the fulness of the gospel of the Lord, of whom the twelve apostles bear record; and they bear record according to the truth which is in the Lamb of God. Wherefore, these things go forth from the Jews in purity unto the Gentiles, according to the truth which is in God.

And after they go forth by the hand of the twelve apostles of the Lamb, from the Jews unto the Gentiles, thou seest the formation of that great and abominable church, which is most abominable above all other churches; for behold, they have taken away from the gospel of the Lamb many parts which are plain and most precious; and also many covenants of the Lord have they taken away. And all this have they done that they might pervert the right ways of the Lord, that they might blind the eyes and harden the hearts of the children of men. Wherefore, thou seest that after the book hath gone forth through the hands of the great and abominable church, that there are many plain and precious things taken away from the book, which is the book of the Lamb of God. And after these plain and precious things were taken away it goeth forth unto all the nations of the Gentiles; and after it goeth forth unto all the nations of the Gentiles, yea, even across the many waters which thou hast seen with the Gentiles which have gone forth out of captivity, thou seest – because of the many plain and precious things which have been taken out of the book, which were plain unto the understanding of the children of men, according to the plainness which is in the Lamb of God – because of these things which are taken away out of the gospel of the Lamb, an exceedingly great many do stumble, yea, insomuch that Satan hath great power over them.

Nevertheless, thou beholdest that the Gentiles who have gone forth out of captivity, and have been lifted up by the power of God above all other nations, upon the face of the land which is choice above all other lands, which is the land that the Lord God hath covenanted with thy father that his seed should have for the land of their inheritance; wherefore, thou seest that the Lord God will not suffer that the

Gentiles will utterly destroy the mixture of thy seed, which are among thy brethren. Neither will he suffer that the Gentiles shall destroy the seed of thy brethren.

Neither will the Lord God suffer that the Gentiles shall forever remain in that awful state of blindness, which thou beholdest they are in, because of the plain and most precious parts of the gospel of the Lamb which have been kept back by that abominable church, whose formation thou hast seen.

Wherefore, sayest the Lamb of God: I will be merciful unto the Gentiles, unto the visiting of the remnant of the house of Israel in great judgment. And it came to pass that the angel of the Lord spake unto me, saying: Behold, sayeth the Lamb of God, after I have visited the remnant of the house of Israel – and this remnant of which I speak is the seed of thy father – wherefore, after I have visited them in judgement, and smitten them by the hand of the Gentiles, and after the Gentiles do stumble exceedingly, because of the most plain and precious parts of the gospel of the Lamb which have been kept back by that abominable church, which is the mother of harlots, saith the Lamb – I will be merciful unto the Gentiles in that day, insomuch that I will bring forth unto them, in mine own power, much of my gospel, which shall be plain and precious, saith the Lamb.

For, behold, saith the Lamb: I will manifest myself unto thy seed, that they shall write many things [in the Book of Mormon] which I shall minister unto them, which shall be plain and precious; and after thy seed shall be destroyed, and dwindle in unbelief, and also the seed of thy brethren, behold, these things shall be hid up, to come forth unto the Gentiles, by the gift and power of the Lamb. And in them shall be written my gospel, saith the Lamb, and my rock and my salvation. And blessed are they who shall seek to bring forth my Zion at that day, for they shall have the gift and the power of the Holy Ghost; and if they endure unto the end they shall be lifted up at the last day, and shall be saved in the everlasting kingdom of the Lamb; and whoso shall publish peace, yea, tidings of great joy, how beautiful upon the mountains shall they be.

And it came to pass that I beheld the remnant of the seed of my brethren, and also the book of the Lamb of God, which had proceeded forth from the mouth of the Jew, that it came forth from the Gentiles unto the remnant of the seed of my brethren. And after it had come forth unto them I beheld other books [Doctrine and Covenants, Pearl of Great Price, …], which came forth by the power of the Lamb, from the Gentiles unto them, unto the convincing of the Gentiles and the remnant of the seed of my brethren, and also the Jews who were scattered upon all the face of the earth, that the records of the prophets and of the twelve apostles of the Lamb [Old and New Testaments] are true.

And the angel spake unto me, saying: These last records, which thou hast seen among the Gentiles, shall establish the truth of the first [Bible], which are of the twelve apostles of the Lamb, and shall make known the plain and precious things which have been taken away from them; and shall make known to all kindreds, tongues, and people, that the Lamb of God is the Son of the Eternal Father, and the Savior of the world; and that all men must come unto him, or they cannot be saved. And they must come according to the words which shall be established by the mouth of the Lamb; and the words of the Lamb shall be made known in the records of thy seed, as well as in the records of the twelve apostles of the Lamb; wherefore, they both shall be established in one; for there is one God and one Shepherd over all the earth. And the time cometh that he shall manifest himself unto all nations, both unto the Jews and also unto the Gentiles; and after he has manifested himself unto the Jews and also unto the Gentiles, then he shall manifest himself unto the Gentiles and also unto the Jews, and the last shall be first, and the first shall be last. [Christ's mortal ministry and the original Christian Church were established among the Jews; the latter came from them to the Gentiles, including Israel; the restored original has been established among Israel and the Gentiles and will come from them to the Jews.]

And it shall come to pass, that if the Gentiles shall hearken unto the Lamb of God in that day that he shall manifest himself unto them in word, and also in power, in very deed, unto the taking away of their stumbling blocks – And harden not their hearts against the Lamb of God, they shall be numbered among the seed of thy father; yea, they shall be numbered among the house of Israel; and they shall be a blessed people upon the promised land forever; they shall be no more brought down into captivity; and the house of Israel shall no more be confounded. And that great pit, which hath been digged for them by that great and abominable church, which was founded by the devil and his children, that he might lead away the souls of men down to hell – yea, that great pit which hath been digged for the destruction of men shall be filled by those who digged it, unto their utter destruction, saith the Lamb of God; not the destruction of the soul, save it be the casting of it into that hell which hath no end. For behold, this is according to the captivity of the devil, and also according to the justice of God, upon all those who will work wickedness and abomination before him. ...

And it came to pass that he said unto me: Look, and behold that great and abominable church, which is the mother of abominations, whose founder is the devil. And he said unto me: Behold there are save two churches only; the one is the church of the Lamb of God, and the other is the church of the devil [all false religion]; wherefore, whoso belongeth not to the church of the Lamb of God belongeth to that great church, which is the mother of abominations; and she is the whore of all the earth.

And it came to pass that I looked and beheld the whore of all the earth, and she sat upon many waters; and she had dominion over all the earth, among all nations, kindreds, tongues, and people.

And it came to pass that I beheld the church of the Lamb of God, and its numbers were few, because of the wickedness and abominations of the whore who sat upon many waters; nevertheless, I beheld that the church of the Lamb, who were the saints of God, were also upon all the face of the earth; and their dominions upon the face of the earth were small, because of the wickedness of the great whore whom I saw.

And it came to pass that I beheld that the great mother of abominations did gather together multitudes upon the face of all the earth, among all the nations of the Gentiles, to fight against the Lamb of God. And it came to pass that I, Nephi, beheld the power of the Lamb of God, that it descended upon the saints [members] of the church of the Lamb, and upon the covenant people of the Lord, who were scattered upon all the face of the earth; and they were armed with righteousness and with the power of God in great glory. And it came to pass that I beheld that the wrath of God was poured out upon that great and abominable church, insomuch that there were wars and rumors of wars among all the nations and kindreds of the earth.

And as there began to be wars and rumors of wars among all the nations which belonged to the mother of abominations, the angel spake unto me, saying: Behold, the wrath of God is upon the mother of harlots; and behold, thou seest all these things – And when the day cometh that the wrath of God is poured out upon the mother of harlots, which is the great and abominable church of all the earth, whose founder is the devil, then, at that day, the work of the Father shall commence, in preparing the way for the fulfillment of his covenants, which he hath made to his people who are of the house of Israel.

And it came to pass that the angel spake unto me, saying: Look! And I looked and beheld a man, and he was dressed in a white robe. And the angel said unto me: Behold one of the twelve apostles of the Lamb [John the Beloved]. Behold, he shall see and write the remainder of these things [the Book of Revelation]; yea, and also many things which have been. And he shall also write concerning the end of the world. Wherefore, the things which he shall write are just and true; and behold they are written in the book which thou beheld proceeding out of the mouth of the Jew; and at the time they proceeded out of the mouth of the Jew, or, at the time the book proceeded out of the mouth of the Jew, the things which were written were plain and pure, and most precious and easy to the understanding of all men. And behold, the things which this apostle of the Lamb shall write are many things which thou hast seen; and behold, the remainder shalt thou see. But the things which thou shalt see hereafter thou shalt not write; for the Lord God hath ordained the apostle of the Lamb of God that he should write them. And also others who have been, to them hath he shown all things, and they have written them; and they are sealed up to come forth in their purity, according to the truth which is in the Lamb, in the own due time of the Lord, unto the house of Israel.

And I, Nephi, heard and bear record, that the name of the apostle of the Lamb was John, according to the word of the angel.

And behold, I, Nephi, am forbidden that I should write the remainder of the things which I saw and heard; wherefore the things which I have written sufficeth me; and I have written but a small part of the things which I saw. And I bear record that I saw the things which my father saw, and the angel of the Lord did make them known unto me.

And now I make an end of speaking concerning the things which I saw while I was carried away in the spirit; and if all the things which I saw are not written, the things which I have written are true. And thus it is. Amen.

A quotation of Nephi taken from 2 Nephi chapter 28 of the Book of Mormon; this excerpt was written by the prophet Nephi about 550 BC.

For it shall come to pass in that day [the last days or the day of the Gentiles: our time] that the churches which are built up, and not unto the Lord, when the one shall say unto the other: Behold I, I am the Lord's; and the others shall say: I, I am the Lord's; and thus shall everyone say that hath built up churches, and not unto the

Lord – And they shall contend one with another; and their priests shall contend one with another, and they shall teach with their learning, and deny the Holy Ghost, which giveth utterance. And they deny the power of God, the Holy One of Israel; and they say unto the people: Hearken unto us, and hear ye our precept; for behold there is no God today, for the Lord and the Redeemer hath done his work, and he hath given his power unto men; Behold, hearken ye unto my precept; if they shall say there is a miracle wrought by the hand of the Lord, believe it not; for this day he is not a God of miracles; he hath done his work.

Yea, and there shall be many which shall say: Eat, drink, and be merry, for tomorrow we die; and it shall be well with us. … and if it so be that we are guilty, God will beat us with a few stripes, and at last we shall be saved in the kingdom of God. Yea, and there shall be many which shall teach after this manner, false and vain and foolish doctrines, and shall be puffed up in their hearts, and shall seek deep to hide their counsels from the Lord; and their works shall be in the dark. And the blood of the saints shall cry from the ground against them.

Yea, they have all gone out of the way; they have become corrupted. Because of pride, and because of false teachers, and false doctrine, their churches have become corrupted, and their churches are lifted up; because of pride they are puffed up. They rob the poor because of their fine sanctuaries; they rob the poor because of their fine clothing; and they persecute the meek and the poor in heart, because in their pride they are puffed up. They wear stiff necks and high heads; yea, and because of pride, and wickedness, and abominations, and whoredoms, they have all gone astray save it be a few, who are the humble followers of Christ; nevertheless, they are led, that in many instances they do err because they are taught by the precepts of men.

O the wise, and the learned, and the rich, that are puffed up in the pride of their hearts, and all those who preach false doctrines, and all those who commit whoredoms, and pervert the right way of the Lord, wo, wo, wo be unto them, saith the Lord God Almighty, for they shall be thrust down to hell.

Wo unto them that turn aside the just for a thing of naught and revile against that which is good, and say that is of no worth! For the day shall come that the Lord God will speedily visit the inhabitants of the earth; and in that day that they are fully ripe in iniquity they shall perish.

But behold, if the inhabitants of the earth shall repent of their wickedness and abominations they shall not be destroyed, saith the Lord of Hosts. But behold, that great and abominable church, the whore of all the earth, must tumble to the earth, and great must be the fall thereof. For the kingdom of the devil must shake, and they which belong to it must needs be stirred up unto repentance, or the devil will grasp them with his everlasting chains, and they be stirred up to anger, and perish;

For behold, at that day shall he rage in the hearts of the children of men, and stir them up to anger against that which is good. And others will he pacify, and lull them away into carnal security, that they will say: All is well in Zion; yea, Zion prospereth, all is well – and thus the devil cheateth their souls, and leadeth them away carefully down to hell. And behold, others he flattereth away, and telleth them there is no hell; and he saith unto them: I am no devil, for there is none – and thus he whispereth in their ears, until he grasps them with his awful chains, from whence there is no deliverance. Yea, they are grasped with [spiritual] death, and hell; and death, and hell, and the devil, and all that have been seized therewith must stand before the throne of God, and be judged according to their works, from whence they must go into the place prepared for them, even a lake of fire and brimstone, which is endless torment. …

Yea, wo be unto him that hearkeneth unto the precepts of men, and denieth the power of God, and the gift of the Holy Ghost! Yea, wo be unto him that saith: We have received, and we need no more!

And in fine, wo unto all those who tremble, and are angry because of the truth of God! For behold, he that is built upon the rock receiveth it with gladness; and he that is built upon a sandy foundation trembleth lest he shall fall.

Wo be unto him that shall say: We have received the word of God, and we need no more of the word of God, for we have enough! For behold, thus saith the Lord God: I will give unto the children of men line upon line, precept upon precept, here a little and there a little; and blessed are those who hearken unto my precepts, and lend an ear unto my counsel, for they shall learn wisdom; for unto him that receiveth I will give more; and from them that shall say, We have enough, from them shall be taken away even that which they have.

Cursed is he that putteth his trust in man, or maketh flesh his arm, or shall hearken unto the precepts of men, save their precepts shall be given by the power of the Holy Ghost. Wo be unto the Gentiles, saith the Lord God of Hosts! For notwithstanding I shall lengthen out my arm unto them from day to day, they will deny me; nevertheless, I will be merciful unto them, saith the Lord God, if they will repent and come unto me; for mine arm is lengthened out all the day long, saith the Lord God of Hosts.

Nephi's parting words ending his writings in the Book of Mormon (2 Nephi 33:10-15) about 544 BC.

And now, my beloved brethren, and also Jew, and all ye ends of the earth, hearken unto these words [of 1 Nephi and 2 Nephi] and believe in Christ; and if ye believe not in these words believe in Christ. And if ye shall believe in Christ ye will believe in these words, for they are the words of Christ, and he hath given them unto me; and they teach all men that they should do good. And if they are not the words of Christ, judge ye – for Christ will show unto you, with power and great glory, that they are his words, at the last day; and you and I shall stand face to face before his bar; and ye shall know that I have been commanded of him to write these things, notwithstanding my weakness.

And I pray [to] the Father in the name of Christ that many of us, if not all, may be saved in his kingdom at that great and last day.

And now, my beloved brethren, all those who are of the house of Israel, and all ye ends of the earth [all people], I speak unto you as the voice of one crying from the dust: Farewell until that great day shall come.

And you that will not partake of the goodness of God, and respect the words of the Jews [Bible], and also my words [Book of Mormon], and the words which shall proceed forth out of the mouth of the Lamb of God [Bible, Book of Mormon, Doctrine and Covenants, Pearl of Great Price, ...], behold, I bid you an everlasting farewell, for these words shall condemn you at the last day. For what I seal on earth, shall be brought against you at the judgement bar; for thus hath the Lord commanded me, and I must obey. Amen.

A quotation of the whole of 3 Nephi chapters 29 and 30 written about 34 AD by the prophet Nephi, a descendent of the above quoted Nephi. Nephi addresses us (the Gentiles today) following a several-day ministry of the resurrected Lord, of whom Nephi was a prophet, among His followers in the New World.

And now behold, I say unto you that when the Lord shall see fit, in his wisdom, that these sayings shall come unto the Gentiles according to his word, then ye may know that the covenant which the Father hath made with the children of Israel, concerning their restoration to the lands of their inheritance, is already beginning to be fulfilled. [The Book of Mormon was published in 1830 and early Mormon leaders were some of the first Zionists.]

And ye may know that the words of the Lord, which have been spoken by the holy prophets, shall all be fulfilled; and ye need not say that the Lord delays his coming unto the children of Israel. And ye need not imagine in your hearts that the words which have been spoken are vain, for behold, the Lord will remember his covenant which he hath made unto his people of the house of Israel. And when ye shall see these sayings coming forth among you, then ye need not any longer spurn at the doings of the Lord, for the sword of his justice is in his right hand; and behold, at that day, if ye shall spurn at his doings he will cause that it shall soon overtake you. Wo unto him that spurneth at the doings of the Lord; yea, wo unto him that shall deny the Christ and his works! Yea, wo unto him that shall deny the revelations of the Lord, and that shall say the Lord no longer worketh by revelation, or by prophecy, or by gifts, or by tongues, or by healings, or by the power of the Holy Ghost!

Yea, and wo unto him that shall say at that day, to get gain, that there can be no miracle wrought by Jesus Christ; for he that doeth this shall become like unto the son of perdition, for whom there was no mercy, according to the word of Christ!

Yea, and ye need not any longer hiss, nor spurn, nor make game of the Jews, nor any of the remnant of the house of Israel; for behold, the Lord remembereth his covenant unto them, and he will do unto them according to that which he hath sworn. Therefore ye need not suppose that ye can turn the right hand of the Lord unto the left, that he may not execute judgment unto the fulfilling of the covenant which he hath made unto the house of Israel.

HEARKEN, O ye Gentiles, and hear the words of Jesus Christ, the Son of the living God, which he hath commanded me that I should speak concerning you, for, behold he commandeth me that I should write saying: Turn, all ye Gentiles, from your wicked ways; and repent of your evil doings, of your lyings and deceivings, and of your whoredoms, and of your secret abominations, and your idolatries, and of your murders, and your priestcrafts, and your envyings, and your strifes, and from all your wickedness and abominations, and come unto me, and be baptized in my name, that ye may receive a remission of your sins, and be filled with the Holy Ghost, that ye may be numbered with my people who are of the house of Israel.

Appendix J

Estimate of the Number of Human Inhabitants of the Earth[part #]

We estimate in this appendix the total number of individual persons who have lived on the earth throughout its history by means of a simple mathematical model also described. The model is simple because (1) a simple model is adequate for an order-of-magnitude estimate and (2) sufficient details are not available to justify a more complex model.

We use the usual, exponential-growth model for describing human population dynamics, namely,

[J1] $$dN/dt = (\beta - \delta)\, N(t) = \gamma N(t),$$

where N(t) is the human population at time t (in years), dN/dt is the rate of change of population at time t, β (Greek "beta") and δ (Greek "delta") are the birth and death rates, i.e., β and δ are the respective average numbers of births and deaths per person per year, and γ (Greek "gamma") $= \beta - \delta$ is the net growth rate. The solution to [J1] (see endnote 27 of Chapter 8) is

[J2] $$N(t) = N_0 \exp(\gamma t),$$

where N_0 is the initial population at time $t = 0$. If we assume that each person lives to age L and dies at this uniform (average) life expectancy, then births at time t must equal deaths at time t + L and the following relationship between birth and death rates must hold.

[J3] $$\beta N_0 \exp[\gamma t] = \delta N_0 \exp[\gamma(t + L)],$$

We adopt this result for *uniform lifetime* L as an approximation for an *average lifetime* L. Dividing by $N_0\exp[\gamma(t+L)]$ gives

[J4] $$\delta = \beta\exp[-\gamma L] \qquad \text{and} \qquad \gamma = \beta - \delta = 1/L \log_e(\beta/\delta).$$

Thus, specification of any two of the four parameters β, δ, γ, and L in this simple model determines all four.

Nevertheless, quantities γ and L, or another pair, are difficult to estimate, being influenced by culture, nutrition, and disease, especially as they affect infant mortality. Moreover, the population history of the earth is not described by simple, straightforward application of [J1] because calamities such as war, flood, famine, and disease periodically upset the smooth population growth predicted by [J1] and, indeed, occasionally cause a sudden, significant decreases in population. Therefore, we assume [J1] applies only locally and only over periods of smooth, continuous population growth.

Considering a single geographical region in which the simple model applies during each of several growth periods, the population of this region at time t may be written

$$[J5] \qquad N(t) = N_{01} \exp[\gamma_1 t_1] - \Delta N_1 + N_{02} \exp[\gamma_2 (t_2 - t_1)] - \Delta N_2 + \ldots,$$

where N_{0i} is the population at the beginning of the ith population-growth era, γ_i is the net growth rate during this era, t_i is the time at which the ith era ends, ΔN_i is a sudden population loss at the end of this era due to some calamity such as flood, famine, war, or plague, and index i = 1, 2, 3, … denotes the first, second, third, … population-growth era. Of course, population-growth eras and calamities following them may be local rather than global so that the sum indicated in [J5] must be added to similar sums for different regions, each with its own population-growth character and growth eras. It is consequently clear that even using the simple growth model [J1], an *accurate calculation* of world population at any time in history is complex and requires detailed information that is not available.

To obtain an *estimate* of world population at any selected time based on the limited information available we must simplify our model considerably. We first assume a general global pattern, eliminating a need to sum over separate regions. Moreover, we assume a continuous population-growth era of duration t dating from the flood in Noah's time, at 2330 BC. (We thus ignore, for instance, the bubonic plague or "black death" epidemics that decimated populations of Europe during the fourteenth- through seventeenth-centuries. In the fourteenth century alone plague killed one-third the population of Europe. In various parts of Europe mortality rate is estimated to have been between two-thirds and three-fourths and even higher in parts of England. In the 1665 "great plague of London" some 69,000 died out of a population estimated at 460,000 of whom a supposed two-thirds had fled the city to escape contagion. We also ignore the not insignificant number of persons who lived before the flood.)

For this single assumed growth period we know the initial population (N_0 = 8), the current population (N = 6 billion) and the time interval (t = 4333 years). Using these values in [J2] we obtain

$$[J6] \qquad \gamma = 1/4333 \log_e(6{,}000{,}000{,}000/8) = 0.0047163 \text{ per year.}$$

We further estimate β/γ, for a reason that will shortly become clear. Using [J3] we write

$$\beta/\gamma = 1/\{1 - \exp(-\gamma L)\}.$$

Since γ is known, a β/γ value can be calculated for any assumed value of average lifetime L. Results for β/γ versus L are shown in the table of calculated values below.

Small average lifetime is considered because of infant mortality and because we assume fertility throughout each individuals lifetime instead of a more realistic period of thirty years.

We can now estimate the total number of persons who have lived on the earth between the flood in 2330 BC up to any later time t. This cumulative number $N_{Total}(t)$ is the number who have been born in the period of duration t dating from 2330 BC. In time interval dt the number of persons born is $\beta N(t)dt$. Thus, by integration, the total number born over interval t is

$$\text{[J7]} \qquad N_{Total}(t) = N_0 \beta \int_{t=0}^{t} \exp(\gamma t)\, dt = N_0 \beta/\gamma \{\exp(\gamma t) - 1\}.$$

The 1 in curly brackets is negligible when $\gamma t > 3$; the value of γt exceeds 20 for the calculations represented in the following table so that this 1 can be neglected. The total number of persons born between the flood and time t later is therefore just β/γ times the number living at time t.

Present N_{Total} values ($t = 4330$ years) of number of persons born since the flood are shown in column 3 of the following table for different values of average lifetime L. They are probably underestimates because they omit persons who died in plague epidemics, wars, and persons who lived before the flood. In order-of-magnitude estimate an N_{Total} value of 100 billion persons is indicated.

However, this number is too small in the scope it implies for Christ's atonement (Maxwell, Neal A., *Not My Will, But Thine,* Bookcraft, Salt Lake City, 1988, 51-52). In the *Pearl of Great Price* (Moses 1:33) God describes Christ as Lord

N_{total} values calculated for average lifetime L.

L, years	β/γ	N_{total}, in billions
10.	21.707	130.
12.5	17.467	105.
15.	14.641	87.8
17.5	12.623	75.7
20.	11.109	66.6
22.5	9.932	59.6
25.	8.991	53.9
27.5	8.221	49.3
30.	7.580	45.5

of the *universe*. So does John (*Bible,* John 1:1-3). So does Enoch (Moses 7:30). The first reads

> And worlds without number have I created; and I also created them for mine own purpose; and by the Son I created them, which is mine Only Begotten.

The last quotes Enoch addressing God. It reads

> And were it possible that men could number the particles of the earth, yea, millions of earths like this, it would not be a beginning to the number of thy creation;

While either (i) a creation and fall or (i) a transplant must occur on every populated world, only one atonement is required because of its infinite scope.

Appendix K

The Doctrine of Christ

A ten-minute sermon preached on 21 May 2005 by Barton E. Dahneke

The Book-of-Mormon-prophet Nephi was taught by an angel and Nephi recorded these teachings in the Book of Mormon about 550 BC. I quote portions of his record.

> And I, Nephi, beheld ... the Gentiles ... that they did prosper in the land [of America]; and I beheld a book ... carried forth among them. And the Angel said unto me: Knowest thou the meaning of the book? And I said unto him: I know not. And he said: Behold it proceedeth out of the mouth of a Jew [the Jews]. The book that thou beholdest is a record of the Jews, which contains the covenants of the Lord ... and it also containeth many of the prophecies of the holy prophets; and it is a record like unto the engravings which are upon the plates of brass, save there are not so many... wherefore [the book is] of great worth unto the Gentiles.
>
> And the angel of the Lord said unto me: Thou hast beheld that the book proceeded forth from the mouth of a Jew; and when it proceeded forth ... it contained the fulness of the gospel of the Lord, of whom the twelve apostles bear record, ... according to the truth which is in the Lamb of God. These things go forth in purity unto the Gentiles.
>
> And after they go forth by the hand of the twelve apostles of the Lamb, thou seest the formation of [a] great and abominable church ... for behold, they have taken away from the gospel of the Lamb many parts which are plain and most precious; and also many covenants of the Lord have they taken away.[1]

We learn from this passage that the Bible has been corrupted by removal of many plain and precious parts from it, parts telling of the gospel of Christ, by a great and abominable church which formed after the gospel record went forth in purity from the apostles of the Lamb. Why were plain and precious parts removed? Because the removed parts prevented priestcraft or domination of the people by wickedness and craftiness of men. They prevented priestcraft by teaching that each person could and should commune with and receive truth directly from God. What would be more frustrating to false priests trying to mislead and abuse people? Such priests simply expunged such teaching from the Bible. Indeed, even the corrupted Bible was thereafter closely held, not commonly available to Christians. What exposure to even the corrupted Bible Christians had was controlled and limited over many centuries to teaching by their priests. Corruption of the Bible was secretly accomplished by those who would thereby gain domination over others, for this is the goal of the enemy who motivates and guides such workings in his church.

Early corruption of the Bible, it being the foundation of all orthodox Christian religion today, means that orthodox Christianity of today is corrupted. This situation was predicted by Nephi, by Bible prophets, and described to Joseph Smith as the condition of Christian churches of our time. When Joseph inquired of

God which church he should join he was answered by the Author of Christianity that he should join "none of them." Only a church eventually restored by the power of God utilizing the young prophet Joseph Smith now finds favor in the sight of God and now possesses the pure and complete gospel of Christ because the Lord restored this church with the original purity and fullness of His teachings. This knowledge is a great blessing and great is the responsibility that comes with it.

What pure and precious parts of the gospel were removed from the Bible? And even though they were removed, does evidence of them remain? The answer to the latter question is *yes* for at least one important part of the gospel of the Lord. This part was called by Christ and early Christians "the doctrine of Christ." And the term doctrine is not used in a generic manner but refers to a specific doctrine of great importance, uniquely identified and set apart by Christ as His own.

Three Bible passages refer to the doctrine of Christ and provide a little information about it. They provide just enough information that we can recognize Christ's doctrine after we learn it from another source, but not enough to fully anticipate it before then.

The first of these three passages, authored by the Apostle Paul, is found in Chapter 6 of Hebrews.[2] Paul identifies the doctrine of Christ by name (verse 1), the principles and ordinances it contains (verses 1 and 2), and indicates its importance (verses 4-6). Because one may utilize the doctrine of Christ to become "enlightened," by "tasting the heavenly gift," by partaking of the Holy Ghost and the good word of God, and the powers of the world to come, it is impossible for those once so enlightened, if they fall away, to again renew themselves unto repentance, seeing [that deliberately and willfully turning from God-given knowledge] they crucify to themselves the Son of God afresh, and put him to an open shame. That is, the doctrine of Christ is so powerful and important that if one falls away after fully partaking of it, the sin is unforgivable. Violation of few, if any, other principle or doctrine carries such a heavy consequence because no other provides such knowledge of God, not just knowledge of facts but knowledge at the level of meaning and feeling. The importance and power of this doctrine, now removed from the Bible, is at the highest possible level.

The second passage provides additional evidence. This passage, only three verses in length, was authored by the Apostle John in his second general epistle to all members of the church, the whole epistle containing only 13 verses. John wrote this passage during formation of a great and abominable church, as prophesied by Nephi who learned it from an angel. John accordingly provides members (saints) with a defense against the "many deceivers who are entered into the world" at that time. Namely, John admonishes the saints to love Christ by keeping His commandments and to love one another. John then provides a test by which true Christians could (and can) detect such deceivers.

> Whoso transgresseth, and abideth not in the doctrine of Christ, hath not [knowledge of] God. He that abideth in the doctrine of Christ, he hath [knowledge of] both the Father and the Son. If there come any unto you, and bring not this doctrine, receive him not into your house, neither bid him God speed: For he that biddeth him God speed is [a] partaker of his evil deeds.[3]

Again, the reference to the doctrine of Christ is brief because the early Christians were quite familiar with it and needed no description. And again, the doctrine of Christ is placed at the highest level of authority and priority.

The third Bible passage that refers to the doctrine of Christ was spoken by Christ Himself using the term "My doctrine." It is found in two verses of the gospel of St. John, but I include the two preceding verses for completeness.

> Now about the midst of the feast Jesus went up into the temple, and taught. And the Jews marveled, saying, How knoweth this man letters, having never learned?
> Jesus answered them, and said, 'My doctrine is not mine, but his that sent me. If any man will do his will, he shall know of the doctrine, whether it be of God, or whether I speak of myself.' [4]

Here Christ speaks of His doctrine and reveals its function: to provide knowledge of its origin, of the station of Christ, and His authority to speak and act for His Father. Moreover, the preceding two verses, included above, suggest from where in the Bible Christ's doctrine was removed. I think it was originally found preceding the verse which says "And the Jews marvelled, saying, 'How knoweth this man letters [and, between the lines, from whence receiveth this man such authority], having never learned?' " It is inconceivable to me that John, as insightful as he was in the full breadth and depth of the gospel – its full meaning, if you will – would have excluded something so important as the doctrine of Christ.

Fortunately, the doctrine of Christ is restored to us today in the Book of Mormon [and the Doctrine and Covenants, where it is summarized in the last 4 verses of section 10]. It was the first thing Christ taught generally to "His other sheep" (John 10:14-16) to whom he appeared in America about 33 AD, and is recorded as given from the lips of Christ in 3 Nephi 11:31-40. The "first Nephi," who lived and wrote in the sixth century BC, also included this doctrine in the final chapters he wrote in about 550 BC.

By the doctrine of Christ we are commanded to repent, to believe in Christ, to be baptized, to receive fire and the Holy Ghost, to taste the heavenly gift and become enlightened, to know Christ and His Father, and to obtain salvation (eternal life) in the celestial kingdom. Anything less than this doctrine, any of these elements missing or embellishments added, any precept or principle not included or implied by Him, is not His doctrine.

For me it began with the Book of Mormon and Moroni's promise. But now it is by the doctrine of Christ, by knowledge I have received by fire and the Holy Ghost, by enlightenment from tasting the heavenly gift, that I have come to know God. I have also learned for myself more surely in this process that the Book of Mormon is genuine scripture, God's pure teachings that contain the pure gospel of Christ including the plain and precious parts that were removed from the Bible. Most importantly, I know that Christ is, that Joseph Smith is His prophet of the Restoration by which Christ reestablished His church for all people in our time who seek to find and follow truth, fully found, as in times of old, in Christ's church alone among all churches in the world.

[1] Portions of *Book of Mormon,* 1 Nephi 13:19-26; these verses are quoted in full in Appendix I but they are not numbered there.

[2] *Bible,* Hebrews 6:1-6.

[3] *Bible,* 2 John 9-11.

[4] *Bible,* John 7:14-17.

Appendix L

A Few Scriptures and their Implications Regarding Evolution of Humans

Human evolution is contradicted by correct interpretation of scripture, a fact that eliminates *the* key argument in today's conflict between science and religion. While modern-day scripture is regarded by most as unorthodox, it is truth rather than orthodoxy that has always been of greater concern to true Christians. Indeed, the "orthodox" interpretation of the Biblical creation account is wrong and sometimes deviously used (Pennock, Robert T., *Tower of Babel,* The MIT Press, Cambridge, MA, 1999). However, endnote 21 of Chapter 10 is brief so we more fully indicate here its scriptural basis and support other assumptions and beliefs invoked.

Vaguely in the Bible (because the original text was corrupted, *Pearl of Great Price,* Moses 1:41 and Appendix I) but clearly in literal interpretation of the Book of Moses (see Table comparing *Bible* and *Book of Moses* texts on page 257), Adam was created by God as the first man and, indeed, the first flesh on the earth. Adam was put in a Garden of Eden prepared by God for him to live in. Adam was commanded to dress and keep the Garden. Eve was later created as an help meet for Adam. Thereafter, God created every beast of the field and every fowl of the air and commanded they come unto Adam that he might see and name them. Whatsoever Adam called each living creature, that was the name thereof. (These facts are taken from Moses 3.)

Dressing and keeping the Garden were not demanding. It contained neither death nor thorns or thistles. Moreover, Adam and Eve were created as little children in reasoning ability for the Gods had not yet appointed unto them their reckoning (*Pearl of Great Price,* Abraham 5:13). Being naked bothered neither Adam nor Eve.

How long were Adam and Eve in this condition? Probably a *long* time. As little children are content to play away each day, Adam and Eve were occupied in dressing and keeping the garden and in naming animals and fowls and all creatures. Moreover, "Abraham saw that in the time (or day that Adam and Eve were to partake of the forbidden fruit and die) it was the Lord's time (or day), wherein one day to God is as a thousand years to us." (Ibid.) One day as a thousand years is a magnification of time by 365,000. Three years of God's time is as more than a million years of our time. If we speculate that time flowed in the paradisiacal Garden as it does in heaven, a few hundred years *in the Garden* would be as over 100 million years on earth *outside of it.*

In Adam and Eve's Garden no death occurred. Indeed, nothing changed in the Garden of Eden. There was no aging and "all things which were created ... remained in the same state in which they were after they were created; and they must have remained [that way] forever and had no end." (*Book of Mormon,* 2 Nephi 2:22) Thus, although we are not told how long their tenure in the Garden was, a long tenure of obedient Adam and Eve in the Garden was both possible and likely.

After Adam left the Garden he lived 930 years and died. When did his death occur? I believe within the last six thousand years. Support for this belief is found in the Book of Revelation, Chapter 5, wherein John saw seven seals on the book of life and each seal represents a thousand year period (*Doctrine and Covenants* 77:7. It is stated in the preceding verse that the history of the earth will last seven millennia [I presume after the fall of Adam and Eve]. In the first six we experience life in the present, mortal condition we now know. Shortly after the beginning of the last millennium the Savior will return and claim His own. We are near this transition.)

The earth and its creatures may have evolved outside the garden over the long period of Adam and Eve's tenure in the Garden. We know little from the scriptures about conditions outside the Garden, but the fossil record suggests a long period of evolution existed where death occurred and survival of the fittest applied. In a literal reading of scripture, humans, the descendents of Adam and Eve, were not involved in this evolution because Adam and Eve, though the first flesh of the earth, were – as it were – out of survival-of-the-fittest play. With no death, survival of the fittest had application to neither Adam and Eve nor any of their posterity, born late in earth's history, i.e., during the relatively brief period of the last few thousand years.

What about evidence of prehistoric humans claimed to date back to a much earlier time than the last few thousand years? I here make three observations.

(1) All dating methods have potential pitfalls and the descriptive sciences are not known for their rigor. Paleontology is inherently difficult; its interpretations often seem to me to be too elaborate for the limited information available. If interpreters form rigid presuppositions, paleontologists exacerbate the difficulty.

(2) Interpretations of evidence and truth do not necessarily coincide, especially when an investigator has strong preconceptions about what things are supposed to emerge from his or her findings. It is difficult to think outside one's paradigm where any other intuition seems foreign and unrealistic. And science has little or no early-human-history evidence about human thought and activity (beyond the mundane) that would survive outside of a sympathetic paradigm. There have been long-unrecognized cases of fraud, on-site speculations before a theory or interpretation is carefully and critically considered, and much controversy among scientists and others on practically every substantive issue. No paleontological knowledge of human thought during early earth history seems to yet be stable and reliable despite vivid descriptions one encounters in magazine articles and elsewhere.

(3) Nevertheless, some life-forms may have evolved to what is now regarded as early humans despite the missing link. It seems none of these forms now survive as recognizable descendents and evidence of their behavior and thought is not known. With many possibilities, any conclusions based on science is tentative and speculative. B. H. Roberts, an early Mormon leader-scholar, referred to early, apparently-human forms as "pre-Adamic man." This label is inconsistent with modern scripture (Moses 1:34, 3:7) which indicates the origin of today's humans was father Adam (and mother Eve) who appeared, in the case of Adam, as the first flesh on the earth.

Thus, literal interpretation of scripture suggests that humans were not affected by evolution because, with no death in the Garden of Eden, Adam and Eve were apparently unchanged for a long period during which the world around them evolved.

Appendix M

Propositions Listed and Supported in the Text

(with page number following)

1. One's *paradigm, system of belief,* or *philosophy* is utilized in and essential to observing, classifying, and storing the facts and in recalling, associating, and interpreting them to obtain understanding and meaning. (35)

2. To expand and enhance a paradigm, one must pay attention to facts which are unexpected, which seem strange, which are non-intuitive. In other words, one must seek to learn at a fundamental level. (37)

3. Knowledge of objective facts provides no comprehension of deeper meaning. Only through interpretation of facts utilizing a higher understanding does one comprehend such meaning. An adopted *paradigm, system of belief,* or *philosophy* used to interpret facts thus strongly influences and, indeed, controls meaning. (39)

4. While logic and mathematics may be used to investigate truth by conclusive elimination of incorrect assumptions and theories, no demonstration that a logicomathematical axiomatic system absolutely or uniquely represents observed reality is possible because any set of logicomathematical axioms must support many diverse models. In science and mathematics no method is known for discovering, specifying, or demonstrating the true nature of the universe. Discovery and demonstration of such truth, if possible, requires a different paradigm. (227)

5. Physics in particular and science in general have not established any unique underlying reality by which material phenomena can be understood at a fundamental level. Recent results indicate that a basic axiom of physics (locality) is inconsistent with quantum processes. Understanding of physics previously thought to be consistent is now in question. (249)

6. Repentance and faith in Jesus Christ are the first two principles of His doctrine with baptism and receipt of the gift of the Holy Ghost (confirmation) two required ordinances that follow. According to the doctrine of Christ, these principles and ordinances and continued desire to follow Christ provide salvation and are the basis of a true vision of reality. (305)

7. While science addresses and provides useful but tentative answers to *how* questions relating to objective, reproducible, lowest-common-denominator, material facts, it neither answers nor even contemplates ultimate *who, what,* and *why* questions relating to existence, to God, and to meaning. Compared to answers to *who, what,* and *why* questions, answers to *how* questions seem incomplete and unsatisfying, preoccupied with tedious detail and lacking comprehensive vision and any feeling of certain, universal connection and joy. (343)

8. Embracing *any* paradigm, system of belief, or philosophy involves an essential "leap of faith." (359)

9. Of all the various faiths, paradigms, systems of belief, and philosophies, one stands above all others in the assurance offered of its truth and the benefits promised to all who will receive it; its champion is Christ and the system is His doctrine. (363)

10. The doctrine of Christ leads one to appeal to the power of God above his or her own power. Only through the power of God may one reach beyond the limits of tentative, mortal knowledge to a level of absolute truth, understanding of meaning, and indescribable joy. (366)

11. Perverted religion is a human product inspired by the enemy and may be recognized by the principles and methods it utilizes contrary to the teachings of Christ. These principles and methods include *active* ones like force, coercion, privilege and power of human over human, deceit, vanity, and pride as well as *passive* ones like distraction through indifference and preoccupation with "higher priority" objectives. Perverted religion, including Godless materialism, is designed and promoted by the enemy to prevent one from finding and following the power of God (i.e., divine guidance) that Christ offers in His doctrine, an offer frequently repeated in scripture. (371)

12. Truths, virtues, and gifts received in the original Christian Church were lost due to an apostasy and many of today's orthodox Christian traditions are corrupted. (394)

13. The pure and complete gospel of Christ has been restored to the earth and is available to whoever will receive it; the promise of God to reveal its truthfulness directly to one who will receive it has been repeated. (405)

14. Christ has demonstrated His devotion to each of us. We can respond to His devotion by showing our devotion to Him. He would have us do so by finding and following His way that we might obtain success and joy. (416)

15. Even without an adequate truth criterion, unavoidable conflict between the elaborate, rigid dogma of the medieval Church and observation and deduction of Galileo and others disproved the dogma. A conflict between science and religion (i.e., that dogma) and a scientific revolution thus arose. Some hold the notion that this conflict reveals an essential flaw in religion but no such flaw or conflict is evident in a careful comparison of the scientific method and the doctrine of Christ. Instead, severe flaws are found to be inherent in only the scientific method. (435)

16. Reality, by its definition as the totality of all real things and events, is comprehensive, universal, and unique. Any means for discovering and establishing the nature of reality and its description – the truth – is universally useful to Christian, scientist, and all others alike. Within science and Christianity the only known means for conclusively establishing absolute truth is the power of God – the only adequate truth criterion – accessible by the doctrine of Christ. (452)

17. Science based solely on objective, material-universe, lowest-common-denominator, value-free facts reliably provides neither truth nor meaning and it is therefore incapable of characterizing reality. Fundamental truth, values, and associated meaning utilized in science must be brought to it from higher understanding and belief. (465)

18. Meaning of the doctrine of Christ may be summarized in the following five gifts received by a devoted Christian: (1) an absolute knowledge of Christ and of reality; (2) an epiphany of joy; (3) growth beyond the natural in personal qualities and capabilities; (4) mutual devotion with Christ and a devotion to all humankind; and finally, (5) a more excellent hope for eternal life in the Kingdom of God where an everlasting fullness of joy is realized. (470)

Index